The Ultimate Guide to Hunting Skills, Tactics, and Techniques

The Ultimate Guide to Hunting Skills, Tactics, and Techniques

Edited by **Jay Cassell**

Skyhorse Publishing

Copyright © 2012 by Jay Cassell

All Rights Reserved. No part of this book may be reproduced in any manner without the express written consent of the publisher, except in the case of brief excerpts in critical reviews or articles. All inquiries should be addressed to Skyhorse Publishing, 307 West 36th Street, 11th Floor, New York, NY 10018.

Skyhorse Publishing books may be purchased in bulk at special discounts for sales promotion, corporate gifts, fund-raising, or educational purposes. Special editions can also be created to specifications. For details, contact the Special Sales Department, Skyhorse Publishing, 307 West 36th Street, 11th Floor, New York, NY 10018 or info@skyhorsepublishing.com.

Skyhorse® and Skyhorse Publishing® are registered trademarks of Skyhorse Publishing, Inc.®, a Delaware corporation.

www.skyhorsepublishing.com

10 9 8 7 6 5 4 3 2 1

Library of Congress Cataloging-in-Publication Data is available on file.

ISBN: 978-1-61608-879-8

Printed in Canada

Table of Contents

Introduction

JAY CASSELL

In *The Ultimate Guide to Hunting Skills, Tactics, and Techniques*, you're going to find detailed information on everything you need to know about hunting big and small game, predators, turkeys, waterfowl, and upland birds. All of the important game species in North America are covered, from rabbits and squirrels to ducks and pheasants to deer, bears, and moose. All of the important tactics are covered as well, from hunting with firearms, to hunting with muzzleloaders, to hunting with bows and arrows.

According to recent statistics, there are almost 17 million licensed hunters in the United States alone. Of them, 11 million hunt whitetail deer, 2.6 million hunt wild turkeys, 2.3 million hunt waterfowl, and 4.8 million hunt small game such as rabbits and squirrels. In the past ten years, predator hunting (coyotes, in particular) has been exploding, with possibly 4 million hunters pursuing that incredibly exciting sport.

Due to their overwhelming popularity among the hunting public, I've devoted the largest section of this gigantic book to whitetailed deer. Taking excerpts from books written by such acknowledged hunting experts as Peter Fiduccia, John Weiss, Hal Blood, John Trout, and others (including a few from yours truly), I've tried to hit on all the important aspects of whitetail deer hunting: calling, still hunting, driving, stand hunting, hunting with the wind, using scents, rattling, tracking, and much more. I've also included an important section on finding wounded deer by John Trout. Obviously, no one wants to wound a deer; the goal is to make one clean, killing shot, allowing the animals to expire quickly. That doesn't always happen; it's something we all need to deal with. John Trout tells you how.

After the large deer section, you'll find valuable how-to-hunt information on elk, mule deer, blacktail deer, grizzly and brown bears, black bears, and more. Then we move into a section on predator hunting by Ron Spomer (to find out how to obtain a copy of Ron's book on predator hunting, please see the author credits on page 783). Spomer's calling tips, as you'll discover, are invaluable.

Small game with rabbit hunting pro Dave Fisher is next, followed by turkey hunting, one of my favorite things to do. After a long winter, what better way to get outside than to get up on an early spring morning, hike out into the woods before sunup, listen to the birds waking up, the squirrels starting to rustle in the leaves, the *thump-thump-thump* of a ruffed grouse drumming on a log. Then, if it all works out, you'll hear a gobble, and the game is one. Ray Eye, easily the best known turkey hunter in the world, and someone I consider a dear friend, agreed to let me use some of his material here, on what to do with silent birds. Read it; you'll learn something.

After the bird hunting section – presented in tip form by veteran editor Lamar Underwood – you'll find a huge section on recipes, from a variety of well-known game chefs (Kate Fiduccia, Monte Burch, J. Wayne Fears) as well as from cooks who specialize in everything from Dutch oven cooking to smoking to crafting incredible side dishes. The section on how to butcher a deer, by Monte Burch, is something you'll want to hang on to.

When I came out with *The Best Hunting Stories Ever Told* in 2010, I had such a great time assembling stories by authors whom I've long admired that I couldn't help but include a few here in the Adventure Reads section. Here, you'll find memorable pieces by the likes of H. G. Tapply, Sigurd Olson (this is a personal favorite, about how a whitetail buck survives another hunting season, as seen through his eyes), Gene Hill, and Thomas McIntyre, a long-time friend and author of *The Shooter's Bible Guide to Optics*. Tom allowed me to use an epic piece about a wolf hunt he took in Nunavit a few years ago. Reading it makes you feel as if you are there with him, crossing the tundra, pursuing a lifelong dream of taking a large, northern gray wolf.

There's more, of course, including a few pieces I wrote about some of my own exploits. I hope you enjoy them.

Finally, you'll come to a huge record-book section, courtesy of the Boone and Crockett Club. Check out the photos of some of the record-book trophies. Amazing. The scores of the top ten animals in each species category are almost hard to believe!

More than anything, though, I hope you learn some things from all of the experts who have graciously contributed their precious works to this compendium. If you like what you read, consider picking up some of their books, and getting their whole story, on whatever species that you like to pursue. Hey, it's all about learning, improving, becoming a better hunter. The process never stops, it just gets better, it just gets more fun.

Jay Cassell
Editorial Director
Skyhorse Publishing
August 2, 2012

The Ultimate Guide to Hunting Skills, Tactics, and Techniques

Part 1
Deer Hunting

Introduction

JAY CASSELL

With a population of almost 30 million in the lower 48 states, the whitetail deer is without question the most popular big-game animal in the United States. From firearms and ammunition; to bows, arrows, and broadheads; to optics and clothing, to footwear, calls, scents, stands, and blinds, all-terrain vehicles, and base layers, to television shows, videos, and of course books, a billion-dollar industry has grown up around this one animal. What is the attraction? What is it that drives us to distraction, waiting for deer season to come so we can venture out into the woods and, with some luck and a lot of skill, take a nice buck…or a doe, if you are focused on putting venison into your freezer.

Whitetail hunting is not easy, as the quarry has keen eyesight, acute hearing, and an uncanny sense of smell. Plus, when you go into the woods hunting, you are entering the whitetail's world, his backyard. You must be at your stealthiest, with the wind just right, your movements quiet and fluid, your scent at a minimum, your eyesight at its keenest – in essence, you must be on full alert 100 percent of the time to succeed. Start to daydream, or think about what's going on at work, or what bills have to be paid – that's when a buck will slip by, perhaps 75 yards away in the dense forest. He's there, he's gone, you blew it.

To help you improve your odds of success, I've picked out excerpts from solid hunting books, written by acknowledged experts in the field. I've attempted to hit all of the important tactical areas of whitetail hunting – from choosing a deer rifle and ammo, to using cover and attractor scents, to working the wind, rattling, tracking, driving deer, still-hunting, stand hunting, and more. I concentrated more on tactics and techniques, and not as much on gear, because the tactics are what will help you score. Gear, which changes every year, is support material, as you can get a buck just as easily using the rifle you bought in 1990, wearing your four-year-old camo clothes and eight-year-old boots, as you can wearing everything that you bought just before the season. But tactics – you learn the tactics, go out in the field and apply them – that's something you'll never forget, that's what will help you become a better deer hunter with each passing year.

The section starts off with some great tactical advice from veteran hunter and writer John Weiss, then moves on from there. Learn it, use it this season.

—J. C.

Surefire Whitetail Tactics

JOHN WEISS

Pick a Winning Stand Area

The greatest impediment to taking a mature white-tailed buck is not being in the right place at the right time. In fact, the legendary Fred Bear once observed that "you can't shoot a deer you don't see."

Not long ago, when researching material for a series of magazine articles, I went straight to today's whitetail experts, hunting with them over the course of several years and picking their brains about their favorite stand-hunting hotspots. The advice I sought had to be relevant to bowhunters and firearm hunters alike, no matter where they live or hunt, and no matter whether they prefer to use portable tree stands or ground blinds.

The hunting luminaries I talked with earn or earned their full-time livelihoods from deer hunting, and collectively have pursued trophy whitetails in every state inhabited by the species. They include long-time friends Harold Knight and David Hale, of Knight & Hale Game Calls in Cadiz, Kentucky; Will Primos, of Primos Game Calls in Jackson, Mississippi; Jim Crumley, of TreBark Camo in Roanoke, Virginia; Larry Frasier, head guide for Deer Creek Outfitters in Sebree, Kentucky; Johnny Lanier and Leo Allen, owners of Bent Creek Lodge in Jachin, Alabama; and Ray

McIntyre, who at the time was owner of Warren & Sweat Tree Stands in Grand Island, Florida.

At the conclusion of this quest, I allowed my computer to digest the countless pages of interview notes. It coughed up seventeen different types of locations where a hunter can place a stand with expectations of taking a larger than average buck.

Incidentally, I also reflected back over three decades of hunting whitetails and, not surprisingly, I could recall taking bucks in every one of the expert's recommended locations. When you take your buck this year, I'll wager it will be in one of the following places.

Major Deer Runways

"Major deer runways serve as travel corridors between bedding and feeding areas," David Hale said.

Major deer runways reveal plenty of all-day deer traffic, but the only time bucks travel such runways is during the beginning of the rut when does are coming into heat.

"While a network of other threadlike trails may criss-cross the terrain, there is no mistaking a major runway. It may be quite wide, due to generations of deer repeatedly using this thoroughfare, and the soil will have become so compacted over the years that little vegetation grows there. Although a major deer runway may course through a tract of forest land, you're more likely to find it in conjunction with restrictive terrain features such as long, narrow hollows, lengthy streambottoms, or where distinctly different cover-types meet, such as pines bordering hardwoods."

According to Harold Knight, in fall and winter major deer runways are predominantly used by doe-family groups (one or two does, their most recent offspring, and perhaps a spike buck, forkhorn, or daughter from the previous season). Mature bucks use major deer runways only during the peak-rut phase of the mating period when they are engaging in trail-transference in order to follow does approaching the peak of their estrus cycles.

Minor Deer Trails

"Minor deer trails are used by mature bucks during the non-rutting weeks of the fall and winter months," Will Primos told me. "Mature bucks do not like to associate with doe-family units at this time, preferring to keep their private lives private. Occasionally, you may find a minor deer trail paralleling a major deer runway on the runway's downwind side and in much heavier cover; this allows a buck to keep tabs on the activities of other deer and to even use them as sentries to forewarn him of danger."

"However, in a majority of cases, mature bucks will adopt their own home-range areas away from doe-family groups," Jim Crumley added. "Minor deer trails can be difficult to identify because they are not tamped down to the same degree as major deer runways, and this allows vegetation to hide them from view in many places."

Minor deer trails are predominantly buck trails, and they are commonly found running parallel to and downwind of major deer runways. Set up your stand accordingly.

A very light skiff of snow on the ground makes the task of identifying such trails infinitely easier. Be especially alert for the absence of very small tracks. When small tracks are found in conjunction with large tracks, a doe-family unit is using the trail, not a lone buck.

Scrape Concentrations

"A mature whitetail buck may create as many as three dozen scrapes during the pre-rutting period, but a majority of them are quickly abandoned and only a very few become elevated in status to primary scrapes," Larry Frasier explained. "Moreover, setting up in the vicinity of clusters of scrapes is generally far more productive than merely standing watch over a lone scrape, because the concentrated nature of the breeding sign indicates the animal's revisitation on a far more frequent basis."

"What most hunters do not understand about the rutting period is that waiting on a stand near primary scrapes is most effective only during the pre-breeding phase of the rut, which is about two weeks before does reach the zenith of their estrus cycles," Jim Crumley said. "During the peak of the rut, scrape hunting continues to be effective, but a much wiser tactic is to occupy a stand overlooking a major deer runway or a doe-family bedding area because anxious bucks will be spending less time tending their scrapes and increasingly more time in the vicinity of does, waiting for the very first ones to become receptive."

Trail Hubs

A trail hub is where two or more trails cross. Intersecting major deer runways always reveal the most deer traffic (in the form of does, their current offspring, and immature bucks).

Conversely, intersecting minor deer trails reveal far fewer sightings of animals; however, since most of the animals sighted will be mature bucks, these are the places to search for during the non-rutting period.

"As the rut intensifies, a trail hub that produces day-long excitement with plenty of various-age animals sighted is a location where a minor deer trail, that is, a buck trail, intersects with a major deer runway being used by doe-family groups," David Hale emphasized. "Keep in mind that the greatest incidence of trail hubs occurs on relatively level terrain where the cover is of mixed species."

Boundary Trails

A whitetail's home range averages less than two square miles in size, with the perimeter often delineated by major terrain features such as lakeshores, rivers, sheer rocky bluffs, deep gorges, and forest edges that yield to wide-open prairieland. "Scout these likely home-range boundary areas and you'll find trails," Johnny Lanier advised. "When deer are engaging in routine daily behavior, boundary trails are infrequently used. But if there are few does in the region and the rut is in progress, bucks will patrol boundary areas, covering many miles per day in search of estrus females."

"If hunting pressure mounts, bucks will filter out of their usual haunts to find seclusion in peripheral areas; now is when boundary trails also become hotspots worth watching," Leo Allen added.

Escape Trails

"Under intense hunting pressure, and especially during the course of drives, deer immediately vacate their areas of normal activity and head for very heavy cover or difficult terrain," Will Primos observed. "Knowing this, and knowing in advance where that hunting pressure is likely to originate, such as from a campground or popular hunter parking area, watching an escape trail can pay handsome dividends."

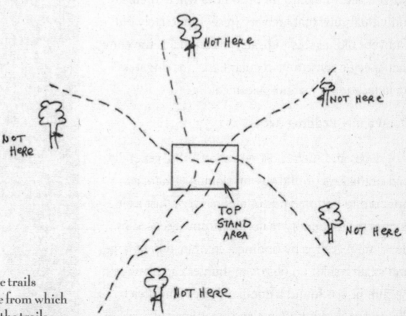

Trail hubs are places where two or more trails intersect. The best stand areas are those from which a hunter has shooting coverage to all of the trails.

"First, locate the most nightmarish cover you can find in the region," Larry Frasier suggested. "It might be a swamp or a spruce bog, but it could also be a ravine choked with brush and jackstrawed logs, a pine plantation, or a jungle of tall vegetation such as phragmites or cane. Next, search for tracks entering the cover. If you can find tracks that are splayed and eight- to ten-feet apart, indicating a bounding animal, you've found an escape trail."

Rub Lines

"Essentially, a rub line indicates a minor deer trail used by a buck. But compared to a minor trail used by a buck on a year-round basis, a rub-line trail is used most frequently during the pre-rut period," Jim Crumley explained. "The foremost purpose of the trail is still a travel route back and forth between bedding and feeding areas, but it's fully within the area where the buck hopes to eventually breed and he is therefore inclined to mark it with visual and olfactory signposts. As the rut gets underway, a rub-line trail may also connect scrapes strung out across the countryside."

"A recent rub will reveal a moist, light-colored Cambium, while one that is weeks old will have begun to dry and turn slightly gray in color," Harold Knight said. "I like to find rub lines where there are individual rubs that are very fresh, moderately old, and very old, as this indicates the animal is traveling that specific route on a regular basis, making it an ideal location for stand placement."

Doe-Family Bedding Areas

Does and their most recent offspring generally bed in thickets or midway up sloping terrain, as opposed to bottomlands or along ridges. Just as it is possible to identify major deer runways used by doe-family groups by finding a combination of large and small tracks, an observant hunter can likewise be sure he has found a doe-family bedding area by the presence of both large and small matted ovals in grass, leaf litter, and snow, and seeing evidence of both large and small droppings.

"The prime time to hunt a doe-family bedding area is the pre-breeding phase of the rut, as amorous bucks will be nearby, anxiously waiting for the first does to enter estrus," David Hale noted. "A stand should be located at least 100 yards away from the actual bedding area, on a main trail leading toward it, to avoid getting too close and spooking the animals."

Mature Buck Bedding Areas

"Mature bucks generally bed higher than doe-family units and in thicker cover. Since mature bucks are usually solitary animals, the discovery of a lone bed in a region pockmarked with numerous rubs on

Mature buck bedding areas are difficult to hunt because one must never violate the resident buck's feeling of security or he'll leave, perhaps forever. Sometimes a quickie ground set-up along a trail leading to the bedding area is less intrusive than hanging a tree stand.

saplings, and a combination of old and fresh tracks and droppings, is what you should be looking for," said Will Primos.

"There are two best times to wait on a stand near a mature buck bedding area," Ray McIntyre added. "The first is very early in the season, well before the pre-breeding period of the rut. The second is during the post-rut phase when exhausted bucks enter a week or more of recuperation and thus spend more time than usual in their bedding areas."

Of critical importance, remember that a mature buck's selection of a bedding area is based solely upon the feeling of safety offered by that place. If you violate the buck's security by installing your stand too close, he'll vacate the region and begin bedding elsewhere. All of my interview experts agreed that a hunter should set up at least 200 yards away from a mature buck's bedding area, on a minor deer trail leading from the bedding region to a prime food source, and he should occupy his stand only on those days when the wind is absolutely in his favor.

Grazing Areas

Early in the season, before killer frosts wipe out lush vegetation, whitetails are primarily grazers. "Search for secluded grassy openings, hay meadows, soybean fields, and native species of greenery that deer in that region prefer. Then establish a stand that will allow you to watch the food site at morning's first light and again at dusk." Johnny Lanier advised.

Browsing Areas

"As the season progresses and vegetation begins turning brown and entering a dormant state, whitetails become browsers and dote upon the tender twigs, buds, and branch tips of regenerative saplings and immature brush," Harold Knight said. "No matter where you live within the whitetail's range, you should be able to find either white cedar, red maple, mountain maple, or black ash, all of

Owing to their generally large sizes, grazing areas such as forage grasses, grainfields, and food plots are more efficiently covered by firearm hunters rather than bowhunters. Dawn and dusk are the best hunting times.

which deer browse upon heavily. Remember, the browse material must be within their reach, and this means finding immature trees with low branches no more than six feet off the ground."

Ice Cream Food Areas

In every region of the country, deer have certain foods that are special treats. Since these treats are usually available for only very brief periods, they draw animals from afar.

"Examples of these ice cream foods include the two- to three-week long acorn drop, the several week period in which orchard fruits are maturing, and fields containing crop-residue spillage immediately after corn, soybeans, carrots, and sugar-beets have been harvested," Ray McIntyre said.

"Occupy your stand early and late in the day, just prior to the arrival of a storm front or, best of all, immediately after the passage of several days of severely inclement weather," he concluded.

Staging Areas

"Staging areas consist of 100- to 200-yard-wide bands of thick cover surrounding grazing areas, browsing areas, or ice cream food areas," Will Primos explained." If a given food site is relatively close to occupied dwellings or roads, deer will mill around in a staging area until darkness sets in before exposing themselves in the open to feed. The same is also true in secluded regions where hunting pressure is intense.

"After finding one of the three types of feeding areas that deer are frequenting, scout the adjacent cover for approach trails and place your stand at least fifty yards back in the cover so you'll be able to see your quarry before evening shooting light fades. Morning stands in staging areas might have to be as much as 100 yards from the actual food site because mature bucks often leave the open feeding grounds before dawn's shooting light arrives."

Clearcuts and Burns

When a forest fire ravages the terrain, everything looks charred and horrible for many months. However, ash deposits reduce the pH content of the soil, and what emerges is extremely succulent, high-quality, regenerative vegetation that draws deer from surrounding areas.

"When logging companies clear-cut a tract of climax forest, the elimination of the trees likewise scars the landscape. Yet with the overhead, shade-producing canopy now eliminated, a profusion of ground-story plants and saplings emerges, providing deer with a cornucopia of feeding opportunities," Johnny Lanier said. "Periodically check with your local Forest Service office or timber company to learn of recent forest fires or logging operations, and

you'll undoubtedly find more deer per square mile in those regions than elsewhere."

Stormy-Weather Bedding Areas

Deer are relatively immune to the effects of precipitation, but when it occurs in conjunction with winds exceeding ten miles per hour, they hole up in protective cover. Every hunter should therefore have at least one stand overlooking a trail leading into or through a stormy weather bedding area.

"Because they retain their leaves year-round, conifers are the most favored stormy weather bedding sites," David Hale noted.

"In the absence of evergreens, look for walls," Harold Knight added. "These are the protected lee sides of thick cover such as multiflora rose, honeysuckle, brush, or steep boulder-riddled terrain, all of which have the effect of blocking the wind and thereby allowing an animal better use of his senses than elsewhere."

Diversion Areas

"A diversion area is any natural terrain feature or manmade confluence that squeezes deer traffic in a certain direction," Larry Frasier observed. "An example of a natural diversion area might be a constricted bottleneck in a steep bottomland. A manmade diversion might be a permanently open gate in a fenceline.

"Also scout for narrow corridors through thick stands of cover, perhaps where a winding band of infertile soil has prevented lush natural growth, or even several blown-down trees which deer are likely to detour around."

Crossings

"Next time you see a precautionary deer-crossing sign along the highway, pull over onto the berm and spend a few minutes studying your surroundings," Will Primos suggested. "Likely as not, you'll see that both sides of the road consist of long stretches of relatively open ground except for that one specific place where two opposing tracts of woodland closely border the road. And that is precisely where the sign has been placed.

"Whitetails are cover-loving creatures, yet they regularly cross fields, meadows, pastures, and even highways during their travels. Naturally, they'll most often cross at a particular location where they need not expose themselves for any longer than necessary.

"So, when scouting, try to find a terrain situation that is similar to a highway deer crossing; that is, a piece of open ground where two opposing wooded points almost meet. When deer want to travel from the one woodlot to the other, their crossing location will undoubtedly be in the vicinity of the wooded points.

"A low saddle crossing a steep ridge can also be a hotspot," Ray McIntyre advised. "In this case, however, it is not the cover per se that affords deer their needed sense of security, but the dip in the contour of the terrain so they are not silhouetted against the skyline."

"Another type of crossing I've found highly productive is a slightly elevated ridge of dry, wooded land separating two swamps," Will Primos said. "Spooked deer will not hesitate to bound away through standing swamp water, but unalarmed animals going about their routine business will consistently use the higher, drier ground instead."

Drinking Sites

Under normal weather conditions, typical whitetail habitat has abundant "sheet water" in the form of streams, rivers, lakes, and springs. But deer are opportunists and will also drink from rainwater puddles, stock tanks, farmponds, roadside culverts, and irrigation ditches.

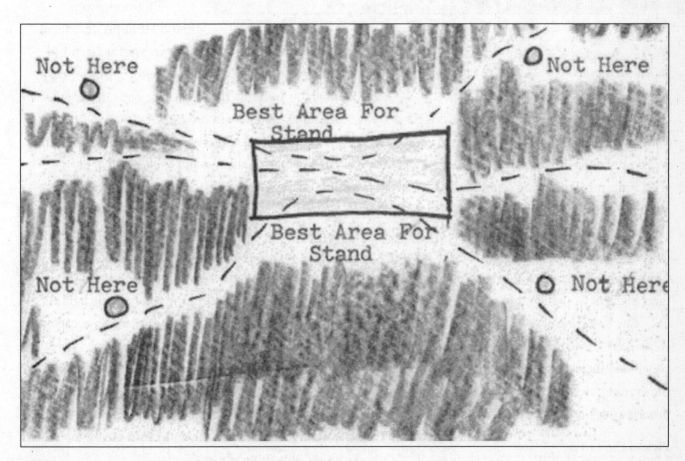

Diversion areas, sometimes also known as funnels or bottlenecks, force deer traffic to squeeze through a narrow area of terrain. Diversion areas are the most popular stand sites among bowhunters because of the generally short-range shots that are afforded.

Drinking sites can be hotspots, but only during periods of severe drought when most of the local water sources are dried up.

Consequently, drinking sites are not good places to establish stands under normal conditions when rainfall has adequately provided the animals with widespread drinking opportunities.

The prime time to sit on a stand near a drinking site is during a severe drought in which all but the largest sources of water are dry. Tracks peppering a drinking site tell you how many animals are visiting it, their frequency of visitation, and their probable sexes.

The best time of day to occupy a stand near a water source is early morning, after the deer have concluded their daybreak feeding; conversely, in the evening, deer do not customarily show up at drinking sites until after full dark.

Pick of the Litter

I've just described eighteen locations which, given the right time of year and/or certain weather

conditions, are sure-fire places for taking a buck. Obviously, few of us have the time to place a stand in every one of the eighteen locations yet, at the other extreme, it would be unwise to put all your hope in only one stand.

A flexible hunter should probably have three to five different stand sites. This will allow him to adapt to changing conditions and also to rest each of his stands now and then, rather than burning out a single stand through continual use.

Of the eighteen stand locations described, it is imperative to have a stormy weather stand. Otherwise, whenever severe weather strikes, you might as well stay home because none of the other locations are likely to produce.

My second choice would be a trail hub, simply because part of the fun and excitement of deer hunting is seeing animals. By the same token, in being able to look over a number of different bucks, you stand a better chance of attaching your tag to something that is really exceptional.

A stand in a diversion area is essential if you live in a region where hunting pressure is light; if hunting pressure is intense, substitute an escape trail stand instead.

A stand overlooking a feeding area is a must. Make use of a portable stand for this type of work so you can easily relocate your stand from a grazing area to either a browsing area or ice cream food area as the season progresses.

Finally, my fifth stand choice would be near a mature buck bedding area, especially if the presence of a rub line, scrapes, or large tracks suggest that the deer in question is a trophy animal.

Failsafe Stand and Blind Set-ups

Many firearms hunters believe that, since they're using a scoped rifle and can pop off a round at an unsuspecting animal up to 300 yards away, things such as scent drift or how deer catalog various sounds become virtually meaningless in terms of stand or blind placement. But guess what. A recent hunter survey by the National Shooting Sports Foundation revealed that, every year, the majority of firearm-killed deer are taken at seventy-five yards or less.

Consequently, I've always advised firearm hunters to use as much care in selecting their stands and blinds as bowhunters do. Who knows, even though your firearm may be capable of reaching way out there, the buck of your dreams may eventually step into view at a distance of only a dozen yards. And if he does, the smallest error in judgment or planning can become magnified to such proportions that it may easily cost you your prize. Actually, two types of error may enter the picture, for there are errors of omission (things we should have done but didn't) and errors of commission (things we did but shouldn't have). And it's usually the errors of commission that prove to be the most detrimental because, when the shooting distance is so close you can see a fly on the animal's coat, even the faint scratching noise of whisker stubble against your collar may send him crashing away through the brush.

That said, it's clear that one thing that distinguishes an advanced hunter is the degree of control he strives to maintain over his hunting and shooting set-ups. Much of this comes about through his learned ability to benefit from past experiences by remembering what worked well before and striving to duplicate those same circumstances time and again.

Bowhunters must select stand sites that afford close-range shots or deer will jump the string. Many experts believe eighteen yards is the ideal shooting range.

As a result, when describing "failsafe" stand and blinds, I'm not referring to specific types of terrain locations as we did in the previous section, but attributes of stand and blind set-ups themselves. And to be sure, the higher the number of these desirable features that can be incorporated into a given stand location and its placement, the greater the hunter's chance of scoring.

Narrowing the Range

Most bowhunting authorities agree that the ideal shooting range is somewhere between ten and twenty-five yards. Even though you may be capable of placing arrows accurately at thirty-five yards or beyond, it's not wise to shoot this far when hunting, due to a deer's ability to dodge the flight of the arrow.

Some hunters claim this is untrue, believing that arrows travel so fast, especially from modem compound bows, that it's virtually impossible for deer to "jump the string," but this is a huge misconception.

First, it is not the sight of the arrow flying toward them that deer react to, but the sound of the string being released. Even if you use string silencers such as cat- whiskers or acrylic yarn puffs, your string will still make a slight thud—like twang, which can cause a deer to instantly duck into a crouch. This is an instinctive reaction whereby a deer coils his legs like springs to propel him into an escape mode; a microsecond later, the arrow flies harmlessly over its back.

As far as arrow speed, most modem compound bows generally chronograph at around 250 feet per second. By comparison, sound travels at 1088 feet per second. Therefore, noises made by you or your equipment will reach the deer five times faster than your arrow. What this means is that it takes a deer only three-tenths of a second to drop a full body size, but at twenty-five yards it takes your arrow at least five-tenths of a second to reach its target; hence, a clear miss. Yet, at eighteen yards or less, it takes an arrow only two-tenths of a second to reach its target; which means there's no chance for the deer to duck before the arrow arrives.

Obviously, many of us would probably be tempted to take a shot at a big buck beyond twenty-five yards. But if you keep in mind the rule of thumb of placing your stand within ten to twenty-five yards of where you expect to see deer, in the long run you'll experience far fewer misses. Then, if an occasional thirty- or thirty-five-yard shot does indeed present itself, and you can't resist taking it, remember to aim low—in the vicinity

of the heart—so that when the animal predictably dives into a crouched position, he'll be moving downward into the arrow's flight path and you'll have a good hit in the lung region.

The Sunlight Factor

One error that both bow and gun hunters make is scouting during midday, when the sun is almost directly overhead, then completely overlooking the fact that, most probably, any shooting opportunity they're awarded will come early or late in the day when the sun is low on the horizon.

This reminds me of a hunt in Rockingham County, North Carolina. I was situated in what I thought was an ideal stand, watching a trail hub. As late afternoon approached and the sun began sinking to the horizon, it became increasingly more difficult to see the trail.

Then, just when the sun had become almost too blinding to look at, an impressive 10-pointer appeared. It was the biggest buck I had ever seen in this particular area, but by this time my burning eyes were squinted almost closed with stinging tears streaming down my face. With no choice, I slowly raised my arm to wipe my eyes with my sleeve. The deer caught the slight movement, and quickly evaporated into the bright haze.

The lesson learned from this experience is that, aside from the difficulty of looking directly into the sun without discomfort, when bright sunlight is shining in your direction it tends to magnify even the smallest of movements.

So why not turn this situation entirely around, and make it work the same way against the deer? In other words, if you're an early-morning hunter, you'll want your stand to be situated so that the rising sun is on your back and its bright rays are slanting in the direction where deer are most likely to approach from. If you're an evening hunter, you'll want your back to the West, to achieve the same end. If you hunt both mornings and evenings,

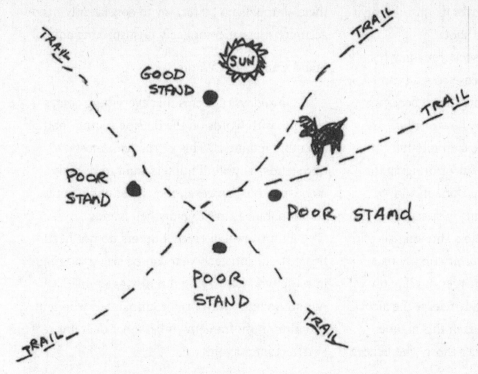

When picking a specific spot for a stand, the prevailing wind direction is the first consideration. Next in importance is ensuring that the sun is on your back or to one side, so you aren't looking into bright light.

you'll probably need two stands in entirely different locations. Sometimes, of course, you might strike it lucky and find a tree where you can compromise by having the sun slightly to your left or right.

With this matter attended to, any deer that approach will have difficulty seeing you because looking in your general direction will mean staring directly into glaring bright light.

Pick the Right Tree

It's possible to situate a stand so that the sun is not in your eyes, yet you're still bathed in bright light as a result of being too close to perimeter cover edges. It's better to be farther back in the cover, where long tentacles of shadows will help to break up your outline. Some hunters like to have a jumbled maze of heavy brush, vegetation, or tree branches immediately behind them. This is certainly better than being out in the open, but it's more

effective to be at least partly encircled by cover.

Many accomplished hunters—bowhunters, in particular—study specific tree species that may best suit their needs. Keep in mind that early in the season, when autumn foliage is still present to obliterate your man-form, virtually any type of tree possessing adequate leafy branches may suffice. The trick is to anticipate what that same tree will look like in weeks to come. After the leaf drop, many tree species become so denuded that not even a sparrow would be concealed from view.

One dramatic exception are the various evergreen species (pines, firs, spruces, cedars), which retain their bushy boughs year-round to afford excellent concealment.

I also like oak trees. Even though an oak's leaves will eventually turn brown and die, they remain securely affixed to their stem attachments long into the dead of winter. The same is true of yellow and tulip poplar, beech, and certain hickory species.

It also pays to select a tree that is not straight-trunked and standing alone like a sentinel, but one which is disfigured, has many gnarled and twisting branches at the intended stand level, and is situated in close proximity to other, similar trees.

Still another important feature I like to see incorporated into both bow and gun stands is moderately thick ground—story vegetation, brush, tag alders, and other growth along the trails leading into my sphere of coverage. The cover should be dense enough so that I have to visually strain to see through it; vegetation this thick hides my presence to any approaching deer, and gives me just the right amount of time to prepare for a shot.

In other words, if I see a buck threading his way in my direction through dense cover, I can rise from a sitting to standing position if necessary, reposition my feet, and raise my bow or rifle. Then, when the deer is about to step into full view, I can begin drawing my bow or bringing the rifle's scope to my eye, all of this done in s-l-o-w motion. Then, when the deer finally steps out of the trailside screening cover and into a shooting alley, no additional movement is necessary on my part. All I have to do is squeeze the trigger or relax my fingertips to smoothly and cleanly release the arrow.

Try engineering your stands in this manner and you'll quickly join ranks with those who believe

there simply is no better way to consistently make accurate shots at completely unsuspecting animals.

Stand Camo That Works

Nowadays, it seems that everything comes in a box with words on the outside stating "partial assembly required." This is true with most tree stands, as well; if hunters want to be truly inconspicuous, however, they must implement additional measures to hide their stands.

Unfortunately, many hunters do not heed this advice, and each year can be seen trudging into the woods carrying recently assembled portable stands with bright, unpainted wooden and aluminum frame members that deer are certain to detect, and avoid.

Pick a tree for your stand that is surrounded by other trees with leafy branches. The branches, and the shadows they cast will help you blend with your surroundings.

After the leaf-drop is complete, relocate your stand to a tree that has many forked trunks and gnarled branches to help absorb your body form.

After many years of hunting experience, I've learned that a properly hidden bow or gun hunter must be virtually absorbed by his surroundings. Serious deer hunters should do everything possible to ensure that their stands melt into the forest's woodwork, so that a wary buck slipping into the vicinity doesn't have a clue that a hunter is in the area.

The first order of business is to hang the stand in your backyard and spray all exposed surfaces with flat black paint. Then, after it dries, use light green or olive drab paint to create vertical bars and stripes to further break up the stand's appearance.

How High is the Stand?

Many veteran hunters aren't climbing as high as they did in previous year. They've discovered that the only time a high stand is advantageous is when they're in a tree that does not have assorted limbs and leafy branches to break up their out- line, or when they're hunting on a steep mountainside and the deer are expected to be coming from an uphill direction. Then and only then is it necessary to be twenty-five or even thirty feet off the ground to be out of a deer's line of vision.

Keep in mind, when bowhunting, that the acute downward angle of the shot increases proportionately with a tree stand's height. In many instances, a portable stand hung no more than ten feet off the ground may be perfectly acceptable if the tree in question has many gnarled, disfigured limbs and leafy branches at that level to adequately conceal the hunter.

If you find an ideal tree but there is little cover at the desirable level, consider gathering some branches, brush, and other cover and attaching it to your stand. Avoid cutting cover from the area immediately surrounding your stand, so you don't eliminate the screens that are needed to block an approaching deer's line of vision.

Since bow and gun hunters both require shooting alleys in several different directions, gather the cuttings from this work and use them.

I like to use a lightweight folding saw for pruning out shooting alleys. Depending upon the location of branches in my chosen tree, I reduce my shooting alley cuttings to straight sapling sections and leafy crown sections. The straight sapling sections can be horizontally tied to my stand, while the leafy crown sections can be inverted and hung upside-down by branch crotches from the horizontals. In just a few minutes, I can make my stand almost completely melt into its surroundings.

Ground Blind Mastery

Few veteran hunters are locked into the mind-set that tree stand hunting is essential to success. Sometimes a savvy hunter will come to the conclusion that he doesn't need a tree stand at all, and that a ground blind is what's really called for.

In fact, one or two ground blinds can save the day when high wind, driving sleet, and plummeting air temperatures make climbing into a tree stand foolhardy.

Unfortunately, many hunters make the mistake of simply tacking a length of camo cloth between two saplings, or piling up brush, and then attempting to merely hide behind the screen of cover. This may suffice for the rifleman who is watching a trail crossing or feeding area 100 yards away. But if a buck slips in close from an unexpected direction, the makeshift blind may cause the hunter to blow his only shooting opportunity. Similarly, such haphazard attempts at blind construction rarely benefit the bowhunter.

Two culprits are at work here. First, when attempting to use such a ground blind, the hunter inevitably finds it necessary to peer over the top edge of the blind to watch for deer traffic, thus exposing his head and shoulders to view. Then, when the moment of truth arrives, the nature of his equipment requires him to rise still higher to draw his bow or shoulder his firearm, which not only exposes still more of his upper body torso but also interjects

A ground blind can save the day when there is no suitable tree for a stand in a hotspot hunting area, or when windy or inclement weather makes climbing trees dangerous.

his search elsewhere in the hopes of finding both sign and a suitable tree for establishing his waiting location.

Conversely, the ground-blind hunter isn't short-changed in this manner. He doesn't need a tree! He can capitalize upon his discovery by simply designing a hiding place right there, even squarely in the open, knowing in advance that deer will very shortly become accustomed to it and no longer register suspicion or alarm over its presence.

This isn't to say that a ground blind can be carelessly situated. As with a tree stand, wind direction is of unquestionable importance because the hunter will want to ensure that his scent is carried away from the area where he expects deer to appear. Also, the hunter will want to build his blinds in locations designed to place the early-morning and late-afternoon angle of the sun in his favor.

Building Your Blind

Like tree stands, no two ground-blinds ever look alike, but a few construction tips will go a long way toward ensuring the hunter remains as inconspicuous as possible.

An unobtrusive blind is one that closely matches the height of surrounding native cover in the immediate vicinity. If the ground cover is low and sparse, it may be necessary to dig a shallow pit to accommodate a hunter sitting on a stool inside. In the case of gun hunters, the pit can be circular in shape, but bowhunters require a diamond—shaped pit to enable them to draw their bows in frontal, right. and left directions.

If possible, I like to gather native brush and branches and build an igloo-like structure, using twine to hold cover in place where necessary. I then use pruning shears to cut out three small openings

undesirable movements into the hunting equation. Consequently, cover placed behind and around you is just as important, maybe even more so, than cover placed in front of you. The reason is because thick screening cover entirely surrounding your position completely hides your presence from all directions and mutes any subtle movements that you may have to make to bring your equipment into use.

I sometimes even think that the diehard treestand hunter is at a disadvantage. Upon locating favorable sign or a high traffic area for seeing deer activity, the tree- stand hunter must next engineer an appropriate set-up within acceptable shooting range in accordance with his choice of equipment, and this entails a myriad of considerations. Yet, as it so often happens, there simply is no tree of suitable size for enacting an elevated hunting strategy. So the hunter invariably forgets about the sign he has found, no matter how encouraging it may be, and continues to shoot through; these can be round, ten-inch diameter holes for gun hunting, and six- by twenty-inch-tall vertical "slots" for bowhunting.

Another option is poking a number of upright sticks into the ground to encircle the blind site, and then stapling camo cloth in place; be sure to obtain a brand that is rot and mildew proof, to withstand many years of use. Place assorted leafy branches or other native cover around the perimeter of the structure to further break up its appearance.

There are also various types of portable blinds on the market. These are fully-enclosed affairs that pop up quickly with interior wands, and have zippered shooting windows. They look conspicuous, but when left in place all season, in locations where they won't be bothered by other hunters, deer eventually pay them little mind.

Finally, with regards to both tree stands and ground blinds, a partner can be invaluable in fine-tuning your hunting site. Have him walk around your stand or blind and study it from different angles in order to suggest areas that need attention. In the case of a tree stand, perhaps just one more leafy branch strategically tied here or there may significantly improve the set-up. If it's a ground blind, have your partner face your shooting openings as a nearby deer might periodically do, to ensure your human silhouette is not back-lighted and making you readily visible; in this situation, you need more cover behind you.

In conclusion, remember that although you may know what hypothetically constitutes an ideal tree stand or ground blind for either bow or gun hunting, there's little to be gained by becoming so obsessed with the word "perfect" that anything less is discouraging and reduces your confidence.

Deer hunting is unpredictable, and in the natural world nothing is ever as precise and exact as we might wish it to be. In fact, many of the deer I've taken over the years have been from tree stands or ground blinds where, given the supreme power,

I would have placed a bush here or there, altered the growth of a particular branch one inch to the right or left, or done something else to fractionally change the picture. Yet in the final analysis I still enjoyed success.

Stalking and Still-Hunting Skills

An old sage once observed that man learns more from his failures than from his successes. This unquestionably applies to my twenty years worth of trial- and-error learning experiences in attempting to sneak up on white-tailed bucks.

For example, take the apparently simple matter of deciding upon the best time of day to be prowling around in search of a deer. For many years I subscribed to the conventional wisdom of sitting on stand early and late in the day when the animals are moving around naturally, then spending the midday hours still-hunting because that is generally when deer are not moving.

During those years, I took plenty of deer from my tree stands during dawn and dusk hours, yet I rarely got close enough to a buck during midday hours to place a telling shot. Invariably, my only reward was catching a fleeting glimpse of the south end of a deer headed north.

Then, one day, the light bulb in my brain experienced an unusual burst of illumination which changed my deer hunting strategy forever, and has since allowed me to successfully close the distance to countless numbers of bucks.

It all boils down to this logical conclusion. When deer are bedded during midday, they are virtually impossible to approach because a mature buck will have chosen a hiding location designed to provide the utmost security. To monitor his surroundings, he'll undoubtedly be on high ground, which enables him to have a good view of everything around him. Due to rising thermal air currents during midday, this high ground also allows him to use his nose to catch wafting tendrils of odors emanating from anything that may attempt to approach from below. Further, he's sure to be sequestered in dense cover, from which he'll have several escape route options because he instinctively knows that anything skulking around will have great difficulty penetrating such places without making forewarning noises.

Consequently, our hypothetical buck has four distinct advantages going for him during the midday hours. He's not moving but laying down, and is therefore difficult to see; and because of his carefully selected hiding location he can quite easily see, hear, or smell anything prowling around that may be a potential threat to his well-being.

Now insert a noisy, smelly, moving human into this picture and there is no question which creature has the upper hand!

Now examine a comparable sneak-hunting scenario as it might unravel during the early morning hours of the day, and then again as evening dusk begins to settle in, and see how various components of the hunting equation dramatically turn around in your favor instead of the buck's.

Early and late in the day, our hypothetical buck is probably on his feet and moving around,

During midday, deer are usually bedded, hidden from view and unapproachable. The best still-hunting success is at dawn or dusk when deer are on their feet, clearly visible, and preoccupied with feeding or other activities.

which makes him far easier to see; not only is his body form better exposed to full view, but the motion receptors in your eyes will quickly draw your attention whenever he moves. Moreover, the reason he's on his feet is because he's doing something such as feeding, drinking, traveling to or from a food source or drinking site, rubbing a sapling with his antlers, tending a scrape, trailing a hot doc, or reaffirming his social ranking with other bucks. It's the very fact that he's engaged in some type of activity that makes him vulnerable because his senses and thought processes are at least partly preoccupied with the activity itself rather than what may be lurking (you) in nearby shadows.

Looking for Deer

Periods of light fog or drizzle, or gentle snowfall, seem to pacify deer and make for ideal conditions for sneaking up on a buck. Yet in the final analysis, a hunter's success hinges almost solely upon his eyes and how he uses them. In fact, I've often thought I'd be willing to trade my most expensive firearm for a far lesser gun and the vision of a hawk; it's been said that if a hawk could read, it could read a newspaper at 100 yards. Since a trade for such superior vision is obviously not possible, the only alternative a hunter has is learning to use the visual capabilities he does have to maximum effectiveness.

The problem with our human vision, as it relates to deer hunting, is that when we look off

into the distance we tend to pinpoint our focus upon a small area, in an attempt to sort out details. As a result, if an animal 100 yards away is just ten yards outside your concentrated area of focus, you probably will not see it, especially if part of the animal's anatomy is concealed by cover. You may

Learn how to see deer by first panning the distance with wide-angle vision to detect movement. Then, pinpoint your focus to determine if it's a deer worth a still-hunting attempt.

then conclude that no deer are around, begin your next forward advance, suddenly hear a loud snort, and only then see the deer for the first time as he bounds away.

All of this occurred because, contrary to the way we customarily view our surroundings, deer do not identify things by first looking at them in pinpoint focus. Instead, they scan their territory with a wide—angle perspective that allows them to catch the slightest movements, even when they are taking place around the outer-most periphery of their visual scope. After that movement is detected, they narrow their focus on it for further classification.

Of course, successful sneak hunters know to move along at a snail's pace, with long pauses in between each step, so that the overall distance they travel during the day equals no more than 100 yards every half-hour. They've also trained them- selves, when panning the terrain ahead, to not intently look at any particular feature, but to move their eyes slowly from right to left, then back again, concentrating upon picking up any movement that may be taking place in the distance. Only after no movement is spotted do they visually take the cover and terrain apart piece by piece. It's then, and only then, that they permit themselves to cautiously take another step or two forward.

Tracking Tips

When there is snow on the ground, many sneak hunters combine their still-hunting efforts with tracking in an attempt to double their chances of spotting deer. But it usually isn't worth it to follow tracks discovered in mid afternoon. As emphasized in a previous section, deer customarily bed during midday, so the tracks probably were made earlier that morning and the animal may now be far away. But even if the deer should happen to be in the immediate area, remember how difficult it is to sneak up on a bedded buck that has all of his senses riveted upon his surroundings. This makes a good case in favor of following tracks only when they are discovered at dawn, because you can presume with a high level of certainty that the deer that made them is nearby, on his feet, and moving slowly.

One mistake committed by many hunters who have elected to follow tracks is to use the same exact route taken by the deer while continually looking at the imprints in the snow at their feet. What such hunters fail to realize is that when deer are traveling, they constantly monitor their back trails, which invites detection of a hunter's presence if he's on the same trail.

A savvy hunter, on the other hand, sneaks along a parallel course to the tracks, staying as far away from the tracks as he can while still being able to note the direction they are going; in most instances this distance will be thirty or forty yards to one side of the tracks or the other. Also, try to stay

When tracking a deer, take a course parallel to the deer's so he doesn't look back and see you. Don't continually look at the tracks; focus your attention up ahead, hoping to spot the animal itself.

When putting on the final stalk to get within shooting range, take it slow and easy, tread on soft ground to make no noise, and use intervening cover to conceal your approach.

within thin cover, plotting each forward movement in such a manner that trees, brush, bushes, boulders, or other cover will help to hide your movements and make you less noticeable when a buck periodically looks back over his shoulder. Also spend a minimum of time looking at the tracks themselves, because the only thing they tell you is where an animal once stood. Where you want to train your attention is far ahead in the distance, where the tracks are leading, in hopes of eventually spotting the deer itself.

Putting On the Stalk

When you finally come within sight of a deer, whether by following tracks or simply during the course of still-hunting, you may be able to successfully conclude the hunt then and there. Yet, just as often, you may spot the deer several hundred yards away. Or, as the animal continues to slowly move onward, it may inadvertently place some cover or terrain between the two of you. In either case, a renewed vantage point must be gained if there is to be any chance for a shot, and this means putting on a stalk.

First, try to second-guess the direction of the deer in the hopes of intercepting it at some point farther ahead. If it's possible to go around the backside of a steep knob, large rock formation, brushy thicket, or several acres of dense pines, and if such cover will hide any noise or movements you may make, it may pay to take off at a trot. Otherwise, since the animal is unaware of your presence, it's better to take it slow and easy.

It is imperative that the primary landscape features between the deer and the stalker not be disturbed or altered. In other words, the bobbing hat of a hunter moving along behind a hedgerow will alert the animal, as will other body movements such as your entire head and shoulders suddenly coming over the crest of a grassy knoll like a jack-in-the-box.

It's important to engage the stalk in such a manner that intervening terrain features may be utilized to block the view of the animal while advance movements are being executed. This means carefully (but quickly) selecting the route ahead, and using cover features such as logs, rocks, stumps, and the like that conceal most of the body most of the time, even if it makes the stalk longer in time or distance. Whenever you take a peek to reorient yourself to the animal's distance or perhaps its slightly changed travel direction, make sure your head is held low and to the side of the cover rather than high and above.

Should the animal be in sight and happen to look in your direction, freeze! Don't move again until the deer has given your general area the once-over and then returned to its previous activity.

What should you do if you make a mistake and snap a dry twig or step upon crunchy leaves that loudly broadcast your presence? The answer is to just accept it as part of the challenge of hunting deer, because it happens to the best of hunters. But also

If you step on a stick and it snaps loudly, freeze. A nearby deer will rivet his attention in your direction, but if there are no more sounds he'll forget what alerted him and go back to his former activity.

remember to immediately come to a halt for at least several minutes, not twitching as much as an eyelid.

Lots of noises occur in the places where deer live, and they become accustomed to hearing everything from falling nuts, to squirrels rustling in ground leaves, to turkeys and grouse flushing from cover, to branches falling to the ground. In other words, deer are continually getting an earful.

However, deer also have the innate ability to catalog what they hear as either normal or potentially unsafe. As a result, if you commit some faux pas that alerts a deer, it will train its senses in your direction and wait for further noises to allow it to confirm what it initially heard. If you immediately come to a halt and make no more noises, the deer will eventually set its mind at ease and return to its former feeding or other activity. Therefore, it's not the occasional, blundering noise a hunter sometimes makes that spells his undoing, but the rhythmic cadence of continuing noises that to a deer signal danger.

Similarly, keep in mind that whitetails have relatively short attention spans. Biologists working with deer in large experimental enclosures say that three minutes is about the limit to their memory or any matter they may be engaging in before turning their attention to other thought processes. So when you make an occasional mistake—and you will—stop for several minutes, and any recognition that nearby deer may be giving that mistake will soon be forgotten.

One of the main difficulties in stalking deer is that decisions must usually be made quickly and accurately. But a hunter must be inventive, resourceful, and willing to put out just that little extra bit of effort that some others might not be so inclined to invest.

I remember one time when I took off my boots and walked in stocking feet across crunchy gravel to quiet my approach as I crossed a dry streambed. Another time I belly-crawled through 200 yards of thorns because the only suitable approach cover was close to the ground; as I field-dressed my buck, I looked and felt like a pin cushion. I can't remember how many times I've had to hold my rifle over my head while fording waist-deep streams.

Once-Jumped Deer

Okay, you've been doing a commendable job of sneak hunting, and you finally spotted a nice buck, but then, while stalking to within acceptable shooting range, things went amiss. The deer momentarily glanced in your direction, apparently caught a slight flicker of movement on your part, and began loping away, white banner astern.

The correct strategy now is to simply sit down and be patient for at least fifteen minutes. Deer that are not outright spooked are often curious about what alerted them, and sometimes will circle around in hopes of identifying whatever it was made them nervous in the first place. This means that you may yet get a shot, especially if you pay close attention not to the direction in which the deer departed, but rather behind you and to either side.

If no deer returns to the immediate area after a full fifteen minutes, I suggest continuing to sneak hunt but making an elliptical loop to the right or left because the animal will certainly be keeping tabs on his back trail. Keep in mind that the deer probably didn't go far. Researchers studying animals wearing radio collars have determined that, unlike elk or mule deer, which may go five miles when spooked, whitetails invariably turn on their afterburners for only 200 yards or so, until they're just out of sight, whereupon they come to a halt, dive back into heavy cover, and resume their slinking behavior.

Exactly how you pursue a "once-jumped" deer also depends upon the nature of the terrain. As a general rule, whitetails hold to the same type of cover and elevation as when you first moved them. Consequently, if you start a deer in a large stand of cedars, chances are the deer will stay in the cedars rather than breaking for nearby hardwoods. And if

If you spook a deer and it dashes off, wait fifteen minutes to let him calm down. Then make a wide arc to get ahead of the deer's line of travel and wait patiently. He may eventually close the distance and provide a shot.

you start a deer in a swamp, it will probably remain in the swamp rather than evacuate for a nearby pine plantation.

Similarly, in mountainous terrain, a deer started on a sidehill bench will predictably follow that bench on approximately the same contour level of elevation. Start a deer on a ridge and he'll probably continue to cling to that high ground for as long as possible. There are exceptions; if the deer comes to a saddle that allows him to slip unseen through a break in the ridgeline to the opposite side of the mountain, for example, count on him to take advantage of that natural escape hatch.

With knowledge of these behavioral traits in mind, you should be able to analyze the surrounding topography and make an educated guess as to where the animal might be farther ahead and, just as important, how to best approach it. Above all, don't rush. Think everything through because a once-jumped deer quite often presents himself for another shooting opportunity at a later time, but a twice-jumped deer is rarely so careless.

Finally, don't allow yourself to develop a fixation on one particular animal. You may be following tracks in the snow that suggest an impressive buck is somewhere up ahead, and you may have even jumped him once. But if you begin concentrating solely upon that one animal, to the exclusion of other deer that may be in the same immediate region, it may cost you. There may even be a bigger buck in the area, but you'll never see him if your focus is solely on the one you're following.

Advanced Deer-Drive Maneuvers

I'd be willing to bet this week's grocery money that the traditional, worn-out deer-drive tactics you and your partners currently are using are largely ineffective.

In the least, the rather standardized deer drives so prevalent among today's whitetail hunters don't have much relevance when it comes to taking big bucks that have become programmed to react to drive situations in an entirely different manner than naive, younger deer. In short, today's big deer are panic-proof, and that means they're lot likely to get up and flee directly away from a conventional drive line.

The Good Ol' Days, Weren't

Unquestionably, driving deer a generation ago was quite a thing. Drivers carried not only firearms, but whistles, horns, and even discarded Halloween noise-makers upon occasion. The drivers dutifully stomped through the woodlands, hooting, hollering, and otherwise saturating the hills and hollows with a fusillade of approaching sounds. The din was supposed to move whitetails in the direction of stand hunters waiting as much as one or two miles ahead on logging roads, near clearings, or sometimes simply behind a tree near a suspected deer run.

Looking back, I wouldn't trade those memories, because they helped to shape my evolution as a deer hunter. But it is now evident that our drives—no matter how much fun and camaraderie we enjoyed—were confused, disorganized, and constituted little more than rudimentary gang hunting.

The drivers rarely had shooting opportunities, which is understandable because the noise they made enabled bucks to pinpoint their locations ahead of time and then sneak back through the spread-out drive line or circle widely and skirt the line altogether. Sometimes deer merely remained hidden in their beds in heavy cover until the drivers passed, and then bounded off in the opposite direction. Other times the commotion stampeded the deer, so that the animals did not follow predictable escape trails but squirted out in random directions. Consequently, even those standers who had been positioned on known deer trails seldom had shots, and those who did indeed see deer nearly always missed because the targets were in full flight.

None of this is to say that our mob-hunting efforts were dismal failures, because "even a blind hog will find an occasional acorn." But compared to the sophisticated drive tactics of today, those of the past were definitely inefficient, overly time-consuming, and sometimes downright dangerous.

Further, there is no doubt in my mind that only a fraction of the bucks living in any given region were ever seen, much less shot at. Moreover, if someone even suggested that bowhunters could stage effective days, he would have been laughed out of town.

The Mini-Drive Concept

Small drive parties have a lot going for them. In these days of increasingly posted lands, a small group of courteous hunters stands a far greater chance of gaining access to private property than

Small drive parties are easier to organize than huge gangs of hunters. Silent drives are more effective than noisy drives because the animals move slowly, providing better shooting opportunities.

what happens when a caravan of vehicles pulls into the driveway of a predictably recalcitrant farmer to ask for drive-hunting permission. Even in the cases of state and federal lands, fewer hunters are easier to organize, position on stands, and keep track of on the drive line, which translates into greater efficiency.

Additionally, a gang of perhaps fifteen or twenty hunters can expect to make only several drives per day, simply because of the logistics involved in trucking so many hunters to their

individual stand locations, lining up the drivers, and then at the appointed time beginning the long march cross-country.

Yet nowadays, with a smaller, hand-picked group of just a few hunters, we commonly stage up to twenty drives per day.

The first order of business is nominating one member of our hunting party to be the drivemaster. He doesn't have to be the best shot or have taken the most deer over the years; his main attribute should be that he's the individual who best knows

Always select a drivemaster. He needn't be the most skilled hunter in the group, but should be the one who best knows the terrain and how the animals move when pushed by drivers.

the property to be driven and where the animals usually go. In this manner, with an aerial photo, he can show each member of the group what the terrain and cover to be driven looks like, where the drivers will begin, where each stand hunter should place himself, and what the animals are most likely to do. Be flexible about this, too. When the hunting party drives one particular area and then moves to a new drive location perhaps a mile or two away, it may be prudent to elect another drivemaster who knows that particular property better than anyone else.

If no one in the group is intimately familiar with the terrain to be driven, hunting permission should be obtained well before opening day. This allows the group to do some pre-season scouting to learn the lay of the land, property boundaries, and anything else that will play a role in their hoped-for success. In fact, if it's private property, the best source of information is the landowner himself; he lives there year-round and probably sees deer almost daily.

Of course, whether it's private or public land, a key element in planning our drives is that we avoid huge, sweeping tracts of real estate. Such places take an eternity to drive but, more important, a small group of hunters simply cannot properly push the cover or guard all possible exits, and this allows the deer far too many escape options.

The terrain situations we particularly like to drive are very well defined. Invariably, each will consist of heavy cover bordered on at least two sides by open ground (such as prairie, pasture, or hay meadow) or some type of natural barrier such as a wide river-course or lakeshore, and seldom is the cover to be driven larger than twenty acres.

These self-imposed restrictions allow us to capitalize upon several different things. First, these little broken segments of private land or fragmented portions of state and federal lands are usually overlooked by other hunters. But we are perfectly happy to have these so-called leftovers, because they are the very places where cagey bucks like to hole-up as hunting pressure continues to mount on larger pieces of nearby real estate. Moreover, since whitetails are reluctant to expose themselves in open places, the well-defined perimeters of such swatches of cover allow us to better second-guess how the animals will move when pushed from their beds.

Examples of these mini-drive situations are almost too numerous to list,

but among our favorites are the following: narrow gullies or ravines that are choked with downed timber but are no more than 200 yards in length; rectangular-shaped pine plantations no more than five acres in size, with immature trees that have dense whorls of branches close to the ground; rectangular-shaped cornfields no larger than five acres in size; willow bars along watercourses, in which the cover is no wider than fifty yards and no longer than 200 yards; narrow hollows with almost impenetrable stands of honeysuckle, laurel, or rhododendron; briar patches or jungles of laurel or multiflora rose that are no larger than ten acres in size; tag alder thickets bordering stream bottoms; swampy lowlands no

Driving small tracts of land is more effective because the deer have fewer escape options. An all-time favorite drive is through a bottomland where stand hunters can watch a constricted area the animals must squeeze through.

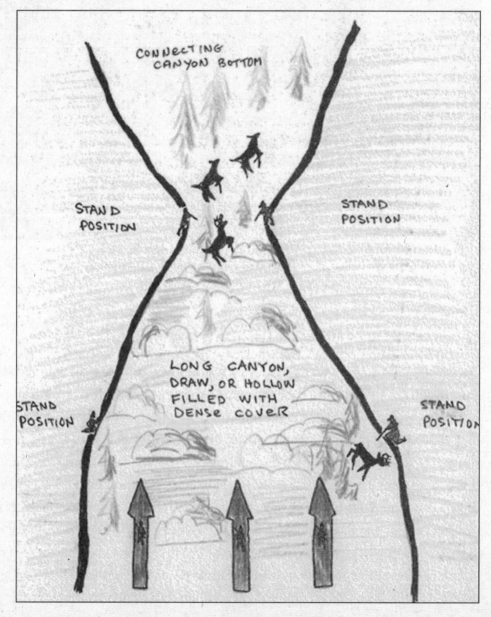

larger than ten acres in size, and which have pole timber, blowdowns, at least several inches of standing water, and occasional dry hummocks; former fields and croplands now laying fallow and which have grown up in brush and thick regenerative saplings such as sassafras, sumac, poplar, and crabapple, no more than ten acres in size; and, finally, former burns and small clearcuts coming back into successive vegetation and thick young trees.

Raucous Drives are Out

We make use of silent drives. There is no hooting, hollering, and whistling. The reason for this is because we stage our drives during both bow and gun seasons. Especially when we're bowhunting, we don't want to risk wounding animals, as would be the case with deer wildly jackrabbiting through the cover. Much more to our liking is to just gently nudge the animals and hope they'll slowly sneak off in the direction of one of our standers.

For the most part, those hunters who are designated as drivers are actually engaging in still-hunting, although they move along a tad faster than what is recommended for a one-man still-hunting maneuver. The net result is that when deer are moved from their beds, they do not panic, which often rewards one of the drivers with a shot. Yet if the driver doesn't even see a particular deer move out ahead of him, his partner on stand farther ahead may have a chance at a slowly loping animal.

We also prefer to enact these mini drives on windy days. When the wind is gusting at more than eight miles per hour, a whitetail's sensory apparatus is greatly impaired. Under these conditions, a buck's ears cannot easily distinguish between the sounds of human footsteps and clacking tree limbs or rustling leaves. Moreover, a deer's eyes cannot easily detect a slowly moving hunter because of the competing movements of swaying stalks of vegetation. And although his nose may pick up the scent of one or more drivers in the distance, the erratic, swirling

nature of the breezes will prevent the deer from pinpointing their exact locations or the routes they're taking.

As a result, the deer knows to lay down and hold tight. But if he is indeed moved from his bed, chances are better than even he'll travel only a short distance before quickly hunkering back down again.

Several years ago, we had an intriguing experience in Kentucky. There were three of us, and we decided to place Bob Murray on stand in a narrow corridor of high ground between two marshy bogs. Bill Jorgensen and I would then sneak hunt through an adjacent stand of cedars, hoping to push something to Bob. The wind was so fierce that I couldn't keep my hat on, so I folded it up and shoved it into my back pocket.

Moments later, a six-point buck got up just a few yards in front of me and, for brief seconds, just stood there, broadside. I loosed an arrow that flew harmlessly over his back. The deer took off, but ran only fifty yards before ducking back down again in waist-high grass. With my attention riveted on the deer's location, I began a careful stalk, eventually put the deer up a second time, and missed him again. The animal slowly ran just another fifty yards, but now was in the narrow corridor. A few seconds later I heard Bob Murray's victory yelp, indicating he had scored a good hit.

Under the windy conditions just described, staging mini drives is not unlike rabbit hunting. Of course, if there is no wind, you can still make drives, but the chances of the drivers having shooting opportunities are greatly reduced, especially if they are using archery tackle.

Games Big Bucks Play

In the past ten years, I'd venture a conservative estimate that I've participated in at least several hundred so-called mini drives. A number of specific happenings and events have so consistently repeated themselves that I now consider them almost axiomatic.

If there's a big buck in the cover, he'll be the first to come out or he won't come out at all. If you suspect he's still in there, drive the cover again, but this time from a different direction.

For one, when a mature buck is hiding in a relatively small piece of cover (less than twenty acres) and the cover is driven, that big buck will either be the first deer out of there or he won't come out at all.

Big bucks are extremely security conscious, and if they have reason to believe that their cover has been blown, they will not hesitate to leave the area, pronto! This insight is invaluable to an enterprising hunting party.

First, a hunter who is designated to wait on stand must exercise great care in hiking to his station. If a buck is bedded relatively close by and hears the hunter moving into position, he will know that general area is a potential source of danger and he will not travel in the stand hunter's direction when he is routed out by approaching drivers.

So, when moving to your stand, take the long, roundabout way if necessary and sneak into position

as quietly as possible. Also, once you've selected your vantage point, do not change your mind later and decide that perhaps somewhere else fifty yards to your right or left might be better. Your partners may have already begun the drive, and if the buck in question decides to leave the area by coming your way, he will be well ahead of any does or younger bucks in the region and therefore may very well detect your movement as you change locations.

If the drivers move one or more bucks through your general area but you are not presented with a shot, don't despair. Simply note the exact travel route used by the deer and file the information away in your memory bank. Then, when you drive the area again several days or weeks later, make the necessary adjustment in where you decide to wait

Hunters placed on stand should not move once they're in position. The drive may have already begun, and if the stand hunter moves, he's sure to be spotted by deer coming his way.

Mature bucks are adept at sneaking around drive lines or remaining bedded until drivers pass and then getting up and slipping off in the opposite direction. Now is when the buttonhook drive pays off.

on stand, for when the buck is moved yet again he'll likely use the same escape corridor as before.

By the same token, those hunters who are to act as drivers should allow their stand hunters plenty of time to get into position. It's simply a wasted effort to begin the drive five minutes too early, before the standers are well situated at their intercept locations.

If a combination of does and small bucks pass a stand hunter's location, the drive party can be certain any larger bucks in the immediate vicinity decided to hold tight; otherwise, they would have been the first ones out.

Actually, this is a far more common occurrence than most hunters realize. Big bucks select their hiding places with craft and cunning, and are reluctant to abandon these security havens because they know that rising from their beds and exposing themselves greatly increases their vulnerability. Consequently, when a hunter filters through their area, such deer quite often lower their chins right down onto the ground and then don't even blink.

Therefore, after a drive has been concluded, if members of your group have reason to believe there still is a buck in the cover somewhere, there's only one

thing to do: drive the cover a second or even a third time until the buck is either routed out or everyone becomes convinced he wasn't there in the first place.

Don't make the mistake of driving the cover in the same manner as before. Try something different, such as driving the cover in the opposite direction with your stand hunters placed in the vicinity of where the drivers began on the previous drive.

It's also worth mentioning that when you're staging drives on succeeding days, you should likewise avoid running your drives in the same manner as you did earlier. The only thing this will accomplish is educating the deer in that area.

Take a ten-acre, rectangular-shaped briar patch. This type of cover offers a buck a myriad of splendid hiding possibilities, but if your drivers consistently approach from the west, it won't take the buck in residence very long to learn where the danger is always going to come from.

The second time you drive the briars, have your drivers approach from the south, the next time from the east, and so on, assuming the nature of the terrain allows for such alterations. This way, especially if you are the lucky beneficiaries of windy weather, the deer will remain totally confused and not know which direction to expect danger. Nor will they ever know the surest escape route to avoid being detected by the hunters placed on stand.

When Deer Double Back

In many instances, a buck will hold tight in his bed, allowing a driver to pass, and then rise to his feet and attempt to slip out the back door, so to speak. He probably will not leave his chosen cover, but simply relocate his bed a slight distance away.

Imagine that you are in a jungle, trying to hide from someone. If that person passes close by, but you know you are well concealed, chances are you'll hunker down and stay put. Then, after that person passes and continues on for some distance, chances are you'll begin moving in the opposite direction in order to increase the distance separating you and your adversary.

White-tailed bucks behave much the same. And there is one trick that will stack the odds in your favor. It's called by various names such as the buttonhook drive, or fishhook drive, but by any description the methodology is the same.

In using a rectangular-shaped pine plantation for purposes of illustration, let's place two hunters on stand along the far border of the pines. At the opposite end, two drivers space themselves a comfortable distance apart and begin sneak hunting through the pines toward their partners in the distance.

However, the two drivers don't actually proceed all the way through the pines to where their partners are on stand. They only travel perhaps two-thirds of the way through the pines, then they about-face' and begin sneak hunting back toward their starting points. Quite often, one of the drivers will have an almost point-blank shot at a deer trying to slip away.

An intriguing aspect to all of this is that any buck that has doubled back to get behind the drivers may figure out what the drivers are up to when they engage in their buttonhook maneuver. Now the buck will double back yet a second time, to get behind the drivers once again. And this will take him in the direction of the hunters on stand!

A one-man drive is effective when a hunter who has filled his tag wants to help his partners. If he slowly wanders around like a farmhand, with no attempt to be sneaky, deer will move out of his way and hopefully expose themselves to the hunters waiting on stand.

The One-Man Drive

A solo drive is just the ticket when one member of a party has already taken his buck, while the rest of the hunters in the group want to wait on stands overlooking deer trails. The hunter who has already taken his buck can now help his partners fill their tags by playing dog.

Standers climb into their perches or ground blinds in pre-dawn darkness for the customary morning watch. But then, sometime in mid-morning, the lone driver begins hiking randomly through the cover without regard to wind direction. He makes no special effort to sneak or quiet his footfalls. I often whistle softly to myself as though I'm a forestry worker doing a routine timber survey or a farmer counting livestock.

Since deer regularly see such people afield, a lone individual going about his business rarely alarms them. They simply get up and move out of his line of travel, using one of their established trails to relocate to an adjacent area. One driver moving in an erratic, snakelike pattern can keep deer slowly circulating all day, and eventually his partners watching various trails should have shooting opportunities.

Mini drives of the type described here can be quite challenging because they tax the ingenuity of all participants. But they're also loads of fun, and often result in new additions to the camp meatpole.

Wind, Scent, and the Whitetail

KATHY ETLING

The whitetail buck moves steadily along the trail, head burdened beneath a huge set of antlers. As he travels, he occasionally pauses to sniff both ground and air, searching for danger. All is well, so the buck continues onward. A twig snaps, and the animal's cupped ears pick up the sound. He halts, every muscle tensed for flight. But when a squirrel begins chattering, the buck twitches his tail and plods ahead. Later, the buck's eyes catch a flash of movement. He stops. Suspicious, he drops his head to scope out the terrain. Again it's nothing, just a turkey trying to locate its flock. He relaxes and moves forward. Then the air currents deliver something his ever-alert senses will absolutely not accept: the smell of a human.

Knowing that his survival depends on an immediate decision, the buck springs into action. He pivots and bounds back the way he just came. He could have snorted, but larger bucks often won't allow themselves the luxury of making noise. This particular buck just disappears, like smoke, back into the forest. Two hundred yards ahead, a lone hunter sits in his stand, oblivious to the fact that a record-book whitetail was so close just a few short seconds ago.

Such is the way of the wary whitetail. We may sometimes fool its ears, occasionally fool its eyes, but only rarely, if ever, can we fool this animal's incredible sense of smell. Some of the best whitetail hunters have given up even trying. Instead, they make what they know about air, wind, and whitetails work for them. Before taking a look at how some super whitetail hunters do this, along with some facts recently discovered by researchers, let's first examine the basics.

Successful hunters like Peter Fiduccia bank on being able to fool the whitetail's eyes, ears, and nose. (Credit: Peter Fiduccia Enterprises.)

Human Scent

A human must smell pretty repulsive to a whitetail. But is it really our smell? Or is it what wild deer associate with it—danger! In either case, even the faintest whiff is enough to send deer into a panic. If they smell humans, most of them run away or hide.

Human scent, or body odor, consists of several components: sweat, breath, **pheromones** (similar to the whitetail's), and faint smells released by other bodily secretions like those from our sebaceous (oil) glands. Many individual scents combine to form an odor that would probably be as identifiable to each one of us as a whitetail's is to him, *if* our sense of smell were as acute as a deer's. Even though it's not, pheromones and our own personal scent are what makes us attractive to prospective mates, or so scientists tell us.

How each of us smells depends, in good part, on our personal hygiene and habits. We can avoid meat, strong spices, alcohol, and tobacco and bathe with unscented deodorant soap to minimize our natural scent. But it's doubtful that we will ever be able to eradicate it completely. Human scent is a problem, but when it comes to hunting deer, it's only a small part of the problem. The real problem lies in how that scent is dispersed.

Air

Air is the culprit here—the air all around us. No matter where we may move, our bodies must travel through air. Even when the atmosphere around us appears to be dead calm, ever-present air molecules combine with the gaseous scent molecules given off by our bodies, so as we move, our scent is left behind. Even if we don't move at all, our scent certainly does. Unfortunately for those of us who hunt, the air is never perfectly still.

Wind

Wind is simply air in motion. It is pure energy that constantly moves across the earth's face. It may move so slightly we can't even feel it, or it may blow in tornado-like gusts. The weight of the air, or **air pressure,** is the driving force behind wind. High-pressure areas around the globe are continuously shifting as they rush to fill low-pressure voids. Wind results. Think of a balloon. If you fill the balloon with air and hold the end shut, all is well: The air is contained. But release your grip on the balloon just a slight degree, and the high-pressure air inside surges violently outward to join lower-pressure air. As the earth rotates, its motion affects both wind speed and direction. And when wind skims over topographic features such as mountains, forests, and deserts, the friction produced also influences wind speed and direction. Tremendous problems confront anyone, whether meteorologist or hunter, attempting to predict what the wind in a given area will be doing in an hour, a day, or a week.

Thermals

Most hunters have had deer smell them when deer seemingly shouldn't have been able to do so. **Thermal currents** were almost certainly to blame. Thermal basics are simple in that, as with wind, thermals aren't always totally predictable. Meteorologists call them **thermal slope winds**. According to theory, as air warms each morning, it flows upward from valley floors to ridgetops. Warm air rises because it is lighter and less dense than colder air. As warm air rises, it carries scent along with it. At sunset, the reverse is true. Ridgetops cool swiftly, while the valley floor remains warm. But while this warmer air continues to rise above the valley, the ridgetop's heavier, colder air displaces it as it flows down the slopes. The result is simply this: each evening, scent should drift downhill, while each morning scent should rise. Even with the prevailing wind in your favor, though, these thermal slope winds can occasionally give you away.

Thermals are especially unpredictable when they contribute to what are popularly known as "swirling" winds. When winds swirl, friction is usually a contributing factor. Try for a moment to imagine a southwesterly wind (one that blows *from* the southwest) as it gathers speed over an open field. The wind gains speed because nothing exists in that field to slow it down. Imagine that wind now slamming into a forest at the field's northeast edge. The resulting friction forces much of the wind up and over the treetops, but some will find its way through the trees. If field and forest are both located in a valley, hunters in the woods near the field's edge would logically believe that when the wind comes over the field like this, their human scent will be dispersed toward the forest. Should they hunt in the morning, they'll think rising thermals will carry their scent up to the ridgetop beyond the forest. But here's the catch: When thermals are confronted by friction, they may do the unexpected. Thermals influenced by friction might carry scent aloft, then drop it back onto the valley floor in the opposite direction from where the wind is blowing. The invisible air eddies thus formed may hold hunter's scents in places they least expect them to be.

Missouri's Jim Holdenried can confirm this. An accomplished bowhunter and firearms hunter, Holdenried has experimented with wind and its currents. To do so, he tosses handfuls of baking soda into the air simply to observe the ways in which it drifts. "You can actually see air currents swirling," he said. "From years of experience, I know deer will readily move when winds are strong. I firmly believe that they gather in spots where air eddies form. They feel safe there, because eddies will concentrate and hold most of the scent in an area."

Holdenried discovered one such spot that seems to attract deer whenever wind conditions are right. To keep deer from detecting him before climbing into his stand, Jim refuses to hunt this stand unless everything is perfect. Because of this, he may only hunt this spot two mornings a year. Yet every time he does, he sees three or four bucks. "One morning I saw two huge bucks, but the wind gave me away before I could draw on either one," he said. Later that morning, however, he killed a nice 6-pointer.

"The bucks that I spooked had approached my stand site from downhill, so the thermals should have been in my favor," Holdenried recalled. "The wind was from the southeast [blowing toward the northwest], while the deer were traveling toward the northeast. No way should they have been able to smell me until they were within bow range, but they did, and I believe it was because of the way the wind was swirling."

Since Holdenried hunts inside a line of woods near the edge of an open field, friction was probably the culprit here. But in the process of investigating the way winds swirl, he learned something else about whitetails: During periods of high wind, deer are often more active than usual. This fact was verified in the landmark four-year Texas whitetail radiotelemetry study mentioned in previous sections. "We divided wind speeds into five groups for this study," study co-author Dr. Steve Demarais explained. "These were: 0 MPH to 4 MPH; 5 to 9 MPH; 10 to 14 MPH; 15 to 19 MPH; and 20 MPH and above. We discovered that deer moved quite readily when wind speeds registered from 0 to 4 MPH. Their activity levels then declined as the speed of the wind increased, until they bottomed out when wind speeds reached 15 to 19 MPH."

But surprisingly, when winds exceeded 20 MPH, deer activity was highest. "High winds aren't common here, so we had fewer observations to base our data on," Demarais noted. "Still, this study definitely revealed to us that deer move the most when winds are strongest."

When pressed for an explanation, Demarais made a guess. "I think that when it's really windy deer lose their ability to sense the environment around them.

Dr. Steve Demarais and Bob Zaiglin discovered in their Texas telemetry study that bucks move readily in winds of between zero and four miles per hour. (Credit: Brad Harris.)

They can't hear, see, or smell as well as they usually can. They move because they're nervous. When winds are highest, deer will even run at strange sounds because they can't figure out what caused them.

"Any reasons as to why deer move more during high winds would only be a guess, but we do have a theory. During moderately high winds, deer probably bed down. They are sound-, sight-, and smell-oriented, and when wind picks up it confuses these senses. They consequently don't move around as much, at least up to a point. But then, when winds really pick up speed, deer get skittish and scared. They get up and move *more*, possibly because they're nervous. Maybe they move

more because high winds often accompany weather fronts. But that brings up another item we were able to verify for the big buck hunter: Bucks move best on the day a weather front moves through an area. And, surprisingly, they move just as well the day *after* the front moves through."

Study data such as these prove that dedicated hunters shouldn't give up when the wind is at its worst. They should just plan to hunt *in the wind.* Why? Because that could very well be the best time to bag a buck.

Two other top hunters have turned whitetail hunting in the wind into a science. One of them, Dr. Bob Sheppard, an internist from Carrollton, Alabama, has been hunting whitetails for thirty years. Sheppard's taken many deer, some of them real trophies. He's killed most of them on public land, too, and lets the wind select his hunting location for the day.

To be fair, someone who does as much scouting and planning as Sheppard does deserves to succeed. Still, his methods—even on a small scale—should work for anyone. He first obtains topographic maps of his hunting areas from the U.S. Geological Survey. Then he buys satellite infrared photos of these areas if they're available for that sector. In Alabama, prime sources for these photos include the county office of the U.S. government's Agriculture Stabilization and Conservation Service (ASCS) as well as various timber companies. Old military photos are another possibility. These photos are both big—forty inches by forty inches covers 3,500 acres—and fairly expensive . . . but worthwhile if you can talk someone into selling them. (Sometimes the ASCS will part with them when an updated version becomes available; Sheppard says you just have to keep trying.) At one time, Sheppard used standard aerial photos from the ASCS, and they'll work, too, but he changed to the satellite infrared versions because they're so much more detailed.

Sheppard scouts during February and March in thousand-acre chunks at a time. "I walk back and forth, from east to west, and then from north to south," he said. "I go over as much as I can to find out how the land lays and what the available cover is like. Then I look for any bottlenecks and funnels that could force a deer to use a certain area, and later log that information on my master map. I'll also note any good deer sign near potential stand locations. I use numbered thumbtacks for each spot and position these on my map. Each number corresponds with a place to hunt. Each numbered location is also entered into my computer database along with all pertinent details."

Some of the details Sheppard enters concern the wind. "I decide which way the wind should be blowing for both the best approach to the stand and the best chance of success while hunting it," he said. "Right now, I own six forty-by-forty maps that have a total of about five hundred thumbtacks stuck in them. Before I go hunting, the first thing I do is turn my radio to the weather channel to find out which way the wind is blowing. If it's blowing from the northeast, I type "NE" into my computer and it prints out a list of all the best places to hunt under those wind conditions."

Sheppard uses a portable computer that goes with him to deer camp. Anyone wanting to adapt this system for personal use could start a manual system using index cards, but it would take a bit longer to access than an electronic one. Another trick Sheppard uses when he's deer hunting is to tie a piece of No. 8 black sewing thread to either his broadhead or the end of his gun barrel while he's in his stand. He also ties a piece of thread to a tree limb down at ground level. By watching both threads, he can tell whether the wind is consistent or whether it's shifting from place to place. If it shifts too much for the stand to be effective, he'll move to a different one.

"It's amazing how much turbulence there is when you're hunting along an edge," he commented. "The air can flow around a steep hill or a clear-cut just like water flows around a rock in a river. The wind may look like it's blowing your scent away from an area when you're twelve or fourteen feet up in a tree. But at ground level, it can be an entirely different story. That's why I use thread, so I'm sure."

One hunter with a less scientific approach—yet one who gets real results—is Angela Vogel of Cottage Hills, Illinois. "Angel" has taken a number of Pope and Young bucks since she started bowhunting in the mid 1980s. "I became addicted to hunting big bucks without even knowing it," she said. "They're what I'm after, and to me they make the hunt worthwhile."

Vogel is another fanatic about wind and her various stand locations. She's been known to spend two hundred hours bowhunting each season, and when she can, she prefers positioning at least twenty tree stands from which she can choose each day. Like Bob Sheppard's, some of Vogel's locations are good only when the wind blows from a certain direction. She got her second Pope and Young buck because she was patient enough to wait for an east wind before hunting a spot that she'd suspected for quite some time had real trophy potential. "I'd found a steep ravine that connected two crop fields," Vogel explained. "It was a natural pathway for deer. But although it was full of sign, I knew the only way I'd be able to hunt it right was if an east wind was blowing. We don't get many east winds, but since I waited until everything was perfect, I shot a big buck the first time I hunted there." Vogel's "east wind" buck scored 159⅜ points, good enough to qualify as a nontypical for Pope and Young.

Vogel bagged her third Pope and Young trophy while hunting during a forty-mile-per-hour wind. "Terribly windy," she remembered, "but the bucks were tremendously active. I'd been using a grunt call, but in all honesty I can't say that the deer were responding to it. I'm not even sure they could hear

Illinois's Angel Vogel won't hunt in a particular stand unless the wind is perfect.
(Credit: Kathy Etling.)

it. But first a 6-point buck came in, and then an 8-point. Both were acting crazy, so I figured a doe in heat was probably nearby. I kept waiting and hoping, and then this big, beautiful buck came in. I shot him from fourteen yards, and he dropped in his tracks." The buck was Vogel's largest to date, with sixteen scoreable points. It tallied up 174⅞ nontypical inches of antler under the Pope and Young scoring system.

It's hard to fool a whitetail's incredible sense of smell. But now, perhaps, we can do what these hunters have done for years. We can make what we now know about air, wind, and the whitetail work for us this coming season.

Scents and Non-Scents

Before hunters can deceive a whitetail's ears or eyes, they must first understand the many ways they can deceive the animal's nose. Some hunters swear by whitetail scents. Others wouldn't use them if their lives depended on it. What most hunters seem to believe, no matter what their predilection, is that whitetail scents will work *on occasion*. Through both

trial and error and paying attention to tips provided here, you should be able to determine the best time and way to fit scents—or the lack thereof—into your own hunting routines.

The first whitetail I ever killed was taken in a spot where I'd sprayed nearly an entire can of apple scent. There were no apple orchards within a hundred miles, so I'm not really sure why the deer was there. Nothing works like success, however, and I, for one, was hooked on scents for years afterward. Other hunters believe that it doesn't really matter if a tasty food source isn't present in a certain part of a whitetail's range. They think that if a food lure smells enticing enough, whitetails will be drawn to it anyway. Whether the smell attracts deer looking to fill their bellies, or simply because the animals are curious, will probably never be known for certain.

What *is* known is this: Should you decide to use scents, choose well-known brands. **Matrix scent,** a combination of urine, glandular matter, and secretions from non-rutting bucks and does, is an all-season scent. It is especially effective during the early season before animals become almost immune to all the new smells wafting through the forest. Other excellent all-season scents include **tarsal gland scent, interdigital gland scent,** and **forehead gland scent,** the latter combining glandular secretions from whitetails' preorbital and sudoriferous glands.

Both **doe-in-estrus scent** and **buck urine** seem to work best just prior to the rut and immediately afterward. Most bucks are so busy chasing does during the rut that bottled scent seems to hold little appeal for them at that time. The exception may occur in an area with low deer densities where bucks are actively seeking does. Enough hunters report success using scent during the rut's peak that many experts put out these scents anyway. They believe that it won't hurt anything, and that it might actually help.

Some hunters will use a *coverup* or *masking scent* such as raccoon urine, fox urine, or coyote urine to mask their human odor, which can linger along the trails they take to get to their stands. Wearing high-topped rubber boots also cuts down on human scent dispersal and may be a wiser tactic. If you are dead set on using a masking scent, however, then use raccoon scent. Not only are raccoons not predators, and therefore not threats to deer, but they also climb trees. A curious deer that follows a raccoon's scent trail won't find it unusual to discover that the "raccoon" has climbed a tree.

I quit using skunk as a masking scent a long time ago, after spooking numerous deer. Once I began thinking about it, I realized that anything that would spook a skunk (and cause it to spray its scent) would probably make a whitetail uneasy, too.

Lures (food attractants) such as apple scent will probably work best in areas where that scent is commonly found. Use acorn scent in a forest of oaks, pine scent in a region of pines, and so on. But never discount the curiosity factor when confronted with the thorny problem of whether or not to use a particular scent. Whitetails may be compelled to check out an unusual or new scent they've never before smelled.

Some hunters carry scent-matching to extremes. They believe that the pine scent contained in a particular bottle may not be the exact same pine scent with which deer in their hunting area are familiar. After all, there are many different species of pine trees. They may all smell the same to us, but what should concern us most is how they smell to a whitetail.

Probably the most valid use of deer scent is for making *mock scrapes.* Mock scrapes continue to be underused tools, probably because they involve so much work. To make an effective mock scrape, scout your locations well before the pre-rut period. A garden claw and long-handled trowel will come

in handy, and always wear rubber gloves. Whenever possible, remove and freeze the tarsal glands from the previous season's deer, but if that's not an option, either buy a good grade of tarsal gland scent or use a freeze-dried tarsal gland that can be rehydrated. The mock scrape is, in effect, simply another method of decoying deer, albeit one that attempts to fool a whitetail's eyes and nose.

The final deceit is the elimination of most, if not all, human scent. There are several ways in which this can accomplished. The first way is time-consuming but inexpensive—a method I used years ago, I collected leaves, branches, and grasses from the area near my deer stand. I placed this vegetation inside a pillow case, tied the case shut, then tossed pillow case and my hunting clothes into the washing machine. I ran through a plain warm water cycle so that the natural scents permeated all my gear, then dried everything—sticks, leaves, and grass included—in the dryer. Once the clothes were dry, I stored them in a large plastic garbage bag tightly tied shut. I then wore those clothes to my stand and tried my best not to get sweaty along the way. (I sometimes changed into my scented clothing at the stand and stashed my sweaty clothing in the plastic bag to prevent the whitetails' keen noses from detecting it.)

Mickey Hellickson, wildlife manager for the King Ranches in Texas, pays strict attention to the wind whenever he hunts the ranch's vast holdings, whether for himself or with a client. "I'm not a big believer in cover scents or attractants," Hellickson said. "When I'm rattling, I pick positions where I'm able to see downwind openings where bucks may come in. I suppose the closest attention I ever paid to masking my scent was before I'd moved down to Texas from Iowa. Back then, I'd store my clothes in a sack with soil I'd gathered from around an old, rotten stump. That soil had such a rich, heavy smell, I thought it would work perfectly as a cover scent."

Although the technology is expensive, odor-eliminating suits and outerwear are worth the investment. Some garments are made to be worn under hunting clothes but over underwear. Other items have been manufactured as outerwear, complete with a soft, quiet microfiber shell. Such clothing has many small patches of odor-eating carbon integrated into the fabric. The carbon literally blocks human odor from reaching the surrounding air. Of course, for the technology to work best, all your other gear, as well as your hair and exposed skin surfaces, should also be as scent-free as possible. I have worn as many as three layers of scent-adsorbing clothing to try to completely beat the whitetail's almost otherworldly sense of smell. The results are worth the time, effort, and money I've spent. I've had bucks nearly step on me while I was hunting on the ground—even when they approached me from downwind!

When clothing made with carbon technology loads up with too much human odor, deer will start smelling you. They may simply behave in a more nervous manner. They may make low snorts, as though trying to clear the scent from their noses. Keep in mind that most whitetails live in relatively close proximity to human activity. It is not unusual for them to occasionally get a whiff of human scent. What your aim as a hunter should be is to reduce your human scent to an acceptable level. Scent-adsorption clothing does this better than anything else. To make such clothes scent-free once again, simply toss them into a clothes dryer set on high for a minimum of forty-five minutes.

Magicians use smoke and mirrors to perform illusions in our everyday world. In the whitetail's world, you can create your own brand of magic, doing what may seem downright impossible: making whitetails appear by making yourself disappear . . . and tricking their noses in the process.

I've worn as many as three layers of scent-adsorbent clothing to try to completely beat the whitetail's phenomenal sense of smell.
(Credit: Bob Etling.)

How to Use Thermals to Your Advantage

My favorite tree stand was a top producer for years. It sat high atop the crest of a ridge overlooking a seventy-five-foot-wide power line right-of-way that was cleared of brush every four or five years by the local utility company. From my vantage point in this stand I was able to observe a number of whitetail travel lanes. Through the years, I took several high-quality bucks from this stand. It was a wonderful spot, complete with an outstanding view, but I used it for so long that local whitetails became wary of it.

Biologists have noted that cultural knowledge plays a critical part in the survival strategies a whitetail adopts. Simply put, if a deer suspects a place is dangerous, it somehow is able to pass that knowledge along to other deer. I believe that is what happened to my power line stand. Since some of the bucks I shot had been chasing does at the time, I believe those same does later spread the news that my power line right-of-way was a dangerous place for deer.

After several years of consistent success, I realized that the local deer had adopted some annoying—to me—habits. When I first set up my stand, they filtered across the right-of-way all morning long. They stopped—presumably to bed down—during early afternoon hours, then resumed crossing at about 4:00 p.m.

Over time, that all changed. The deer slowly became warier. In the mornings, I combated this increased wariness by wearing a camouflage face mask and sitting very still. Deer still looked my way, but if the wind was right and all else appeared normal, they were usually lulled into thinking no one was about.

Evenings presented a dilemma, however. When I first started hunting there, does, fawns, and small bucks traveled down the hillsides that funneled into the gorge in front of my stand. When evening approached, they climbed back out of the gorge to cross the power line right-of-way en route to nighttime feeding grounds. Nothing bothered them—but then their behaviors changed. After about five years, the whitetails started holing up in the gorge until well past shooting hours. The gorge—which is on adjoining property where no hunting is allowed—is extremely deep and thick with brush and timber. I was not unable to see any deer waiting—staging—within it, nor would it have been legal to shoot them if I somehow had seen them. But I sure could hear them.

I believe these deer were making good use of the knowledge that late afternoon, when the sun starts its slide toward the horizon, is the ideal time to lie low and wait. Even under totally windless conditions, even when I was scrupulously clean and wearing scent-blocking clothing, these deer often started snorting. Low levels of human scent, which at one point didn't faze them, now sent them into a panic. They waited in the gorge, constantly testing the air, putting to good use the "zero tolerance" policy they seemed to have adopted for even the merest whiff of human scent.

The best bucks I've taken from this stand were all shot during the morning when thermals were rising. The only buck I ever shot there in the afternoon was a 10-point spooked by a hunter on a neighboring farm. Had the buck not been fleeing another hunter, I doubt if I would have seen him.

I finally got fed up wasting every afternoon on a stand that had never been an evening producer. On the third day of that year's firearms season, I began wondering where I could go to make the most of the dwindling afternoon. I went over in my mind the basics we all learn when we first start hunting whitetails. *Why* were deer lurking in that gorge each evening? And not just small bucks, but even the does that might pull into view a lust-crazed larger buck? The answer was simple: The deer knew about my stand and knew about me. They waited until after dark in the lowest spot available, where evening thermals would deliver any scents of danger.

How could I fool them? I had to adapt, as they had.

I realized that I simply could not get these particular deer. Their staging area was not on our property, nor was it legal to hunt there. But since our farm is full of similar steep-sided gorges and rugged hollows, finding another area where whitetails might also be staging seemed like a viable option. I began to plot a strategy.

That year, the acorn crop had been an almost total bust. The deer I had seen in the power line right-of-way had been browsing on oak brush and grazing on open-country grasses and forbs.

Since the deer had been reduced to browsing and grazing, I decided to hunt close to a pasture where I'd occasionally seen deer feeding in the evening. This pasture followed a gentle ridge line that, at its terminus, dropped steeply off into a small creek bottom. That small creek in turn dumped into another, larger creek. I set up on the ground at the juncture of those creeks, about as low as I could go and still be downwind of the field, yet able to scan its edges.

I settled into position at 4:00 p.m. I made a doe blat, and within ten minutes I saw several does traveling inside the treeline, just outside the field edge. A small buck followed, nose to the ground. The group milled about where the field cornered with the woods, noses scent-testing the air. I wasn't sure that they had heard my call at all. When I squirted some of my wind-check powder into the air, it swirled down to the ground, then streamed down-hollow, away from the deer. Unable to scent me, the whitetails fed up the hill, browsing inside the woods until they were out of sight.

Then I heard a noise behind me, and I slowly turned my head. At the crest of a saddle stood a fairly good buck. He'd crawled under a fence and was heading down the creek bottom toward my position. I wasn't sure at first whether to try for him. He had good mass and some decent width, but his tine length seemed weak. For several minutes, I wasn't sure I would even have a chance, for when he reached the creek bottom he began scent-checking the air. He stood there for ten minutes tossing his head and sniffing, first one way, then the other. It was obvious that he'd performed this maneuver before. Finally, he started walking—straight down the creek. He veered when he was about fifty yards from me, now angling about ten feet above the hollow's floor. I wasn't planning to shoot—until I saw his antlers going away from me. When he paused, looking around, perhaps for the doe that had uttered the bleat, his nearly white rack

suddenly looked very good indeed. I shot and he ran in a circle and fell. My .280 Remington's bullet had pierced his heart.

Deciding to take a buck based on what its rack looks like going away is not a particularly bright thing to do. The 8-pointer was a good buck—sixteen inches wide and sixteen inches high with fairly good mass—but he wasn't a *great* buck. I was grateful, though, for having had the chance to take him after waiting less than an hour on a spur-of-the-moment ground blind. I knew I was onto something important.

Each year I speak to many people about hunting whitetails and hear the same complaint: They have a good morning stand that peters out in the afternoon. Or perhaps they'll see deer in the evening but rarely in the morning. What should they do?

"You've got to really work those thermals," said the late Terry Kayser of Horizons West Outfitting in Dodson, Montana. My husband, Bob, and I hunted with Kayser when he was outfitting in the rugged Cabinet Divide Mountains near Heron, Montana. Each morning, he placed us in lonesome clear-cuts at the top of his world. In the late afternoons he moved us to stands located along river bottoms or in valleys—as low as he could get us. That's how I scored at five o'clock one evening on a really good 10-point buck at the edge of a lowland cedar swamp. At the time, Kayser was rattling for Bob somewhere out of sight of my location. I couldn't hear him rattling, and I'll never know whether the buck could or not. All I know is that the buck came busting out of the bog, stood at the edge of a giant clearing for several minutes alternately scent-checking the wind and refreshing one of his scrapes, then came barreling across a stretch of open prairie. I shot him as he dawdled near a second scrape.

"I learned long ago that whenever you are rattling or calling, or even if you're just waiting in a stand, hunt low in the evenings and high in the mornings," Kayser told me. "If deer are holed up because of bad weather, wait until later in the day and then try working your way downhill, calling as you go, with the wind in your face. That's a good way to jump deer bedded near bottoms, where scent will be swirling on stormy, low-pressure days. You have to learn to work the thermals, because deer always do," he said.

"Hunt high, hunt low" seems like an easy concept to grasp, but it can work against you. First, if you get on stand too early, or if you hunt extremely deep canyons such as those in some western areas, the morning sun may not warm the air fast enough to force thermals upward until eight or nine o'clock.

Second, said whitetail hunting expert Jody Hugill of College Station, Pennsylvania, "You have to watch your scent when you're hunting in bottoms. Scent can sometimes stall in low places. If it seems 'windstill' in a bottom as the air starts to cool, the scent that's already there may actually be pooling. Stay alert to subtle air movement that will carry your scent almost imperceptibly away from any area you plan to watch. Under windstill conditions, scent pools in the deepest spot. If you hunt at the very end of this 'pool,' you might be able to pick off whitetails as they either pass through or stage there before heading to nighttime feeding areas."

Hugill is right. Even in windstill conditions, a good scent-check powder or other wind-testing device (e.g., API's Windfloaters or Pete Richards Wind Detector) may reveal a pronounced air current, often in the direction of the prevailing wind.

"I noticed this tendency of scent to drift on several occasions, even under seemingly windstill conditions when I was sure whitetails would scent me, yet didn't," Hugill said. "Afterward I wondered, how did I get away with that? So I began checking the wind under every possible set of conditions using my own homemade variations of Windfloaters. At summer's end, I'd collect dried milkweed pods or Canadian thistle heads. I broke them open, gripped

the seeds between my thumb and index finger, and yanked with the other hand to separate them from the floating silky fibers. I stored these 'floaters' in plastic bags, then stuffed some into a film canister when I went hunting. They worked great and didn't cost a dime."

Hugill said he has often dropped one of his floaters and watched it drift down a creek bottom, make a large circle, and return. "That's why I know pooling scent can contaminate a large area. By understanding this, you can make certain your stand is properly positioned."

"Steep-sided hollows produce more swirling evening thermals than will more open creek bottoms," agreed master deer hunter Mark Drury. "I'll go low in evenings too, but only if I can locate a consistent wind direction—even if only a subtle one—that helps me take advantage of thermals."

"If there is one thing that is going to negatively affect a hunter who decides to use calls or rattling, that one thing will be not paying attention to scent, wind, and thermals," said Bob Zaiglin. "Even when walking in to a stand site, I'll try always to walk with the wind hitting me in the face. This gives me a chance to walk up on a deer, sure. But it also means I won't be spooking out every deer in the countryside."

"I probably have a different view on the wind than many experts," said Brad Harris. "Other hunters have told me that their deer usually come in from a downwind direction. Now, calling is my passion; it is the one thing that I do all the time. I know I can't see every deer that responds, but I have had very few deer ever try to skirt me and come in from downwind."

Why does Harris think this is so? "Well, once I have a deer on the string, I'm not about to let up. I continue to call or rattle aggressively, doing everything in my power to get it to come in. I don't want it to have the time to think about the situation and decide, *I have to go downwind.* I firmly believe that a deer will do this when a hunter sees a deer on its way, drops the call, and sets up. Heck, yes, that makes a deer nervous. All of a sudden the deer's thinking, *Where did that noise go? Why did it stop? Uh-oh, I'd better go downwind to check up on it.* If any deer stops to look the situation over, that's when I'm going to call or rattle for all I'm worth. I want to reassure it that, yes, I'm right here. I don't want the deer to think it over. I want it to know I'm here and I'm waiting. As long as I'm calling, I'm in control. If you do what many experts suggest, you risk letting the deer's natural instincts take over. It's a lot like playing a big bass. When you've got it on, your best bet is to keep the line tight and reel it right in to where you are waiting."

The science of air, scent, wind, and non-scents isn't rocket science. It doesn't take an Einstein to be able to figure out how to trick a whitetail's nose as easily as we sometimes trick its eyes and ears. What it does require is the willingness to pay close attention to every detail that transpires in the whitetail woods or plains each time you go out the door. Only knowing what worked and why, as well as when to resort to the same tactics again, will pay off in the end.

Getting Started Rattling, Rattling—What to Expect

Does rattling sound like a hunting tactic you'd like to try, yet you're not quite sure where or how to begin? Does it make sense to wait until you get a deer this year, and then saw off its antlers? Perhaps you have a set of antlers from a deer you took last season, or before. Or, perhaps you can prevail upon someone you know for his or her next set of antlers. Should you wait until spring when you can go hunting for a nice, fresh set of matched sheds? And what's wrong with synthetics, anyway? Do they work as well as the real McCoy? Do sheds work as well

or sound as realistic as fresh antlers? What about rattling devices? Surely whitetails must suspect that any "rattling" created by store-bought devices is phony, right?

Through the years I've interviewed many whitetail experts for the express purpose of learning what each believed was the most foolproof way of rattling in whitetails. While each expert's methods are amazingly similar to those of the others, and while even their preferred rattling sequences bear more than a passing resemblance to those of the other experts, and while the parameters they look for when they are preparing to set up are not that much different, it's clear that each of our experts has definite opinions about what another hunter should do and use to create the most realistic-sounding mock buck battles possible.

Synthetic, Real, or Something Else?

I've used both synthetic antlers and real antlers, and I honestly have never been able to tell much difference between the two. I've rattled in deer using both types. If I were asked to put my feelings about the two antler types into words, I suppose I would say that real antlers sound more solid when clashed together. The synthetics I used seemed to be slightly higher-pitched, and they seemed to reverberate a bit more. I can't truthfully say this reverberation is a negative, though. The sound from the synthetic antlers might actually have carried farther because of it than the sound from my real rattling horns. Were I to go rattling at this very moment, whether I would grab the synthetics or authentic would be a moot point. In fact, I'm so impressed with a few of the rattling devices I've recently seen that I just might use them instead. But more about them later.

Some hunters swear that nothing sounds like a fresh set of rattling horns. But if you bring antlers inside at the end of each day and rarely expose them to the elements, even a twenty-year-old set

Jerry Shively used real antlers to lure this fine Montana buck in for Mark Easterling.
(Credit: Jerry Shively.)

Although Bob Zaiglin prefers to use fresh sheds to rattle in bucks, he has done quite well with synthetics, too, as evidenced by the buck in this photo.
(Credit: Bob Zaiglin.)

will sound identical to a set removed from a buck's head today. To get that so-called "fresh" sound, some hunters soak their sheds in water, no matter how new they may be, for several ours. Others rub their sheds down with petroleum jelly to seal in freshness. Still other experts prefer oiling or waxing their sheds with a scent-free product to preserve that "just-off-the-buck" degree of freshness.

Bob Zaiglin uses a large set of real antlers for his rattling horns. Mickey Hellickson looks for the heaviest, freshest pair of shed antlers he can find. "I've been using some massive horns lately," Hellickson said. "I cut off the brow tines and then shaved the surrounding area smooth to the beam so they're easy to grip. A large set of horns produces the greatest volume. My study revealed that volume is more important than any other factor to rattling success. The higher the volume, the greater the distance over which it will be heard. The greater

the distance, the more bucks that will hear it. And if more bucks hear your rattling, more bucks are bound to respond."

Proponents of using real antlers include other successful hunters, too, experts like Peter Fiduccia, Jay Cassell, and Jim Holdenried. "Using smaller antlers won't discourage smaller bucks from investigating," Fiduccia pointed out. "And smaller antlers are far easier to pack around." Cassell agrees. "I want to imitate the sound of smaller bucks fighting," he said. "By doing so, I hope to lure in a larger buck who's hoping to whip both their [smaller bucks'] butts."

Fiduccia noted that synthetic antlers usually don't have to be modified for safety's sake, but that if you don't modify real antlers you could be hurt in an accident while pulling them into your stand, climbing hills, or negotiating bluffs. "Always be cautious when using real antlers in a public hunting area," he warned. Fiduccia modified his set of smaller antlers by trimming off sharp tines and drilling a hole through each base where he threaded a lanyard.

According to Peter Fiduccia, not only will smaller antlers rattle in bucks of all sizes, they're easier to pack around. (Credit: Fiduccia Enterprises.)

Modify real antlers before using them to rattle by cutting off the ends of tines; otherwise you could be seriously injured—or worse—if you fell on them while walking or climbing into a stand.
(Credit: Kathy Etling.)

"I use real antlers for the most part," said Jim Holdenried. "I prefer a set of sheds that would score about 125 Pope and Young points. Smaller rattling horns don't do it for me, particularly not for more intense, 'hard' rattling sequences." Holdenried also removes sharp tines to keep them from cutting or jabbing his hands. "I've used a rattling bag, but I have better luck with real antlers," he concluded.

"I've used real antlers, synthetic antlers, and rattling bags," noted M.R. James. "I like actual antlers, real and synthetic, because of the sounds produced when I tickle the tines together or really grind the beams. Artificial antlers don't sound as true

to me, but the deer don't seem to mind or notice. My favorite set of horns is a pair of sheds I found that score about 135 Pope and Young points."

For ease when packing into a hunting area and climbing into tree stands, James says it's hard to beat a rattle bag. "Rattle bags may have their drawbacks, but they're sure handy to tote," he said. "I prefer rattling bags full of ceramic dowels rather than wooden dowels. Ceramic just seems to work better, especially in wet weather when wood may swell and lose its crisp tones." "I've heard it all, and the best sounds are produced by real antlers or good quality synthetics," said Gary Roberson of Burnham Brothers Game Calls in Menard, Texas.

A nylon mesh rattle bag containing ceramic dowels is both easier and safer to carry than antlers, and sounds authentic enough to fool rutting bucks.
(Credit: M.R. James.)

Rattling "Tricks"

M.R. James will sometimes tie a rope to his rattling horns, then tie the rope to a bush or tree below his stand. He then lowers the antlers on this "haul" line so that they are resting in the bush or next to the sapling. When he jerks on the line, the antlers thrash about in the brush where they might attract a nearby deer.

One thing all of these hunters have in common is a high degree of originality and an ability to take tricks they've learned about and make them their own. "Some hunters will fasten a string to a sapling, then pull on it from their stand, high above, to create the illusion of a buck rubbing the sapling,"

Peter Fiduccia said. Fiduccia sometimes fills a third of a plastic zipper lock bag with fish tank gravel. He places the gravel-laden bag inside another plastic bag. He then makes a small hole through each bag, runs a long string through both, and attaches the bags to his ankle. In this manner he's able to rattle with his foot, with a minimum of movement, while he's waiting in his tree stand. As he rattles, he moves his foot back and forth to drag the bag over the undergrowth and forest litter beneath his stand. "This is just another way of setting the stage so that any buck listening will think a battle is going on," he said. "It provides a realistic sound, right down to the 'hooves' moving back and forth across the forest floor."

A rattle bag can be rolled against a tree trunk—or your leg—to create the sound of sparring bucks with a minimum amount of movement, as Wilbur Primos demonstrates. (Credit: M.R. James.)

Rattling from Ground Blinds

The argument about whether tree stands or ground blinds are better continues to rage among rattling experts. "I prefer ground blinds," said Fiduccia. "Ground blinds work better for breaking up your profile, or as something easy to hide behind. I've often made my ground blinds from stacks of cedar trees."

In agricultural areas, many hunters who rely on rattling report excellent success when set up behind a blind made of straw bales. The advantage here is that the blind is fairly stable, even during high winds, and it provides a great screen for hiding hunter movement. Being able to mask movement is vitally important to trophy bowhunters like Judy Kovar of Illinois.

Scouting for Sparring Circles

"What I'm looking for is an open spot that's surrounded by fairly heavy cover," said Jerry Shively. "The places that seem to work the best are those where I've watched bucks fighting over the years. Bucks seem to have very definite locales where they prefer to fight. You can identify one of these spots by the sparring circle evident on the ground. I've hunted this one piece of property for more than twenty years and I know all the bucks' favorite places to fight." As its name suggests, a sparring circle is a large, round area where you can tell animals were trampling the ground beneath their hooves. Grass may be flattened within this circle, or the earth may be mostly bare because bucks have fought there for many years. Brush and undergrowth may be battered and beaten, too. The ground may also reveal paw marks and antler gouges. The more such sign you discover in a particular location, the better your chances will be of rattling in a buck there.

"I don't really return to certain rattling locations per se," Bob Zaiglin said. "But I get these vibrations about a spot. I know, everybody laughs, but as I'm walking through the brush I really start feeling like *This is an area that I'd be in if I were a buck.* Or, *Man, this looks really deery. Look at all those fresh scrapes.* So, I move on to step two of my process: looking for a good place to station both my hunter and myself. I want to be in a spot where I can see in both directions. I really believe I rattle up more deer due to confidence than technique. I'm so confident when I think I've found a good spot that I'm almost positive that's why I've had such fantastic success." Zaiglin has rattled up whitetails everywhere he's hunted, even back home in Pennsylvania. In Texas, he's rattled up several hundred deer that have been taken by his hunters, and hundreds more that his hunters have passed up.

One Rattler, Two Hunters

Shively's favorite rattling tactic, when guiding hunters, is to position two hunters on stands two or three hundred yards apart. He then splits the distance between them and rattles. "My hunters usually see deer, but I won't," he said. "Since they're elevated they have a better view of the terrain. Since hundreds of yards separate them, one may see one buck while the other sees a different buck. I once had two hunters shoot at two different bucks at the same exact moment. None of us were aware of it until we got together afterward. 'I shot,' said the one. 'No, *I* shot,' said the other. My head started spinning, but then I found out they'd both scored on really nice whitetails."

Rattling from Tree Stands

If you decide to do your solo rattling from a tree stand, choose a tree with a trunk that is large enough to hide you, should the need arise. "It's a good idea to always rattle from the side of the tree where you do not expect the buck to appear," Peter Fiduccia said. "Natural cover to break up your outline is a must. It's particularly helpful beneath your feet so that any deer looking upward will be

Rattling brought both of these bucks into range—on the same morning!
(Credit: M.R. James.)

unable to make out your human silhouette." Deer peering upward are a fact of life when rattling or calling emanates from the treetops rather than from down on the ground. You can sometimes mitigate that effect by rattling from the sides of steep hollows where the sound appears to be coming from farther up the hillside, even if you are in a tree stand. The

Don Kisky keeps his rattling sequences loud but short to pull in trophy bucks like this to within bow range.
(Credit: Don and Kandy Kisky.)

risk in this maneuver is that a deer may come in higher up on the hillside, be on the same level as you, and be able to see you in the tree stand. "Another good ploy is to position yourself where you can whack your rattling horns against a leafy limb," Fiduccia said. "This simulates the sounds of a buck thrashing its rack in a bush or sapling. Don't be afraid to thwack the rattling horns against the tree's trunk, either. Doing so provides an even greater degree of realism."

"I find it hard to get deer to commit to coming in when I'm waiting in a tree stand in an area where deer can see quite well," Don Kisky said. "One of my favorite tricks is to make them think that the rattling is going on just over the hill. Whenever deer can see well, they become extremely cautious. That's why I like rattling from the edge of a bluff or creek where it's difficult for them to circle downwind of me.

Rattling Sequences

"I'll always make a snort-wheeze before I start rattling," Kisky continued. "If I see two bucks in the distance, I'll use the snort-wheeze, too. When I rattle, I really go at it. I think it's impossible to make too much noise when you rattle during the rut. Of course, when you're busy flailing around rattling, it's easy for a buck to spot you. That's one reason I keep my sequences loud, *but short*. My normal sequence lasts just ten seconds. If you rattle too long, bucks may sneak in and spot you and you'll never even know they were there." Kisky has used rattling to take many of his biggest deer. These include bucks that were gross-scored at 197, 181, 179, 177, 171, 167, and 161, among others. To say that Kisky knows what he's doing with a set of rattling horns in his hand would be a major understatement.

"I do all my hard rattling from mid- to late October," Jim Holdenried said. "Prime time for me is from the eighteenth to the thirty-first and perhaps during early November, particularly if the action is

Don Kisky likes to play with a big buck's mind by making him think that the rattling—the "fight"—they hear is going on just over the hill.
(Credit: Don and Kandi Kisky.)

somewhat dead. Those are the days when you might not be ready and suddenly, here they come at a dead run!"

"One thing you have to know about antler-rattling is that it's as much about what you're feeling as anything else," added Bob Zaiglin. "Say a buck is two hundred yards away—or maybe you only think he is. If you have the feeling that you are close to the buck of a lifetime and you want to bring him in, try just tickling the antlers at first. This is a great tactic to use during the cold, early morning hours following a warm spell. Some people like to clash those antlers together as hard as they can, but I can't help but think that this type of noise might inhibit deer from coming in. It's only on the second or third time I grind those antlers together that I begin to get louder and enhance my sequence so that it appears to any buck that may be listening that the ground and the brush are being torn apart by those 'two battling whitetails.' And that's what I want him to think."

"I'll start rattling right before the rut begins, around the first of November," Jerry Shively said. "We'll start with some light rattling and some get-acquainted grunts, nothing dominant or too loud. Our deer aren't yet fighting at this time. They aren't acting really aggressive. When you see them sparring, they're still just tickling their horns. I rattle just enough to work on their curiosity."

Shively doesn't get serious about his rattling and grunting until about a week before the rut starts on November 15. "You can make a tremendous amount of noise out there if you're trying to mimic two deer seriously going at it," he said. "There is no way a single hunter can make enough noise to accurately duplicate it."

M.R. James begins his rattling sequences with buck grunts, and then starts raking a tree trunk with his antlers. "I start off slow, as if the 'bucks' are merely sparring," he said. "I'll mesh the antlers for several periods of ten to fifteen seconds with soundless intervals between the sequences. I let the action build in intensity as the 'fight' progresses, with prolonged grinding of the beams and clicking of the tines, but with occasional pauses. I seldom rattle for more than 90 to 120 seconds per sequence. I conclude by 'tickling the tines' one final time, then finishing off with three or four aggressive buck grunts."

As a bowhunter, James will seldom move on to a different stand site. Instead, he may rattle from the same stand site six to eight times during a four-hour

Kandi Kisky has taken deer as large as some of husband Don's, including this massive 170+ whitetail shot with a muzzleloader.
(Credit: Don and Kandi Kisky.)

period to attract any bucks that may be traveling through his hunting area.

"Do I vary my rattling sequences?" asked Brad Harris, rhetorically. "Yes, quite a bit. The way in which I vary my sequences intrigues hunters. I tell them that you have to get in tune with your surroundings. I rattle the way I feel, the way the weather makes me feel. On some days, it just seems like deer should be more responsive, so I'll rattle or call more often. On doldrum days, I'm more laid back, quieter, and I don't rattle as much."

One of Harris's typical rattling sequences will begin with one loud aggressive grunt in every direction. "That should get the buck's head up," Harris said. "He's now listening, so I pause a few seconds, then start rattling as though one buck has just confronted another, and then the battle begins. I rattle five to thirty seconds, just swiping the antlers together, and then I'll pause, listen, and wait, because you never know if a buck is just over the next ridge. I'll rattle, then pause, then rattle perhaps two times more while pausing and listening. I'll rattle, wait, and then maybe grunt. Even after I've quit rattling, I'll probably make a grunt every now and then in case the buck is coming but I'm unable to see him."

If it's windy, Harris will rattle loudly and more often. "You have to adjust to conditions," he aid. "If I'm in an area where I'm able to see long distances, then I'll probably rattle less. Cold, clear conditions usually mean rattling will be more productive than on warm or hot days."

Peter Fiduccia explained every detail he puts into his rattling sequences. "First, I find a good spot where I can set up," he said. "I'll start by dribbling some buck urine around the area. I then do my best to create the illusion I'm after. This means stomping my feet, stepping hard upon leaves and twigs, adding some aggressive grunts, hitting my horns against tree limbs, and then slamming the antlers against the ground or tree trunks. I'll do this for fifteen

seconds, thirty seconds, forty-five seconds, or even an entire minute. I'll then pause to look and listen in all directions. You must stay alert. If you think it might work, shake a nearby sapling or stomp on the ground to entice any nearby whitetails into showing themselves."

Fiduccia then waits between fifteen and twenty minutes before rattling again. "The next time I'll wait thirty minutes," he said. "Some people move to a new area, but I prefer to stay put. Should a buck appear, try always to be positioned in a place where you're able to shake a sapling or grunt or do both. If you are unable to do this, then try to have a rattling buddy along who can. This simple motion or call may be the last nail in that buck's coffin. What you do is provide him with one final motive to rush in and see what's going on."

Fiduccia warns hunters who are new to the rattling game to remain at high alert for any sign of a nearby buck, including the sound of a snort or grunt, the slight movement of legs beneath nearby brush, sunlight glinting off an antler tine, a silhouette where you don't remember seeing one before. "Deer are shifty critters," he said. "Now you see them, now you don't."

The Best Times to Rattle?

Although all of our experts would rattle all day long, their consensus "best time" was early morning, particularly one that was frosty cold and windstill. Bob Zaiglin qualified his choice when he said, "I've rattled all day long, for many years. It doesn't matter where you might be rattling from—if it's not close to a deer you'd like to take, it will be for naught. Sunup is my favorite time to rattle, but you must be woods-wise enough to figure out where the buck you want is hiding, then decide how best to try to rattle him in. If you can get to within five hundred yards of where that is without disturbing him, your rattling and calling techniques will be perhaps 60 percent effective. If you can close that distance to two hundred yards, those techniques may increase in effectiveness to as much as 90 percent."

"I learned one time-management lesson the hard way," added M.R. James. "I owned this one place in the Indiana suburbs that had some great whitetail hunting. One morning I went in early and climbed up into my stand. It was still dark when I began rattling. I heard something, looked down, and saw a buck. It walked right under my stand. The only problem was it was still dark. I could see antlers, but it wasn't legal shooting time yet. I learned the hard way not to rattle too early or too late. It's difficult passing up a nice buck that you rattled in fair and square because you couldn't wait until it was time to shoot."

"Without a doubt, the first ten minutes of light and the last ten minutes are the very best times to rattle," said Don Kisky. Jerry Shively reports having better rattling luck in the afternoons and evenings. Even so, he admitted, "There are days when I can't do anything wrong—but there are just as many days when I can't do anything right."

From Which Direction Will Bucks Come?

Mickey Hellickson's Texas research study confirmed that bucks are more likely to approach a rattler's position from the downwind side. Surprisingly, as he stated in the previous section, mature bucks were no more likely to approach from downwind than younger animals were. A few bucks from all age classes broke precedent to come in from directions other than downwind. "I've rattled bucks in from all directions," said Bob Zaiglin. "They don't always come in from downwind. What will happen, though, is that the buck will usually circumvent the rattler to come in from the downwind side. That's why rattling with a team works so well.

"Say you have a north wind," he said, to illustrate his point. "One person is in a stand in a mesquite tree that's south of where the other person is rattling from the ground. The person in the stand

to the south of the rattler will always see far more deer than the one who is rattling."

"I've rarely had bucks come rushing in except in Texas," M.R. James said. "The bucks I rattle in in other places usually approach my position slowly, their ears back, hair standing up on the backs of their necks, walking stiff-legged, and posturing. I've watched plenty of these bucks raking trees or brush with their antlers as they came closer to my stand. I've arrowed several that swaggered in and stopped directly beneath my tree. I really believe deer can pinpoint the exact location of any 'buck fight' they hear. It's a big thrill for me to rattle or grunt a good buck close enough to shoot at with a bow."

When rattling or calling, stay alert to any buck that might walk in stiff-legged and posturing, just waiting to work over a sapling with its antlers.
(Credit: Bob Etling.)

To which, I'm sure, the rest of our experts would add a fervent "Amen."

Rattling: What to Expect

Okay, you're out in the field. You've started rattling. What should you expect to happen, and when?

To begin, remember that deer don't *only* vocalize. Nor do they merely tickle, mesh, or clash their antlers together in the sounds of battle, mock or authentic. Deer will also stomp their hooves to communicate with each other. Whether the stomping emanates from a doe that's trying to warn her youngsters or a buck reluctant to continue on the path it is taking, foot-stomping provides not only an aural warning via other deer's ears, but also a visual warning during periods of high winds. In

Create the total illusion when rattling from the ground by using your antlers to rake trees, leaves, and brush and to thump the ground like a buck's hooves.
(Credit: M.R. James.)

Jay Cassell with a buck he rattled out of some heavy mesquite brush on a ranch near San Antonio, Texas. (Credit: Jay Cassell.)

the latter case, nearby deer may be able to see an agitated animal better than they can hear it.

Foot-stomping imparts a chemical message as well. A deer's hooves emit a pheromone—a chemical message—from the **interdigital gland,** a scent gland between the two parts of the deer's cloven hoof. A whitetail stomping on a trail, for example, is providing an olfactory warning to any deer that may follow that something wasn't quite right here. Whether it was the scent of a human hunter carried from afar or something along the trail that seemed out of place and, therefore, potentially dangerous, the interdigital gland does its work subtly and swiftly. Many hunters sweeten mock scrapes and mock rubs with commercial interdigital gland scent or with hooves frozen and preserved from previous seasons. Should a deer you decline to shoot discover your

Avoid moving your rattling setup too frequently, because thick undergrowth can work to a whitetail's advantage and you might not see a deer approaching.
(Credit: Don and Kandi Kisky.)

rattling setup and start stomping its foot because it suspects a human is nearby, your best recourse is to relocate. Any other deer that comes by will immediately be alert to the presence of danger. Move, but do so carefully. Don't stand up, believing that you haven't rattled in a buck, and then be startled to see a white tail bobbing off into the distance.

If an agitated buck races in looking for another buck, his pawing and stomping of the ground will not leave a negative olfactory warning for other deer. Although his hoof-stomping provides an auditory signal, if an olfactory threat or agonistic signal is communicated as well, biologists, at least as far as

I know, are unaware of it. Should a buck race in and stomp prior to a "fight" that never materializes—and you miss your chance to take him—no olfactory warning will be given unless the buck realizes that a human is there. If it fails to do so, you might even be able to rattle him in again. Should he run off unaware that a human was nearby, there's no reason for you to leave.

Moving your rattling location may work wonders, especially if there's a lot of great hunting ground and few other hunters, as in much of Texas and the West. Such a strategy may prove less lucrative in the East, Midwest, and South, where hunter densities are much higher. In states as scattered as Michigan, Missouri, Pennsylvania, and Georgia, staying in one place—even all day—is

In most states, rattling from one place all day is preferable to moving, as archer Holly Fuller demonstrates.
(Credit: Holly Fuller.)

preferable unless you are hunting a large tract of private land with few other hunters. One reason to avoid moving your rattling setup too often is that thick undergrowth can work to a whitetail's advantage by camouflaging its presence until the last possible moment. If you move and reveal your position, you're aiding the whitetail's cause. Stay put. Let *him* make the mistakes.

For every buck that bursts onto the scene in response to your rattling sequences, probably four or five others choose to take a wait-and-see attitude and remain hidden. These deer may be subdominants, their native caution holding them back to see what will transpire next. Or perhaps a dominant buck is biding his time, waiting for the best moment to charge into view. It's always possible that no buck has heard your rattling, but a buck is heading your way as you prepare to give up for the day. Should you leave the stand and risk spooking a possibly responsive buck? Granted, there are no guarantees that this theoretical "buck" will ever make its appearance. But it might also be the buck you bag.

Successful rattlers like Iowa's Don Kisky agree that the one quality that will most help you succeed is patience. (Credit: Don and Kandi Kisky.)

A Rattler's Most Important Quality

Should you decide to give calling, rattling, and decoying a go, you must also work on the one quality that will help you succeed more than any other when using these techniques: patience. The more you rattle from any given stand, the more likely a buck will eventually investigate. Perhaps his curiosity finally maxes out. Perhaps he just traveled into hearing range. Perhaps he's finally bred the doe he was following, and he's looking for another. When he hears the sound of antlers clashing, he might think the "fight" is being waged over another hot doe and come storming in. Or maybe you've finally agitated him beyond all reckoning and he stampedes in to find out what in tarnation is going on. In any event, patience is a crucial part of the art of deceiving whitetails.

Where to Rattle?

If conditions are right, whitetail bucks—unlike turkey gobblers—will come in to almost any location. Bucks responding to rattling will race up hills and down, may storm across creeks, and will even race across bare fields, so great is their desire to view or participate in the "fight" now underway.

"I've experienced some of my best November rattling in eastern Colorado, along the Arkansas River," M.R. James said. "At this one ranch you could see deer at such a great distance you could actually watch as bucks ran across pastures or hopped fences to reach the rattling. That was some of the most exciting rattling I've ever experienced."

Don't be reluctant to set up anywhere you feel there's a halfway decent chance of rattling in a buck. Just be sure there is a good place for you to hide until you or your hunting partner is able to make the shot.

Early in the season, rattle in areas where you have seen bucks moving about in their bachelor groups. Look for core areas where early rubs have been made on small, insignificant saplings and where

Bob Zaiglin team-rattles by setting up in a thicket that will disguise his movement well upwind of where his hunter is positioned in a tree stand. (Credit: Bob Zaiglin.)

platter-sized scrapes roughly mark the animal's semi-territorial boundaries.

As the primary rut approaches, remember that bucks will be traveling. They may return to core areas regularly, but they are more likely to check in only occasionally. No matter what size a

M.R. James's whitetail hunting tools: rattling antlers, a rattle bag, and deer calls. He won't leave home without 'em. (Credit: M.R. James.)

buck's normal home range may be, once the rut commences, all home range bets are off. While some bucks may remain true to their annual home range, others may look for estrous does elsewhere. Some radio-collared bucks have been tracked thirty miles away from their annual home ranges, although this is the exception, not the rule. Don't waste your time targeting a particular buck that may no longer be in the area. Instead, set up close to an area frequented by one or more doe family groups. Whenever does are in estrus, bucks won't be far away.

Stay Alert

Once when M.R. James was hunting in Illinois he set up his stand in a point of woods where three trails converged. "I climbed into my stand and began rattling," he said. "Now, I could see for a long way in every direction. I mustn't have been looking in the right place, because all of a sudden I saw something move out of the corner of my eye. This buck must have run all the way across the corn field in front of me without me seeing it. When I did, the buck was only fifty yards away. He walked in, licking his nose, and I shot him."

Can You Rattle Too Much?

Too much of a good thing can sometimes work against you. That may be as true of rattling as it is of partaking of too many boilermakers on a Saturday night. Don Kisky believes too much rattling during past hunting seasons has worked against him more recently. "I've rattled so much in the past that I honestly think the five- and six-year-old bucks on our farm have become conditioned to the sound. Older bucks don't respond as readily as they once did. Yet I can hunt a farm where deer aren't used to the sound and rattle one right in. I've rattled in most of my larger bucks, but now, when they get to within seventy or eighty yards, I'll rely on grunting to bring them the rest of the way in. Three of my five largest whitetails have been grunted or rattled in."

Common Scents and Strategies

RICHARD P. COMBS

Scent Reduction

Let me begin by admitting a bias up front. I am highly doubtful of the notion that scent can be eliminated. The real question, as I see it, is not if scent can be eliminated, but if it can be reduced sufficiently to give hunters an advantage they would not otherwise have.

Answering that question is difficult for several reasons. Little truly independent research has been done on the subject. Scent, as we have seen, is a matter of volatile (gaseous) molecules being carried through the air to the sensory organs, usually nasal passages, of an animal. While the technology and methodology may exist to determine the concentration of these molecules in a given controlled area, few independent labs with the necessary resources have to date had sufficient motivation to conduct the kind of research that would provide useful information to hunters. Further complicating things, hunters are dealing with biology and uncontrolled conditions, not machines in a lab. A machine may indicate the concentration of various molecules in an enclosed space, but that does not tell us how those molecules behave in a forest or on a prairie. It also doesn't tell us at what level of concentration a given species under given circumstances can detect those molecules, or how they will react to various concentrations of them.

What we are left with then, is common sense and anecdotal evidence accumulated by hunters in the field. (Another bias: I'm highly skeptical of common sense. Common sense would suggest the sun circles the earth. Science tells us it's the other way around, and I'm inclined to go with science.)

Anecdotal evidence is far from perfect, but it is evidence and should not be ignored. And anecdotal evidence suggests that scent reduction can make a difference. Virtually every consistently successful deer hunter I know makes some effort to reduce or control scent in some way. Somewhere out there, I'm sure, is a consistently successful hunter who pays no attention to scent control. I just haven't met him. Imperfect though the evidence may be, thousands upon thousands of hunters who have logged countless hours in tree stands and blinds have come to the conclusion that taking some measures to reduce scent while afield is worth the effort and the expense.

When hunters talk about controlling odor, they are talking about two things. One is the odor produced continuously by their bodies and their breath. (Or more specifically, by various secretions and the action of bacteria on these secretions.) The other involves the various odors with which they or their clothing and gear may be contaminated, including soaps and shampoos, shaving creams, lotions, ointments, smoke, gas fumes, oils, mothballs, foods and beverages, cooking odors, and any other substance that hunters or their gear may come in contact with. We can speculate about which of these odors are more important, and which of these odors animals may or may not associate with humans or with danger, but the simplest and safest course of action for any hunter concerned about scent control is to try and keep all odors to an absolute minimum. Knowing how best to do this requires a basic understanding of how various scent reduction products work.

Starting Clean

While it may be possible to reduce scent, it seems only reasonable to start out with as little scent as possible. That means on our person, on our clothing, and on our gear. Commercial soaps and detergents are usually scented, and most leave behind a residue. Fortunately, the shelves of

A savvy hunter washes prior to each hunt in order to remove any bodily or foreign odors that deer may detect. (Credit: In-Scents.)

most sporting goods stores, and the pages of most hunting catalogs, are well stocked with a variety of commercially produced soaps, detergents, shampoos, and underarm deodorants, all unscented and promising to leave behind little or no residue. There are even unscented cleaners and deodorants for boots.

Brushing teeth and gargling, while it won't eliminate breath odors, can keep down the bacteria that contribute to these odors. Many hunters watch their diets before heading for the woods, avoiding strong smelling foods such as onions and garlic. These not only affect the breath, but their odors can be detected in perspiration. Finally, some hunters advocate taking zinc to reduce body odor.

Properly stored, much of our gear is less likely to be odiferous, one exception being our guns and bows, more specifically the solvents and lubricants we use on them. Best bet here is to use as much of these products as needed, but avoid using excessive amounts. There are, by the way, lubricants on the market advertised as having little or no scent, and there are others with cover scents, such as pine scent.

Avoiding Contamination

At its most basic level, scent reduction means avoiding contamination by foreign scents. When it comes to clothing, that can be as simple as storing clean hunting clothes in a sealed bag or container of some sort, assuming of course that the container itself does not emit an odor. It also means avoiding contamination before and after storage to the extent possible. Many hunters like to dry their clothes outdoors, for instance, to avoid possible contamination from fabric softeners that have been used in a dryer. That's fine, unless your neighbor upwind fires up his grill or his wood stove while the clothes are drying.

Hanging gear in the garage between hunts is a habit I'm working to avoid. The fabric seats and the straps on climbing stands, along with blinds and other items, will surely absorb exhaust fumes and the other odors associated with vehicles. Better to store gear in an unattached shed, if possible. Not all sources of contamination are that obvious, though.

I recently watched in amazement as a hunting buddy of mine, who uses a variety of scent control products on his clothing, climbed into my truck on the way to a hunt and casually lit up a cigarette. I'm not amazed that he smokes, or that he might have decided he'd rather smoke than remain scent free—I'm amazed that he bothers with the expense and effort of reducing scent, then contaminates his clothing and gear with smoke.

Stopping by the diner for breakfast while wearing hunting clothes is another source of contamination. And how many hunters stop at the gas station en route to their hunting spot? If gas fumes don't contaminate their clothes, how about

When keeping your hunting clothes outside, be sure they are away from the outside dryer vent and away from the grill (if you happen to fire it up for some tasty grilled venison steaks).
(Credit: Fiduccia Enterprises.)

the puddles of gas and oil they're tromping around in that will undoubtedly adhere to the soles of their boots? To the hunter trying hard to keep such scent contamination to a minimum, the entire world suddenly becomes one big source of unwanted odors, some of which catch him by surprise. Stopping to pick up a hunting buddy on a recent outing (the same one who smokes), I found him under the hood of his car squirting a lubricant on his fan belt. Remembering a squeaky clutch peddle that was beginning to drive me nuts, I grabbed the spray lubricant when he set it down, leaned under my dash, and sprayed it on the peddle. Big mistake. Instantly the entire inside of my vehicle, and presumably everything in it, smelled like kerosene.

The best way to keep such incidental odors to a minimum is to keep the hunting clothes and boots in their air tight container, and change after exiting the vehicle, at the location of the hunt. At first I considered this a huge bother. Over time, though, it has become a habit I would stick with even if I weren't concerned about scent control. I've discovered that I'm much more comfortable driving, on the way to and especially from a hunt, in street clothes and shoes. Given that, keeping my hunting clothes in a sealed container becomes a convenient way to keep them together and organized, in addition to helping avoid scent contamination.

Scent Reduction Products

Assuming we're as clean as possible, the next step is to recognize that we cannot get entirely scent-free, and even if we could that condition would not last long. That's where scent reducing products come in. To understand which ones to use and when, it's necessary to understand how the various scent reducing products work, and what they are designed to do.

Essentially, there are three types of commercially produced products intended to reduce odors. These are 1) products designed to prevent the formation of certain odors, by killing or inhibiting the growth of bacteria that cause these odors, or by neutralizing acidity 2) products designed to prevent the formation of the gas molecules that form odors, and 3) products with activated carbon that adsorb odors.

Sodium bicarbonate—more commonly referred to as baking soda—is famous for its ability to control odors by neutralizing acids, including the acids present in perspiration. It is the active ingredient in a number of the scent control products being marketed to hunters. If the product suggests that you can gargle with it, odds are the active ingredient is baking soda. The best way to use many of these products is to apply them directly to the skin after showering. Apply them everywhere, if you like, but pay special attention to the areas that perspire the most.

Plain baking soda can be useful, either as a deodorant (mix it with a little corn starch to keep it from clumping), as a toothpaste, or a mouth rinse. For hunters who cannot (or prefer not) to line-dry clothes, a few tablespoons of baking soda in the dryer can dry them scent free.

Another product that acts in a similar fashion is silver in clothing fabric. Silver has long been known for its antimicrobial properties. (In plain language, it kills germs.) The U.S. army has for some time issued to infantrymen socks with silver in the fabric to control the growth of bacteria that give rise to a number of foot ailments. In more recent years, at least one maker of hunting garments offers socks and undergarments including silver. The idea is to prevent the growth of the bacteria that cause body odors.

Stopping odors by controlling the conditions that create them is one approach; another approach entails a chemical interaction with substances to prevent volatility. As we have seen, odors are formed when substances release molecules into the atmosphere. Some substances are not volatile. Steel,

for instance, is not volatile and normally has no odor. A chemical reaction that controls volatility—that is, one that stops the release of molecules into the air—prevents odors. Many of the scent reduction products that are sprayed onto the skin, clothing, or gear, operate on this principle. The disadvantage of these products is that they are in effect consumed as they function, and must be regularly re-applied to continue working.

Finally, among the more recent means of scent control for hunters is the use of carbon-impregnated clothing. Any hunter who has looked at an ad for these garments probably has a basic understanding of how they work. Tiny carbon granules trap and hold odor molecules, preventing their release into the air. Eventually the granules are full up, and can contain no more odor molecules. An application of heat releases some, if not all of these molecules, freeing the carbon granules to trap odors again.

The use of activated carbon has long had industrial and military applications, usually for controlling or neutralizing toxic substances of various kinds. The military often issues carbon clothing to personnel in areas where there is the threat of chemical weapons. It works.

The use of carbon clothing for odor control is more controversial. In industrial applications, carbon that has adsorbed its capacity and will be re-used is heated at temperatures that would destroy any garments. The argument is often made that the temperatures to which carbon clothing is exposed in a clothes dryer are insufficient to achieve the desired results. The case made by the manufacturers of these garments is that heat at these temperatures, while it may not entirely eliminate the scent molecules trapped by the carbon, will eliminate enough of them to enable the garment to work as intended.

In the only truly scientific study of scent control I have found—at least as it might have some relevance to a hunting situation—Dr. John Shivik of the National Wildlife Research Center extensively tested the ability of seven search dogs to find people wearing scent-control clothing, compared to their ability to locate people not wearing such clothing. The people were placed in blinds, the dogs were allowed to sniff a piece of fabric previously handled by the people in the blinds, and dogs and handlers were then given specified amounts of time in which to locate the subjects. In all but one of forty-two trials, dogs found all the test subjects within the allotted time. Dr. Shivik found that persons not wearing carbon suits were detected from slightly greater distances, but did not find the differences in distance to be statistically significant. While noting that he believed it possible for individuals to put on sealed carbon suits in such a way as to remain undetectable to dogs, his overall conclusion was that for practical purposes, carbon suits are ineffective.

In fairness, if we are going to be truly scientific in our approach, we have to concede that the results of one test are never conclusive. It will be interesting to see if other researchers can duplicate these results, or if they arrive at different conclusions. As a side note, it is significant (though not surprising) that Shivik did observe significant differences in the time it took dogs to find subjects, and these differences were related to barometric pressure, humidity, and the variability of the wind. Shivik also speculated that one probable source of contamination of the suits was that wearers handled them in putting them on. Hunters using these suits might want to consider wearing rubber gloves when donning them.

Blinds

Blinds haven't traditionally been thought of as scent reduction products, so I've given them their own category. When I say "traditionally," I mean that few hunters would associate blinds with reductions in scent—but that's not to say the thought has never occurred to hunters. In recent years, with the growing popularity of commercially produced, fully enclosed blinds, a number of hunters have suggested that these blinds could help contain scent. Use of such ground blinds is increasing in popularity, but they have not been commonly used long enough to accumulate the kind of anecdotal evidence that has built up around other scent reducing products, like the clothing and soaps.

Still, it doesn't seem inconceivable that blinds could afford some degree of scent control, if only because they block the wind, thereby preventing it from carrying at least some scent downwind. More recently, some blind makers have been offering in blinds the same carbon—impregnated fabrics that are offered in hunting garments. Clearly these are designed to be scent reduction products, and are one more weapon to consider in the arsenal of hunters committed to achieving every possible edge they can get in the effort to defeat the nose of a whitetail.

Arguably the ultimate in scent-control is the Deluxe Blind from SCENTite. Essentially, this blind is a large, air-tight box that vents scent thirty feet above

This blind from Scentite helps to reduce human scent and includes a vent pipe that extends from the ceiling of the blind up 30 feet (where most times it is secured to a limb of a tree). (Credit: Fiduccia Enterprises)

the blind—assuming the blind is on the ground—and higher than that if the blind is on a quad stand. SCENTite owner Bill Ferguson demonstrates its effectiveness by creating smoke inside the blind. The blind does indeed completely contain the smoke, letting none of it out until it reaches the top of the vent tube at least 30 feet up. Bill's observations using this blind not only demonstrate its effectiveness, but result in some observation about scent and how it is carried that might have a more general application.

"Some common sense has to be used in terms of blind placement and current conditions," Bill explains. "For instance, if you're in a valley and deer are traveling downwind around the hillside at a height of 30 feet or more, they will probably pick up the scent of the hunter in the blind. As far as we've been able to observe, though, a hunter in a more or less flat area, or on or near a hilltop, will remain undetected by deer in his hunting area. Getting the scent up at least 25 feet seems to carry it over the heads of any deer in the area until it dissipates."

What about downdrafts?

"Honestly," says Bill, "the only situation in which I've seen deer detect scent from this blind is when they are on a hillside above it. I have not yet seen deer that were below the level of the vent detect hunters in the blind. In fact, after the season we've often put a line of corn all the way around the blind about five feet out, and had deer come in and eat all the way around with two people inside the blind. We do that just to demonstrate its effectiveness."

The more serious hunters I know tend to employ at least some of the scent-reduction strategies outlined in this section, and many use them all. They wash themselves and their clothing in unscented soaps and detergents, store their garments carefully in sealed containers, use scent-reducing products, and in many cases wear carbon clothing. Few totally ignore wind direction.

My own experiences, which I present here as neither less nor more valid than those of any other experienced hunter, are inconclusive. Depending on circumstances, I use some or all of these products. I have been detected by game when following a rigid scent control regimen. I have also had game downwind of me for extended periods of time, and remained undetected.

In addition I have observed, as have many hunters, that game animals at times appear to detect an odor, but not to a degree that causes them to bolt. The head comes up, perhaps, and they appear to change from a relaxed state to a tense state. They look around, as if looking for the source of a faint odor. It could be that they detect an odor, but think it is at some distance, or are simply unable to locate the source of it. I've even had deer snort, or jump and run a short distance, only to stop. On more than one occasion I've had the opportunity to arrow animals that I'm sure were aware of my presence, but couldn't locate me. It is not unreasonable to speculate in these situations that keeping scent to a minimum is the difference between an animal that becomes alert to possible danger and remains in the

Many hunters believe enclosed ground blinds can help contain scent. Some blinds make use of carbon-impregnated fabrics to absorb scent.

area long enough to provide a shooting opportunity, and one that bolts instantly.

Based on all this, I am inclined to continue using scent reducing strategies unless and until more extensive scientific studies convince me they are ineffective. My thinking, which appears to be in accord with the thoughts of many experienced hunters, is that getting within range of mature big game animals is sufficiently difficult that I want any edge I can get.

Attractor Scents

My friend Rick Dunn was toting his slug gun down a logging road on a farm in south-central Ohio, stopping periodically to apply a few drops of doe-in-heat scent to the pad on his boot. He had only a vague destination in mind, and no particular strategy beyond the use of the scent trail he was laying down. Rick is a high-energy type, and a little on the restless side, and he had spent as many hours sitting in a tree stand as he could tolerate in one day.

He had covered maybe half-a-mile on the long, winding dirt road, and had stopped once again to apply the doe urine, when he caught movement from the corner of his eye. Something was traveling down the logging road behind him, and since the road made a big, winding path, he was catching just glimpses of it through the woods. He stepped off the road, behind a tree, to watch. Eventually it came around the bend and he could see it clearly—a big-racked buck, nose to the ground, following his trail like a hound after a rabbit.

Rick's too experienced a hunter to waste time in a situation like that. He shouldered his gun, put the crosshairs on the sweet spot, and squeezed off a shot. Not long after, he was field dressing his big Ohio buck. And as you might imagine, Rick is sold on the use of doe-in-heat scent when deer hunting, at least when he's hunting close to or during the rut.

There is no question that deer can be lured into shooting position with scents. What is equally clear is that scent doesn't always work. And when it does work, just why is a controversial issue in the case of many scents.

Of course, anything that always worked would have to be illegal. Hunters aren't really looking for something that always works. They're looking for something that gives them an edge—something that makes the odds against scoring on any given day a little lower. How many times would you use scent for one opportunity at a good buck?

The issues for hunters are, what kind of scents work, when do they work, when (and why) do they often not work?

Attractant scents can be divided into several categories, though there may be some overlap. These are Food Scents, Sex Scents, and Curiosity Scents. Urine can also be a category of its own. Though it is often considered a sex scent, and might also be considered a curiosity scent, we'll explain why we list it as a category of its own later in this section.

Why do I say there may be some overlap among these categories? Until we can get inside a deer's head, we really have no way of knowing for certain what motivates it. Was it hungry and fooled by that bottled apple scent, or was it curious about a strange new smell it had never encountered before? Was that rutting buck fooled by the doe-in-heat scent, or was it curious about something that vaguely resembled the scent of a doe-in-heat but wasn't? Some would argue that any time deer respond to a bottled or synthesized scent, they are responding mostly from curiosity. And of course some hunters would say, "Who cares why they come in, just so they come in?"

Manufacturers themselves recognize the overlap. Many refer to their scents as lures. The ingredients are something they prefer to keep secret, but they often indicate that the lure contains a mixture of ingredients designed to appeal to hunger, or curiosity, or both.

Food Scents

First let's distinguish between "food" and "food scents." In states such as Michigan or Texas, where baiting deer is perfectly legal, hunters may put corn, apples, beets, or similar foods out as bait, and it seems reasonable to assume deer that encounter the bait for the first time are responding to smell.

That is not what we are talking about by use of food scents, however. By "food scents" in this context we are talking about the use of bottled scents made from concentrates or synthetic odors, or solid mixtures that are volatile enough to produce food scents that can be detected from some distance, or various products that are heated or even boiled to produce scents intended to resemble foods.

An interesting issue related to food scents is the oft-heard caution about using the scents of foods that do not occur naturally in a given area. The idea is that a deer who suddenly detects the scent of, say, apples, in an area where there are no apple trees, will react with suspicion, or will sense in some way that something is not right and will avoid the area.

Many biologists, and some hunters, scoff at that idea.

"The idea that a deer catches a whiff of com in an area where there is no cornfield and is suddenly on the alert or suspicious that something is fishy, is just ridiculous." Well-known whitetail expert Peter Fiduccia told me recently. "Deer are very wary, but they're not that complicated. They don't think that way. If it smells like something good to eat and they're hungry, they'll check it out."

We can speculate about why deer respond to certain foods at certain times, and others at other times, but ultimately it's something only the deer themselves know. Bottom line for many hunters, though, is that putting out a food scent is unlikely to do any harm, and can sometimes be the ticket to success.

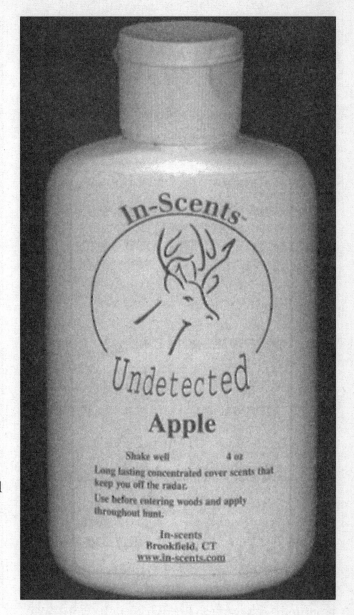

Try using apple scent even in an area where there are no apples. A deer's natural curiosity may cause it to come in to check out the new food scent. (Credit: In-Scents.)

Curiosity Scents

Deer are without question curious creatures, which is the idea behind curiosity scents. They investigate their environment, and one of their chief instruments of investigation is their nose. They've been referred to as one hundred pound noses that run around smelling everything in the woods. Given their curiosity, and their reliance on their noses, it's not surprising that deer will on occasion approach the source of a strong, unusual, or unknown aroma to check it out.

What exactly are curiosity scents? In the case of commercially produced scents, that is a difficult question, since manufacturers are highly secretive about the formulas they claim to have developed after years of study. In one University of Georgia study involving the use of motion-activated cameras placed over a variety of scents, the numbers of deer attracted to car polish rivaled the numbers attracted to several kinds of urine and food scents.

Sexual Attractants

Sexual attractants don't just get deer excited, they get hunters excited. No mystery there—when you consider that close to and during the rut is the one time when even big, secretive bucks allow their obsession with hot does to make them vulnerable, it's not surprising that hunters would seek to take advantage of that vulnerability. Probably the most commonly used sexual attractant is doe-in-heat urine, which may be placed on the ground, or used to saturate a rag or a wick and hung from a tree, or even sprayed into the air. Hunters also frequently use doe urine to lay down scent trails, saturating a rag that can be dragged, or a pad that can be worn on a boot sole.

Dominant buck urine, too, is popular. The idea is that bucks detecting the scent of another buck in their area will feel challenged and will seek out the buck to chase it off. Still others theorize that dominant buck urine can attract and hold does in a given area. It has been demonstrated that does can determine the difference between subordinate and dominant bucks. Though we tend to think of the bucks as seeking the does, does will frequent areas containing dominant bucks, and especially in those areas where the buck to doe ratio is in good balance, does may travel outside their home ranges to find dominant bucks.

Buck Urine is most effectively used during the rut. Bucks high on the pecking order are quick to check out of the urine is from a buck they know, or a strange buck. (Credit: In-Scents.)

Among the more serious trophy hunters I know are several who begin placing dominant buck scents in various forms throughout their hunting area, usually late in the summer, though sometimes earlier, and in one case year-round. The theory is that this brings more does in the area, and keeps them there, and in turn more bucks are drawn into that area as the rut approaches. (More about this approach in subsequent sections.)

Peter Fiduccia discovered in the 1970s that using buck urine on a mock rub helps to complete the illusion, both visually and through the odor.
(Credit: Fiduccia Enterprises.)

Earlier we suggested that urine could be considered a category in itself. Here is why: ungulates, including deer, tend to be fascinated by urine of any kind. It seems to be a means of communication within the species, but may also tell deer about other species, including predators, in the area. There is some controversy regarding how deer react to the urine of predators, but regardless of how they react, they do seem drawn to check out urine. Ordinary doe urine is a commonly used scent. Many hunters believe that it doesn't make sense to use doe-in-heat scent before any does are likely to be in heat, but there are some other reasons not to use it. One reason is that it tends to repel does. The hunter looking primarily to cull does from a local herd or

put venison in the freezer probably doesn't want to repel does. Beyond that, some hunters theorize that does attract bucks, so why drive away does?

The whole issue of how deer react to human urine has generated the widest possible response from hunters. At one extreme are the hunters who use bottles or other devices to avoid contaminating their hunting location with the smell of human urine. At the other extreme are hunters who intentionally "contaminate" their stands sites with human urine, deposit human urine in scrapes, and even create mock scrapes with human urine, in the belief that it attracts deer.

A number of more or less scientific studies in recent years have studied deer response to a variety of scents. The studies aren't always conclusive, but they do tend to point in a couple of interesting directions. One of these is that deer herds confined in pens don't always react to smells the same way wild deer do. The other is that neither penned nor free-ranging deer appear to have strong aversions to human urine, and may exhibit some curiosity about it. Bottom line: human urine may or may not attract

Deer communicate through the odor of their urine during the breeding season. A doe in estrus will leave urine with a very strong odor. Bucks who are in the prime of their breeding season and at a prime age, will also leave urine with a strong musky odor.
(Credit: Ted Rose.)

deer to some degree, but it doesn't seem to repel them. Leave the urine bottles at home and let fly from your tree stand if you want.

The fact is, various studies indicate that deer sometimes show a mild curiosity reaction to a variety of odors from all kinds of urine to oddities such as car wax. One thing hunters don't need a scientific study to confirm: a deer detecting the close proximity of a human or other predator will turn inside out getting away.

Urine is not the only way deer convey sexual messages to one another—various glandular secretions, such as those deposited by bucks on rubs, may serve a similar function, along with the tarsal glands. A buck in rut can be smelled, even by the inferior noses of humans, for some distance under the right conditions, and any hunter who has picked a buck up by the hind legs to lift him into a pick-up truck, or who has ridden in an SUV with a buck behind the seat, is intimately acquainted with that aroma. Various commercial producers have attempted to bottle or mimic tarsal gland scent, and more than a few hunters like to trim off the tarsal glands of a tagged buck, to use as a lure. Many hunters freeze them in plastic bags for repeated use.

Pheromones

We can't address the issue of sexual scents without taking a look at pheromones. Pheromones are organic chemical substances used by various species to communicate with one another, or to produce any of a number of instinctive responses. Many insects, in particular, are known to use pheromones heavily. Pheromones may enable an ant to tell its community the location of a food source, for instance, or allow a colony of bees to coordinate an exodus from a hive to establish a new colony elsewhere. They also stimulate sexual activity. Insects aren't the only species that make use of pheromones. Mammals do, also.

Hunters became very excited about pheromones, more specifically the volatile

As with most mammals in the animal kingdom, pheromones create instinctive responses in both bucks and does. (Credit: Ted Rose.)

substances in rutting buck or doe-in-heat urine that produce sexual responses in deer. A buck detecting these pheromones will instinctively react to them, every time. Hunters first learning about pheromones thought that perhaps they had hit on the holy grail of deer hunting: a scent that would invariably cause any buck encountering it to come to the source of the pheromones. Their hopes were dashed, however, by another incontrovertible fact: after they're released by the deer these pheromones last for anywhere from 15 seconds to, at most, 6 minutes. They work for deer because deer produce fresh pheromones continuously.

Does this mean that, as a practical matter, there is no such thing as, what is commonly referred to as "doe-in-heat" scent? Some experts would argue that that is indeed the case. Consider, though, that scientists have identified at least ninety-three substances in the urine of a doe in heat. It seems entirely possible that a buck can tell a doe is in heat (actually she is in estrus) even without the pheromones. Will a buck respond to a doe even if the pheromones aren't present? We can't say with any certainty, but experiences like those of my friend Rick Dunn suggest that a buck will at least sometimes follow a trail of "doe-in- heat" scent, regardless of what the ingredients may be, and regardless of whether or not it contains pheromones.

Cover Scents

Unexploded land mines are a major problem in war-torn parts of the world, killing and maiming innocent people sometimes many years after conflicts have ended. Proving yet again they are man's best friend, dogs have been trained to sniff them out. They find, them, too—six inches or more under ground, having been buried for years.

That in itself is amazing enough, but considering that the dogs are trained to respond to the explosive materials, which are often encased in a molded, solid block of inert material such as plastic, the feat is even more amazing.

Now consider this: most scientists are of the opinion that white-tailed deer have olfactory capabilities at least matching those of most dogs and, in the opinion of some, exceeding those of dogs. It is not unreasonable to wonder if it is possible for a hunter to mask his scent sufficiently to fool the nose of a deer. It doesn't help that behavioral scientists have observed that white-tailed deer can distinguish between as many as twenty different scents simultaneously.

Before you give up on the idea of cover scents, though, you might want to ponder this question: Why do some dogs seem to delight in rolling in the foulest, rottenest, most disgusting carcasses or other odiferous odors they can find? Biologists tell us that this behavior is common to wild as well as domesticated canines, and theorize that the behavior is an attempt to mask scent, as an aid in stalking prey.

Along similar lines, why do canines, felines, and other critters often kick dirt over their droppings, if not to reduce or mask scent?

Under the right conditions, hunting from a tree stand can carry scent over the heads of nearby game.

If we are correct in assuming that animals engage in these behaviors to reduce scent, then thousands upon thousands of years of evolution would seem to support the notion that it is indeed possible to mask scent to a degree that will make a hunter less easily detected by his prey. While it seems unlikely that scent can be entirely eliminated in this manner, perhaps it can be reduced to such a degree that it cannot be detected for as great a distance, or as quickly, by a prey species. Or perhaps the mixture of aromas causes a momentary hesitation, giving the predator a few extra seconds that can make the difference.

Native Americans were known to sometimes apply cover scents of one sort or another. Some tribes routinely sat in the smoke from campfires, convinced this cover scent gave them an edge when stalking into bow range of their quarry. They may not have understood scientific methodology, but they hunted almost daily all their lives, and for generation

When camping or hunting from remote cabins, scent control can be a real challenge. When possible, leave outer garments outdoors on a porch or in a shed, where they won't pick up odors from fire, cooking, or other sources.

after generation depended on successful hunts for their very survival.

What Kind of Cover Scent to Use?

This is a more complicated question than it might at first appear to be. Typically, cover scents attempt to produce a strong smell that is common in the environment. Earth scent, pine scent, and the urine of common creatures such as foxes and raccoons are probably the most popular cover scents. Usually, earth and pine scents are sprayed on, or attached to an item of clothing in the form of wafers or patches, while urines are usually applied a few

Since foxes frequently inhabit the same areas that deer do, many hunters choose to use fox urine as a cover scent. (Credit: Ted Rose.)

drops at a time to boot soles before entering the woods, to prevent deer from readily discerning the trail.

As in the case of food scents, some hunters feel it's important to use cover scents that are common to the area. In the case of fox or raccoon urine, there are few areas inhabited by deer that are not also inhabited by these critters. Dirt would seem to be a common element, though a hunter might wonder if a generic dirt scent would closely resemble everything from the red clay of Georgia, to the sand of the South Carolina Low Country, to the Arizona desert.

What about the use of urine from predators such as foxes? While some studies suggest that deer may react negatively to the urine of predators, other studies suggest otherwise. Then too, although the urine of various species may have different odors depending on what they have eaten, urine does tend to break down quickly in the environment to the point at which, according to some biologists, all mammal urine smells basically the same. Certainly many successful deer hunters routinely apply fox urine to their boots before entering the woods.

Still other hunters scoff at the notion that a deer is put on the alert by, for instance, the scent of pines in an area where there are no pine trees. My own take on this is that since it is as easy to use a scent that is common to the area being hunted as to use one that is not, why not use the locally common scent, just in case.

Here is another consideration: if half the hunters in the woods are using earth scent (or pine scent, or fox urine), might not a deer learn to associate that scent with hunters? In the West, many hunters, especially elk hunters, hunt from spike camps, where they usually spend at least some time sitting around campfires. More than one successful hunter has suggested the smell of smoke acts as an effective cover scent. In the introduction, I made reference to the hunters who smoke cigarettes on deer stands, putting a smoking butt in the fork of a tree just long enough to shoot an approaching deer, then finishing the smoke before climbing down to take up the trail. Could cigarette smoke be a cover scent?

Assuming cover scents can work, whether or not smoke (or any other scent) can act as a cover would probably depend upon whether or not deer have learned to associate the smoke, or other scents,

ATVs and similar vehicles enable hunters to cover ground without leaving scent. This is especially important when hunting trophy bucks, or when hunting the same area repeatedly.

with humans, and more specifically with danger. It seems unlikely that deer in a big woods, or a more or less remote area, would make that connection—although if they experience pain or a threat from one smoking hunter, the association could be made quickly. At the same time, deer that often come into contact with people, whether in heavily populated suburban areas, farm country, or areas where they are subject to heavy hunting pressure, would be quite likely to associate the smell of smoke with humans.

Hunting Big Woods Bucks

HAL BLOOD

Track Him Down

Nothing quite compares to the satisfaction of tracking down and shooting a big buck on a blanket of fresh snow. Taking on this king of the forest on his own turf—and winning—is a worthy accomplishment. Big-woods white-tailed bucks have developed keen instincts to avoid danger from predators. Unlike herd animals that rely on many eyes and ears to alert them to danger, a big-woods buck is on his own. His very existence depends on his ability to avoid or escape from predators, including humans. If a white-tailed buck survives to his fourth year, he's one of the toughest animals on earth to hunt. He constantly watches for danger and rarely lies down where he can't see his back track. We've all heard a story or two about the hunter who followed a track a few hundred yards and found a monster buck standing there waiting to be shot. That's got to be the purest form of dumb luck! I'm not begrudging anyone who's ever shot a buck that way, because I'd do the same if I had the chance, and I'd count my blessings. I figure any buck standing around waiting to be shot needs to be removed from the gene pool.

Of the hundreds of deer I've tracked over the years, though, I've never been lucky enough to find a monster buck that stood still and let me walk up to him, so I've had to develop the skills necessary to help me get close to bucks and create my own luck. The good news is that anybody with patience and persistence can develop these skills, too. Tracking is not simply the ability to follow in a buck's footsteps. To become consistently successful at tracking you have to develop certain skills: identifying and aging tracks in any weather condition, having a sixth sense to help you become more in tune with your surroundings, being able to move about the woods as if you are a part of them, and knowing the habits of bucks—the when and why of what they do. In essence, you must start to think like bucks do so you can anticipate their moves. Each buck is an individual that has developed his own habits from his life's experiences, but bucks also have habits in common that are part of their genetic makeup. By learning these, you'll have a better chance of anticipating a buck's next move and be on your way to consistently bagging big-woods bucks.

There's something about being in the big woods on the track of a buck in the snow that makes me feel as if I'm in a new realm of hunting that disconnects me from the rest of the world. I can't explain it, and if you've never done it you won't understand it, but once you *do* experience that feeling, you'll be hooked. When I get on a track, I forget about everything and concentrate on nothing else but how I can catch this buck. I guess you could call it living for the moment.

Tracking bucks is the fastest way to learn their habits. When you follow a buck, he'll take you to his hidden haunts—places you might never expect a buck to go. He'll show you where his signposts are and where the does are. Once you've followed enough bucks, you'll start to see the pieces of the puzzle come together. I hope my experiences will help you sort through that puzzle on your way to becoming a big-buck tracker.

Reading Tracks

The first step to becoming a tracker is learning to identify tracks. I've read in books and articles that you can't tell the difference between a buck track and a doe track, but I believe this is false. If you look at the whole picture—and not just at an individual print—you'll be able to tell a buck track from a doe track most of the time. The more experience you have, the better you'll be at distinguishing one from the other. First, look at the print itself.

How Big is the Track?

Size is the first thing to consider. There isn't a doe alive that has a track a big as a hog buck's, but it

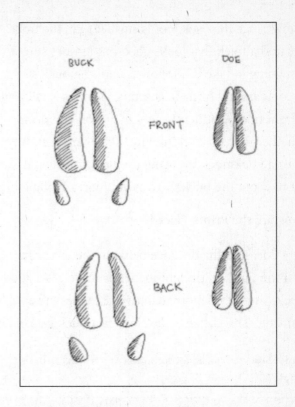

Buck versus doe tracks.

This is the largest buck track I've ever found. This is a walking print and he is so heavy his toes splay out. (The Leatherman tool pictured at the right is eight inches long.)

can be difficult to tell a doe track from the track of a medium- sized buck.

Are Any Dewclaws Showing?

If there is less than two inches of snow, a walking doe usually doesn't leave dewclaw prints, but a good buck always leaves them in any amount of snow and even on bare ground. The heavier a buck is, the deeper the prints will be and the more they'll be set back from the hooves. If they're running or there's more snow, both does and bucks leave dewclaw prints, but bucks' dewclaws are larger compared to the size of their hooves than does' are. Bucks' dewclaws also leave a print as wide as or wider than the print of the hoof itself.

Are You Looking at a Front Hoof or a Back Hoof?

There's a big difference. When a deer walks, its back foot steps in the same spot as its front foot, covering the front track; therefore, the print you see will be that of the back foot. This is important to know, since the back foot is smaller than the front. If I find a track that looks good but I'm not sure if I'm going to take it, I follow it until the buck stops to look around or make a scrape. There he will leave a front hoofprint that I can size up so I can decide whether to keep tracking him. Once you're sure you have a buck track by sizing up the prints, you'll learn more about the buck's size as you start to follow him.

How are the Prints Placed?

Measure the distance between the left print and the right. If it's eight inches or more, it's a good buck—and if it's more than twelve inches, it's a monster. This distance develops as a buck gets older

This shows the back foot stepping directly on top of the front foot.

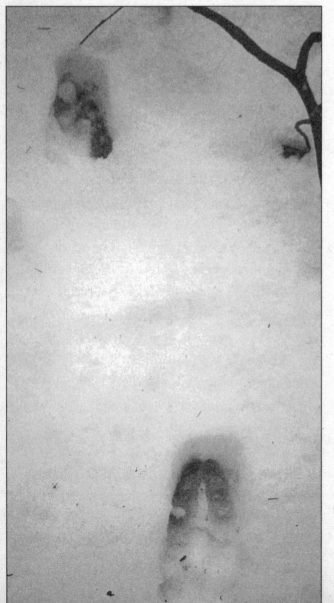

This buck went around the two-foot opening between the trees. This indicates that he is carrying a wide rack.

and his chest gets deeper. Notice whether his hooves are dragging, especially when there is very little snow. The older a buck is, the more he will tend to drag his feet.

How Long is the Stride?

When a buck walks at a normal pace, two feet between prints is a good buck; anything more than that and you've got a real monster. The length of the stride shows how heavy a buck might be. The longer a buck is, the more he weighs. One of the thickest and heaviest-necked bucks I've taken weighed two hundred pounds even and was seven and a half years old. He was very short and compact. Another buck I shot had a thin neck and I doubted he'd weigh two hundred pounds, but he tipped the scales at 235. Hanging up, he was ten feet long from his back feet to the tip of his horns.

Aging Tracks

Knowing how to age tracks is very important, but it can be tricky because there are so many variables to consider. You'll have to look at the temperature the previous night, the daytime temperature, the type of snow, when it last snowed, and whether the snow melted or evaporated. Knowing how to age tracks will keep you from sneaking along on an eight-hour-old track or hurrying on a half-hour-old one.

When to Age a Track

The first time to age a track is when you're deciding whether to follow it. I always pay attention to the weather the night before. I look at the temperature before I go to bed and when I get up. If I hear it snow in the night, I note what time it started. This way, in the morning I have a better chance of figuring out when a track was made. I'll usually take a big track made any time during the night. Many hunters have the idea that if a track

Running tracks.

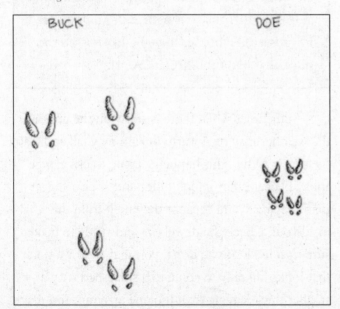

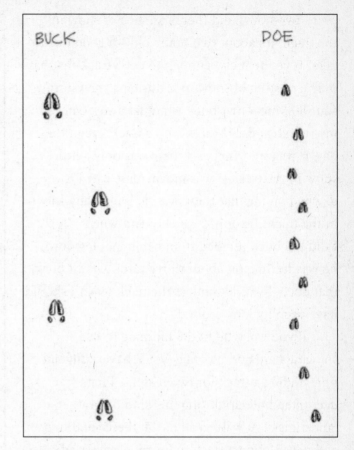

Walking tracks.

wasn't just made, it's not fresh and therefore not worth taking. I go on the assumption that wherever the buck went during the night I can go during the day. I've never taken the track of a buck in the morning that I did not catch up to during the day, and the track of the biggest buck I've taken was two nights old when I started on it!

Aging Tracks in Snow

The type of snow matters when you're aging a track. A damp snow keeps the track crisp for a long time, and sometimes this can make you think the track is newer than it really is. If there's cold, dry snow on ground that is not frozen, a track will probably have ice in it, but don't worry—it takes only a short time to freeze when it's cold. If snow is falling and you have an idea when it started, you should be able to tell the age of a track fairly accurately. For example, if it's snowing an inch every two hours and there's an inch of snow in the track, it's about two hours old—a good one to take. If you're lucky enough to cut a track that has only a dusting of snow in it during a snowstorm, start looking—that buck is not far away. Once in my training years I picked up a track late in the day. It was snowing, and there was only a little snow in the track. I was moving fast when it dawned on me that there was no longer any snow in the track. I stopped quickly, and when I did the buck jumped from behind a blowdown he was feeding on about thirty yards away. I blew that one—I was looking at the track when I should have been looking around.

If you wake up in the morning to find it snowing hard and blowing, you'll have a difficult time finding a track for two reasons. First, deer often hole up during this kind of weather. Sometimes I've walked all day in these conditions and never found a track to follow. The second reason applies if you're trying to find a track from the road. The wind usually blows down roads, and it doesn't take long for drifts to cover tracks that might have been made. I've tracked bucks in conditions like this when I knew I was less than half an hour behind a buck, but his track across the road was already obliterated.

Another thing to consider if you find a track with snow in it is which direction the buck is traveling. If he's walking, it might be difficult to tell. Brush some snow aside and poke your fingers down to the bottom of the track, and you may be able to feel which way the hooves are pointing. You may also see snow pushed ahead of the print as he steps. If you're still not sure, follow the track the way you think it is going, and there will eventually be a place where he jumped to cross a log or stream. His back feet will be farther apart and ahead of his front feet, and you'll be able to tell his direction of travel.

Drifts Cover the Tracks

I took Chris out tracking one morning after a fresh snow the night before. The snow had stopped, but it was quite windy. Chris and I dropped another hunter off and were looking for tracks as we went. We turned around and came back on the same road before turning onto another road where we found a nice track. It wasn't more than an hour old, and we had high hopes as we followed it into a spruce thicket where the buck had been looking for does. We hunted slowly, as I was sure he must be in there because the other road we had driven on was only a quarter mile ahead of us, and we hadn't seen tracks crossing it. Then the track went out of the spruces and right up to the road we had driven on and disappeared—it had drifted over. We picked the track back up on the other side of the road and followed it up the mountain. We had now lost over an hour, so we hadn't gained on him at all. When we got up the mountain, we found where he had spent quite a bit of time feeding and looking for does. Then he crossed the border into Canada and we had to stop. We might have caught up to him before he crossed the border if we hadn't missed the track that had been drifted over in the road.

Sometimes when there is snow on the ground, the weather may turn warm or rain may fall and start melting it. When this happens, aging tracks can be tricky because they'll look older and appear bigger than they really are because they melt from the inside out. Check the dewclaws and stride to make sure it's a buck. If you don't, you may follow a track that looks big only to come to a small bed with a smaller track leaving than the one arriving. You may

This is what you hope to find when tracking. A buck preoccupied with rubbing and scraping will be easier to spot.

even find a track so melted out that you can barely distinguish the hoofprints. If you know the melting happened during the night and the track wasn't there the day before, it's still a good track to take.

Following a Melted Track

I followed a track like that one morning after it had rained all night. It went up a hardwood ridge that I had been on the day before without seeing any big tracks. I cut a good buck track that was washed out to double its normal size. I thought the buck was quite far ahead of me, so I kicked into high gear and started traveling. I hadn't gone a quarter mile before he busted out of some thick slash thirty yards in front of me. He'd been bedded, and I happened to pick up his track at the end of his night's journey. I shot him a few hours later.

Never discount a track in these conditions—it might be fresher than you think. If you're always looking for an hour-old track, you'll do more looking than tracking. If you get on a track made the night before, one thing is for sure—a buck will be at the end of it.

Aging Tracks as You Move Along

Once you've found the track you want, you'll need to keep track of its age as you follow it. This is where knowing the current temperature plays a big role in your tracking. When it's cold, a track that breaks through ice will start to freeze instantly. I check the track by tapping it with the barrel of my rifle to see how thick the ice is. If there's just a skim of ice, I know I'm not far behind. The inside edge of the track also tells you about the age. When a track is made, the inside edges as well as the snow kicked up in front will be soft. As the track ages, the snow will start to become firm. How fast this happens depends on the temperature. I constantly check tracks by feel. I take my glove off and feel inside the track with my bare fingers. When the temperature stays around freezing, it's very difficult to age tracks, because a track will keep its texture and appearance for hours.

Aging Tracks by Examining Droppings

Another way to age a track is to feel droppings. This is often more accurate than feeling

This old buck had a crooked toe on his back foot. It was an easy one to follow when there were other tracks around.

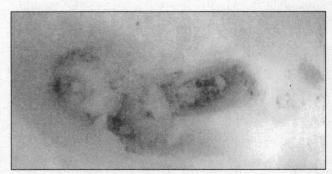

the track itself. Feeling droppings is most accurate when it's cold enough to freeze things. I pick up droppings and squeeze them to see how frozen they are. (I know some people probably think I'm nuts, but let's just call it getting back to nature!)

Hunters tell me all sorts of things they've read about how to tell buck droppings from doe droppings. One even told me he had read that buck droppings are the clumpy ones and doe droppings are the individual pellets. Nothing could be further from the truth. What a deer eats controls the consistency of its droppings. In summer and early fall, when they're feeding on green plants, the droppings tend to clump together. When they start eating nuts and browse, the droppings are in pellet form. Pellet size is also not an indication of the size of a buck—that's an old wives' tale. From what I've observed during years of tracking and killing big bucks, I'd say that four out of five bucks have small droppings—when you field dress enough big bucks, it becomes obvious. This tells me that most of the bigger droppings I see are made by does. Another thing I've noticed is that elongated (capsule-shaped) droppings are made by does. If you're skeptical about any of this, the next time you track a good buck, check out the droppings for size.

What to do Once You Find the Track You Want to Follow

Once you've found the track you want, be aware that the buck you're following is either bedded or up and moving. If you pick up a track in the morning, he'll probably be bedded when you catch up to him. Hunt the track until you feel he's up and moving around. You'll be able to tell he's up if you find a bed with fresher tracks leaving it or tracks that get fresher as you go. If a buck is moving quickly, I'll move quickly, too. I don't want to waste time if

I'm an hour behind him. I'll set a fairly fast pace, but I always look around as I go. I learn something from every buck I track. I may not get him the first time, but if I can learn his habits, I'll have a better chance the next time I encounter his track. I always pay attention to what the buck is doing and where he's going. I note streams I've crossed and ridges I've gone over. I keep a running tally in my head of other buck tracks I cross along the way and which direction they go. This helps me to sort things out if the buck starts circling around searching for does and also makes me aware of other buck tracks I'd rather take. I may find a bigger or fresher track or one heading in a direction I'd rather go, and I'll switch tracks if I think my chances are better with the new one.

It Pays to Switch Tracks

We did just that in the story I told of the buck with the cut foot. We had been following a track made during the night since first thing in the morning. It was about ten o'clock when we crossed the track of another good buck. The new track had been made since daylight, so I figured we had a better chance of catching up to him in a hurry. We took the new track and jumped that buck in about fifteen minutes. Another time my son, Gary, was with me, and we were tracking a good buck. We came to a spot that was torn up where our buck had fought with another buck. I was circling around trying to sort out the tracks when I found a bed with a fresh track leaving it. We started following that one and bumped into the buck in a thicket only a hundred yards away. Every situation is different, but sometimes it pays to switch tracks.

When a buck starts checking on does, he will take some time, and the more time he spends, the faster you'll gain on him. Sometimes a buck will just scentcheck for does as he passes by, but as the rut get closer, he'll spend more time following does around. This creates a jumble of tracks that you would swear was made by a whole herd of deer. When I find a spot like this I make a big circle around the area, looking for my buck's track coming out. I do this for two reasons: first, it saves time, and second, he may still be with the doe. Either way, doing this makes figuring out my next move faster. If you try to follow where a buck and doe fooled around, you'll waste a lot of time and get frustrated. Make the circle and you'll gain time on your buck.

How do You Know if a Buck is Bedded?

I'm often asked how to tell when and where a buck is bedded. It's a good question, because if you know the answer, you have a much better chance of seeing him and getting a shot. You won't be able to tell all the time, but here are some things to look for: Since bucks like to bed in secure spots, they usually choose a bluff. If they

A fresh rub on a beech tree. (Note the shavings on the snow.)

bed in low ground, they'll probably choose a knoll in green growth.

This doesn't narrow the choices much, so here are some other things to check out: When I'm following a buck and his track turns abruptly uphill, there's a good chance he's bedded, so I start looking at the possibilities. I'll usually leave the track and circle around as high as I can get. On this first circle, I look for his track coming out. If I cross a track coming out, I keep following it and haven't lost any time. If it doesn't come out, I go back to my old track and cut the circle a little smaller. Now I take my time and look everything over, hoping to catch him lying down. I have all the time in the world—a buck is within several hundred yards of me and all I need to do is find him.

The scene where two bucks had been fighting. It was torn up in an area fifty-by-fifty feet.

Circling Works!

Once I picked up a track from a road during a blizzard. I had driven to the end of the road and as I came back out, I cut a buck track that had been made since I went in. I followed it high up onto a hardwood ridge. Up ahead I saw a green bluff, and the buck was headed straight for it. I circled above it, and when I peeked over the edge, I saw him lying down about forty yards below me staring down his back track. That was his last day on the mountain.

If you're hunting with a companion, post one person and the other person should circle the track.

By going high and looking down, you keep the upper hand. A buck always watches his back track and won't expect danger from above. I've also used this method when a buck turns and goes uphill. Sometimes he'll pick a place to bed where he can see the spot where he turned. As soon as he sees you turn onto his track, he'll be gone, but if you circle above him, you may catch him looking around.

The best indication that a buck is going to bed down is seeing him feeding. Most of the time a buck will feed just before lying down, especially if he's been on a long journey. Be careful not to miss the signs—sometimes they just nip a twig here and there. Bucks also frequently rub their antlers before bedding, and sometimes they also paw the ground a little. If you see signs of feeding combined with either of the other two actions, your buck will almost certainly be bedded nearby.

By paying attention to what a buck is doing, you'll be able to take a lot of the guesswork out of knowing when he's bedded. If a buck is bedded and hasn't been spooked, you'll have a good chance of getting a shot at him. When you see that a buck has started to feed, start looking for a place

Following the Bedding Signs

Stan and I were working a track through some green bluffs up on a mountain. The buck started to feed as he went down into a hardwood ravine. Then he started rubbing his antlers here and there before heading into some green growth. I knew there was a winter road on the other side of the green growth, and I told Stan to circle around and wait in the road for the buck to cross, as I didn't think we could get a shot in the thicket. I took the track into the thicket thinking I'd spook him out to where Stan was. I was inching along when I heard a little rustle ahead of me. I looked up to see a nice eight-pointer take a jump and stop thirty yards from me. He was looking in my direction and I could see the steam coming from his nostrils. All I could think of was Stan, standing out there in the road and wishing he was with me. The buck finally took off and crossed the road just around the corner from where Stan was standing.

This buck avoided the opening between these saplings.
This tells you he has a wide rack.
(Courtesy: Susan C. Morse)

you think he might be bedded and start circling. Move slowly and silently and look over every inch of the woods trying to catch a glimpse of fur or antler.

If you're tracking with a companion, one of you should wait on the track where you have a good opening to shoot, because often when you spook a buck from somewhere other than his track he'll run or sneak out on his back track. I think they do this because it was safe when they came in that way, so they feel safe running out that way. Once they get away from the immediate area, though, they'll leave their track and go where instinct tells them. Leave the hunter who stays on the track at the place where the other hunter starts circling. That way he or she will be close enough for a shot if the buck chooses his back track as an escape route.

Better Now Than Later

While driving in on a logging road early one morning during a snowstorm, Stan and I rounded a corner and saw a big buck track going down the road away from us. It looked so fresh I thought the buck should still be standing in it! We followed it down the road to where it went into the woods, and there we could see that the buck had started to run. He must have seen us come around the corner in the truck. I figured that since he was up and moving, our best chance was to try to catch him looking. We followed him as he wandered about a mile down into a swampy thicket. Soon we saw signs of feeding and some rubbed saplings, and I told Stan he'd be bedded close by. We found the best opening we could, and Stan waited. I made a two-hundred-yard circle and was swinging back toward Stan when I spotted a bed in front of me. It had been made by our buck, and he had just left, heading out on his back track right toward Stan. I eased along the track, expecting to hear a shot ring out at any time. When I saw Stan up ahead I was bewildered. Why hadn't he shot? When I reached him, he told me that he had seen the buck but felt the foliage was too thick to chance a shot, and thought we might get a better opportunity later. We tried all day to get another chance but never did. This one-hunter-stays-while-the-other-circles tactic has worked often enough for me that I try it whenever I have another hunter with me.

A typical remote deer camp in the north woods.

Once you've discovered a buck's bedding place, there are two possible outcomes. One, you shoot him, and two, you spook him and he hauls away in twenty-foot bounds. If the latter happens, many hunters give up on the track, thinking the buck is long gone. But having this happen actually makes me happy—I got the buck to move out of an area where I wasn't able to shoot him, and now I may have a better chance. It's human nature to take off in hot pursuit of a buck you've spooked. You think he must be right ahead of you waiting to be shot, but he's not. He's waiting, but he's also watching his back track, and as soon as he sees you, he'll be gone again. Once that happens, he'll probably put some distance between himself and you and will continually look back on his track. As you follow him you'll find places where he stood looking back and then a set of running tracks leaving.

For years I immediately followed spooked bucks, and the most I ever got was a quick running shot at a fleeing animal. It finally dawned on me that if I waited a while before following him, he might forget that I was there. This was another patience lesson I had to learn, but it has paid off tremendously over the years. Now if I spook a buck, I sit down to have a sandwich and wait half an hour. I have to check my watch, as it always seems like an eternity. I've tried waiting fifteen minutes, and that doesn't work. Remember that when you're waiting, so is your buck. He'll wait to see if something is going to follow him, and when nothing comes along he relaxes and goes about his business. Often he'll lie down again. Most of the time a buck doesn't know what spooked him. He simply saw movement or heard a noise and wants to get away from the immediate area until he can identify what it was.

Eat a Sandwich First? Are You Kidding?

One morning I left my remote camp with Brian, my hunter for the week. There was an inch of new snow on top of the three inches we already had, and it was still snowing. We were excited about the day's hunt, since we had already seen three good bucks that week but hadn't had a shot. We knew luck would eventually swing our way. We were hoping to find a fresh track but knew it would be difficult—the snow was making all the tracks look the same. We were still-hunting parallel to each other on the side of a green bluff where I knew several does were hanging around. I saw a deer bust out of the firs in front of me and run down the ridge. I walked down to check the bed and found that it had been made by a pretty decent buck.

I went over and told Brian that I had jumped a buck that would weigh about 180 pounds and it was his call whether we went after him or not. He had really wanted a bruiser, but since it was Thursday already, he chose to go after this buck. I said, "OK," pulled a sandwich out of my pack, and started eating it. Brian said, "What are you doing? We have to go after the buck!" When I told him we were going to wait half an hour, he couldn't believe it. He told me that in Pennsylvania, where he's from, if you wait around, a buck will be on another property where you can't hunt. I told Brian to relax, because the buck wouldn't go far. When the half hour was up, we went after him. When I have another hunter on the track with me, I walk in front so I can read the track, and the other person stays right behind me watching off to both sides. The buck ran only about two

(Continued)

Eat a Sandwich First? Are You Kidding? *(Continued)*

hundred yards and then started walking. We walked about two hundred yards more before cresting a spruce knoll. I scanned the woods up ahead, spotted the buck moving behind a blowdown, and pointed out to Brian where he was. The buck walked behind the blowdown, and as he stopped to look back toward us, only his neck showed. Brian fired and the buck dropped like a sack of potatoes. It was ninety paces to where the eight-pointer lay dead with a hole in his throat patch. Brian said this was a special buck for him, as he had always wanted to hunt in Maine and he had shot the buck with the rifle his father, now passed away, had given him.

Brian shot that deer within five hundred yards of where we jumped him. That was the start of a streak where my hunters and I killed three bucks on three hunting days in a row. The day after Brian shot his buck I shot a 220-pound nine-pointer. The next hunter I had shot a 180 pointer on his first day out. With all three of these bucks I used the tactic of waiting a half hour, and the farthest any of the bucks was shot from where it were spooked was about half a mile. If you try waiting patiently, you'll greatly improve your chances while tracking.

Brian with his first big woods buck. An eightpointer taken after a short quarter mile tracking job. We gave the buck a half-hour to settle down after jumping him and he bedded again.

Sometimes when you spook a buck, especially in the afternoon, he may decide to stay up and go on a walkabout. He may start making his rounds, checking for does and freshening his scrapes. This is the best time to get a shot, as he'll be easier to spot when he's moving. He'll also be preoccupied when he's scraping or rubbing and is not as likely to spot you. If I've waited half an hour and find that a buck is still wandering, I move right along for a while to catch back up to him. Once I've caught up, I move more slowly and watch what he's doing. For me this is the most exciting time to track. A buck is close to me, I can "watch" his every move by observing the changes in his track, and I never know when I'll peek around the next tree and see him standing there, as if by magic.

The final point to remember about tracking is to always be watching for other deer as you go. Don't become so focused on the track you're following that you fail to see anything else in the woods. Other deer can be decoys and can often give you information if you examine their actions. When you're tracking a buck, remember that he'll be traveling where other bucks travel, and the chances of seeing a different buck are good.

Opportunity Almost Missed

One day Stan and I were tracking a buck that seemed to be on a mission. We had jumped him late in the morning after working his track for a few hours. Now he was down in a thick spruce tangle where it was hard to see more than thirty yards. We jumped him again, and since it was late in the day we stayed on his track. We had gone only another hundred yards when we came to some tracks wandering around in the thicket and saw signs of feeding. The tracks were the same size as the ones we we'd been following, so at first I thought it was the same buck, but it didn't make sense to me that a buck that had just been jumped would stop to feed so soon. The tracks were fresh, and I was looking around thinking about what to do next when I spotted half of an eight-point rack sticking out from behind a spruce tree twenty yards from us. I could make out the outline of his back and could tell he was standing broadside. Stan was one step to my left and couldn't see him. I thought he was going to get a shot, but instead the buck just evaporated into the spruce, as they often do. If I had been focused just on the running track of the buck we were on, we would have walked right past the other buck and never known he was around.

I've taken you through all the steps and tactics I use when tracking bucks. You have to realize, though, that every situation is different and every buck is unique. No one tactic will work all the time, and if it did, I'd hang up my rifle, because it would no longer be a challenge to hunt the bucks of the big woods. I'll wrap up this section with a story of a hunt with a client on which we used many of the tactics I discussed in this section. See how many you can pick out.

Patience and Persistence Pay Off

It was opening week of deer season and by dinnertime on Sunday night, it had started to snow and it was accumulating fast. All the hunters were a-buzz in anticipation of what the first morning would bring. By breakfast the next morning, over a foot of snow blanketed the ground and the storm was winding down. I told the hunters that finding tracks might be hard, as the deer probably stayed put during the storm. After breakfast we all parted ways, wishing each other luck. I was guiding Sue Morse, as I had the previous five years during this same week. We had decided to hunt some high country where we always seemed to find bucks. As we turned off the highway onto a logging road we noticed that the snow was much deeper here than it was back in town, which is often the case at higher elevations. The snow was up to the truck's bumper, and when we came to a hill we couldn't climb it. I stepped out to size up the situation and went in over my knees. I told Sue we had better go back closer to town to hunt until the snow settled down. I turned the truck around and we headed back. As I drove, I was trying to think of somewhere to go, as I hadn't scouted any places closer to town. I finally decided on a ridge that ran between a swamp and a stream. I pulled the truck down a side road and we jumped out, eager to get going—we'd already lost an hour of our morning.

(Continued)

Patience and Persistence Pay Off (*Continued*)

The plan was to find the track of a good buck and go after him. We started off at a steady pace in a straight line, searching for telltale punch marks in the snow. After walking for an hour without seeing a single track, we concurred that the deer hadn't moved much during the storm. We were continuing along a hardwood ridge when suddenly I caught a flash of brown as a deer jumped off the edge of a bluff. I snorted and we waited a few minutes for a response. When nothing happened we went over to see what size deer I had seen. We found a good-sized bed and a bounding track leaving it. The track coming into the bed was almost completely covered with snow. I figured he must have fed early in the evening and laid up for the night.

I told Sue it looked like a buck worth going after. She agreed and we began our half-hour wait while enjoying the beauty and stillness of the woods. Then we headed out on the track and found that the buck had run only about a hundred yards before starting to walk. Soon we crossed another track heading up the ridge. This track was the same size as the one we were on and was made about the same time the night before. We followed our buck over the ridge and down into a spruce swamp on the other side of it. As we were easing through the spruces I could see a swale opening ahead. As I leaned out to look, I spotted the buck lying under a spruce tree about thirty yards away. He was watching his track intently, and I knew he must have seen me. As I leaned back and pointed for Sue to shoot, he jumped and disappeared into the spruces on the other side of the swale. We sat down and had a sandwich to wait him out a second time.

When we took up his track again, he led us into a maze of tracks where some other deer had recently been. The trees and underbrush were quite thick, so we decided to circle the whole area. As we made our way around, we came to where he had been standing, and we spooked him again. We waited again, and when we took up the track I could see that he had played enough of this game and was going to make time. He was moving fast and circling back toward where we had jumped him. When we got back to the other side of the ridge, where we had started, I realized that the other buck track we had seen in the beginning hadn't gone out of our circle. I told Sue we should go back and get on *that* buck, as he wouldn't already be spooked. We went back to his mostly filled track and followed it up the ridge. When he reached the top, there were green bluffs and ravines everywhere. I decided to circle to narrow down his location. We made a two-hundred-yard circle, scouring every inch of the woods for a bedded buck. When we came back to our own track and discovered that he hadn't come out, we knew things were looking up.

I told Sue to wait in the hardwoods where she could see the buck's back track while I circled again and pushed him out. I went back up his track, and this time I figured there was only one bluff he could be on. I walked to the top of it, and there was his bed with a track leaving it. Just then Sue's rifle boomed, and I was so close I could hear the action work as she pumped another shell into the chamber. The rifle boomed again, and I started down the track to find out what had happened. As I reached Sue, I saw that she was standing over a beautiful buck. She was all smiles, and the first thing she said was that she loved the rifle she had used—I had let her use my rifle to see if she liked it. She told me that the buck had come sneaking down the ridge, and when she put up the gun he spotted her and started running. She swung the bead on him and fired, and he dropped in his tracks. When he tried to get back up, she finished him off.

We took a lot of pictures and I did the dressing chore. Then I rigged up a two-person drag and we headed for the closest road, about half a mile away. I left Sue with her buck and cut cross-country to get the truck. We loaded the buck and were heading for the tagging station by about one o'clock. Sue's buck tipped the scales at just over two hundred pounds, which qualified her for her first entry into the Biggest Bucks in Maine Club.

Sue with her first two-hundred pound buck. I circled the buck and he came out on his backtrack, where Sue was waiting.

Here are the things we did to make our hunt successful. Did you discover all of them?

1. We had the persistence to travel until we found a track.
2. We waited half an hour for the buck to settle down and bed again.
3. We took note of the other track made in the night.
4. We were quiet enough to see the first buck bedded.
5. We waited half an hour again.
6. We circled the thicket when we got into the maze of tracks.
7. As the first buck circled back we noticed that the other track had not gone out.
8. We changed tracks when we thought we had a better chance.
9. We circled where we thought our buck was bedded.
10. We posted Sue on the back track.

If you picked up on most of these points, it's time for you to hit the woods—you're ready to get some practice. I think you'll find that tracking is a very rewarding way to hunt. It's you against the buck on his turf. You match wits with him and you have to be capable of going where he takes you. Once you shoot a big woods buck after tracking him down, you'll be hooked for life.

Carrying a light and sturdy deer drag is an absolute necessity for the hunter who tracks and stalks whitetails in big woods. (Courtesy: Ted Rose)

The Easy Way Out

As the saying goes, once your buck is down, the work begins. This saying is very appropriate in big-woods hunting—especially if you're still-hunting or tracking—because it's possible to find yourself with a downed buck miles from where you're camped or where you parked your vehicle. When hunters ask me how we're going to get a buck out if we shoot one way back in the woods, my usual response is that if we shoot a buck, we have the rest of the week to get him out.

Being worried about getting a buck out keeps many hunters from venturing too far back in the woods. In most places where whitetails are hunted you can drive a truck or an ATV to within a short distance of where a buck was shot. I've heard hunters make a big deal out of dragging a buck a quarter mile, but in the big woods that's a dream drag. I can't tell you how many bucks I've dragged out of the big woods, but I've probably tried every imaginable way to do it. Dragging is work, but by trial and error over the years I've figured out the easiest ways to do it.

First Things First

Before you start to drag your buck, take care of a few other important details. First, take some good photographs. There's no better time to capture the moment and the beauty of your buck than the moment he's down. His hair will be fluffy and his eyes will still have a shine almost as if he were alive. Take photos before you start field dressing to avoid having them show blood. If you hang a photo of your trophy on the wall, nonhunters will be less likely to be offended by it if the deer is clean and beautiful than if blood is running out of his mouth and onto the snow. And photos taken in the natural setting where you took your deer will preserve the memory of the hunt better than those taken in the back of a truck or in the wood shed. The camera I carry has a timer so I can take photos if I'm alone or

An ATV can be a big help in getting a buck out.

get in a picture with another hunter. Take plenty of photos at different angles and then keep the best.

After the photo session, it's time to field dress your buck, and everyone has a special way of going about it. My way is quick and simple. It may go against conventional wisdom with respect to cooling the meat rapidly, but when you hunt in the north, cooling is usually not an issue. First, don't cut the buck's throat. It's a myth that a deer needs to be bled—one that should have been dispelled long ago—but I still hear hunters talk about the need for it. Besides being unnecessary, cutting the throat will make your taxidermist unhappy because he'll have to sew up the cut and try to blend in the hair you cut off. Here are my quick and easy steps:

1. Cut around the anus as deep as your knife will reach.
2. Start a hole through the skin and flank muscle just ahead of the penis. Put your index and middle fingers in the hole, pull up on the flank, and then run your knife between your fingers all the way to the sternum (the point where the ribs from both sides come together).

3. Roll out the stomach and intestines, including the anal tube.

4. Cut the penile cord at the anus and pinch off the bladder and remove it.

5. Cut around the diaphragm to release the liver and stomach. 6. Finally, reach above the heart and lungs and cut off the windpipe to release them. If you want to keep the heart and liver to eat, you can save these last two steps until you get back to camp.

I do not cut the skin between the hindquarters or remove the penile cord, because doing this exposes some of the best meat to dirt and air and has no effect on cooling the meat.

In Maine, the magic number for a buck's field-dressed weight is two hundred pounds. A two-hundred pound buck qualifies you for entry into the Biggest Bucks in Maine Club so you can receive the coveted red-and-yellow shoulder patch. For entry into the club, the field-dressed weight is defined as the weight with all internal organs removed including heart, lungs, and liver. There are hunters who spend a lifetime hunting in Maine in hopes of bagging just one of these brutes.

The last thing to do before dragging your buck is to attach the tag. Each state and province has different regulations about tagging. Maine law requires hunters to attach the tag to the buck before moving it anywhere. Make sure you check the law for the area where you are hunting. Some hunters have told me they also mark their bucks so they can identify them if they are stolen. I guess this is a good idea, but I hope I never have to hunt in an area where other hunters would do such a thing.

Dragging Your Buck

Solo Dragging

If you're alone and capable of doing the job yourself, grab an antler and go. Don't tie a rope around the antlers to drag the buck with, as all of his weight will be on the ground and his antlers will snag on every twig or log you pass. By grabbing the antler itself, you'll be lifting the head and neck off the ground, and you can weave through the brush and over logs more easily. The terrain and conditions will determine whether you should just sling your gun and go or take your gun ahead first. If the buck is exceptionally heavy or the terrain is flat with no snow, walk ahead fifty yards or so, clearing out sticks and blowdowns as you go, and leave your rifle—and your jacket if you're getting too warm. Then go back and drag the buck to where your rifle is. Continue leap-frogging like this all the way out. It's a slow process, but you may not have another choice.

The easiest way for one man to drag. The antlers and front legs won't catch in the brush.

Two Long, Lonely Drags

I've had some long drags by myself, and the longest one was on bare ground. It started at nine in the morning, and I got the buck to camp at four-thirty, just as it was getting dark. I shot the buck in the pouring rain high up on a mountain. When I started dragging him, I moved right along on a downhill slope, stopping for a breather when I needed it. When the terrain started to level out, I switched to taking my gun and jacket ahead. At one point I had to go uphill to cross over to another ravine. It took about an hour to travel the two hundred yards, over and around a maze of blowdowns. By three o'clock I had made it to the back of a chopping, but I was still a mile from camp. Fortunately, though, I was only about a quarter mile from the lake I was camped on, so I hurried back to camp and got my boat and my wheeled cart. I wheeled the buck out on a skid trail to the lake and took him the rest of the way by boat. It didn't take long to drift off to sleep *that* night. The buck weighed 215 pounds, and the drag was about a mile, not counting the cart and boat ride.

I had another long, solo drag with a 235-pound buck I had shot high on a mountain. I had started tracking him on the side of the mountain closer to my camp, but I shot him on the other side. I had to decide whether to drag him up a few hundred yards and then back down to where I started or to go down from where I was, knowing I'd hit a road that was somewhere down below. It was an easy choice: I headed downhill. I started the drag at about one o'clock, and this time there *was* snow on the ground, which made for better sliding. It was fairly steep, and I went about a mile in three hours. It was getting late and starting to snow hard, and I decided to leave the buck in the woods so I could get out before dark. I took off my shirt and put it over the buck to keep any coyote that might wander by from having a midnight snack. I made a mental note that I left him in a skid trail with water running in it and that there was a stream about fifty yards away. By now it was snowing so hard I could barely make out the ridge I was paralleling. I came to another skid trail that took me out to a logging road where I hoped to catch a ride with another hunter, since I was about twelve miles from my truck, which was on the other side of the mountain.

As I walked, I kept coming across fresh tire tracks in the snow where one vehicle after another had left the area—probably minutes before. I had walked a couple of miles when a pickup truck full of Canadian hunters came along. I flagged them down, and they gave me a ride to the paved road in the back of their truck. I was half-frozen by the time we got there. They were turning away from where my truck was, so I started walking again. The highway plow truck passed me going the other way, so I knew I could catch a ride with him on his return trip to town. (That's one thing good about living in a small town—you know everyone and they're willing to help people out.) I kept walking to stay warm, as all I had on was a long-underwear top and a jackshirt, and they were wet straight through. I walked about another mile and came to where a tractor trailer had gone off the road. I knew the sheriff on the scene, and he let me sit in his cruiser to get warmed up while I waited for the plow truck. When it arrived the driver pulled the tractor trailer back onto the road and we headed for town. I got home at eight o'clock that night, and needless to say, Deb was pretty relieved.

I called a couple of friends from town to help me get the buck out in the morning. Then I took a hot shower and crawled into bed pretty well worn out. The next morning we had about a foot of new snow as we headed for the mountain to finish the drag. When we got to the logging road, we had to wait for the grader to plow it out. We followed him for four miles to the turn where we knew we'd have to snowmobile in. Tommy and I snowmobiled in to where I had come out the night before and started walking in. It was as if we had entered a winter wonderland. The trees were bent over from the weight of the snow. It had snowed even more on the mountain than in town, and in the raspberry bushes it was up to our crotches. I was beginning to wonder if I could find my buck, as everything in the woods looked the same. I wished that I had taken the time to spot a trail out with my knife the night before (by slicing off a bit of the bark from small trees), but I hadn't wanted to take the time as it was late.

At least I had made good mental notes all the way out. We walked in just the way I had come out, following the same ridge. I finally felt like we were close and had started looking for the skid road I had left the buck in when I heard the stream to my left. I came to a skid road, looked up it, and saw the tip of an antler sticking out of the snow about three inches.

We started to drag him in the deep snow, but were not making much progress. Then Tommy, who had hunted that area before and recognized the spot, said to wait a minute. He disappeared into the snowcovered trees, but in a couple of minutes he was back with the news that a wood yard was only a hundred yards away, and we could get the snowmobiles to it. We dragged the buck to the yard and went back to get the snowmobiles. By the time we got back to town, tagged him and got home, it was about three o'clock in the afternoon.

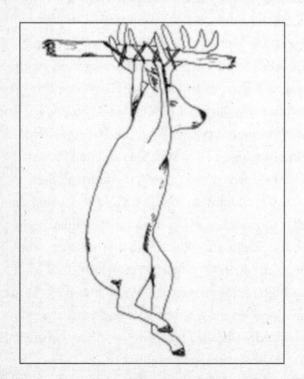

Using a dragging stick will help make the job quicker and easier when two are dragging.

Dragging with a Partner

If there are two of you, dragging becomes a lot easier. By taking a few minutes to rig up a drag stick, two hunters can move along without having to stop as often as one does. First, tuck both of the buck's front feet behind his antlers and lash them there with rope or webbing. Then, break off a dead stick a least two inches in diameter and long enough to give you an eighteen-inch handle on either side of the rack when lashed to it. Lash the stick tight to the beams between two points so it doesn't slip. Now both of you can sling your guns, grab one end of the stick, pick it up to your waist, and push. This method uses the same concept as driving a wagon with a team of horses or oxen. The weight of the head and neck is off the ground, which helps to avoid ruining the cape. It's amazing how easily a buck will slide along like this, especially in the snow.

Dragging in Unfamiliar Territory

If you end up shooting a buck in a place you're not familiar with, check your exit options before you start dragging. Locate your position on a map. Plot it on a GPS if you have one. Look for the closest road, even if it's not the one you came in on. Topographical (topo) maps include most of the old logging roads even if they're no longer in use. They may just look like a path in the woods, but they usually follow the best contour of the land, are a good, flat surface to drag on, and will usually take you to a good road. If you can't find one nearby, pick the best route you can by going downhill if possible. Obviously you will want to take the straightest route you can, so use your compass to keep yourself on track. Avoid going near streams and ponds unless you can get a canoe to them—otherwise you'll be battling the spruce thickets and blowdowns that are common in these areas.

Other Dragging Options

Here are some other methods to consider as you plan your way out.

- Use a four-wheeler if they're permitted, as they can follow old logging roads fairly easily.
- If you're near a lake, use a motorboat or canoe to save time and energy. Remember to wear a life jacket if you're on the water, as the water is very cold and you won't survive long in it if your boat capsizes. I've taken many bucks out by boat over the years. In fact, it would have been impossible to hunt in some places without having a boat available to get the buck out.
- Use a wheeled cart. They are fairly inexpensive (look for them in mail-order catalogs) and easy to take to camp. They're not much good in the woods, but they're great on old logging roads or roads where a bridge is out and you can't get a vehicle past.
- A floatplane is the ultimate buck hauler. One year in my remote camp, Mike shot a buck on the back side of the mountain—the side away from camp. He would have had about a two-mile drag, of which one mile would have been uphill. But he shot the buck about three hundred yards from a pond, and I knew my friend Steve could get his floatplane in to it. We were camped on a

A boat is a good way to get to areas with little hunting pressure. Watch the weather on a daily basis, as storms can blow in quickly.

By using a float plane, we saved a day of dragging when this one was shot in an inaccessible area.

lake, so I asked Mike if he wanted to pay for a plane trip out for his buck or make a really bad drag. It didn't take him long to decide on the plane ride. We dragged the buck to the pond, hung him in a tree, and made the journey back to camp. That night I called Steve from a two-way radio and asked him to pick up the buck in the morning and drop it back at camp. I met Steve where the buck was in the morning and he got the job done, saving Mike and me a lot of sweat.

Leaving a Buck Overnight

If you have to leave a buck overnight, consider taking these precautions:

- Leave a shirt over him to discourage coyotes. Coyotes are usually too shy of human scent to go near anything that smells of it.
- Mark your position with a GPS if you have one.
- Mark the area with flagging ribbon or a handkerchief. Flagging ribbon comes on rolls in various colors and can be found at any hardware or sportinggoods store.
- Mark your trail by blazing small trees by skinning the bark with a knife. The exposed white wood will stand out against the gray-and-green background.

A snowmobile can get you back in on roads not accessible by four-wheel-drive vehicles.

Mike's six-pointer. We were hunting so far back in we had to have him flown out by float plane.

The neck on this buck explains why I call him The Hog. I shot this 260-pound nine-pointer at nineteen paces, before he could get out of his bed.

- When you get to a road, mark the spot where your path meets the road especially well, as most roads already have flagging ribbons hanging along them from forestry use.

Taking these precautions will help you to avoid losing a once-in-a-lifetime trophy and having him rot in the woods or become food for coyotes and ravens.

The way out is not always easy, but it is the culmination of a successful hunt for the nomadic whitetail.

Mastering the Art of Tracking

Tracking big woods bucks is an art. Hunters who track bucks are like artists and have different styles or approaches to their work. Some throw paint on the canvas as quick as possible. Others painstakingly pay attention to every detail with every stroke of the brush. When artists are done with their work, the end result will either be just a picture or it might be a masterpiece.

Big woods buck trackers also have different approaches to their work. The end result of tracking a buck is always going to be a "picture" or a hunting experience, but some of these pictures will end up being a "masterpiece" or a trophy on the wall. Like the artist who has a closet full of pictures for every masterpiece he creates, the tracker has a memory full of experiences for every trophy on his wall. The key to putting the trophies on the wall is learning from all the experiences. Hopefully, some of my experiences will help you to create your own masterpiece.

Finding a Track

Obviously the first step to tracking a buck is to find a track. Sometimes this is easier said than done, especially if you're looking for the old toe draggers. These big old bucks are generally a small part of the deer population and the most reclusive. They are also the most difficult ones to track and kill.

Most hunters try to find a buck track by driving logging roads. There are areas in the big woods that have been logged extensively and there is a maze of these roads. A buck that lives in an area like this is eventually going to have to cross roads. If you drive enough of these logging roads, the odds are that you will eventually find a buck track. When you find a track in an area like this, circle the section of woods the buck went into by driving the roads around it. The buck may have already passed through that section and crossed another road.

If you are not familiar with the area, it's a good idea to have a map that shows all of the roads. By circling the area and not finding the buck's track coming out, you have an idea how far away he might be. If you don't take the time to circle the area, you might spend hours on a buck track only to find that another hunter is ahead of you on it. I know of hunters who will find a track an hour before daylight and wait there so another hunter doesn't get on it. It's kind of like staking a claim during the gold rush. The problem with doing that is, while you're waiting, the buck might still be traveling and cross another road. That makes the chance of another hunter being ahead of you on the track even greater. The upside of finding a track from the road is that you haven't burnt up any energy before starting on it. The downside is that putting time in on a track, you may have another hunter ahead of you when it crosses a road. One year in Maine on the last day of the muzzle-loader season, there was finally some snow to track on. That year there had been very little tracking snow, and since it was my only week to hunt without a client, I was itchy to get on a track. Chris was with me to video and it was going to be our last chance this year to get some footage. The snow that fell in the night was mixed with sleet and freezing rain. There was very little around town, so we drove north hoping to find better tracking snow. As we turned onto a logging road that went north, we found out that there were other hunters with the same idea. There were tire tracks going down all of the side roads, so I knew that taking a track in that area would most likely lead to getting "cut off" by another hunter.

I kept driving north until we reached an area where there were no other tire tracks. Then, just ahead, we could see the telltale pock marks in the snow where a deer had crossed the road. Just as we had hoped, it was the track of a good buck. The buck was heading into a big piece of woods between the road and a river. I didn't think he would cross the river and there were no roads in that area, so we decided to take the track.

The snow was quiet and there was a little bit of wind, making it a perfect day to be on the track of a buck. The track led us down into the green growth where the buck had been checking on does. After about a mile, the buck went up a ridge into some hardwood choppings. There, the buck found another buck that was with a doe and began following them. I was excited knowing that the two bucks might distract each other enough to make it easier to get a shot at one.

Not far from where the tracks came together were running tracks crisscrossing from the bucks chasing the doe. I could see more green growth down below, so I figured the deer had gone into it. The wind was blowing in that direction, and we had just starting to circle around when a deer snorted. I knew the deer had most likely winded us. We made a big circle hoping the deer weren't spooked too bad and we could get around them. Half-way around the circle we cut running tracks heading in the direction of the river.

At that time we were in an old grown-up cut, so I decided to keep moving until I figured out where they might be going. It didn't take long to find out that all three of them jumped into the river and swam across. I was amazed that they did, as the river was 50 yards wide with a lot of current. I guess they just didn't like the smell of us! I knew there was a road about a half-a-mile away from the other side of the river and it would be a good place to check for their tracks.

I marked the spot where the deer crossed the river on my GPS so just in case they didn't cross the road, it would be easier to pick up their tracks again. It was a little discouraging knowing we were going to lose a couple of hours getting back to the truck and driving around. But I didn't think that the deer would go too far once they crossed the river. Usually when deer cross a stream or river they feel safe, because that's how they have been able to escape from coyotes.

We finally made our way to the road on the other side of the river. To my surprise, the deer had walked across it at the top of a ridge and continued along the ridge pretty much in a straight line. I kept seeing running tracks coming back towards us and then circling back. The dominant buck had been chasing the other buck. I kept thinking that it was only a matter of time before I would catch them chasing again. After about an hour I began to realize that the doe was heading to a deer yard that was a few miles away. The deer finally crossed another road and I could see fresh tire tracks in it. My heart sank as I stepped into the road and saw that another hunter was following the tracks. It was a long walk back to the truck knowing my season was over. When there is a fresh blanket of snow on the roads, it's possible to drive along at a pretty good clip and spot tracks, even before daylight. If there is enough snow, though, some of the logging roads are going to be plowed. When they are, snow is thrown off to the sides making it very difficult to see tracks from the road. Tracks are also hard to spot if the snow is wet and vehicles throw snow from their tires off to the side of the road. In either case you will have to drive slowly looking off into the woods for tracks. Even then it's easy to miss them.

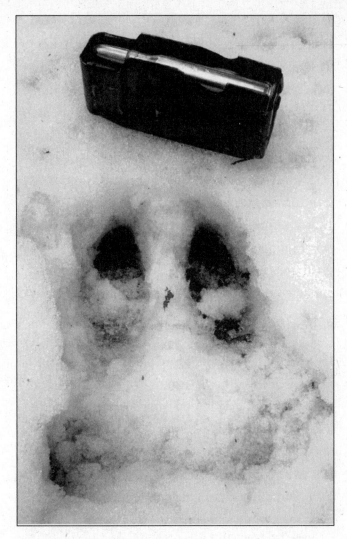

The 7600 .30-06 clip is three-and-a-half inches, so this buck is a monster. Note the dewclaw imprints are way outside of the hooves.

One morning Chris and I were driving a road where we had found a good buck track the day before. I knew there were several good bucks in the area and was hoping to find where one had crossed a road. The snow the day before was wet and had made slush on the roads. The vehicle traffic had thrown the slush way off to the sides, making pock marks in the snow everywhere. Not seeing any tracks on that road, we turned onto a less traveled road that circled back to the first.

Just before we completed the circle, we cut a huge buck track crossing the road—one of those tracks that are as big as they get. The buck track was going into the circle, so I figured that he had to be in there somewhere. The circle was about one mile by two miles. We followed the buck up a ridge, where he began to check on some does. I hunted slowly, thinking that I might catch him chasing a doe. Soon the buck turned towards the first road we had driven and I began to get the sinking feeling that he had crossed it. I picked up the pace, and when we got to the road, there was a truck parked at the track and boot tracks in the buck track. We were so anxious to find a track that I was driving too fast to really scan the woods off to the sides of the road. That was another painful lesson on patience for me!

Those are the reasons that I don't really like to hunt in areas with a lot of roads that can be driven on. I much prefer to strike off through the woods looking for a track. This way I'm hunting and learning something about the area. If you spend all your time riding around looking for a track, you really miss out on a lot. Quite often I will walk back in on a winter road or cart road to see if a buck has crossed. These roads are usually easy walking, making it easy to cover a lot of ground in a hurry. Another reason I like to walk is that bucks have learned to avoid the busy roads as much as possible. Time and time again, I've found where a buck has crossed off the end of a road that is driven on by vehicles.

One time I decided to try an area that I found while moose hunting, though I had never deer hunted it. There was a winter road that circled a ridge and connected two logging roads. There had been snow on the ground for a week, and as I was driving in I could see that there had been vehicles in and out of the road all week. I was thinking about turning around and going somewhere else, but decided to go to the end of the road anyway. When I got to the end of the road where the vehicles turned around, there was not one boot track going down the winter road. It was obvious that everyone in this area was a road hunter.

I started walking down the winter road, and before I was out of sight of the truck, I cut a pretty good buck track that had been made in the night. I decided to continue on and look for a bigger track. About 200 yards farther on, I cut a bigger track going in the same direction as the first. From there I could see another track farther down the road. I walked over to that track only to find that it had been made by another good buck. All three of these bucks had crossed the winter road in the night and were heading in the same direction.

If I don't find a track on one of these winter roads, I turn 90 degrees to the road and head into the woods. Depending on the terrain in the area, I usually will make a big square or a circle, looking for a track. I try to follow a ravine or travel along a ridge hoping to find a track crossing over it. I also check any signpost rubs or scrape lines that I know of in the area. If it's during the rut, I will check around every place I know of where there are does. There are very few days that I do not find a good buck to follow by doing this. The days I don't find a track are usually the ones when there is snowstorm or the day right after one. When it's snowing in the morning, all the hunters in camp get as excited as kids in a candy store, but I know from experience that the odds of finding a track that day are not real good. The reality is that you are going to have to find where a buck has been within a couple of hours or his track will be covered. Once in a while I happen to find such a track, but more often than not I spend a long day searching.

I remember one snowy morning walking back in on an old winter road with a client, hoping to find a toe dragger to follow. There were a couple of inches of snow on the ground and it was coming down steady. About a mile down the road, four deer had just crossed. I suspected one was a small buck and they were heading toward some signposts, so we followed the tracks. We caught up to the does and watched them run off. The buck had split off from them and went to the signposts. There were no big tracks there, so we worked our way along a swamp and back to the road. Just as we got back on the road again, there was another small buck track wandering up it. We followed the track around a corner and a little crotch horn buck was standing there, looking at us. We watched him until he got bored of us and wandered off into the snowy woods. I was beginning to think that it was going to be one of those days when the deer would be moving around everywhere. As it turned out, that wasn't going to be the case. We walked the rest of the day for mile after mile and only found a few other tracks that were made by small deer. As the snow piled up the deer had just hunkered down to wait out the storm.

Picking the Track You Want to Follow

When I look at a deer track, there are three things that I want to determine. They are the size of the deer, whether it is a buck or doe, and when the track was made. These things determine whether or not it's a track that I want to go follow. Sometimes this task can be quite simple by just glancing at the track, but other times it may require following the track for a while to determine these things.

The first thing I look at is the size and shape of the track itself. Keep in mind that when a deer is walking, the rear foot is placed directly into the front foot print, so the track you see is the rear foot.

Guide Mike Stevens was lucky to find this buck's track during a snowstorm, but he was glad he did.

Keep in mind also that the rear foot is smaller than the front foot. If the track is two-and-one-half inches wide and three inches long, and the dewclaws are a half-inch outside of the hooves, it is most likely a mature buck.

I personally like tracks that are three inches wide, as they are usually made by the old monster bucks. I don't recommend that all hunters hold out for what I call a "3 × 3 track" (three inches wide and three inches long), since in most places these tracks are few and far between. As I noted earlier, bucks from different areas may have smaller feet. Make sure you know what is realistic for the size of a foot on the bucks in the area you are hunting. The biggest buck that I have taken so far, which you will read about later in the book, is a good example of that. When I saw the track, I almost decided not to follow it even though I had just jumped the buck. If I had been hunting in Maine I wouldn't have, but I knew that in Ontario not all of the big bucks have big feet.

The shape of a track can help you determine whether or not it was made by a mature buck. As a buck gets older his feet will tend to splay out. This will cause the dewclaws to show more, even in a minimal amount of snow. A mature buck will have

These Ontario bucks' hooves are the same size, but the one on the left is from an older 200+ lb. buck and the one on the right is from a yearling. Note the tips are worn on the older buck's toes.

dewclaws that show one to two inches behind his toes and they will be noticeably wider than the rest of the track. A mature buck's toes will be rounded or blunt in the front from wear over the years. The print of an older buck will appear to be square because as his feet splay, it causes the toes to spread apart. This square shape will be apparent no matter how deep the snow may be.

The next thing I look at is the length of the stride. I like to see the distance between steps to be 24-36 inches. This measurement can vary depending on how fast a buck is walking. Generally speaking, the longer a buck's stride, the longer his body is, which is a good indication of how much the buck might weigh. Long-bodied bucks will typically weigh much more than short-bodied ones.

The other thing I consider while I'm looking at the stride is what I call the stance–the distance side to side between the tracks. On a mature buck this distance will be 8-12 inches. This measurement is an indication of how wide a buck's body is, and another hint of how much he might weigh.

The last thing I look for is if the buck drags his feet in the snow. Mature bucks have a tendency to drag their feet, and the older they get, the more they drag them. I call them the cross-country skiers. These bucks drag their feet so much that the when you see the tracks, it looks like someone was skiing through the woods. I can assure you that I never walk past one of those tracks!

Quite often I am asked if there is way to tell a buck track from that of a doe. The answer is that there is no foolproof way to tell by just looking at the track. That's why we have to combine looking at the track itself and then considering the other indictors like the ones I mentioned previously. That being said, there are still some mature old does in the woods that have big feet. Some of them will even display dewclaws that look like a buck's. These are usually barren does that have no fawns and are alone. This is another reason you may confuse their track with that of a buck. There is also no way to tell a yearling buck track from that of a doe, as the bucks dewclaws have not yet matured. Anyone who thinks he can tell a buck track from a doe track 100 percent of the time has probably not tracked a lot of deer. I have tracked literally thousands of deer in my life, and I'm here to tell you that I will get tripped up once in a while.

Sometimes you may just have to follow the track for ways to determine whether or not it was made by a buck. It shouldn't take you long to figure it out and it might just be worth the time. I rarely go more than several hundred yards on a track before I determine whether or not it was made by a doe. A doe acts totally differently than a buck and there are several things that I will be on the lookout for. If the track is wandering and feeding, especially within sight of a road, it is probably a doe. If the deer goes between trees that are too close together for antlers, it's probably a doe. The one way you will be able to tell absolutely for sure if you're tracking a buck or doe is when they urinate. When a doe urinates, she squats down like a female dog. This will be obvious in the snow, as the back feet will be spread apart and pointed out. The urine spot will be a small round hole in the center of the tracks. When a buck urinates, he stands with his hocks together and the urine will be in an oblong hole and splattered. Then there will most likely be drops of urine in the snow along his trail as he continued walking.

Not all that long ago I followed what turned out to be the biggest doe track that I have ever seen. I picked the track up where it crossed the road in the middle of the day. That morning I had been tracking a buck that had crossed the border and I had to leave it. The conditions were near perfect with wet snow, and I was anxious to get on another buck. This track was a 3 × 3, with huge dewclaws, so I assumed it must be a buck. I had only gone 50 yards on the track when I started having my doubts.

Big does will often have big tracks.

The deer had started feeding within sight of the road. I still didn't believe it could be a doe with a track that big, so I continued on it. Within 100 yards, the track turned towards a green knoll, so I thought the deer was most likely lying down. I circled up onto the knoll and found a bed with a track walking away from it. The deer was feeding again and little did I know that I had already spooked it. I came to the running track which was headed back towards the road. This deer was not acting like a buck, but I still clung onto hope. I followed the track back across the road and up a ridge for about 100 yards, where the deer had stopped to urinate. There, written in the snow as plain as day, was the spread out tracks and round urine hole of a doe. Needless to say I was disappointed, but at least it had only taken about 15 minutes to find out for sure.

Obviously, if you follow a track that you are unsure of and you come to a rub or scrape, you can make an easy confirmation, but quite often a buck will travel a long way without making any. That's the reason it's much easier to look for doe sign. If there is more than one deer traveling together, there is another way to determine if one of them is a buck. If the bigger track is walking on top of the small track, it is most likely a buck following a doe. If the small tracks are walking on top of the bigger ones, it is most likely a smaller doe or fawn following a doe.

Aging Tracks

There are two important reasons to be able to tell the age of a track. The first is to decide whether or not to follow a particular track. If I am going to take a track in the morning, I want to make sure that it was made the previous night. If it was, I will catch up with the buck sometime during the day. The later the track was made in the night the better, but it doesn't really matter as long as it's the buck I want to follow.

The second reason to be able to age a track is so that you can sort through a maze of tracks without losing the buck you are following. Once you become good at aging tracks, you are well on your way to mastering the art of tracking. That being said, figuring out how long ago a track was made is the most difficult part of tracking for a hunter to learn. That is because there are so many variables that factor into it. I relate these factors to figuring out a mathematical equation. Basically it a combination of the type of snow, when it last snowed, current temperature and past temperature.

Obviously, if it had snowed in the night, it is going to be quite simple to guess the age of a track. All you really need to know is when the snow stopped and how frozen the print is. Once the snow has been on the ground for a few days, it becomes critical to know the difference between a track that was made the previous night and one that is two days old. I've heard countless stories by hunters who said they lost a buck track when it got mixed in with other tracks. If those hunters were able to age the tracks, it would have helped them to stay on their bucks.

When a track is made in the snow, the conditions begin to affect it almost immediately. This is where the calculations come into play, and once you learn them it becomes second nature. I look at track in two separate ways: the bottom of the print and the top edge of the snow. Sometimes one will tell me more than the other, but by looking at both of these things I can age a track to within 15 minutes if the conditions are right. A track is either freezing or thawing, depending on the temperature, but in either case it is changing. The only exception is when the temperature is within a few degrees of the freezing point, in which case a track will stay the same for a long period of time.

When I look at the top edge of the track, I'm looking to see how crisp and sharp it is and also how crisp the snow is that was pushed up in front of the track. This edge changes very quickly and is the single most important thing to look for when sorting through tracks. I was tracking a buck with my son Gary one day when I had the opportunity to teach him this valuable lesson.

We had picked up the track from a road just after daylight that morning. Within half an hour we had jumped the buck. The buck took us up on a ridge where there were other deer. Our buck started to walk in the tracks of another buck with the exact same-size track. That other buck's track was made in the night, so both looked similar. When I asked Gary if he could tell the difference, he said that they looked the same to him. I pointed out that the track we were following still had a sharp edge and the one made in the night was just slightly rounded on the edges from evaporation in the cold air. The difference was only noticeable to Gary when we got down and looked closely at the track. Sometimes these subtle differences are the only way to keep you on the trail.

When I examine the bottom of the track, I do most of it by feel when it's cold and by sight when it's warm. When it's warm the print itself will melt until, eventually, there is nothing more than a square hole in the snow with bare ground in the bottom. How long this takes depends on the temperature. When it's cold the print freezes, so by feeling how frozen it is I can get an idea of when it was made. Again, the temperature will determine how fast the print freezes.

These examples are best suited to new snow on bare ground. When there are several layers of snow, the print become harder to see, as the snow falls back into the track. Once this happens, I rely more on looking at the top edge of the track and also feeling its inner edge. The inside edge of the track will get firm or set up when it's cold. This will actually happen quicker than the edge rounding over. Feeling the loose snow on the inside edge of the track is the quickest and easiest way to tell if the track has just been made. Whenever I feel in a track, I always use my bare hand. With gloves on, you just cannot be accurate enough.

The only way to get good at aging tracks is by experience. A good way to get the experience when you can't be in the woods is to make tracks around your property. You can experiment all winter if you live in an area that has snow. It doesn't matter if you make the tracks or your dog makes the tracks; all you need to do is to keep checking on them to see how they change over hours and even days. You can also go out in the woods and track other animals, such as fox or coyote, to get some practice. You'll be surprised at how much you will learn by doing it, and it will give you a head start on your next deer season.

On the Track

Once I decide to follow a buck's track, I'm going to hunt it two different ways. If the track is hours old, I'm going to hunt the track to catch up to the buck. The odds are that the buck is bedded down somewhere and I want to catch up to him as fast as I can. The quicker I can catch up to a buck, the more time I will have to hunt him.

All too often a hunter will move slowly along on a track that was made in the night and never get close to the buck. It's not uncommon for a buck to travel five or 10 miles in one night. If you find his track where he had just begun to travel, it is going to take you a while to catch up to him. Until a buck gives me some indication that he is lying down or the track begins to get fresher, I am going to move along at a fast walk. By moving fast, most of the

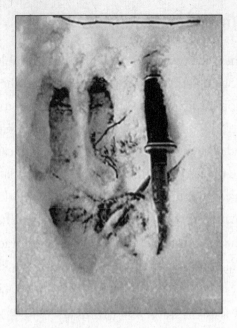

This monster buck track is crisp, clear and fresh.

time I can catch up to the buck within three or four hours.

If I think a track is less than an hour old, whether I have been following it for a while or I have just found it, I will hunt it at a slower pace. This pace will depend on what the buck is doing. If he is moving along in a straight line, I will still move fairly fast, but I will also be looking more closely at the woods ahead. If the buck is checking does or laying down rubs and scrapes, I will move more slowly, really taking the time to search the woods. I want to try to get look at the buck before he gets a look at me.

Whenever you're on a buck track, you have to become a student and learn from that particular buck. I don't care how many bucks anyone has followed, there is always something to be learned from each one. You may learn where one of his secret hideouts is, or he may take you to one of his signpost rub areas. You may also learn places that other bucks are using. By following a buck, you will also find out where all the does in his area are. All of this information is going to be useful the next time you end up hunting in the same piece of woods.

Bucks are born with certain basic instincts, but most of their behavior is learned over the course of their lifetime. That's why an old mature buck is the most difficult one to kill. A buck's whole life is spent trying to avoid danger, and they become good at it. Once a buck is successful at eluding danger by employing a certain trick, he will most likely use the same trick again. In the big woods, predators like wolves and coyotes have the most influence on a buck's behavior. A buck will use the same tactics to escape when being followed by a hunter as he does with a predator. It's important for a hunter to learn these different tactics, and use them to his advantage.

One of the most common tricks a buck will use is to turn around and walk back in his track for a ways and then jump off to one side. This gives the buck time to gain some ground while whatever is following him is trying to figure out where he went. A coyote is going to follow the track to the end and then it will take him a while to find where the track went. Likewise, a hunter on the track might also take some time to figure out where the buck went. Once the buck you are following uses this trick, you should expect him to use it again. As soon as you see the buck's track coming back towards you, immediately look off to both sides for his jumping track. Every time you can catch the buck using this trick, you will gain some time on him. With any luck, you might even catch him coming back on his track.

Another common trick that bucks use to escape danger is to walk in water. They've learned that by walking in water they can lose a predator. It's quite common to follow a buck to a stream and not see the track come out the other side. When this happens, he buck has obviously walked one way or the other in the stream. First, I always look in the direction the buck was traveling. If the stream is shallow enough, I will walk in it and look for water dripped on rocks or ice to confirm that I'm going in the right direction. All the time that I'm doing this, I'm also looking on both sides of the stream bank for his track. If

I come to a log that is lying across the stream or a spot where the ice is frozen across the stream and I do not see any sign, then I know that the buck has probably traveled the opposite way. At this point, I turn around and search the other direction. I have followed bucks in streams for several hundred yards before they left them. The water doesn't have to be a stream for a buck to walk in it; they will quite often walk the wet places in the woods where the snow has melted and left puddles on the ground. This quite often happens in skidder trails and spring seeps. Once you know a buck is using the water like this, it's much easier to pick his track back up. Just walk in the water and keep looking for the track leaving it. No matter what trick a buck uses to try and lose you, the sooner you can figure it out, the faster you can gain ground on him.

The one escape tactic that some bucks use is to run. I don't mean that the buck runs off a ways and settles back down, but that these bucks might run a mile before stopping. My experience with such bucks has been that they are very wary and never let their guard down. You will never gain ground on a running buck until he decides to stop. Usually these bucks give no indication that they are going to lie down, and they will be watching their back track when they do. Once they see movement following them, they are up and running again, and may travel another mile before stopping again.

When I discover that the buck I'm following is one of these running bucks, I know I'll be putting on some miles that day. I hunt these bucks with two objectives in mind. One is to pressure the buck by moving fast on his track in hopes of catching him looking back just long enough to get a shot. The other objective is to find another good track to switch to. Experience has taught me that my odds of shooting a buck that is not a runner are much greater than shooting one that is. Once you figure out a particular buck's bag of tricks, you just might be able to anticipate his next move.

Just when I thought that I had seen every trick that a buck might use, not long ago a buck showed me a new one. It was the last day of the muzzle-loader season in Maine, and there had not been any tracking snow all season. It had rained in the night, so I hoped that there might be some snow in the higher elevations. As I was driving to the place I wanted to hunt, there started to be a covering of wet snow on the ground. Now I just hoped that I could find a good buck track to follow.

I walked back in on an old winter road to look for tracks. About a mile back in the road was blocked with alders, and I went into the woods to get around them. I knew there was a stream not too far ahead, so I decided to walk to it and follow it back to the road. As I was walking along the stream, I stumbled across a signpost rub. It was a nice-looking one, and I decided to stop and take a photo of it. I was kneeling down taking the photo when I noticed the slight dimple of a buck track beside the tree the rub was on. There was only an inch of snow on the ground, and I was wondering if the track might just be an old one in the mud under the snow.

As I carefully scraped the snow out of the track with my finger, I could see that the bottom of the track had packed snow in it. That confirmed to me that the track had been made in the night. I put away my camera and headed out after the buck. Since it was still snowing lightly, I moved quickly on the track not knowing if I could catch up to the buck before the track became totally filled in with snow.

The buck crossed the stream and hadn't gone far when he found some does to check on. There had also been another buck checking those does, and that buck's track was fresher. I took the fresher track and hurried along on it before it filled in with snow. After following the buck for four hours, I knew he must be still up and moving, as the amount of snow in the track didn't change. The buck was still wandering and searching for does, stopping once in

a while to make a hooking. He buck took me to an area that I was familiar with, just as his track was beginning to get fresher. I started to creep along, thinking I would see the buck at any minute. The conditions couldn't have been more perfect for killing him.

The buck walked over to a blown-down spruce and fed on the old man's beard on both sides of it. There was now no snow in the track, so I knew I had missed the buck feeding there by minutes. I continued easing along on the track as it crossed a swale and disappeared into the cedars on the other side. I knew the buck was looking for a place to bed down and I was going to have to try and catch him in his bed. The buck left the cedars and crossed the same swale farther down and went into the dark spruce.

Just inside the spruce I could see where the buck had been standing and then had jumped back to the left. I looked up the swale and thought that the buck might have seen me when I crossed it, following his track. I was bummed out and decided to wait a half hour for him to settle down. The wind was blowing into the woods from the swale, so I decided to move into the spruce and find a log to sit on. I had eased down the buck's track a few jumps when I spotted a round brown patch of fur 30 yards in front of me.

I knew it was the buck, but couldn't tell what part of him I was looking at. There were spruce limbs everywhere, and as hard as tried, I could not make out any part of the buck. I took a step to the left and then one to the right, but still couldn't make anything out. All of a sudden, I saw a thick dark rack with tall tines move back and forth. Then the buck's shoulder came into view and I knew he was going to bolt. I swung the bead onto his shoulder and fired just as the buck bolted. I knew I had missed as soon as the gun went off. My sight picture was high on the shoulder and the buck dropped down when he bolted.

Needless to say, I was sick! The buck was a heavy-bodied one with the antlers to match. I followed the track for about 50 yards, just to make sure I had not hit the buck. Seeing that I had not, I broke off some fir boughs and sat down on a log to wait. I sat there thinking about why I hadn't seen any other part of that buck standing there. The brown spot I did see was his hind quarter. He had been standing in his bed looking back over his shoulder at me and his head was up in the spruce limbs. I guess all the limbs and the blowing snow made good camouflage for him.

I couldn't eat a sandwich, but I did manage to get down a cookie. Then I reloaded the speed loader I had used and had just put it back in my pocket when I looked up to see the buck walking back towards me at about 40 yards. He stopped behind some firs where I couldn't see him. I held the gun on the firs thinking he was going to step out. After 10 minutes of waiting, I knew something wasn't right, so I walked over to the fir thicket where I had last seen the buck. He must have caught wind of me, as he had run straight back away from me for a few bounds and started to walk again.

Now I'm thinking that this buck must have a death wish! I followed him for about another half hour, when his track jumped to the left again. I could see a cow moose up ahead and thought maybe the buck was spooked by her. I followed the running track about 50 yards, and there was the buck's bed with a running track leaving the bed, so I knew that I had jumped him again. That was twice that this buck had jumped off to the side of his track and lain down to watch it. I had never seen this before, but now I was onto him.

This time I went right after the buck without waiting, in hopes of catching him before he lay down again. About a half hour later the buck was back to where he had fed on the blow-down. Then, once again, he jumped to the left and headed into a thick

patch of spruce. This time I left his track and circled slowly around, looking to see if his track came out. When I closed the circle, I knew the buck was bedded down again. I looked at my watch and it was 3:00. It would be dark in an hour and I was about three miles from the truck. Even though the buck was close, it would take me an hour or two to hunt that piece of woods and have a chance of killing him. It was a tough decision, but I headed out for the long walk back to the truck.

As soon as I start to follow a track, I'm trying to figure out where that particular buck might be going and what he is doing. Everything a buck does and everywhere he goes is deliberate. I always try to get into the mind of the buck that I'm tracking, so I might be able to determine what he is up to. The time of the season will also help me determine what a buck might be up to. Before the rut, a buck that is traveling pretty much in a straight line, and not stopping, has someplace in his mind where he wants to be. That place could be the next mountain over or it could be a hideout he has five miles away. In most cases the buck is already there and bedded down, and the best thing for hunter to do is hunt the track as fast as they can and catch up to him. The sooner you catch up to a bedded buck, the more time you will have to hunt him.

Dave Delair poses with his 220-pound eight-pointer. His guide, Tom Hamilton, was on the track when the buck came by Dave.

During the rut, a buck will be checking on does most of the time. Typically, these bucks keep moving until they find where a doe has been and then they begin to wander and search for her by scent or by following her track. When a buck is doing that he is not paying as much attention behind him, and it's a good time to catch him off guard. In either case, the sooner you can figure out what a buck is up to, the better the chance you will have at getting a shot at him.

What a buck has been doing is written in the snow by the tracks he leaves. I got the chance to show a classic example of this to one of my clients during the rut not long ago. There were a couple of inches of snow on the ground and the plan for Ed and I was to find a good buck track to follow. We left the truck and headed for a cedar chopping where I knew there had been some does living. As we worked our way around the chopping, we found the track that we were looking for.

The buck was following a doe's track up the hardwood ridge above the cedars. The tracks were fairly fresh, so we worked our way up the ridge hoping to catch the buck off guard. We hadn't gone far when we came to the doe's bed, with her running tracks leaving it. I knew then that the buck had caught up to her. I told Ed there was a good chance that we might catch them chasing, so we needed to be watching carefully up ahead.

The buck followed the doe up to a shelf on the ridge and then they began to walk parallel along it. Every once in a while the buck would chase the doe around, and then continue walking in the same direction. I knew they would eventually lie down, but I was hoping we would catch them before they did. The wind started to blow and it began to spit snow, making it a perfect day for tracking. Pretty soon another doe got in with our deer and all three walked up a small knoll. There was a ravine on the other side of the knoll and I thought we might catch them in it. As we peered over the top we could see a

deer standing on the ridge across the ravine. When I looked with my binoculars, I could see that the deer was a spike horn. I could also see the tracks we were following had gone past the spike horn and over the ridge. Now we were going to have to get around the spike horn without spooking him or have him spook the other deer. The spike started to feed his way down the ridge, so we just waited for him to get out of sight.

Waiting on the spike horn had cost us about 10 minutes, so we picked up the pace a little. The deer made their way into a hardwood chopping where two more tracks joined in with them. One was a doe and the other was another good buck. Things were starting to get exciting, but the problem we had now was that there were 10 eyeballs to see us. All five tracks stayed in line as they went back down the ridge through the chopping. It was really windy out in the open, and I assumed the deer were going down out of the chopping to bed down.

The deer went across a small clear-cut with a green knob on the other side. The knob was cleared except for a few patches of small firs, so I didn't think the deer would stay out there in the wind. There was also no way to circle around the knoll, as it was open all around it. We followed the tracks to the knob where they started to go up, then turned and went around the side of it. The deer had slowed down and were starting to wander, and I was starting to get that "gut feeling" like something was going to happen.

We were easing slowly along the right side of the knob with thick firs on our left. The tracks were heading down towards another ravine, so I focused out ahead of us, hoping to catch a glimpse of brown. We had moved ahead a ways before I glanced down at the tracks again. When I did, I noticed that the tracks had turned left into the firs. At that instant I knew the deer were right there on the knoll. Too late, just as I looked to the left I could see a doe and a heavy-horned buck sail off the knoll only 30 yards from us. Ed had seen them at the same time and he ran ahead to try and get a shot. When he did, two more does jumped up in front of him and ran down into the ravine. By the time we ran to the other side of the knoll, the buck had disappeared down off the ridge.

I knew Ed was disappointed at not getting a crack at that beautiful buck. My emotions were somewhere between disappointment and disgust with myself for not going with my gut feeling and stopping to think over the situation. When looking things over, we could see that the deer had a good place to bed out of the wind in the first on the back of that knoll. If I had paid more attention to the tracks, I would have seen them turn into the firs. It would have given us a chance to circle back around and get above the deer. It's times like that when an old buck will keep you humble.

Not long ago I read an article that talked about gut feelings and explained what they are. Everybody gets them and for all kinds of reasons. The article said that all of our experiences are stored away in our subconscious minds. A gut feeling arises when our mind pulls together all of our past experiences when we are in similar situations. The article also said that it was a good idea to trust your gut feelings. I knew when I was following those tracks that the buck was going to stay with the doe and they would eventually bed down. I had just talked myself out of thinking that they would be on that knoll. I always seem to have to learn these lessons the hard way!

The Death Creep

The two things that hunters have the most trouble with when tracking a buck are sorting out tracks and knowing when and where a buck might be bedded.

Mature bucks are loners, and unless they are with a doe, they will find a secure, out-of-the-way place to bed down by themselves. Just because a buck heads into a swamp, thicket or up a ridge

doesn't necessarily mean that he is going to bed down. But if a buck does stop to feed before going to one of these places, there is a good chance that he is going to be bedded. When a buck is traveling, he doesn't usually take the time to feed; he will usually feed when he gets to where he wants to lay down.

When a buck that I'm following starts to wander around and feed, if the terrain allows it I will circle the area the buck is heading into and look for his track coming out the other side. By doing this I don't waste any time. If I find his track coming out of my circle, I just continue on it. If I don't find his track when I circle, I have the buck located and can take all the time I need to hunt for him. If I can get the higher ground when the buck is bedded on a ridge, I will go behind the ridge and get above the buck. Then I still hunt slowly in a zigzag manner, trying to catch the buck bedded or get a shot when he jumps.

If the buck goes into a thick area, I know my chances of killing him by staying on his track are much better. I call this the "death creep," and it is the most difficult aspect of tracking to master. Once you close in on a buck and kill him using the death

Roger Kingsley took his first Big Woods Buck while tracking it with his guide, Rocky Achey. One hundred ninety-six pounds and eight points is a good start.

creep, you've accomplished something that very few deer hunters ever will.

The death creep requires the hunter to be alert at all times with eyes and ears. You have to be able to detect the smallest patch of brown that is out of place. You also have to be able to detect the slightest sound of a twig breaking or the dull thud of the buck getting to his feet. Good balance is also crucial to being able to put on a death creep. You will have to be able to stand on one leg until you can get your other foot planted on the ground. All of this is going to require concentration and patience. The death creep is the end game or culmination of all the work you put into catching up to a buck.

When I start my death creep, I take one small step at time. Every step will give me a whole new picture of the woods. Before I take each step I lean forward and scan every inch of the woods in front of me as well as off to both sides. Quite often the buck will walk around a blow down or thicket and watch his track from the side. I also follow the track out as far as I can see it with my eyes to try and figure out where he might be bedded. I play out this whole process as if I were in slow motion, as any quick movements are sure to be spotted by a bedded buck. My entire goal when going into the death creep is to either shoot the buck in his bed or get close enough to him to get a good running shot when he jumps.

The conditions are going to play a big role in the success of a death creep. If it is a still, calm day, it will be a lot harder to get in close to a buck. His hearing is so acute that he will hear the slightest rustle of a branch or twig snap underfoot. The best chance of killing a buck while you are in the death creep is when it is windy, and especially if it blowing snow. These conditions help to cover your sound and your motion. Later in the book you will read about my successful death creep on the Island Buck, but sometimes things don't always turn out as planned.

One morning while hunting out of a remote camp during the muzzle-loader season in Maine, I picked up a good buck track at daylight. It had snowed about six inches in the night and it was still coming down. The track was half filled in with snow, but I knew that it couldn't be more than a few hours old. I had only gone about a quarter of a mile on the track when I came to the buck's bed with no snow in it. At first I thought I had jumped him, but then I saw that his track was walking away. I thought to myself, it doesn't get any better than this.

Big snowflakes were coming down and the visibility was only about 50 yards. I had a good feeling this buck was going to be mine. I followed him across a brook and up onto a ridge, all the while thinking that I would see him at any minute. The buck then went around some softwood knolls, as he looked for does. After a while he dropped back down a hardwood ridge and into a ravine. Then a steep ridge appeared in front of me with the buck's track going up it. It was snowing so hard that I hadn't seen the ridge, and now I was afraid he was bedded on top and might have already seen me. There was a ledge going straight up on my right and a ledge dropping off to the left. The buck was moving up a passage way between them. My only choice was to death creep up his track.

I eased up the steep ridge with every step giving me another view over the top. All of a sudden, the buck stood up in front of me at 25 yards as if he were in slow motion. He had been lying behind a log and must have seen the top of my head. As I started to bring my gun up, I couldn't believe he was going to stand there. The muzzle loader I was using was my old Hawken rifle with a Lyman peep sight mounted on the tang. I kept trying to pull the hammer back, until I realized that I was pulling on the sight instead of the hammer. Just as I reached over and pulled the hammer back, the buck bolted. I got lined up on

Guide Rocky Achey with a 220-pound nine-pointer he shot standing in his bed after a slow death creep.

him to shoot, but my feet slipped and by the time I caught myself, the buck had disappeared over the ridge. It's hard to remember all the thoughts that were racing through my mind, but all I knew was that I had just blown my chance at one of the best bucks I'd seen in quite a while. He would have dressed out at well over 200 pounds and had thick, dark beams and tall points.

My mistake was carrying a gun that I hadn't used in years and was not accustomed to. I hadn't realized until the day before the season that I didn't have enough bullets for my Gonic inline, so I'd dug out the old Hawken rifle. The hammer on the Hawken is on the right side and I'm left-handed, making it awkward in the first place. I guess when

Tim Burnell's first Big Woods Buck was shot while tracking a bigger buck with the author.

my thumb felt the peep sight, I subconsciously thought it was the hammer and started pulling on it. I had two more running shots at that buck that day, but didn't connect with either one. Later that week, I missed another good buck with the Hawken and swore I would have a muzzle loader that felt right to me by the next season. Another hard lesson learned.

Sandwich Time

The one tactic I use that has helped me and my clients kill more bucks while tracking is to wait

There are several factors you must take into consideration before you decide to either follow a wounded buck right away or wait.
(Sue Morse photo)

after jumping a buck. This is the one thing that more hunters have told me helped them kill their first buck by tracking than any other. The subject is important enough to examine carefully.

Nine times out of 10 when you jump a buck, he will run for a short distance and then stop, waiting to see if anything is going to follow him. He may have only run because he heard a stick break or saw movement, and doesn't really know what it is that spooked him. By going after a buck as soon as you jump him, you will most likely find a spot where he stood looking back at you. The tracks leaving that spot will be running, as he spotted you and knows something is after him, and now the buck will always be watching his backtrack. That makes getting a shot at him a lot harder. I've found that by waiting half an hour, the buck will assume nothing is following him and will settle down.

At first I tried waiting 15 minutes, but found that it was not long enough. I usually have a sandwich while I'm waiting to help pass the time. I also make sure to look at my watch, as waiting for 10 minutes can sometimes seem like an hour. Once I take up the track again, I expect that the buck has done one of two things: He is bedded down again, in which case I'll have to figure out where. Or he started traveling, in which case I am going to have a better chance of catching him moving.

I'd like to clarify a few things about this tactic and when I vary from it. There are basically two times that I will forego the wait. One is when I've waited my half an hour and end up jumping the buck again. If I jump the buck a second time, I probably won't wait another half hour, as the buck now knows something is after him. I'll have to catch him making a mistake. The other time I don't wait is when a buck is with a doe, paying more attention to her than what is behind him. The doe will want to keep an eye out behind her, but the buck will have her distracted, making it much easier to catch them off guard.

Once you learn the basics of tracking, you have to keep applying them until you get results. I always tell hunters that if they keep repeating what they know to do, the law of averages will eventually catch up to them. So get out there and find a track to follow. The journey in tracking is all about the experiences along the way. It might be in the woods you explore or the wildlife you see. Whatever it is, once tracking is in your blood, it will be like a virus you'll have to live with.

Hunting Rutting Bucks

JOHN TROUT

Decoding the Rut

Throughout this book, I have mentioned several times that anyone—at just about any location—can kill a buck during the primary rut. Bucks are on the move, making sure that any hunter, regardless of how much they know about hunting deer, can enjoy success.

Some hunters only get in the woods during the primary rut, knowing this is the best opportunity to take a trophy whitetail. That's understandable, but hunting only during the peak-breeding season will not make you a knowledgeable deer hunter. It might make you a better woodsman and all-around outdoorsman, but there's too much left unsaid about deer during the primary rut.

With this emphasized for the 500th time in this book, I should mention that I still love hunting the primary rut. I look forward to it during the pre-rut, and I dread the arrival of the post-rut season. Consider how hard you might work during the pre-rut period, yet never get close to shooting a trophy buck. We're all entitled to compensation for our hard work. The primary rut is the time to be compensated.

In 1996 my son John hunted hard during the archery pre-rut season, hoping to get a crack at a wall-hanger. It didn't happen. However, when the firearm season debuted, which was timed with the peak of the rut, he tagged a buck that grossed just over 164 Boone and Crockett inches.

Photoperiodism refers to the decrease of sunlight with each passing day. A buck's testosterone level rises as the amount of light decreases.

I should point out that you could be the luckiest during the primary rut if you have an understanding of how the rut unfolds. And knowing the habits of breeding whitetails could make you lucky sooner than otherwise.

This section discusses the breeding cycle that occurs during the primary period, which lasts about ten to fourteen days. That's when most of the does are bred. However, every area has one "peak-rut day" governed by latitude, when breeding peaks. It could be mid-November in your area or perhaps December 30, but it typically falls within the same time frame each year, and experienced hunters can narrow it down to within three to five days.

Once the breeding begins, bucks begin start taking chances, moving into open areas at any hour of the day and into open areas in search of estrous does.

In the northern U.S., most of the whitetail breeding occurs between November 5 and 20. It is about thirty to sixty days later in the southern part of the country.

Photoperiodism plays a key role in determining the breeding period. Photoperiodism is the term used to define shorter days, or the decrease of sunlight. It's a gradual and slow process that begins after the longest day of the year in summer. The effects of photoperiodism are two-fold. First, the buck's testosterone level rises throughout the process. As pointed out earlier in the book, bucks will breed whenever opportunity allows; they just need to be in the right place at the right time. But if only the time is right, they will go looking for the right place.

Some hunters wonder if an onset of cloudy days would affect the arrival date of the breeding cycle. I know of no research to support that. In fact, in the forty years I have hunted whitetails and observed their breeding cycle in the Midwest, I can say that the peak has never fluctuated by more than seventy-two hours. Granted, weather might affect deer movement and buck activity, but I don't believe it has any affect on the breeding cycle.

Determining the peak day is not that hard to do. Typically, when the rut peaks the bucks run rampant. You will see them at all hours of the day, often crossing fields and skirting the edges in search of a doe about to breed. All you need to do is be out there in the woods, and in some cases you can determine the peak by way of vehicle.

You should understand that a high testosterone level, most common in dominant, mature bucks, allows them to establish hierarchy prior to the rut. Mature bucks do most of the breeding. When photographing whitetails, I have observed many a doe running away from subordinate bucks, only to allow a dominate buck to breed her a short time later.

Researchers have noted that when mature bucks are in short supply, a doe might leave her home range to find Mr. Right. Keep in mind that many areas are short of trophy whitetails. Thus, traveling does might prevent a big buck from coming into your hunting area. Naturally, the more mature bucks you have around your hunting area, the better the chance a trophy will show up . . . and the does in your area will attract mature bucks.

Just as photoperiodism affects bucks, it also affects does, causing a rise in estrogen, and, eventually, the estrous period in during which they breed.

Does are also affected by photoperiodism. When it peaks, they go into estrus—often termed "in-heat"—due to a dramatic increase in estrogen production. This reaction is timed with ovulation, making certain eggs will be present and fertilized by the buck's sperm. Research has shown that estrus does are, in a sense, like rutting bucks. They become restless and move much more often than they did during the pre-rut period.

There are other factors worth noting about estrus does. They urinate more often and, more importantly, their urine contains a scent that tells bucks they are ready to breed. A doe will stay in estrus for about twenty-four hours. If she is not impregnated when the estrus cycle ends, she will not allow a buck to breed her again until the next cycle in about twenty-seven to twenty-nine days. I read where one Alabama doe had her second estrus cycle twenty-one days after the first, while a doe in Minnesota had her second thirty days after the first.

It's true that poorly nourished bucks and does might not have typical breeding cycles. Most unhealthy bucks will reach a testosterone peak several days or weeks before the peak-rut day. A doe could come into estrus several days or weeks earlier as well.

The primary rut cycle is a short period of about two weeks or less, but that is not carved in stone. One Michigan study of healthy penned deer showed the breeding cycle of 174 does lasted from November 2 to December 21. Worth noting, though, is that more than eighty percent of the does mated during the last three weeks in November.

The breeding cycle always ends abruptly, particularly when it comes to mature does—those one-and-a-half years or older. Fawns, or six-month-old does, sometimes breed their first winter, but usually not as early as mature does.

In his book *Quality Deer Management*, renowned outdoor writer and whitetail consultant Charles Alsheimer divides the rut into three phases: seeking, chasing, and breeding. He claims that similarities exist in each phase, yet different habits are also common. How right he is!

For instance, bucks might cover a tremendous amount of ground just before the breeding begins. Yet once a buck discovers an estrus doe, he might stay in a given area for more than a couple of days.

When a doe comes into estrus, a mature buck will find her. In fact, he usually finds her a day or two before the breeding begins. I once observed a huge eleven-point buck with the same doe three days in a row. I never saw him breed her, but I made it a point to return to the same ambush location daily, assuming the hot doe would get hotter. She did, and I shot the buck on the third day.

Other bucks will be around as well, even if they are not fully mature. Several times when hunting, I have observed as many as five bucks after the same doe. In some non-hunting areas while photographing whitetails, I've seen even more. On one November morning when I left my stand and walked to a field, I saw five bucks hanging around a single doe. One carried a large eight-point rack while the others were still waiting to see their second birthday. I knelt in the bushes for nearly an hour while the bucks chased the doe from one end of the field to the other.

Does are often injured and sometimes killed by the antlers of a mature buck that becomes aggravated while waiting to breed. It is not common, but he might jab her in the backend, causing injury.

As mentioned previously, subordinate bucks seldom breed. However, it does happen, particularly when several does come into estrus simultaneously. In some cases, a mature buck might be particular about his partner (which occurs more often than you think). If no mature buck arrives, an estrus doe might breed with a younger buck. In other words, being a mature buck does not necessarily come with exclusive breeding rights. It only gives him first choice.

A mature buck will keep the other bucks at bay, so to speak, staying close to the breeding doe and leaving her only to chase off a subordinate buck when necessary. Even then, he seldom runs very far. If he forces the smaller buck fifty to one hundred yards away, he's often content. It's also true that sometimes a mature buck won't have to run a small buck away. They often just lower their ears and walk toward the youngster with a ready-to-kill look in their eyes. When showing this aggression, their hair stands up on their backs—an unmistakable message that causes most small bucks to turn and walk away.

Subordinate bucks are usually the ring leaders when most of the doe chasing occurs. This behavior goes on throughout the pre-rut period, but it is strongest just before a doe comes into estrus. Mature bucks seldom chase does until the primary rut period.

A dominant buck will threaten a subordinate buck by displaying aggressive behavior. He lowers his ears and his hair stands up. It's usually enough of a show to send a smaller buck away.

Bucks lip curl after sniffing doe urine. A doe does not have to be in estrous to cause a buck to lip curl, however.

Just before the actual breeding of most does begins, mature bucks move consistently in dense areas where does commonly bed during daylight hours, sniffing beds to see if a doe is "Ready Freddy."

Hunters sometimes claim to have seen a buck trailing a doe, but going the wrong way. I doubt that backtrailing occurs in error, because a whitetail's nose is too good not to know a hot trail and the direction a doe is traveling. I do believe, though, that he will sometimes backtrail a doe in hopes of finding her bed to see if she is about to come into estrus.

Just before copulation occurs, a buck will approach the south end of a doe to scent her and determine how close he is to breeding her. He will often try to stimulate her by licking her vulva.

When a buck mounts a doe, he lowers his chin and slides it along her back. His forelegs rest just behind her shoulders. This does not pin her down, however. Occasionally, she will pull away when he first attempts to breed her.

I have observed whitetails breeding on several occasions. Copulation takes only about ten to twenty seconds, but is often repeated within a few minutes. I saw one buck breed a doe, and then breed her two more times in a ten-minute period. He would have bred her again, except the doe would not allow it—possibly because she felt pain and discomfort. About one hour later, however, he did breed her once more.

Lip curling is a trademark of the primary rut, but not limited to that period. Lip curling is an expression displayed by a buck after scenting a doe's urine. He extends his head upward, opens his mouth and rolls his lower lip forward. However, a doe does not have to be in estrus, or even near estrus. I have seen bucks lip curl after smelling doe urine during the off-season. Hunters often become excited when they see a doe with a tail in the horizontal position, convinced she is in estrus. While it is true that many hunters have shot trophy bucks following a doe with a stiffened tail, I'm not so sure it is always a sign that the doe is willing to breed. Many times, I have seen does with their tails pointing outward, either briefly, when defecating, or just because they favor this position for no obvious reason. It could also be that the doe has already bred.

Research has shown that a doe's vulva has contractions after she has bred, which causes her tail to rise and sometimes stay that way off and on for a long time, up to a couple of days. Thus, when you see a doe with a tail in the horizontal position, you could be, as the old saying goes, "A day late …."

Vocalization is strongest during the primary rut. A buck will commonly send the grunt-snort-wheeze signal to other bucks, especially when breeding is close.

During the primary rut, a mature buck will seldom feed, although water remains important to him. I saw one mature buck walk away from a breeding doe to drink from a ditch about two hundred yards away. The two deer had been in a grown-up field for several hours. They had bred on a few occasions, and both had bedded a couple of times. When the buck left the doe, she was feeding, but he never browsed on the lush vegetation once. When he left to go to water, he was only gone about ten minutes, and she was out of his sight for only about five minutes as he passed through thick

vegetation and walked down a steep bank. After drinking, the buck casually walked back to the doe.

As the rut winds down, mature bucks will move less and less. Subordinate bucks, though, continue to move consistently for several days in areas where hunting pressure is low, seeming to know that the dominant bucks are resting up. They also seem to know that they could stumble onto that late-breeding doe (not likely, however).

Bucks lose a tremendous amount of body weight during the rut—some as much as twenty-five percent or more. When the breeding ends, they go on a feeding binge that opens the door to post-rut hunting tactics. But during those glorious primary rutting days, a little knowledge can lead to a lot of luck.

It has been suggested that bucks typically weigh more and have bigger antlers if they don't breed much. I would think that in areas where there are fewer does, bucks might also lose less weight and sport smaller headgear because the rut is extremely strenuous. They have to move more to find estrus does, and the competition is sure to be a problem because nearly every buck will end up pursuing the same doe.

Your chances of tagging a trophy buck during primary rut might be better if you don't have several

This buck is follows following the trail of a doe. Hunters sometimes spot bucks backtrailing a doe, but this often occurs because a rutting bucks buck will check the beds to locate an estrous doe.

does to every buck, which is precisely why does should be harvested. It boils down to quantity vs. quality. Lots of does (particularly a healthy herd) will produce many fawns. This means you will have more deer in your area, but it doesn't necessarily mean that your chance of intercepting a mature buck is that good. Studies have shown that the fewer does there are, the more bucks move. Hunters have shown that the more the bucks move, the better their chances of tagging a trophy.

Speaking of harvesting does, the best time to do so is not during the peak rut or during the primary rut unless you have tagged your buck. Shooting a doe could promptly spoil an area for a few days. Besides, who's to say the right buck isn't trailing the doe you shoot? You just can't beat the post-rut period for harvesting does.

As for big bucks trailing does, I've always suspected that other hunters have enjoyed more of this good fortune than I have. I consistently hear stories about guys who watched a doe pass, then had a whopper buck come walking through minutes or sometimes hours later. I don't mind telling you, I'm still waiting for that to happen to me. The chances of

the right buck trailing a doe rest a little upon Lady Luck. If you are seeing your share of does, you know you are sitting in the right ambush location. But if you are not seeing the does, you can't blame Lady Luck alone.

Now that you have an understanding of the primary rut, you know that the rutting habits of bucks and does are totally different than their behaviors at any other time of the year. You should also know that there's much more between the lines, such as scraping and other rutting factors. These habits are your ticket to tagging a mature buck during the primary rutting season.

Cold Fronts and Moon Phases

During the primary rut, mature bucks quickly become discouraged when hunting pressure intensifies. This has an effect on morning and evening buck activity in daylight hours, and causes changes in the habits of does. However, there are natural phenomena that occur each year, prompting whitetail bucks to get with the program. If the hunter recognizes the phases that trigger bucks to move, he can enjoy an opportunity comparable to opening day at the peak of the breeding season.

This buck is nervous about something. Note his tightly tucked tail. Even a doe in estrus won't keep a mature buck from seeking cover when he smells danger.

Although most hunters prefer to be out when favorable weather conditions exist, research indicates that bucks may move more as a cold front approaches.

Most hunters share one thing in common—a preference for hunting on days with radiant sunrises and sunsets. Along with these, we like crisp temperatures and no wind. But are these really the ultimate hunting conditions?

Cold Fronts and Barometer Crashes

Ideal weather usually occurs when the barometer is steady. However, research indicates that deer may move more frequently when the barometer is unstable, especially if it drops drastically. Many hunters also report seeing more deer when such a weather front approaches.

I still remember a particular November hunt several years ago. It wasn't what you would have called a good day to be perched in a tree. There had been a warm southerly breeze just the day before, but now I had to fight uncontrollable shivers brought on by a strong north wind, rapidly plummeting temperature and a light drizzle. Perhaps that is why I didn't see the huge buck slithering past my stand until I caught a glimpse of movement in my peripheral vision. I shouldered the gun and attempted to find him in the crosshairs of my scope, but before I could locate him, the deer disappeared into a thicket.

In planning hunts, many hunters of us don't think about the barometer. Research suggests, however, that changing barometric pressure can signal good hunting.

That incident remains vivid in my mind for good reason. A few moments after the buck vanished from my sight, I heard a shot several hundred yards to the east. My dad had also braved the brutal weather, and was rewarded for this daring venture. His gun dropped the huge nine-pointer as it passed by him. In recent years, I have come to look forward to the somber days whenever the rut is close or in progress. In fact, I can hardly resist heading for the woods on a nasty day. It had been no surprise to see that buck sneaking past, and no real shock when I heard dad fire minutes later. The conditions can be almost unbearable when a north wind blows in, but I have discovered that miserable weather can considerably improve my chance of tagging a buck, even if hunting pressure has sent him into hiding. This realization has made it easier for me to stay out there, regardless of what Mother Nature does.

For many years I have kept records of deer sightings, and I've tracked my harvests and the conditions that existed on a given day, including changes in barometric pressure. I've seen a strong increase in buck movement when a big change in barometric pressure occurs.

Dr. Grant R. Woods, a wildlife biologist who has studied deer movement for a number of years, has collected data indicating that deer move much more than usual when the barometric pressure changes by four or five points. Such a change commonly occurs when a cold front approaches. Grant said that hunters should look forward to the first cold front of the season, since deer are always prompted to move. However, he added that deer move and feed heavily only as long as the barometric pressure declines. He bases this fact on studies that show increased deer sightings when the barometer drops. However, a rising barometer usually does not hold as much promise for hunters.

"A rising barometer is trickier than a falling barometer," Woods said. "This can occur when you go from an extended low that has been around for several days to a high-pressure system moving in. Under these conditions, you just don't get a big change in deer movement. In fact, any change is usually a gradual one."

How Bucks Respond

So, how does all this affect bucks? First, consider the rutting activity of bucks and then the hunting pressure that might have set them back. Next, consider the approaching cold front and the falling barometer. The weather conditions trigger deer movement, causing them to feed heavily, and bucks know that the does will be up and moving, which stimulates them to move, too.

While photographing whitetails on numerous occasions, I've seen does in fields feeding heavily as a cold front approached. Watching them, I often spot bucks. Most of the time, the antlered deer cared less about eating than about checking out the does. When hunting, I've observed a similar effect when bad weather approached: does moving and browsing, and bucks moving in search of does. For this reason, I believe that the approaching cold front and falling barometer cause a rise in the buck's testosterone level.

The deer hunter should understand exactly what prompts deer to feed heavily when a cold front approaches. Precipitation and wind are the two primary factors that apply. Deer want to feed before the hardest rain, heaviest snow or strongest wind arrives so they can stay bedded while the nastiest weather prevails. That's not to say that some precipitation and wind will not be present as the front approaches. On the contrary, in the episode I mentioned previously, the cold front had not yet arrived, but it was knocking at the door with the constant drizzle and gusty winds. My idea of prime time to be in the deer woods.

Make no mistake: An approaching warm front accompanied by its own wind and rain will also cause the barometer to fall. Do not count on

An approaching cold front can trigger strong winds and a drop in barometric pressure, causing all deer to move. The does move to feed, and the bucks move because they know the does are out and about.

an increase in buck movement when a Southerly approaches, however. The barometer tends to fall fast before a cold front, but bucks don't move as well when a warm front approaches because the barometric pressure doesn't change as rapidly. Logically, we can also assume that bucks are move comfortable when cooler temperatures exist.

According to a meteorologist I spoke with, the more change there is in temperature, the more rapidly the barometer falls. For instance, let's say the barometer has remained steady for a lengthy period and the temperature has been in the 60s and 70s. Along comes a fast-moving cold front that drops temperatures into the 20s and 30s. The barometer will fall several points rapidly, and the bucks will move.

If, however, it has been in the 40s and 50s, and the approaching cold front drops the temperatures to the 30s and 40s, the barometer will not fall as much or as rapidly. You can be sure bucks will not move as much as they would have if a stronger cold front was on the way.

Timing is Crucial

If you get in the woods as the cold front settles on the area, more than likely you will miss the hottest action. The best hunting occurs when the cold air first bumps against the warm air, and the temperatures start to fall. It could happen at prime hunting time in the morning or afternoon, at night or during the mid-day hours. The point is, you should already be hunting when it hits (excluding the dark hours, of course).

The incident that I mentioned earlier involved perfect timing. The temperature was about seventy-five degrees (quite unusual) and the wind had begun to intensify. I remember talking to my dad earlier that day. We had not seen many bucks, and had blamed that on previous hunting pressure and warm weather. We both arrived on stand earlier than usual that somber afternoon, and I'm convinced that the front had given him a better chance of harvesting a buck than he would have had the next day, after the front settled on the area.

Where to Hunt

It's hard to say exactly where you should hunt when a cold front approaches. Personally, I have had the best results hunting afternoons and sticking to

When the barometer starts falling, deer often start feeding earlier in the day than normal.
Photo by Fargason Technologies/Scentite Blinds.

food sources. When favorable weather exists, deer may not show up close to a food source in daylight hours. But that can change when the barometer is falling. Then deer may arrive at a food source much earlier than normal. The hunting pressure will probably be lighter than usual, which might help get the deer to you without disturbance.

Earlier in this book I mentioned the massive twelve-point Alberta buck I rattled into bow range. A light rain, coupled with wind gusts, did not dampen the spirits of the buck that responded to my rattling. That evening I also watched another buck chase does—something I had not seen previously in the five days I had been pursuing whitetails in this area. My ambush location was along the edge of a field where deer had come to feed.

Moon Effects and Rutting Activity

For many years, deer hunters have wondered how whitetails are affected by moon phases. We've all heard various opinions about the full moon and new moon, but with little research to back up these interesting discussions, we can only wonder what to expect when hunting.

We do know that one full lunar cycle takes about twenty-nine days. During this period, the moon goes through four phases, including the new moon, when the nights are darkest, and the full moon, when the nights are brightest. It is popularly believed that deer become nocturnal during a full moon, which has led many hunters to think that much of the breeding occurs at night. Thus, one could assume the best time to kill a buck is only during the new moon. While this theory makes sense, veteran hunters will tell you there is far more to the story.

Full Moon and New Moon

Many hunters claim that we should never assume that deer become nocturnal during the full moon. Like others, I strongly believe that they will lay up and move less during daylight hours, but timing of the new moon is the real issue.

Let's say the peak of the rut typically arrives November 10. If the full moon occurs in late October, there will be a new moon in early November. Thus, does might come into estrus a few days earlier and cause an increase in buck movement. The same principle applies if the full moon arrives just before the peak of the breeding season. The hottest action will occur a few days later.

Everything can backfire if the full moon falls about one month before the peak of the breeding season. When it does, hunters can count on another full moon during the heart of the primary rut, a scenario that could mean a hunter will see fewer bucks during the daylight hours.

David Hale of Knight & Hale Game Calls once told me that when hunters experience the full moon during the primary rut, they should rely on other tactics. It only makes sense, he says, that hunters consider the rut less visible. Buck movement is likely to become sporadic and inconsistent, as if the primary rut had arrived, but it hasn't.

Many seasoned hunters now say it is no longer the early morning and late evening hours that produce action if the moon is full during the primary rut. In fact, these hunters claim that midday

action can be unbeatable—usually at its best action between 10 A.M. and 2 P.M.

I sincerely believe that we should never decide to hunt or not to hunt based on a particular moon phase. Weather patterns and hunting pressure are probably more significant when it comes to determining when bucks do and do not move (especially during the primary rut).

One individual I discussed this with explained that the guy who can hunt quality private land will see more buck activity during the full moon than the guy who is hunting crowded public lands during the new moon, when the nights are darkest.

Serious hunters should consider reading *"Hunting Whitetails by the Moon,"* by Charles J. Alsheimer. It is a fact-filled book that provides an easy understanding of moon phases and effects, as well as technical information for pursuing deer during all phases of the rut.

When it comes to hunting a full moon, you could fall back on the old saying, "Expect the worst and hope for the best." When it comes to hunting the new moon, think about another proverb: "The right time is now."

I don't plan to forfeit any hunting time in the future, regardless of what moon phase exists, or

If the full moon arrives during the primary rut, try hunting during the midday hours.

Many veteran hunters believe deer move and feed heavily at night during the full moon, laying up before the first light of day begins.

whether the sun shines and the wind blows. You see, I like spending all the time I can in the woods, regardless of which phase of the rut we're in or hunting pressure around me. I might even find myself sitting near a hot scrape or two when the time is right.

Hot Scrapes vs. Dead Scrapes

Veteran hunters are aware that scrapes are not limited to the primary rut. On the contrary, they begin showing up during early autumn. It's also true that big bucks have been harvested over scrapes several weeks before the primary rut. Thus, you might be wondering why you read very little about scrapes in Section I. I can explain that in one paragraph.

Scrape hunting is more productive during the primary rut just before, during, and just after the breeding. That word "just" is the key; the best time to shoot a mature buck over the right scrape, or scrapes, is limited to a few days. During the pre-rut period, I've found it much more reliable to pattern mature bucks in other ways we've already discussed, such as rub lines, food sources and certain trails. With that out of the way, let's get on with how you can determine which scrapes are most likely to attract a mature buck.

Before I go any further about natural scrapes, you should be aware that I won't be discussing mock scrapes here. You can find more in chapter 14 of *Hunting Rutting Bucks*, which provides ways to lure primary rutting bucks into range. For now, though, it's best to assume that scrapes are one of the least reliable ways to hang a trophy whitetail on the wall. Yes, I said "least." But don't jump ahead just yet. You see, natural scrapes offer more opportunities than mock scrapes.

Let's face it, a fresh scrape gets every whitetail hunter's adrenaline flowing and, for just a moment, flips on the "dream switch." Almost involuntarily, we imagine intercepting the ghostly buck that left his mark behind.

Scrapes begin showing up in early autumn, but seldom provide action until the primary rut.
Photo by Vikki L. Trout.

Such was the case a few years ago when I discovered no fewer than a dozen scrapes stretched along two hundred yards of a well-used trail. Several huge rubs were also present, prompting me to hang a stand in preparation for gun season, only days away. The scrape line was truly a sight to behold, and it followed a ridge of white oaks that were dropping acorns and attracting does. Equally important, there was a pocket of dense pines and honeysuckle nearby that, I knew, could well be a bedding area for the mature buck that had made the scrapes. More about what happened in a moment.

Locating scrapes or scrape lines is seldom difficult. If a hunter scouts enough, he or she can usually find buck sign. But coming across a potentially "hot" scrape line is seldom purely the result of luck. In fact, you can bet your luckiest camo hat that hunting near most scrapes will not produce positive results. Several factors determine whether or not a buck will visit the spot again, including where the scrapes are and how cautiously you investigated the area.

A seasonal rise in the buck's testosterone level prompts him to begin scraping, and this usually occurs during the pre-rut. But just how seriously should a hunter take these scrapes?

Territory scrapes, also known as boundary scrapes, typically show up along the fringes and roadbeds. However, seldom do these produce action. The author believes that the best scrapes are those that form a scrape line.

Research has shown that during the late summer and early fall, bucks will show signs of aggression toward each other. They begin scraping, but the scrapes left at this time are seldom more than territory markers used to advertise a particular buck's presence. Hunters generally find them before the primary rut, and they are often along the fringes of agricultural fields, logging roads and similar openings. Some knowledgeable deer hunter first called them "boundary" scrapes eons ago—the perfect name. These boundary or territory scrapes seldom form a true scrape line, nor do they become scent stations revisited by bucks on a regular basis.

Researchers have also determined that as deer densities increase in an area, so do the number of scrapes. I certainly can attest to that. When hunting areas that hold several bucks, I always seem to locate scrapes earlier than I do in areas where there are fewer deer.

As the does approach sexual readiness, usually a few days before the peak of breeding, scrape activity intensifies. Many consistently successful hunters now believe this period is also the time to

locate and hunt the hottest scrape lines for dominant bucks.

Several years ago, Dr. Larry Marchinton and his colleagues at the University of Georgia studied several groups of deer, noting that in pens containing bucks of age three and one-half and younger, the three and one-half-year-olds did most of the scraping. Younger bucks often avoid scraping early in the pre-rut period, because such scrapes serve as territory markers. Scraping close to the peak of the rut is usually done to facilitate scent communication with the does, but young bucks apparently have little or no desire to get aggressive with their elders.

If this is true, we can assume that fresh scrape lines found a few days preceding the peak of rut were made by dominant bucks ready to get down to serious business. But can a hunter count on these scrape lines to provide action?

I don't mind telling you that I have wasted a lot of time sitting in stands near a scrape or scrape lines. Many other veteran deer hunters would admit they have done the same. The bigger bucks just don't show up as often as we'd like.

According to Myles Keller, it could be because we often spoil a perfect opportunity before the hunt even begins. He says that a lot of scrape lines are of no use, because it's too tough to hunt them properly. Hunters must consider their approach to a scrape line and how much scent they leave near by. Moreover, even if they do everything perfectly, they still have to factor in the hunting pressure in that area.

Keller also notes that a single slip is all it takes to spoil a scrape line. Remember, we're talking about mature bucks. Once a dominant buck is alerted to your presence (or someone else's), you can count on him becoming more nocturnal, returning to the scrape line only during the dark hours. The avid hunter who visits the area consistently, meanwhile, sees that the scrape line is being freshened by the buck with some regularity, but fails to see the animal

(Above) The author has had much more success hunting scrapes with when there are overhanging limbs that have been chewed and/or dismantled by bucks. (Below) However, even does will chew on overhanging limbs, sometimes out of curiosity, because they want to know "who" was there, and possibly when they are nearing estrous.

in daylight. Keller readily admits, however, that you can never be too careful when hunting a mature buck near a scrape line. He still finds himself making mistakes and forfeiting a particular location, simply because the buck discovered his presence.

Which scrapes offer the most potential, little ones or big ones? I've often heard hunters talk about finding scrapes as big as the hoods on a truck. I've found a few like that myself. But after spending countless hours hunting over them through the years, I can't say that big scrapes will positively attract more bucks than little scrapes.

Big scrapes are often referred to as primary scrapes, and for good reason. A scrape that is four feet in diameter will be visited and freshened up more consistently than a two-foot scrape. Nonetheless, primary scrapes are still not as reliable as scrape lines.

I've had some of my best luck hunting scrapes beneath overhanging limbs that have been recently chewed and/or dismantled by the antlers of a buck. As you may know, the overhanging limbs I speak of are often rubbed with a buck's pre-orbital gland, which is on his forehead. These limbs, which typically hang about four to six feet above the ground directly above the scrape, are frequently licked, chewed and, many times, beaten to death with antlers. And don't think for a moment that does won't scent, lick or chew on such overhanging limbs. They do so quite often as the breeding gets close to peaking.

Many trees are not acceptable to bucks making a scrape and selecting an overhanging limb. Bucks usually prefer small deciduous trees, such as

The author took this nine-pointer along a hot scrape line on the first day of the gun season. He found the scrapes during the primary rut, just days before the firearm season and the breeding debuted.
Photo by Vikki L. Trout.

maples, pin oaks, dogwoods, fruit trees, ash and many others. Conifers are not favorites, but they are sometimes chosen.

I suspect the overhanging limb(s) are more important than the pawed area on the ground, having watched several deer pay little attention to the scrape itself but stop to smell the limb above. It happens throughout the primary rut and sometimes in the post-rut, several weeks after the scrape had been pawed. The overhanging limbs serve as valuable scent posts to all deer, and their importance to the development of a hot scrape line is greater than the actual scrape on the ground.

One primary scrape with a chewed overhanging limb is likely tobe-come more of a dependable scent post than a big scrape that is only pawed. I would suggest you keep that in mind if you locate and want to hunt a primary scrape. Again, though, the line with several scrapes, where some have chewed and dismantled overhanging limbs, will be more likely to attract a big buck.

The scrape line mentioned near the beginning of this section included several scrapes with mutilated branches overhead, interspersed with other limbs that didn't show as much evidence of mature buck use. It pays to follow scrapes from one to the next to see how seriously bucks have taken the line as a whole.

After locating that line and setting up a portable stand, I avoided the area until opening day. About one hour after sunrise on the opener, I spotted a very respectable buck traveling along the scrape line. My slugster roared before he had a chance to check one of the scrapes less than forty yards from me. The nine-pointer ran only seventy-five yards before piling up within view of my stand.

When hunting scrapes, wear knee-high rubber boots with the pants tucked inside. Also, avoid getting too close to the scrape, and do not brush against foliage and limbs as you pass by. When a buck visits a scrape, his already keen sense of smell is turned on full power.

Because the area around a scrape line is unforgiving in terms of human scent, consider hunting the buck's travel route that connects to the scraping location. Myles Keller points out that dominant bucks are vulnerable when they travel to and from the scrapes, so if a hunter gravitates right to the scrape line, he can't afford to make the slightest mistake.

Therefore, Keller suggests piecing the scrape line together in relation to a buck's bedding site. He warns, however, that many variables can complicate hunting a travel route between a bedding area and a scrape line. For example, the number of does in the region can affect which trails the bucks use, and so can food sources. But you can often count on bucks to lay out a scrape line near or along the same routes does travel consistently.

Keller also noted that too much distance between the scrape line and the bedding area has a significant impact on a hunter's odds of success. An

Although it helps to wear rubber boots whenever you check a scrape, it's still very easy to leave scent behind and spoil a hunting opportunity. There's no need in getting to get too close to a scrape.
Photo by Vikki L. Trout.

educated dominant buck simply will not travel very far during daylight hours to reach a red-hot scrape line.

But even if a mature buck is unlikely to take risks getting to a scrape line, he will travel far when he knows there's a pretty good chance of locating a breeding doe.

Scrape lines near funnels are often more productive, because when bigger bucks move during the daylight, they like to stay in the cover of an existing travel corridor. That is why one west-central Illinois outfitter prefers to hunt scrape lines that connect to funnels and bottlenecks between fields or fencelines. They are natural travel corridors that entice bucks to produce scrape lines. The bucks also know that a scrape line in these areas is more likely to be noticed by traveling does.

It is safe to say that no scrape line guarantees you a crack at a mature buck. I really believe that big whitetails will sacrifice breeding opportunities when they sense their survival is at stake. Even so, although it's safe to say that you could spend

Bucks will take more chances and cover much more ground in search of an estrous doe than they will to visit a hot scrape.

countless hours hunting dead scrapes, hunting a hot scrape line is one way to tag a trophy buck during the primary rut. That's providing you follow the previously mentioned guidelines and the standard set of rules I'll be discussing next.

Whitetail Strategies

PETER FIDUCCIA

Catch Wind of This!

I first learned how unpredictable wind currents could be many years ago. I was posted in a tree stand that was productive only when the wind was out of the west. Around 4:15 pm, a buck came from the swamp and made his way toward my position. A steady breeze blew from the buck to me. Suddenly, 40 yards out, the buck stopped abruptly, lifted his nose and without hesitation–disappeared.

I was confused. The piece of sewing thread that hung from my bow indicated the wind was blowing in my favor. I hadn't crossed his trail, so he couldn't have picked up my odor, and I took a shower and put on clean clothes before the hunt, so I was reasonably sure I had kept my body and clothing odor to an absolute minimum.

Then I remembered the bottle of powder in my backpack. When I sprayed the powder in the air, what I saw would change what I thought about wind currents forever. At first, I watched as the white powder confirmed that my scent was drifting away from the buck. Then about 15 yards behind my stand, the powder dropped suddenly and quickly blew back past me toward the buck. I was astonished that a low wind current could move in the opposite direction of the prevailing winds and was strong enough to even spook a buck.

What I learned from reading and talking about wind and air currents with certified biologists like Jay McAninch, the President and CEO of the Archery Trade Association (ATA), was as profound as it was

This big boy likes what he is smelling. If he was getting a nose full of human odor, however, he would have bolted instantly. (Credit: Ted Rose)

enlightening and helpful. The information below will help you not only understand wind currents better, it will help you see and bag more deer this season.

Prevailing Winds

In every area you hunt, there will be a prevailing wind direction during the hunting season. It is the predictable breeze that we are all told to keep in our faces in order to prevent deer from scenting hunters who are on stand, still-hunting or making a drive. Over most of North America, the prevailing wind is from the north, west, or northwest. This wind can often be the strongest of all the winds that blow during deer season. Other times, it is nothing more than a continuous light breeze. It has been documented that even though deer will move in all directions in relation to the wind, they prefer to move into the wind whenever they can. Seasoned hunters know that deer trails match the prevailing wind direction and customary wind changes.

Knowing the prevailing winds is especially important in more open habitats. Choosing which side of a bottle neck or funnel will be determined by the prevailing winds. When posting along the edges of agricultural fields, pay attention to the prevailing wind because most of the time the does and fawns enter first. If they don't pick up your scent, a buck may soon come into the field as well.

Deflective/Convection Currents

Deflective wind currents are the product of the prevailing wind flowing over an obstruction or flowing into an obstacle that changes the direction of the airflow. For instance, if your stand is in front of a thick group of tall pines or a steep rise or depression, these obstructions can disrupt the flow

It has been documented that deer regularly prefer to move into the prevailing wind. So, when the prevailing wind is out of the north or west, position your stand on the opposite or downwind side of a deer trail to minimize your chances of being winded by deer.

of a prevailing breeze. For hunters, wind current that is deflected downward is trouble because, if the velocity is strong enough, that current can create a back draft much like the undertow on ocean beaches. If you are in a tree stand, you might never know that the wind current deflected after it passed you and actually flowed back "under" the prevailing stream.

Deflective currents result in many "micro" wind currents that become isolated and localized over relatively small areas. Imagine how water directly hitting a surface splashes in all directions until its initial velocity is lost–and that is what happens when wind hits an obstacle. These small pockets of air are called convection cells and are capable of going in any direction–which spells trouble for the unaware hunter.

Deflective currents are prevalent under low pressure centers, which are common as the days cool and cold fronts start pushing south from Canada. Beginning in October, deflective wind currents are the predominant air movements and that means deer hunters should not only know these flows exist but also how they work.

When hunting from the ground or from a tree stand, you should take into account the terrain or structure that lies behind the stand. Consider how the prevailing wind will be deflected in the vicinity of your stand. Be sure to test the currents using a fine spray powder from each stand and record your findings in a daily log book. After noting the wind flows, position each stand to maximize your ability to predict what the air currents will be doing.

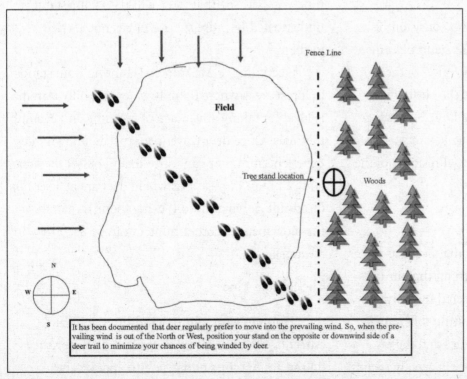

It has been documented that deer regularly prefer to move into the prevailing wind. So, when the prevailing wind is out of the North or West, position your stand on the opposite or downwind side of a deer trail to minimize your chances of being winded by deer.

The rock behind this hunter will definitely cause a deflective current to take place. When posting in places with obstructions, remember your scent may blow against the prevailing wind!

If the airflow in an area seems unpredictable, then you must move completely from the area. Remember, deflective currents don't occur all the time and they vary in speed. After sitting in a stand several times, you will begin to learn how to use a convection cell or deflective wind flow to your advantage.

"The hunters I've known who consistently take mature bucks are guys whose stand placement strategy is dictated first by the direction of the prevailing winds and, second, by the air flows in and around each stand. Knowing how deer will be receiving wind- borne scents is the key to successful hunting," said Jay McAninch, CEO/President of the Archery Trade Association.

Thermal Currents

Thermal winds are airflows that occur as the air temperature increases in the morning (hot air rises—cool air falls). All hunters are affected by thermal winds, which result from temperature differentials between the ground or water bodies and the air close to the earth. Thermal activity is usually highest during the first and last hours of daylight and it lasts until the circulating air and the ground and water are similar in temperature. This means thermals are most active during the prime times that deer hunters are on stand.

At sunrise, the ground and water are still cool from the nighttime temperatures. So, as the sun warms the air, there will be a rising wind current. You will have an advantage if you sit on the high side of a stand on a slope and if you approach your stand from a ridge top; your scent will drift up. Used to your advantage, early morning thermals can contribute to a couple of hours of action-packed hunting.

In the evening, the opposite effect takes place. The air cools quickly as the sun sets, while the ground and water bodies remain warm for several hours. In this situation, a down draft will occur as the cool air sinks (we've all felt that sudden quick chill as we pass by an area that is lower than the higher ground we came from). During this time you should enter your stand from the valley bottoms and not the ridge tops and it pays to take a stand below a hillside trail. Within a short time you will see that deer will pass your stand undisturbed because your scent is not carried to them.

According to McAninch, "Hunting from stands in forest areas where there is water and hilly terrain is ideal for taking advantage of morning and evening thermals. Once deer travel patterns are known, the experienced hunter can move in and out of the area and can hunt in positions where deer are at a serious disadvantage. In addition, using thermals can mean the movements of other hunters can be used to your advantage."

The Bottom Line

Hunters who ignore wind directions and currents often see fewer deer. And, the deer they do see are nervous and quick to spook. The

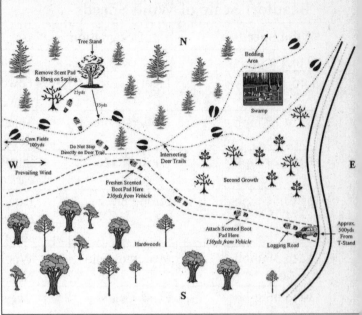

Note how the hunter walks to his stand, against the prevailing wind.

I always check how the wind is blowing before heading to my stand. Once in the stand I check the wind every 30 minutes with a powder to be sure it has not changed direction or that a convection current doesn't have it blowing against the prevailing wind.

In the morning, as the temperature rises, so do the thermal currents...they carry your scent uphill.

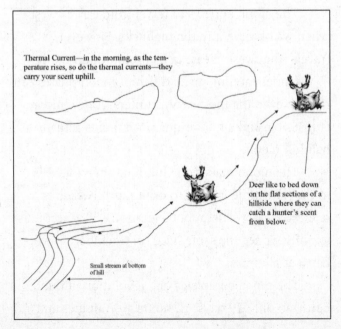

seasoned hunter always keeps wind uppermost in his mind. To consistently see more deer, consider the prevailing winds, deflective winds, and thermals and how they will affect your hunt each time you go afield. If you become wind savvy, you will immediately improve your deer hunting success ten-fold. You will see far more whitetails standing calmly within range, which will be the key to bagging your next trophy buck!

Wind Detecting/Checking Products

- H. S. Archery Accessories–Windicator–www.hunтersspecialties.com
- Primos–Wind Checker–www.primos.com
- Buck-Studs–Wind Marker–www.buckstuds.com
- Turkey Creek Trails–Wind Scout–www.eders. com
- Wind Chaser–www.eders.com
- King-Wind Walker Wind-Detector Orange– www.eders.com
- Contractor's Powdered Chalk–Local hardware store, Home Depot, Lowes
- Common Black Sewing Thread

Beaufort Scale of Wind Speeds

Wind Speeds	Designation	Description
0 to 1 mph	Dead calm	Wind detector powder rises almost vertically
2 to 12 mph	Light Breeze	Powder moves slowly in one direction or another Deer movement natural.
13 to 18 mph	Moderate breeze	Small branches move freely. Deer movement continues to be normal.
19 to 24 mph	Fresh Breeze	Small trees begin to sway. Deer move but begin to use their ears and eyes more to detect danger.
25 to 31 mph	Strong Breeze	Large branches and treetops begin to sway, small trees begin to bend, wind whistles in wires. Deer move more cautiously, stopping often to detect danger.
32 to 38 mph	Moderate Gale	Whole trees move and creak. Deer move, but not as freely. Noises make them more nervous.
39 to 46 mph	Fresh Gale	Twigs and small branches begin to break off trees. Deer movement begins to slow, flee response heightens.
47 to 54 mph	Strong Gale	Larger branches break, small trees bend severely, larger trees are in constant motion. Deer seek cover. Any movement is limited to short distances.
55 to 63 mph	Whole Gale	Trees uprooted, ground debris becomes airborne. Deer remain bedded down.

By the Light of the Moon

Let me start by saying that I'm a firm believer that different phases or cycles of the moon do influence deer activity throughout the year. To some degree, I think that the moon also plays a role in feeding behavior as well. I don't place a lot of confidence in the belief that the moon dictates precise dates of activity levels of the whitetail rut. A moon cycle might coincide with an active rut one year more than another. But I can't base my hunting strategies and hunting time to align with the different cycles of the moon.

With that said, I must admit that I have been a long time enthusiast and student of the planets and other aspects of the solar system. In fact, it is because of my penchant for studying the planets that I accidentally came upon the terms "perihelion" and "aphelion." These two terms describe the continual cycle of the earth slowly moving closer to the sun year by year and then retreating back from it again over an eleven-year period. It is this cycle, I believe, that actually influences whether the whitetail rut will be active or lethargic. But I will cover more about this later.

Here are some moon facts-

The moon appears to travel from east to west when we observe it in the night sky. However, it travels from west to east in its orbit around Earth.

Understanding many different moon phases can mix-up even the most savvy hunters. A new moon isn't visible and a first or quarter moon is actually a half full moon.

The moon makes one full rotation on its axis in the same time it takes to orbit Earth (which is referred to as a synchronous rotation). This accounts for why we see the same "face" of the moon from Earth at all times.

The moon completes one revolution (around Earth) in only 29 days, 12 hours, 44 minutes and

What effect does the moon really have on the activities of deer?

This is a buck I followed and shot on our farm the morning after a night with a full moon.

2.8 seconds, but actually returns to its original position opposite Earth in 27.3 days.

The moon holds an elliptical orbit that varies in distance to Earth from 225,742 miles to 251,968 miles with the average distance being 238,856 miles.

The moon is responsible for creating tidal friction on Earth that slows our planet's axial rotation by .002 seconds, thereby lengthening a day by that much every century. It also keeps Earth from wobbling out of control.

Additionally, it has a day that differs from a 24-hour Earth day, instead averaging a slightly longer day of 24 hours and 50 minutes.

The moon rises and sets at different times every 24 hours.

While Earth turns on its axis the moon moves about 12 degrees eastward in its orbit, causing it to rise an average of 51 minutes later each day.

As if that isn't enough, the moon's height above the horizon varies through the seasons. In early spring, the first quarter moon is highest, the last quarter is the lowest and the new and full moons are about equal. However, in the fall, it changes significantly. Around September, the last quarter is highest, first quarter is lowest, and a new and full moon coincide with the sun's midday high-point. In December, the full moon is highest, the new moon is lowest and the two quarters are in-between. The terms "directly overhead or underfoot," really mean how high or low the moon gets above and below Earth.

So you can see that despite over 20 years of countless articles written about the moon, it remains confusing to most—especially when it includes its influence over white-tailed deer and their movement and breeding. There are volumes of articles, books, calendars, graphs, DVDs and even reference charts to carry afield that are all dedicated to how the moon influences whitetails—especially during their breeding season. By getting to the bottom of this issue, it can help you make better hunting decisions.

For many hunters, the question about planning their hunting time and strategies around the status or influence of the moon's cycle or phase has become of paramount importance to them. Unbelievably, some will not even go deer hunting if they feel the moon's cycle isn't at the right stage to encourage movement or rut activity. How wrong is that? Very wrong! One never knows what can happen once you are afield. I have either seen or killed plenty of bucks that came past my stand by some other hunter moving in the woods, after a deer drive on neighboring properties, and even some that were chased by coyotes. My point is, if the moon's cycle predicts that activity levels will be slow and rutting behavior will be at its lowest level—it doesn't pay to not go hunting.

In fact, on one occasion when the "charts" told me that the moon's cycle predicted a slow rut and

Ralph Somma with a buck shot during a moon cycle when buck activity was supposedly going to be slow. That's why I hunt, rather than worry about what phase the moon is in.

mostly nonexistent activity—I went hunting anyway. On the way to my stand, I accidentally drove a deer to myself as I walked in. The buck was crossing a logging road and when he saw me, he ran back in the direction from which he came. I hid behind a large boulder and waited. Forty minutes later, the eight-point buck reappeared and started to cross the logging road. He never made it to the other side! So there you have it, a day afield hunting beats the hell out of a day at the office or reading about hunting in camp because the moon's cycle is "wrong."

The gravitational pull of the moon is strong. Its pull affects many life forms and natural wonders in our world—there is no doubt in my mind about that. There is also no denying that the moon's pull affects the tides in the oceans. But does the moon's lunar cycle play an important enough role to have hunters plan their entire deer season around the stages of its cycle? This is the question that needs to be answered once and for all.

Many deer stalkers are convinced that significant whitetail activity is greatest during specific moon phases. Many hunters tell me they are certain they see more deer moving during midday after especially dark nights, solely due to the cycle of a new moon.

The assumption is that dark nights make it difficult for deer to move easily within their range, forcing them to move more during daylight hours. Still others are certain the primary rut takes place during the rutting moon (which is close to the second full moon after the autumn equinox).

Many devoted hunters have been convinced by so-called authorities that lunar phases are critical for timing deer movement during specific moon phases, but believe me, there are many facts that suggest that is simply not the case.

Researchers from the University of Georgia's School of Forest Resources examined how the moon's lunar phases affect the timing of the white-tailed deer's breeding behavior. They wanted to find out if deer hunters who strive to bag a buck should concentrate their hunting tactics during a full, new, or partial moon.

David Osborn, Dr. Karl Miller, and Robert Warren, UGA wildlife research biologists, used breeding-date data from a variety of state wildlife agencies to determine if moon phases had any effect on whitetail doe estrous cycles and, therefore, the rutting activities and behavior of bucks. Breeding dates were gathered from captive deer in four states and more than 2,000 free-ranging does in seven others. Believe it or not, this information took between three to nineteen years to compile. It was then compared to lunar cycles throughout the birth date ranges.

"We would expect annual breeding dates for a population to be similar if the calendar date and therefore, the same length of daylight, was the driving influence," explained Osborn. "We would expect annual breeding to be less similar if moon phase is the driving influence because a particular moon phase might vary as much as 28 days across years."

The fact is, and many of you have heard me preach this for years, biologists and scientists have long agreed that photoperiod (the length of daylight) is the overriding influence on whitetail breeding activity. There are no bones about it—the evidence is quite clear. Scientists and biologists agree that the phase of the moon has virtually nothing to do with the timing of whitetail breeding activity.

For years, state wildlife biologists all over North America regularly and confidently use calendar dates to help hunters plan their vacations and time afield to match with the peak rut activities. The state of Virginia shows November 15th as the peak of the rut and Minnesota hunters need to be in their deer stands the first week of November. In my first book, I listed the prime rutting dates in most of the northern states and provinces as November 10th through the 15th give or take a few days on either end.

But while any of the dates provided can be used as reliable guidelines, they should not be taken as the last word on rutting activity. As I have often said, there are just too many other outside factors to consider. The rut can be delayed by extremes. Matt Knox, Virginia's deer project leader said, "It's really impossible to choose a specific date because of a variety of outside factors. I'd say that November 15th is a pretty consistent date for the peak, but it's going to vary a few days on either side."

Dr. Warren of the University of Georgia said, "The timing of the rut is influenced by various factors, but moon phase doesn't appear to be one of them." The study found there was no hard evidence to support theories that breeding behavior is controlled by lunar cycles. Dr. Warren says weather, food availability, human activity and a variety of other factors all play a role in the timing of the rut, but breeding activity typically happens within a relatively predictable period, no matter what the moon phase happens to be. It is controlled more by the length of daylight than anything else.

New England deer biologist Gary Levigne, who works with Maine's Department of Inland Fish and Game, contributed to the UGA study and he also echoed the theory that the timing of the rut is based almost entirely on photoperiodism.

Again, if you have ever heard my seminars, read my articles, or the chapter in my book about the rut, I strongly emphasize that Mother Nature (perfect in her design) has planned through evolution to perpetuate the species. That means making sure the fawns are born during times of good weather and good sources of food availability for the doe. The bottom line is that evolution has developed a plan where the fawn survival rates are maximized. If fawns are born too early in the year, when it may still be too cold or wet, the does may not be able to gather enough food to provide vital nutrition in their milk. If they are born too late, the fawns may encounter early snowfalls and won't have

On full moon nights like this, it seems as though deer wait until much later in the evening to come out into large fields.

enough time to become healthy enough to survive the oncoming winter. So, the 28-day disparity that would coincide with the moon phase theory would mean that fawns could be born 28 days before or after the peak fawn birth date. Most hunters who watch when does drop their fawns, know birthing takes place pretty much the same time every year.

It is important to note that the while the rut may be about the same dates in Montana as they are in Maine, breeding activity in the more northern latitudes like Saskatchewan and Alberta typically takes place over a short period of time, but activity tends to be a lot more intense. On the other side of the coin, deer that live in southern states like southern Texas and Florida have a much longer breeding season, sometimes lasting as long as four or more months. Trying to pin down an actual date of the peak rut may be much more difficult in southern areas because there tends to be less concentrated rut activity around a specific time. But the general

conviction among most whitetail experts and almost all of the biologists and scientists I have talked with, is that no matter where deer live, they don't seem to pay attention to the phase of the moon.

The question about whether the breeding activity is influenced by the gravitational pull of the moon has been answered. There are, however, still other questions hunters regularly pose to me, "What about the moon's influence on other deer activities? Do deer feed more during the day during a new moon phase because they can't gather enough forage during extra dark nights? And do the moon's lunar cycles have any affect on deer movement in general?"

Well, not according to my deer observations over the last 40 years, and not according to the many biologists that I have talked with either. No one I know or have interviewed has found any distinct or predictable patterns in wildlife activity during various phases of the moon. Deer movement in general might remain fairly regular if weather, hunting pressure, and food sources remain constant, but the chances of that are slim as deer live in a world of continual change.

Most biologists agree that the most influential factor not only on breeding patterns, but in a deer's life in general, is the availability of high-quality forage. Again, Mother Nature makes sure that the driving force behind the life of every doe is procreation. Therefore, they are designed to respond to changing food sources in order to provide the maximum amount of energy for their fetuses or fawns, depending on the season.

There have been several studies (both private and public) that have demonstrated without question that breeding activity can take place either very early or very late, depending on the quality of the mast crop. When the mast crop is heavy and very early, does come into heat earlier than normal. If there is a total mast crop failure, breeding activity can be delayed, sometimes by a month or more.

So with all that said, what should a hunter do? My advice is (as it has always been), "A good day afield hunting deer beats one at home!" I strongly recommend that hunters stop worrying about how the moon's cycle or phase affects their deer hunting and forget all the hype that goes along with it. You can take this advice to the deer hunting bank because the information I just shared with you is a good as gold–hunt the calendar, not the moon. Remember this–researchers across the country agree–whitetail breeding behavior is controlled by photoperiodism, not the moon phases.

As many of you know, I start hunting as soon as the season opens. Like many of you, I hunt right through to the end of the season as well. As I mentioned in my first book, if you happen to be on the way to work and you see a big buck out and about at 10:00 in the morning, call in sick! The rut is on and you need to spend all day in the woods if you can.

So, there it is, my feelings about placing too much reliability on the moon cycles or phases and deer activity and the rut. In a sentence–it's nothing to really worry about.

Be a Deer Whisperer

JAY CASSELL

Take a look at almost any deer hunter and chances are he has a grunt call hanging around his neck. Do these devices really work, or are hunters wasting their time snorting and grunting as they make their way through the woods?

Vocalizations

Deer make three basic calls—the snort, the bleat and the grunt. We've all heard deer snort.

When combined with calls, rattling can draw bucks in from long distances.
(Credit: Summit Treestands)

You're tiptoeing through the woods, trying to get close to some heavy brush, and all of a sudden you hear a loud wheezing sound; a second later you see a white flag go bounding off through the trees. That sound is the snort, which deer make when alarmed and to alert each other to danger. For the hunter, making a snort on a deer call is of little practical use.

On the other hand, the bleat, made mostly by fawns and does, can be used to advantage. A hunter calling in an area that does frequent can usually bring a doe by making a pleading, crying bleat. "You have to put feeling into it," says Jim Strelec of Knight & Hale Game Calls. "A lot of hunters just blow into the call and produce a dull, boring bleat. That's not going to attract any deer's attention. For a bleat to work, you have to make it sounds as if a fawn is really in distress. Cry through that call and you'll see the difference. Does will practically come running."

And following the does, one hopes, will be a buck.

Grunt Work

A deep, guttural vocalization made through a tube call imitates the sound bucks make when they're either with a hot doe or actively looking for one. I've seen and heard bucks grunt throughout all stages of the rut. Unfortunately, although I've used the call during that period, I've had limited success. I have come to the conclusion that with all those

Grunt calls can stop a rutting buck in his tracks. Just don't overdo it!
(Credit: Summit Treestands)

This is true especially at the beginning of the season, when the woods are full of grunting hunters, so in the past few years I've remained quiet at this time, during the gun season in particular.

In the early bow season, or in the latter half of the gun season, I use the grunt call fairly often. And while I've spooked deer with the call—they either figured out that I was a human grunter, or else thought I was a larger buck that they didn't want to mess with—I have also called a few bucks in. It really seems to depend upon the individual buck. If a buck is hot after a doe and hears a grunt, he's more likely to investigate than if he were just going about his daily routines. Sometimes rattling antlers in conjunction with grunt calling has worked, too.

Is Calling Worth it?

Yes. There will be times when you spook deer with grunt calls or bleats. And there will be times when deer pay you absolutely no attention. But there will also be times when the call will either draw a buck into range or make him stop in his tracks, giving you an opportunity for a shot.

In short, calling is not a panacea but merely another tool in a deer hunter's arsenal. Don't expect too much from calls, and use them at the appropriate times.

hunters in the woods blowing on grunt calls, many deer now associate the sound with the presence of a human being and have therefore learned to avoid it.

The Still-Hunting Advantage

JAY CASSELL

The buck never knew I was there. I had been pussyfooting down an old logging trail, pausing every five yards or so, stopping every 20. I was standing next to a large hemlock, my body partially obscured by branches, watching the road in front of me, when I saw movement off to the right. A deer was moving down a trail that intersected the logging road 40 yards ahead.

Head down, nose to the ground, the buck was obviously following the scent of a doe. Caution was the last thing on his mind. When he reached the logging road, he skidded to a stop, turned and looked right at me. Too late. I took him with one shot.

Still-hunting. It's a highly effective way of hunting deer, especially if you do it at the right time, in the right place, the right way.

When

Much depends upon the weather. On still days, with crunchy leaves or icy snow covering the ground, still-hunting is out of the question. No matter how quiet you try to be, you'll still make too much noise and spook any deer way before you can get within gun range. Better to remain in a tree stand on still days, and still-hunt on windy days, when gusts conceal your leaf crunching, or on damp or rainy days, when ground cover is wet and won't make noise when stepped on. Deer also tend to bed down on rainy and especially windy days, so your best chance of getting a shot at a buck under such conditions is to go find one, on foot, quietly.

Where

No matter what the weather, I like to still-hunt when I'm in new territory. While I prefer a tree stand when the situation is right, I don't have a clue where to put up a stand when I'm in unfamiliar country. Still-hunting lets me learn the property, plus it gives me a better chance at a deer than just putting up a stand in any old tree.

In damp or windy conditions, when deer are probably bedded down, I head to the thickest cover I can find. Rhododendron stands, hemlock groves, cedar swamps, thickets, steep ledges; anyplace a buck is likely to bed down is where I'll go. When hunting such spots, wear camo if the law allows, and move slower than slow. Deer pick these spots not only because they're sheltered, but also because they can watch for approaching danger.

When hunting tough-to-reach cover, pay special attention to the wind. Even if you're wearing a cover scent that's consistent with the area's vegetation, moving into an area with the wind at your back dictates that you stop and figure an alternative route. The brush may be ridiculously thick, or the ledges perilously steep, but common sense says you should try to circle around and approach from downwind. Being lazy and just barging ahead anyway will only ensure that you won't see deer.

How

This may sound like a cliché, but it's true: If you think you're going too fast, you are. Serious still-hunting means going painfully slow, so slow that it's almost boring. But you're doing this for a number of reasons. With each step you take, you have a different perspective of the woods. A bedded buck can come into view with just one or two steps. Take five or six, and that buck will detect your movement and be history before you even know he's there.

You're also moving slowly because you want to be quiet. Take each step carefully. Watch where you're putting your feet. If you suspect there might be a stick under the wet leaves you're about to step on, put your foot down slowly. Gradually increase the pressure, putting your weight first on your heel, then on the rest of your foot. As you go, if you can put your foot on a rock that won't tip, on moss, on snow—anything that you're certain won't make noise—do it. If you're in an area where you know your footsteps will be silent, then don't watch your feet. Instead, watch the woods in front of you and around you. I'm not talking woods that are 25 yards

When still hunting, always be ready to shoot, as the element of surprise is on your side.

in front of you, either; rather, 100 yards or more. That's where you're likely to see a buck, not close up. Train yourself to look as far as you can see, and you'll start spotting deer you wouldn't have seen otherwise.

As you move through a given patch of woods, be aware of where the large, silhouette-breaking trees are located. Pause by them. The last thing you want to do is pause out in the open, because that's exactly when a buck is going to come walking into view and see you. Pause by trees, as I did on that logging road, boulders, blow-downs, anything to break up your silhouette. And do it no matter where you are; even if you think you're in an area where you know a buck won't be, still-hunt carefully, and pause by large objects.

Be Ready

Three years ago I was hunting in New York's Catskill Mountains. I was way down the mountain, hunting virtually inaccessible ledges. With a lot of hunting pressure up top, I figured deer would be down low, away from the crowds. It was nearing the end of the season, there was snow on the ground, it was late afternoon. The snow was somewhat, crunchy, so I was moving extra carefully, placing my feet on rocks whenever feasible.

Dropping down to another ledge, I stopped next to a boulder. Generally when I stop, I don't move for at least five minutes, usually 10. Just as I was about to end my break and move another 25 yards or so, I heard something crunching off to my right. Sure enough, a doe and yearling appeared, moving along my ledge. To my surprise, they came to within 10 yards of me, then stopped and started to paw the ground, looking for food. They didn't see me at all. And while I was tempted to quietly say *Boo*, I stayed silent and motionless. I wanted to see what would happen.

What happened was that I heard more crunching off to my right. Now antlers came up over the lip of the ledge. It was a 7-pointer, just 30 yards away. He looked at the does and then froze, his widening eyes riveted on me. He had me, but he didn't move; obviously the presence of the does so close to me had him confused. What would he do? I figured I'd better do something, because he'd probably bolt any second. Ever so slowly, I started to raise my rifle. If I could get it just halfway up to my shoulder, I could take a snapshot and maybe get him.

Naturally, it didn't work that way. The retractable scope cap snapped on the zipper of the camo jacket. Both the doe and yearling heard it and looked right at me; then all hell broke loose.

Throwing the gun to my shoulder, I looked through the scope and immediately saw brown. But it wasn't the buck! It was the yearling, running to my left, blocking my view of the buck. And within seconds it was over, as all three deer disappeared over the edge of the ledge. I took no shot at the buck, as the only shot I had, at the last split second, was a running kidney shot. Too risky, in the situation.

Lesson learned? Whenever I stop somewhere now, I never, ever, hold my gun low on my body, no matter how tired I am. Port arms is always my rule now. And so is that time-honored piece of advice: Always be ready, because you never know.

Climb Higher, Hunt Better

JAY CASSELL

Get the most out of your climbing tree stand.

This past season, I used climbing tree stands more than I have in all of the past 10. One reason is that I got permission to hunt some new property, near my home, just before the opening of bow season. I didn't have time to scout the area at all, so I just took my climber into the woods each day and set up in areas that looked promising.

Using a climber helped me learn the new property in a hurry. That's one reason for using a climber. Another is when you aren't seeing anything out of your permanent stand, and want to watch a different spot.

Climbers let you learn new property and set up in areas where deer aren't pressured.
(Credit: Summit Treestands)

The following routines help me get into the woods, up a tree and settled, fast.

Quiet and Quick

The biggest drawback of climbers is that they make noise. You clank into the woods, pull this bulky thing off your back, attach it to a tree by

turning bolts and nuts, then scrape your way up to a vantage point. Yes, climbers do make noise, but you can reduce it. I always strap an extra bungee cord or two around my stand, which keeps the two pieces together and prevents them from banging as I walk. For setting up at the base of a tree, replace wingnuts with large, accessory-type knobs; they are quieter and easily tuned with gloves on. If you drop them in the leaves, you won't lose them. When you go up the tree, go as quietly and rapidly as you can, but do it while keeping an eye out for deer. If you're silent in your approach and setup, you'll be surprised at how many deer may be nearby.

The Right Tree

When I hike through the woods with a climber on my back, I search for trees that overlook frequently used deer trails. I also look for a tree that's at least 10 yards off my chosen trail;

set up too close to a trail and deer will peg you in a hurry. Search for a straight tree, one whose diameter is right for the size of your climber (mine is about 14 inches). Rule out trees that are crooked, that lean, or that have an abundance of broken branches you'll have to deal with. The final variable is to find a tree near others that can break up your silhouette.

If you find a tree you like, hunt it that day. If you plan to hunt out of the tree again, though, consider that you want to get to it as quickly and quietly as possible the next time. Find the best trail leading to the tree, one that you can move along quietly, with concealed movements.

Have a Routine

Devise a routine and stick with it no matter where or when you hunt; if you know where

Camo cloth helps conceal this hunter's movements. (Credit: Summit Treestands)

A good sling will help you make steady shots from a stand. (Credit: Summit Treestands)

Set your stand in a tree large enough to break up your silhouette.
(Credit: Summit Treestands)

When bowhunting from a stand, keep movement to a minimum; draw well before a buck gets too close.
(Credit: Summit Treestands)

everything always is, you have fewer chances for making mistakes. My routine is this: Before I start into the woods, I strap my safety belt around my waist. The part of the belt that goes around the tree is in my left pocket, ready to be pulled out as soon as I get onto the tree. My release (for bowhunting) is in my right pocket. A rope for hauling up bow or rifle is attached to the top part of my stand.

When I get to my tree, I take the climber off my back, undo the bungee cords (these go into my pants pocket), undo the nuts, and attach the blades of the climber around the tree. I next tie my rifle or bow to the haul rope, then climb into the stand,

put my feet in the straps, attach my safety belt, and start to climb. A handsaw is in the right outside pocket of my daypack, if I

A shooting rest is the mark of a quality treestand.
(Credit: Summit Treestands)

need to saw off any tree limbs. Gloves and hand-warmers are in the left.

When I reach my desired height—normally 15 to 20 feet—I tighten my safety belt. Once I'm secure, I attach a bungee cord between both parts of my climber, which ensures that the bottom platform won't fall away, should I take my weight off it. My second bungee goes around the top blade.

Next, I take a screw-in step and insert it into the tree. I hang my daypack on the step, then turn around, strap the release around my wrist if I'm bowhunting, then pull up my bow on rifle. I nock an arrow or chamber a cartridge, then settle down.

Coming Down

To descend, do your climbing routine in reverse. Take your time, and don't step on your bow or rifle when you get out of your stand.

Take a Stand

JAY CASSELL

If you intend to build your own permanent tree stand, first make sure that it's okay in your hunting area. In my case, the land is owned privately, and the owner gave me the go-ahead. If you hunt on state land, you'll have to go with a portable, as it's illegal to build there.

However, if you are in a situation where you can build a permanent stand, the next thing to do is scout the area thoroughly. Once you've found the spot, planning begins. In my case, I found a sturdy, forked beech tree that overlooked the exact area I wanted to watch. Next, I made a sketch of my proposed stand, and then gathered the necessary materials. With the help of two friends (one of whom had an ATV for transport), we set to it.

First we cut down a third, nearby beech, about the same diameter as the forked tree. We topped it so that its total height was about 20 feet, then carried it over to the forked beech and pushed it upright so that it leaned against it. With a flat rock for a support under our makeshift corner post, we chain-sawed some of the 2 × 4s in half. These we nailed into the corner post and then into both living trees, as supports, to form a triangle with the trees.

Moving up the trees, we constructed another level of support, then started on the floor. Here, again, we nailed two halves of a 2 × 4 onto the corner post and real trees, to form another triangle. We then cut the 1 × 6s into three-foot and two-foot sections, which we nailed on top of the 2 × 4s for floorboards. A railing went on next, about three feet above the floor; then, three feet about that, we put

A room with a view. A well-constructed permanent stand will last for years if properly maintained.

on the roof, using the same method we used for the floor. Some shingles on the roof, some trimming of excess woodland overhangs, and the basic structure was complete. There was even enough wood left over to fashion a seat, with two short lengths of 2 × 4s nailed between the back two trees, and a

few pieces of 1 × 6s nailed on top! Spikes were
nailed into the side of one of the live trees to serve
as the ladder. Next year, I may even add plywood
or camouflage-netting sides to block the wind and
further conceal myself.

A few thoughts here. We found it necessary to
cut down the third tree, as I didn't want to change
the location of my stand and there was no third tree
close enough to incorporate into the stand. If you
can find three (or four) trees growing close together,
or one sturdy tree that splits into three trees as it
goes up—"triangle trees," I call them—by all means
use them. Live trees will be sturdier, and last longer,
than dead ones or a combination of live and dead
ones. A large double tree, for that matter, can also
become an excellent tree stand.

On the subject of picking a tree, make certain
that your tree is in good shape before you start
building on it. The last thing you want to do is build
a tree stand in a set of trees that may rot out in a few
years.

When building a stand, do it in spring or
summer. Deer know the forest, and anything out of
the ordinary is going to be suspect to them. If you
build your stand well before hunting season,
they'll get used to seeing it there, and won't view it
as potentially dangerous. Building it during summer
will also give the wood some time to weather, so it
won't stand out once the leaves have fallen.

If you somehow find yourself in a situation
where you must build a tree stand just before or
during hunting season, it might make sense to use
natural wood, as the deer may not notice it as readily.
I generally prefer 2 × 4s from the lumberyard,
however, as they last longer, and are easier to work
with. Natural wood is wet, too, which means it's
more apt to split.

Sturdy rungs ensure safety. Check them often.

Once your stand is completed, go sit in it for
a while. Like the view? If not, it might pay to carry
a limb pruner or handsaw into the woods and clear
shooting lanes and any limbs that obscure your
vision.

Finally, clean up the ground around your
stand. Let the woods revert to its natural state; the
less human odor and evidence of human presence,
the better. Never urinate near your stand, before or
during deer season, as you'll simply be advertising
your presence to the deer. For that matter, you
should use scent on your boots, to further mask your
presence.

Driving Deer

JAY CASSELL

Deer season is on its last legs. If you haven't gotten a buck yet, you have to get serious if you want to put venison in the freezer. Tactics that worked earlier in the year won't cut it now. The rut is pretty much over, so rattling, calling or watching scrapes and rubs aren't the answers. And still-hunting heavy cover, which always gives you a chance, isn't as effective, since deer in most parts of the country are going to hear you crunching across frozen ground before you even see them.

No, if you want to get a buck, then it's time to drive. And to do that, you need planning and proper execution.

Last Chance

Where I hunt, most hunters have hung it up by the last weekend of the season. Some have already gotten a whitetail, others have simply moved on to new activities. In camp, there are often only three or four of us left, but somebody in our group usually fills his tag at the end of the season. The reason for this is that we concentrate our drives where we know deer are located.

With two to four hunters in a drive, we key in on two prime late-season areas: steep ledges, especially those on south-facing (warmer) slopes; and smaller (one- to three-acre) hemlock groves or cedar swamps.

The Ledge Game

When we hunt mountainside ledges, we position two standers downwind of likely deer hangouts, in spots on the slope where they can survey as far downhill or uphill as possible. The uphill stander is placed where deer will be unable to move above him, such as at the base of a rock face or an extremely steep ledge. At the agreed-upon starting time, the drivers begin walking across the ledges, with the wind at their backs, about 75 yards apart. Everyone wears hunter orange, and no one even thinks about shooting in the direction of other people. We move slowly, making minimal noise (too much commotion will spook deer into terrified flight, making any shots difficult; it's better to have deer simply get up and walk away). If any deer are kicked up, they usually move straight away from the drivers, giving the standers easy shots across the ledges; or the deer head downhill, giving the downhill stander a chance.

This type of drive also works well on ridgetops and longish saddles.

Groves & Swamps

When deer are holed up in hemlock groves or cedar swamps, we drive only small patches that we can effectively cover. It makes no sense to drive large hemlock groves, where deer can sneak around the drivers or simply stay hidden. We position two or three standers at the downwind perimeter of a small hemlock stand, usually where it opens up into hardwoods. Then one driver, preferably two, will enter the woods at the specified time; if there are two drivers, they move parallel to each other, never losing visual contact. Deer kicked up from the thick stuff will move either straight away from the drivers, toward the standers or out the sides in an attempt to double back. Either way, someone usually gets a shot.

Woodlots, marshes and small fields can also be effectively hunted with this type of drive.

I Was Almost Shot on a Drive a Few Years Ago

It was a stupid mistake, but most accidents are. I was one of three standers surrounding the perimeter of some hemlocks interspersed with blowdowns and thick brush. We were set out as a triangle, with me on the right corner. The drivers walked right by me. They didn't see me; I didn't see or hear them. Suddenly, there was a shot from just uphill of me; then a bullet came whizzing across the forest floor, kicking up leaves not 10 inches from my feet.

At the end of the drive, one of the drivers said he had taken a shot at a running deer but missed. When I told him that he almost shot me, he was horrified. This is a guy who has been hunting for 40 years, and it was the first time he had ever jeopardized anyone on a hunt. After that, we made a few drive rules that we follow to the letter, every year:

- Everyone—driver and stander—always wears hunter orange.
- Before the drive, we make explicit plans. Everyone knows exactly where the other people will be; and the drivers in particular always keep each other in view.
- No one shoots in the direction of anyone else. The only shots that can be taken will be at deer that have broken out the side of the driven area, or have gotten into an uphill or downhill position where a backstop—ledge, knoll, boulder—will stop any errant bullets. If you are unsure of your target, or of what's behind it, do not even think about shooting.

And a final reminder: Hunters who have already filled their tags always act as drivers since they cannot, by law, carry firearms.

Shotgunning for Deer

DAVID R. HENDERSON

Why Use a Shotgun?

Hunting deer with a shotgun is a lot like going to bat in a baseball game with a broomstick. Both implements may be used somewhat effectively, but neither represents the most efficient nor preferred method. As suburbia continues its relentless expansion into deer habitat and humans and whitetails compete increasingly for elbowroom, more and more municipalities are mandating shotguns for big game hunting rather than permitting the use of long-range modern rifles. This is not to say that shotguns are not effective for deer hunting. In fact, the largest-grossing typical whitetail buck recorded in the history of the

The New York State record typical buck—once the world record—was taken in 1939 with a punkin ball slug fired from a shotgun.

Boone & Crockett Club's scoring system was taken by an Illinois shotgun hunter in 1993. The two largest bucks taken in the history of my native New York, a 198-plus typical and a 267-plus nontypical, were both killed during the 1930s with old "punkin ball" slugs.

Today about 4.1 million of the nation's 10 million whitetail hunters go afield armed with shotguns, and the number is growing every year. More than 20 states mandate the use of shotguns for deer for at least some of their hunters. Eight states limit all of their hunters to shotguns or muzzleloaders for deer. Delaware, Massachusetts, New Jersey and Rhode Island allow buckshot or slugs while Illinois, Indiana, Iowa and Ohio limit everyone to slugs. Connecticut used to prohibit rifles but now allows them for hunting on holdings larger than 10 acres, with written permission from the landowner. Eight other states limit at least 40 percent of their hunters to slugs and/or buckshot. Pennsylvania, historic home of the American rifle, now restricts more than 100,000 of its hunters to slug guns and muzzleloaders by mandating special regulations areas around Philadelphia and Pittsburgh. New York has nearly 400,000 slug shooters. Even such frontier outposts as Helena, Montana, and Edmonton, Alberta, have shotgun-only hunting areas in their outer suburbs.

At last count only about 3 percent of today's shotgun deer hunters must or opt to use buckshot; the rest use slugs of one form or another. Given a

The author cautiously approaches a fallen buck taken with a slug gun. Most shotgun hunters select slugs as their ammunition of choice.

fast-growing market, development of slug loads and slug-shooting shotguns has advanced more in the last 20 years than any other aspect of the firearms industry. Today's high-velocity, high-tech sabot slugs and rifled barrel slug guns have turned shotgun deer hunting from a "wait-'til-you-see-the-whites-of-their-eyes" proposition into an event where the hunter can no longer be faulted for preheating the oven when a rack appears a couple of hundred yards away. Regardless, being of sound mind and body, if I'm given a choice, I'll use a rifle for hunting deer rather than a shotgun. I thus found it surprising when, in my native New York, there was staunch opposition to a legislative proposal to allow rifles in the largely agricultural western portion of the state, which has

been restricted to slug guns ever since deer hunting was regulated in the late 1930s.

There is obviously a core of deer hunters who are satisfied with shotguns for deer, but the majority of us who do hunt with a shotgun probably do so because we don't have any choice in the matter. Most of us do, however, have a choice of loads and guns, and given the recent boom in technology in this area, there are plenty of viable options. Which one is right for you? Let's take a look.

Slugs or Buckshot?

First of all, if you have a choice between buckshot and slugs, there is no choice. Slugs are absolutely the most effective load you can put into a shotgun. Granted, buckshot is a devastating close-range load. In fact, the Germans complained to the Hague and Geneva Conventions regarding the shotgun's horrific effect in trench warfare during World War I. That's the reason shotguns were outlawed under the Law of Armed Conflict, Article 23, by the Hague Convention, a decree that the United States chose not to observe. American armed forces used a variety of pump shotguns in the Pacific Theater during World War II, and later in Korea. While the distinctive patter of the M16 rifle was readily identifiable as an American presence, the lion's bellow of a 10-gauge pump loaded with double-aught buckshot may well have been the most feared sound in the up-close-and-personal jungle environs of Vietnam. Ithaca, Mossberg, Winchester and Remington all built tactical scatterguns for U.S. troops.

Buddy and fellow writer J. Wayne Fears says he favored the companionship of a Winchester 97 while serving in the jungles of Southeast Asia with U.S. Special Forces. Wayne said of the 97 that it was one gun you always knew whether it was ready or not, by the hammer position. Any slug, full-bore or sabot, 20-, 16-, 10- or 12-gauge, has a much, much more extensive effective range

There is obviously a core of deer hunters who are satisfied with shotguns for deer . . .

Shotguns are effective tactical weapons for the military and law enforcement personnel.

Richard Paulli displays the mount of the Boone & Crockett 267-plus buck that he took with a shotgun in Illinois in 1983. It is still one of the largest scoring whitetail bucks taken with a slug.

Modern sabot slugs shoot very flat and perform very well on deer-sized game.

than buckshot in the same gauge and, although the margin for error is slightly less, is every bit as deadly in close quarters. But given the choice, the vast majority of American shotgunners will go with slugs every time.

Types of Slugs

Despite all of the hype about saboted ammunition that you read in magazines and see on television, the conventional full-bore slug still represents more than 60 percent of the retail sales to slug hunters. Does saboted ammunition have a longer effective range? Definitely. Is it more accurate when fired from a rifled bore than full-bore slugs are from a smoothbore? Absolutely. Does everyone need that extra wallop and extended range? Nope. Longstanding (and somewhat outdated) surveys have shown that 97 percent of all deer killed with shotguns are taken at ranges of less than 100 yards. An impressive 94 percent are actually taken inside of 75 yards. Foster-type full-bore slugs, such as those loaded by Winchester, Federal and Remington and

the various non-saboted Brenneke-style designs, are very effective at that range.

If you shoot a smoothbore shotgun and take typical shots within these parameters, you are not at a disadvantage with full-bore slugs. Saboted ammunition, at least before the new high-velocity stuff hit the market, offered little advantage over full-bore slugs at traditional deer hunting ranges (40-80 yards). The high-tech ammunition didn't really show its stuff until it had a chance to stretch out and run at longer distances. At that point the high-tech ammunition's superior aerodynamics and ballistic coefficient and the stabilizing effect of the spin generated by the rifling helped the projectile maintain its velocity, trajectory and energy over a greater distance than did the bulky full-bore slug.

Foster-type rifled slugs and the 23/4-inch Brenneke smoothbore slugs look essentially the same as they did when they were introduced—(*Foster's in 1933 and the Original Brenneke in 1935*)—but have undergone some subtle improvements over the years.

Foster-type rifled slugs and the 2¾-inch Brenneke smoothbore slugs look essentially the same as they did when they were introduced . . .

An extraordinary array of shotgun slugs are available to modern deer hunters.

Buckshot is a very effective deer hunting load when used at limited ranges.

ORIGINAL BRENNEKE   FOSTER

Today's Original Brenneke slug and the Foster-style rifled slug (loaded by Winchester, Remington and Federal) are visually identical to their original 1930s prototypes.

For instance, Winchester redesigned its Double-X load in 1982 by swelling the diameter to fill all bores and by making it more consistently concentric. Federal Cartridge followed with a redesign in 1985 and again in the early 1990s while Remington finally swelled the diameter and made some changes to its venerable Slugger in 1993.

Barrels Make a Difference

What about chokes for slug shooting? Odds are that your smoothbore will shoot a slug more accurately with a relatively open choke. The industry, in fact, used to suggest improved cylinder for slug shooting. But shotgun bores vary in dimension, bore to bore, even in the same brand and model. A slug that has been squeezed tightly throughout its journey down the barrel will react differently when it hits the choke—regardless of the constriction of that choke—than one that fits loosely and tipped slightly as it traversed the same distance. I've seen some modified choke shotguns that were real tack drivers and the post-war Belgian Browning Auto-5 that I inherited from Dad shot Brennekes like they were designed for each other—despite its fixed full-choke barrel.

Will shooting high-tech sabot loads through your smoothbore increase your effective range? Maybe, but certainly not to the point that would justify paying 7 or 8 times as much as you would for full-bore slugs. In fact, you will find that saboted ammunition is less effective in a smoothbore than conventional slugs since, if the slug is not spinning, the sabot sleeves will have difficulty separating from the slug and will actually destabilize the projectile.

Sabot slugs are designed for rifled barrels; the soft material of the sabot sleeves grips the rifling and imparts spin to the projectile, which it needs to maintain stability. Full-bore slugs rely on a nose-heavy design for stability during a relatively short flight.

If you shoot a smoothbore but would like to take advantage of the high-tech loads, your best bet is to add a rifled choke tube. All major shotgun manufacturers offer rifled tubes and they are improving all the time. You can also look into aftermarket tubes from Hastings, Colonial, Cation and others—The length of the choke tube is a factor in how well it stabilizes slugs. After all, asking 2 to 3 inches of spiraled grooves to impart a rotation of up to 37,000 rpm on

a projectile that has already reached terminal velocity is asking a lot. Regardless, I've seen some rifled tubes that shot far more accurately, particularly inside of 100 yards, than the laws of physics should allow.

The fact remains, however, if you want to take advantage of the latest innovations and vast ballistic superiority of today's high-tech slugs, you'll need a rifled slug barrel. Be advised that a rifled barrel dedicates the gun to slug shooting only, it will not effectively pattern shot. It will, however, stabilize any slugs—sabot or full-bore Foster or Brenneke-style—and extend their effective range. In fact, full-bore slugs actually skid a bit in the rifling and leave copious amounts of lead fouling in the grooves in a very short period of time, but they will shoot well in a rifled bore. The best slug gun models will have fixed rifled barrels, which means they can't be used for anything but slug shooting, unlike models with interchangeable barrels. As with rifled choke tubes, all major shotgun manufacturers offer at least one model with a rifled barrel and most offer optional rifled barrels that can replace your conventional barrel for the deer season.

With a stiff barrel, good trigger and solidly mounted scope your rifled barrel slug gun should be able to consistently put three conventional-velocity saboted slugs through the same hole at 50 yards from a solid rest. Accuracy at 100 yards will vary with the wind conditions, trigger pull, load and the shooter's ability. To sum it up, what you need from a slug gun depends entirely on how you are going to use it. There's nothing wrong with smoothbore shotguns and full-bore slugs for the relatively short ranges encountered in most deer woods. If you're looking for long-range performance in your slug gun, however, that option is available in rifled-barrel shotguns and high-tech saboted ammunition.

If you shoot a smoothbore but would like to take advantage of the high-tech loads, your best bet is to add a rifled choke tube.

Knowing what loads are designed for what type of shotgun barrels makes a difference in the deer woods.

There's nothing wrong with smoothbore shotguns and full-bore slugs for the relatively short ranges encountered in most deer woods.

Rifle-sights or optics are a necessity for a slug gun. Slug shooting is a specialty use of a shotgun—you must aim the gun rather than just point it.

More than 60 percent of whitetail deer hunters choose smoothbore shotguns and use full-bore (non-sabot) slugs.

Shotguns for Deer

State-of-the-Art Slug Guns

For three-quarters of the 20th century small game shotguns became deer guns by simply changing the load. The market just wasn't big enough to warrant much innovation and manufacturers made few design concessions for slug or buckshot shooters. Ithaca Gun was the first shotgun company to cater to slug shooters, introducing its 12-gauge Deerslayer in 1959. The Deerslayer was a John Browning Model 37 bottom-ejection pump design that Ithaca pulled off the scrap heap when Remington discontinued its predecessor, the Model 17, in 1936.

A spokesman at the Remington Museum assured me that Big Green had willingly given up the design when the original Browning patent had run out to avoid any charges that Remington held a monopoly in the shotgun market. Ithaca Gun historian Walter Snyder, however, says that Ithaca Gun actually built a few Model 37s while Remington was still producing Model 17s and stored them until

the patent expired. The original Deerslayer featured iron rifle sights on a straight-tube barrel (no forcing cones or chokes) with a tight .704-inch internal diameter barrel (conventional 12-gauge barrels are .729) that firmly squeezed all of the slugs available on the market that time.

"Tolerances were really strict," said former Ithaca Gun service manager Les Hovencamp. "I guess if a barrel came off the reamer at .705 or .706 it was scrapped." Most any slug on the market filled this bore, thus retaining the essential square-to-bore orientation before exiting the barrel. The result was vastly improved accuracy, even though the bore diameter was eventually bored out to .719 in the early 1980s to lessen pressures, as slugs got bigger. All major manufacturers eventually followed by offering optional "buck barrels"—shorter, open-cylinder versions of existing designs fitted with rifle sights.

The length of a slug barrel is of very little importance. You'll find that while the powder burns in the first 16 to 17 inches of the bore, there will be a slight increase in velocity up to about 25 inches.

Shotguns designed and manufactured specifically for slug shooting are a relatively new concept.

Anything longer than that actually begins to work as a brake on the ejecta, slowing it down. Most production guns come with 22- to 25-inch barrels while a few hand-built guns have 20-inch barrels.

Birth of Rifled Barrels

Rifled shotgun barrels have been used by trapshooters and produced by European designers for the better part of a century, but until BRI's Bob Sowash achieved a certified MOA group (*five shots measuring 1 inch center to center at 100 yards*) with his slug and a custom-rifled barrel in the early 1970s, the spiral spout was largely unheard of on these shores. In fact, until the 1980s federal law prohibited rifled barrels over .50-caliber for civilian use. They were deemed "destructive devices." The grandfather of rifled shotgun barrels is probably Olie Olson, head gunsmith for E.R. Shaw Barrels of Bridgeville, Pennsylvania, until his retirement in 2001.

A transplanted Californian living in the shotgun-only environs of Allegheny County, Pennsylvania, Olson was frustrated by the relative

The accuracy of today's slug guns, firing modern loads, is better than ever before.

inaccuracy of conventional slug guns. He toyed with rifling shotgun bores with various twist rates in the late 1970s. When Shaw obtained permission from the feds to build spiral tubes for civilian shotguns in 1982, the door was opened for slug shooting to enter the 20th century. Shaw started producing rifled barrels that could be retrofitted to certain solid-receiver, fixed frame shotguns like High Standard Flite Kings. Today Randy Fritz's Tar-Hunt Rifles uses Shaw barrels on its custom bolt-action and pump slug guns and once toyed with the idea of importing today's version of the High Standard receivers from the Philippines.

Rock Barrels in Oregon and Pennsylvania Arms of Duryea, Pennsylvania, ventured into the fray early but the only company that would have a lasting presence was the Hastings Company of Clay Center, Kansas. Originally conceived as a barrel-maker for interchangeable choke systems, Hastings owners Phil Frigon and Bob Rott began importing rifled Paradox barrels from France in 1985 and quickly became the prime aftermarket source of rifled shotgun barrels. Hastings encountered very little competition in the aftermarket rifled barrel market until Ithaca Gun tested the waters in 2003. The venerable upstate New York gunmaker was famous for its "Roto-Forged" smoothbore barrels until its plant moved in 1989 and the forge proved too expensive to rebuild at the new facility. The company was outsourcing barrels for its own M37 pumps from 1989 to 2002 when it purchased a computerized barrel lathe and, for a brief time, marketed aftermarket barrels for other brands of shotguns. The lathe, however, was lost to a creditor when Ithaca closed its doors in New York in 2005.

There are conflicting schools of thought on rifling twist rates. An inarguable fact is that the faster twist rates *(one turn in 24 or 25 inches)* accentuate expansion of slugs. Hastings' Bob Rott and gun builder Mark Bansner say that they saw no difference in accuracy of sabot slugs between 1-28 and 1-36 barrels. Randy Fritz and Shaw's Olie Olson, however, claimed that the sabots preferred 1-28 and Foster slugs preferred 1-36 with 1-34, a good compromise for both. Fritz, who has been in on the development of Lightfields since their inception, actually builds his custom guns with a special twist rate—I think it's 1-34—to shoot Lightfield Hybreds. I have noticed that the soft Foster slugs, when spun too much (1-28 for example) seem to want to "flow" or fly apart due to centrifugal force. I have also noticed that guns with 1-28 twists (1-24 in 20-gauge) do seem to handle high-velocity slugs better than those with 1-36 twist rates.

twist rates *(at 1,400 fps)*	
1-25 inches	37,440 rpm
1-28 inches	33,428 rpm
1-32 inches	29,250 rpm
1-34 inches	27,528 rpm
1-35 inches	26,742 rpm
1-36 inches	26,999 rpm

When Shaw obtained permission ... to build spiral tubes for civilian shotguns in 1982, the door was opened for slug shooting to enter the 20th century.

The advent of rifled barrels sparked a revolution in slug shooting.

First Production Rifled Barrels

Ithaca and Mossberg were the first companies to offer production guns with rifled barrels in 1987—Ithaca with its Model 37 Deerslayer II and Mossberg introducing the Model 500 Trophy Slugster. Heckler and Koch started importing Benelli autoloaders and affixing them with

Shaw rifled barrels. Thompson Center's custom shop and tiny New England Firearms (H&R) started marketing single-shot rifled-barrel guns in the very late 1980s. Today all major shotgun manufacturers—Remington, Mossberg, U.S. Repeating Arms, Browning, Ithaca, H&R, Marlin, Savage, Beretta, Benelli, Franchi and Traditions— offer at least one model with a rifled barrel. Although smoothbore shotguns and conventional slugs still make up nearly 65 percent of the retail market, rifled barrels and sabot slugs are the most advanced and accurate and represent the fastest-growing segment of the industry.

Slug Gun Shortcomings

The effectiveness of a slug gun is limited by chamber pressure *(shotguns operate at less than 12,000 pounds per square inch, rifles up to 60,000)* and, due to looser construction, vibration. Vibration is not nearly as much of a factor with buckshot guns simply because the whole idea there is to spray a pattern of pellets as opposed to centering a single projectile. Slug guns definitely need to be more precise. That's why the bolt-action and break-action singleshot are the most accurate actions. The barrel is fixed (screwed) to the receiver and the entire function of the gun is in a straight line with nothing hanging off it, which means less barrelshaking, accuracy-robbing vibration. That's also why today's slug barrels

are typically short. A long barrel used to be an advantage since older powders needed more space to burn and efficiency was compromised by gas leaking past undersized wads. But the high-tech powders used to propel today's gas-sealing wads is burned in the first 16-17 inches of barrel length, so any barrel of at least 18 inches should be adequate in that respect.

Slugs, like shotshells, thus gain nothing ballistically from a longer barrel. In fact, unlike

Slugs, like shotshells, thus gain nothing ballistically from a longer barrel.

The author took this 8-point buck with a Remington 11-87 autoloader. The autoloader, however, is the heaviest and inherently the least accurate of any slug gun design.

Despite all the advances in slug guns and loads, the shotgun hunter will never achieve the range and effectiveness enjoyed by rifle hunters.

Ithaca and Mossberg were the first companies to offer production guns with rifled barrels . . .

Introduced in 1959 the Ithaca Deerslayer was the first shotgun built specifically for slug shooting.

shotshells, slugs have characteristics that may actually make the shorter barrels more accurate. Slugs are so slow that the gun recoils nearly 5/8 inch before the slug can get out the muzzle. Because of this phenomenon a longer barrel is actually detrimental to accuracy because the longer the slug stays in the tube the more it is affected by the barrel movement caused by recoil and vibration. Autoloaders are inherently the least accurate action because there is so much movement when the trigger is pulled. At ignition the gun starts recoiling, the bolt slides back to eject the empty hull and a fresh load is levered out of the magazine and up to where it can be slammed into the chamber by the returning bolt.

Pumps, with the fore end slide and magazine dangling from the barrel, which is loosely fitted to the receiver, also experience a great deal of vibration at ignition. Ithaca's Deerslayer II line, featuring a free-floating (*not attached to the magazine*) barrel that is fixed permanently to the receiver, is the only exception among pump guns. Although the single shot is the simplest design, it usually is a very inexpensive model shotgun with a less-than-bank-vault-solid lockup, heavy trigger and cheap barrel—factors that negate the action's accuracy potential. Exceptions are the Mossberg SSi-One, the Thompson Center single shot that was phased out of its custom shop in the late 1990s and the H&R and New England Firearms (*identical except for wood and finish*) 980 and 925 (*20-gauge*) series. These guns used extremely heavy bull-barrels to tame harmonics and offset the effects of the heavy triggers. Mine were both hand-fitted at the factory to maximize the tightness of the lock-up and the triggers were tightened. The result is two simple but extremely accurate test guns that I've toted to deer stands on many occasions.

State-of-the-Art Slug Guns

Bolt Actions

The state of the art in slug guns is the bolt action. Once the least expensive, simplest shotgun action, the addition of the rifled barrel and a few other amenities (*like fiber-optic sights, rifle-style synthetic stocks and scope mounts*) has turned the bolt from a beginner's gun into the most inherently accurate slug gun available. If you're old enough to have seen Vietnam "live" through binoculars or on the evening news or to have voted for McGovern, chances are you're familiar with the concept of bolt-action shotguns for beginners.

Who among we gray-templed outdoors types doesn't remember a sibling or crony who started deer hunting with a slug-loaded, inexpensive bolt action or single shot? Seems like there was always somebody with a Polychoked Mossberg 195, Marlin 55 or Sears 140 bolt gun. Or, by the same token, an Ithaca 66 Super Single—or even a crusty old uncle who put slugs in his "Long Tom" Marlin goose gun or one of the old break-action single-digit model H&Rs. Back then singles and bolts were "starters" reserved for kids, or they were multipurpose ordnance used by folks who weren't as serious about deer guns as they were in simply having something in the truck or the barn that could be of use in all seasons. The bolts and singles of those days were at the lower end of the shotgun spectrum. But you've also got to remember that shotguns and slugs per se weren't accurate back then, either. But, as I say, that was then—this is now. Today's bolt-action slug guns are definitely not reinventions of the wheel. Comparisons between them and yesterday's simple actions are about as valid as racing the *Spirit of St. Louis* against a Stealth bomber.

Seems like there was always somebody with a Polychoked Mossberg 195, Marlin 55 or Sears 140 bolt gun.

Above: A good barrel and a relatively light, crisp trigger are the hallmarks of a good slug gun.

Below: The bolt-action shotgun is the state of the art in slug guns.

While the Steadygrip concept doesn't lend itself to comfortable wing shooting, it'll make a great companion in the turkey woods or deer blind.

"Years ago the bolt action was simply an inexpensive shotgun with little more than reliability to justify its existence," said Mossberg CEO Alan "Iver" Mossberg, whose company was one of the prime providers of entry-level bolt shotguns decades ago. "The growing popularity of the pump and autoloading shotguns nearly retired the bolt action. Oddly enough, when bolt action interest was waning, many states were changing their deer seasons to 'shotgun only,' slug ammunition was improving tenfold. Suddenly the bolt-action was reborn and repositioned." But Mossberg's 695 was discontinued at the end of the twentieth century, leaving the Savage 210 alone in the genre. In the twenty-first century, however, used Browning A-Bolts were routinely selling for four figures and the company brought them back in 2011, just after Savage introduced the Savage 220F (20 gauge) in 2010 and the revamped 12-gauge 212 in 2011.

Marlin's 512 was the first-ever bolt-action rifled barrel gun, starting off in 1994. The story goes that veteran *Outdoor Life* shooting editor Jim Carmichel suggested to Marlin that a rifled barrel on its

Steadygrip

From the "What-Will-They-Think-of-Next?" Department comes Benelli's SteadyGrip system. The company's Super Black Eagle and M1 Field autoloaders offer optional stock system that consists of a soft-rubber coated pistol-style grip that drops away from the stock just behind the trigger guard at a 60-degree rear angle. The concept actually dates back more than a decade. In the late 1980s—before the formation of Benelli USA, when the Italian line came from Urbino to the United States through Heckler & Koch—the company's tactical shotguns were offered with a similar-looking "tactical" grip. But no one has ever put one on a sporter until now. Having extensive experience with M-16/AR-15s, which feature a grip and stock configuration virtually identical to the SteadyGrip, I was well aware of the advantage the system afforded off-hand shooting, but I'd also tried some aftermarket tactical grips on other shotguns in the past and found that their abrupt drop actually accentuated recoil when the gun was fired from a seated position.

It was thus with admitted skepticism that I first approached the SteadyGrip. But after a couple of range sessions and a week-long turkey hunt with the Super Black Eagle on the Nail Ranch in west-central Texas, I came away impressed. The rearward angle and soft rubber grip actually made the inertia system (recoil-operated) Benelli autos comfortable to shoot from a seated position— even when the Super Black Eagle was loaded to the tips with 3.5-inch, 2-ounce Federal Grand Slam turkey loads. The SteadyGrip-fitted guns weigh exactly the same and have the same stock dimensions (in terms of length of pull, drop at the comb and drop at the heel) as their conventionally stocked versions and are priced only moderately more. (*M1 SteadyGrip is $90 more than its conventionally stocked version; the Super Black Eagle just $80 more.*)

When shooting off-hand on the range, the SteadyGrip provided the familiar suppressed recoil and, well, steadiness I remembered from my Service Rifle competition days with the AR-15. In fact, the session engendered a mental note to pick up an optional rifled slug barrel (both the Super Black Eagle and M1 Field have them). Afterall, the SteadyGrip models of guns are drilled and tapped for scope mounting. The SteadyGrip system definitely makes the guns "dedicated use" ordnance. But while the SteadyGrip concept doesn't lend itself to comfortable wing shooting, it'll make a great companion in the turkey woods or deer blind.

bolt-action Model 55 Goose Gun would be a big seller and thus it was born. The 512, which featured unique side-saddle scope mounts, a 1-28 twist rate in its 22-inch barrel and later a synthetic stock and fiber-optic sights, was discontinued due to slumping sales in 2001. The Browning A-Bolt slug gun, essentially that company's bolt-action rifle design chambered for 12-gauge, was probably the best-built production slug gun ever made, but it enjoyed a short life span, being discontinued in 1998 after just three years of production. The gun cost more than twice the price of the Mossberg and Marlin bolts and consumers just weren't willing to pay the difference. If you can find one today in good shape, grab it. The problem is that most people who have them know what they have and aren't going to part with them.

The Savage 210 Master Shot is similarly a rifle design (Savage's inexpensive but accurate 110 series) chambered in 12-gauge. Like the Browning,

Mossberg's 695 and the Savage 210 Master Shot are the only commercial bolt-action slug guns available today . . .

Above: A rack of bolt actions *(left to right)* Savage 210, Tar-Hunt RSG-12, Marlin 512P and Mossberg 695.

Below: The Savage 210 bolt gun was replaced in the line with the clip-fed, Accu-Triggered 212 in 2011.

the Savage 210 uses a rifle-style bolt with front locking lugs and a 60-degree throw. The Mossberg and Marlin are shotgun bolts that lock up when the bolt handle is dropped into a recess cut into the stock. The Savage uses a synthetic stock that is virtually identical to the one on its bull-barreled varmint and tactical rifles, the exception being an integral box magazine that protrudes from the bottom of the receiver like a molded goiter. The Savage has a 24-inch rifled (1-35) twist rate with no sights. The receiver is drilled and tapped to accept scope mounts. Unquestionably, the ultimate in slug guns today is the custom-built Tar-Hunt RSG (Rifled Slug Gun) bolt-action series made by gun builder Randy Fritz of Bloomsburg, Pennsylvania. The RSG-12 Professional and its 20-gauge counterpart, the RSG-20 Mountaineer, are basically Remington 700 rifle clones chambered for shotgun loads. Fitted with Shaw barrels, Jewell triggers, McMillan composite stocks, Pachymar Decelerator recoil pad and the custom-made action, the guns retail for thousands. Fritz also fits custom barrels and does trigger work on Remington 870 pumps, calling that model the DSG (Designated Slug Gun) series.

Single Shots

Single-shot, break-open slug guns such as the H&R 980 and 925 Ultra Slugster (bull-barreled 12- and 20-gauge models) and Mossberg's 12-gauge SSi-One are similarly accurate but tend to be heavier and lack the quick follow-up of the bolt actions. Because the scope rail is mounted directly on the chamber, these guns also tend to be rougher on scopes. New England Firearms, the Marlin-owned sister company to H&R, makes the 980 in a less expensive version and both companies market (NEF Tracker and H&R Topper) light, compact single-shot versions with rifled bores. The very inexpensive Pardner series is a smoothbore version.

Unquestionably, the ultimate slug guns today is the custom-built Tar-Hunt RSG (Rifled Slug Gun) bolt-action series made by gun builder Randy Fritz . . .

The single-shot H&R Topper is available with a rifled barrel.

Pumps

Pumps are the most popular slug guns, probably due to retail price point as well as their light weight, durability and simplicity. The compact, lightweight aspect of the pump makes it the darling of the stalker as well as the stand-hunter. Follow-up shots are easier with a pump than with any action other than an autoloader, but heavier recoil is the price one pays for light, compact design. There are nearly 10 million Remington 12-, 16- and 20-gauge 870s wandering around the country while the 12-gauge Mossberg 500 and 835 Ultri-Mag are among the sales leaders every year. Ithaca's M37 pump comes in several 12-, 16- and 20-gauge configurations for deer hunters, including the 11-pound 12-gauge bull-barreled Deerslayer III, which is available only by special order through the company. Ithaca Gun failed again in 2005 but resurfaced in Ohio under new ownership that changed the face of the company. The newest Ithaca Gun offers the old Deerslayer II but the newer Deerslayer III is a trimmed down version of the New York model, with a lighter bull barrel and new twist rate (now 1-in-28) that, coupled with the free-floating concept, leads outstanding accuracy.

The Browning BPS, Winchester SpeedPump, Benelli Nova, NEF Pardner and a couple of

The compact, lightweight aspect of the pump makes it the darling of the stalker as well as the stand-hunter.

New York hunter Roger Scales took this 13-point doe with an Ithaca Deerslayer using a Brenneke slug in 1994. It was one of the largest-racked does ever recorded.

The Benelli inertial recoil operating system used in the 12-gauge Stoeger Model 2000 slug gun permits the use of a wide range of 2-3/4- and 3-inch loads.

pumps from other companies offer rifled barreled versions.

Autoloaders

The autoloader is popular due to its tendency toward lessened recoil and quick follow-ups. The trade-off is that they are generally much

What's Next?

In the late 1990s, with bolt-action shotguns well established as the state of the art, Remington director of firearms product development Jay Bunting told me that there would never be a slug gun built on the Model 700 rifle action. Bunting noted the whole industry learned a lesson through Browning, which built an excellent bolt-action gun based on its A-Bolt rifle action but with a $700 price tag it simply could not compete with the Mossberg, Marlin and Savage guns that were pouring out of mass merchandisers for less than half that price.

But when Remington brought out its 710 rifle in 2000, a bolt-action designed for Mart sales at $350 including a Bushnell scope, many of us thought the door was open for Remington to enter the bolt-action slug gun market with a competitively priced unit. "No, you won't see a 12-gauge 710," Bunting stated emphatically when questioned on the matter. "But how about a smaller gauge? How about one even smaller than 20—a bolt gun designed around a very flat-shooting proprietary slug? Stay tuned." Intriguing.

Double-barreled shotguns, be they side-by-sides or over-unders, are notoriously inaccurate for slug shooting....

Double-barreled shotguns are notorious for shooting in two different directions and thus are not suitable for slug shooting. Occasionally a buckshot hunter will use a double for short-range shooting.

Is Remington planning a proprietary smallbore slug gun built on the Model 710 rifle frame?

heavier and far more expensive than other actions. They are also more complicated and often less reliable and somewhat less accurate due to the excessive vibration caused by the cycling action. The Remington 1100 is the lightest and oldest autoloading model on the market and is available in both 12- and 20-gauge slug versions. It's a long time favorite with slug hunters, as is its successor, the 11-87 and the newer Versa, Browning's Gold, Silver and Maxus, Winchester's Super X2 and Super X3, Benelli's Super Black Eagle and M1 and Beretta's 12-gauge ES100 (formerly the Pintail),

Weatherby's SAS and Traditions' Spanish-built XL- 2000 autoloaders are all popular with slug hunters in both rifled barrels and smoothbores. Mossberg's 9200 fits that bill until it was discontinued in 2000, as was Winchester's 1400 a few years earlier.

Doubles

Double-barreled shotguns, be they side-by-sides or over-unders, are notoriously inaccurate for slug shooting, since both bores often have their own point-of-aim. For that reason, no doubles are currently made with rifled barrels.

Deer Rifles and Cartridges

Deer Loads to Love

There was no explaining the big buck. Deer like that just don't appear in front of the rifle– surely not in front of my rifle. The other deer, those that had charged out of the thicket at ridgeline, had barreled past me close enough to touch with a flyrod. I'd unwittingly cornered them in a postage-stamp copse of pines. Too steep to draw hunters, the talus slope below was like a moat ringing this promontory.

I could have shot the little buck or turned back after that stampede. The cover was empty. But for some perverse reason, I climbed a few more yards, up past the last tree. The short apron of rock on the cliff face behind the pines had no cover. But there, staring down at me with no place to go, was one of the finest mule deer bucks I'd ever seen. I fired right away, and the .30-06 took him down. Sometimes it pays to go where deer have no business hiding.

A .25 Souper . . . at Last

"This cartridge is quite similar to the Improved .250/3000 but came at a much later date and did not gain popularity to any degree. It is made by necking the .308 Winchester case to .25 with no other change. Coming after the introduction of such fine and popular cartridges as the Improved .257 and of course the very fine standard .257, it [has] little to recommend it over existing .25 caliber cartridges similar in design and capacity."

The .25 Souper (left) comes close to matching the .25-06 ballistically, from a .308 case.

So wrote P. O. Ackley in his *Handbook for Shooters and Reloaders*, first published in 1962. Well, 40 years later, I disagree. Though the .25 Souper differs little, ballistically, from the .250/3000 Improved and won't match the .257 Roberts Improved, it's a furlong ahead of ordinary .257 Roberts factory loads. In short actions, it is also a better fit than the Roberts, which derives from the 2.235-inch 7 × 57 case. The .257 (with the 6mm Remington) is a tad long for actions developed around the 2.015-inch .308 and its offspring. You must seat bullets well into the powder space, negating somewhat the value of the longer hull.

Alice van Zwoll finds the .25 Souper as easy to handle as it is to shoot.

Better, in my view, to use a cartridge that matches the magazine when a midweight bullet is seated with its base at or near the bottom of the neck.

Drivel, you say. Perhaps. But the hunting cartridge field is so crowded now that we're reduced

I had Charlie Sisk build his .25 Souper on a Remington 700 short action.

to conjuring significance from trivialities. If you're satisfied with your .243, .25-06 or .257 Roberts, a wildcat .25 probably has little appeal unless you can be satisfied and curious at the same time. I like those three cartridges, but the .25 Souper stole my heart.

It was a love affair long denied. The late *Field & Stream* shooting editor Warren Page may have written the first text I ever read on this round. The hull seemed nicely proportioned. The useful range of bullet weights and styles appealed to me. So, too, the ease of forming cases. While you can neck down the .308, I prefer to neck up the .243. There's just .014 change in neck diameter—light work for an expander ball. As taken as I was with this cartridge, it was decades before I had one built. Then Charlie Sisk came up with a short Remington 700 action and a 24-inch Lilja barrel with one-in-10 twist. He squared the bolt face, lapped in the lugs, and trued up the receiver face and barrel shank. Before assembling the metal, he installed one of his own recoil lugs.

"It might look like an ordinary Remington washer," he says. "But instead of being stamped out, mine is machined from 416 stainless steel, then bored and surface ground by CNC. The result: a lug that's true and flat and fits the barrel perfectly. Your choice of thickness: .200, .300, and .500. Charlie favors Brownell's Acraglas for bedding, and he used it on this Souper. "My father had an old Farmall tractor whose radiator sprang a leak. Rather than pulling it for repair, we mixed up some Acraglas and dabbed that on the hole. It's held for more than 20 years." Charlie concedes that if Acraglas failed as a bedding compound, he'd keep it around only for tractors. But it helps his rifles shoot very well.

This one, in fact, shoots exceptionally well. With a Timney trigger and a Hi-Tech Specialties stock from Mark Bansner, this rifle is easy to control. One-piece Talley alloy mounts deliver a look consistent with the clean, classic lines of this rifle and put the Swarovski 3-9 × 36 (one of my favorite hunting scopes) right in front of my eye.

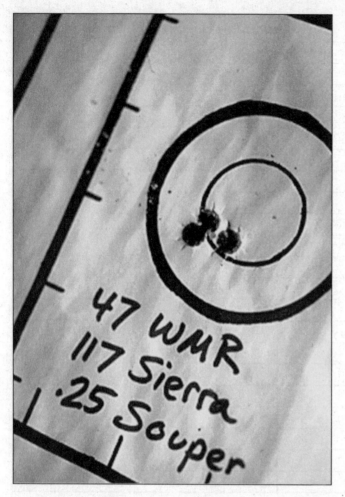

A rifle by Charlie Sisk delivered this group with .25 Souper handloads.

Recoil borders on negligible. The rifle feels like a .243 when I launch a bullet. But the .25 Souper accommodates heavier bullets than the .243. It has significantly more capacity than the .250 Savage, a tad less than the .257 Roberts. You can beat the Souper with the Improved Roberts in long actions, and with the .25-06. But deer won't notice a difference. Here's how this compact wildcat compares to quarter-bore competition, and how it performed with handloads I assembled for the Sisk rifle.

During these preliminary trials, the Sisk .25 Souper gave me seven three-shot groups at or under .75 inch. I did not let the barrel cool or clean it. Loads were tested beginning with the lightest bullets and ending with the heaviest. The last 14

shots from a hot barrel showed that this rifle is one of those jewels that wants to shoot. It will get some field time this winter when coyote pelts thicken up. Incidentally, no signs of high pressures surfaced on the Winchester cases or primers. I got no sticky bolt lifts with these loads—though they are near the top end and should be approached cautiously. Ackley, by the way, lists 87-grain bullets at 3,400 fps, a 60-grain at 4,000, both with IMR 4320.

I shouldn't have waited so long to indulge my wish for a .25 Souper.

Are More .270S Better?

There's no reason for a .277 bullet. By the time the .270 Winchester appeared in 1925, the 7 × 57 Mauser was 32 years old. Its .284 bullet—and that of the 7 × 64 Brenneke, circa 1917—would seem to have been the logical choice for a new hunting round.

But not all having to do with rifle and cartridge design is logical, and perhaps the 7mm's German ancestry figured in. America had, after all, just helped defeat the Kaiser. Probably the diameter of this new sub-.30 big-game number mattered little. The makings for the .270's success were in place: 1) deer hunters freshly enamored of battle-proven bolt rifles, 2) the .30-06 Springfield, with its scintillating reach, and 3) short optical sights that afforded precise aim beyond the reach of traditional deer rounds. Also, smokeless powder, not yet 30 years in the field, was ready to test behind a truly high-speed deer bullet.

When *Outdoor Life*'s gun guru fell for the .270, it already showed promise. Still, Jack O'Connor's writing helped power Winchester's new darling over early bumps, real and perceived. Hunters used to .30-30 bullet action whined that the high-velocity .270 spitzers wrecked a lot of meat. They did—and compared to the .30-30 170-grain soft-nose, still do. The first .270 bullets were particularly troublesome, fragmenting at the breakneck impact speeds

Cartridge	Load	Muzzle Velocity (fps)	Group Size (in.)
.243 Winchester			
	Federal factory, 85 Sierra	3,320	*
	Federal factory, 100 Nosler Partition	2,960	*
6mm Remington			
	Remington factory,100 PSPCL	3,100	*
.250 Savage			
	Remington factory, 100 PSP	2,820	*
.257 Roberts			
	Remington factory, 117 SPCLw	2,650	*
.257 Roberts	Hornady factory, 117SST	2,780	*
.257 Roberts	Federal +P factory,		
	120 Nosler Partition	2,780	*
.257 Roberts			
	Hornady Light Magnum factory		
	117 SST	2,940	*
.25-06	Federal factory,		
	90 Sierra, Varminter HP	3,440	*
.25-06	Remington factory,		
	100 PSPCL	3,230	*
.25-06	Remington factory,		
	120 PSPCL	2,990	*
.25-06	Hornady Light		
	Magnum factory,117 SST	3,110	*
.25 Souper	41 IMR, 4064, 87 Hornady	3,335	.75
	43 H380, 87 Hornady	3,200	1.50
	44 H414, 100 Nosler Ballistic Tip	3,170	.05 (best!)
	48 RL-19 100 Nosler Ballistic Tip	3,325	.35
	46 H4350 100 Speer	3,240	.85
	44 W760 100 Speer	3,140	2.00
	40 Vihtavuori N-150 100 Sierra	3,090	.85
	39 Varget 100 Sierra	3,077	1.15
	43 H4350 115 Nosler Ballistic Tip	3,097	1.00
		2,720	1.00
	44 H4831 115 Nosler Partition	2,917	1.10
	46 RL-22 115 Nosler Ballistic Tip	3,030	1.50
	44 WP Big Game 110 Berger VLD	3,145	.75
	44 Vihtavuori N-160 110 Berger VLD	3,020	.35
	47 WMR 117 Sierra flatbase	2,885	.25
	46 WP Big Boy 117 Sierra flatbase	2,730	.75
	45 NMR 120 Hornady	2,945	.35 (2 shots)

*Accuracy with factory loads varies a great deal depending on the rifle used.

guaranteed by a 3,000-fps launch. Winchester initially sought to mollify meat hunters with a 150-grain load throttled back to 2,675 fps. Not surprisingly, nobody bought it. Market response was what you'd expect for fielding a sports car without a high gear. A better solution—stouter bullets—enhanced penetration. More sophisticated bullets followed, ensuring reliable upset across a wide range of impact velocities.

The .270 made its debut in the Model 54 Winchester, replaced in late 1936 by the Model 70. Among the 70's many chamberings, only the .30-06 has proven more popular than the .270. In 1948, Remington introduced its Model 721 bolt rifle in

The .270 dates to 1925. This box of Winchester Silvertips isn't *that* old.

This buck almost sneaked away, but a .270 bullet found a small alley in the brush…

.30-06, .270, and .300 H&H Magnum—at that time themost revered big-game rounds in use Stateside. A decade later, the .280 Remington cartridge had joined them. It withered in the shade of the .270. The 7mm Remington Magnum came along in 1962. Factory loads didn't have much on the .270, but this belted seven was brilliantly marketed, and chambered in the new Remington M700 rifle. The combination sold like hot cinnamon rolls at a Lutheran fundraiser.

Given the 7mm Remington Magnum's success, you'd think Weatherby would have grabbed the headlines early, with its .270 and 7mm Magnums. First available in 1943, they had essentially the same ballistic potential and were loaded by Norma to reach it. But they were ahead of their time. At the end of World War II, hunters still considered the .30-06 tremendously powerful, and the .270 seemed a veritable hot-rod. Also, Weatherby cartridges were proprietary, chambered only in costly Weatherby rifles. By the 1960s, hunters had powered up, and Remington's 700 made magnums common currency among ordinary deer hunters. Here's what the charts say:

Bullet Weight (gr.)	Type	Velocity (fps)	Energy (ft-lb)
.270 Winchester	130 Power Point	3,060	2,702
	140 Fail Safe	2,920	2,651
	150 Power Point	2,850	2,705
7mm Remington Magnum	140 Pointed SP C-L	3,175	3,133
	150 Swift Scirocco	3,110	3,221
	160 Nosler Partition	2,950	3,091
.270 Weatherby Magnum	130 Nosler Partition	3,375	3,288
	140 Nosler Ballis. Tip	3,300	3,385
	150 Nosler Partion	3,245	3,507
7mm Weatherby Magnum	140 Nosler Partition	3,340	3,443
	150 Nosler Ballis. Tip	3,300	3,627
	160 Nosler Partition	3,200	3,638

My Oehler chronograph shows Weatherby's ammunition to perform as advertised, so handloaders alone can bring the 7mm Remington Magnum even with these two Weatherby rounds from Norma. Well, that's not quite true: High Energy loads from Federal and Heavy Magnum ammunition from Hornady get Remington's 7mm Magnum within 100 fps. High Energy and Light Magnum ammo also brings the .270 Winchester to 100 fps of the 7mm Remington Magnum! Winchester's Power Point Plus runs right behind.

The .270 and 7mm Winchester Short Magnum (WSM) and the 7mm Remington Short Ultra Mag can now be added to that list. The .270 WSM is the first commercial round of that diameter to be offered by a big ammo firm in 60 years. With a case just 2.10 inches long, it does indeed fit short rifle actions, though the body diameter of the case

Bullet Weight (gr.)	Type	Velocity (fps)	Energy (ft-lb)
.270 Win. (Win. PP Plus)	130 Power Point	3,150	2,865
.270 Win. (Hornady LM)	130 SST	3,215	2,983
.270 Win. (Federal HE)	140 Trophy Bonded	3,100	2,990
.270 Win. (Win. PP Plus)	150 Power Point	2,950	2,900
7 Rem. Mag. (Hornady HM)	139 Soft-Point	3,250	3,300
7 Rem. Mag. (Win. PP Plus)	150 Power Point	3,130	3,264

requires magazine changes. The .535 base diameter is essentially a match for magnum bolt faces fitted to the standard .532 bases of most belted rounds. A steep 35-degree shoulder puts fuel capacity close to that of belted rounds. Here are Winchester's factory loads for this potent .270.

I was treated to one of the first prototype rifles, a Browning A-Bolt with 23-inch barrel. Factory-loaded 130 Ballistic Silvertips crossed my Oehler sky screens at 3,290 fps, matching chart speed, even from the relatively short barrel. The 140 Fail Safes left at 3,115, again right on target. Accuracy? That A-Bolt turned out to be one of the most accurate hunting rifles I've ever handled. After bore-sighting, I zeroed the .270 WSM from prone. I've come to trust, even prefer, zeroes established from field positions. You get a true read on the point of impact to expect when you shoot at game. This time, I fired my final two shots prone at 200 yards. Both hit the target's one-inch center ring. A good omen! But repeatable?

My chance to bench this marvel came at Browning's range near Mountain Green, Utah. Two Fail Safes went into a single oblong hole at 200 yards. With no need to shred that target (or to press my luck), I posted another at 300 yards. Three shots later, a one-and-a-half-inch triangle, dead center in the bullseye, stared back through the spotting scope. I can't recall shooting a better long-range group with a hunting rifle. Browning turned down my request to buy the .270 WSM: "It's a prototype. But we'll sell you another." I told them politely I didn't need another hunting rifle but was willing to pay many rubles for this particular rifle. No dice—but I was

allowed to keep the hardware for a do-it-yourself elk hunt in Wyoming.

Two weeks later, I was climbing in snow. Declining a shot at the first bull that appeared, a spike, I bungled the stalk on a fine six-pointer 700 yards across a huge basin. On the last day, still-hunting open timber on the cusp of a storm, I slipped into a sizable herd of elk. A young bull appeared 90 yards away. The crosswire moved onto his shoulder crease. He hunched at the shot, sprinted, and fell dead. The storm broke as I rolled him downslope to a flat place. I didn't have a chance to hand-load for the .270 WSM until I'd returned the A-Bolt prototype rifle. Later, with a Winchester Model 70, I used Redding dies to work up starting loads for the round. Because I had no base data, I proceeded cautiously, using data for the .270 Winchester and .270 Weatherby Magnum as goalposts. Percentage differences in case capacity don't translate directly to percentage differences in propellant charge. Performance and pressure can escalate more or less rapidly, depending on burn rate, case shape, bullet weight, and other variables. Powders between H4895 and WW 760 delivered the best results. A better long-range deer round would be hard to find–should you decide the .270 Winchester doesn't go far enough, or that you want to use heavier bullets but stay above 3,000 fps.

The .270 WSM isn't the first to claim high efficiency. One Remington 78 in my rack chambers the .270 Redding, a necked-down .308 introduced to me by Richard Beebe at Redding Reloading. A cartridge that's easy to shoot and nips close on the

Bullet	Muzzle Velocity	Muzzle Energy	Trajectory (yards)			
			100	200	300	400
130 Ballistic Silvertip	3,275	3,096	+1.4	0	5.5	-16.1
140 Fail Safe	3,125	3,035	+1.4	0	-6.5	-19.0
150 Power Point	3,150	3,304	+1.4	0	-6.5	-19.4

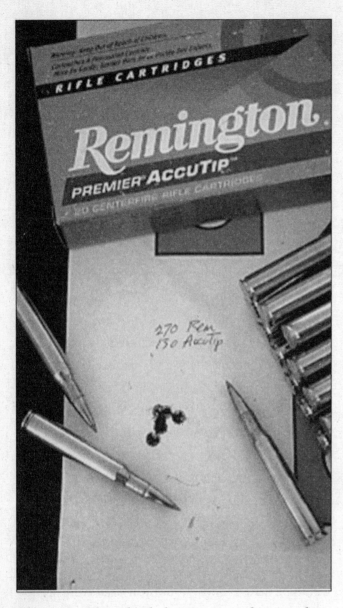

The .270 is perhaps the ideal open-country deer cartridge. The author shot this group with factory loads.

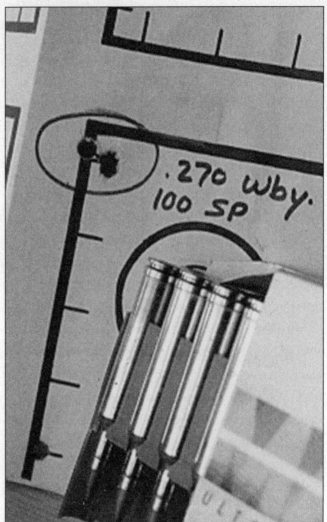

The author's Legacy Mauser in .270 Weatherby Magnum delivered this group from bullets clocking 3,400 fps.

heels of Winchester's star, the .270 Redding in a Brent Clifton rifle stretched across a wide swath of Colorado prairie one evening long ago to nab a mule deer buck about to make its escape into the oakbrush.

Another short but obscure .270 came along in the 1940s, when F.R. Krause of Albuquerque, and Roy Triplett of Cimarron, New Mexico, necked down the .300 Savage. Charles Evans and Bliss Titus also gave their names to this stubby .270. Late-model 99s offered in .308 (the .300 magazines aren't the same length) took the shine off shorter wildcats. The .270

Titus doesn't compete with the 7-08 in modern bolt guns.

One of the criticisms leveled against all .270s is their small selection of bullets. Small is relative. You can shoot only one bullet at a time, and if you can't find a handful of satisfactory .270 bullets amid the dozens now offered by Barnes, Hornady, Nosler, Sierra, Speer, and Swift—not to mention those factory loaded by Winchester, Remington, and Federal—well, you're pickier than me. There could be more .270 bullets around now than there were 7mm hunting bullets in 1962. And, on balance, they're better. Most fall within a narrow but practical weight range; 130 to 150 grains. For deer-size animals, however,

100-grain bullets may be under-rated. A .270 Weatherby Magnum I assembled on a Legacy Mauser action (Shaw barrel, Boyd's stock) shot most bullets well but 100-grain Hornadys superlatively. My first three-shot group with factory ammunition measured under half an inch! While the Weatherby can shoot heavier bullets so fast that at long range they shoot flatter than 100-grain spitzers, there's less recoil with the lightweights. And plenty of killing power.

Best bullets? The .270 established its reputation on deer with ordinary Winchester and Remington soft-nose 130s at 3,100 fps. Those bullets have also taken a lot of elk. Construction matters. One bull I zapped with a fragile 150-grain bullet trotted off because the shoulder stopped penetration. Fortunately, a second hit shattered the animal's neck. Another bull, struck on the run with a 130-grain Nosler Partition, somersaulted—as did one killed by a 140-grain Swift A-Frame that drove from the first rib to the off-side ham. A client once put a 130-grain Hornady through the ribs of a huge six-point bull. The elk reared up, then toppled backward and never twitched. Anyone who says the .270 Winchester is too light for elk, or that .270 bullets won't reliably take big bulls, hasn't gathered much evidence. One Colorado game warden, shooting elk on control missions decades ago, chose the .270 Winchester over other, more potent rounds. He killed hundreds of the beasts.

I suspect one reason this fellow liked his .270 was that it didn't bruise his shoulder or belt him in the chops like rifles chambered to belted magnums. Compared to same-capacity cases with bigger bores, the .270s are well behaved. The .270 WSM's good manners are due partly to bullets of modest weight but also case shape. The short, broad powder column seems to ignite more uniformly and with less violence than a tall stack of propellant. It also permits use of faster powder. Result: less fuel per unit of bullet speed, and less ejecta (unburned powder exiting the case and contributing to recoil).

Compared to 7mms and .30s, there still aren't many .270 cartridges to choose from. But the .270 Winchester, .270 Weatherby, and .270 WSM—with the .270 Howell and wildcat .270 Redding—should be all you need for deer you spot at a distance. Or for just about any animal you'll find in North America.

The Magic of Seven

Numbers can become icons. Between 22 caliber and 35 caliber are lots of numbers designating bullet or groove diameter. Only a few have become standard: .224, .243, .257, .264, .277, .284, .308, .311, .323, .338, .358. The .284, or 7mm, is special because it has become more than a standard. With the .308, it is a most versatile diameter for deer hunting.

You'll find little in the way of black-powder history for 7mms. The obscure .28-30-120 Stevens, a straight, rimmed case, appeared circa 1900. Developed by C.H. Herrick, it was chambered by the J. Stevens Arms and Tool Company in its 44 and 44 single-shot target rifles. Renowned barrelmaker Harry Pope favored it and fitted barrels in .28-30 to other actions. It was said to be an accurate round, better even than the .32-40. But by 1918, Remington had dropped this number from its ammunition list.

The 7mm really got its start in Europe, where Peter Paul Mauser and his brother Wilhelm designed a turnbolt military rifle chambered the 7 × 57 Mauser cartridge (a 7mm bullet in a case 57mm long). The rifle and cartridge were adopted by the Spanish army in 1893. Subsequently, the 93 Mauser and its smokeless round became hugely popular, filling arsenals the world over. Later versions of the Mauser chambered other cartridges, but none have made the jump from battlefield to sporting field as successfully as has the 7 × 57. The world's finest gunmakers have built magazine rifles and double rifles in 7 × 57, and many famous hunters have praised it. W.D.M. "Karamojo" Bell used it on ivory hunts, launching long, blunt 173-grain solids that at 2,300 fps loafed through pachyderm skulls. Stateside between the wars, it proved deadly on all manner of thin-skinned game, shooting lighter bullets almost as flat as the .270, and more gently than the .30-06. The 7 × 57 didn't earn the .270's fanfare, partly because it originated overseas. Also, its listed velocities were considerably lower, due to heavier bullets in standard loadings and pressures kept mild for early Mausers. Its competition steamed up 50,000 psi. Current factory loads (Hornady's Light Magnum in particular) hit hard, and handloaders get a big premium when shoveling the coal to the 7 × 57 in sturdy rifles.

By the time the Spanish Mauser was making headlines, we were already becoming a 30-caliber nation. The .30-40 Krag, adopted by U.S. Ordnance in 1892, was our first small-bore military smokeless round, replacing the .45-70. It was followed a decade later by the .30-03, soon supplanted by the .30-06. In the 1950s, the '06 moved aside for the 7.62 NATO, or .308 Winchester, in the M14 rifle. Not until 1964, with the adoption of the 5.56 Ball Cartridge M19 (.223), did the U.S. Army drift from the .30 bore.

You could argue that the 7 × 57 had all the markings of an enduring big game round. That with the proper bullets it was as versatile as the bigger .30-06. But not all the early 7mms were as popular as the 7 × 57, or as promising. In turn-of-the-century England, F.W. Jones designed a cartridge for Sir Charles Ross and the ammunition giant Eley. It was called the .280 Ross and chambered initially in Canadian Ross straight-pull military rifles. A long rimless case launched 160-grain bullets at 2,900 fps, beating the .30-06, which appeared concurrently in the 1903 Springfield. But the Ross rifle was less reliable. And bullets of the day weren't built to withstand the terrific impact of solid hits at nearly 3,000 fps. Hunters used the .280 Ross in Africa

These 7mm cartridges are all useful for deer. The 7mm Mauser (center) dates to 1893.

on game as big as lions. The hardware and bullets sometimes failed. A few hunters died.

In 1907, English gunmaker John Rigby introduced the .275 Rimless in his magazine rifles. It used a .284 bullet and was very close in dimensions to the 7 × 57. The original bullet, a pointed 140-grain, was replaced by a semi-pointed 140 after the first World War. The apparent reason for this switch: Rigby's Managing Director was once struck in the head by an 8mm German spitzer, and the bullet bounced off. His faith in pointed bullets was badly shaken! The .275 Rimless spawned a rimmed version for double rifles in 1927. The cases differ in dimensions, and the rimmed round was conservatively loaded. It performed much like the 7mm Rimmed H&H Magnum and Lancaster's .280 Flanged Nitro-Express, said to have been a favorite of King George V. The .280 Rimless Jeffery offered a sleeker profile, more speed. It appeared in 1915, pushing a 140-grain bullet at 3,000 fps. Two years later, Germany's gun genius, Wilhelm Brenneke, trotted out his 7 × 64. Ballistically the equivalent of the Ross, it had a brighter future in Mauser bolt rifles and with better bullets. The 7 × 64 (with its rimmed counterpart, the 7 × 65) looks and acts like Remington's .280, a 1957 introduction. Both these sevens are still manufactured.

During the 1920s and '30s, wildcatters concocted several 7mms on the belted .300 Holland case, and on Charles Newton's big rimless .30. Western Cartridge Company produced, briefly, John Dubiel's .276. An improved version came from Griffin & Howe. The .280 Dubiel, with its .288 bullet, delivered stellar performance from its full-length .300 H&H hull. While Newton's own .280 failed, P.O. Ackley drew some attention to his .276 Short Magnum. Later, A.E. Mashburn fashioned a sharp-shouldered 7mm from the long Holland case. Field & Stream gun editor Warren Page killed a lot of game with this super-charged 7mm. Charlie O'Neil, Elmer Keith, and Don Hopkins followed with their .285 OKH. One version of this cartridge used a flash tube and duplex powder charge. These American experimenters might have been inspired by Holland and Holland's .275 Belted Rimless Magnum Nitro, a shortened, reshaped .375 H&H that appeared about the same time (1912 or 1913). It came in a rimmed version for double rifles. Loaded to unexciting levels, the .275 Rimless Magnum was offered by Western Cartridge in the U.S. until 1939.

In 1944, Roy Weatherby added a 7mm to his new line of wildcats on the shortened Holland hull. Like the .270 and .257, it had rounded shoulder junctures. Though it never became as popular as the full-length .300 Weatherby Magnum, it is in some respects a better cartridge. It shoots as flat, with less recoil. You'll get as much speed from a 160-grain bullet as from a 180 in the larger .30–about 3,200 fps. Luckily for Remington, Roy Weatherby kept a proprietary leash on his ammunition, and no commercial rifles were chambered for the 7mm Weatherby Magnum for 20 years. The 1962 debut of Remington's Model 700 rifle was all the more a hit because its list of chamberings included the brand-new 7mm Remington Magnum. A twin to the Norma-loaded Weatherby in case capacity, it is throttled to SAAMI pressures; hand-loaders get the same performance.

The 7mm Remington Magnum achieved almost instant success, mainly because it was advertised in just the right way. Wyoming outfitter Les Bowman had pointed out to the folks at Remington that what they needed was a cartridge that shot as flat as a .270 but carried more punch–one that developed no more recoil than a .30-06 but reached farther. It would fit standard-length actions, as had the .458, .338, and .264 Winchester Magnums already on the market. The ideal cartridge in his part of the world would be a peppy 7mm a hunter could use for mule deer, elk, and pronghorns. And that is the way Remington promoted its new round. Hunters responded with their checkbooks, while Winchester's .264 Magnum languished. With a case identical to the 7mm Remington's and a bullet just .020 smaller, it deserved better. So did the .280 Remington, which could not budge the similar .270 on sales charts. The 7 × 61 Sharpe & Hart, a bit smaller than the 7mm Remington Magnum, was chambered commercially in Schultz & Larsen rifles in 1953 but never had support from a major firearms or ammunition company. It is now long defunct.

Lest you think any 7mm doomed by stiff competition, consider those that have since thrived. The 7mm Dakota, on a shortened .404 Jeffery case, gave hunters a handsome round that upstaged Remington's cartridge a bit. The 7mm STW came along in the 1980s, on the full-length 8mm Remington Magnum case. At 3,325 fps, its 140-grain bullet flies 150 fps faster than the same pill from a 7mm Remington Magnum. Predictably, the edge narrows downrange, because the faster bullet sets up greater the air resistance and drag. More drag means a higher rate of deceleration, all else equal. So at 500 yards the 7 STW is only about 110 fps ahead of the 7mm Magnum. And it's 80 fps behind its successor, the 7mm Remington Ultra Mag. Built on a bigger, rimless case, the 7mm UM kicks a 140-grain bullet out at 3,425 fps and shoots as flat as a Nevada highway. Zero at 250 yards, and you'll see less than

The 7mm-08 in rifles like this short, custom-shop Remington Model Seven, is an ideal whitetail round.

three inches of drop at 300, about a foot at 400. This cartridge bit hugely into demand for the STW. So has the subsequent Remington Short Action Ultra Mag, fashioned from the Ultra Mag case to deliver the punch of a 7mm Remington Magnum.

For decades, Winchester resisted the temptation to field a powerful 7mm. As the Ultra Mag series began its ride about five years ago, Winchester engineers were already considering the concept of a short rimless case with the powder capacity of a traditional belted magnum. The .300 WSM came first, around the time Remington was gearing up to produce its own .300 SAUM. No one doubted that a 7mm SAUM was in the works, but Winchester surprised me when it weighed in with a 7mm WSM. The Remington's case is slightly smaller, to work in a Model Seven action. Performance is nearly identical. I questioned the utility of a short Winchester 7mm magnum on the heels of a short .270 magnum, a

cartridge Winchester had all but promised at the .300 WSM's release. After all, a .270 bullet is only .007 smaller in diameter. In fact, prototype 7mm WSM rifles had to be recalled because the cartridges fit in some loose .270 WSM chambers. The solution was to make the 7mm case slightly longer to the shoulder.

As 7mm cartridges grew to meet demands of hunters for greater reach, less celebrated but perhaps more versatile rounds appeared in the shadows. The .284 Winchester came along in 1963, designed to give that company's Model 88 lever-action and Model 100 auto-loading rifles the punch of a bolt-action .270. A rebated hull, fatter, and a bit longer than the .308's, the .284 case holds about as much fuel as a .270's. In same-length barrels, it can be loaded to the same ballistic level. A real boon to short-action rifles, the .284 got only a luke-warm reception from Joe Deerhunter. Savage offered the Model 99 in .284, and Browning bored the A-Bolt and BLR for it. Custom makers dealing with knowledgeable riflemen get most of the .284 business now. Melvin Forbes, whose Ultra Light rifles feature a 7 × 57-length magazine, has chambered a lot of barrels in .284 and its wildcats. The .284 is a favored parent hull among competitive shooters, who neck it to .264 for 1,000-yard matches. There's less recoil than with .30 magnums; but the 6.5/284 shoots as flat.

In 1980, an unlikely 7mm appeared: the 7-30 Waters. Named after gun guru Ken Waters, who put his ideas into the design, this round is a necked-down .30-30. It was first chambered in Winchester 94XTR rifles. The 7-30 has a shorter neck, sharper shoulder, and more case capacity than its parent; however, you must allow this bullet some barrel time to get advertised velocities (a 120-grain bullet at 2,700 fps).

Three years after the 7-30 slid into Winchester's cartridge lineup, Remington announced the 7mm-08, a .308 necked down. It's an eminently practical design, adaptable to any short-action rifle that handles the .308 and .243. Launching a 140-grain bullet at 2,860 fps, it leaves the 7 × 57 behind, though the Mauser cartridge is .2 inch longer. Hand-loading can wipe out the 7 × 57's 200-fps deficit. The 7mm-08 deserves its popularity. The 7mm-08 Weatherby Ultra Lightweight in my rack ranks among my favorite deer rifles. A 140-grain 7mm-08 bullet gallops right alongside the 150-grain from the .280 Remington.

Some hunters talk about the 7mm cartridges as if their bullets have some magical quality–some innate advantage over bullets .257, .277, or .308 in diameter. Not so! It is true that among the most popular 7mm big-game bullets are a handful with extraordinarily high ballistic coefficients. For example, Hornady makes a 162-grain 7mm boat-tail bullet with a ballistic coefficient of .534. Still, the firm's 190-grain .308 Match bullet registers .530. In hunting bullets, you'll get virtually the same arc from a .277 150-grain bullet as from a 7mm 150-grain bullet driven at identical speeds.

A reader once castigated me for writing that the .30-06 was essentially the equal of the 7mm Remington Magnum. With 150-grain bullets out of the blocks, the 7mm wins. You'd expect it to; it has a bigger case. But comparing the 180-grain '06 bullet with a 175-grain bullet from the Magnum, you'll find the advantage diminishes. In fact, if you pick Hornady's Light Magnum .30-06 load, which launches a 180-grain bullet at 2,900 fps, the Magnum loses in both the velocity category (2,860 fps) and as regards energy (3,361 ft-lbs for the '06, 3,178 for the 7mm). No factory load for the Magnum equals Hornady's most potent .30-06 recipe, or Federal's 180-grain High Energy '06 loads. In fact, potent .270 Winchester factory loads can match what you'll get with the 7mm Remington Magnum.

Of the many 7mm cartridges that have cropped up since 1893, the most useful deer rounds in my view are the 7 × 57 and 7mm-08. One of the biggest bucks I've taken off the mountain fell to a 145-grain Speer hand-load from my Ruger Number One in 7 × 57. A 7mm-08 felled an elk for me not long ago. The .280 is a dandy choice too. My Dakota Model 10 is a .280, and I've dropped both whitetails and mule deer with a plain-jane Remington 78 rebarreled to .280 Improved. My rack holds a couple of 7mm Remington Magnums, and I've killed elk with the 7mm Dakota. An Australian buffalo dropped to a 7mm WSM I was toting when he sprinted from a remote billabong. Still, if I were to buy another 7mm rifle soon, it would be chambered for a round of modest size. I'd shoot 140- and 150-grain soft-point or polymer-tipped spitzers–an ideal weight for all-around deer hunting and in .284-diameter at the top of the charts for ballistic form.

There's no magic in the number seven. And Stateside, we hunters are still a 30-caliber fraternity. For deer hunting, however–no matter where–7mm is all you really need to remember.

The .30-06: Still on Top!

If there's not a .30-06 in your battery, you've probably had to tender an excuse before now. It's not that other deer rifles won't kill as effectively, or that other cartridges aren't as versatile. You own an '06 to pay homage. The cartridge is older than female

The short-lived Ranger version of Winchester's M70 was chambered for several rounds, including the 7mm Rem. Magnum.

suffrage. It went to Alaska when miners were still plodding the Chilkoot trail. With the .30-06 we won two World Wars. It was a charter chambering in the Winchester Model 70 three decades after it appeared in uniform. Seventy years later, it is still arguably the most versatile big-game cartridge ever. And it is probably favored by more deer hunters than any other round. You can live comfortably without a .30-06 and without a towel rack in your bathroom. But why would you?

One of my .30-06s is an M1 Garand, a rare bargain from the U.S. government. I have the restocked Springfield that took the moose, and a Model 70 from the 1940s. There's a Remington 721 in the rack, plain and heavy but with that alluring "gunny" feel of post-war rifles I should have collected when they were new and very cheap. My Model 700 in .30-06 is an uncommon version with European styling, manufactured some years ago. I've owned and relinquished quite a few other rifles in '06, most of which I'd buy back. The pre-64 M70 that slipped away for $180 still grieves me. I'd like to own again an early Remington 760 pump rifle, and that M70 Featherweight of the same era. Long-action lever guns don't appeal to me, but I regret passing up a pristine M95 Winchester. And it's a fact that I turned down a Biesen-built .30-06 for . . . well, you'd question my credibility as well as my sanity.

The .30-06 cartridge was conceived in 1900, when Ordnance engineers at Springfield Armory began work on it and a battle rifle to shoot it. The rimmed .30-40 Krag had served ably in the Spanish-American War. But Paul Mauser's 1898 action was in many ways superior to the Krag-Jorgensen, a more costly mechanism. A prototype rifle emerged at Springfield Armory in 1901. Two years later, the Model 1903 Springfield was in production. Its 30-caliber rimless cartridge headspaced on the shoulder, like the 8 × 57 Mauser. The .30-03 was longer than both this round and the Krag. Powder capacity and operating pressure exceeded the Krag's.

A 220-grain bullet at 2,300 fps made the .30-03 the ballistic equivalent of the 8 × 57, which launched a 236-grain bullet at 2,125.

About a year after the .30-03 appeared, Germany switched to a new bullet: a 154-grain spitzer at 2,800 fps. At that time, such speed was remarkable. The Americans were obliged to catch up, and in short order they introduced the Ball Cartridge, Caliber .30, Model 1906. It launched a 150-grain bullet at 2,700 fps, increasing probable-hit range. The case could have been left as it was; however, someone decided to shorten it .07, to .494. Of course, this meant that .30-03 chambers were a tad long. Soon .30-03 rifles were recalled and rechambered.

The first bullets for the .30-06 were jacketed with an alloy of 85 percent copper and 15 percent nickel. Satisfactory in the Krag, it did not hold up at .30-06 velocities. Bore fouling rendered the rifles inaccurate. Tin plating reduced fouling, but this practice was abandoned when shooters discovered that, over time, tin "cold-soldered" to case mouths, and occasionally caused colossal pressure spikes. An alloy of zinc and copper in 5-95 or 10-90 proportions proved effective and safe. It became known as gilding metal.

The speedy 150-grain service bullet was supposed to pose a threat out to 4,700 yards. But

An easy feeder from any magazine, the .30-06 was developed in the 1903 Springfield.

troops in World War I found the real limit was about 3,400. To increase reach, the Army again changed the bullet, this time to a sleek 173-grain spitzer. Velocity was throttled to 2,647 fps, a minor concession given the substantial increase in ballistic coefficient. Announced in 1925, the new "M-1" round extended maximum range to 5,500 yards. Alas, it also boosted recoil. In 1939, the Army changed bullets once more, to a 152-grain replacement at 2,805 fps. With the "M-2" .30-06 cartridge we fought World War II.

When I was a lad, you could buy surplus military '06 ammo by the bucket. But savvy shooters kept it out of their good rifles. The reason: potassium chlorate primers deposited corrosive salts in the bore. Though Remington developed its non-corrosive "Kleanbore" priming in 1927 (and commercial rounds featured noncorrosive priming exclusively from about 1930), military cartridges were fitted with corrosive FA 70 primers as late as 1952! Corrosive priming, incidentally, does not weaken the case, as does mercuric priming. Conversely, mercuric priming won't damage bores. Since the Korean War, the only domestic .30-06 ammunition to avoid was a run of Western Match cartridges with Western "8 1/2 G" primers. These were corrosive and mercuric.

I still scrounge late-issue .30-06 brass. But I no longer spend hours swaging the primer-pocket crimp on military cases, and for load development I use only commercial brass. Any brand will do; but I don't mix them because case wall thickness, and consequently powder capacity, varies.

There's lots of loading data for the .30-06. Here's some from savvy riflemen who've hunted with it:

Jack O'Conner used 53 grains of IMR 4320 or 4064 behind various 150-grain bullets for 2,950 fps, 56 grains of 4350, and 180-grain bullets for 2,750, 54 grains of 4350 pushing 200-grain bullets for 2,630.

Warren Page claimed fine accuracy with 180-grain bullets and 55 grains of 4350. Townsend Whelen pushed 180-grain bullets to 2,700 fps with 50 grains of 4064. He also used 58 grains of 4831 with those bullets, and 58 grains of 4350 behind 165-grain boattails.

Ken Waters capped 50 grains of Norma 203 with 180-grain Norma bullets and preferred 52 grains of 4320 with 150-grain Sierras.

Alaskan guide Hosea Sarber, whom Jack O'Conner said had shot more grizzlies than he (O'Conner) had seen, used a 172-grain bullet of unspecified make at 2,700 fps.

Not that you have to hand-load for the .30-06. You can get factory loads with bullets weights of 125 to 220 grains. Remington offers a sabot-style Accelerator, a plastic-sleeved 55-grain .224 bullet that clocks over 4,000 fps. Federal High Energy and Hornady Light Magnum loads deliver extra speed with big game bullets–up to 180 fps more. A proprietary (and costly) two-step loading process delivers the premium within allowable pressure limits. If you're recoil-sensitive but still want to shoot big animals, try Remington's Managed-Recoil and Federal's Low Recoil .30-06 loads. Remington halves the kick by pushing a 125-grain Core-Lokt bullet at speeds that are standard for 180-grain bullets. Federal gets there with 170-grain bullets throttled back to 2,000 fps. All major suppliers now market .30-06 ammo with controlled-expansion bullets, which include the Nosler Partition, Partition Gold and AccuBond, Swift's Scirocco, and Reming-ton's Core-Lokt Ultra, the Winchester Fail Safe, and Hornady InterBond, Federal's Trophy Bonded Bear Claw, the Barnes Triple Shock X-Bullet.

Without touching a press, you can use a .30-06 for rockchucks, pronghorns, whitetails, The Wimbledon Cup matches and moose. You can hunt with it for brown bears and buffaloes, too. It has the power to stop big beasts up close, with the speed for flat shooting at distant game. And it won't beat you senseless in a lightweight rifle.

The .30-06 is as common as parking meters. Hunters whose luggage has roamed mindlessly for weeks through the shadows of foreign airports can appreciate such ubiquity. You can buy .30-06 ammo in more out-of-the-way places, worldwide, than any other kind of rifle ammunition. When Winchester altered its Model 70 in 1963, it had, over 25 years, offered this flagship rifle in 18 standard chamberings. Production of .30-06s totaled 208,218–35 percent of all Model 70s made! Incidentally, while standard twist for '06 sporting rifles is one-in-10, Browning 78 and Husqvarna barrels turn one-in-12.

Its versatility and availability have grown despite the proliferation of more potent 30-caliber cartridges and optics that encourage long-range shooting. The chambering of Winchester's Model 70 for the .300 H&H in 1937 didn't dent the popularity of the .30-06. Neither did Roy Weatherby's revamping of the Holland case in the early '40s. But the development during the 1950s of Winchester belted magnums, and the debut in 1963 of Remington's 7mm Magnum, convinced many hunters they could kill more game if they used cartridges bigger than the .30-06. The recent advent of short rimless magnums has kept the .30-06 on

This alpine buck fell to a .30-06, one of the most versatile hunting cartridges ever.

the back pages, and while you'll find more than 80 factory loads for it, versatility no longer sells a cartridge.

"I chamber only one or two .30-06 barrels annually," says Lex Webernick, whose Texas shop, Rifles, Inc., puts about 250 rifles a year into the field. "Most of my customers order .300 magnums of some sort. The .300 WSM was very popular for awhile, but shooters are coming back to the .300 Winchester."

Ballistically, the .30-06 compares well with short and mid-length belted .30 magnums. Figure about 200 fps and 300 foot-pounds difference at 400 yards for the same bullet, depending on bullet weight and type. You can make the '06 look better or worse. For instance, fire at 150-grain Nosler Ballistic Tip at 2,910 fps from a .30-06, and at 500 yards it's still clocking 1,245, within 30 fps of a 150-grain Trophy Bonded bullet shot from a .300 Winchester at 3,280 fps. Or match Federal's High Energy 180-grain .30-06 load at 2,880 fps against standard .300 Winchester 180s at 2,970. Given identical bullets in comparable loads and 200-yard zeros, the .30-06 will strike one-and-a-half to two inches lower at 300 yards than a .300 Winchester. That's a smaller slice of target than you'll cover with the crosswire at 300 yards, a much smaller area than raked by my wobble from hunting positions. Bear in mind that

The .30-06 is still the most popular cartridge among elk hunters.

the .30-06 is more efficient in short barrels than magnums, afflicts you with less blast and recoil, and fits neatly into actions too slender for WSM rounds or even belted magnums. A magazine box that holds five '06 rounds will take only three belted cases at most, maybe only two WSMs. A Weatherby rifle designed to accommodate five .458 Lott cartridges accommodates eight .30-06 rounds.

It's hard to improve on the .30-06, and when you find something that's better, there's a good chance it derived from the .30-06! The .270 Winchester, popular since its 1925 introduction, and the .25-06, a wildcat hailing from that decade but adopted by Remington in 1969, were among the first examples. Then there's the .35 Whelen, another wildcat given a home in Ilion. The .280 Remington also comes from the .30-06; it's been in production since 1957. Among contemporary wildcats, the .30-06 Improved and .338-06 are more popular than the .375 and .400 Whelen. The 6.5/06 has a small following, as does the 8mm/06.

Pushing the '06 shoulder out to 40 degrees increases case capacity slightly, but you'll gain only 50 to 70 fps for your efforts. I own two .30-06 Improved rifles, both carved from 1903 Springfields. One of them took the biggest elk I've shot, a Wyoming bull that dropped to a 180-grain Nosler Partition. Certainly, the .30-06 is an elk cartridge. It and the 7mm Remington Magnum proved equally popular in surveys I conducted among members of the Rocky Mountain Elk Foundation. It also ranked among the top six picks of Washington elk hunters 20 years before the 7mm Magnum appeared. A .30-06 with even ordinary 180-grain soft-points will kill elk handily. And it will shoot flat enough for center holds to 250 yards on both deer and elk. At 300, hold on the topline of a deer and the spine of an elk (assuming a 200-yard zero). At 350, aim six inches above the deer, and right on the topline of the elk. At 400, think hard about crawling closer, no matter what your rifle.

A 165-grain pointed Core-Lokt behaves much like a 180-grain, though its muzzle velocity is higher (2,800 fps) and its ballistic coefficient lower. At 2,900 fps, the 150-grain Pointed Core-Lokt beats the 180 out of the gate by 200 fps; however, its lower ballistic coefficient narrows the gap down-range. To 300 yards there's less than an inch of difference in point of impact between the 180-grain and 150-grain bullets, at 400 only two inches. But the heavier bullet has a 20 percent weight advantage that translates to deeper penetration. During my youth, some hunters preferred 220-grain .30-06 loads for the biggest game. These days, few riflemen want to sacrifice that much speed. A 220-grain round-nose Core-Lokt starts out at only 2,410 fps. A 200-yard zero requires a three-inch lift at 100 yards. Beyond 200 yards, the bullet drops like a stone: 13 inches at 300 yards, 31 inches at 400. Better to sight this load for a 150-yard zero and limit shots to 250 yards.

While the .30 magnums flatten trajectories, the longest shot I've ever made (or attempted) on deer was with a .30-06. As a hunting guide, I learned to relax when hunters showed up with a battered '06. Often as not, they had shot it a lot and shot it well. Crippled animals were more likely when the hunter was packing a magnum with mule shoes on the butt. One of my hunters, Jack, was a .30-06 fan.

A couple of years ago, I decided to buy a really good .30-06. I discovered that one reason the '06 has lost headline space to magnums is that it's chambered in a lot of cheap rifles and is diminished by association. What if an able gunmaker built an elegant, super-accurate .30-06? Feverishly, I scrounged an action: post-war Model 70 metal that had been part of a match rifle barreled to .308. It had never shot particularly well for me.

I phoned Rick Freudenberg, who had built a .30-338 for me some years back and produced rifles for 1,000-yard and National Match competition. Rick is also a hunter and fashions fine sporting rifles. He invited me to his then-new shop near the

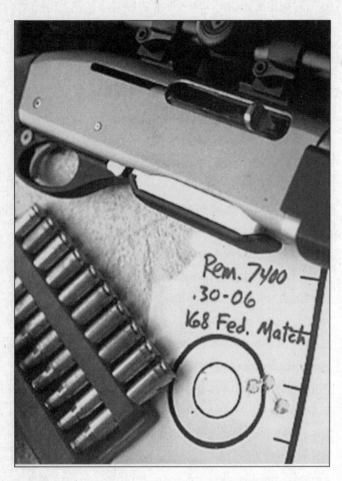

A tackdriver in match guns, the .30-06 showed surprising accuracy in this Remington autoloader.

jobs include Lilja barrels. "Sure, there are other good tubes on the market. But I haven't found any that shoot better than Lilja." He favors a three-groove Lilja with one-11 twist for the .30-06, and commonly gets it to print sub-half-minute groups with Nosler Ballistic Tip bullets.

A pet Freudenberg project is a lightweight hunting rifle with a #4 fluted barrel 23 1/2 inches long. He trims a Remington 700 receiver and flutes the bolt, outfitting it with a Sako-type extractor. The S&K rings and bases add only another ounce, and with a 3-9 × 36 Swarovski scope (11 ounces), the rifle tips the scales at just six-and-a-half pounds. "I call it the Whitetail Special," says Rick. "Winter camo finish makes it look sharp. You can carry it comfortably on long days, but the barrel is long and stiff enough for fine accuracy."

Jim Spradlin, in Texas Creek, Colorado, finishes metal parts for Rick, using a Teflon-like material that comes in 11 colors. Battleship gray looks good with black stocks and protects metal as no bluing can.

I requested a light blue finish on the .30-06, with a 25-inch, medium-weight barrel. "It'll shoot three-quarter inch," said Rick, months later when he phoned to alert me for delivery. "Let me know how you like it."

I like it a lot. The lines, fit, and finish make it as elegant as a synthetic-stocked rifle can be. The comb puts my eye instantly on-axis with the 6× Burris scope I've mounted low over the bore. The grip is long enough for big hands like mine but steep enough that no one should have any trouble reaching the trigger. If I could whine about anything on the stock, it would be that the forend is a bit thick, and that the ledges either side of the barrel are not exactly the same width.

Rick's barrel contour is just right for my taste, his understated logo there appropriate and not at all obtrusive. He reworked the bolt release and checkered it, a classy touch. The bolt handle had already been given a fine stippling—something

I-5 freeway in Everett, north of Seattle. Rick wasn't always this accessible, having spent some of his 50 years in Canada, where he says "there are some very big deer."

Antlers adorn the walls of Rick's machine shop. But if you come just to talk hunting, you'll find that at work he's focused on building accurate rifles. Though he has stocked several in wood, he prefers synthetic stocks: "Mark Bansner's Hi Tech stocks are the best," he says. "They feel good and weigh about 20 ounces—light enough for a featherweight sporter but heavy enough for proper balance in rifles scaling from six-and-a-half to eight-and-a-half pounds with standard barrel lengths."

Rick likes Winchester 70 actions, pre-64s first and current Classics next. He's also built rifles on the Remington 700. Almost all of his custom

I prefer over checkering, which, although it looks better, abrades hands and gun cases and scabbards. I had also stoned the trigger on this rifle before turning it over to Rick, so the pull was a crisp two-and-a-half pounds. The bolt slides smoothly, having already cycled thousands of rounds.

From the start, this .30-06 has wanted to shoot. My first three shots went into three-quarter inch. But in truth I cannot say it's a nail-driver. Often it will start with half-minute intentions, then shake a bullet loose. This recalcitrance is neither unusual nor fatal. The rifle shoots tight enough to kill any deer I target to 400 yards and beyond. On the other hand, it's a custom-built .30-06 with a top-quality barrel, and I'll expect more of it after a reasonable grace period for break-in. I'm confident it will soon corral those occasional fliers that cut one-and-a-half-inch groups from one-holers. Rick prides himself in accurate rifles and has built them for shooters who demand X-ring precision in competition.

A good man to trust with a rifle bored for the best-known big game cartridge of all time.

Notes on Short Magnums

Since metallic cartridges appeared in the late 1800s, the trend has been to more power in smaller hulls. Several black powder cartridges favored by post-Civil War hunters had cases over three inches long: the .38-90 Winchester and .45-120 Sharps, for instance. Smokeless powder permitted smaller cases, because the propellant was more efficient. The first successful small-bore military rounds, circa 1887 to 1891, had cases less than two-and-a-half inches long: the 7.65 Belgian at 2.09, the 7.62 Russian at 2.11, the .303 British at 2.21. The 8 × 57 German Mauser hull miked 2.24, our .30-40 Krag, 2.31.

Hunting cartridges followed the trend of infantry rounds. In 1895, the .30-30 (2.04-inch case) was chambered in the Model 1894 Winchester. In 1913, Charles Newton delivered to Savage a new cartridge with a case 1.91 inches in length.

Seven years later, Savage announced an even shorter round for its Model 1899 rifle. The .300 Savage hull measured 1.87 inches but packed 10 percent more power than a .30-30.

By this time, British gunmakers had designed several long cartridges for the spaghetti-like Cordite powder. Three became important here. In 1910, Jeffery announced a rimless .404. Rigby's .416 came the following year. In 1912, Holland and Holland brought out its .375 Magnum. The .404 had a rebated case 2.86 inches long, with a .544 base and .537 rim. The .416 Rigby was rimless, with a .586 base and 2.90 overall length. The .375 H&H had a .532 belt ahead of the extractor groove and .532 rim; case diameter forward of the belt was .512. The belt served better than the .375's faint shoulder as a headspacing stop.

Unfortunately for the lunch-bucket sportsman, long cartridges required expensive rifle actions like the Magnum Mauser. Then, in the early 1940s, shorter magnums appeared in the workshop of California insurance salesman Roy Weatherby. He reduced the taper on the Holland case to boost capacity, and cut it to two-and-a-half inches. Necking it down produced the .257, .270, and 7mm Weatherby Magnums. They'd fit any magazine built for the .30-06; however, they were proprietary rounds, available only for Weatherby rifles.

Short magnums became popular Stateside in the late '50s, beginning with the .458 Winchester Magnum in 1956. Two years later came the .264 and .338. Cases measured 2.50 inches—as did the hull of the later 7mm Remington Magnum. The slightly longer (2.62-inch) .300 Winchester Magnum case went commercial in 1963, three years after Norma introduced its .308 and .358 Magnums (2.56 and 2.52 inches).

Even shorter high-performance rounds were already popping up. Olin announced a wide-bodied, rebated .284 in 1963. At the same time, a pair of belted short-action rounds incubated at Remington.

The .350 and 6.5 Magnums appeared in 1965 and 1966–in homely 600-series carbines that sold poorly.

On the bench-rest circuit, however, a very short cartridge was about to make history. Competitors Lou Palmisano and Ferris Pindell reshaped the .220 Russian (a necked-down 7.62 × 39) to form what would become the .22 PPC. That was in 1974; a 6mm PPC would soon follow. From base to 30-degree shoulder, these hulls measured barely over an inch, though basal diameter approached that of the .30-06. Palmisano figured that the shorter powder column would yield better accuracy. Proving the PPC's superiority over the established .222 and 6 × 47, in a game dominated by one-hole groups, would be tough. But in surprisingly short order, Palmisano and Pindell convinced colleagues to try the new rounds. Two of the top 20 rifles in the Sporter class at the 1975 NBRSA championship matches were chambered to PPCs. By 1980, 15 of the top 20 shooters had a PPC on the line. In 1989, all of the highest Sporter scores were shot with PPCs, plus every one of the top 20 in the Unlimited class and 18 of the 20 best in Light and Heavy Varmint.

In 1992, short rimless magnum rounds appeared in Don Allen's Dakota line. The 7mm, .300, .330, and .375 Dakotas, based on the .404 Jeffery, measure 2.50 to 2.57 inches, but hold more fuel than belted magnums. The .300's 97-grains (water) capacity is just three grains shy of the full-length .300 Weatherby's. John Lazzeroni's first ventures into cartridge design, in the mid 1990s, yielded a stable of gigantic rimless rounds. Then John embarked on a new project: short cases based on the full-length hulls. Bases for his .243 and .264 short cartridges like .532, standard dimension for an ordinary belted magnum like the 7mm Remington, and same as the head on Lazzeroni's long .257 Scramjet. The short 7mm, .300, .338, and .416 have .580 heads, like their full-length counterparts. John used metric measures to name these hotrods:

- 6.17 (.243) Spitfire: 85-grain bullet at 3,618 fps
- 6.71 (.264) Phantom: 120-grain bullet at 3,312 fps
- 7.21 (.284) Tomahawk: 140-grain bullet at 3,379 fps
- 7.82 (.308) Patriot: 180-grain bullet at 3,184 fps
- 8.59 (.338) Galaxy: 225-grain bullet at 2,968 fps
- 10.57 (.416) Maverick: 400-grain bullet at 2,454 fps.

By then, Winchester had already announced its .300 WSM. Slightly longer and, with a .532 base, not quite as broad as the Lazzeroni Patriot, the .300 Winchester Short Magnum performs like a belted .300.

Winchester Magnum (the "short" magnum introduced in 1963 that now seems quite long!). At 2.76 inches, a .300 WSM loaded round barely clears the mouth of the .300 Winchester case.

Browning apparently approached Winchester with the idea for the WSM early in 1999. Browning and U.S. Repeating Arms Company redesigned their bolt-action big-game rifles for the .300 WSM, initially loaded with a 180-grain Fail Safe at 2,970 fps and a 150-grain Ballistic Silvertip at 3,300 fps. Though it got the jump on Remington with its first short magnum, Winchester did not then register a 7mm. Remington soon announced a .300 and a 7mm Short Action Ultra Mag, the .300 a ballistic twin to the .300 WSM. Just enough shorter to fit comfortably in a Model Seven action, the Remington rounds hold slightly less powder. Promptly, Winchester followed with a .270 WSM and a 7mm WSM, then brought new meaning to "short" with its Super Short Magnums. The .223, .243, and .25 WSSMs are based on the .300 WSM trimmed from 2.10 to 1.67. Next to the .22 WSSM, a .22-250 looks tall. But there's more capacity in the WSSM case, and the round has a 200-fps advantage over the .22-250. Factory loads include a 55-grain Ballistic Silvertip, a 55-grain Pointed Soft Point, and a 64-grain Power-Point. They kill Texas deer like bolts from Zeus. WSSM cartridges were first chambered in super short-action Browning A-Bolt and Winchester M70 rifles.

I like short cartridges. They're efficient, delivering the velocity of longer rounds with less fuel. A shorter powder column means more complete burning inside the case, which means less ejecta, less recoil. Short cases fit in short actions, for a small weight savings and shorter bolt throw. Given the PPC's history, short cartridges can be accurate. But these advantages are mainly academic. You likely won't feel lighter recoil or a couple of ounces less weight; you won't notice faster bolt cycling or better accuracy. You might pick up on bumpy feeding, particularly with the Super Short Magnums.

The .223 Winchester Super Short Magnum accounted for this Texas whitetail.

Winchester's Super Short .243 (left), with the 6mm Remington BR and the .270 WSM.

To my knowledge, I shot the first elk ever killed with a .270 WSM and a .300 SUM, probably the first killed with an 8.59 Lazzeroni Galaxy. I've shot deer with the .223 WSSM and the 7mm SUM, elk and big African antelopes with the .300 WSM. Australian buffalo dropped to Fail Safe bullets from my 7mm WSM. I like the short magnums as well as the belted magnums whose performance they duplicate, but not a lot better. The WSSMs produce top velocities for their diameters; however, they don't feed as smoothly as traditional rounds. We may not be making cartridges too short yet, but we're mighty close.

Winchester and Browning developed extra-short rifle action for the WSSM series of cartridges.

Cartridge	Bullet Weight	Muzzle Velocity	Cartridge	Bullet Weight	Muzzle Velocity
.223 Rem.	55	3,240	.270 Win.	130	3,060
.22-250	55	3,680	.270 AHR	130	3,150
.220 Swift	55	3,800	.270 Weatherby	130	3,200
.223 WSSM	55	3,850	.270 WSM	130	3,275
.243 Win.	100	2,960	7mm Rem. Mag.	140	3,150
6mm Rem.	100	3,100	7mm SUM	140	3,175
.243 WSSM	100	3,110	7mm WSM	140	3,225
.240 Weatherby	100	3,400	7mm Ultra Mag	140	3,425
.257 Roberts	117	2,780	.30-06	150	2,910
.25-06	115	2,990	.300 SUM	150	3,200
.25 WSSM	115	3,060	.300 WSM	150	3,200
.257 Weatherby	115	3,150	.300 Win. Mag.	150	3,250

Shooting Deer Rifles

It was a tiny patch of pines. At one corner it met the Kanitz sugarbush, an open maple hillside. I'd trudged up the fenceline and stopped just shy of the corner. Russet leaves skittered through the hardwoods. I shivered; Michigan's November wind had bite.

The snap of limbs, and then voices, told me the drivers were close. In minutes they were all but a pebble's toss away, boughs sloughing against canvas farm jackets. I relaxed. No deer in this pocket.

But then a snap and a thud and a whitetail buck popped from pines close enough for

Any rifle that takes a buck like this is a good rifle. Marksmanship makes it so.

conversation. He sunfished and jetted straight-away. A .303 bullet caught him in the back of his neck and slammed him to earth. I couldn't remember lifting my rifle. Truly, sometimes muscle memory beats deliberate aim.

Deer Guns that Make You Look Good

Rifles aren't like refrigerators. They don't run by themselves. They're not like televisions that you program with predictable options. Rifles must be carried and shouldered and aimed. How well they perform depends mainly on how well you handle them. In that respect, a deer rifle is a lot like a basketball. Skilled hands can make any basketball do amazing things. But unlike basketballs, all rifles are not the same. Rifles differ in weight, length, balance, operation, and feel. Some are easier to use than others. You're wise to look for one that makes you look good.

A lot of deer hunters think an accurate rifle is the best choice. But a rifle doesn't have to be very accurate to kill deer. A two-inch group at 100 yards means all your bullets will strike well inside deer vitals out to 300 yards—farther than you're likely to shoot. The one-hole groups shooters like to flaunt are evidence of fine intrinsic accuracy, but they say nothing about field accuracy: how the rifle will perform in your hands from field positions.

The Model 94 Winchester became hugely popular with whitetail hunters largely because it pointed so well. In big hands or small, against thin faces and heavy jowls, whether your arms were long or short, a 94 had a wand-like quality. It shot where you looked, almost by itself. The Model 94 and equally lithe 336 Marlin and 99 Savage carbines still make sense for close-cover deer hunting. Now, however, most hunters carry more powerful, more accurate bolt-action rifles. The agenda: longer reach. Big scopes help potent, flat-shooting cartridges nip little groups at long range. At the bench, on targets, and over chronographs, such artillery is impressive. In the field, it often fails. That's because heady ballistic performance comes at the expense of fine handling qualities. Truth is, ordinary deer cartridges in rifles built for easy shooting will give you more success than a high-octane round in a rifle better suited for the bench. Here's what appeals to me in a deer rifle.

A slim profile. Pick up a broomstick and point it as if it were a rifle. Quick, huh? A broomstick is not shaped to help you aim, but it's easy to direct. That's partly because it's slender. Instead of filling your hands like some bulky rifle stocks, a broomstick is free to rotate and pivot in them. Why do you think best-quality English shotguns are so trim? Bulk in a rifle's buttstock puts weight where you must lift it, slowing your shot. Forends contoured for a rest are poorly shaped for your palm.

A long, open grip. A tight, steep grip makes for uncomfortable carry and slow handling. It also forces your trigger finger into a tight curl, preventing a smooth, straight-line pull. The Winchester 94 has a long, straight grip—like British grouse guns. A straight grip prevents the full hand contact that can wed you too tightly to the rifle. Handlebars on racing bicycles could be built thick and shaped to cuddle the fingers. They aren't. Pressure at points of contact is automatically greater, making the bike respond

right away to changes in that pressure. A pistol grip can help you steady the rifle and control it during recoil; but you'll shoot better with one very slim up front, opening slightly rearward in a gentle curve that keeps the lower part of your hand well back from the guard.

Modest weight. Light weight gives you an easy carry but makes the rifle hard to "settle" when you aim. It bounces violently with your pulse, yields readily to gusts of wind. Rifles between six-and-a-half and seven pounds appeal to me. Loaded, with sling and scope, they'll scale around eight—light enough to pack all day but with heft enough to control when you're breathing hard. I favor a center of balance on the forward guard screw, or a slight tip to the muzzle.

A comb for the sight. A stock comb should put your eye instantly in line with the sights or on the scope's axis. Some modern combs are too high for iron sights—just as early bolt guns had combs too low for scope use. Cheek support holds your eye still. The weight of your head on the stock steadies the rifle. If you must lift your head off the stock to find the sight, or press hard to get your eye low enough, the comb is impairing your ability to shoot quickly and accurately.

A sight for fast aim. For deer hunting, I use mostly 3x and 4x, sometimes 6x scopes or variables of modest power. They're lightweight with objective lenses of 22 to 36mm. No need for big front glass or more power than 6x, even if you occasionally shoot beyond 300 yards. You'll want a wide, bright field; you won't want to see every blip that your pulse or muscle twitches impart to the rifle, or a sight so high or ponderous that it makes the rifle top-heavy. Where's the weight in a Model 94 or a carriage-class double shotgun? Low between your hands. Compact, lightweight scopes keep it there.

An adjustable trigger. You can't shoot well if you can't control the trigger. Alas, factory rifles these days commonly wear triggers designed by class-action attorneys and stiff enough to hoist a sack of dog food. Insist on a crisp, consistent pull no heavier than four pounds (make mine two). If you can't get that, install an aftermarket trigger by Timney. Don't fret about over-travel–movement of the trigger after let-off. Adjustments for sear engagement and trigger spring tension are what determine the trigger's feel before the shot. After adjusting your trigger, make sure it's safe by slamming the bolt hard a dozen times. If there's even one failure to cock, increase sear engagement or trigger spring tension or both.

A cartridge that won't beat me up. Sure, I appreciate fine accuracy and supercharged bullets that fly chalk-line flat; but they don't help me shoot deer. In fact, a cartridge that makes a lightweight rifle kick hard is on the deer's side. Flinching makes me miss. You too! A .270 that shoots softball-size groups will knock the stuffing out of any deer at any range you're justified shooting from field positions. Maybe you prefer a .243 or 6mm, a .25-06, 7-08 or .280. The .308 and .30-06 have earned their popularity. All are fine deer cartridges–if you load 'em up in a deer rifle you can shoot well.

Zero

One bitter November long ago, a kid in a hooded sweatshirt took aim at a whitetail buck standing in a stubble field. Shivering in the cold dawn air and shaking from excitement, he couldn't hold the crosswires still, even when he leaned against the snow-capped fence post. "How far?" he wondered. A long shot; the deer looked very small in the Weaver K4. The kid just knew he'd have to hold high. His reticle bobbing above the buck's shoulder, the kid yanked the trigger. The rifle roared, and the buck kept eating. Two more shots drew no reaction from the deer, which, it seemed to the kid, might as well have been cropping wheat on the moon.

Down to his last cartridge, the youngster finally held right on the buck's ribs and forced himself to squeeze. The deer collapsed.

The kid was elated but as embarrassed with his shooting as with his failure to mark where the buck had stood. He scoured the shin-high stubble for 20 minutes before he found the animal only 160 yards from where he'd shot. The fast spitzer bullet would have hit the buck with a dead-on hold out to 250 yards.

Since then "the kid"–me–has been cautious about holding over. I've found that with a 200-yard zero, there's hardly ever a need to hold high on an animal. If my quarry seems too far for a center hold, I work closer. I seldom shade higher than the backline. A backline hold will kill from 250 to 300 yards. Game farther than 300 looks impossibly small, and is almost always approachable.

The confidence to hold center comes from knowing your rifle is precisely zeroed to give you a long point-blank range. Among the deer hunters I've guided were many men whose rifles were improperly zeroed. Consequently, it became routine to ask: "Why don't we shoot that rifle–to make sure it's still zeroed?" This tactful opener generally prompted one of three responses:

A. "Good idea! It might have been bumped in transit. Besides, I could use a warm-up myself."
B. "Well–OK. Ammo's expensive, and I'm sure it's right on, but I suppose one or two rounds won't hurt."
C. "Naw. This rifle has shot down the middle since Poppa gave it to me in '61. I don't want to mess with it."

All these fellows would shoot, because I gave them no alternative. Usually, the man most reluctant to step to the bench turned in the worst performance. It became an easy call. Any hunter unwilling to test his rifle or himself almost assuredly has something to hide. He may also have a distorted view of shooting: that it is a reflection of his manhood, a measure of competence in a field

Zero from a padded rest on the forend. Fire three-shot groups, letting the barrel cool periodically.

where every man is supposed to be competent. Such pitiable souls hang their egos with the targets.

Truly, shooting is a skill that must be learned and honed. It cannot be inherited or bought. Hunters who prefer to talk up their prowess without putting holes in paper are, almost without exception, unskilled. A super rifleman can make a poor shot; an accurate rifle can print a loose group. But there are lessons in errant bullets. An accomplished shooter learns from them and loads up for one more string. Whether testing the rifle or yourself, zeroing is the first step. Zeroing connects the bullet path with your sightline at a certain distance. You determine that distance by manipulating the windage and elevation dials. Once you've zeroed, you know where the bullet will hit in relation to your sight.

Here's the procedure. First, check your scope bases to ensure that they are tightly affixed to the receiver. You may have to remove your scope. Taking the bases off lets you check for rust. To remove rust, scrub lightly with a brass brush and solvent. Finish with an oily cloth, then a dry one. You don't want oil between bases and receiver. Use a close-fitting screwdriver to tighten each base down, cinching screws alternately to evenly distribute pressure. Greasing the dovetail cuts on Redfield-style bases eases ring installation.

Rings should be spaced to support both ends of the scope well. This is especially important if your scope has a big objective bell or the long, heavy ocular housings of some variables. Extra weight and length on the ends add leverage to any force that might strain your scope tube and affect zero. Accidental bumps and long days in tight scabbards can make your rifle shoot where you're not looking. Most modern scopes tolerate lots of punishment, but an extension base or ring can be useful for long scopes. The leggy 6X Lymans on two of my rifles needed wide ring spacing, so I used extension bases to add support up front. Conversely, short-coupled variable scopes often require an extension base or ring reversed, so the power-dial clears.

Many hunters mount their scopes too far back, sometimes because the powerdial of a variable won't allow the scope farther forward. This is like placing a television on its side so it better fits between the sofa and rocker! The scope must be mounted so you can easily look through it to aim. If it is too far back (or too far forward), you must consciously move your head to get the full field of view. This not only takes time; it can force you into an awkward shooting stance, straining your muscles and shifting your center of gravity.

The first step in zeroing a rifle is checking the base screws. Loose mounts are a common problem.

Whatever the scope, it should be mounted so you see a full field at first glance.

Even with no ring-spacing problem, it's easy to mount a scope too far back. That's because at home, where you have no target or sense of urgency, you check scope position by bringing the rifle to bear slowly. You're relaxed. You rotate the rifle to square up the reticle while adjusting head position fore and aft. In the field, you focus quickly on your target and lean into the rifle as you pull it home. You've no time for squaring up reticle or refining head position. You jam that butt into place and your eye toward the scope and hold the rifle firmly as you press the trigger. Often, the ocular housing clobbers your brow.

When placing a scope in its rings, mind the eye relief before you twist the scope to adjust the reticle. After checking for manufacturing burrs and filing them out of the rings, wipe them and the scope clean. Then snug the rings lightly around the scope and, using some distant object as your target, quickly cheek the rifle. Pull it hard into your shoulder. Repeat. You'll find you automatically shove your head forward on the stock. Slide the scope in the rings until you see a full field each time you mount the rifle. Now sit, kneel, and drop to prone. An ocular housing that's too close (or too far forward) will give you a reduced field. Prone will place your eye closer to the scope than will an offhand position. In the field, you may have to use both. Once you've established eye relief, pencil lines on the scope fore and aft of a ring, loosen the rings and, holding the rifle out in front of you, rotate the scope so the vertical crosswire is plumb with the buttpad.

Check those pencil lines for position, then tighten the rings.

Cinch ring screws alternately, as you would the lug nuts on an automobile wheel. You don't need goop on the threads to keep them from backing out, but neither should you leave oil on the tube. I wipe most scopes with a tack rag or oily cloth before installing the rings, but a thoroughly dry scope stays in place best.

Scope weight has a lot to do with the load on rings. Big objective lenses and 30mm tubes increase inertia, so when the rifle recoils it has a hard time getting the scope to come along. When rings lose their grip, you lose your zero. A gunsmith friend who has mounted many dozens of scopes met his match when he tried to affix a husky German variable to a four-fifty-something-caliber magnum bolt rifle. The scope kept slipping, even when he tightened the rings so they dented the steel tube and used tape to boost the gripping power! He finally punted, installing a smaller scope.

Once your scope is properly mounted, you'll want to bore-sight the rifle: align the axes of scope and bore without shooting. If you have no straight-line access to the breech, as with auto-loading or pump or lever rifles, you'll need a collimator. This device has a bore-diameter spud that fits in the muzzle, and a screen that appears in front of your scope. You aim at a grid on the screen, adjusting the sight so the crosswire quarters it.

If yours is a bolt rifle or dropping-block single shot, bore-sighting is easier. You remove the bolt or drop the lever, and set the rifle on sandbags so that looking through the bore you can center a target. Without moving the rifle, you adjust your reticle so it quarters the target. I bore-sight in my living room by placing the rifle on a soft but flat chair cushion and looking through the bore out the window at a rock on a distant hill.

Bore-sighting is not zeroing; it's simply a preliminary step, a quick way to align bore and scope so you don't waste ammunition trying to get "on paper" at 100 yards.

On the range, I use cardboard boxes as target boards. My targets are notebookpaper sized to give me the sight picture I prefer. Medium crosswires in a fixed 4X scope call for a six-inch-square target at 200 yards, but a fixed 6X scope offers the best picture with a four-inch square. It's important that the white squares be big enough to accommodate the movement of your reticle, small enough to help you discern differences in the size of each quarter. Heavy reticles require bigger targets; post and dot reticles work well with circular targets. For iron sights with a bead in front, big circular targets make sense. The light brown cardboard backer and white target both show bullet holes clearly. My 25X spotting scope picks up .243 holes at 200 yards easily, unless mirage is strong. If you use a black target, or a target with black printing, you'll be walking forward frequently to check for bullet holes you can't find.

Zeroing is a bench project. The object is to make your line of sight intercept the bullet path at a given distance. Tremors and other human interference won't do! Shooting for zero, you'll remove as much of your influence as possible. You have to aim, and you must trip the trigger without disturbing the rifle in its cradle of sandbags. That's all. The fundamentals for getting a dependable zero are the same as those for shooting a tight group: Pick a calm day; take your time; be sure the sandbags support the stock the same for each shot.

For deer rifles, it's a good idea to place targets at 100, 200, and 300 yards. The 100-yard target is to check bore-sighting. Adjust the scope so bullets strike roughly two inches above center, then go to the 200-yard line. At 200, shoot three rounds

Adjust the windage dial for still conditions, the elevation dial so you hit point of aim at 200 yards.

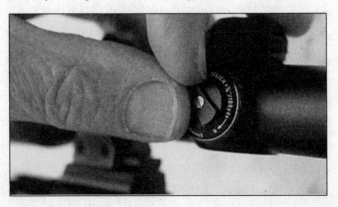

between sight changes, giving the barrel time to cool between rounds. Hot, sunny days are poor times to zero because the barrel heats fast and cools slowly. I allow at least 30 seconds between shots in a group.

When you've moved point of impact to center at 200 yards, let the rifle cool completely, clean it and fire another group. Mark the first shot from the cold, clean barrel because that's the most important shot you'll fire on a hunt. Keep the target to compare with other targets you'll use later to check your zero. If clean-barrel shots leak out of the group, you might want to try another load, or hunt with a fouled bore.

Where you can shoot 300 yards, by all means do so! The more shooting you do at distance, the more precision you'll bring to your sight adjustments. Shooting only at 100 yards and estimating bullet drop beyond that range is bound to bring you to grief. Refine the zero far away, then check it at short range.

A few cartridges are best zeroed at 100 yards because most of the shooting they're designed for will be at that range, or because they lack sufficient energy to be effective much beyond 150 yards. The .30-30 is a woods cartridge. So is the .35 Remington, the .444 Marlin, the .45- 70. Even rifles chambered for 200-yard cartridges can benefit from a shorter zero. The .250 and .300 Savage come to mind. Iron sights don't affect bullet performance; but they can reduce effective range by limiting precision.

The "rule of three" that used to appear in shooting articles from time to time alludes to the idea that if long-range rifle shoots three inches high at 100 yards it will hit about three inches low at 300. This is true only if you have a very flat-shooting rifle. A .30-06 needs a 100-yard lift of three inches to put its pointed 180-grain bullet on the money at 200. It drops three more inches in the next 50 yards or so, and crosses the 300-yard mark about nine inches low. The rule of three, strictly interpreted, applies mostly to 25- to 30-caliber magnums.

After you've zeroed, fire from different hunting positions to ensure the change won't affect point of impact.

Sitting, with a tight Latigo sling, is the form that will give you lethal hits to 300 yards.

Some hunting rifles could well be zeroed for 250 yards. But beyond that you run into mid-range problems. A bullet's arc is parabolic; the highest point above sightline is not in the middle of that arc, but past the middle. For example, the .270 Weatherby zeroed at 300 yards with a 130-grain, pointed bullet will print 3.3 inches high at 100 yards, and 3.8 inches high at 200, where it is nearer its zenith. Four inches is, to my mind, too much lift to ignore—especially if it comes where you can expect a lot of shooting at deer. It is silly to zero for extreme range, where you'll seldom shoot, if by doing so you incur a midrange gap that forces you to adjust your aim.

Not long ago I was sneaking through second-growth Douglas fir. Suddenly, I spotted a whitetail buck 60 yards away. As he turned, I shouldered my Savage 99 and found his forward ribs in the 3X Leupold. The bullet was on its way almost before I realized my finger was applying trigger pressure. The deer ran hard for a short distance and collapsed, both lungs destroyed by the 150-grain Winchester Silvertip. A lot of game is shot like that: right now, right here, with a center hold. A 200-yard zero makes center holds deadly at short and middle ranges so you can forget about shading.

Another time, I found the dot in my 2.5X Lyman Alaskan bobbing around in a tight alley between me and a fine buck that was showing only its ear and eye. Because my zero kept the bullet close to my line of sight at this moderate distance, I was able to hold where I wanted to hit, threading the 165-grain .308 soft-point through the alley to the buck's brain.

Part of the reason many hunters like to zero long is that they overestimate yardage in the field. One fellow told me recently that his .30 magnum could outshoot any rifle between 800 and 900 yards, and that he'd toppled a grand buck at 700 steps by holding a tad over its withers. Now, I'm a country boy, but even a Congressman would have blushed spinning that yarn. The flattest-shooting cartridges around lob their bullets nearly three feet low at 500 yards when zeroed at 200. To keep a .270 Weatherby

Open-country hunting can deliver more venison if you steady your rifle with a bipod.

bullet (muzzle velocity 3,375 feet per second) from sagging more than a foot at 700 yards, you'd have to zero at over 600. That would put the bullet roughly two feet high at 300 and 400. The bullet would be plunging so rapidly at 700 that if you misjudged range by 50 yards, you'd miss the deer's vitals.

A 200-yard zero wrings the most from modern rifle cartridges at the ranges most big game is shot. It lets you aim in the middle for 230 yards or more of your bullet's flight. It complements the 4X scope or low-power variable that's most useful for deer and elk hunting in mixed cover. It enables you to shoot as far as is practical, but also reminds you that to get close is to boost your odds for an accurate shot and a quick kill.

Get Real About Shooting

Accuracy is a measure of consistency. Anyone can hit a bullseye once; hitting it five times in a row shows consistency that breeds confidence.

But confidence in what? If you shot the rifle from a bench, your job was not to disturb the rifle as you pulled the trigger. You had a bit part. If, on the other hand, you had to support the rifle and hold it still and time the shot, you were the main character.

It's easy to shoot tight groups from the bench. That's why most hunters use it so much, and why most shoot poorly from sitting, kneeling and offhand—positions you'll use in the field. It's always a good idea to rest your rifle, but if a stump isn't handy, you'll wish you'd practiced with that rifle in your hands.

On the hunt, you make the shot. After 35 years of hunting, I can't remember a rifle that missed. A rifle that shoots into three inches at 100 yards will keep bullets in a deer's chest to 300 and beyond. Chasing minute-of-angle groups is senseless, because from hunting positions you're quite capable of missing targets the size of a small refrigerator. I have.

Once, at a sight-in day on a shooting range, I asked hunters who'd just zeroed their rifles to take one offhand shot at a six-inch circle at 100 yards. Only five hits showed up. The backing paper, 22

In the woods, steady shooting positions are easy to assume if you've practiced them.

inches square, had 30 holes. More than a dozen riflemen missed the backer.

As you prepare for hunting season, check your rifle's zero by firing two three-shot groups. Clean the barrel and let it cool between strings. If both groups are centered at 200 yards (figure two-and-a-half inches high at 100) and in each case the first shot is close to the other two, get off the bench.

Use paper targets because they show exactly where bullets strike. Distance isn't important–your goal is to master the fundamentals of marksmanship: position, aiming, trigger control. Before you load up, find the rifle's natural point of aim, and adjust your feet to bring that point of aim onto the target. Don't pivot at the waist or force the rifle over with your arms. You can't hold the rifle still, so your object is to hold the rifle where its constant movement is centered on what you want to hit.

A sling helps you steady the rifle with a shooting loop that adjusts independently of sling length. Give the loop a half-turn out, slip your left arm through it, then run the loop above your triceps, snugging it with a keeper. Flip your hand over the sling so it rests flat against your wrist as you grip the forend. Taut up front, the sling pulls the rifle into your right shoulder as it transfers the weight to your left shoulder. The sling is loose from your arm to the rear swivel.

A strap is not a sling. Without a shooting loop, the strap is pulled tight its entire length, tugging at the rear swivel, twisting the stock and pulling it away from your shoulder. A strap can be used as a "hasty sling" offhand, as you have no anchor for your left elbow and thus cannot keep a loop taut.

In all positions, use bone structure to support the rifle. Muscles tire quickly, then twitch. Sitting and kneeling, keep the flat of your elbow against the flat of your knee. Offhand, your right elbow should be horizontal for a straight pull back on the grip and to open a pocket in your shoulder for the butt. Keep the left elbow well underneath the rifle. Place the butt high enough for a straight-ahead aim.

Offhand, keep your left elbow well under the rifle, your right arm horizontal, your head erect.

I typically take a couple of deep breaths before a shot, then let the third leak slowly as I pressure the trigger. My lungs are empty but not collapsed when the shot comes. Trigger control is merely a matter of applying pressure when the sight is on target, and holding it when the sight wanders off. That's easy to explain, hard to do. Resist the urge to squeeze quickly as the sight dives toward the target. Follow through by holding your rifle for a second during recoil, and practice for follow-up shots by cycling the action fast.

I like to fire three-shot groups, one in each of the four positions. Then I rest. Regular practice in small doses helps you more than a long day at the range every two weeks. Keep your targets; assess your progress. As groups shrink, try to eliminate flyers. Dry firing from field positions at home is a big assist.

You may shoot a deer from a rest this fall. But to count on it is to fantasize. Get real. Now.

Shooting Standing

"Stand up and shoot like a man." Bad advice. You'll shoot much better sitting or kneeling because your center of gravity is lower and you have more ground contact. But if you must shoot quickly or over brush, standing may be your only option. Here's how to practice a position you'll try never to use–but one that could someday put venison on the table:

Check your zero at camp. It will give you confidence in the rifle. Result: better marksmanship.

1. Before you lift the rifle, point your feet properly. Place them shoulder-width apart, with your weight evenly distributed. For starters, a line through your toes should cross your rifle's shadow at roughly a 30-degree angle. That will get you close to a comfortable position; but if the sights are off target, adjust your body by first moving your feet. Find your natural point of aim: the direction in which the rifle naturally points. Do not force the rifle onto the target with your arms!

2. Grasp the grip firmly and pull the rifle's butt into your shoulder. Keep your left elbow nearly under the rifle and your right elbow almost horizontal. Your right shoulder will form a nice pocket for the buttpad. Raise the stock comb to your face; drop your face as little as possible for a firm contact with the comb. Touch the trigger with the first joint of your index finger.

3. Keep your head erect so you can look straight through the sight. Squint if you must. Scopes should be mounted so the rear (ocular) lens extends to the rear guard screw. If you must mount the scope so the lens housing extends more than an inch over the grip, the stock is probably too long for you. Your eye should be about three inches from the ocular lens when your face is as far forward as comfort allows.

4. Take two deep breaths—one as you shoulder the rifle, the other as you let it settle on the target. Relax as you release the second breath; do not forcibly empty your lungs. Now the sight should be on the target, and your trigger finger should be taking up slack.

5. Apply pressure to the trigger when the sight is on target; hold pressure when the sight moves off target. The rifle should fire when the sight is where you want it. When you run out of air or if the rifle starts to shake badly, do not jerk the trigger. Start over. Resist the urge to "time" the shot, yanking the trigger as the sight bounces onto the target. Most often, you will miss.

6. Follow through, maintaining position as the rifle recoils. Call your shot—that is, tell yourself where the bullet hit before you look in the spotting scope or retrieve your target. An accurate call means you had your eyes on the target and knew where the sight was when the bullet left. That is very important! Calling your shots is the first step in correcting problems with position, breathing, and trigger control.

7. Practice offhand more than any other position. Dry firing (empty) enables you to practice more often and without recoil. Get good before you try to get fast. Hurrying a shot teaches bad habits. When a big buck forces you to hurry, you'll be faster and more accurate if you've practiced proper form.

When practicing, cycle your bolt as if you needed a quick second shot. You may, someday.

Tumbling Deer Like Grouse

Shooting deer quickly is more like shotgunning than sniping. To roll a buck rocketing through the alders, you can't deliberate. But neither is snap-shooting mindless response. It's the practiced coordination of eyes, mind, and hand—right away. You don't need extraordinary reflexes. You do need discipline. Snap-shooting melds position, breathing, and trigger control. Master these fundamentals first. Speed comes later.

A running deer is like a Sporting Clays target. You have an eye-blink of time to map out a shot path and position your feet as you bring the stock firmly to your cheek, keeping your eye on the target. Already you've shifted your weight to power the swing from your thighs up through your torso. Your arms hold the gun and complete minor corrections to the sight picture, but every shot begins at ground level, where your feet anticipate target direction. Swing "in front of your feet" and you'll miss. Footwork is no more important in boxing or golf.

When a buck breaks for cover, don't delay! On the other hand, your best shot may come a split second after you're ready to press the trigger. Assessing the shot as you mount the rifle is a crucial first step to a hit. Fire as the buck changes direction or ducks a blow-down and you'll have squandered

what may be your only chance. Convince yourself that a shot begins as soon as you see the target. Your decisions from that point do affect where the bullet will strike, and when, and whether the deer will be there for it or not.

Calculating lead takes time and often will put your bullet too far forward. For most shots in cover, move the rifle quickly onto the target from behind, and you'll score with no lead at all.

A bullet gets there right away. Deer must throttle back in thickets, and seldom will they cross at 90 degrees to your shot. So forget the arithmetic. Just swing and shoot. Imagine a grapefruit-size bullseye over the buck's vitals. Up close, hold at the front edge of that grapefruit as you swing. If you're swinging from behind, you probably have more than enough built-in lead. Beyond 50 yards, depending on target angle and speed, hold a grapefruit or two in front of the target grapefruit.

Deer look faster than they are, and it's easy to get snookered into aiming too far forward. Remember also that a bullet is not like a charge of birdshot that forgives excessive lead by killing with

Metallic silhouette matches hone your offhand skills and help you learn to shoot under pressure.

the tail of a long pellet string. Your bullet must hit with its nose!

As a youth, I read far too often about shotgunners firing at the first duck and hitting the last, about deer hunters splintering oak limbs a garage-length behind departing bucks. It happens still, because hunters still stop their swing. But if you shoot with a moving rifle and as soon as the sight covers the forward rib, you will kill deer. You'll get them where big whitetails give other hunters a glimpse too brief. And you'll see bucks tumble like grouse.

Charlie Sisk built the .338/08. Wayne used a 180-grain Nosler Ballistic Tip to down this Missouri buck.

The Facts about Interpreting Deer Sign

STEVE BARTYLLA

During the predawn hours of November 14, Minnesota's Pat Reeve and his cameraman, Jim Musil, climbed into their stands to film another hunt for *Driven 24/7*. Being a veteran of capturing trophy buck hunts on film, memorable experiences are not rare for Pat. Little did he know that this day would turn out to be more memorable than any hunting experience he'd ever had before.

In reality, like many other hunts from stands, the hunt truly began while scouting. In this particular instance, it was almost scouting by accident. Pat had been to Schuyler County Illinois' Sugar Creek Outfitters scouting the previous spring. Based on those findings, he headed out with Sugar Creek's head guide, Chad John, on the rainy afternoon of November 12 to slap up stands for his hunt.

The true irony was that they were actually going out to hang another stand when Pat made a last-second decision about an unplanned addition. The combination of a little luck, a keen eye and his ability to interpret mature buck sign were the keys to his eventual encounter with a truly world-class buck.

The stand they'd intended to hunt was the tip of a cut on a thick side hill. The cut created pinch points on the top and bottom. Because of his findings in the spring, they were headed for the top.

"As we drove ATVs in," recalled Pat, "we passed right by the funnel at the bottom and could see thigh-size rubs. Arriving up top, Chad told me that he'd been in there a little while ago and those rubs weren't there. So, after hanging the stand up top, we went down to take a closer look. I'm glad we did. Not only were the fresh rubs encouraging, but the trails were much more impressive than they appeared in spring."

Jumping forward to November 14, the morning's slow start changed fast when a doe came running in, dragging a buck behind her. With a tree blocking Pat's view, the only reason he knew it was a shooter was because of an excited whisper from his cameraman.

"When the deer finally got to where I could see it," Reeve said, "my first thought was, 'Oh my Gosh. It's a Booner!' He was still about 60 yards away in brush, walking toward us."

After some anxious moments, it all came together. "When he hit my wider 20-yard shooting lane," Pat recalled, "I voice-grunted to stop him. After getting the OK from Jim, I took another second

Pat Reeve and cameraman Jim Musil pose with the huge buck that resulted from Pat's ability to read fresh buck sign.

to be sure my 20-yard pin was on him and let the arrow fly. I knew before I hit him that it was a good shot."

The sweeping beamed, high-tined 10-point turned out to be considerably bigger than Reeve first believed. Even after the drying period, the buck came in as a 203-inch gross typical. Though learning to interpret buck sign doesn't guarantee those types of results, Pat Reeve would be the first to affirm that it played a critical role in his arrowing that buck. Frankly, it plays a critical role in taking many other mature bucks, as well.

Mature bucks are a different species of deer. In most areas, because of the intense hunting pressure they endure, they place a higher premium on safety than other deer must, or they die. Because of that, during most of deer season, they are loners. They most often have different bedding areas, utilize different trail systems and may even sacrifice prime food sources for lesser quality, safer options.

Furthermore, they tend to be more temperamental than other deer. Because they have learned to survive by avoiding daylight encounters with hunters, it often doesn't take as much of a push for them to change their patterns as it does with other deer.

Because of their loner tendencies and propensity to alter their patterns, the ability to read mature buck sign becomes critical to achieving consistent success for much of the season. This is so true that, during all but the chase, breeding and second-rut phases, I'd always much rather set up on a relatively small quantity of fresh, quality big-buck sign than on massive quantities of pure deer sign. To differentiate quality from quantity, the ability to interpret mature buck sign is required.

Reading Rubs

Because most hunters consider rubs the most accurate form of sign for identifying big bucks,

Clusters of rubs back off from open food sources identify staging areas. When the rubs indicate a mature buck's activities, this can be a great spot to set up for afternoon hunts.

let's begin with them. When it comes to reading sign, I've always found that finding it isn't enough. If hunters truly are to interpret sign and use it to their advantage, they must be able to formulate an educated guess as to how it fits in the big picture and if the creator is likely to pass the area again during daylight. To accomplish that, one must understand why the sign was left to begin with—the buck's purpose for making the rub.

Though some early rubs certainly are due to the velvet-shedding process, they are in the minority, and it has been my experience that the few made during velvet shedding aren't nearly as impressive as those made after. Velvet-shedding rubs most often involve the use of branches or small saplings. When one considers that their purpose is to remove velvet, not to stand out as signposts to other deer or to vent aggression, it only makes sense that they often aren't anywhere near as visually obvious as later rubs. It simply isn't their function.

Primarily, non-velvet shedding rubs, referred to strictly as rubs from this point forward, serve as communication tools. Research has strongly indicated that they convey both visual and olfactory messages to other whitetails. In essence, rubs are a means of advertising an individual buck's presence, providing a general indication of his maturity and serving to intimidate other bucks.

Furthermore, the act of rubbing provides an avenue for building the strong neck muscles required for fighting and venting frustrations. As the rut grows closer and testosterone levels rise, a mature buck becomes much like a bomb ready to explode. Something as innocent as hearing another buck grunt in the distance can inspire a mature buck to thrash a tree. Along with venting frustrations and building muscles, this act also displays power to possible observers. That display has the potential to further intimidate a prospective combatant into submission.

As it applies to using rubs to gauge the maturity of the maker, almost every serious hunter knows to

get excited when he finds a shredded tree with the diameter of a man's thigh.

The myth is that immature bucks won't also rub large trees. They do. The difference becomes apparent in the amount of damage they can achieve.

As with immature bucks, the big boys also hit many smaller-diameter trees, saplings and brush. This is particularly true of early-season rubs, when testosterone levels and aggression are both comparatively low. The majority of early-season rubs appear on unimpressive trees.

Because younger bucks will occasionally rub large trees, both the height of the rub and width of the tine gouges can be used to determine a buck's relative maturity on large trees with little rub damage.

When the shiny sides of trees in a rub line either consistently point toward the feeding or bedding area, rub lines can reveal the buck's travel direction and indicate if the travel corridor would be better suited for morning or afternoon hunts.

The key to gauging the maturity of the makers of rubs really lies in the damage done to the tree. During inspection, simply ask yourself if you believe a young buck would do this level of damage to the object. More often than not, the reduced power and testosterone levels result in young bucks creating nothing more than a small bare strip on saplings or two narrowly spaced, relatively low gouges from their bow tines on larger trees.

Conversely, a mature buck's increased bulk and nasty temperament is bad news for saplings. Long peals, twisted branches and snapped trees get me every bit as excited as calf-sized rubs. When it comes to larger trees, the big boys often shred them. Even when they don't explode on the tree in a fit of aggression, the height of the rub and spacing of the tines typically give the maker's size away.

Frankly, the young bucks rarely do much damage and, although mature bucks will sometimes also rub low, their rubs are almost always low. That is due to the increased need to use leverage to their advantage. When using rubs to gauge the maker's maturity, all of these factors must be considered. Of course, if the rub is fresh, it never hurts to check for track size either.

Yet another difference between mature and immature bucks' rubbing tendencies can be seen. In a nutshell, young bucks make far fewer rubs and begin rubbing in earnest much closer to the breeding phase due to their relative inexperience and slower-rising testosterone levels. The combination works to retard the 1.5- and 2.5-year-old bucks' signposting endeavors, so a collection of early rubs typically indicates the presence of a mature buck.

As discussed previously, before the chase phase occurs, most buck travels consist of transitioning between bedding, food and water. Therefore, it stands to reason that most rubs occur around food and water sources, bedding areas and the trails connecting the three.

Ultimately, rub lines are nothing more than a series of otherwise unrelated rubs that a buck makes over numerous trips between these three destinations. In general, the more trees suitable for rubbing that exist along the travel corridors and the more often the buck takes the route, the more defined the rub lines become.

Not only do rub lines indicate buck travel corridors, they can also provide insight into the buck's direction of travel. That is determined by studying the side of the tree that's rubbed; that's the side the buck was coming from.

This can be useful when determining whether a stand placed along a buck's travel corridor is best for hunting mornings, afternoons or both. Take a well-established rub line connecting a bedding area to a clear-cut, for example. If the majority of rubbed sides of the trees face toward the bedding area, chances are good that they were made over the course of numerous evening trips to the food source, as the buck transitioned from bedding to feeding. Conversely, if the shined sides are on the clear-cut side, they were most likely made when the buck returned to bed in the morning. Finally, a somewhat equal mix indicates that he uses the same trail both going to and returning from feeding.

As useful as this can be, basing decisions on one or two rubs can lead to incorrect assumptions. Rubs are made as a buck walks along. When the tree lies in his path, he'll most often trash it from the direction he was approaching, providing an accurate guide to where he was coming from.

However, if it lies off his path, the angle he takes to reach it can create misleading results. Furthermore, I've occasionally witnessed bucks circle a tree before rubbing. And if a tree has an angle to it or large branches that make access to part difficult, the buck commonly adjusts his stance to provide the best access to the portion of the tree most easily rubbed.

It's best to only use rub lines to predict travel direction when the majority of rubs tell the same story. By refraining from making assumptions based on one or two rubs, as well as factoring in the possible need to veer off course and access issues, rub lines can be very accurate indicators of travel direction.

Along with travel corridors, food and water sources and bedding areas, concentrations of rubs can also reveal staging areas. A survival mechanism that mature bucks often use is to hang back from open food sources, such as agricultural fields, clear-cuts and meadows. They will burn time in these staging areas until either darkness arrives or enough other deer expose themselves to this potentially dangerous open area to assure the buck of its safety. When burning time, bucks often mark these staging areas with rubs.

Because of that, when a concentration of rubs are found, commonly twenty to one hundred yards off the edge of an open food source, it's a good bet that it identifies the location as a staging area. When the rubs show that a good buck is burning time here, this can be a great location to pick up his early evening movements. Often, encounters during legal shooting hours can occur in staging areas with bucks that won't step foot into feeding areas until after dark. Clusters of rubs can be used to identify these valuable stand locations.

Understanding Scrapes

Scrapes are yet another valuable bit of sign which hunters must be able to accurately interpret. These large, bowled-out, pawed areas of dirt scream bucks so loudly that few hunters can refrain from getting excited at the sight of them. What many don't realize is the sort of complex messages these signposts relay and the effects they have on other deer.

For years, scrapes were thought of as really nothing more than pickup bars designed for and

When bucks work scrapes, it is very likely that their primary goals are to advertise their presence to all other deer and intimidate rival bucks.

by bucks. Many researchers speculated that a buck made scrapes to attract estrous does for breeding. Although that happens on occasion, many years and countless hours of research later, the popular belief amongst scientists is changing. More and more, studies are indicating that scrapes are utilized to a greater extent as intricate communication and intimidation tools, rather than as meat markets.

In many ways, scrapes are not unlike the whitetail world's version of a billboard. They are an elaborate combination of advertising and information. It is theorized that scrapes communicate a buck's dominance, identity and other information of social importance. It is believed that bucks deposit odor-based messages that convey such information, having physiological and psychological impact upon other deer.

Breaking down a scrape into components can help illustrate how they may be able to provide all this information. Most hunters realize that any serious, hard-hit scrape has a licking branch hovering above it that is repeatedly worked by bucks. This is a key component of the site. They lick it, chew it, rub their foreheads on it and even thrash it about with their antlers. In the process, it is believed that they deposit chemical signals that advertise their presence, as well as their individual identity.

Along with working the licking branch, they also typically paw the ground to create the traditional oval shape that many think of as the scrape itself. Until someone actually holds a conversation with a deer, it is impossible to tell exactly why. However, the theory that this act displays aggression and a willingness to fight to prove dominance does make sense. I also believe that it also has a degree of visual appeal to possibly attract deer from upwind.

Finally, we have the act of urinating on the scrape. Early in fall, deer typically do this without involving their tarsal glands. Later, during the peak scraping phase, bucks perform the act of rub urinating by pinching their back knees together to draw their tarsal glands close and dribbling their urine over them, ultimately depositing it on the scrape. From these odors, it's believed that other deer can decipher the social and physiological status of the maker, which may inform them of such things as the buck's dominance, health and readiness to breed. To further support this, it has been found that the compounds in a buck's urine that relate to age and dominance only appear during the peak scraping, chase and breeding phases of season.

Over the years, I've read and heard other "experts" break scrapes into classes such as breeding, territorial, boundary, core area and about 50 other groups. To this, I say hogwash. Frankly, I don't

buy for a second that bucks purposefully travel the edges of their home range and make scrapes to serve as territory markers. Do I believe they make some scrapes near the edges of their home range? Sure. A mature buck can make over 200 scrapes in a single season. Some are bound to occur along the edges of his home range, as well as in his core area. However, I don't buy that a buck is capable of consciously thinking, "I'm going to create a scrape here for breeding, one there to mark my core area, yet another to show this is my territory and then finish up with a lap of scrapes around the boundary of my home range."

This isn't meant to say that bucks' scrapes can't be grouped into classifications. I believe they can. Essentially, I break them into three groupings: scrapes they'll likely never revisit, scrapes they work fairly regularly, and individual scrapes that numerous bucks all work together.

Because mature bucks can make so many scrapes, it stands to reason that most are spur-of-the-moment, random scrapes. Most likely because they aren't placed where the buck passes often, they're created and forgotten. I also include the scrapes made by immature bucks in this group because, frankly, they have no clue what they're really doing. They have urges and see the cool big guys making scrapes. So they become copycats, really not having the maturity or experience to understand the purpose behind their actions.

Next, there are the scrapes that occur along an individual buck's travel corridor. Because he routinely uses the trail connecting his bedding and feeding areas, "transitioning" from one area to another, he also routinely freshens one or more scrapes he's made along that path. When he's in the right frame of mind and a licking branch is staring him in the face, I don't believe he can help but make or refresh a scrape. If the maker of this kind of scrape is a good buck, such transitional scrapes can be great to hunt.

Lastly, there are primary scrapes—those that occur in specific locations that concentrate high numbers of deer. It may be in the back corner of an alfalfa field, the intersection of two heavily used logging roads, the downwind side of a doe-bedding area or anywhere else that numerous deer frequent. In each case, many deer pass a specific location and it serves as an effective spot to place a billboard for advertising. Young and old bucks alike hit it again and again, most often year after year. When positioned in areas where bucks feel safe, these can also be very exciting places to hunt.

Spring is the best time to locate scrapes for hunting—the time when one can truly evaluate their level of use. After tossing out the ones that weren't used much, one can determine whether the scrape occurs along a specific buck's travel corridor or in a high-use area. From that, you can determine whether it falls within the transitional or primary scrape slot. Then, it's simply a matter of figuring out if the area makes sense to hunt.

Making these determinations on scrapes found during season is a little trickier. When a new found scrape is first opened up, I know of no way to consistently determine whether it will become a heavily utilized scrape or not. I simply rely on the amount of mature buck sign in the area and woodsmanship to decide if it's worthy of hunting.

Finding scrapes that have been open for a while makes the job easier. If the chase phase is still a ways off and the scrape is in an area likely to observe daylight activity, seeing large tracks in the scrape is all I need to give the spot a chance.

Reading Tracks

Speaking of deer tracks, I believe they are often the most-overlooked piece of deer sign left in the woods. How many times do hunters push aside a few leaves to study a trail in detail, looking for large tracks to verify that a mature buck is using it?

A fairly obvious and general, but pretty darn accurate, statement is that big bucks have big tracks. Knowing this can be applied to scouting in several ways. First, because family groups and mature bucks commonly use different trails, finding a mixture of adult and fawn tracks on that cow path of a trail running through the mature section of the woods allows us to easily identify it as a family group trail. When further examination reveals the absence of disproportionately large tracks, it's best to find a different location to hang a buck stand.

On the flip side, extra-large tracks on trails, in scrapes, around rubs, at water holes and anywhere else tracks can be found are a strong indicator of the presence of a mature buck. The benefits of finding these tracks are obvious.

When it comes to track size, I'm sure you noticed that I refrained from giving measurements. The reason for this is that the average size of a big buck track varies from area to area, particularly from north to south. A general rule of thumb is that the

Because bucks have comparatively broader shoulders and narrower hips than does, their back hoof overlaps their front with an inside offset during a relaxed walk.

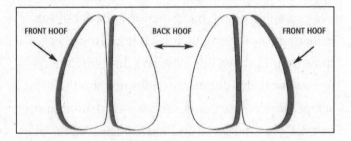

Because does have comparatively broader hips and narrower shoulders than bucks, their back hoof overlaps their front with an outside offset during a relaxed walk.

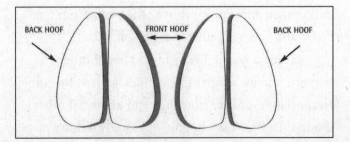

farther north you travel, the larger the subspecies of deer. This is because of the survival advantages of possessing a larger body in colder regions—the larger the body, the less energy is required to heat one body unit—and of having a smaller body in the hotter southern regions, making it easier to shed excess body heat. Heck, in Wisconsin alone, body sizes are noticeably smaller in the southern portions of the state than in the northern regions.

Because of that, providing track measurements would be doing most readers an injustice. About the best gauge I can offer is that a mature buck track is commonly 15-30% larger than that of a mature doe. Using that as a guide, most readers should be able to differentiate tracks. But remember that this is a generalization, and exceptions do occur.

As far as the rest of the popular methods of differentiating buck from doe tracks, I've never found them to be reliable. Dewclaws are evident in buck, doe and even fawn tracks when conditions are right. I've run across numerous does that dragged their hooves and just as many mature bucks that didn't.

However, along with size, there is another trait that can be used to consistently differentiate buck and doe tracks. Because of the advantages it provides for birthing fawns, does typically have wider hips. When walking naturally, the back hoof print overlaps the front track as wider hips cause the back track to overlap the front with an offset to the outside. Much like men having smaller hips and wider shoulders than women, bucks also typically have wider shoulders than hips. That causes their back track to overlap their front with an inside offset. Knowing this enables one to study the tracks of walking deer and gauge their sex. When combined with track size, one can now use tracks to identify mature bucks.

Clues Provided by Scat

As with the myths associated with track size, I've never found any consistency to the old wives tale that bucks defecate in individual pellets, whereas doe scat is clumped. From my experiences, the clumped verses pelleted scat is due to what the deer has eaten and has nothing to do with its sex.

However, as a general rule of thumb, I have found that big bucks leave big piles of seat. As with everything, there are exceptions. Still, the more indicators that point toward the presence of a mature buck, the more it is likely to be a big guy.

One of the better values of deer droppings is the indication of feeding areas. When leaves around oaks are pawed and the area yields numerous piles of deer droppings, you can bet deer have been feeding there on acorns. Surpluses of scat in any potential food source show a high level of feeding.

Droppings also indicate if a food source is currently hot or already passed over. If all the droppings are old, chances are that the deer have moved to greener pastures. In turn, if there are either fresh piles intermixed with old, or exclusively fresh scat, you know that feeding is occurring now.

Making the Bed

As with tracks and scat, one can use certain guidelines to differentiate buck beds from family group bedding areas. As previously mentioned, bucks typically bed by themselves. Therefore, when various sized depressions are found in the leaves it's a pretty safe bet that it reveals a family group bedding area.

On the flip side, when a lone, large depression or a handful of similarly sized large depressions are found, it indicates a buck's bedroom. Though finding several beds can lead one to believe numerous animals are bedding there, the thing to key on is whether they're all large. Many times a buck will lay up in the same area, but not the same bed each time. If all the beds in an area are big, there's a good chance it's the work of a single buck.

When snow is on the ground, urine spots can be another indicator. Often, deer will urinate as soon as they rise from their beds. Because of differences in anatomy, a doe's urine spot is often at the edge of the bed, whereas the buck's urine spot tends to be in the center.

That alone is not enough to base an educated decision on; that's where adding more pieces to the puzzle comes into play. For example, it's a good bet that it's the bed of a good buck if the urine spot is in the center of a bed with large tracks leading away and no small beds are present. The addition of other big-buck indicators is what makes this a reliable trait.

Conclusion

Interpreting deer sign is more of an art than an exact science. When you really boil it down, it amounts to understanding sign and piecing as many bits of evidence together as one can. The more pieces one can put together, the more accurate the conclusions become. With that, we can make educated decisions on what's going on and where our odds are the highest of having a daylight encounter with Mr. Big.

Any location where deer tracks are left provides the opportunity to check for big-buck tracks. Overlooking this bit of sign is a huge mistake.

Following the Map to Trophy Bucks

Studying the topographical-contour (or "topo") map, I knew I'd found a killer stand site. A sharp erosion cut sliced up the side of a steep wooded ridge, stopping about 20 yards short of a deep saddle. It was the merging of three funnel features into one. If the cut was even half as deep or the sides anywhere near as steep as the map indicated, deer would not want to cross it. They also wouldn't want to needlessly climb the extra 50-some feet of steep ridge that flanked both sides of the saddle. With the ridge snaking through the woods for over a mile, it was a safe bet that bucks would be running that as well. As if to add a cherry on top, the map showed that swampland, highly likely to be used as bedding areas, was positioned on both sides of the ridge. There was little doubt that this spot had tremendous potential.

Over a mile and a half from the nearest access point, with map in hand and a stand and set of climbing sticks on my back, I began the walk to see this funnel for myself. Though I'd only have one day I could hunt the spot, I was far from disappointed that I'd have to work this hard to get to the location. Because I was hunting public lands, I wagered the extra work of packing the stand in with me that the local hunters hadn't studied a topo map of the area, and that they'd be hunting much closer to the road. I was right, and I wasn't disappointed with what I'd found.

With the stand set, I made my way back to the funnel well before first light the next morning. Even as I climbed into the tree, I could hear the distinct trotting sounds of an approaching buck. Still well before first light, the large shadowy figure slipped through the saddle within easy bow range of my stand. I won't even pretend to know how big he was, but I can safely say he had a lot of bone on his head.

The rest of the day was one I'll cherish for the rest of my bowhunting days. From my stand, I can't even tell you how many different bucks I saw. As I put in my hunting logs, "somewhere between 12 and 17 different bucks, 2 or 3 of them shooters. Too many to give antler and age stats. The times ranged from before first light to 10 minutes before dark, with spurts of action spread out over the entire sit. They were everywhere, but more passed the stand than anything else. Only change would be to shift to the tree 10 yards down from southeast corner of saddle to pick up shots at where the two slob bucks crossed the cut. Amazing stand location! 9.5 (out of 10 rating)."

As you probably figured out, I didn't shoot a buck that day. I didn't even draw my bow. To be honest, the only reason I didn't was because I ignored some faint sign that occurred in a spot that was comparatively easier to cross than the rest of the cut. One big boy followed the cut up to that point and crossed there, instead of climbing the extra 20 yards to the tip. He may have been the same buck I'd seen before first light. The other was running the ridge side and crossed there. Still, although the property was being hunted heavily, the ability to effectively read topo maps had provided me with one of the best days I've ever had on a stand. If I hadn't had to leave the next day, who knows what it would have produced.

Enefits of Map Reading

As was the case with that hunt, topo maps can be very valuable scouting tools. I personally rely on them so heavily, and have had such success using them to locate potentially hot stand locations, that I feel blind scouting without one.

One of the main benefits of reading topo maps comes from minimizing the risks of missing good stand sites. As the public-land hunters illustrated by missing the funnel stand setup that began this piece, while foot scouting it can be easy to miss stand sites that stick out like sore thumbs on a topo map. The bird's-eye view they provide displays a big picture that can't be seen from the ground.

Spending some time studying topo maps before you go afield can help you determine the best stand-placement sites, and how to reach them.

As beneficial as using maps to uncover stands may be during off-season scouting, it is even more so when in-season scouting is required. When scouting during the season, finding quality stands is certainly a goal. However, keeping deer ignorant of the fact that they're being hunted and not pushing them off their current patterns is every bit as important.

That's where the ability to read topo maps can be worth its weight in gold. Instead of blindly stumbling around the woods, if there is any relief to the property at all, one can find many of the most promising stand-site locations before even hitting the woods.

Of course, one still must foot scout the locations to gauge their true value. However, if you first generate a list of the top-potential spots, the lowest-impact routes to those locations can be determined. The ability to slip in and out, without trashing the entire woods scouting, greatly reduces the disturbances typically required to find a property's hot spots.

Another advantage that topo maps commonly provide is the ability to piece travel patterns together more effectively. Assuming a basic knowledge of the property's food sources, the topography often shows the best routes to and from these areas. Furthermore, many bedding sites are also based on topography. From simply knowing where the deer feed, the ability to read maps often enables savvy hunters to make educated guesses on where the deer bed and how they travel back and forth to feed.

Luckily, all of this can be accomplished through some basic map-reading skills and a little experience. Even for map-reading novices, learning to read topo maps can be relatively easy.

Map Reading 101

The United States Geological Survey's (USGS) 7.5-minute quadrangles (quads) are the basis for most topo maps. The USGS has quad coverage for all of the United States. Luckily, in today's computer age, there are several sources that offer printable versions for free, as well as numerous companies offering maps for sale. Because of USGS quads being so widely used, I'll use them as the standard for our exploration into map reading.

Let's begin by exploring cultural features, such as roads, railroad tracks, buildings and major transmission lines. USGS quads illustrate cultural

Topo maps have the potential to reveal excellent, low-impact routes for accessing a property and stands.

features in black. This information alone can help set the stage for how you can gain access to areas and even suggest possible routes to stand sites. Next, we have the wooded areas that are shaded in green. Aside from that obviously showing us where the woods are, narrowed-down necks of green can show potential funnels.

The hydrological features, such as swamps, rivers, lakes and ponds, also can show funnels. The narrow piece of dry land between those bodies of water could be a good example of that. Rivers and streams often are used as travel corridors for deer, and they can serve as excellent low-impact routes to stands. A swamp is a potential bedding area. Finally, any hydrological feature can create barriers that many other hunters may avoid. For whatever reason, many hunters are unwilling to put on a pair of waders or jump in a canoe to go deer hunting. This often results in mini-sanctuaries existing within areas that are heavily hunted. Studying a map can show you where these areas exist.

As helpful as the bird's-eye view of those features can be, showing the land in relief is often the greatest advantage contour maps provide. Each contour line on a map indicates a line of equal elevation, with a standard contour interval of 10 feet on most quads. That means if the 1250-foot contour is running along the side of a hill, the next contour going up the hill will represent the 1260-foot line, whereas the one going downhill would be the 1240. Although this does show us how far above sea level things are, the real purpose for hunters lies in showing relief.

Because they are lines of constant elevation and are at set intervals, contour lines show how relatively flat or steep the terrain is. When the contours are spaced relatively far apart, the terrain is fairly flat. Conversely, the closer they are together, the steeper the terrain. With this understanding, we can begin to see topographical features emerge.

One of the most basic features is a ridge. With contour lines on both sides stacked close together, increasing in elevation as they reach the top, a ridge is easily identifiable. In wooded areas, ridges often serve as natural travel corridors for deer. Typically, the family groups will have a worn trail on top, with fainter trails just off the sides that are used by bucks. During the rut, it is not uncommon for bucks to run ridge systems for miles while searching out hot does.

When a major ridge splits, the point before it breaks into two is also a good location. Because bucks are likely running the ridge hard, this point is almost like the intersection of two highways. When set up right, a hunter can cover the bucks running all three portions of the ridges, as well as those switching from one to another.

When the contours bulge out to the side of the ridge, it indicates a knob. When small, minor ridges shoot off the side, they show points. Wooded knobs and points are often used as bedding areas. Bucks tend to select the ones that allow them to use their eyes to see the lowland below and the wind to cover their backside. That combination provides bucks with the ultimate in safety.

Ridges pair with other features to create many different topographical funnels. For example, a saddle is nothing more than a dip in a ridge top. If you were to look at the profile of a saddle, you would see the top of the ridge runs fairly horizontally. Then, at some point, the ridge top would dip downward, only to rise back up and continue at its former elevation. It can be thought of almost like something has taken a huge bite out of the top of the ridge. The bottom of the dip is called the saddle.

When we find a location where the contour lines running along the top of the ridge wrap around to its opposite side, as if the ridge came to a tapering end, only to have the contours start up again, we have a saddle. On the map, it resembles two ridge tops in the process of converging and melting into one. As

a side note, both the tapering end of a ridge and the high sides of saddles are potential bedding sites.

Because a saddle is lower than the ridge top on either side, deer often cross the ridge in the saddle. Simply put, they are lazy and don't want to expend extra energy unless there's a good reason to.

Another good topographical funnel are dry washes (cuts) running down the side of the ridge—cuts caused by erosion from years of focused runoff. Once they erode to a certain point, they become difficult for deer to cross. To avoid doing so, many deer will either go up the ridge to cross at the upper tip of the cut or down the ridge to cross at the bottom.

When these cuts are deep enough to discourage crossing and go far enough up the ridge, they can be great stand sites. Sitting above the top of a cut can enable you to cover the traffic around the tip, along with the buck trail common to the upper edge of the ridge and the family group's ridgetop trail. The bottom of the cut, where the runoff begins fanning and the cut dissipates, can also produce good stand sites.

A cut is easily identified on a quad map by the contours V-ing into the side of the ridge, as they

Topo maps provide hunters with the ability to more effectively conduct in-season scouting on new properties while keeping disturbances to a minimum.

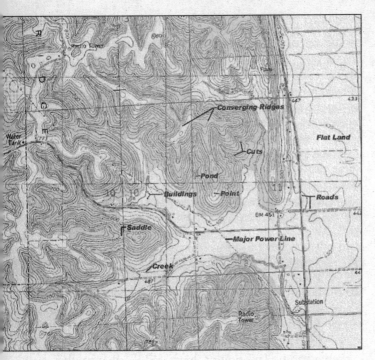

This topo map has two roads, two buildings, a power line, a pond, a creek, a point, two converging ridges, two cuts, a saddle and flatlands that are labeled. Study these features and find other examples on the map.

go up the side. In general, the narrower and more pronounced the V is, the sharper and steeper the sides of the cut are. Conversely, the more the series of contours each resemble a U, the more tapered the out. These cuts are still worth investigating, however, and are often sharper than the map reveals.

Another potentially good stand site is where several cuts come together near the bottom of the hill or ridge sides. Because deer tend to follow these cuts up and down, the convergence of cuts can create a busy intersection of deer trails. Stands placed along the side hills, above where the cuts converge, are good bets. But because swirling winds are the rule in these locations, only those who take odor control very seriously should attempt to hunt them.

A bench, yet another type of funnel, can be one of the best stands for rutting bucks there is. In a nutshell, a bench is a fairly flat strip of ground that runs along the side of a ridge, somewhere around halfway up.

It is common in ridge country to have farm crops planted in valleys that are flanked by wooded ridges on either side. In such a setting, the deer often bed high and feed low. Under these conditions, when a bench runs along the side of a ridge, a buck can scent-check the trail of every doe that's recently transitioned between feeding and bedding. Because of that, and because these flat areas offer easier walking than the steep sides of the ridge, benches often become highways for cruising bucks.

As with every other topographical feature, a bench will show up on a contour map. When looking at the stacked contours along the side of the ridge, keep an eye peeled for a gap somewhere around halfway up the ridge. Remember, tightly stacked contours show steep raises in elevation. When a gap appears between contours that are tightly stacked above and below it, you have a bench. Furthermore, the longer it snakes its way along the side of the ridge, the more productive the bench will likely be.

When it comes to funnels involving ridges, many of the very best are where two of these features converge. As was the case with the stand location at the beginning of this section, a good example is when a sharp cut begins near the base of a saddle. Here, the hunter can intercept bucks running the top of the ridge, those crossing at the saddle and the ones skirting the cut.

Flatland hunters also have the potential to find topographical funnels. Deer like to maintain low profiles; it increases their life expectancy. So they will commonly travel any dips or gullies that keep them hidden. Finding these low-profile areas on contour maps can identify places that deer use as travel routes. Look for areas where contour maps make "U"s as they meander through flatter areas.

Conclusion

As you can see, having the ability to read topo maps can provide tremendous advantages in finding stand sites, as well as keeping scouting and hunting impact at a minimum. The more one studies these maps, the better they become as more potential stand sites emerge.

To help build these skills, simply print out a topo map of your hunting land and put it to use during an off-season scout. When you come across topographical features, find them on the map and note how the contours appear. After no time at all, the features will begin making sense. Trust me, if you get nothing else from this book, the minimal effort it takes to learn how to read topo maps will pay for itself countless times over.

Finding Wounded Deer

JOHN TROUT

Wounded Deer Realities

On a chilly November evening during the late 1960s, a white-tailed doe passed by my stand. Not one to pass up a golden opportunity, I drew the string of my old Bear recurve bow, anchored, and released the fiberglass arrow. The dull thump that followed verified that my arrow had hit the deer in the body cavity. The following morning, I picked up the blood trail and tracked the wounded deer until the trail finally ended 250 yards from the thicket where the incident occurred. Although my search continued the rest of the day, I failed to find the deer.

Losing my first whitetail shot with bow and arrow was almost more than I could bear. It was frustrating, humiliating, heartbreaking and, well, you get the picture. Nevertheless, something good came out of this tracking endeavor. You see, from that day on I became obsessed with learning everything about the behavior and the recovery of wounded deer. I would make it a point to assist friends when tracking their deer, jumping at the chance to discover facts we knew little about.

Fortunately, today we know far more than we knew back then. I have now hunted whitetails with bow and gun for more than thirty-five years, and have participated in countless tracking pursuits. Many of these adventures ended with a filled tag. Some did not. However, all provided insights for future tracking efforts, and for the words contained within this book.

Today, the discussion of tracking wounded deer has become a hot topic. In fact, many publications that once refused to discuss the subject of tracking wounded deer now make it a point to include this subject regularly. Before going on, let me first say that there is both good news and bad news about the coverage of tracking wounded deer. First comes the good news. Publications that do discuss the topic have done a great job of educating hunters. This is necessary as we continue to battle anti-hunters and animal activists, and further our need to learn about wounded deer.

I have often wished that it would be mandatory for hunters to pass a tracking and deer anatomy test before they could receive a deer hunting tag. Imagine if everyone received a booklet with anatomy illustrations, shot placement tips, guidelines for determining hits, and tracking and recovery tactics. Each license applicant would have to study the booklet, then take a basic test. Some people might disagree with this idea, but I see it as a gateway to building more responsible hunters. The more we know about the subject of tracking deer, the better we are prepared to stand up to the antis and activists, the better ethics we will practice, the better shots we will take, and the more deer we will recover.

A bowhunting instructor in Iowa once told me that we must continue educational practices about shooting and tracking deer. He based his opinion on how little some hunters know about whitetail anatomy. One student, who viewed a large illustration of a white-tailed buck, was asked to point out the location of the animal's heart. He selected a spot at the base of the neck where it joins the shoulders. Many students were also surprised to learn about the precise location of the lungs, and had no idea that the lungs of an adult deer were nine inches in diameter.

Now let's get back to the coverage of wounded deer that has taken place in recent years. The bad news is that some writers have misled hunters. Now don't get me wrong, most who write about tracking wounded deer have a good understanding of the subject, and they have done a great job of informing readers. Some, however, did not get the facts straight before passing them along. For instance, one writer who discussed tracking gut-shot deer talked about a kidney hit and compared it to the liver and stomach wound. He claimed a kidney-shot deer would die in a few hours and would bleed very slowly internally. Unfortunately, he failed to realize how much blood flows through the kidneys. A hole in the kidneys causes immediate hemorrhage and death within seconds.

Once a hunter shoots, he has an ethical responsibility to do everything he can to recover the animal.

Other writers have passed along opinions taken from hunter surveys. While statistical information is interesting and sometimes helpful, it does not necessarily tell the whole story. In other words, 500 hunters may give opinions and make guesses to some tracking questions. But consider that many of these 500 hunters may not be very experienced. Some may have tracked only one or two deer; others may have simply misread the questions, and thus answered incorrectly.

I don't claim to know all there is about tracking wounded deer. I keep an open mind and seem to learn something new each time an experience occurs. I also absorb the information I read and give it careful consideration. However, I cannot deny the cliche, "Experience is the best teacher."

Since I have always kept records of hunts, harvests, and tracking occurrences, I have been able to come up with a few interesting and helpful facts. In the past thirty-seven years, I have participated in more than 450 tracking events. Many were deer I have shot, many were deer shot by other hunters. Approximately 300 of these incidents occurred before 1985. Since that time, my tracking pursuits have decreased simply because these days I pass on more shots, holding out for a trophy.

I have seen every wound imaginable, and have seen the unexpected occur on many occasions. Nonetheless, these experiences have helped me to recover many wounded deer. Some were recovered only because others, or I, recognized a certain wound and knew how the animal would react. Yes, I have been fortunate to have the assistance of many friends who know the ins-and-outs of tracking wounded deer. The primary objective is to tag a deer. That's what we all want to do. However, I'm like you, in that I enjoy the hunt. I love to see a beautiful sunrise and sunset, watch all the critters running around the woods, learn the habits of the deer I watch, and just love to feel and breath country air.

However, I doubt any of us will deny the bottom line. We want to kill a deer no matter how much we enjoy the additional pleasures that come with a quality hunt. As I have said before, the kill is like the icing on the cake.

Shot Placement

Of course, before any of us can feel the excitement of a kill, we must first have a good understanding of a deer's anatomy. We must know where to place the broadhead or bullet, and we must know what shots we should and should not take.

There are a few golden rules to remember about shooting at a deer: You must judge yardage with some degree of accuracy and avoid shooting beyond your effective shooting range; you must wait until the animal offers a shot that allows you to make a clean kill; you should shoot only when you are confident of killing the deer; and you must know the precise location of the vital organs if you are to accomplish anything.

Despite these facts, some hunters still take unwarranted shots. Others have also gotten the idea, perhaps from a previous thrilling experience, that they should not shoot at the lungs of a deer – the animal's largest vitals. For instance, I often hear from hunters who prefer to shoot at the heart. Why would anyone prefer to shoot for the heart when the lungs are much larger and may put the animal down as quickly, and sometimes sooner? Another guy told me he always shoots for the neck. He relies on hitting a two-inch-diameter vertebrate, or perhaps the one-half-inch carotid artery, to put the deer down, instead of the nine-inch diameter lungs. Maybe this guy shot a deer in the neck once and dropped it immediately. Maybe he did it twice. Maybe the first time he hit the deer in the neck it was totally accidental. Who knows? But I do know that it makes no sense to select a small target when a bigger target exists. I also know that it is easy for a projectile or

Deer hunters should take only those shots they believe will result in quick, clean kills. This buck is quartering away, allowing plenty of room for a bullet or broadhead to reach the vitals.

broadhead to miss the vitals in the neck and pass through only muscle.

Each hunter must know his equipment and its capabilities. He should also realize the best shot is a broadside or slightly quartering-away shot. Quartering away is best because it allows room for error. Your broadhead or bullet is heading for the vital area. Never consider taking quartering-into and facing-into shots unless the animal is close and you know beyond any doubt that your broadhead or projectile can hit a vital organ. Sometimes it is possible, sometimes it isn't.

A two-season hunter must also know when one weapon will get the job done and another will not. For instance, I will not hesitate to shoot at the shoulder of a deer when I'm using a firearm and the animal presents the perfect opportunity. However, although a few of my arrows have passed through the shoulder blade of a deer and reached the lungs, I make it a point to keep my sights focused behind the shoulder of the animal when bowhunting.

Broadheads and Bullets

Speaking of broadheads and bullets, both are effective when the hunter takes a preferred shot. But there are certain limitations that apply to a bowhunter that may not apply to a firearm hunter. Bone is of primary concern. It has nothing to do with hemorrhage and tissue damage. A razor-sharp broadhead is lethal and, when coupled with the right bow, arrow, and hunter, will usually penetrate completely and kill quickly. In fact, I have found in most cases, when identical wounds exist, the right broadhead produces a better blood trail than a projectile does.

Your choice of broadheads should be taken seriously, however. Although I hunt with bow and gun, I have always had a stronger love for the archery season. Over the years, I have tried countless brands of broadheads in the backyard and in the field. I have found that inconsistent arrow flight and poor blood trails exist from broadhead to broadhead. This should concern all bowhunters. Most of us realize that some broadheads do not fly like field points, and we realize that some cannot be easily tuned. However, the big test occurs when you shoot a deer. You could say that some have it, and some do not. We know a sharp broadhead is necessary, but it's also a fact that even some razor-sharp broadheads are responsible for poor blood trails. It's really a test all bowhunters must go through. All broadheads can kill, but you must still discover those that shoot best, and those broadheads that do the damage you expect.

Every hunter must also realize that blood trails are not always dependent upon the projectile or broadhead used. Poor blood trails are often the result of the wound location. I have shot deer in the stomach with one-ounce slugs and found no blood on the ground. The same has happened when using sharp broadheads. This is common, because organ tissue often clogs the entry and departure holes. The height of the entry and departure hole will also affect the amount of blood that gets to the ground. With this in mind, the hunter must always consider the wound before he decides that his equipment was responsible for a poor blood trail.

The size and weight of the bullet and broadhead may or may not have an effect on the blood trail. You must decide for yourself what works best and what will increase your chances of recovering an animal after the shot. Any projectile and broadhead will kill when it passes through the vitals, but some do it quicker than others, and some do more damage and result in better blood trails.

When hunting with a muzzleloader, I have sacrificed the fine accuracy of some projectiles and went with others that made bigger holes and left better blood trails. These bullets could not group in a one-inch circle at 100 yards, but they can group in a four-inch circle at seventy-five yards. Since my shots are usually fifty yards or less when deer hunting, I go with the projectile that does the most damage, yet has enough accuracy and size to get the job done.

In recent years, bowhunters have seen the introduction of many new types of broadheads. Some have large cutting diameters and some do not. However, a broadhead with a large cutting diameter is not necessarily the best to use. We have also had the opportunity to try mechanical broadheads - made to open on impact. In my opinion, mechanical broadheads are still going through the testing period. Some manufacturers introduced these heads because they felt it necessary to keep up with the competition. Some hunters claim mechanical heads are the greatest, while others claim penetration is severely affected. Again, it comes down to trying what works best for you. Personally, I stick with the common theory: If it ain't broke, don't fix it. If you are dissatisfied with a particular tracking endeavor and believe your broadheads could be to blame, try to find something better. If you like the results of what you have, keep using them.

When a non-vital wound occurs, hunters often wonder which causes the most trauma and damage to tissue - broadheads or projectiles. Although one could come to various conclusions, depending upon the precise location of a non-vital wound, and the broadhead or bullet that hits a deer, it has been determined that less tissue damage and trauma occurs from a sharp broadhead. However, research has determined that many wounded deer that are not found, do recover, regardless of whether the hunter shot the animal with a bow or gun. In fact, if organs are spared and infection is not a factor, a deer will recover.

During the past three decades, I have witnessed the recovery of several deer with previous wounds. These wounds appeared to range from one week to one year old. Most of the deer had previous wounds to a leg, shoulder, or neck. One incident in particular involved a small buck I shot with a bow straight down under my tree stand. The arrow slid along the inside of the rib cage, but apparently missed the vital lungs. We tracked the deer about 100 yards until the blood trail ceased. After a careful search in the hours that followed, I finally gave up the trail. One year later, a friend of mine killed the buck in the same area. We found a sixinch piece of my unmistakable arrow shaft, and the broadhead inside the animal's chest when we field dressed the deer. Tissue had formed around the shaft and broadhead, and the deer appeared healthy.

Be Persistent

Getting back to the realities of wounded deer, we must realize that some deer do not die. Superficial wounds occur, even when an obvious blood trail may lead you to believe otherwise. You will need to know the difference in wounds that are only superficial and those that will result in the deer

succumbing. Equally important, however, is realizing you have an ethical responsibility to do everything you can to recover an animal, despite any belief that the wound is superficial or otherwise. You will feel better with yourself if you do everything you can to recover an animal, even if it is lost in the end. As long as you can see a blood trail, and up to a certain period after the blood trail is lost, the hunter must put a strong effort into recovering the animal. Many hunters recover their deer only because they did not give up. It is not always an obvious blood trail that leads them to the downed deer, but simply a determination to keep looking.

To fulfill our ethical responsibility, the hunter must first consider the little things that begin the moment he pulls the trigger or releases the bowstring. You must watch the animal closely to see how it leaves the scene. Did it run or walk away? Did it stop and stand in one spot? Exactly which direction did it go? Surprisingly, being aware of these little things could make the difference in recovering or not recovering the animal.

Then comes the waiting game. You must know how long to wait before you begin tracking. Tracking too quickly, or too late, could make the difference in finding a downed deer, or causing a deer to go down. Different wounds require different waiting periods. Sometimes it is better to push the deer and other times it is better to wait for minutes, or even several hours, before you begin tracking.

Finally, it comes down to tracking skills. You must know what to look for, and where you will find valuable sign that could lead you to the deer. Will the deer bed down or will it run or walk until it drops? Some blood trails are sparse while others are easy to follow. What does it mean when you find blood in a pool and what does it mean when only droplets or smears are found? Yes, many questions come up when you discuss tracking a wounded deer. The following sections will provide the answers and solutions to these questions, and more. All hunters

Despite the hours of scouting and pursuing it takes to finally get a shot at that certain deer, you may also find yourself needing tracking skills before the hunt ends. It's the last phase of a successful hunt.

wonder what their chances are of recovering a deer they shot. Certainly, the possibility of a recovery depends upon several factors that you are probably aware of. However, to gain a little insight, one could consider one of the few wounded deer studies conducted in North America.

The Camp Ripley Study

During four bowhunts at Camp Ripley, Minnesota from 1992–93, research officials did an extensive wounded deer study. The study was conducted by Jay McAninch and Wendy Krueger of the Minnesota DNR, Dr. Dave Samuel of West Virginia University, and several colleagues.

After the interviews and statistics were completed, it was determined that archers reported hitting 955 deer. Interestingly, 693 bowhunters,

or 86.8 percent retrieved a deer. Surprisingly, only thirteen percent of the deer wounded were not recovered.

Also worth mentioning is the fact that Camp Ripley bowhunters apparently picked their shots wisely during the four hunts. Of the total archers that shot deer, and interviewed by trained officials when they checked out, sixty-six percent said they took "Broadside" shots, while twenty-eight percent claimed they took "Quartering" shots (quartering into and quartering away). Only a small percentage of the hunters said they took "Head-on," "Straight-Away," and "Straight Down" shots.

In ending this section and the final mention of our responsibility as a hunter, each of us must consider his or her actions and how they will reflect on all hunters. Non-hunters, even those that are not anti-hunters, don't want to hear about deer we did not recover. The Camp Ripley study certainly proved positive for hunters and negative for animal activists who have claimed that hunters are losing a large percentage of deer they wound. Certainly, bad hits are occasionally going to happen. We are human and we do make mistakes. Nonetheless, most of us do take warranted shots and recover most wounded deer.

A hunter once told me he had never lost a deer. I must believe he hasn't hunted too long. Anyone who hunts long enough with bow or gun is going to lose an animal someday, even if he shoots accurately and is the best tracker of the area. Regardless of whether you are a beginning deer hunter or a veteran, you will decrease the risk of losing an animal after reading the pages that follow.

Table Camp Ripley: Total deer hit and retrieved at Camp Ripley, Minnesota during 1992-1993.

	1992			1993	
	Hunt 1	Hunt 2	Hunt 3	Hunt 4	Average
Total Deer Hit	331	219	266	139	238.8
Retrieved Deer	248	158	190	97	173.3
Recovery Rate (%)	92.2	83.2	87.6	84.3	86.8
Loss Rate (%)	7.8	16.8	12.4	15.7	13.2

Analyzing the Shot

Before tracking, a hunter should analyze what happened right after the shot. These details are of little importance if the deer drops in its tracks, but can make a huge difference if the deer ran or walked away from the area when hit. The hunter must then decipher the rest of the puzzle, beginning with knowing whether he hit or missed his target.

Reactions of Deer

Consider the hunter who suffered from extreme anxiety when the deer approached to within thirty yards. He nervously and instinctively shouldered his rifle, and then squeezed the trigger. As the deer ran off, he stood in his stand and attempted to figure out exactly what had happened. He could hardly remember shooting and, once on the ground, had no idea where the deer had been standing moments earlier.

Even if the hunter scanned a large area looking for sign, he probably wouldn't be in the right place. He can't remember how the deer reacted to the shot, and has no idea if he hit the deer, or the type of wound he is dealing with. The situation now looks grim, and the chance of a quick, clean recovery appears slim. This scenario happens quite a bit. Many hunters fail to notice what goes on after the shot, and have no idea if they even hit their intended target. This usually leads them to look for their deer prematurely, which can result in pushing away an animal that might have been recovered. The fact is, many deer shot with bow or gun do not always show definite signs of being hit. However, the observant hunter will always notice a few of the finer details, details which can reveal if the deer was hit.

A deer's reaction to a shot varies. Of particular importance are the location of the wound and the nervousness of the animal when the shot was fired will affect its reaction.

Several years ago, my son John prepared to shoot as a nervous doe walked within easy bow range. She spotted his movement and looked up at the tree stand where he was perched. By this time John had already drawn, anchored, and settled his sights behind the doe's shoulder. He released and watched the arrow cleanly pass through the doe's lungs. The deer turned sharply and ran for thirty yards before stopping. Then she turned around, looked back, and snorted. She lunged forward a few yards and fell dead.

Another hunter I know spotted a deer in a food plot made a cautious stalk until he was within easy gun range. Moments later, the rifle roared and the buck jumped straight up in the air, indicating it had been hit. However, the buck did not take off rapidly. Instead, it stood there a couple of seconds, staring across the field, then put its head down and resumed feeding. As the shocked hunter prepared to shoot again, the deer suddenly dropped to its front knees. A second or two later, it rolled onto its side and took a few last kicks. The hunter later discovered he had made a perfect lung shot.

The reactions of these deer were unusual, but they demonstrate that unusual circumstances can happen. Most often, a lung-shot deer will turn and run away at break-neck speed, or sometimes drop instantly when the shoulder is hit. These deer did not, even though one of them had detected the hunter just before the shot.

Most wounded whitetails run away with their tails down. This is particularly true of those that are hit hard. Exceptions always exist, however. Some deer, when shot, only lope off and flag their tail side-to-side, as they would do when spooked from a bed. This is rare, but it does happen. Interestingly, the location of the wound may play a role in the deer's reaction to being hit.

For instance, most paunch-shot deer I have observed loped away, and seldom flagged their tail. In fact, when a whitetail does the unexpected and

Most wounded whitetails leave the scene with their tail tucked. There are always exceptions to the rule, however. For this reason, never assume you missed just because the tail was up.

flags its tail, it is usually one that has been hit in the vitals. About ninety percent of the deer I have seen that were shot in the heart, lungs, or both, ran away with their tail tucked. The remaining ten percent flagged and did not run as hard as those that kept their tail tucked. No one knows why these incidents happen. Wounds to bones or muscles usually send a deer running away hard, with their tail tucked. Seldom do these deer lope away with their tail flagging, even if the wound is only superficial.

It's important to understand the difference between bullet and broadhead wounds. The bullet produces shocking power and trauma, and does some damage to tissue, blood vessels, and organs. A bowhunter relies exclusively on a sharp broadhead and the damage it does to tissue, blood vessels, and organs.

The shocking power of a bullet often knocks a deer to the ground, even when the shoulder blade is untouched. It's also true that shock may cause a deer to stay down temporarily, or permanently. Temporary shock can often cost a hunter, however.

On one occasion, I shot a huge eleven-pointer at sixty yards with a slug gun. I later learned that the slug passed through the base of the neck where it

joins the shoulder, missing the vertebrate. However, when the deer dropped and lay motionless for five minutes, I believed the slug had probably hit the shoulder or spine. As I was on the way out of the tree, I spotted the deer beginning to move. Just as I reached the ground, the buck was on its feet, staggering away but gaining momentum with every second that passed by. Another hunter downed the deer a few minutes later, and I assumed that shock was the only thing that probably kept the deer down after I had shot.

Many bullet wounds result in shock to deer, even if the projectile does not hit vitals. Heavy projectiles, particularly those that expand, seem to hit the hardest and induce the most shock. That is not to say that the heaviest bullets are best to use, however. It only means that we may notice a deer's reaction to a heavier projectile more often than we notice a reaction to a lighter bullet. Keep in mind, bone and heavy muscle usually cause a projectile to expand more than softer areas such as the paunch. Additionally, rib bones are soft and seldom cause a bullet to expand as much as those that hit other bones or heavy muscle.

One shocking (I mean that literally) story I heard involved a Kentucky hunter who participated at a random-draw hunt. He knocked down a buck the first morning with his rifle, climbed down from his stand, and walked away to get his buddy. The two returned and began shooting photos as the proud hunter stood behind the deer and laid his rifle across the huge antlers of the buck. A couple of camera clicks later, the deer came to life, sprung to his feet, and bounded away. Neither hunter ever saw the deer again.

Is this story true? I don't know. Hearsay is usually interesting but the facts are sometimes twisted. Is it possible? Yes.

Shock can occur long after a deer endures an arrow or bullet wound. However, I have also seen deer go into immediate shock due to arrow wounds.

A Pennsylvania buck, that I hit high in the back, lay almost motionless when I approached some fifteen minutes after the shot. As I got within a few feet of the downed animal, it slowly got up and walked away, staggering with each step. Regulations did not allow me to carry a bow as I tracked the deer in the dark, so I could only watch as the deer moved away. The following day, I jumped the deer from its bed and it ran away, very alert. Eventually, the wound proved to be only superficial.

I know of two other loin-shot deer that were hit with arrows that seemed to go into temporary shock just moments after the shot. Paunch-shot deer, on the other hand, never seem to go into an immediate, paralyzing shock, nor do those hit in the vitals.

Some hunters may be more impressed with a gun wound, solely because of the knockdown power. However, this has little to do with overall damage. The sharp broadhead causes hemorrhaging that cannot be matched by a

projectile. In truth, the right broadhead is as lethal as any bullet.

I have already talked about deer running hard when shot. This is particularly common of deer that are not hit in the paunch. When a hit deer runs hard, it usually has its belly low to the ground and appears to be setting a new sprint record for the 100-yard dash. Another indication of a deer being wounded is that it will pass over the top of obstacles. I have seen them crash through brushpiles and other major debris that they would bypass any other time when fleeing from a bed after being jumped. Who knows what is going on in their mind, if anything? However, I must believe that they know survival is at stake when the wound occurs.

If you shoot at a deer that is with other deer, it will usually break away from the others shortly after leaving the scene. It may run with them a short distance, but the wounded deer will probably turn away and travel a different direction.

Blood is not always present at the location the deer stood when you took the shot. Still, a deer will usually leave scuffed areas on the ground when it tears away quickly.

You can safely assume a deer is wounded if it beds down within view of your ambush site. If you see the deer bed down, you should stay put, watch the deer closely, and let it make the next move.

A deer that leaves the scene and beds down within view is probably wounded. Deer often bed down when shot in the liver, stomach, or intestines. However, other wounds may also induce bedding close to the shot location. This commonly occurs when the deer does not know the hunter is there, but sometimes will happen even when it is sure of the hunter's presence. If you see a deer bed down, I would suggest you stay put and watch the deer closely. The idea is to let it make the next move. You can safely assume you have wounded the deer, and the last thing you want to do is send it running away to parts unknown.

Precise Locations

The hunter must make a mental note of the area right after the shot. The precise location where the animal stood is crucial when you attempt to decipher what happened, and you try to find blood. The further away you are from the location, the more difficult it may be to find the exact location.

Always pinpoint landmarks that you can search for later. Such a landmark may be a rock, a certain tree, or perhaps a little thicket. It is probably easier to make a mental note of a location if you are in a tree stand when the shot is taken, but even an

observant ground hunter can get close to the precise location where the deer once stood.

If anxiety clouds your awareness and prevents your seeing the precise location, take notice of the direction in which the deer walked or ran after the shot, and anything it passed by. Being close is better than not knowing at all. You can also assume that the precise location will look different from afar than up close. If this happens and you can't find the location, return to your original ambush site and look again. This tactic has helped many hunters on countless occasions to find the precise location where the deer stood, or the direction in which it ran. I have often returned to my tree stand to look over the area when I couldn't find blood sign or tracks.

Any deer that does not drop will usually kick up leaves at the location where the shot occurred. A careful examination of the area will reveal kicked-up leaves or debris, and sometimes tracks. Tracks may not appear as they do normally, however. The tracks

Always mark the location where the deer stood when the shot was taken. White toilet paper shows up better than clothing, or the accessories you carry.

The location of the wound has a lot to do with how the deer reacts after the shot. Deer hit in the vital organs, bone, or heavy muscle usually leave the scene rapidly. Paunch-shot deer often lunge forward, run a short distance, and begin walking.

of a deer that has fled from the scene usually appear as scuffed or scraped areas in the soil.

Once you find the precise location where you shot the deer, or where it left the area, mark it with something that is easy to see. Bright tissue paper hung on limbs about shoulder height works well, and you can see it for a long distance. I usually tear off one- to two-foot-long piece that can dangle loosely. Remember to remove the tissue paper after you have finished tracking the deer, or if you have determined a miss. The second best thing you can use is trail-marking ribbon. Camouflage hats, bows, guns, fanny packs, and other hunting accessories do not work as well as markers, even during daylight. If you do not have anything with you to mark the spot, clear a large bare spot on the ground. This will be easy to find if you return to the shot location.

Arrow and Projectile Analysis

Unlike the bowhunter who may retrieve an arrow and determine a hit or miss, the firearm hunter cannot rely on positive evidence, such as a clean or bloody arrow. However, the firearm hunter can look for shattered limbs and trees that may have marks which indicate a miss. On some occasions, after not finding blood, I have returned to the location where the deer was standing and analyzed the path of my projectile. Sometimes, I could find the spot where the deer tore away, and then locate something the projectile struck. A bullet that hits a tree or a large limb is sure to do some damage. All you have to do is find it.

A few years ago, during Indiana's muzzleloader season, a buck approached within thirty yards of my tree stand. The respectable eight-pointer walked broadside to me, offering a perfect shot. The crosshairs of my scope settled on the deer's shoulder and I squeezed the trigger. When the smoke cleared, I could see the buck running off with its tail flagging. Knowing I could not have missed, I climbed down and found where the deer had been standing before

it left the scene. Immediately, I could see a large clump of hair, apparently from the brisket of the deer. I could also see scuff marks in the leaves. However, a futile search revealed no blood or deer.

After I returned with friends later in the morning, I climbed back into the tree stand to look over the area in an attempt to pinpoint the deer's travel direction when it left. To my amazement, I could see a huge, shattered limb in a white pine only ten yards in front of my stand, about fifteen feet above the ground. Then I knew what had happened. The projectile had deflected after slicing through the limb, probably hitting the deer on the underneath side of its brisket, resulting in only a superficial wound. In fact, I could then remember seeing the limb in the scope before shooting. I had raised the gun slightly to miss the limb, but in doing so put it in the way of the projectile.

The bowhunter, if he or she does not see the arrow in the deer, usually looks for it beyond the location where the deer was standing. Following the flight of an arrow is not always possible and attempting to do so can lead to a poor followthrough and missed shot. Of course, an arrow may also deflect before it reaches a deer, and might not be found anywhere close. However, common sense usually has us looking for the arrow beyond the location where the deer stood. Upon finding the spent arrow, look it over for blood. If it is covered on all sides with blood, it usually signifies a pass-through. Be aware, though, that debris, particularly wet foliage, may clean an arrow of some or all of the blood. For this reason, a thorough examination is necessary before making a final determination.

The location of the wound will also determine how much blood will be on the arrow shaft. For instance, an arrow that passes through the paunch of a deer may have little or no blood on the shaft, and perhaps only a small amount of tissue. The same goes for an arrow that merely grazes a deer, or deflects on bone. Every bowhunter should look at an

The author examines his arrow for blood, tissue, or tallow. In rare situations, wet foliage and debris can wipe an arrow almost clean. Always examine a spent arrow carefully in good light to determine if you hit or missed. (Photo by Vikki L. Trout.)

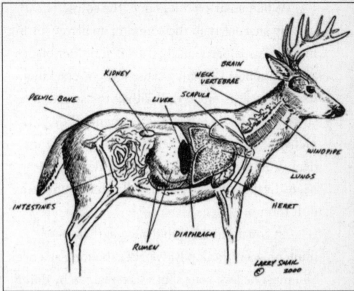

The hunter has an ethical responsibility to know the anatomy of a deer, and to take only those shots that will kill cleanly and quickly. Only then can he become a skillful tracker when a deer is wounded, and travels farther than anticipated.

arrow very closely, and do it under a light whenever possible.

My dad once shot at a doe that showed no signs of being wounded. He climbed down from his tree, found his spent arrow, examined it, and climbed back up in the tree convinced he had missed. As he sat there for awhile holding his bow, he began to see traces of what first appeared to be tallow on the shaft. Looking more closely, he determined it was stomach tissue. Additionally, he smelled an odor on the shaft.

This story had a successful conclusion. Knowing the arrow had passed through the paunch of the deer, he waited a few hours, then started tracking, soon picking up a few drops of blood a short distance from where the deer stood when he released the arrow. Following the trail slowly,

he found the doe 150 yards away where she had bedded down and died.

Both projectiles and broadheads may cut hair, and you may find hair at the precise location the deer stood. When found, it is usually positive evidence of a wound. Thus, if you cannot determine whether you have hit or missed the deer, look over the ground closely. Deer hair tells a very interesting story, as you have read in the previous section. Deer hair varies in size, texture, and color throughout the animal's body. For this reason, a close examination of deer hair may even tell you the location of the wound.

Sound Advice

Certain sounds may also offer positive evidence of a hit or miss. For instance, when an arrow hits the body cavity of a deer (the area behind the shoulder and in front of the hips), it usually produces a dull thump. Arrows that hit limbs or trees often produce a loud crack. This sound is similar to the sounds of an arrow that hits bone, but there is a distinct difference between the two.

When an arrow hits bone, the sound is usually sharper than the sound of an arrow hitting limbs. This is particularly true of shoulder blades and leg bones. Ribs may cause a slight cracking sound, but it is much duller than the sound of a shattering shoulder blade or leg bone. If there is plenty of distance between the shooter and the deer (200 yards or more), a projectile may be heard hitting the animal. Usually, that sound is a dull thump.

In conclusion, I would suggest that every hunter always think positive after shooting at a deer. You must believe your shot was on target. by doing so, you are sure to spend more time looking for sign that will determine whether you really hit or missed it. In fact, you should never give up looking until you are sure beyond any doubt that you missed. I don't have a problem with any hunter who fails to recover a deer they shot. Sometimes this can't be helped, and anyone can hit a deer poorly. However, assuming a miss without a careful examination, only to discover otherwise a few days later, is sure to be detrimental to our sport.

How long should you wait before tracking a wounded deer? Each hunter should make his decision based on the wound.

Blood Trails and Tracking

The best trackers are those who are patient. Following the trail of a wounded deer effectively requires you to do so slowly, cautiously, and quietly. You must consider many factors before starting to blood trail. This section will focus on tracking techniques, beginning with the precise location of where the deer was shot. Following a blood trail can be simple, or it can be difficult. Sometimes we make it more difficult than it is, while other times it is much more difficult than we expected. The location of the wound, the type of terrain, and how soon you begin tracking will all play essential roles in trailing the deer.

Tracking a wounded deer is an art that some have mastered through experience. Others jump right in and do a fine job the first time out. Good trackers do much more than follow drops of blood on the ground, however. A skilled tracker knows to look for blood smears, tissue, and hair. He knows if a wounded deer has bedded, is walking or running, and he can often follow a trail when blood does not even exist. Most important, he does not assume anything.

Before going on, let me say that there is one fact that stands out above the rest. A large amount of external blood does not necessarily mean that a deer is going down. Many of us have experienced these types of blood trails, but they do not always lead to a downed deer. I have seen some superficial muscle wounds bleed extensively for long distances. On the other hand, I have seen wounded deer go down within 100 yards, without leaving one drop of blood on the ground.

First Blood

There are many reasons why you might find blood at the location the deer stood when you took the shot. There are also many reasons why you might not find blood until you have gone a considerable distance from where the deer was standing. Moreover, there are also reasons why a deer may not bleed at all. The location of the wound, angle of the shot, diameter of the entry and departure hole, penetration of the projectile or arrow, and height of the entry and departure hole will decide how quickly a deer bleeds externally.

Extremely low wounds sometimes result in blood getting to the ground immediately, whereas high wounds will seldom result in blood getting to the ground until the deer has run a fair distance. Such was the case when southern Indiana bowhunter Ed Rinehart shot a small buck only a few yards from the base of his tree. The arrow entered high and just behind the shoulder, but did not exit. We spent more than an hour looking for blood of this lung-shot deer, but could not find anything. We finally found the buck piled up 125 yards from where Ed shot it. This deer did not leave one drop of external blood.

My dad once shot a buck from a tree stand, hitting it low in the stomach. Blood was splattered everywhere at the precise location where the deer stood. However, the blood slacked off to pin drops only fifty yards from that spot. After tracking the buck another twenty-five yards, the blood stopped. We later recovered the deer and discovered that the arrow had entered the deer in the bottom of its paunch, and exited in the middle of its underbelly.

I used these examples to give you an idea of why you do or do not find blood quickly. As mentioned previously, every wound will vary. Despite these variations, I will always look for blood at the location where the deer stood when shot. If I don't find blood, I will do my best to locate hair and scuffed marks. Then I will widen the search and attempt to find the first blood. In the following sections, you will read about each type of wound imaginable, and how soon you can expect to find blood. Most tracking endeavors cannot begin until you find the first blood. After finding the first blood, you can examine its color and know when to begin tracking.

Colors of Blood

Blood is not just red. It can be bright or dark. It can be darker than dark, or crimson instead of bright. Each wound gives off a certain color of blood, and that color should guide you when deciding how soon you should track the deer.

For instance, dark blood is the result of an abdomen wound. Muscle wounds result in bright blood, similar to lung-shot deer. However, a lung-shot deer may produce blood that appears almost pink. Heart, some artery, and kidney wounds usually result in bright to crimson blood.

If the hunter does not pay special attention to the color of blood, he may not know how long to wait before he begins to track the animal. The bowhunter, if he or she retrieves the arrow, can often determine the color of blood by looking at the shaft. If the shaft cannot be located, the bowhunter must do the same as the firearm hunter and locate the first few drops to make a determination. However, always consider the angle of the deer and the path of the projectile or arrow shaft. It is possible for a deer to leave both bright and dark blood. For instance, if your arrow or bullet enters the deer near its hip and exits through the paunch, it is possible you could find bright and dark blood. In this case the bright blood is usually more prevalent, but the fact remains that both colors could exist. If a hunter shoots a deer quartering toward him, his broadhead or projectile may enter the animal just behind the shoulder and exit in front of the hip. He will also find bright and dark blood. The bright blood would be from the wound to one lung, and the dark blood would be the result of the wound to the stomach and/or intestines.

Complete arrow or projectile penetration may determine how quickly you find blood. In case you're wondering, two holes are always better than one. First, consider that the path of the arrow or projectile is longer than it would be if it did not exit. The more it penetrates, the better the chance it will hit a vital organ, or artery. Additionally, an exit hole increases the chance of external blood getting to the ground, and the possibility that you will find blood sooner than you would have if only an entry hole existed.

Examining Arrows

Bowhunters can often obtain facts from a spent arrow, facts that can aid them in tracking. First, let's look at penetration.

Some trackers believe that good things come from an arrow that remains in the deer. For instance, it could keep the entry and/or departure hole from clotting. There is probably some truth to this theory, since coagulation can occur. I would much rather see a pass-through, though, simply because I will probably locate the arrow, and there will be a better chance the broadhead has hit vitals.

If tallow is present on an arrow, it indicates certain wounds. These wounds will be discussed in later sections. However, many wounds where tallow is found do not result in easy-to-follow blood trails, or dead deer. Exceptions do exist, however.

You may determine a pass-through by the straightness of the arrow shaft, and the blood you find between the nock and the broadhead. Bent or broken arrows, even when found at the location the deer stood when shot, sometimes indicate the arrow did not pass through. When the arrow hits, the deer often lunges. If the arrow hits a tree or heavy brush, it may break off or bend. You can usually determine penetration by how far the blood comes up the shaft, and by the location of the bend or break. If the arrow is bent or broken on the front half (nock end), you probably did not penetrate totally. On the other hand, if the bend or brake is on the business end, the

arrow has probably penetrated totally. You may also find blood on just one side of the arrow. This may indicate a graze, but not always. Debris and foliage, particularly when wet, can clean an arrow on one side, or all sides. An arrow that is found after you track a deer for a given distance also tells a story. For instance, an arrow that has penetrated totally will usually come out broadhead first, and fall to the ground from the exit hole. This is true whether you shot the deer from a tree stand or the ground. It will not work its way out through the entry hole if it has penetrated totally.

Sometimes, if a deer carries the arrow, it will bump into debris or trees, causing it to break apart and flip away from the blood trail. I can't tell you how many times I have tracked and found a deer, yet failed to see the arrow along the blood trail. Backtracking will usually turn up the arrow, however.

Waiting before Tracking

How long should you wait before tracking a wounded deer? Will waiting increase your chances of finding the animal, or will the delay hinder you? These questions are always sources of debate among hunters. Some hunters say you should push every deer, while others say it's best to go after some deer right away. A few believe you should delay tracking any wounded deer immediately. I will give you my opinions, and in doing so, explain how I have come to these conclusions. Although research has played a part in my opinions, my primary beliefs have come from in-the-field experiences.

When I started deer hunting in the 1960s, hunters always thought it best to sit back and wait twenty or thirty minutes before picking up the trail of a wounded deer. It was believed that the deer would bed down, stiffen, and eventually die if left alone, or be stiff enough so that it couldn't get out of its bed. If you jumped the deer, and it obviously had not stiffened enough to lay there and give you another shot, you should have waited longer before you started tracking.

Today, we know that a wound does not cause a deer to stiffen and die. It is the severity of the wound that will cause the animal to succumb, coupled with the length of time you wait before tracking it.

Rigor mortis is the stiffening of muscles after death. After a deer dies, it will begin stiffening. Various muscles will stiffen first, after a given length of time, although variables may affect the results.

John D. Gill of the Maine Department of Inland Fisheries, and David C. O'Meara, of Maine's Department of Animal Pathology, conducted a survey in the 1960s to estimate the time of death in white-tailed deer. For several days, they observed the carcasses of eighty-five deer shot by hunters. The two gathered data on body temperature, eye appearance, pupil diameter, and muscle stiffness. Their article and findings appeared in the Journal Of Wildlife Management, Volume 29, No. 3, July 1965.

To check rigor mortis, Gill and O'Meara gently flexed various joints by grasping the outer edge of the jaw, the upper end of the neck, the forelimb above and below either the wrist (corpus) or the elbow (humerus), the hind leg above and below either the ankle (tarus), or the knee (femur). The

Rigor Mortis Table: Numbers of observations of rigor mortis in deer. (Journal of Wildlife Management, July 1965, John D. Gill and David O' Meara.)

Rigor Mortis		Hours Since Death					
		1	2	3	4	5	6
Jaw	None	0					
	Partial	6	6				
	Stiff	1	18	28	24	14	18
Neck	None	4	14	6	1		
	Partial		2	16	28	14	20
	Stiff		1	4	10	13	17
Wrist (Carpus)	None	7	23	15	8	2	2
	Partial		5	24	37	33	26
	Stiff			1	5	4	15
Elbow (Humerus)	None	7	10				
	Partial		12	20	12	10	5
	Stiff		3	20	38	29	29
Ankle (Tarsus)	None	4	3	1			
	Partial	1	12	14	11	8	3
	Stiff		2	12	16	16	18
Knee (Femur)	None	4	2				
	Partial	1	12	5	3	1	2
	Stiff		3	20	21	18	20

team made certain they did not reduce or break rigor, and the degree of stiffness present was recorded as "None", "one-quarter inch", "one-half inch", "three-quarter inch", or "complete".

It was observed that muscles gradually stiffened soon after death, but would later relax because of internal chemical changes. Temperatures and other factors contributed to the rate of change in various parts of the body. Although more stiffening occurred in this sequence - jaw, knee, elbow, ankle, neck, and wrist, exceptions were mostly due to these four reasons:

1. Wounds may prevent, weaken, or delay rigor near tissue damage.
2. Rough handling may reduce or eliminate stiffening.
3. Differences due to air temperature (possibly masked by other variables).
4. Freezing confused with rigor mortis.

It was noted that jaws stiffened within two hours. Gill and O'Meara claimed the lower jaw clamped tightly with the lips concealing the teeth, although the tongue protruded. As the jaw relaxed, the front teeth became visible and the outer end of the jaw would flex about inch.

Stiffness, of course, may help you determine how long a deer has been dead, but it is not a factor before death. However, there is another consideration when wondering how long to wait before tracking a wounded deer.

We know that a running whitetail has about three times the heart rate per minute of a bedded deer. Thus, it is safe to assume that a moving deer will bleed more than a bedded deer, whether the bleeding is internal or external. Does this mean that a wounded deer should be tracked right away?

I say no, even though these facts have led some to believe that we should push all wounded deer, regardless of the location of the wound. Some

hunters claim that a moving deer will bleed out and die sooner than one that is bedded. Personally, I believe we should throw this theory out the door along with the stiffening hypothesis.

I will agree that heart rate and bleeding increases with movement. However, keep in mind that a moving deer is getting farther away with each step. I've had times when it took me an hour to follow a deer for 100 yards or less, simply because blood did not get to the ground when the deer was walking. And that's the bottom line: A wound that allows blood to get to the ground, particularly muscle wounds, could call for immediate tracking. On the other hand, a gut-shot deer that may leave very few drops of blood, or no blood at all on the ground for a long distance, should never be tracked immediately. Consider that stomach and intestinal matter may clog a hole in a deer, preventing blood from getting to the ground. A large broadhead or projectile may make a big hole, but that doesn't necessarily mean that an entry or departure hole will remain open and allow blood to reach the ground. I also know that a gut-shot deer will not succumb quickly, and will usually bed down if not pushed.

When tracking a deer, it is primarily a blood trail that will lead you to the animal. Obviously, the tracking becomes more difficult if no blood is present. Now consider the distance a deer may travel. In the case of stomach and intestinal wounds, many deer lay up a short distance from where they were shot. These wounds are fatal, and deer with such wounds will die within a given number of hours depending upon precise location of the wound - organ and artery damage. However, if you push the animal to increase the heart rate and induce bleeding, you still may get no more blood on the ground than you would have if you left the deer alone. Meanwhile, the deer gets farther away, and the chances of recovering it grow slimmer. Consider slowly pushing a deer for five minutes, and how far it could travel. If you allow the gut-shot deer to stay bedded, it will still bleed internally - perhaps slower than it would have if moving, but nonetheless the end result is still death. The best advice I can give is to consider distance. The further you must track a deer, the less chance you have of a recovery.

Fortunately, many hunters do wait to track stomach and intestinal-shot deer. But some insist upon waiting to track any deer, including those with muscle wounds, where increased bleeding could lead the animal to succumb when it other- wise may not have. Thus, you should evaluate every wound when deciding how long to wait. For instance, why wait to track a double lung-shot deer that will probably go down in seconds, a short distance away? Then again, waiting a few minutes and sizing up the situation won't hurt anything since the animal will obviously not be going anywhere. Waiting too long to track a deer with a muscle wound, though, could be damaging when coagulation begins. I have provided a table that you can use as a guide. I have stuck to this waiting schedule, as have other veteran deer hunters I know. The results have been spectacular and have led to the recovery of more than a few deer. Of course, you must know the location of the wound, and be aware of how it will affect tracking. Other factors, such as too many hunters in the area, terrain, weather, and darkness may also affect the length of time you should wait to track a deer. In the following sections, I have supplied anecdotes, and information about specific types of wounds that tell why it is best to wait or delay tracking.

Lack of patience should never tempt you to begin tracking a deer immediately. When I shoot a deer, I'm as eager as the next guy to get after it and see my trophy up close. However, you must be patient and wait if necessary. I would that many hunters who pursue an animal right away do so because they just couldn't stand the agony of waiting. Just as harmful would be waiting, but not waiting long enough. For instance, if you should wait for four hours and you wait for only one hour

Time to Wait Table: The author's schedule for waiting to track a wounded deer, by wound location. Variables may exist that will prompt or delay time to wait.

Location of Wound	Time to Wait Before Tracking
Artery (major)	20 minutes
Heart	20 minutes
Hip (muscle only)	20 minutes
Intestines	8 – 12 hours
Kidneys	20 minutes
Leg	20 minutes
Liver	2 – 3 hours
Lungs	20 minutes
Neck (muscle only)	20 minutes
Shoulder (muscle only)	20 minutes
Spine or Neck Vertebrate	0
Stomach	4 – 6 hours

to track a stomach-shot deer, you will probably push the deer farther away, just as you would have done if you had started tracking at once.

Throughout this book, I suggest that some wounds call for immediate tracking. After viewing the table, you might wonder why these wounds suggest you wait twenty minutes. Actually, staying put for a few minutes after shooting an animal will help you gain composure, and recall a few events that may help to put you on the blood trail. You may not pick up the trail until twenty minutes after the shot, but you are still in immediate pursuit and will probably prevent coagulation. When you do pursue a deer right away, you must move slowly and quietly from one drop of blood to another. Avoid getting ahead of yourself if you lose the blood trail, and keep a constant look ahead for a bedded or moving deer.

Reading Tracks

Just finding tracks when you trail a deer is helpful, but being able to read those tracks will provide valuable tracking insight. Tracks show you if a deer is running or walking. Tracks may indicate other factors, including the sex of the deer, size, and sometimes the type of wound the animal encountered.

Various types of wounds will cause a deer to run differently than it might have otherwise. For instance, a heart-shot deer often runs much more erratically than a lung-shot deer does. The running tracks of a deer with a stomach wound are totally different from one with a hip wound. Joseph Bruner, a German tracker, studied eight different sets of tracks of wounded deer. In 1909, Bruner provided an illustration of the track patterns in a book titled Tracks And Tracking (see table). In recent years, I have attempted to determine the accuracy of the track patterns and wounds depicted in the table. In many cases, the tracks I followed did not stay visible long enough, the deer stayed in woods and thickets and did not produce tracks, or the animal dropped dead before I could evaluate the tracks. Although I have yet to compare precisely the tracks recorded by Bruner and deer I have trailed, I have seen similarities - primarily the track patterns as a result of wounds to the foreleg and hind leg.

The back hooves of a deer are slightly smaller than the front hooves. It is difficult to provide measurements, since the size of the track is dependent upon the subspecies of the deer, age, and size. However, most adult whitetail tracks will be two and one-half to three inches in length when the animal walks. When running, the length and width of the tracks are slightly larger.

When you follow the tracks of a wounded deer, they often lead into other tracks, leaving you confused. This can happen in snow, even when it appears for a moment that you could follow the animal to the end of the continent. When the tracks you follow merge with other tracks, it is best to bend over, get close to the ground, and proceed cautiously. One thing you can bet on is that most wounded deer do not attempt to travel with others unless the wound is minor, such as a scrape under the brisket,

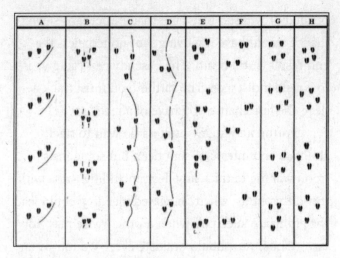

Wounded Deer Walking Patterns: (A) Trail of a deer shot through brisket with leg broken low in shoulder. (B) Trail of a deer shot high through the shoulders. (C) Trail of a deer with a broken foreleg - the lower the leg is broken, the more pronounced the drage mark. (D) Trail of a deer wit a broken hind leg - the lower the leg is broken, the more pronounced the drag mark. (E) Trail of a deer shot through the ham. (F) This trail usually means that the animal was shot through the intestines, liver or lungs. (G) Same as F but did not penetrate to the lungs. (H) The cross jump results from a bullet through the intestines or liver with the animal standing broadside to the hunter. (Joseph Bruner, Tracks And Tracking).

or a nick on the leg. I've also noticed that severely wounded young deer do not attempt to get back with the doe, nor does a severely wounded doe try to find her fawn.

Whenever I shoot a deer that is with others, it may run away with them, but will not stay with them long. After a short sprint, the wounded animal usually separates from the others. Thus, if you can't find blood near the location where you hit a deer, follow all the tracks but pay special attention to a track that suddenly separates from the others, or a track pattern that differs from the others.

When tracking a deer, it also helps to know if a deer is running or walking. For example, if walking tracks suddenly change to running tracks, it could be the deer detected your presence. Alternatively, the deer may have been bedded and detected your approach. Whenever a walking deer suddenly runs,

I evaluate the situation carefully. I may stay on the trail, or I may sit down and wait.

There are two ways to tell if a deer is walking - by tracks and by blood. First, we'll discuss tracks.

A running deer brings its back feet ahead of the front feet. The tracks will appear as a set of four tracks, with the tracks of the back feet parallel with each other, and in front of the tracks made by the front feet. Each set of four tracks will be spaced two and one-half to three feet apart.

When a deer walks, you will find two straight lines of tracks about fourteen to twenty inches apart. That's understandable, if you consider the body width of a deer. The toes of the tracks will also be turned outward slightly. The straight-line appearance of the tracks can differ, as well as the outward angle of the toes when certain conditions exist. For instance, when a doe's udder is filled with milk, the tracks made by the back hooves may be farther apart than the tracks made by the front hooves, and the tracks of the back hooves may curve more outward than the front ones. It is also believed that track patterns of does in estrous, and bucks in rut change slightly. A certain wound may also have an affect on how the tracks appear.

For many years, veteran hunters and trackers have argued about determining the sex of the deer by its tracks. The debate will continue, as some tracks may allow you to determine the sex of the deer, while others will leave you scratching your head.

The size of the track may help, but only when it comes from a big buck, and you are familiar with

A running deer brings its back feet ahead of the front feet. Instead of evenly spaced tracks, you will find set of four tracks each.

A walking deer's tracks will be in two straight lines, those made by the left, and those made by the right hooves.

the size of the tracks of an average adult deer in your area. If you have seen hundreds of tracks in the area made by deer weighing 125 to 150 pounds, and then come across the tracks of a 200-pound deer, you will probably see a noticeable difference, and believe they are that of a buck. However, I have seen one and one-half-year-old, 150-pound bucks with tracks as large as two-and-one-half-year-old, 200-pound bucks. In addition, tracks may appear larger and deeper in snow and soft soil than they would on a dry, dirt surface. And since a running deer's track appears larger than a walking deer's track, it wouldn't be wise to estimate the sex or size of the deer if it is running.

You will often find drag marks in snow when you follow the tracks of a buck, providing the snow is a certain depth. A buck seems to walk more clumsily than a doe, and it's a fact that does raise their hooves slightly higher than a buck's, probably because their pelvic structure differs from bucks. In deep snow, all deer leave drag marks. In fact, when examining the tracks of deer in captivity, I've found that the only way to see drag marks of bucks is when the snow is one to three inches deep.

In heavy leaves, you may also determine drag marks. However, that is very difficult to do since the depth of leaves and terrain can vary every few yards. The best chance of seeing a buck's drag marks in leaves is when the terrain is level, most of the leaves have fallen and are dry, and there has not been heavy deer traffic through that specific area.

A deer's hooves are designed to provide traction, but not on slick surfaces. On ice, a deer

Bucks will leave drag marks behind their tracks when they walk in snow. However, if the snow gets deep, all deer will leave drag marks.

walks very carefully, and appears to know that its hooves could slide out from under him. If the animal goes down, it may not be able to get back up.

Blood Trailing

Tracking a wounded deer, particularly one that does not leave an easy-tofollow blood trail, requires skill. Most hunters, who have mastered the art of tracking, did so because of experience. However, help is advantageous, regardless of your abilities.

I always find myself much more nervous when tracking my own deer. Secondly, it really helps to have more eyes looking for blood and a downed deer. My son and I have shared many tracking experiences in the past two decades, and I am always glad to have his help. He is a patient tracker, as are many of my friends who are proficient trackers. In recent years my wife, Vikki, has also assisted me with trailing, and while she usually stands patiently on the last drop of blood, she often finds more blood in that location while I'm out ahead somewhere.

Just how many should be involved when the tracking begins? I prefer a party of two or three. Four hunters are pushing it. I have often assisted when the tracking party consisted of four, five, or more. I find

things too noisy and careless, which can lead to a trampled blood trail or a spooked deer. When three people track the deer, one can stay on the last blood while four eyes continue looking for the next drop.

Although some blood trails are easy to see and can be followed rapidly, most difficult trailing episodes go from drop to drop. When you find one drop, look closely for another without moving too far ahead. If you can't find another drop within sight of the last, mark the spot before getting too far away. Never get in a hurry and start looking for a downed deer too quickly. Some hunters would rather look for a deer than a drop of blood. Their eyes never focus on the ground and surrounding debris for sign. This leads to careless tracking, and may spoil a recovery opportunity.

Walk to the sides of a blood trail as you follow it. If you walk over the blood, you'll kick up any drops that you've already found. While this may be okay if you find the deer a short distance ahead, it certainly won't do you any good if you have to return to the blood drops later on. For instance, what if the deer you're following suddenly begins backtracking? Surprisingly, some deer do turn around and go back in the same direction they just came from. If you walk a couple of feet to the sides of the blood trail, and mark it consistently, you should have no problem returning to the original trail if the deer turns around and walks back from where it came.

As mentioned previously, it helps to tie white tissue paper or trail-marking ribbon a few feet above the ground each time you find blood. Don't lay your marker on the ground, or tie it a foot or two above the ground, since it would be hard to see from a short distance away.

It may not be necessary to mark the trail if you are finding large amounts of blood, but it is necessary whenever you find blood droplets several feet apart. The markers allow you to return to the last blood, and they allow you to see the directional travel of the deer you are trailing. Many times, after losing a blood trail, I have looked back through the woods to see 100 yards or more of markers. I can then notice if the deer is veering right or left, and can concentrate on looking for blood in another direction. When the tracking ends, return to your location and remove the markers. Tissue paper will decompose eventually, but this may take several weeks. Seeing tissue paper strung through woods is not a pretty sight, and it won't do much for your hunting area.

Speaking of hunting areas, be aware that a major tracking episode will probably hurt your hunting area for several days. Consistently, I have seen areas dry up immediately following a trailing endeavor. However, when you consider the disturbance and the human scent left in the area, it's no wonder the hunting becomes stale. I always hope for a good rain to wash out human scent as soon as the tracking ends.

I've said this before: Despite what you may have heard, the volume of blood you find on the ground has little to do with your chances of recovering a deer. I have heard hunters (myself included) say, "This deer is about to go down." These opinions are often based on a heavy blood trail. However, many scrape and muscle wounds cause excessive bleeding that do not always result in a downed deer. These wounds produce blood trails that would make you believe an artery was severed, but after a couple of hundred yards or less, they begin to tell a different story. On the other hand, many stomach and intestinal-shot deer leave little or no blood, but will result in a downed deer. For this reason, it is best not to speculate when it comes to the amount of external blood, since it could affect your persistence to continue tracking if the going gets tough.

Large cuts across the bottom of the deer may result in excessive bleeding when the broadhead or projectile does not penetrate into the body cavity. They simply make a long incision. You might determine this type of wound at the location the

The amount of blood that gets to the ground often depends upon the location of the wound. Don't be mislead if you find very little blood. Many deer that do not bleed much externally may still be mortally wounded.

deer stood when you shot. A large section of hair, sometimes up to several inches, will be found on the ground after grazing an animal.

When the blood trail becomes difficult to follow, get down on your knees, or bend down to look for blood. You'll be surprised how much more blood you can find when your eyes are only a foot above the ground, particularly when nickel-size droplets suddenly turn into drops the size of pinheads. Getting on all fours is probably better than bending, but it can also damage an existing blood trail.

Many blood trails intensify as you follow them, while others begin to weaken. Several factors will determine the amount of blood that gets to the ground as the deer moves farther away. For example, you may follow the trail of a running deer that received a muscle wound. Each time the deer's heart pumps hard, blood is expelled through an entry and/or exit hole. If this deer begins walking, the blood trail may weaken.

A low hit can also cause more blood to get to the ground early in the tracking than it will later. A high hit works the opposite, since the blood you find on the ground may intensify after the deer travels a short distance. Then, consider a low hit, and blood

Get close to the ground if the blood trail becomes difficult to follow, but make certain you stay to the sides of the trail and don't walk over blood.

in the body cavity. As the deer travels, internal bleeding may occur. This blood soon reaches the hole in the deer and finds its way to the ground. Thus, the blood trail begins intensifying as the deer moves farther along the trail. Later, I discuss specific wounds and what kind of blood trails will occur as a result of these wounds.

You may find two trails of blood instead of one when complete penetration occurs. The possibility of two blood trails depends upon the location of wound, and the height of your entry and exit holes. However, if a single blood trail suddenly turns into two, make certain the deer is not backtrailing.

Previously, I told how you can tell if a deer is running or walking by its tracks. You can also determine if a deer is standing, walking, or running by examining blood droplets. When a deer walks slowly, you will find a line of droplets. Each droplet is round and completely encircled by thin splatter marks. The shape of the droplets is the same as those made by a standing deer, except they are not in a line. Instead, you may find several droplets in one location, perhaps covering a one- or two-foot area. When a deer stands, you might find a pool of blood as each drop merges with another. The amount of

blood you find on the ground depends upon the wound, and how long the deer stood there.

When a deer runs, the blood droplets are oblong. You may find splatter marks on the wide end of the oval droplet, but not on the opposite end. The wider portion of the droplet, which has the splatter marks, also indicates the direction the deer is traveling.

When you find blood in the deer's tracks, it usually indicates a leg, shoulder, neck, or ham wound. The blood ends up in the track after running down a leg, but this usually doesn't occur until the animal has traveled for a distance. It is also possible you may find blood on the ground between the left and right hooves, or about the center of the deer. This often occurs when you track a neck-shot deer, or if your departure hole came out on the bottom side of the deer.

Always examine the blood carefully to make certain it is indeed blood. There's nothing worse than losing a blood trail, then to have someone holler, "Blood," and then discover it isn't blood at all. The woods floor is full of red, maroon, and purple colors.

When you find two blood trails instead of one, it probably means the deer is bleeding out of both sides. However, always make certain the deer hasn't walked back the same trail it came through earlier.

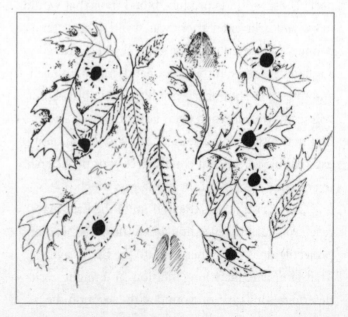

I've seen some maple leaves that had red blotches on them that look exactly like blood. Many types of berries splatter on the ground and appear as blood. When you are uncertain, use your saliva to wet the spot you suspect is blood. If it doesn't wipe off, you know it isn't blood. Another thought is to use hydrogen peroxide or a commercial blood tester.

When blood dries, it becomes darker and is harder to see. The more blood there is in one location, the longer it will stay wet. However, if you follow a dry blood trail and it suddenly turns wet, you probably got close to the deer and sent it moving.

When a blood trail expires, I will begin looking for blood smears on rocks, trees, tall weeds, and other debris. If I don't find smears, I resort to following trails and looking for tracks. If tracks are not visible, I look for another means of trailing the deer. For instance, when a deer runs in leaves, it leaves an obvious trail. The leaves are kicked out and piled up near the locations where the deer's hooves come off the ground. Even if the deer walks in leaves, careful tracking may allow you to follow the trail. When the hooves of a walking deer come down, they curl the leaves under each hoof.

Finally, don't take things for granted when tracking a wounded deer. This can get you into trouble. I try to look at each trailing experience as a unique one. I often know what to expect, but avoid

A deer that walks will leave blood droplets that are round with splatter marks surrounding the drops.

When a deer runs, it leaves a different blood trail. Notice the oval shape of these blood droplets, and that splatter marks are only at one end of the droplet.

Many leaves and berries can resemble blood. If you have any doubt if what you found is blood, test it with hydrogen peroxide or a commercial blood tester.

making guesses. I stay on a blood trail as long as possible, and then resort to tracking the animal the best I can when blood is not getting to the ground. When I can't track the deer any longer by blood or tracks, and all other efforts to locate them have been to no avail, I begin the recovery attempt. For this reason, it's important for you to read the section, "Last-Ditch Efforts."

The String Tracker

The bowhunter who chooses to use a string tracker may find it beneficial when it comes to recovering a deer. However, you should be aware of a few disadvantages.

A friend of mine, Woody Williams, used a string tracker in Ontario while hunting black bear.

After shooting a bear, he nervously watched the string unwind until it stopped. He believed the bear was down.

Shortly after dark, Woody and I got on the trail of the wounded bear. We found blood here and there, but easily followed the line that had unraveled from the string tracker. About 150 yards later, we reached the end of the line (I mean that literally). It had caught in debris and broken. We never recovered the bear.

String tracking line is tough, but it can break. Archers should also be aware that arrow flight and accuracy can change when using a string tracker. The farther you shoot, the more drop you will have. When I used a string tracker for the first time several years ago, I found it necessary to adjust my sight when shooting at twenty yards. My arrows dropped about four inches. At thirty yards, the drop increased dramatically. If you plan to use a string tracker, plan to practice often.

Wind can also cause problems when using a string tracker. The loop of line that dangles loosely from the canister to the business end of the arrow may catch on accessories or limbs, causing the string to unravel.

On the positive side, a string tracker can give you several hundred yards of easy tracking if you make a bad hit. If the line gets to the end of the spool, simply tie on line from an extra spool. This can add another few hundred yards of easy tracking. A string tracker may also help you track a deer if it rains. Finally, a string tracker makes it easy to locate your arrow when you miss, or if it totally penetrates. If the arrow does go all the way through the deer, however, you may find two trails of line when you follow it.

Tracking with Dogs

No hunter will dispute a dog's ability to follow a trail. We also know that a dog will do a better job than we can of tracking a wounded deer. After all, they can follow a trail by scent, while we must use our eyes.

However, the idea of using dogs does not appeal to every hunter. Instead, they believe that it is the hunter's responsibility to do everything humanly possible to recover the animal, without the aid of a dog.

This is a touchy subject, so I might as well jump in and give my opinion. I don't have a problem with using dogs in some tracking situations, but a thin line exists. Where dogs are legal, I often wonder if it can lead to careless shooting on a hunter's part. If they have access to a quality dog, would they take risky shots? Stress is another factor. Is it possible that an unleashed dog would cause undue stress when it trails a deer that has received only a minor wound? I believe so. If I started deer hunting in a state that allowed dogs to trail deer, I might see it from a different perspective. But I have another opinion. If a deer is doomed and will surely die, such as a gut-shot deer, and all tracking efforts by the hunter have failed, it would seem better to use a dog than to not find the animal at all.

At the time of this writing, trailing dogs are legal in fifteen states. In one of these states, however, dogs must be on a leash. There is also an organization dedicated to helping others recover deer with the aid of dogs, but not until the hunter has made a thorough recovery attempt.

I must tip my hat to Deer Search, Inc. (D.S.I.), a New York group of volunteers that uses leashed dogs to track and find wounded deer. There are sixty members in the western chapter, where Mike Coppola is a trustee, and past president. According to Coppola, his chapter received about 550 requests to track wounded deer in 1999. He reported that the chapter assisted in about 200 of the requests. Each request is evaluated when the call comes in. Coppola said that a large percentage of the wounds are shoulder hits. However, D.S.I. makes every effort to help hunters recover liver and gut-shot deer. Even

States that Allow the Use of Trailing Dogs

Alabama	New York
Arkansas	North Carolina
California	South Carolina
Florida	South Dakota
Georgia	Texas
Louisiana	Virginia
Mississippi	Wisconsin*
Nebraska	

*Dogs must be on a leash.

the organization's brochure states, "D.S.I. is NOT a hunter's crutch, it is an agency of Last Resort." After you have tried everything else you know to do and still circumstances prevent you from recovering your wounded deer (or bear), call Deer Search, Inc. For more information, contact Deer Search, Inc., P.O. Box 853, Pleasant Valley, NY 12569, or call 716/648-4355. www.deersearch.org

Tracking Accessories

Deer hunters pack along all kinds of gadgets, from grunt calls and scents to wind-checking devices. Why not prepare a tracking kit? Surprisingly, you can include about everything you could possibly need in a fanny pack or small daypack. If you are hunting close to home or a vehicle, you can leave the pack stored away until duty calls.

The most important items are probably markers to place above blood droplets, a proper light for

Tracking Kit Essentials

Compass	String Tracker
Field Dressing Gloves	Toilet Paper
Hydrogen Peroxide	Topographic Map
Knife	Tracking Book
Light/Lantern	Trail Marking Ribbon
Radio	

Store these items in a fanny pack or daypack, and keep them close by.

To make certain you have everything when tracking becomes necessary, consider packing a tracking kit in a daypack or fanny pack.

tracking in the dark, and hydrogen peroxide, or a commercial blood testing chemical. However, there is an array of other items listed in the Tracking Kit table that you may find useful. Some of the items

© Ted Rose

Taking time to evaluate all the signs and then planning a course of action is often crucial to locating a wounded deer.

you may have with you, but nonetheless the kit makes certain they will be there when tracking a deer. I would also suggest you pack along this book if space allows. This will make it possible for you to recognize the type of wound you are dealing with by blood color and hair. Additionally, you will have quick access to tracking tips.

I consistently pack a tracking kit, hoping that some of the items won't be used. As they say, though, "It's better to have it and not need it than need it and not have it."

Butchering Deer

JOHN WEISS

Bringing Your Deer Out

The act of getting a buck out of the woods and back to one's parked vehicle, camp, or home seems to perennially be riddled with misinformation. It's logical to assume that dragging a deer requires only a strong back and weak mind. But since I've always been adverse to hard work, I've tried every conceivable way of transporting deer in the hopes of lucking upon small tricks that might make life easier. Much of what I tried in earlier years didn't work very well.

One ludicrous idea that never fails to appear in sportsmen's magazines every year is a sketch of two hunters carrying a deer that is trussed upside-down to a long pole they've lifted and are carrying

The only time the animal should be lifted and bodily carried is when there is standing water and swampy terrain. Don't use a single log carried high on your shoulders as sometimes depicted in sportsmen's magazines. Instead, use two sticks to fashion a stretcher-like affair to lower the deer's center of gravity.

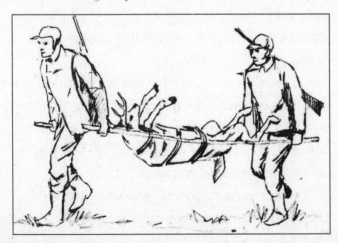

on their shoulders. What I learned is that the high center of gravity of the deadweight mass will cause the carcass to shift and sway around. The end result of that bouncing weight is hunters arriving back in camp with back pains and shoulders rubbed raw.

There is only one situation in which I recommend this or the similar procedure of carrying a deer on a stretcher-like affair between

A simple variation of the stretcher-carry is making a travois so that the lower part of the animal's weight is on the ground.

The most common method of removing a deer from the field is to simply grab the antlers and begin dragging. But there are better ways that are safer and easier on the body.

two poles. That's when a deer is killed far back in swampy habitat and must be bodily lifted and carried to avoid being dragged through water and black muck.

The most common method used by hunters is simply grabbing the deer's antlers with one hand or the other and dragging the animal across the ground. Although the practice is widespread, words of precaution are in order.

If the drag is a long one, and one's youth slipped away many sunsets ago, all kinds of back and shoulder problems may ensue. The reason for this is that the dead weight of the animal on the ground presents a very low center of gravity, requiring the hunter to bend low to grab onto it and remain in his crouched position through the duration of the drag. This results in tremendous strain upon both the vertebral column and its contiguous musculature, often causing you to remember the dragging experience far longer than you would have liked. Also, should you slip on wet leaves or snowpack, there's at least a fair possibility of pointed antler tines going into your calf muscles.

Sensible Methods that Work

One technique is no more complicated than using a short length of rope and a stick of wood that's about two inches in diameter by two feet in length.

First raise the deer's front hooves and place them behind the antlers (or behind the ears if it's a doe) and lash them to the neck so they are up and out of the way, eliminating their resistance against the ground and giving you a somewhat pointed object to pull through the cover.

Next, time the other end of the rope to the center of the stick and begin wrapping it around until it's about two feet from the deer's head. At this time, take a half-hitch around the stick with the rope so it won't unwind.

Now place your hands behind your back, one holding either side of the drag stick, lift the head and front shoulders of the deer slightly off the ground, and begin heading for camp. Compared to grabbing onto the antlers and heaving-ho, this method allows you to stand almost at full height while dragging. And since there is about a one and one-half foot distance from your backside to the antlers, there's little chance of them ever gouging you.

Ideally, the best thing is using this drag method with a partner, each grabbing onto one side of the stick. It is amazing how easy this makes the job, especially if you have gloves to protect your hands. When your right hand and arm get tired (your partner will be on the opposite side, using his left hand and arm), stop to catch your breath and then switch places for a while.

This is the recommended method of removing a deer from the field if the required dragging distance is just a few hundred yards or if most of the route is downhill. If it's a longer drag, or if it will take you uphill, there are easier methods.

One is using some type of shoulder harness. Many varieties are available in sporting-goods

A short, stout length of branch is an easy way to drag deer across flat terrain.

If the drag is a relatively long distance, and part of it is uphill, a shoulder harness allows the back and shoulder muscles to bear most of the workload.

stores and through hunting mail-order catalogs like Cabela's and RedHead/Bass Pro Shops. Most have the same type of webbed seat-belt material used in vehicles. And some of the more common types have a belt that buckles around the waist, or a diagonal shoulder strap with a longer strap or rope going off the backside that is tied to the deer's head.

Not too long ago I tested one of these devices by dragging a heavy log around my backyard and found the going surprisingly easy. Then, later in the season, I archery-killed a fat doe and found the dragging easier still. I was pleased as punch, until the following year when I killed a buck and ran into all kinds of difficulties. The antlers kept digging into the ground or grabbing roots and brush, continually jerking me to a sudden halt.

Then I had a brainstorm. Why not drag the deer by its hind legs instead of its head, so brush and other obstacles would slide right over the natural curvatures of the rack? It works great, with one exception. Since you're dragging the carcass against the grain of the hair, the hide will be ruined.

A somewhat different gizmo is called the Deer Drag. This affair consists of a length of heavy-duty aircraft cable and a comfortable rubber handle that is not hard on the hands. Just slip the cable noose over the head or antlers, snug it up a bit, and when you begin dragging, the short length of cable is designed to lift the head and neck of the animal off the ground.

Still Better Ideas

It's been said that everyone achieves a fleeting moment of fame at least once in his life. And for Jim Matthews of Duluth, Minnesota, that brief moment involved a common sheet of plastic.

The Peter Fiduccia Lifetime Deer Drag is a safe drag to use and easy to carry. This handle-type deer drag, with a short length of cable around the base of the antlers, makes short work of getting deer out of the woods.

As a taxidermist, Matthews wanted to make a full-body mount of a deer for his studio. This meant somehow getting his deer out of the woods without dragging it on the ground and scuffing up the hide.

"If you place the plastic on the ground, lay the deer on top, and then wrap the plastic around the carcass and tie it with cord before you begin dragging, you'll be amazed," Matthews explained. "The slick-surfaced plastic reduces ground friction against the hide by at least fifty percent."

Hearing this, I wasn't surprised the following year when a Wisconsin company introduced the Deer Sleigh'r, available through mail-order hunting catalogs. The Deer Sleigh'r improves upon Matthews' idea because it's made of a special heavy-duty plastic that won't tear when dragged over sharp rocks and brush. I tried it that season and found I could easily drag a one hundred eighty-pound animal with just one hand. Moreover, if it's a drag of a mile or more, the gizmo can easily be towed behind a four-wheeler.

Making Hard Work Easy

When dragging a deer by any method, take it slow and easy, particularly if you're over forty years old. Pace yourself. Stop every fifty yards or so, even if you do not feel overly tired. This rest time allows you to scout ahead a bit for the easiest drag route. In this manner you can find and then take advantage of slight variations in the terrain, avoiding even short uphill drags and following the best trail to skirt rock formations, blowdowns, or other obstacles.

It's usually best to take a slightly longer route if it enables you to stay on level ground or drag downhill. I've even been known to briefly drag my deer in the opposite direction of camp if it means eventually coming to dry, powdery snow, damp leaves, pine needles, or some other terrain surface that allows the remainder of the drag to see the deer carcass effortlessly slide along.

When hunting alone, I like to use the leap-frog method to simultaneously bring out my deer and the hunting equipment I was using that day. Simply drag the deer fifty yards, stop, then go back and pick up your rifle or bow, portable stand, heavy outer coat, and any other gear, and carry the stuff fifty yards beyond the animal. Then return to the deer and drag it up to where the gear is.

This change of pace makes deer dragging far less tiring. But also, you can do a bit of scouting for the easiest drag route and move aside any dead branches or other obstacles that may be blocking the route as you're carrying your equipment forward.

Better still is when there are three or four hunters in the group. Two can begin dragging the deer. The third carries all the rifles and day packs. The fourth works farther ahead, finding the best trail and pushing aside debris. Then, every two hundred yards or so, they alternate positions.

Horse-Packing Your Deer

In most situations, a hunter who has successfully collected his deer will find he's within relatively easy dragging distance of a road or trail. This is typically the case when whitetail hunting east of the Mississippi. There are some situations, however, in which whitetails are taken in remote backcountry places, especially in the northern border states, Canadian provinces, and in many Rocky Mountain states where they often coexist with mule deer and elk.

In such cases, dragging a deer all the way to camp or a vehicle may be impossible, and this leaves only three choices. You'll probably not seriously consider the first option, hiring a helicopter to fly in and hover overhead while dropping a cable down to you and your deer. Don't laugh. I heard of a multi-millionaire computer programmer, who works for Microsoft, who does that very thing every year.

The other alternatives–far more realistic approaches–are using either your back or a horse's back to transport your venison.

Removing a deer by horseback is possible In many deer-hunting situations. Ranchers who live near popular hunting regions commonly offer this service for hire.

The easiest, of course, is leading a packhorse to camp with your deer meat aboard. Most hunters obviously don't own horses (or mules), but in those regions where they are most likely to be needed for hunting work they are widely available for rental. Check the Yellow Pages of a local phone book, the classified ads in local newspapers, or ask the nearest rancher.

Even though horses or mules may not be playing a daily role in your hunting activities, it's wise to learn in advance which ranchers in your hunting area have them available. Most likely you'll be able to navigate your four-wheel-drive truck or ATV close to the kill site and retrieve your deer by dragging it the remaining distance. But it's nice to know where you can obtain four-footed help in bringing out your animal, if your deer runs into upside-down real estate before dropping, or if you sprain your ankle.

Rarely do ranchers simply hire out horses or mules and let strangers drive away with them in transport trailers. It's standard practice that when you rent a horse or mule, you also hire the owner or one of his hired hands for a few hours; that individual knows how to bridle the animal, which types of saddles or pack carriers to use and how to cinch them in place, how to load and distribute the game meat, how to control the animal, and all the rest. It will cost more than just a couple of bucks to remove your deer from the hinterland in this manner, but at the same time you save worry, hassle, and mistakes because the person hired assumes the responsibility of getting your precious venison cargo and antlers back to where you can resume caring for it yourself.

Get a Faux Horse or Mule

Although a live horse or mule does a yeoman's job of removing a deer from the field, we've seen how they involve pre-planning and a good deal of expense. A neat substitute are two items my friend Ray McIntyre conceived. Called The Horse and The Mule, they are far from being hay-burners.

McIntyre used to be the head man of Warren & Sweat, the company that made premium tree stands, and his latest brainstorms are carryalls fitted with one or two small bicycle wheels that can be pushed or pulled to transport deer across even fairly rugged terrain. The Horse's unique design places the weight over the axle, producing almost zero pounds at the handle, allowing one man to simultaneously transport two large deer if necessary. The Mule is designed for transporting one deer and is especially well-suited for use in snow and swamps, and goes over logs and rocks with ease.

Backpacking Your Deer

In situations in which horses (either real or mechanical) are not available, or cannot be used due to the inhospitable nature of the terrain, you must

Hunters who frequently find their quarry in steep or rugged terrain prefer a single-wheel carryall for efficiently removing their deer from the field.

Two-wheeled carryalls are popular with many hunters. They'll carry a heavy load and are best suited for level terrain where there is not much cover blocking the route.

become the beast of burden yourself and carry the deer out on your back. This is why I always have the following items in camp or back in my vehicle: a lightweight, tubular backpack frame, several muslin gamebags, a twenty-foot length of thin nylon lashing cord, a heavy-duty folding knife with a small saw blade in its housing, and a canteen of water. Seldom are these ever needed on an average deer hunt, but when the fateful day arrives, as it eventually will, they're more than worth any inconvenience of having them along.

After field dressing your deer, and with it now laying on its back with its body cavity propped open to allow cooling, hike back to your vehicle to get your packing-out essentials. This allows you to carry out the liver and heart on that first trip and to simultaneously relieve yourself of your rifle, binoculars, and other gear no longer needed that day. You can also exchange your heavy outerwear for lighter-weight garments; just be sure you continue to wear your orange vest.

After returning to the kill site, use your knife's saw blade to remove the deer's four lower legs at the knee joint; this will lighten the overall carcass weight by ten pounds.

Next, cut the head off at the base of the neck where it joins the main body torso. This load, depending upon the weight of the antlers, will probably be around forty pounds.

Finally, cut the deer into two equal halves; the front half will weigh about forty pounds and the back half about fifty pounds. This leaves three relatively easy packloads to carry out.

The only disadvantage to packing out a deer in this manner, other than the physical work involved, is that the hide must be sacrificed. Although the hide could be entirely removed from the carcass before cutting it into three sections, I prefer to leave it attached to serve as protection for the venison. Each carcass section is then slipped into its muslin gamebag to further protect the venison from trail grime and insects, especially where the hide has been cut and meat has been exposed.

A few other tips are also worth passing on. If the weather permits, it's wise to leave the field-dressed deer at the kill site until the following morning before reducing it to backpacking sizes. The cold night air will rigidly firm up the meat, making it easier to handle than when it's warm and soft. Obviously, temperatures warmer than 50°F during midday precludes this approach; when it's hot you'll want to get your venison back to camp as quickly as possible.

Also, when lashing down the large carcass sections on the packframe, take whatever time is necessary to balance the heavy load. You don't want to find yourself carrying a lopsided load, as this invites losing one's balance and falling, or possibly spraining an ankle on the greater weight-bearing foot. Try to distribute the meat evenly, so it is shoving straight down on the centerline of the packframe.

Also try to position the weight as high as possible (within reason) on the packframe. This will allow you to maintain a normal upright stance while hiking, rather than being hunched over. The

In the most rugged terrain, the only option may be to bring out your deer piecemeal by first reducing it to quarters at the field dressing site and then lashing them to a packframe.

advantage here, particularly if you have a waist belt on your packframe, is that your hips and strong upper leg regions can help bear the brunt of the weighty load rather than your back alone having the entire responsibility.

Camp Care of Deer Meat

Outside your mountain cabin the dark chill of night is beginning to settle like a shroud over the landscape and sparkles of frost are littering the ground like bits of broken glass. The wind is howling ominously and there are spits of sleet in the air. But at this moment nothing could dampen your spirits, for only a dozen paces from the front door a single handsome buck hangs from a birch limb in testimony to your hunting skills and hard work. It's the first deer to arrive in camp and you're both proud and satisfied that you've earned every ounce of your winter's supply of venison.

So spend the evening celebrating, but bear in mind that your deer is going to require a good bit of attention during upcoming days. You'll want to ensure that the venison remains cool and protected from flying and crawling marauders, and you'll want to clean the carcass for the trip home. Your mind is buzzing with things to remember and steps to follow. But now is the moment to throw another log on the fire, graciously accept another handshake, and sip once more from your hot mug.

Hanging Your Deer

As soon as deer have been transported back to camp they are traditionally hung from some type of overhead device. I prefer a stout tree limb because

A hanging deer makes a happy camp; many hunters prefer to hang their deer from the head.
(Photo by Tom Slinsky)

little work is involved compared to building a horizontal meatpole of sorts. Also, if it's still early in the season and the weather is warm, leaves on the trees will shade your animal carcass from the bright sunlight.

Whatever the design of the hanging mechanisms, however, their purposes are all the same: namely, to get the animal up and off the ground so it can be worked upon, so the carcass will remain clean of dirt, so ground-crawling critters won't bother it, and so air can circulate to facilitate cooling.

Visit almost any camp and you'll see many deer hanging by their heads while others are hanging by the hind legs, their owners claiming the matter is no more than personal preference.

There are several reasons why I prefer hanging deer by the hind legs. With the carcass in this position, remaining body heat is free to rise and easily escape. Conversely, if you hang a deer by the antlers, rising body heat will find itself trapped inside the chamberlike chest cavity, actually causing the upper half of the carcass to begin slightly warming up again!

Also, the greatest quantity of a deer's blood, lymph, and other body fluids are located in the front half of the body. Most of these fluids have been removed during earlier field dressing activities, but there's still some remaining in the deer's smaller veins and arteries and throughout tiny pockets and intramuscular spaces. When the animal is hung, these body fluids, like all liquids, will begin to slowly drain to the lowest elevation they can find. This is all to the good, but you'll want them to exit the carcass as quickly as possible, not slowly seep down over and through the carcass and perhaps invite the growth of bacterial spoilage or impart the venison with objectionable flavors.

If you'll recall, during field dressing operations the windpipe and esophagus were severed high up in the neck region. Therefore, if the deer is hung by the

The author prefers to hang a deer from the back legs instead of the head. This allows body heat to quickly escape from the carcass so the venison can begin to rapidly cool.

hind legs, any residual body fluids wanting to drain away will simply follow a short, downhill course through the now-wide-open windpipe/esophagus region and quickly pass out through the nostrils and mouth without contacting any valuable cuts of meat. In fact, a day or two later you'll notice a puddle of the stuff on the ground directly beneath the animal's head.

Hanging a deer by the hind legs requires the use of some type of gambrel inserted horizontally through the Achilles tendons. Be sure to hang your deer higher than you ordinarily might if there are coyotes or free-roaming dogs in the region. (Photo by New Hampshire Game & Fish)

There are many ways to lift your deer off the ground. The Armstrong Method, with the help of several partners, is the most common. You can also use an ATV or pickup. If it's a one-man operation, you can't beat a small block and tackle made for the purpose.

To hang a deer by the hind legs, first make a two-inch-long slit with a knife through the thin skin separating the hock of each rear leg from the Achilles tendon. Then insert the opposite ends of a gambrel through these two holes, tie a rope to its top center, and hoist the deer aloft. Gambrels all serve the same function but vary somewhat in design; they're available through hunting mail-order catalogs and at farm-supply stores.

Actually lifting the deer off the ground is most commonly done with the help of partners, using

the Armstrong method. But if alone, a miniature block and tackle makes the work a breeze, as does fashioning a pulley to the overhead tree limb and pulling on the lift-rope with a vehicle or ATV.

Initial Meat-Care Procedures

At this point I'm going to discuss various venison-care activities every hunter must attend to sooner or later. The sequence in which these tasks are performed may vary, depending upon average daily air temperatures, prevailing weather conditions, and so on.

Generally, when my deer arrives in camp, the first order of business, even before hanging the animal, is removing the heart and liver from their plastic bag and placing the two organs in a clean pail filled with water and one cup of salt. It's even wise to cut the liver into two or three large pieces to expose the inside, although this is not necessary with the smaller heart.

Slosh the organ pieces around in the water to remove surface debris, dried blood, and interior blood clots. In a few minutes the water will turn bright red. Dump this water out and add fresh salted water. Rub the liver gently with your hands and poke your fingers inside the large arteries of the heart to further loosen and dislodge blood clots from inside. When the water turns bright red still again, discard it and again replenish the supply with clean salted water.

Now, allow the heart and liver to soak for six to eight hours. This final soaking will thoroughly purge both organs of any remaining traces of blood. If you've never cared for venison liver or heart, perhaps they were never cared for properly in this manner; otherwise, don't leave them in the field because there are sure to be others in camp who would appreciate having them.

After the liver and heart have completed their soaking period, rinse them with clean water and place them on a drainboard for fifteen minutes.

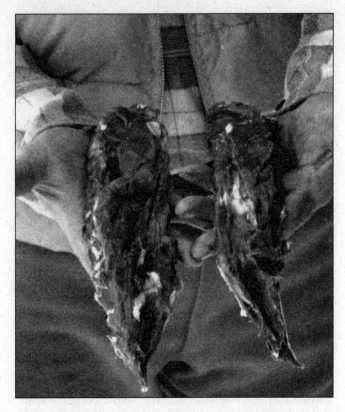

The first venison to be tended to in camp is the heart and liver, which should begin soaking in salt water. Then immediately remove the tenderloins from inside the rib cage; these are the most tender cuts, comparable to a beef's filet mignon.

Then place them in a plastic bag in your refrigerator or camping cooler. Traditionally, liver and heart are consumed in camp for dinner the first night or the very next morning for breakfast. They can also be properly wrapped and frozen for later use, although fresh liver is always superior to that which has been frozen.

At this time, I also like to remove the tenderloin steaks.

These should not be confused with the long backstraps located on the exterior of the carcass along either side of the backbone and which require removing the hide to obtain. Rather, they are much smaller, only two inches in diameter by about twelve inches in length, and they are located along both sides of the backbone inside the chest cavity.

I call them mini-tenderloins, but whatever they're called, they are the most tender venison any deer possesses and anatomically are comparable to the filet mignons of beef steers. The easiest way to remove these prime strips of meat is by using a small knife, even a pocketknife, to separate one end or the other from attachments along the backbone and then filleting them the remainder of the way out. When the deer carcass is hanging by the hind legs, with the body cavity open and exposed, removal of the mini-tenderloins is far easier than when the deer is hanging by the head, which prevents you from easily seeing your work.

Strangely, many hunters leave the mini-tenderloins in their deer until they later begin full butchering operations at home, but I advise against this practice. By that time the tenderloins, since they have no protective hide-covering, will have acquired a glaze or hard casing on their exposed surfaces, which must then be trimmed away, resulting in a significant loss of the prime meat. A much better approach is to remove the mini-tenderloins as soon as possible, trim them of bloodied areas and fat, then quickly refrigerate them.

Another thing in favor of removing the mini-tenderloins in camp is to please any partners who dislike liver or heart but would nevertheless like to share in the celebration of eating venison on the eve of the first deer brought into camp.

With the heart, liver, and mini-tenderloins attended to, your next chore is cleaning the deer carcass still hanging outside. Use a small knife to trim away bloodied, unwanted skin and tissue remnants and fat globs surrounding the field-dressing incision and throughout the abdominal and excretory regions; you're not going to eat these anyway, so why allow them to become breeding areas for bacterial contamination that may spoil adjacent meat areas?

If enough water is available, I like to wash out the inside of the body cavity. Many hunters consider this a cardinal sin, claiming water should never be allowed to touch meat or other parts of the carcass, but according to professional butchers this is merely another old wive's tale. Washing, particularly if a bit of salt is dissolved in the water, facilitates the removal of dried blood and other debris that may not have been entirely removed during field dressing or that found its way inside the body cavity when the deer was being dragged out of the woods. Removal of these potential contaminants is imperative if the carcass is to properly age without spoiling. Just remember to use your water sparingly (most of it will drain downward and exit through the nostrils and mouth) and afterwards use clean rags or paper towels to completely blot up any remaining moisture; the ribs should literally shine.

If the deer was backpacked out in large chunks, be sure to trim and clean them as well. A small terrycloth towel soaked in warm water and then wrung out serves nicely. Dried blood that is too stubborn to remove with a damp rag alone will easily come away by occasionally dipping the towel in a small bowl of vinegar.

All of these measures result in a nice deer carcass that is far more presentable and easy to work with at butchering time than one that is dirty and stained with dried blood. That results in far more venison eventually finding its way to your table.

Protecting Your Deer Carcass

Every year, megatons of prime venison is lost due to a variety of unforeseen events. Warm-weather spoilage and infestation by blowflies are the two leading culprits.

Ideally, deer hanging in camp should not be subjected to air temperatures below 25°F at night or higher than 45°F during midday. If either situation is anticipated or arrives without warning, special measures should be taken to prevent the meat from freezing or becoming too warm and spoiling.

Begin by hanging the deer in a location that is shaded during the better part of the day. In this manner, the carcass will undergo sufficient chilling

Measures should be taken to prevent the carcass from being exposed to wide temperature ranges. Draping the carcass with a heavy tarp will prevent it from freezing at night. Conversely, in hot weather, draping it during the midday hours will allow the venison to retain the coldness it achieved the previous night.

during the night hours to keep the meat cool during the daylight hours.

One hunter I know saved an old sleeping bag that had seen years of use; he literally "bags" his deer whenever it's bitter cold. By cutting the bottom edge of the bag open, he doesn't face the problem of trying to slip the deer inside. He merely wraps the bag around the deer and closes the zipper to insulate the venison just enough to prevent it from freezing. He also does this during extremely hot weather, allowing the deer to chill overnight and then, first thing in the morning, wrapping it with the sleeping bag to retain its cool temperature throughout the day. At the end of each hunting trip he merely tosses the bag into his washing machine, so it's clean for next year's outing.

Other hunters who may not want to go to this trouble should at least have a piece of canvas tarpaulin in camp that can be draped over their hanging deer to prevent it from freezing or being exposed to warm midday temperatures.

Blowflies are the bane of deer hunters. They look like common houseflies but with metallic bluish or greenish colors, and as soon as the daytime temperatures rise into the upper thirties they'll swarm to your deer's hanging location. They enact their dastardly deeds by landing on exposed meat and laying thousands of tiny white eggs. In two or three days, the eggs hatch into larvae that feed upon the meat. By the time a hunter first notices blowflies on his deer, much of the venison may already have to be sacrificed. Consequently, strict measures must be taken at the outset to prevent the flies from ever touching your deer. In warm states throughout the South and Southwest, hunters construct special deer-hanging houses to protect their deer. The buildings resemble outhouses in size but have screened walls, with an overhead roof to shelter hanging deer from inclement weather, and are permanent affairs in annual deer camps.

In hunting situations in which building such structures would be inconvenient or even prohibited, other remedies must be sought.

First, forget the old advice about sprinkling the carcass with pepper. You'll need five pounds of the stuff to cover every square inch; otherwise flies will land in the many tiny places not coated, and there will be countless such places because breezes will blow much of it away.

Gamebags, on the other hand, do an excellent job of protecting deer carcasses from blowflies and other insects, provided they are the right kind and used properly. Don't cheap-out and buy the one dollar cheesecloth gamebags found in many sporting-goods stores. Their thin, fragile, wide-mesh construction is about as effective in warding away insects as waving your arms and cursing.

What you want are heavy-duty gamebags made of porous but tightly woven cotton or muslin. They're shaped like long tubes with a drawstring closure at one end to entirely enclose the carcass in a cocoon. Such bags cost as much as twenty-five dollars (ouch!), but they do the job well and can be washed and reused for many years.

Three final notes. Don't assume that mere chilly weather means the absence of insects; only if it's below freezing is your venison safe from the critters. Don't assume that leaving the hide on the animal will protect it from insects; there are many entrance points they can use to gain access to your venison. Do make a point of checking your hanging carcass several times each day so you can quickly employ any remedies that may suddenly become necessary.

To protect a hanging deer from insects such as blowflies, which can ruin venison in short order, wise hunters invest in a special gamebag made for the purpose. To help keep deer clear, gambags can also be used when transporting deer on vehicles.

Growing and Hunting Quality Bucks

TOM INDREBO

Three Steps to a Grand Scheme

I've never believed that old saying, "It's better to be lucky than good." Far from it. I believe the harder you work, the luckier you get. Everyone can get lucky occasionally, but consistent success is no accident. Our accomplishments at Bluff Country Outfitters result from year-round planning, lots of work, never-ending review and analysis, and trying to learn from our mistakes so we don't repeat them.

Laurie and I didn't come to Buffalo County in 1993 with a long-term plan and business blueprint to launch Bluff Country Outfitters. But this business didn't grow by itself, either. As we saw its potential grow and evolve, we kept feeding the fire while being sure it didn't consume us in the process.

Even today I don't keep a "recipe book" that lays out everything we accomplished since we moved here, or projects that we will accomplish in the years that follow. In fact, the book you're now reading is the first time I've sat down and turned my management thoughts and plans into the printed word. However, I keep my ears and eyes open at all times, and I pay attention to what works, what doesn't work, and how we can make things work even better. I've always been good at improvising and trying new ideas, and before I give up on an idea or expand it, I try to make sure it will work more than once and in different settings.

I also try to be patient. A quality deer-hunting operation can't be created in one or two years. It requires a long-term commitment that pulls you through the mistakes you're bound to make, and keeps things in perspective when a plan exceeds expectations. It's a day-to-day, week-to-week, month-to-month and year-to-year effort. You might not even see many differences each year, but when you look back five or 10 years, the differences are huge.

Meanwhile, you must remain flexible, adapt your plan to unexpected changes, and always blend those ideas into your state's deer- and wildlife-management rules and regulations. Sometimes you'll also need to work with neighbors, local conservation leaders, state wildlife biologists and maybe even local and state politicians. You won't always win disagreements and political skirmishes, and some partnerships end on sour notes, but win or lose, you must push on while complying with the state's larger, overall management programs.

Step 1: Know the Land

So let's get started. At risk of simplifying our approach, I consider Bluff Country Outfitters' deer-, land- and hunting-management plan a three-step program. For Step 1, I stress the importance of knowing the land itself. Before you decide where you're going, you must know what your property is already producing and what's taking place in its every corner and hilltop. Study its terrain, its waterways and drainage patterns, property lines, ownership trends, access issues, local hunting culture, adjoining farming practices and woodland management.

BLUFF COUNTRY OUTFITTERS

Create a library of county maps, topographical maps, aerial photos and county plat books that show your hunting land. Nearby land-ownership patterns and the size of surrounding properties can have more impact on your management plan than your knowledge of your property's terrain and habitat.

With the Internet, it's easier than ever to develop a good library of topographical maps and aerial photos. Buy a county plat book every couple of years from the County Courthouse to watch land-ownership changes, and monitor how neighbors parcel up their lands when they sell out. It's not uncommon to see farmers sell their land by breaking it into 5-, 10-, 20- and 40-acre parcels. The smaller the holdings, the more landowners there will be, and the more complex your challenges will become.

Of prime importance, of course, is your own land and what it's producing. The more you know about its terrain, woodlands, logging operations and agricultural practices, the better you can predict how, where and when deer move about the area. This is especially crucial knowledge for bowhunters, who must take advantage of the deer's natural movements to increase their odds of success. Whether you're hoping to intercept a buck between his bedding and feeding areas, or to waylay him during the rut as he cuts cross-country to search for doe family groups and receptive partners, you'll do more guessing than

bowhunting if you don't have a good grasp of what's taking place on the ground and how it affects deer activity.

That reminds me of "The Wishbone Buck," which Doug Hick of Phillips, Wisconsin killed nearby back in 1991. Doug was hunting along a rub line near the end of October, right before the rut really kicked in. At that time of year, bucks are back in the security of their home areas after leaving their summer hangouts and bachelor groups about a month before. Here in the Bluff Country, they lay up in October while the acorns and maple leaves are falling. They're almost nocturnal in their movements. They'll have a spot where they feel safe, where they'll see or smell you if you try to move in on them.

As October moves along, that buck will get up from his bed, walk a route to a feeding area and rub trees every so often. If he lives a few years, you'll find where he's rubbed the same trees multiple times during those years. If you want a decent chance of shooting him, you must be familiar with that travel corridor and have an idea where he's bedding. At some point, his rutting urge will bring him out of his bedding area in daylight, but he will still be near his bed. If you're not familiar with this spot and stumble right into his bedding area, you'll bump him out and never see him in daylight.

To figure out how close you are to his bedding area, scout in the spring, find his rub line and unravel it back toward his bedding area. He will make a scrape every so often, and his end scrape will probably be about 50 to 60 yards from where he beds. Locate that final scrape, turn back in the direction you came from, and find the next-to-last scrape along his route and set up between those two scrapes.

The challenge is to figure out how to reach that spot and set up on it without alerting the buck when you're there in late October. This usually requires setting up your stand (or stands) before he returns from his summer range. The safest bet is to trim out the site in spring and get everything set. Things will grow in a bit during summer, so maybe in August or September go back in there, do the final preparations, and clear a little trail so you can slip in quietly in late October.

Then, once he's in there again in late September or early October, leave him alone for at least the first three weeks of October. He's not moving out soon enough in daylight to get a look at him. When it's time to go after him, don't force it. Wait for the right wind, slip in there when it's right, and sit so you can watch that end scrape nearest his bedding area. If you've done your homework and you respected the wind, you should be able to get that buck the first time you hunt him.

How will you know when the time is right? You'll have about a five-day window to take a buck on this kind of setup. That last scrape gets all torn up and dished out like a bowl because when that buck starts getting those rutting urges toward the end of October, he might get up and walk that short line from his bed every hour. The trouble is, most guys find that last scrape, get all fired up, and set up on it the first chance they get. They never see the buck because he knows they're there. They're too close to his bed and they made noise putting up their stand. Every time they show up, the buck knows it.

Doug Hick didn't blow his opportunity when he moved into place in 1991 to get the Wishbone Buck, but he had his doubts at first. After he got into his stand, he pulled up his bow with his rope. As he lifted it, he accidentally banged the bow onto his tree steps. That buck came right in! Doug's stand was close to where the buck was bedded, and the buck probably mistook the banging sound for deer messing around in his area. Doug had the right wind and the right situation, and he made the shot when the buck appeared.

We recognized the Wishbone Buck right away. I had seen him for a couple of years and had taped him quite a bit for our Monarch Valley tape. But I first encountered him when he was a 2 1/2-year-old and running scrapes. In one memorable scene in the video, I filmed him as he walked all the way around me, trying to figure out what I was.

Doug shot him with his bow the following year in the situation we just described. The buck was an impressive 8-pointer that scored in the 140s when it was 3 1/2 years old. We named him the Wishbone Buck in 1990 because the end of his beams looked like a turkey's wishbone. We never would have gotten him if we didn't know so much about that piece of ground, and how, why and when bucks use setups like that to their advantage. Those kinds of details are usually the difference between hunting and just hoping.

Step 2: Know the Deer

As the Doug Hick hunt illustrates, it's also important to know what deer are doing year-round on your land. Obviously, that means paying attention year-round, not just when the hunting season is near or under way. Don't just note where you see deer. Try to figure out what draws them to particular sites and when you see them in different locations.

Don't expect to unlock all their secrets the first year or the first two years. Chances are, as long as you're hunting a particular piece of land, you'll always learn a little more about it year to year. Again, you might not realize how much you learn daily, weekly or monthly, but when viewed in three- or five-year increments, the knowledge you compile will be staggering. One reason I included the story about John Sligh and his 160-class bow-kill in September 2005 was to illustrate how easy it is to overlook a good spot for years. I was in my 13th year on our Bone Creek farm when the right circumstances finally coincided to steer me to that setup. Chances are, if I hadn't stumbled onto those two bedded bucks that summer, John never would have been sitting on that site after he arrived from Florida.

As you continue roaming, scouting and hunting your land, you'll learn a lot about the many ways deer use the terrain and cover to their advantage. You'll discover that some individual deer have habits that defy general rules. In some cases, those preferences vary by where you happen to be hunting. You can't discount something found in one place but not the other. In these bluffs, I've seen deer bed in little more than tufts of grass along a fence line where they can see far and wide, almost as if they were antelope. In most cases, though, they bed just over the top of ridges, along shelves in thicker cover where they can look out and down. They

This hilltop shelf offers whitetails a safe place to rest, rub and monitor their surroundings for danger. Deer like to bed just over the top of ridges, along shelves in thick cover that lets them look out and down. They count on the wind to bring scent from over the ridge behind them.

count on the wind to bring scent from over the ridge behind them.

Learn all you can about how winds swirl through your hills and valleys. Where do deer go to find relief from howling winds that make it difficult to hear approaching threats? Pay attention to quiet zones downhill from ridgetops. The wind often comes up from our valleys with such force that it seems to blow right over the top, leaving calm air just beneath the ridgeline on the opposite side. It's not unusual for me to see trees bucking, groaning and popping above me in a stiff wind, even though the woods are quiet where I stand in a hollow below the ridgetop. Each ridge, valley and hilltop can create its own unique wind currents, depending on wind speed and direction, so the more time you spend in the woods, the better you'll know where to hunt under different conditions.

I've also found that mature bucks tend to bed where they can see a decent distance. Some of them like to bed in more open cover than you might expect. I think they do whatever they can to avoid being surprised. In some ways, their behavior resembles that of wild turkeys. They want as much distance as possible between themselves and possible threats.

Step 3: Combining Your Knowledge of Land and Deer

As you increase your knowledge of your land and the deer that live there, the real fun begins. The more you learn about both, the more you can use the ax, saw, tractor and plow to make your land even more productive for deer hunting.

Granted, you can always hunt deer by relying solely on your knowledge of their habits and travel patterns. For some people, though, that's not enough. We also like to work with the land and create plans and projects that make deer hunting even more interesting and productive. As you're learning your land's features and how deer use them, it's time to place food plots and build waterholes, set up long-term forestry plans, learn the deer's food preferences, learn different plants' peak palatability stages, schedule plantings and harvests on your larger fields, and work with neighbors and experts to provide services you can't or won't tackle yourself.

In other words, it's possible to make good hunting sites even better by giving deer more reasons to be there. Again, though, you must know your land to recognize its potential and possibilities. For instance, not too far over the ridge from John Sligh's stand is a spot where we've had lots of luck over the years. Pat Reeve or his father sat there for several years, and the first year I guided hunters, I put a guy in there. A big buck came through, the guy shot it, and I looked like I knew what I was doing.

That spot is a natural travel route that skirts a steep area right uphill from a stream. Deer bed along that hillside all the way out to a point where they can lay and watch everything below them. With good cover, the right terrain and lots of white oaks dropping acorns, deer were always bedding along there. I figured the bucks were always coming through that spot during the rut to look for does, and I wanted to make sure they had another reason to show up.

We'll cover this topic in depth later, but this is the site where I built one of our first woodland waterholes. We used a Caterpillar, built a clay-lined pond in there, and seeded the area around it. Why build a pond inside a thick bedding ground? During the rut, bucks run for hours and get thirsty. When they feel dehydrated they head for water, so I figured I would give them a water source right where they expect to find does.

That decision paid off. Bucks started flocking to that pond. Not only did they come there for water during the rut, they started coming there in September, especially during hot spells. The hotter the weather, the better action you'll have on woodland ponds. Twice now we've killed three

Pope & Young bucks in one season off that pond, which proves you can take a good spot and make it even better.

Not only that, but this example shows you don't need to be a mile from the nearest road to shoot big bucks. The spot is within a quarter-mile of our home. The experience also taught me how tolerant deer can become when they're hanging out near a great food source. During years of good acorn crops, deer bed near that pond and its white oaks, and they just watch us when we go past on the ATV. If they do run off, they seldom go very far.

Adapting and Improving

By using your knowledge of deer and your land as building blocks, you'll never run short of ways to combine those elements to launch new management plans as you tweak, modify and overhaul previous projects and ideas. That's one of the great things about owning your own hunting property and realizing how much fun you can have with plants, axes and shovels during the off-season.

The site where this woodland waterhole is located was already a good place to bowhunt before the pond was built. The pond's presence, however, makes the spot irresistible to whitetails, especially on hot days when a drink of water can lure them from their nearby bedding areas. (SC)

You learn something about yourself in the process. I know lots of people who never realized the satisfaction of planting seeds and seedlings, and then watching plants and trees grow in the years that follow. It adds a new dimension to deer hunting, and creates even more satisfaction when you see deer including your projects in their daily routines.

As you'll see in the next section, you'll find other ways to boost your overall hunting satisfaction as you become familiar with your woodlots and native plants. In some cases, you'll even discover how to make trees and long-range forestry plans pay dividends for you while improving and diversifying the deer's diet and nutritional needs.

Many bowhunters learn something about themselves while doing chores to improve their land's habitat for deer and other wildlife. That is, they find that using an ax, plow and shovel brings satisfaction and a sense of accomplishment as plants grow and deer habitat regenerates.

Knowing Your Land, its Trees and Plants

One aspect of deer and land management often overlooked in books and magazine articles is the importance of a forestry plan that includes your property's trees, shrubs and other naturally growing plants. Too many bowhunters and land-owning deer hunters concentrate on food plots and the latest and greatest seed varieties. Never forget that white-tailed deer in most regions have gotten along for eons without farmers and food plots, but they will always be a species that requires woodlands with lots of young growth, edge cover and thick understory.

Whitetails will never get by on food plots alone, yet when I drive around some regions, I'm amazed to see how many woodlands have become largely unsuitable for deer. I often see mature forests in such advanced stages of natural succession that little sunlight reaches the ground. As the woodland shrubs and bushes that create bedding cover disappear from lack of sunlight, deer move to more favorable habitats.

Mature woodlands support far fewer deer than younger, more diverse woods, and most of them desperately need chain-saw work. But before you jump in and make lots of noise and sawdust, make sure you know the age and health of your woodland, and how best to cure what ails it. Unless you have a sound understanding of forestry practices, it makes sense to hire the services of a trained forester to assess your woodlands. Be sure to ask for references and work with someone with experience in your sort of property.

Explain what you want to achieve with your land to make it suitable for whitetails, and keep an open mind. Don't cringe and protest if he advises limited clear-cutting in some areas. Clear-cuts can jump-start deer habitat by opening the ground to sunlight and triggering dense regrowth. In my area, tree species like poplar (aspen) and oaks literally explode with new growth when given access to sunlight.

The secret for most of us is to perform several small clear-cuts in select spots to create more edge cover. Deer love these "new" areas because of their increased potential for bedding and food. Never forget, deer are browsers, not grazers. They seldom stand long in one spot, preferring to move every few bites to sample something new.

Work closely with your forester and walk along when he inspects your woodlands to assess their potential. Ask questions and make sure he grasps your goals—short-term and long-term. If you pay attention, you'll learn much about your own woodlands by seeing trees through a forester's eyes. You want diversity in your woodlot, not only in tree and plant species but in their ages.

I've found that when I enroll in a forestry program, the forester wants to cut everything with a trunk larger than 18 inches in diameter. Some older trees might look like prime specimens, but they're actually "overripe" and it might be best to harvest them before they reach the point of no return. Others are soft, hollowed by rot and age, and will topple in the first big storm. In the meantime, their trunks and decaying branches make good den trees and food sources for birds and small mammals, like raccoons and squirrels.

I also refuse to remove my best white oaks, especially those near bedding areas, staging areas and woodland ponds. Quality white oaks create prime food sources and often provide great sites for a portable stand. I make a point to get in there and fertilize them each spring to help them reach peak productivity.

Another thing to consider is the type of cover that lies between some of your known feeding and bedding areas. If much of this is fairly open woodland with little underbrush, you probably won't see much daylight deer activity. Also, what kinds of trees are in there? If it's an "early successional" section of woods, such as box elders that filled in long-forgotten fields or openings, you might want to create some extra year-round cover in obvious travel corridors to ensure a thicker understory. I've had good luck planting cedars, pines and spruce to increase this cover so deer feel more comfortable moving through during hunting hours.

The Logging Process

As you work with your woods and a trusted forester, don't be surprised when you learn logging isn't a one-time project. Depending on the size and composition of your property, you might want to log every year, every few years or every 10 years. As we discussed earlier in broad detail, many factors come into play when making forestry-related decisions. Some decisions affect the here and now, but other efforts won't be noticed or appreciated until long after you're gone.

I conducted two logging operations on our 335-acre farm the first 12 years we lived here. And when my neighbors do some logging, I keep abreast of their work to help me understand how it might affect deer and their movements on our land. If there's one thing I've learned about logging it's this: It's difficult for loggers to take out too much! You might think they scalped your land, but that's seldom the case. Most of us can't handle fullblown clear-cuts, but it's often the lesser of evils. Far worse are some select cuts in which unethical loggers remove your prime trees and leave the junk standing. In worst-case scenarios, those trees simply grow more branches and quickly reshade the forest floor.

That's another reason you'll want to stay involved at every step. Not only does your presence keep everyone honest, you can intervene when needed. For instance, if you're considering pond construction, make sure those plans are not overlooked in your forestry/logging planning. And, unlike the woodlands, I want my ponds shaded as much as possible. The shade from surrounding trees helps slow evaporation from the ponds and makes deer feel a little more secure when taking a drink.

Which trees should be logged off and which ones should be left alone? Sometimes it depends on their location. The author likes to build woodland ponds among mature maples and white oaks, knowing that acorns and fallen maple leaves help entice deer to a waterhole.

So, although I insist that loggers leave all white oaks surrounding my woodland ponds or potential pond sites, I have them cut aggressively as they move farther back into the woods to improve nearby bedding grounds.

I also like to leave stands of maples nearby or around woodland ponds. Deer will gorge on white-oak acorns, obviously, but they also love to eat maple leaves shortly before and after they drop. That combination of ponds, white oaks and maples—with thicker underbrush and trees farther back into the woods—provides deer fresh browse, secure bedding areas, and quick access to water. In other words, ideal and diverse deer habitat.

Realize, too, that loggers often have different agendas than landowners and foresters. Unless they know you're watching every step, they'll focus on what's important to them, not you. Their goal is to get the work done quickly and efficiently. They want the wood, they want to remove it quickly, and they don't always care what kind of mess they leave behind. If they slice and dice your woodlands into a tangled pile of scrap branches and severed treetops, all those long-used deer travel corridors will be obliterated or confused beyond recognition.

To address such situations, I invite friends and neighbors to come in and buck that wood, cut firewood, and create or reopen travel corridors. This work must be done soon after loggers leave, however. If you wait for brush, brambles and young trees to spring up, that new growth will make clean-up and corridor-building and restoration a major headache.

Another vital responsibility to yourself is to continually track the cash value of wood leaving your property. This is yet another reason to work with trustworthy foresters and loggers who have strong references. Different woods—both in terms of the tree's species and the quality of its saw logs—bring vastly different prices. If there's significant lag time between the time your contract is signed and when the work is done, check to ensure lumber values didn't jump. Wood prices, especially for hardwoods, can be as volatile as oil!

Trees: The Long-Term Crop

No matter where you are in your planning efforts, another fun project is planting trees. I think of trees as a long-term crop. In many cases, I don't expect to be around when trees I plant pay big dividends for wood, deer and cash. On the other hand, you just might see some benefits faster than you expect.

Either way, success hinges on your forestry plans. You can't plant some trees just anywhere, and you don't want huge stands of the same species. That does deer no good. It's best to intermix your plantings with long-term goals in mind. If you're to maximize your land's qualities and account for its weaknesses, your plans must account for its topography, soil types, and orientation toward the sun. It's important to realize that not all hillsides, ridgetops and valleys are created equal. Some sites grow certain trees and shrubs better than others, and provide better bedding or feeding areas at different times of the year.

For instance, in northern climates it pays to notice which trees and shrubs can handle summer's extreme heat. Those that can't withstand moderate dry spells and hot summer suns will never grow large enough to provide adequate cover when wintering deer seek those south-facing slopes for extra daytime warmth. Such areas are worth improving as bedding grounds. I've noticed several sites in my area where deer bed on sun-soaked ridgeline points. In fact, if you know of anyplace where deer spend lots of time bedding in winter, go there in winter and early spring to search for shed antlers. Deer often like these sites in autumn, too, and bask there in the morning sun.

Tree plantings can serve many purposes, of course. As we mentioned earlier, they can be planted in select numbers and places to increase cover in travel corridors and bedding areas. Also look for areas where you can plant trees to create more borders and edge cover. I often create shelterbelts of spruce and pine, and then I mix in ash, oaks and more pine behind them for every other row. You might want to encircle some

Trees are a long-term "crop," in that they can pay dividends in wood, deer and cash for many years if you follow a good forestry plan. This Bluff Country hillside provides a rich mix of oaks and aspen.

fields, create windbreaks or divide a field into several irregularly shaped sections that you let revert to brush and trees. As you create these new woodlands, you make some fields more secluded and private, which encourages daytime feeding activity.

In still other cases, though, I've converted entire fields into wooded cover. That's why I view trees as a long-term crop. No matter what I plant or the purpose for the plantings, I try to learn all I can about the different tree species that grow well in my region and learn how deer abuse or make use of them.

For instance, it's easy to get poplars to regenerate along field edges. Simply plow or roto-till the soil, and poplar shoots start "suckering" within weeks. Within a couple of years you'll have dense poplar stands that deer and ruffed grouse covet.

Although deer will browse on poplars, they simply hammer white cedars during winter. Deer browse white cedar so aggressively that I must protect them with fencing materials until they grow beyond the deer's reach and maintain themselves. When I first planted cedars around my ponds, they didn't last long. The deer tore them up. I even had trouble with white pine. Deer tear them up early and often by rubbing in autumn and browsing in winter.

When I'm trying to create thermal cover where deer can bed, I often plant Colorado blue spruce because deer pretty much leave these trees alone. In fact, spruce trees, in general, don't suffer much abuse from deer.

Again, stay involved with your forester. I've learned a lot from state and county foresters about how to better plan my tree plantings for diversity. I want oaks, white ash, cedars, various spruce species, Norway pines, red pines and white pines on my land. In one case we planted 87 acres in trees, which required 800 trees per acre to ensure we got enough survival to maintain the stand. We probably planted 100,000 young trees on that site. When big numbers die off in dry years we go back in and replant.

As you draw up your plans, figure in some expenses for replanting, and look ahead a few years to ensure you spend your money wisely and efficiently. In Wisconsin, for example, the state pays up to half the cost of converting certain fields into woodlands if you maintain your reforesting plan a minimum of 15 years. By keeping the land out of agricultural production that long, you pretty much let trees take over while letting the state help you recoup the costs. This benefits the state because well-established woodlands make it difficult for someone to come along later and turn it back into croplands.

Also look into government nursery programs. In many cases you can buy your tree stock in bulk at great prices from your state or county nursery. In addition, you can usually tap into their expertise and advice on how to buy the best trees at the best price, and find out ways to do your plantings as cheaply and easily as possible.

It's difficult to cut down too many trees. The author likes to generate thickets of raspberries and blackberries by using a chainsaw to create a small opening and then roughing up the topsoil. These plants and young trees also provide good browse for wintering whitetails.

Beyond—and Beneath—Trees

As you talk to foresters and deal with nurseries, don't forget to discuss options for underbrush that benefit deer and other wildlife. For instance, I like to encourage the growth of wild raspberries and blackberries. Sometimes it's just a matter of opening the woodland canopy and roughing up the topsoil—a process called scarifying—and let sunlight and rain do the rest. Not only can these thick brambles provide dense, thorny cover for deer, their leaves also provide good nutrition in fall for whitetails. Whenever possible, look for ways to offer deer a variety of naturally produced annual foods. That way, if one crop isn't producing in a particular year or place, you'll be better able to focus your attention when it's time to hunt.

Realize, too, that trees don't have to produce mast crops to benefit deer. Although deer key on white oaks first when they start dropping acorns, they'll hit falling maple leaves next. Red-oak acorns are seldom much of a factor early, and they're easy to identify because they're the last trees to lose their leaves.

I mention maple leaves because I've learned that whitetails gorge on them for a few days each year in early autumn. I think deer like maple leaves because they hold much of the sugar that flowed into them just before dropping. In fact, if you clear shooting lanes in early fall and cut maple branches still carrying leaves, deer never take long to strip every leaf from the cuttings. Whenever possible,

I make sure to get out there and do some final trimming on my stands. Usually the peak color in our region is the first week of October and, soon after, the maples shed their colorful leaves.

Maple leaves start falling—usually in mid-October around here—right about when the first does come into heat. When this happens, those does are often in the maple stands eating fallen leaves. It's only a short time frame, though; maybe a five-day window when you can count on whitetails hitting those leaves. Obviously, if you know it's going to happen, it's a great time to be out there.

That's another example of how the hunting season and the deer's world are made up of many different steps. If you're not in step with the deer, you could be missing your best bet by one or two days nearly every day of the hunting season! That's the downside of creating diverse habitat and food sources. The more you produce, the more you must plan, scout and perform maintenance. Even so, I keep planting, cutting, clear-cutting and scarifying the soil in order to diversify my land's plant and food communities.

That also means keeping track of all the fruit trees scattered about our lands. Many long-forgotten farmers in our region planted apples, plums and other fruit trees throughout their properties. Even though people no longer rely on these trees for fruit, deer have never forsaken them. So, between apples, plums, white oaks, red oaks, maple leaves, poplar buds, maple buds, white-pine needles, white-cedar fronds, and raspberry and blackberry leaves, deer on our farm have no trouble finding a smorgasbord of woodland foods.

Pay attention to all these natural food sources as autumn moves along. If you ignore them and concentrate all your efforts on food plots and agricultural fields, you'll miss some of the hunting season's best action.

With scouting cameras deployed in 15 or more places at any given time, the author captures some remarkable woodland scenes. Whether it's a red-bellied woodpecker taking flight or a red fox hunting mice and voles, scouting cameras capture many award-winning scenes. (SC)

Scouting cameras sometimes capture that unique one-hour time frame when a buck sheds its antler velvet in late summer. Once velvet cracks and starts to bleed, it isn't long before it's in shreds—like on this buck's antlers—and then gone until the buck grows his next set of antlers. (SC)

What to Plant and When to Plant it

Whether the purpose of your food plots is to create more shooting opportunities or provide supplemental foods for your land's whitetails, it's important to develop confidence and knowledge in some basic plants that grow well in your region. Make them the foundation of your food-plot program, and then start experimenting with other seeds and seed varieties as you grow with your program.

Likewise, have a basic planting schedule for each of your seeds/plants, and then experiment by planting some at various intervals. If you're a person who keeps journals—and refers to them later—you'll stay ahead of the game and probably obtain more reliable insights to help steer your seed purchases and planting schedules in the years ahead.

I realize, though, that some people find journals a bore and chore, and want no part of them. I won't try to change your basic personality, but when it comes to later reference, memories are never as reliable as written notes. Even so, journals aren't mandatory, and if you'd prefer to avoid them, just keep your plans consistent and fairly basic. The fewer details you start with, the fewer you must remember months or years later as you plan subsequent feeding areas and food plots.

I now pause to point out something that is obvious to almost everyone who contemplates food plots: Before you start or expand your program, collect soil samples where you intend to plant and get them analyzed. I won't dwell on this point, because every article, book, DVD or TV show I've ever seen that deals with food plots stresses the importance of soil analysis. Likewise, there's no shortage of formulas and local guidance to help determine whether you must spread lime—and how much to spread—to achieve the proper soil pH for your chosen plantings. If you haven't taken this basic, mandatory step to heart by now, my guess is that you don't wear a safety belt in your car or tree stand, either. And if that's the case, I doubt there's anything more I can add to convince you that soil tests are vital and basic to your food plots' long-term success.

Launching Your Program

Another piece of advice I read and hear without fail is to consult local experts to determine which plants and crops grow best, and what deer prefer most in your region. This advice also falls under the "safety belt" category: It's for your own good. So talk not only with your county agricultural agent and/or state wildlife biologist, but neighboring farmers and local bowhunters who work with food plots.

After you get their advice, start with known, reliably productive seeds and plants, as well as basic planting schedules, and save your experiments for the years that follow as you gain experience.

My staple crop for several years has been soybeans. They grow well in my region, deer love them, they're available in nearly endless varieties, and they offer great flexibility regarding when to plant them. I try to approach my program as if I were a professional farmer. I want to achieve the best possible results every year, I want to get it right the first time, and I want to build some flexibility into the plan to account for the possibility of drought and other vagaries of weather.

The best way to address those concerns starts with the soybean seeds themselves. Different beans mature at different times, deal more effectively with competing weeds, and tolerate certain weather

The author has enjoyed much success with soybeans in his feeding fields. No matter which seed varieties you plant, expect positives and negatives. Some plants might be easily maintained, but that doesn't mean deer will love them for their taste. (SC)

conditions better than other varieties. In recent years I've had great success by planting Monsanto's "Roundup Ready" soybeans (and Roundup Ready corn seeds, too, for that matter). What does that mean? Roundup Ready seeds produce plants that won't be killed by Roundup herbicides.

Before I switched to this seed variety, I had to get into my feeding fields and food plots and cultivate them to keep the weeds in check while the plants were growing. If you don't have a way to control weeds, they will take over your fields and food plots and nullify whatever you've invested up to that point. After switching to Roundup Ready seeds, I can now go in there and spray the fields as the plants start to take off, and then they pretty much take care of themselves. Weeds are never again a problem while the beans are growing.

Realize, though, that there will be positives and negatives to nearly every seed variety you use. For instance, Roundup Ready seeds are more expensive to buy and you still have to spray herbicide on your fields. According to various reports, they also produce smaller yields, but I haven't really noticed that because deer, not machinery, "harvest" my soybean crops.

The other downside to Roundup Ready soybeans is that they grow "hairy" bean pods. I've found that whitetails much prefer soybeans with the normal, smooth-skinned pods, but they will eat the Roundup Ready variety. Besides, it seems everyone around here is also planting Roundup Ready beans, so it's not like deer can go somewhere else for the smooth variety. For my small food plots, which can be quickly and easily cultivated for weeds, I still consider planting the old-style varieties when I target a specific site as a food plot for hunting. When you give deer a choice, they will hit that smooth-pod variety first.

Also realize you'll need different seeds for different locations, soil types and available sunlight. These considerations become tricky when planting small food plots inside the woods, or seeding your woodland's logging roads and walking trails.

Again, though, don't be the lone ranger. Ask advice from local experts when planning small or long and narrow woodland openings. In Wisconsin, I've received a lot of help—and financial savings—by working with state-and county-employed foresters. That's how I learned that the state sells a great seed mix for use on trails, access roads and logging roads. The wildlife blend I've been using includes brassicas, winter wheat, red clovers, white clovers, a hardy alfalfa, and plants like lablab and cowpeas.

Is Timing Everything?

Unfortunately, the process of choosing optimum plants and specific seed varieties is one of the easier decisions you'll make for your feeding fields and food plots. I wish every decision were so easy. The fact is, no matter which crop or seeds you select, you can usually make an informed decision relatively quickly after talking to two or three local experts.

But when you ask questions about the optimum time to plant crops to flexibly deal with Mother Nature's challenges, and then you complicate the scenarios by asking them to predict when your plants will produce the most palatable crops for a hunting food plot, you better pack a lunch. You're going to be there a while, discussing an array of "what-if" scenarios. Still, what choice do you have? When it comes to picking seeds, and the ins and outs of when to plant them, your best information sources will always be home grown.

No matter which crop you discuss, your success with it will hinge on timing and conditions, and your ability to stay abreast of your plants' development. Much will depend on rainfall, air temperatures and Mother Nature's many other mood swings. If your plantings run headlong into a drought, you might have to watch helplessly as the crop wilts away. And if your soil wasn't right to begin with, you'll probably

get something far short of expectations. In that case, you'll have only yourself to blame. Remember those soil tests discussed earlier?

But don't give up. No matter what crop you plant, it does indeed have its own unique cycle, and it's often possible to alter the cycle a bit to suit your needs. That means you must now decide if you want these plants to be primarily for the deer's nutritional value, or do you want them to reach peak palatability during a particular two-week window in the hunting season? Or do you hope to achieve a little benefit of both worlds? Or isn't that possible?

If you want to hunt over that soybean patch, expect to make some trade-offs somewhere. When we plant soybeans in a "normal" year—that is, from April to May—we expect that will give us our best

This big buck is eating soybeans in August. Sometimes deer feed heavily on the leaves of soybean plants during summer, but don't eat the plants' pods and beans until much later in the year. In fact, they might not touch the beans until mid- to late winter. (SC)

chance of producing a maximum-yield crop for use as a winter food source. The trade-off is that deer probably won't be interested in that particular food plot during most of the archery season. However, it might attract them during December's bow season.

Another possibility is to plant that same soybean variety a month or so later, from June to July, hoping it will reach its green, leafy, succulent stage during the early bowhunting season. However, when we wait that late to plant soybeans here in west-central Wisconsin, we don't expect them to produce their maximum yield. A later planting ensures a much shorter growing season, and also makes the plants more susceptible to a late-summer drought. We could easily end up with nothing if the drought persists for long. And even if moisture returns while the plants are still viable, the growing season will soon end and the plants won't recover in time to produce a full crop of beans.

Then again, we might not care as much about the beans themselves, as long as the plants reach "peak succulence" soon after the archery season opens. If we haven't had a drought or long cold spell, those plants will be almost mature by then, and even though their beans will be fairly well developed, deer don't miss a chance to move in, ignore the beans, and feast on the leaves. They'll often eat every single leaf on those late-planted soybeans, just like a mower taking off the tops of the plants.

I've seen deer clean an 8- to 10-acre field right down to the stalks, leaving only the stalks and bean pods. If we're lucky, they'll be in there after the season to finish off the beans, too. If we've put enough soybean plants out there for them, they'll keep coming to those beans for much of the winter.

Although some trade-offs are almost certain no matter what you do, you can hedge your bets, play the variables, and possibly stretch your plan to its max. For instance, try planting some of your preferred crops on a staggered schedule each year, maybe waiting two weeks between each planting.

If a field is too small to support a lot of deer, they can wipe it out quickly once plants become succulent. The author has seen deer take 8- to 10-acre soybean fields right down to the stalks during late summer.

That way, no matter what happens with the weather, at least one of those plantings should produce something tasty to monitor during the hunting season and beyond.

You can hedge your bets even more by finding creative ways to water some of your food plots. If your food plots aren't monstrously large, and you're lucky enough to know someone with a water truck, sometimes you can arrange a couple of waterings during summer dry spells. I know guys who pump septic tanks, and I've asked them to come over and help. Their trucks usually have a large tank for freshwater, so they can drive in here, fill up the tank with water from the creek, and spray a large area for me. It's sure a lot cheaper than an irrigation system!

Handing off the Baton

Food plots can be especially fun to monitor when they seemingly take turns feeding deer from late summer through winter. If you've planted a good variety of plants and seeds, and staggered when and where you planted them, the plots will reach peak palatability and production at staggered times. Once again, you're using your food plots to shift deer from one "pasture" to the next as they find one plant or plant variety more pleasing to their tastes and nutritional needs.

The only way you'll know when a food plot is reaching its prime is by scouting and watching it for deer activity. No matter how fast your plants grow, and no matter how green they might look to you, each plant has a peak time when deer find it most preferable. That peak can be difficult to predict or estimate because much depends on when you plant it, how well it converts nutrients while growing, how regularly it receives water, and which farming practices you've followed. A plant's palatability usually improves to a peak level over just a few days,

This buck is feeding in a field of clover and alfalfa. If you plant a good variety of plants and seeds, and stagger when and where you plant them, whitetails will switch to each food source as it reaches peak palatability. (SC)

Deer fed heavily in this turnip field in late fall, just the way the author planned. He needed a couple of years to fine-tune when to plant turnips. One year he waited until the second week of August to plant them. When the plants sent up their leafy tops a few weeks later, deer mowed them down and the turnips never developed.

and when it hits that peak, deer can't resist going there whenever possible.

One year I planted some turnips on one of our farms during the last week of July. Another year I planted them during the second week of August. Once the deer found them, they were thick in there. They mowed the tops off every turnip plant in those fields and the turnips never had a chance. Unfortunately, by the time I happened to swing by to see what had happened, we missed our chance to hunt those sites. Plus, the turnips never matured into the late-autumn and over-winter crop I had envisioned, so that gave me something to fine-tune in the years that followed.

I had a similar experience with a barley field one year. For about three weeks during July—long before archery season, obviously—every buck in the area seemed to be in there, eating barley. Then, after those bucks pretty much cleaned out the barley, they left and they never went back there again. I wondered if they had been eating the barley itself or a new seeding I had planted in a parallel patch. I walked out there and checked, and it was obvious they had been eating the barley when it hit a certain stage in its growth.

The deer's browsing impacts raise another challenging aspect of feeding fields and food plots. If your food sources are too small to accommodate the number of deer using them, they'll remove everything so fast you'll never get a chance to hunt the sites. Neither will the plants bounce back fast enough to provide any winter food. Finding that proper balance between herd size and food production takes constant and attentive effort.

However, some plants handle these tasks better than others, and you might need to work more of these plants into your overall plan. With alfalfa, for instance, it's possible to provide just enough of it that you never have to mow and bale your crop. Deer will do it for you. And as I touched on earlier, if you have enough soybeans planted, deer will come through first to get the leaves and then return later in the year to get the beans. But if you have more deer than your soybeans can support, they might take everything your plants produce and those plants will be finished for the year.

If that's the case, you definitely need to re-evaluate your approach before the next planting season.

Sweet Treats and Junk Food

I'm sure this whole topic of taste preferences and peak palatability has been studied to death by researchers far more skilled than I am. The common key for much of it, though, is probably the period of time when sugars reach their peak levels in a plant's foliage and fruit. Whether it's apples, maple leaves, members of the brassicas family—cabbage, broccoli, turnips, kale, canola (rape), collards, rutabagas, Brussels sprouts, etc.—and a vast array of other plants, when they convert their starches to sugar, they become magnets. Deer are drawn to this irresistible force. It can be like a candy store, with all deer walking in to get something.

I'm also assuming deer get more out of those foods than just sugar. Plants provide lots of protein and nutrients, and deer apparently know when particular plants are most nutritious and beneficial.

Even so, I have to believe a whitetail's food choices aren't simply practical, and that humans aren't the only creatures with bad eating habits. In other words, maybe deer crave a few junk foods and won't turn them down even when their nutritional needs dictate they concentrate on something else.

That doesn't mean whitetails forsake nutrition for long. What we see them eating at one particular hour isn't the only thing they eat all day. They're eating other foods when we're not there to watch, and maybe those unseen feedings address their most vital nutritional needs.

Another intriguing aspect of food choices is that deer don't always switch from one food to the next overnight as plants hit their peak palatability mark. From what I've observed, deer prefer some foods year-round, even long after we would assume there is no more benefit to be gained from particular offerings. For instance, I think deer would eat old corn year-round if they could find it.

On more than one occasion, I've seen deer walk past freshly sprouting plants in late May and early June, and head straight for leftover corn in an unplowed field. When I first noticed deer feeding in one of our old cornfields during a late afternoon, I didn't think much about it. Then I started seeing more and more deer feeding out there in that standing cornfield.

Why were they eating nearly year-old corn when all that fresh greenery was available? I'm just speculating, but my best guess is that maybe all those greens were too dramatic of a diet change in late spring. Maybe the green stuff that was most abundant was causing diarrhea or other digestive problems. Or maybe they just needed some corn, and more starch, in their diet as they headed into summer.

The fact that you see a buck feeding in a field during midsummer might have little or no bearing on his whereabouts in November, but such sights never grow old for bowhunters. Not only is it fun to see antlers developing in July, but it's also fun to see fields of green sprout from seeds you've planted.

The author strives to provide deer a reliable, long-lasting food source to carry them through cold months. By not harvesting all of his corn and soybeans during autumn, he ensures he has an ample supply of standing crops to supplement the deer's winter diet.

Then again, maybe it's that "junk-food" factor. Maybe they were just supplementing their diet, almost like us when we eat crackers with our soup. We don't need those crackers, but their taste complements soup so well that they become standard for certain meals. Likewise, maybe deer don't need that old, dry corn in late spring, but they won't turn it down when it's available.

To prove that point to myself, the following year I left more corn out there over winter. Then, on

June 1, I started mowing and chopping it up with my brush hog. Sure enough, the deer moved right in to clean it up. About a week later, I chopped up another 10-yard patch, working my way closer to my farm buildings. By late June I had worked my way down the field almost to its end. Still the deer kept coming. Finally I chopped the corn right next to my big barn. Soon after, I counted 18 bucks in velvet eating there one afternoon.

Some people might read these observations and wonder how they're relevant to bowhunting. Granted, the fact that bucks are eating old corn in June has no bearing on where they'll be in September or during the rut. But there's a fun element to planting and maintaining feeding fields and food plots that appeals to a broad spectrum of bowhunters. For many of us, whitetails and deer hunting are year-round activities, and their fascinating behaviors only add to the charm.

Part 2

Big Game Hunting

Introduction

JAY CASSELL

North America offers many opportunities for big-game hunters. Black bear populations are exploding in the East, wolf hunting is now available in some of our western states, mule deer are holding their own after a population drop in the 1980s—and there are elk, pronghorns, sheep, moose, and more. In this section, we've tried to hit the major species, ones that are available to many of us and which in most cases don't require some ridiculously expensive tag or a ten-year wait in a lottery. Different methods are covered—with bow, rifle, and shotgun—and different parts of the country are explored. Now you just have to figure out where you want to go.

—J. C.

The Bowhunter's Field Manual

JUDD COONEY

Bears

Bear bowhunting seldom lacks in challenge or excitement, whether you're following a pack of trained bear hounds, spotting and stalking a bruin across a salt grass flat in Alaska, stand-hunting over a bait in Saskatchewan or calling a ravenous bear with a predator call in Arizona.

Bears are unique animals that have habits and many characteristics totally different from other big game. They are the only species of big game that spends the cold winter months in hibernation. They are soft-footed, silent, solitary animals that prefer the most rugged terrain and inhospitable, impenetrable jungles of brush and vegetation, negotiating and surviving in this habitat with ease.

Black bears come in many different color phases, ranging from light blonde to reddish or cinnamon, chocolate brown, and coal black. Black bears on Kermode Island, off the coast of British Columbia, have evolved into a predominantly creamy white color, and the rare "glacier" or "blue bear" phase near Yakutat, Alaska is a beautiful and unusual bluish-gray color.

There are areas of Canada, Alaska, and the eastern U.S. where the bears are predominantly black, and getting a color-phase bear is a rarity, while in central and western Canada and the western U.S., color-phase bears make up about 40 percent of the population. One spring I had a sow bear bring three beautiful blonde-colored yearlings into a bait site with her when she appeared in the early spring.

She abandoned the cubs in mid-June, when she was ready for breeding, and by September, two of the cubs had shed their blonde fur and were dark brown, while the third remained a light-blonde color with dark lower legs, a phenomenon I had never witnessed before.

Grizzlies and brown bears (actually the same species) vary in color as much as black bears, but display the grizzled or variegated-colored hair that gives them their name. I've observed black bears that had a grizzled-color appearance and grizzlies that were solid brown or black, so color is not a reliable species identifier.

The most dependable identification characteristics are the roman nose of a black bear, compared to the dished-in face on the grizzly, and the rounded shoulders of the black as opposed to the grizzly's predominate hump. A black bear's claws are short, and if they show at all in the tracks

Like a lot of other big game, black bears prefer southern exposures for feeding grounds when they first leave their dens.

they will be very close to the toe pads, while a grizzly's claws are long and usually leave a mark at least an inch or more in front of the toe pad.

When a bear first rouses from its long winter's nap, it's pretty lethargic. Its feet are very tender (I've heard that bears completely shed their footpads during hibernation, but haven't observed this personally), and their digestive system needs reconditioning. For the first few days, they stay close to the den, resting and nibbling. As time progresses, they venture farther and spend more time satiating their growing appetite. A spring bear may spend four hours a day roaming and feeding, while a fall bear preparing for hibernation will spend four hours a day resting or sleeping and 20 hours voraciously feeding on anything that doesn't bite it first.

Bears are completely omnivorous and have an amazingly varied diet, from bugs to berries and grass to the grossest carrion around. They are also very efficient predators, and are very capable of killing other big-game critters. There are several studies that show black bear predation on elk calves to have a major impact on elk populations in areas of the west.

One spring, I had a bowhunting client who almost called me a liar when I told him that black bear were very capable game killers and especially effective on elk calves. As we were approaching a bear bait for his late afternoon hunt, I spotted a pile of fresh bear crap in the trail, and right on top of the pile was the small, undigested hoof of a calf elk. The proof is in the poop, you might say.

The black bear's secretive, reclusive nature and preference for impenetrable habitat would make it an exceptionally difficult adversary for a bowhunter, if it weren't for the bear's escalating appetite after it comes out of hibernation in the spring. Spring has long been a favorite time of year for hunting bear. It's generally the only hunting season available at this time of year, and the bear's pelt is thick and glossy after being protected from the elements and light during the winter's hibernation.

Bear Baiting 101

According to the last Pope & Young biennial records, over 60 percent of the bow-killed black bear are taken with the use of bait. Baiting spring bears is not rocket science and it's a technique that can be mastered by most bowhunters. There is, however, a tad of injustice to such mastery.

An accomplished golfer, tennis player or even fisherman is often referred to as a master of his sport. Just think how you'd be referred to as an accomplished baiter.

I never claimed to be a good bear outfitter or guide, but I was a good garbage hauler and scrounger, and that equated to success when it came to killing bears consistently for clients and myself. I've often heard comments that bears like nothing better than a maggoty, rotten carcass to feed on, and

Baiting for black bears still requires a bowhunter to be very careful with movement. Even though a bear is coming in for the food, he is very wary and will spook easily.

I can guarantee you that nothing is further from the truth. Bears are very persnickety eaters when they have a choice.

One spring I worked as a conservation officer for the Colorado Division of Wildlife and was inquisitive about every aspect of bear behavior. I placed the fresh carcasses of road-killed mule deer and elk alongside those of a horse, steer, and sheep at one of my well-used bait sites, where there were several bear actively feeding. The bears completely ate the deer and elk carcasses before touching the horse. I replaced the remaining steer and sheep carcasses with more recently deceased ones, and even with the fresher carcasses, the bears completely cleaned up the rapidly ripening horse before starting on the steer.

They completely cleaned up the bones and bits of meat from the other carcasses before touching the sheep (which shows good taste on their part, as I feel the same way about mutton). I've also watched bears pick through a large box of edible scraps from a café, much as you and I would pick out our favorites on a buffet line. They scrounged out the chicken and meat scraps first and then moved to the fish, fruit, eggs, toast, rolls, pie, cake, etc. Potatoes were generally the last edibles munched.

In my experience with over 30 years of baiting, citrus fruits and lettuce are a total bust for bears. Fish is another item that some swear by, and I suppose if you have an inexhaustible supply it will do the job, but I've found that fish rots quickly and gets ruined in short order by flies and maggots. It's just not worth the effort.

I used to haul several trailer loads of killer ponies from Texas each spring to use as bear bait (probably a felony in this day and age) because I always wanted fresh meat or bait on the site when a client was hunting. A bear that leaves a bait still hungry, with the bait completely gone, is a lot less likely to return regularly, and I wanted them to know there was always something to eat when they came back . . . regardless of the time of day.

My favorite bear baits were edible scraps from the local cafés. I would pay the kitchen help a couple of bucks per five-gallon pail and then freeze the scraps for later use. Bears would walk right past a fresh horse or colt carcass to get to the edible scraps; they were easy to haul and use and didn't rot down or attract flies too badly.

For several years, I got loads of "end-of-run" candy from a company and was afraid I might be creating a population of diabetic bears. One of the best baits I ever used were 50-pound blocks of hard candy from the Jolly Rancher company in Denver. At the end of a production run, they would empty the machines into a plastic bag inside a box, creating a solid block of candy. I put these sweet chunks in the bottom of the barrel, where a bear could scrape off a smidgen of the candy—just enough to pique his taste buds and keep him working the bait, even when all the other goodies were gone. The bears couldn't get the solid blocks through the holes in the barrel, and a block of candy would last all season, making sure there was always a bit of delectable and appealing bait left in the barrel. Unfortunately after a couple years, the company went to computerized candy making and did away with this long-lasting, fly-free, easily handled, un-spoilable, indestructible, and irresistible form of bear bait.

For a number of years, in addition to edible garbage, I hauled pickup loads of outdated pastries and bread for bear bait. To add to the drawing power of these delicacies, I poured old honey, diluted 50 percent with water, over the whole mix. Honey is a great additive to all types of bear bait, and a good supply can be obtained from any beekeeper at a reasonable cost. The old honey keeps well, and if it turns sugary or solid, just adding hot water will make it pourable again. I have burned honey on many a bear bait and had bears walk right up to the dense black cloud of cloyingly sweet smoke and actually burn their noses on the hot honey can. The past few years, I've added smoking scent sticks to my bear-baiting set-ups, as the dense, sweet, berry-flavored or anise-flavored smoke carries for considerable distance downwind.

The pungent smoking scent sticks can also be placed on both sides of the tree stand to help mask your scent or confuse the bear's sensitive olfactory organs at close range. Bears, like other big-game species, require food, water and protective habitat, so confine your baiting (food) to areas near the other two essentials.

I like to have a bait at the edge of, or near, a small clearing or opening for one simple reason. The ravens, crows, and magpies that can raise havoc with loose bait can also be your best advertising agents. When I first start bait, I place loose scraps where the birds can see it from the air. Their raucous racket will often attract bears that cannot see or smell your bait.

I don't want my bait site in the open or where a bear has to cross large open areas to get to it. A bait in such a location might get hit, but only late at night when the bear feels protected by the cover of darkness. Keep your baits close to escape cover and near a source of water, where the prevailing wind can carry the scent into the cover and the birds can advertise the bait's presence to every bear within hearing, and you'll earn your master's badge in baiting in short order.

Stand placement over bait is also critical to the success of a bear bowhunt. Remember, a bear has a very discerning nose and hearing as keen as any big-game animal. Many people would have you believe a bear has poor eyesight, but I don't subscribe to that theory at all. I have had bears pick up my camouflaged form at several hundred yards on numerous occasions. I think their vision is much better than they are given credit for, and will continue to operate under that assumption until I can be convinced otherwise. I feel that a very high percentage of the bears taken over bait are fully aware of the hunter in the stand, but simply don't give a darn, as long as the hunter doesn't make

any quick, noisy, threatening movements. Wind is without a doubt the most critical factor in placing a bowhunting stand. The distance from hunter to bear is generally 20 yards or less, and a slight whiff of pungent human scent at that distance can put even a dominant old boar on red alert. I generally put my bear tree stands 16 feet above the ground and in a position where the least likely avenue of approach is behind the stand. In Saskatchewan, we were hunting along the lakeshore, so it was easy to place stands where we had both the prevailing breeze and the open shoreline working for us.

If you have to make a choice, choose the stand location with the wind in your favor at the time you will be bowhunting from the stand. Quite often the prevailing breeze is from one direction during the day, and then it will switch directions toward evening. Make use of this anomaly to get your stand where the wind works for you. You can use scent blocker or eliminator and wear the best scent-suppressing clothing and all this helps, but the real key to success is hunting with the breeze in your face.

I constantly make use of a small, plastic squeeze bottle filled with scented talcum powder to check the wind currents and breezes from the stand location at a time of day when I will be hunting from the stand. A very simple procedure, but an extremely important one that can make the difference between a huge bear rug on the den wall or a blow-up photo of your mother-in-law.

Another crucial factor in choosing a bear stand location is the light direction. The best time to bowhunt bears over bait is in the late afternoon, so place your stand where it's fully shaded during the prime time. You certainly don't want to be lit up like a store window manikin in the late afternoon light, where your slightest movement will be illuminated and intensified.

Once your stand is in position, inspect it thoroughly for the slightest squeak or scrape and get your bow and gear hangers situated where you can place and retrieve your equipment with a minimum of movement. The less disturbance you make when getting in and out of the stand, the better your chances of success.

'Course there are exceptions to every rule. As a bear hunting guide and outfitter, I'm able to spend much more time working the baits on a regular basis than an individual hunter. Sometimes this can be used to a client's advantage.

In Colorado and Canada alike, both my guides and myself make little attempt to approach a bait site quietly and often drive a truck, boat, or fourwheeler as close to the bait as possible. We rattle the bait cans and barrels noisily while baiting and leave as much scent around as possible before leaving with a maximum of racket. This habituates the feeding bears to both noise and human scent around the bait. It also tunes them into the fact that when they hear the noise, they'll find fresh food at the bait. I make it a point to *never* go to the bait without leaving fresh enticement.

When we take a client to the bait by boat or four-wheeler, we drive as close to the stand as possible and leave the engine running while we bang and clatter around, adding a bit of fresh bait to the can while the bowhunting client slips into the stand. When he is situated, we leave the site, making no effort to be quiet. Numerous times, before our truck or boat is out of sight, a hungry bear will be approaching the bait. Proper advertising pays off.

Anti-hunters have been quick to jump on bear baiting, hound hunting and spring bear hunting in general as unethical, unsporting, and detrimental to the burgeoning bear populations. Which is total hogwash. Unfortunately, they were able to get this issue on ballots in several western states and convince the uneducated and unwashed masses, through lies and misinformation, that bear numbers were declining and spring hunting killed an abnormally high number of females with cubs. Consequently, spring bear hunting of any kind

has been eliminated in many of the prime bear-producing states of the western United States, such as Colorado, Utah, and New Mexico.

Fall Bear Bowhunting

The fall of the spring season has meant a spring in the fall season, with more bears roaming the western states than ever before. bowhunting fall bears is a totally different proposition from hunting spring bears.

When a bear comes out of hibernation, it will spend four hours feeding and moving and up to 20 hours sleeping or resting. In the fall, the process is reversed, with the bear active and feeding up to 20 hours a day, taking minimal down time for rest or sleep. This gives a bowhunter who is willing to put in the time and effort ample opportunity to take a prime fall bear.

Food is the chief motivator for fall bears, so the obvious tactic is to bowhunt near food sources such as berry or acorn patches and grain fields. Water is also a critical element in many areas during the fall season, and man-made tanks, springs, and seeps are also superb places to ambush a thirsty fall bruin. When you can locate a water source adjacent to a food source, your chances of finding and arrowing a fall bear increase dramatically.

The best time to ambush a fall bear in a feeding area or waterhole is during the late afternoon. Even though bears actively feed most of the day and are out and about at daylight, the mature bears likely will confine their feeding and movement to heavy cover during the daylight hours.

The warmer the weather, the less likely a fall bear will be found in the open during the day. The morning dew and dampness of the vegetation will generally fulfill a bear's water needs until later, after his siesta. In hot, dry weather, a bear may slip into a waterhole to slake his thirst mid-day, but the behavior is unpredictable, which makes waiting for one an iffy proposition at best.

Shot placement is critical on a bear, as it has a thick layer of fat and a long coat of hair.

The erratic, swirling mid-day thermals are another reason to stay away from a honey hole until the odds are loaded in your favor. When you find a prime fall bear ambush location, be patient and hunt it only when the conditions are the best possible. A woods-wise trophy bear can be as leery and spooky as a whitetail buck. Let him know you're in the area hunting him and lurking around his favorite feeding or watering spot, and he'll pull stakes and vacate the area in short order.

Calling Bears

Calling bears with a predator call is a way of hedging your bets during the autumn season and adding a whole new challenging dimension to your fall bear bowhunting. I carry several predator calls with me at all times during the fall and have called in a number of bears for clients and myself.

Fall bears are dominated by their appetite, and the alluring sounds of an animal in dire trouble might just bring them within bow range. For fall bear calling I prefer a call with a deep, raspy tone that imitates a deer fawn, calf elk, or big-game animal in distress.

Bears may respond to calling on the dead run or saunter in to the call with aggravating slowness. Bear calling takes a lot more effort than other types of game calling, as the best results come from almost continuous calling. Bears have a short attention span, and when the calls sound stops for extended periods of time, they lose interest and stop coming. When I set up to call bears, I stay for an hour to give a distant bear time to get within sight. Once a bear is spotted responding to the calling, I adapt it to his actions. When he stops or slows down, I call louder and more frantically. As long as he's headed my way, I make my calls just loud enough for him to hear, which keeps his attention focused.

Bear calling can keep the hackles on the back of your neck standing straight up, especially when an approaching bear suddenly disappears in the brush and you know he's close, but can't see him.

My first bear-calling adventure was the most potentially dangerous situation, with a darn good lesson. I was working on Afognak Island, Alaska as a stream guard for the Alaska Department of Fish & Game at the time. I'd seen lots of cross and silver fox on the beaches and along the streams scrounging, and decided to call some in for movies. I picked a bright sunny morning, and as soon as it was light enough for filming, about 4:00 a.m. there, I eased my skiff into a small inlet and hiked a couple hundred yards to the edge of a clearing that was several hundred yards long and about one-hundred yards wide. I scrunched back under a spruce, got my camera ready for action, and ruined the peace and quiet of the morning with an agonizing series of distressed rabbit squealing and squalling calls.

The ear-ringing sounds had barely been absorbed by the impenetrable underbrush and moss-laden trees of the forest when a huge brown bear bounded out of the trees across the clearing from me and stood with his head swinging back and forth, trying to locate the source of the enticing sounds. One look at the size of that huge, hungry predator was all it took for the ignoramus source of those sounds to slither soundlessly and speedily away from the clearing, my tongue stuck to the roof of my mouth, and the predator call buried deep in a jacket pocket. As soon as I got a short distance from the meadow, I ran like heck to my boat, expecting at any minute to be overrun by the 700-pound fox I'd called up. If that bear had come in behind me while I was calling, there's a good chance I wouldn't be writing this book.

Bear Hunting with Hounds

Hunting bears with hounds is an exciting adventure and requires a hunter to be in top physical condition. Also, remember to practice shooting that will simulate shooting a treed bear.

Not many bowhunters are in position or have the time to raise and train a pack of bear dogs. Consequently, they miss out on the challenge, frustrations, camaraderie, and rewards in seeing such endeavors come together in forming an efficient bear-hunting team.

Clients hiring an outfitter that hunts with hounds also do not get to see the hunts average out, the way the dog man does. I've had clients whose hunt was over the first morning after an easy, quick chase and cooperative bear. Several of these unenlightened bowhunters complained they would never hunt with hounds again because the bear didn't have a chance against the well-trained dogs. Little do they know.

The next hunter may spend five days of trudging over mountains and through canyons listening to the distant dogs trailing a hound-wise bear on hot, dry hillsides without ever seeing a hair of the bear. Some of these clients have left camp with their tail between their legs vowing never again to try and hunt the abominable, "un-bayable" black bear unless it's from a tree stand over a bait.

Only the outfitter in any hunting situation gets to see enough action and different situations to have any comprehension of what the "average" hunt is like.

The best advice I can give on preparing for a bear hunt with hounds is to get yourself in good physical condition, 'cause the longer you can last on the hunt, the better your chances of bringing home a trophy bear.

Feet are the first to go on a bear chase. Most bowhunters have probably spent the winter months in front of the TV without tromping around much, keeping their legs and feet in condition. Spend some time climbing the bleachers at the football stadium or up and down the gravel piles at a local gravel pit with a hefty pack on your back. A little conditioning at home will make a big difference when it comes to negotiating rough country on a bear chase. Don't plan on breaking in a new pair of lug-soled boots (a prerequisite on a hound bear hunt) on your hound bear hunt; do it at home where the consequences won't be as disastrous.

I've had pro football players and marathon runners who thought they were going to die on a bear chase because their legs, feet, and muscles weren't conditioned to climbing over logs and rocks while hiking up and down the mountainous terrain that a black bear calls home.

A black bear can outrun a horse on flat ground and has the stamina to stay ahead of a pack of bawling bear dogs all day long, especially if he's survived previous hound hunter encounters. When a mature bruin is being pursued by a pack of hounds, he'll head for the most inhospitable habitat he can find and negotiate the rugged terrain with ease. Most bear chases are determined by Murphy's Law, so you can bet the better shape you're in, the closer to the truck the bear will tree. If you're looking for a tough, day-after-day, ass-dragging bear hunt with hounds, just show up for the hunt out of shape and hoping for a quick, easy time of it.

Practice your shooting on the ground, but also do some shooting that will simulate shooting a treed bear. I've had good bowshots shoot up all their arrows at treed bears without drawing blood, because of the excitement, bear fever and the impossible angles involved.

When you go on a bear chase, take a *full* quiver of arrows, and if you've got any apprehensions, have your outfitter or guide carry an extra handful. My guides and I have walked many miles retrieving extra arrows from the truck or camp because a shook-up bowhunter couldn't seem to get an arrow and a bayed bear in the same place at the same time.

Spot-and-Stalk Bear Hunting

Spot-and-stalk is the ultimate challenge in bowhunting any species. When you're dealing with hairy critters that have the equipment, ability, and often the temperament to do serious damage to your tender young body, spot-and-stalk hunting for bears takes on a whole new dimension. It is the leading method for taking grizzlies, brown, and polar bears, and is equally effective on these species in spring and fall alike.

The first prerequisite for successful spot-and-stalk bear hunting is to see your adversary *before* it sees you. Bears may not have the best eyesight in the realm of big-game animals, but I've seen them pick out a camouflaged hunter at 100 yards and disappear in a heartbeat on more than one occasion.

I've had several grizzly licenses in Alaska when bowhunting other species, and blown several stalks on them. The times I've been in a situation to arrow one of these tremendous trophy animals, they had

me pinpointed. Shooting a black bear at point-blank range when he knows you're there may not be real smart, but doing the same with a grizzly or brown bear is more like suicide.

Good binoculars and a spotting scope are essential to spot-and-stalk bear hunting and the propensity for letting your eyes do the walking until you spot a stalkable bear. Once you spot a shootable bear, be patient, take your time to watch his movements and plan your stalk to the last detail. Keep the wind and sun direction in mind and use your spotting scope to study terrain features you can use to get within bow range of your quarry. I would venture that over 90 percent of the blown stalks on big-game animals are due to impatience and "pushing the envelope" to get the shot. Patience is next to godliness when it comes to spot-and-stalk hunting, especially when your adversary is armed with formidable teeth, claws, and attitude.

When still-hunting black bear in the fall, their color variations blend in well with the tans and browns of fall vegetation. Unlike when you are hunting a deer, you won't see the white flicker of a tail or a white rump patch that gives a deer away.

Judging Trophy Bears

Bears are without doubt the toughest big-game animals to judge for the record book. It's extremely hard to accurately determine the size of a bear's skull under a thick covering of hide and long hair, especially if you haven't encountered many bears in the wild under hunting conditions. When I first started guiding and outfitting for bear hunters, I bought a spring scale to get an accurate weight of all the bears killed. I got rid of the scale after the first season 'cause all the bears weighed less than half what the hunter estimated, and I figured it was better for business if they claimed to have killed a 400-pound behemoth bear rather than one that actually weighed 160 pounds on the scale. "Ground shrinkage" is probably more acute with bear hunters than any other type of big-game hunting. We used 55-gallon drums for bear-bait containers and advised our hunters that if the top of a standing bear's back reached the second ring on the barrel, it was an average-sized bear. If the top of its back was between

When bears first emerge in the spring, they are intent on eating and will be in places where spring growth is abundant, along stream banks, ponds, lakes, and swampy areas.

the second ring and the top of the barrel, it would be close to recordbook class. And if the top of its back was *above* the barrel top . . . shoot quickly.

A large boar bear is easy to judge because of its massive bulk, low-slung build and broad, heavy head. A lean, gangly, leggy young bear is equally easy to judge. It's the large, bulky females with their hefty build and smaller skulls, and the equally bulky mid-sized males with skulls that might just make the record book, that are the stinkers to judge down to the last inch.

To add to the confusion, there are long, lean, lanky bears that aren't very impressive looking, with long skulls that will measure better than they appear, and then there are short, stocky bears that look massive, with short, wide skulls that measure less than appearances indicate.

There isn't any magic formula for accurately judging the difference between a bear with a skull measuring 17 3/4-inch and one with a skull measuring 18 1/4-inch that qualifies for the Pope & Young record book.

Any bear, regardless of skull measurement, is a trophy. The condition and color of the pelt may be more of a determining trophy factor than skull size to many bowhunters, myself included. I've often had clients take a smaller bear with a prime, unblemished pelt or different color phase over a larger animal with a scruffy, badly rubbed hide. Beauty is definitely in the eye of the beholder when it comes to bear pelts. The only person you have to please on your bear hunt is *you.*

Bears are tough critters with tremendous vitality and endurance. Couple these factors with the sometimes impenetrable habitat in which they thrive, and it's not hard to see that a bad hit or inferior equipment is going to lead to a less-than-desirable experience and a lost animal.

I've had bowhunters take bears with longbows, recurves, crossbows. and compounds, so any bow you can shoot well will do the job on a black bear when a good broadhead is properly placed. Several of my lady clients have made clean kills on large bears with 42-pound bows, shooting two-bladed razor-sharp cut-on-contact broadheads.

Bows and arrow shaft type are not critical as long as you can put the arrow where you want it. But broadheads are extremely critical, and so am I. I prefer a cutting type broadhead to penetrate a bear's thick fur, heavy muscle, and fat layers, and my clients and I have made many clean kills with these heads. I do not like mechanical broadheads for anything other than turkeys, and did not allow them in my bear-hunting camp, nor do I allow them in my whitetail camp in Iowa. There are simply too many things that can go wrong for me or one of my clients to take a chance on wounding and losing a bear because a broadhead malfunctioned.

Almost all the wounded and lost bears I have encountered over the past 40 years of bear hunting and guiding have been hit too far forward. I admonish my clients constantly to keep away from the massively muscled and heavyboned front shoulders. The likelihood of recovering a bear hit too far back is much greater than a front-end hit bruin. Bears are built similarly to humans, and their lungs extend much further back than most hunters think. A sharp forward-angle shot behind the shoulder can be deflected by the outside of the rib cage, or can slice along it, exiting the front of the chest. Unless the shooter is lucky enough to cut open the brachial artery down the inside of the front leg, the bear is going to get away.

Several years ago, I had a client make just such a shot on a gorgeous blonde-colored bear while bowhunting with us in Canada. He had a video camera mounted in the tree behind him and got a perfect shot of the hit and the bear running off. After watching the video numerous times and seeing the arrow strike in a seemingly perfect hit behind the shoulder, the hunter was convinced we would find his bear. I wasn't. I'd trailed the bear for a quarter

mile, then lost the blood trail entirely and figured the hit was non-fatal. However, I don't give up on a wounded animal easily, and the following morning, six of us did a grid search for four hours where I'd lost the blood trail. I became even more convinced that despite what it looked like on video, the hit did little damage to the bear.

Late that afternoon, the bowhunter killed the very same bear on the same bait. The previous hit had gone in behind the front shoulder, grazed off the ribs and exited through the front of the chest . . . just what the blood trail indicated. Both entrance and exit holes were sealed over and were starting to heal. If we hadn't seen the bear on video and identified it by its unique markings and color, we might have missed the 24-hourold wounds entirely. Bears are unique and tough animals. Treat them with the respect they deserve and you'll never have an unsuccessful bear bowhunt.

Bears spend time looking for insects in downed trees and under rocks. Still-hunting with the wind in your face in potential feeding areas will get you a bow shot like this.

Proper shot placement and a razor-sharp broadhead are critical to penetrating a bear's thick layer of fat and into its vitals for a clean kill shot.

Elk

Majestic or magnificent would have to be the words that aptly characterize a bull elk, with his head thrown back, colossal, rapier-tined, ivory-tipped, mahogany-brown antlers caging his heaving chest and flanks. His high-pitched bugling whistles and deep, growling grunts echo and reverberate across the valleys and float up the steep mountain slopes. Add a landscape of frost-sparkled meadows corralled by shimmering gold-leaved aspens, intense green spruce and pine against a backdrop of snow-capped mountain peaks, and an azure sky flawed only by puffs of clouds, and it's understandable why thoughts of bowhunting the wily wapiti run rampant in almost every bowhunter's aspirations.

If I really and seriously had to choose a single critter (*heaven forbid*) that is the ultimate bowhunting challenge year after year, and one that I never tire of bowhunting, it would be the bull elk. Elk are large, tough, intelligent beasties with survival instincts unrivaled by any other hoofed big-game animal. A mature bull can sport a set of antlers liable to give even an experienced bowhunter the adrenaline rush of a lifetime and the shakes and shimmies of a Greek belly dancer. Best of all, elk meat is about as delectable a table fare as there is, and there's lots of it.

Elk were originally foothills animals that roamed most of northern and western North America, but due to their size, herd instincts, availability and edibility, the vast herds were quickly decimated by market hunting and the survivors were forced into the most remote reaches of mountains to escape annihilation. Today, through wise and often lucky game management, the wily wapiti have expanded their range and numbers and have been reintroduced to many former haunts where they were previously eradicated.

Present-day elk are broken down into three distinct subspecies groups, the largest and most extensive being the Yellowstone elk, which has recently been re-classified as the American elk as far as the Pope & Young and Boone & Crockett record books are concerned. The Roosevelt or Olympic elk resides in the rain forests of Washington, Oregon, and southern British Columbia, Canada. The Tule elk, whose range is limited to the confines of

Elk country is immense. Your toughest challenge will be conquering the steep and heavily forested land where these majestic animals live.

California, is found in such limited numbers, with equally restricted hunting access, that it is not listed as a separate category in the Pope & Young record books, although Boone & Crockett does have a separate Tule elk category.

The American elk range extends from British Columbia, Idaho, and Nevada eastward through the Rocky Mountains and into the prairie states of North and South Dakota and Nebraska. American elk have been transplanted back into their native haunts as far east as Pennsylvania and southward to Oklahoma. Poaching and lack of the huge tracts of land needed have been the major drawbacks to some of these transplanted herds expanding fully and re-establishing themselves. For the most part, these transplants are holding their own, and in some cases the increasing numbers allow for limited hunting seasons.

American elk are by far the most numerous and widespread members of the wily wapiti family and the most sought after by the bowhunting fraternity. One would think that with hunters, from the earliest native Americans to the current compound-wielding bowhunters, pursuing them, the trophy quality and size of these majestic mountain dwellers would have declined somewhat. Nothing could be farther from the truth. Under modern game management and the wily wapiti's propensity for self preservation and reproduction, American elk are more numerous than ever, and the trophy quality of bulls in many areas has never been better.

I've often heard hunters claiming to have killed a 1000-pound bull elk, but a bull that size is a rarity. One fall on a private ranch in the south San Juan mountains of Colorado, I guided Billy Ellis to a huge 6x6 bull that about did us in packing it out. When we got the four skinned quarters to the processor, minus the legs, head, hide, and antlers, the quarters weighed a whopping 449 pounds.

It's usually figured that the four quarters without hide, head and legs will weigh approximately 50 percent of the live weight. That would put this bull's weight at 898 pounds, which stood as the heaviest four quarters weighed at that processing plant for many years and may still be the record.

Most mature bulls weigh 600 to 800 pounds live, with large mature cows in the 500-700 pound class. You don't really appreciate an elk's size until you get one down three miles from the truck on a hot September morning and wonder how the heck you're going to haul it out before it spoils or gets fly blown. Unfortunately, many elk hunters are not prepared for this chore and end up losing some of the best eating on hooves.

An elk's sense of smell will rival or exceed that of any big-game animal, including a mature whitetail buck. I've had a herd of elk wind me from half a mile away and not even hesitate in getting the heck out of Dodge. Their eyesight is superb, as is their hearing. Elk have the brain capacity and honed survival instincts to instantly add all the input from their superlative senses into an escape and evasion plan that often leaves bowhunters wondering "wha' happen?" Throw in the elk's tremendous strength, stamina, and penchant for covering miles of rugged terrain with ease, and you have a game animal worthy of the best of your bowhunting efforts.

Elk are herd animals, especially during the fall breeding period or rut. Like other antlered big game, the bulls of summer remain alone or in small bachelor herds while their velvet-covered antlers grow to fighting size. An elk's antler growth is one of nature's most phenomenal occurrences. The bulls don't shed their antlers until February or March, and their awesome headgear is fully grown by August. The only other cells that divide and grow as fast as elk antler cells are cancer cells, and much cancer research has evolved from the study of fast-growing elk antler cells. Asian people have long praised the soft velvetcovered elk antler as a cure-all for many things and as a powerful aphrodisiac.

In August, as the bulls' testosterone levels rise and their antlers harden, they move into pre-rut mode by rubbing the velvet from their antlers, fighting trees and brush, and sparring with each other to build up neck and shoulder muscles. The larger bulls move in and start hanging out with small groups of cows and calves and asserting their dominance over any bull that approaches their harem. Their cow-attracting and competitor-intimidating bugling and grunting activity increases and peaks somewhere between September 15 and October 1 in most elk areas of the West.

It's a no-brainer that calling in a belligerent, bellowing bull elk and arrowing it at point-blank range is the epitome of the elk-bowhunting experience. However, elk are out and about 24 hours a day, 365 days a year, and the peak of the rut isn't the only time to bowhunt them. In fact, it may be the toughest time to kill an elk.

Early-Season Elk-Ambushing Tactics

Archery season in most of the elk states generally opens before the bulls are fully into rut mode, filling the countryside with their high-pitched challenges and announcing their whereabouts to anything with ears. Hunting silent elk is a whole different ball game from bowhunting bugling bulls. The weather during the early part of the archery elk season is generally on the warm-to-hot side, and this can be the key to getting your arrow and a bull in the same place at the same time.

Elk will retreat to the deep timber shortly after day break. You may find them in small clearings in basins where the hunting pressure is light or non-existent.

Over the years, my clients and I have had a much higher success rate per elk encounter when hunting from ambush than using any other method. During the early season, elk wallows, waterholes or springs, natural mineral licks, and travel routes are deadly places to set an ambush. Elk are not quite as habitual in their daily movements as some of the other species of big game, but they do have favorite haunts that they use regularly enough to make patiently hunting them a worthwhile endeavor.

Pit blinds have long been one of my favorite methods of ambushing elk. Whether they're in an oak brush thicket where there aren't any trees big enough for a tree stand or in an open meadow at the edge of a wide-open pond, pit blinds are the most deadly elk tactic in the book.

Several years ago, I was bowhunting with outfitter Dick Ray in New Mexico in the early season, when it was hot and dry. I'd passed up several small bulls and called in a nice 5 × 5 for one of Dick's hunters, but still hadn't found the one I wanted. I had several days left to bowhunt when Dick told me that some ranch hands building fence on a high bench covered with dense oak brush motts had seen a 6 × 6 bull watering two afternoons in a row at

a tank dam in the middle of a wide-open pasture. According to them, the bull came from one direction one late afternoon and the opposite direction the following afternoon.

The next afternoon, one of Dick's guides and I drove to the area and found the waterhole pounded by elk tracks. There wasn't a speck of cover within 100 yards of the small pond. We finished the three-hour chore of digging a spacious pit blind into the face of the dam and camouflaging it with oak brush and were settled in its shaded interior by 5:00 p.m. At 5:30, I arrowed a huge 6 × 6 that walked out of the oak brush 200 yards across the meadow and came straight to the waterhole without giving our blind a second glance. I'll trade three hours of digging for a bull like that any day.

Pit blinds can be used almost anywhere you can get a hole in the ground. Elk are accustomed to danger approaching or appearing above ground level, and they tend to overlook things below eye level. A few years ago, my secretary, Dawn Walker, bowhunted a pit blind we'd dug 25 yards from a spring in an open valley within a mile of my house. She wasn't going to be fussy and intended to take the first legal elk within bow range. The first afternoon she sat in the blind, a half dozen elk charged off the oak brush slopes to water just before dark. There were several cows and a nice 4 × 4 bull drinking 20 yards from her, and she couldn't shoot because there was a spike bull (protected in Colorado) standing *five feet* away, right in the shooting lane, and another just a bit farther out. They shuffled around in front of her, almost kicking dirt into the pit, completely unaware of her presence. The others finished watering and wandered into the meadow to feed and then moved in to water. The next afternoon, she arrowed a hefty yearling and had to call on reinforcements to help her get it out.

A pit blind is about as simple and easy an ambush site as you can get. When possible, I dig them to the same dimensions as my antelope blinds and usually cover them over entirely with sagebrush, tumble weeds, oak brush, or pine boughs, so the bowhunter is sitting in the dark. An elk's sense of smell is acute, so choosing a pit blind location downwind is very important. However, I've found that scent control is much easier hunting out of a pit blind. Unless there is a stiff breeze, human scent tends to hang in the cooler confines of the pit. The surrounding covering, sprayed liberally with scent eliminator or scent killer or doused with a potent elk scent, helps dilute or cover the dreaded human odor. On several occasions, my clients and I have had elk munch on the leaves and branches covering a pit blind. Talk about a heart-thumping encounter.

The other end of the elk-ambushing spectrum is the use of tree stands. I've had clients take a number of elk from tree stands over wallows, springs, mineral licks, and well-traveled trails over the years, and they can be one of the most efficient and effective methods of bowhunting elk. Elk won't hesitate to look up, so movement or the lack thereof is a crucial factor.

A lightweight, portable tree stand is an essential item if you're planning an elk bowhunt. Leave the climbers at home, because most western tree types have too many limbs to make them usable, and even though they can be used on quaking aspen, care should be taken to keep your safety belt in constant use because the spongy, soft bark of an aspen can peel out from under the stand and give you a rough ride to the ground.

Background is extremely important when putting up a tree stand for elk. Elk are well-tuned to the dangers associated with the human shape, and getting skylined is a sure way to end your elk bowhunt on a sour note. I've had elk taken from tree stands in cedars and junipers that were only eight feet off the ground because the almost solid background and dense shadows made the bowhunter invisible to the elk. Height isn't nearly as important as good background cover and concealment.

There have been a lot of pros and cons written about how effective it is to bowhunt elk wallows, and there is no pat answer that covers all conditions. I've taken elk bowhunting well-used wallows and spent many fruitless hours sitting over a seemingly "hot" wallow without seeing hide nor hair of a wily wapiti.

Elk are liable to use a wallow at any time of day or night, and there doesn't seem to be a peak time to hunt at one. I've found that during hot and dry weather, bowhunting wallows late morning and early afternoon seems to pay off about as much as any other time. Locating and hunting over a well-used fresh wallow during mid-day is a good way to spend time between your early morning spot-and-stalk or bugling hunt and your late afternoon hunt.

Spot-and-Stalk Elk Bowhunting

Spot-and-stalk bowhunting is the second most productive method of putting an elk on the ground with a bow and arrow, and can be a real test of your bowhunting skill and perseverance.

Elk are big animals and live in big country, and this combination is what gives spot-and-stalk hunters nightmares. I've heard it said that 90 percent of the elk live in 10 percent of the country, and while that may not be true under all circumstances, it's a pretty fair summation of the situation. Most first-time elk hunters can't

comprehend the vastness of elk country and the ease with which these long-legged ungulates roam their home habitat.

Many whitetail bowhunters try the same tactics on elk and come up short because they don't cover enough ground. My spot-and-stalk philosophy is to get into the area I intend hunting in the pre-dawn darkness and try to cover as much ground as I can, until I locate elk, either by sound, fresh tracks and droppings or smell.

Since I am very careful to take advantage of the slightest mountain breeze and hunt with the wind in my favor as much as humanly possible, I can often smell the sweet, licorice-like smell of elk before I see them. I've had clients follow me around for days without realizing that I'm constantly checking the wind with my trusty powder bottle filled with talcum powder. Sometimes all it takes is a small shift in direction to keep the wind in your favor, and it's senseless to try stalking or still-hunting elk if they have the slightest chance of smelling you.

Many times I've glassed elk that spooked at a hunter's scent while the hunter was a half-mile or more away. Doesn't take much human scent to pollute the pure mountain air to the point of spooking a hunter-shy elk. The problem is seriously compounded if you're bowhunting when the elk are

If you hunt public land, let other hunters move the elk around during the mid-day hours. Keep posted during your lunch break where you can glass an area where elk may show.

herded up and the number of eyes, ears, and noses is multiplied. Keep this fact in mind on your elk hunts: *When the sun goes up, so does the wind, and when the sun sinks, the late afternoon breeze flows downhill.*

I'm always amazed when a client shows up for an elk hunt and doesn't have a good pair of binoculars. Many bowhunters feel binoculars are for use in wide-open country and from a stand, but I make constant use of them when spot-and-stalk or still-hunting through the woods. I glass every nook and cranny that might harbor a hidden elk, looking for anything that could possibly be the ear, nose, rump patch or antler tip of a hidden elk.

Even binoculars are not infallible when it comes to dealing with elk. Last fall, I was poking along through a dense patch of thick downfall timber when I spotted a light patch of color against the dark background. I froze in midstride and glassed the patch for a full 30 minutes, trying to tell whether it was an elk or a patch of sunlight against the rotted end of a stump. A dozen times I decided it had to be the side of a bull elk and two dozen times I decided it was the end of a stump. After half an hour, my eyes burned like someone had poured salt in them as I tried vainly to find ears, antlers or anything that resembled part of an elk. Finally my patience gave out and I convinced myself that no self-respecting elk would lay there that long without some hint of movement. Even then I wasn't convinced, and decided to backtrack and approach from a different angle. Hah! The wily elk was more patient than I was, 'cause the instant I took a step backward, a 5 × 5 bull crashed out of its bed and vanished.

Don't waste your money on a small cheapie set of pocket binoculars, 'cause they'll just cause you grief and maybe cost you a trophy elk. Binoculars are a once-in-a-lifetime purchase, so get a second job, save your money, and buy the best set of binoculars you can afford. For elk hunting, I prefer a set of quality medium-sized 7 × 42 or 8 × 32s. These glasses are powerful enough for long-distance glassing, but gather plenty of light for early-morning and late afternoon glassing, and are especially useful in dark-timber situations. Don't just buy them and carry them in your fanny pack or daypack. Get used to using them regularly. They can make a big difference in the success or failure of your spot-and-stalk elk hunt.

High-country, above timberline, spot-and-stalk bowhunting is the epitome of the elk-hunting challenge. There's no way an elk hunt in such country can be anything but successful, even if you never kill an elk.

Fortunately or unfortunately, there are no figures on just how many spot-and-stalk elk hunts are blown by impatience. Judging from my own experiences, I'd say the figure is above the 90 percent level. It seems no matter how long you wait, it's not long enough. If you err, do so on the side of patience.

Spotting elk in the high country can be easy or difficult, depending on how smart you work your spotting. Trying to pick out elk in the early morning or late afternoon grayness of a shadowed mountainside is exceedingly difficult when you're trying to glass *into* the sun. Glassing elk when the early morning or late afternoon sun is at your back, with its gilding rays of warm light lighting up the scenery, and the elk's light-tan hide, is a piece of cake.

There are places where I only glass when the morning sun lights up the countryside and any elk around glow like neon signs, and places where I only glass in the early evening for the same reason. There are places where I have to change locations a few hundred yards as the sun moves up or down to see into pockets, valleys, clearings, and hidey holes with the light working for me. Make the shadows and light work for you, rather than inhibiting your ability to pick out the shape or form of an elk long before it has a chance to pick you out. The key to success in spot-and-stalk bowhunting any critter is to pinpoint your quarry *before* it spots you.

Another key to long-distance high-country spot-and-stalk elk bowhunting is having and making use of a good spotting scope. I have two favorites. The first is my Nikon 15 × -45 × , 72 mm ED Field Scope with an accessory 60x eyepiece for ultra-long-distance spotting, when conditions are optimum and I need the additional power to judge a trophy or pick a foolproof stalking route. This scope is on the heavy side, but is superbly sharp and clear at the higher magnification, and I generally use it with a sturdy tripod or window mount on my truck window.

The second is a lightweight, waterproof, rubber-armored Nikon 16 × - 48 × XL Spotter II. This little scope is also very sharp and clear and easily transported in a fanny pack or daypack into the roughest, back country elk terrain. A small, sturdy tripod increases the scope's effectiveness, but I generally use it supported by my hat or pack over a log or rock with equally good results.

Elk Calling 101

"How the heck can anyone miss an animal the size of a bull elk at 30 yards or less" my client questioned as we sat down to one of my wife's sumptuous suppers the night before his elk bowhunt started.

"Kind of hard to explain," I replied to the point, "until you've been there."

The second day of his bowhunt, we were slipping our way through the dense oak brush on a side slope in the dark when we heard a bull bugle on the slope above and in front of us.

There was a series of small clearings or meadows interspersed with large and small oak brush motts on the slope, and the bull sounded like he was within a couple hundred yards. I put my client in front of a small clump of oak brush where his green camo would blend with the background and slid down at the base of a Ponderosa a few yards behind him. The breeze was drifting down the slope,

One of the best elk calls is a cow call. Keep the calling light and be ready for action if a bull is within calling range.

so we'd have the wind on the bull unless he circled below us, a definite possibility.

The bull bugled every ten minutes or so, and as soon as there was good shooting light, I waited for a bugle, then immediately answered with some seductive (I thought) cow calls. The bull fired back instantly and I could see by my client's body language that he was fully alert and ready for action.

The bull's next bugle left little doubt he was headed our way. Five minutes later, his tan form came drifting silently through the brush 50 yards in front of us. The cautious bull drifted down hill and stopped just out of bow range, where he locked up and bugled several times, trying to get a rise out of the cow he'd heard, and gave us a good look at his tall, massive 6 × 6 rack.

Much to the consternation of my compadre, I never made a sound. I'd been frequently checking the breeze with my powder bottle as the bull approached and figured, if I called, he'd likely sidehill below us, just out of range, and pick up our scent. After ten tense minutes, the bull finally lost interest and moseyed back the way he'd come. The minute he was out of sight, I slithered to my client and motioned for him to hustle forward 50 yards to another clump of oak brush, where we quickly set up in the same relative positions.

Once again I cow called excitedly, getting an immediate response from the bull less than 100 yards up the slope. I quickly cut loose with a challenging high-pitched spike-bull squeal followed by several more beseeching cow mews. The bull came crashing through the bushes, stopped behind a clump of brush 40 yards in front of my client and proceeded to thrash the brush grunting and bugling his sex-crazed fury.

I was keeping one eye on my client kneeling ten feet from me and could see his arrow bouncing on the rest as the bull circled around the brush and headed our way. When he stepped into a small opening 30 yards below us, I chirped sharply and brought him to a halt where my thoroughly shook-up bowhunter put an arrow right over his shoulders. The bull vanished as quickly as he came, and we could hear him crashing brush and rattling rocks for 200 yards up the hill.

"That's exactly how people miss elk at point-blank range," I chortled to my chagrined, red-faced client. "Now you've been there."

Every elk bowhunter dreams of bugling a bull within bow range, and I'll be the first to admit this is as good as bowhunting gets. However, calling elk isn't the same as it was when I killed my first elk in the early '60s. Today's elk hunter is far more knowledgeable, with a better understanding of elk habits and idiosyncrasies, and calling techniques and tactics, than ever before. With the proliferation of magazine articles, videos, television programs and live seminars, the plethora of elk bowhunting and calling information available is phenomenal.

Unfortunately, the elk have learned about as rapidly as their nemesis, and those that didn't learn have been removed from the gene pool.

I bugled in my first bull with a coiled piece of gas pipe that sounded horrible compared to modern calls, but the elk were so uninitiated, they responded readily. Today I call less than ever and rarely bugle, but my percent of response is as good or better than ever.

When I enter the woods, elk hunting during the rut, I try to remain totally undetected by the elk until I am in the best-possible position to seduce or infuriate a bull within bow range. I've observed many bowhunters tooting and chirping their way through the woods like the pied piper of the Rockies, and even if they get a bull to respond to their calling, they don't know it.

During the early part of the bow season in most elk states, the elk are just tuning up for the rut and only bugling perfunctorily. They'll respond to good calling at this time, but guardedly and silently. When I feel I'm close to elk in the early season, I set up and use cow and calf mews and chirps for at least an hour or more without moving.

Later in the season, when the herd bulls have gathered their harems, the rules of engagement change. There are lots of eyes, ears, and noses to defeat getting within range of herd bull, and calling him away from his harem is a tough proposition. I've found the best way to do this is to get as close to the herd without spooking them before making a sound. Start calling too soon and the bull will round up his girls and move them away. By the time the dominant bulls have their harems together, they're ready to forgo the fighting for some *loving*, and if given half a chance will drive their cows away from aggressive bugling.

When I'm hunting a herd bull covered up by cows, I try to sneak as close as possible making sure the wind is in my favor. When I get close (depending on my whims and the conditions), I'll usually cow call softly in hopes of suckering the bull away from his herd. Squealing like a competing spike at this time might just spook him into flight with his harem or bring him on the run.

Several years ago, I slipped to within 75 yards of a herd with a good bull and managed to get between the bull and most of his harem as they crossed an overgrown logging road. I was kneeling behind some serviceberry bushes with the bull just over the ridge above me. When I cut loose with a spike-bull squeal, that dang bull charged down the hill and sideswiped the bush I was behind with his awesome antlers. Try staying in place when that happens. By the time I got my heart off the roof of my mouth and my arrow back on the string, the whole herd had vanished.

As I mentioned, my first elk call was a coiled gas pipe. I went from there to a modified Herters metal-reed deer call that I had to blow so hard to get the breaking bugle, the insides of my cheeks often ended up bleeding at the end of a day of elk calling. A diaphragm turkey call and 36-inch piece of 1 1/4-inch PVC pipe as a grunt tube put the variety into elk calling. With this combo, I could bugle, squeal, chirp, and mew to vary my calling to suit the situation. Today I use the Primos palate plate and Quaker Boy diaphragm calls along with Woods Wise and Quaker Boy Hyper cow calls, with a Primos grunt tube for most of my calling. There are hundreds of superb elk calls of every type to choose from, and all will work some of the time, and none that I know will work all of the time.

Each and every rutting-elk encounter requires its own strategy and tactics, and while you can learn *how* to call and bugle elk from the profusion of available information, learning *when* to call elk is the key to putting that bull at pointblank range, where you can't possibly miss. And that comes from experience.

Decoying Elk

Elk bulls today are much more cautious and circumspect when they respond to calling, and over the past 10 years, I've had few that came on the run looking for trouble. Most will come in slow and easy looking for the cow or bull that is making the racket. When they don't see the sound source, they tend to get spooky and, at best, circle downwind to scent-check the area. At worst, they just get the heck out of Dodge.

I've hunted with decoys of various sorts all my life, and for years I felt an elk decoy would work wonders in allaying an approaching elk's suspicions and bring him the final yardage needed for a good bow shot. However, I didn't relish the thought of carrying a full-body taxidermy mount or archery target through the woods at 9,000 feet to accomplish this purpose.

When I met and discussed this with Dave Berkeley, owner of Feather Flex decoys, it didn't take long to come up with prototype lightweight foam elk decoys that could be rolled and transported easily. The silhouette decoy we came up with was full-sized, without a head for ease of design and portability. The decoy fastened between two trees with lightweight bungee cords, and the elk looked as if its head was hidden by the tree trunk or brush.

Using a two-man approach to calling in a bull elk will allow a hunter to concentrate on the bull and his own movement, while the other partner does the calling. Close encounters like this are not uncommon!

This new decoy worked extremely well and brought a number of elk within bow range for me and my clients, but it still lacked the prime ingredient, extreme portability. I've had several manufacturers approach me for advice on elk decoys, and the one thing I stress is that the decoy has to fit in a daypack or fanny pack. This is a tough requirement, but if you can't take it with you when you leave the truck in the morning and pack it all day every day, chances are you aren't going to have it with you when you really need it.

Jerry McPherson, owner and designer of Montana Decoys, solved that problem with photo-realistic cow elk decoys that collapse in a hoop; small and light enough to be carried all day, every day of your elk bowhunt. And they really do work.

On one of my first attempts to decoy a bull, I left my prototype decoy hanging between two immature spruce bushes along the edge of a meadow while my hunting partner and I went pursuing a bull that had come in behind us. When we returned several hours later, another bull had come along and evidently made a pass at my silhouette decoy, tangling his antlers in the cords and the flip-floppy decoy. According to the profusion of skid marks in the meadow, the bull threw a fit for 50 yards trying to get the clinging decoy out of his antlers.

Adding a decoy to your calling set-up and appealing to both the bull's hearing and sight might just tip the balance in your favor when you're dealing with a curious but cautious or wary bull. As an added attraction, I use elk scent around the decoy to appeal to or confuse the elk's sense of smell.

I make sure my decoy is set where an approaching elk can spot it from some distance, as I've found that a decoy suddenly popping into view will spook an elk or arouse its suspicions. When they can see the decoy for some distance and at the same time they hear elk sounds, it arouses their curiosity and they are much more liable to come

Using a decoy will help tip the odds in your favor. Place the decoy where it can be spotted from a distance as the bull comes in to your calls.

closer. When decoying and calling elk, I try to position myself where it is difficult or impossible for an approaching elk to sneak around behind me, and the path of least resistance puts him in good shooting position.

I try to place me or my client, off to one side and between the incoming elk and the decoy, but not in direct line of sight between the elk and decoy. I've had elk so engrossed with the decoy, I was able to draw and let down several times within 20 yards without them paying any heed to my slight movement. Decoys can be a deadly and effective addition to your elk bowhunting arsenal, but only if you carry it with you each and every time you go elk hunting.

Shot Placement and Equipment

Elk are *tough*! I've bowhunted many species of big-game animals, and in my experience, none are tougher nor more survival-driven than elk. Where a hard-hit whitetail buck will travel 200 yards, a bull elk with the same hit can go half a mile. The heart-lung kill zone on bull elk is roughly twice the size of that on whitetail deer, 20 inches to 24 inches. This

The kill zone on a bull elk is about twice the size as that of a whitetail. Practice shooting at 30 to 40 yards with a kill zone target area of about 20 to 24 inches.

makes little difference. One bowhunter made a clean one-shot kill on a 5 × 5 bull with a 42-pound bow. The bow that you shoot the best is the one you want to use for elk hunting. While there's a lot of latitude in bow type and weight for bowhunting elk, the one equipment factor where there is absolutely no leeway is broadhead dependability and sharpness.

I prefer and have taken many elk with *"cut-on-contact"* broadheads. However, I *do not* like or recommend mechanical broadheads of any kind. Why base the success or failure of your elk bowhunt on a head that may or may not work, when there are many solid and proven heads that leave no doubt?

Bowhunting elk is the supreme western big-game challenge, so make sure you're prepared for the encounter.

means that a 40-yard shot on a bull elk is equivalent to a 20-yard shot on a whitetail, *if* you spend the time practicing at the longer distances.

I've had many eastern and Midwestern clients who stated they wouldn't take a shot over 20 yards. I can appreciate their discretion, but they are cheating themselves and decreasing their chances of success. In the wide-open spaces the wary wapiti call home, shot distances may be extended considerably, and you need to practice, practice, practice at the longer distances to increase your chances of scoring on a bull.

You might surprise yourself at how well you can shoot at 60 yards with lots of practice, and conscientious practice at these distances will make a 35-yard shot seem close. Also, practice from a variety of shooting positions. Shoot from your knees, sitting, twisted sideways and to the off side. Elk have a way of coming from the most unpredictable angles, and practicing these shots will prepare you for such an eventuality.

I've had clients take elk with longbows, recurves, and compounds, and the type of bow

Mule Deer and Blacktail

Taking a trophy mule deer with a bow and arrow just may be today's toughest bowhunting challenge. Throughout much of the west, the mule-deer population is in a drastic decline, and finding a trophy buck that will make the Pope & Young record book is getting tougher with each passing year.

What this boils down to for the bowhunter looking for the best opportunity to arrow a decent mule deer buck is more critical research and care in choosing areas that have a recent history for producing record-class mule deer bucks. It used to be that a bowhunter could head west and hunt almost anywhere in the mountains of Colorado, Utah, Wyoming, or Montana, have a decent chance at seeing lots of mule deer and getting a chance or two at a good buck. Those days are long gone.

A look at the statistical summary of the last P&Y biennial recording period and last record book can provide a wealth of information, not only about where the best bucks were taken, but also the most successful method of hunting them. As a point of comparison, there are roughly eight times the number of whitetails entered into the record book as mule deer. This means putting a mule deer in the book is eight times more difficult than taking a Pope & Young whitetail. These figures should give you an idea of the task you've chosen if you decide you want a mule deer buck for your trophy room wall.

Colorado is still the top trophy-producing state for mule deer (both typical and non-typical), followed by Utah. Wyoming, Oregon, and Idaho also produce many typical and non-typical mule deer, and Kansas is number three in the production of non-typical mule deer.

I can swear by this statistic. Several years ago, I was bowhunting whitetails with my good friends Drew, Mary and Bob McCartney in north-central Kansas, and rattled in a 180-plus, non-typical muley buck. The curious buck came right up to my whitetail decoy and stood broadside at 20 yards, while I cussed Kansas law, that prohibits non-residents from taking mule deer on a nonresident archery deer license.

Today you might have a better chance of arrowing a monster muley off the back porch of an urbanite, living on the edge of one of the small towns in the foothills along the front range of the Rockies, than in one of the remote, hidden, high valleys on the western slope. The mule deer have moved close to human habitation and actually invaded many of the small mountain communities to escape from constant pressure by the escalating mountain lion, coyote, and bear populations.

I used to make an annual trip to Estes Park, Colorado, in late November and early December to photograph the huge bucks that migrated to the lower reaches of Rocky Mountain National Park, then into the city limits as winter and coyotes pushed them down from their high-country homeland. It wasn't uncommon to find 20 to 30 bucks, from a hefty 170 points to monsters well over 200 points, in the area, along with plenty of does and fawns.

During the fall of 2003, I swung through Estes on my way back from Iowa (for Thanksgiving at home) in hopes of photographing some bucks. Ha! In two days of driving around, I found a dozen mule deer (total) and only two small bucks. According to the local conservation officer, Chronic Wasting Disease (CWD) had wiped out most of the deer in the area, and the few that were left by this insidious disease were further hammered by the coyotes and big cats.

Many of the historically famous mule-deer areas are no longer good bets for bowhunters, and some areas that haven't been noted for producing big mule deer are gaining ground. Many of the prairie states and provinces are producing big bucks, simply because they are out of cougar country and the bucks get a chance to grow to trophy proportions, especially on private ranches and areas where there is still predator control of some sort.

Don't overlook eastern Colorado, New Mexico, Wyoming, Montana, and the Dakotas in your search for a prime mule deer bowhunting location. Alberta is also high on the list of trophy mule deer producers, and there are some areas of the province that offer excellent, non-resident bowhunting opportunities. Start planning well ahead of time, so you can thoroughly research your mule deer bowhunt. It will be time well spent.

Mule deer are open-country, migratory critters that live in and roam much larger expanses of habitat than whitetails, with a far less defined home range. The muleys' yen to roam makes them more unpredictable than whitetails and more difficult to pattern and ambush. However, the broken, more open country they call home makes them an ideal subject for spot-and- stalk bowhunting. Roughly 60 percent of the mule deer bucks entered into the Pope & Young record book were taken by the spot-andstalk method.

Spot-and-Stalk Muley Hunting

The key to successful spot-and-stalk bowhunting is just what the words imply. First you have to spot the buck and then you stalk him. Sounds simple, but considering some of the large-scale and inhospitable country the big muley bucks call home, bowhunting them by this method can involve lots of time and plenty of patience, not to mention a good share of luck. For my money, spotand- stalk mule deer bowhunting in the high country, above timberline, is the quintessential bowhunting experience.

If you bowhunt properly using this method, you're going to be spending most of your time spotting, judging, planning, and plotting rather than stalking. The most important part of your bowhunting equipment will be your optics. Good binoculars and a quality spotting scope will make the job of spotting a trophy mule deer much easier and more comfortable. I've often stayed in one location, glassing for a big buck in good mule deer

Wherever you hunt muleys, you'll need excellent binoculars. Your bare eyes won't pick out mule deer (or parts of mule deer) in the draws, gullies, canyons, and other hidey holes they favor.

country, for eight to ten hours at a time. A cheap pair of binoculars with poor-quality lenses will have your eyes feeling like they've been sandpapered and salted after a concentrated couple of hours of glassing slopes and ridges, trying to pick out the well-camouflaged form of a stalkable mule deer buck. Buying a pair of quality binoculars is a lifetime investment, and if you choose carefully, it may just be the most useful and valuable single item of equipment in your bowhunting arsenal.

Any quality binoculars in 7×, 8× or 10× will work for glassing mule deer. For the longer distances usually involved, I prefer 10× binoculars. Mine are sharp, center-focus binoculars that are tough, lightweight, medium-sized, and gather light unbelievably well, all prerequisites for mule deer spotting.

A lightweight, good-quality, variable-power spotting scope is essential for critical long-range spotting, pinpointing deer locations, judging trophy quality, and choosing a stalking route to your quarry. I found that 15 - 45× is the best all-round power. The lower setting isn't too powerful for general scanning and spotting; yet the higher setting is strong enough for critical long-distance trophy judging and picking out details in terrain features. I have a 60× eyepiece for my 60 mm spotting scope, but this is only usable under perfect conditions with a rock solid rest or tripod.

The next most important element of your spot-and-stalk mule-deer hunt is *patience*! It's difficult for any bowhunter in spectacularly open muley habitat to master sitting in one location and have his eyes do the walking and work. Most bowhunters want to move out and comb the countryside in an attempt to locate any bucks in the area. Not good. The essential element to the success of your mule-deer bowhunt is whether you can spot a trophy buck before it spots you. Guess that's why they call it spot-and-stalk bowhunting.

You'll be a lot less likely to give yourself away to a sharp-eyed muley by sitting quietly and comfortably in the shade of a tree, under a rock ledge, or even in the cab of your pickup, and let your eyes cover the countryside. This is much more efficient than traipsing over hill and dale, rattling rocks, filling the air with your pungent scent, and, in general, letting everything with fur and feathers know there's an intruder in the area.

Locating mule deer is best accomplished during the early morning hours, when the deer are most active and time is on your side. Nothing is more frustrating than spotting a good buck in the late afternoon and not having enough time to get within stalking distance before dark. Of course, this will give you an excellent starting point the following morning and certainly narrow down your search area, so early evening spotting is definitely worthwhile.

Mule deer spend much of their time in the open. They will often bed on an open hillside, at the base of a small tree, under a ledge, or in the shade of a bush, where they have a panoramic view of their surroundings. There are many times when a crafty old buck's bedding or loafing location makes for an impossible stalking situation. *Be patient.* A very high percentage of blown stalks are due to one fundamental faux pas: *impatience.*

When glassing for mule deer, it's important to make use of every little trick you can muster. Always try to glass with the sun at your back, lighting up the area you're glassing. The mule deer's gray coloration was designed to blend with his habitat, and it's unbelievable how well this camouflage works against the broken pattern of shadow, rocks, and brush. The golden rays of early-morning and late afternoon sunlight will reduce the effectiveness of this camouflage and make a muley's hide stand out like a diamond against a lump of coal. Plan your glassing to take advantage of this fact.

Don't sit there in blissful ignorance and figure you're always going to spot a full-bodied, magnificent, heavy-antlered buck perfectly outlined against a grassy background in plain sight! It

happens, but you're better off looking for a shape that seems out of place, like an antler sticking up over a bush, a partial rear end patch on the backside of a thicket, or the flick of an ear or tail against a shadowy background. Spot the little things that don't quite fit their surroundings, and then take the time to put together the rest of the pieces and parts with the aid of you binoculars or spotting scope, and you'll locate a lot more mule deer.

The tough part, when patience becomes even more important, is *after* you spot a good buck that has your mouth watering and puts a tremor in your bow hand. This is the time that most spot-and-stalk hunts are blown. The uncontrollable urge to proceed with the stalk often overrides the common sense of taking the time to properly plan it from the first to last step. *Big* mule deer bucks didn't grow to trophy size by being stupid and making mistakes. A mature buck has super eyesight, a keen sense of smell and phenomenal hearing, combined with the survival instincts to get him out of danger in the most expeditious manner possible. Don't overlook the slightest detail when planning your stalk.

This is the aspect of your mule-deer bowhunt when a good spotting scope can pay for itself in short order. You can use your spotting scope to choose every inch of your stalking route. Study the smallest detail of the terrain features between you and your adversary without ever leaving your observation post and taking a chance on spooking the deer.

If you spot a buck or bucks feeding in the early morning, unless they are close and in an ideal location for a relatively quick stalk with everything in your favor, it might be better strategy to wait until they bed down for a mid-morning siesta. There are, of course, times in a spot-and-stalk hunting situation where you may have a chance at success by pushing the envelope a bit, and getting the stalk on without wasting time. On several occasions, I've located mule deer feeding along a slope or flat, and headed for brush or timber that would make an ideal ambush point . . . *if I could*

Big buck mule deer live in rough, rocky, isolated, and lonely places. Don't forget to glass shady spots where they like to feed, bed, and hide.

get there ahead of them. In this situation, go for it, but don't forget the deer's senses of smell, hearing, and eyesight in your stalk and don't rush it.

Once the deer get bedded down and stay put for 15 minutes or so, make sure you know where each and every deer is located. If it's a long stalk over difficult terrain, don't hesitate to draw a rough diagram of the situation and make use of it during your stalk. The countryside and objects look a lot different through binoculars or a spotting scope due to limited depth of field and the compression factor of optics. Make sure you pinpoint the deer's location with a landmark you can identify without question when you get close to where you last saw your quarry. There have been a number of times when failure to fully pinpoint a buck's exact location has let the buck win the encounter. There have been an equal number of times when the untrustworthy deer moved while we were in the process of the perfect stalk, and the buck wasn't where it was expected to be. Stalking mule deer is never cut-and-dried; so don't get overconfident, impatient or careless at this stage of your hunt. It will cost you dearly!

Spot-and-stalk bowhunting can often be better used by two bowhunters working together. Four eyes are always better than two, and once a deer is located, having one set of eyes glued to the deer while the other bowhunter makes the stalk increases the odds of success considerably. Take the time to work out a set of clear and concise signals to communicate from both ends of the stalk, without miscommunication. Leave the slightest opening in this regard, and you can bet Murphy will pop out of the brush and throw the screws to your best-laid plans . . . big time.

Backpack Mule Deer

One of the major reasons for backpack bowhunting mule deer is that it allows you to get into prime mule-deer country that is almost inaccessible by any other method of hunting. One of my favorite mountain bowhunting axioms always has been, "When you get into country where there are no people, you'll find game!" Backpacking for trophy mule deer may just be your best option for that out-west, high-country hunting venture. There's little doubt that a spot-and-stalk bowhunt for a gigantic mountain muley is the epitome of bowhunting challenges, and a backpack high-country hunt has to be the supreme mule-deer bowhunting experience.

Despite what some bowhunters think, a trophy mule deer buck can be as crafty and spooky as a whitetail. Letting such a buck see or smell you in his home area is just inviting him to disappear without a trace. By carefully backpacking into the area, keeping the mountain breezes in your favor, staying on the back side of the ridges in the heavy timber, and setting up a dry camp with a minimum of noise or disturbance, you won't broadcast the fact that you're around to anything bigger than the local pikas and rockchucks.

One of the major drawing cards to a backpack, high-country bowhunt is *cost*! You can't go much cheaper than loading the family car with your

Plan your spot-and-stalk route well in advance. Keep the wind in your face and wait for the right shot. Always keep an eye out for other deer—deer you originally didn't see that would blow your stalk.

hunting equipment—backpack, sleeping bag, 8 × 10 foot piece of plastic, minimum amount of food, an aluminum pot with sterno stove—and driving to the nearest high-country mule deer habitat. Backpack bowhunting can get you into many areas that are not readily accessible by any other method. You can do it on your own or with a bowhunting buddy, rather than having to hire the services of a professional outfitter or guide, thereby saving money, adding challenge and the resulting element of self-satisfaction to your hunt.

The first step in setting up a backpack bowhunt is to pick an area where there is a huntable population of mule deer, in country that's suitable for backpacking. Get hunting info from various western states, listing seasons and dates, to begin the process. Most western state Game & Fish Departments also

provide harvest data or kill figures on the different game management units within the state. With this info and a general state map, you can begin to narrow down your choices.

Look for units that have low density of hunters and a good success ratio in areas with lots of wild and wooly country. There are many areas in the western mountains where you can park the family station wagon (or minivan) along the highway on a high mountain pass, at a mountaintop microwave tower, campground, U.S.F.S. trailhead leading to a wilderness area, or on the end of a logging road at the base of a mountain, and go backpacking. No need for a 4 × 4 pickup, four-wheeler, or horses and trailer to get you close to some of the best big-buck country available.

Another option that's a bit more expensive, but far cheaper than an outfitted mule-deer bowhunt, is a drop-camp high-country bowhunt. This is a great way to get into good mule deer country *if* you do your homework and choose the area you want to be packed into yourself. Leaving the choice of a drop camp up to a horse-packing outfit that doesn't do any scouting, and is more interested in the ease of getting into and out of the back country than its potential for trophy bucks, may not be in your best interest. There are outfitters who have set drop camps in excellent deer country and will pack you in and out for a reasonable price. By far the best plan is to thoroughly research a hunting area and then have a packer cart you and your equipment to *your* chosen location.

Still Hunting Mule Deer

An additional method for bowhunting mule deer bucks is by still hunting, with approximately 15 percent of the Pope & Young entries taken using this method. This totals up to 75 percent of the bucks being taken by spot-and-stalk and still hunting methods.

In my experience, it's really tough to differentiate between the two methods. When you're still-hunting through a pocket of timber, keeping your eyes open for a buck, you're basically spotting on the move. When you locate a buck, your still hunt turns to a stalk even if it's only for a few yards. When you spot a buck from a distance and ease carefully into bow range, are you stalking him or still-hunting him? Who cares . . . as long as you end up with him on the ground?

Still hunting through a piece of likely mule-deer habitat takes the same patience and locating skills as spot-and-stalk hunting, only this time you don't know for sure exactly where you quarry is located. Remember, you're more likely to see only a portion of a deer rather than the whole animal. Key your thinking to this aspect. Many neophyte muley bowhunters don't even consider binoculars for this type of hunting, but I can tell you from experience that good light-gathering glasses are even *more* important for this type of hunting.

Still hunting is hunting "up close and personal," in close quarters where a single step can make the difference between success and disaster. Binoculars will tell in short order if a light patch is a deer's rear end or just a sunlit patch of grass, if that slight movement was the tip of an antler showing from behind a tree or bush or the movement of a pine squirrel. Carry binoculars with you all the time and force yourself to use them constantly. Once you find out their value in close quarter still-hunting, you'll never be without them for any of your bowhunting ventures.

Remember the three main detriments to your getting within bow range of a trophy mule deer buck in still-hunting are wind, noise, and movement. *Always* still hunt through an area with the wind or breeze in your favor. The best way to accomplish this is to use a squeeze bottle filled with talcum powder and let the prevailing breeze dictate exactly how you still hunt through the area. Try to move as slowly and cautiously as possible, stopping often to survey and glass the terrain you're working into.

Tree-stand hunting for mule deer is not a new phenomenon, but it's one that is rapidly gaining popularity, simply because of its proven effectiveness. Only eight percent of the record-book entries for mule deer were taken from tree stands, while a whopping 78 percent of whitetails are taken using this method. Tree stands for mule deer can be deadly when properly placed.

There have been numerous occasions when I have been still hunting or spot-and-stalk hunting and have seen a good buck in an ideal location where a tree stand would work, or come upon a mineral lick or heavily used trail from a feeding area that is an obvious location for a tree stand. A well-placed tree stand with good background cover and good treestand hunting techniques is a highly effective mule-deer tactic. Ideal tree-stand locations are overlooking waterholes, travel ways leading to feeding areas or croplands, in saddles and cuts where deer travel from one range or drainage to another, and other locations where a muley's travels are narrowed down to a specific ambush point. With the mule deer's propensity for open country with sparse tree cover, there are often ideal ambush sites in saddles or along creek beds or meandering streams, on trails leading to a bedding area in the middle of the wide-open spaces, and a million other excellent locations with little cover available and *no* trees. Don't give up!

Get yourself a shovel, pickaxe, and good brush cutter and put in a pit blind or ground blind. This is probably the most overlooked method for bowhunting a trophy mule deer and yet it can be one of the most adaptable and effective methods employed. I have used pit blinds in situations where it would seem impossible to get within bow range of a cautious, open-country, mule deer buck, and had them walk within a few yards of the blind within hours of its construction.

Calling Mule Deer

Two percent (or less) of the mule deer entered into the record books were taken by some method of calling. Mule deer are not territorial like their whitetail cousins, nor are they as aggressive during the rut. The mule deer buck's mild manner makes it tough to get one fired up with rattling antlers or grunt challenges to suck them close enough for a bow shot. I've rattled in a few bucks, but they responded out of curiosity more than anger. Several eventually worked their way close enough for a good shot, but the percentage of responses certainly didn't make this one of my favorite methods of bowhunting muley bucks.

I've had much better results using a coarse-toned predator call to imitate the distress bleats of a deer. This is a viable method for bringing in a buck or doe early in the season, when the fawns are still with the does. I've had several good bucks respond when I was calling coyotes early in the fall and again during the winter.

Again, during the late season, I feel it's more of a curiosity response rather than one of aggression or anger, although my late-season calling has brought in some real trophy bucks. I always carry a predator call with me when bowhunting, and wouldn't hesitate to try to coax up a trophy buck if he was in sight, with no alternative way of getting close enough for a shot. Calling may not work often enough to use it as your main method of bowhunting trophy mule deer, but it does work and might give you a chance at a trophy buck when nothing else seems feasible.

In states with late-season mule deer hunting, driving is another viable method of putting a trophy buck within bow range. This method can be well used where the mule deer tend to congregate in their wintering areas—along river bottoms, shelter belts, or along wooded slopes or valleys. A mule deer's natural tendency is to move uphill or to more open ground, so take this habit into consideration when choosing your ambush points.

It doesn't take a whole crowd of pushers to move muleys out of cover. In fact, one or two bowhunters moving slowly through a patch of prime, late-season mule-deer cover, with the wind at their backs, will be far more effective than a larger group. Wise old bucks have a propensity for sneaking up side draws, small gullies or other inconspicuous escape routes, so keep your eyes open for such locations when setting up your late-season drives.

Columbian Blacktails

Columbian blacktail deer are found in California, Oregon, Washington, and lower British Columbia, with Oregon and California producing a major portion of the record-book bucks. California's archery deer season opens in mid-August, when the bucks are still in velvet; consequently, almost all the record-book Columbian blacktails in velvet are taken in California.

The majority of the Columbian blacktails (like their magnum-eared cousins) are taken by spot-and-stalk bowhunting, with the second most effective method being tree-stand hunting.

Most of the foregoing techniques used for mule deer are equally applicable to Columbian blacktails. However, when I bowhunted them again in Oregon, I found that they responded to calling and rattling far more readily than mule deer.

On one occasion, I was bowhunting a densely wooded ridge overlooking a wide valley where the visibility was severely limited by the dense jungle-like vegetation. At mid-morning, I set up along an overgrown logging road and commenced rattling and grunt calling, as if I were whitetail hunting. Within minutes, a heavy, dark-antlered blacktail stuck his head out of a fern thicket 30 yards from me, trying to locate the source of the sound. What I wouldn't have given for a decoy.

That buck appeared and disappeared in the verdant vegetation in front of me for the next 20 minutes while I tried to coax him into the open for a shot. I'd see patches of hide, antlers, or rump, and occasionally a head, but never enough for a good shot. After half an hour of inactivity, I figured the buck was gone and started rattling again. An even larger buck appeared in a small opening at 40 yards, but before I got my wits working and came to full draw, he melted into the background like his compadre. I bleated and grunted softly and got several momentary glimpses of him twice more before he, too, was engulfed by the green labyrinth.

A tree stand would have put me in position to see down into the dense jungle ferns, vines, and moss-shrouded trees, and given me a good shot at either record-book buck. I did manage to call in a couple of forky bucks, but after an encounter with the two boomers, I just couldn't bring myself to take the shot.

Sitka Blacktails

Sitka blacktails are found in the northern section of British Columbia and the coastal regions of Alaska. Kodiak Island is definitely the place to go for a record-class Sitka blacktail buck. When I worked for the Alaska Department of Fish & Game in the early '60s, there weren't any blacktails on Afognak Island and darn few on Kodiak Island. Their population exploded shortly thereafter, and not too long ago, the limit was seven deer per hunter. The lush vegetation and abundant food supply make for a high population of fat, healthy deer, but the lack of minerals doesn't do much for antler growth. Consequently, a bowhunter needs to look over lots of deer to find a Pope & Young qualifier.

Bowhunters weren't the only ones to benefit from the population explosion of the Sitka blacktails. The humongous predatory brown bears were quick to take advantage of the burgeoning red-meat supply and actually learned that gunfire usually meant a fresh gut pile or carcass. This unusual response added a whole new dimension to hunting blacktails for gun hunters, as the voracious bruins started showing up unexpectedly at the site of a fresh deer kill. These close-quarter encounters in the jungle-like thickets of alder and devil's club resulted in a number of fatalities, both human and bear.

Fortunately, a bow doesn't make much noise when it goes off, but I've talked with a number of bowhunters who have lost deer to brown bears. On one occasion, a bowhunter arrowed a deer a bit far back and watched it move slowly into an alder thicket, where it bedded down. The bowhunter backed off and positioned himself on a hillside several hundred yards above the downed deer, waiting. He spotted a brown bear in the valley half a mile above the deer's hidey hole, but didn't think anything about it.

An hour later, he spotted the bear moving purposefully down the valley with his nose in the air and realized he was wind-scenting the wounded deer and headed right for the thicket. A few minutes later, the frustrated bowhunter watched the huge bear carry his record-book blacktail over the hill and out of sight. He was frustrated but darned glad that he hadn't been in the thicket gutting or quartering his deer when the bear showed up to claim the kill.

Almost all Sitka blacktails are taken by spot-and-stalk bowhunting using the same techniques, tactics, and equipment as mule-deer bowhunters. The coastal areas of Alaska are noted for their atrocious weather, so waterproof rain gear is essential for comfort, as is a pair of quality, ankle-fit hip boots that you'll more than likely be wearing day after day.

According to Ed Russell, a bowhunting compadre residing in Anchorage, Sitka blacktails respond readily to bleats and squalls in imitation of a doe or fawn in distress. Ed was one of the first to seriously bowhunt blacktails on Kodiak and has taken a number of bucks by calling them. His favorite call is simply a blade of grass stretched between his thumbs. A variable-tone deer call would work just as well and be easier to master. However, unless you're bowhunting an area with good distant visibility, hunting with a partner who has a brown-bear license and a *big* rifle, or are crazy; calling Sitka blacktails in brown bear country may not be the best bet for putting a trophy blacktail buck on your den wall.

Summing it Up

In my opinion, the future of mule deer in the west is not good, with everything from predators to human encroachment working against them. However, there are still many good mule-deer areas with enough boomer bucks roaming around to fulfill your wildest bowhunting dreams. Don't procrastinate, start planning that mule deer bowhunt *now*. When planning for blacktails, do your homework, research over the Internet, and plan well in advance.

Hunting Bears

KATHY ETLING

Spot-and-Stalk Hunting

Open Ground Stalking in Canada and Alaska

Outfitters who guide hunters along Canada's and Alaska's northernmost fringes of trees often spot black bears feeding on gut piles remaining from early season caribou or moose hunts. Some outfitters advise caribou hunters to purchase black bear tags to take advantage of a great opportunity for a two-species bag. Spot-and-stalk works especially well if your quarry is a trophy black bear boar. A nearby tree line indicates forest beyond, and the few scattered thickets of trees that extend onto the tundra afford big bears enough cover to make them feel secure. Barren ground tundra is often gently rolling, which also increases the bears' comfort level. Hunters should like this country as well—the dips and swales provide needed cover when they're putting the final stalk on trophy bruins.

Once breeding season ends in June, most adult boars leave the forest to wander about on the open tundra. They pass the time foraging on bush blueberries, bog cranberries, and subalpine blackberries. Bears will eat as much ripe fruit as possible at one location before moving on to another. This lethargic lifestyle suits larger bears just fine, and the animals steadily gain weight until autumn. Their summer weight gain, while substantial, still isn't sufficient for an animal that will soon shut out the world for several months. As days shorten, the looming winter inspires black

bears to go into a literal feeding frenzy. The animals chow down on anything and everything that might increase vital stores of body fat for the long winter's sleep ahead. Gut piles left behind by late summer caribou hunters provide a source of premium protein with minimum effort. The value-to-cost ratio tilts significantly in value's favor, making gut-pile feeding a good deal for the bears. Some trophy black bear hunters book or plan a hunt for both black bear and caribou in areas where seasons overlap just so they have a chance to capitalize on this late-season bruin tendency.

One might argue that open-ground stalking near gut piles is nothing more than glorified baiting. That isn't true. Where gut piles are both many and scattered, there's no telling where black bears may appear. Some may feed only at night. Others may start to feed on one gut pile and then leave for another. Bear movements in areas of wide open spaces are more random and unpredictable than near actively tended baits. This simply adds to the challenge of the hunt.

Knowing that a plethora of gut piles exists as winter approaches means many black bears throw caution to the wind. It's not unusual to spot several of these big, shaggy creatures roaming the open tundra in broad daylight, searching for meat. Wise hunters will outfit themselves with good optics, situate themselves at an excellent vantage point downwind of several gut piles, and start glassing within optical range of the tree line. After bears gorge themselves, they'll usually lie up in the timber while their meal digests. The first twinge of hunger will send them looking once more to the tantalizingly fresh piles of offal.

Whether you choose to spot from one of the huge boulders that commonly litter much of this country or simply perch behind a substantial tundra knob is a matter of preference. The idea is to attain a high enough elevation downwind of the feeding grounds to spot bear movement. There is nothing more thrilling than watching several huge old bruins lumber from their temporary woodland lairs as a brisk north wind ripples their long, silky coats.

Barren ground country is just that: barren ground. This is some of the last land that opened up after the glaciers' retreat at the end of the last ice age. Boulders that were deposited as the glaciers melted dot much of the landscape. After you spot a big bruin in terrain like this, your next task is to keep the wind in your favor as you slip close enough for a shot. Putting a boulder or a small tree between you and the bear as you sneak toward it is one workable technique. So is staying hidden in the folds of the earth as you work your way ever closer. As winter nears in barren ground country, the wind picks up. When you're stalking bears, the wind may be your ally, but it can also be your enemy, because shooting accurately in windy conditions requires you to get reasonably close to your target.

Once the caribou-hunting camps shut down for the season, bears are drawn closer to them by the smell of blood from abandoned meat houses as well as the smell of cooking that permeates the now-empty kitchens. It is common for black bears to break into these camps and wreak havoc. Buying a bear license for a lateseason hunt could buy you a chance at one of the bruiser bruins that are out and about at this time of the year.

Spot-and-stalk for black bears can be used successfully anywhere black bears travel through open ground. The best circumstances occur when a bear is leisurely feeding or grazing in an open area where it won't be harassed by others and possibly chased off before you can put the stalk on it. Larry Heathington, a former bear guide and outfittter from Arizona, sometimes used spot-and-stalk tactics in the fall as bears were gorging themselves on favored foods before denning up for the winter. "I'd cover a lot of territory with my hunters," Larry said. "Early each morning we'd take the pickup and drive to various backcountry spots. I'd park the truck, and then we'd walk to places where from past experience I knew we'd find big prickly pear flats. You have to come at these spots from downwind, and ideally you want to be high enough to be able to look over a lot of country. Bears are fairly easy to spot in such places. They really stand out. Morning is when bears are reluctant to leave the prickly pears they've been feeding on, and some of them just wander in for a while before they lie down for the day. Once you spot a bear you want to take, stay put and watch where it lies down. Then just come back later that afternoon to where

When hunting barren ground black bears, start glassing within optical range of the northernmost tree line. (Courtesy: Jim Zumbo)

Ex-guide and bear expert Larry Heathington used spot-and-stalk tactics each fall when bears were gorging on prickly pears.
(Courtesy: Larry Heathington)

Linda Powell and noted outdoor humorist Pat McManus pose with Pat's B.C. black bear.
(Courtesy: Jim Zumbo)

the bear was that morning and wait for it to get up. That's when you can bust it."

One other place to find bears in the fall is foraging in oat fields. If you know bears have been in a farmer's crop fields, don't be afraid to ask permission to hunt. Most farmers and ranchers regard bears as nuisance animals. Not only will they allow you to hunt, but they may even help you by telling you where to start searching.

Spot-and-Stalk in the Timber

In areas where black bears occur, they range between open and forested areas—they seem to have no "druthers." They go where the food is—or, if it's mating season, where the sows are. And as winter approaches, they search for den sites.

Hunters in the northwest region of the continent often ride back roads or highways where they glass every forest opening or logging trail where bears might be spotted. Black bears seem to like walking along logging roads. When they leave their dens, they often head for these roads to graze on the young sprouting grass or budding clover whose seeds are frequently sown by timber

companies in the fall to prevent erosion. Many timber companies permit hunters access and hunting on their lands, but always double-check beforehand with local game and fish personnel or law enforcement agencies.

Black bears can sometimes be spotted standing or walking in streams or traveling along stream banks, too. The U.S. Forest Service manages vast tracts of timbered wilderness where hunting is allowed in accordance with state wildlife laws. Be armed with an up-to-date map of any area you plan to hunt so that you don't run afoul of private property owners.

When searching for black bears along logging roads and streams, remember that most states and provinces prohibit shooting from the sides of public roads. The statutes in each state are different, so be sure to find out well ahead of your trip what is legal and what is not.

The very nature of the forest makes spot-and-stalk hunting more difficult in densely timbered areas. Most hunters who kill black bears in heavily wooded tracts do so by chance. Deer, elk, and moose were the primary objectives of many successful bear hunters, who bought over-the-counter bear tags as an afterthought. Such hunters sometimes bagged bears after spotting them by chance while searching for their primary targets or after unexpectedly finding themselves within shooting range of them.

In many areas of the country, spot-and-stalk bear hunting in the timber is considered a very chancy proposition. In a few areas, though, black bear outfitters and hunters actually concentrate their spot-and-stalk activities in timbered areas. Such hunts most often find hunters and guides using spotting scopes to survey rock slides where local bears enjoy searching for grubs, lichen, or moss. Such areas also are preferred in the spring, when bears crave shoots of tender, green grass shortly after emerging from their winter dens. Some outfitters have good luck guiding hunters to bears feeding on south-facing slopes in the spring. Bears seek out such areas because that's where the snow melts earliest and the year's first green growth pushes through.

Springtime bruins may also seek out other favorite foods—the buds, leaves, and catkins of aspen trees—so keep aspen thickets in your sights, too, particularly those that are just budding out.

You can use a similar tactic in early fall, when rolling hills are covered with ripe berries. Bears are sometimes so preoccupied with feeding on the berries that you can stalk close enough for a clean shot, but you must pay constant attention to the wind. Getting close enough to make the shot with a bow can be one of the most challenging experiences in all of hunting.

Once you spot a bear, you and your guide put the sneak on it. Such a stalk may pay off, but it may also fail because of erratic, swirling mountain winds that make it almost impossible to predict with accuracy the direction in which human scent will blow. Wearing scent-blocking garments or using

Wearing scent-blocking garments could help you get close enough to make the shot on a black bear. (Courtesy: M.R. James)

scent-elimination products could help get you close enough to make the shot.

Stand Hunting for Black Bears

Never discount the effectiveness of hunting black bears from treestands, even if you are not allowed to use bait. Dalton Carr, a former government bear hunter and one of the country's preeminent authorities on bear hunting, is sold on stand-hunting, especially in the fall. "Bear hunters can really do well when hunting from stands during periods of drought," he said. "That's the time to set up near water holes or other water sources bears use. If the countryside is dry, bears won't be feeding on berries or acorns, because both of these mast crops need water to mature.

"Another good black bear tactic during droughty times is to set up near an elk herd," Dalton continued. "Black bears go into a feeding frenzy for about a month before they hibernate. They have to pack on weight so that they can survive the winter. If other types of forage are scarce, bears will start lurking near elk herds. They'll be forced to kill elk calves and stragglers when the opportunities present themselves, or they themselves will be in danger of not surviving the winter."

Calling Black Bears

The premier caller of black bears in North America is Larry Heathington, formerly of Casa Grande, Arizona, and now living in Texas. Larry is well-known as an outfitter who really knows his stuff, whether it's hunting bears, sheep, pronghorn, or any number of other big game species. Larry accompanied Chuck Adams when that bowhunter killed his record-book Alaska brown bear that squared or measured ten feet, eleven inches. Larry has also guided ex-publishing mogul Robert E. Petersen on most of his hunts, many of which involved Foundation of North American Wild Sheep auction tags or high-dollar governors' tags, and almost all of which resulted in Petersen killing Boone and Crockett record-book rams, pronghorn bucks, or Rocky Mountain elk. "I haven't been hunting as much during the past few years," Larry admitted. "I prefer to arrange and guide two to four high-dollar hunts each year and spend the rest of my time training and showing cutting horses."

During his years as both an outfitter and guide, Larry traveled from Arizona to Canada hunting black bears with clients. Somewhere along the way, he hooked up with Reed Carney, a hunter who had experienced good luck calling bears. "I sure didn't figure bear calling out. Reed pioneered the technique. He was using a varmint call when a couple of bears came in. Bear calling just took off from there."

To call in bears, Larry uses a call that mimics the scream of a rabbit. His favorite brand is Circe. "This call has ejectable reeds, so it's quick and easy to replace them," he said. "Calling bears means doing a lot of calling—pretty much nonstop for about forty-five minutes at one location. You then walk fifteen or

In fifteen years of hunting, Larry Heathington called in over one hundred bears for lucky hunters like this man. (Courtesy: Larry Heathington)

twenty minutes to another place and call from there for another forty-five minutes. If you continue to call like this all day long, you'll find a bear that will come in. Look out, because when they do, their hackles will be standing on end and they will be mad. They sometimes rush in so close, bouncing their front paws off the ground, that the hunter sits there sort of stunned. I always told them, though, if the bear isn't big enough or is not the right color, shoot at their feet or between their front legs. That scares them off.

"Calling works," Larry said. "In over fifteen years of hunting, I called in more than one hundred bears, and more than fifteen or sixteen of them squared eight feet or more. That's a big black bear for Arizona." Terry Paysom, one of Larry's hunters, killed one huge black bear boar with an estimated age of twenty years. The old boar squared eight feet, eleven inches, immense by black bear standards.

"The oldest bear was a twenty-four-year-old sow, well past the age when she could have cubs," he said. "She was blind in one eye. A sow too old to have cubs will really put on weight, so it's difficult to determine whether they're sows or boars. An old three-hundred-pound sow could pass for an eight-year-old boar."

Larry's calling sometimes worked almost too well. "I once guided Wyman Meinzer, the Texas wildlife photographer and writer," he said. "I told Wyman to get ready, but I'm not sure he believed me. He'd said he wanted to get some close-up shots of a big bear. I asked, 'How close?' He said, 'As close as you can get 'em.' Well, okay. I first called in a brown one, but then a blonde bear came in. It came closer and closer and closer, and finally Wyman yelled, 'That's close enough!' Well, he'd said he wanted the bear in his face. I guarantee you, he's got photos of a wild bear from about six feet away."

Larry doesn't feel too guilty about calling bears close enough to make friends and acquaintances distinctly uneasy. "I called in one bear for Bill Cross, a good hunter and one of my best friends," Larry recalled. "That bear came in very close, and did so extremely quickly. It scared Bill so badly he never guided bear hunters or went bear hunting again. He said, 'I'm done. I'm too old. I'm not as fast as the bears are, and I'm done.' He was, too."

Larry has called bears equally well during both spring and fall seasons. "Calling works pretty much by rote," he said. "I'd hunt public land anywhere there was a fairly substantial population of bears. I'd position my hunter or hunters out on the rimrock so that the bears would have to come in from below and the hunter would have a good, unhurried shot. The best laid plans, however, don't always work. Sometimes bears would sneak in from behind, too.

"One day I was guiding Terry Paysom," Larry continued. "I was calling and we both were watching down-canyon. I heard a twig snap and turned around to see a big old sow trying to clamber up the rimrock to get up to where we were. I said, 'Terry, do you want this bear?' He didn't, so we scared her off."

Larry was quick to point out that black bears don't always play by the rules. "Sometimes everything would work perfectly," he said. "You'd spot the bear several hundred yards off and have plenty of time to get into position to make the shot. Other times, though, they'd be on top of you before you even knew they were there. That's why you get up high on that rimrock so you can see into the canyon below. Bears can be sneaky. You must watch everywhere. They'll sometimes come in behind you, or to the side of you, and they'll even come in two or three at a time. That really keeps things interesting."

Larry said that during more than fifteen years of guiding, he called in about fifteen black bears each year. "Calling near a big prickly pear flat where bears can feed works well," he said. "They really love eating prickly pears."

Larry said that calling works well all day long. "There's no best time," he stated. "The first bear I ever called in responded at 2 p.m. What I'd usually do was go out early in the morning, call for four or five hours, then return to camp for lunch and a nap. After we'd slept a while we'd go back out to call and hunt some more. This was very effective, because you were hunting all day long."

Larry rarely guided bowhunters. "Heck, when I was guiding back in the 1970s and 1980s, archery wasn't that big yet," he said. "I wouldn't recommend using a call for a bowhunter. When a bear responds, he's already mad. A bowhunter who made a poor shot would just make matters worse."

Bowhunters shouldn't be upset because Larry feels this way. He's not even too keen about calling in bears for some of the firearms hunters he's guided. "That's the problem when you're guiding bear hunters," he said. "They're not always as quick with the gun as you'd like them to be. That means you have to run into the brush a lot to escape an angry bear."

A tree stripped of its cambium layer proves black bear have been using the area.
(Courtesy: Ron Dube)

When he was still guiding bear hunters, Larry advised them to use any caliber from a .270 Win on up. "I'd pack a .338 loaded with 250-grain soft-nose bullets as a backup gun," he said.

"Bears don't scare me much," Larry continued. "I've had lots of close calls. I once was looking for a wounded bear. I walked right past the place where he was hiding in the brush. He charged out of there and ran at me from behind, busting brush as he came. I spun around and shot and killed him in midair. His momentum carried him past me, and as he rolled by, I had to kick his carcass off me. That was too close. It made me a lot more cautious."

Larry could regale you with exciting bear tales for hours. "One bear tried its best to get me," he said. "It came charging uphill at me. It didn't get there, but he sure did his best. Another time I was guiding Jim Callahan, a gunmaker. Jim had never before killed a bear. We spotted one standing on a ridge about five hundred yards away. I pulled out the call, and before we knew it, here came the bear on a dead run. It came in so fast Jim couldn't get a shot off quickly enough. Before we knew it, the bear had leaped up onto the same rock ledge we were on, and was still running directly for us. When Jim finally shot, the bear was just twenty yards distant."

Larry said bears seem to respond to calls better when the sky is overcast and drizzly. "Bears like cool, cloudy weather better than hot, sunshiny days," he said. "In the springtime, if it starts snowing again, don't give up hunting. Bears will not return to their dens if they've already blown their plugs." That simply means returning is not an option once bears have eaten enough to initiate digestion, which eventually results in defecation. A brown "plug" of fecal matter indicates that that year's hibernation is over for that particular bear.

If Larry has a regret, it's that he never tried calling bears in Minnesota or Wisconsin. "I always

According to Larry Heathington, black bears can see movement farther than most people think.
(Courtesy: Larry Heathington)

wanted to crawl into a treestand and call," he said. "I know it would work."

As for bears themselves, Larry has nothing but respect for them. "Bears can see movement way farther than you think they can," he said. "Move or make noise, and they damned sure will hear or see you." To counteract possible fidgeting by his hunters, Larry advised them to wear camouflage from head to toe, and then told them to sit still.

"I didn't use a spotting scope and I never relied on binoculars," he said. "I always looked with my naked eye. If bears are coming, you're probably going to see them. They really stand out—those big black or brown or blonde blobs coming through the green weeds or trees. The hardest time I ever had making out a color was once when a hunter killed a platinum blonde bear. I could barely see it because in the fall the oak brush was kind of yellow and the bear's coat blended right in."

Larry lived and breathed bear hunting for a good portion of his adult life. His advice on shooting at a bear is simple, and can be broken down like this: "Shoot through both shoulders and bust 'em down if you can," he said. "The bottom line is that you don't want the bear up and moving around. If it can't move but is still alive, you can always shoot it again. If it's moving, though, you'll have a devil of a time finishing it off."

For those who want to try calling, which is probably the most exciting bear hunting experience of all, Larry offered this tip on shooting charging bears: "Use the top edge of the upper scope cap as your sight when a bear is charging at you, and you'll get him," he advised. "This is such a good way to sight on close objects that you can even use this trick to shoot an eight-inch plate at twenty-five yards. Calling bears that may pop up extremely close to you presents real problems to hunters who have scopes on their rifles. Even if the power ring is turned all the way down, there's still enough magnification to

screw you up. That's no good when a bear's about to run right down your throat."

Larry has some tips about how to maintain your calls, too. "When you call this much, number one, you've got to have some pretty good lungs on you," he said. "At first, two hunters should probably switch off, or someone is going to be pretty winded.

"Second, plan on replacing your call's reed—perhaps several times in a day. I always packed spares, and that's why Circe's call is so good. Because the reeds are ejectable, replacing them is no problem. You'll blow lots of reeds out of the calls, too, but I always kept two calls on a lanyard around my neck. When one call would stop working, I'd switch to the second. While using the second call, I'd replace the reed in the first. That way you're giving any nearby bears the constant stimulation they need to provoke them into coming to see what's going on."

According to Tom Beck, a retired bear biologist who formerly worked for the Colorado Division of Wildlife, each year he gets reports of successful bear hunters who bagged their animals after luring them into range with a deer call. "Fawn bleats seem to work best," Beck said, "but the distress call of any animal that shares a bear's range would probably be effective." Although somewhat off the topic, each year a number of Sitka blacktail hunters in northwestern Alaska generally will report various harrowing brown bear encounters after the hunters try to use deer calls to lure a buck close enough to shoot.

Larry didn't have any cut-and-dried advice concerning when an Arizona hunter would get the best bearskin on an animal. "Really, it depends on the bear," he said. "I've seen poor hides in the fall and poor ones in the spring. If you want a good hide, I'd advise you to go as late in the season as possible. By that time their winter hairs are all grown out, and hides should be prime. And if you go hunting in the spring, you probably should go as early as possible to get a hide in good condition. In my experience bearskins are really ratty for only about thirty days each spring."

Larry Heathington has done it all when it comes to hunting, guiding, and outfitting for trophy-class animals of many species. He has nothing left to prove in this arena, so he has left it for a while to devote time to another of his loves, the training and showing of cutting horses. He'll never get hunting totally out of his blood, though, and that's a good thing for us hunters. As long as Larry is willing to share, all hunters will continue to discover exciting tactics like calling for trophy black bears.

Hunting Grizzly Bears

1805 May 5

Capt. Clark and (George) Drewyer killed the largest brown bear this evening which we have yet seen. It was a most tremendious looking anamal, and extreemly hard to kill notwithstanding he had five balls through his lungs and five others in various parts he swam more than half the distance across the river to a sandbar, & it was at least twenty minutes before he died; he did not attempt to attack, but fled and made the most tremendous roaring from the moment he was shot. We had no means of weighing this monster; Capt. Clark thought he would weigh 500 lbs. For my own part I think the estimate too small by 100 lbs. he measured 8. Feet 7 1/2 Inches from the nose to the extremety of the hind feet, 5 F. 10 1/2 Ins. arround the breast, 1 F. 11. I. arround the middle of the arm, & 3.F. 11.I. arround the neck; his tallons which were five in number on each foot were 4 3/8 Inches in length. He was in good order, we therefore divided him among the party and made them boil the oil and put it in a cask for future uce; the oil is as hard as hogs lard when cool, much more so than that of the black bear. The Grizzly Bear is one of the largest and strongest animals in the world, with many external and internal features.

Captain Meriwether Lewis wrote these words almost two centuries ago, during his and Captain William Clark's famed Voyage of Discovery. Grizzly bears of Lewis and Clark's time typically had had confrontations before only with various native peoples. The primitive weapons wielded by Indians never were much of a match for a grizzly, one of the continent's toughest customers. But Lewis and Clark soon discovered that the bears were terribly hard to kill even when wounded by weapons from their arsenal of "modern" weapons. Inexperienced hunters of grizzlies quake in their boots over tales such as the one above, but a well-placed shot at an unaroused grizzly will usually kill the animal as rapidly as a shot at any other large game animal. It's just that a "well-placed shot" can be difficult to make when a hunter is standing within twenty-five yards of one of these big bruisers. And that should the grizzly be aroused, then it becomes a whole different story.

The Inuit call grizzlies Aklaq. Lewis and Clark dubbed them grisly, griz, and grizzly for the grizzled or silvered appearance of their coats, and the name stuck. Settlers often called the bear "Old Ephraim." In recent times these bears have been called "silvertips," again because of the long white- or gray-tipped hairs that give them such a distinctive appearance. Scientists, well aware of the bear's fierce reputation, dubbed the animal *Ursus arctos horribilis*, Latin for "horrible bear." The name accurately describes a grizzly hell bent on mayhem, which on rare occasions some may intend. Yet today's scientists understand that most often these animals choose to retreat rather than take their chances with humankind.

Natural History of the Barren Ground or Tundra Grizzly

Although barren ground grizzlies are smaller in body size than other grizzlies, they are highly aggressive and incredibly fierce—a dangerous combination. During 2000, Alaskan officials credited these animals, also called tundra grizzlies, with ten human fatalities in an area where few humans live. The lesson is simple: Never take the barren ground grizzly too lightly.

Barren ground grizzlies were persecuted—and their numbers reduced—during the peak years of the fur trade, but during the past two decades their numbers have rebounded with vigor.

A big barren ground boar will tip the scales at more than five hundred pounds, while a large sow will weigh about half that. When pelts (pelage) are prime, the guard hairs are long and silky and the underfur is thick. The barren ground's coat can vary in hue from black to pale blond. An intermingling of white or gray hairs serves to give many of these bears the classic grizzled appearance. This grizzling is most obvious on darker-coated bears.

Fewer barren ground grizzlies are found per thousand square miles than grizzlies of other areas simply because tundra habitat is poorer. Coastal areas provide bears with a regular supply of salmon. Logs fallen or dropped amid dark timber yield a feast of termites and grubs. Out on the barren ground or tundra, food is more difficult to find, and so are good denning sites in which to while away the brutal winter.

The country these bears inhabit looks bleak and stark, yet these big omnivores subsist on a surprisingly varied diet of berries, insects, ground squirrels, marmots, lemmings, caribou, muskox, moose, and carrion. During the Arctic spring green-up and well into the early summer, barren ground grizzlies have even more to choose from, including flowers, grasses, sedges, herbs, tubers, corms, and roots.

Rob Gau, a biologist with the Northwest Territories, documented the feeding habits of barren ground grizzlies. He verified that caribou, by far, is the bears' most common food item. The most *important* items, though, are berries: crowberries, blueberries, cranberries, and bearberries. So vital is a generous late summer berry supply to the eventual reproductive success of tundra grizzlies, says Rob, that an absence or general scarcity of berries may be the primary limiting factor preventing barren ground grizzlies from expanding their range and numbers throughout the central Arctic region.

Barren Ground Grizzly Range

The barren ground begins just north of the last tree line and extends up to the edge of the polar ice cap. The land is exactly as described—barren ground—and it represents the very outermost margins of suitable brown bear habitat. From a distance, these barrens appear flat and almost featureless. Some creeks rush and tumble as they journey to the sea, while others slowly meander. Willows crowd the stream banks in many place, and their branches often mesh in a thatched canopy that provides ungulates and bears alike with shade and relief from insects during warmer months. Willows provide great forage for moose, and where moose go bears are sure to follow. Barren ground grizzlies prey on moose, muskox, and the calves of both species in addition to caribou.

Hunting Barren Ground Grizzlies

Hunting barren ground grizzlies in the Territory of Nunavut means booking a spring hunt with an Eskimo or Native Canadian guide. The ideal time for such a hunt is when enough snow still remains that guides can pick up the tracks of big bears and follow them until their hunters get close enough to shoot. Traditional barren ground grizzly hunts are conducted from snowmobiles if there is enough snow or on foot if spring comes early and snow melts.

Hunting barren ground grizzlies in Alaska's Brooks Range, the barrens of the Arctic National Wildlife Refuge (ANWR), the Northwest Territories (NWT), or Nunavut is a task for the spotting scope, particularly during late summer hunts. Hunter and guide spend long hours visually picking apart the vast open landscape searching for bears near willow thickets and along rivers and streams. Several times while hunting in Alaska's Brooks range, I've kicked out bears from streamside willow thickets, both big boars and sows with cubs.

Once you spot a bear, you and your guide hightail it toward a suitable ambush spot. You'll need hip boots in some places, such as Nunavut, with its many lakes, rivers, streams, and bogs. (And be aware that slogging through bogs in hip boots can test your endurance and will, especially when you miss a mossy tussock and plunge into water deeper than the top of your boot.) Also pack plenty of moleskin, because navigating mossy stump tundra, where your feet bobble about incessantly and never seem to get a purchase on solid ground, usually turns into the "agony of da feet" after several days.

As you stalk closer, you and your guide must remain aware of the bear's keen sense of smell, its eyesight, and hearing, particularly as you travel through willows or water. Any time you approach a moving bear, whether it's traveling away from you or not, take nothing for granted. As you slip closer, the bear occasionally may disappear from sight, and at such times you will have no idea what it's doing. It might decide to change course and run straight for you, or it might spot prey nearby. Remember that over a short distance a grizzly is faster than a horse. When in grizzly country, always be prepared to shoot and shoot quickly.

Remaining hidden in the earth's folds or behind rocks is an excellent tactic to use when you attempt to slip closer to a bear. You can also remaining hidden as you sneak along a willow-covered bank or behind an esker snaking its way across a glacial plain. (An esker is a curving ridge made up of rock deposited eons ago by a stream that wound its way beneath a glacial ice sheet.) Another way to approach a grizzly is to partially or completely obscure your movements by dropping down within the banks

One way to approach an open-ground grizzly is to drop down within the banks of a creek to obscure your movements.
(Credit: Kathy Etling)

of a creek or river channel. If the terrain is too flat for any of these tactics, wait until the bear obscures itself before attempting to move closer. When the animal lies down, enters the willows, moves behind an esker, or climbs down into a creek channel, that is your cue to resume your stalk. Move whenever you are unable to see the bear's eyes. If the animal is foraging as it travels, wait until its head is turned away from you or until it seems totally engrossed in feeding before easing forward. Whenever the bear lifts or turns its head, drop back down and freeze low to the earth until it resumes its activity. Because bears' eyes face forward, as humans' do, their peripheral vision is unlikely to tip them off to your presence as long as you remain a reasonable distance away. If you are close to a bear, however, all bets are off.

Grizzly-bear hunters, like black-bear hunters, use a variety of items to check wind direction, including API's Windfloaters, unscented talcum or scent-check powder, or a cigarette-lighter's flame.

The Territory of Nunavut

Barren ground grizzlies seem to be thriving in the new Canadian territory of Nunavut. Most Americans have no idea what Nunavut is, or where it's located, but here's a brief lesson on a government created on April 1, 1999, when a block of land was carved from the eastern portions of the Northwest Territories.

The Territory of Nunavut was proposed in a 1976 document submitted to the Canadian government by the Inuit peoples of the Northwest Territories. This document, the *Nunavut Proposal,* was written by tribal elders to settle the Inuit's long-standing claim to their traditional homeland. Today Nunavut is a territory, but one day Inuit leaders may press for full provincial status.

Other Places to Hunt Barren Ground Grizzlies

Both Alaska and the Northwest Territories have limited barren ground grizzly tags available. (Although some people refer to Alaska's northernmost grizzly population as "barren ground" grizzlies, strictly speaking the bears probably should be termed mountain grizzlies.) Grizzlies in the NWT inhabit land from the tundra barrens above the northernmost tree line to the MacKenzie mountains in the west. Be careful if you hunt there. Arctic weather can be extremely unpredictable and cold spells and high winds may occur suddenly, without warning.

If You Go Barren Ground Grizzly Hunting . . .

The remoteness of the barren ground grizzly hunting areas and limited rescue capabilities increase the risk of many natural hazards. You must be prepared to deal with extreme and rapidly changing weather, unpredictable river crossings, high winds, and dangerous wildlife, including polar bears. If you book such a hunt be prepared to be fully responsible for your own life. Guides or outfitters can do only so much. In extreme circumstances, guides may be able only to take care of themselves. This means that saving your life may be up to you!

A Coastal Grizzly Bear Hunt

In 1997 Stan Godfrey, of the Pope and Young Club, experienced the hunt of a lifetime. Stan was bowhunting for grizzly bear in the Unalakleet River drainages in western Alaska with guides Vance Grishkowsky and Ron Sherer. Stan's hunting partner, Dan Brockman, was also bowhunting the big animals. The two archers were positioned in treestands near active bear feeding sites along the river's shoreline. These sites were scouted out each morning by guides who plied the nearby streams in jetboats.

On day six of Stan's hunt he watched rather disconsolately as a large bear walk past his stand thirty-two yards away. "It was a little too far for me to shoot and feel comfortable about it," Stan said. "I did not want to wound a grizzly, which would put me and my guide in a potentially dangerous situation when we later had to track it into the brush."

Stan knew this bear might have been the best opportunity he'd had. "Just then, I heard a loud splash," he said. "I slowly turned my head to see an equally large bear carrying a freshly caught salmon onto a nearby island in the river." The bear gobbled down the salmon, then started walking toward the man. "I could hear a riverboat approaching," Stan said. "But the bear kept coming."

The bear forded the shallow water between the island and the shore and then walked past Stan at a distance of eighteen yards. The bowhunter released the arrow and watched it enter the bear's body behind the animal's front leg. The bear roared, spun to bite at the spot where the arrow had penetrated, then walked back the way it had come. When the

Beautiful brown bear boars like this one killed by Jim Zumbo can be hunted along the coastlines of Alaska and British Columbia.
(Courtesy: Jim Zumbo)

animal was about thirty yards away, it appeared to topple over in some sparse brush.

"When my guide finally arrived, I told him where I thought the bear had fallen," Stan said. "We slowly approached to find the grizzly dead in its tracks, thirty yards from where I had shot it."

The Alaska Department of Fish and Game aged the old boar at twenty-eight years. Its skull officially scored 24 4/16 Pope and Young points, ranking it among the top three grizzly bear trophies ever taken by an archer.

Merely considering a hunt in which you would pit yourself against the King of the Forest can get your heart thumping, but to score on a bear the equal of Stan Godfrey's seems the stuff of dreams, whether you're toting a .416 Rigby or a seventy-pound bow.

Rifle hunting for grizzlies and brown bears along the Alaskan and British Columbian coastlines relies heavily upon spot-and-stalk tactics. Even Stan Godfrey's success was highly dependent on his guides being able to take him to an area where bears were actively feeding. When you are constrained by

time, remaining aware of bear movements is often an essential component of eventual success.

Grizzlies and Baiting

Baiting is not permitted anywhere for grizzlies, although sometimes guides will set up close to the gut pile of a moose or caribou taken earlier in the season, perhaps by a previous client. Any gut pile that appears to have been claimed by a grizzly presents a prime opportunity for a hunter with a bear tag. If a bear has dragged a gut pile or carcass away and covered it with sticks and leaves, it will probably return to feed some more.

During springtime hunts, guides and clients usually direct their spotting scopes toward south-facing slopes, where grizzly bears congregate to graze on the first green growth of the season.

Mountain Grizzlies

During late summer and early fall, grizzlies may be found in open meadows foraging on berries. One hunter who capitalized on such a situation was Wisconsin's Chuck Schlindwein. "I believe in the American dream," Chuck said. "I hunt with a few doctors, but I never let that stop me even though they have way more money than I do. When they told me they were considering an Alaskan trip, I told them, 'Just give me a few years' notice and I'll go with you.' Three years ago they told me they were going to book with an outfitter. I began working every bit of overtime I could get." Chuck is a slate and tile roofer. It is a skilled profession, one that requires a lot of detail work, and one that is in great demand. As Chuck and his buddies set about the task of choosing an outfitter, they split up the outfitters' lists of references and called every single person that appeared on them.

After hearing nothing but glowing reports on outfitter Curly Warren, of Alaska's Stoney River Outfitters, their minds were made up. "We booked three years ahead," Chuck said.

The hunters anxiously awaited their Alaskan trip. When they finally flew into Stoney River Lodge, they were seriously stoked for their hunt. "After we flew in to Stoney River Lodge, we split up," said Chuck. "A pilot loaded me and my gear in a Super Cub and flew me thirty-seven miles north to where my guide was waiting at spike camp.

"I was mainly hunting moose, although Curly had mentioned that there were good numbers of grizzlies, too. Once we started hunting, we'd get up before light, drink hot coffee, and prepare some freeze-dried food inside the dome tent, then wait until light before leaving the tent. The tent had been set up in a real brushy area to protect us from the wind. We waited for light because we weren't eager to accidentally bump into any bears. Downslope was a big marshy area, which was ideal, since I really wanted a big moose."

The September sun in Alaska rises above the horizon and then remains there for hours. Chuck and his guide settled down where they could watch the swampy area downslope of the tent. In the middle of the bog, there was a big, grassy meadow. As the hunters glassed, they spotted movement to the left of this meadow. "The sun was in our eyes, but we finally decided that the movement was a grizzly feeding on blueberries. I'd purchased a grizzly tag almost as an afterthought, even though the guide had wanted me to buy a second caribou license," Chuck said. "I was interested in grizzlies because I'd never seen one in the wild.

"As we were watching the first bear, a second grizzly came out. I told the guide I saw another grizzly, but he didn't believe me. At about that time the first grizzly saw the second bear and stood up. The second, smaller grizzly started to run, and the first grizzly chased it. Both bears disappeared over the hill.

"My guide continued to blow on his moose call," Chuck said. "The smaller grizzly finally emerged directly below where we were waiting. It walked, stopped, looked back over its shoulder, and then walked some more. It came about 150 yards toward us, stopped, glanced back over its shoulder, and then entered the brush to our left.

"I then saw the big grizzly, farther behind but definitely following the smaller bear. It moved slowly along the same creek where the smaller animal had walked, occasionally 'whuffing.' When it whuffed, the hair stood up on the back of my neck. The bear continued to wander back and forth four or five hundred yards below us. The guide kept saying, 'He is a big bear.'

" 'Maybe that bear is looking to be shot,' I finally said. My guide said, 'That's all I need to hear.' We got up and started walking through the brush toward the grizzly. The guide said, 'Chamber a round.' I said, 'Why? The bear is still four hundred yards away.' The guide replied, 'If we bump into that smaller bear, the big bear will charge. If he does, it will be a false charge. Try to stand your ground, but remember I'll be backing you up.'

"We kept walking, and the guide said that if the bear looked up, I should stop moving. He explained

Hunters spot for mountain grizzlies as the animals forage in open meadows for marmots or grubs. (Courtesy: Jim Zumbo)

that he didn't think grizzlies could see all that well, but that they could distinguish movement. At about that time, the bear looked up. I stopped, but the guide didn't. The bear saw the guide's movement, and here he comes. He jumped the creek and rushed toward us.

"The guide said, 'Where is he?' I pointed toward the grizzly. The guide said, 'Whenever you want him, take him.'

"I dropped down on one knee, shot once, and the bear began biting where I'd shot him. The guide said, 'Shoot him again.' I thought my shot had been good, but I shot again. The bear now moved to the side a bit, then looked away. The guide said, 'Shoot him again.' I said, 'All I can see is his rear end.' The guide said, 'Then shoot him in the butt.' I did, and the bear fell. My first shot, though, was a killing shot. It had taken out both the animal's lungs."

Chuck was using a Browning A-bolt Stainless Stalker chambered for .30-06 Springfield. His ammunition was Federal's Hi-Energy 180-grain Nosler Partition loads. "On several occasions our guide said he liked the way Nosler partitions performed on moose and bear," Chuck said.

Chuck Schindlein bagged his grizzly on the first day he hunted in Alaska. He later learned that his grizzly qualified for Boone and Crockett's all-time records book with a skull measurement of 24 11/16 inches. Four or five days later, he bagged a massive 64 1/2-inch Alaska moose that missed qualifying for the all-time Boone and Crockett record book by about an inch. Two days after the moose, Chuck shot a nice black bear.

Calling Grizzlies

No guide seems willing to intentionally try to call grizzlies to the gun or bow. This tactic can get out of hand even when used for black bears, so that may explain their reluctance to experiment with grizzly calling. Nevertheless, many tales are told of hunters grunting for moose and getting the living daylights scared out of them by charging grizzlies.

Calling grizzlies would probably work—and work well—if guides and hunters were able to set up someplace where the bear could not take them by surprise. Hunters would have to be very aware and extremely brave to attempt to call in grizzlies in prime grizzly-bear range, but if they wanted to try it, the ideal call would be that of a moose. Especially effective would be a moose or elk calf in distress.

Mike Fejes, who has killed six Alaska brown bears, said that using a moose grunt call is a great way to find out if any bears are hiding near a gut pile or carcass cache. "Just call before you get too close," Mike said. "If bears are nearby they should stand up so you can see them." But don't attempt such a foolhardy tactic unless you're ready for the consequences, you can see in all directions for a great distance, or you are backed up by someone you trust who carries a big, accurate rifle.

Mountain Grizzlies

A grizzly bear living in the mountains and traveling along a trail often reaches out with the front paw that's nearest a tree and takes a swipe at it—a side swipe. To do this, the bear stands on its other three legs, and the claw mark on the tree is horizontal. No one knows what side swiping means, although it might be a loose territorial marker or simply a means of communicating the bear's presence to other local bears.

Grizzlies are also known for biting prominent trees within their range. These bite marks may mark an area as "belonging" to a particular bear or advertise the bear's size to other local bears. Hunters who knows their stuff can use the marks of canine teeth to arrive at an estimated size for the grizzly. The distance between the canine tooth centers reveals how far apart those teeth are. Larger bears' canine teeth, as you would guess, are farther apart than those of smaller bears. My good friend Jim Zumbo, who is skilled at hunting every species of North American big game, was hunting grizzlies in Alaska during the 2002 spring season. "It was miserable," Jim said. "Rotten weather every day. I slept cold, ate cold, and was wet every minute of the day. I didn't have dry feet for ten days.

"We were grizzly hunting not far from Aniak, along the Kufko-Quim River," Jim continued. "It was darned good hunting. We'd see three or four grizzlies every day from camp. The mountains we were hunting were full of nasty alder thickets on the lower slopes. Those alders just ripped and tore at you. Above this alder tangle, the mountains looked a lot like golf greens. Low bush blueberries grew everywhere. In springtime, the bears graze on the grass growing on these slopes.

"We'd seen a big griz across the river from our camp. It was brown with gray ears, so I think it was real old. Neither my guide nor I wanted to cross the river and get wetter, so we concentrated instead on a nice grizzly feeding on the open slope of the mountain behind camp. A grizzly in that scrub looks

Hunters spot for mountain grizzlies as the animals forage in open meadows for marmots or grubs. (Courtesy: Jim Zumbo)

immense. There's no way you should lose it. Right before we left, we could see it about a mile away and upslope. We started climbing, dipped down to ford a small stream, and darned if we didn't lose sight of that bear.

"We continued climbing another quarter mile," Jim said. "As we were going up the trail, the bear was coming down the same trail. We saw each other at about twenty-five feet. The bear stood up on its hind legs when he saw us, and from where I stood he seemed about twenty-seven feet tall. An alder bush was in my way so I couldn't shoot. The bear rushed off the trail, ran a few yards away, popped his teeth, and stood up again to stare at us at about sixty or seventy yards. I settled the crosshairs on the center of his chest and slowly squeezed the trigger of my .338 Rem Ultra Mag. The bear went down, then clambered back to its feet and ran about eighty yards. It then dropped fell over and died.

"I was using Remington ammunition," Jim said. "Those Swift A-Frame 250-grain bullets really did some damage. What a bear-killing load!" Jim's grizzly squared out to seven and a half feet. The beautiful bear's pelt was a rich auburn brown. Jim had scored on just the second day of a ten-day hunt.

"The next day we went moose hunting," Jim said. "In that country that meant climbing up to this one ridge where we'd glass, and then glass some more. Glassing was all we wanted to do, too. Venturing into that valley full of alders would be like going straight into hell. You wouldn't do it unless there was a reward.

"That morning, Dwight Van Brunt, of Kimber Rifles, said he thought he saw a black bear. Well, my ears perked up. I would have liked to take another black bear. We started stalking it, but as we got closer the 'black' bear started coming toward us. It wasn't a black bear at all, but a monster grizzly. This big griz walked past us at thirty yards. As nice as the bear was I'd shot the day before, this one was better. It would have squared nine feet if it had squared an inch."

Montana's Mike McDonald traveled to Alaska to bag this high-scoring Boone and Crockett grizzly bear. (Courtesy: Mike McDonald)

Hunting Brown Bears

A brown bear is in a class by itself. Mature brown bear boars are usually quite large, and some are even huge. Brownies are intelligent and cunning, and they possess unbelievable strength. Most are shy, but every brown bear has the potential to be dangerous. Some brownies can be vindictive, and a few have even been reported to plan and enact methods of revenge! In short, brown bears may be more like humans than many of us would care to admit.

Brown bears have been placed high upon a pedestal by hunters who wonder what it would be like to go one-on-one with such magnificent creatures. Since the dawn of time, humans have sought ways to test the limits of their courage. It is not so much bravery that motivates brown bear hunters, but rather respect and admiration for their quarry. Like Native Americans and Native Canadians of an earlier age, today's brown bear hunters seek out the mightiest animal adversaries, not to diminish them by the animals' deaths, but to exalt these bears as opponents worthy of the near fortune the hunters must spend to hunt them, the preparations

A brown bear is intelligent, cunning, and possesses a strength beyond belief. (Courtesy: Bob Beaulieu)

and bad weather they must endure, and the endless introspection that commences as soon as their quest begins: *Why am I doing this? What do I hope to discover about myself? What if I fall short?*

Like the earliest humans, modern hunters are filled with awe at the prospect of walking upon the same terrain as these mighty bears. They are willing to gamble a lot of money for just a chance to see, and possibly kill, a big brown bear. They fly out in small airplanes that rumble to precarious stops along rocky streambeds and sometimes even flip over on sodden, sandy shorelines. Would-be brown bear hunters sometimes wind up hunting from these crippled planes, biding their time until they're rescued.

Weather looms as a possible impediment at almost every moment of the trip. Brown bear hunters far too often see their chances for a bear disappear amid fogs that cover brown bear country for days on end—fog so pea-soup thick that they render even the finest optics unusable. Brown bear hunters may spend an entire hunt in a tent buffeted by high winds and lashed by rain or snow. They must be ready, willing, and able to get wet, sleep cold, slog over long distances—sometimes on snowshoes—and be scared out of their wits by the sometimes-lunatic maneuvers of bush pilots. And always, as they slip cautiously through boggy thickets, clamber over small knolls, or stumble through the willows, they must be prepared to stare Death in its face without flinching.

A brown bear is tenacious. Its will to live is extreme. A brownie whose adrenaline is surging can keep going and going and going, even as shot after shot pierces its vitals. It is the brownie's ability to take and mete out abuse in equal measure that keeps so many big game hunters permanently enthralled by these tremendous carnivores.

Could any other hunting experience compare with the sight of an eleven-foot Alaska brown bear standing erect twenty yards in front of you, its five-inch-long ivory claws curling downward from front paws the width of serving trays? The bear is big enough. It is close enough. You know your weapon intimately. Your guide is ready to back you up. It is, in fact, the moment of truth.

Are you up to it?

Or not? For that is what brown bear hunting is all about, isn't it? Wondering if you will measure up against this magnificent creature. Wondering if, when the chips are down, you are up to the task as so many others have been.

The ones who weren't, well, they didn't live to talk about it. And if they did live, most returned to civilization strangely mute about their experiences. Such is the power of the bear to make you put up or shut up. Talk about *Fear Factor!*

And yet as big and as strong and as courageous as brown bears are, most will go out of their way to avoid people. As formidable as they appear, at least to us puny-by-comparison humans, brown bears will back down from a confrontation with one of us more often than not.

Yet there's always that element of unpredictability when one is hunting brown bears. That "What is it going to do next?" question that is never completely answered until you see it unfold with your own eyes.

A Brown Bear Hunting Tale

My good friend Marlin Grasser, now retired, was an Alaskan Master Guide for fifty years. Marlin lived in Alaska from the time he was seventeen. He hunted big game all over the state, from the Brooks Range far up north to the Wrangells in the south to the Alaskan Peninsula far out west.

Marlin reminds me of a big brown bear himself: fearless, tough, and dogged in his determination. Unlike the brown bear, though, Marlin never backs down from anyone or anything. When one day he came across a set of huge bear tracks in the snow, Marlin and some other men followed them. The bear went up hills and down for more than three hours. It traversed alder patches and creek beds, but always managed to stay out of sight. When the men emerged from one particularly dense thicket, Marlin spotted the huge animal. "It was looking back at us over its shoulder from five or six hundred yards away," Marlin said. "Then it entered another brushy pocket. I told the hunter I'd go in after it and try to push it out the other side."

Remember that part about brown bears being cunning? Some really are. Unfortunately for Marlin, this was one of them. "The bear just wouldn't be pushed," he said. "I crept through the alders, but the bear remained in the thicket. I wasn't worried. I climbed in there with it because a bear will almost always run out the other side. If it had, my hunter would have a shot.

"The bear sat tight. I finally climbed up this one bank and spotted it sitting in a ring of tall grass.

As soon as it spotted me, it charged. I was carrying an old Model 70 Winchester chambered in .300 H&H Magnum. The bear was coming so fast I had to shoot from my hip. The bullet tore into the bear. It fell down in front of me and lay there. I chambered another round and shoved the rifle barrel right against its back and pulled the trigger. Nothing happened. I ejected that round, chambered another, and did it again. All in all, I chambered three rounds and tried to fire them all, but the gun was broken."

At the sound of the last trigger click, the bear was up off the ground and all over Marlin. Marlin shoved the rifle into the animal's face, and it bit the stock and the barrel, which pushed it back a little. Brown bears and grizzlies usually go for the face, and this one was no exception. "It used its paw to slap the rifle out of my hand," Marlin explained. "The force knocked me over. When I flipped down on my back, my legs flew up into the air. The bear grabbed one of my legs with its teeth and bit it hard six or seven times. Then it growled and ran away." Marlin's leg was ripped to pieces. Two puncture wounds had penetrated his shinbone and blood and marrow were oozing out. Marlin finally raised his head and saw that the bear's track leaving the area was full of blood. "I got up and checked my gun," Marlin said. "A tag alder seed had somehow fouled up the firing pin. I cleaned the seed off so that it would shoot, and then I went after the bear. I tracked it to within thirty or forty yards of where my hunter was waiting.

"Didn't you hear that commotion?" I asked the man. "Oh, yes," he said. "I heard you shoot, and then I heard all the racket, but I didn't know you needed me."

Marlin figured that his hunter was just about useless. He told him to follow their tracks back to the hunting lodge and tell Marlin's son to send their pilot to help Marlin locate the bear from above. Marlin then left the hunter as he gave chase to the wounded bear.

"I had quite a bit on my mind at that time," Marlin said. "But my hunter would have given me even more to think about. He went back to the lodge and told my son Eddie that a bear had mauled me and that I was dead. Then he cracked open a bottle of Seagram's Seven and started drinking. When the very next plane landed at our airstrip, my hunter boarded. I never heard from him again."

Marlin was badly wounded but determined to kill the bear. When the lodge's pilot flew low over him later that day, Marlin yelled to him, asking if he could see the bear. The pilot yelled back that the bear was at the top of the next alder patch.

"I climbed up, and sure enough, there's the bear, about sixty yards away," Marlin said. "As soon as he saw me, he charged. He just flew at me with his hind legs lunging. He was really moving, and I raised my gun and shot. The bear fell, scrambled up, and I shot again. It just kept running down the hill and across a creek."

Marlin had one shell left. "I waited a while, hoping it would give the bear time to die," he said. "Then I followed it. I walked down the hill and across the creek, and I cut another bear track. This one wasn't bloody. *Oh, hell,* I remember thinking. *Another bear. That's all I need.* I was pretty worried. I walked up and down the creek, looking. I stopped on a little knoll, and as I was standing there the bear walked out of an alder patch about sixty feet away. I hollered at him, "Hey, bear!" The bear turned, looked at me, and charged. I shot again. The last bullet I had with me. This bullet went in his back just behind the shoulder and dropped him. I sat there on the ground for a good long time before I gathered the courage to see if he was really dead."

Brown Bear Hunting Methods

Stalking Brown Bears in Southeast Alaska's Coastal Rainforest

Alaska brown bears (*Ursus arctos middendorffi*) are hunted both spring and fall, depending on where you plan to hunt. In the spring bears are scattered on side hills after they emerge from their dens. They forage for tender grasses and also sedges near the edges of lakes and streams. The claws of spring bears are longer than at any other time of the year, and their hides are often very nice, too.

In the fall, brown bears concentrate near stream tributaries, where they fish for salmon to gain as much weight as possible before winter sets in.

Many brown bear outfitters hunt their clients out of boats or motorized rafts. Guides and hunters glass the shoreline or tidal flats searching for foraging brown bears. Some also climb hills where they can spot for long distances. When a suitable bear is located, the boat is beached or the hunters simply stalk as close as possible before shooting.

Another way to hunt these bears is to fly over the coast, searching for a big brownie feeding on a kill. If a bear is located actively feeding, there is a good chance it will still be near the kill when hunters return on foot the next day. (In Alaska it is illegal to fly—other than in a commercial airliner—and hunt bears in the same day.)

The Alaska Peninsula

The Alaska Peninsula has been designated a "trophy bear area" since 1976 to ensure the quality of these giant bears for years to come. When this area was first designated Alaska wildlife officials decided that spring hunts would take place in even-numbered years and fall hunts would occur in odd-numbered years. The only North American hunt more costly than an Alaska brown bear hunt is a polar bear hunt, and a polar bear hunt isn't much more expensive.

Senior airman Theodore Winnen, a load crew member with the 18th Fighter Squadron, Eielson Air Force Base, decided during mid-October, 2001, to go Sitka blacktail hunting with his buddy, Staff Sgt. Jim Urban, and two other friends. Their destination: Hitchenbrook Island in the Gulf of Alaska's Prince Edward Sound. Many stories have been circulated

about Winnen's big bear. In fact, within a few weeks' of the animal's encounter with the airman the bear had "grown" in myth to an almost unbelievable 12-feet 6-inches in stature and over 1,800 pounds in weight, neither of which were true.

Winnen and three hunting buddies were dropped off on Hinchenbrook by an air taxi on the morning of October 14. Hinchenbrook, a mere 165-square miles in size, harbors about one hundred Alaska brown bears, a density that is higher than on any other island in the Sound, according to Cordova area wildlife biologist Dave Crowley, who works for the state's department of fish and game.

Winnen had purchased a bear hunting permit just in case he happened to encounter one of the huge bears for which the Alaskan coastal islands are so famous. As the skies cleared on the morning of October 15, Winnen and Urban started hunting. The two men followed a creek bed upstream as they searched for deer. Urban was armed with a .300-caliber Win. Mag., while Winnen carried a .338 Win. Mag. As the hunters walked farther up the creek they noticed a pool full of dying salmon. Both

Many outfitters and guides conduct their bear hunts from boats like this one. (M. R. James photo)

men knew such a scene would be highly appealing to a hungry bear. The two men continued following the creek upstream until they came to a small island ringed with thick brush. Some blueberries still clung to their bushes. On the island grew a huge spruce tree and at its base was what looked to be the start of a large hole.

At about 9:30 a.m., Winnen glanced upstream to see a big brown bear just forty yards away. The bear was flipping over logs looking for salmon.

"He's a shooter," Urban whispered. Both men jacked shells into their guns, then took off their packs and laid them at the base of the huge spruce which was nearby. They then moved a few feet farther upstream. Winnen scanned the small amount of real estate between the two men and the bear. He noticed a large tree that had fallen to the ground, and told Urban, "When the bear crawls over that log we'll take him."

The only problem was that the bear moved so fluidly over the log, as if it had not even been there, that neither hunter was able to get off a shot.

As the bear continued down the creek, the two hunters lost sight of him. They retreated to the big spruce where they had left their packs. As they waited there, a few seconds later the bear appeared just ten yards in front of them. "He was coming toward us," Winnen said. Winnen tried to aim for the bear's chest, but all he could see through his scope was the bear's head. Urban said, "Shoot! Shoot!"

Winnen recalled aiming for the bear's left eye. The bullet, however, hit two inches lower, entering the side of the bear's muzzle and entering its brain. Winnen continued to shoot. All in all, he fired six shots into the big brownie.

In photos, the bear's paw is almost as wide as the hunter's chest and sports threeto four-inch claws. Winnen guessed the bear's hide weighed more than 200 pounds.

Once back at the base, Winnen took the hide and skull to the state Department of Fish and Game

Bob Fromme used his bow to take this big British Columbia grizzly in 2000. The bear's skull scored 24 4/6 using the Pope and Young system. (Courtesy: Bob Fromme)

to get it sealed, as required by law. Fish and Game records reveal the skull's unofficial Boone and Crockett green score of 28 and 8/16 inches, while the hide squared 10-feet, 6-inches. Biologist Crowley said he suspects the bear was 15 to 20 years old. Based on the bear's girth measurement it is estimated that the bear weighed somewhere between 1,000 and 1,200 pounds, far larger than almost any other bear ever taken on Hichenbrook Island.

The Kenai Peninsula

The Kenai Peninsula in south central Alaska is connected to the rest of the state by a narrow, heavily glaciated corridor. Few bears migrate through this corridor, making the Kenai brown bear population essentially a closed group. Alaska Department of Fish and Game biologists estimate that somewhat more than three hundred brown bears inhabit this area, with well over half that number found in the peninsula's western portion. One hundred or more brownies inhabit the peninsula's eastern edge along the Gulf of Alaska and farther north.

The ABC Islands

Admiralty, Baranof, and Chicagof Islands support large brown bear populations. Admiralty holds more than 1700 bears, while Baranof supports more than one thousand of the animals. Chicagof is home to almost 1800 brownies. Kruzof, a smaller island in the same archipelago, has a population of about 125 brown bears. The island with the greatest density of brown bears is Admiralty, where 386 bears can be found on every one thousand square kilometers.

Hunting Kodiak Brown Bears

The name says it all: Kodiak! Any bear hunter, including those who have not yet hunted these animals but would like to, knows that Kodiak brownies are, if not the largest carnivorous land mammal, then among the largest. Some bear hunters believe—and California's Mike Fejes is one of them—that Unimak Island's brown bears are somewhat larger than Kodiak's.

The Alaska Department of Fish and Game, though, votes for the Kodiak. According to Larry Van Daele, biologist in charge of Kodiak Island, "Kodiak bears are the largest bears in the world. A large male can be over ten feet tall when standing on his hind legs and five feet tall at the top of his hump when he is standing on all four legs. A large boar will weigh as much as fifteen hundred pounds." As is always the case, hunters and outfitters tell of unsubstantiated records of bears weighing even more.

Bob Fromme's Kodiak Hunt

Kodiak browns of almost any size, though, are large enough to attract the attention of any serious bear hunter. One such hunter was archer Bob Fromme of San Diego, California. Fromme had been wanting for years to take one of the giants with a bow. He'd booked and gone on a number of combination hunts for caribou and other game that also would have allowed him to shoot a brown bear by paying an additional trophy fee. Fromme never saw a bear on any of these hunts, so he went for broke and booked a hunt with Tom Kirstein, a guide from Fairbanks.

"Timing on any brown bear hunt is critical," Fromme said. "Hunters think of hunting brown bears while they are fishing for salmon like the photos depict from the McNeil River Wildlife Refuge. That may seem ideal, but it isn't reality for anyone hoping to kill a Kodiak brown bear.

"The salmon run from around August 1 to October 1," Fromme continued. "That is an excellent time to hunt brown bears in the Alaskan Peninsula, where hunting season corresponds fairly well with the salmon run.

"On Kodiak, though, the fall season doesn't start until the last week of October, when salmon runs are finished. The spring Kodiak bear hunting season is a month long. It begins on April 15 and ends May 15. Outfitters book hunters on fifteen-day hunts, so you have a choice of hunting from April 15 to April 30 or from May 1 to May 15. Hunters who go during the earlier period have the best chance of taking a boar whose coat is not yet rubbed, but these hunters may not see many bears if spring is late and the animals remain in their dens. Another downside to the earlier hunt occurs when snow still covers the earth. It is quite strenuous to hike around in deep snow and even harder to stalk a bear in it. The later spring hunt, from May 1 to May 15, guarantees hunters that more bears will be out, although many of them will be sows and cubs. The chance that you will have to contend with deep snow lessens as well on a later hunt."

Fromme's outfitter had his clients hunt Kodiak's fabled Deadman Bay area. Fromme's plane was unable to land at the Kodiak airport until the second day of his hunt—not uncommon on Alaskan hunting trips. Once they arrived in camp, Fromme's guide immediately hurried him to a boat for a quick trip across the bay to a spot where the guide knew big boars liked to den up for the winter.

"We set up high on one slope overlooking a large basin," Fromme said. "From where we were sitting I could see another slope, and that's where the boars liked to den." As the pair watched this slope, they spotted a big boar. Before they could move, though, a resident hunter killed the animal. Fromme wanted to move. "I can't stand hunting where someone else has just shot up the place," he noted.

Fromme and his guide returned to their boat. They set out and started glassing the shoreline. It didn't take long for the guide to spot some huge tracks in the snow. He noted how far apart the tracks were as well as the amount of drag. A giant of a boar will plow through some drifts rather than walking or leaping because the animal is so powerful that bulling its way through snow does not even faze it.

"The guide suspected we were looking at a huge boar's tracks," Fromme said. "We could see where the trail disappeared into the island's interior. The time was 8:30 p.m. I knew it would be getting dark at 10 p.m. We waited for a while, and when the bear didn't reappear, I decided to sneak along his trail to see if I could spot him.

"He was feeding in a thick patch of alders only about a hundred yards from his trail along the shoreline," Fromme said. "As I tried to move closer, he must have spotted my movement and spooked somewhat. I roared at him, trying to calm him down by making him think my movement was made by another bear. Then I hit a rabbit call, thinking that might help calm him, too, if not bring him out to investigate the sound. He didn't bolt out of the thicket, so we decided to let him settle down for about fifteen minutes or so before I attempted to go any closer."

Fromme's guide was worried about the amount of remaining daylight. He wondered if there was enough time for Fromme to get off a shot before dark no matter what action he decided on. After the fifteen-minute wait was up, Fromme took off his outermost boot layer. The outfitter had advised his hunters to cut down a pair of neoprene stocking-foot chest waders and wear them inside a pair of ordinary hunting or hiking boots to act as hip boots when crossing creeks or bogs. The hunters wore them rolled down for normal walking and pulled them up thigh-high when they negotiated water hazards.

"Once my hiking boots were off, I pulled up the hip boots and then knelt down in the snow and mud," Fromme said. "I don't know if I'd have gotten away with this if the boar hadn't been groggy after having just left his winter den. I'd sneak closer to him on my knees for about two minutes—about that time he'd lift his head and look around. I'd stop whenever he was watching and then sneak forward again. I was about forty yards away when he rolled over on his side. This gave me the chance I'd been waiting for. He wouldn't be able to see me move, so I stood up and tippy-toed around him from the rear. There was a jungle of alders behind where he was lying, but also a stream. My goal was to make it to a spot with the right angle, so my arrow could take out both of his lungs. I crept closer and closer until I was twenty-one yards from him. Only a bush blocked my shot. I took a couple more steps to get around the bush and was now eighteen yards from this huge boar.

"I had paid for a cameraman to accompany me so he could videotape my bear hunt," Fromme

Bowhunter Bob Fromme stalked into an alder thicket with this big Kodiak brown to shoot it from eighteen yards. (Courtesy: Bob Fromme)

continued. "The cameraman saw how close I was to the bear, and he remarked that if the bear tried to jump me, the guide would not have a good shot at the animal. So the guide began to move closer. He took a couple of steps, and the bear must have suspected something was up, because he pulled his front legs up so that his front end was off the ground. The way he stopped gave me a perfect triangle behind his front legs to aim at. I released, and my arrow hit him in his right side. It went all the way through his body, and the broadhead and six inches of arrow shaft were sticking out on the other side. He felt the pain, bit at his side where the arrow had gone in, and grunted. Then he turned around. I knew he would probably run toward me because I was on the thick side of the alder patch, and he did. I froze until he was about ten yards away, and then I backed up a little. He headed up higher through the alders, but he couldn't go far. He rolled over and died. Only about eight seconds had elapsed from the moment I shot until the bear died."

Bob Fromme killed his Kodiak brown bear in May 2002. The hide squared ten feet four and one-half inches, and the skull's Pope and Young green score was 28 8/16 points. Although not yet officially scored after the drying period, Fromme's bear's green score exceeds the official Pope and Young score of the current record, which was taken by Jack Frost. Fred Bear's brown bear is the current number two brown bear in the world. An estimate of the bear's weight during the fall, when the animal would have been in peak condition, was fourteen hundred pounds.

Fromme was shooting a Mathews Rival Pro with a draw weight of seventy-five pounds and a draw length of thirty inches. He used Blackhawk Vapor All-Carbon arrows tipped with Rocket Ultimate Steel fixed-blade three-blade broadheads. This combination of arrow and broadhead weighed in at 500 grains and traveled at 260 feet per second. Fromme's bow was also fully equipped with Sims anti-vibration products, including dampeners and stabilizer. The archer wore Scent-Lok beneath his camouflage. The camouflage pattern he selected was Bill Jordan's Timber Advantage.

Kodiak brown bears (*Ursus arctos middendorffi*) are a unique subspecies of the brown or grizzly bear. They live exclusively on the islands in the Kodiak Archipelago, where they have been isolated from other brown bears for about twelve thousand years.

Today between 2,800 and 3,000 bears inhabit Kodiak Island at a density of about 0.7 bears per square mile. Kodiak bear populations are healthy, and they enjoy a relatively pristine habitat and well-managed fish populations.

Kodiak Numbers

Even though Kodiak bear numbers are stable, and in some places are increasing, a major mortality factor for Kodiak cubs is cannibalism by adult male bears. Mature boars may not only kill and eat cubs, but they also occasionally kill a mature sow simply because she is not in estrus. There is no way of knowing how such behaviors affect overall bear numbers, but there is little doubt that having hunters kill mature boars helps ensure that more young bears will survive to adulthood. Even so, over twenty-five percent of Kodiak cubs die before striking out on their own.

Kodiak brown bear sows become sexually mature at the age of five and continue throughout their lives to produce cubs. Usually four years elapse between litters, so recruitment is low, one reason cub cannibalism is of such concern. Litters consist of only two or three cubs, although a sow occasionally may be seen with five or six tagging along behind her. Biologists suspect that such sows have adopted orphaned cubs to raise as their own.

Bob Beaulieu's Kodiak Hunt

All facets of the brown bear's life are fascinating, especially to those who hunt them. No wonder people are so willing to pay almost a king's ransom to line up their sights on one of these immense beasts. One who did just that was Bob Beaulieu. Although Bob had retired before he went brown bear hunting in April 2000, he never gave up on his dream of someday hunting the giant brownies.

Using a rather roundabout method of research, Bob found a master guide, Jim Bailey, of Eagle River, Alaska, who had had a cancellation for April. That truly was fortuitous, considering that most brown bear hunts are booked five years in advance.

Bob and his wife traveled from their Florida home to Kodiak, Alaska. "I hunted fairly early in the year," Bob said, "when the whole idea is to glass the hillsides looking for big bears and hope you see enough bears to make a good selection. Jim boated us to an area about an hour from Kodiak. We were put up fairly luxuriously, in shacks rather than tents. The weather didn't cooperate at all. I hunted for three days, and there was only one afternoon when it wasn't raining, snowing, or sleeting.

"The snowline where we hunted that afternoon [I shot the bear] was at about a thousand feet," Bob continued. "When we finally started to glass, we spotted a sow with a cub and another bear with a pretty substantial rub spot.

"My guide was young, but he was a very good guide," Bob said. "We spent a lot of time glassing the snowline, where bear tracks were clearly visible. One set had tracks so big it looked like a truck had made them. When the guide spotted these big tracks, we crawled up closer to them and started spotting from there. It was rough going. The snow was waist-deep in places. I'd taped my gun barrel so I could be certain it would shoot. I was more concerned about my scope, because I had used the gun as a walking stick when it was difficult to negotiate in the snow.

"Finally, we saw a bear about two miles away," Bob said. "It was the first bear we'd seen. It would walk a while, then roll over on its back and play

with its feet. The guide said it looked like a good bear, one that would measure at least eight feet. He also said we had to get ahead of it so I could get a shot at it.

"It took about an hour to get into position," Bob continued. "The bear was walking toward this deep ravine. We walked ahead of it and got onto the other side of that ravine and waited. Pretty soon we could see the bear coming toward us. I'd been winded, but had had time to catch my breath, and I was ready to shoot. The guide told me he'd stop the bear. He yelled once, then again, but the wind caught his words, and I know the bear hardly heard them, but he looked directly toward us anyway. A head-on shot was not what I was hoping for. The bear finally began to go down the ravine, and I was able to shoot it through the back." Bob's Winchester Model 70 (post- 1994) was chambered for .375 H&H Mag. His ammunition was Federal's 300-grain Bear Claw Trophy Bonded Sledgehammer. A Nikon 3–7X variable was atop bob's rifle, mounted on see-through iron sights. When Bob's bullet struck the bear behind its shoulder at 150 yards, the bear immediately started shaking like its spine had been broken. "The recoil caused me to lose sight of the bear, and when I looked again, it was gone," Bob said. "I asked my guide, 'Where's the bear?' He said, 'It dropped like a rock. Keep shooting.' 'At what?' I said, because I was still unable to see the bear. I shot a few times in its direction, but to this day I'm not sure I hit it again."

Bob Beaulieu knew how lucky he'd been. Looking back, he knew he had about a one in five chance of making such a low-percentage stalk without blowing it. "Plus, this was the only bear we'd seen after several days of bad weather," Bob said. "I call it my once-in-a-lifetime bear."

Bob is right in more ways than one. His big Kodiak brown bear really was a oncein- a-lifetime bruin. His boar's skull measured 26 4/16 points using the Boone and Crockett scoring system, so the bear qualified for the club's annual awards dinner.

Although generally solitary in nature, Kodiak bears sometimes gather in large groups where there is an abundance of food. To avoid fights, especially between boars of disparate ranks that could easily be killed in such an altercation, Kodiak brown bears have developed a complex system of body language, facial expressions, and sounds to express their desires and to avoid battles. Kodiak bears were commercially hunted throughout the 1800s. A bear hide brought only about ten dollars at the time, which is no more than what a beaver or river otter pelt was worth.

Farmers at one time tried to raise livestock on Kodiak Island, but bears promptly scrambled their efforts. They then began to systematically kill the big brownies, and bear numbers plunged. Sportsmen became so worried about the drop in bear numbers that they petitioned the federal government to protect both bears and their Kodiak habitats. As a result, the Kodiak National Wildlife Refuge was created in 1941.

Today hunters kill about 160 Kodiak bears annually. Regulations are strict. Each year about five thousand resident hunters apply for a chance at the 319 permits set aside for them. Nonresidents regard as more precious than gold any permit they receive. As of press time, to hunt Kodiak brown bears you need a valid Alaska hunting license, a Big Game Tag Record, a brown bear locking tag, and a registration and/or drawing permit for the area you plan to hunt. If you are not an Alaska resident, you also need proof that you will be guided by a registered guide or a relative within the second degree of kinship.

Registration permits are issued for those who hunt bears along Kodiak's road system. These permits can be obtained only at Kodiak's Alaska Department of Fish and Game office. They issue an unlimited number of registration permits, and the permits can be obtained by either residents or nonresidents.

Drawing permits are issued for bear hunting in all other parts of Game Management Unit 8 (Kodiak Archipelago). There are twenty-nine Drawing Hunt Areas, and the hunts are further divided by season and hunter residency, with a total of 472 permits issued annually. Most of these permits are issued to hunters selected in a lottery. A limited number are also available for nonresident clients of guides with exclusive use areas on the Kodiak National Wildlife Refuge. Bear hunter success averages thirty-five percent for Alaska residents and seventy-five percent for guided nonresident hunters, with spring hunts having a slight advantage over fall hunts.

Trophy-class bears have been taken in nearly every drainage on Kodiak and Afognak Islands. During the last spring hunt for which Alaska officials have complete records, bears with skull sizes exceeding twenty-eight inches were killed in the following hunt areas: Halibut Bay, South Uyak Bay, Uganik Lake, Wild Creek, Aliulik Peninsula, South Arm of Uganik, and Deadman Bay.

Hunting Siberian Brown Bears

Warren Parker is a member of an exclusive club. Warren, a Missouri building contractor as well as the former president of Safari Club International, is one of the few people to have killed animals representing every legal, recognized bear species in the world. Warren's "World Bear Slam" includes an American black bear, an Alaska brown bear, a grizzly bear, a barren ground grizzly bear, a polar bear, an Amur bear, a European brown bear, a Mid-Asian brown bear, a Kamchatka brown bear, and a Siberian brown bear.

As you might expect, Warren experienced some thrilling moments as he collected his Bear Slam. "My Siberian brown died at my feet," he remarked. "I was one of the first hunters ever allowed to hunt Yukitiz, east of the Lena River, in Russia. This was during the

Warren Parker and his Siberian brown bear, which is part of his SCI World Bear Slam.
(Courtesy: Warren Parker)

latter part of the 1980s. We were there in the fall to hunt snow sheep. I really didn't even know the area had any brown bears.

"My guide and I had spotted a small band of sheep up in the mountains," Warren continued. "We made a good stalk, but the sheep weren't what I was after. Luckily, as I'd stalked closer, I'd jacked a shell into the chamber of my rifle. To pull out of that country, we had to cross a small valley. We started across a small plateau and I could barely believe my eyes when I saw a big bear running right at me in a full charge."

Without thinking, Warren aimed and shot his .270 Win, which was loaded with a 130-grain bullet, hardly the load for an enraged bear. In short order, he delivered two quick shots through the bear's lungs.

"The bear started spinning, as bears often will when they're hit hard," Warren continued. "The animal forgot I was even there as he continued to spin rapidly just twelve inches from where I was standing. I finally put one last shot in the boar's skull to put him down for good."

Warren Parker's great Siberian brown bear was ranked number one in the world in SCI's record book for many years. The big boar squared eight feet and sported a lovely dark brown, silver-tipped coat.

Warren Parker's Kamchatka brown bear hunt came about almost by chance as well. Russia's Kamchatka Peninsula is across the Bering Sea from Alaska. "This hunt was an interesting deal, too," Warren commented. "I was there in autumn to hunt the Kamchatka sheep. I'd already bagged my ram, so my guide and I decided to drop down into the lowlands.

"When we arrived there, I couldn't believe what I was seeing," Warren continued. "We walked out upon this huge plateau—perhaps fifteen miles square—and there must have been at least a hundred bears on the plateau feeding on low bush blueberries. To take a bear, all a hunter would have to do would be work the plateau's perimeter until he found a bear big enough to take, then stalk slowly toward the animal until he had a shot."

If only things had been that simple.

"I had a cameraman along to film my hunt," Warren said. "I admit I probably pushed the envelope too hard on this occasion. I tried to get too close to the bear I'd chosen. As I was standing there about a hundred yards from the bear, it turned around and immediately charged me. At that same moment, another big boar, this one about seventy-five yards away, charged me, too. I fired three shells at the one, reloaded, and then shot two bullets into the second.

"Both were simply outstanding animals," Warren concluded. "One squared eleven feet, while the other squared ten feet, six inches." Warren shot his two huge—and quite cranky—Kamchatka brown bears with a .300 Win Mag and 180-grain Nosler handloads.

Bowhunting Western Big Game

FRED EICHLER

Elk

Bowhunting elk can be the ultimate adrenaline rush. They are big, majestic, loud animals that can have massive antlers. The elk is arguably the perfect species for bowhunters who want an action-packed adventure. On the flip side, returning home year after year without fresh elk meat or even a close call can be bitterly disappointing.

As an avid elk hunter who has guided more than a hundred clients on hunts for these awesome animals, I have learned that successfully bowhunting elk requires three main things:

1. Getting in range
2. Drawing undetected
3. Proper shot placement

It sounds so easy, just three little things. However, each one has prerequisites. Before breaking down these three main requirements, let's look at some average success rates.

Anybody can bowhunt elk. Go buy a tag, grab your bow, and head out. Obviously, this is as much effort as thousands of bowhunters put into their hunts, since the average archery success rate—including both bulls and cows—in most Western states hovers around 14 percent for both guided and nonguided hunts. Based on these numbers, your average hunter has only a slim chance of ever harvesting an elk.

I point this out because I feel that most people have the misconception that bowhunting elk out West is pretty easy. Heck, just flip on your TV and watch one of the elk shows, and you can see guys calling in and shooting tremendous elk. Some popular DVDs on the market also show one monster bull after another being called into big, open meadows and harvested. Realistically, unless your pocketbook is extremely deep or you have drawn a limited-tag area, your hunt will not be so easy. Statistics from a three-year period show archery success rates for Colorado, Wyoming, Oregon, Washington, Idaho, Montana, and Utah averaging about 12–15 percent. These numbers include bulls and cows and both guided and nonguided hunts on both public and private land. In states such as Nevada, New Mexico, and Arizona, these numbers are slightly higher due to the limited number of tags available.

What statistics don't show are the opportunities lost—for example, close calls, missed shots, and hunters winded, spotted, or busted while drawing their bows. If lost opportunities were included in the statistics, those success rates would be a lot higher.

So what makes the difference between routinely harvesting an elk and falling into the majority of elk hunters who go home empty-handed every year? There are a lot of factors that come into play, some major and some minute, but they all fall under the three main requirements listed above. My goal in this section is to help you improve your odds on your next elk hunt.

Getting in Range

Getting in range sounds pretty obvious. To be able to shoot an elk you must first get in range. Now let's look at how to get that elk within bow range and how not to screw up once he is there. Let's call bow range from point-blank breathing in your face out to 30 yards. This is the critical distance where everything usually pans out or not.

To get within bow range of elk, the most effective and common methods include:

1. Calling: Emulating the sounds of a calf, cow, or bull to lure an elk into range.
2. Still-hunting: Slipping quietly through the woods, hoping to either sneak into range undetected or spot an elk moving toward you and wait or position yourself for a shot.
3. Stand hunting: Waiting in one location for an elk to come into bow range.

Calling

Let's start with calling. In my opinion, this is the most overrated way to lure an elk into bow range. Any elk that is coming in to a call is ultra-alert. It is looking for another elk, so the odds of getting busted are increased exponentially. Also, since elk use their sense of smell to follow and locate each other, they usually circle downwind of the calls. That said, on those occasions when it does work, when a bull or a cow reacts to your calling and runs into bow range, it is an exciting experience that you will never forget.

Before sharing my suggestions on calling elk, I want to share a story of an elk hunt in Colorado that we captured on video. I was with two friends, and just minutes before we had watched two raghorn bulls sparring in a small clearing about 300 yards away. Now the three of us slipped through the aspens looking for a good spot to set up. I checked

the wind, and then moved into an area where I had enough room to shoot. I slowly knelt down by a small aspen tree and started breaking finger-sized branches off a fallen limb. I cow-called softly while my friend Scott cowcalled from his position 20 yards behind me.

We had cut the distance in half and quickly set up in a small stand of aspens. We knew the bulls were alone and were counting on them wanting to join up with a few lonely and vocal cows. It wasn't going to be easy—Scott was carrying a video camera and my friend Brian was also with us. Brian was set up to my right and Scott was between and behind us, where he could tape the action if the bulls came in. Scott cow-called again and I broke a few more small branches. We were doing our best to sound like a small group of cows grazing through the aspens, softly calling to one another.

Suddenly, through the trees I spotted the top of a rack as one of the bulls made his way toward us through the white-trunked aspens. He was followed closely by the other bull, which stopped to rake an aspen limb with his antlers. The wind was still in our favor, and the two bulls continued toward us, confident they were about to meet up with some cows, not two bowhunters and a cameraman. As the lead bull closed to within about 30 yards, he stopped and looked around. I was sure one of us would be spotted any second. I tried to make myself small as I hid behind my bow and the small aspen tree. Although I couldn't see them, I was sure Brian and Scott were also trying to stay calm and blend into the brush.

The young bull continued slowly forward, heading directly toward me. If he continued on his current path, he was bound to spot one of us at any moment. I slowly started to draw my recurve. The bull was now only about 20 yards away and instantly spotted the slight movement. He jumped and took a few steps to my left, which turned him broadside to me. Luckily the young bull hesitated while I finished

This bull came running into range of my two friends and me. Cow calls lured him in to 20 yards.

my draw and released. The arrow struck the bull just above the heart, and he ran only 40 yards before he stopped and collapsed in front of us. Our setup had worked perfectly, and Scott captured all the action on video.

Although on tape this whole sequence took less than four minutes, it had taken years of botched setups and hundreds of hours afield to help tip the scales in our favor. What follows is a list of tips and tactics I have used to call in elk while hunting and guiding. Just remember that calling does not work all the time. Wind is by far your toughest obstacle, because most elk will attempt to circle or come in downwind.

Noise

It's a fact; elk make noise when they walk through the woods. Don't misunderstand me: they can move quietly when they want to, and I've watched bulls that thundered into a setup sneak away without making a sound. But generally, when

elk are comfortable, they make a lot of noise: branches snapping, antlers scraping brush and trees, legs and hooves breaking branches or hitting logs and rocks as they walk along. Sometimes they really make a racket. Use that knowledge when you are calling. Noise adds realism. It's tough to get used to because generally when bowhunting silence is your main concern. However, if you are trying to convince a bull or cow to come join you and the only noise is your calling, oftentimes they will hold up out of range. So next time you try calling, add a little noise to your routine. Try breaking a few small twigs or raking a tree with a branch. It may just be enough to cause that elk to rush right in.

Stop Calling so Much

Overcalling is a common mistake. It's hard not to scream on that bugle tube again or to send a few more cow calls down into the draw. I've learned the hard way that less is best.

Elk have great hearing, and both their calls and yours travel a long way. If an elk is going to come in or respond, usually just a few cow calls (a few being three or four) or a single bugle is all it takes. This can be especially true on public land, where most elk have already heard the latest in new elk calls long before you ever put on your pack.

I once watched a friend of mine on public land spook a bull into the next county by overcalling. From my vantage point above him, I watched as the whole show played out. A bull was heading up over a ridge, and I was trapped on the opposite ridge so I couldn't move without being spotted. The bull was alone and heading into the timber when we both heard my friend's two cow calls float up from the draw between us. I watched as the bull turned completely around and started heading rapidly down the ridge toward my buddy. He couldn't see the bull from his location and cow-called again three more times. The bull continued heading toward him but slowed down noticeably. The third time he called, the bull bolted back up the slope and into the timber. He had obviously heard too much. I truly believe that had he stopped after the first two calls, the bull would have trotted right down into range. As it was, overcalling blew that elk out of there, and my buddy never even knew the bull was around. I think this scenario happens more than we realize.

The lesson here is to give elk time to respond to your calls. They may be coming in silently from a few hundred yards away, so make sure you give them enough time. I have often been surprised by elk that came in to my calls as much as an hour after I had let out a few pleading cow calls. I try to wait at least 30 to 45 minutes before moving or calling again from the same area. I prefer using a cow call over a bugle and usually use only three to four cow calls at a time.

Diane Kinney is an avid bowhunter who hunts with a recurve. Her story proves how effective calling can be in the right situation.

This bull was busy raking a tree when I slipped up to 19 yards and saved the tree's life.

"It was down to the last hour of the last day of my elk hunt, when two bulls stepped out into the meadow across the valley from where we were. I could tell they were bulls, but not how big. I cow-called to get the attention of my guide, Dick Louden. From where he was he couldn't see them. He understood immediately and started calling; the bulls started our way across the meadow into the valley below us and then they disappeared from view into an arroyo. Not knowing where they would come out, I was standing with an arrow nocked,

Diane Kinney from Pennsylvania and her bull that guide Dick Louden called in.

gait changed, he slowed, went about 100 yards, and went down. He never got back up. It was by far the most exciting fifteen minutes of my life and an experience I will never forget."

Bugling

In my opinion, bugling is probably the most overused calling technique. I bugle only sparingly unless the bulls are really cranked up. More often than not I've seen bulls gather up their cows and run when challenged by another bull. If the bull doesn't run and responds, I try to wait for him to bugle again before calling so I can gauge how worked up he is and mimic everything he does. Occasionally a bull will come screaming in no matter what you do or how often you do it, but generally I try to err on the quiet side. If he wants to fight, don't worry, he will find you.

If you find yourself trying to work one of those stubborn herd bulls that won't come in, try this radical technique. Sneak in as close as you can without spooking the bull or his cows. Then let out your best bugle. If the bull herds up his cows and takes off, you follow. Run up as close as possible without being spotted (terrain obviously plays a role in this method) and then try cow-calling three or four times. Not just a short mew. Stretch it out a bit like a pleading, whining cow. Meeeeeewww. If all goes as planned, the bull will spin around and drop back to pick you up, thinking that he has inadvertently lost one of his cows. In the right situation, this can be a great way to lure in an old bull that usually wouldn't come in to your calls.

Don't forget that most elk coming in to a call will try to circle downwind. So if you're calling by yourself, try to use the terrain to your advantage. Try to force the elk to come in upwind of you, or set up anticipating them to circle downwind. If you practice your calling and hunt during the "prime time" for your location, you may have the most exciting close-range encounter imaginable. When calling, I've had

using a pine tree that made the perfect cover for my 'ground blind.' The sound of rolling rocks in the arroyo was the first thing to give away their position. Suddenly there was an elk rack coming up and out of the arroyo, but I realized it was not a legal bull as he passed. I didn't have time to be disappointed when the second set of antlers came into view. This bull was legal and trotting past me at 11 yards. As the realization that the bull was legal flew through my mind, as if on its own, my recurve came up, the string came back, and the arrow was in the air. I heard a CAWACK as the arrow hit hard. The bull's the best luck with two people, one caller and one hunter. I like using two different cow calls to try to simulate more than one elk.

Setting Up

How you set up when calling will often mean the difference between success and failure. One common mistake is not being set up at all. I have (on more than one occasion) been embarrassed in front of a client when I have gotten busted by a bull charging into range after I had let out just a few calls, hoping to locate a bull. What I have learned is to always be ready and never to call without first being in position to shoot, just in case a bull or cow you don't even know is there charges in. When pair hunting, I like to have the hunter 20 to 60 yards upwind in front of the caller. Exact positioning varies and depends on the elk's position, obstacles, and terrain. In general, if I know the elk's exact position, I like to place the shooter a little farther out between the bull and the caller. If I am calling blind or have no idea if there is an elk within earshot or where it may be located, I prefer to have the shooter within 20 yards upwind of the caller. In certain situations or on heavily pressured bulls, having the shooter downwind of the caller can work great as the bull circles to confirm it's an elk he is hearing.

Using cow elk decoys is a great way to lure in bulls to bow range.

Since most calling for elk is done from the ground, you must use the terrain to your advantage. Most eastern whitetail hunters are used to hunting from tree stands. It is a whole different ballgame when you're on the ground trying to get drawn on an animal that is wired and looking for any movement. My friend and fellow guide Jake Kraus once had one of our clients set up on a bull that was coming in. He told the hunter to kneel by a tree and wait to see if something responded to his calls. Due to cover, Jake was only a few feet away from our client. A bull responded and started coming in. Jake whispered, "Get ready," and to his shock the client stood up! The bull instantly spotted the movement and bolted down the ridge. When Jake asked why the hunter stood up, the reply was, "I always stand up in my tree stand to shoot. I've never shot kneeling down."

If you're going elk hunting, you had best practice shooting your bow leaning, kneeling, sitting on your butt, and standing on one foot. Okay, the last one is an exaggeration, but not by much. Also practice shooting at steep up and down angles. When you do set up to call and stand, kneel, or sit waiting for an elk to come in to your calls, pay attention to your surroundings. I have often kicked myself for setting up in a position that prevented me from shooting when an elk did come in. You want to be concealed, but not so much so that you restrict your ability to turn, draw, and shoot if the shot presents itself. Pay attention to the position of the sun and always set up in the shade or shadows when possible. Whenever possible, I like to set up with my back to a large tree and with a few other large trees directly in front of or off to both sides of me. They can be great vision blockers and can give you the chance to draw quickly without being detected when the bull's eyes are obstructed by them.

Another thing to try to avoid is calling from too open an area. Elk realize something is up real quick when they hear calls and can't see an elk when they know they should. If you must call from an open

Tommy Bender from New York and his water hole bull.

area with little cover, try using a decoy. Even some of the partial decoys that show just an elk rump or head work great.

Another trick for luring in stubborn elk on pressured land is rattling. I like to use a set of 5 × 5 sheds in areas where I don't have to pack them in too far. Since hunters rarely rattle for elk, it can sometimes fool a bull into range.

When trying to call elk, I think the best rule of thumb is to let the elk dictate which calls to use and how often to use them. If a bull or bulls are bugling their heads off, hammer back at them. If they are not really vocal, play the same game and tone it down a bit. Don't worry if your calls don't sound perfect. Like people, both bulls and cows have their own unique sounds. Sometimes the worst-sounding bugles and most terribly pitched cow calls I have heard have come from real elk that I would have sworn were hunters.

Hunting Water

Another method that can be used with great results is hunting water holes. Find water holes the elk are frequenting by looking for well-used trails with fresh tracks leading into the water. Elk will usually head to water first thing in the evening after being bedded up all day. If the weather is warm, I will sit all day over water. Often, you can catch elk slipping in early in the morning or during the heat of the day for a drink and to cool off. If your area doesn't have water holes or small ponds, you can often find certain spots on creeks or rivers that are favored watering areas.

We often set clients up on water holes in warm weather with great success. A few years ago, I was guiding a fellow from New York named Tommy Bender. Tommy is one of those guys who can tell jokes all day long and never repeat one. I wouldn't describe him as a super-patient guy, but he wanted an elk with his bow in a bad way. Problem was that the hunting was slow and the bulls weren't talking much. Since the weather was warm, I suggested he sit at a small water hole I knew about. I could tell the idea of sitting 12 hours didn't really appeal to him, but he said he would give it a try. When I walked in to pick him up that evening, a huge grin met my flashlight beam. He was fired up and talking fast. He explained that a group of elk came in to the small pond just as the sun was setting. He made a perfect shot on the bull and was as proud as he could be with his first archery bull.

Another client, Rob Evans, who is an outdoor writer and avid bowhunter, joined us for an elk hunt. Once again, the conditions were warm and his guide, Cam Keeler, set Rob up in a blind by another water hole.

Rob said: "After just an hour of sitting, I got so warm I stripped down to my skivvies. The heat had

Rob Evans of Wisconsin with his water hole bull and guides Jake Kraus and Cam Keeler.

me nodding off, but I was jogged into consciousness by the sound of thundering hooves. I dove for my bow and came to full draw as the first cow jumped into the water. Nine more followed, but I didn't see a bull. Then I heard the sound of running hooves again, and a bull ran to the edge of the water shaking his rack. The shot was thirty-four yards, and my arrow blew through the bull's lungs. My first elk made a small circle and crashed dead into the water."

These are two perfect examples of what can happen if you find an active water hole and wait patiently. Every year, water hole hunting pays off for bowhunters out West. You just may be surprised how easy it can be.

This big bull has been doing some serious fighting. He is just dropping his head to get a drink. Now, if he would just turn broadside...

Wallows

When scouting or hunting, always look for wallows. They are usually found in swampy areas or sometimes in or near creeks or drainages. Rutting bulls will roll around in these wet depressions and cover themselves in mud and urine. This strong smell helps attract cows and warns other bulls of their presence. Some wallows are used only once, while others are commonly visited and used by more than just one bull.

Wallows are generally easy to spot. The ground and grass around them are usually gouged by the hooves and antlers of rut-crazed bulls. If you don't spot one of these small muddy depressions, you can often follow your nose to them. One of my favorite wallow stories happened while guiding Brian Brochu from New Hampshire. Brian owns an archery shop and is an experienced bowhunter. I had found an active wallow while guiding a client earlier in the season and suggested Brian give it shot. We tried calling a bull in early that morning with no success. So around 10:30 in the morning, we quietly sneaked into the wallow. Brian set up on the ground, and 30 minutes after I left, a beautiful 7 × 7 bull walked in to roll in his wallow. Brian drew back and made a textbook shot on his very first elk hunt.

When you find an active wallow, don't pass on the opportunity to hunt it.

Setting Up on Wallows

Carefully choose the best location to conceal yourself. Take into consideration where you think the elk are coming from and wind direction. Tree stands, ground blinds, and pop-up blinds are all good choices to use for your ambush.

My favorite setup is the Double Bull pop-up blind because it's tough and can be set up quickly. Blinds are also a plus because they help contain your scent.

A bull will come—it's just a matter of time. Although some people like to call from a stand near water or a wallow, I prefer to remain silent. It is easy

I spotted this bull in his bed. After an almost two-hour stalk, I was able to put an arrow into his chest.

to spook a bull that is coming in silently when you rip off a few poorly timed calls.

I don't believe you can ever eliminate human scent, but you can try to reduce and mask it. Clean clothes, rubber boots, and a clean body will help even more. Remember that concealment and scent elimination are the keys when hunting water or wallows because the animals will be close, and more often than not there will be more than one set of eyes and many noses to deal with.

Other Setups for Elk

For other great stand locations, try trails between feeding and bedding areas. Elk, like whitetails, have favorite bedding areas. They also take advantage of agricultural plantings such as clover or alfalfa, where available. Although hunting

My client Wright Harrell shot this 316 bull from a tree stand. He was set up between the bull's feeding and bedding area.

from the ground near these trails works well, a tree stand gives you a huge advantage with elk. Unlike whitetails, which have learned that danger often lurks in trees, elk are still tree stand illiterate. I usually try to set two stands for different wind directions on one trail. Bear in mind that wind direction in the mountains is tricky business. One general rule of thumb is that wind currents are usually going downhill early in the morning, then switching to blowing uphill by mid- to late morning.

When hunting active trails from tree stands, don't be disappointed if you don't see anything for a day or two at a time. Elk rotate and often use different trails to get to and from their feeding and bedding areas. Usually they will have multiple main routes they frequently use. Be patient. If you're on a well-used trail, the odds are you will get your opportunity. I also try to place my tree stands on the fringes of bedding and feeding areas. Too much scent

at either one can ruin your hunt. Elk don't take much pressure before moving to a new area. Stand-hunting near one of these areas is often the most effective way for a bowhunter to harvest an elk. Unlike a calling situation, the elk aren't as wired, straining to spot any movement or hear a noise. A bowhunter can usually take his or her time and shoot at a relaxed elk as it passes by feeding, on a trail, or coming into or leaving its bedding area. It might lack a little of the excitement of calling in an animal, but it is a great way to put a backstrap on your plate.

Escape Routes

This method usually works best on public or private land where there is other hunting pressure. Like most animals, elk have areas they repeatedly use to escape hunting pressure. Finding these areas is sometimes as simple as looking at a topo map of your area and determining where you would go to leave all the people behind. Sometimes it's a matter of trial and error and hunting the same place over and over and noting the differences between where you see elk on opening day and where you find them five days later. Usually these are two totally different locations.

My friend Blye Chadwick and I once lucked into a great escape route on public land when a rifle hunter friend of Blye's told him where the elk usually go to elude pressure from hunters. We decided to try the area on opening day of bow season and watched as at least 60 elk, a few of which were great bulls, all went down the same steep trail heading to another, more remote area. I managed to take a cow out of the group at 5 yards, but more important, I learned an efficient method of setting up and letting the elk come to me. I've had luck hunting escape routes only during the first few days of the season. After that, most of the elk have already moved to their new areas.

When hunting a good escape route, I try to stay on stand all day. Usually these trails lead to more remote areas or areas where the thickest cover or timber can be found.

Still-Hunting

Still-hunting can be an extremely effective way to slip undetected into bow range of an elk. Fortunately for the still-hunter, elk are big animals and therefore usually make noise when going through the woods. Most elk guides I know prefer to stillhunt elk if they are with a client who is in reasonable shape who can move slowly and quietly through the woods or run if need be.

Oftentimes elk may be vocal, which makes them easy to locate, but they won't respond to calls. This happens a lot on heavily pressured private or public land. Being mobile often allows you an opportunity to slip up quietly on vocal feeding elk. I have also run into range of elk that hesitated before running, thinking I was another elk approaching.

I would only try the run technique on elk that are moving away from you that you can't cut off or catch up to quietly.

Still-hunting requires patience. When I am still-hunting, it usually takes me approximately ten minutes to go 50 yards. That's about one minute for every 6 steps. Slow and steady with no sudden movements is the key. I also stop every few yards to slowly scan the area with my eyes for any movement. I have used this method to harvest both bulls and cows for myself and have also used this method with clients to slip into bow range.

Oftentimes, you will spot elk feeding or walking and can wait for them to come to you or move slowly to cut them off. Full camouflage is the key to utilizing this method effectively. That includes a head net or face paint on your head and hands as well.

One of my favorite times to use this method is when it is raining, snowing, or windy. It really tips the odds in your favor. The key is how slow you can go. I have found that I have never spooked an elk by going too slowly, but I have sent a few hauling by getting impatient and going too fast.

I have successfully still-hunted clients into range of a lot of elk. Unfortunately, since I am usually guiding during elk season, I don't have much time to hunt elk for myself. When I do have a little time, I like to still-hunt if the conditions are right. Since I also love elk meat, I am not picky and usually shoot the first elk I slip into range of. My friends have accused me of having a lucky horseshoe . . . I will spare you the graphic details on where they think it's hidden! I just sometimes seem to be in the right spot at the right time.

My largest bull to date was shot while still-hunting. I was being followed by a cameraman because we were trying to capture an elk hunt on video for Easton Bowhunting on The Outdoor Channel. As luck would have it, we slipped up on three bulls feeding in a secluded meadow. It was early in the season, and the bulls were still hanging out together. There was a small, barely legal 4 × 4 and two 6 × 6 bulls in the meadow. The 4 × 4 was closest and I told the cameraman I would happily shoot him if I could crawl into range. While I was crawling closer, one of the bigger bulls swapped places with the little guy and I had no choice but to harvest the big bull. I am convinced that had I not been wearing a head net and crawling slowly, that bull would have lived another day. Remember that when still-hunting, the slower you go, the better off you are.

Another plus to still-hunting is that you can cover more country. I have often found great stand locations while slipping quietly through elk country. As the old adage goes: "There is more than one way to skin a cat." There are also lots of different theories and methods on how to hunt elk. The ones I have outlined here have all worked for me. However, as all elk hunters know, no method is foolproof when it comes to bowhunting elk.

It's not the size of the elk, it's the size of the experience that matters. Here is my wife Michele with her bull that guide Jake Kraus called in to 10 yards. She used a 48-pound bow, and the bull dropped in sight 70 yards away.

Drawing Undetected

Okay, you've done it. Your heart's pounding and you're not sure why, but you're also holding your breath. An elk is within bow range—one of the biggest and most impressive game animals in North America. You can already taste those 2-inch-thick steaks. Geez, wait till your buddies see this elk! All you have to do is draw your bow. The shot is a piece of cake. Wait, oh no, what happened? He's gone!

It's happened to me, and as an elk guide I have watched it happen to a lot of clients: getting busted trying to draw.

In my experience, this happens more often than not when you're on the ground in a calling situation. For example, the bull or cow is coming in with every sense alerted. It's straining its highly tuned ears for any sound. Its huge eyes are searching for any movement. As soon as you try to move or draw, wham, you're busted. It's the exception when you get to draw and shoot undetected.

In talking with other experienced elk guides, I have found that they all share similar experiences. I asked longtime friend and elk guide Jake Kraus about his strategy and success rate on calling. He likes to call elk from the first day of the season to the last. He is the best caller I have ever heard and prefers calling to other methods of hunting elk. Here is what Jake had to say:

"When a bull screams within earshot, it makes the hair on the back of your neck stand up! The ability to interact with a wild animal such as an elk is a blast. Not every animal will come flying in on a string. Calling elk is a sport that requires finesse and strategy. It is all about when to call, when to keep quiet, which call to use, and when to use it. If you do it right, you're on your way to a close encounter. Make a mistake and you won't see a thing.

"As with most big game species, female vocalizations are really what the male is listening for during the rut. My twelve years of guiding experience has taught me to use my bugle tube sparingly. I tend to use bugling most frequently as a locator call, and that's it. Using a cow call is by far my favorite and most successful tactic for rutting and nonrutting elk. I'll often emit soft calls every minute or so as I sneak through the woods with a client, probing new areas or experimenting in spots that I know hold elk. A cow call is the best call to use, particularly if you know the herd is sensitive to calling pressure. Once a bull is located, cow calls can either be used to coax the bull to your position or to instill confidence as you move in on him.

Guide Jake Kraus and Steve Memmott from Hoyt with the bull Jake called in for him.

"This may sound easy on paper, but remember you are dealing with a wild animal whose senses are put to the test every day. Getting elk to respond to your calls is fairly easy. Getting them in bow range, standing still with a clear shooting lane, and getting a shot without being seen can be very difficult. To further complicate things, by calling you have told the elk that there is something out there. Now the animal is coming in looking for the source of the call. Simply put, the odds are not in your favor. Each year I personally guide anywhere from ten to fifteen archery elk hunters and spend every day of the archery season in the woods. In my experience, I would say that only one of every ten encounters ends with success. It's inevitable that you are going to get 'busted,' but if you keep putting yourself in those close encounters, it is going to happen eventually."

When Steve Memmott, the manufacturing manager for Hoyt bows, came out on an elk hunt with us, I sent him with guide Jake Kraus. He loves to call elk, and I knew Steve would be in good hands. The first morning of his hunt, Jake got a bull screaming with his seductive cow calls. The bull was so worked up he jumped two fences to get to them. The bull got nervous when he didn't see his hairy beauty as he closed within range, so he started to turn to leave. Jake turned him broadside with another cow call, and Steve smoked the bull at a little over 30 yards. His first guided elk hunt only lasted about fifteen minutes, but they were all action-filled.

So what can you do to get drawn undetected? Start with camouflage. It doesn't matter if you're on the ground calling, still-hunting, or in a tree stand. This is one of the most important things you can do

to help your odds. It's simple. Put on a head net and gloves or face paint on your head and hands, and also wear a good, broken-up camouflage pattern. Don't wear anything noisy. Cotton, fleece, and wool are tough to beat for stealthy materials. I have watched helplessly as elk have bolted from clients when their noisy clothing gave them up.

Quiet down your bow. I once had a client draw his bow as a bull came walking past him heading toward me. I had just bugled again, and the bull was coming in pissed. My client did everything perfectly. He waited until the bull's head was behind a tree and drew. I was about 20 yards away from him on that cold quiet morning and I heard his aluminum arrow screech across his rest. The bull didn't hesitate. He dropped and whirled out of there without ever presenting a shot.

Use moleskin on rests and risers to quiet contact between arrow and rest and to avoid an accidental "clank" on the side of a wooden or metal bow riser. Also, practice quietly removing an arrow from your quiver. These are small things that can save a hunt from being unsuccessful.

Another common mistake is drawing while the elk is not yet at a good shot angle. When possible, wait to draw until the elk is in a position to shoot. I have sat and watched with sympathy as clients who drew too soon had to finally let the bow down, their arms shaking with fatigue when a bull or cow hesitated before coming close enough or stopped when they caught a glimpse of movement. It happens every year, usually more than once. Waiting to draw until the animal is at a good shot angle increases your odds of getting a shot if the animal locks up for some reason. Whenever possible, it is best to wait to draw until the elk's eyes are completely or at least partially obstructed by trees or brush.

The draw itself should be smooth and controlled. If you can't draw your bow slowly straight back to full draw, you need a lighter bow.

Every year I see hunters who have to put their bow arm up in the air like they are going to shoot at a star. Then they yank the bow down while jerking back the string. I would rather see hunters shoot a 45-pound bow that they can draw smoothly rather than struggle with a 60-pound bow that is too heavy.

The final key to getting drawn undetected is controlling your nerves. It's easy to come unglued around elk. I have had clients do some crazy things when elk walk into bow range. It doesn't seem to matter if they saunter into a water hole or stroll past on a trail. There is just something about elk that can cause even an experienced hunter to come unstuck. Sometimes it's a situation where a big bull is bugling in your face and ripping up trees . . . well, if that doesn't rattle you then you probably need to quit hunting!

My favorite experience where a hunter "lost it," was in southern Colorado. I was guiding a client on a private ranch and we had a bull pretty worked up, but he wouldn't come down to us. So we slipped up the mountain into some aspens. I set the hunter up in front of me and I let off a bugle. I was just putting the tube down when we could hear this bull come running down the mountain bugling and hitting every tree he could on the way down to us. My client got up and started back down the mountain in a hurry. I jumped up from behind a tree as he came past me and said, "What are you doing? He's coming in." He said, "I know," and kept going. As far as I know, he hasn't been out West elk hunting since. Although this was an extreme example, nerves can cause you to freeze up, or act irrationally. They can be found at some archery and/or gun retail shops. Watch elk shows on TV.

The best realistic practice I have seen is one of the "interactive" target systems. or rent elk DVDs. They will help you get used to how elk move and react. Shooting 3-D competitions, or just shooting with people watching you, will also help you shoot under pressure. One coach I knew who trained

These two bulls are probably 3 1/2 years old.

Like whitetails and mule deer, elk calves are born spotted.

some Olympic shooters would throw firecrackers around to help his students practice under pressure. That may be a little extreme, but you get the idea. Improving your shooting will also increase your odds of bringing home some elk meat.

Field-Judging Elk

Field-judging a typical rack is much easier than field-judging a nontypical rack. Since the large majority of trophies have typical racks, I have included tips and score sheets for scoring typical animals only. These should be used as a rough guide only. The best way for you to improve your own judging skills is to guess the score on friends' mounts, or anywhere you can observe different mounts, and see how close you are.

Any elk with a bow is a trophy, but for those looking for a record-book bull, here are some tips on what to look for. To make the Pope & Young record book, an American elk must score a minimum of 260 inches after deductions (see scoring sheet). Although there are many measurements that apply to the total score, field judging must usually be done in a few seconds. For a quick snapshot of whether a bull will make the book or not there are a few references that will help.

First check to see if the bull has six points on each side. The majority of bulls that make the record book minimums have six relatively symmetrical points on each side. Next look at the length of the main beam. Tine length can add a lot of score in a hurry, so look for a bull with good tine length. The third and fourth points are usually the longest so a quick check of these is a good indicator. If you can roughly total 55 inches by adding all the tines on one side you probably have a bull that will make the minimum if his main beams aren't real skinny. You are looking for a main beam that is 40 inches or more. Also look at width or inside spread between the main beams at the widest point. If it looks to be 30 inches or wider you probably have a contender.

I spoke to my good friend Lee Kline about rough judging in the field. Lee has been an Official Pope & Young scorer for over 35 years. Lee said the best way is to count the number of seconds between your breaths after you see the bull.

Each fall, elk grow a complete new set of antlers. This guy is just getting started on his.

If it is less than one second or you stop breathing completely . . . Shoot . . . it's a good one!

Facts about Elk (*Cervus Canadensis*)

Elk are often referred to as wapiti, which comes from an Indian word meaning "white rump." Mature cows average 500 pounds, while bulls average 700. Elk calves are spotted at birth and gradually lose their spots after one to three months. Only the males have antlers, which they shed each year near the end of winter. New antlers are grown every year and can grow at a rate of an inch a day. The rut (breeding season) takes place from mid-September to mid-October. Their average lifespan is 15 years.

Equipment Suggestions

Elk are large, big-boned, tough animals. I advise a minimum of 45 pounds bow weight with a minimum arrow weight of 450 grains. Razor-sharp broadheads are always a must. I also suggest staying away from flimsy, thin-bladed broadheads with less than a one-inch cutting diameter.

Elk meat is also hard to beat on the dinner table. I enjoy elk a lot of different ways, but here's one of my favorite recipes, which is great if you're having some friends over for dinner.

Elk Roast Stuffed with Garlic and Parsley

Serves 6–8

This recipe works best with a boned piece of elk rump.

4- to 5-pound elk rump roast
4 cloves of fresh garlic, chopped
⅔ cup chopped fresh Italian parsley
½ teaspoon salt
½ teaspoon pepper
½ cup olive oil
1 cup red cooking wine
2 cups beef stock
4 to 6 potatoes, peeled and quartered
3 to 4 peeled carrots, cut into 2-inch chunks
2 medium onions, quartered

In a bowl, combine the garlic, parsley, salt, and pepper. With a sharp, thin (1/2-inch) boning knife, make two or three knife-size holes the length of the roast. Push the parsley mixture into the holes the length of the roast, reserving one tablespoon of mixture. Place the roast in a roasting pan, and rub olive oil and leftover garlic and parsley mixture all over the roast. Let sit overnight in the refrigerator.

Preheat the oven to 375 degrees. Place the carrots, potatoes, and onions around the roast and coat with some of the garlic, parsley, salt, pepper, and olive oil. Add red wine and 1 cup of beef stock. Cover and roast using a meat thermometer to the desired doneness. I suggest medium rare (which is usually about 125 degrees F). Remove the roast and let sit for 30 minutes before carving. Remove the drippings and vegetables and process in a food processor. Add leftover beef stock until it is the proper thickness for gravy. Slice thin and serve.

Mule Deer

Of the five huntable species of deer in North America, mule deer, in my opinion, are the most impressive. Besides tipping the scales as one of our largest deer, their antlers can be huge. When you combine these incredible physical characteristics with their keen sense of smell, incredible eyesight, super hearing, and an uncanny ability to avoid humans, it is no wonder that many bowhunters consider a mature mule deer buck to be one of the most difficult species to harvest with a bow.

Before skipping this mule deer section in search of easier prey, read on for tips on how to bring home the bacon and an impressive rack from one of these Western giants.

There are many reasons why a trophy mule deer is a difficult animal to hunt with a bow. One is that mule deer are found in huntable numbers in only 16 states. That is a far cry from the 43 states that have seasons for white-tailed deer.

The upside is that—thanks to stricter management in several Western states—the opportunity for a bowhunter to harvest a mature mule deer is as good as ever. Especially for the bowhunter that is willing to go the extra mile . . . literally.

Spot-and-Stalk

In my opinion, the spot-and-stalk technique is one of the most efficient ways for a patient, slow-moving bowhunter to harvest a mule deer. This method is most successful when the stalk is made on a single animal that is bedded down. In my experience, the two best times of year to stalk bedded mule deer are early in the fall and during the rut. The advantage to early fall is that the heat during the day causes the deer to bed down early and

get up late. When the weather is hot (70-plus degrees during the day) deer usually stay in their beds most of the day, getting up only occasionally to reposition, urinate, defecate, or drink.

The rut is another great time to catch a buck bedded. Oftentimes during the rut, an exhausted buck will bed down during the day for a few hours of badly needed R and R. In most Western states, the mule deer rut falls later than the whitetail rut. In southeastern Colorado, for example, the peak of the rut falls in early December. In any case, a buck that is bedded for a long duration, whether due to heat or exhaustion, offers a great opportunity for a bowhunter. Before stalking, you must first spot the animal you're after. The two ways to find a bedded muley are to watch a deer bed down, or to spot a deer that is already bedded. When glassing for mulies in early fall, I rarely see a "mule deer" as such. It is usually a branch that doesn't look right, the flick of an ear, the twitch of a tail, a horizontal line that isn't a fallen tree, or a black spot that turns out to be a nose.

Guide Cam Keeler harvested this 185-inch buck using the spot-and-stalk method.

Using a spotting scope or binocular efficiently takes practice. Most guides I know, myself included, have a particular technique we prefer. We use a systematic grid to cover an area efficiently. Some prefer scanning an area from side to side or from top to bottom. I usually do a quick scan, first glassing anything that looks suspicious. Then I start to comb the area from side to side, bush by bush, tree by tree, and rock by rock. It takes patience and good optics, but once you master the art of glassing effectively you will feel naked without a good pair of binoculars and a spotting scope.

I harvested this trophy buck using the spot-and-stalk method, and captured the hunt on video.

Although I have taken bucks and also guided bowhunters to bucks that I spotted once they were already in their beds, whenever possible I like to watch deer come into their beds in the morning. One reason is that it is easier to spot a deer that is moving. The other is that watching mulies approach their beds gives you a lot of additional information you can use to your advantage. For example, you get to see where the deer came from. Odds are it will be heading back to that area when it gets up in the evening. Another huge bonus is that you can see if the deer you're after is alone or if there are others that are bedding down in close proximity.

In early fall, bucks will oftentimes hang in small bachelor groups. Spotting two to seven bucks together is not uncommon. Unseen deer are one of the top reasons stalks don't pan out. I have closed to within bow range of several bucks that never knew danger was close by until one of their unseen travel partners blew the whole gig. The key to a stalk working out is to know what you're up against. Multiple animals increase the difficulty level exponentially. Oftentimes, due to wind direction, your target, other animals' locations, or the time of day it is best to pass on a stalk instead of blowing the deer out of the area or alerting them to your presence.

It is usually better to wait until things are right and make one good stalk than to try to force things to happen. Wind is always a huge factor in making a successful stalk. Wind currents can be tricky, especially in the mountains or rough country. A very general rule of thumb is that wind currents usually travel downhill in the morning and start turning and moving uphill as the temperature rises about midmorning. In the afternoon they usually switch and start going downhill again.

Before stalking in on a bedded mule deer, study the terrain and choose the best path that will keep you hidden. Also try to choose a landmark near where your target is located. Once you move, everything looks different. I once made what should have been a perfect stalk on a bedded buck, but somewhere along my route I unfortunately mixed up the rock that the buck was bedded by. When I crept up in range of the wrong rock and the buck wasn't there, I assumed I had been spotted. I quietly headed back across the canyon to my pack and spotting scope and was upset to find that the buck was still bedded in the same spot. I had sneaked up to within approximately 40 yards of the buck while stalking up on the wrong location. I wish I could tell you that this has only happened to me once! A hunting companion can be extremely helpful in situations like this. By working out a series of hand signals, a hunter can often be signaled into range.

Another tip that helps when stalking any bedded animal is to use a rangefinder. I will use a rangefinder to measure the distance between the animal I am stalking and an obvious landmark in front of or behind the animal, depending on my planned direction of approach. The taller the object, the better you will be able to see it. Then, as you are stalking, you can keep track of how far you are from your intended target by checking the range to your landmark.

When stalking, quiet clothing and equipment are a must. Patience is also a good attribute to have. I have watched many bucks slip away unscathed when hunters tried to rush in too quickly.

A few years ago, my guides were impressed when Dwight Schuh (longtime editor of *Bowhunter* magazine) and his hunting buddy Larry Jones pulled off a textbook stalk at our camp. They were taping a mule deer show for *Bowhunter Magazine TV*, and Larry was acting as cameraman. On their third day of hunting, the wind really kicked up. They had seen some great bucks from our tree stand but couldn't close the deal. A few days prior, my guide Jake Kraus had glassed several different rut-weary bucks

Guide Jake Kraus, Dwight Schuh and me with Dwight's trophy buck taken on a spot-and-stalk hunt.

bedding down in a steep draw. The draw was thick with overgrown brush, making it a perfect bedding area. Jake went and grabbed Dwight and Larry from their tree stands and pointed the draw out to them and suggested they try sneaking down along the edge of the draw with hopes of catching a buck in his bed. After a few hours of slipping along and glassing for bucks, Dwight spotted what he thought might be an antler tine in the thick brush. Dwight and Larry took off their shoes and made a great barefoot stalk. On video, Dwight shot what ended up being a record-class buck at 15 yards in his bed.

Six things worked out to make that stalk successful: they had a bedded buck spotted; it was the middle of the day, so the buck was probably going to be down for a while; they had a constant wind in their favor; they took their time; they moved quietly; and Dwight made a great shot. If you're willing to work for it and adapt to the situation, the spot-and-stalk method can help you fill your next mule deer tag.

Hunting Water

Oftentimes out West, the biggest mule deer bucks are found in the high desert badlands. Sometimes these areas look more like antelope country than prime mule deer habitat. There is a line in a song I think of when I am hunting or guiding in the high desert plains: "Where the deer and the antelope play." Rest assured that they were not singing about whitetails in that song. Water can be the key to having a successful mule deer hunt. Even if there is a lot of it, all animals have their favorite places to drink. Mule deer are no exception.

I have spent days trying to find out where mule deer I have seen are drinking. Sometimes it is an obvious location, such as an irrigation canal, creek, river, or pond. But sometimes it is like a treasure hunt trying to find the small seep in the rocks or the last puddle in the bottom of a dried-up old river or creekbed. Some of the biggest bucks I have ever seen were drinking out of windmill-driven, metal cattle tanks that are out on the plains, 30 miles from the nearest tree. I have also watched bucks come into alpine lakes 2,000 feet above timberline. The one constant is that all mule deer have to drink.

They also all have favorite places they return to repeatedly. I prefer to scout these areas from a distance whenever possible. A spotting scope is invaluable when glassing water holes from a distance. Although I prefer to hunt over water in hot weather, I have had luck hunting mule deer over water in single-digit weather as well. I have video taped and photographed mule deer breaking ice with their front hooves in favorite areas on ponds and rivers. The point I am making is that by glassing and scouting for fresh sign and tracks, you can open up more options in your mule deer playbook. River crossings are another water option. By walking rivers or creek edges, you can often find frequently used

areas. Usually these are places where the water is shallow or crossing is easy.

If the weather is hot, after finding a frequently used watering location, I like to set up for an all-day sit. Wind direction, concealment, and being comfortable are my biggest concerns. In open country, just getting into position without blowing the deer out of the country can often be tricky. In these situations, I prefer to set up and leave in the dark. When possible, I take advantage of one of the quick pop-up blinds on the market, such as the Double Bull blind. They help contain scent and make it more comfortable to sit all day. Other times, I will try to take advantage of any natural cover, or build a small, low-profile brush blind. When possible, I also like to have multiple setups for different wind directions. A comfortable chair with a back is also helpful when you are going to be sitting all day. Mule deer drink at all times of the day, especially when the weather is hot.

Sometimes when hunting water, you just have to improvise. Last year, while hunting for

A blind setup near water or an active trail is another great mule deer tactic.

Hunting over water can be a productive way to harvest your deer. Above, a group of does drink in early September and, below, a young buck breaks the ice to get a drink during a frozen December.

mule deer in another location with cameraman Michael Leonard, I spotted a nice buck up and moving in the hot midafternoon sun. I guessed he was heading down toward some water and green grass that were located at the bottom of the ridge he was on. I quickly changed the game plan. I wanted to try to get in range of this buck. It was early in the year and there hadn't been a freeze yet, so all the leaves were still on the willows and other trees by the water. We used the thick cover to sneak around and get between the buck and the water. There was a good trail coming down the mountain, and I felt confident the buck would use it. I set up only about 20 yards from the trail, and Mike set up behind me with the camera. I figured the buck would be on us any minute, so we stayed frozen and quiet in our spots just off the trail.

Time dragged on as the mosquitoes busied themselves making us miserable. In my haste, I had left behind my pack with the repellent in it. When you're dumb you gotta be tough, so we both suffered in silence waiting for the buck to show up. After almost two hours, I figured that the buck had either seen us or winded us. I whispered to Mike that we might as well pack it in. As I stood up to leave, I spotted the buck. He had taken another route and was below us by the water. How long he had been there is hard to say. I drew back and shot quickly. I was rewarded with a resounding thump and a beautiful mule deer whose antlers were still wrapped in velvet.

If you're hunting out West and the weather is hot, consider sitting by a water hole all day. If the weather is mild or cold, try to hunt water in the mornings or evenings. It may help you fill your tag on your next bowhunt.

Go High for Success

Although not the most commonly used method for hunting mule deer, tree stands can be highly effective in certain situations. I often use them during the rut on the eastern plains, where mule deer like to funnel through the few strips of trees found along most waterways. I also like to use tree stands when I am hunting near agricultural plantings. Mule deer, like elk, will often travel long distances to feed on alfalfa, clover, wheat, and other crops.

Visibility is one big advantage to being in a tree stand. Plus, if the deer doesn't walk by within range, you can sometimes slip down when conditions are right and make a stalk. Unlike whitetails, which are becoming educated to tree stands, mule deer are still very susceptible to a well-placed stand. The two downsides to tree-stand hunting for mule deer is that mulies are more nomadic than most whitetails. This makes stand placement difficult, and that's why I use them only in certain situations. The other downside is that, out West, it can be a long walk from the truck to where you are hunting.

As I mentioned, we often use tree stands during the mule deer rut when guiding clients for trophy bucks. When guiding Lon Lauber a few years ago, the day before his hunt started, I showed him a tree stand I wanted him to hunt. Lon is an experienced bowhunter and a highly accomplished outdoor writer and photographer. When Lon saw the tree stand I had set up low in a cottonwood tree, he flat-out told me he didn't want to hunt there. It just didn't look good to him. I encouraged him to try it for one full day, and if he didn't like it, I would move him to another stand or we could try stalking a buck. Lon grudgingly agreed to try my spot out for one day. At about noon on the first day, Lon called me to come get him and the largest mule deer buck he had ever taken. Lon explained that it had been slow all morning when he spotted two bucks chasing a doe. The doe led them right by his stand, and Lon nailed a trophy mule deer. Two days later, I put another client, Tom Rothrock from Indiana, in the same stand. Tom also shot a big Pope & Young mule deer.

Before the week was over, three of my four clients harvested Pope & Young bucks, all out of tree stands. The largest that week was a 181-inch monster taken by Todd Wickens, also of Indiana. Todd had seen a few bucks hanging around near some thickets while chasing does, so we set up another stand. Todd's stand was only about 6 feet up, and he nailed the monster buck with a great shot at only 12 yards. The moral to these stories is that while they're not that popular, tree stands can be highly effective for your mule deer hunt if the situation looks right.

Sit for a Shot

Sitting and waiting can be a highly effective way for bowhunters to get into range. One of my largest mule deer with a bow was taken from the base of a cottonwood tree where I had been sitting patiently waiting for hours. I had seen the big buck on multiple occasions and knew he was a true giant. It was a mid- December morning during the peak of the rut when I spotted him following a doe into a dense weed patch. There was some alfalfa planted close by, and I hoped that the doe would lead him into the field that evening. I slipped into the field's

Lon Lauber harvested this trophy buck with me from a tree stand set up in a large cottonwood tree.

Tom Rothrock of Indiana harvested this trophy mule deer with me from a tree stand. When it was only eight yards away, Tom dropped the string on this Pope & Young buck.

edge and set up with cameraman Chris Butt to try to wait the deer out. The wind was in our favor, and all we could do was hope my guess would pan out.

Before the sun had even hit the horizon, the doe stood up and started leading the giant buck in my direction. The buck hesitated to rake over a small sapling. While he raked the tree, I could see that this was truly a monster deer. When the buck finished, they slowly made their way toward the field's edge where we were crouched. I tried to maintain my composure as they walked into range. I slowly drew my bow and shot. The arrow passed through the buck's lungs in the blink of an eye. I truly think he didn't have any idea what happened. He took a few staggering steps toward the doe and collapsed. The buck grossed just over 191 inches and netted 186 2/8 inches. This buck, and others I have guided clients on, proves that sitting on the ground, on a log, or on a small stool in high-traffic areas can really pay off, especially in open country where cover for stalking or trees large enough for a tree stand are slim to none.

Rattling and Calling

Mule deer bucks, in my opinion, are not nearly as aggressive as whitetails. So some tactics that work great for whitetails do not get the same response from a mule deer. But that doesn't mean that they don't work at all.

I have guided clients who have successfully rattled up trophy mule deer. I have also had some success rattling in bucks myself. From what I have experienced, mule deer

Todd Wickens of Indiana harvested this huge buck with me. He grossed 181 and netted 175 5/8 inches. He was taken from a tree stand at 12 yards.

come in much more slowly than whitetails and often need a lot of coaxing. The bucks I have rattled in usually had to hear multiple rattling sequences before they would come to investigate. I have had a few young bucks run in, but the old guys seem to really take their time. I have had the best results when trying to call in an animal I have already spotted. The advantage to working an animal you can see is that you can gauge the buck's reaction. If he ignores you, keep making a ruckus.

Once a mule deer buck starts coming in, I stop rattling. I only start up again when the buck stops for longer than 30 seconds or changes direction. In the open country where mule deer are generally found, I really work the antlers hard, frequently crashing the antlers loudly together. This helps the sound carry farther. So always remember to include a pair of rattling antlers in your bag of goodies, but be prepared to rattle more than you ever would for a whitetail.

It is also advantageous to try bleating or using a decoy where practical. Whether I am rattling or not, I always include a doe bleat in my pack. You don't need a special mule deer call. Just take along your whitetail doe bleat tube or one of the tip-over

can bleats. I have caused rutting bucks to veer over to investigate when they think a hot doe may be just around the next tree or clump of sagebrush. Mule deer bucks do grunt very similarly to whitetails, and I have heard one snort and wheeze just like a whitetail as well. Although I have tried grunting, I have always had the best luck with a doe bleat or rattling antlers.

Decoying

Just as with decoying any other animal, I have had mixed results trying to decoy mule deer. The deer may react positively to the decoy and come in to investigate, they may totally ignore it, or they may run out of sight. In states where it is legal, I get a lot more reaction with a 3-D target covered with a tanned mule deer hide than any other type of decoy. No matter what type of decoy you use, it is always best to try it on overcast days. Bright sunny days make almost all decoys shine and look unnatural. I like to use a decoy during the pre-rut or rut. I also prefer using a doe over a buck decoy. I feel that more bucks will come in to a situation where they are looking for love rather than a fight.

The biggest drawback in decoying mule deer is the open country they live in. Setting one up without being spotted is the first obstacle. The second is that if mule deer have a long time to look at a motionless decoy, it seems to unnerve them. It is just not

My largest mule deer with a bow. He was taken using the sit-and-wait method. For the curious, this monster's gross score was 191, net 186 2/8.

Guide Cam Keeler sews a green mule deer hide over a 3-D target to make a realistic-looking decoy.

natural. For best results, try setting up where the buck won't see the decoy until it is already within 50 to 100 yards. Also, using a doe bleat in conjunction with a decoy will help improve your odds of luring a buck in.

Setting up on a Rub Line

Mule deer bucks don't make scrapes like whitetails. The biggest scent posts they make are their rubs. You can use this to your advantage if you find the right rub.

Trappers know that if there is only one small bush or tree in a field, every male coyote that passes by will go out of his way to pee on it. Mule deer bucks seem to have the same mentality when it comes to certain rub trees. I call some "one-time" trees, those that have been used only once when a buck was walking by, or it was made early in the season when a buck was working off his velvet. Other rub trees seem to be used as major scent posts, where passing bucks commonly stop to joust and, more important, to leave their scent. I have video taped and watched as multiple trophy bucks have come in over the course of a day to leave their scent on the same rub tree. This is even more applicable in open areas, where there are only so many small trees or bushes for them to leave their marks on. These scent post rubs are usually easy to identify because they get visited frequently, and so the tree or bush gets more ragged-looking every day. These are great spots to hunt, when you can find them. I usually try to set up downwind as far away as I am comfortable shooting, since a lot of bucks will circle or approach these trees from the downwind side.

Field-Judging Mule Deer

For a typical mule deer to make the Pope & Young minimum, it must score 145 inches after deductions (see score sheet in Appendix A). For rough judging, I look for a typical 4 × 4 or larger, not counting brow tines, since these are usually small if the rack has them at all. Next I look at width. An average mule deer has a 21- or 22-inch gap between ear tips if they were laid out horizontally.

If the buck's inside diameter is as wide as his ears, that's a good start—keep measuring. If I can make 30 inches out of the buck's G-2, G-3, and G-4, it is a good one that should make the minimum. Remember that deep, tall forks add score quickly onto a mule deer rack. This is a quick method I use to figure out if a buck is going to make the minimum score. But there are exceptions, and if the buck's main beam or circumference measurements are weak, he won't make it. If he is symmetrical, he should make it just fine. I look at brow tines as bonus inches that, if present, will just add to the score. The main thing to remember is that if you harvest any mule deer—buck or doe—with a bow, you already have a trophy. A big rack is just icing on the cake.

An exhausted buck takes a break during the peak of the rut. Notice his swollen neck.

Facts about Mule Deer (Odocoileus hemonius)

Larger than whitetails, blacktails, or Coues deer, mule deer get their name from their large, mule-sized ears. Mature does average 100 to 200 pounds, while mature bucks average 200 to 300 pounds. Their average lifespan in the wild is 9 to 12 years. Only the bucks have antlers, which they shed every year near the end of the winter. Mule deer antlers usually branch to form two forks. Fawns are spotted at birth and lose their spots after one to three months. The rut falls in late November to early December. Mule deer are often noted for their peculiar, high-jumping gait: all four hooves leave and hit the ground at the same time.

Equipment Suggestions

Mule deer are large, and shots are sometimes in the open. A flat-shooting, fast bow is advantageous. Because of their size, I suggest a minimum bow weight of 45 pounds, with an arrow weight of no less than 400 grains. As always, razor-sharp, sturdy broadheads are a must.

Mule deer meat is excellent. There are a lot of great ways to prepare it, including jerky, roasts, steaks, and stews. The recipe I have included below is just one of many great ways to enjoy your mule deer meat.

Pepper Steak Mule Deer Stir Fry

Serves 6–8
You can use any piece of your mule deer for
   this recipe.
2½ pounds of mule deer meat, sliced across
   the grain into thin, 2-inch-long strips
6 small cloves of garlic, chopped
½ cup olive oil
2 green bell peppers, cut into strips
1 red bell pepper, cut into strips
8 green onion stalks, sliced into diagonal strips
   (use the entire onion, even the white and
   green leafy parts)
8 ounces sliced mushrooms

1 cup sherry
2 cups beef broth
½ cup soy sauce
3 tablespoons cornstarch

In a wok or large fry pan, heat half the olive oil on high heat and sauté half the chopped garlic for half a minute, then add the meat in batches and sauté quickly until medium rare (do not overcook). Remove from pan. Add the rest of the oil, and sauté the rest of the garlic for half a minute, then add the green and red pepper strips, sliced green onion, and sliced mushrooms. Cook for approximately two minutes on high heat. Add sherry and beef broth, and cook for two more minutes on high heat to bring to a boil. In a small bowl, combine soy sauce and cornstarch and stir until fully mixed. Add to boiling vegetable mixture, stirring constantly as it thickens. Add back the cooked meat, stir to cover with mixture and remove from heat. Serve with rice.

Antelope

Imagine sitting in a small blind in the desert, drops of sweat beading on your forehead and the thick, sweet smell of sage hanging in the air. An isolated water hole lies 20 yards out in front of you, its precious contents steadily evaporating in the heat. Tracks made by delicate hooves pockmark the dirt around the water, and you know it is just a matter of time.

If you have never experienced the thrill of bowhunting for antelope or can't wait to go again, read on for tips on how to plan your archery antelope hunt.

Antelope are truly a Western success story. Hunted almost to extinction in the old days of market hunting, pronghorn antelope are now thriving thanks to progressive game management programs.

The great news for bowhunters is that they are now found in huntable numbers in

A lone pronghorn buck silhouetted against a Western sky.

16 states. Of these, the four that generally stand out with the highest population numbers are Wyoming, Montana, Colorado, and South Dakota.

After deciding which state you want to hunt, call the game commission and ask for one of the state biologists or a game warden who works in the plains area. Both can be excellent sources of information and will often give you the locations of the best public land to hunt. I have found that game wardens will

If the weather is hot and dry, antelope hunting at a popular water hole is the way to go.

often give out the names of farmers and ranchers in their area who allow hunting on their property. Once you choose an area to hunt, get a detailed topo map of the region and mark all the natural or manmade water holes. Again, biologists, local wardens, and landowners can be very helpful with this step and save you the extra legwork.

Water Hole Hunting

When choosing a location to set up a blind, my guides and I check all the water holes for fresh tracks and numbers of fresh tracks. Then we rank the different locations on a map according to our findings. We pay special attention to small water holes that are far from any other water sources. These remote places, when found, can be extremely productive. Ranking fresh tracks and numbers of tracks will help you discover which water holes the antelope prefer. Usually it will be where they can check for danger at a distance before coming in to drink.

Also pay attention to where around the water holes the majority of the tracks are. I have found that most water holes, whether they are manmade (dugout ponds or metal cattle tanks) or natural water sources such as creeks, rivers, or springs,

have specific areas where the antelope prefer to drink. Sometimes the reason one area is favored is easy to identify, for example, the terrain or easy access to the water. At other times, it is subtler, for example, firmer ground or better visibility from the antelope's eye level. Whatever the reason, it is always advantageous to learn exactly where on the water source the majority of the antelope drink.

Whenever possible, I prefer to hunt areas with very limited options for water. I also prefer to hunt small dirt tanks or manmade cattle tanks. Smaller water sources are easier to hunt, and blind placement is not so critical. On the flip side, I have hunted large lakes, ponds, and canals where blind placement and scouting the well-used areas is absolutely critical. Make a mistake in these locations, and the closest look you get of an antelope may be through your binoculars.

Pronghorn hunting over water is a game of patience. Big bucks are just as likely to drink at noon as they are at dawn. So arrive early and be prepared to stay until sunset if you are up to the challenge of a day in the desert heat in hopes of arrowing a big buck coming in for a drink. Weather plays a huge role in whether your hunt over water will be successful or not.

My own patience and determination were put to the test a few years ago while hunting antelope over water. My cameraman, Mike Leonard, was sharing a blind with me. We were attempting to tape an antelope hunt over a water hole for an episode of Easton Bowhunting. I explained to Mike that during a normal dry year, odds were high that we would harvest a buck in a short period of time. Sitting in a small, hot space for almost 15 hours a day is not for the faint of heart. It can take a toll on the most determined hunter. Since I assumed the weather would remain hot and dry, I passed up a few pronghorn bucks during the first few days of the hunt.

A few rain showers made things a lot rougher than I had counted on. After nine straight 15-hour days without another opportunity, Mike and I were starting to show signs of the fatigue and mental torture that only an antelope blind can dish out. Whether it was the heat, dehydration, cramping back muscles, or lack of sleep, it mattered little. We were close to giving up. What started out as a trophy buck hunt quickly turned to a "whatever is legal and comes into range" hunt.

Nine days turned into fifteen, and the fifteenth day of our hunt started out as so many others had. We could see quite a few antelope around us in the distance, but nothing was coming in to drink at our small water hole. It seemed that the many small depressions and gullies in the area were still holding water. The day was slowly dragging on when we heard the sound of running hooves. I grabbed my recurve bow while Mike went for his camera. In an instant, our lonely water hole was teeming with antelope. I was starting to draw my bow on a big doe only about 10 yards away when a large buck walked into my shooting hole. He was about 20 yards away

I harvested this antelope when he came to drink at the metal stock tank in the background.

and broadside. My recurve bow jumped in my hand, and my carbon arrow flew right through the buck's chest. The buck bolted from the edge of the pond, dying less than 50 yards from the water's edge. We had spent 15 days—approximately 220 hours—trying to harvest an antelope. I don't advise that type of marathon, but you can bet I was proud of that buck. I'd hunted as hard for him as I had any animal I have ever taken.

Wet weather can shut down water hole hunting in a hurry. If bad weather rolls in, I usually just wait until it dries up before going back out. This is easy for me, since some of my best antelope spots are only a 30-minute drive from my house. For many hunters, however, waiting until it dries out is not an option. In those situations, we either try other strategies detailed later in this chapter, or wait at the water holes anyway, hoping that some antelope will still come in out of habit. I have learned that some antelope get used to drinking at certain locations and will sometimes revisit them even when other water is readily available.

I harvested this 77-inch Pope & Young antelope after waiting 15 full days at a blind near a water hole.

Me and my wife Michele with her first Pope & Young antelope, taken with her recurve bow. The trophy buck was shot when he came in to a cattle tank.

Sometimes pronghorns visit these water holes because the best grass can often be found near areas that have water, even during the driest years. At other times, it seems they come in just out of habit.

In 2006, my wife Michele had been busy during the first few weeks of antelope season. She was helping our cook feed clients and was also busy helping the guides get hunters out to their blinds. When she finally had a few days to hunt herself, the weather was not cooperating. Another big rain left puddles all over the prairie. Every small depression and road ditch had water in it. I suggested she wait until things dried out, but she had only a few days free and decided to try it. On the fifth day, a large buck literally walked around other water holes to drink at the tank where she was hidden. At 18 yards, she harvested her first Pope & Young buck with a recurve.

Some hunts just seem to be easy and quick. Others can be very difficult and long. A few years ago, I was excited to have Michael Waddell from Realtree Road Trips join us for an archery antelope hunt. Michael had never harvested an antelope with a bow, and he was excited to try hunting them. The evening he arrived, I took Michael and his

Keep an eye out for snakes and scorpions when antelope hunting.

Michael Waddell and his beautiful Pope & Young buck, which he took while hunting with me in southeastern Colorado.

cameraman out to try a spot-and-stalk hunt. I found a large buck bedded in some tall sage, and Michael and his cameraman made a great stalk on him. They closed to about 70 yards before the buck spotted them and fled the scene.

The weather was hot, so we advised Michael that we thought their best bet would be to wait it out at a water hole. On the evening of the third day, a nice buck meandered slowly toward the water

hole where they were hidden. Michael said he was as excited as he has ever been with any animal. The buck came in to drink, and Michael made a textbook shot, dropping the animal within sight of the camera. That night he told me that sitting in that blind for 15 hours a day was one of the toughest hunts he had ever experienced. When it comes to sitting over water, it is usually the patient hunter who scores.

Hot Weather Gear

Since pronghorns are usually hunted in temperatures that can exceed 90 degrees, take lots of fluids with you. A small cooler filled with frozen water bottles will help quench your thirst and keep you hydrated as the day heats up. Stick with loose, comfortable, and quiet clothing. You want to blend in with the black background of the blind, so wear black or camouflaged shirts. Camouflage is also important on any body parts that may be close to the opening of the blind, such as your hands or your face. Keep in mind that dangers may include snakes and scorpions, although dehydration and lightning strikes usually pose the biggest risks you will encounter.

Setting up on Water

Ask permission before building a blind on private land, and check hunting regulations before erecting a blind on public land. Most ranchers and farmers won't mind you setting up blinds, as long as you don't build a permanent structure. The three most common blinds used for pronghorn hunting are partial pit, self-constructed above-ground, and manufactured pop-up blinds. Don't worry if your blind seems to stick out like a sore thumb. Pronghorns adapt quickly and will often ignore obvious objects by water holes, provided they aren't overhunted.

My favorite is the Double Bull pop-up blind. It is lightweight and can be set up in minutes. This is an obvious advantage if you decide to move or

In cattle country, antelope blinds must be "cow-proofed." Here a guide strings barbed wire around a blind to protect it from the curious cows (in the background).

stalk. I also advise wearing knee and elbow pads for protection from hot, sun-baked ground and cactus. Broken terrain or pockets of tall sagebrush can be used to your advantage. I have managed to get within range of a few bucks by using deep draws or dry creek beds to slip up undetected.

But getting in range is only half the battle. Drawing your bow undetected is usually one of the most difficult things to do. Practice drawing horizontally and raising your bow slowly. You may have to drop some bow poundage, but it could make all the difference.

set up multiple blinds quickly. Make sure that your blind is as dark as possible inside—any penetrating light makes you easy to spot. After your blind is completed, you should cattle- proof it. Often, where you find pronghorns you will also find livestock that utilize the water holes. A simple and effective way to protect your blind is to drive four T-posts into the ground off the corners of your blind and wrap two strands of barbed wire around them.

For hunters wanting to try another method, there is always decoying. It has been my experience that this is a win-or-lose proposition, with losing being the more common result. Don't misunderstand me: antelope can be and are decoyed in, and it is a rush when one comes charging at you attempting to run off the artificial intruder, often from as far as half a mile away. It is just that the window of opportunity for this method to work is small, and the best results are obtained at the peak of the rut in areas with a high buck-to-doe ratio. So include a decoy in your gear, but be prepared to leave it at camp if your

Spot-and-Stalk or Decoying

Although bowhunters take more antelope over water than by any other means, torrential rain can ruin such a hunt in a hurry. Fortunately, there are other options. The spot-and-stalk method is tough, since the open prairie that antelope generally inhabit usually offers little cover. This makes it difficult for any predator to sneak up on this sharp-eyed animal. Therefore, full camouflage is a must for trying a

Torrential rains flooded the plains, leaving one of my antelope blinds under five feet of water. In rainy weather, try another tactic besides water hole hunting.

timing is off. Another decoy that can work is an artificial cow or horse. I have had mixed results with these "confidence" decoys, but if you're looking for a project give it a shot.

Hunting over Scrapes

Another option for speed goats (a common nickname for antelope) is hunting them over scrapes. As the rut approaches, antelope bucks make a series of scrapes. They also become territorial and constantly patrol their areas to keep out intruders.

These scrapes can be seen dotting the prairie and are commonly found in dirt roads or dirt openings out on the prairie. They are similar in size to whitetail scrapes, and pronghorn bucks usually urinate and defecate in them. We have successfully guided clients by placing blinds within bow range of antelope scrapes. So if the sky opens up and your blind gets flooded, try setting up on an antelope scrape. It may save the day.

Here is a story written by one of our clients, Daryl Quidort, about his scrape hunt:

In the predawn darkness, the pickup lurched and bumped through yet another huge puddle, which was flooding the two-track. It had been raining steadily for days. In fact, this part of Colorado had received more than its average annual rainfall in just the past three weeks! There was standing water everywhere. One rancher told us there were full stock tanks on his land that hadn't held water in 20 years.

"And this is the year I picked to come hunt thirsty antelope at water holes," I thought glumly as we followed the muddy wheel ruts in the truck's dim headlights.

Antelope hunting at water holes is normally a hot, dry ordeal. Spending 14 or 15 hours a day, from daylight to dark, in a blind situated near a desert water hole takes fortitude and dedication.

"It's like being in solitary confinement!" one hunter exclaimed. "You can't leave the blind in this open country without spooking all the game within miles. You just have to stay in there and tough it out." Of course, when antelope are coming to the water and the hunter is having action, the day doesn't seem so long.

Sunrise was a bright pink promise on the horizon as we pulled up to the water hole where I planned to spend the day hunting antelope. The headlights revealed the portable blind sitting in 6 inches of water.

"Look at that," Fred's guide muttered in his slow, Western drawl. "All this rain raised the pond." After a short discussion, we decided I should try another spot near some scrapes.

With my binoculars, I studied the scrapes about 25 yards out in front of my blind. I had seen antelope scrapes several times in the past, but never understood them or considered hunting them. Usually found out on open, treeless areas, they look and smell quite a bit like whitetail deer scrapes. I was sure they played an important part in the antelope rut, but I didn't know how. Hopefully an antelope buck would give me a demonstration before the day was over.

About 1:00 p.m., I saw two white specks appear out on the plains. By 1:10 p.m., two antelope bucks were standing 100 yards away, nervously looking my way. They were small bucks, their horns barely as long as their 6-inch ears. After trotting back and forth a couple of times, they both raced away at high speed. I wondered if they were afraid of the blind or afraid a larger buck might catch them near the scrapes.

Daryl Quidort and his Pope & Young buck taken by waiting at an antelope scrape.

running right at me. Then, swerving gracefully to his right, the antelope sped past the blind and out of my sight. Without moving a muscle, I waited patiently for him to return—but he didn't. "That's it?" I wondered.

After a time, I slowly opened a small peek hole on a side window. The buck was standing about 60 yards away, shaking his ears and kicking a hind foot under his belly, trying to rid himself of the mosquitoes. Suddenly, he ran toward the scrapes again. This time he sped right past the blind, only about 20 yards away, but going at full speed. Fifty yards out, he stopped, whirled around, and came back. Trotting up to the scrapes, he stopped and sniffed the ground. Then he started pawing the earth with a forefoot.

It would have been interesting just to watch him, to see what his scraping ritual consisted of . . . but I came here to hunt antelope. I shot. The buck's reflexes were to drop and spin away at the sound of the shot. But my arrow got there first.

I know I was fortunate (darn lucky, according to my friends) to get a nice Pope & Young antelope during a rainy-season water hole hunt. Hopefully, if I make this type of bowhunt again, I won't run into such wet circumstances. But if I do, at least now I know what to do when it rains. I'll hunt antelope scrapes.

A few hours later, I looked up from my magazine to see a nice antelope buck heading my way. I quickly grabbed my bow and quietly moved the stool out of the way. On my knees, with an arrow nocked and my recurve in ready position, I froze as the buck smoothly picked up speed. He was

Fence Crossings

Fence crossings are the last little gem in my antelope hunting repertoire. These crossings have also saved a few foul-weather hunts for me. In most Western states, antelope will go under a fence—as opposed to over it—90 percent of the time, even when being pursued by predators. This has always seemed odd to me, since antelope are excellent

jumpers and can clear a fence easily. I have heard it theorized that this is because fences in the West are a relatively new addition to the landscape and are still few and far between in many states. Most antelope may simply have not adapted to jumping over any obstacles they may encounter. Sadly enough, in the future, as fences become more frequently encountered obstacles, antelope will probably become accustomed to jumping over them.

Since they prefer going under rather than over fences, there are always certain places along fence lines where you will find well-worn trails. Antelope often walk quite a ways to use these favored crossing spots where, due to the terrain or a broken strand in the fence, it is easier to go under. If you find a good one, don't pass up an opportunity to harvest your buck there. If the farmer or rancher doesn't mind, you can make your own fence crossing. Just use a few twists of bailing wire or twine to raise the bottom wire by tying it to the one above it. It may not be good to hunt until the following year, but you can bet that the antelope will find and use it.

When approaching a fence crossing, antelope usually stop for a few seconds before going under. That is a perfect opportunity for a bowhunter to take a standing broadside shot. Blinds should be set up near the fence, as far away as you can comfortably shoot. For example, if you're comfortable shooting out to 25 yards, set up the blind 25 yards from the crossing.

Years ago, I shot a beautiful young buck at a fence crossing. I found an active fence crossing and set up a blind about 20 yards from the trail. The weather had been pretty bad, so the water hole hunting was slow. I climbed into the blind early the next morning. After only a couple of hours, a group of young bucks came walking across the pasture heading toward my ambush point. When the lead buck reached the fence, he stopped to look things over. My arrow passed through his chest, and a short sprint later he fell within sight of my blind.

I feel that fence crossings are not nearly as productive as water holes in hot, dry weather, but they do provide another enjoyable way to hunt the prairie speedsters.

When hunting antelope, remember that they have incredible eyesight that they rely on to a fault.

Although they have great hearing and olfactory senses, in most cases they just don't seem to believe that danger is there unless they can see it. Their eyes are their main means of defense. If you can fool their eyes, you are on your way to harvesting what is, in my opinion, the most desirable Western big game animal.

Field-Judging Antelope

For bowhunters interested in trophy antelope, it is important to be able to accurately field-judge a buck. To make the Pope & Young record book, antelope must have a minimum score of 67 inches. Antelope can be difficult to judge, because they have few measurements and no width measurement. This means the few measurements that they do get have a large bearing on your final score. Instead of trying to break down the intricacies of measuring, I will detail how to quickly judge whether you are looking at a trophy animal.

On average, an antelope's ear is 6 inches from tip to base. If the antelope has horns that are

A trophy antelope gives me the stare-down.

13 inches or longer, you may have a contender. So the first thing I do is quickly look to see if the antelope's horn is a little longer than twice the length of his ears. Don't forget that an antelope's main horn is often curved at the tip, so this will add to the length. I have seen some with 4 inches of curl-over, so keep that in mind.

Next, look at the prong, or cutter, as it is often called. Again, use the ear for a reference. If there is more than half an ear showing, or 3 inches, keep looking. Circumference is the next thing to look at. Antelope horns are oblong rather than round, making them wide at the sides and thin in the front and back, so to rough judge mass you want to try to get a side view if possible. Instead of looking at and trying to guess all four circumference measurements, I look at the widest or thickest part of the horn, which is between the base and the prong. If it looks like it is 2 1/2 inches wide, it probably has close to a 6- to 7-inch base. Unless it gets really skinny really quickly at the top, it should make the minimum.

Other things I look for are prongs that start above the ears, or really heavy mass that carries the length of the horn. Of course this is a quick, rough

My largest antelope, harvested in Colorado, netted an impressive 79 inches.

way to estimate if what you're looking at will make the record book. I think if you shoot any antelope with a bow, you already have a trophy. Large horns are just icing on the cake.

Facts about Antelope (Antilocapra Americana)

Antelope, or pronghorns as they are commonly called due to their two-pronged horns, are as unique as the open prairies they call home. Evolution helped these animals adapt to the prairies they live in by developing many different distinguishing characteristics. One of the most notable is their headgear, which they shed every year in November or December. Although called a horn, it really isn't a true horn, since true horns—like those of bighorn sheep or Rocky Mountain goats—grow continually throughout the animal's lifetime. Antelope bucks have a bone core that is covered by a black outer sheath made of keratin. Keratin is a tough, insoluble protein substance that is the chief constituent of hair, nails, horns, and hooves. Oddly enough, about 40 percent of mature doe antelope also grow horns, but unlike the buck horns, which average 13 to 15 inches in height, does' horns rarely grow more than 4 inches long. When antelope shed their horns in November or December, a new sheath, wrapped in hair, is already beginning to grow. Unlike antlers, which grow from the base, antelope horns grow their sheaths both up and down, starting from the tip of the core.

Although they appear huge on the open prairies they inhabit, antelope bucks average only 120 pounds, while the smaller does average 105 pounds. They are equipped with lightning speed, which helps them outdistance their predators, since hiding in the open isn't really an option. The fastest land animals in North America, antelope can achieve speeds of up to 60 miles per hour for short bursts, and they can maintain speeds of 30 to 40 miles per hour for long distances over uneven terrain.

These three antelope does are enjoying a drink during the heat of the day.

Pronghorns also come equipped with spongy, hollow hair that provides layering warmth in the subzero temperatures and blistering winds they face in the winter. In the summertime, temperatures on the Western plains and deserts often exceed 100 degrees. When the weather turns warm, antelope shed their spongy coats, which helps to cool them down. Additionally, they can cause their remaining hairs to stand upright, which helps air circulate close to the skin, keeping them from overheating.

Their protruding, side-mounted eyes allow them close to a 270-degree field of view, which makes slipping up on one undetected very, very difficult.

Antelope fawns are born with muted brown and white coats that become more pronounced and obvious as they mature.

As you can see, antelope are uniquely suited for only one type of habitat. If we ever lose the large tracts of open prairies and grasslands, I fear we will lose or endanger one of the most impressive animals that shares the West with us.

Even if you never plan to bowhunt for antelope, next time you're out West, take a drive out to see one. A large herd running in unison across a seemingly endless prairie is truly a sight to behold.

Equipment Suggestions

Antelope are small animals, so arrow penetration is rarely an issue. I advise a minimum of 40 pounds of bow weight, with 9 grains of arrow weight per pound of your bow. For example, a 40-pound bow would require a 360-grain arrow. And as always, a razor-sharp broadhead is a must. Choose a quiet bow that is as short as possible, whether you are shooting a traditional bow or a compound. Shorter bows are easier to maneuver inside a blind.

Grilled Antelope Backstrap

Allow 6–8 ounces per serving. This marinade works great with elk and deer also.

1 cup soy sauce
½ cup olive oil
½ cup A1 Steak Sauce
4 large cloves of garlic, chopped
½ cup chopped onion
1 tablespoon Jane's Krazy Mixed-up Salt or
    similar seasoned salt with garlic
2 tablespoons Grill Mates Montreal Steak
    Seasoning

In a non-metallic container, combine all the ingredients. Add whole antelope backstraps. Make sure the marinade covers the meat. Marinate backstraps overnight. Discard leftover marinade.

Grill to desired doneness. Slice across the grain into 1/2-inch-thick slices. Game should never be overcooked, as it has less fat than beef. Medium rare to medium is our preference.

Moose Hunting

DAVE KELSO

Hunting Methods

Methods for hunting moose are not any different than hunting other members of the deer family. Many different tactics will work at different times, depending on the season and the seasonal activity of the moose. I have hunted moose about every way possible and have had success with all of them.

More often than not, a hunter will employ a couple of the different methods combined in one hunt. For example, still-hunting can be combined with the use of calling, or stand hunting can be done over a baited area. Most all of these methods outlined work well with each other as well as alone.

Road Hunting

Back in the early 1980s, when we started hunting moose in Maine after a forty-five-year closed

An example of a typical clear-cut that was once so abundant back in the 1980s.

season, many moose were easily taken by simply riding the logging roads. All a hunter had to do was wait for a moose to be spotted on or near the road, get out of his truck, load up his rifle, and shoot it. Even after all these years, many hunters still opt for this method because of its ease, and because it allows them to cover lots of ground each day.

However, I have seen the success rate of hunters and guides using this method drop over the years. Many hunters are still taking moose by road hunting; they are just not taking trophy bulls with any consistency. In the 1980s, there were some factors that I think played into making road hunting a successful hunting method.

First off, moose had not been hunted for quite some time, and I believe that the evolutionary process took its toll, eroding the animal's natural wariness. I still remember the stories my great-grandfather told me. To him, the moose was a much tougher animal to hunt than a whitetail deer. He reveled in the idea of being able to fool a moose, and seemed much prouder of the fact he had killed a small bull moose than he was about any of the two hundred-pound bucks he had taken.

I found that during the first few years of our Maine moose hunt, moose simply stood around and watched, probably out of curiosity, as hunters scrambled from a truck and loaded guns. Today, very few of the larger bulls are simply standing around waiting to be shot. Evolution has come full circle, and now I can appreciate Gramp's stories of the moose's wariness.

The second factor that I think played an important role in making road hunting particularly attractive was the vast clear-cuts Maine had in 1980s. The woods were recovering from a severe infestation of the spruce budworm—the larval stage of a moth that caused untold devastation to our commercial forests. With the softwood trees being literally eaten alive and left to die, land managers had no choice but to go into these devastated areas and harvest the affected trees. This caused the massive clear-cuts that dotted our landscape back then.

The clear-cuts made for excellent soil to be rejuvenated with small hardwood browse, such as the maple and poplar trees that moose feed on. This created a magnet effect. Moose were drawn out into the open to feed, and then bedded down in the open, with no fear of man. A moose is no different from you or me; he does not want to work or travel any farther than he has to in order to survive. Hey, put a refrigerator next to a man's easy chair and he is not going to leave it without good reason. Moose are the same.

With the huge clear-cuts available to hunters and easy access via the maintained logging roads, moose hunting in Maine was looked at as way to fill the freezer quickly. Not much of a hunt, if you ask me.

Couple these two factors with the moose's poor eyesight, and you can see why road-hunting for moose became the accepted form here in Maine. Today, road hunting in states where it is legal can still be effective at certain times.

Road-hunters need to look for areas with good visibility. Roads that are grown in tight with alders and other thickly bunched trees are not going to be good. Where clear-cut logging practices are still in use, seek them out as well as the wider secondary logging roads.

There are three basic scenarios that come into play while road hunting. The first one is that the moose is spotted standing in the road. The truck is stopped and the hunter exits the vehicle. If using a clip-loaded weapon, he simply slips the clip into the weapon, chambers a round, takes aim, and fires.

While the hunter is loading the gun, depending on his excitability level, many things are going to happen, and I think, in my experience, I have seen it all. Believe me, depending on the hunter's skill, there is going to be some major movement going on. So the hunter will need to minimize as much movement as possible.

Have the shooter keep the vehicle door open and stand behind it; it will hide a lot of movement from the moose. As I said earlier, if using a clip-fed weapon, slide the clip in and chamber a round. If the weapon uses rounds that must be thumbed into the magazine, make sure the shooter only takes the time to thumb two rounds. This can be done efficiently, as opposed to trying to thumb a complete magazine full into the gun. At best you may only have the opportunity to fire two rounds anyway. Adrenaline will be flowing at this point, so keeping the human error factor to a minimum is a must for a successful road-hunt.

Guide Dan Glidden of Ashland, Maine, brought a neat little trick to my attention during a hunt in the northern part of that state. One morning, under very

This young bull with developing antlers is attracted to a roadside salt run-off.

windy conditions, he had set up and called with a hunter. Nothing happened, so Dan decided to move on to his next spot. After getting in the truck and traveling a very short distance, a bull was spotted in the road and more than likely, coming to Dan's call. The moose, being somewhat stymied at seeing a truck and not another moose, stood in the road and looked at the vehicle.

Dan's hunter exited the truck, keeping the door open as he'd been instructed to do, turned his back to the moose and loaded his weapon. At one point he looked at Dan and asked, "Is he still there?" Dan replied that he was. The hunter took a deep breath and turned, saw his target, took aim, and fired. The moose pretty much died in the road making Dan's work easy.

This hunter knew full well that he might get overly excited, recognizing his excitability limits, and he did not want to be looking at the animal while he was trying to do something as intricate as thumbing rounds into his weapon's magazine.

I have since instructed my hunters to face away from the moose while loading a weapon and it has worked well. I would highly recommend this technique to anyone else who might have a small excitability problem. Hey, we're all human and there's nothing wrong with getting excited about the chance to bag such a magnificent animal.

The next common scenario is a moose that is spotted on the side of the road as you are driving by. This calls for a great deal of composure from both the person who spots the moose and the driver of the vehicle, although sometimes composure and moose hunting cannot be used in the same sentence.

When someone in a vehicle spots a moose, he or she should not say anything to anyone, just allow the vehicle to keep moving at the same speed and in the same direction to minimize everyone's excited reaction. Drive past the moose and keep on moving far enough beyond the site that you cannot see it and you're convinced that it cannot see you. It might be

one hundred feet or one hundred yards, depending on the landscape. Once you feel you are a safe distance away, stop the vehicle, have the hunter get out and load his weapon.

Now, to cut down on the amount of movement, only the person who saw the moose and the hunter should get out and walk back to where the animal was spotted. There is no need to take the entire hunting party.

Chances are the moose will have moved, so be on the lookout for it. The moose may have come closer to the road or walked farther back into the woods. Each moose has its own agenda and is going to react differently.

Hopefully, you will have the moose standing somewhere near where it was first sighted and the hunter will be able to get a shot off. If the moose is gone and nowhere to be found, chalk it up to an educated moose and move on. You may be able to come back another day and work him with a call, but now is not the time. He knows what you are and the danger you represent to his well-being.

Another scenario that often happens while road hunting: You are driving along and you spot a moose running; makes no difference whether it is in the road or off to the side. It does not like what it hears and sees, and it's running. This scenario can go so many different ways. Let's take it from the top.

The moose is running down the road in front of the vehicle and cuts off to the side. My first instinct is to stop and hope the moose will stop and look back, a seemingly common trait among most of the deer family. I have trained myself to avoid this instinct and to keep driving at the same speed as when I saw the moose. Let him cut off to the side, and continue to drive by as if you are no threat to him. Moose are very accustomed to logging trucks, heavy equipment, and other disinterested parties traveling through their range. He may very well stop and want to continue on the pre-planned path that you interrupted. Drive past him far enough and then come walking back. You may very well find him where you last saw him.

Another scenario might go like this: The moose is spotted on the side of the road in a cut or other small opening. He is more than likely already looking at your vehicle. Keep driving at the same speed, do not stop, and do not put on the brakes. It is tough and no one knows that more than me, having done it countless times. Just drive well past the animal, and by well past, I mean at least a quarter of a mile; half a mile may be better. Pull your vehicle to the side of the road and then walk back looking for the animal.

Chances are that if he has spotted you and is looking at you, he's wondering what you're up to. Stop right in front of him and he will more than likely bolt, and you will never see him again. Drive by him and he may dismiss you as one of the vehicles that he sees all year, due to logging. I have done this many times and found the bull standing pretty much where I left him. Other times I have not driven far enough past, and the moose, deciding that I represented some sort of threat, took off for safer ground. It is a judgment call on your part.

Having spent many hours in the woods while both hunting moose and observing them during other outdoor activities, I can tell you that you need to be able to read the moose when you first spot it. But be advised that you are not going to read the animal correctly every time. There are many "between-the-lines" clues that you need to be looking for—more than I could possibly cover in this book. Experience with live animals will be your best teacher. The more time you can spend searching out these animals and noting their behavior, the better a hunter you will become.

Still-Hunting

Still-hunting for moose is not much different than still-hunting for other members of the deer family, and much of the material written in the countless books about whitetail hunting can also be applied to moose—although the moose tends to stand out much better due to its coloring and size. Other than that, you just need to be in an area that holds a good population of them.

During years when our Maine moose season has fallen outside of the rut and calling has not been a major factor, still-hunting has proven to be very effective and hunters should not overlook this method. The key is to get into areas where you know moose live, and have a back-up plan for those times when they do not respond to calls readily.

My own experiences still-hunting for moose duplicates my experience with whitetails: Get into an area that holds your quarry. Go slow. Look over everything that is not in the normal order of Mother Nature's vertical patterns, and pay close attention to horizontal shapes. Also, with moose, take particular note of black stump-like forms. Look over any root formations that may have been created when a tree blew over in a Windstorm. Often these uprooted trees tear away a lot of top-soil and expose the much cooler under-soil. In warm weather, a moose will bed down in damp blackened earth to let the moisture help him cool off.

In the 1980s, many moose were spotted laying in the shade of uprooted trees in the huge clear-cuts that were abundant back then. Not only did these moose feel cooler because of the soil composition, but also, I believe, they felt safe due to the shadows of the root mass.

At one time, while still-hunting for moose, I would go as quietly as I would for Whitetails. Having spent considerable time with Corey and Maryo, and factoring in my own observations, I have changed my opinion about that.

Moose that are moving through the woods tend to make a lot of noise when they are relaxed and everything in their surroundings seems normal. You will hear the cracking of brush as they walk along. With a bull, you will hear his antlers scraping on the trees and bushes as he walks along feeding.

Whenever I have to resort to still-hunting, I walk through the woods as a moose would. I spend more of my time looking for moose than I do worrying about where I am stepping. Also, if I am not the one who has to tote a gun along, then I have my raking antler with me and I will scrape and bang it on trees as I walk. All I want to do is sound like a moose to any other moose that may be in the area.

If, through your scouting, you find an area that has many beds, consider it a good bet for still-hunting. Tall grass and scattered bushes will most likely be the normal vegetation. Hunt through the area slowly and watch for movement in the vegetation. It may not be the wind.

With large areas of tall grass, such as in a clear-cut or a heath, look for places that are dark in color and low to the ground. Scrutinize these closely with your binoculars and pay close attention to any branch or stick rising above the grass. More than one bull moose has been spotted because a portion of his antlers showed above the surrounding vegetation.

Look for older clear-cuts or selective cuts that have grown up in small soft-wood trees mixed with maples and other moose feed. Moose, being lazy, will get a belly full to eat and then just lay down where the mood suits them. You could spend all day walking slowly through these areas, which can be effective, but will take up a lot of your time.

I prefer to find a high point overlooking likely bedding areas. This can be a hill or it may be as simple as the pushed up dirt banking formed when the road was built. In many cuts an old pile of pulpwood will be left behind. Once I get into position on high ground, I make a couple of bull grunts. If a moose is sleeping out in this area you may not be able to detect his presence until he stands up to see what is going on. If you lack the ability to successfully duplicate the bull grunt or are hunting an area that receives a lot of pressure from other moose callers try simply snapping a stick or

two over your knee. The loud crack of the breaking stick is going to sound like another moose moving through the area. This is more than enough to get a moose to stand up and show himself. Just do not over do the stick breaking. One or two loud snaps will get a moose to stand up and look around with out putting him on alert.

When moving into one of these bedding areas, play the wind. I cannot stress this enough. Keep the wind into your face or at least perpendicular to the suspected location of a bedding moose. Nothing is going to make him bolt faster than your scent hitting him in the nose. On more than one occasion during deer season I have worked through a cut over area with the wind in my favor and spotted nothing. After having walked by a bedded moose my scent drifted back to him. The moose have left with a crash and blur of antlers and moose butt. No doubt had I made some noise during my still hunt I would have made him stand and show himself. But since I was not hunting moose it was just another chance to observe their behavior.

Canoe Hunting

Hunting from a canoe has to be the epitome of moose hunting, as close to a perfect way to hunt such a noble creature as there could ever be. The thought of it conjures up images of huge bulls standing on the banks of small ponds or in river backwaters feeding on water-lily roots. If you decide to hunt moose from a canoe, look at it as if you were still-hunting. First make sure the waterway you plan on hunting has moose along it. I would hesitate to canoe a lengthy river that only has one small section of moose habitat. Your time might be better spent using a different method.

You can use calling as your primary way to bring moose to you, or you can rely on the animal's need to feed to bring them out. Depending on the time of the season, you will see moose either way.

At times, hunters in kayaks slip into areas more quietly than on foot. A canoe makes transportation of the moose easier.

Your main concern when you are canoe hunting is to stay quiet. Any noise you make from a canoe is going to be an unnatural in the moose's environment, which is why I do not recommend using an aluminum canoe as a hunting platform. Aluminum banging into rocks and sliding over logs is quite noisy, so a modern canoe made of Royalex or fiberglass, or a traditional canoe made of cedar and glass, is your best bet. Even with canoes made of these materials, I suggest that you place a piece of carpeting on the inside bottom of the craft to muffle the sound of adjusting your feet or anything that you may drop. The carpeting will also create one more layer of insulation between you and the cold water, and that will help keep your feet warmer.

If you are maneuvering your canoe with a pick pole rather than a paddle, use the wood end of the pole rather than the end with the metal pick. When it strikes rocks on a river bottom, the wood will sound more like a moose's hoof than the clickety-clack of the metal end jabbing on stone.

If you are using a paddle for propulsion, get yourself a quality wooden one. There aren't too many good composite paddles on the market. Not only will the wood paddle be quieter in the water, but you can also use it to rattle overhanging alders

to simulate a moose raking his antlers. Many of the composite paddles just sound way too tinny when rattled that way.

Traveling down a stream or river or slowly paddling a lakeshore is the preferred method of canoe hunting. Move along slowly, especially when you are in a known feeding area—and I cannot stress how slow, slow is. At times moving with the current is going to be too fast!

Often, in the early morning hours when sound travels best, you may be able to hear a moose up to a half-mile or more from where you are. Listen closely enough and you'll get an idea about his line of travel, and hear where you might need to be to head him off.

Corey Kinney did a canoe hunt one year on the Allagash River. Before daylight, he and his hunter launched their canoe at Bissonette Bridge, just below Churchill Dam. First light found them just upstream of Umsaskis Lake, adjacent to the big heaths that surround the south end of the lake.

Both Corey and the hunter could hear a moose in the alder swale that borders the heaths. His antlers could be heard scrapping the alder and poplar trees. Once in a while, they could hear a branch snap under the weight of the moose. It was late in the season, post rut, and no amount of calling would interest the bull. He just kept feeding and paying no attention to the calls.

Corey made the decision to go after it by still-hunting. He and the hunter beached the canoe, got a line on the moose's direction of travel, and proceeded to attempt to cut it off. The hunter was trying not to make any noise, and Corey finally told him, "That moose is not worried about noise. He already thinks we are another moose. We are better off slogging along after him just trying to close the distance." With that said, it was now a full push to get near the quarry.

Finally, after about an hour of trying to cut the moose off, Corey stepped around a lonely spruce tree growing amongst the alders and spotted the moose peeking out from behind a poplar. The hunter made a well-placed shot and put an end to a very frustrating hunt.

If you are using the canoe as a method of travel to still-hunt through heaths and bogs along a waterway, you will do well to follow the advice I offer in the still-hunting section.

Be prepared to exit the canoe frequently in order to see over the banking and scrutinize your surroundings. Because of this, I recommend wearing hip boots or at least good knee-high rubber boots, since the hunter often will find himself out of the canoe as much as in it. Murphy's Law comes into play: "What can go wrong will go wrong and at the worst possible time!" Sometimes the best place to stop for a look around is not going to be the ideal spot to beach a canoe. Be prepared!

Safety while hunting from a canoe is very important. Often there will be other people in the canoe, but the man in the bow is the only person who needs to have a loaded gun. The paddler, and if there is a third person seated in the middle, should keep their guns unloaded until they exit the canoe, since a loaded gun in the back of the canoe is going to point forward at the bowman.

Always keep the gun that is loaded pointed in the air and never at the bottom of the canoe. Accidentally shooting a hole in the canoe is not something you want to happen. The water is cold during moose-hunting season, and the occupants of the canoe will be wearing heavy clothes and boots that can fill with water and pull a man under in seconds. Get a good comfortable lifejacket and wear it! Inflatable suspender life vests are ideal for hunting from a canoe. They give you freedom of movement will not interfere with shooting. Even while hopping in and out of the canoe all day, you will soon forget

that you have it on. To me, it is one of the best investments you can make before beginning a canoe hunt.

Always make sure that you know your canoe ahead of time. Know what the load limits are and do not try to surpass them. A canoe loaded to the gunwales going across a flat lake is one thing; add a chop to the water and you have a recipe for swamping. Also, know what your canoe is going to do should you shoot from it. Occasionally you may be forced to hunt from a small fourteen- to sixteen-foot canoe to get back into some small waterways or bogs. If this is the case, a hunter needs to realize that shooting at a right angle to the canoe may cause it to tip precariously with the recoil of the rifle. I learned this the hard way while duck hunting when I was younger. Believe me, everyone in the canoe is rather shocked to find himself or herself underwater after the gun is fired.

Again, remember Murphy's Law: Anytime water is involved, especially cold water, be prepared for things to really go wrong!

A moose that is standing on the bank of a stream when it is shot, if given a chance, will invariably turn and run back into the water to die. When shooting from a canoe, it is very important to pay close attention to shot placement. Anyone planning a canoe hunt would do well to practice shooting as if they were in a canoe. Practice shooting forward, left, and right from a seated position.

The person who is going to be handling the canoe should spend some time before the hunt getting to know the craft and learning what will make it turn right and left, if it is not something he does every day. He or she has to figure out what to do to stop the canoe in moving water with a pick pole, and hold it steady so that the shooter can make the best shot possible.

Stand Hunting

Hunting from a fixed stand, whether it is a ground blind or a tree stand, is not normally my first preference for hunting moose. It does, however, have its place as a hunting technique and should be considered when the opportunity presents itself for a trophy moose.

The key to successful stand hunting is obviously setting up in an area that moose frequent. If a hunter prefers to hunt from a stand, he should look for feeding areas first. No matter what the rut activity, at least the cow moose are going to be feeding, and the cows will draw the bulls. If your hunt falls during the post-rut period, the bulls are going to be putting the feed bag on as well. Clear-cuts and heaths on the water are good first choices because they provide the foods that a moose is looking for, and offer a good field of vision.

Although a good field of vision is important, it is not as important as setting your stand where the moose are going to be traveling, so that the hunter may get a shot at an effective range of the weapon he chooses. I have seen ideal areas to stand hunt when the field of vision was the first consideration. However, getting a moose to come close enough would have been another proposition. So choose your stand site carefully.

Pre-season observation will tell you a lot about where to set your stand. Even if you only have a day or two to watch an area before your hunt begins, it behooves the stand-bound hunter to make sure he is present at prime feeding times to observe where the moose are coming out and feeding.

As is most often the case of heaths or clear-cuts, trees for tree stands are going to be hard to come by. If you can find one that's suitable, by all means set yourself up in it. However, when no trees are present, you will have to resort to a blind of some sort.

In the heaths that I have experience with, moose travel the shortest distance out in the open between point A and point B. They want to stay in whatever cover they can find for as long as possible. Often a hunter can locate a suitable clump of alders or fir trees to set up in. Once there, build a small ground build to further conceal yourself and your movements, and you should do well.

The new pop-up blinds really shine as a moose-hunting tool. Some of them are large enough to conceal three members of a party comfortably. If you take the time and seal the seams of a pop-up blind, it will keep you dry should it rain. During cold weather, I have even used a small propane heater in these mobile blinds and stayed warm all day. Sitting out in the open on a cold, drizzly day is no picnic, but wet, chilly days offer some of the best opportunities for moose hunting, so it is to a hunter's advantage to be well prepared.

This cow moose is at a natural mineral/salt lick. Roadside run-off creates these areas from salt placed on the roads during the winter.

Slush bags can be placed high up in trees to attract moose. A moose wound up pulling this bag down from the tree.

Whether using a pop-up or a ground blind you build yourself, make sure you set up with a background that breaks up the structure's outline. You don't want to be standing out as a silhouette that is not natural to your quarry. Also, make sure your blind blends in with regard to color and material. You do not want to be setting a green blind against a brown background. Place a few branches or small trees in front of and behind a pop-up blind to break up its outline, and use only materials that are present in an area to insure that any blind you may build onsite will blend in.

Bait Hunting

Maine and many other states and provinces that hold a moose season allow baiting. Placing bait for moose can help attract and hold them in a certain area where the hunter can better his chances.

Actually calling this hunting method "baiting" may be a bit of a stretch. Moose normally eat an average of forty pounds of browse a day, and it is doubtful that the average hunter or guide is going to have the time, energy, and money required to actually carry enough bait to feed several moose. Given that, what the hunter is actually doing when baiting is putting out minerals and salts that the moose find attractive.

Moose have a taste for salt, as evidenced each spring when the roadsides start to clear of snow. As the snow melts and runoff pools in ditches, moose can be found drinking the salty water, and as the vegetation starts to regenerate, the grasses and plant shoots leach the salt into their root systems and into the new green growth. Moose that happen to live near roads that are salted during the winter will feed heavily on the seasoned greens.

There are many commercially manufactured baiting products that contain salt, and these can be purchased from sporting goods dealers. If you do not have access to a dealer for these products, you can simply go to any farm-supply store and buy salt blocks or licks to place in your hunting area. If you use these items, be sure to anchor them securely or place them up high, so that bear will have a hard time getting at them.

Old timers have told me that they used to take burlap bags and fill them with canning salt, then hang the bags from tree limbs. Rain would wash through the bag carrying salt to the ground below, where moose and deer would lick it up. Having used "Slush" made by Buck Expert, a salt and mineral product that comes in a burlap bag, I can tell you that the moose will literally eat the dirt beneath a hanging bag.

Pickling or canning salt is non-iodized and is not as refined as table salt. The granules are bigger, and they clump and form large blocks when they get wet. An eighty-pound bag can be purchased from suppliers for around eight to twelve dollars, and at that price, a hunter can afford to place a lot of salt out in an area. There is a drawback to this technique, however. Other hunters could find the salt and move into the area.

I learned a neat trick from a Canadian moose hunter on concealing the salt. He would find a large puddle or ditch of standing water and pour several bags of pick- ling salt into it. The larger the puddle, the more salt he would pour in. For example, a puddle that measured ten feet by five feet and approximately one to two feet deep would get treated with seven to ten eighty-pound bags of salt. Once the moose find such a spot, they will often keep returning to it.

Another baiting product that works well is the so—called "moose candy," which often comes in two parts and requires mixing at the bait site. It will bubble up and form a crust that adheres to the logs or rocks that you use as a mixing platform and creates a candy lick of sorts. Usually these products for moose will have a maple flavor and scent to them because maple is one of the moose's favorite foods.

When using a "candy" bait, do not be surprised if you only observe cows and calves responding to it as the rut gets near. When the rut is in full swing, a bull's attention is not on feeding but on breeding. Do not despair if you are only seeing cow and calf activity at your bait sites; the bulls will come around to check on the cows.

If you decide to place bait in your hunting area, do so well in advance of the season; thirty days or more is not too far ahead. To get the moose to find the bait quicker, I often use a moose lure or urine to help draw their attention, and reapply the scents or urine each time I check the site. Once I see evidence of moose using the area, I do away with the additional scent, as the moose are going to be leaving a lot of their own urine and scent at this point.

I often use baiting, as do the guides I work with. We do it in areas we are familiar with and hunt from year to year because either they consistently hold moose or they are breeding areas. The bait sites give us a good place to begin our search in a more defined section of a larger tract of moose habitat.

Calling Moose

Calling moose is not only most exciting form of hunting there is, but also one of the most effective . . . and the most complex. More variables come into play in calling than in any other hunting method.

Both sexes of moose are extremely vocal—not just during the rut, but also all year long. A bull moose also uses more than just sounds he can make with his larynx. Bulls communicate by raking trees with their antlers and displaying their racks to one another in a menacing manner.

Often, you not only have to try to appeal to a moose's sense of hearing, but his sense of smell. Depending how close you need to get, you may have to appeal to his sense of sight, as well, with the use of a decoy.

All the moose's senses can protect him, or they can help you call him in. In this chapter, I will discuss the individual uses of each type of call—explaining how it appeals to the moose's senses—and offer suggestions for combinations of various techniques that will lead to a successful and exciting hunt.

Many hunters and guides feel that after a certain date, moose will not respond to a call. In Maine, that means after our September hunt, calling is over. I have heard this opinion expressed by guides I consider good woodsmen, for the most part. They just refuse to believe moose can be called in any later in the season.

This is such an old wives tale that I have to wonder what else these guides do not see. Maryo

The bark from this birch tree was cut away and used to make a birch bark moose Call.

and I, and other guides I work with, consistently call in moose each year during the second hunt in October.

Moose respond differently during the off-peak times of the rut, but they still respond to a call. Not all the cows come into heat the exact same week. Those that are not all bred will come in again. Bulls know this.

Through the use of moose urine, you can trigger a bull into thinking there is a cow in heat in the area you are hunting, causing him to go full bore back into rutting mode.

Maryo has observed his captive moose mating as late as January, and he saw a fetus approximately six months along in development in a cow that was killed on a hunt in Newfoundland during the second week of September. She came into heat at an odd time, but she found a bull that wanted to breed. If that bull was willing to breed, he was willing to respond to her calls.

Types of Calls

Moose calls can be broken down to three categories: those that use your own voice, electronic calls, and mechanical calls that you pull or blow into.

Using your own voice as a call has worked for centuries. I am sure it goes back to the very first Native Americans who relied on moose as sustenance. While a human with a little practice can do a good job of imitating a bull grunt or a cow in heat, you will still need an amplifier of some sort to help duplicate that deep sound the bull makes, as well as to project the cow-in-heat call farther than you can with your voice unaided.

On the days when sound carries well, I've watched guides use just their voices and cupped hands to project moose sounds. But most of the good voice callers I have been around will carry some sort of megaphone—and I have seen just about every kind of megaphone.

George Perry, a guide from Lincoln, Maine, uses a traditional birch bark call, which is nothing more than a funnel made of birch bark. Such calls are still used by many Quebec moose hunters, and they are one of the most sought-after items that every moose hunter wants to own. I have used George's birch bark call, and I have to tell you it sounds excellent in both tone and volume enhancement. I have also made them myself, and always ended up giving them away to clients who saw me use them.

There is not much to making one of these. Simply find a large white birch tree at least fourteen or more inches in diameter. Cut the bark all the way around the circumference of the tree, being careful to make the cut deep enough so that you strike the wood. Measure down about fifteen to eighteen inches and make another cut, parallel to the first one. Now connect the two cuts with a vertical cut and carefully peel the bark from the tree in a solid sheet. Roll the bark into a cone shape. Traditionally the ending seam is stitched with a rawhide lace or grass. George's call is held together with black electrical tape, and I have done this as well. It takes a lot less time than hand lacing, and it is just as effective.

Butch Phillips of the Penobscot Nation shows one of his birch bark moose calls. His birch bark calls are some of the most rugged calls on the market today. Note how the ends are reinforced with stitching.

Butch Phillips, of the Penobscot Indian Nation in Maine, handcrafts what has to be the prettiest birch bark moose call ever made. He learned his craft from tribal elders, as this is a heritage that is passed on from generation to generation. I have had the opportunity to try one of Butch's calls and I've met other hunters who rely on them. He takes great care in choosing the proper tree and removes the bark carefully to get the desired thickness, so he can make a call that will last. Butch told me that over his life, he has taken twenty some-odd moose with his calls.

To make your own tin can moose call, use a No. 10 can (often used in commercial food establishments) and knot a leather lace or flat shoelace from the inside.

I saw another unique megaphone that was crafted by Ron Pickard of Frenchville, Maine—a cone of fiberglass with walls thick enough to let him use it as a rattling antler. I've also seen calls made from black tar paper and from the roll-up plastic sled many of us had as kids. One caller I worked with even used a cheer-leader megaphone. It was kind of large to carry around, but it sounded very good.

Commercial manufacturers of calls, such as Buck Expert, make a cone for use by voice callers. But any cone-shaped item will work as a megaphone to a degree. Just make sure that whatever you choose does not have a "tinny" tone. It should produce the bull grunt, deep and flat, and also be able to project the cow-in-heat call with a medium-high pitch, and without any hollow sound.

Electronic calls, made by a couple of different manufacturers, will produce the cow-in-heat call, various bull sounds, calf sounds, tree-raking, a cow moose urinating, along with some other sounds that can be useful when calling moose.

Here in Maine, we are not allowed to use electronic calls at the present time. I am not a fan of these anyway. For the stationary hunter, I think they have their advantages, but the hunter on the move, or speed calling, is going to find them time consuming to set up and take down. With speed calling, you move from one area to the next very fast, often only spending ten to fifteen minutes at each high-percentage spot. With an electronic call, you may be limited to one tone and pitch for the cow in heat. Many times, you'll need to carry a couple of mouth-operated calls by the same manufacturer, as they will all sound just slightly different in tone and pitch. This will allow you to work a bull more than once if you muff him the first time you try calling him.

Another thing I do not like about the electronic calls are their speakers. In some conditions they sound great, other times they seem very tinny. Weather conditions are going to vary greatly day to day. Moisture in the air or no moisture, the temperature is going to affect how a call sounds and the distance that the sound carries. Surrounding trees and vegetation, and any echo effect of the landscape and terrain, are factors that to determine the sound you get. When you consider all of these

When the wet string is pulled and stretched, the sound resonates out from the inside of the can, simulating either a cow-in-heat call or a bull grunt (depending on the length of the pull).

variables, you can see how they can affect a speaker's performance.

Mechanical calls vary in type as well. Hunters use everything from the coffee can to commercially made mouth calls.

The coffee can call is popular with novice moose hunters. With little or no effort, you can produce a cow-in-heat call or a bull grunt. With little-to-no cost, you can have a few different cans to produce varying pitches and tones. A person can easily learn which can to take out, depending on its sound quality for the given conditions.

To make a call of this kind, you need a coffee can or any other tin can of the same size. Use a nail to punch a hole in the center of the bottom of the can and then thread a leather lace or flat shoelace at least twenty inches long through the hole in the bottom, so it comes out outside the can. Tie a knot on the end inside the can, so the cord you've used cannot be pulled through the hole.

Back when I used a can call, I liked the institutional, or number-eleven, size vegetable can for my calls. I would wrap the outside wall with a layer of carpeting and glue it in place. This would remove the tinny sound. For my laces, I preferred a leather rawhide strip. But, I also had a call with a heavy flat shoelace, just to be able to have two different sounds.

To make the call work, you simply wet the string. Hold the can by the lip under your arm or in your left hand. At the outside end of the can, place the lace between your index finger and thumb, and squeeze the string. Pull it tight and allow your fingers to slide down the string. It may take a few tries to determine the correct pressure you need to apply. The sound is made from the string vibrating due to the pulling pressure you are applying, and the knot vibrating on the can bottom. You pull the string the entire length to get a cow-in-heat call, and make short pulls to get the bull grunt.

It is amazingly simple! With a little practice, most of the time you can be reproducing the two major sounds you need to make. Notice I said most of the time.

The wrong pressure, or a string that is too wet or too dry, and you might make a bad sound. Making a bad sound is a bad thing when trying to call any animal, let alone a moose.

I will admit, when I was using the can call, I found it worked great during the peak of the rut. At the peak of the rut, a moose will respond to the distant sound of a wood harvester saw blade screeching through a log. At times of peak rut, I swear you can call a moose with car horn. But during those days prior to peak and after peak rut, the tin can call is an iffy proposition at best. Plus it requires a lot of movement to work the call. Additionally, it cannot be used in conjunction with a hand-held decoy; a can call is just too cumbersome. Although it can work during the peak rut, it just is not a good all-around call.

Mouth-operated calls are by far the best I have found. Back when I used the can call, I could not find a mouth call that sounded like a moose. Some manufacturers actually took a deer call, added a megaphone to it, and sold it as a moose call. I saw one call that was actually a badly tuned elk call. In those days, I used my voice along with the can call.

The first time I heard a Buck Expert moose call demonstrated, I knew it was going to change the way I called. I could not buy one fast enough. It was a little difficult learning to use the first models Maryo came out with. I compared it to mastering a musical instrument. It took practice, and lots of it. But the first season I used the call, I knew that every bit of time I had put into practicing was worth it.

Since Buck Expert moose calls have been so successful, many companies now are copying the concept of the open-reed system developed by Maryo. A number of manufacturers have changed their products to better match the Buck Expert line of moose calls. As with all other calls, some manufacturers have been able to duplicate the proper sounds, while others leave a lot to be desired. You will have to try out various calls and compare them to see what I mean.

Since the introduction of Buck Expert's first moose call, Maryo has strived to make a call that is more user friendly. In 2005, he came out with his X-Treme Moose Call, which has made long practice periods a thing of the past. In field tests conducted during the 2004 Maine moose-hunting season, guides who had never had a chance to practice on this call were calling in moose on their first try with it.

Not a company to leave well enough alone, Buck Expert will be introducing easier calls for the beginner to use in the future.

How Moose Communicate

There is just no way, through the written word, that I can accurately describe the sounds a moose makes, which is why I decided to make a CD of moose sounds, including an explanation of each one. No matter what type of call you may decide to use, you can learn to duplicate the sounds provided on the CD.

These are the types of sounds you should learn, and explanations of the differences between them:

Cow-in-Heat Call

The sound of a cow in heat is one of the top-two communications a moose hunter should know how to reproduce; a good hunter will find himself using it more than any other. It is also one of the most misinterpreted sounds. Many a moose caller has failed to reproduce it correctly and unintentionally pushed moose away or caused them to hang up.

The sound the cow in heat makes differs from that produced by a cow that's not in heat. It will also vary depending on the stage of her heat. A cow-in-heat call sounds off high and the tone actually quivers. It will rise near the end and then fade off softly, varying in duration from three seconds to as much as fifteen seconds, depending on her degree of agitation. The key to a good cow-in-heat call is the quiver in the tone and soft fade out. Many moose callers, when they are just learning this type of call, tend to make the mistake of chopping the sound off abruptly. You may hear this sound in the wild made by an actual cow moose. When a cow ends her call abruptly, she is saying to the bull, "I am in heat but I have a headache right now. Tag along if you want." A bull will come close, then just hang back, waiting for her to call that she is ready to accept him. This is one reason why beginning moose callers have so many bulls hang up on them. They are just saying the wrong words in moose language.

A moose will also vary its volume so a caller can too. As you start off calling, you may want to project the call loudly. It is advisable to use a megaphone to increase the volume. As a bull comes closer to your position, tone your calls down decrease your volume, and discontinue using the megaphone.

Gary Wadsworth, me, and his son Curt on their first Maine moose hunt. This was the first moose I called in with the Buck Expert moose call.

A cow moose is in heat for a twenty-four-hour period. During this time she will call constantly to find a bull. At the Buck Expert Research Center in Quebec, they have found that a cow in heat will call up to six hundred times in a twenty-four-hour period. I know, I have listened to a cow calling in the wild for an hour or more and lost track of the number of times she sounded off. I do not think you can over call in most cases to get a bull started.

Bull Grunts

The bull makes two very distinct grunts. One grunt says to the cow, "I'm in love." The other says, to other bulls, "I want to fight." A caller should learn both. At a distance, the two calls are going to sound the same, but once the bull moose gets within one hundred yards of the caller, the sound will be noticeably different.

The Buck Expert moose call is the only one I have found to date that can successfully duplicate the bull grunt as well as the cow calls. I use it to grunt when a bull is a long distance out from me; the megaphone really increases the volume and sounds much deeper than I can make the sound with my voice.

Once the bull gets within one hundred yards or closer, depending on how the sound is carrying, I may switch over to my voice. The Buck Expert call reproduces the "I'm-in-love" grunt perfectly—just a simple "Orrrhh."

As he gets closer to the cow, the moose will typically lower his volume. If I want to sound like another bull that is with a cow or approaching a cow, I need to tone my volume down as well. I also do not want to sound bigger than the moose I'm calling. A moose will try to intimidate rivals with his grunts. As a rule of thumb, the deeper a grunt, the larger the bull.

If the moose is coming in and wants to fight, I will switch over to do my bull grunts using my voice and a megaphone. There will be an audible "click" before the "I-want-to-fight" grunt. You can duplicate this sound two ways. The first way is to smack your lips as if you were chewing a big wad of gum. Smack your lips loudly. It will sound even more convincing if you have a substantial amount of saliva in your mouth when you do this. The sound should come off as "Smack Orrrhh."

The second method is the one I use: Place your tongue on the roof of your mouth and suck back while pulling your tongue from the roof of your mouth. It will make a very loud sound that should come off as "Click Orrrhh."

Depending on how big and how mad you might want to sound to another moose, you can draw out the sound of your grunt by exhaling more into the mega- phone and extending the "hhhh." It should sound like "Orrrhhhhh . . . ." Taper it down slowly. The madder the bull gets, the meaner he wants to sound. You want to convince the other moose that you are trying to provoke him. So the madder he sounds, make sure you sound just as mad.

Antler Sounds

Bull moose use their antlers to communicate with other moose. The bull will not only use his antlers to provoke rivals—the larger the rack, the more sound it makes—but also to answer cow calls.

It is believed that when a bull moose rakes his antlers in response to a cow call, he is trying to impress the female by showing that he is the dominant bull in the area. His display is telling her, "Hey babe! I am the biggest guy here. Listen to this."

I have had more than one bull respond to a cow call with nothing more than raking. I also believe it may be a sign of sexual frustration. I think they do this, at times, because they can hear and smell the cow, but cannot see her. These actions are often seen when bull moose get close to the caller.

Master Maine guide Hal Blood called in a bull for some clients on a hunt. The bull immediately responded to the cow calls he made and moved right to where Hal and the hunters were waiting, thinking it was where the cow should be. When he did not see a cow, the bull walked up to an alder clump and proceeded to start shredding it. While he was occupied venting his frustration, a hunter was able to shoot it at a distance of less than twenty yards. This bull had clearly been antagonized by the fact that he heard a cow, came looking for her, and could not find her, so he had attempted to lure her out in the open by using his antlers.

Because bulls use their antlers as a form of communication, other moose know the difference between the sounds of a large set and a small set. A caller wants to keep this in mind when including raking as a part of his calling repertoire. If a caller is raking and sounds too much like a large moose, he may scare away a moose that decides he is smaller than the beast making the opposing sounds. (More on this later.)

The most perfect item to duplicate the sound of a moose antler is just that, a moose antler. A hunter who rakes with an actual moose antler is going to sound just like the real thing. I bought and carry a moose shed that weighs five pounds and fits nicely on my hip, where I wear my fanny pack.

A moose with a five-pound antler is going to be in the two- to three-year age bracket on average. Bernard Metivier of Quebec uses an antler lighter than mine because he does not like to sound big at all.

Corey Kinney, on the other hand, used to lug around an antler that weighed in at over ten pounds—equivalent to one on a three- to five-year-old bull, with a larger palm than mine. While Corey was using that huge antler, he never got a small moose to show himself, and I never knew him to kill a bull less than fifty inches. I lugged that antler for him and did the raking on more than one occasion. It took the use of both my hands to make it sound convincing.

The antler I use is approaching ten years old at the time I am writing this. I always make sure that

Rich Dodge (aka Fudge) likes to use a moose shoulder blade for raking bushes when calling. It is lighter than an antler and has good tone.

I soak it in a tub of water prior to the hunting season. The soaking adds close to a half-pound to the weight of the antler, but it takes out the hollow tin sound that is common with a dried antler. Maybe I am just too picky in the sounds that I try to reproduce, but my pickiness has yielded me some good-size moose throughout the years.

Some callers have found other ways of imitating the antler sound, and the items they use to help them are as varied as calling techniques. My great-grandfather talked to me about an ash canoe paddle that was his preferred method of raking. I still have his paddle, and I can tell you that when it's held properly in my hand and raked in a poplar tree, it sounds very convincing.

I have known some Canadian callers to use the brow paddle from a caribou antler as a raking antler. It sounds very hollow, yet not intimidating to other moose as they approach, and is light in weight for easy carrying.

Many callers like to use a dried shoulder blade from a butchered moose as a raking tool. It sounds great, producing good volume and excellent tone, and it can be rubbed on anything from a six-inch popular tree to a stand of alders to get the desired sounds. The drawback to using a shoulder blade is

that they do become brittle and break, and once a shoulder blade develops a split, the sound quality greatly diminishes. If you desire to use a shoulder blade bone, let it soak in water before the season begins to keep it from drying out and breaking, and to take away some of the tinny sound that you may get with an over-dried bone.

The award for the weirdest item used has to go to master guide Dan Glidden of Maine, who was working as a guide for Corey and I. His client had shot an exceptionally large moose with a spread of over fifty inches. Since Dan did not have a cameraman with him at the time of the kill, we did some after-the-fact filming. While the hunter was relating the story for the camera, he mentioned a sports- drink bottle that Danny rattled in the bushes. Corey and I looked at each other and shrugged our shoulders and let the hunter and Dan continue with their story.

As we were taking down the camp, Corey and I cornered Dan and said, "What is the thing with the sports-drink bottle?"

Dan smiled and kicked the dirt at his feet and told us this story:

"You guys all carry those big antlers for raking. I hate to lug more than I have to. I found that a plastic liter-size bottle on a hardwood stick rattled in the bushes sounds as good as an antler. Sheds that I find in the winter are worth a lot of money, so why am I going to keep one for me? I can go to the dump and find a plastic sports-drink bottle, whittle a stick to fit in the end, and I am all set."

Dan then demonstrated his "Bottle Antler," and I must say it sounded good. I am a firm believer in it to this day, and carry one in my truck in case I lose my antler, or loan it out to a starting moose guide.

You can make one yourself from any one-liter plastic bottle; I have used sports drink and liquor bottles made of plastic. Cut the bottom end out of the bottle, leaving a three-quarter-inch lip all around so that it retains some rigidity. Next, whittle

Nine-year old DJ McHugh of Monmouth, Maine, called in this fifty-plus inch bull for his dad Dennis. DJ used a birch bark call he and his father made together. The bull was one of the largest taken in Maine in 2005, weighing in at 1,050 pounds.

a hardwood stick to a tapered point to fit inside the bottle spout. This should extend through the neck and into the body of the bottle, but not come out the end that you have cut off.

Force the bottle onto the stick so you won't lose it. Cut the opposite end off the stick to the length you want. (Dan prefers to leave his long; it doubles as walking stick for him.) And there you have your moose antler on a stick!

Some callers like to hunt as light as they can. Ron Pickard made his fiberglass megaphone call heavy enough so that he can use it as a rattling antler. The sound Ron gets from his megaphone is excellent, and it allows him to carry only the one piece of gear. He uses his voice through the megaphone as a call, and has the megaphone to rake on trees if he needs to.

Buck Expert has taken this one step further. Maryo designed a call that has a megaphone made from a plastic composite, with a serrated edge on it. Due to the plastics composition, when this megaphone is scraped on trees and bushes, it sounds just like a moose antler. Mario went through a lot of trial and error to get the sound right, and the new call was released in 2005.

The first year we tested the call, it was unbelievable. After demonstrating it in the camp yard, guides were leaving their raking antlers in the trucks each morning—they had that much faith in the sound of the megaphone as a raking antler. This innovation by Buck Expert has lightened the load of the guides that I am associated with.

Making the sounds that a moose makes with his antlers calls for some visualization on the caller's part. He or she needs to remember that the moose is a big, lumbering animal.

A moose does not toss his head back and forth as quickly as a whitetail buck. He moves his head as an animal his size would, in a slow and lumbering manner, but with power and strength. When raking an antler, you have to move it as a moose would to get the correct sound: slowly, deliberately, with some force. If you imagine that you are as big as a moose and trying to move all that headgear around, you will make the required sounds that much more convincing. A moose wants to make sure that others are hearing him as well. When he twists his head from left to right with his antlers in an alder bush, he hesitates at the end of his rake just for a second before twisting back in the other direction. Make sure, when you rake, that you duplicate this rhythm, moving from left to right or right to left, pausing at the end of each swing for a split second before coming back the other way.

Also, make note of his vocalization pattern. He will not grunt while he is raking, but rather will stop the procedure, lift his head, and then grunt. A moose does not hear another moose grunting while it is raking, so the hunter should not make grunting sounds when raking, either. Do it after and before the raking sequence.

As a caller, the volume you put out during the raking will also determine whether or not you are going to see the moose. Too much antler noise will drive away a smaller bull, and on more than one occasion I have had moose come in and hang up.

This is a dandy bull I called in during the 2005 hunting season.

The animal in question and I would call back and forth, challenging each other. He would refuse to show himself. I would call. He would call. He would rake. I would rake. This pattern led me to believe that he had doubts about himself being dominant. At this point, a caller must decide what to do.

Hunting in Maine, I usually have an abundance of moose to choose from, and this greatly influences my decision to be more aggressive in my calling. At this stage in my moose conversation, I normally try to sound like I am a bigger moose than he is. I will thrash my antler menacingly in a bush and grunt loudly, wanting him to think that I am a rival bull that is mad with rage, so the other moose will challenge me.

One of two things will happen. He will either say, "Hey! I am bigger than you," and step out, or he will grunt back as he retreats into the woods, as if to say, "Okay, you win."

Calling Tips

If there is one saying that can be applied to moose calling, it is, "Practice makes perfect." Start practicing with your moose call well in advance to the season. If your family does not want you

practicing in the house, do it when you are driving in your car alone. You want to be able to blow into the call each time and get a perfect sound from it. Bad notes when calling will hurt you more than not calling at all.

When first learning to call, do not get discouraged on those days when you get no responses from a bull. It happens to the best moose callers. Just figure that you were not near enough to an animal that wanted to come out and play with you.

Pay close attention each time you call in a bull. Even if it is not a trophy moose, learn from it. Understand what you did to bring that moose to you.

When you finally call in a couple of moose, continue to use that style of successful calling as your primary technique. If you consistently return to an area to call, remember to vary your technique. Let the bull that heard your primary sequence think that he is responding to a different cow.

Never start your calling sequence before legal shooting time. A bull could be very close to you and show up too early. On those dark, overcast days when daylight takes forever to finally arrive, do not call until your hunters tell you they can see into the woods well enough to shoot.

If you feel you must call before legal light to locate your moose, use this trick I learned quite by accident a few years ago. Carry an owl call and blow into it imitating the "who, who, who cooks for you" call of the barred owl. I have heard moose respond to this call in the night and early morning hours before daylight. When I first mentioned this to Maryo, he said that many old-time Quebec moose hunters had told him the same thing.

When I use this trick to locate a moose, I plan on only getting one grunt from him immediately at the end of the owl call, so make sure you and others with you are listening closely to be able to pinpoint his location. You will only get one chance if he decides to respond to the owl call.

Never assume that you know exactly where the bull is going to come from. Instead, play the wind so it works in your favor. At times this might require you to take a longer route into an area to come in on the downwind side.

Carry more than one call with you while hunting. You could lose or break one. Additionally, even though the same company might have made your calls, they will sound slightly different in tone and/or pitch. This allows you to work the same bull more than once and keep him from getting suspicious.

If you make a mistake with a bull one day and go back in on him later in the week, call to him from a different location within his area. Do not give him anything that will make him more suspicious than he already is going to be.

When walking and calling, if you return to your starting spot via the same route, stop at all the places you called on your trip in and call again. A bull may have responded and you did not hear him. He may still be in the area looking for the cow he heard.

Shotgunning for Big Game

DAVID R. HENDERSON

On the Western Plains

"The buck on the left is 191 yards," said outfitter-guide Scott Denny, peering through a laser rangefinder at a group of bedded pronghorns on the high plains (elevation 4,800 feet) of east-central Wyoming. "We can get closer if we stay behind this little ridge to the right." "No. I'll try it from here," said hunter Steve Meyer, readying his gun on a bi-pod for the shot. "How hard do you think that wind is?" "I dunno. Ten [mph], maybe a little more," said Denny, switching from rangefinder to binoculars. Meyer carefully lined up the crosshairs, shifted them for windage, and slowly exhaled while he pressed the trigger. "Boom!" At the report the herd leapt to its collective feet and after the first couple of strides, the animals were running flat-out in the unique gliding gait indigenous to the species. All of them were obviously very intent on getting somewhere else very quickly. All but one, the targeted buck never got out of his bed and was now lying in a twisted pile with one leg in the air.

It was a nice shot—for a shotgun. Meyer was shooting a 12-gauge Browning A-Bolt. The projectile was one of Winchester's Partition Gold slugs. Possessing well over 1,800 feet per second of muzzle velocity, more than one and a half tons of energy at the muzzle and a projectile comprised of a lead core with a partitioned copper jacket, the Partition Gold is only technically a shotgun slug. Sighted-in to be

dead-on at 150 yards, the slug offered a point-blank range (*plus or minus 3 inches of elevation, assuring no need of holdover*) of 178 yards. Meyer, who had been a member of the slug's design team at Winchester-Olin, gave 2 inches of holdover at 191 yards and allowed for about 6 inches of wind drift.

Illinois hunter Steve Meyer took this Wyoming pronghorn at 191 yards with a Winchester Partition Gold slug fired from a Browning A-Bolt shotgun.

"Shotguns?" had been Denny's surprised reaction the day before when Meyer uncased his A-Bolt and I pulled out my Tar-Hunt RSG-12 custom bolt gun. But after watching us both shoot rifle-like 100-yard groups from a makeshift bench at the Table Mountain Outfitters tent camp outside the tiny prairie town of Shawnee (pop. 8. Yeah, 8), he was a convert. Denny was also at my shoulder that first day when I took a pronghorn buck with an offhand shot of 117 yards in a milling herd that we surprised by popping up from a dry ravine bed. "I was impressed," said Denny, whose Table Mountain Outfitters also put on whitetail and mule deer, mountain lion, turkeys, upland birds and buffalo hunts in Nebraska and South Dakota. "I wasn't so sure at first but after seeing those things in action I figure that's all you need anywhere they're legal."

Triple U ranch hand Clint Amiotte was similarly skeptical a few days later when we showed up equipped with shotguns to take a buffalo from the Triple U Ranch's herd located near Fort Pierre, South Dakota. Admittedly, shooting a buffalo shouldn't be confused with hunting, but then it never could. The American bison is horribly myopic and decidedly indifferent to intruders when they approach from downwind. Hunting bison is much the same today as it was 130 years ago when market hunters reduced the herds from an estimated 30 million to near-extinction. Bison may not be wary, but they are extremely tough animals. The typical 6-1/2-year-old bull weighs between 1,800 and 1,900 pounds with massive, heavily furred shoulders and neck and large bone structure. Amiotte was skeptical that a shotgun slug could effectively work its way through the heavy hide, let alone the muscle and bone.

Bison may not be wary, but they are extremely tough animals.

The author took this 1,850-pound plains bison in South Dakota with a Winchester Partition Gold slug and his Tar-Hunt slug gun.

Using the rolling topography of the 62,000-acre Triple U Ranch (where much of the movie *Dances with Wolves* was filmed), we were able to slip within 90 yards of a small group of bulls standing separated from a herd of about 500 animals. Bavarian Eric Fischer, a fellow Table Mountain hunter who traveled with us to the Triple U, borrowed my Tar-Hunt slug gun and felled the first bull with a single well-placed shot to the neck. "Whoa!" yelled Amiotte, who had seen hundreds of buffalo shot on the ranch—but none with a shotgun. "That shotgun slug is a real slobberknocker ain't it?" Well, that's one word for it. My bull took two shots; the first was a quartering-to shot to the shoulder on a walking animal at slightly more than 100 yards. I was then able to move around the hobbled bull and the "slobberknocker" put him down with a 90-yard neck shot.

The Partition Gold is part of a vanguard of impressive new loads that have been pushing the envelope in shotgun slug performance. The new loads have been described as rifle fodder disguised as shotgun slugs. Despite its flashy ballistics and design, the Winchester load isn't even the fastest or hard-hitting on the market right now. "Some say that the fast slugs need a faster twist rate but I think interior barrel diameter is more of a factor," said Randy Fritz, owner of Tar-Hunt Custom Guns and research and development coordinator for Lightfield. "I think you're going to find that most guns made in the last three years will shoot them fine but anything made before that might or might not handle them well. That's because in 1997 SAAMI (Shooting Arms and Ammunition Manufacturers Institute) instituted a standard bore size for 12-gauge rifled barrels (minimum .719, plus .003) and the newer guns will have standardized barrels where as earlier guns may be virtually any size." The bison and pronghorn hunts were, admittedly, done as demonstrations of modern slug performance. No one would purposely pursue those animals with a shotgun when rifles are perfectly legal. But shotguns and slugs are very common ordnance for some other big game. I've taken several black bears over bait, several wild hogs and four caribou with shotguns and slugs and I'm planning a trip to northern Ontario for muskox and another to South Africa for plains game and birds using only Ithaca shotguns. The technology of slug performance and improvements in slug-shooting shotguns have taken giant strides forward and today's hunters are reaping the benefit.

"Whoa!" yelled Amiotte, who had seen hundreds of buffalo shot on the ranch ... "That shotgun slug is a real slobberknocker ain't it?"

The author had to battle with both distance and the wind to take this Wyoming pronghorn with a Winchester Partition Gold slug.

The author has taken several bears over bait with a shotgun. This 6-foot Manitoba black bear fell to a Remington Copper Solid.

Part 3
Predator Hunting

Introduction

JAY CASSELL

Perhaps the fastest growing sector in hunting is with predators, and why not? Predator populations, and in particular coyotes, are surging across the country. Coyotes roam the suburbs, feasting not only on suburban deer and turkeys, but on cats, dogs, and other pets. There have even been coyotes sighted in Central Park in the middle of New York City!

Not only are predators available nationwide, and huntable at times when most other hunting seasons are closed, but they're smart. Wile E. Coyote didn't get that monicker on a whim! Nor did the term 'sly like a fox' just appear for no reason.

Fact is, predators are cunning, smart, alert, and ultra cautious – making them all the more challenging to hunt.

To me, the ultimate predator is the coyote. Not far behind are foxes, cougars, bears, even raccoons and weasels. But coyotes are the number one target for most predator hunters, because they are so numerous, and because it takes a goodly amount of skill to get one. That's why I've focused on coyotes in this short section, with some very good words of coyote hunting wisdom from television personality and renowned coyote hunting, Rom Spomer.

—J. C.

Predator Hunting—Proven Strategies

RON SPOMER

When I'm Calling You: All About the Sounds and Tools That Make Them

There are days when you swear predators have never responded to a call and never will. So to heck with it. Then there are days when you could play "Yankee Doodle Dandy" on a kazoo and bring a pack of drooling canines into your lap. If you blow it, they will come. So why? Why are they all over you one day, seemingly extinct the next? I don't know. But I do know this. It's not the melody.

When I joined this calling club, I listened hard and often to a flimsy 45-rpm recording of a dying rabbit captured by Johnny Stewart of Waco, Texas. In the dim recesses of my memory I can still hear that tinny, monaural voice, the hum of the amplifier, and the shivering wails of that lost bunny. With a brown plastic, square-sided Burnham Brothers fox call, I practiced imitating those screams, their cadence, and duration. Then I mixed in a bit of real rabbit squalls I'd heard over the years while catching young cottontails and jackrabbits in the hay fields. Figured I had nature duplicated. Knew it when my first coyote came a-runnin'. Then another and another. Soon I was a self-proclaimed expert, laughing at the ridiculous sounds my young hunting partner, Tom Lowin, blasted from his call. "You'll scare 'em right out of the county," I said. "Blow like this." But Tom, for all his talents, had a wooden ear. It didn't matter. He still called in a pack of coyotes.

It was late October in Montana. The Gravelly Range. Doug firs, ponderosa pines, sagebrush, and grass meadows. Local coyotes were running in packs, chasing mule deer. Early in the month we saw six of them bring down a doe and tear her limb from limb, polishing her to bone by dawn. I called a single one evening, shot it, and called a pair one morning, but missed my chance when they got my scent. Tom heard their evening chorus in a narrow side canyon dark with pine. He stuck his call to his lips and blew his sorry impersonation of a rabbit in trouble. The coyotes shut up. Seconds later six of them poured from the woods in an all-out charge. "I shot the closest one, and by the time I reloaded, they were gone. But I could hear them running all around me." Tom hustled back to the cabin, whistling past the graveyard, half expecting a mass attack. It had been an eerie encounter, but it proved there was nothing wrong with his calling.

At that time, 1976, my idea of a proper rabbit squall was a series of quavering cries lasting a second or two each with a split-second pause between them. I'd carry on in this manner for roughly a minute, then shut up for a few minutes to watch and listen. I'd blow the next series louder, the third at maximum volume, adding a dramatic crescendo and decrescendo as I imagined the bunny slowly expiring. Some of my performances were Oscar contenders, I tell you.

Then Tom came along with that silly, long, choking scream that sounded like two Buicks mating in a wrecking yard and called more coyotes in a minute than I had the previous month.

In the years since, I've shot predators that responded to a cacophony of calls from various virtuosos who played a variety of instruments pitched from bass to soprano. All I can tell you is there's no accounting for a predator's taste in music. The blamed things will come to durned near any sound. Heck, I once called two in a row with a canoe.

We hadn't planned to "blow" the canoe when we set out for a bear hunt along north Idaho's Dworshak Reservoir. The idea was to paddle along the shoreline, watching spring meadows for grazing bears. Upon seeing one, we would stash the canoe, hike up and shoot it (the bear, not the canoe). Well, we located a bear eventually, high in a lush meadow, so we carried the canoe far up the bank in order to hide it deep in the woods. As we shoved it over a fallen fir, a number of sticks and stobs screeched across the fiberglass bottom like fingernails over a chalkboard. "Hey, here comes a coyote!" my partner Brad Deffenbaugh hissed. I turned in time to see the crazy dog running up from the shore, hot on our trail. When it recognized us, it bounded into the brush. "That was weird. You suppose it had rabies or something?" We chalked the event off to coincidence.

After studying our hiding spot, we decided it was too open, so we hauled the canoe back to the lake and paddled to a brushier takeout. Again we slid the boat into the woods. Again it screeched. But this time we had our rifles out when a second coyote ran up from the beach. One shot from my .30-06 proved adequate. The coyote looked healthy enough (other than the fact it was dead). "Hey wait a minute!" I said. "Did you notice how he acted just like all our coyotes do when they're coming to a call?"

"Yeah."

"I think he was coming to the screech of the canoe. I think they both were."

Brad agreed, and we're sticking to our story.

Two Schools of Calling

The Tom and canoe incidents suggest that anything can work, but most callers try to stick with more natural sounds and cadences. The most popular approach seems to be similar to what I do, as described above. Call a little, wait a lot. We'll label this call-and-wait. The other style involves calling a lot and barely waiting at all. We'll label this continuous calling. They both work.

The theory behind call-and-wait is "That's what rabbits do." They don't wail nonstop. But they usually don't start up again after a three- to five-minute rest, either.

The theory behind continuous calling is "Once you've got 'em coming, keep 'em coming." Don't give them a chance to slow down, get suspicious, or circle. With that helpless bunny crying for attention, they can't resist racing straight in, even though no rabbit ever wailed for ten minutes nonstop. Let's examine these methods in depth.

Call-and-Wait

The typical call-and-wait performer starts with a low-volume series of plaintive cries, each lasting a second or two with just enough interlude for a breath if needed. Some folks blow for only fifteen seconds; some go for a minute. Then they wait and watch for as long as five minutes before playing their second verse, slightly louder. Another wait, verse three, more volume to reach distant ears. Wait again, verse four louder yet. Coyote callers usually give it fifteen to twenty minutes before moving. Cat callers hang in there for thirty minutes to an hour.

The main advantages to this style of calling are improved ability to spot and hear approaching game. When your ears are full of the sound of your own blowing, you aren't likely to hear drumming paws behind you. In brushy habitat this'll cost you a few shots—maybe get you bit. It's also easier to spot distant game if you're not concentrating on the call.

Lastly, you'll shoot better if you aren't gasping and heaving from all that blowing.

The downside to pausing is that it gives critters a chance to lose interest. I've seen this many times, most recently in Texas, when a bobcat ran out of the brush in response to my partner's calls. Because my buddy was covering one alleyway through the brush and I another, he couldn't see the cat or me. When he stopped calling, Miss Kitty stopped and sat down. I eased my own call up and got her restarted with three good cries, but as soon as I dropped the call to grip my shotgun, she stopped again. Then she saw a mouse or vole or something in the grass. Chased it into the brush. End of story. No amount of calling could coax her out.

The staccato cry of a flicker in distress often fools predators leery of over-used rabbit calls.

Similarly, I've had coyotes come on a dead run, but when the calling stopped, so did they. Some looked the situation over and began circling to catch my wind. Some just sat and watched, hoping to see something encouraging. Some just lost interest and trotted away. This is when a moving decoy earns its keep. Restarting the calls in these situations usually restarts the coyotes, but not always. Switching to a higher-pitched squeaker call sometimes turns them back on. Just purse your lips and suck air or kiss the back of your hand. Many callers keep a bulb squeaker taped to their gunstock.

Continuous Calling

This approach also starts out softly, so as not to spook nearby listeners, but instead of pausing, the caller merely gulps air when necessary and gradually cranks up the volume. If you're alone, swing your head slowly back and forth, always watching. When a subject appears, you may change volume, but keep the sound rolling. Move your gun into position early, pick the animal up, and either shoot as it lopes in or stop it with a bark and then shoot.

The downside here is the possibility of a sneak attack. More than one preoccupied caller has been scratched or bitten, unaware that an animal has come into range. Continuous calling may not be ideal in heavy cover where the sound of thumping feet is often your first clue that you have a customer. Oxygen deprivation is another real possibility when continuously blowing. You probably won't faint, but all that huffing and puffing will make it harder to hold steady for a precise shot. This is the major reason I employ the call-and-wait style. It gives my heart a few seconds to slow down for the shot.

Alternate Sounds

The old dying rabbit is the hands-down favorite call nationwide, but not always the most productive. Depending on habitat and local species composition, the distress cries of other critters can be more effective.

The first alternative I ever tried was the staccato cry of a yellow-shafted flicker. Tom Berger was with me at the time. We were standing in a big Kansas shelterbelt, so it seemed only natural to work the bird call. Besides, attempts at calling with a rabbit cry had netted nothing at several sites earlier that morning. This time, however, we knew a coyote was close enough to hear us, because we had seen one about four hundred yards out in a pasture climbing in and out of a dead Hereford carcass. "It's pigging out on beef. Why would it come to a call?" Tom whispered.

"I don't know, but let's find out." Each of us stood against a tree trunk for cover, and I blew while Tom watched through binoculars.

"He's lookin'. Blow it again."

I blew.

"Here he comes!" Belly distended, coat reeking of putrid flesh, that glutton loped right up to us. We had to tie him from a long pole to carry him back to the truck.

The jackrabbit call is probably the second most used sound in the predator caller's repertoire. It's much like the cottontail's call, only lowerpitched. The jack squall has never produced as well for me as the cottontail squeal, even in good jack habitat. I think the higher-pitched call simply reaches farther.

Where deer are common prey, fawn bleats and low-pitched doe calls blown frantically work pretty well. In the Southwest, the squeals of baby javelina can really bring the dogs and cats a-runnin', but beware mama javelina. I've found myself surrounded by popping tusks on more than one occasion. As long as they don't threaten me too closely, I don't scare them off. Real pig snorts and scents just add to the attraction.

Feral pig distress sounds can be hot where those animals are common, and that includes most of the southern states from coast to coast. Again,

Pork chops for dinner? Most big predators will come running if you squeal like a pig in javelina or feral hog country.

anticipate a visit from an upset mama. If a thirty-pound javelina makes you nervous, wait until a two hundred-pound ticked-off sow tries to run you off.

In forested habitats where tree squirrels are common, the high-pitched whistle of a frightened young squirrel can be an effective draw. These calls are designed to attract adult squirrels during the early season when they're still programmed to protect their young, but they'll lure predators, too. The call is a flat disc with a hole in the middle through which you suck air to make the distress whistle.

Many songbird screams and cries also turn the trick if you can mimic them. You won't find mouth calls geared to play these tunes, but they're available on tapes and computer chips for play in electronic callers. These work best during the spring nesting season when fledglings are falling from nests. Not all calls must mimic animals in distress. Turkey hunters regularly call bobcats and coyotes with normal turkey yelps. These can be especially effective in areas where predators have become educated to the usual rabbit calls. If you want to increase the tension and urgency, go with the kee-kee run of a poult. This starts out something like the squeal of a bull elk, then breaks into an excited yelping.

Crows are so common across the country that most predators know them intimately. Try a fighting crow call sometime and see what happens. You'll probably bring in a passel of crows, but their cawing and flapping will only add to the effect. Last but not least are the puppy-in-distress calls. Oh my, are they effective in late summer when pups are wandering but still being guarded by mom and pop! I don't hunt predators in that season because the pelts aren't prime, but those who must control predators around livestock report that the crying puppy call is deadly. I use it in fall as a backup sound immediately after shooting a coyote that has come to a regular call. I start yipping frantically like a hurt pup. This often brings a second coyote that may have been traveling with the first but was hesitant to come in. Sometimes it even brings a third. This call sounds like a domestic puppy yipping or crying.

Semi-closed-reed calls can be manipulated to produce a variety of low or higher pitched cries.

Calling Devices

Virtually one hundred percent of all predators are called with three types of calls: mouth-blown, hand-operated and electronic. Mouth calls can be divided into two categories: those that imitate prey and those that imitate the predators themselves.

Prey Calls

Mouth-blown prey calls are far and away the most popular because they are compact, versatile, inexpensive, and effective. Anyone who can exhale can blow one effectively. No fancy hand controls are necessary. Tone and cadence are not critical. Just make it go waaa waaa waaa and you're in business. These common calls come in seven flavors.

Closed-Reed

The closed-reed variety consists of a wooden or plastic mouthpiece and barrel with a metal reed inside. In many cases this reed is the same as found in toddlers' squeaky toys. These calls are as common as mushrooms after a spring shower and virtually foolproof, but the sound is fixed. They are deadly effective until too many locals start using them. Then the local critters wise up, and it's time to switch to a different sound.

One exception to the nonvariable sound rule is the Mini-Blaster from Burnham Brothers. It's a tiny call consisting of a long metal reed inside a flexible plastic tube stuck into a small walnut barrel. By biting on the plastic tube, you can change the pitch. The volume from this call is enough to hurt your ears. Another closed-reed call you can modify in mid-blow is the Johnny Stewart PC-1, which has its metal reed beneath a rubber button you bite down on to touch the reed and change its pitch.

Semi-Closed Reed

These are based on the crow-call style, which is a reed sandwiched between two long lips of plastic that can be squeezed with the teeth to vary the pitch. These are a bit tougher to master than metal squeaker reed models, but can produce a wider variety of calls—from low-pitched jackrabbit to high-squeal cottontail. If you already have a crow call, just use it. The Primos cow elk call and antelope call with bite-down lips also work nicely.

Open-Reed

Here's one of the most versatile mouth calls. It features a barrel with a plastic reed riding above a curved platform or sounding board at the blowing end. The reed is held in place by a wedge of cork or plastic or sometimes a fat rubber band. By pressing this exposed reed with teeth or lips while blowing, you change tone from the low bawl of a fawn or lamb to a squeal high enough to shatter glass. If you're good, you can make it quack and bugle like an elk. More importantly, you can make it howl like a coyote—thus the open-reed performs double duty. Growl into the call while blowing to make it raspy.

Diaphragm Calls

You guessed it. This is the standard turkey or elk diaphragm caller. Just a bit of tape and latex held in the mouth. Variable tongue pressure against the palate mixed with variable air pressure changes the

notes of this device to nearly anything. Make it cry like a cottontail, bawl like a fawn, howl like a big dog, yipe like a puppy, yelp like a turkey, or bugle like an elk. Since it's contained completely within your mouth, both hands are motionless and free for shooting. You get maximum volume with minimum air pressure, too, so you don't wear out so fast or breathe so hard.

One spring Ken Sandquist and I were scouting turkeys from rimrock above a big, deep Idaho canyon. It was mid-morning and nothing was happening, so when two giant Canadas flew over honking, I did my best to mimic them with my diaphragm call. No cigar, but close. Then Ken pointed out a pair of coyotes climbing onto an overlook about a quarter-mile up canyon. "Think you can call them?"

Plastic funnels or megaphones add resonance to coyote howls and project the sound in specific directions.

he asked. Without missing a beat I howled, and both animals spun to look right at us. I howled again, and here they came. Neither of us wanted to shoot a spring coyote, so we backed out of there.

Many hunters who can't seem to get the hang of operating traditional diaphragm calls or gag on them should try either the Primos Hyper Plate models with a raised metal "roof" over the latex or the H.S. Tone Trough with a plastic roof over the latex. Both are much easier to blow than standard diaphragms and can be held farther toward the front of the mouth. Some manufacturers are now marketing special "predator" diaphragms, but nearly any turkey or elk caller will work. Heavier reeds are usually pitched lower, lighter reeds higher. You may need one of each to mimic old dogs and females or pups.

Rubber Band Squeakers

These are high-pitched, close-range calls with low volume. Two slender strips of plastic hold a strip of rubber band between them under slight tension. A caller can change the tension and raise the pitch by biting down on the plastic. Good for calling bobcats and fox and coaxing coyotes.

Bellows

Rubber air reservoirs are squeezed to activate internal reeds. Small versions are known as mouse squeakers, and they're good for fox and bobcats or coaxing coyotes those last few steps for a shot. Scotch used to make a large bellows call you operated like an accordion to activate the internal reed, but all that hand motion can work against you.

Voice

Some might not consider the human voice a predator call, but it sure can be. I took my brother out to one of my favorite calling sites in South Dakota one evening and blew through four series with no response. Being the joker he is, Bob began teasing me by "showing how it was done" using his voice. You guessed it—a coyote popped over the horizon and trotted right in.

Since then, I've used my voice to call several coyotes. Voice calling is wonderful because there are no devices to lose or forget and no hand movement. Sadly, few of us can call very long without getting sore or ineffective. My throat gets raw in a matter of minutes.

We Never Talk Anymore—Coyote Language

Howling to locate coyotes began long, long ago. Anyone living outdoors with coyotes is inevitably tempted to imitate their howls. Doing so often elicits a reply. Bingo! You've located a coyote. Just as domestic dogs howl at sirens, so do coyotes. By the mid-twentieth century, numerous Westerners had learned to stop every mile or two along county roads and sound a police siren to inspire coyotes to howl. Then they'd move in, set up, and call them with rabbit cries. Such sirens still work and are used by many callers to scout for animals.

In recent years a number of manufacturers have begun selling specialized coyote howlers that are usually nothing more than open-reed prey calls. Just blow through them with the typical coyote howl cadence. Most howlers come with a plastic funnel or megaphone resonator, but these aren't critical to success. Diaphragms produce wonderful howls, too, and can be used with megaphones or an old kitchen funnel for a bit more resonance.

Most naturalists recognize a complex variety of coyote calls and attempt to interpret them. They've identified as many as thirty-three calls, including pair-bonding calls, puppy-feeding whines, yelps of submission and so on. Most are seldom heard and difficult to differentiate, but a few are fairly obvious and of value to the hunter. The following descriptions should serve to introduce you to conversational coyote, but don't cling hard and fast to these descriptions. Combine them with your own interpretations and experience to detect nuances and meanings. A written description of any animal sound is rough at best. Try to "feel" the call as much as hear it. Some calls sound lighthearted and friendly, others angry, others nervous or edgy. Such tones should help you interpret meaning. Mimic them and use them when you deem appropriate.

Territorial or Dominance Call

Can be given by male or female. Males are typically lower pitched. The dominance call is a no-fooling-around, aggressive-sounding collection of choppy barks and abbreviated howls. It's saying, "Keep out." Use it in late winter after most coyotes have paired and established distinct territories in which they'll soon raise pups. Expect a quick and angry response. This call can spook young coyotes.

Warning or Alarm Call

Similar to the territorial call, alarm calls are a series of barks that warn other coyotes of danger. Alarm barks are usually higher pitched than territorial barks, with a rapid, almost frantic delivery. You'll hear it when a suspicious coyote coming to your call spots you or otherwise determines something is amiss. Once this happens, it's virtually impossible to call anything in, but it is possible to sneak around and get a shot at the barker.

Distress Call or Puppy Whines

The yipping and crying of a frightened puppy. Mature dogs will yipe and cry too, so blowing this call after a shot may pull in a nearby mate.

Greeting, Welcome, or Pack Communication

High-pitched short barks, yaps, and happy howls. Two or more coyotes together sound like a choir of sopranos warming up before a concert. Packs may use this to tell other packs of their location. You hear these wild pack singing parties more often than any other calls. They're useful for locating subjects.

Location Howl

A lone, long, classic howl used to locate others. Can be used to call in coyotes, especially territorial males in winter. The howl starts low and immediately rises two octaves or more, where it is held for three to as many as ten seconds before tapering in volume and dropping smoothly in pitch over the course of a few seconds. Like a Hollywood wolf howl but higher-pitched.

Turn Me On—Electronic Callers

Battery-operated mechanical callers began as turntables playing 45-rpm records. The speaker was attached to the player or, more often, set several yards away using a long extension wire. The records played

Electronic callers provide thirty to sixty minutes of prey cries without huffing and puffing. You remain calm and alert. Great for slow-responding bobcats.

An electronic caller's remote speaker concentrates a predator's attention away from the shooter.

actual recorded animal-in-distress cries or an expert's mouth calls until the phonograph needle spun through the record's grooves. The hunter then had to reset the needle to restart the sequence. Obviously this rather delicate mechanism was subject to malfunction due to debris, dust, wind blowing the needle off track, rain, and snow. Cassette tape players improved things dramatically. One tape could play continuously for thirty minutes, and most of the moving parts were protected inside the box, though debris still got inside the tape opening and created problems. An operator could fairly easily change tapes to play different sounds, and since the tapes were compact and lightweight, it was easy to carry a number of them.

Today, tape players are still marketed, but machines that play CDs and MP3 digital files are also being sold. Some of these are quite compact and durable. A handy feature of some digital machines

is the ability to select tracks instantly without rewinding.

While dedicated electronic game callers are handy and ready to rumble, ordinary tape, CD, and MP3 players can be modified to handle the same job. All you need to do is add an external speaker and perhaps an amplifier to a portable player such as a Sony Walkman. Technicians at electronics stores like Radio Shack should be able to advise you on building such a rig.

I've only used electronic callers a few times, so I'm no judge of their effectiveness, but from all reports, they call in virtually the same numbers of predators as do good mouth-callers. Advantages include 1) the ability to play odd critter distress calls not easily imitated with a mouth call (various bird calls come to mind); 2) long, continuous playing—extremely useful when trying to call cats for thirty to sixty minutes. Cats, more than canines, seem to prefer a continuous call without interruption, and an electronic caller can give it to them; 3) infinite volume control. By merely turning a dial, you can drop an electronic call to a whisper; 4) minimum hand movement. Other than adjusting volume and flipping a tape every half-hour or so, you just sit and watch. Keep the machine between your legs and they'll block virtually all hand movement; 5) a remote sound source. This may be the absolute best reason to hire a machine to do your calling. Stick the speaker fifty to seventy-five feet away, and incoming clients will not be focused on you. Place the speaker next to a decoy for ultimate realism.

Because machines can malfunction, batteries die, and tapes break always carry a backup mouth call or two.

Time and Weather Wait for No Man: The Best Conditions and Times for Calling

Whether or not you call in predators depends on weather. Call during a downpour all you want, but you're unlikely to entice any visitors. Blizzards, extreme heat, and big winds will also ruin your chances. Ah, but light breezes, fog, low pressure, high pressure, and something as simple as cloud cover can make or break your day.

Chances are Your Chances are Pretty Good

New callers usually wonder just what the odds of calling a critter are. Some seem to think they're poor, having heard of hunters who've tried calling for an entire season without luck. The answer depends on what you're calling, where you're calling, and how you approach the site and set up to cover it. Don't fret about the sound of the call itself. Location is the key.

If you're working coyotes in high-density areas like parts of Texas, Oklahoma, Arizona, and Kansas and play your cards right, you should average one response for every four or five setups. You could easily call a dozen stands in a row and see nothing, but the next day you might be swarmed at every stand. One morning last February in Texas, we called at six places and pulled coyotes from five of them. Saw six at one stand, killed two at another. It balances out.

For some reason, probably frequent human disturbance, eastern coyotes are more reluctant to chase down every whisper of bunny-in-distress. A realistic average for good callers who know their territory might be one taker in ten tries.

Odds for bobcats are much lower simply because they don't live in the densities coyotes do, nor do they come as far and as aggressively to calls. However, if you set up in known bobcat territory, you should expect a response eventually.

Gray fox generally come eagerly if you call within a few hundred yards of them. Red fox can be equally aggressive if they aren't harried by coyotes. Raccoons are not good candidates for calling in most places. Lions and bears are real trophies. You'll need to prospect long and hard to find just the right location and conditions to entice one of these into range.

Foggy Philosophy

My favorite calling weather is calm fog. I don't know what it is—the increased sense of security perhaps—that fires up predators on quiet, foggy days, but fire up they do, charging the call with enthusiasm. My favorite foggy-morning call-down happened late one November when my partner Tom and I awoke in our pickup camper on the broken grasslands of western Kansas. While Tom heated water for breakfast, I stepped out to water the landscape, whereupon I discovered two things: thick fog and the frantic cries of a cottontail bidding farewell to this cruel world. I was supposed to go deer hunting, but changed my mind. "Let's call the Hell Zone pasture," I suggested. This was a huge flat on which we regularly saw coyotes hunting but couldn't call because there was no place to hide the truck or sneak within range. In the gray soup, we simply drove to the fence, walked out a few hundred yards, and plunked our buns in grass no taller than our left big toes.

"Good a place as any?"

"Yeah." We sat side by side. I covered the southwest, Tom the southeast. We ignored the north, because that's where the truck was. That's also where the first coyote came from—a huge, dark dog that announced its arrival with heavy footfalls drumming the prairie. When they sounded as if they were about to run up my back, I spun on my butt. El Coyote's eyes just about popped past his nose. Rather than waste time turning around, he kicked in the afterburner and veered right, leaning like Lance Armstrong on a hard corner in the Tour de France. I swung through the air, slapped the trigger, and won the yellow jersey in that little race. As I came out of recoil, I caught sight of a pale-colored bitch turning back into the wall of fog. She disappeared before I could get the cross hairs on her. Both coyotes had come from the direction of the truck. I love fog.

Calling in fog–even ice fog–can be pure magic. You can sit in big, open fields and pastures impossible to approach on clear days. They'll never suspect you out there.

Tom quickly cranked out a series of yipes and wounded coyote cries, waited a few minutes, and started up another wounded-rabbit series. This was too much for a little bitch that must have been dying of curiosity. She came sneaking up a fence line from the south, pausing and peering until Tom got a clear sight picture and dropped her at thirty yards. I stepped fifteen paces to the old dog I'd laid out with a neck shot. It weighed thirty-five pounds, the heaviest coyote I'd ever taken.

Before the fog lifted at mid-morning, we had three more coyotes to skin. Have I mentioned I love calling in fog?

If you find yourself in atmospheric soup, use the opportunity to call sites you can't normally approach without being seen. You may be pleasantly surprised. Even coyotes and fox that are slightly call-wary may fall for a distress cry if it comes from an area in which they've never been spooked before. Follow weather reports so you can plan where to hunt if fog seems likely.

Cloudy Outcomes

I have no firm statistics, but personal recollection tells me that cloudy days have produced more coyotes than clear days. A North Dakota Game and Fish Department survey of some three thousand predator callers confirms my suspicions. Respondents claimed they tolled in more coyotes in cloudy weather than bright. Red fox didn't seem to care a whit whether clouds or sunshine ruled the day. They responded equally. No information was available on bobcat response.

What should you do with this information? I wouldn't let either blue or gray skies keep me home, but given the option, I might head for coyote country on gray days, fox habitat on clear days.

Clouds blanketed Kansas on the most productive coyote hunt of my life. Again, I was out with my good buddy Tom Berger, and we could do no wrong. Sit, call, shoot. Sit, call, shoot. We brought in thirteen animals and killed seven. We'd have tallied more, but my rifle was shooting high and I whistled 55-grain slugs over four coyotes. I clipped a big puff of hair off the last one, and that's when I recognized my problem.

I suppose coyotes feel a bit more secure in the dim light that filters through clouds. It's almost as if the entire day is an extended dawn and protracted dusk. Certainly they are harder to see then, blending into grass and brush. They shine like beacons when struck by morning and evening sun. When backlit, they stand out as nearly black semi-silhouettes.

Perhaps hunters are merely seeing more coyotes on clear days and the actual response rate is no different. Either way, cloudy or clear, I'm going hunting.

Don't be a Blowhard

Wind is the mother of all weather curses. The roar of moving air mutes your calls, disguises their direction, and prevents you from hearing howls or approaching feet. Buffeting gusts ruin your aim, blow bullets off course and discourage predators from even getting up. Wind snaps and rattles clothing and gives you away. When the wind blows over fifteen miles per hour, I often stay home or switch to duck hunting. Sometimes, however, you're committed to a hunt, wind or no wind. Your best option then is to search for quiet habitats such as canyons and forested valleys. In flat country, try working the lee sides of long, wide shelterbelts or at least rolling country. I once called half a day in a big wind without ringing up any customers. Then I drove to some sand hills. With all those dips and holes and hollows, I figured the hills might hide a coyote that could hear me. At my first setup, a coyote popped out of a plum thicket less than one hundred yards downwind. I don't think I'd blown more than two notes before it appeared. It must have been lying just to the side of my scent trail.

Sometimes wind in one place means calm in another. I awoke in Dodge City one November to feel the house shaking. Went out anyway. Sixty miles south the wind was sliding along at an unbelievable ten miles per hour. Practically dead calm for Kansas. I brought in five dogs that day.

Let it Snow, Let it Snow

Conventional wisdom holds that one of the most productive calling times is the day after a blizzard. Makes sense. Having been confined for a day or two, predators are hungry and itching to

A good dump of snow buries prey and makes predators hungry and eager to answer your dinner bell.

discovered that it had been curled up behind a little nest of cattails out of the north wind. Doubly encouraging was a second fresh fox trail that had run out of my view along the line of trees. It was late December, so they were probably paired. For the next three mornings I sneaked within two hundred yards of that shelterbelt and called. Nothing. But always fresh tracks in the area. The third morning, after my calling again failed, I quietly walked toward the trees. It was my last day to hunt the area, so spooking my clients wouldn't matter. And spook them I did. Or at least one. The snowy expanse was empty one second, illuminated by a fiery, furry comet the next. Fortunately, that comet made the mistake of interrupting its outgoing trajectory for a quick look back. A 52-grain satellite from my .22-250 made sure it would never make that mistake again.

I suspect that one of the reasons I haven't called many predators in snow is that their ranks have been thinned and the survivors educated by the time snow falls. Early fall critters are much more gullible than late-season veterans. One of these years I'm going to have to skip deer, duck, and bird hunting in order to take advantage of an early snowstorm. First snow of the year—now that should be good!

Under Pressure

If a falling barometer can shut down the bass bite, why not the predator bite? Well, it just might. That North Dakota survey revealed that red fox respond to calling better during a rising or falling barometer than a steady one. Coyotes, however, liked what they heard better during a steady barometer. This is precious little evidence on which to base a hunt, but while you're out giving it the old Yankee try, why not keep track of atmospheric pressure. In time you might discover some firm correlations that can guide you on future hunts. If you're limited to a few hunts per season and can choose which day to take them, choosing a good

travel. The only problem with that theory is that it's never worked for me. My least productive days have been those following snowstorms. Well, guess what? That North Dakota survey mentioned above revealed that coyote responses rated lower in deep snow, so maybe I'm not imagining things. Interestingly, fox responses were higher with deep snow, but you couldn't prove that by my experiences.

A few years ago I walked a South Dakota shelterbelt bordering a natural wetland and jumped a fox. This pleased me, because I hadn't seen a fox in that locale in years. During the 1970s, it had been crawling with the little red devils. Then coyotes moved in. Well, after seeing that fox run off (and missing it with the .22 rimfire I was carrying for potting cottontails), I had to check its trail. I barometer day would be wise. On the other hand, if you're limited to hunting specific days of the week, to heck with pressure, cloud cover, and all the rest. A bad day in the outdoors is better than a good day cleaning the garage.

Time is on Your Side

I don't need surveys and studies to figure this one out. The best time to call is dawn to mid-morning. The second best is dusk. This correlates with high activity times for all predators and minimal activity times for air. Usually. Once the sun rises and begins heating the ground, wind kicks up. Near sunset, it'll often settle down again. So get your licks in early. The only better time would be at night, but that entails either a full moon and snow or spotlights. Where legal, spotlight predator hunting can be quite productive, but it's never been my thing. Watching those dogs and cats come in is more than half the fun for me.

To maximize your effectiveness during prime calling hours, depart early enough to be on site for your first call when it's light enough to see critters

Head for sheltering woods when wind rages and snow blows. Predators, which lay up in the calmer cover, might hear your calls and investigate.

approaching. Go to your most productive areas and hit them fast and hard. Try to plan a route that will take you to a series of calling spots that are close together. The more places you call, the more coyotes you'll toll. If you're working bobcats or red fox, you'll have to stay longer on each site, so pick your best. Gray fox usually respond as quickly as coyotes but don't come as far. It's possible to call cover pockets a few hundred yards apart and get responses in each. Gray fox tend to be fairly concentrated in good habitat, so it should be possible to work several setups within a mile or two.

As your morning progresses, be alert for changing winds. A north zephyr at dawn can switch to a south breeze after sunrise. Choose your stands accordingly.

Midday is traditionally siesta time for predators, but even the sleepiest can be talked into a lunch break. The trick is to get close enough. Lazy critters appreciate a free meal, but walking half a mile to claim it means it's not so free anymore. My buddies and I have enjoyed amazing action at all times of day. A few times we've even gotten more responses at midday than in the early morning. You just can't predict what your quarry is going to do from day to day. The best approach is to keep trying. At the least, you'll learn something.

Cold, especially following a heat spell, can make predators active all day. As mentioned above, so can clouds and a changing barometer. Don't forget midday calling simply because you think it won't work. If you feel like hunting, hunt. If you feel like napping,

Dawn and dusk are prime calling time.

nap. Over time you'll establish a hunting style that works for you.

Season's Greetings

Early fall is consistently the most productive calling season. Following annual brood rearing, populations are at their peak, and young animals are inexperienced and gullible. Once deer and bird hunters begin combing the fields, disturbed predators become more wary. Their routines are interrupted, their refuges invaded, and their senses alerted by shouts, whistles, odors, and shots. More than a few get shot at and killed, too. As fall moves toward winter, other callers go afield, educating the carnivores they don't shoot. By December, most predators are veterans.

Hunting early in the season seems the most logical, but it has a flip side: Pelts aren't prime. Why pick green tomatoes? Why serve a wine before its time? If fur prices are in the cellar, or you're taking predators to alleviate a depredation problem, prime pelts mean little. But when coyote hides fetch fifteen dollars and up, it seems stupid to waste them. Four or five coyotes a day will cover most of your expenses. How many skiers or golfers get that kind of deal?

I personally begin predator hunting in early October in the high Rockies, late October on the northern Plains, and mid-November at the latitude of central Kansas. I don't hit south Texas until late winter. On large private ranches where I know hunting pressure is carefully limited, I'll wait until pelts are fully prime before beginning to hunt. Let me tell you, seeing full-grown, fully-furred coyotes and bobcats racing to your calls in December is the ultimate predator-hunting thrill. Admiring their pelts stretched and dried and ready for the market is pure satisfaction.

Once pair bonding and mating begin, particularly among coyotes, calling can again get hot, but you have to speak their language. Barks, howls, and meows are the magic words. You want a dog to think you're making off with his vixen— or at least invading his territory. Bobcats and lions will respond to caterwauling. If you've ever heard a couple of male house cats engaged in a shouting match over a sweet young thing, you'll know what to say in the bobcat thickets. Yowser bowser—do they make a racket— long, drawn out yeows and rayows and similar angry and anguished permutations of meow. I'll confess I've never employed these to fool a bobcat in the wild, but I tried them on someone's pet free-roaming bobcat once and he bounced right over with hair standing. And when I was a kid on the farm, I regularly called curious tom and female barn cats by imitating their calls.

Here Kitty Kitty Lion

I sincerely believe these calls can work on lions, too, based on a Mexican adventure I had two years ago. I was hunting Coues whitetails in Sonora as a guest of Leica Optics and Rifles, Inc. Outfitter Rick Martin of Jemez, New Mexico, sent us into rugged, isolated, oak/grass/brush mountains with experienced local guides who spoke of cougars in abundance. They weren't kidding. We found tracks regularly, and our third afternoon, while walking a ridge above a deep, wide mountain basin, we heard what sounded like an overgrown house cat pulling whiskers out of its face. My guide and I immediately began looking

for the source of the new calls, knowing that it was a cougar. My instinct was to imitate the calls, but when I indicated this by pointing to the predator call around my neck (I spoke Spanish as well as my guide spoke English), my guide shook his head "no" emphatically. Yet neither of us could see the cat, despite its continuing calls. Again I pointed to my call. No. We glassed. Finally, my guide pointed excitedly. "Coogar! Coogar!"

"Where?" There followed a Keystone Cops pantomime of pointing and leaning and drawing word pictures until I remembered agua (water), meaning a stock pond in the valley below. Agua. I pointed left of the pond. No, señor. Right of agua. No. Downstream from agua. Si. Si. Si. I scoured the

Open-country coyotes usually respond quickly. Stay longer for fox and bobcat.

oakstudded valley bottom with my binoculars and still failed to see the cat. Then my brain kicked in, and I handed my sharp-eyed guide the Leica spotting scope on its tripod. Get the cat in the scope. He quickly did that, I peeked, saw a lion that was way, way farther down the valley than I'd been looking, and again pointed to my call. "I want to call the cat, imitate its calls. Meow. Meow."

"No no no. Tiro. Tiro!" Shoot, shoot. So, reluctantly and regretfully, I put the cross hairs a foot or two over the lion's head—it was walking left to right at some ridiculous distance—and fired. My custom Rifles, Inc., bolt action, chambered for .257 Weatherby, consistently spit three 100-grain Spire Point Weatherby factory loads inside a half-inch at one hundred yards, and that accuracy seemed to carry. I came out of recoil and got the lion back in the scope just in time to see it dart forward as a white rock the size of a softball rolled off the hill and nearly bounced onto its rump. Although there was no sign of a hit, we hiked down just to be sure. The distance was in the vicinity of seven hundred yards. Hindsight is 20/20, but man, I wish I'd defied my guide and called to that mountain lion. The manner in which he (it was a huge, red, pumpkin-headed male) was singing the blues convinced me he was trolling for a hot date.

Romantic Rendezvous—or Turf War?

Coyotes, because they are so vocal, are the easiest predators to talk-in during late winter mating rites. Find the territory of a mated pair,

slip in undetected, and blow a dominant male howl or two. This is the classic howl, fairly low in pitch and drawn out for as many as ten seconds with a smooth slide down the scale near the end. No preliminary barks or yipes are necessary. Just that commanding howl. Then sit and watch. In fall, this call will frighten more coyotes than it attracts. None of the teenagers on the block want to mess with a big dog. But by January and February, every surviving male thinks he's a big dog and should respond with bravado, running in stifflegged, with hair erect, maybe even growling and barking. This is no polite social visit, but a mission to run you out of town. Be prepared to defend yourself. You can usually stop hard-charging coyotes with a loud bark, but sometimes this only encourages them.

If you're doing control work for a rancher in summer, puppy yipes and family greeting calls work well. Adults are quite protective of their young in this season, so if they hear what they think is a pup in trouble, they'll charge right in. A coyote pup in trouble sounds just like a domestic puppy with its foot caught in a fence. You can mimic it with an open reed rabbit call or diaphragm elk or turkey call. Electronic callers play elaborate recordings of pups in distress.

Storms, winds, phases of the moon. A confusing variety of conditions over which we have no control clearly impact calling success. Some we can work around, some we can work to our advantage, but some we just have to tolerate.

Part 4
Small Game Hunting

Introduction

JAY CASSELL

Many of us first learned to hunt by going after squirrels with a .22, then graduated up to rabbits, then eventually moved on to deer and bigger quarry. But let me tell you, if you want to just have a fun-filled, action-packed afternoon, it's tough to beat small game hunting. A few years ago I hunted for squirrels in the Mississippi Delta with a couple of friends and a dog handler who had two feist dogs. Just watching those dogs work the woods, watching the treetops, going nuts whenever they spotted a gray squirrel lying low on a branch, well, that was worth the price of admission alone. And by the end of the day, we had taken enough squirrels to put together quite the barbecue.

On another hunt – this time in Alabama – I had the pleasure of hunting over a pack of well-trained beagles. When those dogs got wind of a rabbit, rooted him out from a brushpile, and took off in hot pursuit, look out! The action was fast and furious, the dogs were just fanatics about the whole thing, and by the end of the day, we again had enough of our quarry to put together a meal for five of us.

Whether you're just starting out hunting, or perhaps looking for another type of hunting than deer or big game, small game is guaranteed to please. The following pages include tips for both rabbits and squirrels. Try them out – you won't regret it!

— J. C.

Rabbit Hunting

Seeking the Quarry

Why a chapter on searching out cottontails? Well, anyone with a little effort can go out and roust a few cottontails and have a fairly successful day. But, how about consistently getting up rabbits and taking them in unknown territory or in bad weather conditions?

Since my dad didn't hunt, I began hunting by myself or with friends from the neighborhood. None of us knew much about it; we just went out, stomped around, and once in awhile killed a few bunnies. At the time, I wish I would have had someone to offer a little advice; hence this chapter on seeking out cottontails. You've probably heard the old saying, "Only ten percent of the lake holds ninety percent of the fish." This is also appropriate when referring to rabbit hunting. About ten percent of a given area holds ninety percent of the rabbits in that area. Why this anomaly occurs is anyone's guess. You would expect it to be tied directly to the type of cover hunted, but I've seen identical cover hold all kinds of rabbits on one side of a hill, yet not hold any on the other.

Of course, early in the season, rabbits are spread out and can be found just about anywhere, but later, as cover dwindles and rabbits receive some hunting pressure, they back off these thin fringe areas and become more difficult to locate. Large weed fields that held rabbits early on become nothing more than dry wastelands, and nothing more than a waste of time for the hunter and his pack. Here in the northern states, where cold and snow become a factor in late-season rabbit hunting, successful hunters pay close attention to food sources available to the cottontail, as well as to heavy cover nearby. This sounds simple enough, but you'd be surprised how many hunters take little notice of why they found a cottontail in a particular spot.

A friend and I were having a disappointing day hunting cottontails one warm November day. It had been extremely dry for weeks, and we just couldn't locate anything. Then the solution hit me in the face. I came over a steep rise hot and sweating, and just the sight of water, and the cool refreshing breeze from a lake in the next valley, made me feel better.

"That's it!" I told my buddy. "There have to be rabbits around that water, where it is cool and wet."And there were. The dogs ran several and we shot most of them standing on the edge of the lake. In this case the rabbits needed something; it wasn't food, but it was something just as important. It should have been obvious, but it just never occurred to us. It does now, and we've since used this experience to our advantage many times.

Since I am fairly well known around my area as an avid rabbit hunter, I'm often asked to take people out on their first rabbit hunt. In some cases they really only want to use my dogs, but that is another story. I'm not sure I enjoy these hunts very much, as I spend most of my time worrying about whether I, or one of my dogs, am going to be accidentally shot, but it does give me a chance to observe fellows who know almost nothing about the sport.

The first thing a novice rabbit hunter should do is tie a 20-pound lead weight around his leg. It's comical sometimes. We enter a heavy thicket side by side and pretty soon we can't see each other. The dogs jump a rabbit, I yell for my new hunting companion, and he's six acres away already through the thicket and standing in an open field! I burst out laughing, and it puts a damper on the whole day.

Seriously, the first thing a hunter must do if he wants to consistently find bunnies is to slow down. And I mean slow down! A rabbit has very few defenses: one is to run, another is to sit still, and this he does extremely well until you simply walk by him. I witnessed a great example of this just a few weeks ago. A couple of friends and I were hunting an area and the dogs had a rabbit up. During the run, three other guys entered the thicket and came our way. I dispatched the rabbit that the dogs were running, and our party decided to head back to the truck for lunch. We passed by the other three hunters who were quickly walking Army-style out through the brush. Although we covered the same ground they had just walked through, we jumped three more rabbits before we reached the road!

A rabbit is small, almost tiny in comparison to his surroundings. He can hide in unbelievably small amounts of cover. If you can hide a softball in it, a cottontail can hide there. That means a hunter needs to look over every single piece of brush, check out every fallen treetop, and kick every stump and bush in sight. Forget patterns. Have no set routine or speed. Zigzag through the area, stop frequently, and kick everything in sight. This haphazard style will make your quarry very nervous, and he is not likely to sit still for it.

While you're stumbling around looking for this hidden softball, your dogs should also be doing something, hopefully hunting. This gives them time to thoroughly work over the area. Don't expect the dogs to find every rabbit, because they won't, and on many hunts I roust far more than the dogs. Remember

you're a team, they do their part when they're needed, but don't expect them to do it all. Yes, I expect them to roust some game and I'm displeased with them (and I let them know it) when I find a rabbit in a clump of brush they've already checked out, but they make up for it many times over. As with yourself, don't rush the dogs. Let them work. On some days I may hunt a ten-acre thicket for several hours, where others would walk through it in 15 minutes.

OK, let's go on a simulated hunt. It is several weeks into the season, a lot of brush is mashed and mangled, and it is a cold 20°F. You've got one partner with you and at least two frisky beagles. If you're lucky, the beagles will find you a rabbit or two, but as I mentioned before, I don't expect them to do everything. The dogs certainly can't look around and judge like I can standing six feet out of the brush. So what do you look for?

Start out by gazing around the entire area and noting areas that are, or at least appear to be, unusually thick, areas that have few if any hunter paths beaten through them. Also hunt the edges along open fields so long as they haven't been smashed and beaten into the ground. The rabbits will use these fields to feed at night, and some will be sitting just off the field about ten to twenty yards in any cover available. When hunting the really thick stuff, make straight entries into the brush while encouraging your dogs to follow you and stick close. Keep penetrating these tangles, getting in as far as you can, then backing out. Find another spot, penetrate again, then back out. In time, you will jump a bunny, or your dogs will pick up the scent and roust him for you. Your partner should stay on the outside in more open terrain, watching for bunnies that may slip out undetected. Take turns and both of you will get some shooting, and hopefully the dogs will get some action by running rabbits that escaped the heavy cover. If hunting alone, you still have to penetrate the brush, but you'll have to rely more on the dogs for your shooting once the cottontail is up and running.

While you're checking out these likely spots, also keep on the lookout for fallen trees. These are probably the most productive areas, as rabbits love to take refuge in the tops of trees, especially after they've been down at least one growing season, and grass and weeds have encased some of the branches. Find a place where someone has been cutting trees for firewood and you'll find cottontails under the tops. Go out of your way to check out these treetops, as it will be worth it. Stay away from places where a bulldozer was used to clear trees and brush; there may be some cottontails there, but the piles will be so tight, and there will be so many holes to hide in, that a hunter can spend a whole day in there and have very little to show for it.

Of course, any veteran cottontail hunter knows that rabbits love ground-growing vines. Rip-shins, multiflora rose, dewberries, and a host of other vines are used by the cottontail for food and cover. His favorite in our part of the world is honeysuckle, in which he sits and eats. It is one of his favorite foods. I have killed so many cottontails from patches of honeysuckle vines that I never leave the woods without checking out every single one I can find- they're that productive.

We're assuming here that you've never hunted this particular area before, and these are the places I would begin my search for cottontails. Sooner or later you'll encounter some, but keep in mind that some areas are simply better for cottontails than others. Since I believe it doesn't take much to feed a cottontail, and they'll eat just about anything, some other factor must be keeping their numbers down in many places. This almost has to be predators, including the winged variety. Domesticated dogs and house cats kill cottontails by the thousands, and I believe that the common house cat is as great a threat to the rabbit population as any wild predator. This type of pressure also turns cottontails into

strictly nocturnal animals, making hunting them nearly impossible. In this situation, the hunter should consider hunting the very first hours after daylight, and the last couple hours before dark. Some cottontails will be up and around at this time of the day, and the hunter may be surprised at his success in areas he thought were devoid of rabbits.

Once you've hunted an area, the search for cottontails becomes a little easier, and each time through you gain more and more knowledge of the habitat. In places where I have hunted for years, I know exactly where I'm likely to find bunnies. In these same areas are places where I have yet to find a cottontail, and I avoid them. It saves time, plus wear and tear on the dogs and on me.

As you become familiar with a spot, mentally mark each location where cottontails were rousted, particularly their escape paths should they get away. More than likely you will encounter the rabbit or another in this same place next time, and nine times out of ten he'll run the same way.

Catching Them Sitting

When you begin to consistently catch rabbits "sitting," you are probably turning into a very good rabbit hunter. This means you're starting to get tuned in to the whole hunting experience and that you're really paying attention. I know some pretty fair rabbit hunters who have never found one single rabbit sitting, and this amazes me. It tells me a lot about how serious they are about rabbit hunting.

Rabbits are not hard to spot sitting, and with a little practice it's easy. To illustrate this, I have included a picture of one "dug in" somewhere. So how can I find rabbits sitting? First off, I expect to find rabbits sitting. That simply means I know every rabbit will not bolt at the sound of my approach, so I can expect to see some hiding if I look around carefully. Remember, the rabbit has only a couple of defenses: run, or sit still. In some cases, he will sit still.

When looking for these sitters, you've got to look at the brush much more intensely. Don't just gaze out through the brush. Look at each bush, each individual weed, and each small sapling. Don't just look at a small grove of trees; look at each individual tree, studying the base carefully. Expect to see a cottontail dug in at the base of every tree, and I guarantee you will begin to see them.

For years, I heard hunters talk about looking for the rabbit's eyeball and how this gives him away when he is sitting. I guess sometimes it does, but it has rarely worked for me. Remember we said the entire rabbit is barely the size of a soft-ball, especially when curled up in a form, so how big do you think his eyeball is? When you can't find an entire rabbit

Hunters talk about looking for the rabbit's eyeball and how this gives him away when he is sitting. When you can't seem to find an entire rabbit sitting, it will do little good to go around looking for eyeballs! The rabbit's ball-like shape and the distinguishing fur texture will stand out better for someone searching out cottontails. It just takes a little practice and getting "tuned in" to spotting them.

sitting, it will do little good to go around looking for eyeballs! Instead, concentrate on seeing a rabbit. Look especially for a clump of rabbit fur, and you'll soon discover that the rabbits' round ball-like shape and the distinguishing fur texture stand out better than you ever imagined. The fur will seem reddish brown, sleek, and shiny, especially if the sun is shining on it. Almost every cottontail has some white on him, and a few white hairs mixed in on his back. These tiny white streaks combined with the familiar texture of brown rabbit fur will betray the bunny's hiding place. Pay attention, and you'll be spotting sitting rabbits in no time.

Sometimes weather conditions, rabbits' seasonal habits, the time of day, the type of brush you're hunting in, and other variables can make rabbits seem as if they're an endangered species. They're not. They're still there, but sometimes you have to work a lot harder to find them. Those who can still manage to get a few up and running in unfamiliar terrain, or in bad weather, are the hunters I enjoy hunting with. In most cases, these hunters have been able to learn something from almost every rabbit hunt. They can spot the ten percent of the area where most of the rabbits will be hiding, and they find their share of sitters.

In rabbit hunting, the game doesn't begin until the rabbit is found. That's why they call it hunting. Pay attention. Be aware of your surroundings at all times, and ask, "Why was that rabbit sitting there?" In searching out cottontails, there's no big secret to it; it's still a lot of hard work. Pay attention! (Did you notice that's the third time I've said that? Or was it the fourth?) If you're really paying attention, finding cottontails should get a little easier each time out.

Why They Circle and Why They Hole Up

Why a rabbit circles, and why he holes up are topics that have been the bases for much discussion and many arguments between rabbit hunters and beagle owners for what seems like eternity. Each topic could be expanded into a chapter, or even an entire book of its own. I don't intend to spend a lot of valuable space and time on either subject, or expect to settle the argument here, as it is impossible to know what's in a rabbit's mind when he suddenly decides to turn the corner, or just as quickly goes to ground. Rabbits circle-that's a fact. They also hole up.

I am convinced, however, that under certain circumstances a rabbit's actions can be fairly predictable. My theories and thoughts concerning both of these inherited bunny traits are derived from spending thousands of hours hunting and studying them. The answer to why a rabbit circles is simpler and easier to understand than why a rabbit holes up, so we'll discuss that trait first. Keep in mind that although I am mainly talking about cottontails, hares and other species also exhibit the same behavior for the same reasons. Although the hare or swamp rabbit may have a larger home territory, he still returns or circles much like a cottontail, it just takes him a little longer.

The Circle Pattern

I may have already given away the answer to why a rabbit circles, and it won't be a surprise to most experienced rabbit hunters. The cottontail and most all his cousins return roughly to the area where they were kicked up because they simply do not wish to leave their home territory.

In articles I have written for various outdoor magazines, I have explained the "circle theory" many times. In my first video on cottontail rabbit hunting, I also went into much detail about it, including showing a cottontail's precise path across a hillside. The key to understanding why a rabbit behaves this way is tied directly to his home territory.

As a child your territory was perhaps the backyard. As you grew it expanded to maybe the neighbor's next door, and finally the entire neighborhood. In this environment (your territory)

you felt safe and secure. Only if chased by the neighborhood bully would you dare be pushed out of your familiar turf. It is the same with a rabbit. Each rabbit has his own particular territory that he calls home. This territory is sometimes clearly marked by some natural boundary–a creek, an old fenceline, or maybe just the edge of an open field. The rabbit has probably spent his entire life inside this territory, and is extremely reluctant to leave it.

When the rabbit reaches one of these imaginary boundaries, even pushed by dogs, he simply turns and runs the edge of his territory, or turns completely around and slips by the dogs. As the dogs continue to push the little critter, he will eventually end up pretty close to where he was first located.

That brings us to another point that should not be overlooked. Many people believe that well-trained

Brian Salley has found that this large tree marking an old fence line and property boundary is also the edge of a rabbit "territory." Reading the terrain and knowing where the cottontail might show up can be a big advantage when hunting.

dogs actually make the rabbit circle, but this isn't the case. Although we wish we could train dogs to circle the bunny, they have nothing to do with the circle pattern. A good trailing hound simply follows the scent trail no matter where it goes. If he does his job right, and the rabbit begins to circle, he (Old Rover) will end up back at the same place as well.

Of course, there are exceptions to every rule, and once in awhile you will encounter a rabbit that takes off straight away and never looks back. These are just that: exceptions. And even the exceptions can be explained sometimes, especially running rabbits in March. The hunter has encountered a buck rabbit that spent the night wandering around in search of receptive does. When the bunny is rousted in the morning he heads straight back to his home territory. In general, however, most rabbits will make a conscious effort to stick to the area they are most familiar with—and thus they develop circle patterns.

The term "circle" is a little misleading in terms of rabbit hunting. In most cases the rabbit arcs or runs a pattern much like the shape of a balloon on a string, or a large oval. Let's say you've just jumped a rabbit at the end of the string. A normal rabbit run will find the rabbit running straight up the string for some distance. As he begins to pull away from the dogs, he slows down and begins to "arc" and run the circumference of the balloon. When he reaches the imaginary string again, he will turn and often come back down the same trail he went up. This is typical, and I have seen this pattern hundreds of times. It is conceivable that the rabbit does this by smell, and it is a way of keeping his bearings inside his territory. It could also be a way of distracting the dogs, but this is unlikely; in most cases, the rabbit is simply using his nose to backtrack his own footsteps, thus keeping him inside his territory.

When hunting cottontails, I do not nail myself down to the exact spot where the bunny was rousted. If I encounter a situation such as the one just mentioned, I will follow the dogs "up the string"

for a little way until I find a good open place for a stand. In areas where I hunt, staying put in heavy brush will net you very few cottontails. They may circle back to within a few feet of where they were sitting, but you'll never get a shot at them.

Also, on some runs or chases, the rabbit pursued by the dogs will soon set up a pattern and pass through certain openings or around certain obstacles several times. This is because during his weeks and months of living in this particular area, the rabbit has marked these boundaries with scent from a gland under his chin. While in the field for reasons other than rabbit hunting, you may have witnessed this behavior of rabbits rubbing their chins on sticks and small trees. Again, if you are out to kill the rabbit, it pays to be a little flexible. If I notice the rabbit starting to run a pattern around these scent markers or obstacles, I quickly move to one of these points. If he has passed through an opening at least twice, I'm there when he attempts it the third time.

So, in most cases, rabbits circle to avoid being pushed out of their neighborhood or territory. And it is a good thing they do, or most of us would kill very few cottontails, and our dogs would be of little use to us. It is apparent, however, that cottontails will adapt and do anything to survive. In areas where they have been pressured by dogs and hunted extensively, their circle patterns have become less pronounced. On the other hand, in the mountainous areas around my home, I find far fewer cottontails, but since most have never been run by dogs before, they stick to their home turf much better, run much truer patterns, and are therefore easier to bag.

Why They Hole Up

Understanding why a rabbit goes into a hole while he is being pursued should be relatively easy, but it isn't. The primary reason that was stated just a few minutes ago is obvious: the rabbit wants to survive. Then why have you seen rabbits pass scores of holes, then suddenly decide to enter one? Well, to understand the rabbits' logic we would have to think like he does, and sort of get inside his head. That is almost impossible, but we can rely on the knowledge at hand, the experience of many hunts, and the actions of hundreds of rabbits. Also, a rabbit may pass several holes and not enter them for the most obvious reason: there is another creature already down there, in some cases a predator that will surely eat him! Remember that the cottontail is not stupid. He lives every minute of his life in the woods. He has a good nose and knows exactly what's hiding in that otherwise great-looking burrow. In a case such as this he'll pass and take his chances with the beagles pursuing somewhere behind him. (Incidentally, rabbits do not dig their own burrows, but use the holes of other creatures.)

Again, I have written about my theories concerning "why they hole up" in many publications over the years, but my opinions have changed little. Keep in mind that you may have formulated some of the same opinions but never realized it, nor stopped to think about it.

Every single rabbit hunt is different, but after awhile a definite pattern to the rabbits' general behavior is noted. A good rabbit hunter learns to evaluate all these different behavior patterns and each situation and files them away to be used later. Sometime, maybe months later, he may say, "Hey, I know what that rabbit will do," and then he goes ahead and does exactly what you predicted. In a sense you have gotten inside the rabbit's head and begun to think ahead of him. Many times it is no accident that we are standing in the exact spot where the rabbit crosses an opening. All of us have done this one time or another, but many of us fail to learn anything from it. But every time a rabbit enters a hole we should learn something from it and at least come up with a reasonable explanation as to why Mr. Cottontail decided to duck out of the picture. We may not be right each time, but remembering the incident, and filing away the information, will make us better rabbit hunters. Following, in order of importance, are the main reasons why rabbits hole up.

Weather

Without a doubt, any change in the weather has a major effect on the cottontails' actions. I'm sure most of us have been on hunts where practically every bunny kicked up went straight to a hole. In many cases, the weather change was obvious, and this situation is common when a storm is moving into the area. We do not know for sure why the rabbit holes up, but it probably goes back to the survival extinct. Again, put yourself in the rabbit's position. Dogs are pursuing him, the air pressure is dropping, and a storm is coming. I would surmise that the rabbit realizes he is in some danger here and, coupled with a storm moving in on him, he does not want to be pushed anywhere he feels uncomfortable. He retreats underground. Always remember that the rabbit is not the most intelligent animal on earth, but he has been blessed with a very strong sense of instinctive reasoning. These instincts have allowed him to survive for a long time when everything on earth is out to eat him.

More subtle changes in the weather can also cause the cottontail to become subterranean. Cottontails do not like to be pushed when it is very warm or extremely cold. A 75° or 80°F fall day will find most cottontails scurrying for holes once kicked up. The reason is obvious when you're wearing a winter fur coat. Related to this is that fact that fewer rabbits will be kicked up in warm weather because flies and other insects and pests drive them underground.

It is also difficult to jump many rabbits in very cold, 0°F weather, and an awful lot of these are likely to hole quickly. The reason is much the same as if a storm were moving in. The rabbit does not trust the weather or the conditions and wants to stick close to home.

Weather, beyond any other reason, is what forces the bunny to ground. In extreme cases I've seen every run end at the entrance of a ground hog hole. These hunts net few rabbits, and the dogs are loaded up and returned to their pens quickly.

The Wounded Rabbit

I can't remember a single rabbit that was wounded by the hunter or the dogs that did not attempt to get to some kind of hole. This is surely one time when a rabbit, after passing all kinds of holes, quickly slips into one. And they always seem to know where every hole is! When the rabbit is wounded, his survival instinct takes over again. He knows he is in big trouble and with dogs and the hunter closing in on him, he'll enter any hole, regardless of whether there is another animal in

Bad or drastic changes in the weather are the single most important reason why a rabbit holes when being chased. Here Brain Salley shows a nice New York cottontail to Ralphie as a snowstorm moves in.

there or not. The rabbit only goes down the hole a short distance in this situation, however. In fact, it is often possible to reach in with a gloved hand and pull him out. This saves the rabbit from being wasted or eaten by the predator.

On a recent hunt, we jumped a big cottontail and he gave the dogs a good chase for ten or fifteen minutes through some fairly open woods. All of a sudden one of my friends cut loose with his double, and yelled, "He's coming down your way, Dave!" Well, the rabbit never showed up, so I walked up and told Jason to walk in where he had shot and look around. As he did this, I saw the rabbit sneak out toward a long fallen tree. Jason fired again and the rabbit disappeared into a hole at the stump end of the tree. Jason believed he hadn't hit the rabbit, but I knew better. There was no reason for him to squeeze into the hole, except for the fact that he was injured in some way.

On a hunt just two days earlier, I rolled two cottontails only to have both escape to holes barely 50 yards away. In each case the dogs and I would have recovered the cottontail if we had had just a few more seconds, but each rabbit knew his territory extremely well and knew the location of every tunnel.

It is rare for me to wound a cottontail, and it may happen only a few times in an entire season. Unfortunately, in the case above, it happened twice in one day. It hammered home the fact that a wounded rabbit, without exception, is going to a hole. If I hit one, or if I only think I hit him, I take up the trail myself and try to stay as close as possible, meanwhile trying to get the dogs there to help me. I have recovered a lot of rabbits this way. If he's wounded, the cottontail is headed for the closest available burrow, and you can bet your new shotgun on it.

No Choice

In some cases the rabbit seems to feel he has no choice but to escape whatever is pursuing him by going underground. In most cases this happens in small woodlots or places where the rabbit has few options. I have noticed that this behavior takes place much more frequently when the rabbit is jumped by the hunter and not the dogs, or the hunter or hunters are talking and making noise. This may sound strange, but rabbits seem to instinctively know that humans are to be feared much more than hounds. If the rabbit does not know the hunter is in the area, he will sometimes institute his normal escape maneuvers and circle the woodlot. But if he knows humans are close by, and dogs are pursuing him, he will often hole up. Sometimes, when I enter a likely looking patch of cottontail habitat, I keep quiet and let the dogs do the work. If the cottontail doesn't know a person is there, the hunter has the advantage and the bunny is less likely to hole up.

Too Much Pressure

Actually this is just another variation of the 'no choice' scenario, but occurs mostly when too many dogs are run in a small area. Dogs are competitive, we all know that. Each wants to be the first to pick up the scent at a check, be the first in line, and so on. This creates a lot of pressure on the rabbit, as dogs become separated, the general pack starts to break down, and hounds flood the woodlot. Too much pressure should not be confused with "dog speed," which is not what we are talking about here. Actually I've also seen rabbits hole up from too much pressure from too many hunters. A rabbit has good ears, he knows when four hunters and a couple of dogs are descending upon him, and he has only an acre or so of good brush in front of him. What would you do? The rabbit quickly decides he had better find a hole, and in most cases he does.

There are many variations on both of these themes of no choice and pressure. Many times the hunter can help the situation by being quiet, running fewer dogs, sometimes hunting with fewer friends, and other things I've mentioned. Of course, it all depends on how serious you want to get about hunting cottontails. Some take the sport more seriously than others, and some are more concerned about just hunting with friends than killing the cottontail, but if you want fewer runs to end with the dogs' noses in a chuckhole, there are a few things you can do about it.

Availability of Holes

There are some areas around my home that I don't even bother hunting anymore. In one place, an overgrown pasture that runs along a railroad bed, cottontail hunting is virtually impossible. There are plenty of cottontails there, but the railroad bed is an easy place for ground hogs to burrow and they have honeycombed the entire bank, as well as the pasture nearby. With so many escape holes, cottontails in the area have learned it is an easy trick to elude any pursuer. You simply cannot hunt there. Other places are almost as bad. The spot where I mentioned wounding two rabbits in a single day is an old overgrown strip mine. Such old mines also get honeycombed by all kind of burrow makers and sometimes offer incredibly tough hunting. The mines offer good hunting only under ideal weather conditions.

On the other hand, rabbit hunting can be extremely easy in cleared areas and places where the ground is hard and rocky. There are fewer ground hogs and creatures that make holes in the earth in these areas and hence fewer places for rabbits to take refuge. There is a large pine thicket in the mountains where I occasionally run my dogs. Over the years, I have walked every inch of the thicket and can count on one hand the holes I have found there. Consequently the pine thicket offers a great place for run-backs and is easy on the dogs. I don't kill a lot of bunnies there, but I have had some spectacular chases. Swampy areas also provide good hunting because there are very few dry holes there. The availability of holes in the area does have a bearing on the rabbit's decision to use them.

Dog Speed

There are at least six distinct reasons why rabbits hole up, and I believe dog speed is the least important. I've heard it a million times in the past, and still hear the phrase today, "That dog's too fast. He pushes all the rabbits in the holes!" I don't believe it. I used to, but not anymore.

For the first 16 years or so that I hunted cottontails, I held a full-time job. Free time for hunting was at a premium. I was also a little younger and always in a hurry. I had little use for slow dogs and their "bark every footprint" mentality. I wanted to kill cottontails, and in a hurry, so I got the fastest dogs I could find. Things have slowed down some, but I still like those speedy dogs. What hasn't changed is the fact that just as many rabbits go in holes today as they did then. I've hunted with slow dogs, fast dogs, and everything in between. It doesn't

Rabbits go to holes for many reasons. Dog speed and pressure, especially from a single dog, is probably one of the least important reasons why a rabbit suddenly decides to call a halt to the chase. Weather, terrain, and running conditions have a greater influence on a rabbit than the speed of the hound pursuing it.

seem to matter to the rabbit what he is being chased by, but it does to the hunter waiting at the other end. If Mr. Cottontail decides he's going to go in the ground today, he goes; if he wants to run all day, then that's what he does; but dog speed alone has little to do with it. I'll admit that occasionally some hounds will pressure a bunny hard enough to force an underground retreat, but usually weather or some other factor helps the bunny decide to go down a woodchuck hole.

I have often said that no dog could ever be too fast for me, and I still hold that belief to some extent. I never worry about the dog's speed pushing rabbits underground; in fact, the only negative thing about a fast dog is that he overruns the checks and loses the trail. So if you have any dogs that are just too fast, give me a call I can probably use them!

When I began hunting rabbits, it wasn't for any particular reason other than the thrill of the chase and the killing of cottontails. I make no apologies for the fact that I enjoy the entire aspect of it, including the killing. When I'm training a dog or just out exercising him, I have no desire to end the rabbit's life, but when I'm cottontail hunting I want to kill the cottontail, it's just that simple. If it weren't, I'd take up golf or field trialing. In all forms of hunting, the most successful hunters are those who know the most about the quarry they are chasing. Learning why a rabbit circles, or why he holes up, will help you become a better cottontail hunter. It's as simple as that.

Making Sense of Scents

Did you ever wonder how the dogs could come across a fresh rabbit track and tear off at full speed in the right direction? Sure you have, and if you've hunted rabbits for more than a couple days, you've no doubt marveled at this peculiar beagle trait. It's obvious we can't ask the dogs, and the most popular solution to this mystery is simply the scent is stronger in the direction the rabbit is going. Well,

that makes sense, but since we can't ask the dogs, I think this particular talent will always be somewhat of a mystery.

Tons of material have been written in these pages about the beagles' conformation, his breeding, running speed, etc., but without a fairly good nose, the beagles' worth as a hunting hound is pretty much zero. There are a few that seem to sneak by while trailing behind some other dog, but most of the time, a beagle without the minimal nasal gear is quickly destroyed.

I read somewhere that a dog's nose can process information (in the form of smells and scents) about a million times better than we humans can. Again, we can't ask the dogs, but if you've ever watched a good dog trail a rabbit over solid, frozen ground or across a hard-topped road, you would have to admit they have some smeller on them!

There are a hundred factors that determine good, or bad scenting conditions, and I won't even begin to try to cover them all here. Experienced beaglers know that terrain, temperature, barometric pressure, type of cover; time of day, wind conditions, and all kinds of other things can affect how well our dogs can run a rabbit. In fact, I write this on a day when I know the rabbits are holed up and scent conditions are so tough, it is simply easier to rest the dogs, wait for a change. It is 11 degrees below zero, and the wind is whipping about 15 miles per hour! Not ideal hunting conditions for me or a beagle!

After many years of hunting, I am still unsure of the ideal scenting conditions. Sometimes when you think conditions are right, no dog is "locked on" like you hoped they would be. If I have my choice, I like to hunt after several days of cold, frosty weather, and with a spotty, melting snowpack. This does two things. First, it assures some rabbits will be sitting out after a few days underground. Second, with the damp ground and melting snow, I know scent will be clinging pretty well to the ground, and the snow will be stuck down enough so the dogs will not suck in up their nostrils. If the snowpack is melting and spotty, as I've described, it's going to allow the dogs to speed up and keep pressure on the rabbit when they hit open ground. To kill rabbits, the dog (any dog) has to keep pressure on the rabbit. A "dawdler" gives that rabbit time to twist, turn, and make the chase far more complicated than it should be. Throw in a nice, overcast day with the temperature about 38 degrees, and you have the ingredients for a perfect rabbit hunt.

I can't speak for those in the south, but our worse scenting days are those when the ground is frozen hard, or we have several inches of icy, grainy-type snow. On these days, the dogs just can't seem to lock onto any scent and we usually have poor hunting days. Some types of snow have much less effect on dogs, and I have noticed my dogs ran rather well during the late 1998-1999 season on three or four inches of soft, almost powdery snow. With mild winters becoming more and more common, this particular winter had snow on for much of the season. I should add here, however, that experience also has much to do with this. As a dog gets older and has been on a lot of hunts, he is more able to unravel the tiny bit of scent he may be getting up his nose. Older dogs with a few brains also learn to simply follow the tracks in the snow, picking up what scent he can, but also sighting the next set of tracks ahead of him. It may not be textbook, but it gets the job done. Generally, snow that will roll up (as in building a snowman!), makes pretty good hunting.

It's pretty clear that scent freezes. Consider deer, or fish frozen solid in the freezer; you don't smell anything when you sniff at the packages, but lay those packages out on the counter and by the end of the day the whole house smells. It's the same with scent or smell given off by game and in this case rabbits.

The bunny hops around during the early morning hours before dawn and as he goes along

it takes only a few minutes to freeze his footprints locking in his scent. The hound comes along a few hours later and as the sun begins to warm the ground the tracks begin to thaw releasing the scent. Sometimes when you are out hunting you can literally see the steam slowly coming up from frozen ground. This is the exact principle and the bunny scent is drifting up from the prints, and although we can't see it, the dog can smell it clearly. He may begin to cold–trail because he has no way of knowing the scent was laid down hours before.

Temperature does have a lot to do with scenting conditions and how the ground reacts to them. My friend Al, from Pine Bush, New York, is a life-long rabbit hunter and likes to get up at the crack of dawn. When I hunted with him, we were in the woods long before the morning thaw and conditions weren't very good for running. Since his winters are much more severe than ours in Pennsylvania, I suggested Al delay the hunt a little. Al has now told me, "We've been going out later in the morning, and doing very well in the afternoon . . . it's easier on the dogs, and it's been keeping us hunting. We'll sleep in a little later next time you come!"

A temperature above freezing, along with a lower barometric pressure is definitely going to make for better scenting conditions. There is a limit to this, however, and it should be no mystery that once the ground gets hard, dry, and baked, scenting is going to go the other way. Here in the north, it's easy to see smoke from wood burners "hanging" in the air and floating into valleys. These are better scenting days. Tough, clear, cold weather conditions make this same smoke go straight up and dissipate quickly. Rabbit scent will do the same thing.

Wind, terrain and lots of other factors also determine how well our beagles can run a rabbit. When I hunted with Zef Selca, in upstate New York, I was amazed to watch his dogs running "downwind" of the actual track. I had never seen this in a rabbit dog, and it took me a few minutes to figure it out.

At first, I thought these dogs can't even stay on the track, but quickly learned that to run the hare at the speed they did, it was the only way they could run him! The dogs simply galloped along in the ten inches of snow grabbing the scent about eight to ten feet downwind. It was something to see. I am sure this is nothing new to guys that run hares a lot.

Two years ago, we had so much snow we rarely ran on bare ground after Thanksgiving. My dogs did better than expected, and late in the season I also saw them running slightly downwind of the actual track. My hounds have always been only fair at best in the snow, but I think it was that "experience" factor again. They were run so much on snow; they adapted and struggled to find someway of keeping the chase going. It worked and we had one of our best seasons ever despite pitiful weather sometimes.

Good dogs will always find some way to adapt to the conditions and terrain. Most of us have seen a pack tearing it up through nice soft weeds, slow down in tough multi-flora rose, and go very slow over hard packed ground or up a dirt road. Sometimes all of these conditions can be found on a single run!

Here in western Pennsylvania where I live, we have some really varied conditions. Some of our hunts take place in and around old strip mines where the dogs may be called upon to start the rabbit in a corn field, press him across a few acres of heavy briars,

A dog can process smells and scents about a million times better than his human counterpart. Did you ever wonder how a dog can come across a fresh rabbit track and tear off in the right direction?

then scale a 30-foot vertical wall, and trail over loose shale rock. It's a crazy chase sometimes, and we hole and lose a lot of rabbits, but sometimes you have to be impressed when the dogs stick to it over all these varied scenting conditions until the rabbit is killed.

On some of these chases, it is not hard to see when the dogs are going well, and when they are having a tough time. Dogs seem to run a few different types of scent that the rabbit lays down. Most of the time the dogs are trailing "footprints" and other times they are running "body scent."

When my dogs are having a tough time running across open ground and I can see they are heading back to thicker brush, I know the chase is going to heat up once they get back to the cover. The rabbit simply leaves more scent as he brushes up against stuff, besides leaving good footprint scent. The dogs are able to get more scent, work less, and simply go faster.

Dogs will run body scent, footprint scent, or air scent or a combination of all depending on the air and ground conditions. The dog has one thing in mind . . . follow the rabbit, and in almost all cases

he'll use his nose to somehow get the job done. I have a couple good "jump dogs" in my pack, and they are useful, but it is the ones with the good noses that make for some spectacular rabbit chases. We all know that a dog that can dig around and produce a rabbit, and is equipped with a good enough nose to push that rascal around is a valuable dog to anyone.

Rabbits also put down a lot of scent, or little at all depending again on weather, and other conditions. I am sure most of us have seen how difficult it is for our dogs to run a young or very small rabbit. On the other hand with some large, buck rabbits it seems like the dogs can never lose them. Again, it's the amount of body odor the rabbit leaves either in prints, suspended in the air or, on bushes and things he makes contact with.

We have run hare in Michigan when the scent was so strong, I swear I could have run that rabbit! We make jokes about it sometimes, but if the conditions are right, and you come across a big smelly hare . . . a poodle could probably bring the thing around to the gun. The wrench in the whole scheme of things is when snow comes and changes everything. So, I would leave the poodle at home!

Before I wrap up this chapter, I would like to reiterate that weather and how it affects the ground conditions is certainly the greatest factor in how much scent the dog can recover and process, transferring this information into his own running style to keep the rabbit moving. I have what I feel are some very good dogs and we kill a lot of rabbits in front of them. But there are days when I would sell the whole bunch for $10! So don't blame the dog, sometimes he's doing the best he can, even though it might not satisfy us.

A good hunting hound should have one goal in mind, to press the quarry hard enough to overtake him. This means see the rabbit, fox, coyote, whatever, killed by the hunter or caught by him or his pack mates. You can disagree if you like, but that's what they were bred for, and a good dog still has this ancient instinct instilled in him. If he doesn't he will never be a great tracking hound.

To do all this that we ask of him, he has to have a good, working nose on him. Can you imagine the scents of pine needles, leaves, old 'possum tracks, swamp water, deer, weeds, flowers, our own aftershave, and hundreds of other smells he has to sift through to pick up that one distinguishable scent of a rabbit!? In the end, he is the only one that can make any sense out of all those scents!

Some rabbits live in brushy, thorny terrain where a dog may get thorns and briar spines in his feet.

Small-bore Muzzleloaders for Small Game

TOBY BRIDGES

Just twenty years ago, there were quite a few well-made, deadly-accurate small caliber frontloaded rifles available to the muzzleloading hunter who enjoyed potting a few squirrels, rabbits and other similar-size game as much as taking an annual whitetail or two. These were, for the most part, .32 and .36 caliber rifles that could be loaded with a light charge of fine black powder or Pyrodex to produce ballistics similar to a .22LR rimfire rifle. For just a few cents per round, the rifles provided a lot of shooting and hunting enjoyment.

Unfortunately, the number of squirrel hunters in this country has definitely been on the decline in recent years. Before the explosion of the whitetail populations just about everywhere this great animal is found, any woods-savvy hunter worth his salt hunted squirrels. Fall bushy-tails are a true test of a hunter's ability to slip undetected beneath a towering hickory or oak and tumble out a squirrel or two that may be feeding in the canopy above. To make the hunt even more challenging, a few would rely on a small-bore muzzleloader.

Today's hectic world often leaves us with too little time to traipse around in our favorite stands of hardwoods. When the muzzleloading hunter can steal time from a busy schedule to escape for a hunt, that time is now usually devoted to hunting more glamorous game, such as the white-tailed deer. Because of this obsession with hunting whitetails, we now enjoy the finest selection of top-quality muzzleloaded big-game rifles ever available.

However, since fewer and fewer of us can now find the extra time to chase squirrels, or other small game, the selection of muzzleloading small-bore small-game rifles has definitely dwindled.

Hunting small game like squirrels with a muzzleloaded rifle means a small bore—and accurate shot placement.

The Hopkins & Allen underhammer .36 caliber rifles, available from about 1963 on through the mid 1980s, could be loaded to be deadly accurate. With a light charge of powder and patched .350 ball, they were great for sniping at sunning cottontails.

Still, there are a few new-made modern reproduction .32 and .36 caliber rifles available that are ideal for sniping at a few squirrels or rabbits. And the hunter who makes the effort just might find one of the older "gems" that were available through the 1970s and 1980s. And in this chapter, we'll look at loading and shooting these pipsqueak-bored muzzleloaders, and how to tap their performance for small game.

Then…

Some of the superb reproduction small-bore muzzleloaders of the past include the .36 caliber Thompson/Center Arms half-stock "Seneca"; that same firm's short and fast-handling "Cherokee" in .32 or .36 caliber; Dixie Gun Works' .32 caliber

version of their long 40-inch barreled Tennessee Mountain Rifle; the unique "Mule Ear" percussion side-slapper Navy Arms offered in .32 and .36 caliber; and even the simple old Hopkins & Allen .36 caliber underhammer "Buggy Rifle." Some of these rifles were produced in fairly large numbers at one time, and the hunter who frequents gun shows and gun shops that deal in used guns may eventually come across one of them. Most out-of-production muzzleloaded reproduction rifles still have not reached real collector status, and one can often be picked up in excellent condition for a few hundred dollars.

Some of the current small-bore muzzleloading rifles available include the Italian-made "Blue Ridge Rifle" imported by Cabela's, and a pair of "Kentucky"- styled rifles that Dixie Gun Works also imports from the same Italian manufacturer—Pedersoli. The 39-inch barreled full-stock "Blue Ridge Rifle" is offered in a choice of .32 or .36 caliber, in flintlock or percussion ignition. Dixie's .32 caliber "Kentucky" rifle comes with a thirty-five and a half-inch barrel, and is also offered in either flint or percussion ignition. The small-game hunter looking for a slightly faster-handling rifle with a shorter barrel might find the .32 caliber Dixie "Scout Carbine" handier in the woods. This one likewise comes in choice of flintlock or percussion ignition.

The criterion for a great small-game muzzleloading rifle is pretty simple—a small-bore rifle that propels a light sphere of lead with a light powder charge. Unlike choosing the best-suited muzzleloaded rifle for hunting big game, which is one that will shoot accurately with lots of energy, the small-game hunter is actually looking for just the opposite. After all, the idea of hunting small game is to turn it into edible table fare! And this is generally best accomplished with a small caliber projectile that is delivered with just enough energy to cleanly harvest the squirrel, rabbit or whatever the target may be.

The long-barreled .32 caliber version of the Tennessee Mountain Rifle that was once available from Dixie Gun Works was a fine small-game muzzleloader.

At one time, quite a few shooters tried to promote the .45 caliber rifles as "do-it-all" muzzleloaders, capable of being loaded hot enough for deer or loaded down with light charges for shooting a few squirrels. Truth is, the .45 caliber is not a great choice for either use. Even with light 20- to 25-grain charges of FFFg or Pyrodex "P" behind a patched .440-inch ball, rifles of this bore-size are simply too destructive for small game, and unless the shooter is an excellent marksman and can pull off a "head shot" every time, not much is going to be left of the target for feeding the family.

Even the .40 caliber rifles are still way too destructive for havesting small game intended for the table. It has always been the rifles with .32 and .36 caliber bores that have been favored by experienced muzzleloading squirrel hunters. And with the loads required to tap the true accuracy of some small caliber frontloaders, even rifles in these two tiny bore-sizes can result in a great deal of meat loss.

So, which is best for shooting game this small—the .32 caliber or the .36 caliber? Let's take a look at some of the benefits and inherent problems associated with loading, shooting and hunting with each. Then you can make that decision for yourself.

Noted black-powder authority Mike Nesbitt and nice pair of cottontails headed for the stew pot, thanks to the accuracy of a good-looking custom small-bore muzzleloader.

First of all, small-bore muzzleloading rifles are known for being finicky. Simply put, the smaller the bore, the faster it tends to foul. In order to maintain pinpoint accuracy with either the .32 or .36 caliber, the small-game hunter will have to run a lightly dampened patch down the bore between each and every shot. Just the fouling left from one shot will cause the next to create higher pressures, and the slightest difference from one shot to the next is enough to move point of impact an inch or two at just twenty five yards.

When loading and shooting larger .50 and .54 caliber rifles, volume measured 90- or 100- or 110-grain charges of black powder, Pyrodex or Triple Seven can actually vary as much as one to five grains

The small-bore muzzleloading rifle and load that can best duplicate the ballistics of a .22 long rifle proves to be the best suited for hunting game as small as bushytails and cottontails.

from charge to charge. The difference really doesn't affect all that much where a heavy 178- to 230-grain ball hits. But when we're talking about loading and shooting a tiny ball that weighs just 45 to 65 grams, a powder charge that varies as little as one or two grains can mean the difference between a *clean hit* or a *clean miss* on targets as small as a bushytail and cottontail.

So when it comes to being "finicky," it's pretty safe to say that loading the smaller .32 caliber bores requires more attention and finesse than stoking the slightly larger .36 caliber rifles. The Smaller bore definitely fouls quicker, and the light 45-grain .310-inch round ball loaded into most .32 caliber rifles is more affected by slight variations in the powder charge than a 65-grain .350-inch ball shot out of a .36 caliber bore. But, what about the destructive nature of the slightly larger bore and projectile?

One of the most accurate percussion .36 caliber rifles I've ever shot and hunted with was the twenty-seven inch barreled T/C Seneca half-stock rifle. With its brass furniture and cap-box, it was also one of the nicest looking. Unfortunately, this rifle featured a relatively slow (for Such a small bore anyway) one-turn-in-forty eight inches rate of rifling twist. To get this rifle to deliver its best accuracy required stoking it up with at least thirty grains of FFFg black powder or Pyrodex "P" grade powder. The load would push the sixty-five-grain patched .350-inch ball from the muzzle at just over 1,700 f.p.s., with close to 500 f.p.e. Now, this is nearly one-and-a-half times the energy levels produced by the .22 Winchester Magnum Rimfire. A soft-lead ball that hits any small edible target with this much wallop isn't going to leave much for the frying pan! Even when the charge was reduced to twenty-five grains, the rifle still produced energy levels that were simply too destructive.

Small .32 and .36 caliber muzzleloader bores are easily fouled by even light charges of powder. To maintain accuracy and to keep the rifle capable of being loaded, it is necessary to run a damp patch through the barrel after every shot.

with the ballistics of standard velocity .22LR ammunition fired from a rifle barrel. Even if a shot from the Cherokee so loaded was off an inch or two, it still did not totally destroy edible portions of a bushytail.

While I do tend to favor the smaller .32 caliber bores for gathering up the makings for a good squirrel stew, I have to admit that I have taken more squirrels with my old long-barreled semi-custom percussion .36 caliber "Hatfield Squirrel Rifle" than any other small-bore rifle I have ever owned and shot. It features a lengthy thirty—nine inch barrel, and when I first got the rifle back in 1983, I found it to shoot wonderfully with a twenty-five grain charge of FFFg black powder and a .015-inch-thick patched .350-inch round ball. However, the combination of the powder charge and the lengthy bore means the load is getting that ball out of the muzzle at around 1,600 f.p.s., for about 375 f.p.e. If you hit a squirrel anywhere other than in the head, you'll be losing some fine eating.

My favorite muzzleloaded small-game rifle of all time has been the percussion T/C Cherokee in .32 caliber. This light little half-stock rifle was built with a short and fast handling twenty-four inch barrel that was rifled with a fast one-turn-in- thirty-inches rate of rifling twist. Thanks to the faster twist, the rifle still shot great with charges of FFFg as light as fifteen grains. With that much powder, the ball was pushed from the muzzle at around 1,100 f.p.s., generating just 120 f.p.e. And this is right on par

After a long snowy stretch, cottontails will often come out to sun themselves, offering the patient small-bore muzzleloader shooter an opportunity to collect some fine eating.

The author prepares to knock another bushytail from the branches above, using the short and light .32 caliber Thompson/Center Arms percussion "Cherokee." He feels this little rifle is one of the best small-game muzzleloaders ever offered.

For a couple of years, I played around with FFFg and Pyrodex "P," but just could not get either of those powders to shoot well out of this rifle with anything less than twenty five grains. Back then, I also did some flintlock shooting, and one day tried loading the .36 Hatfield rifle with just fifteen grains of the super-fine FFFFg priming powder for my flintlocks. Accuracy was excellent at twenty-five yards, and when I ran a couple of the tightly patched .350-inch balls across the chronograph, I found the load was doing just 990 f.p.s., which translates into 140 f.p.e.—or about the same as a high velocity .22 long rifle. Through the years, I have taken more than one thousand bushytails with that rifle and load.

The .32 and .36 caliber Italian imports now offered by Dixie Gun Works and Cabela's feature a one-turn-in-forty-eight-inches rate of rifling twist. Right out of the box, the guns are going to produce best accuracy with anywhere from twenty-five to thirty-five grains of FFFg black powder or Pyrodex "P" grade. Likewise, the energy levels generated will be higher than desired for taking most small game. Hodgdon's new FFFg Triple Seven is noticeably hotter than black powder of the same granulation. A lighter fifteen-or-so-grain charge of the new FFFg

propellant should tame down the velocities and energies to make these rifles better suited for busting a few bushytails.

In the race to have the most efficient, fastest-shooting and hardest-hitting muzzleloaded big-game rifle on the market, even when riflemakers do offer a muzzleloader with a bore small enough to use for small game, they seem to have forgotten that for this type of hunting, less is best. And when the rates of rifling twist are as slow as a turn-in-forty-eight inches and slower, it generally takes a hotter charge to make the rifles shoot accurately. I, for one, would like to see Thompson/Center Arms reintroduce the .32 and .36 caliber Cherokee percussion half-stock rifle—and keep the faster one-turn-in-thirty-inches rate of rifling twist—or see anyone else offer a similarly-styled rifle.

So, there are the basic choices—the more finicky and less destructive .32 caliber, or the less finicky and more destructive .36 caliber. While the current crop of small-bore muzzleloaders may seem less than "optimum" for hunting squirrels and other small critters, just about any of them can be loaded to perform well enough for most hunting situations. The hunter just has to learn to cope with the limitations of his or her choice.

Now, it's not unusual to ease in under a nut tree to discover four . . . five . . . six . . . or more squirrels gluttonously feeding in the limbs above. To take full advantage of these opportunities, it pays for the muzzleloading squirrel hunter to be organized. Since these small-bore frontloaders are finicky about powder charges, it's best to pack them pre-measured in small plastic tubes. Not only does this allow you to load the same exact amount of powder for each shot, it eliminates the time it takes to measure out a charge.

Carrying pre-patched round balls in a handy loading block can really speed up reloading as well. A loading block is nothing more than a half-inch or so thick piece of wood drilled through with a

Outdoor writer Gary Clancy with a fine winter-prime coyote harvested with the same MK-85 he used all through the deer season.

Small-bore .32 and .36 caliber rifles may be a little on the light side for coyotes. The author used one of the .40 caliber Dixie Gun Works "Cub" rifles to take this yodel dog that came in to the sounds of an electronic game call.

number of holes near the size of the rifle bore. Into each of these holes, the hunter can push a ball already wrapped in the proper patching. In use, the loading block is often carried on a lanyard of some sort, and when it's time to get another ball down the bore, it takes only a few second to center one of the pre-patched balls over the bore and shove it on into the barrel with a short starter. Then the projectile is pushed on down the bore with the ramrod. The use of pre-measured powder charges and a loading block with pre-patched balls can cut loading time in half.

The small diameter wooden ramrod that comes standard with just about any small-bore rifle is extremely fragile. It doesn't take much to snap it in half, and this is pretty common when trying to reload quickly to get a shot at another squirrel. For actual hunting, replace the wooden ramrod with one of the tough synthetic rods, such as those available through Mountain State Muzzleloading Supplies (Williamstown, West Virginia). Remember, one good morning of squirrel hunting often produces more action, and more reloading, than an entire season of hunting whitetails. And with

an unbreakable ramrod, you won't be forced out of the hunt.

Whether you're after a brace of bushytails that are feeding on hickory nuts or a limit of cottontails that are out sunning themselves after being holed up during a week-long snow storm, there is no more challenging way to do it than with a small-bore muzzleloading rifle. And, if you want to just hone your shooting and loading skills, all the action this hunting provides can have you more than ready for any upcoming big-game hunt.

Now...

Let's face it, since the in-line ignition rifles hit the market back in the 1980s, all of the interest has been in using these rifles to hunt deer and other big game. During the early 1990s, Knight Rifles did offer, for a very limited time, a .36 caliber version of the MK-85. Likewise, during the mid 1990s, Thompson/Center Arms offered an optional .32 caliber barrel for their System One "interchangeable barrel" in-line rifle. But other than those modernistic two, small-bore muzzleloaders have remained pretty well a traditional thing.

Quite a few modern in-line rifle owners very often use their rifles to take some varmints and predators, but since "eating" these targets is the last thing on their minds, no one seems to worry about meat loss. Consequently, most continue to use the same powder charges and bullets they use to hunt the big game for which they bought the rifle. The varmint or predator "targets of opportunity" simply allow the hunter to practice with the rifle and load under actual hunting conditions. If the intended target happens to be a valuable furbearer, such as a bobcat or fox, it's only a matter of finding a saboted bullet that won't expand and destroy the pelt.

Small Game Hunting

LAMAR UNDERWOOD

Squirrels

Staying Put on Your Stand

When you've selected a good spot to sit and wait for squirrels to show themselves, don't be in a hurry to walk over and pick up the first two or three you down—with shotgun or rifle. Mark them carefully and keep sitting tight and watch for another target to show.

The "Trunk-hugger" Squirrel

When a squirrel hugs the trunk, high in the tree and not moving, it usually is facing up the tree. By hugging the trunk yourself, you can outlast the squirrel into thinking the coast is clear. It will make a move, giving you a shot.

A Squirrel Hunt Can Make Your Day Great

Many hunters get so caught up in the pursuit of deer and "glamour" upland birds like grouse, quail, and pheasant that they forget the simple pleasures of a great day out squirrel hunting. Take a golden autumn day, a small pack with sandwiches and a thermos, a scope-sighted .22 rifle, and local knowledge of an area and you can walk for miles— that is, walk when you wish to. A lot of your day will be spent sitting quietly at the basses of trees, watching the canopy overhead. One caveat: You can't do this hunt when and where firearm deer hunting is in progress.

The Trophy Squirrel

The big, dark fox squirrel is not considered as good on the table as the smaller and more-plentiful gray, but many hunters find ways to enjoy them on the table. They also lend themselves to becoming a beautiful trophy mount. Famed Georgia outdoor writer, the late Charlie Elliott, keep a mounted fox squirrel that drew more comments from visitors than any of the trophy big game heads he had on his walls.

Important Deep-winter Hunting Tactic

The most important tactic to remember about deep-winter squirrel hunting (other than the places to find the squirrels!) is to hunt with your eyes scanning the trees far in the distance. You'll see your quarry at much longer distance in the winter. Once you've spotted a squirrel, make your quiet stalk and try to get into position for a shot with your .22.

Can You Keep Still?

Just as in deer hunting or in a duck blind, staying still—really still—pays off in squirrel hunting from a stand. Some hunters are just too fidgety.

Playing "Hide-and-Seek" with Squirrels

When a squirrel is on the opposite side of a tree, and keeps going around and around as you circle, trying to get a shot, try throwing something noisy over to the squirrel's side. A heavy fallen stick or something. You can often move him to your side this way.

Squirrel for Supper

Don't sell the squirrel short as table fare. I love them fried, in flour and hot fat. Tastes as good as sweet nuts to me. The hell with the Cholesterol Police!

Squirrel Recipe

Among the many ways of cooking squirrel meat add this to your recipes: Cook the squirrel with the same recipe you use for Buffalo Wings.

Those Wonderful Squirrel Dogs

They'll never have the glamour and appeal of labs and pointers and setters, but good squirrel dogs are worth their weight in gold. What kind are they? All kinds! Feists, curs, whatever. A good nose and desire to hunt are the credentials, and the best way to take advantage of them is to have your squirrel dog puppy hunt with an accomplished squirrel dog. The really good squirrel dogs hunt close to the gun and use their nose, eyes, and ears to find squirrels. Easing slowly through the squirrel woods with one of these dogs is a wonderful way to go hunting. In many areas, you'll have a bonus: You'll flush coveys of quail, and send rabbits bouncing away.

Crock Pot Squirrel

Frying your squirrel meat isn't the only way to enjoy it. Try cooking your squirrel meat in a crock pot with sauerkraut. About six hours should be right to have the meat tender and falling off the bone.

Cutting-edge Squirrel Loads

In a comprehensive article called "Cutting-Edge Squirrel Loads" on the *Game & Fish* magazine Web site, www.gameandfishmag.com, writer Mike Bleech gives today's squirrel hunters the latest details on shotgun and rifle loads that do the best job in bringing home a limit of bushytails. Bleech examines the important differences in magnum versus standard shot loads, with emphasis on the all-important velocity considerations. He brings the .22 hunter right up to date with test-firing comparing the venerable .22 Long Rifle against the scorching hot newcomer the .17 Hornady Magnum Rimfire and the newer, but slower, Hornady .17M2. The .17M2 gets Bleech's nod as the best way to go because, as he says, "The light crack of the .17M2 is barely noticed by the squirrels."

Deep-winter Squirrel Hunting

Even when Old Man Winter has a solid, white grip on the woodlands, good squirrel hunting with a scoped .22 rifle can be found. Local knowledge of harvest crop fields like corn, and groves of oaks, hickories, walnuts, pecans, and other foods are essential. Look for the woodland areas with squirrel nests adjacent to areas with food.

Listen Up!

Are the trees too thick to see the squirrels? Perhaps you can hear them "cutting," opening nuts and letting shells drop to the forest floor. You won't

be the first to find and bag a squirrel which has tipped off his position in such a way.

Call Squirrels with Fifty Cents

A cheap and easy way to call to a squirrel in order to get it to give away its location is to strike two quarters together, edge to edge. Done right, this will sound enough like a squirrel barking to get the real thing to bark back.

Mast Crop Low, yet Hunting Great

When the crop of acorns on the white and red oaks is low, look for squirrels to be concentrated in areas where some trees have bucked the trend. Whatever good spots for acorns are available, the squirrels will find them—particularly the white oak acorns. White-tailed deer do the same.

The Pecan Tree Bonanza

The shady, fruit-bearing groves of pecan trees planted throughout the southeast and on into Texas are squirrel magnets. Forested edges of the groves will hold good populations of squirrels. With the landowners' permissions, you'll be set for good hunting.

Shoot Squirrels with Erasers

When hunting squirrels with a recurve or longbow you can keep your arrows from sticking into tree limbs too high for you to retrieve them by using a rubber pencil eraser in place of a metal field point. You can buy these erasers at any art supply shop. Look for the large, arrowhead-shaped kind that slips over the top of a pencil's normal eraser.

The Nests are Off-limits!

Sometimes when squirrel hunting, the thought may cross your mind that firing at one of the lofty nests you're seeing might be a good idea—get the squirrels out and moving. It's a bad idea, and illegal. Your shot into the nest could kill or wound a squirrel you could never retrieve. Don't do it!

You Need the Optics for Just Plain Fun

People have been bagging limits of squirrels for a long, long time without using optics, but that doesn't mean you should. By taking along binoculars and using a scoped rifle, the fun you'll have during the time you spend in the squirrel woods will be greatly magnified (pun intended!).

Midwinter Fox Squirrels

When there's a crust of snow on the ground and the temperatures have dipped into the 20s, Don't expect fox squirrels to be on the prowl in early morning. You'll find the best hunting Doesn't get started until around ten o'clock. Although like gray squirrels, fox squirrels like acorns and other nuts, in midwinter they will always head for corn if it's nearby. Fox squirrels prefer belts of trees near croplands instead of dense forests, more so than grays.

Wait until Later to Pick up Your Squirrels

"Don't pick up a downed squirrel immediately. Moving from a stand to recover downed game will end the hunting temporarily." —Bob Gilsvik, *The Guide to Good Cheap Hunting*, Stein & Day, 1978.

Try More-aggressive Squirrel Tactics

Successful squirrel hunters today have come as many calls and calling techniques as duck hunters. Consider these two examples: On the Hunter Specialties Web site, www.hunterspec.com, pro Alex Rutledge shows how to use the H.S. Squirrel Call to do the "Barking," "Chattering," and the "Young Squirrel Distress Call." All are effective, but "Barking" is one known to set off a chorus of squirrel answering calls and tip off their locations in woods you're hunting for the first time. Outdoor writer John E. Phillips, in his "John's Journal," on his Night Hawk Publications site, www.nighthawkpublications.com, also likes "Barking," along with some other calls he describes in his article, "How to Hunt Squirrels Aggressively."

Rabbits

The Hunter's "Rabbit's Foot" Luck

Rabbits are the Number One game for hunters everywhere—and with good reason. They breed like crazy, which is great since few of them survive the predators they face for even one year. There are still plenty to go around for hunters, who prize delicious rabbit on their tables and like the way rabbits can be hunted with a variety of methods and a minimum of expensive gear.

After the Shot

Even when you think you've missed a rabbit, check around in a circular area of about 20 feet. When wounded, a rabbit may run a little distance and then stop and sit tight.

Watching for the Rabbit You've Jumped

When your dog is running a rabbit, don't keep your eyes locked on the path the dog is taking. Keep looking in other directions, and you may spot rabbits that are trying to slip past all the action, or others that are just sitting tight waiting for you to go past.

Top Tips for Late Season Rabbits

Late season is a great time to hunt rabbits because deer hunters have ceased activities. Hunting can be tough, though. According to writer Ed Harp on the Indiana state site of *Game & Fish* magazine, www.indianagameandfish.com, the most important four considerations in finding late season rabbits are to find the clover, find blackberry and raspberry bushes, find the pine sapling stands where rabbits have chewed the bark in a circle, and find deer hunter food plots. Harp has six more top tips to help you get your limit in the article, "Ten Tips for Taking Winter Rabbits."

Use a Stick to Beat the Brush

When hunting rabbits without a dog, use a brush stick, like a wading staff, to beat on the edges of thick cover where they may be hiding.

Cold and Windy Mornings

On a windy morning, after a very cold night, look for rabbits to be on the sunny and lee sides of ridges, forests, and brush rows.

Hunting the "Slabfoot" Rabbits

He's not called the "Varying Hare" for nothing, possessing two coats of fur to wear as needed. With the fall sun starts riding lower and lower in the sky, the days becoming shorter and shorter, the Snowshoe rabbit starts putting on its white coat whether needed or not by snowfall. Even with nary a flake on the ground, the big hares begin to change color—a dangerous situation for them since they stand out in the forest so starkly. In Alaska, where I spent two teenage winters, Snowshoe rabbit hunting became a big part of my life. I loved hunting them and eating them.

Snowshoes in Winter: The Going Gets Tough

The hunting in the hills not far from Fairbanks, where we lived, was easy until the snows came, then became more difficult with each passing day. The Snowshoe is mostly a nocturnal animal. During the day the rabbits hole up under the endless spruces and don't move until after dark. Kicking them out is tough work without a dog. When we were lucky enough to get one bounding away through the snow, they were remarkably fast and hard to hit in their great leaps over the snow. Old "Slabfoot." I loved them.

The Snowshoes' Survival Plan

When winter grips the great North woods, the icy winds moaning through bare limbs without a scrap of vegetation, the snow piling on the endless spruce forests, the Snowshoe rabbit makes out just fine. Gone are the succulent plants of spring and summer, but the "Varying Hares" do just fine on a diet of willow, poplar, and other saplings of tender green bark. The Snowshoe has four big front teeth perfect for gnawing a bellyful of bark every night. Days are spent in cozy holes back under the spruces. No matter how cold, they make out just fine.

Tactic for Snowshoes: Leave the Feeding Grounds Behind

The area where you find the great crisscrossing webs of Snowshoe tracks may not be the best place to make your hunt. They were there last night feeding; now they're dead certain to be in the thickest cover of the nearest swamps. That's where you want to make your hunt, moving slowly past the beaver dams, humps of brush, fallen trees, and limbs—the places where Snowshoes spend their days, not their nights.

Your Best Rabbit "Scouts"

The best rabbit scout you can find will be the farmer who owns the land you hunt on. Next will be the deer hunters who've been working the area. Many of them aren't interested in rabbit hunting, but they will have seen the spots where rabbits thrive.

Part 5
Turkey Hunting

Introduction

JAY CASSELL

Turkey hunting, to me, is the most exciting type of hunting you can find. You get up at 4:15 in the morning, grab a quick breakfast, put on your camo hunting clothes, grab your 12-gauge and some No. 5 shells, and head out into the pre-dawn darkness. If you've roosted birds the night before, you head to that area, probably a copse of hemlocks where the birds are roosting. Then you set up and you wait – not too close to the roosting trees, not too far. Perhaps you set up a decoy. As the sun begins to brighten the horizon, there is stirring in the trees. Then the early morning silence is shattered by a booming gobble that echoes through the woods. Then another. In response, you tree call softly, just to let that gobbler know you're there. He gobbles some more, you call back softly. Now you hear wings flapping as a hen pitches out of the roost and down to the ground. Quickly you make a few barely audible yelps on your slate call, then you rustle some leaves, or maybe smack your hat against your leg, imitating a bird flapping its wings. More gobbles—and now another one opens up behind you. You call again, this time with a mouth call so you can remain still. You hear more birds hitting the ground. No more gobbles – he's on the ground. You see a fan open in the distance. You call again, he gobbles. He's coming!

And so goes a morning hunt. Will you get the bird? Will you move and scare him off? Will some hens take him away? Will your calling entice the gobbler to keep coming toward you, into shotgun range, or will you sound like a dying seagull at the moment of truth, and scare him away? The possibilities are truly endless.

I live for mornings like that. What's more, such mornings – any mornings – in the turkey woods are educational experiences. Every time you go out, you learn, and as the years go by, you'll become a better turkey hunter if you pay attention to what's going on around you.

*   *   *   *

While I'm at it, I should also suggest that readers consider joining the National Wild Turkey Federation. Founded in 1973 by Tom Rodgers, and dedicated to the conservation and research of the North American wild turkey, the NWTF enlisted the services of biologists and turkey hunters to build a body of science that would ultimately lead up to the largest wildlife trap-and-transfer program in the history of mankind, restoring a species that neared extinction in the early 20th century to more than 7 million wild turkeys throughout North America by the turn of the 21st century. The passion and perseverance of those pioneer supporters elevated the NWTF into one of the most successful upland conservation habitat and hunting rights organizations in the world. www.nwtf.org.

—J. C.

Myth of the Call-Shy Turkey

RAY EYE

Of all the subjects that turkey hunters argue about, nothing increases blood pressure like a debate over how much one should call and that calling somehow "creates" call-shy turkeys. Before we get into the subject of call-shy, I feel it important to tell you that this is not just a rant on my part. I'm not just crying in my milk or whining about how I'm mistreated in hunting camps.

Much of the call-shy information in this chapter will affect you as a turkey hunter. Every year across America, millions of working-man turkey hunters with limited hunting time will not kill a turkey simply because of this call-shy belief. As a professional cameraman, field producer, and guide for outdoor media, I'm faced with the call-shy myth pretty much everywhere I travel to hunt. After a late-night flight into a new state (always after a rough several hours' drive to camp), I'm up early the next morning, with little sleep, then transported to an area in complete darkness, and always someplace I've never seen in daylight before. It would seem I have enough of a challenge to kill a turkey on camera without this call-shy thing, but more times than not, the local guide warns me not to call to his turkeys because they are call-shy.

So, I share with you calling and hunting tactics that work for me that will in fact help you kill turkeys. I have learned them from years of battling this call-shy nonsense, against stubborn guides, outfitters, and local hunters who scorn my calling. Yet we have continued to kill turkeys consistently, regardless of call-shy beliefs. If you are a firm believer in call-shy, all I ask is that you read this chapter with an open mind, think about some of your past hunts, and consider that maybe if you'd used some of this information, it might have worked, especially on a hunt when you did not kill a turkey mainly because you did not call, held back your calling, or called very little.

So, it's time—let's dive in. Some of this might be painful to call-shy believers, but I assure you, it works for me. And for those of you who are new turkeys hunters without strong opinions already in place and who are open to learning from my experience, this information will turn you into a turkey killing machine.

All across the wild turkey's range, there are hunters who subscribe to the notion that you should call just barely enough to let the birds hear you—maybe once, maybe twice, perhaps three yelps every thirty minutes—and then sit back and allow that wily tom's patience to run out, at which point he might show up at the original source of the appropriately subdued calling.

To call more than that, the theory holds, is to poison the air with turkey noise pollution certain to ruin not only that day's hunt, but the prospects of other hunters unfortunate enough to enter that same territory for the rest of the season. "That fancy contest calling crap" is believed to create a negative reaction among turkeys that somehow become conditioned to avoid the sounds of their own kind.

As a professional cameraman, field producer, and guide for outdoor media, I'm faced with the call-shy myth almost everywhere I travel to hunt.

The turkeys are call-shy. As soon as you start calling, they run the other way.

But in reality, turkeys just do not turn into call-shy phantoms. If anything, they become people-shy. It is excessive human activity that shuts down gobblers, not calling, and this is something I learned many, many years ago. It amazes me that any hunter could actually believe wild turkeys can, in the span of a few weeks, or even a few years, learn to "know" it's a hunter making the sounds. They don't know we imitate them. They can't know this. They have no capacity to know this. Sorry, but turkeys do not know we humans are calling to them and are merely duplicating their language. Depending on who you talk to, the case is made that aversion to excited calling gets passed on to turkey eggs before they hatch. What is the bottom line on calling? Is it possible for humans to "educate" wild turkeys,

to cause them to stop gobbling, leave the area (or both), by calling excitedly on a box call? If you really believe this, think about what you're saying.

It just does not seem possible that a wild turkey vocalization, a hen yelp, something that is so very important to turkeys, could somehow create a callshy turkey. But because of this call-shy myth, many turkey hunters are programmed to hold back, or call softly. Many are afraid to call when in fact, if they would call, they could actually kill a turkey. It totally amazes me that hunters really believe that a sound, a vocalization from a distance, would scare a turkey, shut turkeys down.

But quite honestly, I think it's absurd to presume that wild turkeys could evolve—even learn by association—to shy away from the calling of their own kind, a vocalization, a sound, especially when it is essential to the perpetuation of the species to

Outdoor media camp hunters with their "call shy" turkeys.

respond to it, and their survival depends on it. Call-shy, or "caller-shy" as it was labeled many years ago, is nothing new and is something I have had to deal with my entire turkey hunting life. It wasn't as bad back in the old days—I just did what I had to do to call turkeys and took the heat from superstitious, call-shy-fearing local hunters.

So, now let's travel back in time and review a little call-shy history from days gone by, because believe it or not, call-shy is not just a modern-day myth. I know, here I go again, okay, I'm old, but back in my early Ozarks days, turkey hunters gathered at local check stations and restaurants, filling the air with both calling and hunting stories— talk of smart, elusive gobblers, tales cloaked in myth, tall tales of super-intelligent, mystical birds. For me,

these stories are all part of the allure and mystery of my early turkey hunting experiences. I remember a story told many times around our Ozarks campfire. At the old trapper's cabin on Buford Mountain, if someone were foolish enough to light a cabin lantern just before daylight, that "ole bronzeback" wouldn't gobble for a month.

Here's one told many times at the local turkey check-in station: "There is no man alive, near or far, that has a chance against the caller-shy 'Ghost Gobbler' of Clinton Ridge. One soft cluck from any hunter at daylight, and it's over; that mountain ghost will not gobble the rest of the season."

What about "ole long spur" of Dryfork Holler— now there's a challenge. That old gobbler outsmarted every man who ever toted a box call and chalk, and all it took was just one owl hoot at daylight, and he'd go silent the rest of the season. Heaven forbid if anyone ever tried to call in "ole broken toe," the King of Bell Mountain; one soft cluck and he'd be headed off into the next county.

This is one true call-shy story from the 1970s, down in the Ozark hills in the area called Dryfork Holler. After hunting there several days, I noticed turkey gobbling decreasing with every passing day. As the season progressed, especially on weekends when scores of hunters entered the same public-ground holler, gobblers would go silent. So I would pack it in and go somewhere else to find gobbling turkeys. Numerous hunters from the area blamed me for nongobbling turkeys in Dryfork Holler. It was said the turkeys were call-shy, that I and others called too much, too loud, and shut them all down. So I asked my dad if this was in any way possible.

My dad just laughed out loud and said, "Call-shy is just a turkey hunter's excuse. If a turkey doesn't come to his call, it's not the calling you or anyone else did to scare those turkeys into silence or move them away from that area for awhile; it is all of the noise and movement, it's the intense hunter activity in there every day.

"It has nothing to do with calling. It's all those people walking everywhere, running to a gobbling turkey, driving Jeeps everywhere, bumping turkeys, hunters skylighted, and all the head bobbing on a turkey's approach. Wait a couple days after all the city hunters leave the mountain and things settle down, then go back to Dryfork Holler and kill your gobbler."

A few years later, around 1973, I made my turkey camp on the main road through national forest land, with a friend who at the time was fairly new at turkey hunting. He usually hunted with a group of hunters west of Potosi, Missouri. This group and others they hunted with as well as others in the area all firmly believed every turkey hunting myth ever told. I invited another friend, an older,

seasoned hunter from southern Iron County, to join us for a morning of turkey hunting. After his early afternoon arrival in camp and a quick tour of our national forest hunting area, we settled in for a quiet campfire dinner. Not long after dinner, my friend asked if turkeys roosted anywhere close by, especially in the deep holler behind the camp. As I had not heard any turkeys while in camp, and not around camp at daylight, but miles away in a more remote, prescouted area, I really didn't know.

Tom grabbed his old, weather-worn box call and said, "Well, let's find out," as he walked away from our campfire and let her rip with deep, loud, raspy yelps. But before the echo of his call faded away in the distance, and before we had even had time to listen, my other guy in camp went crazy.

"What in the hell you think you're doing?" he yelled at Tom. "I have to hunt around here. What are you trying to do, shut all the turkeys down? Stop calling now!"

I couldn't believe a new hunter had the nerve to yell at a seasoned turkey hunter, someone who probably had killed more turkeys than this new guy had ever actually seen in the woods, someone known for his many years of killing turkeys consistently, not just for himself, but for many others as well. Tom, with a puzzled look on his face at first, shook his head with a big smile as he slowly slid his old call back inside his front pocket. He walked back to camp, loaded his bedroll and gear in his truck, and told me he was sorry, but he had to go—he would go somewhere else where his calling was not judged, and we would have to hunt together another time.

Today, as a hunting professional traveling across America, I find that the call-shy "movement" has grown to huge proportions, to the point of becoming a major roadblock for my many on-the-road turkey hunting adventures. My greatest call-shy challenge is always in Florida. Somehow the Osceola turkey is thought to be the king of call-shy, and Florida seems to be the callshy capital and the national call-shy headquarters.

"Our turkeys are different," some Osceola hunters and guides tell me. "You might get away with that aggressive calling where you come from. But it won't work here. Our turkeys don't like calling. But if you must, just a soft cluck. The only way to hunt our turkeys is to set up and wait for one to walk by going to or coming from the orange groves. Roosting doesn't work with our turkeys." My all-time favorite, though, is local guides sizing up any of us pros when we come to town, just like a Western gunfighter.

The first time I called turkeys in the Florida swamps was back in 1982; I have hunted in Florida many, many times since then, for outdoor media hunts, shooting outdoor TV shows, or just hunting with good friends. Now don't take this the wrong way—I love Florida, I love the people, all the many friends and family I have from all my many years of hunting, and of working seminars and trade shows in Florida. And I have experienced some great hunts without the interference of the call-shy myth, but they have been few and far between.

Here are just a few examples: guides will take my camera crew and me to the very setup where they (for whatever reason) didn't or couldn't call in a

Several years ago, on my arrival in New England I was greeted with "it's over; the turkeys are all call shy." But I really do not have time for this. I have to guide outdoor writers and complete TV shows, so I hunt like I always do and never hold back on my calling.

turkey (are you ready for this?), just to see if I can call the turkey, regardless of the real reasons why they didn't call him in. Many times after the first morning's hunt, because of my calling an outfitter has assigned me an area (which I call the "penalty box") with the least chance of me to "booger" their turkeys with my calling. More than once, outfitters have sent me into an area where "no one has killed a turkey in years," just to see if we can. I really do not have time for any of this—I have to get a TV show done, and I usually just pack up and leave.

But I have not always packed up on my own. I have been asked to leave ranches several times because of my hunting and calling style, even though we had completed a TV show with multiple on-camera kills. Now, I have to admit that sometimes it's my own fault. On a ranch with a huge outdoor media hunt, we were told the turkeys were call-shy and did not like calling. The game plan was to sit and wait for turkeys to walk by. Well, I did the first morning, but in so doing, I listened to turkeys on a roost in the distance. That afternoon I asked a ranch

hand about that area. Given the okay to go in there, I roosted turkeys that evening.

The next morning, I set up tight on the edge of a field, where four of us witnessed unbelievable roost calling, an in-your-face fly-down, fighting, strutting, and an awesome kill for the show. All this involved two of us calling nonstop, to make it happen. Back at the lodge, tired with travel and the callshy battle, as I was reviewing some of my footage for the outdoor writers, the outfitter just happened to walk into the room.

Just as soon as he saw the footage and heard our calling on the big screen, he said: "Boy, what in the world are you doing to my turkeys?"

And I said, "That would be killin' 'em, sir." Yep, that's when I was asked to leave.

My greatest challenge in completing a media hunt or outdoor TV show is not always the weather, time of year, or even the turkeys, oddly enough. It's usually the people I have to deal with. There is always some outfitter, guide, or even local hunter who becomes a stumbling block to complete my hunt because of a call-shy mentality. But more often than not, just after my arrival in a new place, immediately a call-shy warning is delivered by an "expert" guide with about three years of turkey hunting experience, who has never hunted outside his own county much less away from his home state. It's always the same about calling to "their" turkeys, "their turkeys are different," and "because it won't work here."

"You might be able to call like that where you come from," they say. "But if you call like that around here they won't gobble for a month." Hmm, how do they know that? Do they follow the turkey around for a month just to see if he gobbles?

On many tightly scheduled hunts, I only have three mornings to make it happen, and I am more than willing to listen to the outfitter or guide about his turkeys. They usually know where they roost, where they strut, and where they gobble, which is all

very important information, and quite honestly, no one knows the turkeys on their place any better than they do.

Once in the field, as soon as the call-shy thing comes up, I put my plan in place. First morning, I do whatever is asked with how they want me to hunt their place, all the while learning the turkeys' habits in that area. It is on the second day that I start my plan of attack. The last two days, I hunt, scout, roost, and call my way, and we have completed many more shows my way than their way and with a very high success rate, calling so-called "call-shy" turkeys, especially on the last day.

I also find it interesting because it's always that third day when the locals get upset, because they continue to believe my calling is scaring their turkeys. Even after we kill them. (The turkeys, that is.)

Now, I'm not claiming everywhere or everyone I hunt with is into this call-shy phenomenon. I've hunted with some really good outfitters who just tell me to have at it, and I have hunted with guides who turn me loose, and tell me to just do my thing.

But I also have to tell you that after thirty-some years of hunting in Western states, call-shy has never been something I had to deal with during any Western hunt. This includes Rios in Texas, Oklahoma, and Kansas, Merriam's in New Mexico, California, South Dakota, and Wyoming, and everywhere in between. Of all the hundreds of Western hunters, guides, and outfitters I've hunted with over the years, not one of them has ever heard the term call-shy. They don't even know what it is. So is it possible, just maybe, that this call shy thing only affects the Eastern turkey and the Florida Osceola turkey?

The truth is that it's the hunter's mind that creates more problems with killing turkeys than the turkeys actually do. Turkey hunters everywhere need to realize what a huge mind game turkey hunting really is. Something I talk about in my seminars is how during the heat of battle with a gobbler, the hunter is thinking the gobbler is outsmarting him. Hunters think the turkey has a PhD; they give turkeys human characteristics, and all the while the gobbler is out there just being a turkey.

If a hunter thinks a turkey is call-shy, he does not call as he should to kill the turkey. If, before a hunter begins to call, he thinks a turkey will not come to his call, the turkey will more than likely not come to his call. The mind games that so many hunters play actually prevent them from killing turkeys in many situations. A positive approach, confidence, determination, clear thinking, and a never-give-up attitude kills turkeys.

A great example of the turkey hunter mind game came during one of my media hunts in the late 1990s, in the second week of Missouri's spring gobbler season. With two-year-old gobbler numbers down, older gobblers were covered up with hens. There was plenty of breeding and strutting, but little gobbling. Hunters were frustrated with little response from the gobblers, and during this phase, many times when a hunter did get a tom to gobble to his call, hens would lead the gobbler away. With the first week's statewide kill total way down, hunters were preaching the gospel of call-shy. The season was off, something was wrong with the turkeys—this message was spreading like wildfire throughout Northern Missouri.

My media hunt was scheduled to start in the middle of the second week and run through the weekend. With outdoor writers flying in from all across the country and my professional guides from Arkansas arriving in a few hours, I really needed to find an area for them to hunt without a lot of pressure on the turkeys. A good friend who lives in the area located a 3,000-acre tract of rolling timber with a network of small fields, an awesome timbered river bottom, and an assortment of old crop fields. My professional guides driving from Arkansas were to meet one of my local guides in town as soon as they arrived and come straight to the new property to meet me, as we had little time with our media hunters arriving the next day. The good thing was that my Arkansas guides had already hunted four states and were seasoned guides and great turkey hunters—a very important element in having a successful hunt for my outdoor writers.

My friend, the ranch manager, and I drove around the property to scout and to learn the lay of the land, to see property boundary lines, and where he had seen gobblers strutting and heard gobbling.

Idaho gobbler taken by NWTF public relations director Brent Lawrence during a Western media hunt. "Call shy" with Western Guides and Outfitters has never been much of a problem. Photo by John Hafner

As I have done for many years, at each stop I cut and yelped to get an idea of turkey numbers and gobbler locations at around 10 a.m. However, the ranch manager was shaking his head in regard to my calling because these turkeys were so "call-shy," he said. Family members on the ranch had little success the first week of season with the call-shy turkeys and it was the worst season ever on this property.

But, as we stopped on an old dirt road on a big long ridge with multiple spur ridges and deep hollers, from what I'd seen I was excited about the chances of a great hunt. These beautiful rolling ridges are just not the usual type of terrain found in northeast Missouri. As I was walking to the back of the truck while digging out my calls, the manager warned me again about calling, and asked if was I sure I wanted to do this "calling thing" before my hunters arrived. During my very first series of cutting and yelping, two gobblers rifled back a reply, just as my guides pulled up to our truck. I asked the manager not to say anything about "call-shy," and after quick introductions, I told my Southern guides that maybe they should kill a turkey before the writers arrived, and get it out of their systems. Of course they were in disbelief that I would allow any hunting before the writers arrived, but I assured them it was okay. I cut again, and both gobblers down in the holler on a bench, and others somewhat closer, rattled again.

"So guys, why are you standing here?" I asked. "Don't you think you should kill those gobblers?" With wide eyes and in a mad rush to pull their guns from the truck, they were falling all over each other. Down the hill they scrambled, stopping only to call quickly, then keep moving. We heard them close the distance, then set up and cut again. Both turkeys were gobbling nonstop, and now sounded like they were in my guys' laps.

After two quick gunshots echoed down the valley, we heard a little flopping and cheering, then all was quiet. Let's see—this entire deal took around

five minutes from start to finish. The ranch manager seemed to be in shock or in disbelief as my guys topped the ridge, each carrying a big gobbler, and placed both birds in the back of the truck, as they thanked me over and over.

This is when I ask my guys: "What do they think you're doing? Why would you call like that to these turkeys? The season is off, something is wrong with the turkeys. Don't you know all these turkeys are call-shy? That actually the turkeys are call-shy all across north Missouri this season?"

"Nobody told us they were call-shy!" they both replied excitedly.

The moral of the story is that after a twelve-hour drive to get there, no time to talk to anyone, without a clue the season is supposed to be off or that turkeys throughout the area were supposedly call-shy, my guys didn't hold back with calling. They called just as they always do, and with great results.

If hunters believe turkeys are call-shy, they are very hesitant to call, and receive little response to very little soft calling—or no calling—when in fact they actually should be calling. This is the when talk of call-shy spreads like the plague. What it all comes down to is that "call-shy" is just part of the human mind game. It's not the turkeys themselves, but the state of mind of the hunters.

On the lighter side, I've had fun with this call-shy thing many times over the years. Back in the 1990s, while working a turkey media camp in southern Missouri along the Meramec River with some National Rifle Association leaders, talk of the turkeys being call-shy began shortly after my arrival. During the first evening, while our NRA hunters remained at the main lodge relaxing and consuming adult beverages, several of the local guides and I departed for a late evening of roosting. After separating to cover a larger area, the guides and I met right at dark on an old road overlooking a beautiful river bottom. As I walked up, they shushed me, and told to be very quiet because several gobblers had roosted a couple of hundred yards down the main ridge.

I hadn't heard them yet, so I told them I was going to owl hoot. That's when one of the guides grabbed me by the shirt and said: "Listen now, don't you hoot unless you sound just like an owl, or they'll know we're here!"

"So," I asked them, "who are 'they'?"

"The turkeys—they'll know we're here," one of the guides replied.

Shaking my head in disbelief, I said, "Okay, I'll do my best so they won't know we're here."

Several hoots later, and after only a couple of weak gobbles in return, and thinking out loud as I pulled out my mouth call, I said, "Let's warm 'em up a little with some cutting, and a fly-up cackle, and see if there are some other gobblers in this area, too."

This is when one of the guides grabbed me in a bear hug, while frantically reaching for my call case. "What in the world do you think you're doing? If you call, we'll never kill any of our turkeys. Not just tomorrow—but the rest of the week!"

"Okay, okay, I won't call. After all, we don't want them to know we're here," I said. "I'll call when I roost by myself. Sorry, but it works it's something I've done for thirty years. I get a better reaction with a turkey call than with hooting."

As they started walking back to their truck, shaking their heads in disbelief and disagreement, I quickly ran back to the edge of the road and blew out a pig squeal, a mooing cow, and a chicken. Suddenly both turkeys sounded off in multiple gobbles, and three others farther down the ridge joined in. Grinning, I said, "You see, I didn't turkey call to them . . . so we should be all right in the morning."

Can you believe that they actually spewed rocks against my rental car with their truck tires as they sped off in a huff?

During the next morning's hunt, with a different local guide and my two NRA hunters in tow, the call-shy deal came up once again. After our daylight hunt was busted by a trespasser from state land, we moved to a new area and I really got on my call. Even after a turkey in the bottom gobbled right back at me, my new guide said, "Should you really be calling like that?"

"I really do not have time for this," I grumbled as we quickly moved in for a setup.

As we set up in a low corner of an old field next to the river, our turkey was gobbling just over a hump in the field. As soon as I hit my call again, this turkey was on his way—the only problem was a hunter with a box call on state land, closing fast, yelping as he came. I got back on my call just as I saw not one, but two fans come up over the hump. After witnessing a beautiful double gobble from twin toms, I told my hunters to get their guns up and stay ready. We needed only another fifty yards or so, and it would be showtime.

The box-calling hunter was now at the river's edge, and really close to our fence. He called and both turkeys gobbled, but then they kind of slicked down from strut to half-strut, took on an alert posture, and began to moving to our left. One of my hunters and the guide both asked what was going on. As I repositioned both shooters to our left, I calmly explained our current situation.

"Okay guys, here's the deal. We were doing fine once we closed the distance and called from here. The gobblers thought the hen was coming to them. But when the guy on state ground called, it kind of confused them at first. But because of how I can read turkey body language, and since I have done this for so long, I can almost tell you what those gobblers are thinking.

"Once the other hunter reached the river's edge and called much closer, those turkeys knew he was a hunter—especially the lead bird, which promptly told the other turkey; 'We need to move away from here, that is a hunter, not a hen, and what we think is a pretty girl is really a human with a Lynch box call with a rubber band and white chalk.'"

My great friend and hunting buddy Frank Imo holding a late morning Illinois "call-shy" gobbler, called in this turkey with a box call.

My next aggressive set of calls immediately received two very loud, close gobbles, to our extreme left along the field edge, so I quickly moved my shooters several yards up the field edge and slightly farther to our left. Just as my hunters raised their guns, both gobblers appeared at twenty yards, just as they topped a slight rise in the field.

"Kill 'em," I instructed. Both guns roared, and as cool a double kill as you will ever see concluded our morning hunt.

Of course I did not tell them until after the hunt that turkeys do not know we are calling or hunting them, and that it was our box-calling hunter's movements down at the river's edge that had caught the lead turkey's attention as the hunter was

trying to find a way across the river to trespass and get to the gobbling turkeys.

Origins of the Call-Shy Argument

Let's analyze the logic behind the notion that calling can wise up turkeys and make it harder for everybody to score. The flawed assumption by many hunters is that, if they call, and the turkeys don't come, the turkeys aren't coming for other hunters either. They aren't even coming to each other. The mating season has been artificially ended by hunters calling their heads off out there. This is where the belief comes from that those other hunters calling "too aggressively" spoil it for everybody, because they are just adding layers of call-shyness to already educated birds.

For starters, think about the natural progression of spring mating season. Boy turkeys are in the mood and fired up about mating season before girl turkeys are. The system works well, in the sense of producing more baby turkeys, because it ensures that girl turkeys won't be ready first, which would create a problem. It makes sense then that the toms take up positions on the dance floor, fight each other over the best spots, and start the dance by themselves so the hens will really be impressed, once they also get good and ready.

On some hunting days, the natural order of things matches pumped-up gobblers against a lot of not-yet-receptive hens, and lucky hunters just happen to be sitting at the base of a tree, right between them. Talk about being in the right place at the right time! When these fortuitous stars align, when you're crossing a fence, if you just squeak the rusty barbed wire up and down with something that approximates a turkey rhythm, you might not have enough time to get your gun off the ground and reloaded before a lovestruck strutter shows up and begins humping your leg.

On such days (and occasionally at other times), hunters who never practice calling can bring big fat gobblers right into their laps, by squeaking out a few noises on their calls of choice. This confirms, in the minds of those hunters, that calling is not an important aspect of spring turkey hunting—you don't have to be a good caller to kill a turkey. As proof, photos of big toms, tails all fanned out, are submitted as Exhibit A. As long as nobody calls too much, the fragile conditions that allow such hunts to play out remain in full force, according to those who subscribe to these beliefs. But if even one person so much as strings together a little bit of that fancy contest-calling crap, it ruins it for everybody. It shuts up the turkeys. It moves them into tunnels they have dug for such emergencies.

Next let's consider the possibility that, when calling does not produce results, it could be that the calling was not realistic enough to get the hopedfor reaction from the birds. When the stars are not perfectly aligned, as above, a lot of hunters set up, call sparingly, and then nothing happens. They might hear a decent amount of gobbling on the roost and get answers to their tree calls, but the turkeys fly down, shut up, and go the other way. Flawed deduction: it was the calling that shut them up and caused them to go the other way.

What if the calling, on the other hand, had struck a chord with those turkeys? What if, even when toms are not likely to break from the harem and come, the caller had engaged the hens? What if the calling got the birds yacking and excited, and the whole works came marching to the source of the sounds, hens ready to see who the heck is picking at them, rounded tail fans trailing along? Would you believe in the value of calling then?

Many hunters have better luck when they call sparingly than when they give in to an experimental mood and call more aggressively. Think about this. If you cannot produce realistic—truly realistic—turkey sounds, would you expect that making those sounds louder and more often would cause turkeys to just come running? However, this is the foundation of the many arguments that "overcalling" screws it up for everybody. The call-shy thing gets repeated all the time, even by call manufacturers, so it's not surprising that a lot of hunters buy into it. In the enthusiastic marketing of the latest super-secret call, the sell message has been known to include the notion that this new sound will call up wizened gobblers that have become conditioned to more traditional calls.

Wild turkeys know authentic turkey sounds when they hear them. They live with other wild turkeys every day of their lives. They call to each other constantly. They come to each other a lot, but not every time. And they don't run or fly away at the first hint of a real yelp. The call-shy case crumbles in the face of reality if you think about how silly it is to presume that wild turkeys can somehow become conditioned to avoid the voices of other wild turkeys.

Believe what you will, but if you knew how many turkeys good callers can bring right to their boot tops, consistently and regardless of the phase of the breeding season and other mitigating factors, you would sit up straight and start practicing immediately. The mating urge doesn't control gobblers all spring long. From minute to minute, what it takes to call up turkeys changes, and the lifetime study of these variables is an important aspect of spring turkey hunting that many hunters are not aware of.

For example, spring weather that turns cold and stormy (it can snow in the Black Hills in May, and tornadoes and big rains come often enough) can call a sudden halt to the mating urge. Head into the woods in the aftermath of these conditions, call subtly like a sweet hen, and you might as well have pulled your sleeping bag over your eyes back in camp. You are not going to call up a turkey. But go forth under those same conditions, and sound like a strange gobbler who's yelping and cutting and poking his index finger into the chest of every other gobbler in the area, and things can be very different. I challenge toms with gobbler yelps, and many springs I call up and kill many more toms using gobbler yelps than hen yelps. It all depends on the situation.

Even under favorable conditions, being able to size things up and adapt can work wonders. If you get a soft gobble in response to excited calling, consider that it's a subordinate tom that wants you to hear him but not any other nearby gobblers. Slide up a little closer to the soft gobble, give him some excited invitations, and get your gun up.

Do everything you can to engage every hen you hear. Try to call up every one, because you don't know when you'll get a bonus silent strutter hanging onto the tow rope. If you engage hens but the source of the hen calling moves away, take a tip from Hawaii turkey guru Jon Sabati. Reposition, and try to sound like a lost hen that wants nothing more than to join the group, and see if they don't come to gather you up.

This is what it comes down to. Your calling has to sound realistic, and to rationalize away the reaction of turkeys to unrealistic sounds is to blame the turkeys and fellow hunters for your own unwillingness to practice enough so you can make those realistic-sounding calls. This gets to the heart of the matter, to the essence of putting the odds in your favor: You should not even bring calls into the woods that you are not proficient with. It isn't macho to use a mouth call if you cannot make realistic

turkey sounds with it, and it actually hinders your chances of calling up birds.

Counter to the call-shy culture that permeates turkey hunting camps and message boards, there is no question that your chances of getting close to any given turkey are better if you sound excited to get together with them or are challenging their standing in the social order. Let's consider the possibility that other forces—some natural, some manmade—can quiet turkeys down and even move them to other locations. People pressure is huge. So is the natural order of mating season. When dominance is (sorta) settled, and kingpin gobblers sleep tight with harems of hens, you don't hear nearly as much gobbling as you do at other times, and it's harder for anybody, even real hens, to call up a tom.

The true variable when it comes to calling is that wild turkeys are fickle. It does no good to try to read things into it when you make realistic calls and they still don't come. All turkeys do not come to all turkeys calling to them. Don't worry about why the first one didn't come. Just call to the next one and see if he will. And if nothing seems to be working, practice more—both as a woodsman and as a caller.

One last thing—this is not a plea to fill the air with your calling. Everyone should hunt the way they like best. But, please, can we stop blaming excited and realistic calling when things don't go well out there for all those who are just too scared to call because they somehow believe their calling will make turkeys "call-shy"?

Scouting with a Purpose

RICHARD P. COMBS

"Whenever, in the course of the daily hunt, the red hunter comes upon a scene that is strikingly beautiful or sublime—a black thundercloud with the rainbow's glowing arch above the mountain, a white waterfall in the heart of a green gorge, a vast prairie tinged with the blood red of sunset—he pauses for an instant in the attitude of worship."

—Ohiyesa, Santee Dakota physician

Just as hunters should enter the woods on opening day with a strategy in mind, they should undertake pre-season scouting with a strategy as well. Properly done, scouting should enable the turkey hunter to:

1. Confirm the presence of a huntable turkey population in an area.
2. Become familiar with the geography of the area to be hunted.
3. Learn how turkeys use the area, patterning gobblers if possible.
4. Develop specific hunting strategies.

Confirming the Presence of Turkeys

Often, the first objective is achieved before serious scouting is necessary. A hunter might be familiar enough with an area to know that turkeys are present in huntable numbers, or might be able to rely on reports of other hunters or landowners. District offices of state divisions of wildlife, or their local equivalents, along with game wardens, are usually good sources of information on turkey populations. Members of the National Wild Turkey Federation (if you're not a member, you should be), can contact local chapters of that organization for useful information. With computers, hunters can search out hunting forums on the Internet and solicit feedback from local hunters. Local sheriffs can sometimes be good sources of information, also.

What exactly is a "huntable population"? That depends in part on the size of the parcel of land to be hunted, and on hunting pressure. If hunting pressure is very heavy, there cannot (in my opinion) be enough turkeys to represent a huntable population. Not only are chances for success diminished by the presence of too many hunters in the woods, but the quality of time afield is compromised as well, as hunting strategies are dictated more by other hunters than by the turkeys themselves. And nothing is more frustrating to the turkey hunter who has done his homework and caused all of 101 factors to fall perfectly into place than to have the hunt spoiled by another hunter No matter how good an area looks, and no matter how high the local turkey population, do yourself a favor and find a less crowded place to hunt. Better, in terms of both your hunting enjoyment and your chances for success, to hunt a small population of birds that are not heavily hunted than large numbers of birds that must run a gauntlet of hunters every day.

The size of the property you will hunt is a factor here, too. If you are limited to hunting a small parcel of real estate, your chances of success are low if population densities are not very high. On the other hand, if you have thousands of acres at your disposal, and can walk (or drive) to cover a lot of ground, even an area with a comparatively low population of birds can be productive. I tagged my first turkey on a wooded property of less than 100 acres. For several years I hunted the place regularly, and took a tom there every spring. My strategies were limited by the size of the place, but it didn't matter. Habitat in the area was a perfect blend of woodlots, cropland, and pastures. The turkey population was high, and the birds were always there.

By contrast, I also began hunting a state forest covering many thousands of areas at about the same time. Turkeys were dispersed widely throughout the area, and the population density was fair at best. Still, experienced hunters did well. There was plenty of room to spread out, and a hunter could walk for miles along ridgetops, or drive dirt roads, prospecting for birds.

Often, a hunter is aware that turkeys inhabit an area, but needs to determine relative population levels. There is no quick way to do that. If you are fortunate, in one outing you will hear sufficient numbers of birds gobbling, and find sufficient sign, to tell you that the population is high. More often you'll find a track here and there, a few droppings, and a feather or two. In most cases, at least several trips to an area will be required to get a real feel for the number of birds present. It's not unusual to scout an area and see only a little sign on one outing, only to return a few days later and see a great deal of sign. The time of year and recent weather must be taken into account. In late summer, or during the early fall deer season, there should be a fair number of feathers around, since the birds molt in the summer and the feathers are still present. Whatever the time of year, scouting after a recent rain is helpful.

Time of year is important for other reasons, too. Turkey ranges tend to vary between winter ranges and spring/summer ranges, though there will be some overlap. Assuming reasonable numbers of birds in an area, meadows, pastures, natural forest openings, logging roads, or cropfields, especially if surrounded by nesting cover, should draw and hold turkeys beginning some time in March in most parts of the country. In fall and winter, the birds may move into more heavily wooded areas where the mast crop is better, or to farms offering corn, soybeans, and other crops. This means that an area loaded with turkeys in the fall and winter may be nearly devoid of them in the spring. This is one reason it's important to scout close to opening day. If limited to one scouting trip, I'd want it to be within two weeks of the season opener, preferably within a few days.

Turkey feathers can be found anytime, but especially in late summer, when birds are molting.

Learning the Lay of the Land

Gaining familiarity with an area is probably the best reason to scout in the winter, since scouting when the foliage is down allows you to get to know the lay of the land much faster. And just as deer hunters like to scout in late winter or early spring so they needn't worry about spooking deer, the turkey hunter can cover ground freely in the winter, when the birds are flocked up and when he needn't worry about alerting them to human presence.

Topo maps, plat maps, county road maps, and aerial photos all provide valuable information. Not all hunters take advantage of aerial photos, but they are available free or for a nominal fee from most agricultural extension offices. Plat maps are available from any county courthouse. Google Earth is a good source of aerial photos. Coverage is not yet universal, but it soon will be.

While very useful, none of these can substitute for actually walking the property. The aim is to become familiar with every feature of the geography, including hills, ridges, points, creeks, draws, pastures, clearings, oak glades, thickets, evergreen stands, and fences. It is difficult to overstate the value of this knowledge in a hunting situation. The goal is that when he hears a turkey gobble on the property, the hunter will know where the bird is gobbling from, what is between him and the gobbler, which clearings or meadows the turkey is likely to head toward when he comes off the roost, and which logging road, trail, ridgetop, or fenceline, he is likely to use in getting there.

Patterning Gobblers

If turkeys were predictable, coyotes, owls, hawks, bobcats, and other predators would kill them all long before human hunters had a chance at them. Every experienced turkey hunter has found the perfect setup for a gobbler, only to have the bird fly off the roost and wander off, gobbling lustily, in a totally unpredicted direction, ignoring the most seductive yelps, purrs, and clucks. That's turkey hunting. Nonetheless, gobblers do have favorite roosting areas, strutting zones, midday loafing areas, and dusting areas. They tend to frequent these areas at certain times of the day, and in moving between them they tend to use the same haul roads, trails, fence openings, and creek crossings.

Specific knowledge about where these areas are, and how and when turkeys use them, is invaluable. Some forms of sign can indicate turkey patterns. The occasional track, scratching, loose feather, or dropping, indicates little except that a turkey was in the area,

Scouting in winter is the quickest way to learn the lay of the land and cover ground without fear of spooking turkeys.

Turkey tracks—If the middle toe is 2 1/2" or longer, it's a tom.

recently or not so recently, depending on the sign. Clearly a lot of tracks, feathers, scratchings, or droppings, including fresh sign and older sign, suggests an area that turkeys are using heavily and with some regularity.

Experienced hunters have little difficulty distinguishing gobbler tracks from hen tracks. The middle toe of a hen is usually two inches or less in length, though a big hen may be slightly bigger than two inches. By contrast, the middle toe of a gobbler is usually two and a half inches in length or more, and even a very small mature gobbler will have a middle toe at least two inches long. A gobbler's stride is about a foot, but closer to two feet when running. Drag marks in bare dirt or sand indicate that a gobbler has been strutting in that area, and you've probably found a strutting zone. Drag marks are not easily confused with anything else. They tend to be about two feet long, if conditions permit, and are parallel but not very straight. Dusting spots are good finds, since turkeys tend to use the same dusting areas repeatedly.

These are often small, hollowed-out spots in dusty or sandy areas. Close inspection will usually reveal some small feathers in the dust. Because dusting is something turkeys often do at midday or later in the afternoon, these can be good fallback spots when morning strategies have failed. A big concentration of droppings

usually indicates a regular roosting area. These aren't often found, and when they are, it's usually by accident.

Bill Massey, a turkey hunter from Indiana, was the first person to point out one interesting turkey sign to me. Bill, on several occasions, observed turkeys eating the buds from the tops of mayapple plants. Depending on their location, not all patches of mayapples will be budding out in turkey season, but those that are will often get attention from turkeys. Since learning of that, I've gotten in the habit of checking any patches of mayapples I come across. It is easy to see if the buds have been eaten; the plant stems look as if they have been pinched off at the top. As far as I've been able to determine, while skunks, possums, and possibly some other creatures eat the ripe fruit of mayapples, nothing else bites off the buds.

Some hunters find it difficult to distinguish turkey scratchings from the sign left by deer pawing for acorns, or even by squirrels and other rodents digging under the leaves to hide food or find it. Though old scratchings left by one or two birds can be difficult to identify with certainty, fresh turkey scratchings are usually easy to identify. One characteristic of turkey scratchings is that turkeys usually scratch all the way down to

Both gobblers and hens dust frequently. Look for tracks and feathers in dust for positive ID.

bare ground. If they encounter small roots, they like to scratch at the roots, leaving them exposed or broken. Typically, small piles of leaves are left behind each scratching. Some hunters believe they can tell the direction of travel this way, but that is not always easily done, since a flock of turkeys tends to mill about when moving through the woods scratching. It is difficult to confuse the fresh scratchings of a flock of turkeys with any other sign; generally a large patch of woods will be fill ed with scratched over spots, each with a small pile of leaves behind it.

An ability to age sign can be useful. Learning that skill takes time, but hunters coming across sign they know to be very fresh should examine it closely on subsequent visits to the area, keeping in mind rain and other weather patterns intervening between visits. Evidence as subtle as dew can indicate whether a track was made this morning or last night, as can the presence or absence of tiny cobwebs or insect trails in the track. Over time, hunters who examine and re-examine sign can develop an amazing ability to age tracks, droppings, and even feathers.

Sometimes it is possible to encourage fresh sign by creating conditions favorable to it. For instance, hunters can find bare spots of ground at the intersection of two logging roads, a field edge, or another likely spot and soak the spot with water from a nearby stream, pond, spring,

Unlike deer, squirrels, and other woodland creatures, turkeys tend to scratch down to bare soil, often exposing small roots. Leaves piled at one end of scratchings are another giveaway.

or even their canteens, then check the spot a few days later for tracks. In an area that already holds tracks, hunters can eliminate the sign, then check back later for new tracks indicating recent and regular activity in that spot. Depending on the accessibility of an area, it is possible to rake up hard ground, or even put down small patches of fresh dirt or sand in likely areas to look later for tracks, drag marks indicating strutting, or indications birds are dusting there.

The last and perhaps most important step in patterning gobblers is to visit the hunting area close to the season opener. Hunters should seek a good listening spot, usually on a hilltop, ridgeline, or bluff, and be there well before first light. Leave the calls home, except for an owl call, crow call, or other locater, which could prove useful. Be prepared to sit in one spot and lis ten for some time. Locating birds on the roost is fine—it gives hunters a general indication of where birds will be in the morning and, for those in states where all-day hunting is permitted, where they're likely to be in the late afternoon.

Even more important, though, is determining which direction turkeys take when they leave the roost. Obviously, the hunter who knows where the turkeys are going can be there waiting for them. Given that knowledge, it does not matter if the gobblers are henned up. It does not matter if they are subordinate toms afraid to respond to a hen call. It does not matter if they are old loners who will not come near a decoy. It does not matter what the hens are doing or not doing. This is where knowing the lay of the land counts heavily. The hunter who knows the area well can quickly make an educated guess about where a gobbler is headed.

If the birds aren't vocal, or if they clam up soon after fly down, the hunter can use shock calls to try to elicit gobbles. Probably the most effective

tactic is to pick a spot near a large meadow, a big, open wooded area, a logging road, or other vantage point, and glass for turkeys. Spotting turkeys not only reveals likely travel routes and feeding or strutting areas, but also gives hunters an opportunity to observe behavior. Is a boss gobbler alone, or does he have subordinate toms with him? Are gobblers strutting or not? Is there any fighting going on? Are hens coming to the toms in response to gobbling and strutting, or do they appear to be ignoring them? Are the birds in flocks, or do they appear as singles or as two or three birds together? Other sections in this chapter deal with specific hunting strategies for specific situations, but all this information is useful in helping hunters formulate strategies.

It's important not to spook birds as the season approaches. The idea is to learn where the turkeys are without alerting them to your presence. Hiking ridgelines, walking logging roads, and moving from one spot to another in search of birds might be the way to go in large, comparatively remote forests, but a low-impact approach to scouting will serve most hunters on private land better. Any movement between one spot and another should be accomplished as unobtrusively as possible, using routes planned to minimize the likelihood of encountering turkeys.

Developing a Strategy

Turkey hunters typically enter the woods before daybreak, planning to set up on the first gobbler they hear on the roost. When that bird has clammed up or wandered off the property where hunters can't pursue, they begin covering ground, pausing now and then to call and listen for a response. They may call more or less aggressively, depending on nothing more than whether they prefer more or less aggressive calling in general. It is hard to knock an approach to turkey hunting that

Low-impact scouting close to season opener will locate and pattern turkeys.

has filled countless thousands of turkey tags. I've killed more than a few birds using that approach myself. But let's face it, the only difference between wandering around aimlessly and walking down a ridgeline or logging road is that the ridgeline or logging road gives us a sense of direction and hence an illusion that we have a strategy. In fact, it's a nonstrategy.

By contrast, the hunter who has scouted thoroughly and patterned the birds hunts with a strategy. He calls more or less aggressively based on his knowledge of how the birds are behaving in that area at that time. His initial set-up is more likely to result in success because he knows where the birds are, knows how to use the terrain and the cover to get close to birds without crowding or spooking them, and can make an educated guess about which way they will go from the roost. If a gobbler fails to come in, he quickly formulates a back-up plan, relocating to call from another spot, or determining where the turkey is going and getting there first. When gobbling activity falls off, he knows of a good strut zone or two, a place where he can set out decoys and call intermittently, with the knowledge that there is a

good chance a gobbler will show up at some point in the morning. If he is aware of a spot where turkeys tend to seek shade when the sun gets high, he will be there waiting for them. He might know of an afternoon dusting area, and if he knows where the birds roost and can hunt all day, he'll know where to set up late in the day. He may have constructed blinds in some of these areas, allowing him to move in and set up quickly with minimal disturbance, and at the same time creating a well-concealed hide he can remain in comfortably for long periods. In addition, he knows how to move from one of these areas to another with the least risk of spooking turkeys.

Of course there is no guarantee that his strategy will pay off on any given day. Compared to wandering down a logging road, though, or simply sitting down in the woods in a spot that looks good, a well-planned strategy offers better chances for success. In the course of three or four hunts, the odds are on the side of the hunter with a sound strategy. Moreover, having a strategy offers the added advantage of being lower impact, not as likely to alarm birds and make them less vocal or more call shy. Having a strategy is particularly advantageous when the turkeys are not gobbling, whether it is because they are with hens, because the weather is bad, because they are extremely wary, or for whatever reason. That is when the hunter who has patterned turkeys can really take advantage of the knowledge he has acquired. Patterning gobblers is a time-consuming process that few hunters bother with, but done correctly it is one of the most effective steps a hunter can take toward filling his tag.

Advanced Calling Strategies

"Th' real old hunter uses what they call a lion's tongue. Cuts 'em in half an' lets 'em wilt and

Tips

- One good way to find strut zones or other hotspots is to create conditions favorable for tracks or other signs in likely areas. Splash water from a stream or pond onto bare, dry earth nearby, or pour water from a canteen.
- Use a rake or sticks to rake up bare ground in likely spots, then look for tracks or drag marks.
- If the middle toe on a track is two and one-half inches or longer, the track was left by a gobbler.

Wide open spaces often make turkeys easier to locate, but harder to set up on. The turkey below is a Wyoming Merriam's.

puts 'em in their mouth, and they just make a hen ashamed of itself."

—Grady Waldroop, as quoted in *The Foxfire Book,* 1972

Can we lay to rest the myth of the turkey-calling champions who impress judges but can't fool real turkeys? Somewhere there may be such a caller, and it is certainly true that there is a big difference between contest calling and hunting. The thing is, I've had the good fortune to hunt with a number of turkey-calling champions; every one of them was keenly aware of the difference between contest calling and hunting, and every one of them was an excellent turkey hunter. It is, after all, a passion for turkey hunting that usually fuels the inspiration to take up contest calling in the first place.

The endless debate about the relative importance of calling skills is really a complex issue. Most calling champions will tell you that calling skills are not the most important attribute of a good turkey hunter. Some of them are sincere and some, I suspect, are just being modest. At the risk of sounding like a politician, I would argue that the relative importance of calling skills depends in part on how we define "calling skills."

If by "calling skills" we mean the ability to precisely imitate the various sounds of a live turkey, I agree with others that this ability is of secondary importance at best. On some days it seems that gobblers will respond to any sound that vaguely resembles a hen yelp. My daughter, at age nine, once called in a pair of longbeards using a Quaker Boy push-pin box call after about one minute of coaching in the car on the way to the hunt.

Meanwhile, the world-calling champions I have hunted with have demonstrated time and again that there are many days on which even world-class calling will not seduce a wily tom

Box calls have earned a place in every serious turkey hunter's vest. Their downside is the movement required to operate them, which can often be hidden with natural color, a blind, or a piece of camo fabric over the knees.

the recorded sounds of live turkeys, or a mix of live turkeys and expert callers. Even for the experienced caller, recordings can be great refreshers after not calling for many months, especially in learning the cadence and the dynamics of turkey calls. The best sound system, though, is no match for the real thing. Beyond a certain point, calling will not improve until the caller spends time in the woods listening to real, live turkeys.

turkey. On the other hand, if our definition of "calling skills" includes knowing when to call and when not to, when to use which calls, when to call loudly and aggressively and when to call quietly, how to use various "non-vocal" sounds that turkey hunters make to bring in gobblers, then I would have to argue that calling skills are very important. Yes, you can bag plenty of gobblers by yelping on a box call, without resorting to calls other than a plain yelp, and without ever mastering a different style of call. Over the long run you'll bag more gobblers, though, if you expand your calling to include more variety.

Most box calls should be tuned. Mark the screw on the "lid" and try it at different settings, stopping when it elicits regular responses.

Improving Sound Quality

We'll start with this because it is probably the least important. Accurately mimicking the sound of a turkey builds confidence, though, and confidence is important. Beginning callers often make two mistakes: they use recordings exclusively as a source of learning, and they practice indoors.

Audio and video disks are excellent tools to help you learn how to call turkeys, and they are getting better all the time. The best ones feature

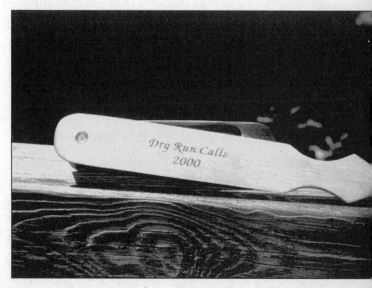

Most callers at some point have experienced the following. They practice for hours at home or in their vehicles and are increasingly satisfied with their calling. Then, on opening day they begin calling in the woods, and find themselves examining their call to see if it's defective. The sound in the open woods is altogether different than the sound at home or in a vehicle. There is much more reverberation indoors, and calls outdoors may seem flat and lifeless by comparison. It's important to spend some time practicing outdoors. The most dedicated callers record their calling outdoors to analyze it later and find ways to improve.

Mastering Various Types of Calling Devices

Assuming the other basic woodsmanship skills are in place, this may be the simplest thing a hunter can do to boost his success rate. For reasons known only to turkeys, a given gobbler on a given day will respond only to a box call, not to a diaphragm call. Or maybe it's a slate call that suddenly inspires him to drop out of a full strut and run 200 yards for a rendezvous with a load of copper-coated No. 6s. Some hunters will not enter the woods without their trusty boat-paddle-style box call because there have been times when it elicited gobbles and nothing else would.

Hunters often believe a certain call is successful because the turkeys in that area have never heard it before. This is why some hunters swear by tube calls or wing-bone calls, which are far less common than box calls and diaphragm calls. There is some evidence of late that turkeys respond best to sounds that are above the range of human hearing, and several manufacturers market calls which work at that level.

Since we can't get inside a turkey's peanut-sized brain to see what is going on there, we'll never be sure of the motivation. It does seem clear, though, that turkeys can be finicky about which sound they'll respond to. That being the case, it is to the hunter's

advantage to master at least several different styles of calls and carry them with him whenever he hunts.

Some are more difficult to master than are others, but any hunter can carry one or two box calls, including a pin-push style, and one or two slate-type friction calls. Wing-bone and tube calls are among the most difficult to master, but they offer the aforementioned advantage of being less frequently heard in the turkey woods.

Diaphragm calls are less difficult to learn than tube or wing-bone calls, though not as easy to learn as friction calls. There are very successful turkey hunters who don't use diaphragm calls, but they do offer several advantages, and every turkey hunter should give them a try. They're small and light, and that makes for a lot of versatility. You can carry a dozen of them in a small container, and no two of them will sound alike. They'll emulate sounds ranging from that of a young, sweet hen, to that of the raspiest old hen in the flock. They'll produce fly-down cackles, purrs, cuts, and yelps.

Perhaps their biggest advantage is that they enable the hunter to call without moving. There are times when a cluck or a few soft purrs will persuade a wary gobbler standing in full view sixty yards away to move in. The hunter with a friction call may be pinned down, unable to move his hands without being spotted, but the hunter with a mouth call can purr away while remaining motionless. And who knows how many gobblers sneaking in silently from an unexpected direction have melted away into the forest upon spotting the hand movements of a hunter working a friction call?

Clearly, there is no one style of call that is essential for turkey hunting success, but the hunter who learns to use a wider variety of calls will be a more versatile, and hence better, hunter.

Non-Vocal Calls

These consist of scratching in the leaves, drumming, and flapping wings. I have heard some hunters talk about fooling turkeys by scraping wings against trees, but I've never heard a turkey do that, and I have not tried it. There is another sound I have heard turkeys make that I have never heard emulated, and that is a kind of rattling sound some gobblers make with their wings, and possibly their tails, while strutting. It sounds like gravel being shaken in a shoebox.

Most hunters have at one time or another been walking through dry leaves only to have a gobbler sound off from very close by. Sometimes gobblers mistake a hunter walking slowly through dry leaves for a turkey walking, which is not surprising, especially if the person stops now and then and changes pace. There have been times when I was sure an approaching turkey was a hunter. It only makes sense, when moving through dry leaves is unavoidable, to walk with a slow, irregular cadence.

Scratching in the leaves is even easier. Turkeys often follow a peculiar scratch, scratch-scratch, scratch cadence when digging after acorns or other foods under the leaves. They scratch first with one foot, then make two quick scratches with the other foot, then scratch again with the first foot. It's easy to imitate, and often fools turkeys. I don't recommend starting with this call, or even using it randomly, since it may put turkeys on the alert. It's a good one to try now and then, though, when a turkey is hung up close by and doesn't seem to be responding to calling. Drumming is probably the most interesting sound turkeys make. Sometimes toms that do not gobble at all will nonetheless strut and drum. The theory is that these are subordinate birds, reluctant to gobble for fear of getting a good flogging from the local boss. Drumming is a way to more quietly advertise for hens. If this is accurate, it is easy to see why drumming can be effective, at least for bringing in a dominant bird. Drumming doesn't always work, of course—anything that always worked would have to be illegal. It is a good ploy to try when other tactics fail to produce. Several manufacturers are now marketing calls that simulate drumming gobblers.

The sound of turkey wings flapping is a common one in the turkey woods, heard when turkeys fly down from the roost, fly up to the roost, or when they fight. There are devices marketed to create this sound, and some hunters carry real turkey wings to do it. For my own part, I'm not convinced that the old technique of yanking a camo handkerchief rapidly taut and loose with both hands doesn't do as adequate a job, and I have brought a few turkeys in after doing this, though I have never done it without also making a fly-down cackle and, in most cases, a few quiet yelps. I'm told that in the case of call-shy old solitary gobblers, the flapping sounds of a bird flying off the roost, to the exclusion of all other sounds, can sometimes be effective. I don't doubt it, but can't speak to that from personal experience.

When to Call Aggressively, Quietly, or Not at All

Years ago, when I first had the opportunity to hunt with some of the better known turkey hunting experts, it was a real confidence builder to spend a day in the woods with them and return empty-handed. That might sound strange, but hunting with these famous turkey hunters and seeing that they did not always succeed was reassuring. They hunted with a confidence that was born not of a feeling that they were sure to bag a gobbler every time out, but with the knowledge that sooner or later their tactics would work.

I was curious to observe their hunting styles, to see who hunted aggressively and covered a lot of ground, who relied more on discipline and patience, who called loudly and often, who exercised more restraint in calling. Certainly there were differences in hunting styles, but what I found over time was that most of them were difficult to pigeonhole. Depending on where they were hunting and how the birds were responding, they changed their

A gobbler approaching silently will often stop and cluck. If he hears a cluck in return, he is reassured and comes in. If not, he slips away.

tactics, sometimes prospecting and covering a lot of ground, sometimes setting up in a likely spot and waiting out birds, sometimes cackling and cutting and lost yelping, sometimes calling only with an occasional cluck or a little purring.

How did they know which strategy to use? They didn't. If they "knew," we'd have killed turkeys every time we hunted. They made educated guesses, based on experience, and they experimented. Sometimes, it seemed, anything would work, and other times nothing would. Over time, though, the hunter who is versatile, adaptable, uses his best judgment, and is not afraid to experiment, will take more turkeys than the hunter who always uses the same strategy no matter what the birds are doing.

There is a greater degree of consensus about how best to approach some situations than others. Here are a few calling strategies about which most experienced turkey hunters can agree.

First, if a gobbler indicates by his reaction that he likes a certain call, keep giving it to him. If loud yelps from a box call have him double-gobbling and moving pretty quickly in your direction, keep giving him loud yelps from a box call.

Most hunters will agree that as the bird moves closer, it's usually smart to back off on the volume and frequency of calls. Turkeys have an amazing ability to determine exactly where a sound is coming from for some distance. When you're working a bird into range, you want him hunting for you, not looking right at you. If the bird knows your precise location, you run the risk that 1) he will be expecting to see a hen there, and may hang up or even slip away if he doesn't, and 2) he will see you.

Loud and aggressive calling has its place, but rarely if ever will that be when a gobbler is on the roost. To begin with, hens rarely call aggressively from the roost. Then too, a gobbler that hears a hen yelping aggressively is expecting that hen to come to him under the roost. Often a gobbler will continue to strut on the roost, pausing occasionally to peek at the forest floor for the hen he knows is approaching, as long as a hunter continues calling. Only when the calling stops for a period of time will the gobbler fly down. For this reason, a few quiet tree yelps are adequate until the gobbler flies down. A fly-down cackle is about as aggressive as a hunter would normally want to be when calling to a roosted bird.

The exception to that might be if you know you are competing with real hens roosted nearby. Then you might try pouring it on. It's a long shot, but probably as likely to succeed as anything under those circumstances.

Toms that seem call-shy, either because they are subordinate birds or because they have been subjected to a lot of hunting pressure, are more likely to respond to quiet, infrequent calling than to loud, aggressive calling. In a similar vein, call-shy gobblers are unlikely to respond to gobbles, to drumming, or to fighting purrs.

The closer you get to a gobbler, the more likely he will respond to your calls. Keep in mind, though, that safety is a major concern here. Apart from that, moving in close to a gobbler risks spooking him, ruining the hunt for that morning, and possibly educating that bird and making him tougher for the rest of the season. When safety concerns are satisfied, and when hilly terrain, thick foliage, and a certainty of the gobbler's location permit it, hunters can sometimes slip to within sixty yards or so of a gobbler. From that location, a cluck or a few quiet yelps will often generate a quick response in a gobbler that paid no attention to calls from more typical distances of 150 yards or more.

Experts often talk of taking a gobbler's temperature, by which they mean determining how fired up and eager the bird seems to be by calling with increasing aggressiveness. If aggressive calling results in more frequent gobbling, double and triple gobbling, and a bird moving steadily if not rapidly toward the hunter, then the callers continues with aggressive calling as long as the bird continues to respond and come in, backing off only as the gobbler gets closer. On the other hand, if the gobbler does not increase gobbling frequency in response to more aggressive calling, it's time to back off, calling less frequently and with less volume.

Is there a time not to call at all? Occasionally you will encounter a gobbler so call shy he is almost impossible to bring in, even with the most non-aggressive calling. One option is to seek a more cooperative gobbler—a smart option in many cases. But if he happens to be a long-spurred old gobbler, or if he manages to get under your skin and you want that particular bird, your only real option is to hunt with minimal calling, or none at all.

You might try a very infrequent, very quiet yelp, or just a cluck. Or you might try setting up to bushwhack the bird, without calling at all. It requires extreme discipline and patience, and there is no guarantee of success, but it can work.

The bottom line on all this is that most experienced turkey hunters these days vary their calling in terms of frequency and volume, letting the birds themselves indicate which kind of calling they prefer on a given day.

Additional Techniques and Tips

We've looked at moving in close to a gobbler when conditions permit. The opposite can work, too. When two or more hunters work together, they can sometimes employ what is variously called the "ghost hen," the "floating hen," or the "fading hen." If a gobbler seems hung up, one caller slips away very quietly and calls from different positions farther and farther behind the hunter. The idea is that when the gobbler thinks his hen is moving away from him, he'll pursue, and this will bring him past the shooter, within range.

This is an effective technique that has put a lot of gobblers on the dinner table. Three caveats: first, moving as a gobbler is approaching is always risky. You want to be sure you are not visible to the bird. If he spots movement, that duel is probably over. Second, this method works best when you know the area well. If an obstacle such as a stream, thicket, or fence is hanging up the bird, success is unlikely. And finally, this is an approach to be used only after you're reasonably sure the bird is hung up, and you've already tried a few other approaches to get him off the spot. The reason for this is that whenever the caller separates himself from the designated shooter, there is a risk that another gobbler will approach from a different direction, out of range of the shooter. It's even possible that the original gobbler will move past the shooter without providing a shot, either because he is just out of range, or because a thicket or obstacles of some sort make a clear shot impossible.

One tactic that is probably not used often enough is the silent treatment. When a bird gobbles in response to calls but seems to hang up or go silent, try putting the call aside and waiting him out. Give him at least twenty minutes. Often he'll come sneaking in to see where his hen went.

A Couple of Final Tips

Clucks can be among the most effective calls. A single, isolated cluck seems to mean "I'm over here, where are you?" I believe that in many cases a hung-up gobbler will remain silent for a while, then cluck one time. If he gets a cluck in response, he is reassured and comes in. If not, he slips away. Stay alert for that single cluck. When you hear it, cluck back and get your gun in position.

Many hunters don't use locator calls, complaining that they rarely work. It is true that locators don't always elicit gobbles. Stick with them, though, and use them regularly, and they will work on occasion. Unless a hunter is seated with his gun in position, it is always better to elicit a gobble with a locator call than with a turkey call. This causes the gobbler to reveal his position without moving toward the hunter. Every turkey hunter occasionally has this experience: he is working his way along a ridgetop trail or a logging road, stopping to yelp occasionally. He walks over a rise and around a bend only to catch a glimpse of a gobbler flushing or ducking into the woods. It's possible, of course, that the gobbler just happened to be there. But more than likely, the gobbler heard the approaching "hen" and was headed for a rendezvous with her. Had the hunter been able to elicit a shock gobble, he'd have been set up and ready. And even if he hadn't, the gobbler would not have been moving toward him and there would have been less chance of spooking it.

In a variation of that theme, the hunter stops and yelps, only to have a gobbler sound off from over a bank or on the other side of a thicket. Before the hunter can finish yanking on his headnet and scampering into position, the bird has peeked over the bank or around the thicket and spotted his frantic activity.

Certainly there are many times when a gobbler will gobble in response to a turkey call, but not to a locator call. That's why, when the locator doesn't work, we reach for the turkey call. It's always worth trying the locator first, though. When you decide to yelp loudly as a locator, better to do it where visibility is good, and in a spot that will allow you to drop and get in position quickly.

Gobblers may respond to any loud, sudden noise. Sometimes less commonly heard sounds, such as the goose call, work best.

Which locator is the best? Every experienced turkey hunter has his favorite. I sometimes use an owl call, especially early in the morning, but generally prefer something louder. Crow calls work for me on occasion, but in areas where there are crows squawking nonstop, I reach for something else. Any loud sound can work, even air horns.

Pileated woodpecker calls can be effective. One morning, digging around in my gear still more asleep than awake, I put a goose call in my vest pocket by mistake. I used it, just for laughs, and it worked!

Locators are typically used to find a gobbler when prospecting, but they can be useful at getting a tom to reveal his location any time. If you've worked a bird in close, and he suddenly clams up on you for ten minutes or so, slip a locator out and give a blast on it. If the bird is close by, he will usually gobble in response to a loud locator.

Sometimes it is necessary to relocate on a gobbler. That is always a tricky maneuver. Every effort should be made to get the gobbler to sound off and reveal his location before moving, or you risk spooking the bird. Once you hear him gobble and determine his position, you can move safely and with a better idea where to go. Pull out all the calling stops if necessary. Cluck, to see if the bird is in close. Yelp, softly a time or two, and then with increasing volume and frequency. Try cutting, then use the locator. Only as a last resort should you attempt to relocate without getting a gobble from the bird.

Gobbling is a controversial call, mostly because of safety concerns. It's probably not a good idea on public land, unless the area is remote and you can be confident there aren't other hunters in the area. Even on private land, gobbling is something to undertake with caution. The situation in which I most often use gobbling is when I'm roosting a bird in an area where afternoon hunting is prohibited. Occasionally, when I'm hunting private land, and am set up in a spot from which I have good visibility and would easily see any nearby hunters, I will gobble to locate a bird. A gobble is more likely to send toms running off than to bring them in, but it can be effective on dominant birds. It should be used sparingly, and with an extra measure of caution.

There is a wide range of calling skills, and calling styles, among the best turkey hunters. Most of the more consistently successful callers have these attributes in common, though: versatility, in terms of being able to use at least several different kinds of calls; confidence that their calling will sooner or later bring in a gobbler; and a willingness to experiment, to try different calling tactics until they hit on the right one to bring a given gobbler on a given day to the gun.

The Optimum Turkey Gun

"I don't believe all turkey hunters will agree on any one subject pertaining to the wild turkey. That's good. It proves that the wild turkey has been, to a marked degree, successful in addling the brain of the people who pursue him with uncertainty."

—Gene Nunnery, *The Old Pro Turkey Hunter,* 1980

While much depends on the individual hunter, it can be a useful exercise to explore the attributes that a good turkey gun should possess. Some of these are very subjective factors, but even the less subjective qualities are open to some debate. Length, for instance, is a measurable, objective quality. The conventional thinking is that short-barreled shotguns—say twenty-six-inch barrels or shorter— are preferable for turkey hunting. The turkey hunter must often swing his gun slowly to track an approaching bird, and must occasionally change positions quickly to move the barrel from, say, the 2 o'clock position to the 9 o'clock position when a gobbler sneaks in from an unexpected direction. It's amazing how often a tree, a low-hanging limb, or a shrub of some kind obstructs that movement, preventing a shot or requiring exaggerated movements that risk spooking the target. It's even more amazing how often a barrel just two or three inches shorter would eliminate the problem.

On the other hand, some very accomplished turkey hunters prefer longer barrels. Why? The longer sight plane makes for more accurate shooting, which is important for tightly choked barrels sending small patterns at a target the size of a turkey's head. As for obstructions getting in the way, say these hunters, that's what pruning shears are for. For my own part, I find the arguments in favor of shorter barrels more persuasive. To the extent that accuracy is a problem, a low-power scope, or even good iron sights, will better resolve the problem, and without the extra weight and length.

Is gauge really a point of debate? My friend and fellow outdoor writer Tony Mandile has taken several turkeys I know of with a 20-gauge O/U. No doubt the old saw 'Beware the one-gun man' applies here, as Tony uses that little 20 gauge almost exclusively for his shotgunning. He shoots it well, and knows its capabilities. Tony and I hunted Osceolas on the Seminole Reservation in the Florida Everglades a few years ago, and I chuckled when I saw Tony's guide looking askance at his choice of firearm. He was all smiles a few hours later, though, as he and Tony emerged from the bush with a fine gobbler. Though Tony is far from the only turkey hunter to regularly fill his turkey tags with a 20 bore, the guide's concern that it would make his job tougher was not unfounded. The added challenge imposed by the 20's limited range is a handicap most hunters choose not to accept, and few hunters would argue that it is the optimum turkey gun.

The big 10 gauge has its proponents. All else being equal, the 10 gauge can reach out a little farther than the 12. The question is whether or not the extra range (which is not that much greater than that of a 12 gauge chambered with three- or three-and-one-half-inch magnum shells) is worth the extra weight and recoil. For a few, the answer is clearly yes. For the majority of hunters, the answer is no.

The 12 gauge is far and away the most popular medicine for serious turkey hunters, for several reasons. Those chambered for 3 1/2", and even 3" shells approach the performance of a 10 bore, but are significantly lighter. Even 2 3/4" shells are available in magnum. The venerable green Remington Express shells in that length and #6 shot are deadly out to 40 yards in my old Ithaca Model 37. Shotgun manufacturers offer a variety of guns designed specifically for turkey hunting, and all the major shotshell makers offer 12 gauge shells designed specifically for turkey hunting. All these options allow hunters to select the combination of range, recoil, and price that they want, and to own a shotgun that is effective for game from quail and dove to waterfowl and turkeys.

How important is camouflage on a shotgun? If the finish is not shiny, blued barrels and brown or black stocks probably blend in well enough with most environments. Certainly thousands of turkeys are bagged each season by hunters carrying uncamouflaged shotguns. It is true, though, that the gun is the one thing that must usually be moved as a turkey approaches. Full camo surely can't hurt, and could conceivably make a difference in some situations. I haven't made up my mind on this one. I often use camo guns, or put a camo gun sock on my shotguns. At the same time, I have a handsome double-bore Pedersoli smokepole that I never cover in camo, and I've taken quite a few birds with it. (Be careful with camo tape, by the way—I have seen taped guns rust in a matter of hours in damp conditions.)

Pump, autoloader, single or double bore? "Pump over autoloader," insist some hunters, "because they're more reliable." Maybe so, and I'd buy that argument if the quarry were Cape Buffalo or lion, but it's not. A good, well-cared-for autoloader is more than sufficiently reliable for turkey hunting. Properly done, turkey hunting is a one-shot endeavor anyway, except for the rare circumstance, so even a jam or a failure to chamber another round should not result in a lost opportunity. I normally hunt with a pump, by the way, but the reason has nothing to do with reliability.

"Autoloaders over pumps," insist some hunters, "because they reduce recoil." They've got a point. If recoil is a real concern for you, autoloaders may be the way to go. Not all hunters are bothered by recoil, and even those who are might reasonably point out that, once the gun is patterned, shooting those shoulder-punishing magnum turkey loads through it is a relatively infrequent occurrence.

Regardless of the kind of shotgun you prefer, one way to substantially reduce recoil is porting. Barrels can be ported for a reasonable cost, and ported choke tubes are widely available. There is some debate about whether or not the ported choke tubes are as effective in reducing recoil as ported barrels are, for technical reasons we needn't get into here. Either ported barrels or ported choke tubes do provide some reduction in recoil, though, and are worth considering, especially if you prefer light, short-barreled guns and insist on the maximum range offered by extra-full chokes and magnum shotshells.

I can see few arguments in favor of the single-bore shotgun other than light weight, economy, and safety for the young hunter. The double bore offers the second shot capability, but so does every other option except the single bore, and often at less weight. My friend Tom Cross, outdoor writer, veteran turkey hunter, and the fellow who helped me along when I was new to the sport, makes a good case for the double bore. Tom points out that of all the options, only the double barrel gives a hunter an instant selection between two choke sizes and two shot sizes. If a gobbler hangs up at forty yards Tom uses one barrel; if it sneaks in from behind and is slipping past at ten steps, he uses the other barrel. Further, as Tom points out, the double bore tends naturally to be shorter because the receiver is smaller than that on pumps and autoloaders.

Certainly there is nothing wrong with the single bore, and it may very well be the ideal gun for the youngster. And as Tom Cross points out, the side-by-side or O/U offers some unique advantages. The hunter who owns a double bore for waterfowling or upland gunning, and who decides to take up turkey hunting, can certainly be well-served in the turkey woods by his favorite double. Still, the battle between the traditional double barrel and the pump gun or autoloader was fought a long time ago, and in this country at least the pumps and the autoloaders emerged the clear victors in popularity.

Should the ideal turkey gun have a sling? I suspect most turkey hunters would say yes. Slings leave the hands free for hiking into and out of the woods, or for climbing steep hills, and they can be used as a sort of brace to steady the aim, in much the way rifle slings are used. I normally don't use a sling, even when the rifle or shotgun I'm hunting with is equipped with one. Over the thirty-plus years I've spent carrying rifles and shotguns afield, I can recall several instances in which I bagged game while entering or leaving a hunting area while my companion, with gun slung over his shoulder, could only watch. Do several such instances over the course of a lifetime outweigh the convenience of using a sling? That's a personal call, of course, but for many serious hunters the answer is no. Since having a sling doesn't require using it, I'll go with the consensus on this one and concede that the optimum turkey gun should be equipped with a sling.

Most turkey hunters will agree that the ideal turkey gun should be tightly choked to achieve maximum pattern density and longer range. Bring up the subject of maximum range for turkey guns at a hunting camp and sooner or later some (presumably) true turkey hunter is sure to point out that the true turkey hunter enjoys the challenge of calling birds in close. The implication, of course, is that real turkey hunters aren't overly concerned with extending the range of their shotguns.

There is some truth in that, and many turkey hunters at some point take up bow or muzzleloader for the added challenge, a challenge resulting in part from reduced range. Thousands of other hunters shoot open-choked or small bore guns, and are perfectly content to limit their shots to the effective ranges of those guns.

On the other hand, part of the challenge of any form of hunting is obtaining maximum performance from the weapon of choice, be it bow, muzzleloader, or shotgun. Heading out to the range to experiment with chokes, loads, and various shot sizes in search of the maximum effective range is part of the fun. I've spent countless hours seeking an elusive additional five yards from my favorite smokepole, when I could easily gain an additional ten yards by pulling my old Ithaca or Mossberg from my cabinet. For that matter, I have at least one other muzzleloader that would increase my range by the same margin. I enjoy experimenting with chokes, powders, wads, shot charges, or shotshells, trying to get the most from my guns.

How important is it that shotguns be chambered for three-and-a-half-inch shells? There is no guarantee that a three-and-a-half-inch shell will produce the best pattern in a given gun, nor is there a guarantee that magnum shells will perform better than their standard counterparts. My old Ithaca Model 37 is chambered for two-and-a-half-inch shells. The venerable green Remington Express outperforms every shotshell I've experimented with in that gun, including the two-and-a-half-inch magnums. The non-magnum load in that gun will kill turkeys cleanly out to forty yards. And there is no denying that those big three-and-a-half-inch shells are punishing. On the other hand, they do add pellets to the count, which can make for denser patterns downrange. They are very popular with a lot of serious turkey hunters. Since guns chambered for the long shells can also handle shorter ones, it's hard to find a downside to guns chambered for them.

Granted, if current trends continue shotgunners may one day be able to take turkeys at ranges that greatly reduce the challenge of the sport and substantially increase the harvest of turkeys. In that case, we might want to take a look at regulating the kinds of loads or guns with which hunters are allowed to pursue wild turkeys. In the meantime, we can head out to the range with patterning boards and targets and shotguns and ammunition and various other paraphernalia and have a lot of fun shooting.

What about sights? Optics, including scopes, red dot, and holographic sights are becoming increasingly popular among turkey hunters, but are still not nearly as popular as open sights. There are undeniable advantages to scopes, especially for hunters whose vision is less than perfect. Expense may be one factor in the continued preference for open sights, but there is certainly something to be said for simplicity. There is little to go wrong with open sights.

Given that turkey hunting requires precise shooting (compared to wing-shooting), the standard single bead sight is inadequate for turkey hunting. Two beads are better, but open rifle-style sights with fiber-optic beads have become the standard for most turkey guns. Our 'optimum' turkey gun, then—if we accept the preceding arguments—would be a short-barreled 12-gauge pump or autoloader chambered for three-and-one-half-inch shells, with an extra-full choke tube, in camo finish, with a sling and either fiber-optic sights or a low-power scope, red dot, or holographic sight.

If your passion for turkey hunting compels you to run out and buy the optimum turkey gun, I fully understand. Wild turkeys not only challenge hunters, they embarrass us on a regular basis. The desire to gain every legal and ethical advantage can be strong. And there is something to be said for pride of ownership, for the sense of pleasure to be derived from owning the best, and for hunting with confidence. Still, 'optimum' is a slippery term, and not to be confused with 'favorite.' My own current favorite turkey gun is my double-bore 10-gauge smokepole. It's too long, it's too heavy, and it does not have the range of a modern shellshucker. Why do I prefer it? Well, I like the way it looks. I like the heft of it, and the way it feels in my hands. I like the sense of tradition I feel when I carry it in the woods, the feeling of connecting with some unknown ancestor who once carried a similar fowling piece afield in search of game, quite possibly on the same hill I'm hunting. I like to hear the shot boom out through the valley and see the gray smoke roll when I let down the hammer. And I never do that without envisioning that other fellow, perhaps a century and a half ago, dropping the hammer on a turkey and waiting for the smoke to clear to confirm that his shot was true and his family will eat turkey for dinner. If I don't grab the smokepole, I usually reach for my old Ithaca Model 37, for no other reason than that I'm comfortable with it. I killed my first turkey with it many years ago, and I remember that event every time I pull that gun from the cabinet. In the final analysis being familiar with a gun, having

confidence in it, shooting it well, and knowing its maximum effective range, is more important than a few extra yards of range, a few inches in barrel length, or the latest high-tech sight or camo pattern. Still . . . I have to admit I've noticed the ads for a certain short-barreled 12-gauge pump chambered for three-and-one-half-inch shells, with a sling, the latest camo pattern, fiber-optic sights, and a maximum range at least ten yards beyond anything I'm currently shooting. Should it catch my eye in a weak moment, I just might have to add it to my collection.

The Shot Size Debate

Disagreements over shotguns tend to be friendly in nature, while for some reason disagreements over the best shot size for turkey hunting can practically lead to fisticuffs. It's just one of those things turkey hunters tend to have strong opinions about. Everyone who has spent some time experimenting with patterning shotguns can agree on one point: There is no predicting pattern density or uniformity based strictly on shot size. A gun may produce a more effective pattern with No. 4 shot than with No. 6, though the shell with No. 6s contains hundreds of pellets more than the one with No 4s.

Though Nos. 4, 5, and 6 are far and away the most popular shot sizes among turkey hunters, Nos. 2 and 7 1/2 have their proponents. I know several turkey hunters who rely on No. 2 shot in states where it is legal, aiming at the wing butt instead of making head shots. I'm skeptical that this is the most effective approach, but can't speak from personal experience, never having tried it. As for 7 1/2s, biologist, writer, and life-long turkey

hunter Lovett Williams has dispatched more than a few gobblers with that shot size.

For some this is a safety issue. According to insurance industry statistics, hunting in general is safer than swimming, soccer, baseball, bowling, and even pocket billiards. Still, though turkey hunting accidents seem to be declining nationwide, there is no denying that turkey hunting accounts for more than its share of accidents. The larger and heavier the shot, the greater the range at which it presents a hazard, and the more damage it can do at close range. Some hunters argue in favor of lighter shot for this reason.

My own preference is for No. 5s, which strike me as a good compromise between additional pellets for pattern density, and good downrange energy for penetration. However, I only use No. 5s when it patterns as well as, or better than, No. 4s or 6s. Between those three sizes, I'll use whichever size patterns best in a given gun.

There is a lot of talk in the shotshell industry about downrange energy. Some charts have been developed indicating that No. 6 shot cannot be

(Continued)

The Shot Size Debate (*Continued*)

relied upon to penetrate adequately at ranges beyond thirty-five yards. I applaud the inclination to be conservative about range, but I have to say I have bowled several turkeys over with No. 6 shot at ranges out to forty yards and slightly beyond, knocking them off their feet and killing them cleanly. There is an old saying among shotgunners that pattern density will become a problem before downrange energy does. Thus far I have let pattern density determine range for me, and I have yet to lose a turkey as a result of inadequate penetration. That is not to suggest that energy downrange is not a concern. Shotgun pellets shed energy rapidly, and smaller, lighter pellets shed them faster than heavier pellets. If you have a pattern that remains adequately dense at very long ranges, you should give some thought to this, particularly if you are using No. 6 shot or smaller.

Energy is something to keep in mind when considering magnum shells. In the past, magnum shotshells lacked the velocity of comparable non-magnum shells, because they contain proportionately more shot than powder. Manufacturers in recent years have addressed this discrepancy by producing high-velocity magnums.

A related aspect of shot selection is not size but hardness of shot. Shot may be deformed as it travels down the barrel and through the choke. The fewer deformed shot, the better the pattern. All else being equal, hard lead shot performs better than softer lead shot. Simply switching to copper- or nickel-coated shot can significantly improve a pattern. In addition to patterning better, hard, round shot penetrates better than soft or deformed shot.

Chokes, Extended Forcing Cones, Backboring

Shot charges flow through a barrel like water through a hose. The choke is often compared to the nozzle on a hose, constricting the shot charge into a smaller pattern. A key difference is that the results are far less predictable in the case of shot. There is a point, varying from one gun or shotshell to another, at which additional choke ruins a pattern.

Two points hold true about tightening shot patterns, though. First, it is the degree of choke relative to the bore size that determines pattern, as opposed to any absolute size. That is why a full-choke 20 gauge does not necessarily pattern tighter than a full-choke 12 gauge, though the diameter of the choke is much smaller in the case of the 20 gauge.

Second, all else being equal, shot that is more gradually constricted patterns better than shot that is constricted abruptly.

This explains why the modern, super-full-choke tubes extend beyond the barrel. It also explains the increasing popularity of lengthened forcing cones, a highly touted feature on many new shotguns. The forcing cone is the transition from the chamber to the bore-traditionally about three-eighths-inch long. Extending the forcing cone to at least two and one half inches can produce better patterns and somewhat reduce felt recoil. It is doubtful that extending the forcing cone beyond that length achieves any real benefits.

Back-bored barrels have become more popular in recent years as well. Simply put, a back-bored barrel is one that has been enlarged from the chamber forward to the choke. This can benefit patterns in two ways: First, a bigger diameter barrel means less deformed shot. Second back-boring makes the choke smaller relative to the bore, in effect increasing the choke. In fact, barrels that have had the choke removed can in effect have it restored by back-boring.

All these features-lengthened forcing cones, back-boring, and the installation of choke tubes-can be performed by gunsmiths on most modern guns and some older ones. Are they worth it? For the competitive sporting clays shooter looking for every edge, these are all important features. For the turkey hunter? That depends. The installation of choke tubes, if your gun doesn't already feature them, will make it more versatile, and will in all likelihood result in tighter patterns (probably much tighter patterns) with extended, extra-full tubes. The improvements offered by lengthened forcing cones and back-boring will usually be less dramatic. The cost for both would be less than the cost of a new pump shotgun. How badly do you want a slightly better pattern and slightly less recoil? How badly do you want a new pump shotgun that might already feature these options and would probably be shorter and lighter, handle three-and-a-half-inch magnum shotshells, and come decked out in the latest camo pattern?

The Muzzleloader Turkey Challenge

TOBY BRIDGES

Taking a big twenty-five pound wild turkey gobbler with a muzzleloading shotgun could prove to be the greatest challenge the muzzleloading hunter can tackle. Season-wise, older gobblers possess the uncanny ability to give a hunter the slip, making this big bird as much a trophy as any big-game animal. Those who have spent a number of years pursuing this great upland bird often refer to the wild turkey as *"America's Big Game Bird."* One thing is for certain, the hunter who has matched wits with this bird . . . and lost . . . will quickly learn to give it the same respect given to a trophy-class whitetail buck or bull elk.

Any hunter who underestimates the survival instincts of a wily older turkey gobbler is generally destined to go home empty handed. Accept it; the wild turkey is no dummy. It takes a hunter with woods savvy to be consistently successful season after season, especially when going after this tremendous game bird with a close-range muzzleloaded scattergun.

Success with a muzzleloading rifle for whitetails and other big game has encouraged an ever-growing number of hunters to turn to muzzleloading guns for hunting other species as well. And thanks to continually growing wild turkey populations, this big bird is high on that list. In this chapter, we will take a look at the guns and loads, both old and new, that are up to the task of cleanly downing a huge bird that can run thirty m.p.h. and fly fifty m.p.h.

Then . . .

Thirty or so years ago, many states offered very limited turkey hunting opportunities. Hunters often had to enter into a special lottery drawing for one

There is a lot of satisfaction in walking out of the turkey woods with a fine muzzleloaded gobbler thrown over your shoulder.

of a few thousand permits that were to be issued. Today, in many of these same states, the turkey hunter can easily purchase a permit right across the counter. Plus, in quite a few states, the hunter can now harvest two or three turkeys during the course of the season, and many hunters are turning to the Challenge of hunting with a muzzleloading shotgun to harvest at least one of those birds.

Get a gobbler close enough and you can cleanly take the bird with just about any muzzleloading shotgun and load. I once dumped a big Texas

There is something special about taking a wild gobbler with a muzzleloaded shotgun, as twelve-year-old Zack Opel experienced. It's doubly rewarding when it's your first turkey.

Rio Grande gobbler at just twelve yards with an extremely small twenty eight-gauge muzzleloader! But I most definitely wouldn't recommend it as the ideal choice for hunting an adult bird that can easily top twenty pounds. Even at thirty or forty yards, a wild turkey may seem far too large to miss. However, keep in mind that a big gobbler can be a tough target to put down. You see, the target isn't the whole turkey—but rather just the head and neck. In other words, the "kill zone" the muzzleloading shotgunner has to go for measures roughly two inches wide by ten inches tall. A shotgun and load that can put a dozen or more pellets into this zone will better increase your chances of that turkey laying there flapping his last as the smoke thins.

Taking my first muzzleloader turkey was every bit as important to me as taking my first muzzleloader whitetail. That first spring with a muzzleloader, I was hunting the rough Ozarks hill-country of south-central Missouri, and by the third morning of the season, I had enjoyed several close opportunities. But for one reason or another, I felt the birds were just a little farther than I cared to shoot at with the circa 1850s original English built "William Moore" twelve-gauge percussion double I carried for the hunt.

The shotgun was a favorite of mine, and threw nice even patterns when stuffed with a 95-grain charge of FFg black powder and a one and three eighths-ounce charge of No. 5 shot. Now, since the thirty-four-inch barrels did not exhibit the first hint of choke constriction, the patterns were far from being tight. But by carefully loading the big double with near equal volumes of powder and shot, plus the proper combination of traditional muzzleloader shotgun wads, the patterns were very evenly dispersed. At twenty-five yards, I found that I could easily keep ten or so of the No. 5 pellets on a 2" × 10" strip of construction paper, used to

Toby Bridges with the first gobbler he ever took with the Dixie ten-gauge double, a fine tom from Missouri.

Father and son double—author Toby Bridges, right, and son Adam enjoy a little conversation about the morning turkey hunt. Bridges' muzzleloading twelve-gauge Knight MK-86 performed every bit as well as his son's three-inch magnum twelve-gauge pump.

duplicate the target I would be going for if and when I got a big gobbler within that range.

At the first crack of daybreak on the fourth morning, a roosted gobbler answered back to my owl hooting. The bird was just one hundred and fifty yards away. Slowly and quietly, I cut the distance in half and settled down next to an old logging road. The tom continued to gobble on his own, and just before I felt it was time for him to fly down, I gave a very light hen yelp on my slate call. I heard the bird leave the roost and hit the ground, so sat the call on the carpet of leaves and rested the big double on an upraised knee. I had just drawn the right hammer to full cock when I spotted the gobbler coming on at a half walk, half run. At twenty yards, the bird stopped, raised its head and

started looking around. When the hammer fell, the nearly one hundred and seventy-five-year-old shotgun roared. That gobbler was floored by the load.

I took several more gobblers with that old shotgun before retiring it. The gun was replaced with a modern ten-gauge reproduction percussion double Dixie Gun Works still offers today, sold as their "Ten-Gauge Magnum." Shooting a hefty 100-grain charge of FFg black powder and one and a half ounces of No. 6 shot, this gun performed well on wild turkey. However, it still threw relatively open patterns, limiting shots to twenty to twenty-five yards. So, I played around with developing a wad (of sorts) that would help maintain tighter patterns at thirty and maybe thirty-five yards.

Back then, I did a lot of modern shotgunning as well, and reloaded my own 20-, 16- and 12-gauge shot shells. I discovered that a crimped sixteen-gauge hull would slip right into the muzzle of the Dixie ten-gauge, and the experimenting began. The version of the homemade wad that produced the best patterns was made by filling a fired sixteen-gauge hull with shot, then running it under the crimper of my reloader. Once the hull had been crimped, I would take a sharp knife and cut the plastic hull all the way around just above the brass head. And once the plastic had been cut free, I would dump out the shot, then take the cup produced and cut three evenly spaced one-inch cuts at the open end. This formed the petals or sleeves needed to pull the homemade shot cup back from the shot charge.

I worked my load up to 110 grains of FFg black powder. Over the powder charge, I would seat a single .125-inch *over-powder* card wad, and top that with a half-inch-thick *fiber cushion wad*. Right on top of that, I would set the homemade plastic shot cup, then poured down the one and three-quarters ounces of No. 6 shot it took to fill it. The entire load was then topped with a .030-inch-thick over-shot card wad. So loaded, the Dixie ten-bore proved to be a very effective thirty- to thirty-five-yard turkey gun. At the longer distance, the gun and load would consistently keep ten or twelve pellets on the 2"×10" strip of construction paper I used for my target.

Muzzleloading shotgunners today don't have to go to this much effort to work up such a turkey load for any open-bored frontloading shotgun. Ballistics Products (Corcoran, Minnesota) now offers several different twelve- and ten-gauge shot cups that come without any slits for forming the petals, or sleeves. These can be loaded the same as my old homemade shot cup, allowing the shooter to determine the length of petal or sleeve that results in the best patterns from a particular smooth-bore. And if you go this route, just be sure to slit the cups, because without the sleeves to pull the shot cup away from the shot charge, at under twenty yards a still shot-filled cup can hit an old turkey gobbler with the same devastating effects as a rifled slug!

Now . . .

Just as the modern-day muzzleloading big-game hunter has taken to the futuristic in-line muzzleloading rifles and top-performing loads, the serious turkey hunter looking to use a frontloaded smooth-bore is now turning to similarly styled muzzleloading shotguns. Like the modern rifles, these guns are built with an efficient in-line percussion-ignition system that greatly reduces any chances of a misfire—as long as the hunter has snapped a cap on the ignition system before loading, and loaded the shotgun properly.

Tony Knight with a big twenty-seven pound Iowa tom take with a 12-gauge MK-86 and a healthy load of No. 5 shot.

Introduced in the early 1990s, the Knight MK-86 was the first of these in-line muzzleloading smooth-bore wonders. Aside from the modern in-line ignition system and modern safety system found on this shotgun, the one other feature that has made this front-loading twelve-gauge so effective on wild turkey is the .665-inch "extra-full" screw-in choke that came standard on this shotgun. When a shooter takes the time to build a precise load, this modern muzzleloading shotgun is fully capable of matching the performance of a modern three-inch magnum breechloading shotgun.

The muzzle of the twenty-four-inch Knight MK-86 barrel is threaded to accept screw-in interchangeable chokes of the "Rem-Choke" variety. The one Knight shipped with the gun was a .665 Hastings choke, which immediately lets everyone know that this was intended to be one serious turkey gun. Another feature I really liked about the modern smooth-bore was that the receiver came drilled and tapped for easy installation of a low-power scope, or a simple rear peep sight. That first season with an MK-86, I relied on a 1X scope that allowed me to adjust the center of my pattern to print dead on a gobbler's head and neck. Since then, I've replaced the scope with a William's receiver sight. Both approaches sure take the guesswork out of aiming.

The extremely tight constriction of the .665 Hastings choke requires that the choke be removed in order to get properly fitting wads into the barrel. However, it took only once for me to learn that you should first dump in your powder charge, then remove the choke for the remainder of the loading sequence. If the choke is removed and a powder charge dumped in, quite a few powder granules will end up in the threads for the choke found inside the bore. This makes threading the choke back in place after the shotgun has been loaded extremely difficult.

The Knight MK-86 that I have hunted with since the gun was first offered seems to perform best when loaded with a hefty 110-grain charge of Pyrodex "RS/Select." Over that, I load a .125-inch heavy *over-powder* card wad and two of the one quarter-inch thick lubed Ox-Yoke Originals felt shotgun wads. Next, I push down one of the Ballistic Products "Turkey Ranger" twelve-gauge shot cups, and fill this with a one and three-quarter-ounce charge of No. 6 lubaloy copper-coated lead shot. The load is topped with one of the twelve-gauge styrofoam Knight over- shot wads. Now, the "Turkey Ranger" wad is one of the Ballistics Products shot cups that comes non-slitted. I usually slit mine down about a half-inch, which is enough to form an airfoil that will pull the cup away from the shot charge shortly after leaving the muzzle.

Once the loading process is completed, the extra-full choke tube is threaded back into the muzzle. And so loaded, this shotgun will keep nearly one hundred per- cent of the shot load inside that magic thirty-inch circle at thirty yards. At forty yards, the load is good for around ninety percent patterns. At fifty yards, the MK-86 so loaded has proven capable of hitting with right at eighty percent of the pattern inside a thirty-inch circle. And while I don't really condone "long-range" shooting at wild turkey gobblers, I can remember one stubborn old Iowa bird that refused to come any closer, and the MK-86 reached out and tapped him at nearly fifty yards. The gobbler turned out to be the largest I've ever taken—a twenty-eight and a half pounder!

Knight Rifles has more recently replaced the MK-86 with an all-new in-line model known as the TK-2000. For this very modern in-line percussion shotgun, Knight actually reverts back to some very old technology. Instead of a constricted choke, the company installs a new "screw-on" jug choke. Other than the fact that this choke screws on, the concept is not all that different than the jug chokes that showed up in some shotgun bores during the second half of the 19th century.

The TK-2000 is a true twelve-bore, and is still loaded pretty much the same as the old MK-86—except the shooter now does not have to remove the choke to get proper fitting wads into the gun. The jug choke found in the screw-on choke tube actually opens up larger than true twelve gauge, then returns to the actual bore-size of the barrel a little more than an inch from the muzzle. This allows the shot charge to move along parallel with the bore all the way to the choke. Then the expanded internal dimension lets the shot follow the surface, outward and away from the center of the shot load. However, as the surface turns back in and returns to actual bore size, the shot is then redirected in toward the center of the shot charge. Many shooters who have hunted with this shotgun report exceptional turkey-taking patterns out to forty or more yards.

Another of my personal favorite muzzleloading shotguns is the Lenartz "Turkey Taker" produced by Lenartz Muzzleloading, a small semi-custom gunmaking operation located near Alto, Michigan. The gun is actually a twelve-gauge version of the Rdi-50 (Radial Drop Ignition) in-line ignition rifle also produced by this company. Both feature an effective, easy-to-use ignition system that utilizes a hot No. 209 primer. To prime, the shooter simply lifts a small handle on the gun's "primer cover," exposing a primer-shaped opening. A .209 primer is dropped in, and the handle pushed back down to enclose the primer.

The "Turkey Taker" I've used now for a number of seasons is a great performer with the same load I shoot in my old Knight MK-86, and loaded in the same manner. The feature I like about this light six

Muzzleloading gun maker Tim Lenartz with a fine Illinois gobbler he took at forty yards with one of his own twelve-gauge "Turkey Taker" in-line shotguns. This one features a .665-inch extra-full screw-choke.

and a half pound in-line muzzleloader is its short, easy-handling length thanks to the short receiver and twenty-two-inch barrel. Lenartz also installs a set of great Williams adjustable rifle sights on the barrel, allowing a shooter to sight the center-density of a load to print right where the gun is aimed. The Lenartz muzzleloader is a delight to carry all day in the turkey woods, and really performs when its time to pull the trigger.

The turkey hunter who likes a blend of modern performance and a bit of old-fashioned tradition should look at the Cabela's twelve- and ten-gauge doubles that also come with screw-in chokes. These great side-by-sides allow the turkey hunter to have a "modified" choke in one barrel for those birds that often run in almost too close for the tight pattern of the "extra-full" choke—in the other barrel for those stubborn old birds that won't step an inch closer than thirty yards. Like the in-lines with constricted chokes, the tubes must be removed for loading proper-fitting wads.

It's hard to believe that a muzzleloading shotgun can throw a thirty-yard pattern such as this. However, the Knight MK-86 shown here comes with a screw-in "extra-full" choke tube that will outperform many three-inch magnum-pump and semi-auto 12-gauge turkey guns.

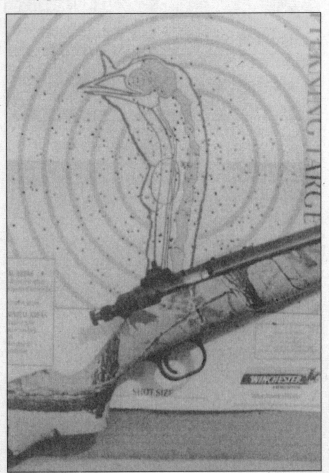

My most memorable morning of hunting wild turkey was one I hunted with one of the Cabela's twelve-gauge doubles. Work had kept me from hunting the last week of the Missouri season, but as daybreak broke that last Saturday of season, I was standing in a pasture only a mile or so from my home. I waited to hear the first gobble of the morning, and when a gobbler greeted the coming day from a ridge a half-mile away, I hooted like an owl. And another gobbler answered less than one hundred yards away.

I eased down next to big white oak and called once very lightly with my old Rohm Borthers box call, and that gobbler went ballistic. It had rained through the night and that bird was apparently very lonely. I heard him fly down, and called lightly again. The turkey cut me off with a gobble before I ended the third note. I sat the call down and waited. Only a couple of minutes passed and there he was, just fifteen yards away. I waited for the tom to move behind a tree, then corrected the direction of the muzzles of the Cabela's double. When the bird stepped out, I putted lightly on the diaphragm call

The short, easy handling length of the Lenartz "Turkey Taker" has made the shotgun one of the author's favorite muzzleloading turkey guns.

This Iowa tom was taken with a Thompson/Center Arms muzzleloading 12-gauge in-line, topped with a scope for easy centering of a pattern on a gobbler's head and neck area.

Well, I had an Iowa tag in my pocket as well, and lived only fifteen miles from the state line. The season was open and I knew a farm I could hunt, so I jumped in my Jeep and made the twenty-minute drive. As I climbed out of the vehicle, I could hear two birds gobbling back and forth to one-another. A few minutes later, I slipped in between them and did some excited calling. When I first sat down to call, I was about one hundred and fifty yards from each of the birds. But after a few series of cuts and clucks, and a few excited yelps, both were coming to me. And they were coming fast. I reached up and cocked back the hammer of the left barrel, and waited. Both showed up almost simultaneously, and in range. When the better of the two stepped clear of the other gobbler, I centered the bead on the base of the tom's waddles and brought the trigger back. At thirty five yards, the "extra-full" choke tube and 100-grain charge of FFg black powder behind one and a half ounces of No. 5 shot dumped that bird where he stood. The turkey was almost identical in every respect to the one I had taken just forty-five minutes earlier in Missouri with the right barrel.

in the roof of my mouth and up came his head—and back came the trigger. Ten minutes later, I was back home with a beautiful twenty-four-pound gobbler and the sun wasn't even all the way up yet.

A two-state double in less than an hour. And it was done with a slow-to-load muzzleloading shotgun.

Weather-Proofing the Muzzleloading Turkey Shotgun

Spring turkey seasons just happen to take place during what is usually the wettest time of the year. In fact, many short two-week long seasons are often cut nearly in half due to inclement weather. And if you've ever hunted turkeys, you know what it's like to get really soaked.

Unfortunately, the number one reason for a misfire with any muzzleloaded gun is due to rainy weather. So, when faced with hunting during damp weather, what precautions can the muzzleloading turkey hunter take to insure that when the opportunity presents itself that a muzzleloading shotgun, whether of traditional or modern design, will belch fire, smoke, and a healthy charge of shot when the trigger is pulled?

(Continued)

Weather-Proofing the Muzzleloading Turkey Shotgun *(Continued)*

Easily the most vulnerable part of a load is the percussion cap that produces the fire for ignition. This is especially true with the traditional side-hammer guns, where the cap is right out in the open, and most vulnerable to wet weather. The solution is actually pretty simple. Just run down to the local archery shop and pick up a tube of bowstring wax. Then take a few seconds to rub down the cone of each nipple. And once a percussion cap has been pushed down onto the waxed surface, rub a little more wax around the base of the copper cap. This really seals the ignition primer inside from the weather. Now, RWS percussion caps are some of the most waterproof on the market, but even when using these, I still use the bowstring wax to insure that moisture stays out. And getting to the nipple of an in-line rifle does take a little more effort, but the time spent to coat the nipple and base of the cap with wax could mean the difference in just the hammer falling or the shotgun firing.

Another good loading habit to get into when going after spring gobblers with a muzzleloaded smooth-bore is to squirt a dab of grease-based black powder lube onto the bottom of the fiber cushion wad. Then, when this wad is seated down over the heavy over-powder card wad, this lube will be "squished" into as thin protective barrier that will keep moisture from reaching the powder charge. Plus, when the shotgun is fired, the lube will help keep the fouling from the burning powder charge soft, making the reloading of that barrel easier.

Some muzzleloading turkey hunters also stretch something thin over the muzzle, to keep rain and dampness out of the barrel altogether. I've seen everything from a small balloon to several strips of vinyl electrician's tape used. All such precautions will keep the load dry from the weather, and the muzzleloaded turkey shotgun as close to 100-percent sure-fire as a muzzleloader can get.

Part 6
Bird Hunting

Introduction

JAY CASSELL

Last year I had the opportunity to duck hunt out of Bay Flats Lodge, south of Corpus Cristi in Seadrift, Texas. After airboating to blinds strategically placed on small islands throughout San Antonio Bay, just off the Gulf of Mexico, we'd hunker down and wait as the sun slowly came up. You could hear birds overhead, their wings whistling in the dark as they flew out to feed. But then, once the sun came up, the action got fast and furious, as huge flocks of redheads and small groups of pintails pitched into our decoy set. The shooting was fast, everyone in our group of 10 got birds (I shot my first bull sprig, or male pintail), and just watching the Labs retrieve those birds was worth the price of admission.

Redheads in Texas, black ducks in Maine, mallards in Arkansas, geese in Manitoba – you can go just about anywhere and find good duck and goose hunting. And the good news is that duck populations in particular are now at record levels across much of the country – thanks in large part to strong conservation work by groups such as Ducks Unlimited and Delta Waterfowl.

If waterfowl aren't your birds of choice, we included hunting information in here on many other types of birds as well – from pheasants to quail to doves to grouse, with some shotgunning and wingshooting tips added to help you hit what you're shooting at.

—J. C.

Bird Hunting Tips

LAMAR UNDERWOOD

Duck Hunting Tips

Wind and Your Decoy Setups

The truth is that you can spread your duck decoys just about any way you wish, as long as you leave an open area for the birds to land into the wind. No matter which way they come from, or how much they circle, their final move down will be into the wind. No wind at all? It becomes a guessing game.

The Toughest Shot in Duck Hunting

Shooting a cripple on the water is duck hunting's toughest shot. You'll see your shot pattern absolutely smother the bird, yet it will swim on.

How Fast are They? Let's Ask Hemingway

" . . . You can remember duck shooting in the blind, hearing their wings go *whichy-chu-chu-chu* in the dark before daylight. That is the first thing I remember of ducks; the whistly, silk tearing sound the fast wingbeats make; just as what you remember first of geese is how slow they seem to go when they are traveling, and yet they are moving so fast that the first one you ever killed was two behind the one you shot at, and all that night you kept waking up and remembering how he folded up and fell."

—Ernest Hemingway, "Remembering Shooting— Flying," *Esquire* magazine, February 1935

"Special Effect" Decoys

Decoy makers today have waterfowl hunters covered from every possible angle, including sleepers (actually resembling sleeping birds), feeders (with necks outstretched), and bobbers (rear ends of ducks feeding under the surface).

Mack's Prairie Wings: Don't Miss it!

Down in Stuttgart, Arkansas, the Command Center of classic, tall-timber mallard gunning, the waterfowl emporium Mack's Prairie Wings has everything the serious waterfowl hunter could hope for. Named after Richard Bishop's classic Prairie Wings book about the area, Mack's options include fantastic links that just take you into the current state of waterfowling everywhere.

—www.mackspw.com.

Guide's Advice I Don't Want to Hear

In the duck blind, you'll often hear your guide urge you to, "Stay down. Keep your head down. Don't watch the birds! I'll do the watching." Well, if you're not watching the birds, you're losing part of the joys of the hunt. Your blind should be good enough for you to peer through the stalks or brush just as the guide is doing. When the ducks are passing right overhead, neither one of you should be looking skyward. You'll spook the birds for sure.

Take 'Em? or Let Them Circle?

"Mallards, blacks, gadwalls, widgeon, and pintails all like to circle a decoy set once or twice before they decide to come in. Two or three birds may leave the flock and pass in nice range. Take 'em! Never mind the flock."

—Ray P. Holland, *Scattergunning*, Knopf, 1951

A Waterfowl Hunter's Classic Book

A Book on Duck Shooting by Van Campen Heilner is the magnum opus of waterfowl hunting books. Illustrated in color and black-and-white by the legendary Lynn Bogue Hunt and complete with a huge selection of photographs, the book is a total portrait of duck hunting from the far North to South America and even Europe. Originally published by Penn Publishing, Philadelphia, in 1939, the book can be found on used book sites like Amazon (www.amazon.com) and Alibris (www.alibris.com) and others. A new edition has been published by Premier Press, Camden, South Carolina, with an introduction by Jim Casada.

Local Birds: Use Small Decoy Spreads for Small Bunches

Make a distinction between the resident ducks you hunt in early season and the large flocks that migrate in later on. You'll spot resident birds in pairs and small flocks, so decoy them accordingly and don't burn out any one place by hunting it too often. Save the big spreads for when the birds from up north show up.

Why Cans are Number One

"Now, the canvasback is the king of ducks in the old hunter's book, and an epicure's delight in the bargain. He is the hardest of them all to hit as he hurtles hell-bent across the sky. The big bulls remind you of a jet fighter with their bullet heads and sharp, small, swept-back wings. Those wings claw air at such a furious clip that they send the big, fat bodies racing along faster than any other duck. They are straightaway speedsters made for a big track, and they never flare or dodge."

—Jimmy Robinson, "Bull Cans of the Delta," *Sports Afield*, 1938, referenced in *Autumn Passages*, Ducks Unlimited and Willow Creek Press, 1995

The Making of a Duck Caller . . . Sort of

You might say I'm a Clint Eastwood-Dirty Harry, sort of duck caller. Clint said, "A man has got to know his limitations." My own call rests in my pocket mostly, because I'm not very good with the thing and because, like Blanche in *A Streetcar Named Desire*, "I've always depended upon the kindness of strangers," meaning guides and hunting-camp hosts who really know their stuff when it comes to tooting on a duck call. In Arkansas and Tennessee, the calling lanyards these guys wear aren't just for showing off duck bands.

Pothole Sneak Attack

If you've scouted out a promising pothole or small pond and you're planning to jump-shoot the ducks that are resting there, try to sneak up on them with the wind at your back. When the ducks jump into the wind (which they most certainly will do), you might get a shot before they re-orient themselves and fly the other way.

Mix 'Em up if You Want to

So you're thinking about adding some bluebills or canvasbacks (diving ducks) to your decoy setup of mallards, pintails, and gadwalls (puddle ducks) to give your spread more visibility. Go right ahead. It won't hurt your chances a bit.

Gloves for Setting out Decoys

Gloves that stretch almost to your elbows and keep your hands dry are a must for setting out decoys. Shuck 'em off and wear your regular gloves when you get into the blind. See the "Midwest PVC Decoy Glove" at Mack's Prairie Wings, www. mackspw.com. Check other favorite waterfowl gear vendors for other options.

Too Hidden for a Good Shot

When you're hunkered down in a blind so that you can't see the ducks you're working, when it comes time for someone to exclaim, "Take 'em!" you come up with your gun and have to find the birds before you get down to pointing and swinging the barrel. It won't be an easy shot.

Wait out Those Gadwalls

Gadwalls can be tricky when they're working your decoy. In his classic book

Scattergunning, legendary *Field & Stream* editor and waterfowler Ray P. Holland advises, "Gadwalls are particularly prone to circle and circle. Keep your head down and don't move, and they will come within range when ready."

Jump-shooting Joys

Jump-shooting ducks from a canoe or john-boat is a great way to hunt some creeks and small rivers. The best way is with a partner, one hunter with the gun at the ready, the other on the paddling. Stay quiet, anticipate the sharp bends where you may surprise a few mallards, blacks, or other puddle ducks. Listen carefully as you go. You just might hear the birds before you get to them.

Pond Shooting at Sunset: The Way it Used to be

Waiting for ducks at sunset beside ponds where the ducks would be coming to roost was

once a mainstay of hunting tactics. Local wood ducks, mallards, and black ducks, puddle ducks of all sorts that had migrated into a particular area—they all come hurtling into the ponds after sunset. Sometimes the shooting was so late, the birds had to be outlined against the western sky. Today, shooters who try this are easy marks for wardens waiting nearby to hear the sounds of gunshots after legal shooting hours. If you want to just watch the show (and you should!) leave your guns in the truck.

Northeast Arkansas: They've Got the Ducks

I've had wonderful duck hunting with Charles Snapp around Walnut Ridge and the Cache River area of northeast Arkansas, near the Cache River. The region has tremendous rice-producing activity, and today is said to "short-stop" a lot of the ducks that would be heading on down to the famous Stuttgart area. Look for duck guides and camps in Northeast Arkansas.

Movement—Not the Blind—Wrecks Your Chances

Most of the time, when ducks working toward your decoys decide to flare away, it was movement that spooked them, not your blind, no matter how flimsy.

Dreams of a Duck Caller

I admit to being a card-carrying Calling Wannabe, bitten by the bug in my youth when I opened a package from Herter's. Inside were my first duck call and a 78-rpm record on using it—complete with the recorded sounds of an actual hunt. That big, beautiful wooden call became a prized possession. I played that record constantly,

soaking up the notes of the Highball, the Comeback Call, the Feeding Chuckle, even the harsh Brrrrr, Brrrrr used on diving ducks. Suddenly, duck hunting became more fun than ever—even on blank days when not a duck turned to my call or fell to my gun.

It's All about Visibility, Visibility, Visibility

Unless you're gunning a tiny creek-bottom or river location, surrounded by high trees, most of your duck-hunting locations will be in open areas where you hope passing birds can see your decoys and come on in. Anything you can do to increase the visibility of your spread will make a difference. Black decoys show up better from a distance. Magnum-size adds visibility. Canada geese decoys add visibility, whether you're hunting geese or not. Movement devices (the ones that are legal where you hunt) are critical if there's no wind blowing: spinners, battery-driven shakers, pull-cord movers—whatever you've got.

Using Double-barreled Guns in the Blind

Despite their status as classic smoothbores, side-by-side and over-and-under double-barrels have two issues with some waterfowl hunters. First is the two-shot limit. Some consider that a liability. They want three shots. Next is the fact that doubles must be broken open for feeding, and that can sometimes by cumbersome in the blind.

Take My Hand!

Duck and goose hunters are around water, docks, boats, slick boards to walk on, slick steps to climb—all sorts of uneven, unsteady spots to negotiate. Seniors who hope to keep enjoying hunting as long as they can should not hesitate in asking someone to "Take my hand!" It's a lot better than ruining your day.

The Great Blue Heron Decoy Trick

Many of the old-time waterfowl market hunters swore by the trick us having a Great Blue Heron decoy in their spread. The Heron is a wary bird that won't allow anything to approach it very closely, therefore the old-timers felt a Heron in the decoys was a real confidence booster. Today you can buy a heron decoy from several major waterfowl gear providers and try out the trick yourself.

Speaking up for Mallards

"I glowed with elation at the prospect of matching wits again with the mallard. One does well to select it as his favorite duck. . . .There are faster ducks and those less reluctant to decoy. The mallard lacks some of the patrician qualities of the canvasback, the bluebill's dash and the brilliant flight performance of the teals. But its intelligence seldom sleeps. When it spills from the skies, wing-bars flashing iridescently, a feather or two floating in the wake of the charge that struck it down, no gunner, no matter how often he has centered such a target, fails to respond in a feeling of satisfaction and achievement."

—Kendrick Kimball, "Pintail Point,"
Field & Stream, 1935, reprinted in *The Field &*
Stream Reader, Doubleday, 1946

Duck Hunting's Outer Edge

Maine sea duck hunting, in coves of freezing rough water and along rocky coasts of pounding surf, can be so risky that I once ran an article when I was editing *Sports Afield* called "Ducks of the Deadly Ledges." Despite the dangerous implications, this can be fantastic hunting for eiders, scoters and assorted puddle ducks. The eider, by the way, makes a wonderful trophy mount. Just type the words "Maine sea duck hunting" into Google and you'll get lots of sites.

When it's Bluebills We're after

"Into this rocket-minded world the speedy bluebill fits most admirably. If there is jet propulsion among birds it all started with him. As he rides the northern gales he comes with the speed of a bullet, and he is gone before the slow-minded hunter can get his gun to his shoulder. For those who love duck hunting the time of the bluebill is the high mark of the year. Few birds are speedier, few offer a more sporting target. And, above all, few are more obliging in responding to decoys. For the bluebill, 'scaups' to the hunters on the Eastern Shore, is a gregarious little bundle of energy. He loves company and he will arrow into your stool with the greatest of confidence, even eagerness. Another high recommendation for him is his edibility."

—Jimmy Robinson, "Rockets of the North,"
Sports Afield, 1937, referenced in *Autumn Passages,*
Ducks Unlimited and Willow Creek Press, 1995

Magnum or Super-Magnum?

Over-sized decoys certainly increase the visibility of your spread. The choice of Magnum or Super- Magnum boils down to visibility versus carry. You can carry more Magnum decoys in your bag than Super Magnum.

The "Hole" is the Thing

No matter what shape of decoy spread you decide is right for your hunting location and conditions, it must contain a hole or two for the birds to land. If the water in front of the blind is

certain conditions and situations. The big waters, the swift rivers, the wind and rain and ice and fog, all that gear to be managed—it's not always easy hunting. If you're a senior or disabled, you have to consider hunting only when you have a buddy along.

The Outer Gun: The Key Position

The Outside shooter on the upwind side of permanent duck blinds or lay-out blind setups is in the key position and can absolutely ruin the shooting for everybody with him. It's happened to me more times than I can remember. The ducks, or geese, are coming into the spread against the wind, from his side. If he starts shooting too early, around the corner, the guns in the center and other side will get no shots, or shots at widely flaring birds only. Sometimes, to top off this little drama, the outside offender will turn to the other guys and say, "Why didn't you guys shoot?" Advice: Put an experienced shooter in that outside position, a shooter with the judgment and nerve to wait until the birds are into the spread enough so everybody can shoot.

solid with decoys, the birds will land on the outside of the spread, at long range or even out of range.

Winchester's Model 12: A Waterfowling Treasure

The Winchester Model 12 pump is one of the greatest guns that ever went duck hunting. If you possess one of the originals, consider yourself a lucky gunner.

Waterfowl Hunting's Most Important Tip

You won't bag any ducks or geese unless you're hunting where (choose one, or all) they're flying, feeding, or resting. Today! If you don't see birds in the fields, in the water, or in the air, you'll have to set up at a spot where you've seen them before (like yesterday, perhaps) and hope for the best.

Considering the Risks

The reality of waterfowl hunting is that it can be rather daunting—even downright dangerous in

Where'd the Mallards Go?

When you're on a marsh in the early morning where you reasonably expect a flight of mallards, don't be surprised if they don't show up until later in the morning. Your local birds, or even visitors from the north, may be feeding in the fields.

Black Ducks—Red Letter Day

My calling aspirations reached a sort of pinnacle years later. I was hunkered on an icy creek on the marshes of the Chesapeake Bay, near the famous Susquehanna Flats. A pair of black ducks flew down the creek, very high and in a big hurry, headed somewhere with express tickets. They clearly were not interested in my modest decoy spread, but when I hit them with my old Herter's call and the Highball, they turned like I had 'em wired. Interested then, they circled warily while I scrunched down. Now I started rattling off my Feeding Chuckle, and a few moments later they were cupped and committed. I could finally say that I knew how to call ducks.

Waterfowl Hunting with Sean Mann

From his headquarters on the Eastern Shore of Maryland, Champion caller and call-maker Sean Mann runs waterfowl hunting adventures on the Shore and hunting ducks and geese in Alberta that is some of the finest this author has ever seen. Some of the photographs in this book taken by photographer Tim Irwin were made when hunting with the author and Sean in Alberta, at his camp outside Edmonton. Sean runs a quality operation, with leases that put the gunner where the birds are regardless of the time and conditions. Bag limits in Canada are generous, and the shooting simply spectacular. For complete details, go to Sean's Web site, www.duck-goosecalls.com, or phone Sean Mann's Hunting Adventures for brochures at (800) 345-4539. Sean starts hunting in Canada in September, so book early.

As the Season Goes on . . .

If you're a serious duck hunter and you don't already know this, you soon will: As the season progresses the ducks will fly higher and higher, and you will keep having to add decoys to your spread to attract their attention.

Remington's 870 Wingmaster Pump

As a "working man's" choice for a great waterfowling gun, the Remington 870 Wingmaster pump has brought down a lot of ducks and geese for a lot of folks without breaking the family budgets. It was the favorite gun of Sports Afield's legendary Jimmy Robinson.

An Unusual Duck-hunting Safety Reminder

Bangor, Maine outdoor writer and waterfowling veteran Tom Hennessey received what may be the ultimate reminder on duck-hunting safety. Although the subject is dead serious, as we've pointed out above, this one is funny. On the way out the door with his lab Coke, Tom heard his wife Nancy say, "Who are you going hunting with?" He answered, "I'm going alone." Tom says Nancy's pause and reply were as chilling as the pre-dawn darkness: "If something happens to you, how will Cokie get home?"

Jump-shooting on Western Rivers

"So you jump the islands by floating down from above, scanning carefully with binoculars to see if any mallards or Canadas are resting in the lee water down at the tail . . . Then you paddle like hell to put the island between you and the birds, beach at the upper end, then sneak down through the mini-forest."

—John Barsness, Western Skies, Lyons & Burford, 1994

Where the Birds Want to be

Pushing into a cove in the marsh or along a big river or lake, in the first pre-dawn light, you flush a big bunch of ducks or geese. Away they go, gabbling and honking. Never mind trying to follow them or heading for another spot. Set up right there. It's the place the birds want to be.

"Take 'Em!"

Few moments afield are as thrilling as those when a big flock of ducks sweeps into your decoys. You'll shoot a lot better when you are aware whether your birds are diving ducks—like bluebills and canvasbacks—or puddle ducks—like mallards and pintails. Diving ducks will bore straight past when the shooting starts, while puddle ducks will bounce skyward as though launched from a trampoline.

Tall-timber Trick

When gunning the hole in the tall timber with a few decoys out, give the water around your tree a good kick when birds are passing or circling to imitate splashing and feeding activity.

You Really Ought to Join DU

There are so many good reasons for a serious waterfowl hunter to join Ducks Unlimited (DU)

that we can't list them all. Their Web site for hunters, www.ducks.org/hunting, will tell you all about membership benefits, including a wonderful magazine, hunting tips, videos, and the great work DU does to preserve waterfowl habitat. You can phone them at (800) 45-DUCKS.

When Ducks are on the Way in

When your calls have gotten the attention of a passing flock, and the birds have turned and are in the way in, there are two opposing views on what to do with your call next. One (the majority, by the way) says to cease all calling and let them come on. The other warns that if you've been doing the feeding chuckle, keep it up as the birds come on. To stop now might spook them.

Don't Forget to Plug That Gun

The most frequent ticketed waterfowl hunting violation is failure to plug pumps and autos to three shots. Many hunters have this happen simply because they haven't checked their gun properly.

Tell Your Guide about Your Calling

When you've been putting in a lot of time and practice on your duck calling, don't let the guide's obvious skill keep you from doing your thing. You've paid for the trip, and you ought to have a chance to see what you can do while you're in an area where the ducks are flying.

Avoiding a Deadly Leap

"To see a retriever hit the water in one of those long, hell-bent leaps is, without question, an impressive sight. Fact of the matter, though, is that it can be downright dangerous. Often waterlogged and floating just beneath the surface, long splinters and stubs of stumps and fallen trees can impale your dog. Common sense dictates that deadwood snags or other such obstructions should be removed from the area in front of the blind."

—Tom Hennessey, *Feathers 'n Fins*,
The Amwell Press, 1989

A Different Type of Decoy Setup

Guide Rick Nemecek told writer Wade Bourne that he doesn't believe in standard decoy patterns like a J-Hook or U: "I believe these patterns become familiar to ducks that see them day after day. Instead, I set my stool in small family clusters with three to six decoys per cluster. Now the overall pattern may be a J or a U, but it's loose. These clusters don't run together to form long strings." (For more tips from Rick Nemecek and other top guides see Wade Bourne's book, *Decoys and Proven Methods for Using Them*, Ducks Unlimited, 2000.)

A Cut Above

Freelance duck and goose hunters can run into a lot of stuff that needs cutting fast. Avery Outdoors Avery Quick Cutter is a powerful ratchet-style cutter

that will take out the toughest brush or even stray wire. With it you should carry the Avery Speed Saw, with seven razor-sharp teeth per inch. It could help you build you blind anywhere. Break-Up camo pouches or you can get a combo patch that hold both.

—www.averyoutdoors.com

Early Morning Pothole Tactic

When ducks are on a pothole in the early morning and have not left for their day's feeding, you have a choice: Try to sneak up on the pothole before they leave, OR try to get a shot pass shooting as they fly over on their way to the fields. The later approach depends on your scouting abilities. Have you discovered the route they take from the pothole to the fields?

The First Decoy Spreads—Ever!

In his wonderful book *Decoys and Proven Methods for Using Them*, Wade Bourne reports on the discovery by anthropologists in 1924 of a basket of eleven canvasback-shaped, woven, tule-reed decoys made by Indians in the Humboldt Sink area of west-central Nevada, carefully wrapped and buried 2,000 years ago.

Decoy Choices of a Top Guide

In his book *Decoys and Proven Methods for Using Them*, writer Wade Bourne reports on the strategies of Rick Nemecek of Port Clinton, Ohio, longtime guide on the Sandusky Bay marshes on the south shore of Lake Erie. Nemecek says, "I've talked to biologists who fly aerial waterfowl surveys, and they've told me the first thing they notice when they see ducks on the water is their black profiles. So my early season spread will include one-third to onehalf black duck decoys. Then the next thing biologists tell me they see is white, so I always set two or three pintail drakes in my spread. My typical early season spread of eighteen decoys includes seven or eight black ducks, three pintail drakes—and the rest mallards. In later season, my spread of thirty-six decoys includes twenty-four black ducks, three pintails, and nine mallards."

Choke Tube Add-on

A waterfowl gun decision that comes up all the time is whether to stay with your factory choke tubes or purchase one of the highly-touted add-ons. In an article on the Cabela's Web site, www.cabelas.com, writer Adam Bender says he's been getting patterns more effective than factory tubes with Carlson's Black Cloud Choke Tubes, using Federal's Black Cloud steel shot loads. The Cabela's site offers other choke tube choices as well.

Picking up the Decoys the Easy Way

Here are a couple of nifty ways to pick up your duck decoys without having to lean out of the boat. For one, cut a notch in the blade of a paddle. Hook onto the decoy anchor line and lift. As an option, create a special pole from a 5- to 7-ft. dowel rod with a metal hook screwed into the end.

The Wind Rules the Direction

Like airplanes, ducks and geese will land into the wind—whatever wind there is, a wisp of breeze or a gale. Plan you blind location and decoy setup accordingly, because this isn't a maybe. They will come in into the wind!

Some Realities of Sea-duck Hunting

"Sea-duck shooting—eiders and coots—brought into vogue by the one-a-day limit on black ducks, is educating hunters to dangers that neither they nor their dogs have encountered on sheltered bays and marshes. Make no mistake about it, sea-duck shooting is rough business, and a dog fetching eider ducks from an offshore ledge takes a beating."

—Tom Hennessey, *Feathers 'n Fins,*
The Amwell Press, 1989

A Must-see Waterfowling Museum

Located on the banks of the historic Susquehanna Flats, at Havre de Grace, Maryland, not far from I-95, the Havre de Grace Decoy Museum houses one of the finest collections of working and decorative Chesapeake Bay decoys ever assembled. The museum was established in 1986 as a private, non-profit institution existing to preserve the historical and cultural legacy of waterfowling and decoy making on the Chesapeake Bay. There are also displays of blinds, boats and shooting rigs. Every serious waterfowl hunter will want to visit this one: www.decoymuseum.com.

Jump-shooting without a Boat

You don't necessarily have to use a boat to jump-shoot creeks and small streams. If you can stalk the banks quietly, you might get within range of puddle ducks using the stream as a sanctuary during the day when they're not feeding in the fields.

Tricks of the Freelance Hunter

With the development of the so-called "Mud Motors," such as the Go-Devil, and portable boat blinds like Avery, freelance duck hunting has been made a lot easier. With your johnboat (a 16-footer ought to be about right) on a trailer, you can go to whichever locations the ducks are using. Use the afternoon hours to scout, scout, and scout—looking for locations where the ducks might be loafing during the day, or an inviting spot along a flyway where you expect them to be crossing the next morning on their way to feed or loaf. (See the fantastic Macks Prairie Wings store and Web site, www.mackspw.com, for mud motors, boats, portable blinds—the works. Also, Cabela's at www.cabelas.com.)

Late Season Timber Tactics

"We've learned one thing that's really important for hunting in late season. When the ducks are extremely wary, they'll work into little bitty openings in the thickest, brushiest woods in the area. These are places where we won't use more than 15 decoys plus our shakers. . . . I'll make one short highball on their first pass, then I'll shut up and let 'em work on their own. Once I tell them I'm there, I don't call anymore. I think the biggest mistake hunters make in flooded timber, especially from Christmas on, is calling too much."

—Arkansas Guide George Cochran, interviewed by writer Wade Bourne in Bourne's book, *Decoys and Proven Methods for Using Them,*
Ducks Unlimited, 2000

It's Not Just Wood Ducks Anymore

Used to be a time when local ducks were almost entirely wood ducks. Mallards and others were visitors from the North. No more. Plenty of mallards and other puddle ducks spend their summers in areas where they can be well scouted prior to opening day. Wood ducks the same.

The Romance of Sea Duck Hunting

"You'd have thought the tollers were trespassing on property owned by eider ducks. Flock after flock swung in to investigate. Spent shells twirled in the tide, and Bubba retrieved until his feet were sore from the barnacle-encrusted rocks. In between, we talked about seals and shags, eagles, deer, snow squalls and black ducks and whistlers, and shotguns and steel shot—which, I have to admit, will shoot effectively when you learn to use it."

—Tom Hennessey, *Feathers 'n Fins,*
The Amwell Press, 1989

Add a Few Decoys to Your Jump-shooting Boat

When you're heading for a day's jump-shooting on a likely stream, don't forget to take along a few decoys. On a day when you're seeing a good number of birds on the move, at a cove or quiet spot, especially on a braided river, you might have the chance to put out your decoys, wait a while, and pull in a flock or two.

Don't Push Your Luck with Decoys

Positioning your decoys closer to the blind so your shots will be easier may sound like a tempting idea, but it's not a good one. You won't be getting any shots! Put the closest decoys at least 30 yards from the blind, the others even farther out. If you gun can't handle that distance, it's not a very good duck gun.

The Right Time, the Right Place

One of the greatest experiences on earth is to be in your duck blind before daylight, with your decoys out, on a frosty morning without cloud cover. As you sip your coffee or tea, you'll watch the stars fade away as the shadowy shapes of the nearby terrain begin to take form and color. Hopefully, birds will be flying, heading out to their feeding grounds, or spooked by other hunters somewhere. It's the Grand Parade starting, and you are there.

Using the Wind with Your Decoy Spread

Ducks often want to land outside a spread of decoys—even when the setup has left an inviting hole. That's why you want to set your decoys upwind—not directly in front of the blind—so that you'll still have a good shot at the birds coming in against the wind and trying to land on the outside of the decoy spread.

Origin of the Word "Decoy"

"The word decoy is a shortened version of the Dutch word EndeKooy, which was a cage-type trap for snaring wildfowl."

—Wade Bourne, *Decoys and Proven Methods for Using Them,* Ducks Unlimited, 2000

Fighting Back on Those Bluebird Days

When there's not a cloud in the sky or a breath of wind blowing—a notorious "bluebird"

day—even when ducks are moving (which won't be very often!), it's tough to get their attention. Battery-driven shaker decoys and jerk-strings attached to some of your decoys can save the day on bluebird days. If you don't have a chance to study how pro guides set up their jerk decoys, check out Wade Bourne's book, *Decoys and Proven Methods for Using Them.*

The Freelance Duck Hunter

It's not easy to be a freelance duck hunter today, hunting on your own, finding good places to put out your decoys, bagging some birds. It takes skill, energy, gear, and planning—and the cold fact is that many hunters just can't pull together all those necessary ingredients. They join clubs that have leases, and they book guides.

Yes, Indeed, Ducks are Hard to Hit

In his classic book *Scattergunning*, Ray P. Holland points out that ducks are harder to hit than any other gamebird because: They are taken at longer ranges, they fly faster, the shots come at more angles, and their protective feathers make them tougher to kill.

Sea Duck Hunting: Get the Picture?

"In the lee of the ledge, a dozen of Al's handmade eider-duck tollers bobbed like a string of lobster buoys. To our right, smooth-running swells turned white as they stumbled over a stoop of submerged ledge. Spruces picketed the shores to our left. Gulls skirled, and a sea-tossed salad of kelp and rockweed was so salty you could smell it."

—Tom Hennessey, *Feathers 'n Fins,*
The Amwell Press, 1989

Tiny Camera, Big Memories

Attach a tiny digital camera to the same lanyard from which you hang duck calls and dog whistles. It will then be at your finger tips to capture the action.

Foggy Morning Timber Hunting

In the School of Hard Knocks I've attended, fog means lousy duck hunting. Double and triple that in timber hunting, where bright sunny weather always seems best. (Probably because the ducks can see the decoys in the open pools in the trees but can't see you standing in the shadows.)

Don't be a "Skybuster"

A "skybuster" is the most hated person on any marsh or field where there's duck or goose hunting. The Skybuster blazes away at birds that are clearly out of range, thereby frightening the birds away from the area and ruining chances others might have had on the incoming birds.

The Best Decoys Ever

Before they were banned in 1935, live decoys were used by waterfowl hunters, particularly commercial hunters. The decoy birds, which had to be fed and kept all year, were small domestic ducks, resembling mallards, prone to frequent calling.

They Love Those Sandbars

Sandbars on the edges of shallow water in clam bays and coves of big rivers will be a good drawing card for ducks and geese to loaf and pick up grit, especially when you've got open water while most region's ponds and lakes are iced-up. When scouting for such locations, one of the most rewarding sights you'll ever see will be birds dropping down over the trees in a bend in the river ahead. That's where you'll want to be setting up.

What Discourages Most Duck Hunters

Finding a good place to hunt is the Number One issue for all duck hunters today. Even with special management areas open to hunters, finding a good place to hunt ducks simply isn't easy. In most areas, goose hunting is much easier.

You've Got to Lead Them

The legendary duck hunter George Bird Grinnell is often referenced for his famous quote, "Shoot ahead of them . . . Shoot farther ahead of them . . . Shoot still farther ahead of them." And it's a fact: Most ducks are missed by not leading enough.

Silhouette Decoy Hole Punchers

The job of putting out dozens of silhouette decoys on hard or frozen ground becomes a lot easier when you use a hole punch like the Real-Geese Stake Hole Punch, available from waterfowl emporiums like Mack's Prairie Wings, www.mackspw.com, and the Smart Stick, available from www.smartstick.com.

Beating the Crowds in Public Hunting

Ducks quickly wise up to blinds on public hunting areas. You score more ducks if you seek out remote corners that see much less pressure. Use just a half dozen or so decoys and call only enough to get passing birds' interest.

The Chesapeake Style: Big and Tough

Just as the Chesapeake Bay retriever is generally bigger and stronger than a Labrador retriever, the early-style Chesapeake decoys were heavier and blockier than those being carved elsewhere in the early years of decoy making.

The Magic of Calling Your Birds

"To the avid waterfowler, no moment of truth can match the instant when a flock first responds to his call and decoys, the time when this wild, free bird of unsurpassed grace begins a descent from the sky down to gun range. It is a stirring spectacle . . ."
—Grits Gresham, *The Complete Wildfowler*, 1973

"Flasher" Decoys—Great but Not Guaranteed Successful

Where legal, the "flasher" movement decoys, like the original "RoboDuk," catch the eyes of ducks flying high and wide off your spread. While deadly in early season, they are considered by most experts to not be as effective in later season on down the flyways, when ducks have been seeing them in just too many decoy spreads. In fact, some hunters go so far as to say they believe the flashers can actually spook ducks.

Shooting Ducks in the Decoys

You have to want to shoot a duck awfully bad to let the incomers land in the decoys, and then you blast them on the water.

What Shot Hitting the Water Tells You

When you see your shot string hit the water behind a low-flying duck, your most-likely reaction will be that you shot behind it. Not necessarily so. The shot string is hitting the water well beyond the bird and could have been right on target, except too high.

Avery's Got the Stuff

Avery Outdoors Inc. in Memphis is where you kind find waterfowling mainline gear like layout blinds, plus gizmos and accessories you've never thought of that will make your waterfowling easier. Check them out at www.averyoutdoors.com.

Fetch That Bird!

If you have to hunt ducks on big water without a dog, bring along a spinning rod and a big surface plug. You can cast the big plug a long way, long enough to retrieve down ducks you can't wade to.

Your Face is a Dead Give-away

When using layout blinds in most duck and goose setups, you've got to do something about your shining face. To incoming ducks, it will stand out like a neon sign. Wear a face mask or dab on some camo makeup.

Goose Hunting Tips

The Most Effective Way to Set out Goose Decoys

Veteran Maryland call-maker Sean Mann guides early season duck and goose hunting in Alberta and is one of the most successful and experienced in the business. He told DU's Wade Bourne, in a tip for the DU Web site: "To finish more geese when hunting over a field spread, set decoys 10 feet apart (three long steps), and face them in random directions. This set provides a natural, relaxed look, and it also offers incoming birds plenty of landing room inside the spread. By setting my decoys so far apart, I use half the number I used to. I can set up and tear down faster, and most of all, the geese work better.

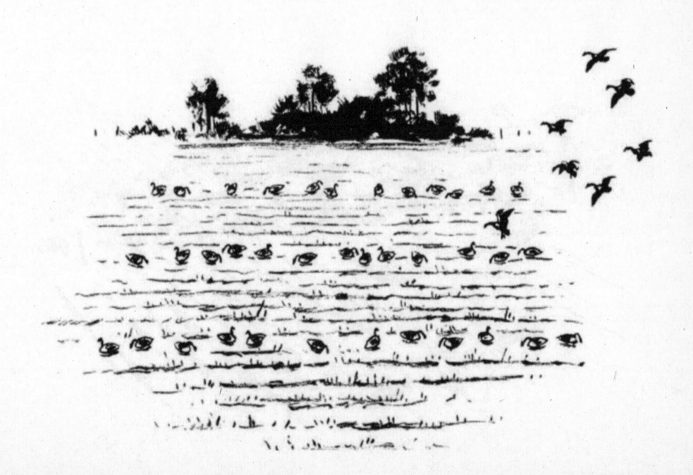

Our hunts are much more productive than when I set decoys closer together. Less really can be more."

How to Change Your Luck with Snow Geese

In the October '08 *Field & Stream,* author Dave Hurteau, in an interview with veteran guide Tracy Northup, Up North Outdoors, www.huntupnorth. com, presents a deadly method for changing your luck with those tough, high-flying flocks of snow geese. In a tip called, "Play the Wind," Northup says. "Snow geese typically fly high and circle straight down, making it difficult to shoot them anywhere but right over a good spread. But a 30–40-mph wind keeps them flying nice and low." Northup recommends scouting out a location of snows where there are ditches or hedgerows a hundred yards or so from the fields where you can sneak into position to pick off the low-flying snows as they pass—without spooking the main flock.

Birds in Flight: Looks are Deceiving

Because they are big, Canada Geese appear to be slow in flight, compared to ducks. And because of their long tails, pheasants appear to be slower than they really are. Swing your gun properly, lead the bird, and keep swinging as you pull the trigger. Or you'll be shaking your head, wondering how you missed.

Snow Geese: Playing the Numbers Game

Those large flocks of snow geese weaving across the horizon, clamoring constantly, are hard to pull into normal decoy spreads of just two- or three-dozen birds. The flying geese can see great distances, and they are looking for big groups of feeding birds. Savvy hunters have learned to cope with this by putting out decoys by the hundreds, if necessary, and to do this they'll use all the silhouettes they can haul to the site, plus whatever "rag-type" decoys they can

fashion themselves from things like baby diapers and white garbage bags attached to a stake.

Layout Blinds Take Getting Used To

When using a layout blind, before the birds start flying take some time to try practicing the move it takes to rise into a shooting position. It takes some getting used to. If you don't practice it, you may not be in a good position with your face well down on the gun during the first critical seconds when it's time to, take 'em!

Local Geese, Local Knowledge

We live in an age where many (most!) Canada Geese have never been to Canada and are never going. They have become local birds, and the generous limits and seasons reflect that. Hunting them in early season is pleasant and rewarding, but you have to do your homework in finding a place to hunt where the birds are feeding, resting, or flying past.

When the Canadas Sleep Late

In below-zero weather, sleep in an extra hour or two. When it's that cold Canadas will stay roosted and fly out to feed only after the sun has come up and warmed things up a bit. It might be 10 am before they leave the roost. The only thing you'll get by showing up at dawn is cold.

Keep Those Silhouettes Visible

When using silhouette decoys for geese, take care to position them so many of them appear broadside at every angle. When edge-on to the viewpoint of the flying birds, they become invisible.

Layout Blinds: You're Part of the Action

You're lying in a field, totally hidden right among the decoys. No brushy blind, no boat, no pit blind, no elaborate box blind, no blind on stilts. Instead, you're tucked comfortably into a well-camouflaged layout blind, made further invisible by attaching brush to the blind's convenient straps and holders. You're wearing camo yourself, including a hat and mask. Even your gun is camouflaged. Unlike hunting from a brush blind where you have to keep your face down—and thereby miss part of the spectacle of flying birds on the way in—you're seeing the whole show, from the time birds appear in the distance, until they coming right into your face. There's nothing like it!

Skip Knowles of Peoria, Illinois, takes aim at a Canada goose while hunting from a layout blind in a field north of Winnepeg, Mantoba.
Photo © Jay Cassell

Hiding Your Boat in Plain Sight

The john-boat or canoe you can put into the water and go wherever the ducks and geese are flying has gotten a lot easier to hide with the introduction of today's synthetic camo material. The material, imitating different shades and textures of marsh grass, comes in manageable mats you can attach to your boat, then roll up and put away after your hunt. Cabela's, www. cabelas.com, has a bunch of different patterns, including the excellent Avery, and there's a popular one called Fast-Grass that's available at the Knutson's waterfowling store and site, www.knutsondecoys.com.

Don't Let Those Incoming Geese Fool You

"The approach of wild geese to a blind is one of the neatest optical illusions in nature. The geese just keep on coming. You think they are one hundred yards away, and they are two hundred. You think they are fifty yards away, and they are one hundred."

—Gordon MacQuarrie, "Geese! Get Down!,"
Field & Stream, 1941, reprinted in *The Field & Stream Reader,* Doubleday, 1946

Ruffed Grouse and Woodcock Hunting Tips

Good Hearing Can Pay Off Big

When the leaves in the woods are dry and crinkly, say on a perfect Indian Summer day, you can actually hear the few steps ruffed grouse take to launch into flight. The sound is a sort of dry, "tick, tick." Once you've heard it a couple of times, followed by a flushing bird, you'll know what to listen for.

Lend a Hand to Your Bird Hunting

When your upland bird hunting—quail, grouse, pheasant—takes place in thick cover, an

old glove worn on your left hand (for right-handed hunters) enables you to ward off vines, limbs and briars as you work through the cover while your gloveless right hand holds your smoothbore ready for the flush.

Grouse Hunting Teamwork

It's fun to hunt grouse with a buddy, but you must know each other's location at all times, and even then you may not be able to take a shot. (That's the very reason most grouse hunters shoot better when they're hunting alone.) In keeping track of one another, use a simple call-out, like, "Ho!" or "Over Here!" instead of constantly shouting sentences like, "I'm over here, Bob, on your right." The more grouse hear of such talk, the more likely they are to flush wild.

Spring Training for Rookie Dogs

"Spring woodcock provide the perfect opportunity to steady a young dog up . . . a high percentage of these birds are willing to sit so tight. A secondary reason is that the dog is fairly easy to see due to the lack of vegetation in early spring . . . Seeing the bird depart is of particular good for youngsters. It fills them with more fire and desire for the future . . . tells them inwardly every time that this, bird hunting, is why they're here on earth."

—Nick Sisley, *Grouse Magic,*
self-published, 1981

A Startling Grouse-kill Discovery

"I kept track for my next 20 grouse kills. I don't like to keep statistics while I'm grouse hunting. . . . However, I did keep track for 20 birds and quit. I found that I killed 16 of those ruffs on what I figured were reflushes, four of them on the original flush. Those statics were startling, even for a guy who has chased the thunder birds for almost two decades."

—Nick Sisley, *Grouse Magic,* self-published, 1981

How Far Do Grouse Roam Every Day?

Despite the amount of boot leather hunters wear out in pursuit of their favorite bird every season, grouse are really "stay-at-home" gamebirds, seldom roaming more than a half mile from its home range.

Second Shots on Early Season Grouse Coveys

When you flush a couple of early season grouse, and fire only one shot, don't break your gun to reload right away. You may be into an entire group of birds hatched that year, and one of the birds that's been sitting tight will jump late—just when you break open your gun. On the other hand, if you've fired both shells, try to reload as quickly as possible.

The New England Grouse Gun Classic

William Harnden Foster, author of the classic *New England Grouse Shooting,* shot a 28-gauge Parker DHE with a straight stock.

Keep Track of Where You Shot From

Woodcocks are small birds and their feathers make for excellent camouflage on the forest floor. This can make finding one you've shot hard to retrieve, especially if you're hunting without a dog. After you knock one down, hang your hat on a branch or drop a spent shell on the ground where you were standing when you pulled the trigger. If you get confused about where you thought the bird landed you'll be able to return to the exact place you shot from to restart your search.

What are Your Chances?

"I've kept a detailed journal of my days afield . . . Here are the hard facts: For every twelve grouse flushed, four escape unseen; of the eight the hunter glimpses, four are out of range, disappear too quickly, or otherwise evade getting shot at; of the four shots that the hunter takes, three are misses."

—William G. Tapply, *Upland Autumn: Birds, Dogs, and Shotgun Shells,* Skyhorse Publishing, 2009

Burton L. Spiller's Grouse Feathers

When one first opens the pages of Burton L. Spiller's *Grouse Feathers,* the immediate effect is startling. Opposite the title page, which, in addition to Spiller's name, informs us that the book's illustrations are by Lynn Bogue Hunt, there is a full-page drawing of a ruffed grouse huddled against a pine trunk while a great horned owl passes below. The effect is startling. Instantly, one knows you're about to read a book produced by a writer and artist who love grouse and know what they're talking about. The edition I have was published by The Macmillan Company in 1947, but the original was a Derrydale Press edition in 1935. *More Grouse Feathers,* also illustrated by Lynn Bogue Hunt, followed from Derrydale in 1938, but a new edition was published by Crown Press in 1973, with an introduction by *Field & Stream*'s H. G. Tapply. Burton

L. Spiller wrote other books, but he will always be best remember for these two chronicles of hunting the golden New England hills for grouse and woodcock.

Cock Bird or a Hen? How to Tell

The black band on the tail of all ruffed grouse tells you whether you've bagged a male or female. The cock bird always has a continuous band, while the hen's is broken. As in all things in nature, there are exceptions sometimes, mostly among young birds.

Those "Fantasy" Grouse

Sporting scene painters—even the very best of them—invariably picture ruffed grouse flying through the open—clearings in the trees, even along the edges of fields. The artists do that, no doubt, so the audience can see the bird. The reality is that you'll almost never have a chance to look down your gun barrel and see a grouse in huge openings like those in your favorite paintings. You might have a glimpse of a bird in a small gap in the trees and brush, just for an instant—if you're lucky.

Noise Flushes More Grouse

Yes, grouse can be a tight-holding bird, but when you're approaching their location with a lot of chatter and constant commands to your dog, you're almost guaranteeing you'll get a wild flush, out ahead of the point.

Flushing Dogs as Grouse Dogs

It makes a lot of sense to use flushing/retrieving dogs like Labs, Springers, and Goldens as grouse and woodcock dogs. (Pheasants too, by the way.) In addition to flushing the birds, they retrieve and make great family dogs. When trained properly to hunt close to the gun, these dogs can do a good job for you in grouse and woodcock covers. When not properly trained, running wide distances and out of control, they are worse than useless. You'd be better off walking up your birds alone.

Signpost to Good Woodcock Hunting

Look for white splashes on the ground of the covers where you're hoping to find good woodcock hunting.

Back on That Legendary "Road"

Field & Stream writer Corey Ford's grouse story "The Road to Tinkhamtown" has become a sort of cult classic, revered in anthologies and close to the hearts of an army of grouse hunters who love the literature of the sport. The story originally appeared in the October 1969, issue, with a superb illustration by the artist Howard Terpning. Ford died of a stroke on July 29, 1969, prior to the publication of the story. As this is written, the original unedited version of the story [written in 1963], returned by writer/editor Laurie Morrow from Ford's handwritten manuscript, is now being featured on the *Field & Stream* Web site, www.fieldandstream.com. Laurie Morrow is the editor of the Corey Ford anthology of stories, *The Trickiest Thing in Feathers*, Wilderness Adventures Press, 1996.

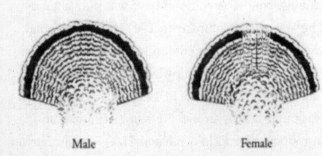

Male   Female

The New Englander—Found Just about Everywhere

Although the traditional home of the ruffed grouse is New England, you will find them and their subspecies all over the northeast, down the Appalachian chain to Georgia and Alabama, in all the Rocky Mountain states, and on west to Oregon and Washington. They are found all over Canada, the Yukon, and Alaska.

Aspens and Grouse: The Late October Key

Grouse hunting and shotgun expert Nick Sisley tells us that where grouse thrive in aspen country—like the Upper Midwest—look for fantastic gunning in 13–17-year-old aspens in late October, and the grouse are feeding on hazel catkins that thrive in this particular aspen-age stage.

Going it Alone

"I like to hunt alone, when there's no one to blame but myself. I have found that picking my way through birdy cover without a dog taps into something atavistic and important that absent when dogs are doing the hunting for me. Hunting without a dog is . . . hunting. I find myself thinking like a grouse, scanning the cover, imagining where a bird might be lurking, how close he might let me approach, which direction he'll choose to fly."

—William G. Tapply, *Upland Autumn: Birds, Dogs, and Shotgun Shells*, Skyhorse Publishing, 2009

Walk 'Em Up!

Grouse hunting with no dog is better than grouse hunting with a poor dog. The untrained or poorly training dog will run too far from the gun, flush every bird in the area, then chase them down and flush them again.

The Perfect Grouse and Woodcock Gun

When it comes to grouse guns, arguments may rage over the bore—12 or 20 gauge—but you'll find general agreement over these details: lightweight, short barrel, fast swinging, and with a stock that fits so perfectly that it instantly becomes part of you when your face touches the stock.

Keep Your Favorite Covers as "Top Secret"

It may go without saying, but this tip is a strong reminder: You must not take someone to your favorite grouse covers unless they are an absolute trusted friend for life. No exceptions! Be warned! If you break this rule, you're going to someday arrive at your favorite cover to find more SUVs than a dealer's lot.

Stay after Them!

"Reflushing grouse is a key to success in more ways than one. It's a cornerstone to good, sound, basic grouse hunting."

—Nick Sisley, *Grouse Magic,* self-published, 1981

He's Not Alone!

Flush one woodcock, and you're likely to find others not far away. When the flight is on, there should be a good number of birds in the vicinity.

The Quiet "Getaway"

In rainy or snowy weather when they're holding tight in the spruces, hemlocks or other conifers, ruffed grouse can launch into flight with hardly a sound, far less noise than the familiar whirr of wings you're expecting. As a bonus, the bird may be eight feet over your head.

Avoid Over-training Your Dog

"Because Sam [a setter] was so 'birdy' and easy to handle, I made the mistake of over-training him. I realized it when he began pointing birds other than game species. Whenever we got into a cover where partridge or woodcock were scarce, he would start slamming into stylish but unproductive points. The pup was, of course, trying to please me. I had worked him so often on planted pigeons that he figured whenever I hung a bell on him he'd best point something—and soon."

—Tom Hennessey, *Feathers 'n Fins,*
The Amwell Press, 1989

Finding Woodcock Covers

"All alders do not attract woodcock, but I have seldom found woodcock in large numbers far from alders . . . On the migratory flight, if it is not alder cover that is used, it will be cover close to water or damp ground . . . I have found woodcock in large numbers on a mountain top, but, as in lowland coverts, it was flat land with alders."

—George Bird Evans, *The Upland Shooting
Life,* Knopf, 1971

How Grouse Survive the Winter Woods

During the golden days of autumn hunting, ruffed grouse will be found near their favorite foods—among wild berries, in old apple orchards, among acorns and beechnuts. As the snows come and the winter deepens, you'll find them "budding,"

actually surviving by eating the buds of next year's greenery.

The Great Grouse Dog Secret

"The secret to acquiring a great grouse dog doesn't rest in buying one, for the truly great ones are seldom if ever for sale at any price. Nor does the secret lie in selecting a puppy from one of those mythical 'long bred lines' of pure grouse dogs. The secret to great grouse dogs centers around one heck of a lot of both hard work and outright luck."

—Nick Sisley, *Grouse Magic,*
self-published, 1981

Number One on the Table: It's the Ruffed Grouse

As far as I'm concerned, all upland gamebirds are great on the table, but there is one that stands out as better than the rest. It's the ruffed grouse. No, I don't want to argue about it. It's the ruffed grouse! (Of course the wild turkey is better than anything, but I'm not comparing turkeys to our upland birds.)

Marking down Flushed Birds

"Generally, grouse tend to fly farther when they're shot at, not fly as far if they flush wild . . . There was a time when I shot at every bird possible—the old theory that shooting makes them sit tighter on the reflush. Hogwash. The father a bird flies, the less your chances are of flying him again. Birds sit tighter because they're not in familiar territory, not because they've been shot at."

—Nick Sisley, *Grouse Magic,* self-published, 1981

The Flight-bird Woodcock Myth

There's an old woodcock saying that will never die, even though it's a complete myth. It's the idea that flight birds are bigger than local birds. They're not. In a particular instance, one bird might be older and bigger than a local bird. But later, when the local birds leave, they too become flight birds.

Woodcock Flights and the Full Moon

"Thank God for the moon. Since day one, sportsmen have attributed their success or lack of it to the phases of that celestial sphere. Woodcock hunters are no exception. In fact, if you could produce a deed to the melon-like moon that illumines October nights, I guarantee you, a woodcock hunter would be the first in line to buy it. Why? Because theory has it that the nocturnal travelers always migrate on the full of the moon. I don't buy it. For my money, you can place that theory in the same category as the one claiming that flight birds are bigger."

—Tom Hennessey, *Feathers 'n Fins,*
The Amwell Press, 1989

Hitting More Grouse: The Big Secret

Here it comes, the grouse-hunting technique that will put more birds in your coat than any other: When

you hear the flush, don't stand there looking for the bird, then raise your gun. Your gun should be coming to your shoulder as you look toward the direction of the flush. At the first glimpse of the bird, the barrel should be coming onto what you're seeing, and you fire instantly. There's no tracking, no aiming. It's a "throw" shot, as I prefer to call it, instead of the oft-heard "snap" shot. Of course, this method is assuming a hunting buddy is behind you, out of harm's way.

Out of Circulation—and Staying That Way

When the temps really drop and high winds are raging through woods, ruffed grouse—just like the white-tailed deer—can remain holed up in conifers, not using much energy, waiting it out.

Equipped on "Stayin' Alive"

The ruffed grouse is one tough dude, well equipped to withstand tough winters and predators. His legs are feathered with hair, and even his feet have fine feathers which act like snowshoes. His plumage so matches the woodlands that he is almost impossible to spot on the ground. In deep winter during storms, the grouse is not adverse into diving into snow banks and spending the night out of harm's way. Sometimes, this move is fatal when the crust freezes on top and they cannot break back through come morning.

What Grouse Really Weigh

A serious grouse hunter in Tennessee weighed every bird he ever shot for many, many years. They all weighed between 1 pound, 12 ounces, and 1 pound, 14 ounces.

Woodcock Flights: The Real Deal

"Take my share of moonbeams. To get these grand gamebirds moving, give me a good oldfashioned line storm of wind-driven rain. You know, the kind that lacquers leaves into your windows and shimmies the shade of the lamp post across the street. Next morning, let me hunt covers in a river valley where fresh young alders are crowding out tired old fields. Come afternoon, give me birch knolls and poplar hillsides that are mounded with ant hills and moist with spring creeks. Give me that, Sport, and it's a sure bet that on Saturday there's be a woodcock cooking in the beans."

—Tom Hennessey, *Feathers 'n Fins,*
The Amwell Press, 1989

The Dead "Giveaway" on Woodcock

"Going into strange woodcock terrain 'cold' can be disappointing. Two coverts may look alike, yet only one many attract 'cock. Whitewash is the best clue, next to seeing actual birds. The white splashing disintegrate rapidly and when you see them you can almost count on woodcock being nearby."

—George Bird Evans, *The Upland Shooting Life,* Knopf, 1971

The Penultimate Upland Gunning Experience

The autumn day has been crisp and tangy. The hills and valleys were aflame with color, but now, at dusk, the shadows have dulled the splendor. Your dog's work has not been error-free, but neither has your shooting. Nevertheless, as you walk back to your truck, you feel the puffy heft of a pair of grouse and three woodcock against the small of your back. The day has been filled with exciting action and the deep satisfaction of being a part of the autumn uplands. You're hoping it will be the same on your next time out. But you never know. There are no guarantees, and you don't want any. Just another chance.

Grouse Sit Tighter on Reflushes

A grouse biologist shared a theory with outdoor writer and grouse expert Nick Sisley that he believed grouse definitely sit tighter on reflushes. The reason: because they're not in the spots they usually frequent. In their more-familiar, favorite spots, like the one where you first flushed them, they know the best escape routes and use them every time they're disturbed. On the reflush, they're probably in less-familiar cover.

Stop Spooking the Grouse

My friend Jay Drake is a superb grouse hunter who is convinced that noise is the greatest problem in getting good shots at grouse. Jay has many times noted tracks in the snow where grouse simply walked away, never flushing, as he approached. Jay likes to hunt alone to reduce the noise of bells, whistles, commands to dogs, shouts between hunters, and even boots on dry leaves and cracking sticks. In Jay's view, you have to use more stealth to bag grouse than you ever thought necessary.

Join the Ruffed Grouse Society

For the serious grouse and woodcock hunter, the Ruffed Grouse Society offers a serious list of benefits that include: four issues each year of their very fine magazine; the opportunity to take part in a strong nationwide effort to improve grouse habitat; the camaraderie of associating with serious hunters like yourself; travel opportunities; info sharing; and others too numerous to mention here. Basic opening membership costs $25 a year. Check them out online at www. ruffedgrousesociety.org or call them at 1-800-JOIN-RGS (873-5576).

It's an Uphill Climb

Most authorities and experienced grouse hunters agree: a grouse flushed on a hillside will fly uphill almost every time.

Best Way to Cook Woodcock: In the Beans

Veteran outdoor writer Tom Hennessey of the *Bangor Daily News*, with several books to his credit, is a grouse and woodcock hunter without peer. Woodcock can be difficult to turn into a great meal he admits, but he has a favorite way of doing just that. Cook a big pot of baked beans just the way you like them, then add in several woodcock breasts to soak and simmer. You'll have a woodcock feast fit for a king.

The Woodcock Gourmand

"How I feel about woodcock breasts, quickly sauteed in wine and brown butter, then salted and peppered, can be quickly surmised by the admission that one evening I ate nine birds by myself, washed down with a fine 1959 Saint Emilion. I would have eaten a few more but my wife had her greedy hands in the platter."

—Gene Hill, "Bad Cooks," *A Hunter's Fireside Book,* Winchester Press, 1972, now offered by Skyhorse Publishing

Pheasant Hunting Tips

When Ringnecks Sit Tight

Despite their reputation for being track stars, running ahead of the dogs and hunters, pheasants are capable of making themselves invisible and sitting tight when they feel pressured enough. They can hide in the smallest clump of grass, letting you walk right past them.

Don't Let That Tail Fool You

Compared to gamebirds like quail and ruffed grouse, the takeoff of a pheasant, while exciting, is rather slow. However, in its initial, vaulting leap, the rooster pheasant's long tail and gaudy colors make the bird seem even larger than it really is, and the shooter fails to take a lead, but merely pokes the barrel at the body of the bird.

How "Cackles" Betray Cockbirds

When a pheasant "cackles" as it flushes, it's a cockbird. Every time. Hens do not cackle. This doesn't mean that cockbirds cackle every time they flush. They don't. Sometimes they fly away in silence. But when you hear a cackling bird, even if it's in the sun and you can't see its colors, you know it's a cockbird.

Once is Not Enough

Don't hesitate to hunt a productive piece of pheasant cover once in the morning and again late in the day. Often, more birds will move into the prime habitat throughout the day.

Go Late for Western Ringnecks

While the typical western ringneck hunt involves following short tails though long, golden grass in shirt-sleeve weather, some of the best pheasant hunting on prime habitats in the Dakotas, Nebraska, and Montana occurs after Thanksgiving. There is less pressure then, and the winter weather tends to push birds into flocks. Gaining access to great hunting spots is often easier then, with big game seasons ended. So consider a late season pheasant hunt in the West.

When Pheasants Fly High and Fast

After the initial flush, when a pheasant gets some distance between itself and the ground, the bird will be flying high and fast. If you're lucky enough to have a bird flying your way that's been flushed by another hunter, you should be ready to take your shot with a smooth, fast swing and lots of lead. On a stand in driven bird shooting, tower shoots, or as a "blocker" at the end of a cornrow, this

is the shot you'll be getting all the time. When in full flight, pheasants are fast, and you've got to get your gun barrel out in front.

The Key Maneuver

When you work pheasant cover, always work toward a distinct end point, be it an irrigation ditch, road, creek, or open field. The birds will eventually figure they can't outrun you. As you and your dog approach that end point, the birds will flush.

You're Walking Past the Birds

Pheasants tend to sit tighter in wet weather, so work cover more thoroughly than you would on a bluebird day.

Boots: Made for Walking

If you don't break in that new pair of hunting boots before the season, you're making a big and painful mistake. One that could even ruin your hunt for big game and birds in rough terrain where you can expect to do a lot of walking.

Coming up Empty!

Always reload quickly after shooting a flushing rooster; he may have compatriots with him. While you're patting yourself on the back for a great shot, other birds may flush as you stand there with an empty shotgun.

The Fox That Flies

Pheasants have been around for centuries and

know all about avoiding man once the hunting season opens and the shooting starts. These are foxy birds, with lots of "smarts" and survival instincts.

Pheasant "Benefit" Shoots: Watch for Them

On the *Field & Stream* magazine Web site, www.fieldandstream.com, in an article called "Deep in the Heart of Roosterland," T. Edward Nickens describes shoots in the Texas Panhandle where communities sponsor "Community Hunts," held for donations of $150 to $250. The money goes to community needs, and the hunters get shooting over thousands of acres of prime private pheasant land—some shoots for weekends, some fees for access the entire pheasant season. Nickens's hunt takes place in the area around Hart, Texas, but the idea is cropping over in many other prime pheasant areas.

Late Season is Special

"But later pheasant hunting may be as pure a form of hunting as there is. The hunter then becomes a classic searcher and stalker, shooting less and hunting much, much more."

—John Madsen, "Pheasants Beyond Autumn," *Outdoor Life,* October, 1977

They Need to Take a Drink

Like four-legged critters, pheasants need a water source to thrive. In dry months in the fall, work cover near watering holes late in the afternoon to find birds.

Late Season Escape Hatches

"I don't have much late-season cunning, but one practice that's worked out well is simply getting as far as possible from roads. An obvious reason is that the birds have faded away from roadsides and roadside field edges. Then, too, the very center of a square-mile section of Midwestern corn-land may be the untidiest part. It's where a farmer tends to sweep stuff under the rug, back where passersby can't see small farm dumps, weed patches, messy fence-corners and junk machinery."

—John Madsen, "Pheasants Beyond Autumn," *Outdoor Life,* October 1977

After the Season Opens . . .

Hunting pheasants on opening day and then a week later will seem like the difference between night and day. The pheasant's "disappearing act" after opening day is one of the most remarkable in all upland bird hunting.

The Slower, the Better

If you are hunting pheasants without a dog, go super-slow. Walking slowly and stopping frequently will make the birds nervous and can key a flush when they're holding tight and waiting for you to walk past.

Find the Roosts for a Shooting Treasure

Out on the prairie, pheasants have limited roosting options. Find those roosts and you've got a wing-shooting gold mine early and late in the day.

Pheasants in the Tracking Snow

Got snow? Then go track up a pheasant. You don't need a dog, and you'll quickly learn the birds' favorite hiding spots and get a good feel of how many birds are in the area.

Quail Hunting Tips

Shooting the Covey Rise

A good covey rise—say twelve to fifteen birds—is one of the most exciting events in all wingshooting. Alas, it's also the time when many shooters miss on their first shot, then hastily throw their second shot into thin air. From Day One, quail hunters are urged, "Pick out one bird and shoot it." But they have a hard time doing it. The sight of all those birds, particularly wild birds, hurtling toward the trees—or even through the trees—keeps their face from getting down on the stock, which will result in a miss every time. Some hunters do well on coveys by telling themselves that they're going to shoot the first bird that flies—just as though they were shooting singles. In my case, my scores on covey rises improved when I started really hunkering down on the gun, swinging toward one bird, and telling myself, "I'm going to kill that bird." That's the kind of focus shooting covey rises requires, at least in my view.

Another Good Reason to Love Bobwhite Hunting

"Apart from his courage and trickiness in the field, the bobwhite has the power of inspiring magnificent nostalgia in the evening, when the fire snaps and the bourbon melds gently with the branch-water."

—Robert C. Ruark, "The Brave Quail," *Field & Stream*, December 1951

Point! Be Ready for Wild Birds

If you're fortunate enough to do some quail hunting for wild birds, you'll soon learn that they don't always act like the birds you've seen in paintings. Instead of being right under the pointing dog's nose, they may be some distance out in front, even as much as 10 yards or more. Be ready for that "out-front" flush.

Leave That Safety on until the Shot!

In my formative gun-handling years, I learned to leave the safety on until the gun is moving toward my shoulder to make a shot. Many quail hunters take their safeties off when walking in to a point to flush the birds. The practice is dangerous. The birds may have moved, the dog will have to relocate, and you might have a lot more walking before the birds take flight (if indeed they ever do take flight). Walking around through briars and tangles with a loaded gun with the safety off is a prescription for disaster. Train yourself to leave the safety on until a bird is in the air and the gun is moving toward your shoulder.

Hunt "Inside" the Field Edges

When your pointing dogs run back and to along a field, staying in the open ground, they may be pretty to look at but will only find coveys of birds that are actually in the field, feeding. By carefully working through the woods bordering the field, the dogs will have a chance to trail and find where coveys have been walking to and from the field, and where they spending most of their daytime hours.

Let Your Dog Work the Cripples

When it's time to "hunt dead!" the best thing you can do for your dog is to avoid walking through the area where you have dead birds or a cripple. Stay out to the side and let the dog find the birds.

Wet-weather Preserve Birds

Rain and wet weather are usually bad news for preserve quail hunting. Quality preserve hunting, with strong-flying birds, always depends on the place you're hunting. Some are great. Some are un-great! But, generally speaking, the flight qualities of preserve birds in the rain will be disappointing.

Marking down the Singles

After a covey rise, many hunters make the mistake of diverting their attention to downed birds too quickly, instead of carefully watching the escape routes of the covey's survivors. Even after these escaping birds are seen to cup their wings and sail in a certain direction, they bear careful watching, for they can sail a long way and change direction quickly.

Cold Front Moving in—Great Hunting!

There's nothing quite like being in the field in an afternoon when low clouds are scudding about, it's starting to spit just a bit of snow or icy rain, and the temperature has been dropping sharply. Quail will be feeding like there's no tomorrow, leaving strong trails of scent your dogs can easily find. You can bag your limit on a day like this.

Make Mine a Side-by-Side

All right, call me "old-fashioned" if you wish. But to me, a side-by-side 20-gauge double is the gun of choice for bobwhite quail. Barrels 26 inches, bored modified and improved cylinder. You can tramp a long time with a light double, enjoying its

sweet feel of balance and sleekness, and when the gun comes to your shoulder, the broad sighting plane seems to flow onto the target. I like double triggers, and a straight stock, but again, I'm old-fashioned. For many hunters today, the over-under seems to be the favorite, especially when it's the same gun used for sporting clays. Makes all the sense in the world. But it's not for me in the quail woods.

Cancel the "Dawn Patrol"

The "dawn patrol," so popular and necessary in waterfowl and deer hunting, isn't necessary when you're out for bobwhites. Particularly on cold or frosty mornings, quail like to remained huddled together on their roosts until the sun is well up and warming the landscape. Then the birds will be out and about, and your dogs will have a much better chance of picking up scent.

Preserve Shooting Dangers: They're for Real!

Every year it happens: A quail shooter on a preserve shoots a companion or a dog. The reason: Preserve birds often run or walk around in plain sight (completely unlike wild birds!), and when they fly they may be so low they're barely fluttering over the bushes. Add to all this the fact that these birds may fly in a direction behind the hunter. If he turns to shoot, he will be blasting his companions, the guides, and the dog wagon, if there is one. The preserve shooter must be calm, cool, a n d disciplined to only take off the safety and raise the gun on strong-flying birds out front. Low birds and birds escaping to the rear are *not an option*.

Leave Some for "Seed"

Shooting a covey of wild bobwhites down to two or three birds doesn't make any sense. From a covey of say twelve birds, set your personal take as five or six. No more. Now leave that covey alone for the rest of the season. There's always next year.

When You're Headed for a Tough Day

One of the toughest days you can have in quail hunting will be when the temperature is very low and a stiff breeze is blowing over the frozen ground. These conditions make finding birds a tough proposition for even the best dogs.

Keep Your Head down on the Stock

Hunters sometimes wonder why they missed a seemingly easy shot—a covey of quail bursting into flight, a flock of mallards right over the decoys, even a wild turkey strutting into plain view. Often the reason is simply because your were so excited and enthralled by what you are seeing, that you lift your head slightly from the gunstock. When you do, it's all over! You're going to miss the shot.

Take it Easy, Get More Shots

With a good bird dog willing to "hunt close" under today's tough conditions, quail hunting is not the place to be in a hurry. Instead, just mosey along and take your time, working every nook and cranny along the edges of the fields thoroughly. You'll find lots more coveys than the hunter in a hurry.

Why We Miss Them

Although wild quail are fast, they aren't that fast—so fast that it's "now or never" as in ruffed grouse hunting. Far and away, most bobwhite quail are missed by shooting too fast.

When Birds are Running, Keep up with Your Dog

When your dog is pointing for a few seconds, then moving ahead, then moving again and relocating as you come up, you've obviously got some running birds ahead. Try to keep up with the dog as he moves along. Chances are high that this covey is going to flush wild, well ahead.

They're Closer Than You Think

"Most quail are killed within sixty feet of the gun. Before you say I am wrong, measure the next ten you kill. The bobwhite fades away so fast on the flush that many men won't shoot at a bird thirty to thirty-five yards away, believing that he is beyond good killing range."

—Ray P. Holland, *Scattergunning*, Knopf, 1951

The Best Snakebite Kit

If you're worried about rattlesnakes where you do your quail hunting, remember that the best snakebite kit ever invented is a set of car keys.

Havilah Babcock, the Quail Hunting Man

Just as the name Burton L. Spiller is synonymous with grouse and woodcock, the name Havilah Babcock is the one you will see on several classics of bobwhite quail hunting. A South Carolina school teacher with deep love and respect for the Carolina low-country, Babcock wrote about quail and quail hunters with wry humor and deep insight. Beginning with the book, *Tales of Quails 'n Such*, Babcock's main interest was bobwhite quail, but he did not shy away from other low country subjects with which he was deeply familiar—everything from catalpa worm fishing to possum hunting. His stories were mainstays in *Field & Stream*, and they are collected in several books available today. Check www.amazon.com.

Western Grouse and Quail Hunting Tips

The Best of the West

Wingshooting in the American West—from desert country to mountain valleys—includes an agenda of birds to warm the hearts of avid bird hunters and their dogs. You have the scaled quail, often called "blue quail" by the locals; the Gambel's quail, the true desert bird; his cousin the California Valley quail, found more in cultivated areas; the mountain quail, the largest quail of all, with a plume that is sharper shaped and stands straight up instead of bending forward like the other western quail; and the Mearns's quail, a colorful, full-bodied quail that hangs out in smaller coveys than the other western quail and lives in the grassland canyons amid brush and scattered trees. All of these quail are a joy to study in photographs and illustrations in books or on the Internet.

The Sage Grouse: Now a Trophy Bird

Due to the loss of quality sagebrush habitat, the big, colorful sage grouse has become a trophy bird, available on open-season lists in nine states. They are found in the high sagebrush areas of the Western United States and Saskatchewan and Alberta in Canada. Going back to the time of Lewis and Clark, groups of sage grouse were a common sight throughout the West. Today, they have become a rare sight, except in certain areas. And what a sight they are. With some of the cocks weighing from six to eight pounds, they look as large as turkeys when crossing open ground.

The Rattlesnake Question

In a lot of bobwhite quail hunting in places like Texas and Mexico, snakebite-proof boots are preferred. In general, most western quail hunting does not require this precaution. Check with the local hunters.

Huns vs. Bobwhites: Which is Faster?

When bobwhite hunters take their first crack at Huns, they'll usually will say the gray partridge is faster. Most of the experienced hunters who have put in their hours with both birds feel the wild bobwhites are faster. The Huns look faster because they're larger and jump at longer ranges.

Sharptails and Gun Dogs

If you'd love to see your dogs work on a great gamebird in open country, then try to take them sharptail hunting. A covey of eight to ten sharptails is a stirring sight to encounter with your dog, then following up the singles will give you a different kind of action, with slow, careful work in cover and tangles.

The Ups and Downs of Chukar Hunting

Once you've located chukars, you literally chase them uphill and down, over steep, tough terrain that can stop your heart if you're not in good shape. When the birds are flushed along the bottom of the hills,

they fly uphill. Going after them, you'll reach the top only to have them fly back downhill. And so it goes.

Here Today, Gone Tomorrow

It helps to remember that Sage Grouse are desert birds, and like desert forbs they can disappear almost completely during drought, only to replicate madly with a little rain . . . some years you find none, while in others they bloom like an irrigated desert, with hundreds of grouse startling local ranchers, who think such numbers of birds must migrate south, or "up the crick," or somewhere in other years.

Something Else You Might Need

Carry a tube of Super Glue in your bird vest. A few drops of adhesive can make emergency clothing or gear repairs. In a pinch, it can even close a wound.

Made for Walking

Hunting western quail will require the best, well-fitted, completely-broken-in boots can you afford. Rocky, uneven ground, sprinkled with cactus that bites, will challenge your every step. Gun dogs will need constant attention, and many western hunters equip their dogs with special boots.

How to Miss Western Quail

They may look like they're flying straight and level, but western quail are almost always rising as your gun comes up for the shot. Blot the bird out and fire, and you'll miss every time. You've got to hold over them slightly.

Just like the Name Says

"Sage grouse habitat can be summed up in a word—sagebrush. To say that the shrub is important to the grouse is a great understatement. The grouse eat it, they hide in it, they nest in it, and they perform their annual, age-old courtship displays near it. Without sagebrush, they cannot exist."

—Craig Springer, *"The Sage Grouse,"* Cabela's
Field Guide Story, www.cabelas.com

Sharptails vs. Ruffed Grouse on the Table

It's no contest: The ruffed grouse not only beats the sharptail but beats almost everything else as well. Still, sharptails are a prize worth bringing home, and there are several ways to enjoy them. One of the most often quoted from hunter-campers is to broil the birds over hot coals in the field.

When Bobwhite Man Meets Western Quail

The first sight of western quail by a seasoned bobwhite hunter like this writer is apt to be a bit disconcerting, as well as memorable. Try to picture twenty to fifty closely-bunched blue-tinted bodies literally flowing over the ground in a stream-like motion. The covey seems to disappear as it leaves open ground and melds into the cover. Then, as you hurry forward, you spot them emerging from the cover in the distance, still on the run . . . and now you are on the run yourself, trying to get them to flush. These are scaled quail, or possibly gambel's, the track stars of western quail hunting.

The Disappearing Chukars

Sometimes chukars can be heard and spotted calling on the tops of hills. Off you go to pursue the covey up the steep slope. When you reach the top, you find they've departed—probably for the cover at the bottom of the other side of the hill.

The Great Treasury of Western Bird Hunting

Imagine an entire book devoted exclusively to western bird hunting. Well, it not only exists, but it's written by veteran writer and hunter John Barsness, whose prose is a hallmark in *Field & Stream*, *Sports Afield*, *Gray's Sporting Journal*, and many other publications. The book is *Western Skies*, published by Lyons & Burford in 1994. Look for it at sites like www.amazon.com. Reviewing the book in *Shooting Sportsman* magazine, Robert F. Jones said, "Anyone planning to gun the Great Plains, whether for sharptails or widgeon, ringnecks or teal, should read this evocative book at least twice—once for the fun of it and again for technique. It's all here—told in the wry, loving voice of a native-born Plainsman who knows both his birds and his country."

You'll Need Water Out There

Every western quail hunter needs to consider the availability of water in his plan for his hunt. Or to put it another way: Consider the non-availability of water. You, and especially your dogs, are going to need it.

Another Way to Carry Water

Photographic supply stores offer collapsible quart and half-gallon jugs made for darkroom chemicals. They make great canteens because you can squeeze the air out of them after you take a drink, which eliminates noisy sloshing.

Gambel's or Valley?

Found in similar terrain, the valley and gambel's quail can be hard to tell apart. The valley quail has scaled markings on the breast. Another difference, pointed out by Ray P. Holland in *Scattergunning*, is that the head of the male gambel's is bright chestnut.

Habit That Betrays Sharptails

Wherever they are found, sharptails have a strong habit that often betrays them: In the early morning and late afternoon they fly to the fields where they like to feed. They can be spotted at that time, even ambushed if you know their route. I've had great sharptail shooting in Manitoba by waiting behind hay bales for the previously-spotted flock to appear.

Sage Grouse on the Table

How do sage grouse taste; Well, it all depends on the way you prepare and cook them, but to many the sage taste is too strong. In the Lewis and Clark expedition in 1805, William Clark wrote, ". . . the flesh of the cock of the plains is dark, and only tolerable in point of flavor."

Sharptails in Flight

When a bunch of sharptails bursts into flight, the birds don't explode skyward in the manner of bobwhite quail or ruffed grouse. They're more like pheasants, a little slow on the takeoff but gathering speed quickly once away from the ground. When pass-shooting opportunities come your way, look for the birds to fly in an alternate flapping/sailing manner.

Tapping into the Alaskan Ruffed Grouse Bonanza

I lived in Alaska for two years—Fairbanks to be exact—attending my last two years of high school while my father was assigned to Ladd Air Force Base as an officer commanding antiaircraft radar installations during the Korean War. North of Fairbanks, the gravel Steese Highway wound through hills and tundra toward the Yukon. The stretch from Fairbanks to a place called "Eagle Summit" harbored the best grouse and ptarmigan hunting covers I shall ever see. When one thinks of these northern forests, ptarmigan come immediately to mind, and, of course, spruce grouse. Now "spruce hens" are terrific as a gamebird when you flush them, but they're nowhere even close to being as wary and fast on the wing as ruffed grouse. But we had ruffed grouse too! Yes, real ruffed grouse, up there in Alaska. And while they were not as wary as the grouse you'll flush in, say, Pennsylvania, they were plenty wary enough to provide us some great hunting and legendary table fare.

Using Calls to Find Chukars

Coveys of chukars sometimes reveal their locations by calling. Chukar calls and instruction are readily available from Cabela's and others.

Chasing down a Hun Covey

You could, in theory, bust an entire covey of Hungarian partridge if you mark their landings after every flush. But you'll have better hunting long-term if you satisfy yourself with three or four flushes. Then go find another covey to work.

Uphill? Downhill?

Unlike ruffed grouse, which almost always will fly uphill when flushed on a hillside, western quail will take off downhill, creating a very difficult shot, since most hunters are not accustomed to holding below the bird.

The "Ground Sluice" Tactic

Many western quail hunters, frustrated by the running birds and anxious to get the covey airborne and scattered, fire a shot that rake the ground in front of the birds and causes them to flush. Of course, if you're hunting with a dog, this tactic is not an option.

Hun Country: Hunting the Prairies

The great prairies of Alberta and Saskatchewan and western states like Montana are home to the European gray partridge (Hungarians, or Huns, as

they are known), first introduced in the very early 1900s. Here big-going bird dogs can do their thing, roaming far and wide as you walk the endless-seeming, rolling land beneath the big sky. In some places, the Hun's range is shared by sharptail grouse, and a mixed bag is possible. To top things off, you might even just some ducks from a prairie pothole and have some swing your way.

Out to Get Some Chickens

The Greater Prairie Chicken, the pinnated grouse, or "squaretail" as hunters familiar with sharptail grouse call it, is hunted in North Dakota, South Dakota, Nebraska, and Kansas. The "chickens" once thrived in the weedy areas of the western prairies in such numbers that hunter like Theodore Roosevelt commonly had fifty-bird days. You won't find any such numbers today, due to the loss of habitat—not the shooting—but in areas when the chickens are still present in huntable numbers, you'll find a gamebird worthy of pursuit and great on the table.

Out for Revenge

Writer Rafe Nielsen got the title of his great chukar story on the Cabela's Web site from his observation, "There's an old hunting adage that claims the first time you hunt chukars, it's for sport. After that, it's for revenge."

Find the Water, You'll Find the Chukars

Water is scarce in the desert country where chukars live, Find the water, you'll find the birds— open springs, river and

creek bottoms, even guzzlers built by state wildlife agencies are home to chukars.

Are You Ready for Chukars?

In a wonderful article on the Cabela's Web site, www.cabelas.com, Rafe Nielson writes: "By far, chukars are the most challenging and difficult North American gamebird. . . . What makes the chukka a difficult gamebird to hunt is the country they inhabit. The steep, rocky slopes of barren deserts are preferred habitat. . . . This most resembles the native land they come from [Afghanistan and India, introduced in the early 1900s] and provides excellent cover when the birds are pressured. Vegetation is also important, and the birds favor the round mountain brushes and grasses such as sagebrush, saltgrass and especially cheatgrass."
—Rafe Nielsen, "Chukar Hunting—This Time Is for Revenge," Field Guide Story, www.cabelas.com

With Ted Trueblood to Back up the Grouse Claims

Whenever someone challenges me on my Alaska ruffed grouse experiences, as they often do, claiming I was not hunting real ruffed grouse, I put

their criticism to the sword by a column late Ted Trueblood devoted in *Field & Stream* to the exact same hunting I had been doing above Fairbanks. As I did, he found the Ruffed Grouse shooting, on the same hunts as the spruce grouse, to be amazing.

After the Covey Flush: Time to Start Scoring

When a covey of western quail has been busted, and the singles are scattered, you can reasonably expect these birds to sit tight and flush close to the gun. Hunting down the singles after the covey flush is what it's all about it western quail hunting.

The Snap Shot on Hun Coveys

Some hunters claim more success on Huns by taking a fast snap shot at the entire covey just as the birds jump. They follow up this "shoot and hope" blast at the covey en masse with a fast swing on one bird.

The "Easier" Chukar Hunting

The steep high-country hills and mountain draws that have chukar hunters gasping for breath and frustrated by the up-and-down escape routes of the birds aren't a factor in a lot of chukar hunting today. The chukar has become a favorite for preserve hunting, providing a hefty greattasting bird to bag and holding well for pointing dogs on preserves. Many preserve hunters and managers favor stocking chukars over pheasants.

What to Expect on Hungarian Partridge

They're twice as large as bobwhites, and the coveys usually jump much farther from the gun and

dogs than Bob does. When Huns jump 30 yards or more from the gun, they seem unbelievably fast, sure to be out of range in just an instant. Feeling somewhat panicky, the gunner may throw two fast snap shots at the birds, and will probably miss. A fast swing on a certain bird works better. The kind of swing and shot duck hunters are used to—not the quick snap of the bobwhite hunter.

Focusing on Mountain Quail

Mountain quail are larger than bobwhites, weighing about nine or ten ounces to bob's seven. Their daily range is larger than the bobwhite's also, as they move between food, water, and sheltered brush that protects them from their enemies. They particularly like canyons with streams in the bottoms, and their strong legs carry them on wide patrols for seeds and berries on the adjacent hillsides.

How We Hunted Ptarmigan with Spruce Hens

Driving along the gravel Steese "highway" we hunted these spruce grouse and ruffed grouse by parking the truck and working into the cover about 50 yards and paralleling the road. Even without a dog, we flushed spruce hens and ruffed grouse with such regularity that we actually had to pace ourselves on bagging a hefty limit. (Ten birds, as I recall, but don't quote me. The time was 1952–'54.) We always wanted to save some action for the pinnacle of the trip—a place called Eagle Summit where the hills rose above the tree line and flocks of ptarmigan could be found in almost every direction. The snow came early up here, and sometimes we were able to walk close enough to kick up flocks of twenty-thirty birds, trying for a double on the flush, then hunting down the singles, just as in quail hunting.

Why Mearns's Quail are Special

The Mearns's quail lives in gentler, kinder terrain than his cousin desert quail. I've hunted them in the grassland canyons near Tucson, Arizona, in country once frequented by Apaches like Cochise. Found in smaller coveys than other western quail, the Mearns's is a hefty bird, great on the table, which feeds on seeds and tubers found in certain types of terrain. My hunts were in January from a motor home with the late Pete Brown, guns editor of *Sports Afield* for many years. During the day the air had a slight chill that made hunting a pleasure, and at night you felt you could grab a handful of stars, and one fell asleep listening to the sounds of coyotes. Great country, great hunting!

When it's Sharptails You're After

Sharptail grouse, a prime gamebird hunted in the prairies of Canada and several western states, can be bagged with pointing dogs, retrieving and flushing dogs, and plain old walking them up.

Tighter Chokes Take More Huns

Your wide-open favorite bobwhite quail gun may not get the job done on Huns. They jump so far out that you need modified and full tubes, rather than improved cylinder and modified.

"Cast-and-Blast" Chukar Hunting

On many western rivers, fishing can be combined with hunting, and chukars are the game. While floating trout and smallmouth rivers, anglers can spot chukar groups on the hillsides between casts, then off they go, scrambling up the mountain. They're guaranteed to be breathing hard when they return, with or without birds in their game vests.

Midday Sharptails: It's "Pick-and-Shovel" Work

Sharptails will spend most of the day dusting, loafing and staying out of sight in everything from brushy tangles to the deeper woods. Digging them out, even with a dog, is slow going compared to the action you can expect to get in the morning or late afternoon.

The Joy of Sage Hen Hunting

"When I lived in the East, I hunted grouse and woodcock in New England. The birds were grand and the country was beautiful, but I could never escape the feeling that I was cramped for room. Everything seemed small and pinched together. I can show you places in the West where you can stand on a hill and see nothing but sagebrush, clear to the horizon in every direction. Not a house nor a tree is in sight, and you know there isn't another living person within twenty miles except, perhaps, for a stray sheepherder or cow puncher . . . There is something in the air that is mighty good. It's sharp, clean, dry, almost brittle, and always there is the faint undertone of sage. It is exhilarating. You're high, so it often freezes at night in September, but the days are warm and you hunt in shirt sleeves. It's grand country for a man who likes a bit of room."
—Ted Trueblood, "Bird of the Wide Open Spaces,"
True Magazine Hunting Yearbook, 1951

Gravel Roads: Where the Game Wardens Stay Busy

When I lived in Alaska, I took note that the Fairbanks paper sometimes wrote about game law offenders. Constantly leading the list were people busted for shooting spruce grouse and ruffed grouse on the few gravel roads through the wilderness.

Since grouse like gravel roads to pick up grit, the wardens kept busy, as certain individuals saw the birds standing in the roads, stopped their trucks, got out, and blazed away, collecting some grouse for the table. Today, the practice of shooting birds in the road is no doubt a leading cause of the demise of many ruffed grouse in the Maine and Canadian bush country, where dirt roads and logging lanes and skidding trails cut through some wild country and grouse come out to get grit on them.

Dove Hunting Tips

Those "Power Line" Doves

When you see doves sitting on power lines, you're not going to stop your truck and start blazing away. The sight is, however, a true indicator that doves are using fields in the area. Keep a close watch as the afternoon progresses and see if you can spot the fields they are using and the routes to and from resting areas and waterholes.

White-Wings Like it Hot

The white-winged dove of the southwest is larger than the mourner and prefers much, much hotter weather. In fact, the birds along the Texas, Arizona, and New Mexico borders shove off for Mexico when the weather turns the slightest bit down from sizzling. I gunned white-wings along

the Arizona border on an annual basis back in the '70s, and found them to be strong fliers and great on the table. White-wings seem to bore ahead in a steady, more-determined nature than mourners, which twist and jink around a lot. Bag limits have declined steadily since that time.

The Perfect Dove Gun

You can shoot doves with any kind of smoothbore you have—from tight-shooting 12-gauge duck guns to wide-open 20-bore quail doubles. But let's say you really want to enjoy the experience to the ultimate, and that includes using the ultimate shotgun. So . . . what is it? And what do you feed it? What follows is a personal opinion, based on considerable experience. First, I want a side-by-side or over-and-under double. Pumps and autos throw their shells, which, in my opinion, must be retrieved and not left lying in the stubble. Next, the gauge. The 20-bore seems perfect to me, although the 28 will certainly do the job in the right hands.(In case you didn't know, 28-gauge guns throw a highly-effective pattern.) Even though some good shooters use the .410, I don't see it as a good dove gun. I've seen just too many cripples and missed birds with the .410, which has a pattern I don't trust. For chokes, I like improved cylinder and modified for my double, but if you can find—or order—one with improved cylinder and full, you might be better off. Number 8 shot seem right for most shooting, but in second seasons, colder weather, 7. might bring down more long-range birds.

Marker Trees: Where Doves Fly Most

Doves often use prominent, single trees as a sort of intersection guidepost when crossing large expanses of fields.

They fly past these positions frequently before fanning out for other sections of the fields. Sometimes these "markers" can be a low clump of small trees at an intersection of fence rows. If you can pick out one of these sites in your scouting, you should have great shooting.

The Pleasure of Small Hunts

Although most dove "shoots" are a big community affairs, with many shooters spreading out over the fields, there's still a place for smaller hunts, the kind two friends can take. Careful scouting over land you have permission to hunt can reveal excellent sites along flyways to set out your shooting stool and get consistent pass shooting. These two- and three-man hunts are especially fun and effective during the winter portions of the dove season, when the birds are bigger and faster.

Doves Like Clear-ground Walking

Wherever they feed, water or pick up grit for their craws, doves like walking over spots of clear ground. They may be flying over thick, tangled brush a lot of the time, but they do not favor walking around in the thick bushes. For watering places, look for open, sandy ramps along the water's edge. In fields, they will be landing in clearings or in the open ground between the rows of feed like sunflower seeds or millet.

Low Birds Spell Danger!

At every well-run dove shoot, you'll hear the person in charge point out the danger of shooting at low-flying birds with good reason: Low-flying birds are dangerous in the extreme. I personally will not even raise my gun to track a bird unless I have about a 45-degree angle.

Those Tough Overhead Shots

One of the toughest shots in dove hunting occurs on a bird flying straight overhead. It's hard to get your gun barrel ahead of one of these speedsters and keep it moving—and still be able to see the bird. Most of the people who are good at making this kind of shot preach the gospel of having the barrel overtake the bird in a rapid swing, then pulling the trigger just as the barrel blots out the bird. Of course, you have to keep that barrel moving (rapidly!), even after the trigger pull. Whatever you do, it's a tough shot.

A Box of Shells, a Limit of Birds

Wherever you go, you'll hear it said that shooting a limit of doves (usually twelve birds) with a box of twenty-five shells is the mark of a really good shooter. In my view, it all depends. If a lot of birds are flying, and you're a cherry-picker, taking only the easiest shots, bagging a limit of birds with a box of shells is no big deal. If a lot of the shots you're getting are long, high and far out and on strong, fast birds—the kind you get in the later half of the dove seasons—you might even consider yourself lucky to bag a limit of birds with two boxes.

Wear Camo for Dove Hunting

Yes, when there's a heavy flight of birds in the area, with plenty of chances to get some shots, you can bag your share of doves wearing just about any kind of shirt—as long as it's not white or solid black. But in normal conditions—and especially in tough conditions when not many birds are coming your way—you'll do a lot better by wearing at least a camo shirt and hat, and even better with camo trousers. Especially after opening day, and especially during the second seasons, doves can be skittish, veering off at the sight of a crouching figure in the bushes.

Dove Hunting's Finest Moment

For this old hunter, the finest moments—with images I can replay in my thoughts with great clarity—are those when five or more doves come slanting in from a side angle, then fly directly across my position. If you're ever going to bag a double, this is the moment. You usually settle for one, of course. And the sight of those sleek, beautiful birds in full flight over the field will come back to you often.

The Sunset Fliers

There's a moment in the dove fields when time after time I wish I could paint. It occurs in the slanting sunset light, when we've finished shooting and the birds are still flying. The setting sun gives them a sort of rosy tint makes the scene unforgettable, while filling one with confidence that there will be plenty of birds around for our next hunt.

Be Alert for Killdeer

Killdeer—those swooping, swerving, and constantly screaming dark-grey birds with pointed wings—are usually very much a part of the terrain where doves are found. If you mistake one for a dove and shoot it, you may face a fine. Be alert and learn to recognize these birds that can look remarkably like doves at times.

Eye Protection is a Must in Dove Hunting

When dove season opens, chances are the sun will be bright, and seeds and all kinds of dry bits of trash will be blowing around. You'll be looking skyward constantly, and there's always a possibility of a stay shot pellet dropping on your stand—and

into your eye. You need protection! Yes, sunglasses are a must. You might need two pair, one with lenses for cloudy days, another for the more-typical bright days.

Bad News Dogs in Dove Fields

Seems innocent enough: a guy wants to bring his retriever along on a dove hunt. He figures to get some good action for his lab, or whatever. Trouble is, the dog isn't trained properly. From the moment the guy gets in the field with his dog, bedlam ensues. The dog runs through all the fields, past everybody's stand, ignoring the master's screams and commands. The afternoon is spent trying to bring the dog under control, to no avail. If you—or a pro!—hasn't had the time to properly train your dog, leave Old Jake at home. And hope that everybody else does the same.

How Not to Take a Tumble

Your favorite dove-hunting stool—Kool-Stool or whatever—is a great place to perch while waiting for birds to come your way. When you're presented with one of those high, fast birds heading straight for you, passing dead overhead, you ought to be aware of leaning back too far. You'll tumble over backwards, for sure. It's a bad, dangerous deal with a loaded gun, and your back isn't going to enjoy it either. If it happens to you, remember to keep the gun pointed skyward, no matter how embarrassed you are, and get the safety back on as soon as possible, definitely before you start trying to get up.

Late Can be Great in Dove Hunting

The second dove seasons—where and when they are scheduled—usually take place during days that seem more like real hunting season than the steamy, hot days of September. In the second seasons, the birds are now all (in September, some are not) full-grown, full-feathered, and in general fly faster than their September kin. The days can be blustery, the birds skittish, and your shooting ability will be challenged to the fullest. You may have bagged a limit of birds with a box of shells in September, but November or December will be a different story. Try it!

New Jersey Hunters: Cross over the River

Years ago, in a display of legislative weakness, anti-hunters managed to get mourning doves placed on the songbird list in New Jersey and dove hunting was banned. Still, all is not lost for enterprising hunters. Just across the Delaware River in Pennsylvania and Delaware, hunting is allowed and there are plenty of doves in places. Yes, you'll have to buy a non-resident license, yes you'll have to do lots of scouting, and perhaps you'll even take a lease. But if you're serious about doves, you'll find good hunting.

Light Loads, Better Shooting

At the tail end of the good old summertime, when dove shooting in your camo T-shirt, you don't want high loads banging your shoulders into a pulp—and bringing on an acute case of flinching. Doves don't take a lot of killing power. Use the lightest loads possible for the gauge you're shooting.

The Ultimate Dove Seat?

Over the years, I've watched dove-hunting (shooting!) seats evolve from canvas lawn chairs to Kool-Stools and beyond. Now perhaps the ultimate has come along. Cabela's, www.cabelas.com, has the Action Products Deluxe Super Seat, which is a padded seat with comfortable back, on top of a box that is a cooler with lift-out trays for gear. There's

also a pouch on the side of the box for more stuff, all for $50. If you want less, that costs less and weighs less, you can opt for Ameristep's High-Back Chair for $19.99.

White-wings are Down Mexico Way

For good white-winged dove shooting today, you'll be looking to book your hunt for one of the many outfitters in Mexico. Type in "White-winged Dove Hunting in Mexico" on your favorite search engine, and you'll see a lot of listings to choose from.

Flying the "Gauntlet"

Some of the most thrilling moments in dove hunting take place at a shoot that's going strong and a dove flies over the woods into the field and immediately meets a barrage of gunfire. Instead of turning back over the woods, the bird bores straight on across the field, unwavering, with more and more shots booming out until it passes out of sight at the other end. It's really something to see—and hear!

Dove Hunting in Mexico: A Look Back

Although this account by Tom Hennessey describes dove hunting in the Yucatan Peninsula of Mexico in the 1980s, you can find much the same kind of shooting today, in an area where there are so many doves they're actually considered to be pests: "You use an overused expression, 'You had to be there.' Far to our right, an immense undulating flock of doves moved across the horizon, like a wind-driven cloud. Like swarms of bees, more flocks arrived. Within seconds they reached the field and were greeted with snappy statements from 20-guage guns, punctuated by belching blasts from the heavier l2s. A fusillade followed, and few birds fell. Wheeling and flaring, the flocks scattered. Doves in every direction."

—Tom Hennessey, *Feathers 'n Fins,*
The Amwell Press, 1989

The Toughest Shot of Them All

Perhaps the toughest shot in all upland gunning occurs when a dove, riding a tailwind, flying high, whips across your stand. Some of these birds actually rock their bodies from side-to-side, seemingly sensing your column of shot whistling past. This is prime-time, great shooting.

Doves are Hard to Hit

More ammunition is expended shooting at doves than any other gamebird. Get the picture?

What to Expect from White-wings

"Coming into a field, white-winged doves are using at cruising speed—which ain't exactly slow. At the first shot, however, they switch on their afterburners and accelerate to a speed that is sickening—to the shooter, this is."

—Tom Hennessey, *Feathers 'n Fins,*
The Amwell Press, 1989

Shoot Lighter-kicking Loads

Dove hunters should know that the 1-ounce "Dove and Quail" loads you see for $3 a box at the marts in August are loaded to almost 1,300 fps to ensure that they'll cycle in autoloaders. Spend a few more dollars and shoot light trap loads instead. When you're wearing no more padding than a camo T-shirt, 1-ounce target loads at 1,180 fps deliver excellent patterns and less bang for the buck, which is what we're after. If you want speed,

try International target loads, which are quite fast at 1,325 fps, but low-recoil thanks to their 7/8-ounce payload.

—Philip Bourjaily, "Reducing Recoil,
Part I," www.fieldandstream.com

Wingshooting Tips

Don't Mix That Ammo

Mixing 12-, 20-, and 28-gauge shells—and even other gauges—in your gunning coat or shell box is a bad idea. The 20 and 28 can drop into the chamber and lodge in the barrel. Bam! Very bad things happen, like losing your hand or your life. We know of one prominent lady shooter who lost a thumb in just such a way during the excitement of crow hunting.

A Cheap Alternative to Clay Pigeons

"A cheap target for shotgun shooting is a Frisbee. . . . About 9 inches in diameter, it's larger

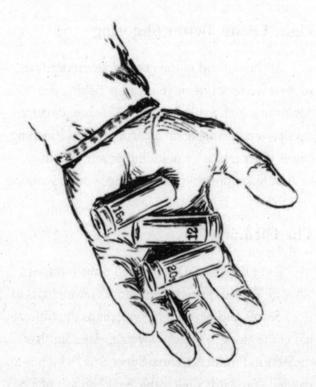

than a clay target, and tougher. The Frisbee will still fly flawlessly at the end of the day with light streaming through countless shot hoes, and it's considerably easier to hit than conventional clay targets . . . a blessing for the beginning shooter."

—Bob Gilsvik, *The Guide to Good Cheap Hunting,* Stein & Day, 1978

Gauges, Chokes, and Pattern Density

The misconception that gauge-size determines shotgun pattern size should have been put to bed long ago. A full-choke pattern, or improved cylinder, or modified . . . whatever . . . is the same diameter and circumference regardless of gauge. It is the gauge that determines the density (the number) of shot within the pattern. Got it? The 12-gauge has more shot than the 20, the 20 more than the 28, and so on.

Steel Shot in Full Choke

There's a myth out there that steel shot won't perform properly in a full-choke gun. *Field & Stream* writer Philip Bourjaily takes it on as part of a wonderful article he did in 2004, "Shotgun Myths Explained," posted on the *Field & Stream* Web site, www.fieldandstream. com. Bourjaily writes, "Manufacturers discouraged the use of Full chokes in the early days of steel for fear of barrel damage. However, almost any load of BB or smaller steel with shoot tight, deadly patterns through a Full choke and won't harm choke tubes, either."

The Straight-stock Bird Gun Preference

According to grouse and shotgun expert Nick Sisley, the straightstock preference on classic upland bird doubles, and others being made today, is not simply for the racy, clean lines. The increased angle

in the wrist of the shooter as the gun comes up results in the face achieving a tighter cheeking on the stock. In addition, the straight stock makes twin-trigger doubles easier to operate.

An Alternate Technique to the "Sustained Lead"

In many schools for serious shooters in the United Kingdom and even in the United States, a different technique than the "Sustained Lead" is taught. Instead of starting the swing with the gun ahead of the bird, the shooter is urged to start the gun barrel behind the bird, catch up with the bird, swing on past the bird, then pull the trigger while the gun keeps swinging. These shooters report that with this technique, the shooter is forced to swing the gun fast and keep it swinging fast throughout the shot. The fact that the gun has to catch up with the bird by a fast swing creates a swing that won't break down or pause as the gun whips on past the bird.

The Truth about the "Sustained Lead"

Whether they're aware of it or not, many shooters—most in fact—learn to shoot with what's called the "Sustained Lead." The gun comes up

ahead of the bird and stays there swinging and tracking, even after the shot. Many serious shooters who put a lot of time and practice (skeet, trap, sporting clays) into their skills come to realize that the "Sustained Lead" is tough to sustain. Something causes the gun barrel to stop swinging fast enough, and the shot is missed. Sometimes, anyway.

The Deadliest Shooting Technique

In an article he wrote for me in the magazine *Waterfowl Hunter*, outdoor writer Tom Huggler described the swing technique favored by many shooters who don't like the so-called "Sustained Lead." In this technique, described in the "Alternative Technique" tip above, the gun starts behind the bird and comes on through. But Tom has a better way to describe it, a way to remember it in the field. As he swings the gun, he's thinking, "Butt . . . belly . . . beak . . . bang!"

Fast Fliers Take a Fast Reaction

On the kind of explosive flushes you're apt to be getting on birds like quail and grouse, getting the gun on your shoulder then swinging the muzzle toward the bird won't get the job done. The muzzle should be moving toward the bird as the gun is moving toward your shoulder and cheek.

Heavy Guns for Practice, Light for Hunting

You can't shoot round after round of sporting clays, skeet, or trap with a shotgun so light you can trudge through grouse, woodcock, and quail country all day carrying it in one hand. The light, fast-pointing guns can be used for a round or two to give you a "feel" for mounting and swinging them, but for serious clay-target shooting, a heavier gun is needed.

Clay-target Practice, and Real Birds

"Any shooting helps us become better, but a 100-straight in trap or skeet or gaining Master Class in sporting clays, using a pretty heavy gun, is not grouse or woodcock shooting— no semblance of it. There's no calling, 'Pull' and here comes the real bird. Instead, it's tramping mile after mile—and maybe you'll get a shot. If you do it's almost bound to be unexpected, even sometimes behind a good dog. Call 'Pull' all you want, but the bird is going to fly when it wants to."

—Nick Sisley, in an article for the
Ruffed Grouse Society

Sorting out the Light Gun Debate

Although it's most unanimous among upland bird hunters that a light gun is needed in the field, the question of "Just How Light?" stirs some debate. Shotgun expert and writer Nick Sisley sheds considerable light on the subject: "The don't-go-too-light camp claims that light shotguns bob around too much, and are hard to control in making a steady smooth swing . . . The go-light-shotgun camp says that a heavier gun does not permit them to carry the gun in a ready-to-shoot manner for hours on end. . . . I've been in the go-light camp for decades. . . . I still can't carry a 7-pound shotgun for hours on end—just can't. So I don't try. Don't have to when carrying a grouse gun of about 6 pounds."

—Nick Sisley, in an article for the
Ruffed Grouse Society

Ain't No Such Thing as "Straightaways"

"How can I possibly miss that shot?" a hunter exclaims. "It was dead straightway." We've heard that one many, many times and will keep on hearing it. But the truth is this: A real straightaway doesn't exist. The shift may be subtle, but your bird is either rising, dipping down, or moving from one side to the other. Dead straightaway, he's not!

Fine-tuning Your Skeet Practice

Skeet shooting is not only fun while improving your smoothbore prowess, it offers certain stations that really resemble the angles you get in all forms of wings-hooting. For the best practice on flushing upland birds like, quail, grouse, pheasant, and woodcock have someone pull for you while you concentrate on stations Low Five, Low Six, and Low Seven. Don't mount the gun. Have it in your bird-shooting carry when you call, "Pull!"

Picking out a Lighter Bird Gun

"Back in 1964 there weren't a lot of light-gun choices. This is not true today. There are a myriad of light ones available from Orvis, Browning, Caesar Guerini, Franchi, Benelli, Remington, Krieghoff (yes, Krieghoff), Kimber, Perazzi, Smith & Wesson, Cortona, Winchester, Connecticut Shotgun Manufacturing Company (Winchester Model 21 reproductions), Beretta, CZ-USA, Ruger, and others. Obviously, some of these makers also offer heavier shotguns. Don't forget the used market—for treasures like small-gauge Parkers, Fox, L. C. Smith, Browning (Superposed), Ithaca, and certainly small-gauge English doubles. (Editor's note: A tip for those who don't know their computers well, just type in the names of these makers on Google and you'll get the home Web site. Say you're interested in a Kimber shotgun. Type "Kimber Shotguns." You'll get the link to go right to Kimber.)"

—Nick Sisley, in an article for the
Ruffed Grouse Society

Just One More

"I've come to recognize collecting as a form of undiagnosed disease. Like the alcoholic who thinks he can just have one and he'll be fine, the gun collector kids himself. . . . The world's greatest easy mark is no longer the pushover he used to be. . . . But if you know of where I could get my hands on an old Model 21 in 16 gauge, bored about improved and modified with a straight-hand stock and checkered butt, at the right price, of course, you know where you can reach me. Just don't call me at home, if you can manage it—and if a lady answers, hang up."

—Gene Hill, "Shotgunners Anonymous,"
Hill Country, E. P. Dutton, 1978

How Far Was That Bird? You Don't Want to Know

Shotgunners, waterfowl hunters in particular, sometimes talk about making 60-yard shots, even 65. OK, I'll believe you. But sometimes before you go much further with such boasts, do yourself a favor and visit you local school's football field. Stand on the goal line and put a box or marker on the 60-yard

line. Was the duck you shot that far out? Thank you, I thought not. For you bird hunters, put the box at 35 yards. Does that range feel familiar? I thought it would.

A Short Course in Spanish Shotguns

"Most of the shotguns made in Spain did not have a great reputation until some time in the 1960s, when a few of the top Spanish side-by-sides were discovered by outdoor writers Jack O'Connor of *Outdoor Life* and Colonel Charles Askins. One of the outstanding Spanish makers they discovered was AyA, acronym for Aguirre y Aranzabal. The 'y' in Spanish is the same as 'and' in English. Since then many excellent Spanish double gunmakers have emerged or were already in production, like Arrizabalaga, Grulla, Arietta, Ugartechea, Garbi, and others. All of these makers are in and around Eibar in the Basque country of northern Spain, and they all concentrate on make side-by-sides in the finest English quality."

—Nick Sisley, in an article for the
Ruffed Grouse Society

Checking out a New Spanish Double

"The shotgun the Ruffed Grouse Society and the Spanish maker AyA have collaborated on is the Model 4/53 in 20 and 28 gauge. The test gun I've been shooting is the 28-bore and it wears 29-inch barrels . . . There has not been one hiccup in the gun's performance, although the back trigger is a bit squishy. The trigger can no doubt be easily remedied by a gunsmith. This little 29 has ejectors, and it tosses spent empties with real authority. I say little 28 because the gun is so light. I assume this one is built on a true 28-gauge frame because it only weighs 5 pounds, 11.5 ounces."

—www.ruffedgrousesociety.org and
www.aya-fineguns.com.

Want a Light Double? Check This Out

"The Dea Duetto is a new side-by-side from Stefano Fausti in Italy. The model designation means something like 'twin goddesses' in Italian, no doubt the 'twin' referring to this model always coming as a two-barrel set . . . one set of barrels is in 28 gauge, the other in .410, and both sets fit to a very tiny frame. The single trigger is non-selective. The right barrel will always fire first. It's going to be right at home when you are hunting the thickest of brambles, when you constantly have one one-hand the double to ward off briars, tiny saplings, aspen whips and alder branches with the other hand. With a so-called 'swing' seldom involved, its shoulder the Dea Duetto in lightning-fast action, point and shoot—all of the latter done in less than a heartbeat. The overall weight gets one's attention. With the 28-gauge set of barrels attached, this one sent my digital postal scale to 4 pounds, 15 ounces. With the .410 barrels the weight was 5 pounds, 1.5 ounces. The .410 set is 2.5 ounces heavier, no doubt, due to the slightly increased mass of metal at the monobloc—the part of the barrels next to the receiver. Ejectors. Screw-in chokes. $4999. Web site: www.faustiusa.com"

—Nick Sisley, in an article for Sporting Clays

"Patternmaster": A Choice Aftermarket Choke Tube

If you're happy with the patterns you're getting from the choke tubes that came with your latest shotgun acquisition, fine. But a lot of hunters keep looking for absolute perfection, and that's what makes the aftermarket choke tube offerings so hot today. There are several out there, but one we're hearing a lot about is Patternmaster, www.patternmaster.com. Philip Bourjaily, on the

Field & Stream Web site, writes, "The Patternmaster, popular among waterfowlers, actually contains little studs near the end of the choke that grab the wad and slow it, producing extremely tight patters with little to no constriction."

"Hey, Dude, You Missed!"

In a column on the *Field & Stream* Web site, www.fieldandstream.com, expert shooter Philip Bourjaily says many shooters just can't admit it when they've made a bad miss: "The first thing he'll do is to look down at the ground." Pro shooting instructor Gil Ash told Bourjaily, "Look up at the spot where you missed the bird, replay what happened, and figure out why. Make a change and move on."

Try Straightening out Your Left Arm

In his classic *New England Grouse Shooting*, William Harden Foster makes a strong recommendation for right-handed shooters to hold the left hand far out on the forearm. If you're not used to this position, try it for repeated practice sessions and then on clay targets, and you might find your shooting greatly improved. Foster felt that the extended hand position made the gun steadier.

Muzzleloader Shotgun Hunting

RANDY D. SMITH

In spite of what has been written in the media my nomination for "The Gun that Won the West" is the common shotgun. The United States may be a nation of riflemen but it was the shotgun that was called upon to do first duty as a provider of game for the table and defender of the family. Shotguns were formidable and deadly when loaded with buck and ball. Shotguns were available to the general public at low cost and when the going got tough they would shoot almost anything a pioneer had to shove down the barrel.

The muzzle-loading shotgun has lagged behind the rifle during the rebirth of black powder. Replica scattergun choices are not nearly those of the rifle. This is unfortunate because, while the black powder rifle lags behind modern rifle ballistics, the properly loaded percussion shotgun will rival modern shotguns in the field. Only the time involved in loading is the muzzleloader's weakness.

The muzzleloader shotgun's loading process presents a new opportunity for the shooter who desires more challenge. I've found that my wing shooting has actually improved with a muzzleloader. Knowing that I do not have backup rounds, I have taken a split second longer to properly point and lead the gun and passed up many marginal shots. This has greatly improved my first hit success rate.

Muzzle-loading Shotgun Selections

In the early years of the rebirth of muzzle-loading several companies offered excellent sidelock percussion and flintlock shotguns. Since there have never been special muzzleloader only upland game, waterfowl, and varmint seasons these shotguns never sold in numbers approaching the rifles. Many of these models are still available on the used gun market and often in pristine condition.

Thompson/Center sold a nice percussion single shot called the New Englander. It was available with either a walnut or weather resistant Rynite stock. This was my first muzzleloader shotgun because of price and availability. I hunted with one for several seasons. It was quick to point and dependable. Its size makes it an excellent choice for a small framed shooter.

CVA marketed a Trapper single shot sidelock shotgun equipped with interchangeable chokes. Its balance and handling was quite similar to the New Englander. Mowrey's Ethan Allen 12 gauge single shot was an unusual shotgun that appealed to the eye and the pocketbook. It is a dependable shotgun.

Dixie Gun Company still sells the Mortimer flint shotgun. It is a 12 gauge with a 36" barrel and it is a beautiful piece to handle and admire.

Today the black-powder sidelock shotgun market is dominated by the Davide Pedersoli percussion double barrel. This gun is sold by nearly all the black powder marketers. Some double-barrel black power shotgun models feature chrome-lined barrels for use with steel shot. Some 10 and 12-gauge models use screw-in choke tubes for greater flexibility and come with X-Full, modified

Cabela's Double — The author has carried this Cabela's 12 gauge double barrel percussion shotgun for fifteen years. With proper care and regular maintenance this gun will last a lifetime.

and improved cylinder chokes. The 20-gauge has a fixed improved cylinder and a fixed modified choke. This shotgun had deep, slick bluing, engraved locks and checkered American walnut stocks.

I have owned and hunted with a Davide Pedersoli 12 gauge double for fifteen years. I have worn out one set of locks and had to have them rebuilt. It has proven to be an excellent turkey, varmint, and upland game gun. I have not hunted waterfowl with it but it is designed for steel shot.

The problem I always had with the single barrel shotguns was for pheasant and turkey hunting. There were situations especially when a pheasant was flying straight away from me, that one shot was not enough to bring the bird down. I needed that

second shot that a single barrel couldn't supply. There were also a couple of times when my load misfired on turkeys and an instant second shot would have been the difference between taking and losing a Tom. When I switched to my Pedersoli double those problems were eliminated.

Those who want an authentic replica of the most common scattergun on the early plains should look for a flintlock Northwest Trade Gun in 12, 20 or 24 gauges. This was the all-purpose weapon of the Indian and the early plainsman. Its popularity is evident by the fact that it was commonly marketed in the early twentieth century to Canadian Indians and Eskimos.

A beginner should consider a percussion shotgun over a flintlock. The delayed firing reaction of the flint gun demands skill and patience for accurate shooting. I often hunt with Dr. Gary White who uses a flintlock shotgun for turkeys. Doc has often demonstrated that a good, well-tuned flintlock shotgun is just as quick on ignition as any percussion or inline gun with virtually no delay. He uses guns that he has made himself and is an expert on touchhole and pan alignment. He is fastidious about flint maintenance. Most beginners are not and do not have access to a finely crafted flintlock smoothbore. A good Trade Gun is the way to start down that road.

Keep it Simple!

One of the reasons for the muzzle-loading shotgun not enjoying the popularity of the rifle has is that many potential buyers are concerned about was seems to be complicated loading procedures. Buyers hear of ounces versus drams and grains, overshot wads and overpowder wads. It seems complicated and slow.

This does injustice to a very simple and efficient gun. Do like the old timers did and keep it simple. Most of you will never know the difference if you follow some simple advice about shotgunning.

First of all the terminology of ounces of shot, drams of powder and grains of powder is confusing. A dram of powder is equal in volume to 27 ½ grains of powder in a rifle. Call it 27 or 26 and forget about it. The measurement of ounces of shot refers to the weight of shot for individual loads.

The easiest solution is to load a shotgun on a one to one ration for game or when you begin patterning. A good 12 gauge upland load is ninety grains of #6 shot over niney grains of FFg black powder. I am referring to volume amounts that are measued with a common measuring device. A one-to-one ration is easy to remember and just as effective as anything else you can dream up.

I use Federal ½ inch thick 12-gauge cushion fiber wads in front of both shot and powder and have never experienced a blown pattern. Normally I will split the over shot wad with my thumb nail but it is not necessary. Over shot cards are fragile and difficult to align properly past tight chokes. When chokes are especially tight I often use a short starter to force the wads past them. I keep my fiber wads loose in my loading bag so that I do not have to fumble for a specific kind. It greatly speeds reloading time.

Support Equipment—Managing powder, shot charges, and caps demands for minimum support equipment. Shown are shot snake and charger, powder measure, nipple pick, capper and shot wads.

You can have too much of a good thing when shotgunning. Guys are always trying to develop "Magnum" loads for turkey hunting and ending up with terrible patterns from hard recoiling powder charges. Ninety grains of powder and an equal volume of shot for a 12 gauge, eighty five grains for a 16 gauge, and seventy five grains for a 20 gauge are excellent field loads and easy to gauge and remember. You'll get a bigger boom with more powder and shot but little else. Keep your loads simple and moderate and you will enjoy successful shooting.

I prefer #5 shot for turkeys, #6 shot for most pheasant, small game, and quail, and #7½ for morning doves. If you don't have interchangeable chokes, you can use a plastic shot collar wad to increase pattern density. I have often done this for turkey and coyote hunting but not for upland game or rabbits because it slows the loading process.

Make certain that your loads are well packed and remain that way. Loads can work loose, especially with a double barrel that is being shoot a great deal with one barrel and not the other. It is also a good idea to cover the barrel you are not loading to help prevent double loading. I generally pull my ramrod and rest it in the unfired muzzle while loading.

Never load a double barrel with the percussion cap still on the un-shot barrel. When I load two barrels at a time, I always charge the left barrel first. No reason for that other than developing the habit of doing things the same way every time which is important for safe shooting.

Backup Supplies

For years I carried my shot in one horn and my powder in another and used the same measure for both. There are a number of shot pouches on the market if a horn doesn't interest you. Many of them have attached pre-measured scoops and chargers. This will save reloading time. My current bag has a shot pouch attached to the shoulder strap with a shot charger.

Many suggest using pre-measured charges. This will save bulk and time. It is a very effective practice for turkey or coyote hunting where you don't expect a lot of shooting. For a day afield, however, I prefer a shooting bag and shot snake.

Tips for Successful Shotgunning

In order to overcome the disadvantage of only having one or two immediate shots develop the practice of holding your position and carefully reloading before taking another step especially when hunting upland game. I have often flushed a pheasant or covey of quail, knocked birds down, reloaded on the spot, advanced with a freshly charged load and brought up another bird with the next step. Getting two birds from the same area with a single shot muzzleloader is not a pipe dream. It can be regularly done, especially in cold weather when the birds are less likely to run or fly. The shooter needs to develop an deliberate attitude and control his actions. This is the challenge of muzzle-loading. Taking a large number of birds is not the idea. Even a single shot cartridge shotgun will reload much quicker than a muzzleloader. It is the challenge of muzzle-loading that is the appeal. Once you develop that attitude, you will be surprised at how many birds you will take.

Pheasant

The king of the game birds on the Plains is the Chinese Ringneck pheasant. They are an import from China and do very well in mixed agricultural and grazing lands. The bird is hunted by flushing him from cover. He is slow to take off and usually noisy. He is perfect for beginning muzzleloaders because he is relatively easy to fine and shoot. And, if you haven't had pheasant and noodles then you just haven't et! Season are from early fall through the end of January. Hunting is best when it is cold or snowy and the birds are holding tight. They are most active in the late morning, early afternoons and early evening. Hunting is usually best during the very early morning when the birds are warm and do not want to leave their positions. Try heavy cover nest to harvested fields of grain, fence rows, waterways and weedy fields for best luck. I recommend a 12 gauge using ninety grains of powder and from #4 to #6 shot of equal volume. As the season progresses and the birds become wilder the heavier shot will do better at longer ranges.

Quail

Bob White and scaled quail make for excellent hunting in the West. These are small birds that move in covey of six to twenty. These little guys prefer thick brush and plenty of cover. The best shooting technique is to pick up one bird with your sight point and stay with him until you shoot. If you don't you are liable to find yourself shooting wildly in confusion.

T/C New Englander—A single barrel muzzleloader such as this Thompson/Center New Englander 12 gauge is an excellent small game, turkey and small bird hunter. It falls short where backup shots are necessary.

Don't feel too bad if you get rattle when flushing the first few coveys. It happens to most of us.

This is my favorite muzzleloader upland bird. Where pheasant hunting is usually done with a large group of hunters who want to keep shooting lines even, quail hunting is perfect for a single hunter and a good dog. I often feel pressured by others to reload quickly when pheasant hunting but that is not the case on a cold Saturday in December and January when everyone else is watching the ball game and I am out alone with my dog. There is an almost leisurely aspect to muzzle-loading for quail in spite of the ruckus of a covey rise.

Walking the edges of waterways and dry streams will produce good populations, especially when near thick brush. A 12 gauge load of #7½ shot and eighty grains of powder is a good quail choice. I usually use #6 shot and ninety grains of powder because of the likelihood of also flushing the occasional pheasant.

Doves

Morning dove hunting is good for the shooting skills but not so great for the frustration level. The little gray flyers are fast and fleeting. They are a migrating bird that is hunting in the late summer and early fall before the weather forces them further south. In the western plains you will have the most success in the early morning and late evening when the birds come to water. Shelter belts next to windmills and ponds are excellent spots for hunting doves. Plan on quite a bit of shooting before you get very many. It is great fun and a good way to sharpen the shooting eye before the later bird seasons. Use a light load of seventy grains of powder and an equal amount of #7½ shot.

Prairie Chicken

There are only five states that allow prairie chicken hunting. Kansas has the largest population and its season usually is time with pheasant and quail seasons. Prairie chickens are about the same size as pheasants but they are much faster and higher flying. They must have a habitat that is at least thirty percent open grassland to flourish. A good hunting method is behind cover on the edges of fields during the morning and evening, and pass shoot as the birds work from grass to grain.

The more common method is to flush them from tall grass. Be prepared for the possibility of a great deal of walking with sporadic success. Try to locate populations by scouting and stalk them early in the morning. Prairie chickens are fast and wary, and the open grassland is their perfect environment. They are excellent table fare. A ninety grain powder charge and equal measure of #5 or #6 shot is my suggested load.

Turkey

I have read chronicles of the early Santa Fe Trail that told of inexperienced hunters mistaking great flocks of turkey for their first bison sightings. It must have been a sight to behold. I did not see a turkey in the wild in Kansas until about thirty years ago. They had been virtually wiped out on the plains by the turn of the twentieth century. Their numbers have increased steadily since re-introduction in the 1960s.

The turkey is the Plains game management success story second only to the whitetail deer. These birds are wary survivors and probably the greatest game bird challenge on the Plains today. They prefer the river bottom overgrowth but can be found in well-watered valleys. The turkey hunter must conceal himself and uses calls to try to lure the old Toms into range. Camouflage clothing is an advantage for turkey hunters. Hunting these birds demands a lot of pre-season scouting to determine where the birds are roosting. A great variety of calls are available. Pick your call and practice as this is one effort that will take skill and patience. A box call is necessary to counter the winds of spring. A hunter needs his call to be recognizable up to a mile on the Plains.

Too many hunters call too much. Once a turkey responds to the call, wait several minutes before calling again. Calling too often makes it easy for the birds to spot your position and it does not entice the bird to come toward you except in certain circumstances. I've witnessed too many hunters immediately respond to a gobble with a call without waiting for them to close the distance. Henned gobblers will be very vocal and not come in. Better to wait until later in the day when the hens have broken off contact.

Breeding season for Rio Grandes can be very short on the Plains so it is often necessary to establish ambuscades. Glassing from ridge tops and moving into position as turkeys pass along narrow creek channels is a very effective strategy. Decoys can also be very good for distracting turkeys as cover is often slight in these areas.

I recommend #2 or #4 shot over at least 100 grains of black powder in a gauge. A 10 gauge is not out of line for these birds. Use a full or extra full choke and plastic shot collars to tighten your pattern. I have killed turkeys at 50 paces using muzzle-loading shotguns with guns that patterned at tightly as any modern gun . . . and with less recoil. A muzzle-loading shotgun is ideal for turkey hunting. Use a fresh load each day to reduce the chances of a misfire.

Waterfowl

Modern Hevi-shot and tungsten shot have changed muzzle-loading for ducks and geese into a fine pursuit. A good 12 or 10 gauge double choked full and extra full with a load of 100 grains of black powder and an equal volume of #4 shot is my normal choice for ducks. I use #2 shot for Geese. A Pedersoli shotgun recommended for steel shot will do well with BB steel shot and 100 grains of FFg black powder. Use plastic shot collars to extend range and pattern density if you do not have chokes.

I recommend a 10 gauge for ducks and geese if they are your primary hunting goals. I like the extra shot a 10 gauge offers in its loads. Try to shoot from a blind where you can reload easily from a standing or sitting position as muzzleloaders do not do well with prone loading positions.

Muzzleloader Turkey—This nice Rio Grande was taken at thirty yards using the Cabela's double with the right barrel choked full and the left choked extra full with standard pheasant load of 90 grains of FFg and an equal volume measure of #6 shot. The right barrel was used and the left barrel held in reserve for a longer shot or a misfire.

Shotgunning: The Art and the Science

BOB BRISTER

Forward Allowance

The easiest way to hit flying game is to swing the barrel through the bird as if to paint it out of the sky.

That rash recommendation comes after more than twenty years of taking the trouble to watch directly over the shoulders of some of the world's finest shots and that is how most of them do it. Precisely when they pull the trigger depends upon distance, speed of target, and angle, the judgment of all three being one of the main reasons for moving the gun barrel through the target at the last instant before firing. It's like giving the mental computer a last-minute readout on all the variables.

I suppose this could be called the swing-through system, because most shooters start their movement of barrel with the target, then swing through it. But to be really precise in long-range pass shooting, it helps to actually start behind the bird, because the gun is then forced to speed up to pass him and in doing so provides added insurance against slowing or stopping the swing. The momentum of the gun will keep it moving even if the shooter fails to follow through consciously.

Fred Kimble, believed by some shotgun historians to have been the greatest

duck shot of all time, must have used the swing-through system. Certainly I did not watch over his shoulder because he did his market hunting in the 1800s, but I've read everything I could find about him or by him on the subject of forward allowance. That information, compared with shooting in the field and testing on crossing targets at known speeds and yardages, convinces me that Kimble used the swing-through system—or some derivation of it—because he had to in order to hit ducks with the leads he said he saw ahead of the bird.

In *The Shotgunner's Book* by Col. Charles Askins, Kimble is quoted as saying that his most common lead on mallards was one duck length ahead of the bird's bill at 40 yards, at 60 yards two duck lengths. Unfortunately he didn't mention what the duck was doing at the time, whether cruising over the treetops or hovering over decoys, but if the duck happened to be passing at the rather common mallard speed of 35 miles an hour, the only way Kimble could have killed him would have been to swing past him rather swiftly.

The reason I can say that is that for months I have been shooting at life-sized silhouettes of ducks (including mallards with measurements taken from real ducks) and the only way I can hit one while

Starting the barrel behind the bird and swinging through him to judge angle and speed is the best insurance against aiming or stopping the gun. The barrel speed required to pass the target provides additional forward allowance, thus reducing the lead the shooter must see ahead of the bird.

holding the gun one duck length ahead of his bill at 40 yards and 35 miles an hour is with the same swing-through system I use hunting.

Computers show that a shot load leaving the muzzle at 1,235 feet-per-second requires a forward allowance ahead of a duck crossing at 40 yards and 35 miles an hour of about 6.2 feet. Judging by the loads he was supposed to have used, 1,235 fps would have come close to the correct velocity for comparison, and if Kimble saw a one-duck lead, and the duck was the same as our mallards nowadays (about 24 inches), somehow or other he had to make up the difference in required forward allowance.

He did it, I believe, by taking advantage of his gun's lock time. His eye perceived the distance ahead of the bird to be one duck length, but with the gun swinging fast, by the time the trigger finger responded, ignition occurred, and the load left the barrel, the barrel was pointed farther ahead of the bird than Kimble realized. That is the beauty of the swing-through system. It provides built-in lead, added allowance, overthrow, or whatever one wants to call the phenomenon of shooting farther ahead of a target than the eye realizes.

This phenomenon can be tested by simply shooting at the ground. Start a fast swing from left to right and pull the trigger when a predetermined spot is reached. The load will not go to that spot, but will impact beyond it in the direction of the swing. This does not mean that you have sprayed the shot, nor physically overthrown the load past the point where the trigger was pulled. It means there is a tiny delay between the message sent by mind to trigger finger and the actual pulling of the trigger, another tiny delay between pulling the trigger and falling of hammer, another tiny delay of primer ignition of the powder charge, and then the elapsed time required for the load to get out of the barrel. Throughout this process, the fast moving gun barrel has been moving. And it requires very little movement to make a decided difference downrange. One degree of barrel movement translates to about 25 inches at 40 yards. This is part of the theory of Robert Churchill, who claimed no such thing as forward allowance is necessary; the shooter should simply point at the target and swing fast.

One great competition shooter of Kimble's day claimed he could swing his gun so fast he needed absolutely no lead ahead of a duck at 40 yards. Adam H. Bogardus, who was by no means a shy fellow, often took out ads in newspapers proclaiming himself to be the greatest shooter of all time. So it is not surprising that he might consider himself able to hit crossing ducks at 40 yards by pointing at them.

Perhaps he could do this, and maybe Churchill could, too. But I certainly wish they were alive today so I could watch over their shoulders as they fire at my moving duck target at 40, 50, and 60 yards. Several of the best shooters of my acquaintance have tried that target, some with the firm conviction they never consciously lead a crossing duck. But their average pattern placement as revealed by pellet holes in the target crossing at 40 miles per hour—at a precisely taped-off 40 yards—revealed they were hitting from 1 to 3 feet behind the duck when they fired just as the barrel passed the bird.

I have tried the same thing myself, at various speeds and yardages, in some cases using

This is the sight picture, barrel swinging with leading duck, used to test the sustained lead required at various speeds and yardages. On this shot, the load struck the fourth duck from the front. Thus a three-duck forward allowance would be required for a sustained-lead shooter. A swing-through shooter would need from one half to one third less to hit the same duck.

the full Churchill drill of pointing the left hand at the target as the gun is mounted, swinging as fast as I possibly could, in effect literally lurching the barrel past the bird's bill, and the best I can do is hit slightly behind the duck at 40 miles an hour and 40 yards.

Now at 25 to 30 yards or so, and 25 to 30 miles per hour, this fast swing will indeed hit the bird with virtually no observed lead if the swing is fast enough. But I found it more difficult to concentrate on fast swinging than simply to see a little daylight ahead of the bird.

English writer Gough Thomas shrugs off Churchill's no-lead theories with the observation that it is simply impossible to move the gun fast enough for long-range hits on fast moving objects. Before him, Major Sir Gerald Burrard wrote: "The truth of the matter is that with shotguns a big forward allowance will always be necessary . . . we must face facts as they are and bow to the inevitable."

Having studied the various theories of forward allowance and marveled at how the Churchill system could circumvent laws of physics, it was revealing to try it on the moving target. From those tests I have decided, at least to my own satisfaction, that the works of Thomas and Burrard on the matter of forward allowance are full of plums of wisdom and that Churchill on this subject was full of prunes.

In attempting to determine how much a fast-swing system can reduce lead at long range, I first had to determine what smooth swing or sustained lead forward allowances would be at given yardages. To do this I would swing with barrel pointing at the lead duck on the target and fire while swinging along with it as the target passed. At 40 yards and 40 miles an hour, the loads struck between 6 to 8 feet behind point of aim, which translates into 7 foot or more lead ahead of a bird crossing at that speed with a smooth swing at target speed. Then, by swinging fast as I usually do in duck shooting in the field, I could cut the observed lead about in half. But as distances

Although a fast swing worked fairly well at 35 yards, long ranges required seeing a great deal of daylight ahead of the target no matter how fast the barrel was moved.

became longer, even the fastest swing I could make required more and more daylight ahead of the bird.

For an example of how much forward allowance we're talking about—say with the gun swinging smoothly the same speed of the bird at 60 yards—I had to hold on the rear bumper of the car to place the center of the pattern on the middle of the target 12 feet behind the bumper! And in case you wondered about some of the many stories you've heard of clean kills on ducks and geese at 70 yards, I've measured the sustained lead required for me with the target moving at 40 miles an hour and it is approximately 18 feet! The pattern, by the way, will have strung out well across my 16-foot board target at that range with most duck or goose loads.

Obviously birds do not all fly at right angles to the gun, nor are they all going 40 miles an hour. Tom Roster did some studies that convinced him that waterfowl fly around 35 miles an hour crossing country, and up to 50 miles an hour when they're really in a hurry or have a tailwind. Then he cranked the necessary data into a computer and determined the actual forward allowance required for birds crossing at 35 to 50 miles per hour and various yardages. Those tables, through special permission from Roster, are shown at the end of this chapter as converted into bird lengths relative to the waterfowl species size.

I was surprised at how closely my computations made on the moving target tallied with those of the computer; maybe more surprised at the consistency with which the human trigger finger can each time pull off a shot and place a pattern on a moving duck at essentially the same spot it did before with the same load. I had expected much more human error variance, but then I had not expected to get so much practice, either. Tests expected to take 1 month took 6. What really surprised me are memories of some long shots I've made at distances I was positive were beyond 60 yards, yet I certainly did not recall being 14 feet ahead of the bird.

Obviously what appears to be 14 feet at arm's length and how 14 feet of spread looks over a gun barrel at 60 yards are entirely different. At 60 yards, 14 feet may appear to be little more than half that; maybe to some shooters it looks even less. This is why I believe it is easier to estimate forward allowances in bird lengths rather than feet and inches. But even if the shooter knows the number of bird lengths and exactly the distance and angle of the target (which he never will out hunting) there remains more art than science to long-range waterfowling because human reaction times and trigger times vary widely.

The late Nash Buckingham wrote that he would envision "a moving spot out in front" of the bird and swing to it, touching off when he reached it. Although Buckingham referred to a spot, he was not

A shotgun is not aimed at moving targets, but must be pointed and kept swinging; the "aim" here was used to show where gun was pointed to put pattern 10'9" back on the target. Such long leads cannot be made by simply swinging faster; at least in the author's tests, no one could do so. The sight picture with a swing-through lead at this yardage at 40 miles per hour was approximately 4 mallard lengths (96 inches).

Geese at this distance should not be skyblasted; they are more than 70 yards away, and at this crossing angle shot-strings are long and patterns relatively inefficient no matter what the gun or load.

a spot shooter. He was a swinging shooter, because he specifically referred to the place he pulled the trigger as "that moving spot out in front." Years of experience had taught him just where that "moving spot" has to be at the angle, speed, and distance of the bird.

Certainly there are other systems of shooting that may work for some. The so-called sustained lead, as advocated by skeet and trap champion D. Lee Braun, simply amounts to starting out in front of the target and staying there, measuring up and if necessary correcting the distance in front, continuing the same steady speed of swing, and firing. This works very well at skeet, fairly well at trap, and may be the easiest way to learn to shoot these American-style games. This is particularly so at skeet, where the path of the targets and their speed are known and the shooter can get locked into his gun, put the barrel out in front the required distance, and start swinging the minute he sees the bird emerge from

Forward allowance for the incoming, rising bird is easiest achieved by starting beneath him, swinging fast, blotting out the target, and continuing the swing. If the bird is close, no observed lead is necessary; if he's high, some daylight between gun and bird becomes imperative with most shooters.

the house. With this system it is easy to keep the barrel ahead of the target.

But skeet shooting and field shooting are different things, and calls to mind an incident by no means disrespectful of the shooting talents of the great D. Lee Braun. Lee, as we called him, was a friend of mine and a longstanding friend of one of the greatest all-around shots of all time, Grant Ilseng, and he once came down to hunt ducks and geese with us in the marsh country of the Texas coast near Ana-huac. The snow and blue geese were flying by the thousands; trouble was they were way up there, and Lee was having a tough time. For one thing, his feet were mired in the marsh, and his sustained-lead system required a lot of distance out in front of the bird. He was trying to measure sustained lead, which had to be around 8 to 10 feet, while looking back out of the corner of his eye to see what the goose was doing back there. Often the goose would see Lee just about the time that long, long lead had been computed, and would flare back with the wind without getting touched. Ilseng, a swing-through shooter, was starting with the geese, painting the

barrel fast through them, seeing (as he told me) about four goose lengths ahead of the bird as he fired.

It was very much like watching an artist paint birds out of the sky. We came in with the limit, although I cannot say who got all those geese. I do know that Lee took a lot of joshing that day.

Now had Lee Braun, one of the greatest shotgun shooters of all time, wanted to master goose shooting in a Texas marsh, he would indeed have mastered it. But he concentrated on making a living with his shotgun as a professional for Remington Arms Company, and as a instructor primarily devoted to skeet and trap where he was all but unbeatable. One of my prize possessions is a copy of his book *Trap-shooting with D. Lee Braun* which he autographed and personalized with a little notation that means a lot to me.

But the story underscores why I like Ilseng's (or Fred Missildine's) swing-through system best; they cut down the daylight I must see ahead of a duck or goose at long range.

On birds that suddenly appear—say a duck that comes whipping past the blind while you're looking the other way—the swing-through system is almost automatic. You're behind that bird to begin with; you frantically try to catch him with the barrel, pull out in front, see some forward allowance in that split second, and pull the trigger. The odds are that bird will fall. But then along comes a lumbering goose or duck that you have watched grow from a tiny dot on the horizon. When he is finally within range, you carefully estimate the yardage, mount the gun, measure up the same lead you saw on the previous bird whipping past the blind—and miss.

How can that be when the forward allowance seemed perfect?

The main difference is that the first bird caught you off guard and you began your swing from behind. This meant the gun was accelerating fast as it passed him, and you could not stop it if you wanted to during the interval of reaction time and lock time.

But with the bird you've watched all the way in, the tendency is to start partially out in front of him, swing slower (because you want to be precise about it) and slow the swing as you shoot. The difference in a continued swing and a slowed swing translates into several feet at 40 yards. The way around the problem, I believe, is to force yourself every time to start out behind, swing the gun through, (not yank it ahead, just pass him) and see a little more daylight ahead than you think necessary.

In long-range pass shooting, birds appear slower than they are, particularly geese which seem even slower because they are big. Watch a jet passing high overhead; it will barely seem to be moving. Thus, the longer the range the greater the optical illusion as to the speed of target. Always swing past a goose far enough to center the pattern on his head rather than his body. If you misjudge his speed, the extra allowance often provides enough error margin to center the pattern in the body. If you're perfect it should still kill him, because there are invariably plenty of pellets behind the front portion of the shotstring at long range.

In experimenting with speed of swing (relative to leads obtained) I asked my wife to drive the moving target past at varying speeds, keeping records on each run and the actual speed the vehicle crossed the shooting position. Since I would not know target speed, I would have to estimate it, the same as in the field. Several times, on a target run that I suddenly realized was faster than I'd thought, I would accelerate the gun to gain added forward allowance, and those were times I best centered the bird. The times my pattern went behind the bird were almost invariably those in which I tried to be too careful, or thought I might be a little too far ahead of the target.

Since I've been making the same hits and misses in field hunting most of my life, I'm inclined to believe the moving target told a fairly accurate tale of what happens to many shooters. However, it must be remembered that a shooter cannot swing as suddenly, nor follow through as perfectly, with his feet mired in marsh mud. Nor can he do so in a duck boat, or sitting in a blind, or on his knees in a rice stubble. Thus, any demonstration of methods of forward allowance must be taken with the shooter's position in mind, or maybe with a grain of salt. I have seen advocates of the fast swing move rather deliberately when standing in mud. They still hit birds, but they did it more deliberately. Otherwise, in yanking the barrel around too abruptly they'd probably have fallen flat—and I've seen, and done, that too.

Thus the shooter must make allowances for shooting conditions as well as speed and distance. He'll need a little more lead when conditions force a slower swing. But never slow down, look back, and try to measure up to see how far ahead you are. That's the easiest way to miss.

I've heard and read statements to the effect that the same lead can be used at 60 yards as 35 yards because what appears to be 3 feet of lead at 35 will actually be much more than that at 60. This can be easily proved by propping up a yardstick on the ground, backing off, and looking at it over the gun. The farther back you go, the shorter the stick will seem to be.

But this is an optical illusion directly consistent with distance, whereas the shot load's speed is not consistent with distance but is slowing up much more rapidly at 60 yards than it was at 35. Therefore, if one sees what appears to be the same forward allowance at the two yardages, it would seem to me that the load would have to hit behind the target at 60 yards due primarily to changes in its time of flight.

I tried this out on my moving target, and had others do the same. Firing was done at markers that had been put out in advance at distances from 35 to 60 yards, but the shooter did not know the exact distance. Target speeds were kept standard

The late Norman Clarke demonstrates the English system for dealing with fast incomers such as driven grouse or pheasant. Weight is shifted to rear foot, gun shouldered quickly, and trigger pulled as the bird is blotted out by the barrels. Since the faster the bird the faster the swing required to catch him, the system is somewhat self compensating. But on very high, fast overhead birds, such as waterfowl, author prefers seeing some lead in addition to the fast swing.

at 35 miles per hour. On the longer shots, even though we concentrated on swinging faster when the yardage was longer, we shot behind unless we saw considerably more daylight ahead at long range than short range. This system may indeed work for some shooters, but I have never observed anyone in the field hitting long shots consistently who was not pointing his barrel well out in front of the bird. I have thus become convinced that I must go on shooting the same way I always have, seeing a great deal more lead ahead of a bird at long range than I see at close range.

When I perceive a bird is really a long way out, at the very edge of clean-killing range, I try to get the gun out in front of him a little farther than I believe necessary, trying to force myself to remember that the shot are slowing down out there. I was taught that system by a one-time market hunter who believed the shot load slowed so fast the lead had to be doubled between a 40-yard bird and a 60-yard bird. In those days I had much more faith in ammunition than I do today, and I doubted the old man's theory. But I could not doubt his ducks, since he killed more of them than I did. So I tried more lead, a lot more than I figured I needed, on the long crossing shots and ducks and geese started falling.

In looking at computer readouts of actual required leads at various speeds and yardage, it seems the old man was closer to correct than I had imagined. The computer claims a forward allowance of 6 feet is required for a crossing target at 35 miles per hour, and a forward allowance of 10½ feet at 60 miles per hour. While 10½ feet is not double 6 feet, it's pretty close. And when you add to that the natural tendency to slow the swing a little while trying to measure up a longer lead, the old man's computations could have been quite close. Obviously they were, because birds quit flying and fell when he shot.

The old man did not condone pass-shooting ducks or geese at long range except in certain situations where he was reasonably sure they could be retrieved. Over open water, or an open field, he would do it. But not in the marsh where a long bird might be very difficult to find if not dead. I believe he was right about that, too.

The conscientious shooter will have studied his gun and loads, have a good idea of what they can do and he can do, and will be in a situation (ideally with a good retriever) that permits recovering the occasional gliders or long cripples that eventually crash a long way from the blind. Just standing and shooting at anything that flies over, trying to guess whether the bird is 60 or 100 yards, is the sort of skyblasting that costs all waterfowl hunters in terms of crippling. And I have no intention of contributing to it by suggesting that any shotshell load, even the 10-gauge magnum, will consistently kill (without crippling as well) at 70 to 80 yards. My moving-target tests show that the finest loads made will string out pitifully at 70 yards and will not have the density they show on the stationary target. Also, the long shotstring at that distance is likely to hit other birds in flight with stray pellets.

No matter what fancy shooting system is employed, it is difficult to center birds in the pattern

The fast swing and follow through is often impractical, even impossible, with one's feet mired in marsh. A fast incomer here could send the shooter backwards into the mud. In this case it is better to take incomers out front rather than overhead. Shooting from a duckboat, on one's knees, or mired in mud requires more gun control with the arms and is usually more effective with a slower, more deliberate swing and more forward allowance. This gives the shooter a better likelihood of maintaining his balance.

at long range, and the longer the range the more difficult it becomes. Most of the hunters I have observed over a lifetime of hunting some of the finest duck and goose country in America are pretty good at 35- to 45-yard shots; beyond that they miss a lot and cripple. And no amount of computer studies can make long-range shooting a simple thing.

The computer's estimates, for example, relate to targets crossing at a 90° angle. This is a quite common angle in long-range pass shooting, and certainly the one requiring the most forward allowance or lead. But not all birds fly at 90° angles, particularly birds that have just been shot at. Second or third shots into a flight of mallards, pintails, or geese may require much less lead because the birds often flare backward with the wind, or climb, or vary their speed and angle in several ways. A bird just starting to climb requires very little forward allowance; in fact, if the wind is strong you may need to point over him and even behind him slightly, because he can actually move backwards in the air for a short distance flaring back out of trouble.

Such things are learned only by practice, and I am reticent to even mention computers or sustained leads in the same sentence with ducks or geese. Yet there are laws of physics that cannot be circumvented, and the same computer expertise that put men on the moon can be used to accurately compute where a gun barrel must be pointing to hit a crossing object. Some shooters can attain that point by swinging fast, some by swinging more deliberately but farther ahead. It doesn't really matter how the allowance is achieved so long as it *is* achieved.

Sometimes it seems almost ridiculous to swing the gun so far ahead of a distant bird, as if you are purposely trying to miss him in front. If that's the way it seems, then try to miss some long-shot gander by shooting in front of him, and see how hard he falls.

Forward Allowance Calculated in Bird Lengths (by Species) Crossing at 90°

35 Miles Per Hour

YARDAGE	20 YD.	25 YD.	30 YD.	35 YD.	40 YD.	45 YD.	50 YD.	55 YD.	60 YD.
Teal	2.2	2.6	3.4	3.8	4.5	5.3	6	6.8	8
Mallard	1.5	1.8	2.3	2.6	3	3.6	4	4.6	5.4
Pintail	1.3	1.5	2	2.2	2.7	3	3.6	4	4.7
Scaup	2	2.5	3	3.5	4	5	5.6	6.3	7.4
Lesser Snow Goose	.9	1.4	1.8	2	2.5	2.9	3.3	3.7	4.3
Greater Snow Goose	1.1	1.3	1.7	1.9	2.3	2.6	3	3.4	4
Canada Goose	.96	1.1	1.5	1.6	1.9	2.2	2.6	2.9	3.4
Western Canada Goose	1	1.2	1.6	1.7	2	2.4	2.8	3	3.7
Lesser Canada Goose	1.3	1.5	1.9	2	2.5	2.9	3.4	3.8	4.4

50 Miles Per Hour

	20 YD.	25 YD.	30 YD.	35 YD.	40 YD.	45 YD.	50 YD.	55 YD.	60 YD.
Teal	2.8	3.8	4.7	5.6	6.5	7.7	8.8	10	11
Mallard	1.9	2.5	3	3.8	4.4	5.2	5.9	6.7	7.4
Pintail	1.7	2.2	2.7	3.3	3.9	4.5	5.1	5.9	6.5
Scaup	2.6	3.5	4.3	5.2	6.1	7.1	8.1	9.3	10.2
Lesser Snow Goose	1.5	2	2.5	3	3.6	4	4.7	5.4	6
Greater Snow Goose	1.4	1.9	2.3	2.8	3.3	3.9	4.4	5	5.5
Canada Goose	1.2	1.6	2	2.4	2.8	3.3	3.7	4.2	4.7
Western Canada Goose	1.3	1.7	2.1	2.6	3	3.5	4	4.6	5
Lesser Canada Goose	1.6	2	2.6	3.1	3.6	4.2	4.9	5.5	6

These allowances are for a smooth sustained lead based on computer readout of mathematical lead in feet. Swing-through shooters can reduce leads one-third to one-half depending upon speed of swing.

The Fine Art of Waterfowl Shooting

BOB BRISTER

The fine art of waterfowl shooting is a fading one, and most of the old masters are gone. We may never see such artists with duck guns again, because any art is perfected with practice and modern laws do not permit such feats (on wild birds) as those of market hunter Fred Kimble, who in 17 days of hunting in early 1872 took 1,365 ducks and 5 brant.

The oldtimers accomplished such feats with relatively primitive guns, mostly muzzle-loading single shots. But with the skies full of game, they perfected the whole of waterfowl hunting. Not only did they know what they were doing, they knew what ducks could be expected to do. Kimble, before witnesses, dropped 57 straight ducks on the wing without a miss, and he probably made longer runs than that. A sensitive man, who handled his violin almost as well as his shotgun, he may well have been the best of them all.

There were many more masters of the waterfowl gun who, because of where or how they lived (often outside laws they could not understand) never achieved reputations beyond the backwoods areas where they hunted. As a boy, I was privileged to hunt with two such men, both getting on in years but still capable of remarkable skill at taking waterfowl. Fortunately they were also full of tales of earlier days, complete with lessons for a wide-eyed youngster who preferred their lessons to algebra class on a good duck morning.

These men, like Kimble, were not just duck butchers in overalls. They were intelligent men who had chosen their way of life in the flooded timber rather than walking behind a plow or clerking in a store. Times were hard but they loved every moment of it, I believe, until the day they died. Most of the great ones were market hunters at a time when this was a legal and well-looked-upon occupation.

One old gentleman, whose name must remain anonymous due to family considerations, continued market hunting long after laws were passed against it. He saw no reason not to—where he hunted there were plenty of ducks. He carved his own duck calls and with them he could speak mallard about as well as any susie. I have watched him converse with ducks on the water 10 yards away, when any mistake by the man with the caller would have exploded mallards like quail.

One morning we were standing knee deep on a flooded pinoak flat, calling and sloshing water under the trees to make ripples as if a lot of ducks were there and suddenly there was a great swishing sound and the sky was literally black with mallards, hens calling, drakes geezing, dropping in around us with wings back pedaling to slow their splash into the icy water. How many ducks we could have killed, emptying two guns into that melee of wings, would be impossible to estimate. But the old man didn't like shooting ducks that way; he liked calling ducks, decoying ducks, and then taking them as they climbed out of the timber with his shiny-worn old Model 97 Winchester pumpgun.

Make no mistake, though, the old man was thinking duck strategy as much as sportsmanship when he failed to shoot into that swarm. One shot and every duck there would have been spooked from that particular slough where we'd set out decoys. As it was, they came trickling back in small bunches and singles, working beautifully to the call. It was one of the greatest days of my life, not only because of the great numbers of ducks but because the old man was in a particularly good mood and took time out to teach me some things.

One of them was how to watch decoying ducks as they lined up coming down through a hole in the timber, and at the instant two crossed or were in perfect line, swinging and leading them both for a one-shot double. This was an old trick of market hunters requiring split-second timing and considerable knowledge of the flight characteristics of ducks. But it can still be done. Many guides in the deep-marsh country of Louisiana and in the flooded timber around Stuttgart, Arkansas, can do it quite often.

A concentration of mallards takes wing from a woodland slough. Rarely will a hunter stalk this near, and a long shot taken into such a flock may cripple several birds for every one killed. Instead, permit the birds to leave and then set up decoys. Chances are good the ducks will return in small flights and decoy well. If shot when flushed from such a spot, the chances are they will be spooked from it the remainder of the day.

Don't believe that? Neither did some contestants in the North American Duck Shooting Championship at Center, Texas, in 1972, when in the first round of competition (game-farm mallards flighted in pairs over a blind in the timber) I managed to kill both my birds with one shot. Whispers of "accident" and "luck" emerged from the gallery behind the judge's table. But after I had managed to do the same thing over again every day of competition, several times in side-bet shooting after the main event each day, some shooters began asking how that trick is done.

The answer, of course, starts with trying to do it, studying the flight speeds of birds in the air so as to anticipate when one is catching up to pass the other. Mallards and pintails often cross each other as they swing back and forth with wings cupped to lose speed. Decoying teal, swift little birds plenty tough to hit normally, usually offer one split second in their decoying procedure when doubles or triples can be made. They will pass low over the decoys downwind, then suddenly whip back and hesitate almost in a wad before dropping in. A shot at that instant may take several birds, but it really isn't recommended unless shooting is slow and a hunter wants to fill out his limit in a hurry. A couple of times, without intending to, I've finished my limit prematurely on teal when the intention was to wait for mallards or pintails.

As much of an art as the shooting is reading the birds, being able to estimate what they'll do and when they'll do it. Diving ducks, such as scaup, bluebills, redheads, and canvasbacks, will often come barreling past in a relatively straight line of flight, even though the hunter reveals himself by sitting up or standing to shoot. Thus, it is fairly safe to take the first bird as soon as the bunch is within good range, leaving more time for second and third shots as the flight passes. But on puddle ducks such as mallards, pintails, gadwall, widgeon, and black ducks, an entirely different strategy is required. Raise

Veteran waterfowl guide Morgan LaFour has hunted the Trinity River bottomlands on the Texas coast for some 50 years. Although never a market hunter, LaFour was an artist at waterfowl shooting until his eyesight began to fail in the late 1960's. At the time of this photograph, about 1961, he could consistently kill two crossing ducks with one shot as they worked the decoys.

a gun to shoot just as a flight of mallards enters range and they may flare backwards with the wind and climb out of range before even a second shot can be fired.

In winning the North American Duck Shooting Championship of 1972 the author makes a double on mallards using the swing-through system. Note the follow through on the second bird and the relatively short distance the first bird has fallen before the second is dead in the air. The gun was a 26-inch-barreled Winchester 101 over-under (improved cylinder and modified choke).

This is the most common mistake of inexperienced waterfowl hunters, and one way to avoid it is to set a stake or a lone decoy as a marker about 40 yards in all directions from the blind. Don't shoot at any duck beyond that marker, and for that matter don't shoot at any mallard or pintail until you know he's within range; let him come as close as he will.

The toughest decision is judging whether the birds will make one more pass nearer the blind or whether they'll take a look at the decoys and go on their way. Here the oldtime market hunter had the advantage. He had enough experience to judge the birds and enough confidence in his calling and decoy setup to wait them out. And he also didn't have to worry so much as we do now about some other shooter close by firing just in time to spook the decoying birds.

Modern shooters for the most part do not take advantage of the chances they have to learn waterfowling. There is no law against putting out decoys when the season is closed and simply watching ducks work them. Much can be learned that way. Pintails, for example, may seem to be leaving the scene, going straight downwind and well past the decoys, when they have actually made up their minds to come in. They make that characteristic last long swing downwind and then whip back bellied up over the decoys. When a pintail is losing interest in a decoy spread (which many of them will) he shows it by hanging high with cupped wings and looking down on the blocks, refusing to lose altitude. He is the one, if ever he comes within range, you'd better take when the chance occurs because he is most likely to drift off elsewhere. But any flight that approaches the decoys low, or loses altitude rapidly,

In typical diving-duck fashion, a flight of redheads comes barreling over blind despite hunters obviously visible to them. Once divers have made up their minds to swing over the decoys, they are likely to keep coming even after first shots are fired and thus first birds can be dropped well out front leaving easy second or third shots as they pass.

should be permitted to let work until they are set up for multiple shots, rather than firing at them too soon and letting them flare back out of range.

Once birds are close over the decoys, it is best to pick out one of the trailing drakes (shoot drakes only, if possible) rather than the front bird. Take the front bird and the more distant birds are likely to flare out of range by the time you get around to them. For another reason, your partner probably will have picked one of the front birds, usually the most obvious one in the bunch. It is very common for two men in a blind to shoot the same duck, winding up with just that one well-ventilated carcass while the rest of the bunch gets away.

The secret of getting several is for both men to pick trailing birds on their respective sides of the blind, take care to drop them, then mop up on the nearer birds which will by then have stabilized to provide relatively easy straightaway climbing shots.

It sounds more difficult to take the longer birds first, but is actually easier. The pattern has more chance to spread and more margin for error on the longer bird (provided he is within range to start with)

and the close birds aren't as easy as they look anyway. The nearer a duck or goose is to a hunter rising to shoot, the more erratic the bird's evasive movements are likely to be. That bird is much more spooked than one farther out over the decoys. And since a spooked duck can make some very erratic moves, and the hunter's pattern at close range is quite small, it actually becomes easier to take one of the more distant ducks.

In pass shooting geese that are bucking strong frontal winds, let them pass over and shoot only when they're past the blind. Then, when they flare back with the wind as they invariably will when shot at, they will still be in range.

I often reverse the firing sequence of a double or over-under, firing the tight barrel first at one of the trailing birds in the bunch and leaving a climbing shot for the open barrel on the closer birds.

I used this tight-barrel-first technique throughout the aforementioned North American Duck Shooting Championship, and was fortunate enough to set a record that still stands: 37 mallards out of 40 shots, all birds fired at as doubles. Since these were game-farm mallards flighted in pairs toward a waterhole some distance beyond the blind, they did not stop to climb as wild ducks would have and it was imperative to drop whichever duck of the pair seemed inclined to go wide out of range, then quickly turn and get the closer bird. This was not easy, because the blind was located in a stand of tall pines, and most ducks were flying slightly higher than the treetops while a few were dodging in and out through the trees. I watched a number of very good shots, who obviously had not hunted many ducks in timber, take a close easy bird while letting the second, already the more distant one, either flare out of range or go behind a screen of limbs.

But the most common miss made by duck and goose hunters today is what would seem to be a very easy shot—the duck or goose that can be seen coming from some distance away, giving the shooter plenty of time to get ready. This bird will be

Limit filled, hunter watches pintails and widgeon over the decoys. Much can be learned about when (and when not) to shoot by observing the decoying characteristics of the various species.

The most commonly missed waterfowling shot comes when shooter attempts to aim rather than swing at big birds that appear to be barely moving. The trick is to start behind the bird and swing through smoothly. As it is more difficult to swing a heavy gun from a kneeling position (or with feet mired in the mud) marsh hunters often do better with lightweight guns they can swing with arms and shoulders.

Hunter in pit blind remains motionless to let low-flying Canada geese pass over decoys. They are bucking a strong wind (note decoy in foreground almost blown over) and to shoot at this point would mean most of flight would flare back with wind out of range.

missed more consistently than the one that suddenly appears from the side of the blind forcing the shooter to make a quick swing.

The reason the "easy" bird is so often missed is that the shooter tried to take dead aim on him, and although he may be conscious of seeing a relatively long lead ahead of the bird, he's likely to stop his swing and try to perfectly measure up the bird. Stopping, or even slowing, the swing is fatal, not to the duck but to the chance the shooter had at that bird.

The slower a bird appears to be coming, such as a big Canada goose lumbering along straight for the shooter, the more likely the tendency to aim rather than swing. Actually that big goose may be moving as fast as a teal; he just looks slow because he is so big.

The way to avoid stopping the swing on any seemingly easy shot at waterfowl is to force yourself to start either with the bird or behind him and swing the gun past him. This is particularly important on high, incoming birds that seem to be barely moving against the wind.

Such birds may be moving slower in ground speed, but the wind resistance slowing them is also drifting the shot load. A 15-mile crosswind will drift No. 2 shot 26 inches at 60 yards, 11.5 inches at 40. Number 4's drift 10 inches at 40 yards, 22.5 at 60. No. 6 lead and No. 4 steel drift 11 inches and 12.7 inches respectively at 40 yards, 25.4 and 28.8 at 60 yards. So additional lead is needed on birds hovering into the wind.

Start behind (in this instance, behind would translate to beneath the incomer) and swing right through him until you achieve the proper lead. Never lead a goose or duck by his "body" but lead as if you were trying to put the full load into his head. This provides added insurance your pellets will arrive at the front end of the bird (where he can be easiest killed) rather than tailing him and possibly crippling. Very few ducks and geese are missed in front; most shooters really have little idea of how much forward allowance is required at long range.

The reason such old masters from the 1800s as Fred Kimble and Adam Bogardus wrote that they saw shorter leads ahead of ducks than my moving target tests indicate may partly have been in the speed of their swing, but more likely in the relatively slow

The late J. R. (Jimmy) Reel of Eagle Lake, Texas, was one of the originators of the white-spread technique of attracting geese and ducks to large numbers of white rags spread out on rice-field stubble to simulate concentrations of feeding snow geese. A lifetime guide and past master of calling as well as shooting, he is shown calling geese for Olympic trapshooting silver medalist Tom Garrigus.

lock time of their black-powder percussion guns. As the fast-swing shooter passes the bird, his barrel continues moving faster than the bird, and the slower the lock time (delay between the pulled trigger and the departing load) the farther out front of the duck the barrel has moved when the load leaves it. Thus the forward allowances the oldtimers saw and the leads they were actually obtaining through their system of shooting were probably entirely different distances.

However they did it, they did it very, very well.

Upland Gunning

BOB BRISTER

Certain gauges and barrel lengths are often referred to as best for doves and quail, others for pheasants and grouse, with size and toughness of game the overriding consideration as if one were selecting an elephant gun. But shooting conditions are more important, and the gun effective on Dixie quail may have little in common with one suited for prairie quail or pass-shooting doves.

I learned that a long time ago, losing a gentlemanly wager in the process. A group of competitors at a live-bird shoot in Mexico were talking hunting, and I made some comment that my 28-gauge quail gun made up for whatever it lacked in firepower with greater speed at getting on game.

Bill Price, one of the fastest guns around, suggested weight is not always that significant a factor in speed of handling and that such theories, projected far enough, could mean a toy popgun with cork and string would be a good quail gun.

"I'll take you and that 28 gauge hunting in the high plains country," he suggested, "and I'll bet you'll be wishing for more gun."

Two weeks later we put down the dogs at dawn 60 miles north of Amarillo, Texas, with an icy Panhandle wind howling across the buffalo grass. The low, rolling ridges contained very few trees; and it seemed the only thing between us and the North Pole was a barbed-wire fence.

Bobwhites rarely hold well to dogs in high winds, and the first covey came roaring up 15 yards ahead of Price's pointers. In a split second they had flared off downwind, picking up speed like jets, and before my second shot they were out of range. Price made what I considered to be an incredible long second barrel kill and the score was instantly two to one in his favor. After that it got worse. The little 28, which had killed like lightning in my native piney woods timber, seemed to be spitting sleet instead of shot.

There was nothing wrong with that 28, custom-bored skeet in one barrel and improved cylinder in the other, except that the conditions where it had worked so well were entirely different than those on the bald, wind-howling prairie. Price was shooting a 20-gauge bored improved cylinder and modified and I'm not sure he wasn't shooting 3-inch magnum 7½'s in his top barrel. Before the day was over, I was indeed wishing for more choke, more gun, or both.

Quail supposedly are not really fast birds, normally attaining only about 25 miles an hour. But they get it all at once. Give them a 40-mile tailwind and they become a bird of an entirely different feather—mostly tailfeather. Doves vary even more in gun requirements. Floating in cautiously over a waterhole they can be taken cleanly with small gauges and open chokes. But cruising high over a feeding field, a tightly choked 12 gauge more commonly associated with pass shooting waterfowl becomes a very fine dove gun.

Pheasants also sometimes require a lot of lead. At the 1975 "One Box" pheasant hunt at Broken Bow, Nebraska, I talked (the night before competition) with a gentleman who assured me he had killed many, many pheasants and that by far the best combination was a skeet-choked 12 gauge and No. 7½ shot. Seems he had been doing quite a bit of practicing on game-farm pheasants at a shooting preserve. The next day the wind blew and the pheasants flew and I was lucky enough to get my limit without missing a bird. I was using No. 6 high-brass loads with the full-choke tube screwed into my Perazzi Mirage over-under 12 gauge.

Every shot in that event is recorded by judges, and I made it a point to find out how the man with the skeet gun fared. To put it in a nice way, he had not seriously reduced Nebraska's pheasant population. Yet I have hunted pheasants near Lethbridge in Alberta, Canada, when a skeet gun would have been just fine; birds were sticking tight along canal banks in heavy cover and often wouldn't flush until almost stepped upon. Pheasants will often do that, and in such cases I believe it is easier to try and center the bird's head with a gun with some choke and range than to gamble the next cock won't come cackling up at 40 yards.

One of the most important tricks to taking pheasants is remembering that the bird's bulk is mostly tail; to hit him low is almost certainly to cripple. A tail-shot cock pheasant, or any other pheasant that comes down with his head up, is likely to disappear and never be seen again unless you have a good dog and a great deal of knowledge of pheasant hunting—they'll run like ostriches and can hide under a pencil.

I've found exactly the opposite shooting technique applies to woodcock, quail, and ruffed grouse in heavy cover. There you can't very well concentrate on the bird's head because you'll be doing well to see the bird at all, and you either shoot at what you see or forget it. Blink once and he's out of sight behind the brush. This is fast, close gun pointing where a skeet shooter's beautifully executed swing and follow through may merely bang his gun barrels against a tree.

Typical Southern quail country—piney woods with grass savannas—where the 20 gauge, or smaller, is perfectly adequate for gentlemanly bird shooting. Ranges are seldom long, and open chokes are best.

I have never advocated spot shooting because it is a poke-and-punch sort of thing rarely dependable on anything but a straightaway. But on close-cover woodcock I probably spot shoot to some extent because I just try and get off some kind of shot in the general direction the bird seems to be going. Sometimes that will turn out to be a tree, but it is remarkable how many birds fall when shot through what seemed to be dense foliage. Shot pellets get through somehow, and I've observed that the most efficient woods hunters do not stand around computing sustained lead.

No matter how open the barrel may be, this sort of shooting usually puts the hunters into an overchoked situation. And the best constriction I've found is none at all. One afternoon in Louisiana our party put up over 100 woodcock, and I cannot remember ever having cursed a firearm so severely as I did the lightweight little 20 gauge that kept connecting with vines, limbs, and tree trunks more often than birds. In theory, this was a fine upland gun. It had 26-inch barrels bored improved cylinder and modified and was being used primarily because I was doing some field testing of that model.

Pheasants sometimes flush underfoot, sometimes at the outer edge of shotgun range. With large shot and fairly tight choke, it is easier to permit a close bird to gain a little distance before firing (or concentrate on a head shot) so as not to ruin the meat than, because of inadequate pattern, to cripple birds that jump at longer range.

There's a woodcock in this picture, but neither camera nor hunters picked up the fleeting shape clearly or quickly enough. In such cover a timberdoodle or quail can be gone in a wink, and the problem is getting gun on bird, not range nor penetration. For such cover, the author favors no choke at all, cylinder barrels.

I liked the feel of it, and killed I believe every quail I shot at that afternoon. The quail were mostly in grassy openings alongside a little bayou and all we got were relatively open shots because the singles would go on across the flooded bayou where we couldn't get to them. But the woodcock were right along the water's edge in thick brush, concentrated along a ridge by high water on either side. That was why we found so many woodcock in one small area and also why I nearly wore out the barrels of that little gun on tree trunks.

It didn't take long for a decision to be made. I'd buy the gun rather than send it back, and did anybody have a hacksaw? I knew the risks. Just whacking off a few inches of barrel is safe enough at producing broad, even cylinder-bore patterns because it effectively removes all choke. But many gun barrels are not the same wall thickness a few inches back of the muzzle that they are at the end, and if the barrels are not bored perfectly concentric, or maybe had been bent or regulated at the muzzle, there's a good chance patterns will not converge perfectly after the tubes are shortened.

I took that chance, bobbed off the barrels to 22 inches, and they shot to point of impact well enough

for the job to be done. Since then I've killed a great many close-cover quail and woodcock with that gun. It is no longer a beautifully balanced firearm. It does not swing so much as it pokes. I would not use it on crossing doves or open-country quail. But it is very good for shooting around trees.

In a lifetime of fooling around with shotguns I've bobbed off quite a few barrels, and circumsized some, trying to retain a little choke by leaving a half inch or so of the start of the choke constriction intact. Most of the time this has worked. When it didn't, I've had to back bore or jug-choke the gun to get acceptable patterns and sometimes wound up getting rid of the gun to someone who needed a poker more than I did.

I once cut back the barrel of a beautiful-handling little Ithaca Model 37 Featherweight 20-gauge pump to 22 inches, trying to create an even faster gun. It turned out to be a fast gun indeed, but one so out of balance and so quick that when a quail got up I'd swing past him, stop and try to get back, and usually miss. I never could shoot that gun again. The moral is that the makers of firearms have some vague idea of how shotguns

Never gamble with an expensive gun by cutting off the barrels; impacts may not be true and balance often will change sufficiently to ruin the gun for anything other than close cover spot shooting. This fine old Parker 20-gauge double should be left as is, although boring out some choke can help for Southern-style quail shooting.

For larger upland birds such as pheasant, prairie chicken, and open-country grouse, modified choke in a 12 gauge is a fine compromise that can be made to pattern improved cylinder with brush loads but tighten to full with extra hard shot trap or pigeon loads.

should balance, and it's wise to think twice about the type of hunting to be done before making radical changes.

Unfortunately, standard borings often fall short of being ideal for upland gunning. For all-around upland hunting, from quail to pheasants, I suppose I'd probably pick an over-under with one barrel bored improved cylinder and the other improved modified (almost full). The English, of course, learned that years ago and many of their guns for rough shooting (what we'd call walk-up hunting) are bored quarter choke and three-quarter choke, which translates into just about improved cylinder and improved modified. For large upland birds modified is a good all-around choice. For closer quarters, and particularly if the gun is a 20 or 12 gauge with considerable pattern density to work with, a gun bored skeet in one barrel and modified in the other is deadly indeed. These borings can be obtained by opening up one barrel of a common improved cylinder/modified gun.

For shooting a wide variety of game in Mexico, including tough wild pigeons, this shooter's gun has Baker choke tubes which screw into barrel to change choke. Exterior twist-type chokes are OK, but shooter must test to see which settings produce the patterns desired; markings cannot be completely trusted.

For the one-barrel man, improved cylinder is hard to beat. Many upland shooters try to compensate for the single barrel's single choke by adding a variable choke device, the most common being the twist-type, which supposedly will provide anything from wide open to extra full. There is nothing wrong with this except that the devices do not always deliver the choke spreads indicated.

By twisting and shooting, each time checking the pattern, the shooter should determine where that particular device must be turned to give the pattern desired. When this is determined, mark the spot with fingernail polish or a scratch or something to show where the "sweet spots" are. Some shooters use different colors of nail polish. Line up the red marks and you have improved cylinder, the white marks mean full, etc.

One other word of advice about adjustable chokes of this type; many guns do not shoot straight after having one installed. This is no fault of the device but of the gunsmith who installed it. Due to differences in barrel wall thickness or other factors a barrel cut back for variable choke installation may be shooting a foot or more off center unless the gunsmith checks it for alignment and preferably shoots it to determine impact. It is the rule rather than the exception that adding a choke device will raise the front sight and tend to lower impact.

If you're considering such an installation, first shoot the gun to see where it impacts. If it's OK, inform the gunsmith that you know where it shoots and that when the job is finished you'll shoot it again to check him out. He may offer to correct the impact if the installation changes it; if he doesn't do so, take it to another gunsmith. An off-shooting gun is to be avoided like a case of colic.

Another thing the short-barrel shooter needs to know is whether he is getting full velocity and penetration from his ammunition. Various loads contain various powders, some of which burn faster than others. This may be no big deal in a 30-inch barrel that offers plenty of time for slow-burning powders to be consumed. But go back to 24 inches or less and in the late afternoons you may find you're using the equivalent of a flame thrower. When the gun is throwing out a long blaze of fire at the muzzle it is not burning its powder completely. Some flame throwing can be expected; it's just a part of shooting a very short barrel. But it can be minimized (and penetration improved) by finding out which loads do the best job.

Matching loads to conditions is a big part of the secret of getting more upland game. Say you have an improved-cylinder barrel and you want it to throw the broadest possible pattern for close cover. Try using a brush load (which has separators in its shot column to distribute the pellets more rapidly). Best of all for this are square shot loads—that's right, little cubes of lead—which really open up in a hurry and can convert a full-choke gun to about improved-cylinder performance at 25 yards. They're called Desperante loads and unfortunately are available only in Europe. The well-known gun writer Roger Barlow provided me a few for loading and testing.

In general, the inexpensive field loads sold in this country contain soft, easily deformed shot that spread faster because they deform more pellets. This is fine for quail or close-range game of any kind because shot stringing doesn't matter much at close range, certainly not so much as pattern spread. Heavier powder charges tend to open up patterns quicker than light loads.

Federal offers special loads (designated T-22) in No. 7½, 8, and 9 shot that do not have plastic shotcup wads and thus open patterns quite quickly. Although they also deform more shot pellets, the advantage in close cover is significant.

But say you want your improved-cylinder barrel to pattern as tightly as possible for pass-shooting doves or maybe those wild-flushing prairie quail

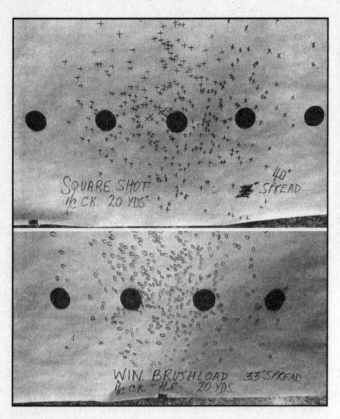

Jump shooting, even with birds as small as doves, often requires tight patterns and good penetration. An excellent choice is 3 1/4 × 1 1/4 7 1/2's in hard shot 12-gauge pigeon load, which patterns much better than standard high-velocity loads but has equal penetration at 50 yards.

Special brushloads, so-marked on the box, broaden patterns as shown. New special skeet loads without the shot collar also open patterns at close range. But the most effective pattern spreader is the square (cube) shot used in Europe. Possibly they will someday become available in the U.S.

that happen to be the common variety in some parts of Texas, Oklahoma, and Kansas, three of the best bobwhite states I've hunted.

The tightest, most efficient-patterning upland loads currently available are traploads and pigeon loads. In many guns you'll get about a 20 percent tighter pattern than the common upland load in the same shot size. Traploads are available only in 12 gauge and come in 1⅛ ounces of No. 7½, 8, or 8½ shot. Pigeon loads have 1¼ ounces of 7½, or 8. For doves I like 7½'s, because the larger pellets are less affected by wind drift and have sufficient shocking power to put down birds that might be feathered with 8's. I've taken a great many doves, many of them with 8's from open-choked, small gauge guns, but over the years, I've settled on 7½ if I'm using 1⅛ ounces or more of shot. For quail in ordinary conditions, a No. 8½ trapload first, followed by 8's,

is a fine combination. For wild-flushing quail in high winds I often use 7½'s; for thicket birds, brush load 8's.

I lean toward larger shot than may be generally recommended for many upland situations because I've learned that prettiness at the pattern board does not always prove out on birds. If dense distribution were the whole story, I'd shoot nothing but 9's. And indeed many shooters swear by them. But I've found they put too many pellets into the flesh of birds I plan to eat, feather too many going-away birds due to lack of penetration, and are more susceptible to wind drift than 8's or 7½'s.

A friend of mine who hunts quail in some of the most fabulous hunting country in America, the south Texas brush country, uses a .410 with No. 6 shot. His theory is that one or two 6's will instantly put down a quail that might flutter off into the brush when hit with several 9's. He also doesn't like small shot in his teeth, and says the 6's will drive on through and lodge against a bird's breastbone. I have never fired at a quail with No. 6 shot, but the man knows what he's talking about. He and his friends (who started out using 9's years ago and worked up to 6's) annually harvest well over 1,500 quail from his shooting lease and in the process possibly have learned something about shooting quail on that lease. Admittedly they have a problem different than most other shooters in that their birds must be shot very quickly while flying across openings in the brush (called senderos) and if the bird is not dropped instantly in the opening he becomes very difficult to find in the dense, thorny brush. Dogs sent into such brush to search for cripples run the risk of rattlesnakes, so these shooters have a situation requiring sudden death to quail, usually at short yardages and with quick shots.

If the .410 seems a great handicap, note the illustration in the chapter Choosing Chokes and Loads in *Upland Gunning* that shows that at very close range a 3-inch .410 pattern is often larger than that of a 12 gauge. This is true because the little gun generates more chamber pressure (13,000 psi compared with around 11,000 for the 12 or 20) and deforms a lot of shot that quickly spread. The pattern may be as full of holes as a rusty bucket beyond 25 yards, but at quick, close range it gets the job done.

For dove shooters looking for a little extra range for really highflying doves or wild-flushing quail, one of the finest and tightest patterning loads available is the pigeon load, containing 1¼ ounces of shot and the equivalent of 3¼ drams of powder. Federal Cartridge Company for some years had the tightest patterning load of this type; although marked "field load," it also carries the pigeon-load notation elsewhere on the box. The reason it is good is that it contains very hard shot, while most field

In this situation quail must be dropped dead instantly or likely will be lost in brush beyond the open "sendero." Note trail of feathers left by the fast-moving bird centered by .410 load of No. 6 shot, a rare combination but one that works at close range due to little gun's shot deformation and quick opening of pattern.

Waterhole dove shooting is usually best with relatively open chokes; the birds aren't far but tend to be erratic when they see the shooter and are not always easy to hit. Author favors improved cylinder. No. 7½ or 8 shot.

Different dove-shooting situations require different loads: the top shooter needs a tight pattern because bird must fall instantly in the opening or be lost in brush. The shooter below, in shade at a waterhole, has a clean area around him where winged birds can easily be found and he can thus utilize benefits of broader pattern without losing cripples.

Around the world, versatility has made the 12 gauge the sportman's top choice. Here Spanish secretario shows red-legged partridge taken with improved-cylinder doubles, the most popular choice from Scotland to Spain for driven birds.

loads contain soft. Therefore I would recommend it for long shots, but not in close-range upland situations where more pattern spread is needed. Remington has made 3¼ × 1¼ loads with extra-hard nickel shot that are great performers. Winchester in 1976 put on the market a new and highly efficient pigeon load offering extra hard 1¼ ounces of No. 8 or No. 7½ shot, and I would far rather shoot such loads—if I had to take my pheasants or ducks with 7½'s—than the standard high-velocity load. Patterns

are tighter and penetration is often actually slightly better at 50 yards than with the high-velocity loads, due to the fact the hard pellets stay round and fly with less atmospheric resistance than deformed pellets. Also, the faster a load is started, the faster its percentage of velocity declines. At 40 yards, the high-velocity loads I've tested penetrate farther than the pigeon load; at 40 yards they were about equal with the pigeon load or slightly better. Recoil is less in the pigeon load.

Because of the many options of factory loads, including everything from brush loads to tight-patterning traploads and pigeon loads, the 12 gauge remains the most versatile of all upland guns. And if weight is a problem, there are 12 gauges that heft and handle about the same as ordinary 20 gauges. The 12-gauge Franchi autoloader (non-gas) weighs a little over 6½ pounds as does the Ithaca Feather-light pumpgun and the Franchi over-under. The Ithaca "XL" model autoloader is gas operated and weighs only very little more than the Franchi long-recoil action. Such guns, with short barrels, carry and handle more like standard 20 gauges but have the load options of the 12.

Certainly the 20 gauge is lighter in the same makes and models (the Franchi non-gas autoloader weighs about 5½ pounds) and 20's in almost any model seem to have a little better balance and quicker handling, plus trimmer looks, than comparable 12's.

Most versatile of the 20's are doubles and over-unders with 3-inch chambers. I hunt a great deal with standard 20-gauge loads, but in a back pocket someplace there are usually some 3-inch magnum

In Botswana, Africa, the author's versatile Perazzi over-under (with interchangeable choke tubes) took doves, sand grouse, ducks, and geese from same waterhole.

7½'s in case a little more range or "authority" is required. Fortunately most modern two-barreled 20 gauges come with 3-inch chambers.

Whatever your choice of an upland gun, just remember that shooting conditions, not toughness of game, are likely to be the important factor—unless you're hunting elephants.

Trap and Skeet

BOB BRISTER

A young cafe waitress one morning noticed the padded shoulder of my shooting shirt and asked the reason for it. When I told her I was on my way to a trapshoot, she stiffened and became quite cool, perhaps envisioning the blasting of some poor creature in a trap.

Somewhere in my files is a clipping from an antihunting publication quoting statistics on how many skeet shooters there are in America, the tone of the article seeming to imply "skeet birds" may be going the way of the passenger pigeon.

To me these were classic examples of the general lack of public understanding of the use of sporting firearms in general, and the games of skeet and trap seem particularly misunderstood even by a large segment of the nation's hunters.

How many times have you heard some hunter say that the reason he doesn't bother with clay targets is that he can beat "any of them hotshots" at ducks or quail?

Maybe he can, maybe he can't. So what?

Skeet and trap are great off-season fun, and shooting a shotgun can do nothing but help the field performance of any shooter no matter how good he may be. Compared with the prices of everything else nowadays, target games are relatively inexpensive, particularly when friends pool resources and acquire reloading equipment to reduce ammunition costs.

Since the clay-target games would each require a full-length book for adequate instructional discussion—and since there are some fine books that do just that—this chapter will hit just a few of the high spots.

Now then, for the many who may not know, those clay targets thrown by hand devices are not skeet nor are they trap; they are clay targets thrown by hand devices. Many shooters erroneously refer to such practice as skeet.

Skeet is the game requiring two houses to launch targets, a high house and a low house, and the average distance of shots at targets passing at 50 miles an hour between those houses is 21 yards. Trap is the one in which all the targets come out of one house, but the shooter does not know exactly at what angle. Handicap trap requires a shooter to fire from yardage longer than 16 yards, that being the distance from which singles and doubles are shot.

If you have never seen either game (and believe me I had not until I killed many a mallard, dove, and quail) it might be worth visiting a gun club just to smell the powder burn. You also might get interested enough to try one or the other, and if so could get sufficiently hooked to become eventually a better all-around shot.

Why there is much controversy around sporting-goods stores over whether some skeet or trap champion could beat ol' so-and-so at doves or quail I'll never understand. That is sort of like arguing over whether the current champion at the

Indianapolis Speedway could beat some backwoods mail carrier at driving in deep mud or snow. The clay-target games, like driving or anything else, have become highly specialized. So, for that matter, are the various forms of hunting. I've seen terrific quail shots who can't lead ducks worth a darn.

Both skeet and trap are to some extent trick shooting, in that once you learn the trick you can certainly smoke a lot more clay than when you first walked out on the field attempting to shoot as you would at real birds. For this reason, no good field shooter who fares poorly his first round of either game should give up and go home. Nor should any sharpie at skeet or trap come to believe he must automatically be better on birds than the man who follows bird dogs all season.

For one thing, the clay target games contain optical illusions.

Trapshooting is an optical illusion in which the target appears to be going almost straight away but really is rising quite swiftly. And that is why special stocks are needed for shooting trap really well; the higher stock (or lately, the bent-up barrel) provides some built-in compensation for the optical illusion inherent to the game. No matter how great the field shooter, if he must hold high over every fast-rising trap target, blotting it out with his gun in order to make a hit, he's at a disadvantage with shooters whose guns are set up so the bird can be seen and broken at the same time. But often the addition of an inexpensive cheek pad to the comb of the field stock is sufficient to make it a trapstock.

A dove at 50 miles an hour is flapping his wings pretty regularly; he lets you know he's moving on. So does a teal or bluebill or band-tail pigeon. But a skeet target sort of sneaks out of the house looking as big as a basketball (or maybe for beginners more like an aspirin). The illusion often is that the target simply cannot be going as fast as the required forward allowance in front of it indicates. This is particularly true of the long stations (positions 3,

American-style trapshooting as seen from the mouth of the traphouse. The clay target, always going away from the shooter, is launched by a single machine at varying angles. The trapshooters are shooting from 16 yards behind the trap, which is standard distance for singles competition. At handicap, depending upon scoring average and ability, shooters may be required to fire from as far back as 27 yards, meaning their targets must be broken at 50 yards or so. With every yard of increased distance, the game gets tougher.

4, and 5) where sustained leads of 3 to 4 feet in front of the target will break it. Otherwise you have to swing to beat sixty, pass it, and still see some daylight ahead. Most shooters, when they finally break a target from one of those stations, estimate

With a movie camera mounted on his gunstock D. Lee Braun smashes one of the toughest targets on the field, low house 4. Starting out ahead of the target (left) he then pulls ahead to establish what he sees as 4 feet of forward allowance ahead of the target (center) which is shown breaking (right) as the ejected hull is thrown from the autoloader. It is difficult for many shooters to visualize forward allowances ahead of targets; the actual lead ahead of this target was 4 to 4 1/2 feet (as Braun saw it) but it does not look that way over the gun barrel. For this reason, the book Skeet Shooting With D. Lee Braun, precedes each over-shoulder visual lesson with a view of a measuring device showing precisely how three feet, two feet, etc. actually look over the barrel at skeet yardages. (Sequence photographs from Skeet Shooting With D. Lee Braun, courtesy of Remington Arms Co.)

As seen from above, this is the basic layout of a skeet range for either American-style or international-style sheet. Note that the targets do not go straight across between high house and low house, but at a distinct angle. The longest distance from any station to the crossing point of the target is 21 yards, and average target speed in American sheet is about 50 miles an hour, for international, 60 miles per hour or more. The shooter begins each round at Station 1. Singles and doubles are fired from Stations 1, 2, 6, 7; all others offer one high-house target and one from the low house.

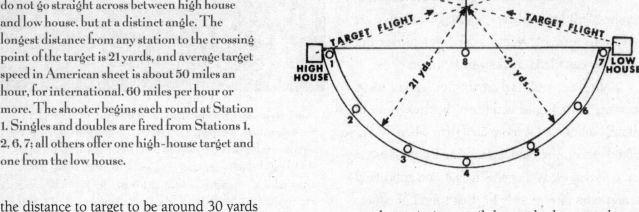

the distance to target to be around 30 yards or more. It is actually 21 yards to the center crossing point, but the speed is roughly 50 miles an hour at that point—another couple of optical illusions.

I believe the biggest mistake made by the beginning skeet or trap shooter is in equating his first score with his ability. The guy who so casually smokes 25 straight has done it before, a lot of times probably. I've seen shooters who couldn't break 10 targets out of the first 25 turn out to be champions once they realized how to equate the optical illusions with their field-shooting experience.

The second biggest mistake, I believe, is made by the shooter who is not serious about taking up championship skeet or trap but who tries to learn to shoot precisely the way the current champions do, with a rigidly mounted gun. It's all in what you're after. If you are interested in improving your field-shooting and game-hunting skills, forget locking into the gun at skeet. Drop the gun to the position you'd

approach a pointing quail dog and take your shots as you would in the field. You may not break quite as many targets, but your hunting skills should increase significantly. But even if you do shoot skeet locked in, your field shooting also will improve to some extent.

The international skeet and trap games contribute more, I believe, to field-shooting proficiency than do American skeet and trap. Both international games are shot as the standard form of skeet and trap virtually everywhere else in the world, despite the fact that both games originated in America. They are more like field shooting in the following respects: At international skeet you can't shoulder the gun; it must be down at waist level with stock touching hipbone and must stay there until the target emerges from the house. And believe me those international targets do emerge! They are moving almost one-third faster than American skeet targets, and they do not necessarily appear.

Part 7

Cooking

Introduction

JAY CASSELL

One of the best parts of hunting is that you get to eat what you have taken. Here we have assembled a variety of mouth-watering recipes, from such well-known wild game cooks as Kate Fiduccia, Monte Burch, J. Wayne Fears, Mary Bell, Marie Lawrence, and John Weiss. We've touched not only on traditional ways of preparing deer, caribou, quail, turkey, and other game, but also such methods as food drying, dutch oven cooking, and making jerky. Plus, you'll find side dishes that work extremely well with game. Enjoy!

—J. C.

Mouthwatering Venison

PETER FIDUCCIA

In all of the *Whitetail Strategies* books I have written, I have always included a chapter with my favorite wild game recipes prepared by my wife and hunting partner Kate. As many of you know, Kate is not only an excellent big game hunter she is also a heck of a wild game chef.

Kate has written four wild game cookbooks and is finishing two more. The recipes I selected in this chapter have been quality-controlled by yours truly and have passed my venison palate with flying colors!

They are all quick and easy to prepare and will make you the hit of deer camp or at home when you make them for family or friends. Remember that you can visit our website at www.woodsnwater.tv to get more of Kate's free wild game recipes and her gourmet sauces to share with your family or friends. Good eating!

Tex-Mex Egg Rolls

Serves: 8 (2 egg rolls each)
Prep Time: 10 minutes
1 pound ground venison
1 medium onion, finely chopped
2 cloves garlic, minced
½ cup medium salsa (preferably a smoother type such as Pace Picante)
½ teaspoon chili powder
¼ teaspoon cumin
Salt and pepper
⅔ cup shredded cheddar cheese
1 package egg-roll wraps
Vegetable oil
Sour cream and guacamole for serving, optional

In large skillet, cook venison, onion and garlic over medium heat until venison is no longer pink and onion has softened, stirring occasionally to break up meat. Drain grease. Add salsa, chili powder, cumin, and salt and pepper to taste. Simmer for about 5 minutes. Add cheese and stir until mixed thoroughly. Lay 1 egg-roll wrap on work surface; cover remaining wraps with plastic to keep them from drying out. Place a large spoonful of venison mixture on center of wrap and roll as directed on package. Place filled egg roll on platter and repeat with remaining ingredients.

Heat 2 inches oil to 375°F in deep fryer or large pot. Fry egg rolls, two at a time, until golden brown, about 2 minutes. Drain on paper towel–lined plate. Serve with sour cream and guacamole.

Venison Filet Wellington

Serves: 5 to 8
Prep Time: 45 minutes
Cooking Time: 10 to 15 minutes

Here's an elegant dish that will knock the socks off your deer-camp buddies. It may look complex, but it really is quite simple. From start to finish, Venison Filet Wellington will take about an hour. Read the directions at least once before preparing this dish, and you will see how quickly it comes together. Have all your ingredients ready, to make the assembly smooth and quick. Don't miss trying this recipe; it is well worth the effort.

2- to 3-pound venison loin, well trimmed

2 tablespoons clarified butter, room temperature

2 to 4 slices bacon

2 tablespoons butter

3 tablespoons olive oil

2 tablespoons chopped shallots

½ pound fresh white or straw mushrooms, finely chopped

1 egg, separated

2 tablespoons cold water

1 sheet (half of a 171 4-oz. pkg.) frozen puff pastry, thawed per package directions

Flour for rolling out pastry

1 cup shredded fresh spinach leaves

½ cup shredded Swiss cheese

Hunter's Sauce

Heat oven to 325°F. Heat a large, heavy-bottomed skillet over medium-high heat. While skillet is heating, rub venison with clarified butter. Add loin to hot skillet and sear to a deep brown color on all sides. Transfer loin to dish and set aside to cool to room temperature. Meanwhile, add bacon to same skillet and fry until cooked but not crisp. Set aside on paper towel–lined plate.

While the loin is cooling, prepare the filling. In medium skillet, melt the 2 tablespoons butter in the oil over medium heat. Add shallots and sauté until golden, stirring constantly; don't let the shallots brown or they will become bitter. Add mushrooms and sauté until most of the liquid evaporates. Set mushroom mixture aside to cool.

Beat egg white lightly in small bowl. In another small bowl, lightly beat egg yolk and water. Set both bowls aside.

To prepare the shell, roll out pastry on lightly floured surface to a rectangle 1 to 2 inches larger on all sides than the loin. Spread cooled mushroom mixture over the pastry, leaving 1 inch clear around the edges.

Layer the spinach, cheese and bacon in a thin strip over the center; the strip should be about as wide as the loin. Place loin on top of bacon. Brush edges of pastry with egg white; this will help hold the pastry shell together while it is baking. Wrap pastry around loin and crimp edges very well to seal. Turn pastry-wrapped loin over so the seam side is down. Place onto baking sheet. Brush pastry with egg yolk mixture; this will provide a beautiful glaze to the Wellington.

Bake for 10 to 15 minutes, or until pastry is golden brown. The loin should have reached an internal temperature of 130°F. Remove from oven. Slice into individual portions and serve immediately with Hunter's Sauce.

"Too Late" Venison Cutlet Gruyere

Serves: 6
Prep Time: 10 minutes
Cooking Time: 10 to 15 minutes

One of the fun parts of hunting is naming deer stands. We have one we call "Torn Shirt" because Peter tore his shirt while putting it up. Another is named "Big View" because the stand overlooks several fields and has a . . . big view! The "Too Late" stand is near a pine-covered ridge and got its name because once the deer reach the peak of the ridge and come out from the cover to cross to the other side, it's too late. I first prepared the following tasty recipe with a buck taken from this stand.

¼ cup all-purpose flour

Salt and pepper

2 eggs

½ cup milk

3 cups seasoned bread crumbs

¼ teaspoon garlic powder

venison cutlets (about 4 ounces each), pounded as needed to even thickness

½ cup olive oil (approx.)

1½ cups seasoned tomato sauce

2 large beefsteak-type tomatoes, thinly sliced

12 slices Gruyere or Swiss cheese

Heat broiler. Place flour in large plastic food-storage bag; add salt and pepper to taste and shake well to mix. In medium bowl, beat together eggs and milk. Combine bread crumbs and garlic powder in wide, flat dish and stir to mix. Blot cutlets with paper towel.

Working with one cutlet at a time, add to bag of flour and shake to coat. Tap off excess flour, then dip floured cutlet into egg mixture. Dredge in bread crumb mixture; set aside on a plate. Repeat with remaining cutlets.

In large skillet, heat about ¼-inch of the oil over medium heat until it is hot but not smoking. Fry cutlets in batches, adding additional oil as necessary, until cutlets are golden brown on both sides and not quite done to taste; transfer cutlets to sheet pan as they are browned.

In small saucepan, heat tomato sauce over low heat; cover and keep warm. Place 1 or 2 tomato slices and 1 cheese slice on top of each cutlet. Place sheet pan under broiler just long enough to melt the cheese.

Ladle about ¼ cup warm tomato sauce on each of 6 plates and place 2 cutlets on top; or, place 2 cutlets on each plate and drizzle tomato sauce around the cutlets. Serve hot.

Venison Tamale Pie

Serves: 6
Prep Time: 20 minutes
Cooking Time: 40 minutes

Here's a dish that takes a little bit of extra time because of the cornmeal crust. But it's well worth the effort! It was during a whitetail hunting trip to south Texas that I first tasted true tamales. We were hunting at the Lazy Fork Ranch and the cook prepared many dishes native to her Mexican homeland. Although I wasn't able to get the exact recipe from her, this one comes close—and I haven't had any complaints on the receiving end when I serve it!

Filling

1 tablespoon canola oil

1 pound ground venison

4 scallions, chopped

1 can (8 ounce) tomato sauce

1 cup whole-kernel corn, drained

¼ cup chopped Anaheim peppers

¼ cup cornmeal

1 teaspoon chili powder

1 teaspoon salt

½ teaspoon pepper

½ teaspoon cumin

¼ teaspoon crumbled dried oregano leaves

Cornmeal Pie Crust

1 cup all-purpose flour, plus additional for rolling
     out crust

2 tablespoons cornmeal

⅓ cup vegetable shortening

3 to 4 tablespoons cold water

Topping

1 egg, lightly beaten

¼ cup evaporated milk

½ teaspoon dry mustard

1 cup shredded Monterey Jack cheese

1 cup shredded cheddar cheese

6 pitted black olives, sliced

Heat oven to 425°F.

To prepare filling: In large skillet, heat oil over medium heat. Add venison and cook until no longer pink, stirring to break up. Drain. Mix in remaining filling ingredients. Let simmer for 5 minutes, then remove from heat.

To prepare crust: In small bowl, blend together flour and cornmeal. Cut in shortening with pastry blender or two knives. When mixture resembles coarse meal or very small peas, add water a little at a time, mixing with fork until dough is formed. Roll out pastry on floured surface until it forms a 15-inch circle. Fit pastry into deep-dish 9-inch pie pan and crimp edges.

Spoon filling into pie crust. Place pie pan on baking sheet and bake for 25 minutes. While it is baking, prepare the topping for the pie: Combine egg, milk and mustard in medium bowl; mix well. When pie has baked for 25 minutes, remove from oven, sprinkle cheeses over filling and pour milk mixture on top. Decorate with sliced olives. Return to oven and bake for an additional 5 minutes. Let stand for 10 minutes before serving. Serve with sour cream and chopped tomatoes.

Escarole Soup with Venison Meat-a-Balls

Serves: 6
Prep Time: 15 minutes
Cooking Time: 45 minutes

My mother, Lucy, introduced Kate to many different Foodstuffs—escarole, broccoli rabe, scungilli and calamari, to name a few. She often reminded her about the way many Italian dishes are prepared: "Use garlic, garlic and more garlic." Both her escarole and broccoli rabe dishes started by sautéing plenty of garlic; the greens were added as the garlic was cooking. After this, chicken broth was added to finish cooking the greens.

When Kate shared with her this venison version of her Meatball Escarole Soup, she was quite pleased, and Kate was happy that she had passed her test. Then she cautiously whispered in her ear, "But next time, use a little more garlic!"

½ cup bread crumbs
½ cup milk

Kate takes a break in our kitchen where she often "Goes Wild" with her delicious cooking!

1 pound ground venison

1 egg, beaten

2 tablespoons grated Parmesan cheese, plus
    additional for serving

1 tablespoon chopped fresh parsley

7 cloves garlic, minced, divided salt and pepper

3 tablespoons olive oil

1 pound escarole, washed and chopped

4 cans (14½ ounces each) chicken broth

Italian bread for accompaniment, optional

In medium bowl, mix together bread crumbs and milk; let stand for about 5 minutes. Add venison, egg, Parmesan cheese, parsley, half of the garlic, and salt and pepper to taste. Mix well. Shape into small meatballs (small enough to fit on a spoon and pop into your mouth) and place on a plate. Cover and refrigerate while you prepare the rest of the soup mixture.

In large saucepot or Dutch oven, heat oil over medium-high heat. Add remaining garlic and sauté until golden; do not let it brown. Stir in escarole and continue sautéing until escarole has wilted down. Add chicken broth. Cover pot and simmer for about 30 minutes. Gently add meatballs to the simmering broth. Leave them untouched for a few minutes so they can set, then stir gently and continue simmering for 7 to 10 minutes longer, until the meatballs are cooked through. I always sample a meatball at about 7 minutes to see if it's done yet.

Serve hot, with grated Parmesan cheese and Italian bread.

Horseradish Cream Sauce

Yield: 1 cup

Prep Time: 10 minutes

Chilling Time: 1 hour or longer

This makes a great dipping sauce for fondue, and also works well as a side for roasts or steaks.

1 cup heavy cream

2 scallions, minced

2 tablespoons fresh
grated horseradish

¼ teaspoon paprika

⅛ teaspoon salt

In large bowl, whip cream until soft peaks form. Stir in scallions, horseradish, paprika and salt. Transfer to glass bowl and chill for 1 hour or longer to allow flavors to blend before serving.

Hunter's Sauce

Yield: 2 cups

Prep Time: 35 minutes

This classic sauce is delicious with venison roasts
    and pan-fried steaks.

3 tablespoons butter

1½ teaspoons vegetable oil

10 ounces fresh mushrooms, cut into quarters

3 shallots, minced

2 tablespoons all-purpose flour

1 tablespoon finely chopped scallion

2 tablespoons brandy

Salt and pepper to taste

½ cup dry white wine

1 cup brown sauce or canned beef gravy

2 tablespoons tomato sauce

1 teaspoon finely chopped fresh parsley

In small saucepan, melt butter in oil over medium heat. Add mushrooms and shallots and sauté. until golden brown. Stir in the flour to absorb the juices. Add scallion, brandy, and salt and pepper to taste. Cook over low heat for 2 minutes. Add wine and simmer until liquid is reduced by half. Add brown sauce, tomato sauce and parsley. Heat until sauce starts to bubble, stirring occasionally. Pour into serving dish and serve hot.

Modern Ground Jerky

MONTE BURCH

Although sliced jerky is the easiest to make, ground-meat jerky has become increasingly popular, not only with commercial jerky makers but with home jerky makers as well. Ground-meat jerky has several advantages. It's less chewy, and it can be made from lesser cuts of meat, as well as the small pieces of meat trimmings from butchering. To use all your butchered meat effectively, you might like to make both sliced and ground-meat jerky. Ground-meat jerky does require a bit more effort, and you'll need a means of grinding and extruding or shaping the ground meat.

The Meat

As with any jerky making, it's important to carefully follow safe meat processing methods,

even more so with ground meat, as pathogens can be spread throughout ground meat. Also, as with all types of jerky making, it's important to cut away all fat and as much sinew as possible, especially with venison. Venison fat turns rancid, and sinew makes even ground jerky tougher to chew. Because the meat used is often butcher trimmings from carving out other choice cuts, including meat from the legs with lots of sinew and flank steak from the ribs with quite a bit of fat, it does take a bit more time and effort to ensure a good, lean meat for the jerky.

Grinding

Regardless of whether you use a hand or powered grinder, the meat should be cut up

Ground-meat jerky has become extremely popular. It's easy to do if you have a grinder, and it utilizes the less-choice cuts of meat.

Make sure you follow safe meat-processing procedures with ground meat because it's more easily contaminated. Cut away all fat and sinew.

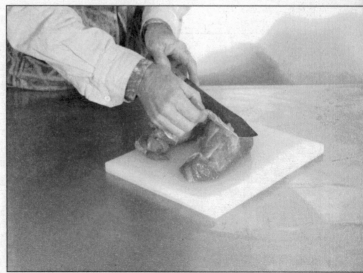

into chunks or strips that will fit readily into the grinder opening or throat. For hand grinders, the smaller you cut the chunks or strips, the easier it is to grind. Make sure there are no bones in the meat to stop an electric grinder or damage the worm gear and grinding plate and blade. A bone will definitely stop a hand grinder, but it is less likely to cause damage. The meat should be 40°F or colder and free of gristle and sinew. Using the meat stomper, slowly feed the meat into the throat of the grinder head. Do not force the meat, and never use your fingers to push the meat into the head. Used properly, today's grinders are very safe, especially when compared to older versions like my granddad's big grinder with a big, wide, open throat. The family joke, "Don't get your tie in there," was really a reminder to all users to be extremely careful.

Grind the meat through the coarse plate first. We prefer our jerky made from coarse ground. If you want a finer grind, turn off the motor, and unplug the grinder. Next, remove the coarse plate, and clean the head of any sinew, fat, and gristle that has accumulated during the first grind. Reassemble the unit with the fine plate, plug the grinder in, and regrind the meat. If the meat mashes instead

of coming through the plate in strings, unplug the grinder, remove all the meat from the grinder and plate, reassemble and tighten the grinder ring, making sure it's tighter than it was before, and begin to grind the meat again. When you're through grinding, run some saltine crackers through the grinder to help clean it out, then unplug the grinder, and disassemble the head. Wash all parts in hot, soapy water, and thoroughly rinse in hot water. Allow parts to dry completely. Spray parts with food-grade silicone to prevent rust and keep your grinder in like-new condition while stored.

The Cure

Although you can simply dry the meat, adding cure and seasonings not only provides a better means of preservation, but it adds taste as well. As with sliced-muscle meat, you can make up your own recipes or use any number of commercially prepared mixes. Many of the recipes in the muscle-meat chapter can also be used for groundmeat jerky. The following are a couple of homemade

Regardless of whether you're using a homemade or commercial recipe, make sure you weigh the ground meat and use the correct amount of cure and seasonings.

Grind the meat using a hand or powered grinder. The LEM/Bass Pro meat grinder makes short work of the chore.

ground-meat recipes that we enjoy. As with muscle-meat jerky, ground meat must also be weighed for proper curing.

Burch Ground Meat Jerky

2 lb. ground venison
2 teaspoons Morton Tender Quick
1 teaspoon each garlic powder and onion powder
½ teaspoon each dried red pepper and ground black
   pepper, or to suit
¼ cup brown sugar

Mix all the cure and spices together. Place the meat in a glass or plastic container. Sprinkle a little of the spice over the meat, and mix well with your hands. Then, add more spice, and mix until you have all the meat well coated with the cure mix. An alternative method is to dissolve the cure and spices in ½ cup of cold water. Pour this over the meat and mix thoroughly. Place a cover over the dish or pan, and refrigerate overnight to allow the cure and seasonings to work into the meat. Extrude or roll the meat out onto the waxed side of freezer paper, a jerky rack, or dehydrator tray.

Burch Ground Meat Jerky 2

2 lb. ground venison
2 teaspoons Morton Sugar Cure (Plain)
1 tablespoon Worcestershire sauce
¼ teaspoon each black pepper, garlic powder, onion
   powder, Liquid Smoke

Another, less spicy ground meat jerky recipe is also a favorite. Again, mix the spices with a little water and then thoroughly incorporate into the meat using your hands. Extrude and dry as mentioned.

Commercial Mixes

A number of commercial cure and seasoning mixes are also available. The following are some of the mixes I've tested and liked.

Curing and seasoning adds to the flavor and preservation. First mix the spices and curing agents together.

Thoroughly mix the meat and cure/seasonings together.

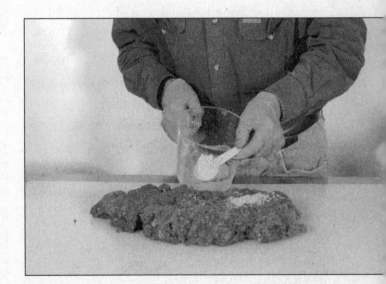

Next, spread the mixed cure and seasoning over the meat.

Bass Pro Shops Uncle Buck's Regular Jerky Seasoning and Cure

Up to 10 lb. meat

4 teaspoons seasoning per 1 1b. of meat

¼ teaspoon cure per 1 1b. of meat

1 oz. water per 1 1b. of meat

The package will do 10 pounds of meat. Mix 4 teaspoons of seasoning, ¼ teaspoon of cure, and 1 ounce of water for each pound of ground meat used. Mix thoroughly until the mixture becomes tacky. Using a Jerky Cannon, squeeze strips on to a jerky rack. Place jerky rack on a cookie sheet, and dry strips in an oven at 200°F for 75 minutes on each side. Or, squeeze strips onto the racks of a dehydrator and dry, following dehydrator directions. The finished product must be refrigerated.

Bass Pro Shops Uncle Buck's Snack Sticks

Up to 5 lb. meat

4 teaspoons seasoning per 1 1b. of meat

¼ teaspoon cure per 1 1b. of meat

1 oz. water per 1 1b. of meat

Another great tasting jerky is made with the Bass Pro Uncle Buck's Snack Sticks Seasoning. Extruded out into round sticks, this is a great homemade Slim Jim. The packet will treat 5 pounds of meat. According to the instructions; "Dissolve 4½ teaspoons of seasoning, ¼ teaspoon of cure, and 1 ounce of water to mix with each pound of meat. Mix thoroughly until the mixture becomes tacky. Process using one of the following methods: Stuff into natural or collagen casings and smoke in smoker until internal temperature of meat reaches 165°F. Or make Slim Jims with a Jerky Cannon and shoot them onto a cookie sheet. Dry in an oven at 200°F for 75 minutes per side or until internal temperature of meat reaches 165°F. Finished product must be refrigerated."

Eastman Outdoors Jerky Cure and Seasoning

5 lb. lean meat

1 oz. seasoning

1 oz. cure

1 cup cold water

Use the leanest meat possible. To each 5 pounds, add 1 ounce seasoning, 1 ounce cure, and 1 cup of ice-cold water. Mix in a nonmetallic bowl for

Purchased cures and mixes, such as the Bass Pro Uncle Buck's Snack Stick mix, are also available for making ground-meat jerky.

The cure and seasonings are added to cold water.

Hi Mountain has a wide line of cures and seasonings.

The ingredients are mixed well, and then the cure and seasoning mix is poured over the ground meat and thoroughly mixed.

5 minutes or until sticky. Cover the bowl, and refrigerate for at least 4 hours. Use the Eastman Outdoors Jerky Gun to extrude the meat into perfect strips or sticks. Package will do 5 pounds of ground meat.

Hi Mountain Jerky Cure and Seasoning

1 to 3 lb. meat
½ cup water per pound of meat
Cure and seasoning according to weight

Make 1 to 3 pounds at a time. Hi Mountain suggests you start with a small batch at first. Mix cure and seasoning according to weight chart. Add ½ cup ice water per pound of meat. Mix meat, water, and seasoning thoroughly for approximately 5 minutes or until sticky.

Mix well, and allow to cure overnight in a non-metallic container in the refrigerator.

Shaping the Ground Meat

Ground-meat jerky is commonly formed into thin strips or round sticks. You can shape the meat into a jerky product in a number of ways. One of the simplest methods is to place a ball of meat on a piece of waxed paper or the waxed side of a piece of freezer paper. Place another piece of waxed paper over the meat ball, and use a rolling pin or straight-sided drinking glass to roll the meat patty out to a uniform thickness of about $\frac{1}{8}$ to $\frac{3}{16}$ inch. Peel back the top paper, and use a kitchen knife to slice the rolled-out patty into strips about 1 inch wide. Take care not to slice through the bottom piece of waxed paper.

Place another piece of waxed paper over the meat, and use a rolling pin to roll the meat out flat to about a 1/8-inch thickness. Remove the top waxed paper piece.

Ground-meat jerky can be shaped into strips or sticks. Shown here are Slim Jim-style sticks.

Ground-meat jerky can be shaped into thin jerky-style strips quite easily with waxed paper or the waxed side of freezer paper. Flatten a ball of cured and seasoned meat onto a piece of waxed paper.

Use a kitchen knife—not a sharp knife—to separate the meat into thin strips. The meat strips can be flipped over onto a dehydrator tray for drying.

Line a jerky rack or cookie cooling rack with freezer paper with the waxed side up. Transfer the strips to the jerky rack by flipping the waxed paper over onto the freezer paper and peeling the waxed paper from the back side. If using the freezer paper, dry the strips until the surface is sealed, flip this over onto a drying rack, and peel off the freezer paper. This gives the ground meat strips a little stability for each of the handling steps. When completely dry, tear or break apart the strips on the cut lines. The strips can also be flipped onto a dehydrator rack for drying.

Another method of creating the strips from ground meat is to line a sheet-cake or other baking pan with plastic wrap. Press the ground meat into the pan to a suitable thickness. Partially freeze the pan, remove meat from the pan, peel off the plastic wrap, and slice into strips. The partially frozen meat is much easier to work with and slice.

Extruding ground meat through a hand-held, ground-jerky-meat extruder is a very common and popular method. These tools resemble caulking guns, and most come with interchangeable tips—both a flat tip for jerky strips and a round tip for stick jerky.

With the meat ground and cured, wet your clean hands in cold water, then take about a cup

With wet hands, roll the cured and seasoned ground meat into thin rolls that will slide easily down into the jerky extruder.

Continue filling the tube.

A jerky extruder, such as the Hi Mountain Jerky Gun, can also be used to shape the meat. These normally come with two tips: one for strips and one for sticks.

Gently squeeze the handle to extrude the ground meat onto a jerky screen, such as that from Hi-Mountain.

The resulting extruded ground-meat jerky ready to dry.

The LEM Patty and Jerky Machine is an attachment that fastens to the LEM/Bass Pro grinder and extrudes sticks or strips of ground-meat jerky. You can grind and extrude at the same time or grind, mix, and extrude.

We found it better to grind, then extrude. As you grind, the meat is forced out onto waxed paper.

When the sticks are the length needed, cut the paper and sticks with the stainless-steel scissors.

of the ground meat and roll it between your hands to form into a roll small enough to slide down into the barrel of the jerky gun. Make sure the roll is wet enough to easily slide down into the barrel. Add more rolls until the barrel is full. Gently push the plunger down into the barrel, making sure to properly align the plastic plunger tip with the barrel so you don't damage the tip. Spray a jerky screen, such as the one from Hi Mountain, with a light coating of cooking oil. Pull the trigger gently to squeeze the strips or sticks onto the Jerky Screen, or extrude the sticks or strips out onto jerky racks lined with freezer paper following the directions above. Now you're ready to dry the jerky.

The ultimate extruder is the LEM Patty and Jerky Machine, an accessory that fits onto the LEM/Bass Pro Grinder. The unit allows you to grind and then extrude large quantities of ground patties or jerky in either strips or sticks, depending on the plate chosen. The accessory extrudes four sticks or strips at a time. The Jerky Machine comes with a special extruding plate; a holder for a roll of waxed butcher paper; one roll of waxed butcher paper; and a pair of stainless-steel scissors. If you grind meat only one time, assemble the jerky machine head, and attach it to the grinder before you start grinding. If you grind twice, attach the machine head before the second grind and use the extruding plate. The first step is to select the appropriate extruding plate, either the patty, jerky strip, or snack stick plate. Fasten to the front of the unit with the stainless steel screws.

The resulting jerky snack sticks on waxed paper and in pans, ready to dry.

Remove the retaining ring from the grinder. Attach the grinder adapter to the grinder using the retaining ring, as you would a stuffing tube. Mount the jerky machine head to the adapter and secure it with the winged bolts. Place the meat chute in position, and secure it with the winged bolts. Attach the waxed paper roll to the jerky machine head using the paper rod and winged nuts. Thread the paper between the jerky machine head and the meat chute. Make sure the paper unrolls counter-clockwise from the back of the roll to place the waxed side up onto the chute. Pull the paper down the meat chute about 3 inches. Start grinding or extruding. The extruded material will push the paper down the meat chute. When the meat reaches the end of the chute, stop the grinder. Use the stainless steel scissors to cut the strips and waxed paper to the desired length and slide them off onto cookie sheets.

Drying

Ground-meat jerky can be dried using an oven, dehydrator, or smoker capable of reaching at least 200°F. Disease-causing microorganisms are more difficult to eliminate in ground meat than whole meat strips. Be sure to follow the dehydrator manufacturer's directions when heating the product at the end of the drying time. An internal temperature of 160°F is necessary to eliminate disease-causing bacteria such as E. coli 0157:H7, if present.

If drying in an oven, place the strips or sticks on jerky racks, positioned over cookie sheets to catch drips. We have also used cookie cooling racks as jerky racks. Preheat oven to 200°F and, with the oven door slightly open, heat for 1 to 2 hours or until the strips crack but do not break when bent. Increase heat to 275°F until internal temperature reaches 160°F.

Ground-meat jerky strips tend to stick a bit more than muscle-meat strips. It's a good idea to turn the strips over to ensure even cooking and to prevent sticking. If using a dehydrator, make sure you follow the manufacturer's directions on drying jerky.

Small Game and Wildfowl Jerky

Upland gamebirds, waterfowl, and small game can all be made into jerky. The type of jerky—muscle

Ground-meat jerky can be dried in an oven set at 200°F. Make sure the meat attains an internal temperature of 160°F.

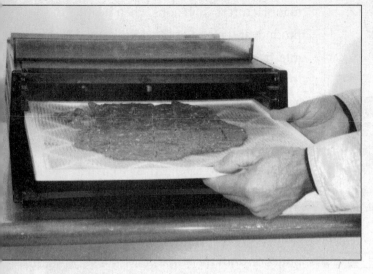

If using a dehydrator to dry the meat, follow the manufacturer's instructions. Shown here is a section of waxed-paper-shaped ground-meat jerky, ready for the dehydrator.

meat or ground meat—depends on the species being used. Small game such as rabbits, squirrels, groundhog, and others, as well as ducks and geese, are best made into ground-meat recipes. Small game often don't provide large enough cuts of meat for slices. The dark meat of ducks and geese, especially snow geese, usually tastes better when ground with other, milder meats or when made into a spicy ground-meat recipe. In fact, a great way of cleaning out your freezer is to make up a smorgasbord of ground-meat jerky from whatever overabundance

of game meat you have on hand at the end of the season.

Ground-Meat Smorgasbord Jerky

2 lb. wild game meat, ground
2 tablespoons Morton Tender Quick
1 teaspoon lemon pepper
1 teaspoon onion powder
1 teaspoon garlic powder
1 tablespoon soy sauce
½ cup water
3 to 4 drops hot sauce (or more if you prefer more heat)

As with all other types of meat, make sure you use safe field dressing and butchering processes, especially when making ground-meat jerky. Pathogens can easily be spread throughout the ground meat. Also, make sure you use meat only from healthy animals. Debone all the meat from the game animals or birds, and remove all fat and gristle.

The first step is to debone the birds and small game. Then, grind the meat. Add the cure and seasoning, refrigerate, and dry.

Geese, ducks, and small game can all be made into excellent jerky.

Cut away all bloody meat, and remove any shot from gunshot game. Ground-meat smorgasbord jerky is a case where you can use even the tougher, lesser cuts, including the thighs of birds such as wild turkeys or geese. If you use the legs, make sure you remove all the tiny, flexible tendons and bones. It's a good idea to first soak all the deboned pieces in salt water overnight in a refrigerator. This will help remove some of the gaminess and also tenderize some of the tougher pieces. If the meat hasn't been frozen, freeze it for 60 days. Partially thaw the meat, then grind it.

Mix the ingredients together, making sure the spices are dissolved in the liquid. Pour the seasoning and cure over the ground meat in a non-metallic bowl, and mix well until tacky. Refrigerate overnight, extrude or form, and then dry. This seasoned and cured ground meat can be made into an excellent snack stick.

Turkey Jerky

Domestic and wild turkeys are large enough to be made into jerky in the sliced-muscle meat method. Only the breast meat is used for this procedure. As with other types of muscle-meat jerky, remove all fat and connective tissue. Also, remove the skin. Then, slice into ¼-inch-thick strips. Partially freezing to firm the meat will help with slicing it into uniform, thin strips. Some of the best jerky I've tasted is the Hi Mountain Turkey Hunter's Bourbon Blend Jerky Cure and Seasoning. After cutting the meat into strips, weigh the meat so you know the exact amount of cure and seasoning mix needed. Mix the spices, and cure according to the mixing chart (per weight) included with the instructions. Mix only the amount needed. Be sure to store the remaining unmixed spices, and cure in an air-tight container until needed. Lay the strips flat on an even surface, and pat dry with a paper towel. Apply the mixed spices and cure to the prepared meat, using the sprinkler bottle included in the package. Sprinkle the first side of meat with approximately half of the

Turkey breast, both wild and domestic, can be made into a mouth-watering muscle-meat jerky.

mixture. Next, turn the meat over, and sprinkle the remaining mixture on the meat. Put seasoned strips in a large mixing bowl, and tumble by hand until the mixture has been spread evenly on all sides of the meat. Stack the strips, pressed together tightly, in a non-metallic container or sealable plastic bag. Refrigerate for at least 24 hours. Hi Mountain Jerky Cure and Seasoning is formulated to penetrate the meat at the rate of ¼ inch per 24 hours; do not cure the meat any less than that. You're now ready to dry or dehydrate the jerky.

Sliced-Meat Turkey Jerky

2 lb. wild turkey breast strips
2 teaspoons black pepper

The Hi Mountain Turkey Hunter's Bourbon Blend Jerky Cure and Seasoning Mix creates a great-tasting, wild turkey jerky.

1 teaspoon onion powder

1 teaspoon garlic powder

2 tablespoons Morton Tender Quick

4 tablespoons brown sugar

1 teaspoon Liquid Smoke

1 cup water or bourbon

You can also make up your own turkey-jerky cure and seasoning mix per the recipe above. Make sure cure, liquids, and seasonings are well mixed together. Pour the cure and seasoning mix over the strips, and then place the strips in a non-metallic

Weigh the sliced strips.

Lay the strips on a flat surface, and sprinkle with the proper amount of cure and seasoning mix according to the weight of the turkey strips.

Debone the turkey breasts; remove skin, fat, and sinew; and then slice the meat into ¼-inch-thick strips.

Mix the cure, seasonings, and weighed strips in a non-metallic bowl; cover; refrigerate overnight; and then dry or dehydrate.

container. Mix well, making sure all surfaces of the meat are well coated. Cover and refrigerate for 24 hours. Remove, pat dry, and dehydrate or dry.

Drying

Small game jerky can be dried in a dehydrator following the manufacturer's instructions. It can also be dried in an oven set at 200°F. The ground-meat jerky can be dried with any of the methods mentioned throughout this book. The turkey jerky strips can be placed on wire racks or suspended in the oven. Make sure you have a pan below the jerky to catch drippings. It's also a good idea to spray racks with cooking oil to prevent sticking. Wild turkey meat tends to dry quicker than red meat, so check the meat after about an hour's drying time. Properly dried jerky should bend but not break. Meat made from fowl must be heated to an internal temperature of 165°F to kill pathogens. There also tends to be more oil, especially in domestic turkey meat. This

Perfectly dehydrated turkey jerky is not only great looking but makes great eating as well.

will bead up on the meat during the drying process. When the jerky is done, pat dry any oil from the surface. After jerky has dried completely, store in airtight containers in a dry, cool area. You can also freeze and/or vacuum pack turkey jerky for longer storage.

The Joy of Smoking and Salt Curing

MONTE BURCH

Wild Game Recipes

For many hunters, salt curing and smoking is a favorite means of preserving or, more commonly, cooking game, including venison, big game, and game birds. As with other types of meats, different methods of cure application can be used, depending on the cut of meat and the desired end result. This includes dry cure and injection cure or stitch or artery pumping, or a combination of the methods. Small cuts, such as loins and cuts from the hams and shoulders, are commonly cured using the dry-cure method. Larger pieces, such as hams, are best cured with a combination of dry cure and injection. Salt-cured game meats may or may not be smoked, but all must be hot-smoked or cooked. As with all meats, it's important to start with clean, fresh, safe, and well-chilled meat.

Corned Deer Loin

The loin is one of our favorite cuts to corn. It tastes almost like corned beef, with a mild game flavor, and there is no fat to be removed. It is, however, a bit dryer because there are no connective fat tissues or marbling. This recipe is easy using Morton Salt Tender Quick.

5 lb. deer loin, boneless venison roast, or combination
2 to 3 quarts water, to cover
1 cup brown sugar
6 tbsp. Morton Tender Quick
1 tbsp. garlic powder
1 tbsp. onion powder
2 tbsp. mixed pickling spices

Place the brine ingredients in a large saucepan. Bring to a boil, reduce to simmer, and stir until all ingredients are dissolved. Place in a large food-grade plastic container and place in the refrigerator to chill. Once chilled, add the chilled meat, cover the container, and keep refrigerated 5 to 7 days, depending on the thickness of the meat. Turn the meat once each day. Remove, wash in cold running water, and place in a large pot. Cover with water and simmer for 3 to 4 hours. Remove, chill, thin-slice, and serve. This makes an excellent Reuben sandwich. Freeze excess for future use in vacuum-seal bags.

Venison Ham

A cured ham from a deer is mighty tasty. The cured deer ham can be smoke-cooked, oven-roasted,

Venison and other big game meats can be corned as easily as beef. The same methods are used.

or boiled. A deer ham is best cured using the combination dry cure and injection. The same basic recipes and techniques for curing a pork ham can also be used on a deer ham. In this case, the deer ham is cut from the carcass by making a cut similar to that for long-cut pork ham, cutting through the aitchbone and pelvic arch.

Trim and smooth up the butt end and cut off the shank fairly short, as the shank of a deer has little meat. A simple method is to use Morton Salt Sugar Cure (Plain) mix. Make up the sweet pickle cure first by combining one cup of the Morton Salt Sugar Cure (Plain) mix with 4 cups of clean, cool water and mix until dissolved. Weigh the ham and make up enough pickle to have 1 ounce of pickle for each pound of meat. Pump the pickle into the ham, using a meat pump and injecting along the bone structure. After the ham has been pumped, apply a dry cure to the meat surface. Again, Morton Salt Sugar Cure (Plain) mix makes the chore easy. Since deer hams are usually not aged, use 1 tablespoon of mix per pound of meat. Measure out enough cure mix to do the ham and divide into 3 equal parts. Apply ⅓ of the mix on the first day and place in a large covered food-grade plastic container or bag and then place in a refrigerator with a temperature of 38°F. After 7 days, apply another third of the cure, and then on day 14, apply the last third. The deer ham should be cured after 14 to 15 days, followed by an equalization period.

To equalize, remove from the container and soak the ham for about an hour in clean, cold water. Lightly scrub off the excess cure and place in a clean food-grade plastic bag or container. Place in the refrigerator and allow the salt to equalize throughout the ham. This will take about 14 days. Remove from the bag, soak again in cold water, and then hang to dry. The ham can be smoked or cooked, but the ham must be heat-treated to 160°F internally before being consumed.

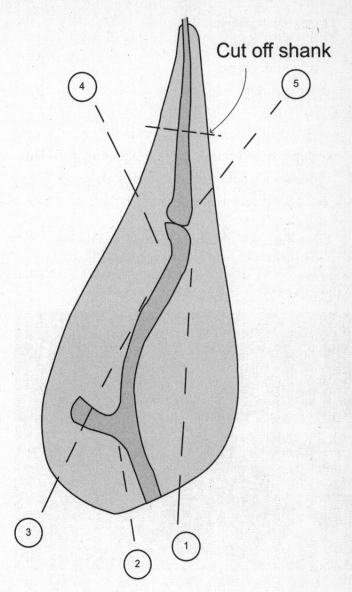

A ham from a deer can also be salt-cured just like a pork ham. The best method is the combination-cure method of injecting a pickle cure along with using the dry-cure method. Follow the numbered diagram for the injection sequence.

Bacon Smoked Quail

If you're looking for a unique quail dish, this is it. The same recipe can be used with pheasant, quail, or chukars. First step is to make up a weak brine solution.

1 quart water
3 tbsp. non-iodized salt
1 tbsp. lemon juice concentrate
1 tsp. dried parsley

1 tsp. onion powder

1 tsp. garlic powder

1 tsp. black pepper

½ tsp. paprika

Dissolve the salt and spices in the heated water, then place the brine in the refrigerator to cool. Place the cleaned whole birds in a food-grade plastic bag and pour the mixed (cold) brine into the bag. Place

Upland game—such as quail, pheasant, and chukars—can all be lightly brined and smoked. Clean thoroughly, removing all feathers and pinfeathers. Cut off feet. Dig out any shot and cut away any bloody areas.

Cure upland birds in a mild brine for 4 to 6 hours, then hot-smoke in a smoker with a water pan to an internal temperature of 170°F. Bacon strips added across the breast can add moistness.

in a plastic food container and place in a refrigerator. Allow to cure for 4 to 6 hours, turning frequently to make sure all pieces are thoroughly soaked.

Remove, rinse the brine, and place on paper towels. Pat the birds dry with paper towels. Drape bacon pieces over the breast of the birds and pin in place with toothpicks. Smoke using apple or alder at 200°F to 225°F until the internal temperature reaches 165°F.

Apple-Soaked Mallard Breasts

Just about any duck can be used—including teal, wood ducks, and gadwalls, one of my favorite eating ducks. The bigger ducks provide a more moist breast, and of course, more meat. Breast out the ducks and remove the breast skin. Cut away any bloody areas and dig out any shot. Steel shot can be mighty hard on the teeth. Prepare the following brine, and soak the breast overnight. This will brine about 2 pounds of duck breasts, or the breasts from 2 mallards.

1 quart water

1 can or jar applesauce

3 tbsp. non-iodized salt

¼ to ½ cup brown sugar

2 bay leaves (crushed)

1 tsp. garlic powder

1 tsp. onion powder

1 tbsp. lemon pepper

Thoroughly mix all ingredients, except for the lemon pepper, in hot water and allow the brine to cool. Place duck breasts and brine in a food-grade plastic container and leave overnight in the refrigerator. Remove from the brine, rinse, and dry with paper towels. Sprinkle each duck breast with lemon pepper and place bacon strips across the breasts. Secure in place with toothpicks. Smoke with applewood in a smoker at 225°F for a couple of hours. Duck is normally best eaten medium rare, but can be smoked until the internal temperature reaches 165°F. To keep duck breasts moist, place in aluminum foil after the first hour of smoking. Slice and serve with baked apples.

Smoked Sky Carp

Snow geese are called sky carp for good reason—they're plentiful, with large limits, tough to bag, and tough to cook. The meat is extremely dark and dry. Salt curing and smoking can, however, provide delicious goose meat, and is a good choice for the big Canada honkers as well. Only the breasts are used. Remove the breasts and remove the skins. Clean up any bloody spots and remove all steel shot. Slice the breasts into ½-inch strips. Make the following brine and soak the strips overnight in a refrigerator.

1 cup soy sauce

1 cup water

1 cup brown sugar

2 tbsp. non-iodized salt

1 tbsp. black pepper

2 tbsp. Worcestershire sauce

1 tsp. garlic powder

1 tsp. onion powder

1 tsp. ground red pepper, or to taste

Remove the strips, rinse under cold water, and dry on paper towels. Smoke using hickory at 200 to 225°F for a couple of hours, or until the internal temperature reaches 170°F. After the first hour of smoking, place the goose strips in aluminum foil to prevent drying.

Wild Game Summer Sausage

Summer sausage is an excellent way of salt-curing and smoking wild game meats. Although venison is probably the single most common meat used, just about any big game, small game, and waterfowl can be used to make summer sausage. The recipe used is easy, with Morton Salt Tender Quick mix. You will need some pork trimmings to add a little fat to the wild game meat. This is a good recipe to use with electric smokers.

3 lb. venison or other wild game

2 lb. pork trimmings

1 tbsp. black pepper

5 tbsp. Morton Tender Quick mix

1 tsp. ground coriander

½ tsp. ground ginger

½ tsp. ground mustard

1 tsp. garlic powder

4 tbsp. corn syrup

Weigh the meats separately. Cut chilled meat into 1-inch cubes and grind through a 3/16-inch grinder plate. Mix the dry spice ingredients in a glass bowl and sprinkle over the ground meat. Dribble the corn syrup over the ground meat and thoroughly mix all. Place in a plastic or glass bowl

Wild game can also be used to create great-tasting summer sausages. Smoking in an electric smoker adds to the flavor.

and refrigerate overnight. Spread the meat out to about a 1-inch depth in a shallow, flat pan and freeze for an hour or so or until the meat is partially frozen. Remove and regrind the partially frozen meat through a ⅛-inch plate. Stuff the ground meat into synthetic casings. If your meat grinder has a stuffing attachment, the final grinding and stuffing can be done in one step.

Hang the stuffed casings on drying racks and dry at room temperature for 4 to 5 hours, or hang in a smoker on sticks, with the damper open until the casings are dry to the touch. Set the temperature of the smoker to 120°F or 130°F, add wood chips, and smoke for 3 to 4 hours. Raise the temperature to 170°F and cook until the internal temperature reaches 165°F. Remove from the smoker and shower the casings with cold water. Place back in the cooled-down smoker and hang at room temperature for 1 to 3 hours or until dry. Freeze sausages that will not be consumed within a week. For more sausage recipes, see Monte Burch's *The Complete Guide to Sausage Making*.

Memorable Meals from Premier Wild Chefs

KATE FIDUCCIA

Over the eighteen years that l have been co-host of the Woods N' Water Outdoorsman's Edge television series, I have been fortunate enough to travel throughout North America to hunt a variety of big game. Not only have I been able to enjoy some of the most exhilarating hunting opportunities a hunter could hope for, but I have been exposed to an added bonus as well: the home-cooked wild-game dishes of each outfitter I hunted with.

Some of these memorable meals were prepared by seasoned wild-game chefs in unique, five-star lodges, and some equally as unforgettable were prepared by camp chefs in cook tents located hours by horseback from civilization. Whether in a commercial kitchen or with the barest of essentials, each chef showed the same inspiration in preparing wild- game meals for their guests.

The meals I enjoyed on these hunts have proved, to me, to be as important as the hunt itself, and they solidified in my mind that for most hunters, preparing and eating wild game is as much a tradition as the hunt itself. Wild game cooking is—in the end—the element that binds the hunt and the eating of game together. Both would be less without the other. Following are some of my favorite outfitter recipes.

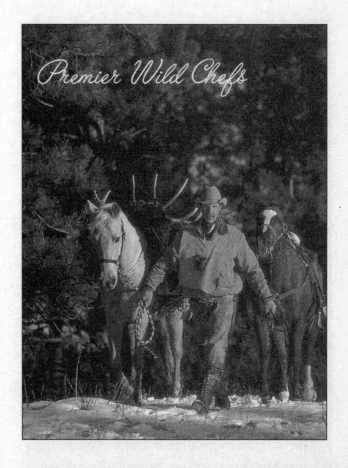

> *Any sportsman who can kill his deer without the tingling spine, the quick clutch at his heart, the delicious trembling of nerve fibers when the game is finally down, has no place in the deer woods.*
> —*Lawrence R. Koller,* Shots at Whitetails *(1948)*

Anticosti Outfitters Braised Deer

Serves: 12 to 15
Prep time: 15 minutes
Cooking Time: 2¾ hours

The recipe for this delicious braise was graciously provided by the chef at Anticosti Outfitters, and reflects the fine culinary tradition of this lodge.

5-lb. venison roast
¼ cup butter
2 carrots, chopped
1 large onion, chopped
Salt, pepper and garlic powder
1 can (14½ oz.) beef broth
⅓ cup red wine
2 tablespoons all—purpose
flour

Heat oven to 325°F. Pat roast dry. In Dutch oven, melt butter over medium-high heat. When it stops sizzling, add roast and brown well on all sides. Transfer roast to plate; set aside.

Add carrots and onion to Dutch oven and cook for 3 to 4 minutes. Season roast with salt, pepper and garlic powder to taste, and return to Dutch oven. Add broth. Cover and bake for 1½ hours.

Add wine and bake for about 1 hour longer, or until roast is cooked to your liking. Transfer roast to serving plate; tent with foil and set aside for 10 to 15 minutes. Meanwhile, sprinkle flour into juices in

Safari Anticosti Outfitters

Emerging from the prehistoric Champlain Sea, the 3,200-square-mile Anticosti Island spreads across the entry to the majestic Gulf of St. Lawrence. In 1895 the French chocolate magnate Henri Menier bought Anticosti Island for $125,000. He went on to invest another 5 million dollars to turn his island into a paradise. in 1974 it was sold to the Quebec Government for 26 million dollars. In 1984 Anticosti Outfitters Inc., which is owned by Jean Gagnon, obtained an exclusive lease of 400 square miles on the southeastern sector of the island from the government. This area has an estimated population of 15,000 white-tailed deer! The rest is history. Safari Anticosti Outfitters has developed the most prestigious deer- hunting grounds in the province of Quebec, investing over 12 million dollars along the way to accomplish its goal.

I was first invited to hunt at Safari Anticosti Outfitters in 1990. Besides getting my two whitetails, I also had the rare opportunity to see seals, whales and uncountable numbers of birds in a variety of colors. The accommodations were top-shelf, but what really impressed me was the food. After each day's hunt, the guests would gather at the log lodge, which was perched on the edge of a sandy cliff overlooking the Atlantic Ocean and mouth of the St. Lawrence Seaway. There, with white-linen table service, we dined on five-course French gourmet cuisine including smoked salmon and oyster appetizers, fine French wine, melon soup, prime rib and mouth-watering homemade desserts. Peter has hunted with Anticosti Outfitters several times since and assures me that with each passing year the hunting, service, and food only get better.

(450) 359-1113

www.safarianticosti.com

batches, transferring to slow cooker as they are browned.

In small bowl, combine tomatoes, peppers, onion, mushrooms, soy sauce, molasses, and salt and pepper to taste. Mix well. Pour mixture over venison. Cover and cook on HIGH for 1 hour, then reduce heat to LOW and cook for 9 to 10 hours longer.

Susan and Lee Carlbom
Sun Canyon Lodge,
Augusta, MT

Dutch oven, whisking constantly; cook over medium heat until thickened. Serve gravy with roast.

Jean-Marie Chretien, General Manager
Safari Anticosti

Sun Canyon Ranch Crock-Pot Pepper Steak

Serves: 6 to 8
Prep Time: 15 minutes
Cooking Time: 10 to 11 hours
For a great meal, serve this stew over grilled polenta
slices or corn bread.
2 lbs. venison steak (deer or elk)
½ cup all-purpose flour
2 tablespoons canola oil (approx.)
1 can (14½ oz.) tomatoes, undrained
2 green bell peppers, sliced
1 large onion, sliced
6 oz. fresh mushrooms, sliced
3 tablespoons soy sauce
3 tablespoons molasses
Salt and pepper

Cut steak into strips and dredge with flour. In medium skillet, heat oil over medium-high heat until hot but not smoking. Brown venison strips in small

Lucky Star Ranch Venison Stew

Serves: 6
Prep Time: 20 minutes
Cooking Time: 2 hours

Sun Canyon Ranch

I first met Lee and Susan Carlbom in 1987. Their outfit is uniquely western, invoking a true feeling of wilderness hunting. Located in the eastern gateway to the Lewis and Clark Forest and the unique Bob Marshall Wilderness Area, Sun Canyon Ranch provides excellent hunting opportunities for both mule deer and elk. It also gives clients a chance to revitalize their spirit as they venture into the last of the true mountain wilderness areas of the continental United States. What struck me most about this facility is that no matter where we were, either at the lodge or in the wilderness, Lee and Susan somehow managed to prepare delicious meals indigenous to the West.

1-888-749-3654

www.suncanyonlodge.com

Tuckamore Lodge Salisbury Moose Steak with Mushroom Sauce

Serves: 4
Prep Time: 15 Minutes
Cooking Time: 15 Minutes

With this recipe, Peggy Mitchelmore turns what seems like just another Salisbury steak recipe into something quite memorable. Serve this with baked potatoes and green beans or steamed broccoli.

We serve this stew with sour cream, baguettes and a nice fresh green salad. It is an ideal menu for a large crowd, because the stew can be prepared beforehand and gently reheated just before serving.

2 lbs. venison stew cubes
1½ cups all-purpose flour
1 tablespoon butter
1 tablespoon oil
Salt, pepper, paprika and chili powder
4 onions, cut into quarters
1 or 2 cans (14½ oz. each) tomatoes, undrained
1 cup heavy cream, or a little more as needed
½ cup ketchup
½ cup red wine, or a little more as needed
1 package (2.4 oz.) Knorr goulash mix, optional
Tomato juice, optional

Pat venison cubes dry; dust with flour. In large skillet, melt butter in oil over medium-high heat. Brown venison cubes in small batches, transferring to Dutch oven or stockpot as it is browned. Season browned venison with salt, pepper, paprika and chili powder to taste. Add onions, tomatoes, cream, ketchup and wine, and goulash mix if using. Cover Dutch oven. Simmer for 2 hours, stirring every 30 minutes; make sure stew meat is always covered with liquid, adding more cream (at room temperature), wine or tomato juice, depending upon your taste.

Baron Josef von Kerckerinck
Lucky Star Ranch, Chaumont, NY

Lucky Star Ranch

As the founder of the North American Deer Farmer's Association, Baron Josef von Kerckerinck knows a lot about deer. On his stately 5,000-acre Lucky Star Ranch in upstate New York, Josef has raised and managed all types of game—European red stag, fallow deer and a host of other non-native deer. Over the last several years, he has been steadily convening the ranch to a strictly white-tailed deer hunting ranch. A native of Germany, Josef brings the European aspect to all his client's hunts with true European shooting houses for the hunt and, most importantly, European-style meals for the guests.

There are few that can come close to Josef's hospitality at his multi-faceted facility. He has always made my family and me feel more than welcome whenever we visit. Over the years, Peter and I have enjoyed great deer hunting at the Lucky Star, and it was here that my son Cody, at the age of nine, shot his first deer—a memory we'll cherish forever.

(315) 649-5519 at www.luckystarranch.com

Patties

1 lb. ground moose

¾ cup cracker crumbs

1 tablespoon Worcestershire sauce

½ teaspoon onion powder

½ teaspoon steak spice

½ teaspoon salt

¼ teaspoon pepper

¼ teaspoon garlic powder

Sauce

2 tablespoons butter

1 can (8 oz.) mushrooms, drained and chopped

2 tablespoons all-purpose flour

1 teaspoon curry powder

1 cup hot water

1 beef bouillon cube

In a bowl, combine all patty ingredients. Mix gently but thoroughly. Divide evenly and shape into 4 patties.

In small saucepan, melt butter over medium heat. Add mushrooms and sauté for 2 to 3 minutes. Blend in flour and curry powder. Add hot water and bouillon cube. Cook, stirring constantly, until smooth and thickened.

While sauce is thickening, either pan-fry or grill the patties for 2 to 3 minutes per side. Pour sauce over each patty and serve.

Peggy Mitchelmore

Tuckamore Lodge

Main Brook, Newfoundland

Conklin's Lodge Venison Roll-Ups

Serves: 8 to 10 as appetizers, 4 to 6 as
main dish

Prep Time: 15 Minutes

Cooking Time: 10 Minutes

2 lbs. boneless venison steaks

Garlic powder, salt and pepper

1 lb. sliced bacon

Barb Genge is the president and owner of Tuckamore Lodge, a first-class operation with Scandinavian-style accommodations in the heart of rugged Newfoundland wilderness. Whether you are there to whale-watch, observe towering icebergs, visit the ancient Viking settlements, or, as we were, to hunt moose, you will experience Tuckamore's hospitality and professionalism. This facility is world renowned in adventure tourism and is recognized as one of the six best lodges in all of Canada. Guests are treated to three sit-down meals a day in the luxurious comfort of the main log cabin lodge. Prepared by a culinary staff headed by Peggy Mitchelmore, each meal, especially dinner, is exquisitely prepared and scrumptious. During our stay, we dined on meals fit for a king, as well as a wide array of fabulous desserts like Death by Chocolate and Gooseberry Pie. Peter and I hunted moose with Barb on two occasions and came home with enough moose meat to try many of the moose recipes the staff so generously shared with us.

1-888-865-6361

www.tuckamore-lodge.nf.net

Slice steaks across the grain into ¼-inch-thick strips. Arrange strips in a single layer on work surface. Sprinkle the tops with garlic powder, salt and pepper to taste. Roll each slice jelly-roll-style with the seasoned side in. Wrap each roll with a portion of bacon, trimming bacon according to the thickness of the roll, and secure with a wooden toothpick. Cook rolls in skillet over medium heat until bacon is cooked, turning to cook evenly. Remove toothpicks before serving.

Marie Conklin

Conklin's Lodge and Camps, Patten, ME

Conklin's Lodge and Camps

Located in the gorgeous deep woods at the north entrance to Baxter State Park (which boasts nearly 205,000 acres of wilderness), Conklin's Lodge and Camps offers excellent year-round hunting, fishing and outdoor activities. Registered Maine Guide Lester Conklin and his wife, Marie, have been operating their lodge since 1987. In addition to highly successful guided bear and white-tailed deer hunts, guests of Conklin's also enjoy pursuing grouse, woodcock, snowshoe hare or even winter coyotes, with or without a guide. Whether you're with a top-notch guide or you adventure out on your own, you'll feel the true spirit of the deep northern backwoods in this area. While on stand, you may see moose, bobcat, lynx, red fox, marten or even a fisher. When you return to camp, you'll be treated to one of Marie's delicious meals, which include favorites such as glazed baked ham, roast pork with gravy, homemade lasagna and stuffed Cornish hen.

(207) 528-2901 at www.conklinslodge.com

Cedar Ridge Outfitters Red Stroganoff

Serves: 8 to 10

Prep Time: 10 minutes

Cooking time: 3 to 4 hours

Here's one of Debbie Blood's camp favorites. Serve it with a heaping bowl of hot white rice.

3 tablespoons vegetable oil (approx.)

3 lbs. boneless venison, cut into ¾-inch cubes

2 cans (14½ oz. each) whole tomatoes, drained, juices reserved

2 cans (14½ oz. each) beef consommé

4 cans (8 oz. each) tomato sauce

2 cups sliced fresh mushrooms

1 large onion, sliced

1 green bell pepper, sliced

Cedar Ridge Outfitters

Hal and Debbie Blood own Cedar Ridge Outfitters. They have been successfully guiding deer, moose and bear hunters in the woods around Jackman, Maine for 20 years. Deer hunting at Cedar Ridge is typical of Maine. You don't see a lot of deer every day, nor bucks in a week. But when you do see a buck, more often than not it's a dandy!

Peter and I first met Hal in the mid-'80s, and later got to know his wife, Debbie. She is a licensed and expert Maine guide who also commands the base operation. On our last visit, we thoroughly enjoyed both the Bloods' hospitality and some of the finest home-cooked meals I have had the pleasure of eating. All meals are served family-style, and Debbie always makes sure they're served piping hot and delicious.

(207) 668-4169 at www.cedarridgeoutfitters.com

Cedar Ridge Outfitters Red Stroganoff

Heat oven to 350°F. In large skillet, heat 1 tablespoon of the oil over medium-high heat until hot but not smoking. Brown venison cubes in small batches, adding additional oil as necessary. Transfer venison to a Dutch oven as it is browned.

When all venison has been browned, slice drained tomatoes and add to Dutch oven with venison. Add remaining ingredients including reserved tomato juice; stir gently. Cover and bake for 2 hours, then check consistency. If the mixture seems to have too much liquid, remove the lid before continuing; if the mixture seems too thick, stir in a little water and recover. If the venison is tender at this point, bake for 1 hour longer; if it is a little tough, bake for 2 hours longer, or until venison is tender.

Debbie and Hal Blood

Cedar Ridge Outfitters, Jackman, ME

Legends Ranch Herbed Venison Rolls

Serves: 5 to 8
Prep Time: 1¼ Hours
Cooking Time: 30 Minutes

When we visited, the side dishes served with this entrée included basil pesto-stuffed tortellini with tomato sauce, fresh steamed asparagus spears and a fresh garden salad. The recipe below has been halved for home use.

Cheese Filling

8 oz. cream cheese, softened
3 large cloves garlic, minced
1½ teaspoons Italian herb blend
¾ cup shredded mozzarella cheese
2 small eggs, beaten
Jalapeno pepper, minced
2- to 3-lb. boneless venison sirloin tip or tender
   rump roast, well trimmed

Breading

3 cups all-purpose flour
¼ cup seasoning blend of your choice (if using
   seasoned salt, use a lower-sodium type)

1½ cups Italian-seasoned bread crumbs
4 eggs, beaten
½ cup milk

Make the cheese filling: in glass bowl, combine cream cheese, garlic and herbs; mix well. Add remaining filling ingredients; mix until creamy. Reserve in refrigerator.

Prepare the venison: Cut roast across the grain into ¾-inch-thick steaks. You should get 5 to 8 steaks, depending upon the size of the roast. Place steaks on lightly oiled work surface (the oil prevents the meat from sticking). Place plastic wrap over steaks to prevent splattering. Gently pound steaks with tenderizing mallet to about ⅛-inch thickness. At this point, each steak should be about 6 inches in diameter.

Place a large spoonful of the chilled cheese filling on a steak, an inch from the edge nearest you; use only as much filling as the steak can hold. Fold the sides of the steak over the filling. Then, roll up the steak jelly-roll-style and place, seam-side down, in a single layer on a sheet pan. When all rolls are complete, place in freezer for about 20 minutes to harden the cheese.

While rolls are in the freezer, combine flour and seasoning in food processor and pulse to mix well; alternately, stir together in large bowl. Place flour mixture in large pan. Place bread crumbs in a separate pan. Mix eggs with milk and place in shallow container.

Heat oven to 275°F. Remove venison rolls from freezer and let stand for about 5 minutes, which will allow the meat to "sweat" prior to being breaded. Coat each venison roll with the flour mixture, then place in egg wash and coat well. Roll in bread-crumbs and set aside.

In deep skillet over high heat, melt enough shortening to cover several rolls; heat shortening to 350°F. Fry rolls, a few at a time, for about 1 minute each. This will seal the meat and turn the crust a light golden brown. Transfer rolls to a jelly-roll pan

(large baking sheet with sides) as they are fried. When all have been fried, place pan in oven for 10 to 15 minutes, until rolls are a rich brown.

John Eye
Legends Ranch, Bitely, MI

Whale River Lodge Caribou Stroganoff

Serves: 4
Prep Time: 10 Minutes
Cooking Time: 2 hours

The head chef at Whale River shared many caribou recipes with me, and I have used them to prepare meat from the two trophy-class bulls I took at the camp. The recipe that has received the most

Legends Ranch

Legends Ranch is owned and operated by Skipper Bettis and Keith Johnson. Between them, they have nearly 75 years of deer-hunting experience. The deer hunting at this ranch is truly legendary. My son, Cody (who was 11 at the time), and I were invited to hunt at Legends Ranch in 2000. We both shot terrific 8-point bucks and saw some real wall hangers during our hunt, too.

Lodging and meals at the Legends Ranch are as outstanding as the hunting. Chef John Eye treats all guests to gourmet meals you would normally find at the finer restaurants across the country. During our stay, Chef Eye and I had many conversations about his experiences as a professional chef, and his love for preparing wild game. During these conversations I decided that one of John's wild-game recipes would be a valued addition to this book.

(231) 745-8000 at www.legendsranch.com

acclaim is this delicious caribou stroganoff. Serve over cooked rice or noodles, accompanied by a salad.

2 lbs. caribou steak
2 tablespoons butter
4 cups water

1 package (1 oz.) onion soup mix

2 tablespoons chopped fresh parsley

1½ teaspoons garlic powder

¼ teaspoon crumbled dried oregano

Pepper

½ cup sour cream

¼ cup cornstarch

Cut steak into 1-inch cubes. In Dutch oven, brown cubes in butter over medium-high heat. Add water, onion soup mix, parsley, garlic powder, oregano, and pepper to taste; stir well. Heat to boiling. Reduce heat to low and cook for about 1½ hours, stirring occasionally. When caribou is tender,

Whale River Lodge

The vast openness of the northern Canadian tundra is both beautiful and stark. Across thousands of miles each year, a distant cousin of the white-tailed deer makes its annual trek. Alain Tardif, owner of Whale River Lodge, has been in the caribou outfitting business for 30 years and has mastered the secret of bringing clients to the areas where the caribou are. On top of that, he has built and staffed lodges that cater to every hunter's needs in areas that are so remote, the only population is native Inuits. I knew we would be traveling far into northern Quebec, but it wasn't until we traveled by jet plane for 2½ hours north of Montreal, then flew by floatplane for another 2 hours, that I realized how far north we were really going! How they get the equipment needed, especially for the kitchen, to these remote places is mind-boggling. But, according to Alain, having the comforts of home is all-important to the hunt, especially when it comes to mealtime.

(800) 463-4868 at www.whaleriverlodge.com

remove about 2 tablespoons of the liquid from the Dutch oven and stir into the sour cream, along with the cornstarch; this raises the temperature of the sour cream to prevent curdling. Stir sour cream mixture into liquid in Dutch oven and cook, stirring frequently, until sauce thickens.

Alain Tardif

Whale River Lodge Outfitters, northern Quebec, Canada

Midwest Venison Casserole

Serves: 6 to 8
Prep Time: 15 minutes
Cooking Time: 1¼ to 1¾ hours

The home-cooked meals at Midwest USA are just as memorable as the hunting. I have made this recipe several times for family and guests. Every single guest has asked me for the recipe. So, here it is.

2 lbs. ground venison

One-quarter of a medium onion, diced

4 cans (10¾ oz. each) condensed cream of
    mushroom soup

1 bag (24 oz.) frozen vegetable of your choice

1 bag (32 oz.) frozen Tater Tots

Heat oven to 375°F. In large skillet, cook venison and onion over medium heat until venison is no longer pink and onion has softened, stirring occasionally to break up meat. Drain any fat. Spread venison on bottom of 9 x 13 x 2-inch baking dish. Spread 2 cans of the undiluted soup over venison. Next, distribute frozen vegetables on top. Spread remaining 2 cans of undiluted soup over vegetables. Finally, top with frozen Tater Tots. Cover with foil and bake for 45 minutes. Uncover and bake for 15 to 30 minutes longer. Let sit for about 10 minutes before serving.

Rodney Hughes

Midwest USA Outfitters, Cantril, Iowa

Midwest USA

As most deer hunters know, Iowa is among the top states in the nation for bagging a trophy-class whitetail buck. Rod Hughes owns Midwest USA Outfitters in Cantril, in the southeastern portion of the state. The whitetail hunting here is exciting because a hunter never knows when the next Iowa Boone & Crockett record-book buck will walk into the sights. I always enjoy hunting in Iowa because of this anticipation.

(888) 530-8492

Hunter's Sauce

Yield: 2 cups
Prep Time: 35 Minutes
This classic sauce is delicious with venison roasts
    and pan-fried steaks.

3 tablespoons butter
1½ teaspoons vegetable oil
10 oz. fresh mushrooms, out into quarters
3 shallots, minced
2 tablespoons all-purpose flour
1 tablespoon finely chopped scallion
2 tablespoons brandy
Salt and pepper
½ cup dry white wine
1 cup brown sauce or canned beef gravy
2 tablespoons tomato sauce
1 teaspoon finely chopped fresh parsley

In small saucepan, melt butter in oil over medium heat. Add mushrooms and shallots and sauté until golden brown. Stir in the flour to absorb the juices. Add scallion, brandy, and salt and pepper to taste. Cook over low heat for 2 minutes. Add wine and simmer until liquid is reduced by half. Add brown sauce, tomato sauce and parsley. Heat until sauce starts to bubble, stirring occasionally. Pour into serving dish and serve hot.

Game Accompaniments

Oh give me a home where the buffalo roam, Where the deer and the antelope play, Where seldom is heard a discouraging word, and the skies are not cloudy all day.
    —Dr. Brewster Higley (19th Century)

As a lifelong lover and reader of cookbooks, I am always trying the latest recipes, experimenting with new ingredients or tweaking old recipes. Sometimes, when I'm trying to come up with a side dish for a new recipe, nothing hits me right away. That's why I like those cookbooks that include a section on side dishes. I often think, "Well, if this is one of the author's favorites, it should be good enough for me!"

So, here are some of my favorite side dishes to serve with venison. Some, such as the Wild Rice Casserole or the Broccoli Casserole, can be placed in the oven alongside a roast; others, such as the Brown Rice Salad or Corn Relish, can be made in the morning to be served at lunch or dinner time.

Fusilli Salad

Serves: 6
Prep Time: 15 Minutes
Cooking Time: 15 Minutes

1 tablespoon plus 1½ teaspoons salt

1 lb. fusilli pasta

1½ lbs. plum tomatoes, seeded and chopped

1 small red onion, minced

3 fresh basil leaves, chopped

2 cloves garlic, minced

12 black olives, sliced

1 cup julienned romaine lettuce

½ cup olive oil

Salt and freshly ground pepper

2 tablespoons grated Parmesan cheese

In stockpot or Dutch oven, combine salt and 4 quarts cold water. Heat to boiling over high heat. Add pasta and cook until al dente according to package directions; stir frequently to prevent sticking.

While pasta is cooking, combine tomatoes, onion, basil, garlic, olives, lettuce and olive oil. Toss to coat well. Season to taste with salt and pepper.

When pasta is al dente, drain in colander and rinse with cold water; drain well. Combine with vegetable mixture and toss to mix thoroughly. Garnish with Parmesan cheese and serve immediately.

Broccoli Casserole

Serves: 6

Prep Time: 10 Minutes

Cooking Time: 55 Minutes

I usually serve this side dish with roasts, since it can cook in the same oven as most roast recipes.

3 eggs

1½ cups light cream

½ teaspoon dry mustard

½ teaspoon salt

¼ teaspoon pepper

2 cups chopped cooked broccoli

1 cup shredded cheddar cheese

Heat oven to 350°F. Lightly grease medium casserole or glass baking dish; set aside. In medium

---

Kate's Grilling Tips

My favorite way to grill corn is to remove some of the outer corn husks and slightly open the inner husks to remove the silk. Then I spread butter (or margarine) on the corn and close the husks around the corn again. I wrap each ear of corn in heavy-duty aluminum foil and twist the ends.

Then I place the ears on the grill for about 20 to 30 minutes, turning frequently. I season with salt and pepper once they are cooked and the husks are removed.

* * * *

If you love eggplant, try this grilled recipe. Peel eggplant (small ones are more tasty than larger ones) and cut off the ends. Cut into slices about 1 inch thick, but don't cut all the way through the bottom (as you might slice a loaf of garlic bread). Between the slices, add a little butter, salt, pepper, oregano and thin slices of mozzarella cheese and tomato. Wrap tightly in foil. Grill for about 20 minutes, turning every 5 to 7 minutes.

---

bowl, lightly beat eggs. Add cream, mustard, salt and pepper; mix well. Add broccoli and cheese; stir to combine. Pour broccoli mixture into prepared baking dish. Place baking dish into a larger baking pan. Pour hot water into larger pan to reach halfway up sides of baking dish. Bake for 45 to 55 minutes, or until mixture is set. Serve warm.

Pungent Caramelized Onions

Serves: 12

Prep Time: 5 Minutes

Cooking Time: 2 ½ hours

These go well with steaks, medallions and roasts.

¼ cup plus 1 tablespoon olive oil, divided

7 large onions (about ½ lb. each)

½ teaspoon salt

2 tablespoons red wine vinegar

Heat oven to 325°F. Brush 1 teaspoon of the oil on shallow-sided baking sheet. Slice onions into quarters, leaving skin on. Place onions, skin-side down, on prepared baking sheet. Brush with one-quarter of the remaining oil, and sprinkle with the salt. Cover baking sheet with foil and bake for 30 minutes.

Uncover; brush onions with one-third of the remaining oil, and sprinkle with the vinegar. Turn onions so the outside is down. Bake for 1 hour longer. Brush with half of the remaining oil and turn onions again. Bake for 1 hour longer; brush with remaining oil before serving.

Cheesy Garlic Mashed Potatoes

Serves: 6 to 8

Prep Time: 15 Minutes

Cooking Time: 25 Minutes

1 head garlic

3 lbs. baking potatoes, peeled and quartered

1½ teaspoons salt, divided

½ cup unsalted butter (1 stick), melted

1 cup shredded cheddar cheese

½ cup heavy cream, room temperature

1 teaspoon white pepper*

Separate and peel the garlic cloves, then crush them gently with the side of a large, heavy knife. In large saucepan or Dutch oven, combine potatoes, garlic, and 1 teaspoon of the salt. Add water to cover. Heat to boiling over high heat; reduce heat and simmer until potatoes are tender, about 20 minutes. Drain in colander. Press potatoes and garlic through ricer or food mill.

---

*You don 't have to use white pepper. I use it to make the dish look nicer. Black pepper will work just as well.

Place hot potatoes in large bowl and beat in butter and cheddar cheese.

Gradually mix in cream, pepper and remaining ½ teaspoon salt. Serve hot.

Corn Relish

Serves: 6

Prep Time: 10 Minutes

Chilling Time: 2 hours

I like to serve this as a side dish with burgers during the late summer when corn is at its peak!

3 tablespoons white wine vinegar

2 tablespoons sugar

1 teaspoon salt

½ cup canola oil

1½ cups cooked whole-kernel corn, prepared from fresh or frozen

½ cup sliced celery

¼ cup pickle relish, drained

¼ cup diced red bell pepper

¼ cup chopped scallions

In small jar with lid, combine vinegar, sugar and salt. Cover and shake until salt and sugar dissolve. Add oil; re-cover and shake well to blend.

Kate's Cooking Tips

When preparing a large meal with many side dishes, get your serving dishes out ahead of time and label them accordingly. I write "potatoes," "gravy," "mushrooms," "venison roast," etc., on small pieces of paper and place them into each dish. This way, all my serving dishes are out and ready when the time comes to plate. There is no confusion (amidst entertaining your guests) as to what goes where when it's hot and ready to be served.

Remember to taste your dish just before serving. This is the last time you can adjust the seasoning.

In medium bowl, combine corn, celery, pickle relish, pepper and scallions. Mix well. Pour dressing over the top and mix again. Cover and refrigerate mixture for at least 2 hours. This relish can be made a day ahead.

Brown Rice Salad

Serves: 6
Prep Time: 10 Minutes
Cooking Time: 1 hour
Chilling Time: 1 hour
1 cup brown rice
2¼ cups water
1 teaspoon butter
¼ cup canola oil
¼ cup red wine vinegar
1 teaspoon balsamic vinegar
1 teaspoon salt
¾ teaspoon sugar
½ teaspoon dried dill weed
1 cup cooked whole-kernel corn, prepared from frozen
1 cup cooked peas, prepared from fresh or frozen

Combine rice, water and butter in medium saucepan. Heat to boiling; stir once and cover. Reduce heat and simmer for 45 minutes. Remove from heat and let stand, covered, for 5 to 10 minutes. Fluff with fork and transfer to large bowl. Let stand until cool.

In small bowl, combine oil, vinegars, salt, sugar and dill. Mix well. When rice has cooled, add corn and peas to rice and toss to mix well. Pour dressing over mixture and toss to mix well. Cover and refrigerate mixture for at least 1 hour. This salad can be made a day ahead.

Rummed Sweet Potato Casserole

Serves: 4
Prep Time: 15 Minutes
Cooking Time: 40 Minutes
1½ cups thinly sliced apples
4 cooked medium sweet potatoes, thinly sliced
½ cup light brown sugar
Cinnamon and allspice to taste
¼ cup butter, cut up
¼ cup light rum
¼ cup water

Heat oven to 350°F. Heat medium saucepan of water to boiling. Add apple slices and cook for about 2 minutes. Drain and rinse with cold water. Lightly grease medium casserole or glass baking dish. Fill dish with alternating layers of potatoes and apples, sprinkling each layer with brown sugar, cinnamon and allspice. Dot top with butter. Mix rum and water and pour over the top. Cover casserole with foil and bake for 40 minutes. Serve warm.

Wild Rice Casserole

Serves: 6
Prep Time: 10 Minutes
Cooking Time: 2 hours
¾ cup uncooked wild rice
¼ cup uncooked brown rice

2 stalks celery, chopped

¼ cup chopped onion

1 quart chicken broth

½ cup white wine

2 tablespoons butter

Salt and pepper

Heat oven to 350°F. In medium bowl, mix together the rices, celery, and onion. Transfer to casserole. Add chicken broth, wine, butter, and salt and pepper to taste; stir gently to combine. Cover and bake for 2 hours.

Roasted Herbed New Potatoes

Serves: 8

Prep Time: 10 Minutes

Cooking Time: 1 hour

2 lbs. small new potatoes (red bliss, fingerling, banana)

2 onions, out into chunks

⅓ cup olive oil

¼ cup butter, melted

¼ teaspoon crumbled dried thyme

¼ teaspoon crumbled dried rosemary

¼ teaspoon crumbled dried marjoram

½ teaspoon salt

¼ teaspoon pepper

Heat oven to 425°F. Combine all ingredients except salt and pepper in medium mixing bowl. Toss to coat. Transfer to large roasting pan and bake until potatoes are done, about 1 hour, turning potatoes every 15 minutes with wooden spoon. Season with salt and pepper before serving.

Summertime Vegetable Pie

Serves: 6

Prep Time: 25 Minutes

Cooking Time: 45 Minutes

When vegetables are fresh from the garden, this dish is at its most piquant. My grandmother used to prepare this, and I now serve it with venison burgers, grilled steaks or shish kabobs.

1 medium eggplant, peeled and cubed*

2 medium zucchini, cubed*

1 large onion, chopped

¼ cup canola oil

4 medium tomatoes, peeled, cored, and chopped

3 large eggs

1 cup grated Parmesan cheese, divided

1 tablespoon minced fresh parsley

½ teaspoon crumbled dried basil

½ teaspoon crumbled dried oregano

Salt and pepper

⅓ lb. shredded mozzarella cheese (about 1⅓ cups)

Heat oven to 350°F. Lightly grease a pie plate or baking dish; set aside. In large skillet, sauté eggplant, zucchini and onion in oil over medium heat until vegetables are soft. Add tomatoes; cover and simmer for about 15 minutes. Transfer to large bowl; set aside to cool.

In medium bowl, combine eggs, ⅓ cup of the Parmesan cheese, the parsley, basil and oregano.

Summertime Vegetable Pie

Beat with fork until well blended. Add to vegetables, along with salt and pepper to taste; stir to combine. Pour half of mixture into prepared pie plate. Top with half of the remaining Parmesan cheese. Top with remaining vegetables and Parmesan cheese. Sprinkle the top evenly with the mozzarella cheese. Bake for 40 to 45 minutes, or until mixture is set. *For a pretty presentation, eggplant and zucchini can be sliced length-wise into thin ribbons, as shown in photo.

Super Herbed Italian Bread

Serves: 8 to 10
Prep Time: 10 Minutes
Cooking Time: 10 Minutes

Having grown up in a non-Italian household, I often ate garlic bread that was dressed to the hilt. Mom used all sorts of toppings: garlic, Parmesan or mozzarella cheese, oregano, paprika, butter,

and even mayonnaise. Later, when I came to know Peter's Italian family, I realized that while bread was included with the pasta in a true Italian meal, it was usually served hot and plain, or with butter on the side. As a lover of all types of bread, I found this acceptable, but not quite as desirable as what I grew up with. So, here's a recipe for Italian bread with the works. This goes well with Venison Bolognese, charbroiled steaks, or chops.

½ cup butter (1 stick), preferably room temperature
4 cloves garlic, minced
½ cup mayonnaise
½ cup grated Parmesan cheese
1 loaf Italian bread, split lengthwise
½ teaspoon crumbled dried oregano
½ teaspoon paprika

Set oven to broil and/or 550°F. Melt butter in small saucepan over medium heat. Add minced garlic and cook for about 5 minutes (longer won't hurt); do not let the garlic brown. While that is cooking, combine mayonnaise and Parmesan cheese in small bowl; mix well and set aside.

Place halved Italian bread on baking sheet, crust side down. Drizzle garlic butter over bread. Place bread under broiler and let it brown slightly. Remove from broiler. With spatula, spread mayonnaise mixture on bread. Sprinkle oregano and paprika over mayonnaise mixture. Return bread to broiler and cook until edges are nicely browned. To serve, slice bread into 2-inch-wide strips.

Dutch Oven Cooking

J. WAYNE FEARS

Longhunter Meatloaf

This is a simple meatloaf recipe that works well with almost any type of lean ground meat. I prefer venison, elk, caribou, or moose, but beef will do, and when cooked in a loaf pan cleaning up the dutch oven is quick and easy.

Portions: 4-5 Dutch Oven: 12-inch
INGREDIENTS

⅔ cup dry bread crumbs
1 cup milk
1 Pound Ground Meat
2 beaten eggs
½ cup grated onion
1 tsp. salt
Dash of pepper

½ tsp. sage
½ tsp. thyme
½ tsp. rosemary

Method

1. Soak bread crumbs in milk.
2. Add meat, eggs, onion, and seasonings mix.
3. Form into a loaf and place in non-stick 8½ x 4½ x 2½-inch loaf pan.
4. Spread with catsup or favorite sauce.
5. Place pan in Dutch oven on a cake rake.
6. Bake at 350°F for 45 minutes to 1 hour.

Tender Roast

I discovered this recipe when I owned hunting lodges. Often I had clients who complained of venison roast being tough. Using my Dutch ovens I tried different recipes for roast until I found this one. It can take less-than-tender roast, whether it be venison or beef, and make it tender.

Portions: 4-5 Dutch oven: 10-inch
INGREDIENTS

4 pounds venison or beef roast
hot water
1 package Lipton dry onion soup mix
1 tbsp. Worcestershire sauce

Method

1. Place roast in Dutch oven.
2. Make a thick paste from one package of dry onion mix and water.
3. Brush paste over the roast.
4. Sprinkle roast with Worcestershire sauce.
5. Place 1 cup of water in Dutch oven.
6. Cover and bake for two hours at 300°F.
7. Cook approximately 3 hours.

Side Dishes

Side dishes are as varied as cooks, and what appeals to one group may not to another. The good thing about cooking with Dutch ovens is that whatever the taste of your guests, side dishes can be prepared in the black pot just as easily as in the home oven, whether it is corn on the cob, squash casserole, or asparagus fingers on a bed of wild rice.

For the purposes of this book, I selected three side dishes that seem to please every guest for whom I cook. These are old recipes that have been proven with time and are just as easy to prepare in a remote mountain camp as on your patio at home.

Macaroni and cheese is a favorite with the younger guests and when you prepare it the way my mother does, it becomes Aneeda's Macaroni & Cheese, and youngsters and adults alike will keep going back for more until it's gone.

High Plains Hominy is a favorite cowboy side dish that city folks take to real fast, especially cheese lovers. The mild chilies add a lot to the dish as well.

Beans are always a favorite side dish, and Miss Pam French, up in Maine, prepares the best. She uses kidney beans, but I have used pinto beans and

What is your favorite side dish? The Dutch oven can do it.

Jacob's cattle beans as well. You just need to adjust the cooking time a little for these other beans.

Use these side dishes to get you started but don't be afraid to try your favorite sides using the magic of the black pot.

Aneeda's Macaroni & Cheese

This is a recipe of my mom's that all who have ever eaten her cooking want. She was a school teacher in a remote country school when she met and married my dad, who was a trapper. She has always been a great cook, and I think it was from her that I got my desire to write and cook.

Portions: 4 Dutch Oven: 10-inch
INGREDIENTS

1 cup macaroni
2 eggs, beaten
1 cup milk, or a little more
1 tsp. salt
plenty of Velveeta cheese
1 cup bread crumbs
pepper to taste

Method
1. Cook macaroni in boiling water with 1/2 teaspoon salt until tender.
2. Beat eggs slightly, add milk and salt.
3. Add egg mixture to this.
4. Pour macaroni in 7" cake pan.
5. Put a lot of sliced cheese on top.
6. Put bread crumbs over this.
7. Dot with margarine.
8. Sprinkle pimento or black pepper on top.
9. Bake at 350°F for about 35 minutes.

High Plains Hominy

This could be classified as a cowboy side dish as I got the recipe from a chuckwagon cook in Texas. A lot of people that do not like hominy say they would not want to try the dish. But once they did they usually came back for seconds.

Portions: 5-6 Dutch Oven: 10-inch
INGREDIENTS

2 cans yellow hominy

3 strips bacon, cooked and broken into pieces

½ cup chopped onion

5 tbs. salsa

1 cup grated cheddar cheese

1 small can chopped chilies

3 whole chilies

Method

1. Mix hominy with onion, salsa, cheese, bacon, and
   1 small can chopped chilies.

2. Place ingredients in an aluminum cake pan.

3. Arrange the three whole chilies on top.

4. Place in Dutch oven and bake at 350°F for 20
   minutes.

Miss Pam's Bean Hole Beans

In the chapter of this book on bean hole cooking, I discussed Ken and Pam French's permanent bean hole at their cabin in Maine. Miss Pam is famous for her bean hole beans recipe. She uses aluminum foil to seal in the moisture of the dish and I have found that the double aluminum foil seal does work some magic. Also, you will note that this dish cooks for a long time. Sometimes Ken puts it in the hot bean hole the night before they plan on serving the beans

Portions: 8 Dutch Oven: 12-inch
INGREDIENTS

2 pounds dry red kidney beans

½ pound bacon, cut into pieces

½ cup molasses

1½ cups brown sugar

2 medium onions

2 tsp. dry mustard

salt and pepper

Method

1. Soak beans in water for approximately 12 hours before putting them in a cast iron Dutch oven. Do not drain beans.
2. Bring beans to a boil and stir in all the above ingredients.
3. Stir well.
4. Cover and seal top of pot with aluminum foil. Leave enough slack for top to fit properly.
5. Place the lid on the foil, then cover tightly with aluminum foil again.
6. Bury in a hot bean hole and cook approximately 15 hours.

Cowboy Biscuits

The world is full of biscuit recipes, some good some not. I have learned, after a career of travelling the world, if you want a good biscuit recipe, go to a working ranch in the American West and get the biscuit recipe that keeps cowboys happy.

I didn't find this recipe at any one particular ranch, I found it being used on several. I thought if it is that good, it is a recipe I need for my collection. I like it because it is simple and you can have hot biscuits quickly.

Portions: 7 Dutch oven: 12-inch
INGREDIENTS

1 cup flour
1½ tsp. baking powder
1½ tsp. sugar
⅛ tsp. salt
½ cup butter
⅓ cup milk or buttermilk

Method

1. Stir together flour, baking powder, sugar and salt. Cut in butter until mixture resembles

coarse crumbs. Make a well in the middle of the mixture and stir in milk.

2. Knead on floured surface a few times. Work dough as little as possible.

3. Roll dough to ½-inch thickness.

4. Cut with a 2-inch cutter.

5. Transfer to aluminum pan in Dutch oven.

6. Bake at 450°F for 10–12 minutes.

Food Drying

MARY T. BELL

Jerky

Humans have benefited from eating dried meat since the Cro-Magnon era. Our ancestors learned about the natural drying process by observing and copying animals that cached their game in trees where it dried in the wind. Today, making jerky is the number one reason many people purchase a dehydrator.

Jerky Talk

Jerky is a popular low-carbohydrate, high-protein, low-fat snack and selling it is big business! In stores, a single-ounce can cost $2, making it more expensive than spiny lobster from the coldest waters of Maine.

Not only is jerky a tasty snack, it is also a great ingredient to use in baking and cooking. Outdoor enthusiasts have long known the benefit of adding jerky to a pot of soup.

Jerky is raw meat that is either:

cut into ⅛ to ¼-inch thick strips that are marinated and then dried,

or

made with ground meat (like hamburger) that is flavored, shaped, and then dried.

Note that when I refer to meat, I'm including all categories: fish, poultry, or any other muscle meat. Some choices suitable for jerky include: beef, buffalo, venison, elk, moose, antelope, lamb, goat, chicken, turkey, duck, goose, ostrich, most fresh and salt water fish, commercial luncheon meats, pepperoni, leftover cooked ham, cooked turkey, sausage, pastrami, and even tofu strips.

Jerky is considered raw meat. Since jerky is dried and not cooked, people always ask if jerky is safe to eat. The answer is yes, it is safe if it's been dried at a high enough temperature, long enough, and stored properly.

Although there is debate regarding the correct temperature to dry meat, the consensus is that it must be dried at a consistent temperature of at least 145°F and preferably 160°F . When drying precooked foods, such as ham, temperature is not as important. Meat needs to be dried at a higher temperature than fruits and vegetables because you must destroy the microorganisms that can survive at lower temperatures.

It's essential to be able to determine when jerky is dry. Water in meat must be removed, and the jerky must be dried enough so that it will not spoil. The time it takes to dry meat into jerky depends on the type of dehydrator, the amount of jerky you are making, water content, thickness of pieces, amount of humidity in the air, and the drying temperature.

Warm food always feels more pliable, so let jerky cool, then feel it in order to determine how dry it is. Squeeze a piece of dried jerky between your thumb and forefinger to detect moisture and soft spots. Finished jerky will bend like a green willow but is firm and will break when folded.

Although it is safer to over-dry than to under-dry, jerky that is dried too long or at too high a temperature becomes crisp and snaps clean like a dry stick.

One pound of raw meat will yield ⅓ to ½ pound of jerky. Strips 10 to 12 ¾ inches wide and 5 inches long that are dried at 160°F will generally dry in four to six hours. A round dehydrator tray that is 15 ½ inches across generally holds ¾ to 1 pound of ¼-inch thick strips.

Proper storage of jerky is also important. If your finished jerky feels oily, wrap it in paper towels to absorb the excess oil. This will help prevent rancidity and encourage longer storage. If the paper toweling gets saturated, discard it and wrap again with fresh paper towel.

I store jerky in sealable plastic bags or airtight jars with tight-fitting lids. Although our ancestors dried meat and fish and kept it from year to year without refrigeration, good packaging and cold temperatures promote longer shelf life. When I plan on keeping jerky longer than one month, I store it in the refrigerator or freezer. For a backpacking or camping trip, I package it in small self-sealing plastic bags.

If jerky is not completely dried, mold can develop. If mold is found in a container of jerky, the entire contents must be discarded.

Strip Jerky

Making strip jerky can be as simple as sprinkling salt, pepper, and garlic on meat strips and then drying them. Although that is a valid way to make jerky, my goal is to introduce you to a bolder dimension in flavor blending. Jerky can be like fine wine: a mingling of characteristics, some subtle, others robust. Imagine a sweet jerky that is a result of adding root beer to a marinade or a spicy tomato jerky that is excellent paired with a vodka and tomato juice cocktail.

Start by choosing lean cuts of meat, such as flank, round, or loin, because they have less bone, connective tissue, and fat.

On a clean, flat cutting surface, use a sharp knife to remove excess fat, gristle, and any membranes and connective tissue. Eliminating as much fat as possible helps prevent jerky from turning rancid and reduces some of the gamey taste of wild meat.

Meat cut across the grain produces a jerky that is easier to break apart and chew. Cut ⅛ to ⅜-inch thick strips. Thin strips dry faster than thick ones.

Frozen or semi-frozen meat is easier to cut than meat that is at room temperature. An electric slicer is great way to cut semi-frozen meat into uniform size strips that all dry in the same amount of time. Naturally thawed meat will have better flavor and texture than meat thawed in a microwave.

Marinating

Marinades are seasoned liquids that can be as thick as molasses or water-thin. Marinating ingredients are mixed together and left for about fifteen minutes so that flavors have an opportunity to blend before adding strips. The amount of time it will take strips to absorb flavoring can vary from a few minutes to several days. The longer the strips are in the marinade the more flavor they will absorb. Scoring meat allows a marinade to penetrate easier

Caution—it is not a good idea to reuse a marinade as during the marinating process blood leaches into the marinating liquid.

and deeper. When marinating less than one hour, there is no need to refrigerate, but when marinating for more than one hour, cover the container and place it in the refrigerator. Big, thick strips will take longer for the marinade to penetrate. Make sure that all strips remain in contact with the flavorings, so stir or turn the strips at least once during the marinating process.

Once the strips are marinated, a colander can be used to drain the marinade off the strips. To dry, lay the flavored strips on a mesh-lined dehydrator tray with no overlapping of pieces so air can reach all surfaces. Dry at 160°F until the jerky bends like a green willow.

Flavoring Ingredients

There are endless combinations of flavoring ingredients to use when making a marinade. A marinade usually includes salt, an acid, a sweetener, herbs, and spices combined in various amounts. When concocting a marinade, smell, taste, and make adjustments before adding the meat.

Generally 1 cup of marinade is used per 1 pound of strips.

SALT is the most common ingredient in a jerky marinade. Salt acts as a preservative and inhibits the growth of microorganisms that cause spoilage. Salt draws water and blood from the meat cells, induces partial drying, lengthens storage life, and adds flavor. Salt, sodium chloride (NaCl), is essential to human life to maintain our equilibrium of liquids. A lack of salt increases the dangers of dehydration. Salt can be used for marinades in the form of soy sauce, tamari, Tabasco, and Worcestershire sauce.

SUGAR: white, brown, or maple sugars and honey, corn syrup, molasses, and artificial sweeteners add flavor and moderate the salt.

OIL does not dry, but small amounts of oil, such as olive and sesame, add flavor and enhance the texture of jerky.

LIQUID SMOKE, especially hickory, is a popular flavoring. In my opinion, most people use too much liquid smoke and produce jerky that tastes like smoke and nothing else. However, used in moderation, it can add a pleasing "campfire" flavor. Liquid smoke is made by burning sawdust, then condensing the smoke and separating out the carcinogenic tars, resins, and soot. Interestingly, it is safer to use liquid smoke than real smoke, and more convenient. Smoke, including liquid smoke, is a natural antioxidant, has an antibacterial effect, and serves as a preservative.

HERBS AND SPICES add interest and flavor. Consider using both fresh and dried. Try adding basil, bay leaves, chervil, chives, dill, mint, oregano, parsley, rosemary, sage, savory, tarragon, or thyme. Some of my favorite spices are cardamom, cayenne, chili powder, cloves, coriander, cumin, curry, garlic, ginger, horseradish, juniper berries, mustard, nutmeg, paprika, and black, green, white, or pink peppercorns. Steep herbs like tea, strain, and add to marinades.

Use 1/8 to 1 teaspoon herbs or spices per 1 pound of meat.

Tenderizers help break down the cell structure of meat to make it more porous and tender. Piercing meat with a fork can help tenderizers penetrate deeper. Vinegar serves as a tenderizing agent and helps meat reach its lowest water holding capacity so that it dries faster.

Alcohol and jerky flatter each other. I understand how jerky and beer became good companions. Beer, wine, vodka, whiskey, etc. add flavor and have a tenderizing effect, but the alcohol itself evaporates when used in jerky. I concentrate and release the flavor of alcohol by simmering it about ten minutes. Use a high-sided pan to minimize the chance of it catching on fire; however, if it does flame, the flame will die when the alcohol is gone. One cup of alcohol reduces to about ¼ cup.

Use ¼ cup beer, wine, or liquor per 1 pound of meat.

Fruits and Vegetables can be juiced, puréed, grated, minced, chopped, and added to marinades. Consider using lemon, orange, pineapple, apple, or tomato juice. Minced cooked onions add a rich sweetness to a marinade. Try adding celery, garlic, papaya, and horseradish powder.

Use 1 teaspoon fruit or vegetable to ¼ cup per 1 pound of meat.

> *Use 1 teaspoon salt per 1 pound of meat.*
> *Use ½ teaspoon liquid smoke per 1 pound of meat.*
> *Use 1 teaspoon to 1 tablespoon sugar per 1 pound of meat.*
> *Use 1 tablespoon oil per 1 pound of meat.*
> *Use ¼ cup vinegar per 1 pound of meat.*

Marinating Containers

Earthenware crocks, glass bowls, and self-sealing plastic bags make good marinating containers. Plastic bags take up less space than bowls and make cleanup easy. By squeezing any excess air out of the bag, you can force the marinade into the strips. When using bowls or other containers, stir the strips every couple of hours to make sure the marinade is able to penetrate all the strips.

Marinating Options

Vacuum it

If you have a vacuum packer, place the strips and the marinade in the special vacuum bags or

in a canning jar (jars are best), and pull a vacuum. The vacuum will force the marinade throughout the cell tissues and help shorten the marinating time.

Brush it

After the marinated strips have been placed on mesh-lined dehydrator trays and dried for an hour or so and the surface moisture has evaporated, you can intensify the flavor by dipping a brush into a bowl of molasses, honey, or barbecue sauce. Apply a thin coating to the surface of the meat, then continue the drying process.

Note

Make small batches the first couple of times you make jerky. Then, over time, tweak your recipes to satisfy your palate and gradually make larger quantities. Keep notes on the recipes you like, what you don't like, and the adjustments you want for the next batch. Include weight of fresh meat, flavoring changes, and how long it was marinated. Jerky making may turn into your most creative culinary expression.

Spray it

Fill a spray atomizer with a thin marinade and spray the top and bottom of the drying strips as many times as you like during the drying process. Try using a little teriyaki sauce and fresh garlic that's been twirled in a blender.

Do the Double-Dip

If the finished jerky is dried too hard or crisp, or has too little flavor, or it's simply a failure and you'd rather fix it than throw it away, try the double-dip trick. All you have to do is to soak your rejected jerky for 10 minutes in another marinade and then dry it again. Not only has this rescued my failed jerky, it has resulted in some very tasty creations.

Do the Two-Step

Marinate any meat strips in whatever marinade you like. Drain and lie on mesh-lined dehydrator trays, but dry only half way. Remove the drying strips and soak again in a marinade for at least one hour, drain, and finish the drying process.

Teriyaki Jerky

This popular jerky should maybe be called "Everybody Likes This Jerky." The following two recipes are basically the same but with different quantities of meat strips to give you an idea of how to adjust ingredients when increasing poundage. Over the years we have all agreed that this family favorite is best when marinated at least 12 hours.

In a bowl, combine all the ingredients except the strips and stir until well blended. Add meat and stir with a sturdy fork. Marinate at least 1 hour. When marinating longer, place in the refrigerator. Drain in a colander. Place strips on a mesh-lined dehydrator tray and dry at a minimum temperature of 145°F to 160°F. To check for doneness, first turn the dehydrator off and let the jerky cool, then feel it to determine if it is dry.

Bloody Mary Jerky

Chew on this jerky or add a handful of small pieces to spaghetti sauce.

For 1 Pound Strips

½ cup V8
⅓ cup vodka
1 tablespoon Worcestershire sauce

For 1 Pound Meat Strips

⅔ cup teriyaki sauce
1 teaspoon brown sugar
1 teaspoon olive oil
1 teaspoon garlic, minced
½ teaspoon fresh ginger, finely grated
¼ teaspoon black pepper, coarsely ground
¼ teaspoon salt
¼ teaspoon liquid smoke

For 5 Pounds Meat Strips

3 cups teriyaki sauce
2 tablespoons olive oil
2 heaping tablespoons brown sugar
1 heaping tablespoon garlic, mined
1 tablespoon black pepper, coarsely ground
1 tablespoon salt
1 tablespoon liquid smoke
1 tablespoon fresh ginger, finely grated

1 teaspoon honey
1 teaspoon lemon juice
1 teaspoon celery salt
½ teaspoon hot sauce
½ teaspoon fresh horseradish, grated
½ teaspoon black pepper, ground

In a bowl, combine all the ingredients except the strips and stir until well blended. Add meat and stir with a sturdy fork. Marinate at least 1 hour. When marinating longer, place in the refrigerator. Drain in a colander. Place strips on a mesh-lined dehydrator tray and dry at a minimum temperature of 145°F to 160°F.

Root Beer Jerky

This sweet and tangy marinade works well with wild meats.

For 1 Pound Strips

3 cups root beer
1 tablespoon garlic, minced
1 teaspoon black pepper
1 teaspoon salt
1 teaspoon liquid smoke
¼ teaspoon pepper

Over medium heat, reduce root beer to 1 cup. Remove from heat and add all remaining ingredients. Let strips marinate at least 1 hour. When marinating longer, place in the refrigerator. Drain in a colander, place on a mesh-lined dehydrator tray, and sprinkle the top of the strips with a little salt. Dry at a minimum temperature of 145°F to 160°F.

Cajun Jerky

Add zip to this marinade by adding more cayenne pepper, and if still not hot enough, add finely chopped jalapeño or habanero peppers.

For 1 Pound Strips

1 cup tomato juice
2 teaspoons cayenne pepper
1½ teaspoons dried thyme
1½ teaspoons dried basil

tray and dry at a minimum temperature of 145°F to 160°F .

Wine Jerky

For 1 Pound Strips

1 cup Burgundy wine

¼ cup soy sauce

2 tablespoons molasses

1 tablespoon garlic, chopped

1 tablespoon olive oil

1 tablespoon black pepper,
coarsely ground

In a bowl, combine all the ingredients except the strips and stir until well blended. Add meat and stir with a sturdy fork. Marinate at least 1 hour. When marinating longer, place in the refrigerator. Drain in a colander. Place strips on a mesh-lined dehydrator tray and dry at a minimum temperature of 145°F to 160°F.

Making Ground Meat Jerky

Making jerky out of ground meat has advantages over making it from strips of meat. Ground meat jerky:

- Tastes great;
- Is cheaper to make than strip jerky;
- Takes less time to make than strip jerky;

1½ teaspoons onion powder

1 teaspoon white pepper

½ teaspoon black pepper

½ teaspoon garlic powder

In a bowl, combine all ingredients except strips and stir until well blended. Add meat and stir with a sturdy fork. Marinate at least 1 hour. When marinating longer, place in the refrigerator. Drain in a colander. Place strips on a mesh-lined dehydrator

meat. Joe likes to combine half venison and half beef, or half venison and half buffalo, because venison alone can be too lean. A little fat will give meat more fl avor and better texture. Sometimes we sprinkle the top of the wet jerky with a little salt and pepper.

Seasoning Ground Meat

The same marinating ingredients can be used with strip and ground meat jerky. The difference is that all the marinade is absorbed when added to ground meat; therefore, use no more than ½ cup of liquid with 1 pound of ground meat.

Once flavorings are added to ground meat, allow at least 15 minutes for all the ingredients to blend before shaping it into jerky.

Shaping Ground Meat

After the ground meat is flavored it needs to be forced into a shape. One pound of ground meat will

> *Did you know that half of commercially processed venison is made into venison jerky or sausage? Processing a medium-sized deer can cost over $100.*

- Can be made by combining various meats—like half venison and half beef;
- Uses all of the meat—there are no leftover scraps like when making strip jerky;
- Does not waste flavorings or marinades, because it is all absorbed in the meat;
- Dries uniformly because all pieces are the same size;
- Dries faster than strip jerky;
- Can be made in different shapes, like bears or cows;
- Is easier to chew;
- Is easy and fun to make!

My husband Joe hunts, and we make jerky to give away as Christmas presents. Plus, during the hunting season, friends and family give us their venison to make into jerky. We find that using commercial flavorings along with a few added ingredients is a very easy way to process a lot of

make between ten and twelve strips, each ¾ inch wide and 5 inches long.

Take Aim With a Jerky Gun

"Jerky guns" or "jerky shooters" are devices used to extrude ground meat into uniformly sized pieces. These gadgets look like caulk guns or cake decorators and have various shaped nozzles for making jerky into strips or sticks. Jerky guns are generally available from dehydrator manufacturers

> *When thawing frozen ground meat, break up any clumps larger than ¼ inch so the flavorings can penetrate. Large clumps can jam up extruding devices.*

or catalogs that sell to hunters and fisher-people. To use, fill the chamber or barrel with the flavored ground meat, then pull the trigger to force the meat into uniform pieces.

Hand Made

Meat mixtures are easier to handle if your hands are wet and the mixture is cold.

The longer you mix the ground meat mixture the better the finished jerky will hold together. With your hands, shape the flavored ground meat into 1-inch balls. Place each ball on top of a piece of plastic wrap or waxed paper. Cover with another piece of wrap or paper. With a rolling pin, flatten the balls into ⅛ to ¼-inch rounds that are about 2 inches in diameter. Uniform thickness is necessary so the jerky dries evenly. If the center of the patty jerky is not completely dry, the jerky can mold.

Fun Jerky

Spread a sheet of waxed paper on your kitchen counter. Spoon the flavored meat mixture on the waxed paper. Lay another sheet of wax paper on top of the mixture. With a rolling pin, flatten the meat to ¼ inch thick. Press animal shaped cookie cutters down firmly to make deep impressions. Choose a deer shaped cutter for ground venison and a cow shape for ground beef.

Carefully remove the shaped mixture and place on top of a lightly oiled leather sheet. Dry at 155°F until it firms up. Remove the drying jerky from the sheet and place on a mesh-lined dehydrator tray to make it easier for dry air to get to it. Return to the dehydrator and complete the drying process. When checking for doneness, make sure the center is completely dry.

Gun-Less Jerky

Spoon the flavored ground meat mixture on to a leather sheet. With a large spoon, a greased

rolling pin, or the palm of your hand, spread and evenly flatten the mixture. Place the meat-filled leather sheet in a dehydrator and dry at 155°F, long enough so the meat can be cut and still hold its shape (usually 1 to 2 hours). Use a pizza cutter or a serrated knife to make indentations or cut lines 1 to 1½ inches apart in the drying meat. Return the tray to the dehydrator and dry until the strips can be broken apart at the cut lines. Remove the strips from the leather sheets and place on a mesh-lined dehydrator tray so air can easily move around the jerky and the meat can finish drying.

Family Fun

This is another way to shape meat and make jerky. I learned this technique from a Boy Scout dad. While I was packing up after a presentation to a Scout troop about why food drying is great for outdoor adventuring, one of the dads offered to help me schlep my stuff to my van. He said, "I'd like to share an idea with you." Then he told me how his whole family participated in making ground meat jerky. "We home school our kids and we like to approach life in a creative way," he said. "We use a Play-Doh Fun Factor to shape our jerky," he chuckled. "It's fun to make jerky in all those shapes. Try it!" he encouraged.

Teriyaki Ground Meat Jerky

Since this recipe uses ground meat, the quantity of liquid is reduced. Too much liquid in a ground meat marinade can make the finished jerky crumble and fall apart.

For 1 Pound Ground Meat

⅓ cup teriyaki sauce

1 teaspoon brown sugar

1 teaspoon olive oil

1 teaspoon garlic, minced

1 teaspoon black pepper, coarsely ground

½ teaspoon fresh ginger, finely grated

¼ teaspoon salt

¼ teaspoon liquid smoke

For 5 Pound Ground Meat

2 cups teriyaki sauce

2 tablespoons olive oil

2 heaping tablespoons brown sugar

1 heaping tablespoon garlic, mined

1 heaping tablespoon black pepper, coarsely ground

1 tablespoon salt

1 tablespoon liquid smoke

1 tablespoon fresh ginger, finely grated

In a bowl, combine all the ingredients except the ground meat, and stir until blended. Let the ingredients blend at least 15 minutes. Add meat, and stir with a sturdy fork or by hand. Marinate at least 1 hour. If marinating longer, place in the refrigerator. Form into shapes and place on a mesh-lined dehydrator tray. Dry at a minimum temperature of 145°F to 160°F. To check for doneness, first turn the dehydrator off and let the jerky cool, then feel it to determine if it is dry.

Joe's Jerky

Commercially prepared spice mixtures can be used with other ingredients to make terrific jerky. For over thirty years I have done business with the NESCO/American Harvest dehydrator company and as a result I have the most experience with their line of spices. Please feel free to substitute your favorite spices for those mentioned in my recipes.

For 5 Pound Ground Meat

2 packages Nesco's original spice

1 package Nesco's pepperoni spice

1 cup soy sauce

2 tablespoons olive oil

2 tablespoons brown sugar

1 tablespoon garlic powder

½ teaspoon black pepper

For 10 pounds ground meat

3 packages Nesco's original spice

3 packages Nesco's hot and

spicy spice

3 cups soy sauce

⅔ cup brown sugar

¼ cup olive oil

3 tablespoons garlic

2 tablespoons pepper

In a bowl, combine all the ingredients except the ground meat, and stir until blended. Let the mixture sit at least 15 minutes. Add meat and stir with a sturdy fork. Marinate at least 1 hour. If marinating longer, place in the refrigerator. Form into shapes and place on a mesh-lined dehydrator tray. Dry at a minimum temperature of 145 to 160°F.

Spicy Tomato Soy Jerky

For 1 Pound Ground Meat

⅓ cup tomato sauce

3 tablespoons soy sauce

2 tablespoons Worcestershire sauce

1 tablespoon brown sugar

½ teaspoon garlic powder

½ teaspoon black pepper, freshly ground

½ teaspoon horseradish, freshly grated

½ teaspoon Tabasco

½ teaspoon liquid smoke

½ teaspoon salt

Put all ingredients, with the exception of meat, in a blender. Put ground meat in a bowl, add blended ingredients, mix, and marinate at least 1 hour. If marinating longer, place in the refrigerator. Form into shapes and place on a mesh-lined dehydrator tray. Dry at a minimum temperature of 145 to 160°F.

Whiskey Jerky

What could be better than booze and a hunk of meat all in one bite? Vary the booze; try rum, scotch, and brandy. Once the meat is dry, add more flavor by dipping the jerky in whiskey and drying again.

For 1 Pound Ground Meat

2 cups cheap whiskey

1 tablespoon soy sauce

1 tablespoon brown sugar

1 tablespoon olive oil

1 teaspoon salt

½ teaspoon liquid smoke

½ teaspoon garlic, minced

¼ teaspoon black peppercorns, crushed

Reduce whiskey to 1/3 cup in a pan with high sides to prevent the fumes from flaming. Be careful. If a flame does appear, it will subside when the alcohol is gone. Cool and then add remaining ingredients to the whiskey; stir; then add ground meat. Marinate at least 1 hour. If marinating longer, place in the refrigerator. Form into shapes and place on a mesh-lined dehydrator tray. Dry at a minimum temperature of 145 to 160°F.

In a bowl, combine all the ingredients except the ground meat, and stir until blended. Let the mixture sit at least 15 minutes. Add meat and stir with a sturdy fork. Marinate at least 1 hour. If marinating longer, place in the refrigerator. Form into shapes and place on a mesh-lined dehydrator tray. Dry at a minimum temperature of 145 to 160°F.

Turkey Jerky

People like saying "Turkey Jerky," and then after they try it they usually smack their lips with delight.

For 1 Pound Ground Meat

2 tablespoons lemon juice

2 tablespoons onion, freshly grated

2 tablespoons teriyaki sauce

1 tablespoon white sugar

1 tablespoon olive oil

1 tablespoon lemon peel, fresh grated

2 teaspoons paprika

1 teaspoon garlic, crushed

1 teaspoon salt

1 teaspoon black pepper, freshly ground

½ teaspoon liquid smoke

¼ teaspoon Tabasco

1 pound ground turkey

Salt, to sprinkle

Hot Jerky

If you want your upper lip to sweat, use habanero peppers.

For 1 Pound Ground Meat

⅓ cup teriyaki sauce

2 tablespoons hot peppers, seeded and finely chopped

1 tablespoon olive oil

1 tablespoon minced garlic

2 teaspoons brown sugar

1 teaspoon black pepper, freshly ground

1 teaspoon horseradish, freshly grated

1 teaspoon salt

½ teaspoon paprika

½ teaspoon chili powder

½ teaspoon Tabasco

In a bowl, combine all the ingredients except the ground meat and stir until blended. Let the mixture rest at least 15 minutes. Add meat and stir with a sturdy fork. Marinate at least 1 hour. If marinating longer, place in the refrigerator. Form into shapes and place on a mesh-lined dehydrator tray. Sprinkle salt on the jerky while it's still moist. Dry at a minimum temperature of 145 to 160°F.

Ham Jerky

Our friend Judy Lynch specializes in conducting horse pack trips throughout North America. After one trip to the Bob Marshall Wilderness in Montana she was discouraged by the response to the trail food she had provided. "I didn't know if I'd ever be able to go on another pack trip unless somehow it got easier," she recalls. Judy loves to cook and takes pride in serving good food. "I want everyone to smack their lips and say, 'WOW! That meal was incredible!'" Judy attended a food drying class and afterward dried all the food necessary for a five-day pack trip. "Drying food was the key," she said happily. "I experienced less stress, my food budget was reduced, the horses packed lighter loads (all the food supplies fit in one large duffel bag), and everyone loved the food, including my husband, who enjoys traditional home cooking." She paused, "Dan said it was the best trail food he'd ever eaten. Ham jerky was the biggest hit. Everybody loved it." She continued, "Riders always want something salty to snack on, and the ham jerky satisfied that desire. Bringing chips on a pack trip is not an easy task, and it's a good idea to eat something salty because it makes the riders drink more water. I also liked that it was different." Choose cooked lean ham slices for jerky and cut ¼-inch thick. Making ham jerky can be as easy as mixing mustard and honey together, painting the ham slices, and then drying. Ham jerky is also a great addition to any split pea soup.

For 1 Pound Ham Slices

¼ cup honey
2 teaspoons Dijon mustard
2 teaspoons dried pink peppercorns, crushed
2 teaspoons dried green peppercorns, crushed
½ teaspoon black peppercorns, coarsely ground

Mix all ingredients together, wait 15 minutes and then add ham slices. Marinate at least 12 hours before drying on mesh-lined dehydrator trays at 145°F.

Sweet Ham Jerky

For a twist, you can substitute maple syrup or brown sugar for the honey in this recipe and sprinkle a little black pepper on the slices right after laying them on the mesh-lined dehydrator tray.

For 1 Pound Ham Strips

⅔ cup frozen orange juice concentrate
½ cup honey
⅓ cup whiskey
1 teaspoon black pepper, freshly ground

Mix all ingredients together, wait 15 minutes and then add ham strips. Marinate at least 12 hours before drying. Place on a mesh-lined dehydrator tray and dry at 145°F.

Traditional Pemmican

Pemmican is one of the earliest and most important high-protein, portable foods. Not only did pemmican nourish the Native Americans, it also served as a compact staple food for the pioneers in their westward ventures. Pemmican is a combination of powdered or finely chopped dried meat, dried berries, and melted animal fat that is mixed into a thick paste and stuffed into airtight animal skins. Dried wild fruits such as strawberries, blueberries, huckleberries, raspberries, cherries, buffalo berries, grapes (raisins), and plums were pounded into a chunky powder. Cracked bones were boiled in water

and the rich, sweet, salty butter-like fat was skimmed off and added to pemmican, as was animal fat that was cut into small (1-inch) chunks and heated in a pan over a slow fire. To store pemmican, casings from animal innards (intestines and stomach linings) were scraped clean and stuffed with the meat, fat, and dried fruit mixture.

Modern Pemmican

This pemmican can be made using either strips or ground meat jerky. Feel free to vary the ingredients. Add a pinch of ground red pepper, chopped peanuts, a touch of honey, and dried apricots, apples, peaches, prunes, pineapple, kiwi, raisins, and strawberries. If you add dried rose hips (vitamin C) you will get an almost completely life-sustaining portable food.

1½ cup powdered jerky
1 cup dried fruit, chopped in ⅛-inch pieces
1 cup peanut butter
Plastic wrap

Grind a few small pieces of jerky at a time in the blender or food processor, set aside, and then grind the dried fruits. Combine all ingredients and mix well. Spread a 12-by-14-inch sheet of plastic wrap flat on the counter. Spoon half the mixture onto the wrap and form a log shape. Firmly pull

the wrap around the pemmican mixture to force and compress it. Repeat with the other half of the mixture. Make sure it's wrapped well to keep air out. Store in the refrigerator until you leave for an outdoor adventure where it can be carried in a pack; up to one month or so.

Jerky Parfleches

As you are dining on this fancy dish, think back to the time when wild buffalo roamed the land and people regularly dried their food. Makes 4 servings.

1 cup jerky, coarsely chopped
1 cup dried cranberries, coarsely chopped
¾ cup dried wild plums, coarsely chopped
¾ cup dried cherries, coarsely chopped
1½ tablespoons red wine vinegar
1 tablespoon fresh thyme, finely chopped
1 tablespoon fresh rosemary, finely chopped
¼ cup frozen orange juice concentrate, thawed
¼ cup butter, melted
30 sheets (12 by 17 inches each) phyllo dough
2 cups butter, melted
1 cup breadcrumbs

Topping

⅔ cup frozen orange juice concentrate, thawed
⅓ cup honey

Combine all but last 3 ingredients and stir. Set aside and allow time for the ingredients to moisten. Place one phyllo sheet on a clean, dry work surface. Brush a light layer of butter, starting with the edges and covering the entire surface. Sprinkle a pinch of breadcrumbs over the sheet. Crumbs serve to ensure the phyllo dough remains flaky between each layer. Use 5 sheets phyllo dough to build 5 layers in this manner. Cut this stack into 4 pieces, 6 inches wide and 8 ½ inches long. Place one rounded tablespoon of jerky mixture in the center of each square and fold phyllo edges into the center to form a "purse." Use melted butter to bind the dough together. Repeat this process with remaining phyllo sheets. Place on a cookie sheet and bake 15 to 20 minutes at 400°F until golden.

Mix orange juice and honey together and drizzle over the parfleches while they are still warm.

Jerky Bread

An entire meal can be packed inside a loaf of bread.

1 loaf raw bread dough
½ cup jerky, chopped into
¼-inch pieces
3 tablespoons water
1 tablespoon dried tomato pieces

1 tablespoon dried onion pieces
1 teaspoon black pepper, finely ground

In a small bowl combine all ingredients except dough. Let the ingredients sit at least 15 minutes. Knead the rehydrated ingredients into dough. Place dough in an oiled baking tin and bake at 350°F. When the crust browns, remove from oven, spread butter on top, and set the loaf on its side to cool.

Jerky Hash

This is a great way to use leftover baked potatoes. Makes 4 servings.

½ cup jerky, cut in ½-inch pieces
¼ cup water
½ cup celery, chopped
3 green onions, chopped
½ teaspoon garlic, minced
1 tablespoon olive oil
3 cups leftover baked potatoes, cubed
Salt
Pepper

In a bowl, rehydrate jerky in water 10 minutes. Drain and save jerky-flavored water. Over high heat, sauté celery, oil, and onion and reduce heat to medium. Add saved jerky water, cover, and cook.

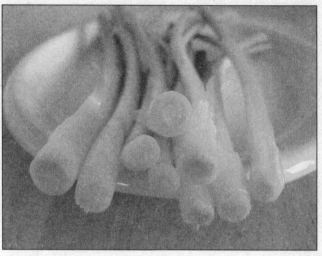

Pasta Con Carne Seca

This is an elegant, yet simple, rich, and pretty dish that works really well with wild meat jerky. Makes 2 servings.

1 cup jerky, cut in ¼-inch pieces
1 cup white wine
½ cup half dried mushroom pieces
½ cup dried pepper pieces
¼ cup dried tomato pieces
3 tablespoons butter
1 cup whipping cream
1 teaspoon basil, finely chopped
1 cup thin pasta
½ cup Parmesan cheese
⅛ teaspoon black pepper, coarsely ground

Remove lid and add potatoes, jerky, salt, and pepper. Stir to prevent sticking.

Jerky Rice

Makes 4 servings.
1 cup short-grain brown rice
¼ cup jerky, cut in ¼-inch pieces
2 tablespoons dried tomato pieces, broken in ¼-inch pieces
1 tablespoon olive oil
¼ teaspoon dried basil
¼ teaspoon dried oregano

Jerky is a wonderful base for making rice and veggies. Just add small pieces of fresh vegetables for crunch, such as bell pepper and carrots.

2 ¼ cups water
Combine all ingredients and simmer uncovered
    20 to 30 minutes.

Put jerky and wine in a saucepan and let sit for 15 minutes. Bring to a simmer, add mushrooms, pepper, and tomato pieces and cook until wine disappears. Reduce to low heat, add butter and add cream. Stir until thick. Prepare pasta according to directions, then drain and add to jerky mixture. Add basil. Serve over the cooked pasta and top with cheese and pepper.

Farmer's Recipes

MARIE W. LAWRENCE

Roast Saddle of Venison with Cumberland Sauce

*A*s with all such meats, the tenderloin or saddle of venison is the prime cut, so you'll want to treat it with due respect. It should be roasted in a similar manner to beef tenderloin, although the accompanying sauce reflects the venison's unique flavor. I haven't prepared a saddle of venison in a while, but when I did, I larded it with bacon and roasted it quickly in a hot oven. Although the entire saddle can be in the vicinity of 5–8 pounds, I'm utilizing a smaller roast, which is more manageable and more affordable. Some folks like to sprinkle on a few crushed juniper berries when roasting venison, but I prefer it without; use sparingly if you decide to.

2 lb. boneless venison tenderloin, trimmed of all fat
4 slices bacon, halved
Salt to taste
Pepper to taste

Season the venison with salt and pepper to taste and drape the half slices of bacon over the roast at intervals along the length of it. Roast the venison in a 475°F oven for about 30 minutes. This should produce a medium-rare roast. If you're one of those people who prefer your venison still roaming around the woods blatting when you cut into it, start checking your roast after 20 minutes. Again, an instant-read thermometer is an excellent investment; try 140°F for a rare roast, 160°F for medium. Remove to a serving platter to rest for 5–10 minutes.

This allows the juices to remain in the meat rather than running all over the platter when it is sliced.

Cumberland Sauce

Cumberland sauce is a traditional English recipe containing currant jelly, port wine, and citrus. Homemade crab apple jelly may be substituted for the currant, if you prefer, and/or a sweet wine such as blackberry merlot for the port. Cumberland sauce is also a good accompaniment to turkey, duck, or pork.

1 c. red currant or crab apple jelly
2 t. grated orange rind
¼ c. orange juice
1 t. grated lemon rind
2 T. lemon juice
½ c. port wine
1 t. Dijon mustard
1 t. fresh grated ginger, or ½ t. powdered ginger
Salt to taste
Pepper to taste

Combine all ingredients in a small saucepan and bring to a boil, stirring until the sauce is smooth. Serve at room temperature; cover and refrigerate leftovers. This will make about 1½ c. sauce.

Venison Stew

I freely admit to not being as much a fan of venison as is my husband, Bruce. Therefore, when he'd proudly drag his harvest of the year home from the woods surrounding Brattleboro, I'd spend much of my time trying to convince myself it was beef. With this recipe for venison stew, I was almost able to succeed.

1 lb. venison, trimmed of all fat and cut in stewsized pieces

2 T. corn oil

2 T. flour

2 c. 1" potato chunks

1 c. carrot slices

1 c. ½" cubes rutabaga

1 T. Worcestershire sauce

1 lg. onion, chopped (1 c.)

2 stalks celery, sliced

1 t. salt

¼ t. pepper

2 c. beef broth

2 bay leaves

½ c. dry red wine (optional, or add more broth)

6 juniper berries, tied in cheesecloth, optional; they add a slightly bitter, "wild" taste

Combine the flour, salt, and pepper in a medium bowl. Dredge the venison in this mixture, coating it well. In a heavy kettle or Dutch oven, brown the venison in the hot oil. Add the onions and celery and continue to cook a few minutes longer. Add the bay leaves, juniper berries, broth and wine. Bring to a boil, reduce the heat, and simmer, covered, for half an hour. Add the vegetables and cook for another half hour, until everything is tender and the stew has thickened somewhat. Remove the bay leaves and juniper berries before serving the stew. This easily serves 4–6.

Venison Mincemeat

My father hunted when he was a younger man, at one time bagging a semi-legendary 10-point buck. Sadly, as the story went, he sold his trophy head to some collector from down country, so I never was able to view the magnificent beast. By the time I came along, our

main supply of venison was courtesy of the local game warden, a man who just happened to have the same last name as we did. Perhaps it was his way of thanking my dad for taking all those wildlife nuisance calls directed to the wrong person. Because this venison was from deer that had been hit and killed by cars, some of it was quite young and tender—good enough to cook as steaks. However, the odd, tough portions were plopped into my mother's trusty pressure cooker therein to process until the meat literally fell off the bones. Then she would be ready to make one of her specialties— venison mincemeat. Mother used to can hers in glass jars—dark, foreboding little vessels of spiced meat and fruit waiting to cover vanilla ice cream or to be plopped into pie shells. If the thought of it all is too overwhelming, I've also included a smaller recipe for those of a more timid persuasion.

3 lb. venison or beef shoulder meat, boiled tender and chopped fine (not ground)

6 lb. tart apples—pared, cored, and chopped

1 lb. suet (beef fat) chopped fine

1 lb. diced citron*

1½ c. candied diced lemon peel

1½ c. candied diced orange peel

¾ c. cider vinegar

2 lb. dark seedless raisins

2 lb. dried currants

6 c. apple cider or apple juice

2 lb. brown sugar

2 T. cinnamon

1 T. allspice

1 T. nutmeg

1 T. salt

1 T. cloves

2 c. brandy, optional

Combine all ingredients except the brandy and portion them into one or two large, heavy pans. Cook over low heat for about an hour, until the liquid is mostly absorbed and everything is quite tender. This will burn easily, so be vigilant! Stir in the brandy at the end of the cooking process. Although old recipes for mincemeat call for keeping it in a crock in a cool cellar, pressure canning is a safer mode of preservation. Follow the directions for canning meat found in your pressure canner guidelines, checking seals to make sure everything is properly canned. Pressure canning is necessary because of the meat in the mincemeat; the pressure canner reaches a higher temperature (240°F) than a boiling water bath is capable of. Alternatively, place your mincemeat in pint or quart freezer containers, seal, and freeze. The texture of the mincemeat may be slightly altered from the freezing process. This recipe will produce about 6 quarts or 12 pints of mincemeat.

Mini Mincemeat

Here's the promised mini-recipe for mincemeat. For this version, simply cook the meat right along with the fruits and spices, another time saver. Although it's possible to substitute ground beef or venison for the diced meat, the texture and taste may suffer somewhat; make sure to invest in top-quality low-fat ground meat if you do and break it up really well during the cooking process.

½ lb. venison or beef, chopped fine

1 lb. tart apples—peeled, cored, and chopped (3 c.)

3 T. unsalted butter *or* 6 T. diced suet

½ c. citron*

¼ c. candied diced lemon peel

¼ c. candied diced orange peel

1 c. raisins

1 c. dried currants

1 c. cider or apple juice

2 T. cider vinegar

1 c. packed brown sugar

1 t. cinnamon

½ t. nutmeg

½ t. allspice

½ t. salt

½ t. cloves

⅓ c. brandy, optional

Stew beef works well for this amount of mincemeat. Mincing the meat while raw is easy to do when working with such a small amount and will cut down on cooking time; partially freezing it first makes the process even easier. (Although it's possible to substitute ground beef, the texture and taste may suffer somewhat; make sure to invest in top-quality low-fat beef if you do and break it up really well during the cooking process.) Combine all ingredients in a large, heavy pan. Bring to a boil, reduce the heat, and cook slowly until the liquid is mostly absorbed, stirring frequently to prevent burning, about ½ hour. Add the brandy, cool, and use as desired. This amount should produce about 4 cups of mincemeat—enough for one solid-citizen pie, a couple of more modest ones, or several tarts. You could also serve it warm over ice cream. Keep unused portion refrigerated, covered up to two weeks.

*A note about citron: Citron is the candied peel of an ancient citrus fruit indigenous to India and later the Mediterranean regions. It's perhaps best known as an ingredient in fruitcake or certain sweet Christmas breads. Although it's now also grown in the Southern United States, citron is not as popular or widely available as many ingredients; around here we're most apt to find it during the months of November and December. Although another dried or candied fruit such as apricots or pineapple may be substituted in a pinch, the flavor of your mince will be somewhat altered.

Mashed Potatoes

Because we always had a garden, we always had plenty of homegrown potatoes. We'd carefully dry and then store them, away from light, in a cool closet room on the north side of the house. There are a number of potato varieties, each suited to one or more uses. In order to get the best results from your recipe, it's important to know your potato types well enough to choose the right one. At least we've only a few main varieties to choose from in the United States, unlike Peru, land of the potato's origin. At last count, I believe that country boasted over a thousand different kinds. Imagine trying to sort that collection for your mashers; it would take until the next New Year's just to get through them all! My favorite potato for mashing is a variety called purple Viking; it's a beautiful round potato with purple skin and snowy-white flesh. However, chances are you won't be finding any of those little guys unless you grow your own. Some folks may prefer one of the mild-flavored "gold" potatoes now increasingly available, although because their moisture content is somewhat higher than many varieties, it's easy to make that type of potato too mushy when mashed with this ratio of ingredients. Therefore for this recipe, I recommend a russet-type potato, both for flavor and texture. They're widely available and won't disappoint.

1 lb. potatoes—washed, peeled, and quartered

½ t. salt

1½ c. water

½ c. milk *or* half and half

2 T. butter

¼ t. seasoned salt *or* ¼ t. pepper

Place the potatoes in a medium saucepan. Add the salt and enough of the water to almost cover the potatoes; you don't want to drown them. To me, there's nothing more pathetic than a pan full of waterlogged, anemic potatoes staring sadly at you. Bring the potatoes to a boil, reduce the heat, and boil gently, covered, for 20–30 minutes, until the potatoes are very tender and the liquid has partially cooked away. Just don't let the liquid totally cook down; a pan of dried-out, burned potatoes staring at you is almost as depressing as their waterlogged cousins. Here is where my years of 4-H cooking lessons come into play; when you drain your potatoes, save the cooking water for use in gravy, soup, or even making bread. Don't throw all those valuable nutrients down the drain! With the potatoes still in the pan over low heat, add in the milk, butter, and seasonings; cover; and let the mixture heat through for a minute or so. Now it's time to mash or whip your potatoes until they're as smooth or lumpy as you wish. Add another pat of butter to the top, if you wish, and serve them while they're hot! If you must make these a little in advance, place the covered pan into a larger pan of simmering water. Once the potatoes start to cool down, they become hard and not nearly as appetizing. This recipe is very easy to halve or double, as you wish.

Rabbit Casserole Provencal

The white wine adds a bit of an exotic flavor, although you can as easily substitute water or chicken stock. Serve the rabbit as is with an accompaniment of crusty bread, or top it with herbed drop biscuits.

1½ –2 lb. rabbit parts (white meat, backbone, and ribcage, or add some leg meat)

½ c. dry white wine

1½ c. water

2 bay leaves

3 small sprigs fresh thyme

3 slices bacon

1 small onion, chopped: ½ c.

1 medium carrot, sliced in rounds: ½ c.

A nice casserole of rabbit Procencal is waiting to warm you up.

½ t. salt
¼ t. white pepper
1 c. sliced mushrooms

Dice the bacon and place in a large skillet or saucepan. Fry it gently along with the rabbit, onions, celery, and carrot. After the vegetables have softened and browned somewhat, add in the water, broth or wine, seasonings, and mushrooms. Bring to a boil, reduce heat, and simmer for 30–40 minutes, until the rabbit meat is very tender. Remove the rabbit from the broth and allow it to cool enough so that you can pick it with the meat off the bones. Add the rabbit back into the pan. You may now either reheat the rabbit in the pan and serve with crusty bread or turn the hot mixture into a casserole dish, top with the herbed biscuits, and bake at 375°F until the biscuits are browned and cooked through—about 20 minutes. This serves around 4.

Country-Fried Rabbit

A good presoak in salted water is the trick to producing moist fried rabbit. Set your rabbit to soaking early on the day you plan to serve it.

1½ lb. rabbit legs
1 qt. water

2 t. salt
¼ c. corn oil
½ c. flour
½ t. paprika
½ t. salt
¼ t. poultry seasoning

You may wish to cut the much-larger hind legs of the rabbit in half, using a good, sharp knife. Place the rabbit legs, water, and salt in a plastic or stainless steel container, preferably with a tight cover, and refrigerate for 8 hours. Drain the legs well, patting them lightly to somewhat dry them. Combine the flour and seasonings in a bowl or plastic bag and dredge the rabbit legs, coating them well. Heat the oil in a heavy skillet over medium, adding the rabbit pieces when it is hot. Fry the rabbit, covered, until it is deep golden brown on one side. Turn the rabbit and brown the other side. Keeping the pan covered during the frying process will help the meat to cook more evenly and to retain moisture. Remove the rabbit to a serving plate. If you wish gravy, add a tablespoon or two of flour to the cooking pan. Cook and stir a minute or two and then deglaze the frying pan with a cup or so of chicken stock or water. Serves 3–4.

Collops

Round steak is a lean and flavorful but rather tough cut of meat. This recipe for collops comes from sunny California, courtesy of my brother and sister-in-law, John and Naomi Wheelock. They've been West Coasters for a good many years now but still have an old-fashioned recipe or two up their sleeves. The word "collops" refers to thin slices of meat and is probably of Swedish origins, although the recipe here actually has Scottish roots, occasionally utilizing lamb or venison in place of the beef. For a more traditional take, you may substitute a bit of diced suet for the butter, an option John and Naomi included in the original. I've adjusted the salt down slightly for my taste, although their version calls for the greater amount; personal preference will dictate.

1 lb. round steak

1 lg. onion, chopped: 1 c.

1–1½ t. salt

½ t. pepper

2 T. flour

2 T. butter *or* diced suet

2 t. Worcestershire sauce

1½ c. water

Slice the steak very thin and then cut it into about 1" dice. This is easier to do if you allow the steak to partially freeze first—maybe an hour in the freezer while you're doing something else. Once it's been diced, place it and the onions in a medium bowl or plastic bag and toss them with the flour. Preheat the butter in a large, heavy frying pan until it's quite hot but not burned; add the meat and onion mixture and fry, turning and breaking it up, until everything is nicely browned. Add the water, Worcestershire sauce, salt, and pepper, stirring to blend thoroughly. Bring to a boil and then lower the heat and simmer, stirring occasionally, for about 15 minutes. At this time you should have a nice gravy to go with your meat; add a bit more water if necessary. Mashed potatoes and toast points are the traditional accompaniments to collops, although buttered rice will also do. Serve to 4 folks looking for a bit of comfort food.

Brunswick Stew

If you consider squirrel hunting to be part of your repertoire, this is the recipe for you. Personally, I've never eaten squirrel meat, although I'm sure the little critters squabbling over the corn and seeds at our bird feeders would provide tender morsels were I so inclined. However, I'd rather just watch their antics than consume them. Fortunately for all concerned, the Brunswick stew recipes I've come across all indicate you can exchange

a chicken or two for the squirrel meat, so to each his or her own! It's still a savory combination of tastes and textures, ready to curb the heartiest appetites. I've find some recipes overflowing with barbecue sauce entirely too sweet; to me this one is "just right."

3 lb. chicken, cut up; *or* 2 squirrels, cleaned and dressed

3 slices bacon, diced; *or* 2 T. oil

1 lg. onion, chopped: 1 c.

2 c. diced red-skinned potatoes

6–8 peeled, diced tomatoes

1. c. whole kernel corn

1½ c. fresh or frozen lima beans

1 T. Worcestershire sauce

1½ t. salt

½ t. pepper

½ t. marjoram

2 T. brown sugar

2 T. cider vinegar

¼ t. Tabasco sauce

In a large, heavy skillet with a cover or a Dutch oven, cook the diced bacon over medium heat until it is brown and has rendered out its fat. Remove the bacon bits from the pan and set aside. Season the chicken or squirrel on both sides with the salt and pepper. Brown the pieces, skinside down first, in the bacon fat or oil. Once it is golden on one

Brunswick stew accompanied by buttermilk biscuits makes a hearty autumn supper.

side, turn it over and add the chopped onion while the meat finishes browning on the other side. Stir in the tomatoes, marjoram, brown sugar, vinegar, Worcestershire, and Tabasco sauce. Bring the mixture to a boil and simmer, covered, over medium-low heat until the meat is almost tender, about 20–25 minutes. Stir the mixture and add in the potatoes, bacon, corn, and lima beans. Cover again and boil gently about 20 minutes longer, until the potatoes are tender and the meat thoroughly done. Buttermilk biscuits go nicely with this stew. It will serve 6 nicely.

Let's Talk Turkey . . .

America's favorite Thanksgiving fare is a true American native. The North American wild turkey, *Meleagris gallopavo*, is one of only two species of wild turkey in the entire world. Its cousin, *Meleagris ocellata*, lives in a relatively small area around the Yucatan Peninsula in Central America. There are five subspecies of *gallopavo*, of which the most numerous is *sylvestris*, the Eastern wild turkey. When Europeans first traveled to the Americas, turkeys roamed in great bands throughout the countryside. Unfortunately, overhunting and loss of habitat brought the turkey uncomfortably close to extinction by the beginning

of the twentieth century. Thanks to the Pittman-Robertson Act of 1937, and extensive reintroduction programs, wild turkeys again roam the United States, their numbers grown from only about 30,000 in the 1930s to over 7 million today. The turkey we're so fond of eating is descended from a domestic Mexican subspecies that was brought back to Spain in the early 1500s. Same ancestry, but bred into a bird of an entirely different demeanor than its wild cousins. Benjamin Franklin wanted the turkey to be our national bird rather than the bald eagle. Who could blame him? The turkey is an American original loved and devoured by almost everybody. Still though, can you imagine a turkey proudly straddling our national seal? Food for thought indeed.

Roast Turkey

The instructions here are for a 15-pound turkey, although ingredients are easy enough to adjust for different sizes. I prefer to roast my turkey at a slightly higher temperature than many instructions call for and have never had it turn out anything but tender and juicy. Methodology is what's important here—coating your bird well with a lubricating agent such as bacon or butter, and roasting it covered until near the very end, at which point a briefly uncovered rendezvous with a hot oven turns the skin to a crisp brown. I also prefer to stuff my turkey before roasting; the stuffing adds flavor and moistness to the turkey, which returns the favor to the stuffing. However, you must be careful not to undercook your bird; the stuffing must be properly heated through to a safe temperature. Prompt removal of any extra stuffing is also an important step to safely enjoying leftovers.

15 lb. turkey, neck and giblets removed
6 strips bacon
¼ c. butter
2 t. parsley flakes
1 t. paprika
½ t. thyme
Salt

Pepper

Stuffing

14–16 slices stale or toasted bread

½ c. butter

1 T. poultry seasoning

1 lg. onion, diced: 1 c.

2–3 stalks celery, diced: 1 c.

Water or low-sodium broth to moisten

First prepare your stuffing. If you have had the ambition and freezer space, you will have been saving odds and ends of bread for just this purpose. If not, no problem; one loaf of most types of bread should fit the bill nicely. I prefer bread with some texture to it, such as a nice oatmeal loaf, although you're limited only by personal preference here. I frequently fit all the slices onto a large cookie sheet and bake them a few minutes, either the night before or the morning of preparation, while preheating the oven for the turkey. You can also briefly toast each in a standard toaster, although this can be time-consuming. I do think the toasting process adds an extra depth of flavor to the stuffing. Melt the butter in a 4 qt. pan or Dutch oven over medium-low heat. Add the onion and celery and cook, stirring occasionally, until they become tender but not brown. Meanwhile tear the bread into pieces and mix it with the poultry seasoning. Add 2 cups of water or broth to the celery/onion mixture and stir in the bread. You will now decide how much more liquid you wish to add to your stuffing; some prefer a moister stuffing, while others like it more crumbly. Once it's moistened to your preference, remove from the heat and prepare the turkey.

Rinse the turkey with cold water and drain. I Don't worry about patting it dry, although some recipes may call for this. Place 2 strips of bacon in a large roasting pan and position the turkey on top of it breast-side up. Add the neck to one side. Stuff both cavities loosely, as the filling tends to expand during cooking. Tuck the neck skin under the bird and tuck the drumsticks into the loop of skin near the tail, if it's intact. Combine the melted ¼ c. of butter with the herbs and seasonings and brush over the entire surface of the turkey. Drape the remaining bacon strips over the breast and drumsticks. Cover the turkey with the vented top of the roasting pan. If for some reason you don't have a top, make a tent of heavy-duty foil instead. Covering the turkey during this phase of cooking will help ensure a moist, tasty bird. Roast in a preheated 350°F oven for about 20 minutes per pound. For approximately the last half hour, increase the heat to 425°F, and uncover the turkey to finish roasting. The turkey will be deep golden brown, and the skin will be crispy as opposed to moist appearing when it is done; a fork inserted near the thigh joint will cause clear juices to run. Allow the turkey to rest in the pan for 15–30 minutes, which allows the juices to remain in the bird rather than running all over the serving platter. It's also a nice time to finish up all the side dishes you're serving with the turkey.

Once the turkey is removed to the serving platter, it's time to make the gravy. I frequently add leftover vegetable cooking water to the pan drippings for more flavorful and nutritious gravy; just don't overwhelm the base with them. I like to heat this mixture in the roasting pan for a minute or two to scrape up all the savory brown goodness left from the roasting process, discarding the neck once this is accomplished. You may also either pour or use a bulb syringe to transfer the juices to another cooking pan prior to this step, if your roasting pan is not stove-top worthy, although by all means add some hot liquid and swish it around if it helps loosen up any bits of goodness. Around 3–4 cups of extra liquid would be sufficient for this size bird. At any rate, either measure or guesstimate the total amount you subsequently have, adding 1 T. flour whisked into a small amount of cold water for each cup of gravy base. Cook and stir over high heat until it is lovely and bubbly, adding salt and pepper to taste

Wild turkeys are true American natives. They provide much leaner fair than their domestic cousins.

only if necessary. Strain through a wire mesh sieve if need be for a nice smooth gravy and serve hot.

Turkey Divan

Turkey divan is another one of those delicious dishes that has too frequently been corrupted by canned cream-of-something soup. Mind you, I occasionally use cream soups myself, but as with the advent of so many convenience foods we've sometimes allowed ourselves to forget what the "original" tastes like. In this case, it's well worth revisiting. Putting aside a little turkey stock in advance will give you just the right amount for this recipe, although prepared chicken broth substitutes nicely.

1 lb. leftover sliced turkey breast

¼ c. butter

¼ c. flour

1½ c. milk

1 c. chicken or turkey broth

2 egg yolks

½ t. dry mustard

1 t. salt

¼ t. pepper

½ c. shredded cheddar cheese

¼ c. grated Parmesan cheese

3–4 c. lightly cooked broccoli florets, well drained

Thinly-sliced French bread, buttered

Melt the butter over low heat. Add the flour and seasonings, cooking for a minute over low heat. Add the milk and broth all at once, increase heat and bring just to a boil. Reduce heat again and add the well beaten egg yolks and the cheddar cheese, stirring just until the cheese melts; do not boil. Remove from the heat. Place the bread slices, buttered-side down, in a greased casserole or baking pan. Layer the turkey and broccoli, topping with the sauce. Sprinkle with the Parmesan cheese and bake in a preheated 375°F oven for 35–45 minutes, until the top bubbles and browns slightly. Serves 6.

Turkey Mole

This dark, spicy Mexican sauce is a nice contrast to the traditionally milder Thanksgiving flavors. I've tried to balance the complexities of a good mole with products readily available further north. Again, I'd recommend white meat, although in a pinch dark will do. If you happen to have chicken floating around instead, it will substitute very nicely.

Turkey Base

3–4 lb. turkey; breast or thighs
½ t. onion powder
½ t. garlic powder
½ t. paprika
1 T. salt
6 c. water
2 T. corn oil

Sprinkle the turkey evenly with the onion and garlic powders and the paprika. Brown in the oil, covered, in a Dutch oven over medium heat until the turkey is golden brown on both sides. Add the salt and the water. Bring to a boil, lower the heat to a simmer, and cook, covered, for about an hour, until the turkey is cooked through and tender. Remove the turkey from the broth and allow it to cool separately while preparing the rest of the sauce. If you prefer, the turkey and broth can be refrigerated overnight, then separated out, and utilized for the mole the next day.

Sauce

4–6 dried ancho chilies
½ c. sliced almonds *or*
¼ c. each sliced almonds and *pepitas* (pumpkin
   seeds)
6 T. corn oil, divided
2 T. sesame seeds
¼ t. anise seeds
¼ t. ground cloves
¼ t. ground allspice
¼ t. black pepper
½ t. cumin
½ t. cinnamon
½ t. oregano
1 medium onion, peeled and chopped
4–6 cloves garlic, peeled and chopped

1 slightly green banana, peeled and chopped
1 lb. tomatoes, peeled and chopped
½ c. raisins
¼ c. packed brown sugar
2 squares unsweetened chocolate
1 c. crushed corn tortilla chips
½ c. dry bread crumbs

Place the ancho chilies in a small saucepan along with 2 c. of the turkey broth. Bring to a boil, reduce the heat and simmer for about 1/2 hour, until the chilies are tender. While the chilies are cooking, prepare the rest of the sauce. In a medium cast-iron skillet, sauté the almond in 2 T. of the corn oil until they just begin to brown. Add the sesame seeds and all the spices, stirring over medium heat a minute or two longer until they are warm and fragrant. Remove them from the pan and set aside. In the same pan, again add 2 T. of oil, the onions, and garlic, and cook over medium heat until they begin to brown. Add the banana and chopped tomatoes and continue to cook, occasionally mashing the vegetables down with a spoon, until the tomatoes and onion are tender. Add the raisins and remove the pan from the heat. Strain the liquid from the cooked chilies, reserving it, and remove and discard the stems and seeds from them. Add broth to the chili cooking liquid to total 4 cups. In a blender, combine approximately half each of the spice/nut mixture, the veggie/fruit mixture, and the broth. Blend until smooth. Repeat with the remaining mixtures, combining them all in a large saucepan. Brown the bread crumbs slowly in the remaining 2 T. of corn oil. Bring the mole mixture slowly to a boil and then stir in the grated chocolate, brown sugar, crushed tortilla chips, and the bread crumbs. Allow it to simmer and thicken for about 5 minutes. Serve over the sliced or cubed turkey, accompanied by cooked rice. This will make a least 6–8 servings. Extra mole sauce may be sealed in a small container, labeled, and frozen to be used with a couple of months.

Oriental Turkey Soup

Since we've already established turkey to be a Native American bird, this title seems a bit of a misnomer. However, the flavor of the turkey blends well with the other ingredients and will provide you with a nice little contrast from more traditional post Thanksgiving fare. Options for the turkey-broth base include your choice of a cooked or raw turkey thigh, or a meaty turkey carcass including whatever odds and ends of the Thanksgiving bird might still be hanging around.

1 turkey thigh, about 1 lb. or the rough equivalent
    of leftovers
1 large onion, chopped
1 lg. carrot, chopped
2 T. peanut or corn oil
Optional: paprika and salt
12 c. water
1½ t. salt
1½ t. soy sauce
2–3 lg. cloves garlic, peeled and halved
¼ t. red pepper flakes
1–2 t. grated fresh ginger root
1 lg. star anise
5 oz. can of water chestnuts
1 lb. ground turkey
1 t. salt
1 t. grated ginger root
1 egg
½ t. garlic powder
1 bunch scallions, sliced
1 bunch bok choy, chopped
1 c. julienned carrots
8 oz. snow peas, halved lengthwise
Crispy Chinese noodles

If using a raw turkey thigh, season the skin with a bit of salt and paprika. Pour the oil into a Dutch oven set over medium heat. Place the turkey skinside down, in the heated oil, adding the chopped carrot and onion around the edges.

Reduce the heat to medium low, cover the pan, and brown slowly, turning the turkey once and stirring the vegetables as needed. If you are using leftover cooked turkey, brown only the vegetables, adding in the turkey once they are dark golden. Now add the water, garlic cloves, 1–2 t. ginger, star anise, salt, soy sauce, and red pepper flakes. Increase the heat to high until the mixture begins to boil. Again reduce the heat to medium low and allow it to simmer until the turkey is very tender, about an hour. While it is cooking, combine the ground turkey, the drained, diced water chestnuts, 1 t. salt, 1 t. ginger, the egg, one scallion, diced, and garlic powder, mixing well. Form into small meatballs; set aside (refrigerate if for longer than 1 hour). Once the turkey is sufficiently cooked, strain the mixture, putting the broth back in the Dutch oven and discarding the vegetables and spices. Pick the cooled turkey meat from the bones and add it back into the broth. Bring the broth back to boiling and gently add in the turkey meatballs, simmering them for about 10 minutes. I use a measuring teaspoon to form them, which will give you small uniform meatballs. Add the chopped and sliced bok choy, carrots, snow peas, and scallions.

For an intriguing twist on turkey leftovers, how about concocting a pot of Oriental turkey soup?

Bring the soup to a boil, to just tender cook the veggies. Serve it at once, topped with crispy Chinese noodles. This makes quite a bit of soup—enough for a crowd or some to freeze for another day.

Turkey Burgers with Sweet Potato Fries

If you prefer your turkey ground rather than roasted, here's the recipe for you! Turkey burgers are easy to prepare, nutritious, and another little reminder of how versatile and delicious this bird can be. Add the tang of cranberry mayonnaise and the mellow crunch of sweet potato fries for a satisfying light meal.

1 lb. ground turkey

2 T. minced onion

2 T. minced celery

1 t. salt

½ t. poultry seasoning

¼ t. pepper

2 T. oil

4 hamburger or bulky buns, toasted

4 slices tomato, optional

4 leaf lettuce leaves, red or green

½ c. finely shredded red cabbage

4 slices mild cheddar cheese, optional

Sweet Potato Fries

2 sweet potatoes: about 1 lb.

Corn oil for frying

Salt

Pepper

Cranberry Mayonnaise

½ c. cranberry-orange dipping sauce ("May")

½ c. mayonnaise

1 t. grated horseradish, optional

Combine the dipping sauce, horseradish, and mayonnaise, stirring to blend well. Refrigerate until serving time. This is also good with ham or meat loaf sandwiches; or use the dipping sauce as a spread by itself. Trim the sweet potatoes, removing any irregularities. Peel or not, as you wish. Cut them lengthwise into ¼" sticks. Chill them briefly in ice

water while heating 2" of oil in a large, heavy skillet over medium-high heat. Allow the oil to heat up to between 375°–400°. Drain the potatoes, patting them dry with paper towels, and fry them a few at a time until they are golden and tender. Transfer them to a paper towel-lined baking sheet, sprinkle lightly with salt and pepper, and place them in a 200°F oven to stay warm while preparing the rest of the fries.

Combine the turkey, onion, celery, and seasonings, mixing lightly. Form into 4 thin patties and fry in the 2 T. hot oil over medium heat until they are lightly browned on both sides and cooked through. If you're using cheese, top the cooked burgers with a slice each and allow them to hang out, covered, in the skillet with the heat turned off; the cheese should melt from the retained heat. Brown the hamburger buns in a little butter, or broil them until just golden. To assemble, place a burger on each bun, topping with tomato, cabbage, and lettuce. Place a generous swirl of cranberry mayonnaise on the upper bun half before sandwiching everything together. Serve the extra cranberry mayonnaise alongside for dipping the fries in. Add some homemade dill pickles and enjoy a meal for 4!

Roast Duck with Autumn Berry Sauce

In my childhood, our neighbor around the corner was an elderly bachelor who mostly made his living raising poultry and sheep. He also augmented his income by running a trap line along the Ames Hill Brook and off in the swampland adjacent to his property. One year in particular, he had a run of luck with his traps at the same time he had planned to butcher off some ducks he was selling to grace holiday tables. Thrifty New Englander that he was, he skinned the mink from his traps with the same knife he then used to butcher his ducks. Although minks have sleek and lovely pelts, they also have scent glands that are not pleasing to smell, let alone taste. Suffice to say, his customers did not remain loyal. Fortunately, duck purchased from a supermarket, butcher, or farmer more conscious of hygiene than my late neighbor can be a classic fall treat, so don't be afraid to try it! It's one of the easiest birds to roast, since the fat in its skin makes the duck self-basting. The richness of the meat pairs well with a slightly tart berry sauce.

4–5 lb. duckling, giblets and neck removed

1 t. salt

1 small onion, chopped

1 small apple, chopped

If the duck is frozen, allow it to thaw approximately 2 days in your meat keeper, 2–3 hours before you plan to begin roasting it, rinse it well with cold water, removing any extra clumps of fat adhering to the underside of the skin. Pat the duck dry with paper towels and puncture the skin multiple times with a skewer, knife tip, or sharp fork. This will enable the fat to more freely render while it's roasting. Stuff the duck with as many apple and onion chunks as will fit. Sprinkle it with salt, place it in the roasting pan, and allow it to stand, uncovered, in the refrigerator until ready to cook. The salt will begin to draw out moisture and help the duck's skin to crisp up a little better while roasting. Preheat the oven to 375°F and place the uncovered duck in the roasting pan on a middle shelf. Roast it for approximately 30 minutes per pound, basting it occasionally in its own juices, until the internal temperature registers 170°F, or until juices run clear when a knife or fork is inserted into the duck's thigh.

Autumn berries are cooked into a spicy sweet sauce to accompany roast duck.

The skin should appear browned and crispy. Remove the duck from the roasting pan and allow it to rest for about 15 minutes before carving.

Autumn Berry Sauce

This sauce is also good served with chicken, turkey, pork, or rabbit. The salt is optional, although you may prefer that hint of it with the meat. If you do omit it, this sauce is also quite nice with pancakes or French toast.

1 c. blueberries, preferably wild

½ c. cranberries

1 c. orange juice

¼ c. honey

1 T. diced candied ginger

¼ t. allspice

¼ t. salt, optional

2 t. cornstarch

2 T. water

Frozen fruit works just fine for this recipe; another great time to enjoy the largesse from your summer's labor. Combine everything except the cornstarch and water in a small saucepan. Cook over high heat until it comes to a boil. Reduce the heat and boil gently for five minutes, until the cranberries have all popped and the sauce has slightly thickened. If you'd prefer a smoother sauce, carefully place in the blender and run it until smooth. Be cautious if the liquid is too hot; you don't want an exploding blender! Return the sauce to the cooking pan and stir in the combined cornstarch and water. Bring to a boil once more and then remove from the heat. This can be served warm or chilled, although it will pour easier when warm.

Roasted Potatoes

These are especially good with roast beef. My preferred potato for roasting in this manner is a red-skinned variety. The thin skin adds texture and color appeal and the flesh is a nice, mealy consistency. Scrub

your skins well, leaving potatoes whole if small or cutting into halves or quarters. Mixing and matching is fine, as long as you're consistent about size so that they all cook in approximately the same amount of time.

1 lb. prepared red-skinned potatoes

2 T. olive oil

2 T. butter

¼ t. cracked black pepper

½ t. crumbled rosemary

Melt the butter in a 9" × 9" baking pan. Stir in the olive oil, pepper, and rosemary. Add the potatoes, stirring to coat them all evenly. Place in a 375°F oven for approximately 45 minutes, stirring and turning them once or twice. You will notice this recipe does not contain salt; I prefer to add it at the table, as the potatoes will crisp better without it.

Potatoes Au Gratin

There are probably as many ways to prepare potatoes au gratin as there are types of potatoes and cheese with which to prepare it. In the variation here, we're emphasizing Continental flavors such as thyme and garlic, along with the mellowness of Swiss-type cheese. Simmering the raw potato slices a few minutes in the infused milk draws out their natural starches to provide creaminess without added flour. Utilizing a mandolin, food grater, or food processor will enable you to produce the extremely thin slices you'll need for this recipe. Layering cheese and potatoes with the cheese on top will result in a nice-browned crust to top things off.

Peeled russet potatoes, sliced paper-thin,
    to equal 4 c.

¼ c. butter

2 c. milk

1 clove garlic, peeled and halved

¼ t. dried thyme

¼ t. nutmeg

⅛ t. white pepper

2 c. shredded Jarlsburg or Swiss cheese

Melt the butter in a large saucepan over medium heat. Add the milk, garlic, salt, nutmeg, thyme, and white pepper and heat to just under boiling. Add the thinly sliced potatoes, stir to blend, and heat to just boiling. Reduce heat and allow the potatoes to simmer for about 5 minutes. They should turn the milk into a nice creamy consistency but still be a bit crisp. Butter a 6-cup casserole and spread half the potatoes evenly over the bottom. Sprinkle with half the shredded cheese and repeat layers. Place in a preheated 350°F oven for approximately 45 minutes, until the potatoes are fork tender and the top browns nicely. Allow to cool about 5–10 minutes before serving. This will serve 8.

Rich with cheese and butter, potatoes au gratin will enhance a variety of winter meals.

Steaks, Chops, and Roasts to Brag About

JOHN WEISS

Every serious hunter should have a collection of wild game cookbooks. I've written five myself and have more than forty others in my kitchen library that I regularly consult. Understandably, I've experimented with, refined, and even created hundreds of venison recipes over the years. One interesting thing I've learned is that it's more often the cooking method, not the particular selection of ingredients, that determines the outcome.

With that in mind, I'll first describe cooking methods for various cuts of venison, with the actual recipes that follow being of less importance to

Serious hunters who take at least one deer every year, plus assorted other species, should have a library of game cookbooks. This is Jackie Bushman, founder of Buckmasters.

the outcome. That way, no matter which recipe is selected, the meat should turn out tender, flavorful, and delicious.

Roasting is a technique in which a venison roast is placed (fat-side up if draped with bacon or other fat) on a rack in an open, shallow roasting pan. The rack holds the roast out of the grease, and the bacon or other fat dribbles down slowly and bastes the roast as it cooks.

In such cooking, it is imperative that a meat thermometer be used to monitor the progress of the roast. Insert the thermometer so the bulb is in the center of the thickest part of the meat, and make sure that the bulb does not touch bone or the bottom of the pan. A venison roast should be cooked only until it is medium-rare to medium on the inside, with a blush of juicy bright pink to the meat's color. Forget that you may like your beef roasts well done. Venison is not beef!

If you look at your meat thermometer, you'll see a graduated temperature scale paired to the desired "doneness" of various types of meat such as beef, pork, and fowl. Venison won't be listed on the scale, meaning that you have to go by temperature alone, and to achieve a roast that is medium-rare to medium you should cook it until its internal temperature registers 140° to 150°F (by comparison, a well-done beef roast has an internal temperature of 160° to 170°F).

Ideally, your roasting pan should sit on the middle shelf-rack in your oven, and the temperature

Roasts such as rolled shoulder roasts should be cooked only until medium-rare with a blush of pink in the middle. Cook beyond this point, and the venison steadily becomes tougher.

When broiling, as with sirloin tip steaks, whether over coals or under the oven's broiler, use high heat to briefly sear both sides, never allowing the inside to go beyond medium-rare.

dial of the oven should be set at 300° to 350°F, depending upon the size of the roast. Very large roasts (more than six pounds) should be cooked at the lower temperature and mid-size roasts (two to five pounds) at the higher temperature. You should never use a dry-heat cooking method with roasts smaller than two pounds because they will turn out tough and dry, so always use a roast of ample size; if it's larger than what your family can consume at one meal, the leftovers can be served in sandwiches, soups, or stews.

Broiling is another dry-heat cooking method, but this technique is generally reserved for tenderloin steaks, backstrap steaks, or sirloin tip steaks. Steaks to be broiled should be at least three-quarter-inch thick, but not more than one and one-half inches thick. Turn your oven's regulator dial to broil, or to its highest setting (generally, 500°F), and remember that the oven door should be left slightly ajar.

Place your venison steaks on the rack of your broiler pan so the juices can drain away (otherwise, they may flame up) and situate the pan so the meat will be from two to five inches from the heat source. Here is where each cook will have to temper his

decisions with good judgment because the heat output of gas broilers, compared to electric, can vary quite a bit; also, thicker steaks should be placed farther away from the heat than thin ones.

Broil the steaks just until their top sides begin to brown, then flip them and broil on the other side for about one-half the previously allotted time. You may wish to barely slice into one of the steaks to check its progress. Those who broil beef steaks claim this heresy, that cutting into them will allow their juices to escape. True, but in the case of venison this small loss is better than relying purely upon guesswork and perchance allowing the steaks to broil just one minute too long and become overdone.

I advise against cooking a venison steak beyond the point of medium-rare, as this stage is when it's at its best. In cooking outdoors over a propane or charcoal grill, simply use the same method as with beef steaks but, again, never permit the meat to cook beyond medium-rare.

Pan-broiling is a splendid method of cooking steaks, but few people are familiar with it. A heavy, cast-iron skillet or griddle is necessary; it should be sparingly brushed with just a bit of cooking oil. One-half teaspoon of oil should be plenty to prevent the meat from sticking; if you add more than this you are no longer pan-broiling but panfrying.

Lay your steaks in the pan and then cook them over very low heat. Since the meat is in direct contact with the skillet or griddle, it is essential to turn the meat occasionally to ensure even cooking. The steaks are ready to serve when they are slightly brown on both sides and pink and juicy in the middle.

Panfrying is similar to pan-broiling in that a heavy skillet or griddle is used. However, substantially more cooking oil is used and the meat is cooked at a much higher temperature. While pan-broiling is ideally suited to thick steaks, panfrying is best accomplished with thinner steaks that have been floured or breaded.

Panfrying typically results in the outer surfaces and edges of steaks achieving just a bit of crispness, which, depending upon the recipe ingredients in

Pan-broiling (or pan-frying), which can also be done on a griddle, is best reserved for sirloin tip or backstrap steaks. Sprinkle just a bit of salt on the cooking surface and you can reduce the amount of cooking oil by half.

the breading, enhances the flavor of the meat. In achieving this desirable result, there may be some sacrifice of tenderness. So, beforehand, you may desire to treat your meat (especially sirloin tip steaks) to a dose of commercially prepared meat tenderizer.

One thing to guard against in panfrying is a burner temperature that becomes so hot your fat or grease begins to smoke. Another axiom of panfrying is to turn the meat frequently to ensure even cooking but, still again, venison steaks should never be cooked beyond medium.

Finally, one trick that ensures success, no matter which cooking method you decide to use, is that your intended serving platter and dinner plates be preheated. I like to simply slip them into the oven for five minutes before the meal is served.

The necessity of hot dinnerware has to do with the fat content in venison compared to beef. Remember that beef has a good deal of interstitial fat, or marbling, which gets extremely hot during cooking and therefore helps to retain the temperature of the meat long afterwards. Because venison does not have much fat woven between its tissue fibers, it cools quickly.

As a result, if you remove a venison roast from the oven, or steaks from the broiler or skillet, and place the meat on a cold platter straight from the cupboard, and then those seated transfer meat from the platter to their cold dinner plates, you're in for an unpleasant experience. Before anyone is even half finished eating they'll begin remarking upon how their venison is becoming colder and tougher with each bite. A hot serving platter and preheated dinner plates are the answer.

Now let's look at a number of recipes that call for roasting, broiling, panbroiling, or panfrying the tender cuts of venison. Keep in mind that you can vary any of the following recipes, especially those calling for roasts, by first soaking your venison in a marinade.

The tenderloins and backstraps are also perfectly suited to being cubed and then grilled or broiled as shish-kabobs.

Sautéed Steaks or Chops

¼ cup butter (½ stick)
1 teaspoon Lawry's Seasoned Salt
4 inch-thick steaks or chops

Melt the butter in a skillet, then blend in one teaspoon of the seasoned salt. Place the steaks in the pan and cook them slowly over medium heat until they are browned on all sides and pink and juicy in the middle. Serves four.

Spicy Deer Steaks Marinade

flour
3 tablespoons butter
3 tablespoons cooking oil
4 inch-thick steaks or chops

Use a marinade that contains wine, vegetable juice, or citrus juice, pour it over the steaks in a bowl, and refrigerate overnight. Drain and pat dry with paper towels. Flour the steaks well, then panfry in a skillet over medium heat containing the butter and cooking oil. Serves four.

Georgia-Style Steaks

4 steaks or chops
1 cup ketchup
1 tablespoon salt
1 tablespoon chili powder
2 tablespoons tarragon
1 onion, chopped
⅓ cup A-1 Steak Sauce

In a skillet, sear the steaks in just a bit of cooking oil on medium-high heat. Meanwhile, in a saucepan, bring all the remaining ingredients to a boil, stirring continually. Transfer the steaks to a shallow roasting pan, pour the sauce over the top and bake for one and one-half hours at 350°F. Serves four.

Venison Teriyaki

2 pounds tenderloin steak
3 tablespoons olive oil
3 tablespoons soy sauce
½ teaspoon garlic powder
1 tablespoon lemon juice
1 tablespoon brown sugar
2 cups uncooked Minute Rice
1 green bell pepper, sliced into strips
1 sweet white onion, sliced
1 cup sliced mushrooms
1 cup beef broth or bouillon

Slice the tenderloin into thin strips. Add the olive oil and soy sauce to a wok or high-sided skillet, then stir in the garlic, lemon juice, and brown sugar. Heat the wok or skillet on medium-high heat until the liquid begins to steam. Add the tenderloin strips and stir-fry them until they are almost cooked. Meanwhile, prepare the Minute Rice according to the package instructions. Now add to the wok or skillet the green pepper, onion, mushrooms, and broth. Turn the heat down to medium, cover, and slowly cook until everything is steaming. Ladle over a bed of the rice. Serves four.

High-Country Buttermilk Venison

4 backstrap or sirloin tip steaks
1 cup buttermilk
cooking oil
flour

Cut the steaks into one-inch cubes, then pound each with a meat hammer to about one-half-inch thick. Place the meat in a bowl, cover with the buttermilk, and allow the steak to soak for two hours. Then dredge the pieces in flour and panfry. Serves four.

Pepper Steak

4 backstrap or sirloin tip steaks
black pepper
2 tablespoons butter
2 tablespoons olive oil
4 teaspoons brandy

Sprinkle a bit of the pepper on both sides of the steaks and then gently pound it into the meat with a meat hammer. Add the butter and olive oil to a skillet and quickly sear the steaks on both sides. Turn the heat down to low and continue cooking until they are medium-rare. Meanwhile, warm the brandy in a small saucepan. When the steaks are ready, transfer them to a preheated platter. At tableside, pour the brandy over the steaks and ignite it. It will briefly flare up and then burn out. Serves four.

Kate's Venison Cutlets

2 pounds steak meat, ¼-inch thick
1 cup seasoned (salt & pepper) flour
2 eggs
1-½ cups milk

1 cup Italian-seasoned bread crumbs
¼ cup Parmesan cheese
1 teaspoon garlic powder
olive oil
1–10-ounce can whole, cooked asparagus
½ pound crisp bacon, crumble
½ pound sliced Swiss cheese

Preheat oven to 400°F. Dredge the cutlets in the seasoned flour. Dip each into a bowl of blended eggs and milk, then coat with a mixture of the bread crumbs, Parmesan cheese, and garlic powder. Heat one-half inch of olive oil in a skillet and fry the cutlets for one minute on each side. Transfer to paper toweling to briefly drain. Place on a cookie sheet. Place two whole asparagus spears on each cutlet, top with bacon bits and one slice of Swiss cheese. Place in the oven until the cheese melts. Serves six.

–Kate Fiduccia

Cracker-Fried Steaks

4 backstrap or sirloin tip steaks
2 eggs, beaten
1 cup saltine crackers, finely crushed
    cooking oil

Dip each steak into the beaten egg, roll in the cracker crumbs, then pound gently with a meat hammer. Dip the steaks a second time in the egg, then roll again in the cracker crumbs. Fry in the cooking oil until the cracker coating has a toastlike color and appearance, no more! Serves four.

Sirloin Tip Roast

1 - 2½-pound sirloin tip roast
2 cloves garlic, slivered
2 tablespoons Dijon-style mustard
1 tablespoon chopped fresh thyme
½ teaspoon black pepper

Preheat oven to 325°F. Using the tip of a knife, cut small, evenly spaced slits in the roast and insert the garlic slivers. Rub the roast with the mustard, then sprinkle with the thyme and pepper. Place on a roasting pan, then place in the oven until the temperature reads 140° to 145°F. Transfer to a warm serving platter, remove the string ties, and slice thinly. Serves six.

Iron Range Venison Roast

1 3-pound rolled rump or shoulder roast
1 teaspoon fennel seed
1 teaspoon sage
1 teaspoon sugar
1 teaspoon salt
½ teaspoon black pepper

Carefully remove the string ties so you can open the roast. Spread the venison out as much as possible and make numerous scoring cuts across the meat with a knife. In a bowl, blend all the remaining ingredients, then sprinkle evenly over the meat. Roll the meat back up into its original shape and make new string ties. Insert a meat thermometer, drape the roast with bacon, and set in a roasting pan. Roast at 325°F until the internal temperature registers 145°F. Serves six.

Steak Sandwiches

1-½ pounds loin steak meat
cooking oil
1 green bell pepper, sliced
1 sweet white onion, sliced

Slice the tenderloin or backstrap meat thinly, then briefly sear in a frying pan containing a small amount of hot oil. Add the pepper and onion slices, cover, and continue cooking over low heat until the vegetables are cooked but still crisp. Toss briefly and then serve on hard-crusted sandwich rolls or warmed tortilla-fajita wraps. Serves four.

Terrific Pot Roasts and Braised Venison

While the dry-heat cooking methods described in the last chapter are designed chiefly for very tender cuts of venison, moist-heat cooking methods work best for not-so-tender cuts that need a bit of help if they are to provide toothsome fare.

We're referring here to venison cuts from the front legs, such as rolled shoulder roasts, blade roasts, and arm roasts. But we can also include rolled roasts from the neck, and even venison from the otherwise tender rear legs but when taken from an old, grizzled buck that is likely to be on the tough side.

These meals traditionally are done in a pot or deep pan on top of the stove, in the oven, or even in a vessel such as a Crockpot. In any of these cases, the idea is to cook the meat in a closed environment so that steam is trapped and softens the meat's connective tissue. The steam comes from a small amount of liquid added to the cooking vessel in accordance with the particular recipe you're following. Generally the liquid is water, vegetable juice, soup, or wine.

Virtually any cut of venison from the front or back legs, or from the backstraps, is suitable for braising. These are backstrap steaks that have been cooked to tender perfection.

As a rule, pot roasts usually are first browned over high heat in a skillet.

The pot roast is then transferred to a pot along with seasonings and the other ingredients a recipe may call for.

The pot is then covered and transferred to a pre-heated oven, or it can slow-cook on a stovetop burner.

What I especially like about cooking pot roasts or using a braising recipe is that you can often put potatoes, vegetables, and other items right in with the meat, which vastly simplifies meal preparation. And, depending upon the recipe, you frequently obtain a rich, sumptuous gravy as a special bonus. Still other times, only vegetables are added to the meat while it cooks, and the mixture is then served over a bed of potatoes, rice, or noodles.

Five-Minute Pot Roast

1 2-pound shoulder or neck roast
1 cup water
1 envelope dry onion soup mix

This is the fastest, easiest pot roast I know of and, happily, one of the most delicious. Place your roast in the center of a square sheet of heavy-duty aluminum foil and bring the edges up and around the sides to form a pouch. Pour one cup of water over the top of the roast, then sprinkle on the dry soup mix. Now pinch together the edges of the foil to form a tight seal to trap steam, and place the pouch in a shallow roasting pan. Place in a 325°F oven for one and one-half hours. When you open the pouch to slice the meat you'll find it tender beyond belief and, as a special surprise, you'll have a good quantity of perfect gravy you can ladle over noodles or potatoes. As with all venison, remember to serve on a hot platter. Serves four.

German Pot Roast

1 3-pound shoulder or neck roast
2 onions, chopped
1 teaspoon garlic powder
4 tablespoons butter
¼ cup vinegar
1 cup tomato sauce
½ teaspoon poultry seasoning
¼ teaspoon nutmeg

The beauty of pot roasts is that you can throw potatoes and other vegetables right in with the meat to produce a one-pot meal. This one is being prepared in a cast-iron Dutch oven over campfire coals.

1/4 teaspoon cinnamon
1/4 teaspoon allspice

In a skillet, sauté the onions with the garlic powder in the butter, then transfer to a plate where they will stay hot. In the same skillet, sear the roast until it is brown on all sides. Transfer the meat to an oven-proof pot, spoon the onions over the top, pour the vinegar and tomato sauce into the pot, then sprinkle the seasonings on top of the meat. Cover the pot with a lid and cook slowly in a 300°F oven for two hours. After placing the meat on a hot platter and slicing it, pour the juices from the pot over the meat. Serves four (with leftovers for sandwiches the next day).

Pot Roast Elegante

1 2-pound shoulder or neck roast
salt and pepper

1 medium can condensed cream soup
1 onion, sliced

In a skillet, brown the roast on all sides in a bit of cooking oil. Transfer the roast to a pot or oven-tempered glass casserole dish and sprinkle with a bit of salt and pepper. Pour on top of the roast and around the sides a can of condensed soup (cream of mushroom, cream of celery, or some other favorite). Lay the onion slices on top, cover, and slow-cook at 325°F for one and one-half hours. Transfer the roast to a hot platter, slice, then pour the cream gravy from the cooking pot over the top. Serves four.

Pot Roast Italiano

1 2-pound shoulder or neck roast
1 medium can condensed cream soup
½ cup dry red wine
2 tablespoons parsley flakes
½ teaspoon thyme
1 bay leaf, crumbled
salt and pepper

In a skillet, brown the roast on all sides in cooking oil. Transfer the roast to a pot or oven-tempered casserole dish. In a bowl, blend the soup (I like cream of mushroom) with the wine and then pour the mixture over and around the roast. Sprinkle the seasonings on top of the roast, cover, and place in a 325°F oven for one and one-half hours. Transfer the meat to a hot platter, slice, and pour the sauce over the top. Serves four.

Hungarian Pot Roast

1 3-pound shoulder or neck roast
1 large clove garlic
salt and pepper
1 onion, chopped
2 carrots, sliced thick
½ teaspoon oregano
½ teaspoon parsley flakes
1 stalk celery, chopped

1 cup beef broth or bouillon
1 teaspoon Hungarian paprika
½ cup sour cream

Slice the garlic clove into thin slivers, then insert them into thin knife slits made into the roast. Rub the roast with salt and pepper, then brown the roast in a skillet using a bit of oil. Place the roast in a pot and add all the remaining ingredients except the sour cream. Cover the pot and with the stove burner on low heat slowly simmer the roast for one and one-half hours or until it is tender. Transfer the roast to a hot platter and slice, then ladle the vegetables over the meat, using a slotted spoon. Add the sour cream to the broth in the pot, turn the heat up, and cook until the sauce is steaming, then pour over the sliced pot roast. Serves four to six.

All-in-One Pot Roast

1 2-pound shoulder or neck roast
salt and pepper
4 potatoes, cut into large chunks
4 carrots, cut into large chunks
1 can green beans, drained
flour or corn starch, as needed

In a skillet or deep pan, sear the roast on all sides until it is brown, then transfer to a pot. Pour hot water into the pot until it comes up halfway on the side of the roast. Sprinkle with salt and pepper, cover the pot with a lid and begin slow cooking with the stove burner heat turned on low. After forty-five minutes of simmering, place the potato chunks in the pot. After another thirty minutes, add the carrots and green beans. Continue to simmer until the vegetables are tender. Transfer the meat to a hot platter and slice. Use a slotted spoon to transfer the vegetables to a hot dish. Then thicken the gravy with just a bit of flour or cornstarch and pour over the pot roast slices. Serves four.

Creamed Sirloin Tips

2 pounds sirloin tip steak
meat tenderizer
1 onion, finely chopped
2 tablespoons butter
½ cup water
2 tablespoons flour
½ cup sour cream
1 4-ounce can mushrooms

Sprinkle meat tenderizer over the steak meat, then gently pound it into the meat with the sharp edge of a meat hammer. In a skillet, sauté the onions in the butter until they are clear. Now use a knife to cut the sirloin tip steaks into triangular- shaped wedges and sear these in the skillet, over medium heat, with the onion until the venison is brown on all sides. Reduce the heat to low, add one-half cup water, cover the pan, and slowly simmer for half an hour. Meanwhile, stir the flour into the sour cream. When the meat is tender, add the cream mixture and mushrooms to the skillet, cover, and allow to slowly bubble for another twenty minutes. The creamed sirloin tips can be served as-is, or ladled over a bed of noodles. Serves four.

Venison Scaloppini

2 pounds round steak
6 tablespoons olive oil
2 teaspoons garlic powder
1 12-ounce can tomatoes
1 teaspoon oregano
1 teaspoon parsley flakes
1 teaspoon salt
½ teaspoon black pepper
4 slices mozzarella cheese

Cut the round steaks into four equal portions. In a skillet, blend the garlic power into the olive oil, then brown the steaks on both sides over medium-high heat. Add the tomatoes and sprinkle the

In braising venison, the meat is first seared on both sides in a pan. The temperature is then reduced to a slow-bubble, other ingredients are added, and then the pan covered and allowed to simmer on low heat.

seasonings over the tops of the steaks. Reduce the heat to low, cover the pan, and slowly simmer for forty-five minutes. Spoon the tomatoes and juices into an oven-proof platter, arrange the steaks on top, then lay a slice of mozzarella cheese on top of each of the steaks. Slide the dinner platter into an oven preheated to 400 °F until the cheese is melted and just beginning to brown. Serves four.

Venison Swiss Steak

½ teaspoon salt
¼ teaspoon black pepper
flour
2 pounds round or sirloin tip steak
1 cup cooking oil
1 green pepper, chopped
2 onions, sliced
1 8-ounce can tomatoes with liquid

Blend the salt and pepper with flour, then gently pound the mixture into both sides of your steak with a meat hammer. Now cut the meat into four equal portions. In a skillet containing several tablespoons of oil, brown the meat on both sides. Add the pepper, onion, and tomatoes (with packing juice), cover the pan, reduce the heat to low, and

slowly simmer for one hour. Check after one-half hour and add a bit of water to the pan if necessary. Serves four.

Barbecued Round Steak

2 tablespoons butter
2 tablespoons cooking oil
1 onion, chopped
2 stalks celery, chopped
2 pounds round steak
barbeque sauce
1 cup beef broth or bouillon
2 tablespoons brown sugar
4 tablespoons Worcestershire sauce
1 medium can tomato soup

Blend the butter and cooking oil in a skillet and sauté the onion and celery, then set aside briefly. In the same skillet, brown the round steak. In a separate saucepan, add all the remaining ingredients and simmer for 15 minutes. Place the browned steak in a deep casserole dish, spoon the sautéed onions and celery over the top, then pour the barbecue sauce over all. Cook, uncovered, for one and one-half hours in a 350°F oven. Serves four.

Sumptuous Soups, Stews, and Casseroles

Soups and stews with venison as the main ingredient undoubtedly date back to the first primitive uses of fire and food cooked in clay vessels. However, it wasn't until the medieval 14th-century reign of King Henry that "stuwe" acquired its official name to identify the nature of the feast.

Some cooks proclaim that a stew is nothing more than a thick soup. Others say soup is nothing more than a thin stew. But there are differences worth noting. There are also many similarities, and there truly is no such thing as an original or secret recipe. By simply adding a pinch of thyme, subtracting the celery, splashing the pot with just

Is a stew really only a thick soup, or is a soup really only a thin stew? The debate goes on, but in either case venison is one of the most popular main ingredients.

Casseroles generally are stew-like concoctions baked in the oven, often with a topping of breadcrumbs or biscuits. Hearty stews are terrific one-pot meals. Leftovers re-heat easily and freeze well.

a hint of sherry, or doing any number of countless other small things, we could concoct supposedly "new" recipes until the end of time.

Incidentally, casseroles loosely fit into the category of stews, and so they'll also be included in this chapter. By definition, a casserole is a very thick stew with a basis of rice, noodles, or potatoes, but unlike a stew, which is generally prepared in a pot on a stove burner, a casserole is prepared in a glass or earthenware vessel and baked in one's oven.

But let's first get back to soups and stews and the main differences between them. For one, the typical assortment of vegetables comprising a soup are generally diced while those going into stews are generally cubed or chunked. The reason for this is that soups traditionally are made on short notice and designed to be eaten just as quickly. Hence, you want to speedily combine all of the ingredients.

Stews, on the other hand, are long-term love affairs that are best eaten only after hours of slow simmering. Consequently, the use of small, diced vegetables, as in soups, would see the stew transform

itself into mush; thick hunks of vegetables hold together longer to give the stew body and integrity.

Another difference between soups and stews is that soups typically have a broth color ranging from semi-clear to amber, while stews usually reveal a rich, dark, gravy-like color. The reason for this is that in preparation of soup the venison chunks are either placed in the soup pot raw to steamcook, or they are just briefly seared in a bit of cooking oil before going into the pot. But in preparation of stew, the venison chunks are usually first dredged with seasoned flour and then browned in a skillet.

Finally, don't make the mistake of using your most tender cuts of venison in soups or stews. The lengthy cooking period, especially with stews, which is necessary to harmonize the flavors of their various components, will turn already tender cuts of venison into soft, limp meat lacking any substance. Instead, use tougher cuts that will hold together through the duration of the cooking and only later become tender.

Last, there are two other important points. Never allow a soup or stew to come to a rolling boil because this will cause the meat to shrink, the

Hearty stews are terrific one-pot meals. Leftovers re-heat easily and freeze well.

vegetables to wilt, and the spices to commit suicide. What you want is an almost arthritic simmer, which reveals faint wisps of steam as tiny bubbles barely pop on the surface. And never allow soups or stews to cook so long that their liquid content begins to

Virtually any combination of vegetables can be used to create a soup or stew. As a rule, stews cook longer, so vegetables should be cut into chunks; soups are cooked more quickly, so vegetables should be diced.

Don't use your most tender cuts of venison for soup or stew because they'll fall apart. Use the tougher cuts from the front legs and neck: the slow-cooking process will tenderize them and their coarser texture will hold them together. The first step with nearly all recipes is to dust the meat chunks with flour and then brown them in a skillet.

evaporate significantly. If this happens, adding a bit of water, stock or wine is the usual remedy.

Stormy Weather Soup

1 pound venison, cubed
3 carrots, diced
4 potatoes, diced
2 onions, diced
2 bell peppers, diced
1 large can tomatoes
3 celery stalks, diced
1 large can V-8 Juice

Stews are traditionally served as complete evening meals while soups are usually served as quick, high-energy lunches accompanied by breads or crackers. But it's not necessary to become a conformist; do as you like.

2 tablespoons Worcestershire sauce
2 teaspoons Tabasco sauce
salt and pepper to taste

In a skillet, brown the venison cubes in a bit of oil, then transfer to a large pot. Cover the meat with cold water, then add the remaining ingredients and slowly simmer for one hour. Serves four.

Venison Minestrone

4 cups dry pinto beans
water 1-½ pounds venison, cubed
1 large onion, chopped
6 carrots, chopped
6 stalks celery, chopped
6 tablespoons olive oil
1 large can tomatoes
3 potatoes, cubed
2 teaspoons garlic powder

2 tablespoons basil
½ cup parsley, chopped
½ cup macaroni, cooked
½ head cabbage, chopped
Parmesan cheese

Place the beans in a deep bowl, completely cover with cold water, and allow to soak overnight. Simmer the meat in one quart of cold water until it is tender, then refrigerate overnight. The following day, drain the beans and add them to the pot containing the venison and broth and simmer two hours or until the beans are tender. Meanwhile, in a deep skillet, sauté the onion, carrots, and celery in the olive oil. When the vegetables are fully cooked, add the can of tomatoes and simmer until the liquid is almost evaporated, then add this skillet of vegetables to the soup pot along with three quarts of water. Allow the soup to simmer for one hour, then add the potatoes, garlic, basil, and parsley and allow to simmer for one hour longer. Just before serving, stir the macaroni and cabbage into the soup, cover and let sit for at least five minutes. After ladling the soup into bowls, sprinkle about one tablespoon grated Parmesan cheese on top of each. Serves four (with plenty left over that can be frozen for another meal).

Savory Bean Soup

1 pound venison, cubed
1 8-ounce can tomato sauce
1 large can tomatoes
2 tablespoons dried onion flakes
10 cups water
1 medium can red kidney beans
½ teaspoon chili powder
2 teaspoons salt
½ cup uncooked Minute Rice
½ cup shredded American cheese

Add all of the ingredients, except the rice and cheese, to a deep pot and simmer on low heat for one hour. Five minutes before serving, stir in the rice. Ladle the soup into bowls, then sprinkle the cheese on top of each. Serves four generously.

Venison Cider Stew

2 pounds venison, cubed

1 teaspoon dried onion flakes

2 teaspoons salt

¼ teaspoon thyme

¼ teaspoon nutmeg

3 potatoes, cut into chunks

4 carrots, cut into chunks

1 apple, chopped

1 cup apple cider

Brown the venison in a skillet in a bit of oil, sprinkling on the onion, salt, thyme, and nutmeg while stirring continually. Transfer the seasoned meat to a crockpot or stew pot, add the vegetables and apple, then pour the cider over the top. Slow-cook on low heat for at least three hours. If too much of the liquid begins to evaporate, replenish it with a mixture of one-half cup water blended with one-half cup cider. Serves four.

Venison-Mushroom Stew

1-½ pounds venison, cut into chunks

seasoned flour

2 tablespoons olive oil

1 teaspoon salt

½ teaspoon black pepper

2 medium onions, quartered

5 potatoes, cubed

3 stalks celery, cut into wide slices

2 green peppers, sliced

2 carrots, cut into wide slices

3, 4-ounce cans of mushrooms, liquid discarded

1 can mushroom soup

Toss the venison chunks in seasoned flour and brown in a skillet with olive oil. Place the meat in a crockpot. Add the remaining ingredients, except the mushroom soup. Cover the ingredients with water and cook for three hours. If the water begins to evaporate, add a little more. About thirty minutes before done, add the mushroom soup and stir in thoroughly. Serve over hot white rice or buttered noodles.

–Kate Fiduccia

Winter Day Stew

2 pounds venison, cubed

¼ cup bacon drippings

1 onion, cut into chunks

2 carrots, cut into chunks

2 stalks celery, cut into chunks

1, 4-ounce can mushrooms

3 potatoes, cut into chunks

2 medium cans beef or chicken broth

1 cup port wine

2 tablespoons Worcestershire sauce

1 teaspoon brown sugar

½ teaspoon cloves

½ teaspoon cinnamon

In a skillet, brown the venison and onion in the bacon drippings. Transfer the onion and venison to a stew pot, add the remaining ingredients and simmer three hours. If the stew becomes too thick, add more broth or wine. Serves five generously.

Deer-Me Casserole

2 pounds venison, cubed

1 medium can condensed cream of mushroom soup

1 cup canned tomatoes, with juice

1 envelope dry onion soup mix

½ cup seasoned bread crumbs

Arrange the meat cubes in the bottom of a casserole dish, then pour the mushroom soup (undiluted) over the top. Sprinkle the onion soup mix, then pour the tomatoes and juice over the top. Cover the dish and bake at 325°F for two hours.

During the final fifteen minutes of cooking, remove the cover from the dish and sprinkle the top of the casserole with the breadcrumbs. Continue baking until the breadcrumbs are nicely browned. Serves four.

Venison Stroganoff

½ cup butter

1 teaspoon garlic powder

1-½ pounds venison, cubed

1 cup flour

1 onion, chopped

1 tablespoon salt

¼ teaspoon black pepper

1-½ cups water

1 cup fresh mushrooms

1-¼ cups sour cream

In a skillet, melt the butter and then stir in the garlic powder. Flour the venison chunks and then brown them in the skillet. Add the onion, salt, and pepper, then stir in the water, cover the pan, and simmer slowly for forty-five minutes. Now add the mushrooms and sour cream and continue to cook another fifteen minutes, but do not allow the sauce to come to a boil. Traditionally, stroganoff is served over a bed of thick Pennsylvania Dutch noodles, but for variety you can use thin oriental noodles or rice. Serves four.

West Texas Venison Casserole

2 pounds round steak or sirloin tip steak

¼ cup flour

1 teaspoon salt

½ teaspoon black pepper

¼ cup bacon drippings

1 stalk celery, chopped

3 onions, sliced

2 tablespoons Worcestershire sauce

2 cups tomatoes, with juice

1 8-ounce package wide noodles

Cut the venison into four or six equal pieces, then dredge in a mixture of the flour, salt, and pepper. Brown the meat on all sides in a high-sided skillet containing the bacon fat. Add the celery and onions and continue cooking over low heat until the onions are clear. Add the other ingredients, except noodles, cover the pan, and cook slowly for one and one-half hours or until the meat is tender. Prepare the noodles according to the package instructions. Then place the noodles on a hot serving platter, carefully lay the venison pieces on top, then pour the sauce from the pan over the top. Serves four.

Cheddar-Noodle Casserole

1 pound venison, cut into cubes

1 stick margarine

1 small onion, minced

1 4-ounce can mushrooms, with liquid

1 teaspoon Worcestershire sauce

1 bay leaf, crumbled

1 8-ounce package noodles

1 cup milk

1 teaspoon salt

¼ teaspoon black pepper

½ cup grated cheddar cheese

1 cup seasoned croutons

In a skillet, brown the venison cubes in two tablespoons of the margarine, then stir in the minced onion and cook over low heat until it is clear. Drain the mushrooms and set aside, pouring the packing juice from the mushroom can into the skillet with the meat and onions. Add the Worcestershire sauce and bay leaf, stir well, cover the pan, and simmer on low heat for thirty minutes. Prepare the noodles according to the package instructions, then drain. Stir the remaining margarine into the hot noodles until it is melted, then add the venison cubes, pan juices, milk, salt, and pepper. Transfer to a buttered casserole dish, then sprinkle the cheddar cheese

Although casseroles are stew-like concoctions, they're unique in that venison burger is usually used instead of meat chunks, and some type of pasta is added such as rice or noodles.

on top. Now sprinkle the croutons on top. Bake at 325°F for one hour. Serves four.

Hunter's Favorite Pie

2 pounds venison, cubed

2 tablespoons butter

2 onions, diced

1 teaspoon garlic powder

1 large can tomatoes

1 tablespoon paprika

½ teaspoon red cayenne pepper

1 bay leaf, crumbled

¼ teaspoon thyme

1 cup beer

3 carrots, sliced thinly

1 package frozen peas

1 tube biscuits

In a skillet, brown the venison in the butter. Then stir in the onions, garlic powder, tomatoes, seasonings, and beer. Cover the pan and simmer slowly for one hour. Stir in the carrots and peas, cover, and simmer fifteen minutes longer. Transfer the mixture to a deep casserole dish and arrange biscuits on top. Now bake at 400°F for fifteen minutes or until the biscuits are nicely browned. Serves four.

What To Do With All That Burger and Sausage

Of all meat products grown in this country, hamburger is the most widely consumed. According to the American Beef Council, every adult consumes an average of thirty-one pounds of hamburger per year in one form or another. Deerburger is equally versatile. And because it's lower in fat and cholesterol than beef, it's more healthy. Use deerburger in any manner in which you'd use hamburger.

Although not as widely used as burger, bulk venison sausage and links also are popular in hunting households. Our favorite uses for them are included in this chapter, as well.

Before offering specific burger recipes, we should point out a few important aspects of using this particular ground meat. First, because of its fat content (which we added at grinding time, usually in the form of suet), it is not necessary to add any cooking oil to a skillet or griddle before frying burgers. It is wise, though, to sprinkle just a bit of salt onto your cooking surface, as this will prevent the meat from sticking and scorching until the fat in the meat has had a chance to render-out slightly for the remainder of the frying.

Second, most grocery stores and meat markets that grind burger use the tougher cuts of beef. Likewise, hunters commonly use scraps, trimmings, and tougher cuts in their burger. But many hunters also commonly use their most tender cuts of venison, throwing into the burger-to-be pile pieces of rump meat and end-cuts from backstraps. This can result in burger that is so tender it may begin to fall apart in the pan. This poses no problem if you're merely browning the meat before adding it to spaghetti sauce, chili, and the like, but it's annoying when you're trying to fry deerburgers.

The solution is to add some type of flavorless binder to the burger just before forming the burger patties with your hands. The best binder combination I've come across is one slice of fresh, crumbled bread, an egg, and a bit of cold water for every one pound of burger. Add the burger and binding ingredients to a bowl and knead them together with your hands; then make each individual burger patty in the usual way.

If your family begins to tire of deerburgers prepared in the customary manner, try adding a little flare to your burgers. Before forming them into

Some hunters have been known to push their entire deer through a meat grinder. But even if you grind only the tougher cuts, scraps, and trimmings, you'll still have upwards of forty pounds of burger and sausage.

Venison burgers, especially when a fancy recipe such as Burgers Al Fresco is used, produce eventful meals to be proud of.

patties ready for the skillet, add a splash or two of Worcestershire sauce, A-1 steak sauce, or barbecue sauce, kneading it thoroughly into the meat. For still different variations of burgers, knead into the ground meat a bit of finely chopped sweet onion and garlic powder, or a combination of sweet basil and thyme. One of the simplest and yet most delectable ways to enjoy your burgers is to sprinkle them with nutmeg while they're frying for a unique nutty flavor.

Other popular uses for all that deerburger you've created include the following:

Venison Burgers Al Fresco

1 pound deerburger
1 egg, slightly beaten
½ cup sharp cheddar cheese, shredded
¼ cup fresh broccoli, finely chopped
1 teaspoon Worcestershire sauce
1 clove garlic, finely chopped
1 tablespoon onion, finely chopped

Mix all ingredients together and make into four patties and fry or grill for five to six minutes per side. Serves four.

–Kate Fiduccia

Venison Meatloaf

1-½ pounds deerburger

2 slices fresh bread, crumbled

2 eggs

1 8-ounce can tomato sauce

1/2 cup onion, chopped

1-½ teaspoons salt

1 medium bay leaf, crumbled

dash thyme

dash marjoram

In a bowl, combine all ingredients and knead together with your hands. Dump the works into a bread pan and tap to settle the contents. Bake at 350°F for one hour. Serves four.

Deerburger Chili

2 pounds deerburger

1 green pepper, chopped

2, 16-ounce cans red kidney beans, with liquid

2, 12-ounce cans whole tomatoes with liquid

1 tablespoon red cayenne pepper

2 tablespoons garlic powder

1 teaspoon ground cumin powder

4 tablespoons chili powder

2 bay leaves, crumbled

Brown the deerburger in a skillet, then spoon off the grease. Add the burger and remaining ingredients to a deep pot along with one quart of cold water. Slowly simmer on low heat for two hours. Serves eight.

Venison Meatballs, Noodles, and Gravy

1-½ pounds deerburger

3 slices fresh white bread

2 teaspoons salt

¼ teaspoon black pepper

⅛ teaspoon basil

⅛ teaspoon oregano

⅔ cup chopped onion

¼ cup butter

1 10-ounce package wide noodles

1 cup milk

1 tablespoon flour

Crumble the bread and knead it into the deerburger with the salt, pepper, basil, oregano, and onion. Now form one-inch-diameter meatballs with your fingers. Place the meatballs on a cookie sheet and chill in your refrigerator for one hour, then brown the meatballs in a skillet containing the butter, turning them frequently. Reduce the heat under the skillet to low, cover with a lid, and let the meatballs continue to cook slowly for another fifteen minutes. Meanwhile, cook the noodles according to the package instructions, then drain. Transfer the meatballs from the skillet to a plate in your oven to keep them hot. Add to the drippings in the skillet the milk and just a pinch of the flour at a time, constantly stirring on medium-high heat until it turns into a rich gravy. Add the meatballs to the gravy, stir gently, then ladle over the top of the bed of noodles on a hot platter. Serves four generously.

Venison Goulash

1 4-ounce package wide noodles

1 pound deerburger

1 onion, chopped

½ cup ketchup

3 stalks celery, chopped

1 4-ounce can sliced mushrooms

1 14-ounce can tomatoes, with liquid

2 teaspoons salt

½ teaspoon black pepper

Cook the noodles according to the package instructions. Meanwhile, brown the deerburger in a skillet. Drain off the grease, then add the onions and continue cooking until they are clear. Stir in the cooked, drained noodles, ketchup, celery, mushrooms, tomatoes, salt, and pepper. Cover the skillet with a lid and simmer on very low heat for one-half hour. Serves four.

Chicago!

1 pound deerburger

2 teaspoons butter

2, 8-ounce cans tomato sauce

½ teaspoon salt

½ teaspoon Worcestershire sauce

1 8-ounce package cream cheese

1 8-ounce carton small-curd cottage cheese

¼ cup sour cream

1 green pepper, chopped

¼ cup scallions, minced

1 6-ounce package wide noodles

In a skillet, melt the butter over medium heat and brown the deerburger, then spoon off grease. Stir in the tomato sauce, salt, and Worcestershire sauce, and allow to simmer on very low heat. In a separate bowl, blend the cream cheese, cottage cheese, and

Grill venison sausages the same way you would those made of beef or pork. They're also terrific when added to casseroles.

sour cream, then stir in the green pepper and a bit of the scallions. Prepare the noodles according to the package instructions, then drain. Stir the noodles into the cheese blend. Butter the inside of a casserole dish, then spread the noodle-cheese mixture in the bottom. Spoon the meat and tomato sauce on top of the noodles and sprinkle with the remaining scallions. Bake at 350°F for forty-five minutes. Serves four generously.

Favorite Ways to Cook Sausage

Venison sausage, whether in bulk form, links, or rings, can be cooked and served exactly the same as you would their beef or pork counterparts purchased at your grocery store.

To make sausage sandwiches, form patties from bulk sausage and fry as you would burgers, then serve on sandwich rolls. As a pleasing variation of this, melt two tablespoons of butter in a skillet. Then knead into the equivalent of each intended sausage patty one egg, one teaspoon of water, and one-quarter teaspoon parsley flakes. Form into patties and fry in the usual way. When the sausage patties are almost done, top each with a slice of mild cheddar cheese and cover the pan briefly. When the cheese is melted, serve each sausage patty between two slices of buttered rye toast.

When using sausage links or ring sausage for sandwiches, I like to fry them slowly on low heat and, when they are cooked all the way through, slice them lengthwise and serve in Italian buns with a heap of green pepper strips and onion slices that have been seared in a bit of olive oil.

Link and ring sausage can also be slow-cooked in a skillet, refrigerated, sliced thin, and served as hors d'oeuvres with assorted cheeses and crackers.

Try these favorite recipes:

Sausage Supreme

1 pound bulk sausage

1 onion, chopped

2 teaspoons Worcestershire sauce

1 teaspoon garlic powder

3 carrots, grated

1 8-ounce package "curly" noodles

1 can condensed cream of mushroom soup

½ cup Parmesan cheese

In a skillet, brown the sausage, pour off the grease, then stir in the onion and Worcestershire sauce. When the mixture begins to bubble, stir in the garlic powder, then turn off the heat. Prepare the noodles according to the package instructions, then drain. Now stir the noodles, sausage mix, carrots, and soup together until they are well blended. Pour into a buttered casserole dish and bake in a 350°F oven for twenty minutes. During the final four minutes of cooking, sprinkle the Parmesan cheese over the top. Serves four.

Country Casserole

1 pound bulk sausage

1 onion, chopped

1 green pepper, chopped

1 16-ounce can baked beans

1 8-ounce package elbow macaroni

½ cup tomato juice

½ teaspoon salt

½ cup grated mild cheddar cheese

In a skillet, brown the sausage in a bit of cooking oil, spoon off grease, then stir in the onion and green pepper and continue to cook on low heat until they are tender. Meanwhile, cook the macaroni according to the package instructions, and drain. Blend the macaroni and sausage mix, then transfer to a large casserole dish. Stir in the beans, tomato juice, and salt. Mix thoroughly. Bake in a 400°F oven for twenty minutes until the casserole begins to bubble. Then sprinkle the cheddar cheese on top and bake five minutes longer. Serves four.

Espagnole

8 large sausage links

3 cups white rice, cooked, keep warm

¼ cup chopped onion

¼ cup chopped green pepper

1 12-ounce can tomatoes, drained

1-½ teaspoons salt

½ teaspoon black pepper

Fry the sausage links in a skillet containing a bit of oil until they are thoroughly cooked. Remove the sausage links from the pan and slice them into half-inch thick "rounds." Add the onion and green pepper to the drippings in the pan and cook until the onion is clear. Now stir in all the remaining ingredients and cook, uncovered, over low heat for fifteen minutes. Serves four.

Venison Ragout

8 large sausage links

1 cup chopped onion

½ teaspoon garlic powder

1 green pepper, cut into half-inch strips

1 12-ounce can tomatoes, drained

2 tablespoons paprika

¼ teaspoon black pepper

½ teaspoon salt

Gently fry the sausage links until they are thoroughly cooked, then cut them into one-half-inch thick "rounds." In the same pan, sauté with the onions and garlic powder until the onions are clear. Add the green pepper, tomatoes, sausage pieces, and seasonings. Cover and simmer over low heat for thirty minutes. Meanwhile, prepare a bed of boiled new potatoes, white or brown rice, or noodles, and transfer to a hot serving platter, then ladle the ragout on top. Serves four.

I hope you will find butchering and preparing your own venison to be a satisfying way to enjoy nature's bounty. May it bring many scrumptious meals to your family and friends.

The Second Best Part of Turkey Hunting

RICHARD P. COMBS

"I went to the woods because I wished to live deliberately, to front only the essential facts of life, and see if I could not learn what it had to teach, and not, when I came to die, discover that I had not lived."

— Henry David Thoreau, Walden, 1854

That would be eating the turkey, of course. Wild turkey is superior to any farm-raised turkey, with a flavor that is fuller and at the same time more subtle and complex. Two caveats apply to the preparation of wild turkey, regardless of the cooking method. First, as with any game, proper preparation begins in the field. That means cooling the bird down as quickly as possible. Hanging the turkey by one leg in a shady area for fifteen or twenty minutes will cool it considerably. If it will be more than two hours or so before the bird can be fully cleaned, eviscerating it in the field is a good idea. Pluck some feathers around the vent, carefully make a cut between the vent and the sternum, then slice down toward the vent and cut a hole around it, removing the intestines and taking care not to cut them or tear them open.

Second, wild turkeys are not self-basting. If they get dry, they become tough and flavorless. Preventing this does not require extraordinary measures, but wild turkeys require a little more attention than do their domestic counterparts, which stay moist because they are fat or because they have had oils or fats injected into them.

For reasons that mystify me, it is common to smoke, barbecue, marinade, or heavily spice wild turkey; my own belief is that the wild turkey's delicate flavor may be judiciously enhanced or complemented, but it is doubtful it can be improved upon. With that in mind, here are some recipes that I believe best bring out the naturally delicious flavor of wild turkeys.

The first two recipes will impress any dinner guests, and they're easy to make. They involve classic

Deep frying whole turkeys, a traditional method in the South, keeps turkeys juicy and makes for a golden brown, appetizing presentation. It's also quick and easy.

crepes, so we'll start with a basic recipe for those. Keep in mind that after it is made, crepe batter can be stored in the refrigerator for at least two days, and can be thinned as needed with milk. Finished crepes can be refrigerated or frozen. It is not necessary to put waxed paper or similar materials between crepes, but they are easier to separate if they are offset, and not stacked precisely atop one another.

Classic Crepes
INGREDIENTS

2 eggs
2 tablespoons melted butter
1-⅓ cups milk
1 cup flour
dash of salt

Place all the ingredients in a blender in the order listed, and blend on high for about 25 seconds. Scrape batter down the sides of the blender and blend for a few more seconds. Prepare a crepe pan (a small, 6- or 7-inch skillet will work) by seasoning or using no-stick spray shortening. Put ½ teaspoon of butter in the pan for the first crepe only. The crepe batter should not be too thin, but should run freely enough to cover the bottom of the pan when about 3 tablespoons of batter are poured in and the pan is tilted. (If you pour in too much, the excess can be poured back out. If the entire crepe pours out of the pan, the temperature is not yet high enough.) The temperature is right when a crepe will cook on one side in one minute or so. Color should be tan or pale brown, not dark.

When it begins to get crisp around the edges, loosen it with a spatula, pick up an edge carefully with your fingers, and flip it. Don't worry if there is a flap; it won't show when the crepe is rolled. If it tears when you lift it, it's not ready to turn.

If the pan sticks, wipe it with a paper towel and put butter or more non-stick spray shortening on it. If this is your first time making crepes, you might need to experiment a little to get the temperature and consistency of the batter just right, but soon you'll be turning them out like a pro. This recipe should make about a dozen 6-inch crepes.

Wild Turkey and Broccoli Crepes

You won't find this recipe anywhere else. I won't claim to have invented it. Like most recipes, I suppose, it evolved over time; in this case an adaptation of an earlier recipe for a more common fowl, with a slight change here, an addition there. Serve it with a crisp white wine.

INGREDIENTS

1-½ cups grated sharp cheddar cheese
8 crepes
Salt and pepper
3 tablespoons butter
2 cups cooked, cubed turkey
3 tablespoons flour
8 tablespoons sour cream
1-½ cups milk
8 pieces cooked broccoli
2 tablespoons Worcestershire
Parmesan cheese

Melt butter in saucepan over medium heat, add flour and stir, cooking about 2 minutes. Add milk slowly and stir until thick, then add Worcestershire, cheese, salt and pepper lightly. Add turkey cubes. Mix thoroughly.

Spread each crepe with a tablespoon of sour cream, and place a spear of broccoli on sour cream, cover with turkey and sauce, roll up crepe, and place in a buttered or seasoned ovenproof serving dish. Sprinkle Parmesan cheese over the crepes, and bake in oven 375° F for 10 to 15 minutes. Serves 4.

Note: *If the pan sticks, wipe it with a paper towel and put butter or more non-stick spray shortening on it.*

Turkey Mushroom Water Chestnut Crepes

This is NOT how the pilgrims served turkey—but what did they know? You'll need a wine sauce for this recipe, but it's quick and easy:

WINE SAUCE INGREDIENTS

¼ cup butter
¼ cup flour
¼ cup dry sherry or dry vermouth
2 cups milk
1 tablespoon Worcestershire sauce
Salt and white pepper

Melt the butter over medium heat and add flour, stirring 2 minutes. Slowly stir in sherry, milk, Worcestershire, salt and pepper, until sauce thickens. Keep warm.

FILLING INGREDIENTS

8 crepes, above
¼ cup chopped pimientos
Wine sauce
4 water chestnuts, diced
¼ cup butter
2 cups diced cooked turkey
2 cups sliced button mushrooms
Paprika
6 green onions/scallions, slice thinly

Melt butter in skillet, add mushrooms, and sauté for 4 minutes. Add onions and cook until translucent-about 3 minutes. Add pimientos, water chestnuts, and turkey. Add enough wine sauce to moisten, then fill each crepe with turkey mixture. Roll and put in buttered oven-proof serving dish, top with rest of wine sauce, sprinkle with paprika. Bake for 10 minutes at 375°F. If desired, turn on broiler after baking to brown top lightly. Serves 4.

Wine-Braised Wild Turkey

Coq Au Vin is a classic French dish. This recipe substitutes wild turkey for chicken. Don't be intimidated by the long list of ingredients—this dish is as simple as adding ingredients to the pot and cooking. First, fillet turkey breasts and cut into serving-size cutlets.

Melt 3 tablespoons of butter, then add and brown:

¼ lb. minced salt pork
½ cup pearl onions
3 minced shallots
1 carrot, sliced
1 peeled garlic clove
Add turkey and brown, then stir in:
2 tablespoons flour
2 tablespoons parsley, minced
½ bay leaf
1 tablespoons marjoram
½ teaspoon thyme
Dash salt
⅛ teaspoon pepper
Add and stir in:
1-½ cups dry red wine
Cook over low heat, covered, for about 1 hour, then add:
⅓ to ½ lb. sliced mushrooms
Cook mushrooms for 5 minutes or so, skim off excess fat from salt pork, then serve turkey topped with sauce and other ingredients.

Simply Stuffed Wild Turkey

Everyone has a favorite turkey stuffing, but sometimes the simplest recipe is the best.

INGREDIENTS

1 dressed wild turkey
3 sliced apples
Lemon juice
½ cup chopped celery
⅓ cup butter
½ cup vegetable oil
3 tablespoons flour
Salt and pepper

Clean turkey thoroughly with cold water, rub salt and pepper on inside of bird. Melt butter and stir in flour and pepper to make a paste. Spread paste over turkey. Stuff turkey with apples and celery, and tie.

Baste frequently with vegetable oil and lemon juice mixture. Roast about 2 hours, depending on size of the bird.

Wild Rice Turkey Soup

Here's one excellent way to use leftover turkey, or the parts that are often discarded.

INGREDIENTS

Turkey legs, neck, giblets, or carcass with meat
4 cups cooked wild rice
¼ onion, chopped
9 cups water
2 carrots, chopped
Pinch of parsley
Bay leaf
½ teaspoon thyme
Salt and pepper

Cut carcass apart, and place in a pot with water. Bring to boil. Add rest of ingredients except rice. Simmer two hours.

Remove carcass from water, strip meat, and put back into soup. Skim fat from surface. Add rice. Simmer another 20 minutes. Leftovers freeze well.

Cream-Roasted Turkey

Season it lightly and serve it by candlelight with a full-bodied Chardonnay if you wish, but it's hard to beat with biscuits and beer in a cabin after a cool, rainy spring day of turkey hunting.

INGREDIENTS

Dressed turkey
Butter
Flour
Cream
Salt and pepper

Cut turkey into serving sizes, rinse and pat dry. Dredge in flour, salt, and pepper. Fry in butter until lightly browned. Put in roasting pan, add just enough cream to cover pieces of turkey. Bake at 350°F, about 20 minutes for each pound of turkey.

Turkey Stuffed with Wild Rice
INGREDIENTS

Dressed turkey
1 teaspoon salt
Lemon juice
2 cups mushrooms
3 cups water
¼ cup chopped celery
1-½ cups wild rice
¼ cup butter
½ cup onion, chopped
1 tablespoon poultry seasoning
1 tablespoon bacon fat
½ cup stewed tomatoes

Rinse and dry turkey, then rub inside with lemon juice. Rinse rice under cold water, drain, put in pot. Bring 3 cups water to a boil, and pour over rice, then add salt and simmer for one hour, adding more water if necessary. Drain rice.

Over low heat in frying pan, melt butter and bacon fat. Sauté mushrooms, onions, celery. In a mixing bowl, pour in tomatoes and seasonings. Add rice and mushroom mixture. Stuff the turkey, then put in roasting pan. Pour 2 cups of water over turkey, cover bird loosely with aluminum foil, and bake at 350°F until tender.

Turkey season coincides with mushroom season in many areas, and it only makes sense to take advantage of that happy coincidence by collecting fresh morels when turkey hunting. (Morels are the easiest to identify and safest to pick of all the mushrooms, but you'll want to be confident about picking morels before trying these recipes.) The simplest recipe: throw 10 morels, fresh or dried, along with a cup of water, into the pan for the last hour when you bake a turkey for great gravy. That advice comes from mushroom expert Larry Lonik. The next two recipes are adapted from Lonik's book *Basically Morels*. See www.morelheaven.com for additional morel recipes.

Pan Turkey and Morels

INGREDIENTS

3 pounds turkey pieces
4 cups heavy cream
Seasoned flour
1 large egg yolk
4 tablespoons butter
Salt
2 tablespoons oil
Freshly ground black pepper
⅓ cup dry white wine
Lemon juice (optional)
1-½ pounds morels cleaned, sliced

Dredge the turkey in seasoned flour and brown lightly in butter and oil. A sauté pan of at least 14" would be preferable. Add wine and cook until wine is almost evaporated, turning the turkey occasionally. Add morels and cream and cook, uncovered, until turkey is done. Remove, with as many morels as possible, to a hot serving dish. Boil down the sauce by half, and thicken by beating the egg yolk with a little of the sauce, then cook it all together, just below boiling, for about 5 minutes. Season to taste with salt and pepper. Lemon juice may be added. Pour over turkey and serve. Rice goes well with this dish.

Roast Turkey and Morels

INGREDIENTS

1 roasted turkey Salt
1-½ cups morels, sliced lengthwise
2 tablespoons flour
2 tablespoons turkey drippings

1 teaspoon lemon juice
2 tablespoons butter
1 teaspoon chopped fresh parsley
1½ cups heavy cream

Carve turkey into servings, keep warm. In a skillet, sauté morels in drippings and butter over low heat for 5 minutes. Sprinkle with salt and push to side of pan. Stir in flour until smooth, then mix together with morels and continue to cook another 2 minutes. Stir in cream until it thickens. Add lemon juice and parsley. Pour over turkey and serve immediately.

Southern-Style Deep-Fried Turkey

Deep frying turkeys, a tradition in the South, is catching on elsewhere. Deep fryers are made specifically for this, but however you do it, keep safety in mind when working with a large container of hot oil. Here's one simple but delicious technique.

INGREDIENTS

Turkey
Seasonings (salt and pepper)

Determine the right amount of oil to use by putting the turkey into the pot, and covering it with water, leaving a minimum of 4 inches below the rim. (If covering the bird leaves less than 4 inches to the rim, the pot is not big enough.) Take the bird out and mark the level of the water with the bird out of the pot. Then pour out the water and dry the pot, add oil (peanut oil is a favorite) up to the mark, and heat it to 350°F.

Make sure turkey is completely dry. Season the turkey inside and out while the oil is heating. Wire the drumsticks together with good, sturdy wire. You must be confident the wire will support the weight of the turkey and not slip off.

When the oil is hot enough, use a long hook to carefully lower the turkey into it. Cook 3 minutes per pound, then use the hook to lift the turkey, letting it drain over the pot. Place it on paper towels to catch oil.

As a variation on the above, turkeys needn't be fried whole. Slice turkey breast into finger-size strips, dredge in seasoned flour, and fry in hot oil in a skillet.

Here's a delicious way to use those inevitable little scraps of turkey that have to be picked off the bones after you slice the bird.

Fruited Turkey Salad

INGREDIENTS

1-½ cups cut-up cooked turkey

½ cup mayonnaise

1 cup seedless green grapes

½ teaspoon salt

1 8-oz. can water chestnuts, drained & chopped

¼ teaspoon curry powder

1 11-oz. can mandarin orange segments, drained

Combine turkey, grapes, water chestnuts, orange segments. Mix remaining ingredients and toss with turkey mixture. Serves 4.

Turkey-Vegetable Fondue

Ever notice how guests congregate in the kitchen while you cook? With a fondue, you cut to the chase and everyone cooks his or her own. It's a fun, easy, and sociable way to serve a medium-size group.

INGREDIENTS

2 lbs. turkey breasts in bite-size pieces

4 -5 cups cooked rice

1 lb. broccoli flowerettes

8 cups chicken broth

8 oz. mushrooms, sliced

Lemon-soy sauce (½ cup soy sauce, 1 bunch green onions, cut in ½-inch pieces, ½ cup lemon juice, ¼ cup dry white wine)

Put turkey, broccoli, onions, and mushrooms on serving tray. Put hot rice in 8 small bowls.

Heat broth in fondue pot. (An electric skillet will work. I find one pot or skillet ideal for 2-4 people, and prefer to separate into two pots for 6 or 8.) Guests spear turkey or other foods with fondue forks or chopsticks, and hold food in hot broth for 2 or 3 minutes until done, then dip in lemon-soy sauce. After main course, ladle broth over any rice remaining in bowls and eat as soup. Serves 8.

Part 8

Adventure Reads

Table of Contents

Gobblers in Paradise—Hunting Birds in Hawaii is Magical and Memorable

JAY CASSELL

At 5:30, in the pre-dawn darkness, I found myself hiking up the side of a volcano, trying to get closer to a gobbling tom. Wind swirled down from the top of snow-covered Mauna Kea, making me shiver in my much-too-light camo clothing.

"It blows pretty good up here in the morning," said John Sabati, Hawaiian outfitter and president of

Calling, early morning, Mauna Kea. Incredibly, the temperature at 5:30 was 38 degrees!

the Volcano Chapter of the NWTF. "Oh, it's also 38 degrees."

Having left 16-degree weather in New York, he didn't have to tell me. It was seriously cold, and I was seriously underdressed, not having anticipated that Hawaii could actually have temperatures below 70 degree.

"Don't worry, it'll be 70 by 10 o'clock," John added.

Jet-lagged, my mind wandered. Just yesterday, I had landed at Keahole-Kona International Airport, after a 45-minute flight from Honolulu. When I walked to the baggage claim, the first person I saw was long-time friend and turkey hunting megastar Ray Eye. Ray had invited me, and a few colleagues, to come hunt Hawaii, to see for ourselves how magical the islands are.

"It's not just beaches, palm trees, surfers and hula skirts," he told me over dinner at Bubba Gump's in Kona that night. "You'll see, we're going to be climbing volcanoes, it's going to be 35 to 40 degrees, there will be snow on the peaks, and the air will be so thin up there that you'll be sucking wind."

After dinner, we made our way back to the rental house where, after having traveled for 11 hours, I promptly fell into bed and was sound asleep in minutes.

Dreams of the Ages

In my dreams, my subconscious wandered to the book *Hawaii* by James Michener. The author had

On the Big Island, the fog rolls in every morning, without fail, making for some challenging hunting.

written that millions of years ago, scores of millions of years before man appeared, the earth consisted of continents and vast oceans. Beneath one ocean, 2,000 miles west of what is now North America, more than five miles down, a fissure appeared in the ocean floor. From that fissure seeped hot, molten rock which, upon contact with the water, created a huge steam column that surged to the surface.

It's been speculated that this steam kept rising out of the ocean for millions of years. Down below, the molten rock kept slowly building up, reaching ever upward. Every once in a while—1,000 years? 10,000?—a rumble would occur from within the earth, followed by a violent uplifting that forced great masses of lava up through the fissure, up through the molten rock that had already cooled and solidified ahead of it. The rock, a subterranean volcano, pushed ever upward, miles from the bottom.

One time, one of the eruptions pushed the molten rock so far up that it broke the water's surface. Now an island had been formed, a lifeless rock in the middle of an endless ocean. And so it stayed, still growing. Other islands eventually developed. In time, soil formed from the eroding lava. Plant life followed, with seeds perhaps carried to the island by wind or birds. In time, human

adventurers come to the islands from the west. The Polynesians were first, but were followed by others.

Volcanic Turkeys

A gobble shook me out of my daydream. Where was I? Oh, wait, Hawaii. I was turkey hunting on the Parker Ranch. Looking down the mountain, I could see vast grassy expanses that stretched all the way to the ocean, just now starting to glisten in the sun's strengthening rays. Huge mounds, some rising 50 feet high, dotted the valley below. "They're called Pu'u," John told me. "They formed when lava seeped out of the ground. That's happening on the other side of the island, at Kilauea, right now."

Just then, Ray let out a loud, staccato owl hoot that pierced through the darkness and wind. Within seconds, there were responding gobbles from all over the mountain. We were surrounded! We also heard some laughing and chuckling coming from below.

"Erkel's francolins," Ray whispered. "I think they're making fun of me."

"The trick here is to not chase every gobbler you hear," John said. "You'll wear yourself out if you do that. It's better to wait until you get a bird that's answering on a regular basis, to up your odds."

When you're hunting in Hawaii, hiking way down and way up is all part of the program.

Who says decoys don't work? These jakes came in and hung around for half an hour.

Giving up on the gobbler that was now moving farther uphill from us, we hopped back in the trucks. Ray and I followed John up the volcano, bouncing along on a dirt and grass road that went up and up. An hour later, we had reached a long ridge. The sun was peaking over 13,792-foot Mauna Lea when we pulled to a stop and got out.

I couldn't believe I was here, hunting. Or that there were Erckel's francolins. Or, as I'd later find out, that the big island of Hawaii is also home to California quail, chukars, mourning doves, wild boar, blue and ring-necked pheasants, mouflon sheep, and wild goats, all huntable species.

"We've even got mongooses on Hawaii," John told me later. "They were brought here to kill the rats that came off the old sailing ships. Unfortunately, the rats are nocturnal and mongooses move about in the daytime, so that plan didn't work."

What's different about wild turkeys in Hawaii, Jon also told me, is that they don't all breed at the same time. With temperatures pretty much the same year-round, some birds mate in spring, some in summer, fall, or winter. "That's what makes this hunting challenging," he said, "because only so many gobblers are breeding right now. You can't call in the others because they aren't interested."

Jon Sabati using a box call. If you want to hunt turkeys in Hawaii, look no further than Sabati.

A Lava Belly Crawl

With the sun now up, Jon and I went hiking down the road, calling and listening. Coming around a bend, we both saw three birds 150 yards in the distance and hit the dirt. As we watched through binoculars, at least 20 more birds came pouring out of a gully, headed across a grassy knoll, and dropped over its edge. The last three birds in the flock were longbeards.

Glassing the terrain, we figured we could belly-crawl over to a ditch, drop down and run 100 yards toward the flock, then crawl another 75 yards to the edge of the knoll. Then it was just a question of whether the birds had kept going, or maybe were resting and feeding right there.

Ten minutes later, we were set up behind some clumps of lava, at the lip of the knoll. "They're right there," Jon whispered. "I see them. Don't move. Let me see if I can call one away from the flock."

All it took was three yelps to elicit a gobble from one of the birds. Slowly raising my head off the ground, I peered around my lava hiding spot in time to see a red head pop up no more than 15 yards away. "He's got a good beard," I heard Jon whisper from behind me. I flipped off the 1187's safety, lined up my beads on that tomato-sized target, squeezed the trigger, and I had my first Rio Grande and my first Hawaiian turkey, a handsome bird with a 9-inch beard and 1-inch spurs.

After congratulations, handshakes, and photos, we hiked back up to truck. It was 10 o'clock. Hawaii has a two-bird limit, so there was no time to rest. I wanted to get that second bird so I could go lie on a beach somewhere.

Pigged Out

Some hunters in my group ended up getting two birds during our three days of hunting, but not me. One day Willie-Joe (Jon's buddy) and I must have called in 25 jakes, all of which I passed on. One hot longbeard did come within 50 yards of our position, but we couldn't see him in the brush, and he wouldn't show himself.

Another time, we had a gobbler talking back to us from way out in the middle of a field. We figured we could sneak through the brush, get to within 75 yards of him, then try to call him away from his hens. We didn't figure on the pigs, though. Just as we were setting up, a line of 40-plus pigs—jet-black sows, boars, and eight piglets—came running out of the brush and started grazing on the tall grass.

"They're dangerous with all those piglets," Willie-Joe said. "Especially those sows; they'll attack if they think their babies are threatened."

The author with his Hawaiian Rio – this one is going up on the wall!

When I asked what they could possibly do to you, his response was simply, "Those teeth can crack through the husks of macadamia nuts. What do you think would happen if they got hold of your leg?"

Parkerized

The remainder of my hunt was spent driving the 130,000-acre Parker Ranch, hoping to spot a gobbler, then get out to put a sneak on him. While that didn't happen, I got to see a part of Hawaii that most people don't have a chance to see. Hawaii is not all beaches and palm trees, but rolling, pastoral hills broken up by brushy patches and low scrub oaks. It reminded me of parts of Montana and Wyoming: open land as far as the eye can see, blue sky, green hills.

Willie-Joe glassing a hillside. As with all open country, glassing carefully is critical.

On the last day of our hunt, we gathered at a cowboy cabin perched halfway up the volcano. A 20-knot wind whipped through the trees as we sat down on the porch and were treated to a lunch of pulled pork and grilled chicken. Diana Quitiquit, vice president of the ranch, gave us a brief history of the spread. The story began in 1809, when a 19-year-old Massachusetts-born sailor named John Parker jumped ship. His presence was soon brought to the attention of the great King Kamehameha I, who at the time was trying to figure out how to control all of the wild cattle that had taken over the island since their introduction in 1793. Parker, musket in hand, volunteered to reduce the herd and start up a supply of beef for trade in the process.

Parker's influence began to spread. Not only did he start getting rich by selling beef to passing ships, but he was also building his own herd. The Parker Ranch was established not long after he married Kipikane, the chief's grand-daughter. Buying two acres at first, Parker slowly enlarged the property, which in time was taken over by his son, Richard Kaleioku Parker Smart. Smart grew the ranch to more than 300,000 acres at one point, making it one of the largest working cattle ranches in the United States.

Hunting in Hawaii

What to Hunt

All of Hawaii's game animals are introduced species. There are six species of big game mammals and 14 species of gamebirds in the state.

On the big island of Hawaii, where I hunted, big game animals include mouflon sheep, feral sheep, feral goats, and feral pigs. Gamebirds include ringneck and blue pheasants; chukars; Erckel's gray, and black francolins; California, Gambel's and Japanese quail; barred, spotted, and mourning doves, sand grouse; and Rio Grande wild turkeys.

Hunting License

All hunters must present a hunter safety card in order to buy an Hawaiian hunting license. There are no exceptions; if you don't have a hunter safety card, you must take a safety course in your home state before going to Hawaii. Merely presenting a current hunting license will not get you a license n Hawaii. The cost is $95 for a nonresident, $10 for a resident. Licenses may be purchased on line at www.state.hi.us/dlnr; 808-695-4620.

Where to Hunt

As a preserve, the Parker Ranch does not require an Hawaiian hunting license, only a signed permit, available at the ranch. To hunt the Parker Ranch, contact Jon Sabati at jonkona@hawaii.rr.com; 808-896-0972.

The ranch also offers ATV rides, horseback riding, nature tours, and historic home tours. Parkerranch.com; 808-885-7311.

Jon Sabati also guides hunters on the 20,000-acre Kealia Ranch in the western part of the big island. Again, contact him at 808-896-0972.

Smart eventually leased some of his land to Lawrence Rockefeller, who started resort development along the coast. When Smart passed away in 1992, some of the ranch was sold off to the U.S. military, but the rest was left in a trust for the Waimea community. Since then, the ranch has been open to the public, offering hunting, nature tours, historic home tours, and ATV and horseback riding.

Tourist Time

Hunting done, Hapuna Beach was my next stop. Called "one of the nicest beaches on the island and possibly anywhere" in the tour guides, it had white sands, gentle water, sea turtles swimming along the beach—exactly what you would imagine, when conjuring up images of Hawaii.

But I was on a schedule. A two-hour drive to the tip of the island took us to the quaint town of Kapaau, which was a bustling community before the sugar cane plantations all went bust 20 years ago. Since rebuilt with craft shops and a funky little restaurant, Bamboo, it was the perfect place for my last meal on Hawaii.

Before I knew it, Ray had driven me back to the airport, then I was back on a 777, flying east, back to New York, back home. As the plane soared above the Pacific, I thought about the frozen turkey breasts, tail feathers and beard in my dufflebag. When I got home, I'd have to dig out some cookbooks and try to figure out some kind of roast turkey and pineapple feast. I also realized I'd better take out *Hawaii* from the library. I don't think Mitchener said anything about hunting in Hawaii, and I know he didn't mention wild turkeys. I wonder what else he missed.

A Dangerous Game—Hunting at a Higher Level for Trophy Blacktails

JAY CASSELL

The concepts of fear and hunting have always seemed incongruous to me. No matter where I hunt, I always know I'm the most dangerous creature in the woods. Whether I'm hiking back to deer camp in the dark, with coyote song pulsing through the darkness; or I'm walking across a field on my buddy's upstate farm, bow in hand, headed to my treestand in the predawn darkness; no matter where I go, I know that other creatures will shy away at my coming. I am armed; I have nothing to fear.

With that imperious view of the natural order of things, I stepped ashore on Kodiak Island last fall, and faced a new reality. It didn't make any difference that I had a Remington Model 700 .300 Ultra mag, loaded with 200-grain Swift A-Frame bullets, over my shoulder; that I had some of the best optics available; that I had a topo map, GPS unit, and compass with me; or, finally, that I had a can of bear repellant (range – 10 yards; spray duration – 5 seconds). What made a difference was this: I was not the top-of-the-line predator here. That title belonged to the many Kodiak bears that inhabit this 150 – by 50-mile-long island in the Pacific Ocean, 20 miles across the Shelikof Strait from mainland Alaska. And that made all the difference in the world.

On the beach, looking at the 12-inch-long bear tracks in the black gravel, gazing at the head-high grass thickets I had to hike through to get up the mountain, toward the snowline, I knew that I could be the prey at any moment. Some hunters have been mauled on this island, others have been charged by bears intent on either stealing a dead deer or fending off perceived danger to their cubs. Could I be next? What would I do if a bear charged? Would a bullet really stop an oncoming, enraged brown bear at 10 yards? Could pepper spray do anything other than piss a bear off? I might find out.

Planning a Hunt Like No Other

The pieces for this trip started to come together two years earlier, when Doug Jeanneret of the U.S. Sportsmen's Alliance and Joe Arterburn of Cabela's asked if I'd like to join them on their annual blacktail hunt on Kodiak. There would be eight of us (six hunters, the captain and mate) living on a houseboat based in Larsen Bay at the southwestern tip of the island. We'd each have two deer tags. Bonus hunting would be jump shooting for ducks, including mallards, buffleheads, and gaudily colored harlequins. We could also fish for halibut and go crabbing for Dungeness and Tanner crabs.

I'd have to take a long flight from New York to Anchorage and then on to Kodiak; live on a cramped boat for a week with a bunch of guys and what might generously be called a shower; hunt on a island with approximately one brown bear per square mile, at a time when they are all feeding heavily in preparation for the upcoming winter; plus, hike and climb every day until I become aware of muscles I didn't even know existed. I told them to count me in.

Time flew, and before I knew it, I was packing my gun and gear and confirming airline reservations. In late October, our group of six convened at the Best Western in the city of Kodiak, where a 1200-pound-plus stuffed brown bear lords over the lobby, dined at a local steak and burger joint, then flew on down to Larsen Bay the next morning, in a crammed Turbo Beaver.

Flying over Kodiak was worth the trip by itself. Snow-covered, jagged peaks soared into the azure blue sky, while frozen-over lakes and tributaries dominated the valleys. The shadow of our plane etched its way across the whiteness below. ("This is my office," our pilot confided to me with a knowing grin.) In time, we came out of the mountains, crossed an unusually tranquil bay, then began our approach to the dirt strip at Larsen Bay. The landing went smoothly, we piled our gear into a waiting F250, then drove the mile to the docks, where the 56-foot houseboat, "The Sundy," was moored. Our home for a week, the boat had a cabin up front with six bunks, three to a side; a kitchen and dining area with two tables; and a large open area to the stern, where we would grill meals, hopefully hang deer, and socialize. The cabin up top, the domain of Capt. Al Henderson, was equipped

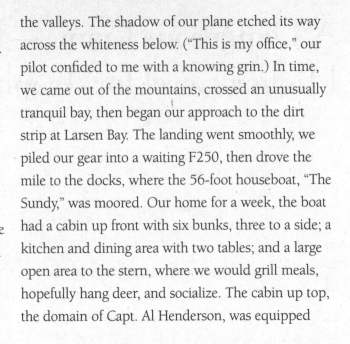

Loading up the plane for the flight to camp.

The author in the Kodiak Holiday Inn lobby. Kodiak bear in the background was a haunting reminder of what lay ahead.

The flight to our destination, Larsen Bay, took us over beautiful and desolate land.

Once on the ground, the first order of business was making sure that our rifles were still zeroed.

Our home for a week – the Sundy.

Our taxi – a Zodiak inflatable.

with a GPS-depthfinder and a sat phone, should anyone need to make calls. We were on our way.

After a stop on a deserted beach to sight in rifles, we cruised down a jagged coast lined by snow-capped mountains that rose from the beach to almost 5000 feet. After an hour, the engines cut out and Capt. Al started barking orders. "I need two men up front to man those crab pots," he yelled. "And a third down here to pass up more of them."

I liked this concept – potential surf (crabs) and turf (venison). With fish heads and skeletons for bait, we tossed five large traps overboard, spaced but 100 yards apart, then proceeded down the bay. Another half hour, and the boat slowed again. This time, word came that it was time for two hunters to get in the skiff and head to shore. This would be a short hunt, as we only had about three hours until dark, but it made sense to try for something. Jeanneret and I were soon in the inflatable skiff, headed toward shore. Show time.

On the Ground

Once ashore, my pent-up bear fears from the past two years somewhat in check, Jeanneret and I headed uphill, toward an area where he'd seen blacktails on previous hunts. As I climbed, I thought things through. Being bear-scared 100 percent of the

time was not an option. Better to channel that fear inward, make it work for me, not against. Better to be on total alert 100 percent of the time, to be the best hunter I could be. As I was to discover, hunting with this frame of mind, your adrenalin always pumping, is a form of elevated consciousness, one that you start to thrive on. At the end of the day, when you relax, you feel completely exhausted.

Jeanneret and I hiked halfway up a ridge above Uyak Bay that afternoon, gaining vantage points where we could, glassing a ravine, watching a well-used bowl like any deer hunters would do. By dusk, we had seen five does and one spike, none of the trophy blacktails that some say literally hide behind every bush on the island. This hunt, I thought to myself as we rode the skiff back to our houseboat, this hunt was going to be a tough one. This would be a test.

Onboard, we wolfed down burgers from the grill, and chased them with a couple of beers. It had been a long day, and I could barely stay awake. I scrambled into my upper bunk, slipped into my sleeping bag, and put my head on the pillow. The sounds of waves gently lapping against the hull soon had me sound asleep.

Next morning, hunting partners remained the same, and Jeanneret and I headed back toward the same area, planning to hike way above where we

Glassing high, glassing low – you keep looking until you see something. Good high-power binoculars are a must.

had been the previous evening. It was a straight 45-degree climb from the beach to the top; at one point I remember thinking I was glad I had spent time at the gym, preparing for this hunt.

Bulling our way through head-high grass, we paused to watch a thick clump of brush that opened out into some hardwoods. In time, a doe emerged from the brush, headed uphill. There was more movement in that thick stuff, and I slowly raised my rifle, hoping this second deer might have antlers. It didn't; we kept climbing.

Two hours later, we crested the ridge, crossed a 500-yard-long open area, and reached a bowl Jeanneret had been talking about. Fresh deer tracks crisscrossed the snow in every direction. It looked promising, but with 50-mph gusts whipping in off the Pacific, we lasted about half an hour, then had to retreat into the lee of the ridge. We eventually set up by some thick brush and glassed a lake below. Deer trails lead from the lake up the mountain on its far side, stretching up onto the snowline and beyond. Somewhere in the distance, cutting through the howling wind, I thought I heard a gunshot. I wondered if one of our group had shot.

When darkness started to enshroud the mountain, we slowly made our way downhill, not wanting to hike out in the dark in the middle of

bear country. Below, out in the bay, we could see the spec that was the Sundy, anchored, waiting for her hunters to radio in for a pickup. Soon we were back in the Zodiak, motoring over whitecaps as the bay started to churn with the wind. The lights of the boat in the distance beckoned with warmth, camaraderie, and good food.

First Blood

Onboard, one of our group, Luke, had a heavy-bodied, wide-racked 9-point buck hanging near the stern. The mood was festive, beers were opened, and everyone congratulated Luke, whose smile beamed that this was a day he'd never forget.

"Joe and I hiked up this ravine, then cut inland for maybe half a mile before setting up to watch a game trail. In time, this guy came ambling by, head to the ground, obviously looking for does. I took him at 48 yards.

"That was the easy part," Luke continued. "Getting him out of that thick stuff, then down the ravine, that was work. I'm still sweating."

What went unsaid was that both he and Joe had been dragging as hard as they could. It's not that the bears are always attracted to the sound of gunshots, as is popularly believed. In truth, the bears also zero in on all the jays and magpies that flock to the gut pile, once you've field-dressed your animal. The trick is to dress your deer and then get out of there fast. "There were so many downed trees and hummocks, the drag took forever," Luke concluded.

Later, Arterburn pulled me aside and said, "Listen, that's a good spot where Luke took that deer. There are always deer up there. You and I should go there tomorrow."

After a venison and salmon dinner, and celebratory cigars all around, we piled into our respective bunks. As happened every night for the whole week, I was asleep the minute my head hit the pillow. I slept the sleep of exhaustion, and didn't wake until the sun was coming up.

My Turn

Arterburn and I hiked up the same ravine that Luke and he had the day before. The temperatures were in the 40s, but this was a straight-up climb, over mud and rocks made all the more slippery from spray from a nearby waterfall. Even stopping every 20 yards, it was tough work. Soon I was stripping off outer layers, trying to cool down. My glasses kept fogging up. I was gasping for air. If a bear or deer had come out of the thickets that clawed at us from

The author checking a rub at treeline.

either side of the trail, I wouldn't have been able to see it anyway.

An hour went by before we reached the top, coming out into a bowl edged by a jagged cliff on one side and a sloping ridge on the other. Arterburn pointed the muzzle of his rifle at bear track in the mud.

"It's old," he said. "Probably a couple of days."

Now we went into hunting mode, easing up the trail, stopping only near trees or rocks, moving slowly, glassing. At this point I was focused on deer, watching for movement, looking for brown horizontal lines or satellite dish ears hidden in brush.

"There's one," Joe whispered, pointing up the side ridge. I looked and there, silhouetted against the sky at the top of the cliff, stood a large-bodied blacktail. I pulled out my 8x42s. Spike.

"I've got two tags," I whispered, "so I could shoot him. But we're so far from the coast that the only thing I'd want to drag out of here is a trophy."

Which is what happened. Coming into an open park, we eased along a game trail that sidehilled up the ridge, then settled back into some thick grass. We agreed to sit there for at least an hour, glassing and watching. I wolfed down a sandwich and water as we waited, then saw movement in the brush on the opposite side of the park, 100 yards away. I eased my .300 Ultra Mag onto my lap, then froze. Now I could see a big, racked buck emerging from the thicket and moving down the trail. Even without my glasses, I could tell he was a keeper: big body, 8 or 10 points.

"Joe," I whispered. "I'm seeing a nice buck right now."

"Shoot him," Arterburn growled as he looked through his glasses. He passed me his shooting stick.

The buck was now out in the open, moving with a purpose across the meadow, directly toward us. The wind blew in my face—perfect—as I eschewed the shooting stick and instead got down on my belly and crawled 8 yards to a lip by the trail we had just come up.

The buck disappeared, out of my view, but then I saw a small tree 40 yards away thrashing back and forth, and watched with delight as the 10-pointer raked it with his antlers. Now he started coming toward us again. He had no idea we were there. At 30 yards, he veered to his right, heading up the meadow. I had a broadside shot.

"Shoot him now!" Arterburn pleaded. He hadn't finished before my rifle boomed, and the buck hunched over and ran, heartshot. He went 15 yards, and piled up in some hummocks. My tag was filled with the blacktail buck I had been hoping for.

After the Shot

Walking over to the deer, the two of us slapped each other's backs, shook hands, and did all the rejoicing that successful hunters do. But we also knew we had a job to do, and we had to do it quickly.

After admiring the buck, a thick-bodied deer with a rut-swollen neck, chocolate antlers, the double throat patch typical of the species, plus a distinctive black crown, we started in with the field dressing, making sure our loaded rifles were within

The author with a heavy-bodied 10-pointer, the result of a slow still hunt.

arm's reach. One man stood guard, the other man worked, and within a few minutes the guts were out, the photos taken, the drag rope affixed to antlers. As we pulled the deer, all 200 pounds of him, the first magpie came soaring in, squawking all the way. Others were right behind him.

"We need to get out of sight of the gutpile," Arterburn said as we pulled the dead weight around hummocks, through water, up and over deadfalls, then onto the game trail. The work was excruciating, with each pull harder than the previous. We were both sweating, both watching our backtrail constantly, both pulling as far as we could before stopping to catch our breaths. It took 20 minutes to get away from the gutpile, which by now had become a feeding frenzy for every bird within a mile. Soon we had the deer in the stream, where the dragging was easier except for all the deadfalls and rocks. Twenty minutes more brought us out of the park, into the ravine. Now we were at the top of the waterfall. We went over the edge, headed down the falls. At times we had to hold the deer to prevent it from falling. Other times we had to hold the drag rope with one hand while grasping at saplings to keep ourselves from sliding down, a long drop to the beach below.

As we neared the bottom, we stopped, panting for breath, muscles screaming. Arterburn pulled out the radio and called the ship.

"Two hunters ready for pick up," he huffed into the radio. "Plus one extra passenger."

"Roger that," came the reply. "We'll come and get you."

We pulled the deer down to the beach and waited, rifles loaded, keeping an eye behind us. There would be no place to go were a bear to come down the trail, following our scent, as the beach was short, and blocked at both ends by rockpiles. I had heard a hunter back in town telling a colleague that a bear had stolen a buck from him at the end of a long drag, right on the beach. "Picked it up the way a Lab picks up a duck," he'd said.

After a mile-long drag through all that thick stuff up above, I'm not sure I was ready to give up my deer to any bear. Fortunately, I didn't have to make that decision, as we heard and then saw the Zodiak headed our way. A few more photos, then we were back in the boat, headed to the mother ship. My trip was a success, and it wasn't over.

A Fitting Finale

The next four days were spent doing all the things you'd ever want to do in Alaska. The following day, a soggy, windy mess, was spent jump shooting mallards, buffleheads, and harlequin ducks, an oddly beautiful bird found mostly in the Pacific Northwest. At the end of the day we picked up our crab traps,

by now overflowing with Dungeness and Tanner crabs. That night, we cleaned and boiled all the keepers in Old Bay seasoning, then had a once-in-a-lifetime feast of fresh crabs, venison, and red wine, eight grubby men in camo eating a natural, wild meal you couldn't get at the finest restaurant in New York.

The week passed quickly: hunting low along the coastline for blacktails one day with Len Nelson; then high, up above the snowline, the next day with buddy Skip Knowles; then finally, on the last day, catching halibut, skinning deer, cutting meat into steaks, fillets, and roasts, then grinding the rest into hamburger. With a vacuum packer on board, we bagged everything and divvied it up into freezer boxes, ready for the plane rides home.

In time, we were steaming out of Uyak Bay, headed to Larsen, where we loaded everything into a

Tanner crabs – part of the game smorgabord.

Along with halibut.

waiting pickup and drove to the landing strip. Snow was falling and the wind was starting to really blow as the Beaver burst out of the clouds, ready to take us back to civilization. We took off into the wind and headed out over the mountains as the squall moved in, bouncing the plane up, down, and sideways, the windows obscured by snow. But we made it – back to the airport, back to the Kodiak Best Western, then back to Anchorage and on home.

It's a strange feeling, sitting here at a computer, poring over my trip notes, remembering an adventure that I had looked forward to for so long, and which went by so quickly. But, it was one of those trips you'll always remember, along with your hunting colleagues who now hold a special place in your memories.

I ran into four members of our group at a recent trade show. We all went out for a few beers, to relive old times. Len told about the bear, always out of sight, that kept growling at he and Jeanneret on the day they hunted together. It followed them for more than 400 yards, crunching through the snow, snarling, roaring, keeping pace with the two hunters. They eventually called the skiff to get them out of there.

Skip and I reminisced about hunting above the snowline together, and glassing a draw where a forkhorn practically walked over me as I stood motionless behind a tree. Twenty yards from there, we came upon sow and cub tracks, prints so fresh that the snow was still tumbling from the rims down into the prints. I remember being glad I hadn't shot

---

Packing for a Kodiak hunt requires some thought. You don't want to overpack, yet you need to be prepared for different situations. The weather, for example, can change in a heartbeat. In the week I was there, we had one day that was sunny and in the 50s; the next it was snowing; and the next it was raining and blowing 50-mph gusts. You've got to be ready for all of it.

For firearms, a deer-sized caliber is fine, although you do want something that packs enough power should you find yourself in a situation with a 1200-pound guy in a brown suit. Following is a partial list of some of the gear I took along.

- .300 Remington Ultra Mag, Model 700, topped with a Cabela's Alaskan Guide riflescope, 3 – 10x40, duplex reticle.
- .300 Remington Ultra Mag cartridges with 150-, 200-grain Swift A-Frame bullets
- Cabela's Alaskan Guide full-size binoculars (8x42)
- Bushnell Legend rangefinder
- Shockey Fannin caping knife
- Remington skinning knife
- Surefire E2L AA Outdoorsman flashlight
- Saint Minmus white LED headlamp
- Cabela's MTO 50 jacket, pants (this raingear is the bomb: it's quiet, comfortable, and kept me dry no matter what the conditions.
- 2 pair gloves
- Two pair Cabela's Alaskan Guide Microtex shirts & pants
- Fleece pullover, pants
- Polartec watch cap
- 3 pair base layers, different weights.
- 2 pair boots (Cabela's Meindl Perfekt boots, Columbia Omni-Heat boots)
- Cabela's Elite Scout Hunting Pack
- Cabela's XPG backpacker sleeping bag
- 3 pair socks, liner socks.
- Scent Killer body soap, field wipes, antiperspirant (Wildlife Research)

that small buck with bears obviously close by. We went in the other direction.

Luke was still beaming about the trophy buck he took, and kept talking about the "best day of his life."

Looking back, it was the best week for all of us.

The Men That Don't Fit In

By Robert Service

There's a race of men that don't fit in,
  A race that can't stay still;
So they break the hearts of kith and kin,
  And they roam the world at will.
They range the field and they rove the flood,
  And they climb the mountain's crest;
Theirs is the curse of the gypsy blood,
  And they don't know how to rest.

If they just went straight they might go far;
  They are strong and brave and true;
But they're always tired of the things that are,
  And they want the strange and new.
They say: "Could I find my proper groove,
  What a deep mark I would make!"
So they chop and change, and each fresh move
  Is only a fresh mistake.

And each forgets, as he strips and runs
  With a brilliant, fitful pace,
It's the steady, quiet, plodding ones
  Who win in the lifelong race.
And each forgets that his youth has fled,
  Forgets that his prime is past,
Till he stands one day, with a hope that's dead,
  In the glare of the truth at last.

He has failed, he has failed; he has missed
  his chance;
  He has just done things by half.
Life's been a jolly good joke on him,
  And now is the time to laugh.
Ha, ha! He is one of the Legion Lost;
  He was never meant to win;
He's a rolling stone, and it's bred in the bone;
  He's a man who won't fit in.

Howl and Barbaric Yawp

Reprinted with permission from *Field & Stream Magazine*.

THOMAS MCINTYRE

The author and guides glass the horizon for caribou. If a herd is present, wolves won't be far behind.

I t was a hunt at first sight, but it would be forty years before I fired a shot.

It began when I saw them from the air over the Alaska Range. Crammed into the rear of a Super Cub in August, I watched the silver foil of reflected sun slide off the surface of a pond as we passed, and there was a caribou cow, brisket deep in the water. She wasn't swimming, and the pond was small enough to have walked around in ten minutes. But she was in the middle, motionless, almost resigned. Then I saw them. Seven or eight, their fur shaded from near black to the gunmetal color that gives them their name, lying on crossed paws on the tundra, like dogs on a rug in front of a fire, ringing the pond, watching the caribou, biding their time, the essence of patience, and fate. And something about all that showed me an animal worth hunting. And though we never touched down or came back, in my mind I was already hunting gray wolves.

Over the years, I saw wolves where I could hunt them, but did not have a tag (and had to overcome serious temptations to violate various wildlife ordinances), or had a tag and did not see them, only hearing the tolling of their howls. I actually live in wolf country (with dead cattle to prove it), in the Northern Rockies where more than 240 individual packs of gray wolves are at large, and where no one is indifferent to their presence. To hunters here, *Canis lupus* is either a rampant slaughterer of elk or a top North American trophy species. I believe that the wolf *is* a rampant slaughterer of elk–*and* a top trophy species. And one I cannot hunt here, yet, for a variety of reasons, none of them reasonable. So to try to complete a forty-year-long hunt, I had to travel 1250 miles to Nunavut.

In Inuktitut, its first language, *Nunavut* means "our land." As large as Western Europe, it has a population of just over 30,000 people—half as many as Greenland—who have lived with and hunted the wolf (*amarok*) continuously for forty centuries.

With only one human for every twenty-five square miles, there's room in the land for 10,000 wolves. And for the wolves, and humans, there are a million central Canada barren-ground caribou. Probably 50 to 60 percent of world's 25,000 polar bears inhabit Nunavut, along with a significant population of tundra grizzlies, most of the world's muskoxen, an unknown number of wolverines, Arctic foxes, Arctic hares the size of tomcats, assorted fur-bearers, waterfowl in the multimillions, ptarmigan, incalculable fresh- and saltwater fish, marine mammals like whales, narwhals, walruses, seals, plus the odd black bear and moose.

For twenty five years I have hunted in Nunavut, for caribou, muskoxen, walrus, and seals. Mostly, though, it has not been what I hunted as much as with whom I hunted, the Inuit. Hunting with them in nightless summer or forty-below March, I've seen the country through their eyes in a way my eyes, alone, would never be capable. When I landed in Arviat ("place of the bowhead whale"), a village of two-thousand on the western shore of frozen Hudson Bay, I saw an early-May Sunday afternoon. But for the Inuit, like the thirty-something wolf outfitter Ryan St. John, it was the last days before the winter snow rotted and there would be no overland travel until summer. So we had to be going.

Around Ryan's house caribou racks poked out of the snow like some antler garden. Ryan's father was a Christian missionary who came north almost 40 years ago and remained in a place he loved, marrying and prospering, almost inadvertently, in business in Arviat. (He ordered wood to repair the house he lived in, and ended up selling the entire load before he hammered a nail; then ordered more.) Now there was a family lumber yard and a shipping-container dock. And Ryan's guiding business. Among the bare antlers sticking out of the drifts, the other Inuit guides in their fur-fringed hooded anoraks loaded the *kamotiks* with what would be needed for them and four US wolf hunters, including me, for up to a week out on the snow-covered lowlands, seventy miles to the west—sleeping bags, tents, lanterns, stoves, spaghetti, frozen caribou, and rifles in sealskin scabbards. Ryan had some dried caribou hides for me lie on, on top of the load in the kamotik he had roped behind his snow machine. After I climbed in, and after one last look around, the machines were started; and I was bouncing along as the kamotik's long wooden runners keened across the bumps and dips in the snow.

In the cloudless sun the temperature was in the teens; and I was in windpants and parka under a white fleece anorak, my feet in Muck Arctic Pro boots. I had goggles over my eyes and beaver mitts on my hands and a dried caribou hide wrapped around me; and the pounding over the snow of the long wooden false runners, with the plastic runners on the bottoms, was surprisingly soothing, and I was soon snoring. I awoke when we stopped, about ten miles from town, where we saw the first *tuktu*, caribou.

I had heard that the herds outside Arviat were big this year, which promised good wolf hunting. Now there were a few hundred caribou, cows and yearlings with the bulls still behind, passing north in front of us, moving across these Hudson Bay Lowlands to the spring calving grounds, feeding on the move as they pawed the snow off the tundra (*caribou* said to mean "snow shoveler" in Mi'kmaq), leaving black circles on the white plains. And as we watched them pass, nearly oblivious to our presence, each of the Inuit opened the cowling of his snow machine and disconnected the headlight.

I asked Ryan why, and he explained that the lights could be seen by wolves fifteen miles across the tundra. Then he smiled and added, with almost no irony, "This is the way our grandfathers taught us."

We went west, the numbers of caribou growing exponentially. The herds were no longer big, but enormous. Hundreds became thousands, then many thousands, ringing the horizon, until I was in the midst of the greatest concentration of large mammals I had ever been in on earth. It was even more telling that the Inuit were almost as enthralled, not having seen caribou like this in many springs.

A modern dog sled.

Some seventy miles from Arviat we reached a low bluff with a field of black, lichened rocks exposed on it, the broken runners of an old sled lying crossed on the ground. This was camp, and we soon had two small tents, one for the guides and one for the hunters, raised and the floors spread with foam mattresses and caribou hides, our sleeping bags rolled out on them. We ate the spaghetti for dinner, then the darkness comes, then the aurora, while the caribou moved past.

Hunting wolves on the tundra meant mile after mile of travel each day. We moved mostly south, looking for fresh tracks, glassing the caribou to see if the wolves have come down on them. If each human had twenty-five square miles to himself, each wolf had seventy-five. And Ryan had guided hunters in past years who saw, when there were fewer caribou, only one wolf in the five days of the hunt. The tracks we found were old, and at midday we stopped, made tea, and ate sandwiches, along with slices of the frozen raw caribou.

As we hunted again for wolves, Ryan asked if I minded if he took a caribou. No, I said. Please do. Caribou season in Nunavut stretches across much of the year; and Ryan looked to be doing more grocery shopping than predating. He spent ten minutes looking over a few hundred cows, looking for a fat one whose hide had not been riddled by warble fly "wolves," the name for the burrowing larvae. Finally he settled on a round-bellied one about 70 yards away. He pulled out his .22 Hornet and knelt on the snow. The shot landed farther down the neck than he wanted, but the dry cow ran only a few yards before staggering, circling, then falling. We went over to it, and Ryan began field dressing.

He cut off the first chamber of the stomach and turned it inside out, shaking out the contents. Now he filled it with bits of organs and caul fat. This was for his grandmother, who particularly enjoyed these cuts of the caribou, boiled.

The liver lay on the snow, steam rising, and Ryan asked if I minded if he ate some now. By all means, I said; and Ryan sliced off a piece of liver, then a slice of tripe, wrapped them together, dabbed them into the stomach contents of chewed tundra, and ate. Four-thousand years of living here have taught the Inuit that they could digest the tundra tuktu had chewed first for them, and that they could find in it the vitamin C needed to prevent scurvy, the bane of so many European Arctic and Antarctic explorers who either because of ignorance or punctilio could never get to eating guts, and died because of it.

After a time, I hunkered down across from Ryan and asked if I could have a bite. He wrapped up some tundra sushi for me, and I took a deep breath and put it in my mouth. The warm liver was delicious, and the tripe added chewy texture. The surprising flavor was the stomach contents which were actually savory, Nature's own *umami*, the elusive "fifth taste." I had seconds, thinking what sophisticated palates wolves must have—because this is what they ate first, too, whenever they made a caribou kill. Snack time over, we lashed the caribou to the back of the kamotik and hunted on.

At mid-afternoon we saw a massive herd of caribou stretching like a bank of low tawny smoke across the horizon, four or five miles away. Even through binoculars, individual animals couldn't be distinguished; but then, like a ball of baitfish in the ocean as a marlin slashes through, or a skein of ducks in the air as a peregrine stoops into them, the herd parted in the center, the two halves separating in opposite directions; and even without seeing them, we knew the wolves were there.

Ryan and I crossed the tundra. One of the reasons for hunting here, to the south, were the trees—man-tall spruce, the wolves using them as cover from which they could ambush caribou. Now they covered us, too, until we swung around them, and found four wolves in front of us. The wolves were yellowish and gray, the biggest, alpha dog a solid *gray*, gray wolf. As our eyes met, the wolves scattered, the big dog loping, tail out, up a white ridge and over a rocky spine. We ran up the slope and were off the snow machine and out of the kamotik. I had my New Ultra Light Arms .243 WSSM with 95-grain Ballistic Silvertips. When we made the crest, the wolf was out to 250 yards, going

The author and his long-awaited trophy.

away. I was down with a round bolted, following the wolf in the Weaver Super Slam scope. All he had to do was keep running. But then he slowed, then stopped, and looked back. I thumbed off the safety.

The big, gold-eyed, thick furred wolf was down at the shot, and somewhere the fifty caribou he wouldn't be eating breathed a collective sigh of relief, at least for this year. When we got to him, I knelt and ran my ungloved hand through his guard hairs and down into the soft undercoat. Nose-to-tail he stretched out six feet and weighed about 120 pounds, and his cleaned skull would score over 16 inches.

"Are you happy?" Ryan asked, admiring the wolf.

And even though it was an utterly inadequate answer, I could only say, "Oh yes."

A few days later, the kamotiks carrying bundles of wolf hides and quarters of caribou, we headed back to Arviat. A forty-year hunt was done for me,

and that one wolf would probably be enough for my lifetime, leaving 10,000 behind in Nunavut. Neither sentimental nor hate-filled toward wolves, I would count myself an admirer, who believes that if it is right to hunt anything, it's right to hunt wolves. Especially in a place as wild as Nunavut.

We pushed our way through caribou all the way back to Arviat, cutting fresh wolf tracks and hearing their howls. Just outside the town we ran across the new track of a polar bear. Ryan stopped the machine; and we walked up to the tracks, taking a line heading north, up the shore of the bay. Ryan set his foot beside a rear paw print, the track exceeding the length of his boot sole.

"Big bear," he judged, "better than nine foot." Looking off to where the tracks disappeared, he trailed the white bear in his mind.

I looked at the track, pressed clean and sharp in the snow, the first I'd ever seen. And wondered if that was enough to begin another hunt, on which I could gladly spend another forty years.

The Rack

JAY CASSELL

"I found his antler, Dad," the throaty voice of my six-year-old son, James, crackled over the telephone. "I saw it in the woods when Mom was driving me home from school, right near where we went hunting! Are you coming home tonight?"

When I told him that my flight wouldn't get in until 11:00, and that I wouldn't be home until midnight, there was a disappointed silence over the phone. Then, "Well, okay, but don't look at it until morning, so I can show you. Promise?"

I promised. We had a deal. I told him I'd see him soon, then asked to talk with his mother.

"Love you, Dad."

"Love you too, James."

Unbelievable. My son had found the shed antler of the buck I had hunted, unsuccessfully, all season. The big ten-pointer I had seen the day before

deer season, the one with the wide spread and thick beams. He had seen me that day, having winded me as I pussyfooted through some thickets for a closer look. I think he somehow knew that he was safe, that he was far enough away from me.

I had scouted the 140-acre farm and adjoining woods near my home in suburban New York, the farm that I had gotten permission to hunt after five years of asking. "You can hunt this year," Dan the caretaker had said to me during the summer, when I asked my annual question. "I kicked those other guys off the property. They were in here with ATVs and Jeeps, bringing two and three friends every day they hunted, without even asking. Lot of nerve, I thought. Got sick of 'em, so I kicked 'em off. Now I'll let you hunt, and your buddy John, three other guys, and that's all. I want some local people on here that I know and trust."

When Dan had told me that, I couldn't believe it. But there it was, so I took advantage of it. Starting in September, I began to scout the farm. I had seen bucks on the property in previous years while driving by, but now I got a firsthand look. There was sign virtually everywhere: rubs, scrapes, droppings in the hillside hayfields, in the mixed hardwoods, in the thick hemlock stands towering over the rest of the woods. I found what were obviously rubs left by a big deer. In a copse of hemlocks near the edge of the property, bordering an Audubon nature preserve, were scrapes and, nearby, about five or six beech saplings absolutely ripped apart by antlers.

With James's help, I set up my tree stand overlooking a heavily used trail that seemed to be a perfect escape route out of the hemlocks. James and I also found an old permanent tree stand, which he and I repaired with a few two-by-fours and nails. This would officially be "his" tree stand—or tree house, as he called it.

Opening day couldn't come fast enough. James and I talked about it constantly. Even though he's only six, and can't really hunt yet, he couldn't wait for deer season. He knows what deer tracks and droppings look like; can tell how scrapes and rubs are made; can even identify where deer have passed in the leaf-covered forest floor. My plan was to hunt the first few days of the season by myself while James was in school, and then take him on a weekend. If luck was with me, maybe I'd take the big buck and could then concentrate on filing my doe tag with my son's help.

Opening day came and went, with no trophy ten-pointer in sight, or any other bucks, for that matter. A lot of other days came and went too, most of them cold, windy and rainy. Three weeks into the two-month-long season, on a balmy Sunday in the 50s, James and I packed our camo backpacks with candy bars and juice boxes, binoculars and grunt calls, and at 2:00 p.m. off we went, on our first day of hunting together. When we reached the spot where I always park my car, on a hillside field, I dabbed some camo paint onto James's face, which he thought was cool. Then we started hiking up the field and into the woods, toward the hemlocks.

We saw one white tail disappear over a knob as we hiked into James's stand. I didn't really care, though. This was the first time I was taking my son hunting! It would be the first of many, I hoped. I wouldn't force it on him, just introduce him to the sport, and keep my fingers crossed.

At James's stand, we sat down and had a couple of candy bars. "Can I blow on the deer call now, Dad?" I said yes, and he proceeded to honk away on the thing like a trumpet player.

"Do it quietly," I advised. "And remember, always whisper, don't talk loudly. And don't move around so much!"

What with James honking on the call and fidgeting—checking out my bow, looking around, pointing to the hawk soaring overhead, crumpling up his candy bar wrapper and stuffing it into his pocket—I was sure no self-respecting deer would come within a mile of us. None did, not to my son's stand, or to mine, or to the rocks where we later sat, overlooking a trail and those ripped-up beech saplings, until darkness finally settled over the woods. But that was okay.

Hiking out of the woods, we met my friend John coming from his tree stand.

"I saw that ten-pointer today," he began, giving James a poke in the ribs with his finger.

"Where?"

"Up near those hemlocks, the same area you and I have been hunting. We were probably 100 yards away from each other."

"Well, what happened?" Part of me was saying, *Great, he got the buck!* The other part of me was saying, *Pleeeease tell me you didn't shoot him.* John looked at me sheepishly.

"I was watching that trail, and I saw a doe headed my way, right where I always put my climbing tree stand. Then, right behind her, I saw a buck—you know that six-pointer we've seen over by the lake? Well, I started to draw back on him—he was only 30 yards away—but then I saw some movement to my left. It was HIM! Cutting through the hemlocks. That six-pointer and doe got out of there fast, and the ten-pointer got to within ten yards of my stand, stopped broadside to me, and then looked up straight at me!"

"Did you shoot? Did you shoot?"

"I couldn't. I was shaking too much. I mean, I could even hear the arrow rattling against the rest. Eventually, he just took off down the trial. Man, he was something. Must weigh 200 pounds!"

Later, driving the short ride home, James said, "Hey, Dad, how come. John didn't shoot that deer?"

"Shooting a deer is a lot harder than many people think. Even if everything else is right, sometimes you can get so nervous that you just can't shoot, no matter how much you want to. John's time will come, though. He works at it."

I didn't see the buck until two days after Christmas. Hunting by myself, I left my normal tree stand and circled around to the backside of the hemlocks. At 4:00 p.m., I was wedged between some boulders that overlook a well-used trail. It was 20oF, getting dark, and I was cold and shivering uncontrollably. But I kept hearing a rustling behind me. *Another squirrel.* But it wasn't. Suddenly, 60 yards through the trees, I could see a big deer headed my way. It was moving with a purpose. It stopped at what appeared to be a scrape, and I could see a huge symmetrical rack dip down as the buck stuck his nose to the ground. Then he stood up, urinated into the scrape, turned, and headed back into the hemlocks. If he had kept coming down the trail, I would have had a clean 15-yard shot. It wasn't meant to be.

That was my season. I didn't see that ten-pointer again, and I missed my only shot of the year, a 35-yarder at a forkhorn that sailed high. Such is deer hunting.

So now I was returning home from my trip. I walked in the door at midnight, quickly read through some mail on the counter, soon slipped into bed. My wife rolled over and whispered, "Don't forget to wake up James before you go to work. He really wants to show you that rack."

The alarm went off at 6:30, and I got up to take a shower.

"Psst, Dad, is that you?" came a sleepy voice from my son's room.

"Yes, buddy, how are you?"

"Wait here, Dad!"

Before I could say another word, he jumped out of bed, put on his oversized bear-paw slippers, and went padding down the stairs to the basement. When he returned, he had the biggest grin on his face that I've ever seen.

"Look, Dad!"

And there it was, half of the ten-pointer's rack. A long, thick main beam, four long, heavy points, the back one eight inches. Amazing. And that buck will be there next year.

"Dad, can I put it on my wall?"

"Of course."

"And can we go look for the other half of his antlers tomorrow, because tomorrow's Saturday, and I don't have school, and you once told me that their antlers usually fall off pretty close together. Please?"

"Sure, James. If you're good in school today."

The deal was made. We never found the other half of the shed, though. It snowed, and we couldn't really look. Mice probably ate the other half.

But you know what? I think maybe my future hunting companion was born this past season.

On Stand

JAY CASSELL

The air is still and cold. The breath rolls out of my mouth like a wisp of fog, hanging there as if frozen before finally dissipating. My gloved hands, tucked deep inside my pockets, have had no sensation in the fingertips for almost an hour. My toes are numb little clubs, stored in boots that seem detached from my body; if I wiggle them, needlelike sensations stab through them. I shiver uncontrollably for a minute, then force myself to stop. Something is coming.

Swish, swish. Swish, swish, swish. Ever so slowly, I roll my eyes to the left, toward the direction of the sound. Now I swivel my head, an eighth of an inch at a time. After what seems an eternity, I'm looking

toward the old rock wall just uphill from me. The deer trail comes through a broken-down part of that wall, straight in front of me, 15 yards away. This is where the buck will come, when it's time. *Swish, swish, crunch.*

A doe appears, cautiously headed down the trail. She's followed by two smaller does. No buck. Their gray, ghost-like forms move at a deliberate pace in the fading light. They stop ten yards from me and look around nervously. The last doe stares directly at me. I avoid eye contact and don't move and, eventually, she pays me no more attention. I'm not a threat. They continue down the trail. The sounds of their hooves *swishing* through the frozen leaves grow farther and farther away, then are gone. I'm alone again.

I've been sitting in this stand from 2:00 until dark for the past four days. I've seen eight does, more squirrels than I care to count, one red fox and a red-tailed hawk overhead, screeching. I did see one large deer body moving through the woods some 70 yards away, but my grunt call made it run from me, tail up.

I think about my family, my job, friends, places. Christmas is coming soon and, once again, I've put off shopping until the last minute. I've got to put up the Christmas tree, put the lights up outside; I haven't even taken the screens out of the windows yet. Yet here I sit, a frozen man in a frozen tree.

I've logged a lot of days in a lot of tree stands over the years. There was the stand up on the Neversink, the one that I built after patterning a buck for more than two years. I shot that ten-pointer the third year I was after him; he was five and half years old.

Then there's the stand I use in the Catskills during rifle season. It's an old one, one that I found and fixed up. I've hunted there for two years now and still haven't taken anything from it. But it overlooks a well-used trail, and I've got a good feeling about it. It just looks too good not to produce. If I'm persistent, sooner or later I'm going to take a deer out of it. I know.

I remember the V stand, made out of cut saplings wedged between two trees and a boulder, the one with the red Dellwood milk crate as a seat. I shot a seven-pointer out of that stand five years ago. A new hunter in our group, Ken, came over at the shot and helped me drag that buck back to camp, and we've been friends ever since. But the days I really remember in that stand are the cold ones, the 10°F days when the wind was howling. That stand was out in the open, and it seemed as if every wind in the mountains funneled through that spot, whistling between the cut saplings, before continuing up the mountain. One day it snowed hard for four hours, yet I didn't budge because deer were moving all around me. When Ken came by to pick me up for the hike back to camp and lunch, he laughed at my appearance. Said he thought I was dead, totally covered with snow, ice-rimmed beard and mustache, and not moving.

It's 4:20 now. The last faint glow of the sun has disappeared from the leaden winter sky. I survey my surroundings. This is a mixed hardwood forest, grown up on land that was farmed 60 years ago. It's hard to imagine how anyone could have scratched a living out of the rocky soil in this area. In the fading light, all the trees appear the same—vertical black lines stretching upward, lines that blend together as one if you stare at them long enough.

I refocus my eyes, moving them from right to left across the drab forest floor, searching for

movement. Darkness is setting in. When you're in these stark December woods, and you're watching daylight slowly turn to gray and then black, the feeling is almost as if you're going to sleep, except your eyes are open. There are maybe 15 more minutes of shooting light, and then I'll have to lower my bow and pack to the ground, climb down, and hike out to my car in the dark. I can hear the noise from the interstate a mile away. Traffic's picking up, people are heading home from work. A train whistle knifes through the stillness. I wonder if my wife is on that train.

I wiggle my toes, move my fingers, suppress another shiver. The cold is freezing on my beard, and I suspect that I again must look as if I'm frozen dead . . . .

To me, the one thing that all stands seem to have in common is that they're cold. Maybe in the beginning of the season the weather will be warm, and there will be pleasant days spent watching the woods, seeing the sun rise, the wildlife start to move. But as the season moves on, the cold creeps in, inevitably, uncaring. And those are the days you remember, the days you suffered, pinning your hopes on the chance that this might be the day he will come down the trail. You can envision him coming now, a big buck that walks right in front of your stand, his rack magnificent, his coat thick, his visage majestic. You can see the cold air billowing from his flared nostrils. You picture yourself slowly settling the sight pin on his heart. Then you let go and . . .

I fish a Milky Way out of my pocket, pulling the paper off with one hand to minimize my movements. Inching my hand to my mouth, I pop the candy in and slowly force my hand back down into my pocket. The bar is frozen, but I work it with my teeth and soon finish it.

Swish, swish. Another sound, one I didn't hear over my teeth crunching the candy bar. It's almost dark, but something is definitely coming . . . not down the trail, though, but through the thickets behind me. I deliberately remove my hands from my pockets and wrap them around my bow. My arrow is nocked. *Swish, crack, swish* . . . stop. He's right behind me now, maybe 15 yards away, probably with his nose in the air, warily checking the wind, maybe catching my scent. He's probably looking right at me. Should I try to move? Try to swivel around slowly? Should I stay still, on the chance he'll keep coming and walk right under my stand?

I decide to pivot around, slowly, very slowly. Maybe I'll get a chance at a shot. First my eyes, then my head. My heart is in my throat. *Swish, swish,*

swish, swish. The tension is unbearable, but this is a feeling that only hunters know, a feeling that hunters live for. My fingers tighten on the bowstring. . . .

The gray squirrel suddenly decides to run down a log next to my tree. He hops on the crunchy, leafy ground and bounds away. I relax and let out a deep breath. The shivering returns. It's almost too dark to see now anyway. I put the arrow into my quiver and stand up, letting the blood flow down my legs, making them tingle unbearably. I tie my bow to the rope with stiff fingers, then lower it to the ground. I undo my safety belt and begin to climb down.

Tomorrow he'll come. I'll be here.

Hunter's Fireside Book

GENE HILL

November

November is almost at the end of the road. You start out where it's warm and still in the lingering pause of summer, go through the part where leaves that are left are seared orange and look down into the valley where November lies.

There are many paths in the valley of November. Some lead to the marshes, others to the convoys of bobwhite, or wander to the hardwoods of turkey and whitetail deer.

Follow the dog or let the horse lead the way to where you can just listen for a moment or so and then go softly to where you hear the scratching of the ruffed grouse or the scolding of the squirrels.

Now stop. Wait here a minute or so and look around. There's a sumac where a buck has rubbed the velvet off his horns. Over by the spring you can see the little borings where the woodcock probed for worms; there are still some fox tracks in the mud.

The old chestnut log has lured a drumming grouse for years, the coons that live in the hollow oak nearby have watched him, sleepy-eyed, and somewhat bored. In the clearing, where the farm once was, is a 12-bird covey waiting for the wind to still so they can feed in quiet and keep a watch out for the Coopers hawk.

I know it's hard to wait. The dogs are anxious, the horse frets at the bit, and the boat down by the marsh is bobbing at the line as if it's anxious to get free.

But take just a minute more—you were a long time getting here, you know. Sit still and smell and taste and get the feel of this November.

Soak it up. Go into it softly and thoughtfully, with love and understanding, for another year must pass before you can come this way again. For neither you nor next November will ever be the same.

Keeping Warm

In the process of exchanging winter clothes for summer clothes in the storeroom in the attic I luckily ran across some old hunting clothes that gave me an excuse to sit down and wool gather (no pun intended) about the days before there were insulated boots and underwear.

Some things are better. It is a lot easier to spray your hunting shirts with some silicone waterproofing than to concoct a smelly mess of beeswax and paraffin to dip stuff in. I was of the school that would rather get soaked than walk around smelling like the

inside of a lamp chimney. But the biggest and the best arguments were on how to keep warm. There was the "layer of newspapers" school, where the weekly paper was tied around your body underneath the next to last shirt. You could hear who opted that way. Then there was always one tough-skinned old badger who just wore one, that's right, just one heavy wool shirt—mind you the weather often got down to zero and at 5 or 6 o'clock a.m. it was often far below. The "Mother's School" is the one I guess I got trapped in—both figuratively and literally. Mothers didn't want to see any skin showing, except maybe a little around the eyes. You wore everything you could stagger under and that was topped off with bib overalls that were cut-downs of your father's. After a half hour of walking, say to a deer stand, you were soaked through with sweat and promptly froze. You could not, however, convince your mother of this fact and consequently a boy risked pneumonia all winter long until he got big enough to win the argument, or tough enough to take four or five layers off and stand the consequences when he was found out—which he always was. Another problem, social as well as thermal, was whether or not it was "sissy" to wear the ear flaps down. We all had caps that were usually corduroy with car flaps that tied at the

top in a bow knot, letting the flaps loosely caress your frozen ears, but no torture on earth could have persuaded me to appear in a deer gang with the knot tied underneath my chin! Mittens of various materials: buckskin, or best of all a heavy homemade yarn, or all kinds of gloves. None of which ever worked to my certain memory. You simply walked around with your hands in your pockets as much as you could. I don't remember anyone who escaped a touch of frostbite on at least one of two fingers.

I guess that originality and conviction really started out at the bottom—with the feet. Erd Reeves either wore sneakers-in two or three feet of snow: all day long—or a tattered pair of hip boots with no socks. Did his feet ever freeze? No. But I have no idea why not. No idea at all. The local loggers wore their stupid knee high, tight laced leather boots that not only cut off most of the circulation but were instantly wet and unbearably cold. But I must admit I envied the dashing appearance they made and I'm sure I made out more than one imaginary order to Sears for a in case I ever got the money; which luckily I never did.

Outside all this variety was some sort of coat so you'd have pockets available. Nine out of ten wore near identical faded blue denim farm coats that smelled of sweet Holsteins or Jerseys. If you had the money—and it wasn't too much in those days, unless you didn't have it, which was the rule-you bought a red and black plaid Woolrich hunting coat with its magnificent high collar. I never could afford one, and by the time a friend of my father's wore his out to where he'd got a new one and passed the old one down to me, I was too long in the arms to wear it.

We may have looked and smelled funny, stuffed with paper and crammed into the bib overalls until they stretched tight like homemade sausage casings, but the reasons for being out are still the same. And the arguments about what to war still go on. But now, when the weather nudges bottom,

I stand patiently in the kitchen and wait until my wife's more nimble fingers have tied the ear flaps underneath my chin.

Friends?

There comes a time in every man's situation when he has to try to lie a little to his children to protect them from certain ugly sides of life until they are old enough to understand. For example, at this time of the year when I'm getting my stuff together to go out and have a few friendly rounds of skeet or trap or shoot a few patterns testing out a new reload I've concocted that mixes 85 with gs, one of my little girls will ask "Why isn't Mr. Zern or Mr. Rikhoff going with you?"

I simply say that my friends Mr. Zern and Mr. Rikhoff have horrible hangovers and couldn't stand the noise . . . but the truth is that these otherwise good family men are "fishing." I once tried to explain to Patty, my seven-year old, what "fishing" was. I explained that Mr. Zern would put worms on a hook, that the hook was tied to a pole of wood with a piece of string and Mr. Zern or Mr. Rikhoff would then dangle this in front of a small trout or has in an effort to catch him. I instantly realized my mistake

when Patty, who has been reading the Waterfowl Regulations, along with wholesome stories from Churchill's "Game Shooting" and Greener's "The Gun and Its Development" instantly saw the thing clearly and burst into tears. I asked her what was the matter and she said sobbing "But Daddy, that's against the law." I asked her what law and she said Section so-and-so paragraph so-and-so.

I hurriedly looked it up and found that she was referring to the Federal laws against baiting. I tried to explain to her that it did seem like that but it really wasn't. And to further clear her mind I went out and got some hair bass bugs Jim Rikhoff had forgotten the night he was helping me test the specific gravity of some apple cider (the same night he drove all the way home with the emergency brake on and had to have the drums freed with a welding torch). I told Party that certain men thought that if instead of using real bait, they used what they called artificials, as hair bugs certainly are, that this is the epitome of being sporting. She got the idea right away, although not at all pleased that the men she had admired for their ability to make light of her fathers whiskey and endure the rigors of pre-dawn goose pits and blistering August afternoons at Vandalia, Ohio, had this character flaw. So a little depressed at my lack of success at shielding her from these ugly facts of life, I watched her disappear into her playroom. A few hours later she came running into my study where I was busily putting a little Linseed on a few scratches in my Krieghoff stock.

"Daddy, we're rich, we're rich!" she shouted. And opening a cigar box she showed me what she'd been working on. In the box were some beech nuts, and some corn kernels, perfectly made of colored modeling clay and even a long roll of serrated earth-colored clay that made a fairly good imitation of an earthworm. I asked her what she thought she had. She said that if we made artificial corn, artificial beech nuts and fake worms, why couldn't we attract ducks, grouse and woodcock. That really wouldn't be baiting, it would be using artificials, and we could go into business and make bushels of money, which she thought, having listened to my wife's frequent discussions on the subject, we sorely needed. I explained to her that it wasn't the sort of thing a real bird shooter would stoop to doing, legality notwithstanding. I also pointed out that she had once seen Mr. Rikhoff drink a rum cola and so he was not to be trusted with an idea like plastic corn and that we would just forget it. But somehow the picture of Jim Rikhoff and Ed Zern holding up a brace of pintails and saying how they "took them over half a peek of hand-made plastic Golden Bantam" sticks gloomily in my mind. Will the Federal authorities please advise?

Memories of Misses Past

It's sort of traditional at the end of the year to look back and take stock of what has happened during the last 12 months. One friend of mine keeps a diary. The regular kind, you might have seen one, for hunters and shooters. But a diary is pretty matter-of-fact. You sit around with a couple of your shooting buddies and one of them says, ". . . that was the day you had the double on green-wing teal . . ." Without a diary you can agree and return the compliment with something along the line of

". . . yes, that's right; I remember it well because it was just two weeks later you had a 94 at Grouse Ridge Gun Club . . ." and the evening is warm with the passing of such soft and sweet memories. But with a diary this never happens. The diary reveals that not only did you not double up on green-wing teal on that particular day (you did not one time double on anything, all year), you missed four easy incomers flaring out over the decoys and went home with two sea ducks. The diary would also reveal that George M. did not get a 94. The diary would read that as usual George M. was stopping his gun and lucked into an 87. The diary is to the shooter as the scale and the tape measure are to the fisherman— irrefutable proof that the judgment and memory of the outdoorsman improves, like a fine wine, with the passing of time. We're not in the business of facts and figures, anyway. Nobody's keeping score. Our end of the year inventory can have anything on the shelf we want. Two ruffed grouse can become eight or even ten or twelve. If you count the near misses, perhaps even a trifle more. The weather along the Chesapeake can get a lot colder and windier when you're sitting in front of a log fire a month later.

So instead of taking a long. hard look at the times gone by, let's take a softer dreamy one. Why not put your feet up on the good furniture and see what you'd like to have happened. This is nowhere near any form of lying-that's an art in itself. We're just looking at the truth from a variety of angles. Did Old Ben break into a covey of birds and flush them out of sight or do you suspect that he hit a running bunch of birds and did damn well to put them up so you could mark down the singles?

Did you really miss that huge old gander that came sailing in on set wings or did you just lire way behind him on purpose-sort of a parting salute? Did you really end up with only a 17 on your last round of trap or were you "working" with the gun to test the width of the pattern? Give it a little thought and you'll discover some nice smooth lines to shore up

your story. I know one shooter who can barely hit the ground with his hat and after his usual two- shot miss he waves his gun barrel around very happily and says "Boy. that's what I'm out here for . . . just to see 'em fly!" He's carried on like this for so long that even I'm tempted to believe him. Trapshooters who have a long string of zeros will talk about how they're just polishing timing and rhythm. And one of the stupidest bird dogs I have ever seen is constantly praised by his owner for his "range."

So, look back and see what fits—from a different perspective. And next year start giving your Christmas presents early. Comment in admiration on some shooter's rhythm and timing. Slap your buddy on the back next time his dog busts every bird for a square mile and tell him how much you hate those close-working dogs that are always right there almost under your feet. And when we're together and it's one of those days when I'm a little bit off, it would be a kind thing for us to chat about sportsmanship and the bigger meaning of being out-of-doors.

Getting Ready

Along about now when the first of the cooling evenings sends the fog sliding thickly through the meadow—so heavy that I can barely see the top of the split rail fence—I feel the urge to get ready. My wood ducks are itchy to leave and now and then from somewhere high a Canada goose reminds me to get moving. The odd woodcock has already been seen along the lane. The shaggy bark hickory is shrugging off its summer green and I can start walking across the lawn without feeling guilty that I'm not pushing the mower. And when I can really forget that I forgot to take down the storm windows last spring; it's time to get ready.

I guess everybody starts a little differently. In the back closet, most with a few tooth marks from times when Tip or Ben or Judy was a pup, and often with a touch of last year's mud, are the boots.

I always want to use the English waterproofing method of half filling each of the leather boots with warmed neatsfoot oil and let them sit—but I never seem to have any neatsfoot oil handy. So I do the next best thing. I light a little fire in the room where my books are and let the boots get warm then give them a good coating of waterproof paste. I'll read a little bit while that soaks in. If I remember to buy them, I'll thread in a new set of laces; if not I'll tie new knots in the old ones. I've got an old toothbrush to get the gunk down in around the soles and worry the briar scratches the best I can. Some would say they look pretty down and out- but I know briars put character in a boot and I like that.

After the boots are done the next step is the hunting coats. With me hunting coats are always somewhat of a problem. The fact behind that is that I shift back and forth (for no really good reason) between a 12-gauge, a 16-gauge, and a 28-gauge. So, by the end of the year, each coat has an assortment of shells of various sizes. I originally started out, very logically, by having a 12-gauge coat, a 16-gauge coat, and a 28-gauge coat. But I got to grabbing the 16-gauge coat and the 12-gauge gun and have ended up rummaging around general stores trying to find something smaller than magnum fours (which is all they ever seem to carry) in order to have a pass or two at ruffed grouse. If you try to find 28-gauge shells in most of the back-water gas stations or groceries they just plain think you're bonkers. Anyway, I have to sort shells and point out the necessary mending to the Queen Bee. After the 12-gauge shells are restored to the 12-gauge coat and so on down the line, the brush pants are separated from the old red handkerchief: wadded up in the hip pockets, the lost pocket knives are found and the nickels and dimes are swooped up by the girls for their banks, order is seen to be taking form. The britches are let out their annual inch in the seat and the annual question "Why don't you throw these old pants out?" is answered by the annual "I will, after I get one more season's wear."

This ritual over, borne patiently but disinterestedly by the dogs, the guns are seen to. Everything in the gun rack is shifted. The trap and skeet guns are moved to the end of the row and the three bird guns put back up front. The dog whistles are found and hung back on their pegs. The gunning glasses are cleaned and the folding cup washed. To the eye of a casual visitor I am now READY. And on the surface, all things in order, it would, indeed seem a neat and meticulous chap is ready to step under his cap and set out. Not yet. For it is only September—teasing us a little with soft fog and a cool evening.

For in the coming weeks the earnest work goes on. The long walks to slim the overfed dogs and the overfed feeder of dogs. The long walks delicious in the prospect of searching out a new or at least long-forgotten cover and reassurance that the natural order of things is in good shape for at least one more fall.

There has come a time in my life when the planting of the tree is at least as enjoyable as the picking of the fruit. We do not see the later chores of pruning. Nor the invasions of leaf borers nor the weight of ice too great for limbs to bear. Only when you plant an apple tree can you honestly imagine perfect apples.

When you prepare early for fall then, and only then, do you have fall perfect; fall without worms. The October seen in September is the October of the landscape artist. It is the October of a small boy, an eager hunting dog or a middle—aged bird hunter.

So, I think, it is with we who live to be outside. No day is ever separate from the tomorrow to come. If we miss now, we'll hit the next time out. That's why dogs bury bones—for tomorrow. If I buried a bone I'd probably forget where I did it. But as long as it's on my mind, I think I'll get up and sprinkle a few 28s in my 12-gauge coat and some 165 in my 28-gauge coat. No old dog can outsmart me when it comes to getting ready.

Hunter's Moon

An English astronomer once commented to the effect that the slight changing of the redness of a distant star could alter a hundred years of our mathematical calculations. This was his way of saying that the works of man are insignificant when faced with the whims of nature. Civilizations have been born or lost in earthquakes and the coming and going of volcanos and tidal waves. A degree or two of temperature change over a few thousand years melted away the ice cap that covered much of North America and a slight shifting in the rain

patterns of the world has created bare and torrid deserts where years ago lay tropic jungle. Hairy mammoths that were born and raised in long-lost humid swamps are now chipped out of the light blue ice of our polar lands.

And you and I stand now in the coming of the fall speculating on the possibilities of an early frost that hopefully will skim the leaves from tenacious oaks . . . and yet not be severe enough to chill the ground so as to send the Woodcock flying on to warmer soils and softer breezes. The slim balance of our sport so hangs on the vagaries of the unseen winds, the unknown seas—mysteries in their causes no les to us than to our apelike ancestors.

Yet, we will grow restive in the weeks ahead. The Hunter's Moon will see the shadow of a sleepless man who paces up and down his plot of grass, a morsel of dog as curious and as expectant as he is, tagging at his heels. He will stare at scudding clouds . . . wet his fingers to predict the vagrant wind . . . and hope that tomorrow will be kind enough to offer him a touch of frost or a heavy rain or a tracking snow. (And don't forget the days you have all three between the dawn and dark!)

But we'll go on out, if I know you, regardless. And come home wet or cold or both ten times to the single day we come home smiling at the red god's toss of dice. But that's all part of sport . . . small creatures are the birds and sheep and deer to us . . . and we, small creatures too, our wishes merely hopes sent up at night, cast out on the winds, in the light of the Hunter's Moon.

Why I Hunt (and Other Stories)

WILLIAM G. TAPPLY

I hunt because my father hunted, and he took me with him, and so we built a bond that has endured past his death, and because his father hunted, and his father's father, and all of the fathers in my line and yours, as far back as those fathers who invented spears and axes and recorded their adventures with pictures on the walls of caves.

I hunt because it links me with the boy I used to be and with the young man my father was then.

I hunt because it keeps my passions alive and my memories fresh and my senses alert even as my beard grows gray, and because I fear that if I stopped hunting I would become an old man, and because I believe that as long as I hunt I will remain young.

I hunt because I don't buy futures or sell cars or swing deals or negotiate hostile takeovers, or litigate or prosecute or plea bargain, but because I am nevertheless, like everyone else, a predator. So I go to the woods where I belong.

I hunt because I love ruffed grouse and woodcock and pheasants and quail and ducks, and because I can imagine no more honorable way for them to die than at the hands of a respectful hunter. As Thoreau understood, ". . . the hunter is the greatest friend of the animals hunted, not excepting the Humane Society."

I hunt because the goldenrod and milkweed glisten when the early-morning autumn sun melts the frost from the fields, and because native brook trout spawn in hidden October brooks, and because New England uplands glow crimson and orange and gold in the season of bird hunting.

I hunt because when I stumble upon overgrown cellarholes and family graveyards deep in the woods, it reminds me that I'm connected to the farmers who cleared the land and grew their crops and buried their wives and children there, and who in the process created ideal grouse and woodcock habitat, and because I like to believe that I am the first man in a century to stand in those places.

I hunt because Burton Spiller and Gorham Cross hunted, and Corey Ford and Ed Zern and Lee Wulff and Harold Blaisdell and Frank Woolner, and because they invited me to hunt with them, and because they were men of my father's generation who treated me like a man when I was a boy, and because they were writers who knew how to tell a story, and because they inspired me to try it for myself.

I hunt because Art Currier and Keith Wegener and Jason Terry and Rick Boyer and Skip Rood and Tony Brown and Marty Connolly hunt, and because these are generous and intelligent men who don't take themselves too seriously, and who are saner than most. They love and respect the out of doors and Nature's creatures, and their friendship has made me a better man than I otherwise would be.

I hunt because the ghosts of beloved companions such as Bucky and Duke and Julie and Megan and Freebie and Waldo prance through the woods, snuffling and tail-wagging, making game and pointing, and especially Burt, my beloved Brittany, who all loved to hunt more than to eat, and whose enthusiasm and indomitable spirit will forever inspire me, and because hunting dogs make the most tolerant friends. They are smarter in many ways than we are, and they can teach us things we otherwise wouldn't understand if we'll just pay attention.

I hunt because I believe Thoreau was right: "Fishermen, hunters, woodchoppers, and others, spending their lives in the fields and woods, in a peculiar sense a part of Nature themselves, are often in a more favorable mood for observing her, in the intervals of their pursuits, than philosophers or poets even, who approach her with expectation." I hunt because I'm convinced, as many anthropologists argue, that prehistoric man was a hunter before he became a farmer, and because this genetic gift remains too powerful in me to resist. I do not need to hunt in order to eat, but I need to hunt to be fully who I am.

I hunt because it teaches me what it taught our earliest ancestors: the benefits of cooperation, inventiveness, division of labor, sharing, and interdependence. These are skills that bird hunters must master. Without these derivatives of hunting, our race would still be primitive. As the psychologist Erich Fromm observed, "[Humans] have been genetically programmed through hunting behavior: cooperation and sharing. Cooperation between members of the same band was a practical necessity for most hunting societies; so was the sharing of food. Since meat is perishable in most climates except that of the Arctic, it could not be preserved. Luck in hunting was not equally divided among all hunters; hence the practical outcome was that those who had luck today would share their food with those who would be lucky tomorrow. Assuming hunting behavior led to genetic changes, the conclusion would be that modern man has an innate impulse for cooperation and sharing, rather than for killing and cruelty."

I hunt because if I didn't, I would have seen fewer eagles and ospreys, minks and beavers, foxes and bears, antelope and moose, and although I do not hunt these creatures, I do love to enter into their world and spy on them.

I hunt because I love old 20-gauge double-barrel shotguns, and scuffed leather boots with rawhide laces, and canvas vests with a few old breast feathers in their game pockets.

I hunt for the scent of Hoppe's gun oil and camp coffee and wet bird dog and frost-softened, boot-crushed wild apples.

I hunt for the whistle of a woodcock's wings and the sudden explosion of a ruffed grouse's flush, for the tinkle of a dog's bell and for the sudden, pulse-quickening silence when he locks on point, for my partner's cry of "Mark!" when he kicks up a bird, for the distant drumming of a grouse, like a balky engine starting up, for the high predatory cry of a red-tail hawk, for the quiet gurgle of a deep-woods trout stream, for the soft soughing of the breeze in the pines, for the snoring of my companions, human and canine, in a one-room cabin, and for the soothing patter of an autumn rainstorm on a tin roof.

I hunt because it is never boring or disappointing to be out of doors with a purpose, even when no game is seen, and because taking a walk in the woods without a purpose makes everything that happens feel random and accidental and unearned.

I hunt for the keyed-up conversation, for the laying of plans and the devising of strategies, for the way memory and experience spark imagination and expectation as we drive into the low-angled sunshine on an autumn morning, for the coffee we sip from a dented old Thermos, and for the way the dogs whine and pace on the way to the day's first cover.

And I hunt for the satisfying exhaustion after a long day in the woods, for the new stories that every hour of hunting gives us, and for the soft snarfling and dream-whimpering and twitching of sleeping dogs on the back seat as we drive home through the darkness.

I hunt because it reminds me that in Nature there is a food chain where everything eats and is, in its turn, eaten, where birth, survival, and reproduction give full meaning to life, where death is ever-present, and where the only uncertainty is the time and manner of that death. Hunting reminds me that I am integrated into that cycle, not separate from it or above it.

I hunt with a gun, and sometimes I kill. But, as the philosopher Jose Ortega y Gasset has written, "To the sportsman the death of the game is not what interests him; that is not his purpose. What interests him is everything that he had to do to achieve that death—that is, the hunt. Therefore what was before only a means to an end is now an end in itself. Death is essential because without it there is no authentic hunting: the killing of the animal is the natural end of the hunt and that goal of hunting itself, not of the hunter. The hunter seeks this death because it is no less than the sign of reality for the whole hunting process. . . . one does not hunt in order to kill; on the contrary, one kills in order to have hunted."

I hunt to prevent myself from forgetting that everything I eat once lived, and that it is important to accept responsibility for living at the expense of another life, and that killing is half of the equation of living. I hunt because it is hard and demanding and sometimes dangerous work, and because performing difficult work well gives me pleasure. And I hunt because it is fun, an intense kind of artistic game, and I like to challenge myself to do it well. As Aldo Leopold wrote: "We seek contacts with nature because we derive pleasure from them . . . The duck-hunter in his blind and the operatic singer on the stage, despite the disparity of their accouterments, are doing the same thing. Each is reviving, in play, a drama formerly inherent in daily life. Both are, in the last analysis, esthetic exercises."

I hunt because, in the words, again, of Ortega y Gasset, it gives me "a vacation from the human condition," which, all by itself, is a full and satisfactory reason.

Five Aces

When I visited my father during the last autumn of his life, we liked to talk about how when he was feeling better we'd pile into my truck and spend a day or two driving the back roads and see if we could track down our old string of grouse covers. They were loaded with indelible memories that both of us cherished.

Somewhere along the line Dad had lost his priceless set of topographic maps where those old partridge hotspots were marked. We hadn't hunted them for close to forty years, but we figured between the two of us, we'd recognize the old landmarks. We'd find them.

We'd run Burt, my Brittany, through the familiar old orchards and alder runs and field edges and piney corners, just for old time's sake. Dad would walk along, and if we got a point, I'd hand him the gun and let him walk up the bird, the way he did with me when I was a kid and those old covers were busting with grouse.

In his day, my father was a crack wingshot. I liked to imagine him dropping one last bird cleanly, and Burt hustling over, picking it up in his mouth, and bringing it to Dad's hand.

I guess we both knew it wasn't going to happen.

During those visits, I made it a point to urge my father to reminisce. He'd always been a pragmatic, stoical Yankee. He'd had a rich and fulfilling life, but a hard one, and he knew that the good old days hadn't always been so good. Nostalgia didn't come naturally to him.

But when it came to upland hunting, he admitted that those old days really had been awfully good.

"Remember Five Aces?" he'd say.

"A magical grouse cover," I'd say. "The best one ever."

"I'd like to see it again." He'd close his eyes and smile, remembering. Then he'd look at me and shrug. "No, actually, I guess I wouldn't. It won't be the same."

*   *   *   *

My father's New England encompassed the southern halves of Maine and New Hampshire. This, naturally, has been my New England, too. The countryside was different in the decade before World War II when he began hunting ruffed grouse. Winding roads, most of them dirt, connected dairy farms to villages. Otherwise it was mostly young secondgrowth forest and meadows and stone walls and recently-abandoned farmland—pastures and orchards and woodlots growing thick with blackberry and thornapple, alder and poplar, pine and hemlock, oak and beech.

As Dad remembered it, it didn't much matter where you hunted. Grouse were scattered everywhere. A day of hunting meant wrapping a corned-beef-and-cheddar-cheese sandwich in waxed paper and stuffing it in your game pocket, cramming your pockets with 20-gauge shotgun shells, tucking your Winchester Model 21 under your arm, whistling up your setter, and setting forth. You'd put the morning sun on your back and head off in a westerly direction, following the dog wherever his nose led him.

Around noontime you'd stop, eat your sandwich, drink from a springfed brook-trout stream, and munch a wild Baldwin apple. If it was one of those warm October days, you'd lie back on the pine needles with the sun on your face, lace your fingers behind your neck, and snooze for an hour with your dog's chin on your thigh. Then you'd load up your shotgun, put the afternoon sun behind you, and wander easterly until you got back to where you started from.

All along the way, Dad said, you'd find grouse—singles, pairs, sometimes whole broods. Even an average dog would point some of them, and even a mediocre wingshot would bag a few. My father always insisted that knocking down a flying grouse in thick brush was surely a triumph, but not really the main point of it. Grouse hunting was more about finding birds than shooting them. A good day was never measured by the heft of your game pocket.

*   *   *   *

By the time I started hunting with my father in the late 1950's, the New England landscape had changed, and grouse were harder to find. The meandering old dirt roads had been straightened and widened and paved over, the abandoned farmland was being reclaimed by developers, and houses were popping up everywhere. Civilization was spreading over the countryside, and we couldn't just set off into the woods for a day's hunt. We did almost as much driving as we did walking. A day of grouse hunting meant six or eight stops at pockets of cover that we'd learned to depend on to hold a few birds. Dad called them "our string o' pearls."

A few of our covers sprawled over several square miles and occupied us for the better part of an afternoon. But most of them took little more than an hour to hunt. They were apple-and-pine corners, grape tangles, alder runs, poplar hillsides, brushy edges bordering dense evergreens. They were usually good for a grouse or two, and when the woodcock flights were down, we'd sometimes find the ground whitewashed with their chalking.

Every season we lost a few of our old covers to housing developments, to power lines, to highway cloverleafs, to strip malls. Others just stopped producing. So we were always scouting for new covers. We scoured our topo maps for clues. We drove the back roads, always ready to take the one less traveled. Any break in a stone wall might signify an ancient cartpath that led to an abandoned farmyard or an old woodlot. We looked for apple orchards gone wild, alder-edged streambottoms, pastures grown to clumps of pine and thornapple, hillsides thick with second-growth poplar and birch—anything that looked birdy, which meant anything that reminded us of someplace where we'd found birds in the past. We didn't have much science for it. A birdy cover had a feel to it that was more than the sum of its parts.

Whenever a new spot produced some grouse, we circled its location on our topographic map, gave it a name, and added it to our string o' pearls.

* * * *

We were munching corned-beef-and-cheese sandwiches and sipping coffee beside a little New Hampshire brook. Duke, our old setter, snoozed on his side in a patch of October sunlight. Our open shotguns lay in the grass beside us. After a day and a half of hard hunting, all four barrels were still clean.

"Slim pickins," murmured Dad.

I nodded. "Mighty slim."

"First Chance, empty," he said. "Ditto Bullring. That one wild grouse in Mankiller. What was it, two woodcock in all of Tripwire?"

"Maybe three," I said. "Duke bumped 'em. Never saw them."

"I dunno," he said. "Maybe our covers are just petering out. They don't look as birdy as they used to."

"They'd probably look birdier if we were finding birds in them."

Dad smiled. "Hand me that map, will you?"

He spread our topographic map on the ground between us. Circles had been inked on it, marking the locations of our secret string of grouse covers. Mankiller, Clumps, Schoolhouse, Jackpot, County Line, Long Walk In, Tap's Pines, Bill's Folly, Traitorous Owl.

Dad squinted at the map, moved his forefinger over it, paused, then looked at me. "You up for an explore?"

* * * *

Brush scraped both sides of our station wagon as we crept over the old rutted roadway. It paralleled a rocky little stream that surely held native brook trout. The road, we happily observed, did not appear to have been driven on for a long time—perhaps, or so we wanted to believe, not since the farmer who cut it through the woods had loaded his family and his belongings into the back of his pickup and left for the last time decades earlier.

It ended at an abandoned farmyard on the edge of a sloping field grown to milkweed and goldenrod and sprinkled with gnarled Baldwin apple trees and clumps of juniper. The farmhouse on the hilltop was long gone. The roof and walls had caved into the cellarhole, but the fieldstone chimney still stood, and an ancient lilac grew in the dooryard.

We got out to look it over. The field rolled down to a stand of poplars that gave way to a screen of evergreens. Off to the right, a hillside thick with brush and briar and birch rose to a ridge lined with oaks, and behind the cellarhole, the glimmer of a brook wended through a string of alders.

"Well," I said. "What do you think?"

"Looks kinda birdy," said Dad. "Worth a look-see."

By the time we got our shotguns loaded, Duke was pointing in the poplars that rimmed the bottom of the field. Dad shot that grouse. A minute later he dropped another one that rumbled out from a clump of hemlocks. He doubled on a pair of woodcock that helicoptered up from a patch of alders, and then he nailed another grouse that we surprised pecking apples in the corner of the old orchard. In between, half a dozen grouse and at least as many woodcock escaped. I shot at several of them.

When we got back to our car, Dad emptied his game pocket, picked up one of his grouse, and stroked its crest with his forefinger. "Eureka," he said softly.

It had been the best three hours of bird hunting that we could remember.

"Do you realize," I said, "that you just went five-for-five?"

He grinned "Of course I do." He reached into the back seat, pulled out our topographic map, drew a circle on it, then arched his eyebrows at me.

I took the pen and wrote "Five Aces" on the map.

*   *   *   *

Hippie House, Stick Farm, John's Knoll, Arnold's Picker, Red Bloomers, Lost Eyeglasses, Marilyn Monroe, The Old Hotel. Five Aces, especially. Just reciting their names floods me with half a century's worth of memories. Dad, of course. Burt Spiller, Gorham Cross, Frank Woolner, Harold Blaisdell and Corey Ford, the men of my father's generation who shared their wisdom and their grouse covers with me. Keith, Art, Skip, Tony, Marty and Jason, bird-hunting partners of my own generation. Macko, Bing, Duke, Cider, Bucky, Waldo, Freebie, Burt, Lilly, bird dogs both mediocre and gifted, all lovable. Points and retrieves, flights of woodcock and broods of grouse, shots made and shots missed.

*   *   *   *

I don't suppose my hunting partners and I will ever find another Five Aces, but we keep looking. We scour our topo maps, drive the back roads, track down rumors. And every year we manage to come up with a few new grouse covers.

This past season we found a brood of grouse at the end of a rocky road that crosses over a river and cuts through some woods. We're calling it Grandma's House.

Curse Buster is the little pocket of apple and evergreen where Jason dropped his first grouse after nearly two seasons of shooting and missing.

And the old pasture where a grouse caught me—literally—with my pants down and my empty shotgun on the ground, and the only thing I could shoot at it were words as it glided brazenly across the open field, we've named Expletive Deleted.

*   *   *   *

The October after my father died, I piled Burt into my truck and we went hunting for Five Aces. I finally found the narrow, rutted old dirt roadway . . . except it had been paved and widened and straightened and lined with mailboxes. The rocky stream that ran alongside it now flowed through culverts and concrete gutters. Half a dozen more-or-less identical colonial-style houses had sprung up around a cul-de-sac in the field, and they'd bulldozed the hilltop flat where the old cellarhole had been. More houses were scattered along the new roads that had been cut through the woods.

I'm glad my father wasn't with me to see it.

Opening Day

"Fishermen, hunters, woodchoppers, and others, spending their lives in the fields and woods, in a peculiar sense a part of Nature themselves, are often in a more favorable mood for observing her, in the intervals of their pursuits, than philosophers or poets even, who approach her with expectation."

—Henry David Thoreau, *WALDEN*

I went to bed at ten and set my alarm for 2:15. I read for a while before I turned out the light. Then I stared at the ceiling, waiting for the alarm to go off. I never sleep the night before Opening Day of the duck season.

We called our secret pond Tranquility, after the book by Col. Harold Sheldon. We'd found it on a topographic map, where it had a different name. We'd followed the lumpy old tote road to Tranquility's muddy banks in Keith's 4WD truck, and, yes, it was loaded with mallards and woodies and blacks. At sunrise and again at dusk they traded back and forth to the swamp over the hill.

We'd had a lot of fun all summer, watching the ducks fly over our pond and anticipating Opening Day. Now it was upon us.

Tranquility is shallow and weedy and mud-bottomed, the product of an ancient milldam on a little trout stream in the hills of southwestern Maine. We made countless trips across the pond in Keith's Old Town canoe to the site we'd chosen for our blind—on the tip of a point on the east bank, so the morning sun would rise behind us, with the head-high cattails at our backs. We loaded the canoe with plywood and two-by-fours and stainless-steel stakes and chicken wire, and we sweltered under August skies, up to our hips in water, to cobble our blind together. We paddled the creek channel so many times that its meandering course was imprinted on our brains, and we knew we could find our blind at four o'clock on a moonless October morning.

The streets were dark on the drive to Keith's house. I felt foolishly virtuous, being up and around while the rest of the world was squandering that magic time. The orange glow from Keith's kitchen window was a beacon in the night. I tapped softly on the back door, found it unlocked, and went in. The mingled, evocative aromas of frying sausage and perked coffee greeted me.

I sat at the table. Keith slid a mug of coffee in front of me. Raisin, his old brown Lab, shuffled over and plopped his chin on my knee. I scratched the special place on his forehead. He whimpered and thrashed his tail. He knew it was Opening Day, too.

We ate two-handed—a fork for stabbing hash browns and sausage, a biscuit for sopping up egg yolk. "Three-duck limit, you know," mumbled Keith. "Hardly worth it."

"That's how everyone else will figure it," I said. "They figure, buy a license, federal duck stamp, state waterfowl stamp, give up a night's sleep and a day's work. For a lousy three ducks? It ain't worth it,

they'll figure. So we'll have the birds all to ourselves. A three-duck limit sounds good to me."

"If they're flying," he said, "it'll be all over in the first fifteen minutes."

"So?"

He nodded. "Valid point."

The moon had set, and except for a billion stars, the October sky was black when we got to Tranquility. We loaded decoys and camouflage netting and shotguns and shotgun shells and Thermos bottles of coffee and bags of donuts and Raisin and ourselves into Keith's canoe, and we paddled across to the blind by starlight. We were careful not to thump the gunwales with our paddles, out of deference to the quiet. We could hear ducks gabbling softly in the potholes. They were all around us. Raisin whimpered, and I thought I heard Keith whimpering, too.

By the time we got to the blind, the stars had started to blink out and the sky was turning sooty. We shoved the canoe under some bushes, and I began draping the netting around the blind, cutting some cattails and sticking them across the top to break our silhouettes. Raisin sat beside me scanning the horizon.

Meanwhile, Keith was in his hip boots setting out the dekes. I looked up when I heard him whistle. A big flock of mallards came skimming over the blind, turned, and splashed into the decoys all around Keith. He quacked at them. They ignored him. Then he laughed, and the birds jumped and flew away.

We were all set up by six o'clock, a half hour before legal shooting. "We probably won't see any more ducks all day," Keith said. "Just those dumb ones that didn't even notice me muckin' around out there."

"They weren't that dumb," I said. "They knew it was too early to shoot."

Just then about a dozen black ducks materialized in front of us. They dropped into the decoys and noodled around for a while before they paddled off. A pair of wood ducks circled a couple of times but didn't set in. They sky continued to brighten, and as it did, we saw skeins of ducks passing back and forth over the pond. Some of them tilted toward our decoys, then continued on their way. Others turned for a closer look. A number of them set their wings and skidded in. They stayed long enough to figure out that the decoys were fake before they wandered away.

In that half hour before legal shooting, we could have killed several limits apiece. "It's gonna be too easy," said Keith. "It's gonna be over before it starts. All that work for ten minutes of shooting."

"Since when," I said, "did easy ever bother us?"

"I got an idea," he said. "Let's get our money's worth. Let's watch the birds fly for a while before we start shooting."

I liked that idea, so that's what we did. The air was full of ducks—blacks and mallards, woodies and teal, pintails and redheads. We hunkered in our blind, drank coffee, and watched them fly while the sky brightened and the sun came up behind us and set the autumn foliage across the pond afire.

Finally Keith said, "We probably ought to shoot our ducks pretty soon."

We loaded up, and Raisin, who knew what that meant, shivered.

The ducks had stopped flying, of course. We sat there until nine-thirty, while the dawn turned into a bluebird October morning, and we never fired a shot. Then we shrugged, collected the decoys, took down the netting, piled everything into the canoe, paddled back across Tranquility, loaded Keith's truck, and went home.

We laughed about it. But we agreed that it had been a memorable Opening Day, and when we got to Keith's house and told his wife about all the ducks we'd seen, she said, "So you *don't* need to go hunting and shoot guns and kill things to have your fun, then."

"You miss the point, sweetie," said Keith. "If we hadn't gone hunting, we wouldn't have been there in the first place."

Last Hunt

Nick pulled his truck against the snowbank beside the mud-frozen road and turned off the engine. Last night's snow layered the dark hemlocks, and the scattering of old Baldwin apple trees on the hillside were black and gnarly. Here and there a wizened fruit still hung from a branch.

"Ah," said Nick's father from the seat beside him. "The Treacherous Owl. We had some fun here. I wondered where you were taking me."

"Looks different in the snow, huh?" said Nick.

"We never had any reason to come here in January," said the old man. "It was woodcock season when that owl showed us this place, wasn't it?"

Nick nodded. "October. The leaves hadn't dropped yet. That was a long time ago. I was just a kid, still trying to keep up with you in the woods."

*   *   *   *

They'd been driving the back roads that day, headed from one grouse cover to another one. Nick had been sitting in the passenger seat and his father was driving slowly, as he always did when they traveled the New Hampshire dirt roads. In the back seat, Duke, their old setter, had his chin on Nick's right shoulder and his nose poking out the open window. All three of them had their eyes peeled for road birds.

When the dark shadow glided across the roadway in front of them, Nick's father hit the brakes. "Did you see that?"

"What was it?" said Nick.

"Big old horned owl. Now what do you suppose he's up to?"

"Hunting," said Nick. "Like us."

"You suppose he knows something we don't know?"

"Bet he doesn't know the ten main exports of Bolivia," said Nick.

His father chuckled. "That knowledge wouldn't do him any more good than it'll do you. But I bet he knows where to find a good meal."

"You think he's hunting for grouse in there?"

"I think," said the old man, "that I see alders and old apple trees and birch whips and hemlocks, and I think I detect the ruts of an old cart path at that break in the stone wall, and I bet we'll find a cellarhole in there where some old farmer made a nice grouse cover for us."

"We better take a look," said Nick.

His father backed up and pulled into the ancient roadway. Fifty yards in at the top of a little round hill they found the cellarhole. The farmhouse had collapsed into itself, but the fieldstone chimney still stood, and out back were a dozen toppled granite gravestones, so eroded by decades of wind and weather that Nick couldn't read the dates on them.

He hadn't yet begun carrying a gun in the woods in those days. His father called it his grouse-hunting apprenticeship. Nick had learned a lot, slogging through the woods behind his father, trying to match his old man's long-legged stride. He'd learned where grouse lived and how they flushed with a sudden explosion of wings, and he'd learned how his father's shotgun came up to his shoulder and began swinging at the sound before he saw anything.

When he thought about it, Nick realized he couldn't begin to enumerate the things he'd learned from trailing his father through the woods.

That owl had showed them a sweet little grouse cover. The apple orchard, which mingled with briar and juniper and thornapple and patches of poplar, dribbled down the hillside behind the cellarhole to a boggy little brook bordered by alders. Duke busted a couple of grouse as they worked their way through the orchard. Nick's old man yelled halfheartedly at the dog. They figured that on balance, Duke did more good than harm, though it was a close call. The old setter never could figure out grouse, but he was death on wing-tipped birds and didn't mind pointing a woodcock now and then.

When the dog locked on point in the alders, Nick's father handed the boy his shotgun. "Most likely a woodcock," the old man whispered. "When he flushes, take your time, let him get out there. Make sure you keep your head down. And don't forget the safety."

Nick nodded. His old man told him the same thing every time he let him try a shot. So far, Nick had never hit a flying bird of any kind. His father always said, "Tough shot," or, "That bird zigged when he should've zagged," or, "I thought you were right on him," as though he actually expected the boy to connect. "The law of averages will catch up with you," his father would say. "When it does, watch out birds." Personally, Nick wondered if he'd ever hit anything.

Nick had observed that when they flushed in thick alders, woodcock tended to helicopter straight up and kind of hang there for a minute before they darted off in some unpredictable direction. But this time, when Nick walked up behind Duke and the bird took flight, it stayed low. Nick's gun came up to his shoulder and his thumb flicked off the safety and he remembered to snuggle his cheek against the stock, but the way the bird was weaving back and forth through the alders, Nick couldn't get on him.

His old man always said, "You can't kill anything you don't shoot at," so just as the bird was about to disappear out of range, Nick pulled the trigger.

"Hey," his old man yelled. "You got him." Nick could hear how he was trying not to sound surprised.

A minute later Duke came back with the dead woodcock in his mouth. Nick's father said, "Thank you," and took the bird from the dog. He held it in his hand and stroked its head with his forefinger. "A lovely little bird," he said softly. "Sometimes I wish we could put them back, like trout." He handed the woodcock to Nick. "Congratulations. Good shooting."

"Thank you, law of averages," Nick said on that October day more than forty years ago when the horned owl flew across the road.

* * * *

"Look how tall those beeches are now," Nick's old man said as they sat there in the truck looking out at the snowy January landscape. "The Treacherous Owl's way past its prime."

Nick found himself smiling. "Aren't we all."

"We packed away a lot of memories here, though, didn't we?"

Nick nodded. "That's why I thought this was where we should come today. To remember. My Bucky pup made his first point right in there." Nick pointed into the woods.

They both looked out the window of the truck. "That was a lovely sidehill of birch whips when we first started coming here," said the old man. "Not much taller than a man's head. There was always a woodcock or two in those birches. Look at 'em now."

Now they were grown-up trees as thick through the trunk as a strong man's arm.

"Bucky was what, six months old that season?" said Nick's father.

"Tiny little thing. All ears and enthusiasm."

"Right," said Nick. "The birches had grown a little taller by then, but it was still a good spot for woodcock. That was the only time I remember feeling as though I absolutely had to shoot a bird. To reward Bucky for his point."

Nick's father chuckled quietly, and Nick understood that he was remembering what Nick was remembering. Bucky had skidded into a point in the middle of the birches, and Nick had pushed in, flushed the woodcock, and missed it with both barrels, and then his father had shot once and dumped the bird. The old man had always been

a better wingshot than Nick, even at the very end of his shooting days. He had never once gloated about it.

When that woodcock dropped amid the birches, Bucky had toddled over to it, sniffed at it, then put his paw on it and stood there proudly. Nick had never been able to persuade Bucky to retrieve woodcock.

"This was the place where you quit hunting for good," Nick said after a few minutes. "It was the last cover you carried a gun in."

"I don't remember it that way," said the old man.

"I do," said Nick.

* * * *

It was one of those gray November afternoons, Nick recalled, twenty or twenty-five years after the day the owl had flown across the road. Bucky was an old dog by then. He'd slowed down a lot, and he'd finally begun to point grouse fairly regularly. So when he locked on a point in a brushy corner on the edge of the old pasture, Nick and his father had moved up quickly on either side of the dog.

The grouse flushed on the old man's side, and instead of darting through the thick stuff and heading for the distant stand of pines, the way any self-respecting grouse would do, this one chose to fly across the open field. Nick watched his father's gun come up and swing on the bird, and in his head he uttered a little benediction for the doomed grouse. The old man never missed an easy crossing shot.

"Bang-bang," Nick's father had said conversationally.

The bird kept flying.

The old man lowered his gun, blew imaginary smoke away from its barrels, and grinned at Nick. "Got him."

"Huh?" said Nick. "You didn't even shoot at him. What happened?"

"Safety stuck."

Nick rolled his eyes. "That's a damn lie."

The old man smiled, then nodded and tapped his forehead with his fingertip. "Got him here, in my imagination. Then I put him back, like a trout." He shrugged. "I've killed an awful lot of birds. More than my share, I figure. One more or less doesn't matter to me. Now we know he's still here."

"What're you trying to say?" said Nick.

The old man dismissed the subject with a flip of his hand. "Nothing very profound."

Bucky died the following spring, and Nick was in no hurry to replace him. When the bird season rolled around, Nick's father kept turning down invitations to hunt with other men's dogs. Nick didn't push him. Grouse hunting wasn't the same without your own dog.

That winter the old man gave Nick his fifty-year-old Winchester Model 21, the only gun he'd ever carried in grouse cover. "It's the arthritis," he said. "I just can't get around the way I used to."

Nick didn't believe that. But he knew his old man too well, and respected him too much, to argue with him.

*   *   *   *

They sat there in the front seat of the truck, looking out the window at the way the cold afternoon sunlight angled in through the trees, not saying anything. Nick, for one, was in no hurry to get on with it, and he guessed his old man was feeling the same.

Nick's mind was whirling with memories. "That time you said 'bangbang' to the grouse wasn't the last time we came here together," he said finally.

"I remember," the old man said quietly. "You talked me into it."

"I wanted you to see Burt work." Burt was Nick's new Brittany, barely eight months old that fall, but already pointing woodcock like a veteran. "You finally agreed to walk through one cover with me. We came here."

"Burt was a precocious bird dog, all right," said the old man. "The cover had grown up and gone to hell by then, though. It was sad to see. Made me feel old."

Nick smiled. "You *were* old."

*   *   *   *

They'd made a short hunt of it. The only part of the Treacherous Owl cover that looked any good was the alder run, and anyway, Nick's father was pretty hobbled with his arthritis. Nick carried the old Winchester Model 21, and Burt darted and pranced ahead of him on his short puppy legs, and the old man limped along behind. Nick tried to keep his pace slower than normal, and every now and then he looked back over his shoulder and said, "How you doin'?"

"I can still keep up with the likes of you," the old man answered.

Burt pointed the only woodcock they found in the Treacherous Owl that day, and Nick missed it both barrels.

"He zigged when he should've zagged," the old man said, still making excuses for him.

*   *   *   *

Now Nick gazed out at the snowy landscape and said, "That day I brought you here to see Burt work—did it remind you of anything?"

"Oh," his father said, "it reminded me of a whole lifetime of things."

"I mean, you following behind me, trying to keep up," Nick said. "Me carrying the Model 21. Me being the one who yelled at the dog."

Nick's father was quiet for a long time. Then he said, "Full circle, huh? I was the kid that day, and you were the father."

"No," said Nick. "You've always been the father."

"Well," Nick's old man said a few minutes later, "we going to sit here all day?"

"I guess it's time," Nick said.

They got out of the truck and crunched through the crusty ankledeep snow on the old woodsroad to the cellarhole on the hilltop. A big old hemlock—it probably had been a sapling that day forty-odd years ago when the owl flew across the road—grew behind the garden of toppled gravestones, and under its lowermost boughs the earth was bare. The afternoon January sun came streaming in, and from the top of the hill you could see over the treetops to some distant New Hampshire mountains.

"This okay?" said Nick.

"This is perfect," said the old man.

Nick knelt down and spread his father's ashes under the hemlock boughs. He thought he should probably say something, but he couldn't think of anything that had been left unsaid between them. They'd finally and truly come full circle, and that was that.

Trail's End

SIGURD OLSON

It was early morning in the northern wilderness, one of those rare, breathless mornings that come only in November, and though it was not yet light enough to see, the birds were stirring. A covey of partridge whirred up from their cozy burrows in the snow and lit in the top of a white birch, where they feasted noisily upon the frozen brown buds. The rolling tattoo of a downy woodpecker, also looking for his breakfast, reverberated again and again through the timber.

They were not the only ones astir, however, for far down the trail leading from the Tamarack Swamp to Kennedy Lake browsed a big buck. He worked his way leisurely along, stopping now and then to scratch away the fresh snow and nibble daintily the still tender green things underneath. A large buck he was, even as deer run, and as smooth and sleek as good feeding could make him. His horns, almost too large, were queerly shaped, for instead of being rounded as in other deer, they were broad and palmate, the horns of a true swamp buck.

The eastern skyline was just beginning to tint with lavender as he reached the summit of the ridge overlooking the lake. He stopped for his usual morning survey of the landscape below him. For some reason, ever since his spike-buck days, he had always stopped there to look the country over before working down to water. He did not know that for countless generations before him, in the days when the pine timber stood tall and gloomy round the shores of the lake, other swamp bucks had also stopped, to scent the wind and listen, before going down to drink.

As he stood on the crest of the ridge, his gaze took in the long reaches of dark blue water far below him; the ice-rimmed shores with long white windfalls reaching like frozen fingers out into the shallows, and the mottled green and gray of the brush covered slopes. His attention was finally centered on a little log cabin tucked away on the opposite shore in a clump of second growth spruce and balsam. Straight above it rose a thin wreath of pale blue smoke, almost as blue as the clear morning air. The metallic chuck, chuck of an axe ringing on a dry log, came clearly across the water, and a breath of air brought to him strange odors that somehow filled him with a vague misgiving.

He was fascinated by the cabin and could not take his gaze from it. On other mornings, it had seemed as much a part of the shoreline as the trees themselves, but now it was different. A flood of almost- forgotten memories surged back to him, of days long ago, when similar odors and sounds had brought with them a danger far greater than that of any natural enemy. He rubbed the top of a low hazel bush and stamped his forefeet nervously, undecided about what to do. Then, in a flash, the full realization came to him. He understood the meaning of it all. This was the season of the year when man was no longer his friend, and it was not safe to be seen in the logging roads or in the open clearings near the log houses. He sniffed the air keenly a moment longer, to be sure, then snorted loudly as if to warn all the wilderness folk of their danger, and bounded back up the trail the way he had come.

Not until he had regained the heavy protecting timber of the Tamarack Swamp, north of Kennedy Lake, did he feel safe. What he had seen made him once again the wary old buck who had lived by his cunning and strength through many a hunting season. Although he was safe for the time being, he was too experienced not to know that before many days had passed, the Tamarack Swamp would no longer be a haven of refuge.

As he worked deeper into the heavy moss-hung timber, he stopped frequently to look into the shadows. The trail here was knee-deep in moss and criss-crossed by a labyrinth of narrow rabbit runways. Soon his search was rewarded, for a sleek yearling doe met him at a place where two trails crossed. After nosing each other tenderly, by way of recognition, they began feeding together on the tender shoots of blueberries and still green tufts of

swamp grass underneath the protecting blanket of snow.

All that morning they fed leisurely and when the sun was high in the heavens, they worked cautiously over to the edge of the swamp. Here was a warm sunny opening hedged in by huge windfalls grown over with a dense tangle of blackberry vines. They often came here for their afternoon sunning, as the ice-encrusted ovals in the snow attested. Leaping a big windfall that guarded the entrance to the opening, they carefully examined the ground, then picked their beds close together. There they rested contentedly with the warm sun shining upon them, little thinking that soon their peace would be broken.

The snow had fallen early that autumn and good feed had been scarce everywhere, except in the depths of the Tamarack Swamp, where the protecting timber had sheltered the grass and small green things. The plague had killed off most of the rabbits, and the few that survived were already forced to feed upon the bark of the poplar. The heavy crust, forming suddenly the night after the first heavy snow, had imprisoned countless partridge and grouse in their tunnels. As a result, small game was scarce and the wolves were lean and gaunt, although it was yet hardly winter. The stark famine months ahead gave promise of nothing but starvation and death, and the weird, discordant music of the wolf pack had sounded almost every night since the last full moon.

The swamp buck and his doe had not as yet felt the pinch of hunger, but instinct told them to keep close to the shelter of the Tamarack Swamp, so except for the morning strolls of the buck to the shore of Kennedy Lake, they had seldom ventured far from the timber. They had often heard the wolf pack, but always so far away that there was little danger as long as they stayed under cover.

Several days had passed since the buck had been to the shore of Kennedy Lake. As yet the silence of the swamp had been unbroken except for the crunching of their own hooves through the icy crust on the trails, and the buck was beginning to wonder if there was really anything to fear. Then one day, as they were again leisurely working their way over to the sunning place in the clearing, they were startled by the strange noises far toward the east end of the swamp. They stopped, every nerve on edge. At times they could hear them quite plainly, then again they would be so faint as to be almost indistinguishable from the other sounds of the forest.

The two deer were not much concerned at first. After satisfying themselves that there was no real danger, they started again down the trail toward the clearing. They could still hear the noises occasionally, but could not tell whether they were coming closer or going further away.

Then just as they neared the edge of the swamp, the sound of heavy footsteps seemed suddenly to grow louder and more distinct. Once more they stopped and stood with heads high, ears pricked up, listening intently. This time they were thoroughly alarmed. Closer and closer came the racket. Now they could hear distinctly the crunching of snow and the crackling of twigs, and then the whole east end of the timber seemed to be fairly alive with tumult, and the air reeked with danger.

The buck ran in a circle, sniffing keenly. The same scent that had come to him from the cabin now rankled heavily in the air, and he knew the time had come to leave the shelter of the Tamarack Swamp. He hesitated, however, not knowing which way to turn. Back and forth he ran, stopping now and then to paw the ground, or to blow the air through his nostrils with the sharp whistling noise that all deer use when in danger.

A branch cracked sharply close at hand, and the scent came doubly strong from the east. With a wild snort the buck wheeled and led the way toward the western end of the swamp followed closely by the doe. Their only hope lay in reaching a heavy belt of green hemlock timber which they knew was separated from the western end of the Tamarack Swamp by a broad stretch of barren, burned-over slashing. As they neared the edge of the swamp they stopped, dreading to leave its protection. From where they stood they could see the dark wall of timber half a mile away. A brushy gully ran diagonally toward it across the open slashing, offering some protection, but the hills on either side were as stark and bare as an open field.

Again came the crack and crunch, now so close that the very air burned with danger. It was time to go. They bounded out of the timber, their white flags waving defiance, and were soon in the brush gully, going like the wind. Just as they sailed over a windfall, the buck caught a glimpse of something moving on a big black pine stump on top of the ridge to their right. Then the quiet was shattered by a succession of rending crashes, and strange singing and whining sounds filled the air above them.

Again and again came the crashes. Suddenly the little doe stopped dead in her tracks. She gave a frightened baa-aa-a of pain and terror as the blood burst in a stream from a jagged wound in her throat. The buck stopped and ran back to where she stood, head down and swaying unsteadily. He watched her a moment, then, growing nervous, started down the trail again. The doe tried bravely to follow, but fell half- way across a windfall too high for her to clear. Again the buck stopped and watched her anxiously. The snow by the windfall was soon stained bright red with blood, and the head of the little doe sank lower and lower in spite of her brave efforts to hold it up.

Hurriedly the buck looked about him. Several black figures were coming rapidly down the ridge. He nosed his doe gently, but this time she did not move. Raising his head he looked toward the approaching figures. Danger was close, but he could not leave his mate.

A spurt of smoke came from one of the figures, followed by another crash. This time the buck felt a blow so sharp that it made him stumble. Staggering to his feet, he plunged blindly down the gully. His flag was down, the sure sign of a wounded deer. Again and again came the crashes, and the air above him whined and sang as the leaden pellets searched for their mark. The bark flew from a birch tree close by, spattering him with fragments. In spite of his wound, he ran swiftly and was soon out of range in the protecting green timber. He knew that he would not be tracked for at least an hour, as his pursuers would wait for him to lie down and stiffen.

He was bleeding badly from a long red scar cutting across his flank, and his back trail was sprinkled with tiny red dots. Where he stopped to rest and listen, little puddles of blood would form that quickly turned bluish black in the snow. For two hours he ran steadily, and then was so weakened by loss of blood that at last he was forced to lie down.

After a short rest, he staggered to his feet, stiffened badly. The bed he had melted in the snow was stained dark red from his bleeding flank. The cold, however, had contracted the wound and had stopped the bleeding a little. He limped painfully down the trail, not caring much which direction it led. Every step was torture. Once when crossing a small gully, he stumbled and fell on his wounded leg. It rested him to lie there, and it was all he could do to force himself on.

While crossing a ridge, the wind bore the man scent strongly to him, and he knew that now he was being trailed. Once, he heard the brush crack behind him, and was so startled that the wound was jerked open and the bleeding started afresh. He watched his back trail nervously, expecting to see his pursuer at any moment and hear again the rending crash that would mean death.

He grew steadily weaker and knew that unless night came soon, he would be overtaken. He had to rest more often now, and when he did move it was to stagger aimlessly down the trail, stumbling on roots and stubs. It was much easier now to walk around the windfalls than to try to jump over as he had always done before.

The shadows were growing longer and longer, and in the hollows it was already getting dusk. If he could last until nightfall he would be safe. But the man scent was getting still stronger, and he realized at last that speed alone could not save him. Strategy was the only course. If his pursuer could be thrown off the trail, only long enough to delay him half an hour, darkness would be upon the wilderness and he could rest.

So waiting until the trail ran down onto a steep ravine filled with brush and windfalls, the buck suddenly turned and walked back on his own trail as far as he dared. It was the old trick of back tracking that deer have used for ages to elude their pursuers. Then stopping suddenly, he jumped as far to the side as his strength would permit, landing with all four feet tightly bunched together in the very center of a scrubby hazel bush. From there, he worked his way slowly into a patch of scrub spruce and lay down, exhausted, under an old windfall. Weakened as he was from loss of blood and from the throbbing pain in his flank, it was all he could do to keep his eyes riveted on his back trail, and his ears strained for the rustling and crunching that he feared would come, unless darkness came first.

It seemed that he had barely lain down, when without warning, the brush cracked sharply, and not 100 yards away appeared a black figure. The buck was petrified with terror. His ruse had failed. He shrank as far down as he could in the grass under the windfall and his eyes almost burst from their sockets. Frantically he thought of leaving his hiding place, but knew that would only invite death. The figure came closer and closer, bending low over the trail and peering keenly into the spruce thicket ahead. In the fading light the buck was well hidden by the windfall, but the blood-spattered trail led straight to his hiding place. Discovery seemed certain.

The figure picked its way still nearer. It was now within 30 feet of the windfall. The buck watched, hardly daring to breathe. Then, in order to get a better view into the thicket, the hunter started to climb a snow covered stump close by. Suddenly, losing his balance, he slipped and plunged backwards into the snow. The buck saw his chance. Gathering all his remaining strength, he dashed out of his cover and was soon hidden in the thick growth of spruce.

It was almost dark now and he knew that as far as the hunter was concerned, he was safe. Circling slowly around, he soon found a sheltered hiding place in a dense clump of spruce where he could rest and allow his wound to heal.

Night came swiftly, bringing with it protection and peace. The stars came out one by one, and a full November moon climbed into the sky, flooding the snowy wilderness with its radiance.

Several hours had passed since the buck had lain down to rest in the spruce thicket. The moon was now riding high in the heavens and in the open places it was almost as light as day. Although well hidden, he dozed fitfully, waking at times with a start, thinking that again he was being trailed. He would then lie and listen, with nerves strained to the breaking point, for any sounds of the wild that might mean danger. An owl hooted over in a clump of timber, and the new forming ice on the shores of Kennedy Lake, half a mile away, rumbled ominously. Then he heard a long quavering call, so faint and far away that it almost blended with the whispering of the wind. The coarse hair on his shoulders bristled as he recognized the hunting call of the age-old enemy of his kind. It was answered again and again. The wolf pack was gathering, and for the first time in his life, the buck knew fear. In the shelter of the Tamarack Swamp there had been little danger, and even if he had been driven to the open, his strength and speed would have carried him far from harm. Now, sorely wounded and far from shelter, he would

have hardly a fighting chance should the pack pick up his trail.

They were now running in full cry, having struck a trail in the direction of the big swamp far to the west. To the buck, the weird music was as a song of death. Circling and circling, for a time they seemed to draw no nearer. As yet he was not sure whether it was his own blood-bespattered trail that they were unraveling, or that of some other one of his kind. Then, suddenly, the cries grew in fierceness and volume and sounded much closer than before. He listened spellbound as he finally realized the truth it was his own trail they were following. The fiendish chorus grew steadily louder and more venomous, and now had a new note of triumph in it that boded ill for whatever came in its way.

He could wait no longer and sprang to his feet. To his dismay, he was so stiffened and sore, that he could hardly take a step. Forcing himself on, he hobbled painfully through the poplar brush and clumps of timber in the direction of the lake. Small windfalls made him stumble, and having to walk around hummocks and hollows made progress slow and difficult. How he longed for his old strength and endurance. About two-thirds of the distance to the lake had been covered and already occasional glimpses of water appeared between the openings.

Suddenly the cries of the pack burst out in redoubled fury behind him, and the buck knew they had found his warm blood-stained bed. Plunging blindly on, he used every ounce of strength and energy that he had left, for now the end was only a matter of minutes. The water was his only hope, for by reaching that he would at least escape being torn to shreds by the teeth of the pack. He could hear them coming swiftly down the ridge behind him and every strange shadow he mistook for one of the gliding forms of his pursuers. They were now so close that he could hear their snarls and yapping. Then a movement caught his eye in the checkered moonlight. A long gray shape had slipped out of the darkness and was easily keeping pace with him. Another form crept in silently on the other side and both ran like phantoms with no apparent effort. He was terrorstricken, but kept on desperately. Other ghost-like shapes filtered in from the timber, but still they did not close. The water was just ahead. They would wait till he broke from the brush that lined the shore. With a crash, he burst through the last fringe of alders and charged forward. As he did so, a huge gray form shot out of the shadows and launched itself at his throat. He saw the movement in time and caught the full force of the blow on his horns. A wild toss and the snarling shape splashed into the ice rimmed shallows. At the same instant the two that had been running alongside closed, one for his throat and the other for his hamstrings. The first he hit a stunning blow with his sharp front hoof, but as he did so the teeth of the other fastened on the tendon of his hind leg. A frantic leap loosened his hold and the buck half-plunged and half-slid over the ice into the waters of Kennedy Lake. Then the rest of the pack tore down to the beach with a deafening babble of snarls and howls, expecting to find their quarry down or at bay. When they realized that they had been outwitted, their anger was hideous and the air was rent with howls and yaps.

The cold water seemed to put new life into the buck and each stroke was stronger than the one before. Nevertheless, it was a long hard swim, and before he was halfway across, the benumbing cold had begun to tell. He fought on stubbornly, his breath coming in short, choking sobs and finally, after what seemed ages, touched the hard sandy bottom of the other shore. Dragging himself painfully out, he lay down exhausted in the snow. All sense of feeling had left his tortured body, but the steady lap, lap of the waves against the tinkling shore ice soothed him into sleep.

When he awoke, the sun was high in the heavens. For a long time he lay as in a stupor, too weak and sorely stiffened to move. Then with a mighty effort he struggled to his feet, and stood motionless, bracing himself unsteadily. Slowly his strength returned and leaving his bed, he picked his way carefully along the beach, until he struck the trail, down which he had so often come to drink. He followed it to the summit of the ridge overlooking the lake.

The dark blue waters sparkled in the sun, and the rolling spruce covered ridges were green as they had always been. Nothing had really changed, yet never again would it be the same. He was a stranger in the land of his birth, a lonely fugitive where once he had roamed at will, his only choice to leave forever the ancient range of his breed. For a time he wavered torn between his emotions, then finally turned to go. Suddenly an overwhelming desire possessed him, to visit again the place where last he had seen his mate. He worked slowly down the trail to the old Tamarack Swamp and did not stop until he came to the old meeting place deep in the shadows where the two trails crossed. For a long time he did not move, then turned and headed into the north to a new wilderness far from the old, a land as yet untouched, the range of the Moose and Caribou.

Part 9

Records

Records of North American Big Game

BOONE AND CROCKETT CLUB

The following excerpts from *Records of North American Big Game, 13th Edition*, have been reprinted with permission of the Boone and Crockett Club.

Black Bear

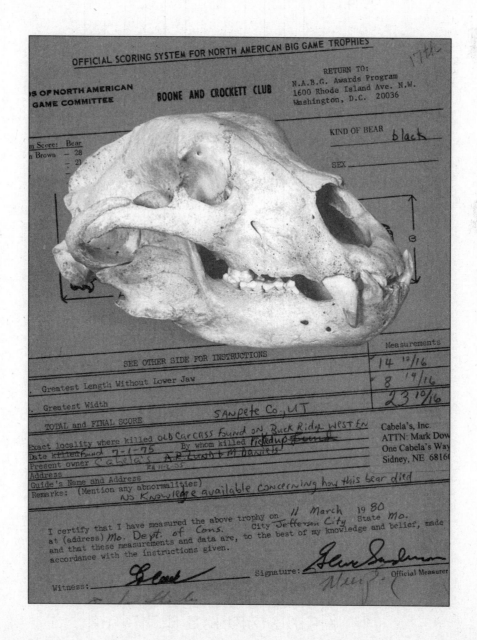

OFFICIAL SCORING SYSTEM FOR NORTH AMERICAN BIG GAME TROPHIES

RETURN TO:
N.A.B.G. Awards Program
1600 Rhode Island Ave. N.W.
Washington, D.C. 20036

...S OF NORTH AMERICAN
...GAME COMMITTEE

BOONE AND CROCKETT CLUB

KIND OF BEAR black

SEX

...m Score: Bear
...n Brown — 28
— 2...

	Measurements
SEE OTHER SIDE FOR INSTRUCTIONS	14 12/16
Greatest Length Without Lower Jaw	8 14/16
Greatest Width	23 10/16
TOTAL and FINAL SCORE	

Exact locality where killed old carcass found on Buck Ridge, WESTEN Sanpete Co., UT

Date killed/found 7-1-75   By whom killed Picked up found

Present owner Cabela's A.P. Lund & M. Daniels

Address RA 11-2-55

Cabela's, Inc.
ATTN: Mark Dow...
One Cabela's Way
Sidney, NE 68160

Guide's Name and Address

Remarks: (Mention any abnormalities) No knowledge available concerning how this bear died

I certify that I have measured the above trophy on 11 March 19 80
at (address) Mo. Dept. of Cons. City Jefferson City State Mo.
and that these measurements and data are, to the best of my knowledge and belief, made in accordance with the instructions given.

Witness: _____   Signature: _____ Official Measurer

Score	Skull Length	Skull Width	Locality Killed	Hunter	Owner	Date	Rank
23 10/16	14 12/16	8 14/16	Sanpete Co., UT	Picked Up	Cabela's, Inc.	1975	1
23 7/16	14 8/16	8 15/16	Lycoming Co., PA	Picked Up	PA Game Comm.	1987	2
23 3/16	13 15/16	9 4/16	Mendocino Co., CA	Robert J. Shuttleworth, Jr.	Robert J. Shuttleworth, Jr.	1993	3
23 3/16	14 9/16	8 10/16	Fayette Co., PA	Andrew Seman, Jr.	Andrew Seman, Jr.	2005	3
22 15/16	13 14/16	9 1/16	Kuiu Island, AK	Craig D. Martin	Craig D. Martin	1996	5
22 15/16	13 14/16	9 1/16	Monroe Co., PA	Jeremy Kresge	Jeremy Kresge	2004	5
22 15/16	14 6/16	8 9/16	Bedford Co., PA	Jesse L. Ritchey	Jesse L. Ritchey	2006	5
22 14/16	14 5/16	8 9/16	McCreary, MB	John J. Bathke	John J. Bathke	1998	8
22 14/16	14 2/16	8 12/16	Carbon Co., PA	Brian J. Coxe	Brian J. Coxe	2003	8
22 13/16	14 1/16	8 12/16	Ventura Co., CA	Loren C. Nodolf	Loren C. Nodolf	1990	10
22 13/16	14	8 13/16	Luzerne Co., PA	Joseph E. Mindick	Joseph E. Mindick	1998	10
22 13/16	14 1/16	8 12/16	Riding Mt., MB	Robert J. Evans	Robert J. Evans	2008	10

Grizzly Bear

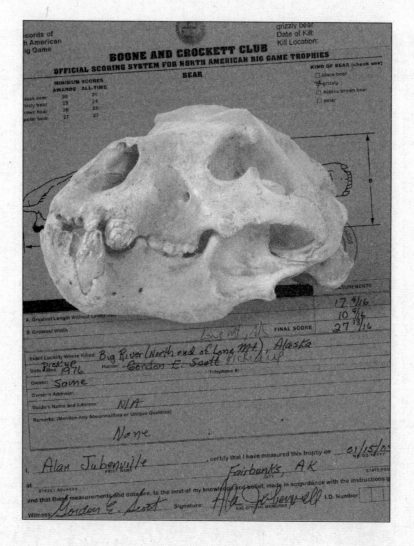

Score	Skull Length	Skull Width	Locality Killed	Hunter	Owner	Date	Rank
27 13/16	17 4/16	10 9/16	Lone Mt., AK	Picked Up	Gordon E. Scott	1976	1
27 3/16	16 13/16	10 6/16	Unalakleet River, AK	Rodney W. Debias	Rodney W. Debias	2009	2
27 2/16	17 6/16	9 12/16	Bella Coola Valley, BC	Picked Up	James G. Shelton	1970	3
27 2/16	16 14/16	10 4/16	Dean River, BC	Roger J. Pentecost	Lynn Allen	1982	3
27 2/16	17 3/16	9 15/16	Inglutalik River, AK	Theodore Kurdziel, Jr.	Theodore Kurdziel, Jr.	1991	3
26 14/16	16 14/16	10	Teklanika River, AK	D. Alan McCaleb	D. Alan McCaleb	1989	6
26 14/16	16 6/16	10 8/16	Anahim Lake, BC	Denis E. Schiller	D.E. Schiller & K. Karran	1990	6
26 14/16	16 11/16	10 3/16	Kala Creek, AK	Eugene C. Williams	Eugene C. Williams	2001	6
26 13/16	16 11/16	10 2/16	Wakeman River, BC	Harry Leggett, Jr.	B&C National Collection	1980	9
26 13/16	16 9/16	10 4/16	Devil Mt., AK	Russell J. Lewis	Russell J. Lewis	1993	9
26 13/16	16 5/16	10 8/16	Otter Creek, AK	James C. Blanchard	James C. Blanchard	2001	9

Alaska Brown Bear

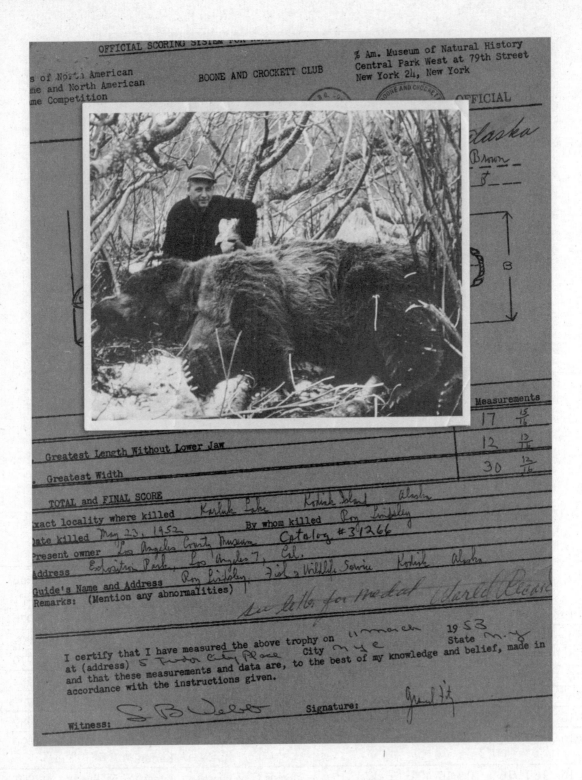

Score	Skull Length	Skull Width	Locality Killed	Hunter	Owner	Date	Rank
30 12/16	17 15/16	12 13/16	Kodiak Island, AK	Roy Lindsley	Los Angeles Co. Mus.	1952	1
30 11/16	18 10/16	12 1/16	Kodiak Island, AK	Erling Hansen	Erling Hansen	1961	2
30 9/16	18 7/16	12 2/16	Kodiak Island, AK	Fred A. Henton	Los Angeles Co. Mus.	1938	3
30 8/16	18 12/16	11 12/16	Bear River, AK	Cap Wagner	Univ. of CA Museum	PR 1908	4
30 8/16	18	12 8/16	Kodiak Island, AK	W.S. Brophy, Jr. & W.E. McClure	William S. Brophy III	1966	4
30 7/16	19 13/16	10 10/16	Port Heiden, AK	Herschel A. Lamb	Herschel A. Lamb	1961	6
30 5/16	18	12 5/16	Deadman Bay, AK	Grancel Fitz	Mrs. Grancel Fitz	1955	7
30 4/16	18 12/16	11 8/16	Kodiak Island, AK	Donald S. Hopkins	Unknown	1940	8
30 4/16	18 12/16	11 8/16	Kodiak Island, AK	Jack Roach	Jack Roach	1947	8
30 4/16	18	12 4/16	Kodiak Island, AK	T.H. McGregor	T.H. McGregor	1960	8
30 4/16	18 5/16	11 15/16	Kodiak Island, AK	Will Gay	Will Gay	1997	8

Polar Bear

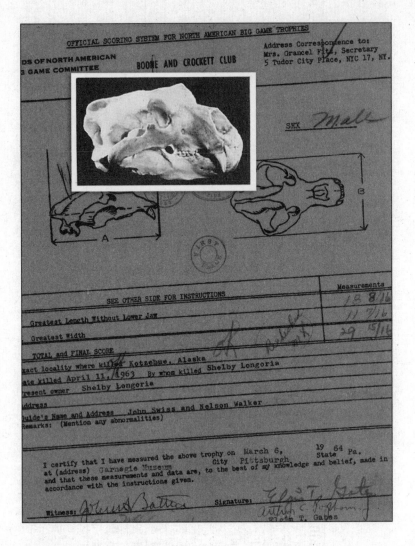

Score	Skull Length	Skull Width	Locality Killed	Hunter	Owner	Date	Rank
29 15/16	18 8/16	11 7/16	Kotzebue, AK	Shelby Longoria	Shelby Longoria	1963	1
29 1/16	18 2/16	10 15/16	Kotzebue, AK	Louis Mussatto	Louis Mussatto	1965	2
28 12/16	17 13/16	10 15/16	Point Hope, AK	Tom F. Bolack	Tom F. Bolack	1958	3
28 12/16	17 11/16	11 1/16	Kotzebue, AK	Bill Nottley	Bill Nottley	1967	3
28 10/16	18	10 10/16	Little Diomede Island, AK	Richard G. Van Vorst	Richard G. Van Vorst	1963	5
28 10/16	17 8/16	11 2/16	Chukchi Sea, AK	Jack D. Putnam	Jack D. Putnam	1965	5
28 9/16	17 6/16	11 3/16	Kotzebue, AK	E.A. McCracken	E.A. McCracken	1966	7
28 8/16	17 6/16	11 2/16	Kotzebue, AK	Curtis S. Williams, Jr.	Curtis S. Williams, Jr.	1967	8
28 8/16	17 10/16	10 14/16	Kotzebue, AK	Winfred L. English	Winfred L. English	1968	8
28 7/16	17 5/16	11 2/16	Point Hope, AK	Rodney Lincoln	J.A. Columbus	1954	10

Cougar

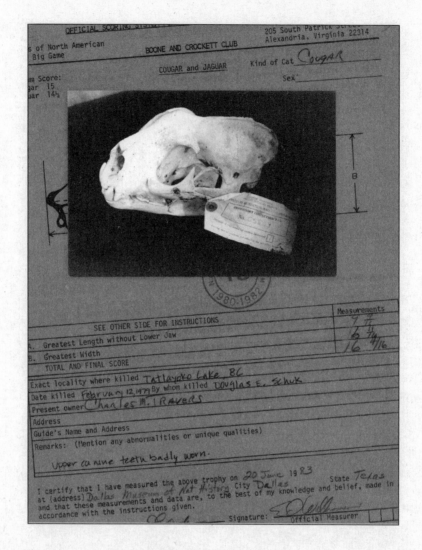

Score	Skull Length	Skull Width	Locality Killed	Hunter	Owner	Date	Rank
16 4/16	9 9/16	6 11/16	Tatlayoko Lake, BC	Douglas E. Schuk	Charles M. Travers	1979	1
16 3/16	9 8/16	6 11/16	Idaho Co., ID	Gene R. Alford	B&C National Collection	1988	2
16 2/16	9 8/16	6 10/16	Sundance Lake, AB	Joseph Gore, Jr.	Joseph Gore, Jr.	2005	3
16 1/16	9 7/16	6 10/16	Park Co., WY	Scott M. Moore	Scott M. Moore	1993	4
16	9 4/16	6 12/16	Garfield Co., UT	Garth Roberts	R. Scott Jarvie	1964	5
16	9 7/16	6 9/16	Tongue Creek, AB	T. Klassen & J.D. Gordon	T. Klassen & J.D. Gordon	1999	5
16	9 4/16	6 12/16	Archuleta Co., CO	Brian K. Williams	Brian K. Williams	2001	5
15 15/16	9 1/16	6 14/16	Clearwater River, AB	Walter R. Weller	Walter R. Weller	1973	8
15 15/16	9 5/16	6 10/16	Hinton, AB	Roy LePage	Roy LePage	1999	8
15 14/16	9 2/16	6 12/16	Walla Walla Co., WA	Robert A. Klicker	Robert A. Klicker	1988	10
15 14/16	9 3/16	6 11/16	Canim Lake, BC	Alejandro Vidaurreta	Alejandro Vidaurreta	1992	10
15 14/16	9 4/16	6 10/16	Idaho Co., ID	Rodney E. Bradley	Rodney E. Bradley	2007	10

American Elk (Typical)

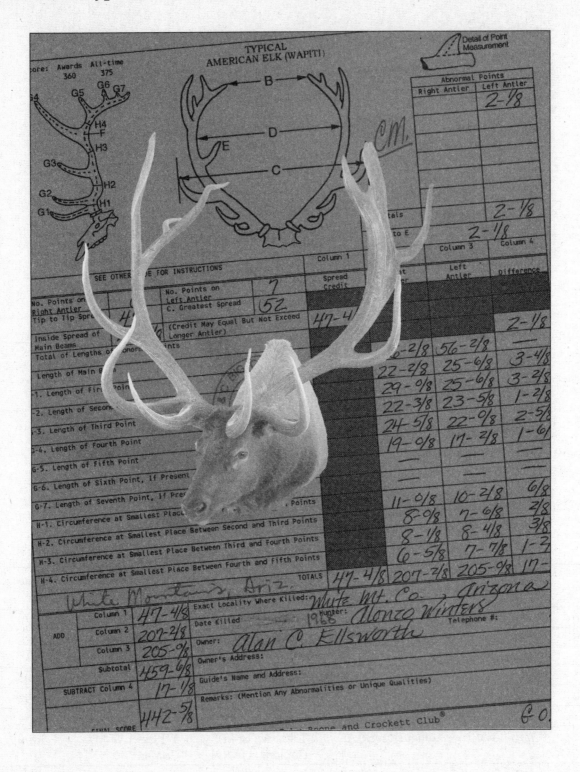

Score	Gross Score	Length of Main Beam		Inside Spread	Circumference Between 1st and 2nd Points		Number of Points		Locality	Hunter	Owner	Date	Rank
		R	L		R	L	R	L					
442 5/8	461 7/8	56 2/8	56 2/8	47 4/8	11	10 2/8	6	7	White Mts., AZ	Alonzo Winters	Alan C. Ellsworth	1968	1
442 3/8	462 4/8	55 5/8	59 5/8	45 4/8	12 1/8	11 2/8	8	7	Dark Canyon, CO	John Plute	Ed Rozman	1899	2
441 6/8	459 6/8	61 6/8	61 2/8	47	10 2/8	9 7/8	8	7	Big Horn Mts., WY	Unknown	Jackson Hole Museum	1890	3
425 3/8	437 2/8	56 7/8	60 2/8	54 6/8	10 3/8	10 7/8	6	7	Nye Co., NV	Jerry McKoen	Jerry McKoen	1999	4
421 4/8	433 2/8	55 4/8	58 2/8	39	11 2/8	10 6/8	7	7	Gila Co., AZ	James C. Littleton	James C. Littleton	1985	5
420 4/8	436 4/8	56 4/8	56 2/8	45 6/8	9	9 2/8	7	7	Yakima Co., WA	Charles F. Gunnier	Charles F. Gunnier	1990	6
419 5/8	434	62 3/8	62 2/8	49 2/8	10 3/8	10 3/8	6	8	Panther River, AB	Clarence Brown	Clarence Brown	1977	7
419 4/8	425 1/8	59 7/8	60 1/8	53	9 2/8	9 3/8	7	7	Madison Co., MT	Fred C. Mercer	Rocky Mtn. Elk Found.	1958	8
418 7/8	440 3/8	58	55	43 1/8	10 5/8	11 3/8	6	7	Wyoming	J.G. Millais	Raymond J. Hutchison	1886	9
418	427 4/8	63 2/8	64 2/8	38 2/8	10 1/8	9 6/8	7	7	Crook Co., OR	Hugh P. Evans	Joseph S. Jessel, Jr.	1942	10
418	429 5/8	54 1/8	50 4/8	44 2/8	8 4/8	8 4/8	6	6	Muddywater River, AB	Bruce W. Hale	Bruce W. Hale	1971	10

American Elk (Non-typical)

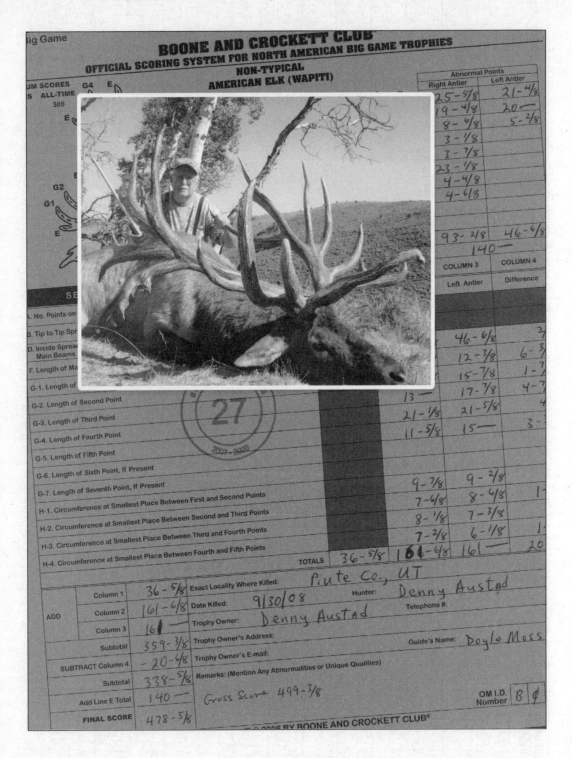

BOONE AND CROCKETT CLUB
OFFICIAL SCORING SYSTEM FOR NORTH AMERICAN BIG GAME TROPHIES
NON-TYPICAL
AMERICAN ELK (WAPITI)

Abnormal Points	
Right Antler	Left Antler
25-5/8	21-4/8
19-4/8	20—
8-6/8	5-2/8
3-1/8	
3-7/8	
23-1/8	
4-4/8	
4-6/8	
93-2/8	46-6/8
140—	

	COLUMN 3	COLUMN 4
	Left Antler	Difference

		Column 3	Column 4
A. No. Points on			
B. Tip to Tip Spr			
D. Inside Spread Main Beams		46-6/8	2
F. Length of Ma		12-3/8	6-3
G-1. Length of		15-7/8	1-7
G-2. Length of Second Point	13—	17-7/8	4-7
G-3. Length of Third Point	21-1/8	21-5/8	4
G-4. Length of Fourth Point	11-5/8	15—	3-
G-5. Length of Fifth Point			
G-6. Length of Sixth Point, If Present			
G-7. Length of Seventh Point, If Present	9-7/8	9-2/8	
H-1. Circumference at Smallest Place Between First and Second Points	7-6/8	8-4/8	1-
H-2. Circumference at Smallest Place Between Second and Third Points	8-1/8	7-3/8	
H-3. Circumference at Smallest Place Between Third and Fourth Points	7-2/8	6-1/8	1-
H-4. Circumference at Smallest Place Between Fourth and Fifth Points			
TOTALS	36-5/8	161-6/8	161—	20

ADD	Column 1	36-5/8	Exact Locality Where Killed: Piute Co., UT
	Column 2	161-6/8	Date Killed: 9/30/08 Hunter: Denny Austad
	Column 3	161—	Trophy Owner: Denny Austad Telephone #:
	Subtotal	359-3/8	Trophy Owner's Address: Guide's Name: Doyle Moss
	SUBTRACT Column 4	-20-6/8	Trophy Owner's E-mail:
	Subtotal	338-5/8	Remarks: (Mention Any Abnormalities or Unique Qualities)
	Add Line E Total	140—	Gross Score 499-3/8 OM I.D. Number B Ø
	FINAL SCORE	478-5/8	© 2006 BY BOONE AND CROCKETT CLUB®

Score	Gross Score	Length of Main Beam		Inside Spread	Circumference Between 1st and 2nd Points		Number of Points		Locality	Hunter	Owner	Date	Rank
		R	L		R	L	R	L					
478 5/8	499 3/8	46 4/8	46 6/8	36 5/8	9 7/8	9 2/8	14	9	Piute Co., UT	Denny Austad	Denny Austad	2008	1
465 2/8	479 3/8	49 2/8	46 3/8	51 1/8	8 5/8	8 6/8	9	11	Upper Arrow Lake, BC	Picked Up	BC Ministry of Environment	1994	2
450 6/8	467 4/8	59	52 6/8	39 4/8	9 1/8	9 3/8	8	8	Apache Co., AZ	Alan D. Hamberlin	Alan D. Hamberlin	1998	3
449 7/8	457 2/8	55 1/8	53 7/8	44	8 7/8	9 4/8	8	7	Golden Valley Co., ND	Kevin D. Fugere	Kevin D. Fugere	1997	4
447 1/8	462 6/8	54 1/8	52 5/8	39 7/8	11	10 2/8	9	9	Gilbert Plains, MB	James R. Berry	D.J. Hollinger & B. Howard	1961	5
445 5/8	455 6/8	58	57 7/8	41 6/8	9 2/8	10	8	8	Apache Co., AZ	Jerry J. Davis	Jerry J. Davis	1984	6
444 4/8	456 3/8	54 6/8	52 6/8	52 2/8	9 4/8	9 4/8	9	10	Coconino Co., AZ	Ronald N. Franklin	Ronald N. Franklin	2003	7
442 3/8	454 6/8	53 7/8	49 7/8	44	8 7/8	9 2/8	7	8	Gila Co., AZ	Dan J. Agnew	Dan J. Agnew	2001	8
441 6/8	460 3/8	55	50 3/8	37	8 2/8	7 5/8	11	10	Clinton Co., PA	John A. Shirk	John A. Shirk	2006	9
439 5/8	477 5/8	58	57	65 6/8	9 6/8	11	10	10	Laramie Co., WY	Joseph C. Dereemer	Bass Pro Shops	1971	10

Roosevelt Elk

Score	Gross Score	Length of Main Beam		Inside Spread	Circumference Between 1st and 2nd Points		Number of Points		Locality	Hunter	Owner	Date	Rank
		R	L		R	L	R	L					
404 6/8	417 1/8	54 1/8	57 5/8	40 6/8	8 2/8	9 4/8	9	8	Benton Co., OR	Jason S. Ballard	Jason S. Ballard	2002	1
396 5/8	418 3/8	46 3/8	46 7/8	32 3/8	8 7/8	9 5/8	10	9	Campbell River, BC	Karl W. Minor, Sr.	Karl W. Minor, Sr.	1997	2
388 3/8	400 2/8	44 2/8	46 7/8	36 1/8	11 2/8	11 2/8	11	8	Tsitika River, BC	Wayne Coe	Wayne Coe	1989	3
384 3/8	391 2/8	48 4/8	49	41 1/8	8 7/8	9 4/8	9	8	Clatsop Co., OR	Robert Sharp	Robert Sharp	1949	4
380 6/8	388	52 3/8	52 6/8	45 1/8	8 3/8	8 1/8	8	8	Jefferson Co., WA	Sam Argo	Sam Argo	1983	5
380 4/8	386 1/8	54 3/8	53 1/8	39 5/8	9 4/8	9 2/8	7	7	Columbia Co., OR	Clifford M. Hayden	Clifford M. Hayden	1991	6
378 5/8	385 4/8	53 2/8	51 3/8	37	8 7/8	8 5/8	7	9	Clatsop Co., OR	Fred M. Williamson	Rusty Lindberg	1947	7
376 3/8	382	53 2/8	52 3/8	41 5/8	10 1/8	10 3/8	8	7	Clallam Co., WA	Picked Up	Roy C. Ewen	1912	8
376 1/8	383 4/8	51	49 1/8	38	10 1/8	10 3/8	8	7	Wahkiakum Co., WA	Norman G. Williams	Norman G. Williams	1948	9
374 3/8	384 3/8	50	47	42	9 2/8	8 5/8	8	8	Bonanza Lake, BC	Ronald K. Bridge	Ronald K. Bridge	2002	10

Mule Deer (Typical)

Score	Gross Score	Length of Main Beam		Inside Spread	Circumference Between 1st and 2nd Points		Number of Points		Locality	Hunter	Owner	Date	Rank
		R	L		R	L	R	L					
226 4/8	235 2/8	30 1/8	28 6/8	30 7/8	5 2/8	5 3/8	6	5	Dolores Co., CO	Doug Burris, Jr.	Cabela's, Inc.	1972	1
218 4/8	230 1/8	27 5/8	27 5/8	29 5/8	5 5/8	5 5/8	6	5	S. Saskatchewan River, SK	Lars Svenson	Larry Svenson	PR 1950	2
217	228 7/8	28 4/8	28 2/8	26 6/8	5 5/8	5 6/8	6	6	Hoback Canyon, WY	Unknown	Jackson Hole Museum	1925	3
216 2/8	222 7/8	28 2/8	28 3/8	26 2/8	4 7/8	4 7/8	5	5	Coconino Co., AZ	Picked Up	B&C National Collection	1994	4
215 5/8	231 1/8	26 7/8	28 1/8	29 4/8	5 3/8	5 3/8	5	7	Uinta Co., WY	Gary L. Albertson	Cabela's, Inc.	1960	5
215 5/8	221 4/8	27 3/8	27 1/8	28 6/8	5 4/8	5 4/8	5	6	Franklin Co., ID	Ray Talbot	David Talbot	1961	5
215 3/8	218 3/8	29 6/8	30 1/8	36 1/8	5 4/8	5 3/8	5	5	Delta Co., CO	Robert L. Ingels	Fred Ferganchick	1958	7
214 3/8	218 2/8	27 5/8	27 4/8	31 3/8	4 7/8	4 7/8	5	5	Gypsum Creek, CO	Paul A. Muehlbauer	Paul A. Muehlbauer	1967	8
213 1/8	216 6/8	25 7/8	24 7/8	26	5	4 7/8	5	5	Moffat Co., CO	Unknown	Cabela's, Inc.	1982	9
212 7/8	217	27 1/8	26 6/8	28 4/8	4 5/8	4 6/8	5	5	Garfield Co., CO	Errol R. Raley	Errol R. Raley	1971	10

Mule Deer (Non-typical)

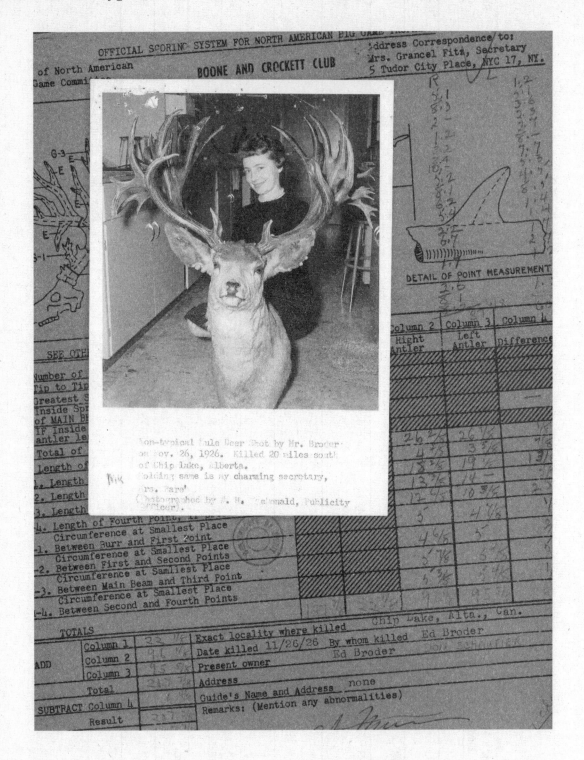

Score	Gross Score	Length of Main Beam R	L	Inside Spread	Circumference Between 1st and 2nd Points R	L	Number of Points R	L	Locality	Hunter	Owner	DATE	Rank
355 2/8	361 6/8	26 2/8	26 1/8	22 1/8	5	4 7/8	22	21	Chip Lake, AB	Ed Broder	Don Schaufler	1926	1
339 2/8	349 6/8	20 6/8	20 4/8	14 7/8	6 4/8	6 2/8	24	23	Okanagan, BC	Unknown	D.J. Hollinger & B. Howard	PR 1890	2
330 1/8	343 3/8	23 2/8	22	9 4/8	8 2/8	8 3/8	21	28	Box Elder Co., UT	Alton Hunsaker	D.J. Hollinger & B. Howard	1943	3
325 6/8	327 7/8	24 5/8	23 5/8	21 6/8	4 6/8	4 7/8	21	21	Nye Co., NV	Clifton Fauria	Cabela's, Inc.	1955	4
324 1/8	329 7/8	25 5/8	25 1/8	32 7/8	6 5/8	6 5/8	16	17	North Kaibab, AZ	William L. Murphy	Michael R. Karam	1943	5
321 1/8	328 6/8	28 1/8	25 4/8	26 5/8	6 7/8	6 7/8	17	25	Umatilla Co., OR	Albert C. Peterson	Cabela's, Inc.	1925	6
320 4/8	327 2/8	23 5/8	24 7/8	25	6	6 2/8	17	20	Madison Co., ID	Grover Browning	D.J. Hollinger & B. Howard	1960	7
319 4/8	329 7/8	24 2/8	24	23 5/8	7 7/8	7 1/8	27	23	Mariposa Co., CA	Harold R. Laird	Cabela's, Inc.	1972	8
311 6/8	321	26 7/8	24 7/8	24 1/8	6 1/8	6 5/8	22	21	Kaibab, AZ	Vernor Wilson	Cabela's, Inc.	1941	9
307 6/8	314 3/8	23 7/8	22 1/8	21 5/8	4 4/8	4 5/8	23	16	Idaho	Unknown	D.J. Hollinger & B. Howard	1935	10

Columbia Blacktail (Typical)

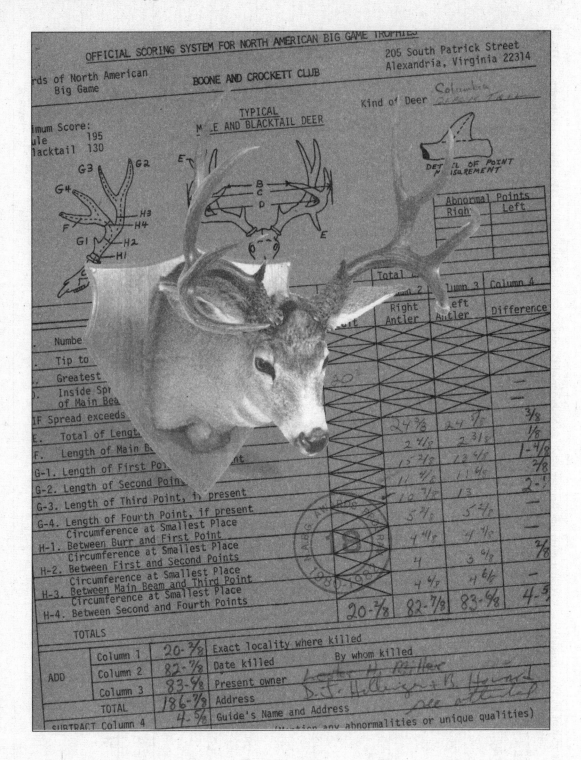

Score	Gross Score	Length of Main Beam R	L	Inside Spread	Circumference Between 1st and 2nd Points R	L	Number of Points R	L	Locality	Hunter	Owner	Date	Rank
182 2/8	186 7/8	24 2/8	24 5/8	20 2/8	5 2/8	5 2/8	5	5	Lewis Co., WA	Lester H. Miller	D.J. Hollinger & B. Howard	1953	1
179	182 2/8	25	24 5/8	19 4/8	4 7/8	5 1/8	5	5	Coos Co., OR	Robert E. Irving	Robert E. Irving	1953	2
178 4/8	184 3/8	23	23 6/8	23 2/8	4 5/8	4 7/8	5	5	Jackson Co., OR	Picked Up	Mervyn R. Thomson	PR 1950	3
175 2/8	181 2/8	22	22 5/8	17 1/8	4 6/8	4 6/8	6	5	Mendocino Co., CA	Clem Coughlin	D.M. & J. Phillips	1981	4
172 5/8	178 4/8	23 1/8	23 6/8	21	4 7/8	4 6/8	6	5	Washington Co., OR	Fred Wolford	Gary A. French	1919	5
172 2/8	183 1/8	26 3/8	25 7/8	20 4/8	5 2/8	5 3/8	7	7	Marion Co., OR	B.G. Shurtleff	B.G. Shurtleff	1969	6
171 6/8	178 1/8	24 3/8	24 2/8	22 2/8	5 6/8	5 2/8	5	6	Skagit Co., WA	Harry M. Kay	Dan Heasley	1939	7
170 6/8	179 7/8	24 2/8	24 3/8	20 7/8	5 1/8	5 2/8	5	4	Clatsop Co., OR	Larry Naught	Allan Naught	1955	8
170 6/8	176 4/8	23 1/8	24	21 4/8	5 3/8	5 4/8	5	5	Elk City, OR	Clark D. Griffith	Clark D. Griffith	1962	8
170 6/8	174 4/8	24 2/8	23 7/8	21	4 1/8	4 3/8	5	5	Siskiyou Co., CA	Frank G. Merz	Frank G. Merz	1979	8

Columbia Blacktail (Non-typical)

Score	Gross Score	Length of Main Beam		Inside Spread	Circumference Between 1st and 2nd Points		Number of Points		Locality	Hunter	Owner	Kill Date	Rank
		R	L		R	L	R	L					
208 1/8	211 5/8	21 7/8	20 4/8	17 5/8	4 2/8	4 3/8	9	9	Polk Co., OR	Frank S. Foldi	Bass Pro Shops	1962	1
197 4/8	202 6/8	23 7/8	22 6/8	19 1/8	4 1/8	4 1/8	11	11	Trinity Co., CA	Newt Boren	Richard Shepard	1955	2
188 6/8	199 4/8	23 4/8	19 7/8	17 4/8	4 3/8	5 1/8	7	9	Shasta Co., CA	Brad E. Wittner	Brad E. Wittner	1981	3
187	192 1/8	21 5/8	22 6/8	18 4/8	4 2/8	4 2/8	9	8	Douglas Co., OR	Alva J. Flock	Alva J. Flock	1967	4
185 1/8	189 1/8	23 5/8	24 5/8	16 1/8	3 7/8	4	8	8	Trinity Co., CA	J. Peter Morish	J. Peter Morish	2005	5
179 4/8	187 6/8	24 1/8	23	22 1/8	5 2/8	5	6	12	Mendocino Co., CA	Russel F. Roach	Russel F. Roach	2002	6
177 6/8	183 6/8	23 7/8	25	22	4 7/8	5 1/8	6	6	Josephine Co., OR	Roxie Smith	Aly M. Bruner	1940	7
177 4/8	183 4/8	22 7/8	23 5/8	17 2/8	4 6/8	4 7/8	6	6	Washington Co., OR	John Susee	Randal P. Olsen	1954	8
176 5/8	179 3/8	20 4/8	20 3/8	13 4/8	4 7/8	4 6/8	8	10	Trinity Co., CA	Harland C. Moore, Sr.	James A. Swortzel	1947	9
176 5/8	184 5/8	21 4/8	22	16 5/8	4 2/8	4 3/8	8	8	Clackamas Co., OR	Ronald G. Searls	Ronald G. Searls	1970	9

Sitka Blacktail (Typical)

Score	Gross Score	Length of Main Beam		Inside Spread	Circumference Between 1st and 2nd Points		Number of Points		Locality	Hunter	Owner	Date	Rank
		R	L		R	L	R	L					
133	136 6/8	20 4/8	19 4/8	19 6/8	3 6/8	3 6/8	5	5	Juskatla, BC	Peter Bond	D.J. Hollinger & B. Howard	1970	1
128	134 1/8	19 6/8	19	19 4/8	4 7/8	4 7/8	5	5	Kodiak Island, AK	Unknown	Craig Allen	1985	2
126 5/8	129 3/8	18 1/8	18 2/8	18 1/8	4 7/8	4 7/8	5	5	Prince of Wales Island, AK	Joseph R. Jeppsen	Joseph R. Jeppsen	2007	3
126 3/8	129 2/8	18 5/8	19 4/8	14 5/8	4	4 1/8	5	5	Sunny Hay Mt., AK	Harry R. Horner	Harry R. Horner	1987	4
125 7/8	128 5/8	17 7/8	18 6/8	13 5/8	4	4	4	4	Tenakee Inlet, AK	Donald E. Thompson	Donald E. Thompson	1964	5
124 2/8	127 1/8	19 1/8	18 2/8	14 4/8	4 3/8	4	5	5	Exchange Cove, AK	Daniel J. Leo	Daniel J. Leo	1986	6
123 4/8	130 4/8	21 4/8	20 3/8	17 6/8	3 6/8	3 6/8	4	4	Uganik Bay, AK	Donna D. Braendel	Donna D. Braendel	1983	7
123 2/8	125 2/8	18 4/8	18 3/8	14 4/8	4 3/8	4 1/8	5	5	Prince of Wales Island, AK	Kenneth W. Twitchell	Kenneth W. Twitchell	1987	8
122 3/8	126 2/8	17 7/8	18 6/8	16 1/8	3 6/8	3 6/8	5	5	Prince of Wales Island, AK	Picked Up	Jack A. Adams	1989	9
122 1/8	127 5/8	18 1/8	19 2/8	15 1/8	3 6/8	3 6/8	5	5	Prince of Wales Island, AK	Picked Up	James F. Baichtal	2004	10

Sitka Blacktail (Non-typical)

Score	Gross Score	Length of Main Beam		Inside Spread	Circumference Between 1st and 2nd Points		Number of Points		Locality	Hunter	Owner	Kill Date	Rank
		R	L		R	L	R	L					
134	140 3/8	19 6/8	20 3/8	16 3/8	4 5/8	4 4/8	5	6	Control Lake, AK	William B. Steele, Jr.	William B. Steele, Jr.	1987	1
126 7/8	130	17	17 5/8	13 7/8	4 2/8	4 4/8	6	8	Prince of Wales Island, AK	Dan L. Hayes	B&C National Collection	1984	2
124 2/8	129 3/8	18 3/8	16 6/8	15 4/8	3 6/8	3 6/8	6	7	Prince of Wales Island, AK	William C. Musser	William C. Musser	2005	3
126 4/8*	137 5/8	18 7/8	20 3/8	17	4 3/8	4 2/8	6	5	Little Coal Bay, AK	Charles Escoffon	Charles Escoffon	1985	
120 1/8*	125 3/8	18 1/8	17 5/8	13 7/8	3 6/8	4 2/8	5	6	Revillagigedo Island, AK	Dick D. Hamlin	Dick D. Hamlin	PR 1970	

Whitetail (Typical)

Score	Gross Score	Length of Main Beam		Inside Spread	Circumference Between 1st and 2nd Points		Number of Points		Locality	Hunter	Owner	Date	Rank
		R	L		R	L	R	L					
213 5/8	223 7/8	28 4/8	28 4/8	27 2/8	4 6/8	5	8	6	Biggar, SK	Milo N. Hanson	Milo N. Hanson	1993	1
206 1/8	209 3/8	30	30	20 1/8	6 2/8	6 1/8	5	5	Burnett Co., WI	James Jordan	Bass Pro Shops	1914	2
205	213 4/8	26 6/8	25 4/8	24 2/8	4 6/8	4 6/8	6	6	Randolph Co., MO	Larry W. Gibson	MO Show-Me Big Bucks Club	1971	3
204 4/8	212 7/8	27 5/8	26 6/8	23 5/8	6 1/8	6 2/8	7	6	Peoria Co., IL	Melvin J. Johnson	Bass Pro Shops	1965	4
204 2/8	231 4/8	26 4/8	22 6/8	25 1/8	5 1/8	5 1/8	7	10	Beaverdam Creek, AB	Stephen Jansen	Stephen Jansen	1967	5
203 3/8	208 4/8	25 7/8	27 2/8	19 3/8	5 7/8	5 5/8	6	6	Sturgeon River, SK	Hubert Collins	Hubert Collins	2003	6
202 6/8	216 4/8	28	27 1/8	21 2/8	5 3/8	5 3/8	9	8	Barrier Valley, SK	Bruce Ewen	Bass Pro Shops	1992	7
202	223 3/8	31 2/8	31	23 5/8	5 7/8	6	8	8	Beltrami Co., MN	John A. Breen	Bass Pro Shops	1918	8
201 4/8	216 1/8	27 5/8	29 1/8	23	5 5/8	5 2/8	6	6	Hamilton Co., IA	Wayne A. Bills	Bass Pro Shops	1974	9
201 1/8	209 7/8	29 6/8	29	24 1/8	5	5	6	5	Warren Co., OH	Bradley S. Jerman	Bradley S. Jerman	2004	10

Whitetail (Non-typical)

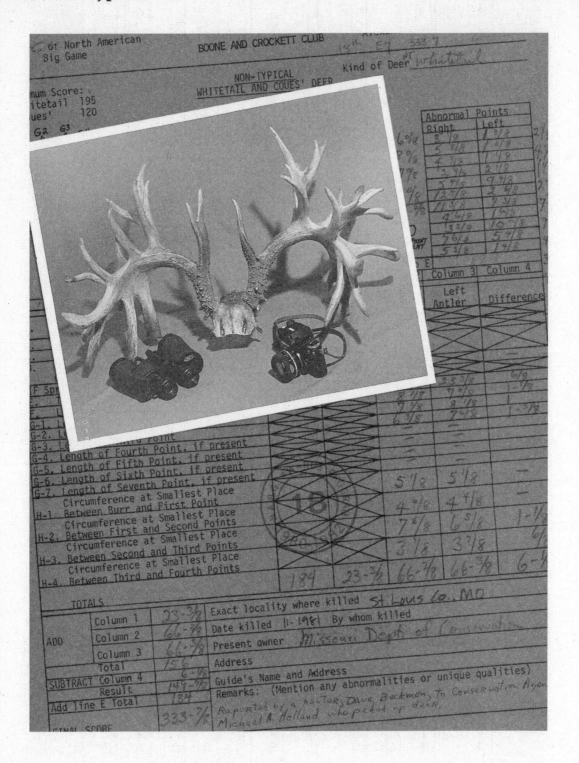

Score	Gross Score	Length of Main Beam		Inside Spread	Circumference Between 1st and 2nd Points		Number of Points		Locality	Hunter	Owner	Date	Rank
		R	L		R	L	R	L					
333 7/8	340	24 1/8	23 3/8	23 3/8	5 1/8	5 1/8	19	25	St. Louis Co., MO	Picked Up	MO Dept. of Cons.	1981	1
328 2/8	343 7/8	25 5/8	24 4/8	24 3/8	6 2/8	5 6/8	23	22	Portage Co., OH	Picked Up	Bass Pro Shops	1940	2
307 5/8	324	26 3/8	23 5/8	22	8	6 4/8	21	17	Monroe Co., IA	Tony W. Lovstuen	Bass Pro Shops	2003	3
304 3/8	317 3/8	27 3/8	27 2/8	23 1/8	5 1/8	5 7/8	17	20	Fulton Co., IL	Jerry D. Bryant	Bass Pro Shops	2001	4
295 6/8	312 4/8	21 2/8	18 2/8	22 3/8	5 5/8	5 3/8	21	24	Winston Co., MS	Tony Fulton	Tony Fulton	1995	5
295 3/8	304 4/8	21 6/8	24 5/8	18 4/8	6 5/8	6 6/8	25	22	McDonough Co., IL	Scott R. Dexter	Scott R. Dexter	2004	6
295 3/8	304 7/8	30 2/8	29	25 1/8	5 4/8	5 7/8	18	17	Adams Co., OH	Jonathan R. Schmucker	Jonathan R. Schmucker	2006	6
294	306 4/8	25 7/8	25 6/8	26	6 5/8	6 2/8	18	21	Greene Co., OH	Michael D. Beatty	Bass Pro Shops	2000	8
284 3/8	291 7/8	21 4/8	19 6/8	16 2/8	4 4/8	4 4/8	21	26	McCulloch Co., TX	Unknown	Buckhorn Mus. & Saloon, Ltd.	1892	9
282	288 5/8	26 1/8	27	24 3/8	6 5/8	6 2/8	15	14	Clay Co., IA	Larry Raveling	Bass Pro Shops	1973	10

Canada Moose

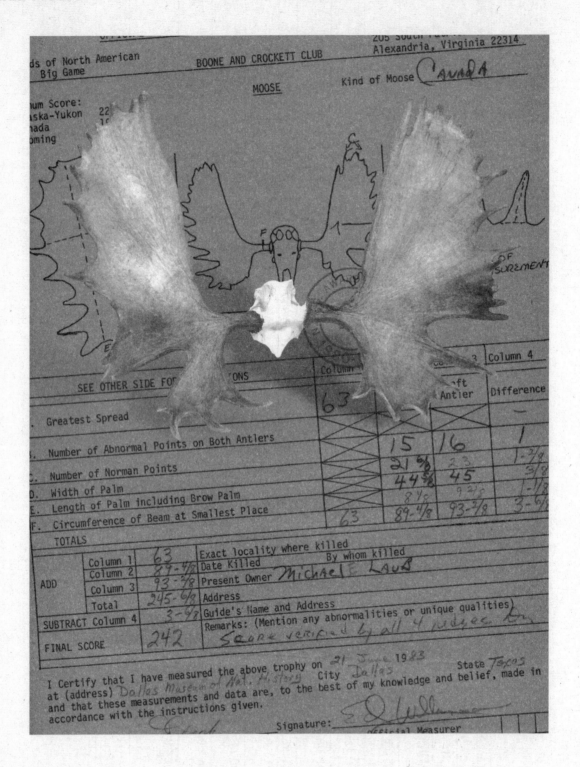

Score	Gross Score	Greatest Spread	Length of Palm		Width of Palm		Circumference of Beam at Smallest Place		Number of Normal Points		Locality	Hunter	Owner	Date	Rank
			R	L	R	L	R	L	R	L					
242	245 6/8	63	44 5/8	45	21 6/8	23	8 1/8	9 2/8	15	16	Grayling River, BC	Michael E. Laub	Michael E. Laub	1980	1
240 6/8	246	63 4/8	48 7/8	47 2/8	18	19 4/8	7 7/8	8	16	16	Kinaskan Lake, BC	Doug E. Frank	Cabela's, Inc.	2002	2
240 2/8	241 6/8	66 6/8	46 3/8	45 4/8	19	18 6/8	7 4/8	7 7/8	15	15	Teslin River, BC	Albertoni Ferruccio	Albertoni Ferruccio	1982	3
238 5/8	243 6/8	65 5/8	44 6/8	43 1/8	21	18 6/8	7 5/8	7 7/8	18	19	Bear Lake, QC	Silas H. Witherbee	B&C National Collection	1914	4
229 2/8	232 4/8	66 2/8	45 4/8	45 4/8	14 6/8	16	8 2/8	8 2/8	13	15	Muncho Lake, BC	Roger J. Ahern	Cabela's, Inc.	1977	5
228 6/8	234 5/8	70	39 6/8	42 2/8	16 4/8	17 5/8	8 1/8	8 3/8	17	15	MacEachern Lake, NS	Brenton Holland	Glenwood Holland	1997	6
227 6/8	233 2/8	59 2/8	45	46	18	16 5/8	7 5/8	7 6/8	15	18	Kawdy Mt., BC	Frank A. Hanks	Frank A. Hanks	2004	7
227 4/8	231 3/8	58 4/8	44	43 4/8	17 3/8	17 5/8	7 6/8	7 5/8	19	16	Cook Co., MN	Donald F. Blake	Donald F. Blake	1985	8
226 7/8	229 5/8	63 1/8	48 5/8	47	16 4/8	16 4/8	8 4/8	8 3/8	11	10	Whitecourt, AB	Tim Harbridge	Tim Harbridge	1978	9
226 6/8	229 5/8	63	44 3/8	42 2/8	18 1/8	18 7/8	7	7	15	15	Halfway River, BC	Richard Petersen	Richard Petersen	1977	10

Alaska-Yukon Moose

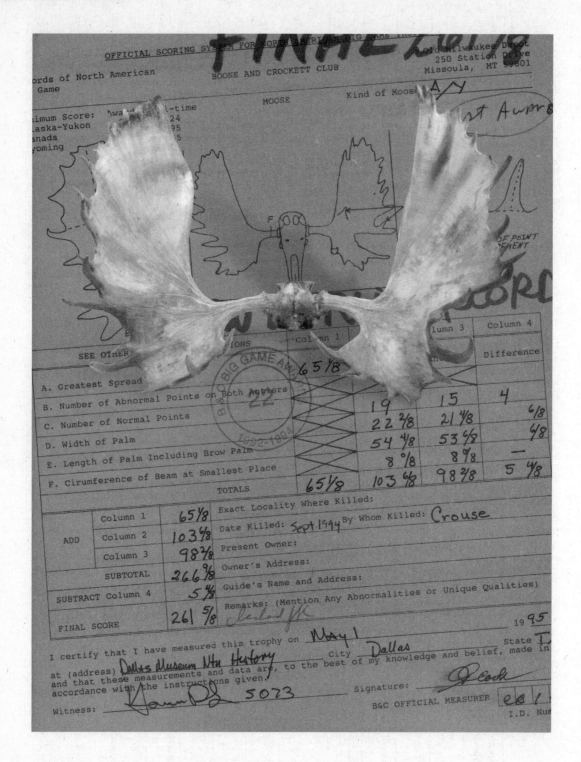

Score	Gross Score	Greatest Spread	Length of Palm		Width of Palm		Circumference of Beam at Smallest Place		Number of Normal Points		Locality	Hunter	Owner	Date	Rank
			R	L	R	L	R	L	R	L					
261 5/8	267 1/8	65 1/8	54 4/8	53 6/8	22 2/8	21 4/8	8	8	19	15	Fortymile River, AK	John A. Crouse	John A. Crouse	1994	1
256 6/8	261 5/8	78 2/8	49 6/8	50 5/8	17 3/8	18 2/8	7 5/8	7 6/8	16	15	Beluga River, AK	William G. Nelson	William G. Nelson	1997	2
255	262 3/8	77	49 5/8	49 6/8	20 6/8	15 6/8	7 7/8	7 5/8	18	16	McGrath, AK	Kenneth Best	Kenneth Best	1978	3
254 5/8	258 5/8	70 7/8	46 4/8	48 2/8	22 2/8	23 1/8	8 1/8	8 4/8	15	16	Kvichak River, AK	Franz Kohlroser	Franz Kohlroser	2005	4
251	269 5/8	77 4/8	46 3/8	51	17	29 6/8	7 7/8	8 1/8	18	17	Mt. Susitna, AK	Bert Klineburger	Bert Klineburger	1961	5
250 3/8	259 4/8	65 1/8	55 2/8	49 2/8	21 1/8	20	8 3/8	8 3/8	18	16	Kenai Pen., AK	Dyton A. Gilliland	Unknown	1947	6
249 6/8	251 3/8	67	47 7/8	48 2/8	22 1/8	21 1/8	7 3/8	7 5/8	15	15	Mother Goose Lake, AK	Josef Welle	Josef Welle	1967	7
249 6/8	256 6/8	71 6/8	49 3/8	49 1/8	26 4/8	22 2/8	9 1/8	9 5/8	11	9	Pedro Bay, AK	David W. Boone	David W. Boone	1996	7
249 3/8	253 4/8	75 3/8	51 6/8	53 1/8	17	18 6/8	7 2/8	7 2/8	11	12	Tikchik Lake, AK	John R. Johnson	John R. Johnson	1995	9
249 2/8	254 3/8	72	48 4/8	49 6/8	19 2/8	17	8 1/8	8 6/8	15	16	Alaska Range, AK	Henry S. Budney	Henry S. Budney	1967	10

Shiras Moose

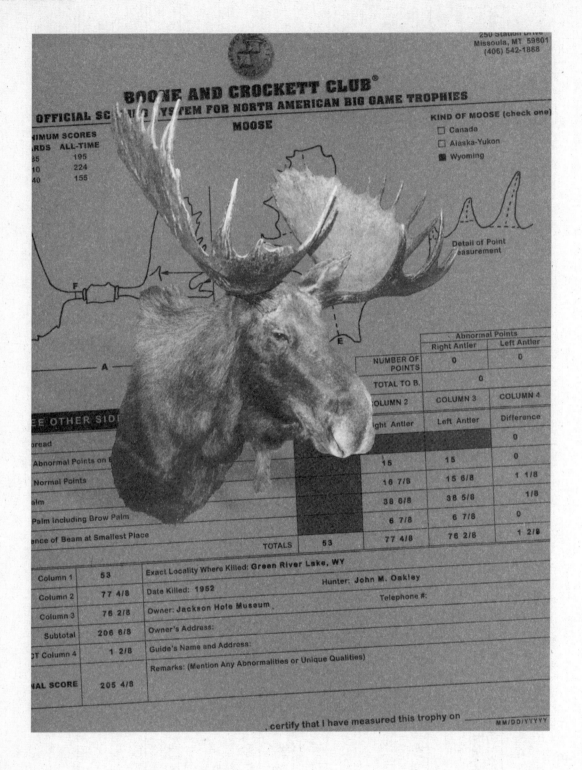

BOONE AND CROCKETT CLUB®

250 Station Drive
Missoula, MT 59801
(406) 542-1888

OFFICIAL SCORING SYSTEM FOR NORTH AMERICAN BIG GAME TROPHIES

MOOSE

KIND OF MOOSE (check one)
☐ Canada
☐ Alaska-Yukon
☑ Wyoming

MINIMUM SCORES

	AWARDS	ALL-TIME
	85	195
	10	224
	40	155

Detail of Point Measurement

SEE OTHER SIDE

	Abnormal Points	
	Right Antler	Left Antler
NUMBER OF POINTS	0	0
TOTAL TO B.	0	

	COLUMN 2	COLUMN 3	COLUMN 4
	Right Antler	Left Antler	Difference
Spread			0
Abnormal Points on B			0
Normal Points	15	15	0
Palm	16 7/8	15 6/8	1 1/8
Palm Including Brow Palm	38 6/8	38 5/8	1/8
...ence of Beam at Smallest Place	6 7/8	6 7/8	0
TOTALS	53	77 4/8	76 2/8	1 2/8

Column 1	53	Exact Locality Where Killed: Green River Lake, WY
Column 2	77 4/8	Date Killed: 1952
Column 3	76 2/8	Owner: Jackson Hole Museum
Subtotal	206 6/8	Owner's Address:
...T Column 4	1 2/8	Guide's Name and Address:
...AL SCORE	205 4/8	Remarks: (Mention Any Abnormalities or Unique Qualities)

Hunter: John M. Oakley

Telephone #:

, certify that I have measured this trophy on _____ MM/DD/YYYY

Score	Gross Score	Greatest Spread	Length of Palm		Width of Palm		Circumference of Beam at Smallest Place		Number of Normal Points		Locality	Hunter	Owner	Date	Rank
			R	L	R	L	R	L	R	L					
205 4/8	206 6/8	53	38 6/8	38 5/8	16 7/8	15 6/8	6 7/8	6 7/8	15	15	Green River Lake, WY	John M. Oakley	Jackson Hole Museum	1952	1
205 1/8	206	56 5/8	40	40	13 3/8	14 2/8	7 7/8	7 7/8	13	13	Fremont Co., WY	Arthur E. Chandler	Arthur E. Chandler	1944	2
200 3/8	204 1/8	55 7/8	38 4/8	36 6/8	13 1/8	13 4/8	7	6 3/8	16	17	Lincoln Co., WY	Aldon L. Hale	Aldon L. Hale	1981	3
199 3/8	209 1/8	62 3/8	38 1/8	36 2/8	12 5/8	16 4/8	7 5/8	8 5/8	12	15	Elk City, ID	Reed T. Fisher	Reed T. Fisher	1957	4
199	202 7/8	48 4/8	40 4/8	42 1/8	12 1/8	11	7 7/8	7 6/8	17	16	Teton Co., WY	Amos E. Hand	B.W. & M. Smith	1946	5
196 5/8	199 6/8	53 1/8	39 6/8	40 4/8	14 5/8	14 2/8	6 6/8	6 6/8	13	11	Larimer Co., CO	Brad B. Schwindt	Brad B. Schwindt	1997	6
195 5/8	200 3/8	52 1/8	41 4/8	40	13	11	7	6 6/8	14	15	Atlantic Creek, WY	Alfred C. Berol	Alfred C. Berol	1933	7
195 1/8	203 1/8	55 7/8	43 1/8	35 6/8	15 1/8	14 5/8	7 3/8	7 2/8	14	14	Beaverhead Co., MT	C.M. Schmauch	C.M. Schmauch	1952	8
194 4/8	198 2/8	58 4/8	39	40	13 5/8	13	7 1/8	7	11	9	Jackson Co., CO	Jack A. Anderson	Jack A. Anderson	1995	9
193	199 3/8	51	40 4/8	42 2/8	14 1/8	11 7/8	7	6 5/8	12	14	Bingham Co., ID	Richard K. Smith	Richard K. Smith	2000	10

Mountain Caribou

Score	Gross Score	Length of Main Beam R	L	Inside Spread	Length of Brow Points R	L	Width of Brow Points R	L	Number of Points R	L	Locality Killed	Hunter	Owner	Date	Rank
459 3/8	490 5/8	51 7/8	48 7/8	40	21	21 5/8	14 5/8	3 5/8	18	20	Pelly Mts., YT	Paul T. Deuling	Paul T. Deuling	1988	1
453	465 1/8	48 2/8	49 5/8	45 6/8	20	17 1/8	13 1/8	4	23	21	Prospector Mt., YT	C. Candler Hunt	C. Candler Hunt	1998	2
452	469 5/8	43 1/8	42 2/8	30 3/8	16 4/8	16 1/8	11 2/8	5	22	19	Turnagain River, BC	Garry Beaubien	Cabela's, Inc.	1976	3
449 4/8	464 5/8	37 2/8	37 4/8	30 2/8	17 5/8	13 6/8	10 6/8	9 3/8	40	33	Fire Lake, YT	James R. Hollister	James R. Hollister	1989	4
448 6/8	458 6/8	51 3/8	51 5/8	40 2/8	18	4	10 6/8	1	24	20	Great Salmon Lake, YT	John Tomko	John Tomko	1965	5
446 2/8	461 3/8	55	53 5/8	40 2/8	14 7/8	13 2/8	9 3/8	5	20	14	Atlin, BC	Irvin Hardcastle	B&C National Collection	1955	6
445 3/8	454	48 7/8	46 2/8	27 4/8	17 6/8	20 2/8	4 5/8	17 6/8	19	20	Cold Fish Lake, BC	John I. Moore	Buckhorn Mus. & Saloon, Ltd.	1958	7
444	454 6/8	44 2/8	45 2/8	36 1/8	13 7/8	20 4/8	4	15 6/8	17	21	Quiet Lake, YT	Russ Mercer	Cabela's, Inc.	1965	8
444	459 1/8	52	52 1/8	38 2/8	8 6/8	20 2/8	1/8	15 7/8	16	25	Mountain River, NT	John A. Kolar	John A. Kolar	1984	8
444	477 1/8	42	43 1/8	35	15 6/8	17	8 1/8	7 3/8	20	23	Kechika Range, BC	James C. Johnson	James C. Johnson	1988	8

Woodland Caribou

Score	Gross Score	Length of Main Beam R	Length of Main Beam L	Inside Spread	Length of Brow Points R	Length of Brow Points L	Width of Brow Points R	Width of Brow Points L	Number of Points R	Number of Points L	Locality Killed	Hunter	Owner	Date	Rank
419 5/8	433 6/8	50 1/8	47 3/8	43 2/8	20	17 7/8	17 6/8	12 2/8	19	18	Newfoundland	Gift of H. Casmir de Rham	B&C National Collection	PR 1910	1
405 4/8	416 3/8	45	44	30 3/8	20 1/8	20 1/8	19 4/8	19 5/8	22	21	Gander River, NL	George H. Lesser	Harold Pelley	1951	2
405 1/8	423 2/8	38	39 6/8	34	21 7/8	20 3/8	18 7/8	18 4/8	22	25	Millertown, NL	Robert V. Knutson	Robert V. Knutson	1966	3
384 2/8	400	39 2/8	39 1/8	39 3/8	14 1/8	18 4/8	10 2/8	17 3/8	16	19	Sam's Pond, NL	James H. Holt	James H. Holt	2005	4
380 2/8	391 2/8	47 3/8	45 7/8	36 7/8	21 7/8	22	17 4/8	16 6/8	22	18	Bonavista Bay, NL	Unknown	Crow's Nest Officers Club	1935	5
375 3/8	390 3/8	42 1/8	43 3/8	37	17 1/8	15 5/8	15 2/8	13 5/8	16	15	Ten Mile Lake, NL	Picked Up	Baxter N. House	1999	6
373 6/8	382 2/8	39 7/8	43 3/8	22 1/8	24 4/8	22 3/8	20	21	21	22	Newfoundland	Gift of J.B. Marvin, Jr.	Unknown	PR 1924	7
359 2/8	374 5/8	40 1/8	42 3/8	34 3/8	16 2/8	14	11 1/8	11 2/8	18	13	Main Brook, NL	Picked Up	Gerard R. Beaulieu	1996	8
357 6/8	368 2/8	39 4/8	41 7/8	46 3/8	16	17 2/8	1 6/8	12 7/8	13	15	Gull River, NL	Picked Up	Gerard R. Beaulieu	1988	9
357 4/8	362 4/8	43 4/8	43 6/8	45 2/8	19 7/8	12 2/8	17 1/8	3 2/8	23	15	Mt. Peyton, NL	Picked Up	Harold Pelley	1968	10

Barren Ground Caribou

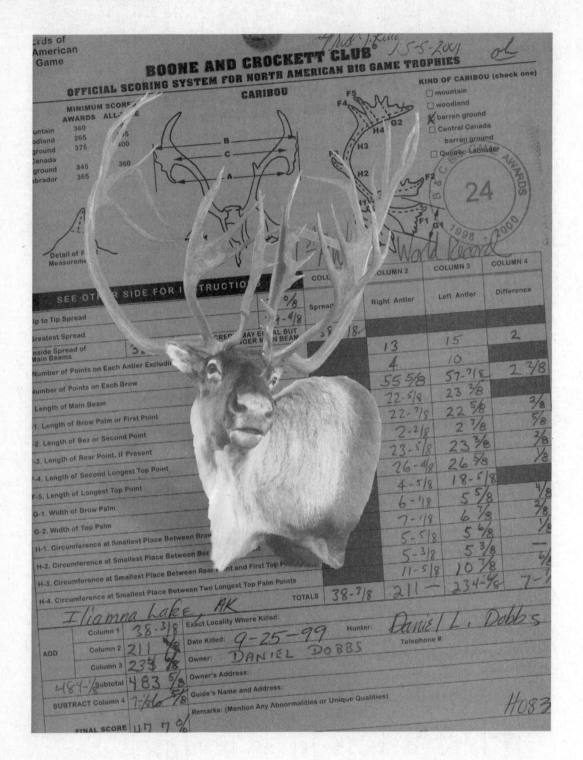

Score	Gross Score	Length of Main Beam R	L	Inside Spread	Length of Brow Points R	L	Width of Brow Points R	L	Number of Points R	L	Locality Killed	Hunter	Owner	Date	Rank
477	484 1/8	55 5/8	57 7/8	38 3/8	22 5/8	23 2/8	4 5/8	18 5/8	17	25	Iliamna Lake, AK	Daniel L. Dobbs	Daniel L. Dobbs	1999	1
465 1/8	493 3/8	50 6/8	49 7/8	40 1/8	19	20 4/8	9 7/8	14 5/8	24	23	Mosquito Creek, AK	Roger Hedgecock	Loaned to B&C Natl. Coll.	1987	2
463 6/8	471 7/8	51 2/8	51 5/8	46 7/8	18 2/8	24 6/8	12 7/8	21 4/8	22	23	Ugashik Lakes, AK	Ray Loesche	Ray Loesche	1967	3
461 6/8	485	53 2/8	55 3/8	35	20	18 2/8	16 4/8	12 4/8	29	21	Post River, AK	John V. Potter, Jr.	John V. Potter, Jr.	1976	4
461 4/8	476 3/8	59 1/8	61 4/8	44 4/8	22 5/8	21 1/8	15	6	19	15	Kenai Pen., AK	Buck D. Mantsch	Buck D. Mantsch	1994	5
459 6/8	473	58	59 3/8	40 6/8	19 4/8	18 3/8	16 5/8	4	30	17	Slana, AK	Floyd A. Blick	Floyd A. Blick	1954	6
459 3/8	472 5/8	53 5/8	55 3/8	33 3/8	19 5/8	19 3/8	8 5/8	13 3/8	19	17	Sharp Mt., AK	Frank Lobitz	Bass Pro Shops	1988	7
458 6/8	473	68 2/8	68 6/8	41 6/8	18 6/8	15 7/8	9	2 3/8	21	17	Alaska Pen., AK	Joseph Shoaf	Joseph Shoaf	1968	8
458 2/8	470 1/8	55 2/8	54 4/8	45 3/8	20 6/8	21 3/8	10 6/8	15 2/8	15	21	Cinder River, AK	Josef Meran	Josef Meran	1967	9
458 1/8	471 2/8	54 1/8	56	38 6/8	15 1/8	20 5/8	1/8	20 6/8	21	29	Gulkana River, AK	W.J. Krause	W.J. Krause	1953	10
458 1/8	474 2/8	49 7/8	50	31 2/8	17 6/8	15 2/8	13 2/8	8 7/8	18	17	Alaska Range, AK	Bobbie E. Robinson	Bobbie E. Robinson	1963	10

Quebec-Labrador Caribou

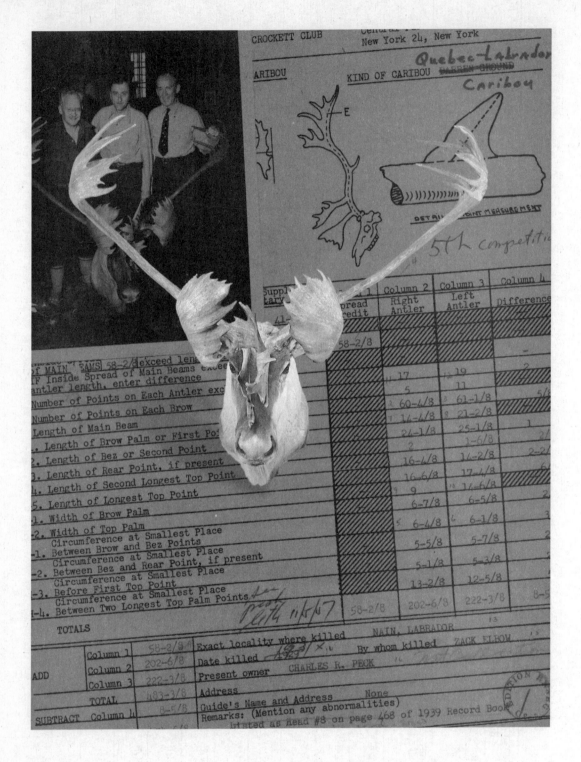

Score	Gross Score	Length of Main Beam		Inside Spread	Length of Brow Points		Width of Brow Points		Number of Points		Locality Killed	Hunter	Owner	Date	Rank
		R	L		R	L	R	L	R	L					
474 6/8	483 3/8	60 4/8	61 1/8	58 2/8	14 4/8	21 2/8	9	14 6/8	22	30	Nain, LB	Zack Elbow	B&C National Collection	1931	1
464 4/8	471 7/8	55 7/8	54 2/8	54 5/8	19 2/8	19 5/8	2 1/8	14 1/8	18	23	Tunulic River, QC	James A. DeLuca	James A. DeLuca	1983	2
460 6/8	475 1/8	59 4/8	56 5/8	49 2/8	16 6/8	21 4/8	13 6/8	18 4/8	22	24	Ungava Bay, QC	Lynn D. McLaud	Lynn D. McLaud	1978	3
441 7/8	452 7/8	52 3/8	51 7/8	44	21 6/8	20 5/8	6 7/8	14 5/8	25	23	Lake Arbique, QC	Larry R. Waldron	Larry R. Waldron	1993	4
439 1/8	449 6/8	56 6/8	59 1/8	42	17 7/8	20 2/8	12 3/8	13 7/8	11	22	Ungava Bay, QC	Don Tomberlin	Don Tomberlin	1985	5
438 2/8	450 3/8	59 3/8	55 4/8	52 7/8	8	21 1/8	1/8	19 1/8	17	25	Beach Camp, QC	Ronald R. Ragan	Ronald R. Ragan	1975	6
434 7/8	445 4/8	51 2/8	52	44 5/8	16 3/8	20 6/8	14 7/8	8 6/8	25	22	Mistimibi Lake, QC	Don L. Corley	Don L. Corley	1983	7
433 3/8	442	50 6/8	53 7/8	54	16 5/8	20 1/8	9 7/8	16 1/8	22	28	George River, QC	Dewey Mark	Dewey Mark	1973	8
433 2/8	451 1/8	46 5/8	44 2/8	41 1/8	20 1/8	20 3/8	14 5/8	17 4/8	22	24	Lake Otelnuk, QC	Robert E. McNeill	Robert E. McNeill	1986	9
431 6/8	450 2/8	53 4/8	56	46 1/8	16 5/8	20 5/8	3 6/8	15 1/8	19	18	Tunulik River, QC	Carol A. Mauch	Carol A. Mauch	1984	10

Pronghorn

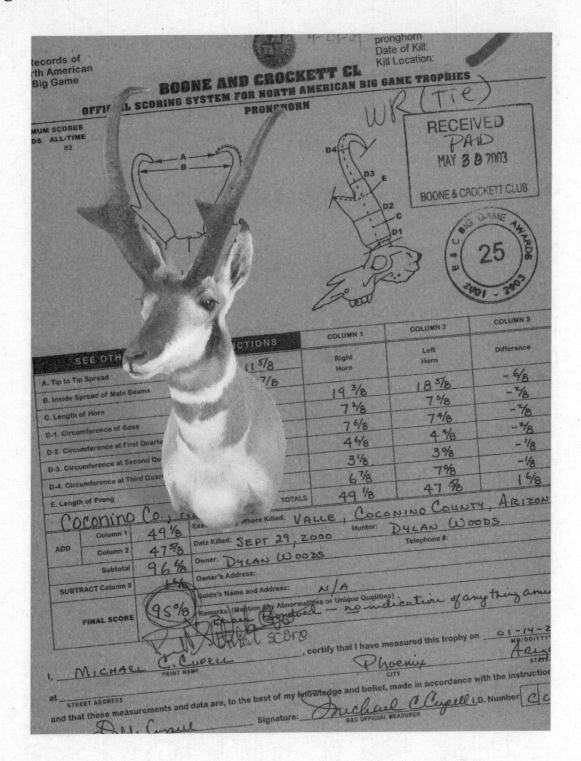

Score	Gross Score	Length of Horn R	Length of Horn L	Circumference of Base R	Circumference of Base L	Circumference of Third Quarter R	Circumference of Third Quarter L	Inside Spread	Tip to Tip Spread	Length of Prong R	Length of Prong L	Locality Killed	Hunter	Owner	Date	Rank
95	96 6/8	19 3/8	18 5/8	7 2/8	7	3 1/8	3	11 7/8	11 5/8	6 7/8	7	Coconino Co., AZ	Dylan M. Woods	Dylan M. Woods	2000	1
95	96 4/8	17 2/8	17 2/8	7 2/8	7 2/8	3 7/8	4	10 1/8	4 3/8	7	6 1/8	Mohave Co., AZ	David Meyer	David Meyer	2002	1
94	94 3/8	17 2/8	17 1/8	7 2/8	7 3/8	3	3	15	13 5/8	7 5/8	7 5/8	Washoe Co., NV	Sam S. Jaksick, Jr.	Sam S. Jaksick, Jr.	2006	3
93 4/8	94 6/8	17 6/8	17 4/8	6 7/8	7	3 1/8	3 2/8	12 5/8	8 1/8	8	8 2/8	Coconino Co., AZ	Michael J. O'Haco, Jr.	Michael J. O'Haco, Jr.	1985	4
93 2/8	93 4/8	18 4/8	18 4/8	7 2/8	7 2/8	2 6/8	2 6/8	8 1/8	1	7	6 7/8	Humboldt Co., NV	Todd B. Jaksick	Todd B. Jaksick	1999	5
93	94 2/8	18 1/8	18 2/8	7 2/8	7	2 5/8	2 6/8	10 1/8	6 5/8	7 6/8	7 2/8	Yavapai Co., AZ	Edwin L. Wetzler	Loaned to B&C Natl. Coll.	1975	6
92 6/8	93	16 4/8	16 4/8	7 2/8	7 1/8	3 1/8	3 1/8	12 4/8	9 5/8	7 3/8	7 4/8	Coconino Co., AZ	Sam S. Jaksick, Jr.	Sam S. Jaksick, Jr.	1991	7
92 6/8	94 2/8	16 6/8	17 3/8	7 5/8	7 4/8	2 5/8	2 6/8	11 4/8	7	7 5/8	7 1/8	Harney Co., OR	Sam Barry	Sam Barry	2000	7
92 2/8	92 7/8	16 3/8	16 3/8	7 7/8	7 6/8	3 5/8	3 5/8	10 2/8	4	6 4/8	6	Yavapai Co., AZ	Denny Austad	Denny Austad	2006	9
91 6/8	93	17 2/8	17 1/8	7 6/8	7 6/8	3 3/8	2 7/8	13 4/8	9	7	7 3/8	Coconino Co., AZ	Steven E. Hopkins	Steven E. Hopkins	1992	10

Bison

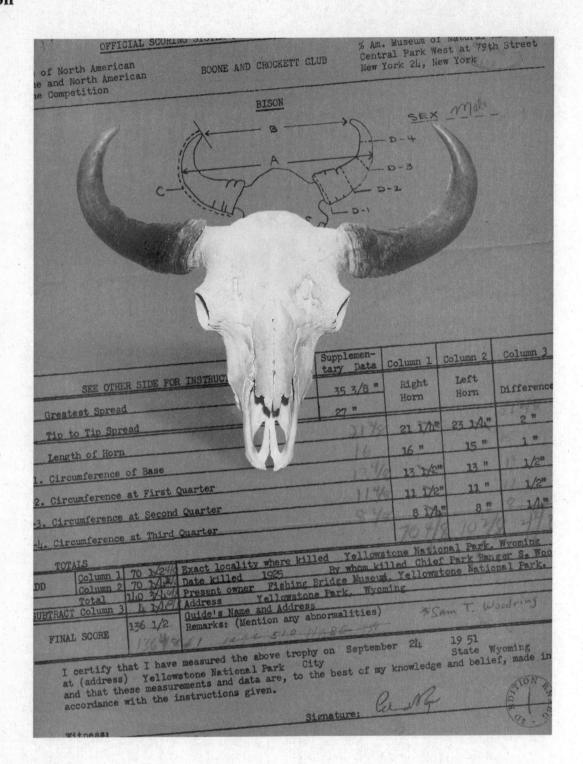

Score	Gross Score	Length of Horn		Circumference of Base		Circumference of Third Quarter		Greatest Spread	Tip to Tip Spread	Locality Killed	Hunter	Owner	Date	Rank
		R	L	R	L	R	L							
136 4/8	140 6/8	21 2/8	23 2/8	16	15	8 2/8	8	35 3/8	27	Yellowstone Natl. Park, WY	Sam T. Woodring	Yellowstone Natl. Park	1925	1
136 2/8	137 3/8	19	18 6/8	18 4/8	18 4/8	6 5/8	6 7/8	30 1/8	22 3/8	Northwest Territories	Samuel Israel	Samuel Israel	1961	2
135	136	18 2/8	18	16	15 4/8	8 6/8	8 7/8	32 2/8	28 4/8	Custer Co., SD	Remo Pizzagalli	Remo Pizzagalli	1995	3
135	139 2/8	23	24 4/8	14 4/8	14 1/8	6	7	31 3/8	20	Park Co., MT	Picked Up	Glenn M. Smith	1997	3
134 2/8	136 6/8	21 2/8	20 6/8	14 4/8	14 7/8	8 6/8	7 6/8	33 7/8	26 2/8	Park Co., WY	Picked Up	H.A. Moore	1977	5
133 4/8	134	19 2/8	18 6/8	17	17	7	7	29 2/8	21 2/8	Great Slave Lake, AB	Mike Dempsey	Natl. Mus. of Canada	1935	6
133 2/8	135 2/8	17 6/8	18 5/8	15 1/8	15 7/8	8 4/8	8 3/8	34 5/8	26 5/8	Teton Co., WY	Edward D. Riekens, Jr.	Edward D. Riekens, Jr.	2007	7
132 2/8	135 7/8	21 2/8	22 2/8	16 4/8	16 7/8	6	7 5/8	35 2/8	26 6/8	Unknown	James H. Lockhart	Carnegie Museum	PR 1939	8
132 2/8	133 5/8	20 5/8	21 7/8	14 1/8	14 1/8	6 6/8	6 5/8	32 6/8	24 3/8	Sweet Grass, AB	Ken Cooper	Univ. of Sask.	1961	8
131 6/8	132 1/8	20 6/8	22 7/8	15	15	7	7	30	20 7/8	Hell Roaring Creek, MT	Picked Up	Philip L. Wright Zool. Mus.	1945	10
131 6/8	133 1/8	21 5/8	21 4/8	16	15 1/8	5 4/8	5 4/8	30	19 5/8	Coconino Co., AZ	Duane R. Richardson	Duane R. Richardson	2002	10

Rocky Mountain Goat

Score	Gross Score	Length of Horn		Circumference of Base		Circumference of Third Quarter		Greatest Spread	Tip to Tip Spread	Locality Killed	Hunter	Owner	Date	Rank
		R	L	R	L	R	L							
56 6/8	57	12	12	6 4/8	6 4/8	2	2	9 2/8	9	Babine Mts., BC	E.C. Haase	B&C National Collection	1949	1
56 6/8	57 7/8	11 7/8	10 6/8	6 4/8	6 4/8	2 1/8	2 1/8	8 7/8	8 2/8	Bella Coola, BC	G. Wober & L. Michalchuk	Gernot Wober	1999	1
56 2/8	56 3/8	11 5/8	11 5/8	5 6/8	5 5/8	2 1/8	2 1/8	7 2/8	6 4/8	Helm Bay, AK	W.H. Jackson	B&C National Collection	1933	3
56 2/8	56 5/8	11 3/8	11 3/8	6 3/8	6 4/8	2 1/8	2	8 6/8	8 3/8	Hedley, BC	Picked Up	Robert Kitto	1969	3
56	56 5/8	10 4/8	10 6/8	6 1/8	6	2 5/8	2 6/8	6 7/8	6 4/8	Kenai Pen., AK	Peter W. Bading	Peter W. Bading	1963	5
55 6/8	55 7/8	10 5/8	10 4/8	6 1/8	6 1/8	2 2/8	2 2/8	7 6/8	6 3/8	Blunt Mt., BC	Picked Up	Jack Adams	1970	6
55 2/8	56	10 6/8	11	6 2/8	6 3/8	2	2 1/8	7 6/8	7 2/8	Oliver Creek, BC	Patrick P. Moleski	Patrick P. Moleski	1994	7
55	55 1/8	11 7/8	11 7/8	5 4/8	5 3/8	2	2	8 3/8	6 4/8	Cleveland Pen., AK	Elmer W. Copstead	Jonas Bros. of Seattle	1939	8
55	55 3/8	12 1/8	12 1/8	5 2/8	5 1/8	2	2 2/8	7 7/8	5 6/8	Alex. Archipelago, AK	James Wilson	James Wilson	1969	8
55	55 3/8	11 4/8	11 2/8	6 2/8	6 2/8	2	2	7	5 5/8	Cleveland Pen., AK	David K. Mueller	David K. Mueller	1997	8

Muskox

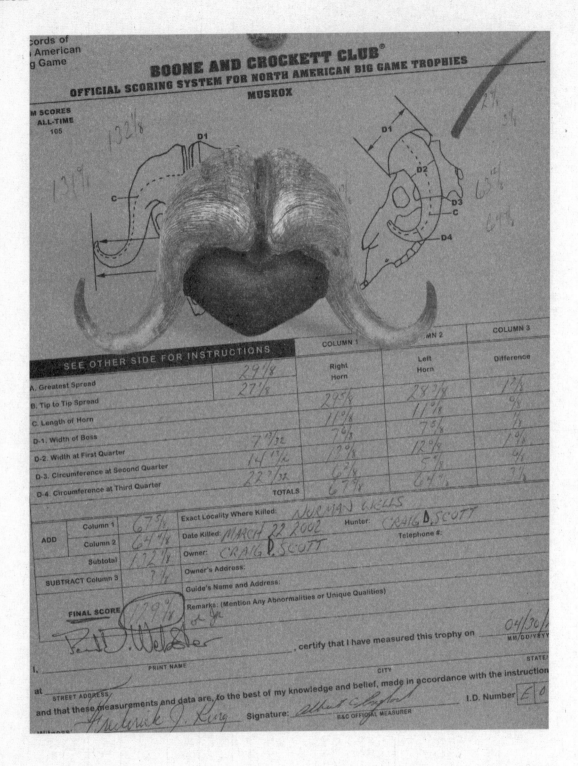

Score	Gross Score	Length of Horn R	Length of Horn L	Circumference of Base R	Circumference of Base L	Circumference of Third Quarter R	Circumference of Third Quarter L	Greatest Spread	Tip to Tip Spread	Locality Killed	Hunter	Owner	Date	Rank
129	132 1/8	29 5/8	28 3/8	11	11	6 2/8	5 4/8	29 1/8	27 1/8	Norman Wells, NT	Craig D. Scott	Craig D. Scott	2002	1
129	131	28 2/8	28 6/8	12 1/8	11 3/8	5 7/8	6 3/8	31 4/8	30 4/8	Coppermine River, NU	Jim Shockey	Jim Shockey	2006	1
128 6/8	130 4/8	29 4/8	30 4/8	11 1/8	10 7/8	6 2/8	6	27 1/8	25 4/8	Kugluktuk, NU	Tony L. Spriggs	Tony L. Spriggs	2004	3
128 2/8	129 3/8	31 5/8	31 7/8	10 4/8	10 4/8	5 5/8	6	29 6/8	29	Coppermine River, NU	Jim Shockey	Jim Shockey	2006	4
127 2/8	128 2/8	29 2/8	29 7/8	10 6/8	10 6/8	6	5 6/8	29 6/8	28 6/8	Kugluktuk, NU	Vicente S. Sanchez-Valdepenas	Vicente S. Sanchez-Valdepenas	1999	5
127	127 2/8	29 7/8	29 6/8	10 1/8	10 1/8	6	6	30 4/8	29 5/8	Kugluktuk, NU	Robert A. Black	Robert A. Black	1996	6
127	128 2/8	29 1/8	29 1/8	11 2/8	10 6/8	6 4/8	6 3/8	28 6/8	26 4/8	Kugluktuk, NU	Ben L. Mueller	Ben L. Mueller	2007	6
126 4/8	127 5/8	30 6/8	30 7/8	10 3/8	10 5/8	5 7/8	5 4/8	29 7/8	28 6/8	Coppermine River, NU	Robert M. Ortiz	Robert M. Ortiz	2003	8
126 2/8	127 2/8	29 2/8	29 4/8	10 5/8	11	5 4/8	5 5/8	27 7/8	27 4/8	Kugaryuak River, NU	M.R. James	M.R. James	2000	9
126	128	30	29 1/8	10 1/8	10 2/8	6 2/8	6	29 7/8	29	Kugluktuk, NU	Eric Llanes	Eric Llanes	1997	10

Bighorn Sheep

Score	Gross Score	Length of Horn R	L	Circumference of Base R	L	Circumference of Third Quarter R	L	Greatest Spread	Tip to Tip Spread	Locality Killed	Hunter	Owner	Date	Rank
208 3/8	209 3/8	47 4/8	46 5/8	15 7/8	15 7/8	12	11 3/8	23 1/8	23 1/8	Luscar Mt., AB	Guinn D. Crousen	Guinn D. Crousen	2000	1
208 1/8	209 3/8	44 7/8	45	16 5/8	16 5/8	11 2/8	11 7/8	22 6/8	19 3/8	Blind Canyon, AB	Fred Weiller	Clarence Baird	1911	2
207 2/8	208 3/8	45	45 2/8	15 6/8	16	11 6/8	11 7/8	23 1/8	19 3/8	Oyster Creek, AB	Martin K. Bovey	Aly M. Bruner	1924	3
206 3/8	206 4/8	44 4/8	44 3/8	15 7/8	15 7/8	12 1/8	12 1/8	21 4/8	21 4/8	Burnt Timber Creek, AB	Picked Up	Gordon L. Magnussen	1955	4
204 7/8	205 7/8	43 1/8	41 6/8	17 1/8	16 7/8	11 4/8	11 7/8	23 4/8	18 6/8	Granite Co., MT	James R. Weatherly	James R. Weatherly	1993	5
204 2/8	204 3/8	44 4/8	44 2/8	16 4/8	16 4/8	10 5/8	10 6/8	25 1/8	25 1/8	Fergus Co., MT	Toni L. Sannon	Toni L. Sannon	2008	6
204	204 6/8	49 4/8	48 2/8	15 2/8	15 3/8	10 5/8	10 2/8	23 7/8	23 7/8	Sheep Creek, BC	James Simpson	Am. Mus. Nat. Hist.	1920	7
203 5/8	205 7/8	43 2/8	41 5/8	17 2/8	17 4/8	11 3/8	10 2/8	20 7/8	23 4/8	Beaverhead Co., MT	Picked Up	MT Dept. of Fish, Wildl., & Parks	1992	8
203 4/8	204 2/8	43 1/8	42 5/8	16 4/8	16 4/8	11 3/8	11 1/8	25 4/8	19 4/8	Sheep River, AB	Katherine A. Pyra	Katherine A. Pyra	1992	9
202 7/8	204	43 1/8	46 2/8	16 7/8	16 7/8	9 4/8	10 1/8	24 4/8	22 6/8	Blaine Co., MT	Debby L. Perry	Debby L. Perry	2008	10

Desert Sheep

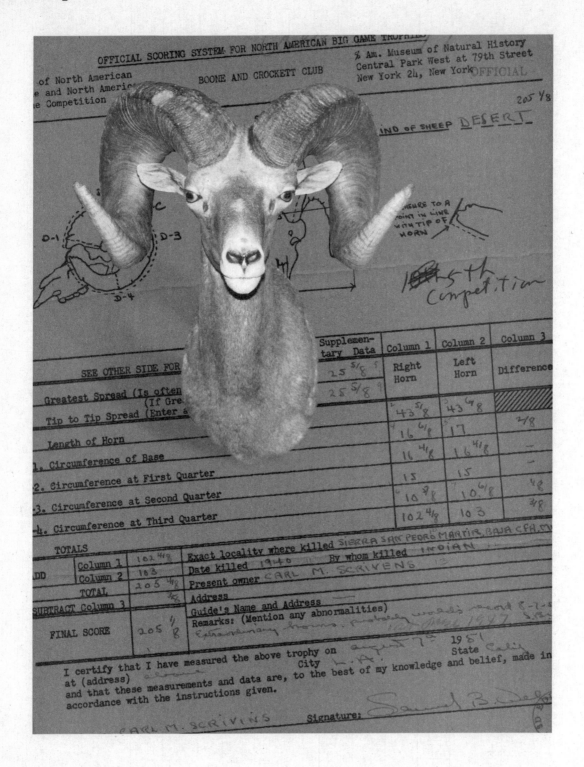

Score	Gross Score	Length of Horn		Circumference of Base		Circumference of Third Quarter		Greatest Spread	Tip to Tip Spread	Locality Killed	Hunter	Owner	Date	Rank
		R	L	R	L	R	L							
205 1/8	205 4/8	43 5/8	43 6/8	16 6/8	17	10 5/8	10 6/8	25 5/8	25 5/8	Lower Calif., MX	Native American	Loaned to B&C Natl. Coll.	1940	1
201 3/8	202 6/8	45 5/8	46 2/8	15 5/8	15 5/8	11 2/8	11 5/8	20 4/8	20	Pima Co., AZ	Picked Up	Greg Koons	1982	2
197 4/8	198 4/8	44	43 4/8	15 7/8	15 7/8	10 5/8	10	23 7/8	23 7/8	Lower Calif., MX	Gift of H.M. Beck	Cabela's, Inc.	1892	3
197 1/8	197 6/8	42 3/8	41 6/8	16 1/8	16 1/8	10 5/8	11	26	26	Graham Co., AZ	Arthur R. Dubs	Arthur R. Dubs	1988	4
192 5/8	193 5/8	41 6/8	42 3/8	15	15 1/8	10 6/8	10 4/8	25 4/8	25	Baja Calif., MX	Javier Lopez del Bosque	Javier Lopez del Bosque	1979	5
191 6/8	192 6/8	42	43 4/8	15 4/8	15 3/8	9 6/8	9 3/8	23 4/8	23 4/8	Baja Calif., MXz	Lit Ng	Lit Ng	1968	6
191 3/8	192 1/8	40	41 3/8	16 5/8	16 5/8	9 1/8	9 5/8	24 1/8	24 1/8	Mexico	Picked Up	Snow Museum	PR 1952	7
191 2/8	192 7/8	38 4/8	40 4/8	16 2/8	16 2/8	10 3/8	10 7/8	21 6/8	17 2/8	Baja Calif., MX	Claude Bourguignon	Claude Bourguignon	1982	8
191 1/8	191 4/8	39 3/8	39 2/8	16 3/8	16 4/8	10	10	19 3/8	19 2/8	Baja Calif., MX	Bruno Scherrer	Bruno Scherrer	1981	9
190 3/8	191 1/8	41	43 7/8	15 3/8	15 5/8	9 1/8	9 1/8	23 7/8	23 7/8	Arizona	Unknown	Bruce R. Kemp, Sr.	1903	10

Dall's Sheep

Score	Gross Score	Length of Horn		Circumference of Base		Circumference of Third Quarter		Greatest Spread	Tip to Tip Spread	Locality Killed	Hunter	Owner	Date	Rank
		R	L	R	L	R	L							
189 6/8	190 3/8	48 5/8	47 7/8	14 5/8	14 6/8	6 5/8	6 7/8	34 3/8	34 3/8	Wrangell Mts., AK	Harry L. Swank, Jr.	Mrs. Harry L. Swank, Jr.	1961	1
185 6/8	186 5/8	49 4/8	44 2/8	14	13 7/8	6 6/8	7 3/8	24 3/8	24 3/8	Chugach Mts., AK	Frank Cook	Craig A. Cook	1956	2
185 4/8	185 7/8	43 6/8	40 4/8	14 7/8	14 7/8	9 4/8	9 3/8	20 7/8	20 7/8	Chugach Mts., AK	Jack W. Lentfer	Jack W. Lentfer	1964	3
184 5/8	185 2/8	44 7/8	47	14 1/8	14	7 1/8	7 2/8	26 6/8	26 6/8	Jacksina Creek, AK	Sherwin N. Scott	Foundation for N. American Wild Sheep	1984	4
184 4/8	186 2/8	43 6/8	46	14 1/8	14 3/8	9	7 6/8	21 6/8	21 6/8	Wrangell Mts., AK	B.L. Burkholder	B.L. Burkholder	1958	5
184	184 1/8	44 6/8	44 4/8	14 2/8	14 2/8	7 1/8	7 2/8	24 5/8	24 5/8	Chugach Mts., AK	Thomas C. Sheets	Thomas C. Sheets	1962	6
183 7/8	184	46 5/8	47 4/8	13 6/8	13 6/8	6 4/8	6 4/8	31	31	Wrangell Mts., AK	Tony Oney	Tony Oney	1963	7
183 6/8	184 3/8	48	47 4/8	14	13 6/8	6 2/8	6 5/8	33 4/8	33 4/8	Alaska Range, AK	Jonathan T. Summar, Jr.	Jonathan T. Summar, Jr.	1965	8
183 4/8	185	45 7/8	45 1/8	13 7/8	14	7 1/8	7 6/8	27 7/8	27 7/8	Whitehorse, YT	W. Newhall	Robert E. Barnes	1924	9
183	183 2/8	42 3/8	39 3/8	14 6/8	14 6/8	9 5/8	9 5/8	22 5/8	19 4/8	Wrangell Mts., AK	Gene M. Effler	Gene M. Effler	1959	10

Stone's Sheep

Score	Gross Score	Length of Horn		Circumference of Base		Circumference of Third Quarter		Greatest Spread	Tip to Tip Spread	Locality Killed	Hunter	Owner	Date	Rank
		R	L	R	L	R	L							
196 6/8	197 3/8	50 1/8	51 5/8	14 6/8	14 6/8	6 6/8	7	31	31	Muskwa River, BC	L.S. Chadwick	B&C National Collection	1936	1
190	190 4/8	46 6/8	46 6/8	15 2/8	15 1/8	6 5/8	6 6/8	30 6/8	30 6/8	Sikanni Chief River, BC	Norman Blank	Norman Blank	1962	2
189 6/8	190 3/8	48 2/8	46 2/8	14 7/8	14 7/8	7 2/8	7 4/8	28	28	Blue Sheep Lake, BC	G.C.F Dalziel	G.C.F Dalziel	1965	3
187 4/8	187 5/8	43	44	14 6/8	14 6/8	8 4/8	8 4/8	22	22	Ospika River, BC	Paul D. Weingart	Paul D. Weingart	1970	4
185 3/8	185 6/8	45 6/8	44 3/8	15 7/8	15 7/8	6 1/8	5 7/8	29 3/8	29 3/8	Prophet River, BC	Felipe Palau	Felipe Palau	1970	5
184 6/8	185 2/8	43	43 4/8	15 6/8	15 6/8	7	7 1/8	28 4/8	28 4/8	Prophet River, BC	Joseph H. Shirk	Mrs. C. Barnaby	1948	6
184 4/8	185	44 4/8	45	15 4/8	15 3/8	6 3/8	6 4/8	26 3/8	26 3/8	Hudson Hope, BC	John W. Pitney	Am. Mus. Nat. Hist.	1936	7
184 3/8	186	44 3/8	46	14 1/8	14 2/8	8	7	28 6/8	28 6/8	Colt Lake, BC	Lloyd E. Hall	Lloyd E. Hall	1963	8
184 2/8	184 4/8	42 1/8	42 3/8	16 2/8	16 2/8	7 1/8	7 1/8	24 4/8	24 4/8	Blue Sheep Lake, BC	G.C.F Dalziel	G.C.F Dalziel	1964	9
184 2/8	185 1/8	47 5/8	45 3/8	14 2/8	14 4/8	6 6/8	6 3/8	31 3/8	31 3/8	Colt Lake, BC	Herb Klein	Dallas Mus. of Natl. Hist.	1965	9
184 2/8	184 3/8	45 7/8	42 7/8	15	14 7/8	7 3/8	7 3/8	22 5/8	22 3/8	Kechika Range, BC	Arthur R. Dubs	Arthur R. Dubs	1966	9

Part 10

Contributors and Their Works

A ll short stories, articles, recipes, and other works appearing in this compendium have been reprinted courtesy of the authors listed below. To buy any of their books, go to the websites indicated.

Steve Bartylla (http://www.amazon.com/Steve-Bartylla/e/B001JRZT5E)

Bowhunting Tactics that Deliver Trophies

Mary T. Bell (http://www.amazon.com/Mary-T.-Bell/e/B001JP2LCK)

Food Drying with an Attitude: A Fun and Fabulous Guide to Creating Snacks, Meals, and Crafts*

Just Jerky: The Complete Guide to Making It

Mary Bell's Complete Dehydrator Cookbook

Hal Blood (http://www.bigwoodsbucks.com)

Hunting Big Woods Bucks: Secrets of Tracking and Stalking Whitetails*

Hunting Big Woods Bucks, Vol. 2

Toby Bridges (http://www.lobowatch.org/)

Hunting Record-Book Bucks

Muzzleloading

Muzzleloader Hunting: Then & Now

Muzzleloading for Whitetails and Other Big Game

Pronghorn Hunting

Bob Brister (http://www.amazon.com/Bob-Brister/e/B001JP8JY4)

Moss, Mallards, and Mules

Shotgunning: The Art and the Science*

Boone and Crockett Club (http://www.boone-crockett.org/)

A Whitetail Retrospective: Classic Photos and Memorabilia from the Boone and Crockett Club Archives

An American Elk Retrospective: Vintage Photos and Memorabilia from the Boone and Crockett Club Archives

American Big-game Hunting: The Book Of The Boone And Crockett Club.

Boone and Crockett Club's 27th Big Game Awards 2007-2009

Vintage Hunting Album: A Photographic Collection of Days Gone By (Vol. 1)

Legendary Hunts: Short Stories from the Boone and Crockett Awards

Legendary Hunts II: More Short Stories from the Boone and Crockett Awards

Records of North American Big Game

Records of North American Elk

Records of North American Mule Deer

Records of North American Sheep, Rocky Mountain Goats & Pronghorn

*Records of North American Whitetail Deer, 5th Edition: Decades of Trophy Listings for Wild, Free-Ranging Whitetails**

Monte Burch (monteburch.com)

Backyard Structures and How to Build Them

Black Bass Basics

Building Small Barns, Sheds & Shelters

Cleaning and Preparing Gamefish

Country Crafts and Skills

Denny Brauer's Jig Fishing Secrets

Field Dressing and Butchering Upland Birds, Waterfowl and Wild Turkeys

Lohman Guide to Calling & Decoying Waterfowl

Lohman Guide to Successful Turkey Calling

Making Native American Hunting, Fighting and Survival Tools

Mounting Your Deer Head at Home

Monte Burch's Pole Building Projects

Pocket Guide to Bowhunting Whitetail Deer

Pocket Guide to Field Dressing, Butchering & Cooking Deer

Pocket Guide to Old Time Catfish Techniques

Pocket Guide to Seasonal Largemouth Bass Patterns

Pocket Guide to Seasonal Walleye Tactics

Pocket Guide to Spring and Fall Turkey Hunting

Solving Squirrel Problems

*The Complete Guide to Sausage Making**

*The Complete Jerky Book**

*The Hunting and Fishing Camp Builder's Guide**

*The Joy of Smoking and Salt Curing**

*The Ultimate Guide to Growing Your Own Food**

The Ultimate Guide to Making Outdoor Gear and Accessories

The Ultimate Guide to Skinning and Tanning

Jay Cassell (http://www.amazon.com/s/ref=ntt_athr_dp_sr_1?_encoding=UTF8&field-author=Jay%20 Cassell&ie=UTF8&search-alias=books&sort=relevancerank)

North America's Greatest Big Game Lodges & Outfitters: More Than 250 Prime Destinations in the U.S. & Canada

North America's Greatest Whitetail Lodges & Outfitters: More Than 250 Prime Destinations in the U.S. & Canada

Shooter's Bible: The World's Bestselling Firearms Reference*

The Best Hunting Stories Ever Told*

The Gigantic Book of Hunting Stories*

The Little Red Book of Hunter's Wisdom*

The Quotable Hunter

The Ultimate Guide to Fishing Skills, Tactics, and Techniques: A Comprehensive Guide to Catching Bass, Trout, Salmon, Walleyes, Panfish, Saltwater Gamefish, and Much More*

Richard P. Combs (http://www.amazon.com/Richard-Combs/e/B001KMGYQQ/ref=sr_ntt_srch_ lnk_1?qid=1341340136&sr=1-1)

Canoeing and Kayaking Ohio's Streams: An Access Guide for Paddlers and Anglers

Guide to Advanced Turkey Hunting: How to Call and Decoy Even Wary Boss Gobblers into Range*

Turkey Hunting Tactics of the Pros: Expert Advice to Help You Get a Gobbler This Season

Judd Cooney (http://www.juddcooney.com/)

Advanced Scouting for Whitetails

Decoying Big Game: Successful Tactics for Luring Deer, Elk, Bears, and Other Animals into Range

How to Attract Whitetails

The Bowhunter's Field Manual

Fred Eichler (http://www.fulldrawoutfitters.com)

Bowhunting Western Big Game

Kathy Etling (www.amazon.com/Kathy-Etling/e/B001K8D1XE)

Bowhunting's Superbucks: How Some of the Biggest Bucks in North America Were Taken*

Cougar Attacks: Encounters of the Worst Kind

Denise Parker: A Teenage Archer's Quest for Olympic Glory

Hunting Bears: Black, Brown, Grizzly and Polar Bears

Hunting Superbucks: How to Find and Hunt Today's Trophy Mule and Whitetail Deer

The Art of Whitetail Deception

The Quotable Cowboy

The Ultimate Guide to Calling, Rattling, and Decoying Whitetails*

Thrill of the Chase

Ray Eye (http://www.rayeye.com/)

Practical Turkey Hunting Strategies: How to Hunt Effectively Under Any Conditions

*Ray Eye's Turkey Hunting Bible: The Tips, Tactics, and Secrets of a Professional Turkey Hunter**

J. Wayne Fears (http://www.jwaynefears.com/)

Backcountry Cooking

*How to Build Your Dream Cabin in the Woods: The Ultimate Guide to Building and Maintaining a Backcountry Getaway**

Hunting Club Guide

Hunting North America's Big Bear: Grizzly, Brown, and Polar Bear Hunting Techniques and Adventures

Hunting Whitetails East & West

Scrape Hunting from A to Z

*The Complete Book of Dutch Oven Cooking**

The Field & Stream Wilderness Cooking Handbook: How to Prepare, Cook, and Serve Backcountry Meals

*The Pocket Outdoor Survival Guide: The Ultimate Guide for Short-Term Survival**

Kate Fiduccia (www.amazon.com/Kate-Fiduccia/e/B001K8AD58)

Cooking Wild in Kate's Camp

Cooking Wild in Kate's Kitchen: Venison

Grillin' and Chili'n: Eighty Easy Recipes for Venison to Sizzle, Smoke, and Simmer

The Quotable Wine Lover

*The Venison Cookbook: Venison Dishes from Fast to Fancy**

Peter Fiduccia (http://www.woodsnwater.tv)

101 Deer Hunting Tips: Practical Advice from a Master Hunter

North America's Greatest Whitetail Lodges & Outfitters: More Than 250 Prine Destinations in the U.S. & Canada

Whitetail Strategies: A No-Nonsense Approach to Successful Deer Hunting

Whitetail Strategies: The Ultimate Guide

Whitetail Strategies, Vol. II: Straightforward Tactics for Tracking, Calling, the Rut, and Much More

Dave Fisher (http://www.amazon.com/Dave-Fisher/e/B001K8VADC/ref=ntt_athr_dp_pel_1)

I'd Rather Be Rabbit Hunting

*Secrets of a Master Cottontail Hunter**

David R. Henderson (http://www.hendersonoutdoors.com/)

Campsite to Kitchen Cookbook

Gunsmithing Shotguns: A Basic Guide to Care and Repair

Modern Shotgunning

Shotgunning for Deer: Guns, Loads, and Techniques for the Modern Hunter*

The Ultimate Guide to Shotgunning: Guns, Gear, and Hunting Tactics for Deer and Big Game, Upland Birds, Waterfowl, and Small Game

White Tails: A Modern Look at Deer Hunting

Gene Hill (http://www.amazon.com/Gene-Hill/e/B001K816UE)

A Hunter's Fireside Book: Tales of Dogs, Ducks, Birds, & Guns*

A Listening Walk...and Other Stories

Hill Country: Stories About Hunting and Fishing and Dogs and Guns and Such

Mostly Tailfeathers

Outdoor Yarns & Outright Lies

Passing a Good Time

Shotgunner's Notebook: The Advice and Reflections of a Wingshooter

Tears & Laughter: A Couple of Dozen Dog Stories

Tom Indrebo (http://www.amazon.com/Tom-Indrebo/e/B002EID7K6)

Growing & Hunting Quality Bucks: A Hands-On Approach to Better Land and Deer Management*

Dave Kelso (http://www.davidkelso.com/)

Moose Hunting: Calling, Decoying and Stalking

Marie W. Lawrence (http://www.amazon.com/Marie-W.-Lawrence/e/B0052XZJEM)

The Farmer's Cookbook: A Back to Basics Guide to Making Cheese, Curing Meat, Preserving Produce, Baking Bread, Fermenting, and More*

Thomas McIntyre (http://www.amazon.com/Thomas-McIntyre/e/B001HP8JUU/ref=sr_ntt_srch_lnk_9?qid=1341495212&sr=1-9)

Days Afield: Journeys and Discoveries in Hunting and Fishing

Seasons & Days: A Hunting Life

Dreaming the Lion

Shooter's Bible Guide to Optics*

The Field & Stream Hunting Optics Handbook: An Expert's Guide to Riflescopes, Binoculars, Spotting Scopes, and Rangefinders

The Way of the Hunter: The Art and the Spirit of Modern Hunting

Wild And Fair: Tales of Hunting Big Game in North America

Sigurd Olson (http://singingwilderness.net/wordpress/)

Listening Point

Lonely Land

Meaning Of Wilderness: Essential Articles and Speeches

Of Time And Place

Open Horizons

Reflections from the North Country

Runes Of The North

Spirit Of The North: The Quotable Sigurd F. Olson

The Hidden Forest

The Singing Wilderness

Wilderness Days

Randy D. Smith (www.amazon.com/Randy-D.-Smith/e/B004KT4K0S)

Bohanin's Last Days

Dodge City

Fort Larned

Heroes of the Santa Fe Trail: 1821-1900

Hunting Modern South Africa with Powder and Ball

Lovell's Prize

Scott City

Sunday's Colt and Other Stories of the Old West

The Black Powder Plainsman: A Beginner's Guide to Muzzleloading and Reenactment on the Great Plains

The Red River Ring

Ron Spomer (http://www.ronspomeroutdoors.com/)

Big Game Hunter's Guide to Idaho

Big Game Hunter's Guide to Montana

Big Game Hunter's Guide to Wyoming

*Predator Hunting: Proven Strategies That Work From East to West**

Rifle Bullets for the Hunter: A Definitive Study

Rut: Spectacular Fall Ritual of North American Horned and Antlered Animals

The Big Book of Whitetail: Strategies, Techniques, and Tactics

The Complete Hunter's Advanced Whitetail Hunting

The Hunter's Book of the Whitetail

William G. Tapply (http://www.williamgtapply.com/)

A Fly-fishing Life

Bass Bug Fishing

Gone Fishin'

Home Water Near and Far

Opening Day and Other Neuroses

Pocket Water

Sportsman's Legacy

The Orvis Pocket Guide to Fly Fishing for Bass

Those Hours Spent Outdoors

Trout Eyes*

Upland Autumn*

Upland Days

John Trout (www.amazon.com/John-Trout/e/B001JP29BI)

Ambushing Trophy Whitetails: Tactical Systems for Big-Buck Success

Finding Wounded Deer

Hunting Rutting Bucks: Secrets for Tagging the Biggest Buck of Your Life

Solving Coyote Problems: How to Coexist with North America's Most Persistent Predator

The Complete Book of Wild Turkey Hunting

Lamar Underwood (www.amazon.com/Lamar-Underwood/e/B001K8CZK4)

1001 Fishing Tips*

1001 Hunting Tips*

Bowhunting tactics of the Pros

Classic Hunting Stories

Classic Survival Stories

Classic War Stories

Into the Backing

Man Eaters

On Dangerous Ground

Tales of Mountain Men

The Bobwhite Quail Book: Classic Upland Tales

The Deer Hunter's Book: Classic Hunting Stories

The Duck Hunter's Book: Classic Waterfowl Stories

The Greatest Adventure Stories Ever Told

The Greatest Disaster Stories Ever Told

The Greatest Fishing Stories Ever Told

The Greatest Flying Stories Ever Told

The Greatest Hunting Stories Ever Told

The Greatest Submarine Stories Ever Told

The Greatest Survival Stories Ever Told

The Greatest War Stories Ever Told

The Quotable Army

The Quotable Navy

The Quotable Soldier

The Quotable Writer

Theodore Roosevelt on Hunting

Whitetail Hunting Tactics of the Pros

Wayne van Zwoll (http://highcountrywomen.com/)

America's Greatest Gunmakers

Bolt Action Rifles

Deer Rifles & Cartridges*

Hunter's Guide to Long-Range Shooting

Elk and Elk Hunting

Elk Rifles, Cartridges and Hunting Tactics

Leupold & Stevens... First Century

Mastering Mule Deer

Modern Sporting Rifle Cartridges

Shooter's Bible Guide to Rifle Ballistics*

The Complete Book of the .22

The Gun Digest Book of Sporting Optics

The Hunter's Guide to Accurate Shooting

The Hunter's Guide to Ballistics

John Weiss (http://www.amazon.com/John-Weiss/e/B001HMQ12Q)

Advanced Deerhunter's Bible

Planting Food Plots for Deer and Other Wildlife

Sure-Fire Whitetail Tactics

The Bass Angler's Almanac: More Than 750 Tips & Tactics

The Whitetail Deer Hunter's Almanac

The Ultimate Guide to Butchering Deer: A Step-by-Step Guide to Field Dressing,

Skinning, Aging, and Butchering Deer*

*A Skyhorse publication

Notes